CRIMINAL PROCEDURE

UNITED KINGDOM
Sweet & Maxwell
London

AUSTRALIA
Law Book Co.
Sydney

CANADA and USA
Carswell
Toronto

HONG KONG
Sweet & Maxwell Asia

NEW ZEALAND
Brookers
Wellington

SINGAPORE and MALAYSIA
Sweet & Maxwell Asia
Singapore and Kuala Lumpur

CRIMINAL PROCEDURE

Professor Dermot Walsh

LL.B. (QUB), Ph.D. (NUI), Barrister-at-Law
Professor of Law,
Director of Centre for Criminal Justice,
School of Law, University of Limerick

Patrick MacEntee S.C., Q.C.

Consultant Editor

THOMSON ROUND HALL
DUBLIN
2002

Published in 2002 by
Round Hall Ltd
43 Fitzwilliam Place
Dublin 2
Ireland

Typeset by
Carrigboy Typesetting Services
Co. Cork, Ireland

Printed by
MPG Books, Cornwall

ISBN 1–85800–223–0

FOREWORD

It is commonplace to remark on the transformation of many areas of Irish law over the past two decades by the publication of first class textbooks. Criminal law is perhaps the last legal area of general importance to receive this treatment, and has indeed been afflicted by the publication over the years of a number of notably bad books. But the last three years have seen the publication of two volumes of superlative quality by Irish criminal lawyers, both practitioners and academics. These are *Criminal Law* by Mr Peter Charlton S.C., Mr McDermott and Ms Bolger; and *Criminal Liability, A Grammar* by Professor McAuley and Professor McCutcheon. Anyone familiar with those outstanding works will understand that it is indeed high praise of the present volume to say that it is a worthy companion to them, an appropriate completion of a trinity which seems likely to dominate the literature of Irish criminal law for the foreseeable future.

The development of a proper literature of criminal law is a matter of national importance, for the reasons identified, with reference to the law of Torts, by the late Mr Justice Walsh in his 1981 preface to McMahon and Binchy's *Irish Law of Torts*. Without a substantial literature of high intellectual quality, and a proper system of law reporting, no area of the law can aspire to consistency, transparency and orderly development.

In fact, Irish criminal law has made considerable strides in those directions, at an increasing pace, over the last thirty years or so. This is substantially the work of a new generation of Irish criminal lawyers, better educated than their predecessors, who have concentrated most their attention on criminal law. Of this generation Mr Patrick MacEntee S.C, Q.C., a consultant on the present work, is widely recognised as the *doyen*.

This book is a marked contribution, from the academic side, to the consistency and transparency of the criminal law. Its scope is enormous, as a glance at the table of contents will show. Its treatment of each topic is the most thorough I have seen anywhere. The author is not content with the descriptive treatment but includes a good deal of historical and analytical material as well. At the same time, the book is entirely practical work: the subjects covered are those which arise daily and hourly in the criminal courts. For solicitors and counsel and (speaking for myself) judges who are concerned with these matters this book will be an indispensable *vade mecum*.

I hope the book will have a wider readership as well. No area of the law receives more media attention than criminal trials, but the coverage is extremely uneven in quality and sometimes serves to confuse rather than enlighten a reader or viewer. One learns the result of the case, but often with little sense of the process leading to that result. Any commentator who troubles to read Professor Walsh's book on, for example, Sentencing cannot fail to become aware that an individual sentence is the end result of a process with specific stages and rules, and with a primary focus on the individual case. I hope that this book will be consulted by those professionally concerned with reporting the courts and with commenting on criminal law and practice.

Since about 1990, few areas of the law have changed more rapidly by statutory innovation and by judicial decision than criminal law and procedure. The task of keeping up with these changes is not an easy one and any book on the subject is likely to be overtaken in particular respects almost immediately. For these reasons I am glad to hear that the publishers are considering, instead of a second edition of this work, an Archbold type publication capable of updating as and when necessary. This would be a great service to the legal profession. In terms of practical utility, this work is fully the equal of *Archbold* or *Blackstone* in the neighbouring jurisdiction; in terms of intellectual quality it is considerably their superior.

Reading this work by an academic on an important aspect of legal practice gives rise to a final thought. For a number of decades there has been in Ireland a quite excessive degree of separation and non-communication between academic and practising lawyers. I hope this book will play a role in the erosion of that division, already well under way. It is undesirable that law should be taught by some who have never had a client and practised by some who rarely read an academic article. Sir Robert Megarry, formerly Vice-Chancellor of the Supreme Court in England and Wales and himself a prolific legal author, remarked in one of his prefaces that argued law was tough law and that nothing could replace the sharpness of focus created by the distinctive facts of an individual case. The academic risks missing this. On the other hand, the practitioner who is unduly narrow in his approach risks losing his sense of place in a coherent and evolving legal universe, like a sailor who can navigate his native bay but cannot use compass or sextant so that his travels are gravely limited. Professor Walsh has skilfully avoided these extremes. His conspicuous success will, I hope, inspire others.

ADRIAN HARDIMAN,
The Four Courts,
October 30, 2002.

PREFACE

The criminal justice system which had been shaped and developed in Ireland primarily in the second half of the nineteenth century was carried over into the new State on its establishment in 1922. While some changes were effected in the first few years, particularly in policing structures, no attempt was made to effect any fundamental redesign. Indeed, if one can ignore the various public safety and other such temporary emergency measures, the legislative history of the Irish criminal justice system right up until 1990 has been one of slow incremental change. After an initial flurry of activity in 1924 and 1925[1] the system settled down until 1939 when it was deemed necessary to enact the Offences against the State Act primarily to deal with a perceived increase in the threat of subversion. It was another 12 years before the next significant measure appeared in the form of the Criminal Justice Act 1951. By comparison, the 1960s was a period of hectic legislative activity with the enactment of the Criminal Justice Act 1960, followed in quick succession by the Criminal Justice (Legal Aid) Act 1962, the Extradition Act 1965 and the Criminal Procedure Act 1967. The 1970s kept up this measured pace with the enactment of three measures primarily in response to the violent situation affecting Northern Ireland: the Offences against the State (Amendment) Act 1972, the Criminal Law (Jurisdiction) Act 1976 and the Criminal Law Act 1976. A fourth, the Prosecution of Offences Act 1974 established the office of Director of Public Prosecutions. Of four significant measures enacted in the 1980s, at least two, the Criminal Justice (Community Service) Act 1983 and the Criminal Justice Act 1984, represented significant milestones in the Irish criminal justice system.

These were not the only legislative measures impinging upon the criminal justice system from 1922 up to the end of the 1980s. Others, such as the various Courts Acts and two Juries Acts, clearly had an input as well but they were not confined to criminal justice matters. There were also a number of substantive criminal measures which touched on procedural matters,[2] or which were confined to one particular aspect of the criminal justice system.[3] Chief among these is probably the Criminal Justice Act 1964 which abolished the death penalty for all offences subject to a few exceptions, most notably capital murder.[4]

---

[1] See the enactment of the Garda Síochána Act 1924, the Criminal Justice (Administration) Act 1924, the Criminal Justice (Evidence) Act 1924 and the Police Forces Amalgamation Act 1925. Relevant temporary measures were enacted in 1923, notably the Garda Síochána (Temporary Provisions) Act 1923 and the District Justices (Temporary Provisions) Act 1923.

[2] See, *e.g.* the Criminal Law Amendment Act 1935, the Treason Act 1939, the Criminal Justice Act 1964 and the Road Traffic Acts.

[3] See, *e.g.* the Prisons Act 1970 and the Criminal Justice (Verdict) Act 1976.

[4] The death penalty was abolished in Ireland entirely by the Criminal Justice Act 1990.

The picture which emerges from this brief survey is one of slow deliberate change in the basic principles, structures and processes of the criminal justice system. Indeed, an examination of the contents of these measures reveals that many of them are either declaratory of the pre-existing law or practice, or make minor incremental changes. Only a few introduce permanent root and branch reforms. Of those that do introduce fundamental changes, most are clearly meant to function within the established norms and processes which have been a distinctive hallmark of the criminal justice system in Ireland for the past 150 years.

That, of course, is what one would expect of criminal law and criminal procedure. Given their role in expressing and enforcing the basic standards of behaviour expected of each citizen in society, coupled with their associated consequences for the fundamental rights and freedoms of the individual, it is highly desirable that our criminal law and procedure should be accessible, transparent and reasonably constant over time in the sense of not being subject to multiple, radical and complex changes in rapid succession. In any healthy democracy based on the rule of law, the average person must always be in a position to know in advance whether his or her proposed course of action in any matter will attract criminal liability. Equally important is for the average person to be in a position to know in advance how, when, to what extent and under what conditions the State, particularly through the medium of the police, can intrude coercively on his or her personal liberty, bodily integrity, property rights, privacy rights and his or her basic right to be left alone. The rules of criminal procedure must also be sufficiently transparent and stable for the average person to make informed decisions at each stage of his or her criminal investigation, prosecution and trial, and generally to appreciate what is happening to him or her.

With one or two exceptions it would seem reasonable to conclude that the Irish criminal justice system satisfied these basic standards up until the beginning of the 1990s. Since then, however, everything has changed utterly. The vehicle for that change has been legislation. If the pace of legislative change in criminal justice matters from the establishment of the State to the end of the 1980s can be likened to a gentle breeze, that in the 1990s will have to be described as a hurricane which shows little sign of abating. More significant statutory enactments have been introduced in the last 10 years than in the previous 60 years. The decade of the 1990s opened with no less than two major criminal procedure enactments and three substantive criminal law measures.[5] The pace slackened in 1991 and 1992 with only one substantive criminal law enactment and one procedural enactment as the hurricane gathered its strength.[6] Nevertheless, the single measure enacted in 1992 was sufficient in itself to introduce a radical new development in the Irish criminal justice system. The pace quickened in 1993 with the enactment of two

---

[5] Criminal Justice Act 1990; Criminal Justice (Forensic Evidence) Act 1990; Larceny Act 1990; Firearms and Offensive Weapons Act 1990; and the Criminal Law (Rape)(Amendment) Act 1990.
[6] Criminal Damage Act 1991 and Criminal Evidence Act 1992.

criminal law measures and two procedure measures.[7] A similar pattern prevailed in 1994 with a further four major enactments, at least two of which effected radical changes in the justice system.[8] In 1995 there was only one criminal procedure measure as against two criminal law measures.[9] In 1996 the balance was turned on its head with the enactment of at least four major procedure measures; two of which introduced arguably the most radical change in the Irish criminal justice system this century, while the other two introduced merely radical changes.[10] This radical transformation of the criminal justice system continued apace into 1997 with the enactment of no less than five major procedure measures and one substantive criminal law measure.[11] There was no let up in this frenetic legislative activity in 1998 with the enactment of five more major measures; three were concerned with international obligations while the other two were driven by events connected with the situation in Northern Ireland.[12] Superficially, it appears that the legislature took a breather in 1999, but the single measure enacted in that year once again effected complex and radical changes to the justice system.[13] Although there was significant legislative activity in 2000 impacting upon criminal law and justice matters, the net effect was not as dramatic as that achieved in many of the other years.[14] However, the pace picked up again in 2001 with the enactment of at least four major criminal procedure measures and two major criminal law measures.[15] All of them effected radical changes to our criminal law and justice system. So far in 2002 there has been at least one significant procedure measure, namely that introducing the "penalty points" system for road traffic offences.[16] There have, of course, been many other measures which do not deal directly or solely with criminal law and procedure, but which nevertheless have contributed to the growth and complexity of the law in these areas. In addition, there has been a very rapid and substantial growth in the body of criminal justice rules and regulations supporting these enactments.

---

[7] Criminal Law (Suicide) Act 1993; Criminal Law (Sexual Offences) Act 1993; Criminal Justice Act 1993; and the Criminal Procedure Act 1993.

[8] Criminal Justice (Public Order) Act 1994; Extradition (Amendment) Act 1994; Road Traffic Act 1994; and Criminal Justice Act 1994.

[9] Road Traffic Act 1995; Criminal Law (Incest Proceedings) Act 1995; and Transfer of Sentenced Persons Act 1995.

[10] Criminal Justice (Drug Trafficking) Act 1996; Proceeds of Crime Act 1996; Criminal Assets Bureau Act 1996; and Sexual Offences (Jurisdiction) Act 1996.

[11] Criminal Justice (Miscellaneous Provisions) Act 1997; Criminal Law Act 1997; Bail Act 1997; Europol Act 1997; and Transfer of Sentenced Persons (Amendment) Act 1997.

[12] Child Trafficking and Pornography Act 1998; Geneva Conventions (Amendment) Act 1998; Criminal Justice (Release of Prisoners) Act 1998; Offences against the State (Amendment) Act 1998; and International War Crimes Tribunals Act 1998.

[13] Criminal Justice Act 1999.

[14] Criminal Justice (United Nations Convention against Torture) Act 2000; Criminal Justice (Safety of United Nations Workers) Act 2000; Illegal Immigrants Act 2000; and the Wildlife (Amendment) Act 2000.

[15] Customs and Excise (Mutual Assistance) Act 2001; Sex Offenders Act 2001; Children Act 2001; Extradition (European Union Conventions) Act 2001; and Criminal Justice (Theft and Fraud Offences) Act 2001.

[16] Road Traffic Act 2002.

Some of this explosion in legislative activity can be attributed to a desire to respond to matters such as child sexual abuse and organised crime which have shot up the agenda of public concern in recent years. It can also be explained, however, by a desire to secure changes in the criminal justice system which will make it easier to secure convictions and the co-operation of suspects and generally to render that system a harsher experience for those who come in contact with it either as suspects or offenders. On the police front these include a substantial growth in the nature and extent of powers regarding: stop, search and question; arrest, detention and interrogation; entry, search and seizure; the abstraction of forensic samples from the bodies of suspects; and the production of confidential information in the hands of third parties. On the procedural front they include: inroads into the right to silence; the growth in adverse inference provisions; obligations of advance disclosure on the defence; more frequent resort to provisions which shift the evidential burden onto the accused; proof by certificate and documentary evidence; the admission of deposition and video-taped evidence; dilution of the right to bail; and the abolition of the preliminary investigation. These developments are complemented by the introduction of much stiffer custodial penalties for certain crimes. To all of this must be added the inclusion of a modified civil procedure to target property which is suspected of being the proceeds of crime. Finally, reference must be made to the growing tendency for the contents of our criminal law and procedure to be driven by developments outside the country. Of particular importance here are the demands of the European Union which, increasingly, are being expressed in the form of legislation which, although enacted in Brussels, is directly binding on Ireland.

It is submitted that the combination of these developments has, in the space of less than 10 years, achieved a radical re-alignment in the balance which had characterised the Irish criminal justice system during the previous 150 years. The heavy emphasis on due process values which imposed a heavy burden on the State to prove guilt against a passive defendant has been replaced by a model in which, at the very least, the State can coerce a much greater degree of co-operation from the suspect, both directly and indirectly, in the investigation of his or her own guilt than had been the case previously. Arguably, the development of a civil procedure to target the confiscation of suspected criminal assets has created a situation in which the suspect effectively has to prove his or her innocence in order to avoid losing his or her property. While all of this may not amount to a "crime control" model of criminal justice in Packer's classic typology, it does represent a significant departure from his "due process" model.

It would be a mistake to focus exclusively on the impact of legislative developments in recent years. The judges have also made a very profound contribution to the growth of the criminal justice system. Indeed, there were long periods throughout the history of the State when their output far outstripped that of the legislature in terms of substantive impact. Even throughout the 1990s the judges have not been left behind by an over-active legislature. It is surely no exaggeration to say that the volume and quality of judgments emanating annually from the Supreme Court, the Court of

Criminal Appeal and the High Court in criminal justice matters are unprecedented in the history of the State. For the most part these judgments are playing a vital role in taming some of the wilder excesses of the legislature and the executive. In that respect they are making a vital contribution to upholding the due process rights and the basic freedoms of the individual. The richness of the judgments also play a very valuable role in interpreting and making sense of the legislation enacted in recent years. On the other hand, the sheer volume and frequency of the judgments can increase the burden on busy practitioners who are already hard pressed to keep up with the legislative developments.

The legislative developments outlined above have come at a heavy price in terms of transparency in the criminal justice system. We have moved very rapidly from a situation in which the essential substance of police powers and criminal procedure was firmly established, stable, familiar and reasonably comprehensible to the average citizen, to a situation where even the experts are experiencing acute difficulty in just keeping abreast of developments. To some extent this is an inevitable by-product of the speed and frequency of legislative developments over the past 10 to 12 years. The real problem, however, stems partly from the fact that these measures effect wide-ranging, radical and innovative changes to the criminal justice system and partly from the sheer length and complexity of many of the measures. Particularly troublesome is the fact that some of the most important enactments, in terms of criminal practice, effect fundamental and far reaching changes across a broad spectrum of the criminal process by amending pre-existing legislation instead of introducing a new self-contained code. Worse still is the fact that several of these reforming amendments introduced over the past 10 years have in themselves been amended; some on several occasions. Equally disturbing is the fact that many of the measures which have the greatest implications for the rights and freedoms of the individual are expressed in very broad terms.

These developments pose a very real threat to basic values in a democracy based on the rule of law. As expert practitioners and academics experience increasing difficulty in advising citizens on their position in criminal matters the power and control of the State, which is the primary source of the complexity and lack of transparency, are enhanced by default. The first and most essential protection against this risk is the availability of a text or texts which provide the practitioner and the citizen with a reasonably comprehensive, up-to-date and accessible account of criminal law and criminal procedure. We have been well served in the area of criminal law with the publication of at least two excellent texts within the past decade. Unfortunately, there has been no equivalent on the criminal procedure front. Ryan and Magee's *The Irish Criminal Process* made a major contribution to our understanding of the criminal justice system when it was published in 1983, but that was clearly much too early to take account of the fundamental and far reaching changes which have characterised the criminal justice system in the 1990s.

The primary motivation behind the writing of this book on criminal procedure is to fill the vacuum identified above. The object of the book is to set out as clearly and as comprehensively as space and time permit the principles and rules governing the key elements of the criminal justice system in this country. It is targeted primarily at practitioners, including: judges, prosecution and defence lawyers, members of the Garda Síochána, probation and welfare officers, the courts service, the prison service, government officials dealing with aspects of criminal justice policy, academics and others whose work involves interaction with the criminal justice system on a regular basis. Every effort has also been made to write the book in a style which will make it accessible to members of the public who have an interest in knowing the law on police powers and criminal procedure or who wish to read up on the law governing a particular issue. It is freely admitted, however, that there are areas which are so arcane and complex that they are destined forever to remain the preserve of the expert.

The focus of the book is very much on an explication of what the law is. While there was always a strong temptation to engage in a critical and policy analysis, it was considered that the most pressing need was for a text which would serve the needs of the busy practitioner and others who need to know what the law is on criminal procedure. I was also conscious of the fact that the very existence of such a text was an essential precondition to the development of an informed critical and policy-oriented literature.

Given the very broad scope of the subject and the interactions which are inherent among the various stages of the criminal process, devising a logical and coherent structure for the book was always going to be problematic. Ideally, each relevant topic would be treated comprehensively in a distinct section. That, however, would result in the book consisting of a discrete collection of sections lacking in any overall coherence or system. In any event there are many topics relevant to the criminal justice system which cannot properly be discussed fully without overlapping with other topics. In the end, I opted for a structure which does not differ essentially from the standard in most criminal procedure texts. For the most part the subject and order of each chapter reflects the progression of a case through the criminal justice system from beginning to end. Accordingly, chapters 1 to 3 deal with basic introductory, institutional and jurisdictional factors relevant to the functioning of the system as a whole. Chapters 4 to 8 deal with police powers in the investigation and detection of crime, while chapter 9 deals with the rules governing the admissibility of evidence secured by the police through their investigative efforts. Chapter 10 deals with bail, while chapter 11 deals with legal aid and representation for the defendant. Chapter 12 deals with the prosecution and the decision to prosecute, while chapter 13 deals with the District Court and the initiation of a criminal prosecution. Chapter 14 deals with the decision to send the accused forward for trial on indictment, together with obligations on the prosecution (such as disclosure) and various pre-trial applications that might arise. Chapter 15 deals with the indictment, while chapter 16 deals with the arraignment and pleas. Chapter 17 deals with the jury, while chapters 18 and 19 deal with aspects of trial evidence and trial procedure respectively. Chapter 20 deals with the Special Criminal Court. Chapter 21 deals with sentencing and chapter 22 concludes the book with appeals.

Even with this structure there are awkward elements. The chapters on police powers, for example, are not and cannot be set out in an order which makes absolute chronological sense. Inevitably, some issues are suitable for discussion in more than one context. In some cases this has resulted in topics being assigned almost arbitrarily to one chapter as opposed to another, and in other cases to a degree of repetition and split treatment between chapters. While I have attempted to keep such instances to a minimum I have not managed to exclude them entirely. The law of evidence has been particularly problematic in this context. Although the text is on procedure, as distinct from evidence, some aspects of procedure cannot be dealt with adequately without some reference to evidence. Accordingly, aspects of evidence are dealt with in diverse places throughout the text. An attempt is also made to include in a separate chapter aspects of evidence which are not dealt with elsewhere but which would be useful to know in order to understand some of the procedural issues which might arise in the trial. It is not very tidy, but it was considered that on balance it would be better to include the additional chapter.

Patently size has imposed a constraint. There are only so many pages that can be bound together in a single volume of this nature. It follows that it has not been possible in this instance to include illustrations of official forms and documents to which there are footnoted references throughout the text. Equally, it has not been possible to include sample indictments, etc. Also for reasons of space it has not proved possible to include separate chapters on some specialist topics, such as the confiscation of criminal assets. There are plans, however, to publish subsequent editions of this text in looseleaf form. Not only will that provide scope to include these extra elements, but it will also facilitate a more detailed discussion of some specialist topics which are touched upon in the text but which could not be developed further due to space constraints.

Inevitably, in researching and writing a book of this size many unrepayable debts are incurred. This has been no exception. There is a danger, of course, in attempting to name all those who contributed as, almost invariably, some names will be inadvertently omitted. Nevertheless, there are a few individuals who have made such a huge contribution to bringing this book to fruition that I cannot contemplate not acknowledging my debt to them. I am very grateful to Mr Justice Adrian Hardiman for taking the time out from his onerous duties to write a most generous foreword. Mr Patrick Mac Entee S.C., Q.C., the consultant editor, has been an inspiration in the development of the book from an early draft through to the final production. Aengus O'Hanrahan B.A., LL.M, has provided research assistance of superb quality at the most critical times. Pattie Punch, Law and Humanities Librarian at the University of Limerick was always available to track down the most obscure texts within impossible time constraints. Dave Ellis and Martin McCann of Round Hall worked wonders in the editing process and managed to retain their cool despite the exceptional pressure they were under. I owe a special word of thanks to commissioning editor, Catherine Dolan. Without her endless patience and constant encouragement this book might never have been completed. I am also grateful to the School of Law and the College of

Humanities at the University of Limerick for their continued support throughout the writing of the book. Most important of all, however, is the debt I owe to my wife Alice and children Orla and Niall. I strongly suspect that they believe that the book does not actually exist and that I only use it as an excuse to escape my share of family duties. After having been out of practice for so long I shall have to crave their indulgence for a gradual return to the fold.

Responsibility for any errors in or omissions from the text rests fully on my shoulders. I have attempted as best I can to state the law as it stood on June 1, 2002. While some legislative and case law development subsequent to that date have been included it has not proved possible within the publishing time frame to include all such developments.

DERMOT WALSH
Newgarden North,
Lisnagry,
November 1, 2002.

TABLE OF CONTENTS

TABLE OF CASES

TABLE OF LEGISLATION

UNITED KINGDOM

Acts

International Conventions

CHAPTER 1

GENERAL PRINCIPLES AND PRELIMINARY MATTERS

A. Basic Foundations

1. Introduction

The basic foundations of the Irish criminal justice system can be traced at least as far back as the nineteenth century when Ireland was still part of the United Kingdom of Great Britain and Ireland. These basic features are: its adversarial and accusatorial nature; its attachment to trial by jury; the centrality of the trial through oral procedure; the independence of the judges, prosecutors and police; and due process values.   **1–01**

2. Adversarial and Accusatorial

The Irish criminal justice system has inherited the English adversarial and accusatorial model. This is probably the feature which distinguishes it most from its inquisitorial counterparts on the European continent. The Irish system is based on a contest between the State and a person suspected or accused of a criminal offence. In that contest the onus is on the State to prove beyond a reasonable doubt that the accused is guilty of the offence in question in accordance with the requirements prescribed by law. The onus of proof rests on the State throughout the contest. If it fails to establish beyond a reasonable doubt that the accused is guilty in accordance with the law the accused is entitled to an acquittal. There is no obligation on the accused to establish his or her innocence. Indeed, the accused can remain silent and non co-operative throughout and will still be entitled to an acquittal if the State fails to establish his or her guilt beyond a reasonable doubt.   **1–02**

The process is not an inquisitorial search for the truth surrounding criminal allegations against the accused which he or she disputes. It is an exercise in determining whether the accused satisfies the legal requirements of guilt. The object is to determine whether the State has established beyond a reasonable doubt that the accused's acts or omissions satisfy the legal requirements for

1

guilt of the offence charged. The determination of what it is that the accused has done or failed to do must be reached in accordance with the rules of evidence and procedure governing this fact finding contest. It must then be determined whether the acts or omissions as proved by these rules satisfy the requirements of the offence as prescribed by law. Frequently, this will result in a determination of the truth of the allegations against the accused. That, however, is not an essential precondition for a finding of guilt, nor even the primary object of the process. Equally, it may happen that the allegations against the accused are shown to be true, but nevertheless he or she is acquitted because the State has not proved in accordance with the rules that he or she satisfied the legal requirements for guilt.

3. Attachment to Trial by Jury

1–03   Since the criminal trial is conducted as an adversarial contest there must be an adjudicator to determine who wins. Traditionally, in these islands, the fact-finding function has been separated from the function of declaring and policing compliance with the rules of the contest. The latter function is the preserve of the judge. His or her role has been equated with that of an independent umpire whose role it is to ensure that the rules of evidence and procedure applicable to the criminal trial process are understood and obeyed. The judge remains aloof from the adversaries and the contest in the sense that he or she does not engage actively in the search for the truth. The onus of adducing evidence and presenting arguments to advance their case rests squarely on each of the parties.

The task of making the factual determination of whether the accused is guilty or not guilty, at least in respect of serious offences, normally rests with a jury randomly selected from the accused's peers. In a jury trial, the jury will listen to all of the admissible evidence presented and tested by the parties. It will be instructed by the judge on how they must approach their task. This will involve an explanation of the elements of the offence charged against the accused and how they should go about determining, on the basis of the evidence they have heard and seen, whether the accused is guilty or not guilty. The jury will then retire and consider their verdict in private. Neither the jury as a whole nor any of the individual members can be asked to explain their decision. When an accused has been put in their charge the determination of whether he or she is guilty or not guilty is a matter for them alone, subject of course to the possibility of their decision being upset on appeal.

The jury can be described as one of the most cherished institutions in the criminal justice systems in these islands. It can trace its history in England back to the thirteenth century. While in purely numerical terms the vast majority of criminal cases, mostly concerning minor offences, are dealt with by a judge sitting alone, the continued role of the jury in the trial of most serious offences has ensured that it remains a central pillar of the Irish criminal process. It is the one major component of the criminal process which remains in the hands of citizens, as distinct from the legal professionals and

State agents. Proposals to cut back on the range of offences which qualify for jury trial have generally provoked stout opposition.

4. Importance of Oral Procedure

The trial in common law systems has always been synonymous with a heavy **1–04** emphasis on oral procedure. This is particularly true of the criminal trial. Generally, allegations of fact against the accused have to be proved by the presentation of oral evidence from witnesses who are in a position to speak from first hand knowledge or experience of the facts they are relaying to the court. These witnesses can then be cross-examined by the other side, with the further possibility of re-examination by the side which called them as witnesses. Submissions on the law governing the offence charged, the admissibility of evidence and matters of procedure are all made orally to the court. Equally, the summing up and/or address to the jury are made orally. Indeed, the presence and role of the jury are primary factors in ensuring that the emphasis on oral procedure remains a hallmark of the trial in common law jurisdictions. While there have been developments in recent years to permit facts to be proved by written certificate in certain circumstances, these fall very far short of signifying a move away from the centrality of oral procedure.

5. Independence and Impartiality

Although the criminal trial in Ireland can be described as a contest between **1–05** the State and the accused, the key players from the State are required to act with complete impartiality and independence from outside influences. In effect their primary mission is to uphold the authority of the law without fear or favour to any side or interest. Ultimately, they are accountable to the law as distinct from the government. Traditionally this has been reflected most emphatically in the independence of the judiciary. Although appointed by the government, judges in these islands have always been distinguished by their reputation for independence from the government and the prosecution in the conduct of criminal trials. This characteristic is so engrained that any direct attempt to curb that independence would surely provoke a constitutional crisis. There is, of course, an argument for saying that the method for appointing judges is heavily weighted towards ensuring that judges will generally reflect a bias in favour of "establishment" values favoured by the government and prosecution. That, however, does not necessarily contradict the assertion that the independence of the judiciary in the conduct of criminal trials is one of the hallmarks of the criminal justice system in these islands. The judges are entirely separate from the prosecution in any individual case. They are expected to, and do, maintain complete impartiality between the prosecution and the defence in the conduct of a criminal trial. Their independence is now entrenched in Article 35.2 of the Constitution which reads: "All judges shall be independent in the exercise of their judicial functions and subject only to the Constitution and the law." Article 35 goes on to protect judges of the Supreme Court and the High Court from being

3

removed from office except for stated misbehaviour or incapacity and even then only by resolutions passed by both the Dáil and the Seanad.

The independence of the judiciary is complemented in the independence of the prosecution and the police. Traditionally, both the prosecution and the police are independent from the government of the day and other partisan interests in their handling of a criminal investigation and prosecution. While this may not always be apparent in practice, particularly in the case of the police, the theory is that both the police and the prosecution are entirely independent in the exercise of their respective powers in the criminal process. In such matters they are accountable only to the law.[1] Indeed, it is generally recognised that both the police and the prosecution should not aim to secure a conviction at any cost. Not only must they operate within the law and rules of the criminal process, but if information which casts a doubt about their case comes into their possession during the course of a criminal trial they should bring that information to the attention of the court. Although they represent one side in an adversarial contest and although the onus is on them to prove the accused's guilt beyond a reasonable doubt, their duty to uphold the law means that they also have a duty to ensure that the other side is not denied due process. As officers of the State they have a duty to uphold the Constitution and, in particular, Article 38.1 which states that "No person shall be tried on any criminal charge save in due course of law." It is also worth noting that the Prosecution of Offences Act 1974 guarantees the independence of the DPP in the performance of his functions.[1a] While there is no specific equivalent for the Garda Commissioner it is firmly established in law and practice that both he and individual members of the force are independent in the exercise of their police powers and law enforcement duties.[1b]

6. Due Process Values

1–06   The adversarial and accusatorial nature of the criminal process in these islands is underpinned by a firm commitment to due process. While this commitment is now given concrete expression in the Irish Constitution, the European Convention for the Protection of Human Rights and Fundamental Freedoms and legislation, it can find much older roots in the common law.

At the heart of this due process concept is the notion that an individual can be exposed to the risk of punishment for criminal infraction only pursuant to a procedure which respects his or her dignity as an autonomous human being within a civilised society.[1c] Merely because an individual may in fact be guilty of a criminal offence deserving of punishment is not in itself sufficient to justify subjecting that person to punishment. If the individual's guilt has

---

[1]   For discusssion of police independence, see D. Walsh *The Irish Police* (Round Hall Sweet & Maxwell), chap. 4.

[1a]   Prosecution of Offences Act 1974, s.2(5).

[1b]   See generally D Walsh *The Irish Police: a Legal and Constitutional Perspective* (Round Hall Sweet and Maxwell, Dublin, 1998).

[1c]   The classic account of the due process model of the Criminal Process is presented in H. Packer, *The Limits of the Criminal Sanction* (Stanford University Press, 1969)

been determined through methods or procedures which would not be considered "fair" then that will preclude his or her punishment for the crime in question. Not only must the individual's guilt be determined in accordance with fair procedures, but it is also considered essential that the agents of the State abide by the basic rules and values which inform those procedures in their investigation and determination of guilt. It is considered that it is less damaging for the body politic to let an offender go free than it is for the State to take advantage of wrongdoing by its agents in order to secure a conviction.[1d]

Before saying a few words about what is meant by "fair procedures" in this context it is worth drawing attention to another fundamental aspect of due process, namely the requirement that an individual should not be exposed to the risk of punishment unless his or her guilt is established transparently and beyond doubt. This reflects the notion that it is better for 10 guilty persons to go free than to convict one innocent person. Accordingly, guilt must be established beyond all reasonable doubt. Closely associated with this is the requirement that the individual's guilt should be established by objective proof in a public trial. Reliance on the knowledge or opinion of the police or other professionals for proof of guilt has no place in due process norms. Guilt must be established on the basis of factual evidence presented and tested in a public trial in which the onus is placed firmly on the State to prove guilt objectively and beyond a reasonable doubt.

1–07

What constitutes fair procedures in our adversarial and accusatorial criminal justice system is heavily shaped by the assumption that the State and the individual do not stand in a position of equality with respect to each other. The State is considered to be equipped with virtually limitless resources for the investigation, detection and prosecution of the individual's guilt. The nature and extent of these resources are such that they simply cannot be matched by the private individual, and especially by the vast majority of individuals who become enmeshed in the criminal justice system. Satisfying the requirements of fair procedures in this context requires a range of balancing measures in favour of the individual suspect or accused so to as to create, as far as possible, an "equality of arms" between the two sides in the adversarial contest. Placing the burden on the State to prove guilt beyond a reasonable doubt is not considered sufficient to strike an acceptable balance. Further measures are necessary. Typically these have included: the right to silence and freedom from self-incrimination, the right to legal representation including the right of access to a solicitor while in police custody, the right to know the case one has to meet, the right to test the prosecution evidence and the right to trial by jury. The contents of this list and more particularly, the compass of the individual measures within it, have never been set in stone. There has always been, and will continue to be, debate about where the balance should be struck between the right of the State to detect and punish crime and the rights of the individual when under investigation by the State.

[1d] The common law has not always endorsed this aspect of due process; see, for *e.g.*, *Kuruma v. R.* [1955] 1 All E.R. 236.

The scope and contents of the measures necessary to achieve equality of arms between the two sides will vary from time to time in response to movements in that debate. The underlying concept of due process, however, remains constant.

B. The Constitutional Context

1. Background

1–08 When Ireland was established in 1922 as a separate State it inherited the criminal justice machinery, principles and values which had existed immediately prior to 1922. As might be expected, legislative, executive and judicial activity over the following 80 years in both Ireland and the United Kingdom has resulted in a growing divergence in the contents of their criminal laws, their machinery of criminal justice and even in some of the basic principles underpinning their criminal justice systems. It would be fair to say, however, that the nature and extent of these changes have not been sufficient to obscure their common heritage. Indeed, some developments over the past 80 years, most particularly their membership of the European Union and common endorsement of the European Convention for the Protection of Human Rights and Fundamental Freedoms, have served to strengthen their common core values and promote re-convergence. Nevertheless, the adoption of a written constitution with its protection for fundamental rights has resulted, arguably, in placing Ireland ahead of its neighbour in respect of due process values in criminal justice.

2. Centrality of Justice in the Constitution

Today the "due process" character of the Irish criminal justice system is anchored in the 1937 Constitution,[2] through the requirement in Article 34 for justice to be administered by courts established by law, the explicit Article 38 prohibition on trying a person for a criminal offence otherwise than in "due course of law", the guarantee of trial by jury for non-minor offences in Article 38.5, the positive obligation on the State to defend and vindicate the personal rights of the individual in Article 40.3, and the protection of other disparate rights such as freedom of expression. Over past thirty years and more the Irish judges have used these constitutional provisions to help shape, give force to and uphold basic due process values in the Irish criminal justice system. They have been unequivocal in their view that justice, in the form of due process, is the central and dominant value in the criminal process. This is clearly reflected in the following passage from the judgment of O'Higgins C.J. in *State (Healy) v. Donoghue*.[3] Although handed down more than twenty

---

[2] Bunreacht na hÉireann.
[3] [1976] I.R. 325.

five years ago it remains the classic statement of the fundamental values at the heart of the Irish criminal process:

> " . . . the concept of justice which is specifically referred to in the preamble in relation to the freedom and dignity of the individual appears again in the provisions of Article 34 which deal with the courts. It is justice which is to be administered in the courts and this concept of justice must import not only fairness, and fair procedures, but also regard to the dignity of the individual. No court under the Constitution has jurisdiction to act contrary to justice . . . (Article 38.1) must be considered in conjunction with Article 34; with Article 40.3.1 under which the State guarantees in its laws to respect, and as far as practicable, by its laws to defend and vindicate the personal rights of the citizen; and with subsection 2 of the same section under which 'the State shall, in particular, by its laws protect as best it may from unjust attack and, in the case of injustice done, vindicate the life, person, good name and property rights of every citizen.' Being so considered, it is clear that the words 'due process of law' in Article 38 make it mandatory that every criminal trial shall be conducted in accordance with the concepts of justice, that the procedures applied shall be fair, and that the person accused will be afforded every opportunity to defend himself. If this were not so, the dignity of the individual would be ignored and the State would have failed to vindicate his personal rights."[3a]

3. Primacy of Constitutional Values

This passage also confirms that rules, practices and procedures in the criminal justice system will not avoid constitutional challenge merely because they are authorised by the bare terms of some statutory enactment or common law rule. The enactment or rule itself must also accord with the basic concepts of justice and fairness. What these concepts require depends very much on the context in which they are considered. Broadly speaking, it can be said that they aim to strike a balance between the interests of the State in the efficient prosecution and punishment of criminal offences and the fundamental rights of the individual to liberty, privacy and dignity. Statutory enactments which impinge upon the traditional freedoms or which strengthen the hand of the State in the criminal process will be scrutinised closely and interpreted strictly to ensure that they do not impinge any more than is necessary on the rights, freedoms and dignity of the individual. If it is impossible to interpret and apply them in a manner which upholds basic due process values they will be struck down as null and void.

1–09

4. Extension to the Investigative and Prosecutorial Process

The judges have not confined due process requirements to the criminal trial. They have recognised that the growth in police powers, together with certain evidential and procedural developments, impinge directly upon the shape and direction of the criminal trial in individual cases. All too often the

---

[3a] *ibid.* at pp.348–349

determination of guilt has effectively been settled in the police station before a case ever gets to the courtroom. If due process values are not to lose much of their practical relevance for the individual in such cases, it is essential that their reach extends to the pre-trial investigative and prosecutorial processes. The Irish judges have not been slow to go down this road. Significantly, the European Court of Human Rights has been equally diligent in finding that the right to a fair trial as protected by Article 6 of the European Convention for the Protection of Human Rights and Fundamental Freedoms applies to pre-trial matters which impact upon the fairness of the criminal trial.

5. Unspecified Rights

1–10   In their application of constitutional due process values to the criminal process, the courts have recognised a number of unspecified or unwritten constitutional rights which are either implicit in or additional to those expressed in the Constitution. These include: the presumption of innocence, the right to silence, the right against self-incrimination, the right of access to a solicitor in police custody, the right to legal representation, the right to be heard, the right to a trial in public, the right to a trial free from bias, the right to a speedy trail and the right to proportionality in sentencing. These and others are considered at appropriate places throughout the remainder of the book. Equally important is the judicial enforcement of these rights through the exclusion of evidence which has been obtained by their conscious and deliberate breach by the agents of the State. This too is dealt with later in the book.

6. Preliminary Matters

In this introductory chapter it is appropriate to look more closely at the right to a speedy trial and the basis for the right to jury trial. Both can be classified as preliminary matters because of the context in which they have been developed in the case law. The right to jury trial is intimately tied up with the classification of criminal offences which, in turn, affects a number of issues in criminal procedure. It is convenient, therefore, to address the recognised offence classifications at the outset including, in particular, that which determines the right to jury trial. The right to a speedy trial is intimately associated with the whole issue of delay in the criminal process. If the prosecution delays too long in pursuing criminal charges against an individual it can deprive the courts of jurisdiction. If the court lacks jurisdiction in a case it cannot be dealt with through the criminal process. It is convenient, therefore, to deal with delay and the associated right to a speedy trial at the outset. Before addressing these matters, however, it is necessary to say something about the rights of victims.

7. Victims

1–11   Crimes are considered to be wrongs committed against the State. It often happens, of course, that the State is either the direct victim or stands in the shoes of the victim because there is no direct victim. More often than not, however, the actual victim is an identifiable person or persons who have suffered loss or injury directly as a result of the crime. Nevertheless, even in these cases it is normally the State which is the prosecuting party. Criminal infractions, particularly when they are serious, pose a threat to society which is considered too serious to leave the consequences to be resolved by a private action between the victim and the offender. Accordingly, the State assumes the mantle of victim in the prosecution of the crime. This, in turn, relegates the actual victim to the status of a mere witness whose personal situation and interests can be sidelined in the contest between the State and the suspect. Traditionally, in this contest the focus of debate has concentrated on the balance between the powers of the State on the one hand and the rights of the suspect on the other. This has generated intense frustration among victims who feel victimised twice over; once at the hands of the offender and again at the hands of the State by their virtual exclusion from involvement in the State's handling of the prosecution against the accused. Moreover, victims frequently interpret concern for due process as the State and society showing greater concern for the suspect offender than for the actual victims of crime.

Growing recognition of the rights of victims in recent years is beginning to impact on the shape and contents of criminal procedure. Initially, this has been felt most in sentencing where judges can now seek and consider victim impact reports and award compensation to victims in criminal trials. Lately, there is evidence of an impact on other elements of the process. In rape trials, for example, there is now provision for the appointment of separate legal representation for the victim. Such developments are considered at the appropriate places throughout the book. At this point it is worth noting that the traditional focus of the debate on the appropriate balance between the interests of the State and the suspect will have to be adjusted to take on board the legitimate interests of victims.

C. The Classification of Criminal Offences

1. Introduction

Criminal procedure is concerned first and foremost with the enforcement of the criminal law. It is not directly concerned with the definition of crime or individual criminal offences, matters which are properly the subject of the criminal law. Nevertheless, any treatment of criminal procedure must take cognisance of some of the classifications traditionally applied to criminal offences. For example, classifications which distinguish between indictable and summary offences, between minor and non-minor offences and between felonies and misdemeanours have, or have had, practical implications for criminal procedure. It is necessary, therefore, to explain the substance and consequences of such classifications.

1–12

2. Felony and Misdemeanour

1–13   The common law traditionally has classified offences into treason, felonies or misdemeanours. In practice, the primary distinction was that between felonies and misdemeanours. Originally the former were considered to be serious offences and the latter minor. Gradually, however, this distinction became less meaningful as Parliament created statutory offences which it classified as felonies or misdemeanours without any consistent appreciation of the concomitant distinction between serious and minor offences. The practical importance of the difference was confined primarily to the scope of police powers of arrest, the distinction between principals and accessories to crime and the severity of punishment that could be imposed on conviction. Even these consequences faded in importance as Parliament increasingly adopted the distinction between indictable and summary offences when it created new offences.[4] The common law consequences that would otherwise have flowed from the felony-misdemeanour distinction in any individual case were catered for in the legislation creating the offence. Now the distinction has been abolished formally by the Criminal Law Act 1997. This Act also makes consequential provision for police powers of arrest, punishment and secondary participation.

3. Indictable and Summary Offences

1–14   The distinction between indictable and summary offences is of major importance in criminal procedure. Broadly speaking, it categorises offences by reference to the manner in which they may be tried. Summary offences, therefore, are those which are tried by courts of summary jurisdiction. In Ireland that means the District Court. Indictable offences are those which may be tried on indictment before a judge and jury, *i.e.* in the Circuit Court or the Central Criminal Court. This classification on the basis of summary trial and trial on indictment generally reflects a division between serious and minor offences.[5] It is not always possible, however, to determine whether an offence is serious or minor from its definition alone. Inevitably, there are offences the seriousness of which depends not so much on their definition but on the circumstances in which they were committed. Accordingly, there is a range of indictable offences which statutorily can be tried summarily in certain circumstances.

Some of the offences in question are listed in the first schedule to the Criminal Justice Act 1951 (as amended). These cover a motley collection ranging over common law offences of public mischief, perjury, obstructing

---

4   Ryan and Magee state that the last Irish statutory enactments to apply the felony-misdemeanour distinction to the offence which they created were the Infanticide Act 1949 and the Registration of Title Act 1964, see also, Criminal Law Act 1976, s.11(1) and Criminal Law (Jurisdiction) Act 1976, s.20(8); *The Irish Criminal Process* (Mercier Press, Dublin, 1983), pp.2–3.

5   For a useful outline of the development and scope of summary jurisdiction in Ireland see the judgment of O'Higgins C.J. in *State (McEvitt) v. Delap* [1981] I.R. 125 at 129–130.

the administration of justice and an attempt to commit a summary offence, as well as statutory offences such as impeding the enforcement of court orders, fraud in obtaining vehicle insurance, unlawful broadcasting and unlawful carnal knowledge and attempts to commit summary offences. The list has been whittled down in recent years as a result of the abolition of some assault and larceny offences which had originally been listed in the schedule. Indeed, the schedule is probably now of lesser importance in practice as a result of the tendency to create statutory offences which can be tried either on indictment or summarily in certain circumstances. Nevertheless, where a person is before the District Court charged with one of these offences and the court is of the opinion that the facts alleged or proved constitute a minor offence fit to be tried summarily, it may proceed with a summary trial where both the accused and the DPP consent.[5a] The accused must be informed of his right to trial by jury before his consent will be valid.

It is now common practice when a new criminal offence is being created by statute for the enactment to provide for maximum punishments which differ depending on whether conviction resulted from a summary trial or from trial on indictment. The choice between summary trial and trial on indictment in such cases would appear to lie with the prosecutor. If he opts for the former then the offence is summary, and if he opts for the latter the offence is indictable. It is almost as if they are two distinct criminal offences sharing the same substantive definition and differing only in the degree of punishment that may be imposed on conviction. The accused would not appear to have a right to opt for jury trial in such cases where the offence in question is minor. However, where an individual case has commenced as a summary trial and in the course of the proceedings the District judge forms the opinion that the offence in question is not a minor offence, he or she can decline jurisdiction and send the accused forward for trial on indictment providing that the statutory preconditions are satisfied (see chapter 14).

4. Minor and Non-Minor

Constitutional Context

The importance of distinguishing between minor and non-minor offences in Irish criminal procedure stems from Article 38.5 of the Constitution which states: **1–15**

> "Save in the case of the trial of offences under section 2 or section 3 or section 4 of this Article no person shall be tried on any criminal charge without a jury."

Sections 3 and 4 refer to trial by Special Courts and Military Tribunals respectively and, as such, are not directly relevant here. Section 2, however, states:

> "Minor offences may be tried by courts of summary jurisdiction."

[5a] Criminal Justice Act 1951, s.2, as amended by Criminal Justice (Miscellaneous Provisions) Act 1997, s.8.

The combined effect of these provisions has been interpreted as conferring a constitutional right to trial by jury upon every person charged with a criminal offence which is not minor. Any attempt to try an accused summarily with a non-minor criminal offence, therefore, will be vulnerable to constitutional challenge unless it comes within the scope of the Special Criminal Court or Military Tribunal exceptions. Offences are only triable summarily if they qualify as "minor" within the meaning of Article 38.2 of the Constitution.

The Applicable Criteria

A substantial body of judicial decisions on the meaning of a "minor" offence in the context of Article 38.2 has built up over the past forty years. Unfortunately, it cannot be said that they offer a clear and comprehensive test which can be readily applied to the diverse situations that arise from time to time. The Supreme Court first had to deal with the issue in *Melling v. O'Mathghamhna*[6] in 1961. Although both the Supreme Court and the High Court have had to return to the subject on several occasions since, its approach in that case is still the appropriate starting point. The accused was charged with smuggling butter contrary to section 186 of the Customs (Consolidation) Act 1876 which stipulated that the offence was triable summarily and that the penalty was £100 or three times the value of the goods at the election of the Revenue Commissioners.[7] Default in payment of the fine could result in the offender being committed to prison for a period of not less than six and not more than nine months. For a second offence the maximum period of imprisonment increased to 12 months. The Revenue Commissioners elected for a penalty of £100 on each of the 15 charges in the case and the accused responded by instituting proceedings in the High Court claiming that the offences in question were not minor and therefore were triable only by judge and jury.

1–16   On appeal from the High Court, the Supreme Court identified four criteria which were relevant in determining whether an offence was minor: severity of punishment, moral guilt, the state of the law in 1937 when the Constitution was adopted, and public opinion.[8] Of these by far the most important was the severity of punishment which could be imposed. By this the court seemed to have in mind the maximum punishment that could be imposed for the offence in question, as opposed to that which was actually imposed or which was likely to be imposed, in the case. Although this would appear to be a critical point it has not yet been settled definitely one way or the other.[9] Unfortunately, there

---

[6]   [1962] I.R. 1.
[7]   This power of election in the hands of the Revenue Commissioners was later declared unconstitutional in *Deaton v. Attorney General* [1963] I.R. 170, but was not specifically challenged in *Melling*.
[8]   See summary by Walsh J. in *Conroy v. Attorney General* [1965] I.R. 411.
[9]   In *Rollinson v. Kelly* [1984] I.R. 248, for *e.g.*, both O'Higgins C.J. and Hederman J. looked to the maximum punishment that the offence might attract for the accused in the trial. Henchy and Griffin JJ. expressed a preference for the punishment actually imposed. McCarthy J. did not deal with the matter.

has been less clarity and uniformity on the critical issue of when the maximum sentence applicable takes an offence over the border from minor to non-minor. In *Melling*, the majority took the view that a penalty of £100 in 1922 when the Constitution was first enacted was not sufficiently heavy. Similarly, they were of the opinion that a possible sentence of 11 months imprisonment would not be sufficient to produce a non-minor offence, as in 1922 some offences which were triable summarily could attract such a punishment. Kingsmill-Moore J. by comparison felt that the question should be approached primarily from the perspective of what the individual accused might consider to be non-minor. The interests of the executive in channelling more offences through the summary procedure should be consigned to second place. O'Dalaigh J. (as he then was) took a similar approach and both concluded that the offences in question were not minor. However, their emphasis on the circumstances of the individual accused and the context in which the offence was committed make it difficult to put a figure on a fine or term of imprisonment which they consider might trigger the right to a jury trial. O'Dalaigh J. seemed to incline towards a figure in excess of six months in the case of imprisonment and a sum in excess of the value of £100 in 1922 in the case of a fine.

Maximum Sentence of Imprisonment

Since *Melling* the maximum sentence of imprisonment that can be imposed in the case of minor offences would appear to have settled at 12 months.[10] Offences which carry possible sentences of, *inter alia*, terms of imprisonment for a maximum period of six months have consistently qualified as minor.[11] By contrast, offences which are punishable by a period of imprisonment for an indefinite period cannot qualify as minor.[12] The same applies to offences which can be punished by detention in St Patrick's institution for a period of three years.[13] It was significant, however, that St Patrick's was classified as the equivalent of a prison. In *J v. District Justice Delap*,[14] the offender was directed to be detained at Trinity House School in Lusk until he reached the age of 19 years old. This was equivalent to a period of detention of three years and four months. Nevertheless, the High Court found that the offence in question was still minor. Trinity House was a place of education and training as opposed to punishment. The period in question, therefore, could not be considered as the equivalent of three years and four months in a prison or similar place of detention.

1–17

---

10 As yet there has been no firm decision on this point, although there are *dicta* in the Supreme Court decision in *Mallon v. Minister for Agriculture* [1996] 1 I.R. 517 to the effect that a term of imprisonment not exceeding one year would not breach the non-minor category whereas a term of two years would.

11 See, for *e.g.*, *Conroy v. Attorney General* [1965] I.R. 411; *Cullen v. Attorney General* [1979] I.R. 394.

12 *In re Haughey* [1971] I.R. 217.

13 *State (Sheerin) v. Kennedy* [1966] I.R. 379.

14 [1989] I.R. 167.

There are now several statutory offences which are punishable by maximum terms of imprisonment for 12 months and are stated to be triable summarily. None of them has been successfully challenged as infringing the constitutional right to jury trial. It is also worth noting that the District Court cannot impose a term of imprisonment longer than twelve months on conviction for an indictable offence which is tried summarily.[15] However, where two or more offences are charged it can impose consecutive sentences resulting in an aggregate term of imprisonment not exceeding two years.[16] It remains to be seen whether the exercise of this power to produce an aggregate term of imprisonment in excess of 12 months will pass constitutional muster. In *Mallon v. Minister for Agriculture*,[17] the High Court held that a single sentence of two years in prison renders the associated offence non-minor. In the case of consecutive sentences the current judicial approach is to consider the punishment imposed for each offence in isolation from the other.[18] In other words, if none of them considered individually is sufficient to render the associated offence non-minor, they cannot have that effect collectively.

Maximum Monetary Penalty

1–18   There is even less certainty on the issue of what might constitute the maximum permissible monetary penalty for a minor offence. In part this is due to the fact that the value of money changes over time. The courts are agreed that the relevant date for assessing the severity of the monetary penalty is the date on which it is imposed, as opposed to the date when the enactment in question was made.[19] In *Kostan v. Ireland*,[20] a fine in excess of £102,000, not surprisingly, was held to bring the associated offence out of the minor category. In *O'Sullivan v. Hartnett*,[21] it was held that a fine of £10,000 would have the same effect. Both cases involved fisheries offences committed on a commercial scale. At the other end of the scale it would appear from *Melling* that a fine of about £1,500 imposed today would not signify a non-minor offence, even for a small scale smuggler. The maximum figure, therefore, must lie somewhere between £1,500 and £10,000. Unfortunately, it is not really possible to be any more precise than that.

Secondary Punishments

Another complexity associated with the severity of punishment test is the whole issue of secondary punishments. These can, of course, vary enormously. Most of the cases which have come before the courts have concerned the automatic forfeiture of goods and equipment or some sort of automatic disqualification. The problem, however, has been not so much one of assessing

---

[15] Criminal Justice Act 1951, s.4.
[16] Criminal Justice Act 1951, s.5, as amended by Criminal Justice Act 1984, s.12(1).
[17] [1996] 1 I.R. 517.
[18] *State (Rollinson) v. Kelly* [1984] I.R. 248. See also, *Charlton v. Ireland* [1984] I.L.R.M. 39; *State (Wilson) v. District Justice Neylon* [1987] I.L.R.M. 118
[19] *State (Rollinson) v. Kelly* [1984] I.R. 248.
[20] [1978] I.L.R.M. 12.
[21] [1983] I.L.R.M. 79.

the contribution that the secondary penalty makes to the overall punishment, as in determining whether it can be taken into account at all. The general rule is that secondary penalties are irrelevant. In *Conroy v. Attorney General*,[22] the issue was whether the automatic disqualification from holding a driving licence imposed on conviction for drunk-driving could be taken into consideration. Walsh J. explained:

> ". . . the punishment which must be examined for the purpose of gauging the seriousness of an offence is what may be referred to as 'primary punishment.' That is the type of punishment which is regarded as punishment in the ordinary sense and, where crime is concerned, is either the loss of liberty or the intentional penal deprivation of property whether by means of fine or other direct method of deprivation."[23]

Despite the severe consequences that the disqualification would have for the accused it could not be taken into account in assessing the severity of the punishment for the purposes of determining whether the offence was minor. A similar approach was taken, and decision reached, in *State (Pheasantry Ltd) v. Donnelly*[24] with respect to a liquor licence disqualification for repeated infringements of the liquor licensing laws.

The relativity simplicity of this rule is thrown into confusion by the **1–19** conflicting decisions of the High Court in *Kostan v. Ireland*[25] and *Cartmill v. Ireland*.[26] The issue in the former case was the provision for the mandatory forfeiture of the catch and fishing gear on conviction of a summary offences under the fisheries legislation. In this case the gear forfeited was valued in excess of £102,000. McWilliam J. found that the forfeiture was part of the primary punishment and, as such, took the offence out of the minor category. In the latter, the issue was the power to order the forfeiture of gaming machines on conviction for summary offences under the gaming legislation. The machines forfeited in this case were valued at £120,000. Nevertheless, Murphy J. concluded that the forfeiture was analogous to the driving disqualification and as such was too remote to be taken into consideration in assessing the severity of the punishment. *Kostan* does not appear to have been cited to the court in that case. To complicate matters further, in *Cullen v. Attorney General*[27] the High Court ruled that a provision which enabled a District Court, in certain circumstances, to impose an additional fine equal to the amount that the injured person would be entitled to receive in compensation brought the offence into the non-minor category. The offence in question was using a vehicle in a public place without a policy of insurance. The court considered that this additional fine, which was really compensation under another name as it was paid to the injured party, formed part of the primary punishment.

---

[22] [1965] I.R. 411.
[23] *ibid.* at 441.
[24] [1982] I.L.R.M. 512.
[25] [1978] I.L.R.M. 12.
[26] [1987] I.R. 192.
[27] [1979] I.R. 394.

Other Criteria

It is difficult to deduce from the case law what effect, if any, the other criteria are supposed to play in the assessment of whether an offence is minor or non-minor. In *Conroy* it was intimated that some offences were of such grave moral guilt that they could never qualify as minor. Similarly, there was some indications to the effect that the scale on which smuggling offences were committed could have implications for the moral guilt involved and by extension the question of whether they were minor or non-minor. For the most part, however, it would appear that the other criteria play a very minor role relative to the severity of punishment. They might have most influence in pushing the court one way or the other when the arguments on the severity of punishment are evenly balanced.

D. Delay

1. Introduction

1–20 Delay in the prosecution of a criminal case can be unfair to the accused. Excessive delay in the initiation of a prosecution can render it difficult for the accused to prepare his or her defence as the passage of time will make it more difficult to assemble evidence, locate witnesses and recall events relevant to the allegations. Equally, delay in the expedition of proceedings once they have commenced can exacerbate the inevitable stress and anxiety that a person will experience while waiting for criminal allegations against him or her to be determined. Accordingly, it is now firmly established that delay can provide a basis to prevent a prosecution from proceeding, as well as for a defence to the charges or for an appeal against conviction. In practice, it is most likely to feature in a judicial review application for an order of prohibition to prevent the prosecution from proceeding. Indeed, where a trial has been excessively delayed so as to prejudice the accused's chance of obtaining a fair trial the appropriate remedy to protect his constitutional rights is an order prohibiting the trial.[28]

There is now a substantial body of case law on the whole issue of delay as a ground for prohibiting a prosecution.[28a] The most that can be done here is provide an outline of the key general principles established by that case law, followed by an outline of further special factors that have arisen specifically in the context of sexual abuse cases.[29]

---

[28] *State (O'Connell) v. Fawsitt* [1986] I.R. 362.

[28a] For further discussion see Doherty and O'Keeffe "Justice Denied, Delay in Criminal Cases" (1998) 49 N.I.L.Q. 385; S O'Keeffe *The Issue of Delay in Criminal Proceedings* (Limerick, Limerick Papers in Criminal Justice No.4, 2000).

[29] Note that Kelly J. in *Gibbs v. President of Dublin Circuit Criminal Court* unreported, High Court, May 16, 1996 provides a very useful summary of the case law up until May 1996. The cases covered include: *State (Healy) v. Donoghue* [1976] I.R. 325; *State (O'Connell) v. Fawsitt* [1986] I.R. 362; *State (Cuddy) v. Mangan* [1988] I.L.R.M. 720; *DPP v. Byrne* [1994] 2 I.R. 236; *Cahalane v. Murphy* [1994] 2 I.R. 262; *Hogan v. President of the Circuit Court* [1994] 2 I.R. 513; *Fitzpatrick v. District Justice Shiels* unreported, High Court, November 27, 1987; *D v. DPP*

It is worth noting at the outset that a distinction is sometimes drawn between delay and lapse of time.[29a] In this context "delay" generally refers to delay in progressing the prosecution and trial after a formal complaint has been made, while "lapse of time" refers to delay by the complainant in making a complaint sufficient to trigger an investigation. For the purposes of the following account "delay" is used indiscriminately to refer to either or both, although a distinction is drawn between delay by the State and delay by the complainant.

2. Constitutional Right to a Speedy Trial

Although there is no express constitutional right to a speedy trial, the courts have interpreted the Article 38.1 right to a trial in due course of law to embrace an entitlement to a trial with reasonable expedition.[30] The fact that the entitlement to a trial with reasonable expedition is implicit rather than explicit in the Constitution does not dilute its weight.[31] Indeed, Keane J. (as he then was) in his judgment in *P.C. v. DPP* highlighted the importance and long pedigree of the right to a reasonably expeditious trial as follows:

> "The right of an accused person to a reasonably expeditious trial has been recognised as an essential feature of the Anglo-American system of criminal justice for many centuries. In *Klopfer v. North Carolina* (1967) 386 US 213, Warren C.J. traced it to the assize at Clarendon in 1166, to chapter 29 of the Magna Carta and to Coke's Institutes. He pointed out that, not merely did it enjoy a prominent position in the sixth amendment as a discrete right 'to a speedy and public trial': it was also expressly guaranteed by the constitutions of several individual States which formed the new Union."[32]

Similarly, in *DPP v. Byrne*, Finlay C.J. said that:

> "The right to reasonable expedition in the trial of a criminal charge would appear clearly to precede, as a natural right, not only the Constitution of Ireland, but the Constitution of the United States as well, and from an historical point of view would appear to derive directly from the Magna Carta and to be part of the common law."[33]

Nevertheless, the fact that the right is closely associated with the right to a trial in due course of law has meant that it has featured primarily, but not

1–21

1–22

---

unreported, Supreme Court, November 17, 1993. In *J. O'C v. DPP* [2000] 3 I.R. 478. Hardiman J. also offers a comprehensive analysis of civil and criminal cases since *O Domhnaill v. Merrick* [1984] I.R. 151.

[29a] See, for *e.g., DPP v. Byrne* [1994] 2 I.R. 236; *PC v. DPP* [1999] 2 I.R. 25; and *PP v. DPP* [2000] 1 I.R. 403.

[30] See, for *e.g., PM v. District Judge Miriam Malone and the DPP* unreported, Supreme Court, June 7, 2002; *JL v. DPP* [2000] 3 I.R. 122; *P O'C v. DPP* [2000] 3 I.R. 87; *PC v. DPP* [1999] 2 I.R. 25; *B v. DPP* [1997] 3 I.R. 140; *DPP v. Carroll* unreported, Supreme Court, March 2, 1994; *Hogan v. President of the Circuit Court* [1994] 2 I.R. 513; *Cahalane v. Judge Murphy* [1994] 2 I.R. 262; *DPP v. Byrne* [1994] 2 I.R. 236; *State (O'Connell) v. Fawsitt* [1986] I.R. 362; *E O'R v. DPP* [1996] 2 I.L.R.M. 128.

[31] *DPP v. Byrne* [1994] 2 I.R. 236, *per* Finlay C.J. at 244; *Gibbs v. President of Dublin Circuit Criminal Court and the DPP* unreported, High Court, May 16, 1996.

[32] [1999] 2 I.R. 25 at 65.

[33] [1994] 2 I.R. 236 at 245.

exclusively,[34] in the context of whether the accused's right to a fair trial has been prejudiced as a result of delay.[35] On several occasions the Supreme Court has emphasised that:

> ". . . the public interest in ensuring that every person charged with a criminal offence receives a fair trial must, where a conflict arises, take precedence over the unquestionable public interest in the prosecution and punishment of crime."[36]

Painful though it will be to victims this means that a prosecution cannot proceed in the absence of a guilty plea where the accused's right to a fair trial has been prejudiced by the passage of time between the crime and the commencement of criminal proceedings.

3. Impact of Delay on Right to a Fair Trial

1–23   In his dissenting judgment in *J O'C v. DPP*,[37] Hardiman J. presented a graphic illustration of the injustice that can flow from delay in the determination of criminal allegations against an individual.[38] Although he was dealing specifically with delay in triggering the criminal process his remarks apply with equal force to delay by the prosecution in progressing a case through to a conclusion. The primary problem is the "fade factor". Since proof of guilt in a criminal matter will often depend very heavily on the oral testimony of witnesses, it is of vital importance that that evidence is given and tested at the earliest opportunity. Even relatively short passages of time can result in witnesses forgetting crucial facts or, perhaps even more damaging, giving false evidence which the witness believes to be true as a result of faulty recall. This memory problem can also afflict the accused in that he or she may experience great difficulty in recalling his or her own movements, actions and associations on certain dates or even periods many years previously.[38a] If he or she is advanced in years he or she may also suffer the disadvantage of having to cope with preparing a defence to serious criminal allegations in conditions of poorer physical and mental health than would have been the case had he or she been called upon to do so at or closer to the time when he or she was alleged to have committed the offence in question. The passage of time can also result in the loss of witnesses or material evidence which would otherwise have been available had there not been a

---

[34]   See *PM v. District Judge Malone and the DPP* unreported, Supreme Court, June 7, 2002.

[35]   Murphy J. has preferred to separate the constitutional right to a trial with reasonable expedition from the right to a fair trial. He considers that the former relates to the timescale which commences with the DPP or other appropriate State agencies obtaining sufficient information and evidence to prosecute the crime. The latter is broad enough to encompass delay from other sources. See *SF v. DPP* [1999] 3 I.R. 235 and *J O'C v. DPP* [2000] 3 I.R. 478.

[36]   *P O'C v. DPP* [2000] 3 I.R. 87, *per* Keane C.J. at 96–97. See also *D v. DPP* [1994] 2 I.R. 465; *Z v. DPP* [1994] 2 I.R. 476; *JL v. DPP* [2000] 3 I.R. 122.

[37]   [2000] 3 I.R. 480.

[38]   Hardiman J.'s treatment of this issue was approved by McGuinness J. in *JL v. DPP* [2000] 3 I.R. 122 at 133.

[38a]   See also, *McNamara v. MacGruairc* unreported, Supreme Court, July 15, 2001.

delay in bringing the case to trial. These factors can combine to deprive the accused's right to be heard of any substantive meaning.[39]

4. Impact on Personal Rights

It is worth emphasising that the relevance of delay is not confined to the accused's right to a fair trial. It can have other consequences which, in appropriate circumstances, will infringe the constitutional rights of the accused to the extent that it would be improper to proceed with the trial.[40] In *PM v. District Judge Malone and the DPP*,[41] Keane C.J. identified anxiety and stress as well as extended loss of liberty as possible consequences. While the latter may remedied by *habeas corpus* the former can only be remedied by a speedy trial. Generally, stress and anxiety are associated with the effects of a public accusation of serious criminality and, as such, arise only in the context of post-charge delay.[41a] The Chief Justice, however, went on to explain that stress and anxiety can arise not just where there has been delay between the initial charge and the trial, but also where there has been a delay in preferring a charge in the first place. The circumstances of the case may be such that the accused will still suffer stress and anxiety even during the period when no formal charge has been laid against him or her. On the facts of this case, for example, the victim made a complaint to a psychologist and a social worker who, in turn reported the matter to the gardai. A formal criminal complaint was not lodged until nearly 10 years later. In these circumstances, Keane C.J. considered that the accused could suffer stress and anxiety:

> "There may be stigmatisation of the accused, loss of privacy, disruption of family, social life and work, legal costs and uncertainty as to the future. In the present case, it is reasonable to infer that the applicant was subjected to anxiety and concern as from the time the investigation began in 1991."[42]

Accordingly, Keane C.J. concluded that both pre-charge and post-charge delay could be considered in determining whether an accused's right to a trial with reasonable expedition could be infringed by stress and anxiety attributable to the delay.[43]

1–24

1–25

---

[39] For further discussion of the legal problems which can arise in prosecutions many years after the offence in the specific context of child sexual abuse, see P Lewis and A Mullis *Delayed Criminal Prosecutions in Childhood Sexual Abuse: Ensuring a Fair Trial* (1999) 115 L.Q.R. 265.

[40] In *Barker v. Wingo* (1972) 407 US 514 at 532, Powell J. identified the following three interests of defendants in securing a speedy trial: "(i) to prevent oppressive pre-trial incarceration; (ii) to minimise anxiety and concern of the accused; and (iii) to limit the possibility that the defence will be impaired." This quotation has been approved on several occasions by the Irish courts. See, *e.g.*, *DPP v. Byrne* [1994] 2 I.R. 236; *State (O'Connell) v. Fawsitt* [1986] I.R. 362. See also Judicial Committee of the Privy Council in *Bell v. DPP* [1985] A.C. 937.

[41] unreported, Supreme Court, June 7, 2002.

[41a] see also *McNamara v. McGruaire* unreported, Supreme Court, July 5, 2001.

[42] *ibid.* at 38.

[43] Disapproving *Mills and The Queen* [1986] 29 D.L.R., and distinguishing *O'Flynn v. Clifford* [1988] 1 I.R. 740.

The Chief Justice went on to explain that in determining whether the stress and anxiety occasioned by the delay are sufficient to justify prohibiting the trial, the court must engage in a balancing exercise:

> "The essential issue for resolution is, accordingly, as to whether the stress and anxiety caused to the applicant as a result of the violation of his constitutional right to a reasonably expeditious trial justifies the prohibition of the trial proceeding at this stage. If this were a case in which it could be said that his ability to defend himself had been impaired and, as a result, there was a real and substantial risk of an unfair trial then, as pointed out by Denham J. in *D v. DPP* [1994] 1 I.L.R.M. 435, the applicant's right to a fair trial would necessarily outweigh the community's right to prosecute. Where, as here, the violation of the right has not jeopardised the right to a fair trial, but has caused unnecessary stress and anxiety to the applicant, the court must engage in a balancing process. On one side of the scales, there is the right of the accused to be protected from stress and anxiety caused by an unnecessary and inordinate delay. On the other side, there is the public interest in the prosecution and conviction of those guilty of criminal offences. In all such cases, the court will necessarily be concerned with the nature of the offence and the extent of the delay."[44]

5. Impact on Children

1–26
The issue of delay takes on a special importance in the trial of children. In *BF v. DPP*,[45] for example, a 14 year old child was charged with sexual offences against two young girls in mid-1995. Due to local hostility the defendant's family moved to England; a move which was not discouraged by the gardai. Subsequently, extradition proceedings were commenced in July 1997 but no attempt was made to progress them until February 1998. The defendant returned voluntarily in August 1998 and criminal proceedings were commenced. He was returned for trial in January 1999 at which point he sought order of prohibition on the grounds of delay. In effect, although the necessary evidence for a prosecution was available by May 1995 the prosecution was not initiated until two years and nine months later. The question for the Supreme Court on the case was whether the delay was excessive and inexcusable.

> "This was a case where on all the evidence it appears to have been a somewhat marginal decision as to whether a prosecution should have been brought at all. While from the point of view of the parents of the victims, the offences understandably seemed horrific, it may well be that there was no serious criminal intent on the part of the appellant. It is obviously impossible to predict how the evidence would unfold at a trial, but even upon conviction it might well be a case where a custodial sentence would not be imposed. A case of this kind should be handled by the prosecuting authorities with the utmost sensitivity, and it is only fair to say that some sensitivity was shown in this case. But in one area there was default. It was of the utmost importance that if it was decided to proceed with charges, there should be no delay so that a trial would take place

---

44   *op. cit.* at 42–43.
45   [2001] 1 I.R. 656.

while memories were fresh and while the appellant was reasonably close to the age at which he is alleged to have committed the offences. A trial of an adult in respect of an offence which he committed as a child, and particularly a sexual offence, takes on a wholly different character from a trial of a child who has committed such offences while a child. This is true quite independently of the different penal provisions applicable to a child or young person, a point also relied on by the appellant. There was, in my view, a special obligation of expedition in this case, but that obligation was not complied with in that the extradition proceedings were allowed to take an excessive length of time, and this delay appears to be inexplicable."[46]

6. Delay by the State

Introduction

A delay sufficient to result in a denial of the accused's right to a trial with reasonable expedition can result either from a failure on the part of the State to progress the prosecution with reasonable expedition or from a failure on the part of the victim to lodge a complaint within a reasonable time. There may, of course, be cases in which delay on the part of both the complainant and the State combines to deny the accused his or her right to a trial with reasonable expedition. While the general principles applicable to delay do not differ markedly depending on the source of the delay, the application of those principles can differ in some important respects depending on whether the source of the delay is the State or the victim. For ease of explication, therefore, delay by the State and the victim will be dealt with separately and in that order, even though the basic principles are common to both.

1–27

Source of Delay

Excessive delay on the part of the State in commencing or progressing proceedings against the accused can be fatal to the accused's right to a fair trial.[47] The delay can result from the acts or omissions of any one or more of the State authorities involved in the investigation, detection, prosecution and trial of the offence, including the Garda Síochána and the courts service. It does not matter that the DPP has no power of direction or control over the authority responsible for the delay.[48] In *DPP (Coleman) v. Mc Neill,* [49] the Supreme Court declared that "there is a solemn responsibility on anyone having anything to do with prosecuting cases to make sure that they are brought to court with all due expedition."[50] Similarly, in *DPP v. Arthurs,* the High Court declared that:

---

[46]   *ibid.* at 663–664.
[47]   *BF v. DPP* [2001] I.R. 656; *B v. DPP* [1997] 3 I.R. 140; *DPP v. Byrne* [1994] 2 I.R. 236. See *DPP v. Arthurs* [2000] 2 I.L.R.M. 363 for a summary of the relevant legal principles extracted from the case law.
[48]   *DPP v. Byrne* [1994] 2 I.R. 236.
[49]   [1999] 1 I.R. 91.
[50]   *ibid.* at 96.

" . . . a necessary corollary of that right [to a speedy or expeditious trial] is that there rests upon the State a duty to ensure that all reasonable steps are taken to ensure such a speedy trial is provided. This must necessarily mean conducting the investigation and prosecution in a manner which, in so far as it is reasonably practicable, eliminates unnecessary delay, and must additionally mean that such resources as are necessary for the orderly and expeditious processing of criminal cases through the courts are provided."[51]

Onus on the Accused

1–28   The onus is on the accused to establish that there has been unreasonable delay in his or her case.[52] Even if the accused discharges this onus it does not follow that he or she will succeed in his or her application to have the trial prohibited. He or she will have to go on to show that: (i) he will suffer actual or presumptive prejudice as a result of the delay; or (ii) that the delay is so inordinate or excessive as to give rise to a necessary inference that the trial will be unfair. If he succeeds in establishing either then the court must prohibit the trial on the grounds that the accused's right to a fair trial was necessarily infringed. In this event it would not matter what explanation the prosecution advanced for the delay. Even if the delay is not sufficient to satisfy (i) or (ii) the accused may still succeed in prohibiting his trial if he can show that there has been inordinate delay in his case and that the cause of that delay can be traced to neglect on the part of the State. Much will depend on the facts of the individual case. Basing himself on the Supreme Court judgments in *DPP v. Byrne*[53] and *DPP v. McNeill*,[54] O'Neill J. stated the law as follows in *DPP v. Arthurs*:

> "The judgments of the Supreme Court in these two cases seem to me to establish that where an accused person proves to the satisfaction of the court that there has been excessive delay in bringing his case to trial caused by the State, he must thereafter satisfy one or other of two tests before a court would exercise its discretion to refuse to proceed with the trial. The first of these tests is that the accused person must show that he has or is likely to suffer an actual specified prejudice or that the length of the delay is so inordinate or excessive as to give rise to a necessary inference that there is a real risk that the trial will be unfair. Where an accused person satisfied the above test, it would seem to me that regardless of what reasons may be advanced by the prosecution to justify the delay, be they good or bad, that the accused person's right to an expeditious trial would necessarily be infringed, and hence the accused's constitutional right to an expeditious trial is to be preferred as against the right of the community to prosecute the alleged offence.
>
> The second test is one which focuses directly on the causes for the delay or the reasons or excuses that are advanced in order to justify it as distinct from the effect, specific or inferred, which the delay may have on the accused's defence, and would apply in circumstances where in the words of Finlay C.J. at pp.246/96 of the report in the *Byrne* case:

---

51   [2000] 2 I.L.R.M. 363 at 376.
52   [1994] 2 I.R. 236.
53   *ibid.*
54   [1999] 1 I.R. 91.

'. . . failure to establish actual or presumptive prejudice may not conclude the issues which have to be determined . . .'

Here what is envisaged, as is clear from the judgment of Finlay C.J. are circumstances where the conduct of the proceedings on behalf of the State might range from at one extreme conduct amounting to downright mala fides across a range including gross carelessness or simple negligence, or as was mentioned in the *Barker v. Wingo* case and, as in fact occurred in this case, overcrowded courts. These factors are relevant because in themselves they can constitute breaches of an accused person's constitutional right to a speedy or expeditious trial."[55]

Relevant Factors

The longer the period of unexplained delay in bringing the accused to trial the **1–29** more likely it is that it will be considered unreasonable and a breach of the individual's right to an expeditious trial. A delay may be so inordinate or excessive that it gives rise to a necessary inference that there is a real risk that the trial will be unfair.[56] Each case, however, will depend on its own particular circumstances to the extent that relatively short periods of delay may be considered unreasonable, while much longer periods may be considered reasonable. In *DPP v. Byrne*,[57] for example, the Supreme Court made it clear that the question whether there had been excessive delay would depend on the circumstances of the case, and especially factors such as the nature of the offence, the cause of the delay and the possibility of prejudice to the defence. The court also accepted that the period of delay may be so long that prejudice could be inferred without the need for proof of specific prejudice. It went on to hold that a period of 10 months from the commission of the offence of drunk driving to the summary trial was not sufficient to prohibit the trial, in the absence of evidence of specific prejudice to the accused.[58] Similarly, in *DPP v. Kilbride*,[59] the High Court was not persuaded that a period of 12 months between the alleged commission of a drunk driving offence and the date of trial, which involved a delay of over six months, was sufficient to prohibit the trial in the absence of specific prejudice to the accused.[60] In *Mulready v.*

---

[55] [2000] 2 I.L.R.M. 363 at 375–376.

[56] *DPP v. Carlton* [1993] 1 I.R. 81; *DPP v. Arthurs* [1999] 1 I.L.R.M. 452. In *Arthurs* a delay of well over two years, while considered to be inordinate and excessive for summary proceedings, did not automatically qualify as being sufficient to raise a presumption of prejudice. In *DPP v. Rice* [2000] 2 I.L.R.M. 393, a series of delays which cumulatively would result in the accused being re-tried in summary proceedings five years after he had been acquitted on the merits was considered to be unfair without the need for proof of actual prejudice.

[57] [1994] 2 I.R. 236.

[58] This was a majority 3:2 decision. The minority considered that even a 10 month delay would be unreasonable in respect of a straightforward summary charge of drunk driving, especially where the consequences of conviction were such that the accused would suffer from anxiety and stress while awaiting the outcome. The minority were also extremely reluctant to overturn the trial judge's assessment of what was unreasonable in the circumstances of the case.

[59] [1999] 1 I.L.R.M. 452.

[60] In *DPP v. Carlton* [1993] I.R. 81, the Supreme Court held that a period of eight months to issue a summons for a road traffic offence was not excessive as it was only two months more than the statutory period of six months permitted for submitting a complaint; unreported, Supreme Court, March 2, 1994.

DPP,[61] it was held that a gap of 21 months between the date of commission of the offences and the date that they were listed to be heard was undesirable, but not sufficiently excessive to prohibit the trial. Only four months of the delay was attributable to the State.

1–30   In assessing whether the delay is excessive the courts can take into account the period from when the accused could first have been charged to the commencement of proceedings, as well as the period from commencement to trial.[62] This will be particularly relevant where the complaint of delay is directed primarily at a failure on the part of the Garda Síochána to conduct the investigation with reasonable diligence coupled with a failure on the part of the DPP to prefer charges when they could have been preferred. However, where the delay is due to the authorities not having sufficient information with which to charge the accused it will not normally be sufficient to prohibit the prosecution on the ground of a breach of the accused's constitutional right to a fair trial. Indeed, in *Lynch v. DPP*,[63] both the High Court and the Supreme Court accepted that gardai were entitled to postpone charging until they were sure that the grounds for laying charges were justifiable and reasonable. The courts also accepted that a delay of 15 months between the earliest date upon which a charge could have been laid and the date upon which it was laid could constitute grounds for prohibiting the prosecution from proceeding. Such delay could hamper the accused's capacity to recollect events for the purpose of preparing his defence. Nevertheless both courts refused to prohibit the trial as, on the facts, the accused had failed to establish that he would suffer prejudice as a result of any such delay.

In *Cahalane v. Judge Murphy*,[64] the Supreme Court upheld the High Court's decision to prohibit the trial on the basis of excessive delay. In that case the period from when the applicant was first questioned by gardai to the return for trial was seven years. During that period there had been substantial delays in taking the decision to charge the accused and subsequently in taking deposition statements from witnesses. The latter delays were occasioned by a desire not to inconvenience the situation with regard to judges of the District Court and with regard to the availability of court accommodation. Although the case was quite complex, involving an alleged conspiracy to defraud the Revenue, the court found that the delays lacked any reasonable explanation. This, coupled with the fact that the defendant suffered anxiety and possible financial hardship due to the delay, meant that it would not be fair to the accused to proceed with the trial. By comparison in *McNamara v. Judge Uinsin MacGruairc*,[65] the Supreme Court concluded that there had been excessive and unexplained delay on the part of the State in preparing the book of

---

[61] [2001] 1 I.L.R.M. 382. See also *DPP v. Carroll* unreported, Supreme Court, March 2, 1994.

[62] *Hogan v. President of Circuit Court* [1994] 2 I.R. 513; *SF v. DPP* [1999] 3 I.R. 235; *PM v. District Judge Malone and the DPP* unreported, Supreme Court, June 7, 2002.

[63] SC, June 10, 1999. See also, *O'Flynn v. Clifford* [1988] 1 I.R. 740; but note *PM v. District Judge Malone and the DPP* unreported, Supreme Court, June 7, 2002.

[64] [1994] 2 I.R. 262.

[65] Unreported, Supreme Court, July 5, 2001.

evidence and bringing the case to trial. Nevertheless, it found that the accused were never led to believe that they would not be prosecuted, they were not left in a particular state of anxiety or concern by the delay and they could not point convincingly to any specific prejudice suffered as a result of the delay. Accordingly, the court upheld the High Court refusal's to grant an order of prohibition restraining their trial.

By comparison in *McKenna v. Presiding Judge*[65a] the High Court broke up the periods of delay into their constituent parts and examined the State's justification for the delay at each stage. It found that the delay of 14 months between the date of complaint and the first arrest of the accused was justifiable as the charges and associated investigation were quite complicated. Then there was a delay of four years and four months between the first arrest and the second arrest of the accused. This period was divided into three sections. The court found that some parts of the delay during this stage were justifiable while no justification was offered for other parts. It concluded that taken as a whole the delay was inordinate and inexusable.

The State cannot avoid the consequences of excessive delay by pleading a **1–31** shortage of judges or overcrowded courts. While a delay occasioned by an overcrowded court timetable in a summary case may be excusable on one occasion, repeated delays in the same case will not, particularly where they are coupled with other delays in bringing the case to trial. In *DPP v. Arthurs*, an additional delay of over nine months caused by a lack of resources in the District Court was considered sufficient in itself to amount to a breach of the accused's constitutional rights:

> "The failure on the part of the State to have made adequate provision for the expeditious conduct of cases in the District Court in question resulting, as it did, in the adding to an already excessive delay a further five months delay, bringing the total delay to two years and three months, was in my opinion, an unwarranted invasion of the accused's constitutional right to an expeditious trial. In that circumstance, notwithstanding the absence of evidence of prejudice, actual or presumptive, the learned district judge was obliged to prevent such an invasion of the accused's constitutional right and should have acceded to the accused's request not to allow the trial to proceed."[66]

If the delay is occasioned by the actions of the accused himself it will not normally be sufficient to prohibit the prosecution from proceeding.[67] This is dealt with further below in the context of sexual abuse cases.

7. Delay by the Complainant

Introduction

For summary offences a complaint must normally be lodged within the period **1–32** of six months from the date of the alleged offence, otherwise it becomes time-

---

[65a] Unreported, High Court, January 14, 2000.
[66] [2000] 2 I.L.R.M. 363 at 377.
[67] *JL v. DPP* [2000] 3 I.R. 122. See review of the case law by Hardiman J. in his dissenting judgment in *J O'C v. DPP* [2000] 3 I.R. 478.

barred. For indictable offences, however, there is no statutory period of limitations.[68] Nevertheless, it is now firmly established that excessive delay in lodging a complaint can provide a basis to prohibit the prosecution on the ground that it would be unfair to the accused to proceed with a trial due to the lapse of time from the commission of the offence. It is not possible to be precise about what constitutes an excessive delay for this purpose. The period of delay may be so long that it automatically raises an inference that the accused's right to a fair trial would be infringed.[69] It is not possible to be prescriptive about what length of time will be sufficient to raise the inference. A delay of 13 years from the date of the alleged offence to the lodging of the complaint, for example, has been described as "inordinate and inexusable" in the absence of extenuating circumstances.[70] There may, however, be factors which render an even longer period of delay excusable,[71] and factors which render a much shorter period inexcusable.

The primary factors which can excuse even very long periods of delay concern the nature of the crime and the actions of the accused in preventing a complaint from being made earlier. These factors have featured most prominently in recent years in the context of sexual offences where the offender was in a position of authority or dominance over the victim. Indeed, such cases are now treated as a special category in this context, although not to the extent that excessive delay in making a complaint will be automatically excused where the complaint relates to child sexual abuse.[72] It is also worth noting at the outset that the principles governing the impact of delay on the trial of indictable offences involving child sexual abuse cases do not differ depending on whether the case is tried on indictment on summarily.[73]

Impact of Dominion

1–33   If the victim can establish that he or she did not make a complaint for many years because of the psychological impact of the crime on him or her, and/or because of the extent to which he or she was subject to the dominion of the offender, then the delay will not of itself be sufficient grounds to halt the trial.

---

[68] This is the case even where an indictable offence is tried summarily; *DPP v. Logan* [1994] 3 I.R. 254; *S v. DPP* unreported, Supreme Court, December 19, 2000.

[69] *J O'C v. DPP* [2000] 3 I.R. 478.

[70] *P. O'C v. DPP* [2000] 3 I.R. 87 at 95, *per* Keane J. See also *JL v. DPP* [2000] 3 I.R., *per* McGuinness J. with respect to 21 years. But note views of Murphy J. in *SF v. DPP* [1999] 3 I.R. 235.

[71] In *B v. DPP* [1997] 3 I.R. 140, for *e.g.*, the trial was allowed to proceed even though the alleged offences had taken place over 20 to 30 years earlier. The delay was due entirely to the brutal dominance which the accused father had exercised over his family and three daughters who were the victims. In *S v. DPP* unreported, Supreme Court, December 19, 2000 a delay of 20 to 30 years did not prevent the trial from proceeding where the delay was due to the dominion of the accused over the victims and there was no specific aspect of his defence which was prejudiced by the delay to the extent that it presented a real and serious risk of an unfair trial.

[72] *G v. DPP* [1994] 1 I.R. 374; *B v. DPP* [1997] 3 I.R. 140; *PC v. DPP* [1999] 2 I.R. 25; *J O'C v. DPP* [2000] 3 I.R. 478; *JL v. DPP* [2000] 3 I.R. 122; *PM v. District Judge Malone and the DPP* unreported, Supreme Court, June 7, 2002; *S v. DPP* unreported, Supreme Court, December 19, 2000; *E O'R v. DPP* [1996] 2 I.L.R.M. 128.

[73] *S v. DPP* unreported, Supreme Court, December 19, 2000.

This is most likely to arise in the context of sexual offences committed by an adult against a young child,[74] and particularly where the adult is in a position to exercise authority or control over the child.[75] The obvious example is the relationship between a child and his or her parent,[76] guardian, older sibling[77] or other close adult relation. Equally, however, it can encompass relationships such as a teacher and child, a priest and child or a doctor and child.[78] In *J O'C v. DPP*,[79] the Supreme Court accepted that the accused was an authority figure for this purpose in the eyes of the victim on the basis that the accused was a sergeant in the Garda Siochana, a next door neighbour and a close friend of the family while the victim was a child of tender years. In *PC v. DPP*,[80] it was accepted that a bus driver who took children swimming and helped to teach them to swim every week was a sufficient authority figure to establish dominion over the children. Even a disparity in age may be sufficient in appropriate cases.[81] In *PC v. DPP*, Keane J. (as he then was) explained:

> "There are cases, however, of which this is one, where the disparity in age between the complainant and the person accused is such that the possibility arises that the failure to report the offence is explicable, having regard to the reluctance of young children to accuse adults of improper behaviour and feelings of guilt and shame experienced by the child because of his or her participation, albeit unwillingly, in what he or she sees as wrongdoing. In addition, of course, in individual cases there may be threats, actual or implied, of punishment if the alleged offences are reported."[82]

As the child gets older and more independent of the dominating adult, it will become progressively more difficult to justify a failure to make a complaint. Nevertheless, the circumstances may be such that delay well into adulthood will be excusable. This is most likely to happen where the adult has exercised such a dominant control over the victim during his or her childhood days that the victim has not been psychologically able to make a complaint until many

---

[74] In *Hogan v. President of the Circuit Court* [1994] 2 I.R. 513 at 521, Finlay C.J. said that "... cases consisting of charges by young children in regard to assaults on them at an early age which are not brought to the attention of the authorities by such children until many years after they occurred involve wholly different considerations from those applicable to [other cases]"

[75] *PC v. DPP* [1999] 2 I.R. 25. In *P O'C v. DPP* [2000] 3 I.R. 87, Denham J. was prepared to cast the net widely to include: the relative ages of the accused and victim, the issue of dominance, the relationship of the parties, the place of the alleged abuse and the nature of the abuse. She also notes that as knowledge of the nature and effects of child sexual abuse grows and as medical, psychiatric and psychological evidence is expanded and presented to the courts other factors may become more apparent; *op. cit.* at pp.98–99. See also, *B v. DPP* [1997] 3 I.R. 140; *P.C. v. DPP* [1999] 2 I.R. 25.

[76] *B v. DPP* [1997] 3 I.R. 140.

[77] Age difference and the surrounding circumstances can be important here. If both parties were children when the abuse started and there was only a few years age difference between them then it is highly unlikely that dominion could be established; see *PM v. District Judge Malone and the DPP* unreported, Supreme Court, June 7, 2002.

[78] *P. O'C v. DPP* [2000] 3 I.R. 87; *SM v. DPP* unreported, High Court, December 20, 1999; *S v. DPP* unreported, Supreme Court, December 19, 2000.

[79] *J O'C v. DPP* [2000] 3 I.R. 478.

[80] *PC v. DPP* [1999] 2 I.R. 25.

[81] *JL v. DPP* [2000] 3 I.R. 122.

[82] [1999] 2 I.R. 25 at 67.

years after the formal relationship with the adult has ended.[83] It may also happen that there are circumstances which convinced the victim that there was no point in making a complaint as she would not be believed. If, for example, the victim reported the matter to a trusted adult, such as a parent or teacher, and no action was taken at the time, this might be considered a factor justifying further delay on the part of the complainant.[84] On the other hand, delay will not be excused where the victim has exercised a free will not to make a complaint, only to decide years later, for whatever reason, to initiate the criminal process. Even if the complainant opts not to complain earlier in order to avoid difficulties within the family or because of a fear that she would be ostracised from the family, that will not be sufficient to bring the case into the exceptional category where the delay can be excused as resulting from the actions of the accused.[85]

Repressed Memory

1–34   More controversially, there have been suggestions in some of the cases that repressed memory can be a factor justifying delay. This refers to the situation where a person blocks out all memory of an event or events in his or life because it is too traumatic to face up to it. The memory is then triggered many years later, usually as a result of counselling to deal with psychological problems. As of yet there is considerable controversy in the psychiatry and psychology professions whether repressed memory is an actual phenomenon and, more particularly, whether events recalled from a repressed memory due to counselling are reliable.[86] In his carefully researched judgment in *JL v. DPP*,[87] Hardiman J. urges caution in the acceptance of repressed memory as a justification for delay in sexual abuse cases. At the very least the expert psychological evidence must be sufficient, detailed and factual to facilitate an assessment of the reliability of the recalled events:

> "Certainly, it seems to me that the whole factual background, including full details of the circumstances in which the allegations came to be made, whether the nature of the allegations changed over time, whether other allegations were made against other persons, and whether repression in the clinical sense is or is not alleged should I believe form part of the report for the purpose of a case such as this."[88]

Later in the same judgment, with specific reference to the expert psychological evidence implying that a repressed memory was an operating factor justifying delay in the case, he goes on to say:

---

[83]   *PC v. DPP* [1999] 2 I.R. 25; *B v. DPP* [1997] 3 I.R. 140.

[84]   *J O'C v. DPP* [2000] 3 I.R. 478; *PC v. DPP* [1999] 2 I.R. 25.

[85]   *PM v. District Judge Malone and the DPP* unreported, Supreme Court, June 7, 2002. Even an acute compassion for the mother who has already suffered immensely at the hands of the father may not be a sufficient excuse in a case where the victim claims to have been abused by her father; *B v. DPP* [1997] 2 I.R. 140.

[86]   For further discussion see: P Casey and C Craven *Psychiatry and the Law* (Oaktree Press, Dublin, 1999), chap. 5.

[87]   *JL v. DPP* [2000] 3 I.R. 122.

[88]   *ibid.* at 151.

"I have discussed the psychological evidence in this case at some little length for three reasons. First, I think it expresses a view as to the excusability of delay or lapse of time in these cases which has not been expressly argued or pronounced upon by the courts and which may require further attention. Secondly, in order to emphasise the need for provision of a comprehensive factual history of the circumstances allegedly leading to disclosure. In practice, it appears to me that this will often require that at least part of such evidence be that of a counsellor or other person to whom, it is said, the disclosure was first made, and the details of the content of the initial disclosure. Without this it seems to me that psychological evidence will often be at an unacceptably theoretical level. And thirdly to indicate the controversies which surround theories of repression and blocking out in the hope that these, if thought to be relevant by the advisers to any party, may be further explored in a suitable case."[89]

Suspending Presumption of Innocence

When the court has to determine whether the delay was the result of the impact of the accused's conduct on the victim, it is placed in an invidious position. Either it must embark upon an inquiry into the truth of the victim's allegations of domination by the accused, or it assumes for the limited purpose of determining the impact of the delay on the victim that the allegations are true. The former option is a non-starter as it could result in the accused effectively having to establish his or her innocence in order to prevent a trial in which the prosecution would otherwise have to establish his or her guilt. Moreover, the inquiry would have to be conducted in the absence of the jury which, in turn, would mean that the accused's innocence or guilt would effectively be determined by the judge alone. By proceeding on the assumption that the allegations against the accused are true the court runs the risk of denying the accused's entitlement to the presumption of innocence, albeit in the limited context of the determination of whether the delay is sufficient in itself to halt the trial. Some members of the Supreme Court have expressed considerable unease at any such encroachment on the presumption of innocence. In his dissenting judgment in *P O'C v. DPP*,[90] Hardiman J. mounted a stout defence of the presumption of innocence and its central importance at all stages of the criminal process in child sexual abuse cases. He also seemed to reject the proposition that it was necessary to assume that the allegations against the complainant were true in order to determine whether the victim's delay in making a complaint was sufficient to prohibit the trial.[91] In doing so, however, the learned judge does not explain how the court can determine this preliminary matter without effectively embarking upon a trial of charges themselves.

In another powerful judgment in support of the presumption of innocence in *P O'C v. DPP*,[92] Murray J. suggests an approach which would treat delay

1–35

---

[89] *ibid.* at 152.
[90] [2000] 3 I.R. 87.
[91] In *JL v. DPP* [2000] 3 I.R. 122, however, the learned judge intimated that the presumption of innocence applied throughout all stages of the process, subject to the assumption that the complaint is true for the limited purpose of determining whether the delay could be attributed to the accused's conduct.
[92] [2000] 3 I.R. 87.

in the making of a complaint as an inherent feature in any case of child sexual abuse at the hands of an adult:

> "I conclude therefore that the right of the State to proceed with the prosecution of offences involving sexual abuse on young people derives from the fact that delay is an inherent feature of such crimes and is explicable by reference to the nature of the offence. Consequently, it is not based on any presumed criminal responsibility or culpability of the accused for bringing about that delay in the particular case."[93]

1–36   Despite these eloquent arguments in favour of an absolute presumption of innocence, the current position would appear to be that it can be put on hold temporarily for the limited purpose of determining whether the delay was caused by the actions of the accused. This takes the form of an assumption that the allegations are true, but only for the purpose of establishing whether the delay can be attributed to the actions of the accused.[94] This would be followed, where necessary, by a full reinstatement of the presumption of innocence in the inquiry into whether the accused's right to a fair trial would be prejudiced by the delay.[95] Delivering the lead judgment in *P O'C v. DPP*, Keane C.J. was forthright in adopting this approach. In his view there was no other way in which the court could realistically embark upon the inquiry into whether the conduct of the accused was responsible for the victim's delay in making the complaint:

> ". . . the inquiry conducted by the court which is asked to halt the trial necessarily involves an assumption by the court that the allegation of the victim is true. Without such an assumption, it would not be possible for the court to conduct any such inquiry and the court would be obliged automatically to halt the trial of a person because of the expiry of a lengthy period of time, even though the failure to make a complaint was due to domination exercised by the adult over the young child during the period of abuse and even where – as happened in a number of cases – the abuse has been perpetrated over many years by a parent or step-parent of a child actually living in the family home with the perpetrator. Since that patently cannot be the law, the presumption of innocence which applied in its full rigour to a criminal trial cannot apply to inquiries of this nature."[96]

Having embarked upon the inquiry the court must determine whether on a balance of probabilities the failure of the victim to report the offending conduct earlier was the result of the conduct itself and/or domination of the victim by the adult. Expert evidence from a psychologist who has interviewed and assessed the impact of the alleged abuse on the complainant will often play a central role.[97]

---

[93]   *ibid.* at 106.
[94]   In making this determination the accused must not be criticised or prejudiced by a failure to deny the allegations or assert his innocence in the course of an application to prohibit the trial on the grounds of delay; *S v. DPP* unreported, Supreme Court, December 19, 2000.
[95]   See *J O'C v. DPP* [2000] 3 I.R. 478.
[96]   [2000] 3 I.R. 87 at 94.
[97]   See the judgment of Hardiman J. in *J O'C v. DPP* [2000] 3 I.R. 478 for a critical analysis of the

Inquiry into Possible Prejudice

Even if the court decides that the victim's delay in making the complaint was **1–37** the result of the actions of the accused it does not inevitably follow that the trial will proceed. It may be that the delay has been such that the accused is prejudiced in preparing his or her defence. As noted above, the accused's right to a fair trial must, in the event of a conflict, take precedence over the public interest in the prosecution of crime. Accordingly, it may be necessary for the court to embark upon a further inquiry aimed at determining whether the delay will cause the accused to suffer prejudice in preparing his or her defence. In this inquiry the full presumption of innocence is re-instated.[98] Keane C.J. explains the position as follows in *P. O'C*:

> "There remains, however, a further inquiry which must be conducted by the court in every case, i.e. as to whether the degree to which the applicant's ability to defend himself or herself has been impaired is such that the trial should not be allowed to proceed. The assumption made solely in the context of the earlier stage of the inquiry that the delay is the result of the applicant's own conduct ceases to have effect once that stage of the inquiry has been concluded. In the final stage of the inquiry, the applicant is presumed to be innocent of the offence with which he has been charged and, if he or she can demonstrate to the court that it is probable that a specific defence which might otherwise have been open to him or her is now no longer available because of the passage of time, the court may then halt the trial on the ground that there is now a real and serious risk of an unfair trial which cannot be avoided by the giving of necessary directions or rulings by the trial judge."[99]

Burden on Accused

The burden of establishing that the preparation of the defence is prejudiced by the delay rests on the accused. He or she must establish on the balance of probabilities that there is a real and serious risk of an unfair trial resulting from the delay in the making of the complaint. In determining whether he or she has discharged this burden the court will have to bear in mind the presumption of innocence. Accordingly, if the accused can show on a balance of probabilities that the delay has prevented him or her from adducing evidence about a matter which could raise a reasonable doubt about his or her guilt, the trial will have to be halted. It is not necessary for the accused to establish that there is a flaw in the prosecution case, just that he or she has been prevented from adducing evidence which, if adduced, could raise a reasonable doubt about an essential part of the prosecution case.

---

value and limitations of such expert evidence and what it should contain. See also his judgment in *JL v. DPP* [2000] 3 I.R. 122.

[98] Note, however, that Denham J. considered that the proceedings were civil as distinct from criminal and as such the presumption of innocence had no application. See also her judgment in *PC v. DPP* [1999] 2 I.R. 25.

[99] [2000] 3 I.R. 87 at 94.

Relevant Factors

1–38   The accused cannot discharge the burden merely by a bald assertion that some specific prejudice has resulted which would give rise to a real and serious risk of an unfair trial. He or she would have to support that assertion with some supporting evidence. This can be done by indicating to the court the nature of the defence which he or she had hoped to make and presenting evidence to the court which shows that the delay has prejudiced his or her ability to pursue that defence. Since the accused is entitled to the presumption of innocence he or she cannot be required to go further and establish that there is a reasonable doubt about his guilt. In *P. O'C*, for example, a key element of the prosecution case was the allegation that the accused locked the classroom door from the inside immediately before subjecting the victim to sexual abuse. The applicant asserted that the door could not be locked from the inside at the time of the alleged incidents. If the applicant could establish that that was the case it would raise a reasonable doubt about his guilt. To that end the applicant presented the court with a letter from the director of the school at the time which stated that as a result of the passage of time he had no recollection as to whether the room would have had a lock fitted at the relevant time, nor would there be records which could establish the matter one way or the other. Had the complaint been made much earlier this difficulty would not have arisen. In the absence of any evidence from the prosecution to the effect that the difficulty presented by the accused did not exist, the Supreme Court accepted that he had done enough to establish that the delay in making the complaint had prejudiced his defence.

Similarly, in *JL v. DPP*[99a] the allegations against the accused related to one incident only which took place in the accused's mobile home. The accused submitted that he had delivered the mobile home to third parties and moved into a house at least three months before the date of the alleged incident. Due to the passage of time he was unable to trace the persons to which he had delivered the mobile home. Nevertheless, the Supreme Court accepted that he had done enough to discharge the onus of proof on him to show that his prospects of a fair trial were prejudiced due to the passage of time. Twenty years later he could hardly be expected to provide material evidence that he had moved three months earlier. It was a matter for the prosecution to establish that he was still living in the mobile home at the time of the alleged incident.

1–39   The unavailability of key witnesses due to the passage of time will be a strong factor supporting the accused's argument that he cannot get a fair trial.[100] It would have to be shown, however, that the witness or witnesses would have been in a position to give direct evidence which could undermine the truth of the allegations against the accused.[101] It may not be enough, for example, for

---

[99a] [2000] 3 I.R. 122

[100] *State (O'Connell) v. Fawsitt* [1986] I.R. 362.

[101] See *PW v. DPP* unreported, Supreme Court, June 24, 1998, but see incisive criticism of this decision in the minority judgment of Hardiman J. in *J O'C v. DPP* [2000] 3 I.R. 478.

the accused to have lost the opportunity of calling his wife as a witness where the most that she could do was to give evidence about opportunities (or lack of them) for the accused to have been alone in the house with the victim where the offences were alleged to have taken place.[102] Similarly, the difficulty of securing alibi evidence after a long passage of time is not considered a strong factor, as such difficulties can be present even where the complaint is lodged after only a relatively short delay.[103]

The accused's argument that he or she cannot get a fair trial as a result of the long passage of time will be strengthened if the allegations are vague about the manner and circumstances in which the offences were committed. If, however, the allegations provide concise detail about such matters, then it will not avail the accused if they do not specify precise dates.[104] Particularly, where a victim alleges regular abuse over a period of time the courts will not look for specific dates of each incident, so long as the periods and frequency of abuse are specified and sufficient detail is provided about the incidents of abuse in order to avoid the situation where the accused's capacity to mount a defence would be reduced to little more than asserting a bald denial.[105]

Excessive Delay

Even if the accused cannot establish that his or her defence will be prejudiced **1–40** by the absence of any specific piece of evidence as a result of delay, it does not follow that his or her right to a fair trial will not be affected by the delay. It may be, for example, that the period of delay is so long that the court can infer prejudice in the absence of specific proof. Much will depend on the length of the delay and the factors of each individual case. In *P O'C v. DPP*,[106] Hardiman J. indicated that exceptionally long periods of delay, such as 40 to 50 years would probably be sufficient in themselves to render a fair trial impossible. He also intimated that the courts should be aware of the dangers of an unfair trial where the passage of time has resulted in the absence of independent evidence and the trial effectively becomes an exercise in the credibility of witnesses.[107] Account should also be taken of the impact of the passage of time on the memories of third parties, as well as the accused and the complainant. Every effort should be made by the prosecuting and investigating authorities to avoid a situation where bare assertion can be countered only by bare denial.

---

[102] *J O'C v. DPP* [2000] 3 I.R. 478. See, however, Hardiman J.'s dissent on this point in the same case.

[103] *J O'C v. DPP* [2000] 3 I.R. 478.

[104] In *PC v. DPP* [1999] 2 I.R. 25 the allegations referred to a pattern of abuse over a period of time, and as such were lacking in particularity about dates and times. Nevertheless, the Supreme Court was of the opinion that the difficulties that would have been created for the accused were not exacerbated by the delay. He would have faced the same difficulties had the complaint been made years earlier.

[105] *J O'C v. DPP* [2000] 3 I.R. 478.

[106] [2000] 3 I.R. 87.

[107] See also his minority judgment in *J O'C v. DPP* [2000] 3 I.R. 478.

Judge's Directions

1–41   There have been suggestions from time to time that the effects of a lapse of time on the capacity of the accused to prepare his or her defence might be cured by suitable directions from the trial judge. As yet, however, there is no guidance from the Supreme Court as to the nature of such directions and when they should be given.[108] In *P O'C*, Hardiman J. highlighted the practical difficulties which would arise in attempting to frame any such guidance. In particular, it can result in the judge inviting the jury to consider the case on what the evidence might have been rather than on the evidence they have heard. The accused is entitled to be tried on the basis of the evidence actually heard and not on the basis of what the evidence might have been many years earlier. If there is a real risk that he or she will be prejudiced by the difference between the two then there is also a risk that he or she will be subjected to an unfair trial.[109]

See chapter 2 for further discussion on delay in the context of extradition.

---

[108] See , *e.g. P O'C v. DPP* [2000] 3 I.R. 87 at 114, *per* Hardiman J.; and *J O'C v. DPP* [2000] 3 I.R. 480, *per* Hardiman J.
[109] See also comments of Keane J. (as he then was) in *E O'R v. DPP* [1996] 2 I.L.R.M. 128 at 140 on the difficulties of giving suitable directions.

CRIMINAL JUSTICE INSTITUTIONS

A. Introduction

Criminal procedure encompasses those rules and principles governing the enforcement of the substantive criminal law. A full appreciation of the contents of these rules and principles, including how they are applied in practice, requires a knowledge of the structure, composition, status, powers and functions of the primary institutions engaged in their application. In Ireland these institutions are: the courts, the police force, the prosecution and the prisons. Before proceeding to a consideration of the substance of the rules and principles of criminal procedure it is necessary, therefore, to outline the main characteristics of these institutions in so far as they are not covered in a later chapter or chapters. For a fuller treatment, reference should be made to the relevant specialist texts.[1] **2–01**

B. Garda Síochána[2]

1. Statutory Basis

One of the first tasks of the government of the new Irish State in 1922 was to establish a police force to replace the Royal Irish Constabulary which had policed the country outside Dublin since 1836. The new police force, designated the Garda Síochána, made its first appearance in September 1922 **2–02**

---

[1] See D Walsh *The Irish Police: a Legal and Constitutional Perspective* (Round Hall Sweet & Maxwell, Dublin, 1998); G Hogan and G Whyte *Kelly's The Irish Constitution* (4th ed., Butterworths, Dublin, 2002); J Casey *Constitutional Law in Ireland* (3rd ed., Round Hall Sweet & Maxwell, Dublin, 2000); M Forde *Constitutional Law of Ireland* (Mercier Press, Cork, 1987); D Morgan *Constitutional Law of Ireland* (2nd ed., Round Hall, Dublin, 1990); J Woods *The District Court Practice and Procedure in Criminal Cases* (2nd ed., Woods, Limerick, 1994); R Byrne and P McCutcheon *The Irish Legal System* (4th ed., Butterworths, Dublin, 2001); J Casey *The Irish Law Officers* (Round Hall Sweet & Maxwell, Dublin, 1996); P McDermott *Prison Law* (Round Hall Sweet & Maxwell, Dublin, 2000).

[2] See D Walsh *The Irish Police: a Legal and Constitutional Perspective* (Round Hall Sweet & Maxwell, Dublin, 1998).

but was not put on a statutory footing until 1923. Even then the measure in question, the Garda Síochána (Temporary Provisions) Act 1923, was designed to expire after one year. A permanent statutory basis was provided by the Garda Síochána Act 1924. In 1925 the Garda Síochána and the Dublin Metropolitan Police were merged by the Police Forces Amalgamation Act 1925 to form the current Garda Síochána. Its statutory basis, therefore is to be found in a combination of the 1924 and 1925 Acts.

2. Legal Status

Body of Peace Officers

The force was established on a model of police first introduced in these islands in Dublin 1786 and which has become standard since the establishment of Robert Peel's London Metropolitan Police in 1829. In effect it is a body of peace officers organised together in the interests of efficiency under the direction and control of a Commissioner (the chief officer).[3] The individual member is the basic and primary unit. He or she occupies an independent, common law office to which is attached a whole range of peace-keeping powers, duties and privileges.[4] Under the legislation these individual members are organised together in a series of hierarchical ranks with the Garda Commissioner at the apex.[5] The senior officers are appointed, and are removable, by the government,[6] while the members in the ranks below superintendent are appointed, and can be dismissed in accordance with the discipline regulations, by the Commissioner.[7] The overall complement of the force, and the numbers in each individual rank, are determined from time to time by the government.[8] Currently, the authorised strength of the force is 11,650. This does not include 1,744 civilian support staff.

A force of Police

2–03 The legislation establishing the Garda Síochána does not confer any police powers, or impose any police duties, on the force as a whole. When new police powers and duties are being introduced by statute the practice is to confer them directly on each individual member of the force, thereby supplementing the body of police powers and duties that already inhere in the individual members at common law. This has the important implication that the exercise of police powers in any individual case is first and foremost a matter for the individual member concerned. He or she must decide in the exercise of his or her discretion whether, for example, to effect an arrest or to conduct a coercive search in any situation where the circumstances are such

---

[3] See Halsbury's *Laws of England, vol.30* (London, 1959), p.43 for equivalent English definition.
[4] See D Walsh, *op.cit.*, chap. 3.
[5] The ranks are: Commissioner, Deputy Commissioner, Assistant Commissioner, Surgeon, Chief Superintendent, Superintendent, Inspector, Sergeant and Garda.
[6] Police Forces Amalgamation Act 1925, ss.6(2), 7(2) and 10(4).
[7] *ibid.* s.10(5) and the Garda Síochána (Discipline) Regulations 1989.
[8] Garda Síochána Act 1972, s.1.

as to bring the requisite power into play. It does not follow, however, that the force cannot function as a collective body in the discharge of its primary law enforcement role. The Minister for Justice, Equality and Law Reform is conferred with the power to make regulations on the internal management of the force, including discipline.[9] This power can, and has been used, to weld the individual members of the force into a structured and disciplined police force capable of functioning efficiently as a cohesive unit. Even more important in this regard is that the Commissioner is statutorily conferred with the power of general direction and control over the force, subject to the internal management regulations made by the Minister.[10] This, coupled with his disciplinary authority over the members of the force, enables the Commissioner to organise and direct the force in the discharge of its functions. He can assign members to particular duties, set operational law enforcement priorities, lay down operational policies, enforce discipline and generally manage the force in the manner of the chief executive of a state agency.[11]

Remit

Just as the legislation does not confer any police powers and duties on the force as a whole, it also fails to define the remit of the force. To some extent this is the inevitable consequence of the fact that the force is established as a body of officeholders under the general direction and control of a Commissioner, as opposed to a corporate body with legal personality separate and distinct from its individual members. It is not possible, therefore, to consider the remit of the Garda Síochána in the manner of the remit of a state agency or limited company. In the case of the Garda Síochána there can be no equivalent of the force acting *ultra vires*. The closest equivalent is an individual member (including the Commissioner) acting beyond the scope of the powers conferred on his or her office at common law or by statute. It follows that the general role of the Garda Síochána must be deduced indirectly from the substance of the powers and duties conferred upon the individual members at common law and by statute, the internal management regulations issued by the Minister and, most importantly, the standing orders issued from time to time by the Commissioner in the exercise of his power of general direction and control and promulgated in the Garda Síochána Code. These reveal that the role of the force embraces: crime control, public order, state security, economic and social regulation, public administration, and accident and emergency response. Unfortunately, the Code is not published, and the only information about the activities and priorities of the force which is published on a regular basis is to be found in the Garda Commissioner's Annual Report. However, there are plans for the Commissioner to publish an annual policing plan.

---

[9] Police Forces Amalgamation Act 1925, s.14.
[10] *ibid*. s.8(1).
[11] Unlike the chiefs of other major state agencies the Garda Commissioner was not designated the accounting officer for the force; this position being occupied instead by the secretary of the Department of Justice, Equality and Law Reform. However, that situation is about to change as the Commissioner is soon to be designated the Accounting Officer; see D Walsh, *op.cit.*, pp. 128–139 for the significance of this change.

Powers

It is beyond the scope of this text to offer a comprehensive account of police powers and duties. Nevertheless, it is necessary to focus in some detail on the contents of those powers which are most relevant to criminal procedure; namely the powers of stop, arrest, detention, interrogation, entry, search and seizure. These are considered later. At the outset it is important to point out that these powers derive from a combination of the powers of the constable or peace officer at common law, the powers conferred on the constable in Ireland by statute prior to 1922 (1925 in the case of the DMP),[12] and the powers conferred by statute on a member of the Garda Síochána since 1922.

3. Co-operation with other Law Enforcement Agencies

2–04   Increasingly, the Garda Síochána has to co-operate with other law enforcement agencies, both in Ireland and abroad, in order to combat crime more effectively. For the most part this co-operation is conducted on an informal or administrative basis.[13] Nevertheless, it is worth noting two significant examples where the co-operation is underpinned by a statutory basis. The first, chronologically, is the establishment of the Europol National Unit. This is provided for by the Europol Act 1997 which was enacted to give effect to Ireland's obligations under the Europol Convention.[14] The Act empowers the Minister for Justice, Equality and Law Reform to designate a unit within the Garda Síochána to be known as the "National Unit" for the purposes of the Act and the Convention. The Garda members of the Unit are appointed by the Garda Commissioner, while the non-Garda members are appointed by the Minister. At least one of these members must be sent as the liaison officer or officers to the Europol Headquarters at the Hague. The Act also makes provision for the appointment of a "Head" of the Unit in whom the day to day management of the Unit is vested. The Unit operates under the control and superintendence of the Commissioner. While its members do not acquire any special powers or duties by virtue of their membership, it is clear that their function is to service the needs of police co-operation among Member States in the European Union.

2–05   The second example, the Criminal Assets Bureau (CAB), is much more innovative in terms of police structures and methodology. In effect it represents a new kind of police force; a multi-disciplinary and inter-agency force, compared to the single-disciplinary and single agency Garda Síochána. Nevertheless, it is based primarily within the Garda Síochána. Given the innovative and distinctive characteristics of CAB and its increasing importance, it is worth outlining its structure and functions in a little more detail.

---

[12]   These were carried over by Garda Síochána Act 1924, s.19(1) and Police Forces Amalgamation Act 1925, s.22.

[13]   See, *e.g.,* S Dunn, D Murray and D Walsh *Cross-Border Police Co-operation in Ireland* (University of Limerick, Limerick, 2002).

[14]   See D Walsh *Europol Act,* 1997 (Irish Statutes Annotated, 1997).

4. Criminal Assets Bureau

Establishment and Composition

The CAB was established as a body corporate by the Criminal Assets Bureau **2–06**
Act 1996.[15] While its composition is not formally prescribed by the Act, there
is provision for the appointment of a Chief Bureau Officer, Bureau Officers
and Bureau staff. The Act obliges the Garda Commissioner to appoint a Chief
Bureau Officer from time to time.[16] The Chief Bureau Officer must be
appointed from the members of the Garda Síochána of the rank of Garda
Chief Superintendent.[17] He or she shall manage and control generally the
administration and business of the Bureau,[18] and is responsible to the Garda
Commissioner for the performance of the functions of the Bureau.[19]

The multi-disciplinary character of the CAB is reflected in the composition
of the Bureau officers. The Minister for Justice, Equality and Law Reform
may appoint, with the consent of the Minister for Finance, Bureau officers from
members of the Garda Síochána, officers of the Revenue Commissioners and
officers of the Minister for Social, Community and Family Affairs.[20] In each
case the appointments can be made only from members and officers nominated
for the purpose by their respective authorities. The officers from the Revenue
Commissioners and the Minister for Social, Community and Family Affairs
are given special protection in the Act to conceal their identities.[21] The power to
remove a Bureau officer from his or her appointment to the Bureau vests in the
Chief Bureau Officer, acting with the consent of the Garda Commissioner.[22]

Powers and Status of Bureau Officers

The Bureau officers do not automatically acquire any additional powers on **2–07**
their appointment to the Bureau. However, they do retain the powers vested in
them by virtue of their status as members of the Garda Síochána, officers of
the Revenue Commissioners or officers of the Minister for Social, Community
and Family Affairs, as the case may be.[23] It is expected that they will use
these powers in the service of the Bureau. Indeed, the 1996 Act specifically
states that their exercise or performance of any power or duty for the purposes
of the Act shall be exercised or performed in the name of the Bureau.
Moreover, a Bureau officer is under the direction and control of the Chief

---

[15] Criminal Assets Bureau Act 1996, s.3 and Criminal Assets Bureau Act 1996 (Establishment Day)
Order 1996.
[16] Criminal Assets Bureau Act 1996, s.7(1) & (2). There is provision for the appointment of an
Acting Chief Bureau Officer in the event of the incapacity through illness, or absence otherwise,
of the Chief Bureau Officer; s.7(5). The Commissioner also has the power to remove the Chief
Bureau Officer from his or her appointment as such.
[17] Criminal Assets Bureau Act 1996, s.7(6).
[18] *ibid*. s.7(3).
[19] *ibid*. s.7(4).
[20] *ibid*. s.8(1)(a).
[21] *ibid*. ss.10 and 11.
[22] *ibid*. s.8(9).
[23] *ibid*. s.8(2).

Bureau Officer when exercising or performing any powers or duties for the purposes of the Act.[24] The Chief Bureau Officer also acquires those powers of direction and control to which Bureau officers were subject prior to their appointment as Bureau officers. So, for example, if it was lawful for the officer (prior to his or her appointment to the Bureau) to exercise any power or perform any duty on the direction of any other person, then it shall be lawful for the officer to exercise that power or perform that duty at the direction of the Chief Bureau Officer.[25]

It is also worth noting that a Bureau officer may be accompanied or assisted in the exercise or performance of his or her powers or duties by such other persons as he or she considers necessary.[26] Where this other person is also a Bureau officer he or she shall have the powers and duties of the Bureau officer whom he or she is assisting.[27] These additional powers are available for the purposes of that assistance only. It follows, for example, that a Bureau officer from the Revenue Commissioners who is assisting a Bureau officer from the Garda Síochána under these provisions will acquire the powers of a member of the Garda Síochána for the purposes of the assistance. The same, of course, applies in reverse if it is the officer from the Garda Síochána who is assisting the officer from the Revenue Commissioners. In practice, the most likely scenario is officers of the Revenue Commissioners and/or the Minister for Social, Community and Family Affairs assisting an officer from the Garda Síochána.

Most police powers in Ireland can be exercised only on the basis of a reasonable suspicion that certain specified circumstances are present. A police officer who entertains a relevant suspicion on reasonable grounds can decide lawfully in the exercise of his or her own discretion to exercise the power in that individual case. It would not normally be lawful, however, for a police officer to exercise the power in any individual case simply because he or she was directed to do so by another police officer who entertained the relevant suspicion on reasonable grounds. In order to lawfully exercise his or her powers on the basis of instructions from another police officer, the instructions in question would have to be sufficient to raise a relevant reasonable suspicion in the mind of the officer under instruction. The Criminal Assets Bureau Act 1996 makes it clear that a Bureau officer is permitted to exercise the powers or duties vested in him or her on the basis of information received by him or her from another Bureau officer in the exercise or performance of that other Officer's powers or duties.[28] Equally a Bureau officer may exercise his or her powers or duties on the basis of any action taken by another Bureau officer in the exercise or performance of that other officer's powers or duties. Any information, documents or other material lawfully obtained by Bureau officers pursuant to these provisions is admissible in evidence in any subsequent proceedings.[29]

---

[24] *ibid.* s.8(3).
[25] *ibid.* s.8(4).
[26] *ibid.* s.8(6)(a). There is also a suggestion that a Bureau officer may be equipped with firearms to assist him or her in the exercise or performance of his or her duties; see s.8(6)(b).
[27] *ibid.* s.8(6)(c).
[28] *ibid.* s.8(5).
[29] *ibid.* s.8(6)(d).

The combined effect of these measures suggests that the Bureau is meant to function as a collective body under the direction and control of the Chief Bureau Officer. This compares with the situation in the Garda Síochána where each individual member of the force exercises his or her powers in any individual case on the basis of his or her own discretion. While the Garda Commissioner is responsible for the management of the force as a whole and the general performance of each individual member in his or her duties, he does not have the power to direct or control how a member exercises his or her powers in any individual case.

The collective identity of the Bureau members is also reflected in the provisions for the sharing of confidential information. The 1996 Act states that any information or material obtained by a Bureau officer for the purposes of the Act may only be disclosed to: another Bureau officer or a member of staff of the Bureau; any member of the Garda Síochána for the purposes of Garda functions; any officer of the Revenue Commissioners for the purposes of the Revenue Acts; and any officer of the Minister for Social, Community and Family Affairs for the purposes of the Social Welfare Acts.[30] Any such information, documents or other material shall be admitted in evidence in any subsequent proceedings.

Bureau Staff and Legal Officer

In addition to the Chief Bureau Officer and the Bureau officers there is a **2–08** provision for Bureau staff. The 1996 Act empowers the Minister for Justice, Equality and Law Reform, with the consent of the Minister for Finance, and after such consultation with the Garda Commissioner as may be appropriate, to appoint persons to be professional or technical members of staff of the Bureau.[31] The legislation does not elaborate further upon what is meant by professional or technical staff in this context. It is certainly wide enough to include accountants, computer technicians and experts in any field relevant to the work of the Bureau. Each member of staff will assist the Bureau officers in the exercise and performance of their powers and duties. He or she shall perform his or her functions at the direction of the Chief Bureau Officer.[32] It is the Garda Commissioner, however, who is invested with the power to remove a member of the Bureau staff from his or her position as a member of the staff.[33] The Commissioner may exercise this power at any time, subject of course to the requirements of natural justice. A member of staff holds his or her employment on such terms and conditions as the Minister for Justice, Equality and Law Reform determines with the consent of the Minister for Finance.[34]

---

[30] *ibid.* s.8(7). Subject to the consent of the Chief Bureau Officer such information or material may also be disclosed to any other officer of another Minister of the Government or a local authority for the purposes of that other officer exercising or performing his or her powers or duties; s.8(7)(e).

[31] *ibid.* s.9(1)(b).

[32] *ibid.* s.9(2).

[33] *ibid.* s.9(4).

[34] *ibid.* s.9(5).

2–09 There is a separate provision for the appointment of a Bureau legal officer. The Minister for Justice, Equality and Law Reform, with the consent of the Minister for Finance and the Attorney General may appoint a Bureau legal officer.[35] This officer is a member of the Bureau staff and reports directly to the Chief Bureau Officer. His or her role is to assist the Bureau in the pursuit of its objectives and functions. The legal officer performs his or her functions under the direction of the Chief Bureau Officer.[36] It is the Minister for Justice, Equality and Law Reform, however, who is invested with the power to remove the legal officer from his or her appointment at any time.[37] The Minister can only exercise this power with the consent of the Attorney General and the Minister for Finance. The legal officer holds his or her office on such terms and conditions as the Minister for Justice, Equality and Law Reform determines with the consent of the Minister for Finance and the Attorney General.[38]

Bureau officers and staff also benefit from certain statutory measures aimed at protecting them from violence or intimidation from the individuals targeted by the Bureau. The Act states that all reasonable care must be taken to ensure that the identity of a Bureau officer who is an officer of the Revenue Commissioners or an officer of the Minister for Social, Community and Family Affairs is not revealed.[39] The same applies to a member of the Bureau staff. Even where one of the Bureau officers is exercising his or her powers or duties in the company of a Bureau officer who is a member of the Garda Síochána, the former shall not be required to identify himself or herself. When exercising any power or duty in writing, he or she shall do so in the name of the Bureau.

The anonymity of non-Garda Officers of the Bureau and Bureau staff also extends to court proceedings. Where the officer or staff member is required to give evidence in any such proceedings, whether by affidavit, certificate or orally, the judge or person in charge of the proceedings may, on the application of the Chief Bureau Officer, if satisfied that there are reasonable grounds in the public interest to do so, give such directions for the preservation of the anonymity of the officer or staff member as he or she thinks fit.

The 1996 Act makes it a criminal offence to identify non-Garda Bureau officers, Bureau staff and their families.[40] It is equally an offence to publish their addresses. The Act also introduces specific offences of assault, obstruction and intimidation with respect to officers, their staff and families.[41]

Bureau Objectives

2–10 The 1996 Act spells out the objectives and functions of the Bureau. There are three objectives. The first is to identify the assets of persons which derive or

---

[35] *ibid.* s.9(1)(a).
[36] *ibid.* s.9(2).
[37] *ibid.* s.9(3).
[38] *ibid.* s.9(5).
[39] *ibid.* s.10.
[40] *ibid.* s.11.
[41] *ibid.* ss.12, 13 and 15.

which are suspected to derive, directly or indirectly, from criminal activity.[42] It does not matter where the assets are situated. They could, for example, be located outside the jurisdiction. The emphasis is very much on the status of the assets as distinct from the person who owns or possesses them. So long as the assets derive or are suspected of deriving, directly or indirectly, from criminal activity, their identification is one of the objectives of the Bureau. It does not matter that the owner of the assets has not been, or is not suspected of having been engaged in criminal activity. Nor does it matter that the assets were not acquired through organised crime, as distinct from other forms of criminal activity. Assets are not defined in the legislation. Undoubtedly, it covers real property and chattels. Presumably, it also covers intangible assets such as choses in action.

The second objective of the Bureau is the taking of appropriate action under the law to deprive or deny those persons of the assets, or of the benefit of the assets, either in whole or in part, whichever is appropriate.[43] Once again the focus is on the assets as distinct from the person who owns the assets. The objective is to deprive the person of the assets rather than to secure a conviction against the person who owns the assets.

The third objective is ancillary to the first two. It is the pursuit of any investigation or the doing of any other preparatory work in relation to any proceedings arising from the first and/or second objectives.[44] This could, of course, embrace the investigation and/or prosecution of persons who own the assets which the Bureau is seeking to identify and confiscate.

Bureau Functions

Although the legislation sets out four distinct functions of the Bureau, they really reflect the functions of the three constituencies of the Bureau, namely the Garda Síochána, the Revenue Commissioners and the Minister for Social, Community and Family Affairs in connection with the proceeds of crime or suspected criminal activity. The first is the taking of all necessary actions, in accordance with police functions, for the purposes of the confiscation, restraint of use, freezing, preservation or seizure of assets deriving or suspected of deriving, directly or indirectly, from criminal activity.[45] The second function is the taking of all necessary actions under revenue legislation to ensure that the proceeds of crime or suspected criminal activity are subject to tax and that the revenue legislation is fully applied to such proceeds or activities.[46] The third function is the taking of all necessary actions under the social welfare legislation for the investigation and determination of any claim for social welfare benefit by any person engaged in criminal activity.[47] The fourth function is the taking of all necessary actions, at the request of the Minister

2–11

---

[42] *ibid.* s.4(a).
[43] *ibid.* s.4(b).
[44] *ibid.* s.4(c).
[45] *ibid.* s.5(1)(a).
[46] *ibid.* s.5(1)(b).
[47] *ibid.* s.5(1)(c).

for Social, Community and Family Affairs, to investigate and determine any claim in respect of welfare benefit where the Minister certifies that there are reasonable grounds for believing that, in the case of a particular investigation, officers of the Minister may be subject to threats or other forms of intimidation.[48] The Bureau's actions pursuant to these specific functions can include co-operation with any other police force, tax authority or social welfare authority of a territory or state other than Ireland.

Although the Bureau is popularly associated with the fight against organised crime it is worth emphasising that the statutory statement of its functions links it to criminal activity generally, as distinct from organised crime which can be considered a particular type of criminal activity.

2–12 The Minister for Justice, Equality and Law Reform may, following consultation with the Minister for Finance, confer additional functions by order on the Bureau or Bureau officers.[49] These must be connected with the statutory objectives and functions of the Bureau. Functions in this context are defined as including "powers and duties".[50] The Minister may also make provision in relation to ancillary matters arising out of the conferral of any such additional functions.

The combination of the Bureau's objectives and functions confirm that it is designed to employ an inter-agency approach to tackling crime. The Garda Síochána, the Revenue Commissioners and the Minister for Social, Community and Family Affairs will pool their expertise, resources and competencies in targeting the assets of those suspected of being engaged in crime and those enjoying the benefits of such assets. The traditional police approach of securing convictions against the offenders has been complemented by a strategy which focuses on the wealth which is believed to derive, directly or indirectly, from crime. The wealth, as distinct from the offender, is the primary target. The objective is to deprive criminals of the proceeds of their crime and thereby take away the incentive of engaging in such activity. By combining the knowledge and skills of the Revenue Commissioners and the social welfare officers with those of the Garda Síochána, it will be easier to identify suspects who appear to be enjoying a life-style which grossly exceeds their publicly declared income and capital. The resources and competencies of all three services can then be used to ensure that the individuals in question are denied social welfare benefits to which they are not entitled, are taxed on their undeclared income and capital and, where appropriate, are deprived of wealth which is suspected of deriving directly or indirectly from criminal activity.

---

[48] *ibid.* s.5(1)(d).

[49] *ibid.* s.6(1).

[50] *ibid.* s.6(4). It is submitted that a ministerial power to confer powers by order on the Garda Síochána, revenue officers or officers of the Minister for Social, Community and Family Affairs which constrict the personal rights of the individual is constitutionally suspect by virtue of the terms of Art. 15 of the Constitution.

Civil Process

One of the most striking features of the CAB is that it relies heavily on the **2–13** civil, as distinct from the criminal, process to confiscate the proceeds of crime. This involves an application to the High Court under the Proceeds of Crime Act 1996 for an interim, interlocutory or final disposal order in respect of property which is suspected to be, directly or indirectly, the proceeds of crime or acquired through the proceeds of crime.[51] A criminal conviction is not a precondition for triggering an application for one of these orders. There is provision for an interim or interlocutory order to be made on the basis of the opinion evidence of a member of the Garda Síochána not below the rank of Chief Superintendent or an authorised officer of the CAB. If such an officer states, either in a affidavit or in oral evidence, his or belief that:

(i) the respondent is in possession or control of specified property and that the property constitutes directly or indirectly the proceeds of crime; or

(ii) the respondent is in possession or control of specified property and that the property was acquired in whole or in part with or in connection with property that directly or indirectly constitutes the proceeds of crime; or

(iii) the value of the property is not less than €13,000;

the court must grant the order unless the respondent introduces evidence to the contrary or the court is satisfied that there would be a serious risk of injustice. The application procedure also includes provision for an order to be granted compelling the respondent to file an affidavit in the Central Office of the High Court specifying the property in his possession or control, or his income or sources of income during such period as the court may specify. The period may not exceed 10 years ending on the date of the application.

Although the CAB is not the only authority which may seek interim, interlocutory and disposal orders under the 1996 Act, in practice it is the source of virtually all applications.[52] For the purpose of gathering the evidence necessary to sustain an application for any of the court orders, Bureau Officers can exercise the powers vested in them by virtue of their status as members of the Garda Síochána or as officers of the Revenue Commissioners. In practice, Garda powers such as the powers of arrest and entry, search and seizure, as well as the powers to access financial records are of particular importance in this context. The Criminal Assets Bureau Act 1996 provides an additional power of entry, search and seizure for this purpose.[53]

It is worth emphasising that the CAB's activities are not confined to a confiscation of assets deriving or which are suspected to derive from criminal

---

[51] For further detail on these and other powers of confiscation and forfeiture see chapter 21 on Sentencing.

[52] The applicant must either be an authorised officer of the CAB or a member of the Garda Síochána not below the rank of Chief Superintendent.

[53] Criminal Assets Bureau Act 1996, s.14.

activity. It also tackles such assets by ensuring that they are subject to tax. To this end the Revenue Officers in the Bureau are empowered and obliged to charge to tax profits or gains from an unlawful or unknown source, and to deal with the assessment and collection of any tax following an investigation by the Bureau. The necessary additional powers are provided primarily by the Disclosure of Certain Information For Taxation and Other Purposes Act 1996 which permits the exchange of information between the Revenue Commissioners and the Garda Síochána in certain circumstances.

C. The Prosecution

2–14   This is dealt with fully in chapter 12.

D. The Courts

1. Introduction

2–15   The ordinary courts with criminal jurisdiction in Ireland today are the District Court, the Circuit Court, the High Court, the Court of Criminal Appeal and the Supreme Court. They are established by the Courts (Establishment and Constitution) Act 1961. To these must be added the Special Criminal Court provided for by the Offences Against the State Act 1939, Courts-Martial provided for by the Defence Act 1954 and the Courts-Martial Appeal Court provided for by the Courts-Martial Appeals Act 1983. It is also worth noting the Court of Justice of the European Community and the European Court of Human Rights. Although not an integral part of the Irish court system their separate jurisdictions are such that they can and do have an impact on criminal litigation being conducted before the Irish courts.

The jurisdiction of the Irish courts is derived ultimately from the Constitution. Article 34.1 stipulates that justice is to be administered in courts established by law by judges appointed in accordance with the Constitution. Indeed, the Constitution specifically requires the establishment of courts of first instance and a court of final appeal.[54] The former must include a High Court with full original jurisdiction in and power to determine all matters and questions whether of law or fact, civil or criminal,[55] and courts of local and limited jurisdiction with a right of appeal as determined by law.[56] The court of final appeal is designated the Supreme Court[57] and is given appellate jurisdiction from all decisions of the High Court subject to such regulations and exceptions as may be prescribed by law.[58] Its decisions are declared to be final and conclusive,[59] although this must

---

[54]   Art. 34.2.
[55]   Art. 34.3.1.
[56]   Art. 34.4.
[57]   Art. 34.4.1.
[58]   Art. 34.4.3.
[59]   Art. 34.4.6.

now be interpreted in the light of the jurisdiction of the Courts of the European Community established by the Treaty of Rome.[60] The Constitution also envisages the establishment of special courts and military tribunals. The former can be established by law for the trial of offences in cases where it may be determined by such law that the ordinary courts are inadequate to secure the administration of justice and the preservation of public peace and order.[61] The latter may be established for the trial of offences against military law alleged to have been committed by persons while subject to military law, and to deal with a state of war or armed rebellion.[62] Both types of court share the distinctive feature that they can sit without a jury to try persons charged with offences within their jurisdiction.[63] Similarly, the provisions in Article 34 of the Constitution (the structure of the ordinary courts) and those in Article 35 underpinning the appointment and independence of the judiciary do not apply to them.[64]

The Constitution clearly envisages the establishment of courts in addition to those specifically mentioned in its text.[65] It follows that the constitutionality of the Court of Criminal Appeal cannot be called into question simply because it is purely a creature of statute. This Court was established by the Courts (Establishment and Constitution) Act 1961 and its jurisdiction is regulated by the Courts (Supplemental Jurisdiction) Act 1961. The latter also regulates the jurisdiction of the other ordinary courts to the extent that they are not already regulated by the Constitution.

The general management and disposal of court business is the responsibility of the courts themselves. In the case of the Supreme Court it is handled under the direction of the Chief Justice and, in the case of the other courts, by their respective Presidents. Up until recently, the general administrative and political responsibility for the court system as a whole has been vested in the Department of Justice, Equality and Law Reform. While political responsibility still resides with the Minister for Justice, Equality and Law Reform the day to day central administration of the courts has been transferred to an independent Courts Service.

2. The Courts Service

In November 1995 the Minister set up a Working Group on a Courts **2–16** Commission under the chairmanship of Mrs Justice Susan Denham, Judge of

---

[60]   See also, Bunreacht na hÉireann, Art. 29.4.3–5.
[61]   Art. 38.3.
[62]   Art. 38.4.
[63]   Art. 38.5.
[64]   Art. 38.6. The Constitution Review Group was of the view that special courts should be brought within the ambit of Arts. 34 and 35 (Pn.2632) at 198. This was also the view of the All-Party Oireachtas Committee on the Constitution in its 4th Report, *The Courts and the Judiciary* (Pn.7831) at 34–35. See *Report of the Committee to Review the Offences against the State Acts, 1939–1998 and Related Matters* (Stationery Office, Dublin, 2002) at 9.45–9.56 for discussion on the specific context of the Special Criminal Court.
[65]   *People (Attorney General) v. Conmey* [1975] I.R. 341; *State (Boyle) v. Judge Neylon* [1986] I.R. 551.

the Supreme Court. Its remit was to review and report to the Minister on the operation of the courts system having regard to:

- the level and quality of service provided to the public; staffing, information and technology, etc.;
- the financing of the courts system including the current relationship between the courts, the Department of Justice and the Oireachtas;
- any other aspect of the courts system which the group considers appropriate; and
- the establishment of a Commission on the management of the courts as an independent and permanent body with financial and management autonomy.

The Working Group's First Report was submitted in April 1996 under the title "Management and Financing of the Court System". Its principle recommendation was the establishment of an independent and permanent body to manage a unified courts' system. This body, to be known as the "Courts Service", would be created as a state agency on a statutory footing. It would consist of members of the judiciary, representatives of courts users, those involved in the work of the courts and a chief executive. The chief executive would be responsible for the day to day administration of the courts and the implementation of the policy of the Board. The Minister for Justice, Equality and Law Reform would remain politically accountable for the financial and administrative management of the Courts system and for policy matters such as courts legislation, court jurisdiction and the number and terms of appointment of the judiciary.

The Working Group's recommendations were given statutory effect with the enactment of the Courts Service Act 1998 which makes provision for the establishment of a Courts Service as an independent corporate entity. The Act prescribes the primary functions of the Courts Service which shall be to:

- manage the courts;
- provide support services for the judges;
- provide information on the courts system to the public;
- provide, manage and maintain court buildings; and
- provide facilities for users of the courts.[66]

The Courts Service was formally brought into being on November 1, and established on November 9, 1999.[67]

---

[66] Courts Service Act 1998, s.5.
[67] Courts Service Act 1998 (Commencement)(Remaining Provisions) Order 1999. See Annual Reports of the Courts Service 2000 and 2001 for an account of its structure, functions, activities and a range of courts statistics.

3. The District Court[68]

Establishment and Composition

The District Court is a single court composed of the President of the Court **2–17** and 52 District Court judges.[69] For operational purposes, however, the country is divided into the Dublin Metropolitan district[70] and 23 District Court districts[71] to each of which individual judges are assigned by the government.[72] The President of the District Court is permanently assigned by statute to the Dublin Metropolitan district.[73] Districts can be created, varied or abolished from time to time by ministerial order.[74] Each district is divided up into a number of District Court areas and a court must be held in each area.[75] The Minister must appoint one or more convenient places in an area, or within one mile of the boundary of such area, at which the court shall be held. These areas can be altered from time to time by ministerial order[76] and the transaction of summary jurisdiction in criminal matters, together with the days and hours when the court will sit, are set out in the First Schedule to the District Court (Areas) Order 1961 as amended.[77]

Time and Place of Sittings

Generally, sittings of the court must be held at a place on the day and hour appointed from time to time under the relevant statutory and regulatory

---

[68] For a detailed account of the District Court and its practice and procedure, see J Wood *District Court Practice and Procedure in Criminal cases* (Woods, Limerick, 1994)

[69] The number is fixed by statute from time to time; Courts (Establishment and Constitution) Act 1961, s.5(2), as amended by Courts and Court Officers Act 1995, s.11 which in turn has been amended by Courts and Court Officers Act 2002. The current permanent establishment of 52 plus the President of the Court does not include an additional position which may be filled while a former President of the District Court serves as a judge of the Court; Courts (No.2) Act 1997, s.5(5).

[70] Courts (Supplemental Provisions) Act 1961, s.32(1) and Courts of Justice Act 1953, s.22.

[71] Courts (Supplemental Provisions) Act 1961, s.32(1) and Courts of Justice Act 1953, s.22.

[72] Courts (Supplemental Provisions) Act 1961, s.32(3) and the 6th Schedule. The Minister for Justice may assign judges to Areas from time to time in consultation with the President of the District Court; see Courts (Supplemental Provisions) Act 1961, s.39 as amended by Courts and Court Officers Act 1995, s.38. The President of the District Court must determine the class or classes of business to be transacted in the places appointed by the Minister (now the Courts Service) under s.40 of the 1961 Act for the transaction of the business of the District Court in that district, and the days and hours at which such class or classes of business shall be transacted in such places; s.42.

[73] Courts (Supplemental Provisions) Act 1961, s.35. The President of the District Court must arrange for the distribution of the business of the District Court in the Dublin Metropolitan District among the judges assigned to that District; s.42.

[74] Courts of Justice Act 1953, s.26, as amended by the Courts Act 1971. See District Court (Districts) Order 1961 as amended, and District Court Districts (Dublin) Order 1945, as amended.

[75] Courts (Supplemental Provisions) Act 1961, s.32(1) and Courts of Justice Act 1953, s.21.

[76] Courts of Justice Act 1953, s.26 as amended by the Courts Act 1971. See District Court (Court Areas) Order 1961 as amended. In respect of an area created or varied he may, after consulting the President of the District Court, appoint one or more places within the area or within one mile of the boundary of such area and the days and hours at which sittings are to be held for that area.

[77] See Courts Service *Annual Report 2001* (Dublin, 2002) Appendix 2 for a table of recent changes to District Court districts in order to align them with county boundaries to the greatest extent possible. Note also that the Minister can vary the class or classes of business for which any area is delimited, alter the places and vary the days or hours appointed for sittings; Courts of Justice Act 1953, as amended by Courts Act 1971, s.16.

provisions in force.[78] However, a judge may also hold a sitting of the court within his or her district. This may occur at a time not so appointed for the purpose of hearing any proceedings adjourned from a sitting so appointed; and at a place or time not so appointed for the hearing of such summary offences as may be specified from time to time by order of the Minister pursuant to section 15 of the Courts Act 1971.[79] It is also worth noting that there is a statutory provision permitting the Minister to declare by order that the early trial or disposal by the District Court of summary offences of any specified kind is desirable.[80] When such an order has been made a District Court judge, within whose district an offence of the specified kind has been committed, will have jurisdiction to deal with the offence in any court area within his or her district and at a place and time not standing appointed for the hearing of cases of summary jurisdiction.

Special provision is made for the Christmas, Easter and August vacations.[81] No sitting of the District Court will be held in the period of nine consecutive days commencing on December 23, of each year. Similarly, there will be no sitting of the court in the period of six consecutive days commencing on the Thursday before Easter Sunday. For the month of August each court district, apart from the Dublin Metropolitan district,[82] is treated as a court area and a weekly sitting of the court will be held in each such area at a specified place for the transaction of summary business which cannot be deferred until after August.[83]

In addition to the substantive limits on its jurisdiction as a District Court, each sitting of the court is generally confined to dealing with defendants from, or criminal matters arising within, its area.[84] It is in this sense that the District Court can be described as a court of local jurisdiction. Because of this local jurisdiction it will happen from time to time that a judge will be familiar with the defendant before the court because of frequent previous appearances by the same defendant before the same judge in criminal matters. It does not follow that the judge should consider himself or herself unsuitable to try the

---

[78] District Court Rules 1997, Ord.1, r.1. A judge may, when sitting at a a place, on a day, and at an hour appointed for the transaction of any particular class of business of the court, transact at such sitting any other class of business of the court; Ord.1, r.2.

[79] District Court Rules 1997, Ord.1, r.1. This also permits a judge to hold a sitting of the court at a place and time not so appointed for the preliminary examination of indictable offences. With the abolition of the preliminary examination by the Criminal Justice Act 1999 this provision is now defunct.

[80] Courts Act 1971, s.15. Woods says that the measure was introduced to deal with summary offences under the Diseases of Animals Act 1966 ("foot and mouth diseases control orders"), but no orders have been made under it to date. Woods at p.26.

[81] See District Court Districts (Amendment) Order 1970 and District Court Areas (Amendment) Order 1970.

[82] The President of the District Court makes arrangements for the discharge of business in the Dublin Metropolitan District during the month of August.

[83] The place will be specified in the Schedule to District Court Areas (Amendment) Order 1970. In Cork City two sittings are held.

[84] See Chap. 13. It is also worth noting that there are several situations in which, by statute, a District Court Judge has jurisdiction over offences committed in Irish territorial seas or abroad; see Chap. 2.

defendant as a result. Adherence to his or oath of office is considered
sufficient protection against the risk of prejudice in such cases.[85]

Summary Jurisdiction

The District Court is a court of summary jurisdiction.[86] Accordingly, it has   **2–18**
jurisdiction to dispose of all summary offences. It also has jurisdiction, in
certain circumstances, over indictable offences if they are of a minor nature or
if the accused pleads guilty (see chapter 2). Apart from these "hybrid"
offences, the court does not have jurisdiction to dispose of indictable
offences. Nevertheless, persons tried on indictment, or sentenced on a plea of
guilty to charges on indictment, will normally have been sent forward for trial
or sentence by a judge of the District Court.[87] There is also provision for
depositions to be taken from witnesses before a District Court judge for use in
a trial on indictment or in an application to dismiss the charges (see chapter
14). The jurisdiction of the District Court extends to the remand in custody or
on bail of an accused and to the extension of detention in Garda custody for a
person who has been arrested under section 30 of the Offences against the
State Act 1939 or section 2 of the Criminal Justice (Drug Trafficking) Act
1996 (see chapter 5).

Juvenile Court

Unlike some other countries, Ireland does not yet have a wholly separate
Juvenile Court. Instead, the District Court doubles as a Juvenile Court for
both summary and many indictable offences where the defendant is under 17
years of age.[88] It sits in camera for this purpose and follows a modified
procedure. It must also sit in a different room or building, or at a different
time, from the ordinary District Court sittings. Part 7 of the Children Act
2001 provides a new statutory basis for the Children Court in Ireland and
extends its jurisdiction to persons under 18 years of age.[89] Nevertheless, it is
still based on the District Court.

Constitutional Issues

Although the District Court is a court of local and limited jurisdiction it can,   **2–19**
and indeed must, rule on constitutional issues in certain circumstances. Where
an accused alleges that his constitutional rights have been infringed in the
course of the proceedings by which he was brought before the court to answer
a criminal charge, the District Court " . . . has a duty to act constitutionally
and to act in such a manner as to preserve the individual's constitutional

---

[85] See comments of Smyth J. in *DPP (Stratford) v. O'Neill* [1998] 1 I.L.R.M. 221.
[86] Courts (Supplemental Provisions) Act 1961, s.33. See *State (McEvitt) v. Delap* [1981] I.R. 125 for
an account of the development of the summary jurisdiction of the court.
[87] The requirement for a preliminary hearing prior to being sent forward for trial indictment has been
abolished by the Criminal Justice Act 1999.
[88] Children Act 1908, s.111, as amended by Children Act 1941, s.26.
[89] Pt 7 has not yet been brought into force.

rights."[90] In the Supreme Court decision of *People (DPP) v. Lynch* Walsh J. stated:

> "It is important to recall that the District Court and the Circuit Court, which deal with the great bulk of criminal trials in the State, are courts set up under the Constitution. Like their brethren in the Supreme Court and in the High Court, each judge of the Circuit and of the District Court is obliged by Article 34.5 of the Constitution to make and subscribe in open court to the solemn and sincere promise that he will uphold the Constitution and the laws. Therefore, the judges of the District Court and judges of the Circuit Court are not dispensed from, or expected to overlook their constitutional obligation to uphold the Constitution in the discharge of their constitutional and legal function of administering justice. It would be most incongruous if they were to apply a general test of basic fairness because the Constitution requires it, and not to rule on questions of the admissibility of evidence obtained as a result of breaches of the constitutional rights of the accused. The judicial obligation is to uphold all of the Constitution."[91]

Accordingly, the court has jurisdiction to exclude evidence if it has been obtained in a manner which breached the constitutional rights of the accused. Similarly, the court ought to entertain submissions where a summons used to secure the defendant's presence before the court was obtained in a manner which breached his or her constitutional rights.[92] The court also has jurisdiction to rule on the constitutionality of a pre-1937 law. While this is not the equivalent of a jurisdiction to declare the pre-1937 law unconstitutional, it is sufficient to disapply it in the proceedings before the court on the ground that it conflicts with the 1937 Constitution.

2–20 There are limits to the extent to which the District Court can act to protect the constitutional rights of a person appearing before it, particularly in circumstances where the constitutional issues being raised are more suitable for an application to the High Court. The District Court has no jurisdiction to entertain an argument that a post-1937 law is invalid having regard to the provisions of the 1937 Constitution.[93] That jurisdiction is constitutionally reserved to the High Court, and on appeal to the Supreme Court. Equally, the District Court has no jurisdiction to submit a consultative case stated for the opinion of the High Court on the constitutionality of a pre-1937 statutory provision.[94] Nor can it seek to achieve the same result indirectly by submitting a consultative case stated where the nature of the question is such that the High Court is in effect being asked to rule on the constitutionality of

---

[90] *Coughlan v. Patwell* [1993] 1 I.R. 31, *per* Denham J. at 37. See also Walsh J. in *Ellis v. O'Dea* [1989] I.R. 530; *DPP (Stratford) v. O'Neill* [1998] 1 I.L.R.M. 221, *per* Smyth J. at 223; *People (DPP) v. Lynch* [1982] I.R. 64.

[91] [1982] I.R. 64 at 84.

[92] *Coughlan v. Patwell* [1993] 1 I.R. 31. See *Ellis v. O'Dea* [1989] I.R. 520 for the duty of the District Court judge to protect the constitutional rights of a person in extradition proceedings before the court.

[93] *DPP (Stratford) v. O'Neill* [1998] 1 I.L.R.M. 221.

[94] *Foyle Fisheries Commission v. Gallen* [1960] Ir. Jur. Rep. 35.

a post-1937 statutory provision.[95] In *People (DPP) v. Dougan*,[96] for example, a District Court judge submitted a consultative case stated for the opinion of the High Court on whether, having regard to the compulsory disqualifications attached to a conviction, the offences of drunk-driving and/or refusing to provide a specimen could be considered minor offences in the circumstances of the case before the judge. Given the compulsory nature of the disqualification on conviction, coupled with the fact that the legislation provided only for summary trial, a ruling that the offences were non-minor would be tantamount to a ruling on the constitutionality of the statutory provisions creating the offences. The circumstances could be distinguished from those in *O'Sullivan v. Hartnett*[97] where a summary offence was punishable by, *inter alia*, the confiscation of equipment used in the unlawful capture of fish. The offences in that case were found to be non-minor, but only because of the value of the equipment confiscated. It did not follow that the value of the items confiscated in every such case would be sufficiently high to take the case into the non-minor category. Accordingly, the decision in *Hartnett* was not tantamount to a ruling that the statutory provision creating the offence was unconstitutional. In *Dougan*, however, the minimum period of disqualification was compulsory in every case. A ruling that it was sufficient to render the offence non-minor, in circumstances where there was no provision for trial on indictment, would be tantamount to a ruling on the constitutionality of the statutory provision creating the offence.

Although the District Court has jurisdiction to take whatever steps it considers proper when the defendant alleges that his or her constitutional rights have been infringed in the procedures adopted for bringing him to court,[97a] the court will not normally be deprived of jurisdiction to proceed to hear a case purely on the basis that there has been such an infringement.[97b] Even if, for example, the defendant alleges that his appearance before the court was secured through an unlawful arrest and detention the court will not normally be precluded from proceeding to hear the charges. Equally, defects in the warrant or summons will not deprive the court of jurisdiction so long as the person is actually present in court to be charged on foot of a valid complaint (see chapter 13, para.13–15). Exceptions will arise where, for example, the defendant's arrest and subsequent detention was unlawfully contrived for the purpose of bringing him or her before the court, or if proof of a valid arrest is an essential ingredient to ground the charge for which the person is before the court.[97c]

For further discussion see chapter 13.

---

95 *People (DPP) v. Dougan* [1996] 1 I.R. 544.
96 [1996] 1 I.R. 544.
97 [1983] I.L.R.M. 79.
97a *DPP v. Delaney* [1997] 3 I.R. 453; *Coughlan v. Patwell* [1993] 1 I.R. 31; *Ellis v. O'Dea* [1989] I.R. 520.
97b *Keating v. Governor of Mountjoy Prison* [1990] I.L.R.M. 850; *DPP (Ivers) v. Murphy* [1999] 1 I.L.R.M. 46; *DPP (McTiernan) v. Bradley* unreported, High Court, December 9, 1999; *DPP v. Byrne* [1998] 2 I.R. 417.
97c *DPP v. Forbes* [1993] I.L.R.M. 817; *DPP (McTiernan) v. Bradley* unreported, High Court, December 9, 1999.

A "Drug Court"

Some progress has been made towards the establishment of "drug courts" in Ireland.[97d] In 1997 the Minister for Justice, Equality and Law Reform requested the Working Party on a Courts Commission to investigate and report on the establishment of a drug courts system in Ireland. Months later the Working Group presented proposals for the establishment of "drug courts".[97e] Subsequently, the Minister set up an expert committee to consider the establishment of such a court. The Committee reported with a recommendation that a drug court should be set up initially on a pilot basis.

A drug court, based on the District Court, was established on a pilot basis on February 1, 2001 in Dublin's north inner city.[97f] Its jurisdiction is confined to persons over the age of 17 years who have been convicted of or pleaded guilty to certain non-violent offences in circumstances where their offending was driven by the need to feed a drug habit. On conviction they will have been presented with the option of a prison sentence or going before the drug court for the purpose of submitting to a programme aimed at weaning them off their drug habit. On their appearance before the court, which is chaired by a District Court judge, they are assessed for their suitability for such a programme. Typically, this will include hearing the views of a probation and welfare officer on the offender's circumstances and a member of the Garda Síochána on the offender's criminal record and, in particular, whether there are any outstanding charges pending against the offender which could render a programme irrelevant.

The programme will involve a very stringent regime aimed at keeping the offender drug free. There are three phases stretching over a period of 12 to 18 months. During the first phase, the offender will come back before the court on a weekly basis for a review of his or her progress. In the second phase, he or she will appear every two weeks and in the third phase every month. The court is supported by a multi-disciplinary team drawn from probation, education and medicine. There is a heavy emphasis on education and rehabilitation, with regular medical checks to ensure that the offender is staying drug free. Sanctions are imposed for a failure to comply with the requirements of the programme.

It is apparent from this brief outline that the "drug court" is not the District Court exercising criminal jurisdiction in the conventional manner. In effect, it is a sentencing court exercising a novel sentencing jurisdiction. The emphasis is on therapeutic rehabilitation as distinct from punishment. That, however, should not be mistaken for leniency. The regime imposed by the court is rigorous and demanding. Indeed, in the first year of its operation fewer than

---

[97d] For a discussion of the "drug court" concept see S Butler "A Tale of Two Sectors: A Critical Analysis of the Proposal to Establish Drug Courts in the Republic of Ireland" in *Criminal Justice in Ireland* edited by P O'Mahoney (IPA, Dublin, 2002), p.407.

[97e] Working Group on a Courts Commission Fifth Report: Drug Courts (Stationery Office, Dublin, 1998).

[97f] I am grateful to Noel McNaboe, Drug Court Co-ordinator for the information on which the following account is based.

one hundred offenders opted to submit to its jurisdiction *in lieu* of imprisonment. This was significantly less than anticipated. It is intended to extend the court's trial basis before a decision is taken on whether to establish it as a regular part of the criminal justice system.

4. Circuit Court

Establishment and Composition

Like the District Court, the Circuit Court is a single court consisting of the President of the Circuit Court and, currently, 30 Circuit Court judges.[98] For the purposes of this court the country is divided by government order into seven circuits,[99] and most of these judges are assigned to an individual circuit.[100] Some circuits will have two or more judges assigned. Unlike the District Court districts, the individual circuits are not further subdivided into areas. Nevertheless, the Circuit Court does move around the principal towns and cities within a circuit from time to time.[101] Moreover, a sitting of the Circuit Court is normally confined to dealing with offences committed within the circuit in question or with defendants who reside or who have been arrested within it.[102] Accordingly, it is described as a court of local jurisdiction. However, outside Dublin, either the prosecution or the accused can apply to have the case transferred to the Dublin Circuit Court (previously the Central Criminal Court)[103] if, for some reason, it was considered undesirable to have it tried on the local circuit.[104] The usual reason given here is that the offence in question has attracted such local notoriety and attention that the accused might not get a fair trial from a local jury.

2–21

Time and Place of Sittings

The location of the sittings of the court within a circuit, and the times of the sitting, shall be prescribed from time to time by the judge of that circuit.[105] Notice of such sittings in counties outside Dublin shall be published in *Iris*

---

[98] The number of ordinary judges is fixed from time to time by Act of the Oireachtas; Courts (Establishment and Constitution) Act 1961, s.4(2). The current number of 30 is fixed by the Courts and Court Officers Act 1995, s.10, as amended by the Courts and Court Officers Act 2002, s.26. It does not include an extra position which may be filled where a former President of the Court serves as a judge of the court; Courts (No.2) Act 1997, s.5(4).

[99] Dublin, Cork, Eastern, Northern, Western, Midland, South-Western and South-Eastern; Courts of Justice Act 1953, s.16; and Courts (Supplemental Provisions) Act 1961, s.20(2).

[100] Courts Act 1977, s.1(2). Ten are permanently assigned to the Dublin Circuit and three to the Cork Circuit; s.2, as amended by s.36 of the Court and Court Officers Act 1995.

[101] Although there may be two or more circuit judges in a given circuit, there will not normally be simultaneous sittings of the court at different venues within the circuit. However, there can be two or more judges sitting simultaneously in different courtrooms at the same venue.

[102] Courts (Supplemental Provisions) Act 1961, s.25(3). See also Circuit Court Rules 2001, Ord.2(g).

[103] See *Tormey v. Attorney General* [1985] I.R. 289.

[104] Courts and Court Officers Act 1995, s.32. This provision would appear to conflict with Dublin Circuit Court's status as a court of local jurisdiction. Nevertheless, this argument failed in a constitutional challenge to a similar provision in *State (Boyle) v. Judge Neylon* [1986] I.R. 551.

[105] Circuit Court Rules 2001, Ord.1, r.1.

Oifigiúil and in a newspaper circulating within the county not later than two months before the date of the sitting. However, if it proves impracticable to hold a sitting as published, the judge, or in his absence the County Registrar by direction of the judge, may adjourn the sitting to a future date. Such notice as may be practicable in the circumstances should be given. Equally, the judge may adjourn proceedings to a future date where he or she is of the opinion that any cause, action or matter cannot be conveniently heard or disposed of in the time allocated for the sitting or for any other sufficient reason.

In the Dublin Circuit the times and places of the sittings shall be prescribed by the President of the Circuit Court, if he or she is assigned to the Dublin Circuit, or the Senior Judge of the Circuit.[106] Notice of the sittings shall be published in *Iris Oifigiúil* no later than two months before the date of sitting. This notice must set out the day of commencement and day of termination of each sitting. However, the President or Senior Judge, as the case may be, may with the consent of all the judges permanently assigned to the Dublin Circuit extend any sitting beyond the date of sittings. There is no need to publish notice of any such extension.

Although there may be two or more Circuit Court judges in a given circuit, there will not normally be simultaneous sittings of the court at different venues within the circuit. However, there can be two or more judges sitting simultaneously in different courtrooms at the same venue.

The court does not normally sit during the months of August and September.[107] In the case of the Dublin Circuit there is provision for judges to sit and promptly hear all such applications and cases as required.[108] Sittings outside of Dublin during these months may be fixed by the President of the Circuit Court where such sittings are, in his or her view, necessary or desirable. Other applications of an urgent nature can be made at any time to the President of the Circuit Court or a judge nominated by him.[109] Notice of the intention to make any such application should be submitted to the County Registrar.

Substantive Jurisdiction

The Circuit Court is described as a court of limited jurisdiction because its original jurisdiction does not extend to all criminal offences. Nevertheless, its jurisdiction is extensive. It is competent to try all offences with the exception of certain treason, murder, sexual and subversive offences (see below under Central Criminal Court).[110] It also has full appellate jurisdiction with respect to convictions and decisions on sentence from the District Court.[111] Although an appeal against conviction takes the form of a full re-hearing of the case, it is conducted before a Circuit Court judge sitting alone. By contrast, when the

---

[106]   *ibid.* Ord.1, r.2.
[107]   *ibid.* Ord.1. r.3.
[108]   *ibid.* Ord.1, r.4.
[109]   *ibid.* Ord.1, r.5.
[110]   Courts (Supplemental Provisions) Act 1961, s.25.
[111]   Courts of Justice Act 1928, s.18 and Courts (Supplemental Provisions) Act 1961, s.22(3)(a)(ii) and 50.

Circuit Court is exercising its original jurisdiction to try an offence on indictment it sits with a jury.

5. Central Criminal Court

The Central Criminal Court is the name given to the High Court when exercising its criminal jurisdiction[112] The court consists of the President of the High Court, the Chief Justice, the President of the Circuit Court, *ex officio*, and such number of ordinary judges as fixed from time to time by an Act of the Oireachtas.[113] Currently that number is fixed at 22. Normally the court sits with a single judge, although the President of the High Court may direct that two or more judges should sit together in a particular case.[114] It follows that two or more Central Criminal Courts can, and often do, sit at the same time. Invariably, all of these sittings are held in the Four Courts in Dublin. It follows that all murder, serious sexual and treason offences, and offences under the Offences against the State Act 1939 are heard in the Four Courts in Dublin.

    The Central Criminal Court enjoys full original jurisdiction in all criminal matters.[115] It enjoys exclusive jurisdiction in: treason, treason-felony, conspiracy to commit treason, the major offences created by the Offences against the State Act 1939, murder,[116] attempt to murder, conspiracy to murder, rape, aggravated sexual assault, piracy and genocide.[117] Since the Circuit Court has jurisdiction in all other criminal offences, relatively few prosecutions are actually brought in the Central Criminal Court.[118] It must sit with a jury,[119] and does not exercise any appellate jurisdiction with respect to conviction or sentence in the Circuit Court or the District Court. It does, however, have jurisdiction over appeals by way of a case stated from a decision of the District Court.

2–22

6. High Court

Although the High Court's original jurisdiction in criminal matters is exercised through the medium of the Central Criminal Court, some incidents of its general jurisdiction, *qua* High Court, feature prominently in criminal

2–23

---

112   Courts (Supplemental Provisions) Act 1961, s.11.
113   Courts (Establishment and Constitution) Act 1961, s.2; Courts and Court Officers Act 1995, s.9(1), as amended by the Courts Act 1997, s.1. The number may be increased to 23 if a member of the Court is a member of the Law Reform Commission; see Law Reform Commission Act 1975, s.14(1) as amended by the Courts Act 1997, s.1.
114   Courts (Supplemental Provisions) Act 1961, s.11(2)(a).
115   Bunreacht na hÉireann, Art. 34.1.
116   This included capital murder; see Criminal Justice Act 1964, s.3(5). It is by no means certain that it includes murder to which s.3 of the Criminal Justice Act 1993 applies.
117   Courts (Supplemental Provisions) Act 1961, s.25(2), as extended by the Genocide Act 1973, s.2(4), and Criminal Law (Rape)(Amendment) Act 1990, s.10.
118   This does not conflict with Art. 34.3.1 of the Constitution which gives the High Court full original jurisdiction in criminal matters. See *Tormey v. Attorney General* [1985] I.R. 289.
119   *Re Haughey* [1971] I.R. 217. However, it exercises summary jurisdiction over criminal contempts.

matters. Chief among these must be the court's jurisdiction over habeas corpus applications. Usually, but not invariably, an application for habeas corpus will be brought by a person who claims that he is being unlawfully detained pursuant to the exercise of a police power or the decision of a court in criminal proceedings. It is also worth noting that if the Central Criminal Court purports to issue an order of discovery in a criminal case it will be exercising its jurisdiction as the High Court as distinct from the Central Criminal Court.[119a]

7. The Court of Criminal Appeal

2–24   The Court of Criminal Appeal is purely a creature of statute.[120] It is provided for by the Courts (Establishment and Constitution) Act 1961 and the Courts (Supplemental Provisions) Act 1961. It is convened in accordance with directions given from time to time by the Chief Justice. It consists of not less than three judges,[121] although the Chief Justice or a single judge of the Supreme Court may deal with interlocutory applications in the exercise of the court's jurisdiction. One of the three judges must be the Chief Justice, or an ordinary judge of the Supreme Court nominated by him. The other two must be any two judges of the High Court nominated by the Chief Justice. One of these two must be the President of the High Court if he is willing to act. Additional members from either the High Court or the Supreme Court, may attend at the request of the Chief Justice.

The Court of Criminal Appeal has only an appellate jurisdiction. It can entertain appeals against conviction or sentence from the Circuit Court, the Central Criminal Court and the Special Criminal Court.[122] Equally, it has jurisdiction to review convictions or sentences on the grounds of a miscarriage of justice, and to review sentences on the ground of undue leniency. Although there is scope for calling fresh evidence before the court, an appeal is normally conducted on the basis of the transcript of the trial at first instance. At the conclusion of the appeal the court can affirm the conviction, reverse it in whole or in part, quash the conviction and order a re-trial, enter a finding of guilty of another offence, or quash, reduce or increase the sentence.[123] On a review application there is greater scope to admit fresh evidence.

The jurisdiction and procedure of the Court of Criminal Appeal is dealt with fully in chapter 22 on Appeals. Accordingly, reference should be made to that chapter for further detail on the court. It is also worth noting that there is statutory provision for the abolition of the court. The Committee on Court Practice and Procedure recommended its abolition and the transfer of its jurisdiction to the Supreme Court. The Courts and Court Officers Act 1995 gives effect to this recommendation.[124] However, the relevant provision can

---

[119a] *People (DPP) v. Sweeney* [2002] 1 I.L.R.M. 532.
[120] See *State (Woods) v. Attorney General* [1969] I.R. 385 and *People (AG) v. Conmey* [1975] I.R. 341 for challenges to the constitutionality of the Court.
[121] Courts (Establishment and Constitution) Act 1961, s.3.
[122] Courts of Justice Act 1924, s.28; Courts (Supplemental Provisions) Act 1961, s.48(2); Offences against the State Act 1961, s.44.
[123] Criminal Procedure Act 1993, s. 3.
[124] Courts and Court Officers Act 1995, s.4(1).

only be brought into effect by government order and as of yet that has not happened.[125]

8. The Supreme Court

The Supreme Court consists of the Chief Justice, the President of the High **2–25** Court, *ex officio*, and seven ordinary judges.[126] Although there are occasions when the court must sit with a minimum of five judges, three judges are sufficient when considering a criminal appeal.[127] The Courts and Court Officers Act 1995 makes specific provision enabling the Supreme Court to sit in two or more divisions at the same time.[128] This is intended to prepare the ground for the abolition of the Court of Criminal Appeal and the transfer of its jurisdiction to the Supreme Court.

The Supreme Court, like the Court of Criminal Appeal, has appellate jurisdiction only in criminal matters. By virtue of Article 34 of the Constitution it has appellate jurisdiction from all decisions of the High Court, with such exceptions and subject to such regulations as may be prescribed by law. It follows that there would be a right of appeal against conviction and/or sentence in the Central Criminal Court direct to the Supreme Court, if it had not been abolished by statute.[129] This is in addition to the right of appeal to the Court of Criminal Appeal.[130] By the same token there is a right of appeal to the Supreme Court from a decision of the High Court on a case stated from the District Court.[131] It is also possible for a Circuit Court judge to refer for decision to the Supreme Court any question of law which has arisen in proceedings before him or her.[132] Morgan comments that this is rarely used as it necessitates the adjournment of the Circuit Court proceedings pending the Supreme Court's decision.[133] Finally, an appeal lies to the Supreme Court from a decision of the Court of Criminal Appeal, but only if that court or the DPP certifies that the decision "involves a point of law of exceptional public importance and that it is desirable in the public interest that an appeal should be taken to the Supreme Court".[134]

For further discussion of the Supreme Courts appellate jurisdiction in criminal matters, see chapter 22.

---

[125] *ibid.* s.1(2).
[126] Courts (Establishment and Constitution) Act 1961, s.1, as amended by the Courts and Court Officers Act 1995, s.6(1); Courts (Supplemental Provisions) Act 1961, s.4(1). The number of ordinary judges shall be 8 where one of them is appointed to the Law Reform Commission; Law Reform Commission Act 1975, s.14(1), as amended by the Courts and Court Officers Act 1995, s.6(2).
[127] Courts (Supplemental Provisions) Act 1961, s.7(4). It cannot sit with four judges.
[128] Courts (Supplemental Provisions) Act 1961, s.7, as amended by the Courts and Court Officers, 1995, s.7.
[129] In *People (DPP) v. O'Shea* [1982] I.R. 384 the Supreme Court ruled that this right of appeal extended to the right of the prosecution to appeal an acquittal. This has been subsequently abolished by the Criminal Procedure Act 1993, s.11(1).
[130] *People (Attorney General) v. Conmey* [1975] I.R. 341, confirmed by *People (DPP) v. O'Shea* [1982] I.R. 384
[131] Courts (Supplemental Provisions) Act 1961, s.52(2).
[132] Courts of Justice Act 1947, s.16.
[133] D Morgan *Constitutional Law of Ireland* (2nd ed., Roundhall Press, Dublin, 1990), p.203
[134] Courts of Justice Act 1924, s.29; Courts (Supplemental Provisions) Act 1961, s.48(3).

9. Special Criminal Court

2–26 Article 38.3.1 of the Constitution makes provision for the establishment of special courts where it is determined in accordance with law that the ordinary courts are inadequate to secure the effective administration of justice and the preservation of public peace and order. Once established, such courts are not bound by the provisions of Articles 34 and 35 of the Constitution.[135] In practice, their most distinctive feature is that they can sit without a jury to try defendants on indictment. A Special Criminal Court established pursuant to these provisions has been sitting continuously since 1972 and, in the light of the Report of the Committee to Review the Offences against the State Acts 1939–1998 and Related Matters, it is likely to remain sitting for the foreseeable future.

The establishment, status, composition and procedure of Special Criminal Courts is dealt with fully in chapter 20. Accordingly, nothing further need be said about them here.

10. Courts-Martial

2–27 Article 38.4 of the Constitution permits the establishment by law of military tribunals to try persons subject to military law for offences against military law.[136] The right to trial by jury enshrined in Article 38.5 does not extend to such tribunals. Part V of the Defence Act 1954 provides for the convening of military tribunals, known as courts-martial. Their membership is confined to officers of the Defence Forces.[137] Their jurisdiction is limited to offences against military law committed by a person while subject to military law.[138] Persons subject to military law in this context are members of the Defence Forces, members of the Reserve Defence Forces in certain circumstances, and civilians attached to or accompanying any portion of the Defence Forces which is on active service.[139] Although the jurisdiction of these courts-martial is confined to offences under military law it does not follow that they deal only with offences against military discipline.[140] An offence against military law also includes an offence against the civil law when committed by a person subject to military law.[141] It follows that a member of the Defence Forces charged with assault or theft, for example, is liable to be tried before a courts-martial. It should be noted, however, that the courts-martial cannot try

---

[135] Bunreacht na hÉireann, Art. 38.6.
[136] The same provision also permits the establishment of military tribunals to deal with a state of war or armed rebellion. Casey suggests that it may be possible to establish these without any statutory basis; see J Casey, *op.cit.,* p.266 and chap.7.
[137] Defence Act 1954, ss.189 and 190.
[138] *ibid.* s.192(1).
[139] *ibid.* ss.118 and 119. For this purpose a portion of the Defence Forces is deemed to be on active service when engaged in operations against an enemy or engaged in military operations in a place wholly or mainly occupied by an enemy (defined as including armed mutineers, rebels, rioters and pirates). A portion of the Defence Forces is also on active duty during any period covered by a government order declaring the forces to be on active service; see s.5.
[140] See Defence Act 1954, Pt V, Chap.2 for the list of offences against military law.
[141] Defence Act 1954, s.169.

any person for treason, murder, manslaughter or rape unless that person was on active service when the offence was allegedly committed.[142]

Appeal from a courts-martial lies to the Courts-Martial Appeal Court, which is really the Court of Criminal Appeal sitting under another name.[143] It is also possible to appeal from the Courts-Martial Appeal Court to the Supreme Court, but only if the former, or the Attorney General, certifies that the decision involves a point of law of exceptional public importance and that an appeal is desirable in the public interest.[144]

Further treatment of courts-martial and the Courts-Martial Appeals Court is beyond the scope of this work.[145] It must be noted, however, that like the Court of Criminal Appeal provision has been made for the abolition of the Courts-Martial Appeals Court and the transfer of its jurisdiction to the Supreme Court.[146] As of yet the necessary government order has not been issued.

11. Court of Justice of the European Community[147]

Introduction

The Court of Justice of the European Community is one of two courts serving the needs of the European Community based on the Treaty of Rome. The second court is the Court of First Instance. European Community law, including the decisions of these two courts, are binding in Ireland in accordance with the provisions of the Treaty of Rome, Article 29.4.3 of the Constitution and the European Communities Act 1973 (as amended). Nevertheless, neither court has any direct role in the enforcement of criminal law within this State. The Court of Justice, however, can play an indirect role through its jurisdiction under Article 234 of the Treaty of Rome. It is necessary, therefore, to sketch its composition, procedure and the operation of its jurisdiction under Article 234.

2–28

Establishment and Composition

The court consists of 15 permanent judges, one from each Member State. They are appointed for a renewable term of six years by common accord of the governments of the Member States. To qualify for appointment to the

---

142 *ibid.* s.192(3). See s.192(2) for further restrictions on the jurisdiction of a "limited" Court-Martial.

143 See, generally, the Courts-Martial Appeals Act 1983 and, in particular, ss.14 and 15.

144 It is worth noting that the certificate must come from the Supreme Court or the Attorney General. The DPP is not given a similar power to certify; Courts-Martial Appeals Act 1983, s.14.

145 See further, C Craven and G Humphries *Military Law in Ireland* (Dublin, Round Hall Sweet & Maxwell, 1997).

146 Courts and Court Officers Act 1995, s.5.

147 See generally: L Neville Brown & T Kennedy *The Court of Justice of the European Communities* (5th ed., Sweet & Maxwell, London, 2000); D Lasok *The European Court of Justice – Practice and Procedure* (Butterworths, London, 1994); G De Burca (ed.) *The European Court of Justice* (Oxford University Press, Oxford, 2001); B McMahon & F Murphy *European Community Law in Ireland* (Butterworths, Dublin, 1989); T C Hartley *Foundations of European Community Law* (4th ed., Clarendon Press, Oxford, 1998); D Lasok & J W Bridge *Law and Institutions of the European Communities* (7th ed., Butterworths, London, 2001).

court a judge must be eligible for appointment to the highest judicial office in his or her Member State or be a jurisconsult of recognised competence. Much of the business of the court, particularly the preparatory stages of a case can be conducted by one of the six chambers of the court, or even by a single judge. Generally, the procedure of the court reflects the civil law preference for written submissions compared with the common law emphasis on oral testimony and argument. If it proves necessary to examine and cross-examine witnesses this will normally be done before a single judge or a chamber. The formal oral hearing of the case before the plenary session or chamber, as the case may be, is usually confined to submissions by the parties' legal representatives for the purpose of emphasising key points in the detailed written submissions which are already before the court.

The court is assisted by eight Advocates General appointed by common accord of the governments of the Member States. Generally, one is appointed from each of the big four Member States (Germany, France, Italy and the United Kingdom), while the remainder are rotated among the other Member States.[148] The Advocate General is a transplant from civil law legal systems, particularly France. It has no direct counterpart in the Irish or British legal systems. He or she sits with the court in a case, but does not actually form part of the court for the purpose of adjudication. At the conclusion of the case for the parties the Advocate General makes an independent submission to the court on what he or she considers to be the correct interpretation of the law at issue and how it should be applied to the case at hand. Typically, the submission will reflect a considered and wide ranging assessment of how the law on the subject in question has been developing and how it should be interpreted in order to protect and promote the integrity of the law as an integral part of the broader European Community scheme. The Treaty of Rome defines the role of the Advocate General:

> "[I]t shall be the duty of the Advocate General, acting with complete impartiality and independence to make, in open court, reasoned submissions on cases which in accordance with the Statute of the Court of Justice requires his involvement"[148a]

The court is not bound to follow the opinion of the Advocate General, but in practice it usually does.

The court deliberates in private and delivers a collegiate decision. It is never disclosed whether there were majority and minority opinions. Both the decision of the court and the opinion of the Advocate General are published. The latter is usually found to be much more revealing and informative than the former on the state of the law and on the issue in question.

Jurisdiction on Referrals from National Courts

2–29   Actions can be initiated in the Court of Justice by Community institutions, Member States and, in certain limited situations, natural and legal persons.

---

[148] Nial Fennelly, currently a judge of the Supreme Court, has served as an Advocate General.
[148a] Treaty of Rome, Art. 222, as amended by Treaty of Nice, Art. 2(28).

Invariably, however, such actions will be based on civil, as opposed to criminal law. While the European Union is rapidly developing a corpus of criminal law, as yet there is no criminal code which is directly binding within the Member States. Nevertheless, the court can exert an indirect influence on the course of a criminal case before municipal courts. This is achieved through its very important jurisdiction under Article 234 of the Treaty of Rome. The Article 234 mechanism is a very practical and necessary consequence of the fact that directly effective Community law is enforceable in the national courts of the Member States by natural and legal persons. If Community law is to be interpreted uniformly throughout the Member States it is essential that some central mechanism should be available for a national court to obtain an authoritative interpretation of a relevant point of Community law which has arisen in proceedings before it. Article 234 provides this mechanism.

Article 234 of the Treaty of Rome states:

> "The Court of Justice shall have jurisdiction to give preliminary rulings concerning:
>
> (a) the interpretation of this Treaty;
> (b) the validity and interpretation of acts of the institutions of the Community;
> (c) the interpretation of the statutes of bodies established by an act of the Council, where those statutes so provide.
>
> Where such a question is raised before any court or tribunal of a Member State, that court or tribunal may, if it considers that a decision on the question is necessary to enable it to give judgment, request the Court of Justice to give a ruling thereon. Where any such question is raised in a case pending before a court or tribunal of a Member State against whose decisions there is no judicial remedy under national law, that court or tribunal shall bring the matter before the Court of Justice."

Broadly speaking, the effect is that a national court or tribunal can refer to the Court of Justice for a ruling on the correct interpretation of a provision of Community law or the validity of acts of the institutions. Where the Community law issue arises for decision before a national court from whose decision on the matter there is an appeal within the national court system, the court in question will have a discretion to refer. In other words it is free to decide the Community law issue itself or to refer the matter to the Court of Justice as it sees fit.[149] If the issue arises for decision before a court from whose decision on the matter there is no appeal within the national court system, that court must normally make a referral to the Court of Justice. In either case the decision to refer should not be taken until all the relevant evidence has been presented before the national court.

---

[149] The Irish Supreme Court has decided that the exercise of this discretion by the High Court does not amount to a decision which can be appealed to the Supreme Court; *Campus Oil v. Minister for Industry* [1983] I.R. 82. For commentary on this decision, see F Murphy Casenote on *Campus Oil* (1984) 21 C.M.L.R. 28; and D O'Keeffe *EEC Law Preliminary Deference: The Supreme Court and Community Law* (1983) 5 D.U.L.J. 286.

Expansion of Jurisdiction

2–30
As the competences of the European Community and European Union have expanded with successive amendments to the Community and Union Treaties so also has the jurisdiction of European Court of Justice expanded. Title VI of the Treaty on European Union (the Maastricht Treaty) gave the Union competence in Justice and Home Affairs. This provides for, *inter alia*, co-operation at the level of the European Union in matters of police and criminal law. The Treaty of Amsterdam transferred several of the Title VI matters, principally those relating to the removal of internal borders and the free movement of persons within the Community, from the inter-governmental structures of the Treaty on European Union to the Community structures of the Treaty of Rome.[150] Co-operation in pure police and criminal law matters remains within the inter-governmental structures of the Union. The relevant provisions empower the Union to enact criminal justice measures which are binding on Member States in the same manner as Community Directives, without the element of direct effect. The Union has exercised this power to create a substantial body of European Union criminal law and justice measures (including a number of important Conventions), which is expanding at a rapid pace. There is a legal obligation on Ireland, in common with each other Member States, to ensure that its criminal law and justice measures comply with the requirements of these Union measures.

It is also important to note that the former Title VI matters which have been transferred from the Union to the Community sphere can be an important source of legislation and decision-making in criminal justice matters. Such legislation and decisions will have the same status as other Community law instruments. These can have direct effect in administrative and judicial processes within the criminal justice system, in the sense that they can be applied for and against the individual without the need for any executing measures on the part of the State.

These developments are accompanied by further provisions for national courts and tribunals to make references to the European Court of Justice for interpretation of the relevant Treaty and legislative enactments, where such interpretations are necessary to determine cases before the national courts or tribunals. There are some differences between these provisions and the Article 234 reference procedure described above. Equally, there are some differences depending on whether the reference relates to a Community or a Union provision.

For the matters which have been transferred from Title VI of the Union Treaty to the Community sphere, the reference procedure is very similar to Article 234. The essential difference is that the reference can be made only by a national court or tribunal from which there is no appeal within the national system. Also, the State may ask the court for an interpretation of one of the

---

[150] For further discussion and analysis, see S Peers *EU Justice and Home Affairs Law* (Longman, Harlow, 2000); E Regan (ed.) *The New Third Pillar: Co-operation against Crime in the European Union* (IEA, Dublin, 2000).

Treaty provisions or an act based upon it. However, the European Court of Justice is specifically not competent to rule on any measure or decision pertaining to the abolition of internal border controls where such measure or decision relates to the maintenance of law and order and the safeguarding of internal security. This may limit the usefulness of the referral procedure on criminal matters.

The amendments effected to the Treaty on European Union by the Treaty of Amsterdam make provision for references to the European Court of Justice for rulings on the interpretation of the provisions of Title VI of the Treaty on European Union (police co-operation and criminal law). It would appear that such references can be made on the same basis as references under Article 234 of the Treaty of Rome. Equally, there is provision for references for rulings on the interpretation and validity of Conventions established pursuant to Title VI,[151] legally binding measures adopted pursuant to Title VI and measures implementing them. It would appear, however, that it is a matter for each Member State to declare whether it accepts this jurisdiction and how it can be exercised. Ireland has accepted the jurisdiction with respect to the Europol Convention, but confines it to national courts and tribunals from which there is no judicial remedy within the national legal system.[152]

It is worth noting that the European Court of Justice cannot review the validity or proportionality of operations carried out by the police or other law enforcement services of a Member State, nor can it exercise the responsibilities incumbent upon Member States with regard to the maintenance of law and order and the safeguarding of internal security.[153] That, however, should not inhibit the court from giving a ruling on the meaning or validity of a relevant Treaty provision or measure in the context of facts which have arisen before the national court or tribunal. It will then be a matter for the national court or tribunal to apply such an interpretation when ruling on the correct interpretation and/or validity of the national measure or action.

Procedure before National Court

Where a dispute arises over the interpretation or, if relevant, the validity of a **2–31** Community or Union measure in proceedings before an Irish court or tribunal, the court or tribunal will hear submissions from the parties on the need for a referral and, where it decides to make a reference, on the formulation of the question to be referred. The actual formulation of the question to be referred is critical as it will have a major bearing on the usefulness of the interpretation provided in response by the Court of Justice. In the context of Irish criminal law and procedure the issue is most likely to involve a dispute over the compatibility of an Irish measure with a provision or provisions of the Treaty of Rome, general principles of Community law or secondary legislation of the Community. Equally, however, it could involve the correct

---

[151] See, *e.g.*, the Europol Convention and the provisions of the Europol Act 1997.
[152] Europol Act 1997, s.10(1).
[153] Treaty on European Union, Art.35(5).

interpretation of the national measure in the light of applicable Community law provisions. The firmly established principle of the supremacy of Community law precludes the national court from applying a provision of national criminal law or procedure which is incompatible with a provision of directly effective Community law. Even where the Community law provision in question is not directly effective, the national court is bound to apply an interpretation of the national measure which is compatible with the Community law provision. It follows that the national court should try to formulate the question to be referred in a manner which clearly identifies the relevant provisions of Community law and national law and the circumstances of the case in which they fall to be decided.

2–32   Another critical factor to be borne in mind when formulating the reference is that the Court of Justice does not actually decide the case which is before the national court. It merely gives an authoritative interpretation of the Community law issue at stake. It is then a matter for the national court to apply that interpretation to the facts of the case before it. The most useful reference, therefore, is one which asks the Court of Justice how certain specified rules, principles or provisions of Community law are to be interpreted in the context of the facts of the case before the national court, including the contents of the relevant provisions of national law.

Where a reference is made under Article 234 the proceedings before the national court in question must be adjourned until the Court of Justice has given its ruling. In the interim, a period of least one year and possibly more than two years, the parties must argue the Community law issue before the court in Luxembourg in accordance with the procedure of that court. When the national proceedings recommence the national court will apply the ruling of the Court of Justice to the case before it. The net effect, of course, could be that the national provisions are relatively unaffected by the Community law dimension. If, however, the effect of the court's ruling is that the national provisions are incompatible with Community law the national court will have to treat them as null and void. It is worth noting that the national court must do this automatically. There is no requirement or option for it to wait until the national provisions have been struck down or repealed by a higher court or the Oireachtas. An alternative possibility which could result from the ruling of the Court of Justice is that the national provisions could be given an interpretation by the national court which is quite different from that which they would otherwise have borne.

Referrals from Irish Courts

For the most part references from Irish courts and tribunals to the European Court of Justice have covered issues arising in the context of: equality between the sexes in employment and social welfare matters, the common agricultural policy, competition policy, state aids, the free movement of goods and workers, the freedom of establishment and the freedom to provide services. Very few references have been made in the context of criminal proceedings.[154] Equally, there are very few reported examples of the "Euro-defence" being utilised in criminal proceedings in this jurisdiction. Perhaps this situation will change as criminal law is used increasingly to fulfil Ireland's obligations in the enforcement of the Community's policies on agriculture, fisheries, the environment, transport, competition and fiscal matters. The rapid development of a body of European criminal law should also have a significant impact in this context.

12. European Court of Human Rights[155]

Establishment and Composition

The European Court of Human Rights is provided for by the European Convention on Human Rights and operates under the auspices of the Council of Europe. It is not part of the institutional framework of the European Community or Union. The court consists of one judge from each of the Member States which have signed and ratified the Convention. Currently, the number stands at 41.[156]

2–33

Convention Rights

By signing the Convention, the Member States undertake to uphold in their domestic law the human rights set out in the text of the Convention. These include the protection for the right to life; the freedom from torture, inhuman and degrading treatment; freedom from slavery and forced labour; right to liberty; right to a fair trial; the non-retroactivity of the criminal law; right to privacy and family life; freedom of thought and religion; freedom of expression; freedom of assembly and association; right to marry, right to a remedy for breach of the Convention rights and freedom from discrimination in the enjoyment of those rights.

Although the Convention does not yet form part of Irish law, individuals enjoy the right to pursue a complaint against the State through the Convention. The substance of the complaint might concern, for example, a police power or an aspect of criminal procedure or criminal law provided for by statute, statutory instrument, common law or even the Constitution, which was in breach of one or more of an individual's rights under the Convention. Equally, the complaint could concern an administrative or judicial decision or an administrative practice.

---

[154] See *Minister for Fisheries v. Schonenberg* [1978] E.C.R. 473; *Attorney General v. Burgoa* (1979) J.I.S.E.L. 73; *Pesca Valentia Ltd v. Minister for Fisheries* [1985] I.R. 193; [1988] E.C.R. 83 and *Pesca Valentia (No.2)* [1990] 2 I.R. 305; *Beara Fisheries Ltd v. Minister for Marine* [1987] I.R. 413. See also the Northern Ireland case *Pigs Marketing Board v. Redmond* [1978] E.C.R. 2347.

[155] See, *e.g.*, F Jacobs, C Ovey and R White *The European Convention on Human Rights* (3rd ed., Oxford University Press, Oxford, 2002); Leach *Taking a Case to the European Court of Human Rights* (Oxford University Press, Oxford, 2001); J Hedigan *Revolution in Strasbourg* Irish Law Times (January 1997) 6.

[156] The Irish judge is John Hedigan S.C.

Admissibility Criteria

2–34   Before a complaint can be processed through the Convention it must concern an alleged breach of one or more of the rights protected by the Convention. Equally, it must satisfy the following admissibility criteria:

(A) Domestic remedies must have been exhausted. Accordingly, the complainant must first avail of any administrative or judicial remedies, including rights of appeal, which are available in the Irish legal system before resorting to the Convention machinery. If, however, domestic law on the point at issue has been firmly settled, for example, by a pertinent decision of the Supreme Court, the exhaustion requirement will not be strictly applied;

(B) The application must be made within a period of six months from the date on which the relevant final decision was taken within the domestic framework. This is strictly applied;

(C) The complaint must not be anonymous;

(D) The complaint must not consist of a matter which has already been examined by the Court of Human Rights or a matter which has been submitted to another procedure of international investigation or settlement, unless of course it contains relevant new information; and

(E) The complaint must not be incompatible with the provisions of the Convention, manifestly ill-founded or an abuse of the right of application.

Court Structure and Procedure

The European Court of Human Rights is at the heart of the enforcement machinery.[157] It has jurisdiction to hear and decide all questions relating to the interpretation and application of the Convention. This includes the jurisdiction to give advisory opinions when requested by the Committee of Ministers (see below) as well as hearing and determining complaints brought by individuals and signatory States. The court sits in committees of three judges, chambers of seven judges and a Grand Chamber of 17 judges. A complaint is initially considered for admissibility by a committee of three judges. Its decision in any individual case must be unanimous and a decision to exclude an application is final. Where a case is declared admissible it then proceeds to a chamber or the Grand Chamber for a consideration of its merits.[158] This also involves a decision on admissibility and the possibility of brokering a friendly settlement. The judge elected to the court from the originating State sits *ex officio* on the chamber (or Grand Chamber) dealing with the case so that his or her expertise in the domestic legal system will be available on the hearing of the case.

---

[157]   From the commencement of the Convention procedure in September 1953 until the coming into force of Protocol 11 November 1, 1998, there was also a European Commission of Human Rights which had a vital role in filtering complaints through the admissibility criteria and in making substantive rulings on admissible complaints. Its functions have been subsumed into the court.

[158]   There is provision for a case which commenced in a chamber to be relinquished to the Grand Chamber.

Where a case has been heard and determined by a chamber the judgment does not become final for a period of three months, unless the parties in the meantime declare that they will not seek a referral to the Grand Chamber. In the absence of such a declaration, one of the parties can refer the case to the Grand Chamber within the three month period. In this event, a panel of five judges from the Grand Chamber will decide on whether to accept the referral. If they reject the referral the judgment of the chamber becomes final. It can be expected that a referral will be accepted only where the case raises a serious question of interpretation or application of the Convention, or a serious issue of general importance.[159]

Status of Court Decision

Where the court decides that a State has breached the Convention it will **2–35** declare accordingly. The court's judgment is not sufficient in itself to strike down the domestic act or measure in question. However, the court's judgment is binding on the State in international law. The State, therefore, is under an obligation to bring its law and/or administrative practice (as the case may be) into line with the Convention requirements as elucidated by the court in its judgment. A failure to do so constitutes a breach of the Convention in itself. The court also has the power to award just satisfaction, which normally means damages, to the injured party. Indeed, on the facts of some cases an award of damages is considered sufficient in itself to uphold the requirements of the Convention. The task of policing compliance with the judgments of the court rests with the Committee of Ministers of the Council of Europe.

Although the Convention has not yet been incorporated into Irish law, Irish courts will frequently entertain submissions based on Convention rights and decisions of the European Court of Human Rights on matters relevant to the issue or issues arising before them. While the Irish courts will not (and cannot) strike down statutory provisions on the ground that they breach a Convention right, they will usually seek an interpretation which is consistent with Convention requirements.[160] If the European Convention on Human Rights Bill 2001 is enacted into law as it currently stands, the courts will be obliged to interpret statutes and other rules of law in a manner which is consistent with the Convention. It stops short of conferring a power on the courts to strike down or even disapply a statutory enactment which is found to be in breach of the Convention. However, there is provision for the High Court or, on appeal, the Supreme Court to make a declaration of incompatibility in respect of a statutory provision or rule of law where it decides that it is impossible to interpret the measure in a manner compatible with the Convention. This does not affect the validity or continued operation of the measure but it does, however, afford the injured party grounds to seek *ex*

---

[159] J Hedigan *Revolution in Strasbourg* (1997) 6 I.L.T. at 9.
[160] For discussion of some of the more recent case law which suggests a greater willingness to seek an accord with Convention case see D O'Connell *The Constitution and the ECHR: Belts and Braces or Blinkers* Irish Human Rights Yearbook (2000). See also L Flynn *The Significance of the ECHR in the Irish Legal Order* Irish Journal of European Law 1 (1994).

gratia compensation from the government. It is also worth noting that the Bill imposes an obligation on organs of the State (excluding the courts) to perform their functions in a manner compatible with the Convention. Breach of this obligation affords a cause of action for damages in the Circuit Court or the High Court.

The enactment of the European Court of Human Rights Bill into law, despite its limitations, will enhance the importance of the Convention and associated case law of the European Court of Human Rights in the criminal justice process in Ireland. It is also worth emphasising that its enactment will not detract from the individual's right, in appropriate cases, to pursue a remedy through the Convention machinery. Since the coming into force of the Convention there have been several successful and unsuccessful applications from Ireland in matters relating to criminal law and criminal justice. It can be expected that there will continue to be more such cases in the future.

E. Prisons[161]

1. Introduction

2–36   The State has the power to imprison a person who has been duly convicted and sentenced to a term of imprisonment by a court.[162] The legal authority for a prison governor to receive and imprison an individual is the warrant of committal issued by the sentencing court in respect of the offender and addressed to the governor.[163]

2. Location of Prisons

Ultimately, the place where a prisoner is to serve his or her sentence of imprisonment is a matter for the executive.[164] Equally, however, there is an implied obligation on the executive to provide a sufficient number of prisons suitable to give effect to the orders of the courts.[165] Currently, there are seventeen prisons and places of custodial detention in the State, some of which cater only for remand prisoners. These are: Arbour Hill, Castlerea, Cloverhill, Cork, Curragh Place of Detention, Dochas Centre, Fort Mitchel, Limerick, Loughan House, Midlands, Mountjoy, Portlaoise, St Patrick's, Shanganagh, Shelton Abbey, Training Unit and Wheatfield. The regime can differ from one prison or place of detention to another, and even within

---

[161]   See P McDermott *Prison Law* (Round Hall Sweet & Mawell, Dublin, 2000).

[162]   *Murray v. Attorney General* [1985] I.L.R.M. 542.

[163]   *R v. Fitzgerald* (1920) 55 I.L.T.R. 60; *State (Caddle) v. McCarthy* [1957] I.R. 359.

[164]   Criminal Justice Administration Act 1914, s.17(3); *State (Holden) v. Governor of Portlaoise Prison* [1964] I.R. 80.

[165]   The Prisons Act 1970 makes provision for the Minister for Justice, Equality and Law Reform to provide places of detention (other than prisons and St Patrick's Institution) for the purposes of the rehabilitation of offenders. Enactments relating to prisons or St Patrick's Institution, or to persons serving sentences in such prisons or institutions, generally apply to these places of detention and persons detained in them.

distinct parts of a single prison or place of detention depending on the category of prisoner. Equally, some prisons cater only for certain defined classes of prisoner.[166] In addition, there are a number of training and educational institutions to which offenders can be referred. These are not classified as prisons or places of custodial detention. They are the responsibility of the Minister for Education and Science, while the prisons and places of detention come under the responsibility of the Minister for Justice, Equality and Law Reform.

3. Minister's Management and Rule-making Powers

The Minister for Justice, Equality and Law Reform inherited the "jurisdictions, powers, duties and functions" of the General Prisons Board for Ireland which was established by the Prisons (Ireland) Act 1877.[167] Accordingly, all the existing prisons were transferred to the Minister who is also empowered to improve them and build new ones. In addition, the Criminal Justice (Miscellaneous Provisions) Act 1997 empowers the Minister to make rules for the regulation and good governance of prisons which are defined as places of custody administered by him. The rules may provide for the following: the duties and conduct of the governor and prison officers; the classification of persons detained in a prison; the treatment of persons detained in a prison, including the diet, clothing, maintenance, employment, instruction, discipline and correction of such persons; the provision of facilities and services to persons detained in prison, including educational facilities, medical services, and services relating to the general moral and physical welfare of such persons; the imposition of penalties by the governor of a prison, or an officer of that prison acting on his or her behalf, for such breaches of prison discipline as may be specified in such rules, by persons detained in a prison; remission for good conduct of a portion of a convicted person's sentence; and the photographing and measuring of persons detained in a prison and the taking of fingerprints and palm-prints from such persons during their detention in prison.

Until rules have been made under this power the rules and regulations current at the time of the enactment of the 1997 Act remain in force.[168] The most important of these are the Rules for the Government of Prisons 1947.[169] These rules serve the dual purpose of protecting prisoners and providing for the proper administration and running of a prison.[170]

2–37

---

[166] For a brief description of each regime and class of prisoner, see *Irish Prison Service Report 1999 and 2000* (Stationery Office, Dublin, 2002).

[167] The General Prisons Board (Transfer of Functions) Order 1928. The Board itself was abolished in 1928.

[168] These were made under the General Prisons (Ireland) Act 1877, s.12; Penal Servitude (Ireland) Act 1891; and the Prisons (Ireland) Act 1907.

[169] See *The Management of Offenders – A Five Year Plan* (Stationery Office, Dublin, 1994) for a set of new draft rules.

[170] *State (Gallagher) v. Governor of Portlaoise Prison* unreported, High Court, May 18, 1977; *State (Richardson) v. Governor of Mountjoy Prison* [1980] I.L.R.M. 82.

4. Status of the Prisoner

While in prison a prisoner " . . . must accept prison discipline, and accommodate himself to the reasonable organisation of prison life as laid down in the Prison Rules."[171] In effect this means that the prisoner must abide by the prison rules and the directions of the prison governor who is also the source of disciplinary authority within the prison. Complaints can be made to the relevant Visiting Committee.[172] The Minister must appoint a Visiting Committee. A committee generally functions as an independent inspectorate of the prison with the power to hear complaints from prisoners. Previously they had powers to hold disciplinary inquiries on oath and to impose special punishments on prisoners, but these were abolished by the Criminal Justice (Miscellaneous Provisions) Act 1997.[173]

5. Inspector of Prisons and Parole Board

2–38 Pursuant to the recommendations of the Expert Group on Prisons, a new position of inspector of prisons has been established.[174] The first incumbent is Dermot Kinlen, a retired High Court judge. At time of writing the office was established on a non-statutory footing. A parole board has also been established on a non-statutory basis.

6. Prisons Service

The Minister for Justice, Equality and Law Reform is still formally responsible for the general management and administration of the prison service as well as policy matters pertaining to the service. This is about to change with the implementation of the recommendations of the Expert Group on Prisons. Broadly, these envisage the establishment of an independent agency to carry on the general management and administration of the prisons service, leaving the Minister to concentrate on policy matters.[175] A non-executive Prisons Authority Interim Board was established in April 1999, and the first Director-General of the prison service was appointed in July 1999. The functions of the Board are to advise the Minister on: guidelines in relation to the management, administration and business of the prison service; steps involved in the transition to the statutory prisons authority, including the senior management structure for the authority; strategic and business planning in the prison service; and the service's annual budget.[176]

As its title suggests, the Board is preparing the way for the eventual establishment of a statutory prisons authority, akin to the independent courts service agency.

---

[171] *State (Richardson) v. Governor of Mountjoy Prison* [1980] I.L.R.M. 82, *per* Barrington J. at 89.
[172] See Prisons (Visting Committees) Act 1925 and Prisons (Visiting Committees) Order 1925.
[173] See s.19(5) which repeals s.3(3) of the Prisons (Visiting Committees) Act 1925. In its place there is a power to hear appeals from prisoners against penalties imposed by the governor.
[174] *Towards an Independent Prisons Agency* (Stationery Office, Dublin, 1997). Previous similar recommendations were made in *Report of the Committee of Inquiry into the Penal System* (Stationery Office, Dublin, 1985) and in *The Management of Offenders – A Five Year Plan* (Stationery Office, Dublin, 1994).
[175] *Towards an Independent Prisons Agency* (Stationery Office, Dublin, 1997).
[176] *Irish Prison Service Report 1999 and 2000, op.cit.*

JURISDICTION

A. Introduction

Just because a person is before an Irish court charged with an offence known **3–01** to Irish law it does not follow automatically that the court will have jurisdiction to try him. It has already been seen, for example, that both the District Court and the Circuit Court are courts of local and limited jurisdiction (see chapter 2) while all trial courts can be deprived of jurisdiction due to the passage of time in certain circumstances (see chapter 1). In addition, the jurisdiction of Irish courts is limited by the critical factor of where the offence was committed. As a general rule Irish courts are competent to try only those offences which were committed on Irish territory. It is important therefore, to define what is meant by Irish territory for the purposes of criminal jurisdiction. That will be addressed in this chapter.

There are some important exceptions to the general rule of territorial jurisdiction. Diplomatic immunity, for example, can operate to prevent offences committed on Irish territory from being tried in an Irish court.[1] More important in practice is the growing list of situations in which offences committed outside Irish territory are subject to the jurisdiction of an Irish court. In addition, it must also be recognised that Irish courts will co-operate with foreign courts within the parameters of established rules and principles to bring suspected offenders to justice in other jurisdictions. The classic example is, of course, extradition. Increasingly, however, this co-operation is being extended to the collection of evidence on Irish territory for use in criminal proceedings in foreign courts and *vice versa*. This chapter, therefore, will also examine the circumstances in which Irish courts enjoy extra-territorial jurisdiction in criminal matters and the rules and procedures governing judicial co-operation with foreign courts in criminal matters.

---

[1] See, *e.g.*, the Diplomatic Relations and Immunities Act 1967 giving effect to the Vienna Convention on Diplomatic and Consular Relations.

B. Territorial Jurisdiction

1. Introduction

3–02 As a general rule Irish courts have jurisdiction over every criminal offence committed within the territory of the State. For this purpose the State does not include the six counties of Northern Ireland. It will be seen later, however, that there are circumstances in which the Irish courts can be seised of jurisdiction over an individual offence committed in Northern Ireland. It is also worth noting that the Irish courts may have jurisdiction over a conspiracy to commit an offence in Ireland even though the conspiracy has occurred outside the State. The position is described as follows by Finlay C.J. in *Ellis v. O'Dea*:

> " . . . it is a fundamental principle of the Irish common law, applicable to the criminal jurisdiction of the Irish courts, that a person entering into a conspiracy outside Ireland in furtherance of which an overt act is done in Ireland is amenable to trial in the courts of Ireland. I am equally satisfied that a person who, though located outside Ireland, does an act which either in itself or by reason of the conduct of an accomplice has the effect of completing a criminal offence in Ireland, is amenable to the Irish courts."[2]

2. Territorial Waters

Definition

Criminal jurisdiction also extends over the territorial waters of the State. Section 10(1) of the Maritime Jurisdiction Act 1959 states that:

> "Every offence committed within the territorial seas or internal waters is an offence within the jurisdiction of the State and may be dealt with by a court of competent jurisdiction although committed on board or by means of a foreign ship and a person who commits such offence may be arrested, tried and punished accordingly."

The territorial seas of the State are defined as that portion of the sea which lies between the "baseline" and the "outer limit".[3] In this context the "baseline" is normally taken as the low-water mark on the coast of the mainland or of any island[4] or on any low-tide elevation[5] situated wholly or partly at a distance not more than three nautical miles from the mainland or an island.[6] The

---

[2] [1991] I.L.R.M. 346.

[3] Maritime Jurisdiction Act 1959, s.2.

[4] Defined as "a naturally formed area of land surrounded by water which is above water at high water"; Maritime Jurisdiction Act 1959, s.1.

[5] Defined as "a naturally formed area of land which is surrounded by and above water at low water but submerged at high water"; Maritime Jurisdiction Act 1959, s.1.

[6] Maritime Jurisdiction Act 1959, s.4(1). The government may by order prescribe the charts which may be used for the purpose of establishing low-water mark, or the existence and position of any low-tide elevation, or any other matter in reference to the internal waters, the territorial seas, the exclusive fishery limits or a fishery conservation area, and any chart purporting to be a copy of a chart of a kind or description so prescribed shall, unless the contrary is proved, be received in evidence as being a prescribed chart without further proof; s.13.

"outer limit" is defined as "the line every point of which is at a distance of twelve nautical miles from the nearest point of the baseline".[7] These definitions are subject to the government's power to prescribe, by order, straight base-lines in relation to any part of the national territory and the closing line of any bay or mouth of a river.[8] Any line so prescribed shall be taken as the baseline. The internal or inland waters of the State extend to all sea areas which lie on the landward side of the baseline of the territorial seas.[9] These internal or inland waters are subject to the jurisdiction of the State to the same extent as its ports and harbours, bays, lakes and rivers, subject to any right of innocent passage for foreign ships in those sea areas which had previously been considered as part of the territorial seas or of the high seas.

Jurisdiction

Every offence committed within the territorial seas or internal waters is an offence within the jurisdiction of the State.[10] As such it may be dealt with by a court of competent jurisdiction irrespective of whether the offence was committed by a foreign ship[11] or on board a foreign ship, and a person who commits such an offence may be arrested, tried and punished accordingly. For the purpose of effecting the arrest the territorial seas and internal waters shall be deemed to be within the jurisdiction of any court or judge having power to issue warrants for the arrest of persons charged with offences within the juris-diction of that court or judge.[12] This would appear to confer the necessary power to issue an arrest warrant on any competent court or judge throughout the State, irrespective of where on the territorial seas the offence is alleged to have been committed. The Act says nothing about the power to issue a warrant to board and/or search a vessel. Nor does it confer any summary powers of arrest, entry, search and seizure. These, however, are conferred by other statutory provisions dealing with specific offences or categories of offences.

3–03

Aliens on foreign ships

Where an offence is alleged to have been committed by an alien on board, or by means of, a foreign ship, the prosecution (apart from the taking of depositions) cannot be instituted in the absence of a certificate from the Minister for Foreign Affairs to the effect that the institution of the proceedings is in his opinion expedient.[13] It is not entirely clear when a prosecution is

---

[7] Maritime Jurisdiction Act 1959, s.3, as amended by the Maritime Jurisdiction (Amendment) Act 1959, s.2.

[8] Maritime Jurisdiction Act 1959, s.4(2). The government may by order revoke or amend any such order; s.4(3).

[9] *ibid.* s.5

[10] *ibid.* s.10(1).

[11] Defined as "a ship which is not a ship of the Naval Service of the Defence Forces or an Irish ship as defined by section 9 of the Mercantile Marine Act 1955". A ship is defined as including "every description of vessel used in navigation whether on or under the surface of the water, howsoever propelled, and also includes a seaplane while it is in contact with the water", Maritime Jurisdiction Act 1959, s.1.

[12] Maritime Jurisdiction Act 1959, s.10(2).

[13] *ibid.* s.11(1). Note also the possible effects of diplomatic immunity.

deemed to commence for the purposes of this provision. In the case of an offence to be tried summarily it would appear to be the commencement of the trial itself. In the case of an offence to be tried on indictment it is at least arguable that the operative moment is when the decision is being taken to send the accused forward for trial.[14] More significant is the fact that a certificate is not required in respect of an offence against Part XIII of the Fisheries (Consolidation) Act 1959 or an offence against the conservation of the living resources of the sea.[15] These exceptions are particularly important in practice given the incidence of fisheries offences committed by vessels from other member states of the European Community while fishing in Irish territorial waters. Moreover, it is worth noting in the context of fishery offences under the Fisheries Acts 1959–95 that the exclusive fishery limits of the State have been extended statutorily to all sea areas within the line marking a distance of 200 nautical miles from the baseline.[16] This exclusive limit can be extended by government order.[17]

3. Airspace

There is no statutory definition of the extent of Irish airspace for the purposes of criminal jurisdiction. Reasoning by analogy from the position at common law, however, it would seem reasonable to conclude that it consists of the airspace above Ireland and Irish territorial waters. Indeed that would appear to be the assumption upon which certain statutory offences are based. Under the Broadcasting (Offences) Act 1968, for example, it is an offence for any person to broadcast from any ship or aircraft which is in or over waters adjacent to the State as defined in the Maritime Jurisdiction Act 1959.[18] It is also worth noting that offences committed by persons on aircraft, or through the use of aircraft, while the aircraft is passing through Irish air space come within the jurisdiction of the Irish courts. This remains the case even if the alleged offender was not on the aircraft at the time. Indeed, the offence may not necessarily involve an aircraft at all, it may stem from the passage of any object through Irish airspace.

4. Other Possibilities

Simply defining the territorial jurisdiction of Irish courts in criminal matters will not always resolve the question of whether an individual offence is within the jurisdiction of the Irish courts. Problems can arise in establishing whether the offence was actually committed within the territory. This is most likely to

---

[14] Ryan and Magee suggest that it occurs after the accused has been sent forward for trial; see Ryan, E., and Magee, P., *The Irish Criminal Process* (Mercier Press, Dublin, 1983) at p. 28.

[15] Maritime Jurisdiction Act 1959, s.11(2).

[16] *ibid.* s.6(1) as amended by the Maritime Jurisdiction (Amendment) Act 1964, and the Maritime Jurisdiction (Exclusive Fishery) Limits Order, 1976.

[17] Maritime Jurisdiction Act 1959, s.6(2)-(5).

[18] Broadcasting (Offences) Act 1968, s.2. Note that it is also an offence for any person to broadcast from any ship or aircraft registered in the State which is outside the territorial waters.

happen where the substantive offence has been committed in another jurisdiction, but an element of planning or preparation has been carried out on
Irish territory. Furthermore, the legislature is increasingly providing for the
prosecution in Ireland of certain offences which have been wholly committed
abroad. This is considered next.

C. Extra-territorial Jurisdiction

1. Introduction

As a general rule offences committed outside the State, even by Irish citizens,   **3–04**
do not come within the jurisdiction of Irish courts. This is, of course, subject to
a number of statutory exceptions.[19] These might be classified for convenience of
exposition under three headings: (i) jurisdiction derived from the universality
principle; (ii) jurisdiction derived from the nationality principle; and (iii)
jurisdiction conferred by the Criminal Law (Jurisdiction) Act 1976 over certain
offences committed in Northern Ireland. Each will be considered in turn.

2. The Universality Principle

Introduction

The universality principle is one of four principles generally recognised at   **3–05**
international law as explaining the jurisdiction of municipal courts in criminal
and other legal matters.[20] It determines jurisdiction by reference to the custody
of the person committing the offence, irrespective of where the offence has
been committed. The main offences which might be classified under this
heading for Irish purposes are: piracy, certain aircraft offences, drug-trafficking
offences on ships, breaches of the Geneva Conventions and, to a limited extent,
perjury.[21] Irish jurisdiction over piracy offences is assumed by analogy from
English authorities. These assert jurisdiction over offences of piracy contrary
to the laws of nations committed upon the high seas.[22] In the case of offences
against the Geneva Conventions, the jurisdiction of the Irish courts is conferred
by the Geneva Conventions Act 1962. This stipulates that Irish courts have
jurisdiction in respect of major breaches of the Conventions relating to sick
and wounded in the field, civilians in time of war and internees, irrespective
of the nationality of the offender or where the offence was committed.[23]

---

[19] *R. v. Page* [1954] 1 Q.B. 170.
[20] The other three are: the territorial principle, the nationality principle and the protective principle.
See Starke, J.G., *Introduction to International Law* (9th ed., Butterworths, London, 1984), Chap. 8.
[21] The Court of Justice of the European Communities (Perjury) Act 1975, s.1 exposes any person,
irrespective of nationality, to the risk of prosecution in Ireland for the equivalent of perjury before
the Court of Justice of the European Communities.
[22] See Ryan and Magee, *op. cit.*, p. 29.
[23] Geneva Conventions Act 1962, s.3(1). Irish citizens may also be prosecuted for minor breaches
wherever committed; s.4(2).

Aircraft offfences

The aircraft offences which are classified under the universality heading are found primarily in the Air Navigation and Transport Acts 1973 and 1975. Any person who commits on board any civil aircraft in flight an act of violence endangering the safety of the aircraft is triable in Ireland for that offence irrespective of his nationality, the place of registration of the aircraft or the jurisdiction in which the offence was committed.[24] The same applies to any person who destroys or damages any civil aircraft in service, or places any destructive device on board, or interferes with navigation facilities or communicates false information so as to endanger an aircraft in flight. The hijacking of an aircraft, or the commission of any act of violence on board which would be an offence if committed in Ireland, is also triable in this State under the universality principle.[25] This does not apply, however, if the aircraft's place of take-off and place of landing are both in the State of registration of the aircraft or some State designated in an order made pursuant to a notice communicated to the State under Article 5 of the Hague Convention for the Suppression of Unlawful Seizure of Aircraft 1970.

Drug-trafficking offences

3–06   The offences concerning drug-trafficking on ships reflect Ireland's obligations under the United Nations Convention against Illicit Traffic in Narcotic Drugs and Psychotropic Substances as implemented by the Criminal Justice Act 1994. Broadly the Act creates two offences which can be classified under the universality heading. First, anything which would constitute a drug trafficking offence[26] if done on land in Ireland is an offence if done on an Irish ship.[27] Although it is not actually stated in the Act the implication is that the offence can be committed even though the ship is outside Irish territorial waters at the time. Second, it is an offence for a person to have in his possession a controlled drug,[28] or to be knowingly concerned in the carrying or concealing of a controlled drug, on a ship where he knows, or has reasonable grounds to suspect, that the drug is intended to be imported or has been exported contrary to certain regulations made by the Minister for Health[29] or the law of any other state.[30] The ship must be an Irish ship, or registered in a Convention state[31] or not registered

---

[24]   Air Navigation and Transport Act 1975, s.3.

[25]   *ibid.* s.11.

[26]   See s.3(1) of the Criminal Justice Act 1994 for a definition of a "drug trafficking offence" in this context.

[27]   Criminal Justice Act 1994, s.33. For this purpose an "Irish ship" has the same meaning as in s.9 of the Mercantile Marine Act 1955.

[28]   See s.2 of the Misuse of Drugs Act 1977 for the definition of a "controlled drug."

[29]   The regulations in question are those issued by the Minister for Health under s.5(1)(a)(ii) of the Misuse of Drugs Act 1977.

[30]   Criminal Justice Act 1994, s.34(2). A certificate purporting to be issued by or on behalf of the government of any state (other than Ireland) to the effect that the importation or exportation of a controlled drug is prohibited by the law of the state shall, for the purposes of a prosecution for this offence, be evidence of the matters stated in that certificate without further proof; s.34(3).

[31]   A Convention state is a state (other than Ireland) which is a party to the UN Convention against Illicit Traffic in Narcotic Drugs and Psychotropic Substances, 1988. See Criminal Justice Act 1994 (s.37(1)) Order, 1997 (No. 63 of 1997) for a list of the states.

in any country or territory.[32] For this offence the legislation states explicitly that it does not matter where the ship is located at the time. Proceedings for either of these offences can be taken in any place within the State, and the offence may be treated for all incidental purposes as having been committed in the place it is tried within the State.[33] However, no such proceedings can be instituted without the consent of the DPP.[34] Moreover, no proceedings can be taken in the State for the second offence (possession, etc) where it is alleged to have been committed outside the landward limits of Irish territorial seas on a ship registered in a Convention state, unless the proceedings are taken pursuant to the exercise, with the authority of the Minister for Foreign Affairs, of the enforcement powers conferred by the First Schedule to the Act.[35] The First Schedule to the Act confers on an enforcement officer a range of powers for the purpose of detecting and taking appropriate action in respect of the drug-trafficking and possession offences on board a ship.[36] They include powers: to board, divert, detain and search the ship as well as powers of arrest and seizure. The powers cannot be used outside the landward limits of Irish territorial seas in respect of a ship registered in a Convention state, except with the authority of the Minister for Foreign Affairs.[37]

Broadcasting Offences

It is also worth noting that unlawful broadcasting from a ship or aircraft registered in the State is triable in the Irish courts even though the offence occurs outside Irish territorial waters.[38] Similarly, an act or omission on board an Irish controlled aircraft in flight outside the State is an offence if it would constitute an offence had it taken place in the State.[39]

Moneylaundering Offences

An interesting variation on the extra-territorial application of Irish criminal **3–07** legislation arises in the context of moneylaundering offences. The Criminal Justice Act 1994 creates a number of moneylaundering offences. Broadly speaking they concern the concealment, conversion, transfer or removal from the State of any property for the purpose of avoiding prosecution for an offence or the making of a confiscation order,[40] where the property in question wholly or partly, directly or indirectly, represents the proceeds of drug trafficking or other

---

[32] Criminal Justice Act 1994, s.34(1). For this purpose a "ship" includes any vessel used in navigation; s.3(1).
[33] Criminal Justice Act 1994, s.36(1).
[34] *ibid.* s.36(2).
[35] *ibid.* s.36(3).
[36] *ibid.* s.35(1).
[37] *ibid.* s.35(2). The Minister cannot give his authority unless the other state has, in respect of the ship in question, requested the assistance of the State or authorised the State to act. When giving his authority the Minister may also impose such conditions or limitations on the exercise of the powers as may be necessary to give effect to any conditions or limitations imposed by that State; s.35(3).
[38] Broadcasting (Offences) Act 1968, s.2.
[39] Air Navigation and Transport Act 1973, s.2(1).
[40] A "confiscation order" in this context means an order made under s.4(4) or s.9(1) of the Criminal Justice Act 1994.

criminal activity.[41] Handling such property is also an offence.[42] The key feature of these offences in the current context is that the "drug trafficking" or "other criminal activity" need not have taken place within the State. It will be quite sufficient that it occurred outside the State so long as it corresponded to an offence under Irish law and an offence under the law of the country or territory in which it occurred.[43] Although this is not quite the same thing as permitting the prosecution of any person in Irish courts for a drug trafficking offence or for certain "other criminal activity" committed abroad, it comes very close. The offence committed abroad can be punished indirectly by the Irish courts through the medium of a moneylaundering offence in which the commission of the former offence is an essential component.

Proceeds of Crime

It is also worth noting that the Proceeds of Crime Act 1996 which makes provision for the forfeiture of the proceeds of crime through a civil process has been given an extra-territorial dimension. Although the Act itself does not specifically extend the reach of the process to the proceeds of crimes committed abroad, O'Higgin's J. in *DPP v. Hollman*[43a] held that it applied where the proceeds of the crime were held in this jurisdiction.

3. The Nationality Principle

The General Rule

3–08   The nationality principle determines jurisdiction by reference to the nationality or national character or place of residence of the offender. As a general rule offences committed by Irish citizens outside the State are not triable in the Irish courts. There are, of course, a number of important exceptions to this rule whereby Irish citizens can be tried in Irish courts for offences committed abroad. Before outlining these exceptions, it is worth noting that foreign nationals ordinarily resident in Ireland are, by virtue of their residence, subject to some of these exceptions.

Homicide and Treason Exception

Traditionally, the primary exceptions concern the offences of murder, manslaughter and treason. Under the Offences Against the Person Act 1861 an Irish citizen can be tried in Ireland for murder or manslaughter committed abroad irrespective of whether the person killed was an Irish citizen. The accused may be the subject of investigation, trial and punishment within any county or place where he is apprehended or detained in custody within the State as if the offence had been committed in that county or place.[44] This particular

---

[41]   Criminal Justice Act 1994, s.31(1) and (2).
[42]   *ibid.* s.31(3).
[43]   *ibid.* s.31(11).
[43a]   Unreported, High Court, July 29, 1999.
[44]   Offences Against the Person Act 1861, s.9.

provision is confined to Irish citizens. It does not extend to foreign nationals who are ordinarily resident in Ireland. The position with respect to individuals who can claim dual nationality is not quite clear. Any Irish citizen or person ordinarily resident in the State can be prosecuted for treason irrespective of where it was committed.[45]

Other Exceptions

More recently, there is evidence of a greater willingness to criminalise certain acts done outside the State by Irish citizens and persons ordinarily resident in Ireland. In this context the word "criminalise" refers to the fact that the act in question is made a criminal offence under Irish law and is triable as such in the Irish courts. The offences in question stem partly from Ireland's obligations under international conventions and partly from public reaction against the spectacle of Irish residents travelling abroad specifically for the purpose of engaging in the sexual abuse of children.

The Sexual Offences (Jurisdiction) Act 1996 makes it a criminal offence for an Irish citizen or person ordinarily resident in the State to do an act outside the State involving a child if it constitutes an offence under the law of the place where it was committed and, if done within the State would constitute an offence under one of the Irish enactments listed in the Schedule to the Act.[46] An attempt to commit such an offence is also made a criminal offence when committed outside the State by an Irish citizen or person ordinarily resident in Ireland.[47] Aiding, abetting counselling or procuring outside the State the commission of such an offence is in itself a criminal offence when done by a citizen or person ordinarily resident in the State.[48] The same applies to conspiracy or incitement outside the State.[49] These offences are aimed at making it a criminal offence under Irish law for an Irish citizen or person ordinarily resident in Ireland to commit, or be involved in a secondary capacity or inchoate manner in the commission of a sexual offence against a child while outside Ireland.

For the purpose of these offences a child is defined as a person under 17 years of age,[50] and a person is "ordinarily resident in Ireland" if he has had his "principal residence within the State for the period of twelve months

---

[45] Treason Act 1939, s.1(2).
[46] Sexual Offences (Jurisdiction) Act 1996, s.2(1). The enactments in question are: s.1 of the Criminal Law Amendment Act 1935; s.2 of the Criminal Law Amendment Act 1935; s.2 of the Criminal Law (Rape) Act 1981; ss.2, 3 and 4 of the Criminal Law (Rape)(Amendment) Act 1990; and ss.3, 4 and 5 of the Criminal Law (Sexual Offences) Act 1993. See *Hatchell v. DPP* unreported, High Court, April 6, 2001
[47] Sexual Offences (Jurisdiction) Act 1996, s.2(2).
[48] *ibid.* s.2(3).
[49] Conspiracy or incitement inside the State to commit the principal offence is an offence generally; *i.e.* it is not confined to persons who are Irish citizens or who are ordinarily resident in the State. Sexual Offences (Jurisdiction) Act 1996, s.2(5).
[50] Sexual Offences (Jurisdiction) Act 1996, s.1(1). In proceedings for an offence under these provisions the court may have regard to a person's physical appearance or attributes for the purpose of determining whether that person is under the age of 17 years or was, at the time of the alleged commission of the offence to which the proceedings relate, under the age of 17 years; s.8.

immediately preceding the alleged commission of the said offence."[51] Proceedings for the offence can be taken in any place within the State and the offence may for all incidental purposes be treated as having been committed in the place within the State where the proceedings are taken.[52] If, however, the accused has been acquitted or convicted of an offence in a place outside the State he shall not be proceeded against for an offence under these provisions in respect of an act constituting the offence of which he was convicted abroad.[53] It is also worth noting that the Act creates a number of offences aimed at criminalising certain acts done by any person (including a corporate body) within the State to facilitate or promote the commission of the principal offence abroad.[54]

There a few other disparate offences which are worth noting under this general heading. An Irish citizen who commits certain explosives offences outside the State is triable in the Irish courts.[55] Unlawful broadcasting offences committed by Irish citizens on the high seas from any ship or aircraft not registered in the State are triable in the Irish courts.[56] Minor breaches of the Geneva Conventions relating to sick and wounded in the field, civilians in time of war, prisoners of war and internees committed by Irish citizens are triable in the Irish courts irrespective of where they were committed.[57]

D. Northern Ireland

1. Introduction

Historical Background

3–09   Ireland and Northern Ireland constituted a unitary criminal jurisdiction until separated by the common land border in 1922. It might be expected, there-fore, that special arrangements have existed since then for the prosecution in one jurisdiction of offences committed in another. Indeed, it will be seen later that special procedures apply to the extradition of alleged offenders from one jurisdiction to the other. With the minor exception of the Foyle Fisheries scheme,[58] however, it was not until 1976 that formal arrangements were put in place to facilitate the prosecution of offenders in one jurisdiction for offences committed in the other. Ironically, these arrangements were largely the result of difficulties experienced by the Irish authorities in complying with requests from Northern Ireland for the extradition of persons accused of

---

[51] Sexual Offences (Jurisdiction) Act 1996, s.2(7).
[52] *ibid.* s.7.
[53] *ibid.* s.9.
[54] *ibid.* ss.2(3), 2(5), 3, 4 and 5.
[55] Explosive Substances Act 1883, ss.2 and 3, as amended by the Criminal Law (Jurisdiction) Act 1976, s.4.
[56] Broadcasting (Offences) Act 1968, s.2.
[57] Geneva Conventions Act 1962, s.4(2). Major breaches can be tried in the Irish courts irrespective of the nationality of the accused; s.3(1).
[58] Foyle Fisheries Act 1952, s.62.

offences associated with the political violence which erupted in Northern Ireland in 1969.

As will be seen later, in the early 1970s the Irish courts took the view that offences committed by persons in pursuance of an attempt to overthrow the government of Northern Ireland by force of arms were political offences. They also took the view that it was an established principle of international law that there should be no extradition for political offences. Since Article 29.3 of the Constitution bound the State to abide by the generally recognised principles of international law, the courts concluded that they had no power to order the extradition of a person to Northern Ireland for a political offence. For the same reason the government was equally of the opinion that the Oireachtas could not introduce legislation permitting the extradition of such persons. This position was politically embarrassing for the Irish government in its relations with the government of the United Kingdom. A political compromise was eventually hammered out in the Sunningdale discussions between the two governments in 1973.[59] This compromise resulted in legislation being enacted in the two Parliaments to enable persons to be tried in Ireland for certain offences committed in Northern Ireland and vice versa.

The Criminal Law (Jurisdiction) Act 1976

The Irish legislation is the Criminal Law (Jurisdiction) Act 1976.[60] It makes provision for the possibility of prosecuting a person in the Irish courts for certain acts done in Northern Ireland where those acts constitute an offence scheduled to, or created by, the Act. There is also provision for the taking of evidence in a court in Northern Ireland for the purpose of a prosecution under the Act in the State. Equally, there is provision for the taking of evidence in a court in the State for the purpose of a prosecution under the United Kingdom legislation in Northern Ireland. Prior to their enactment into law these novel provisions were referred as the Criminal Law (Jurisdiction) Bill 1976 to the Supreme Court under Article 26 for a ruling on their constitutionality. The court upheld the constitutionality of the Bill essentially on the ground that it provided for the peace, order and good government of the State.[61] Although the provisions in the Act dealing with the taking of evidence in one State for the purpose of trial in the other are more properly the subject of judicial co-operation, clarity of exposition demands that they should be dealt with in this section.

2. Extra-Territorial Jurisdiction

Definition

In order to facilitate the criminal prosecution in this State of certain acts done **3–10** in Northern Ireland, the Criminal Law (Jurisdiction) Act 1976 makes those

---

59 See *Boland v. An Taoiseach* [1974] I.R. 129 for a challenge to the constitutionality of the declarations resulting from these discussions.
60 The legislation for Northern Ireland is the Criminal Jurisdiction Act 1975 enacted by the U.K. Parliament.
61 *Re Criminal Law (Jurisdiction) Bill 1976* [1977] I.R. 129.

acts part of the criminal law of this State even when they are done in Northern Ireland. Its provisions, however, are so complex and detailed that they must be read very carefully. To some extent this complexity results from the fact that the offences created by the Act are not confined exclusively to acts done by persons in Northern Ireland. They also embrace certain acts done by persons in this State which are connected in specified ways with offences committed, attempted or planned in Northern Ireland.

At the very heart of the arrangements introduced by the Act is the concept of a scheduled offence. This refers to any offence listed in the schedule to the Act. By virtue of the 1976 Act it is an offence in this State for a person to do an act[62] in Northern Ireland which, if done in this State, would constitute an offence specified in the schedule to the Act.[63] The person shall be liable on conviction on indictment in the State to the penalty to which he would have been liable had he done the act in the State. Aiding, abetting, counselling or procuring such an offence in Northern Ireland is also an offence, as is an attempt, conspiracy or incitement to commit the offence.[64] This is so irrespective of whether the aiding, abetting, counselling, procuring, attempt, conspiracy or incitement occurs within the State or in Northern Ireland. Aiding, abetting, counselling or procuring in Northern Ireland the commission of an offence specified in the schedule is also an offence in this State.[65] The same applies to an attempt, conspiracy or incitement in Northern Ireland to commit such an offence.[66] It does not matter in either case whether the commission of the scheduled offence was to be committed in Northern Ireland or in this State.

The 1976 Act makes it an offence in this State to do any act without reasonable excuse with the intent to impede the apprehension or prosecution in this State or in Northern Ireland of a person who has done an act in Northern Ireland which, if done in this State, would constitute an offence specified in the schedule or an attempt to commit such an offence.[67] It does not matter whether the person aiming to impede the apprehension or prosecution is in this State or in Northern Ireland. Similarly, it is an offence for any person in Northern Ireland who, without reasonable excuse, does any act with intent to impede the apprehension or prosecution in this State or in Northern Ireland of a person who has committed, or attempted to commit, an offence specified in the schedule to the 1976 Act.[68] In this case it would seem, although it is by no means certain, that it does not matter whether the scheduled offence has been committed or attempted in this State or in Northern Ireland.

---

[62] References in the Act to an "act" include references to an omission; Criminal Law (Jurisdiction) Act 1976, s.1(1).

[63] Criminal Law (Jurisdiction) Act 1976, s.2(1).

[64] *ibid.* s.2(2)(a) and (3)(a).

[65] *ibid.* s.2(2)(b).

[66] *ibid.* s.2(3)(b).

[67] *ibid.* s.2(4). See s.2(5) for the possibility of convicting an accused under s.2(4) as an alternative to a conviction for an offence under s.2(1) or s.3.

[68] *ibid.* s.2(6). See s.2(7) for the possibility of convicting an accused under s.2(6) as an alternative to a conviction for an offence specified in the Schedule or an attempt to commit such an offence.

The Scheduled Offences

The list of offences scheduled to the 1976 Act (as amended) are broadly: the **3–11** common law offences of murder, manslaughter and arson, the offences of causing serious harm and false imprisonment created by the Non-fatal Offences against the Person Act 1997;[69] certain arson and damage to property offences;[69a] interference with a railway under the Malicious Damage Act 1861; making and possessing explosive substances and causing explosions under the Explosive Substances Act 1883;[70] robbery and burglary under the Larceny Act 1916;[71] a range of firearms offences under the Firearms Acts 1925–64;[72] unlawful seizure of aircraft under the Air Navigation and Transport Act 1973;[73] and unlawful seizure of vehicles under the Criminal Law (Jurisdiction) Act 1976.[74] The enactments and rules of law governing when a person charged with an offence committed in the State may be convicted of another offence are applicable so as to enable a person charged with a scheduled offence allegedly committed, or attempted, in Northern Ireland to be convicted of another scheduled offence, or attempt to commit such an offence.[75]

Escaping from Custody

The terms of the 1976 Act extend to escaping from custody in Northern Ireland. It is a criminal offence in this State for a person charged with or convicted of an offence under the law of Northern Ireland to escape from any lawful custody[76] in which he is held in Northern Ireland.[77] This applies only if the offence with which the person has been charged, or of which he has been convicted, in Northern Ireland consists of acts[78] which constitute an offence specified in the Schedule to the 1976 Act[79] or an offence which can be tried in this State under the Act.[80] It is also an offence in this State for any

---

[69] Non-Fatal Offences against the Person Act 1997, ss.4 and 15.
[69a] Criminal Damage Act 1991, s.14(4).
[70] Explosive Substances Act 1883, ss.2, 3 and 4.
[71] Larceny Act 1916, ss.23 and 23B.
[72] Firearms Act 1925, s.15 and Firearms Act 1964, ss.26, 27, 27A and 27B.
[73] Air Navigation and Transport Act 1973, s.11.
[74] Criminal Law (Jurisdiction) Act 1976, s.10.
[75] *ibid.* s.2(9).
[76] This refers to any lawful custody in which the person concerned is held for the purpose of the proceedings in relation to the offence under the law of Northern Ireland at any time between the bringing of a charge in relation to that offence and the conclusion of his trial (including any appeal or retrial) for that offence or in which he is held while serving a sentence imposed on his conviction for that offence; s.3(1)(c).
[77] Criminal Law (Jurisdiction) Act 1976, s.3(1)(a). It is also a criminal offence in this State for a person to escape from lawful custody while in Northern Ireland pursuant to an order under s.11(2) enabling the accused to be present in a court in Northern Ireland to observe the taking of evidence in a court in Northern Ireland which will be used in proceedings against him in the Special Criminal Court in this jurisdiction.
[78] It does not matter whether the acts were done in this State or in Northern Ireland.
[79] Included are: aiding, abetting, counselling or procuring the commission of such an offence, and attempting, conspiring or inciting another person to commit such an offence, and doing without reasonable excuse any act with intent to impede the apprehension or prosecution of a person who has committed such an offence; s.3(1)(b).
[80] Criminal Law (Jurisdiction) Act 1976, s.3(1)(a)(i). Also covered is an offence under the law of Northern Ireland corresponding to these provisions; s.3(1)(a)(ii).

person in the State or in Northern Ireland to aid, abet, counsel or procure the offence of escaping from lawful custody in Northern Ireland.[81] The same applies to any person in the State or in Northern Ireland who attempts, conspires, or incites another person to commit the offence of escaping from lawful custody in Northern Ireland.[82] It is an offence for any person in the State or in Northern Ireland to do any act without reasonable excuse with the intent to impede the apprehension or prosecution in this State or in Northern Ireland of a person who has escaped, or attempted to escape, from lawful custody in Northern Ireland.[83]

Impact on Domestic Criminal Law

The efficient operation of the arrangements introduced by the 1976 Act depends substantially on reciprocity in the laws of the State and Northern Ireland governing the substance of the offences concerned. To this end it has proved necessary to amend a number of existing offences in Irish law and to introduce some new ones. Accordingly amendments have been made to the Explosive Substances Act 1883 to make provision for the offences of causing an explosion, doing an act with intent to cause an explosion, conspiring to cause an explosion, and making or possessing explosive substances.[84] The Larceny Act 1916 has been amended with respect to robbery and burglary offences,[85] and the Firearms Act 1964 has been amended with respect to offences of possession of firearms in suspicious circumstances and carrying firearms with intent.[86] Finally, the Act introduces a completely new offence of unlawful seizure of vehicles. It arises broadly where a person unlawfully, by force or threat of force or by any other form of intimidation, seizes or interferes with the control of any vehicle ship or hovercraft.[87] In this context it is presumed, unless the contrary is shown, that a purpose which is unlawful in this State is also unlawful in Northern Ireland.[88] Indeed, it is worth noting generally that where the law of this State is applied by virtue of the 1976 Act to acts done in Northern Ireland, the law shall be read for the purposes of the Act with any necessary modifications and, in particular, as if references to what is lawful or unlawful included what is lawful or unlawful under the law of Northern Ireland.[89]

These amendments and innovations have general application in Irish criminal law in the sense that their application is not confined to the operation of the machinery in the 1976 Act. Accordingly, their substance is primarily a

---

[81] Criminal Law (Jurisdiction) Act 1976, s.2(2)(a).
[82] *ibid.* s.2(3)(a).
[83] *ibid.* s.2(4).
[84] Explosive Substances Act, 1883, ss.2 and 3.
[85] Larceny Act 1916, ss.23, 23A and 23B.
[86] Firearms Act 1964, ss.27A and 27B. In applying s.27A to acts done in Northern Ireland the absence of any licence or other authority requisite under the law of Northern Ireland relating to firearms, or a breach of a condition attached to any such licence or other authority, is a circumstance that may give rise to a reasonable inference that possession is not for a lawful purpose; s.20(7)(b).
[87] Criminal Law (Jurisdiction) Act 1976, s.10(1).
[88] *ibid.* s.10(2).
[89] *ibid.* s.20(7)(a).

matter for a text on substantive criminal law. It is worth noting, however, that the explosive substance offences are defined to include an element of extra-territorial application within the nationality principle.

3. Prosecution of Offences

Restrictions

The Criminal Law (Jurisdiction) Act 1976 confers powers of arrest with respect to offences which are triable in this State by virtue of the arrangements introduced by the Act.[90] Proceedings for any such offence may be taken in any place in the State, and the offence may for all incidental purposes be treated as having been committed in the place where it is tried.[91] For the most part these offences will concern acts done in Northern Ireland. It must be remembered, however, that the arrangements also extend to acts done in this State in certain circumstances. Nevertheless, the likely political ramifications associated with a prosecution for such an offence is reflected by the fact that, where a person is charged under these provisions, no further proceedings can be taken in the case unless by or with the consent of the Attorney General.[92] This restriction does not apply to remands in custody or on bail. There are also restrictions on the extent to which a person can be proceeded against in this State for an offence within the scope of the 1976 Act arrangements where he has been extradited to the State from any place in the United Kingdom, Isle of Man or Channel Islands for an offence other than that specified in the warrant of extradition.[93]

3–12

Taking Evidence

In practice the major difficulty associated with a trial in this State of an offence committed in Northern Ireland is likely to be obtaining evidence from Northern Ireland. Witnesses resident in Northern Ireland may be reluctant to travel to this State for the purpose of giving evidence. Security considerations may also prove an insuperable obstacle in practice, particularly in the case of members of the security forces from Northern Ireland. The 1976 Act anticipates such difficulties by making provision for evidence to be taken in Northern Ireland for use in a prosecution in this State.[94] These enable the Special

---

[90] *ibid.* s.19. Any person may arrest without warrant any person who is or whom he, with reasonable cause, suspects to be in the act of committing an offence under s.2(1). Where an offence under s.2(1) or s.3 has been committed any person may arrest without warrant anyone who is or whom he, with reasonable cause, suspects to be guilty of the offence. Where a member of the Garda Síochána, with reasonable cause, suspects that an offence under s.2(1) or s.3 has been committed, he may arrest without warrant anyone whom he, with reasonable cause, suspects to be guilty of the offence. He may also arrest without warrant anyone whom he, with reasonable cause, suspects to be about to commit an offence under s.2(1). For the purpose of arresting a person under any of these provisions, a member of the Garda Síochána may enter (if need be by force) and search any place where that person is or where he, with reasonable cause, suspects him to be.

[91] Criminal Law (Jurisdiction) Act 1976, s.20(1).

[92] *ibid.* s.20(2).

[93] *ibid.* s.20(5).

[94] Note also that the 1976 Act specifically provides that s. 4F of the Criminal Procedure Act 1967

Criminal Court, when trying an offence under the arrangements introduced by the 1976 Act, to provide by order for the issue of a letter of request to the Lord Chief Justice of Northern Ireland for the taking of evidence in Northern Ireland by a judge of the High Court of Justice in Northern Ireland from a witness specified in the order.[95] The court can issue the order of its own motion or, unless satisfied that it is not in the interests of justice to do so, at the request of the prosecution or the accused. An appellate court may also issue such an order for the purpose of any appeal in relation to the trial of an offence which comes within the 1976 Act arrangements. In either case, the members of the court making the order will be present for the taking of the evidence before the judge in Northern Ireland.

The accused must be informed of certain rights which are available to him where a court makes an order for the taking of evidence in Northern Ireland. For example, he must be told that he has the right to be present in the custody of the Police Service of Northern Ireland (PSNI) at the taking of the evidence.[96] He must also be told that if he exercises this right he will be delivered into the custody of the PSNI. If the accused exercises the right to be present the court must issue an order directing that he be delivered into the custody of the PSNI so often as may be necessary.[97] Of course, if the accused is wanted in Northern Ireland on any criminal or civil matter, his right to be present will be little more than a sham. The Act deals with this problem by stipulating that the accused must be told that while he is in custody in Northern Ireland for the purpose of taking the evidence, he will be immune from detention, and any kind of suit or legal process, in respect of any cause or matter, whether civil or criminal, arising before his arrival in Northern Ireland for that purpose.[98] The accused must also be told that he has the right to be represented at the hearing in Northern Ireland by the counsel and/or solicitor representing him in the proceedings in the State or by another counsel and/or solicitor entitled to practise in Northern Ireland.[99] This right of representation is available whether or not the accused exercises his right to be present at the taking of the evidence.

---

shall not entitle a judge of the District Court to require the attendance of a person before the court for the purpose of taking the person's evidence by way of a sworn deposition if it appears to the judge that the person is outside the State and that it is not reasonably practicable to secure his attendance before the court; Criminal Law (Jurisdiction) Act 1976, s.18 as amended by Criminal Justice Act 1999, s.14.

[95] Criminal Law (Jurisdiction) Act 1976, s.11(1).

[96] *ibid.* s.11(2)(a).

[97] For this purpose, the accused shall be brought as often as may be necessary by the Garda Síochána to some convenient point of departure from the State and there delivered into the custody of the PSNI. If he is on bail he must be taken into the custody of the Garda Síochána not more than 24 hours before the time of any such delivery and kept in custody until the delivery is effected. On his return to the State he will be taken into the custody of the Garda Síochána. If he is subject to a court order remanding him in custody he will be returned to that custody as soon as may be. If he escapes from such custody he is liable to arrest and punishment in this State pursuant to ss.7 and 6(2) respectively of the Criminal Justice Act 1960; see Criminal Law (Jurisdiction) Act 1976, s.13(3). If he is on bail he must be released on that bail. Criminal Law (Jurisdiction) Act 1976, s.11(4).

[98] Criminal Law (Jurisdiction) Act 1976, s.11(2)d).

[99] *ibid.* s.11(2)(b).

Finally, the accused must be told that if he is not represented by counsel or a solicitor he may question directly any witness giving the evidence in the proceeding in Northern Ireland.[100]

Admissibility Issues

A statement of evidence taken from a witness in Northern Ireland pursuant to **3–13** these provisions is admissible as evidence in certain circumstances in the associated trial or appeal of the accused.[101] The statement must be certified by the judge who took it to be a true and accurate statement of the evidence taken.[102] Moreover, it will only be admissible if all of the members of the court were present throughout the taking of the evidence in question. If these requirements are satisfied the statement will be admissible as evidence of any fact stated therein of which evidence would be admissible at the trial or appeal, as the case may be.

Publicity Restrictions

Where a court in this State is conducting proceedings for an offence pursuant to the arrangements introduced by the 1976 Act, it may prohibit or restrict the publication of the names and addresses of any witness or the maker of any oral or written statement tendered in evidence to the court.[103] It may equally prohibit or restrict the publication of the name and address of any person from Northern Ireland whose evidence is to be taken pursuant to the provisions introduced by the Act.

Double Jeopardy

Trying a person in this State for an offence committed in Northern Ireland risks exposing that person to the danger of being punished twice for the same acts. Accordingly, there is provision in the 1976 Act to protect against the risk of such double jeopardy. If a person has been acquitted or convicted of an offence which consists of an offence under the law of Northern Ireland, he can plead his acquittal or conviction as a bar in any proceedings in the State for an offence consisting of the acts that constituted the offence of which he has been acquitted or convicted.[104] There are also consequential provisions for extradition. Where a person has been acquitted or convicted in this State of an offence within the ambit of the arrangements introduced by the 1976 Act, an order cannot be made for his extradition to Northern Ireland for an offence consisting of the same acts.[105] Similarly, a person who commits an

---

[100] *ibid.* s.11(2)(c).
[101] *ibid.* s.11(3)(a).
[102] A document purporting to be a certificate of a judge of the High Court of Justice of Northern Ireland and to be signed by him shall be deemed, for the purposes of this provision, to be such a certificate and to be so signed unless the contrary is shown; Criminal Law (Jurisdiction) Act 1976, s.11(3)(b).
[103] Criminal Law (Jurisdiction) Act 1976, s.17.
[104] *ibid.* s.15.
[105] *ibid.* s.20(4)(a).

offence in this State cannot be extradited to Northern Ireland in respect of that offence solely on the ground that it constitutes an offence in Northern Ireland pursuant to the Criminal Jurisdiction Act 1975 (the United Kingdom equivalent of the Criminal Law (Jurisdiction) Act 1976).[106]

4. Trial in Northern Ireland

3–14　The primary motivation behind the enactment of the Criminal Law (Jurisdiction) Act 1976 was to circumvent the perceived constitutional impediment to extradition for political offences. The assumption was that an alleged offender would take advantage of the political offence exception in order to block any attempt to extradite him from this State for trial in Northern Ireland. Nevertheless, the 1976 Act includes a provision which gives an accused an option of trial in Northern Ireland for an offence which would otherwise be triable in this State pursuant to the arrangements introduced by the Act. A person charged with such an offence must be informed of his rights associated with this option by the District Court on his first appearance before that court in conection with the charge.[107] He must also be informed of his rights by the court by which he is to be tried for the offence before entry of his plea on arraignment.

The option of trial in Northern Ireland is exercisable only if, at any time before the accused has entered a plea on arraignment, the court[108] is satisfied that a current warrant has been duly issued in Northern Ireland on an information laid by a member of the PSNI.[109] The court must be satisfied that the warrant authorises the arrest of the accused for an offence which, broadly speaking, is otherwise triable in this State under the provisions of the 1976 Act. If the court is also satisfied that the accused has requested trial in Northern Ireland, it must make an order directing that he be delivered into the custody of the PSNI. Where such an order is made the person affected must be brought by the Garda Síochána as soon as may be to some convenient point of departure from the State and there delivered into the custody of the PSNI.[110] In the meantime he must be kept in Garda custody or in a prison. However, if the person is charged with, or convicted of, another offence in the State while waiting to be sent to Northern Ireland pursuant to an order, his delivery shall be postponed until the conclusion of the proceedings for that other offence and of any sentence of imprisonment or detention imposed in respect of it.[111]

---

[106]　*ibid.* s.20(4)(b).

[107]　*ibid.* s.14(1).

[108]　The "court" means: (i) the High Court; (ii) during the preliminary examination, the District Court; and (iii) when the accused is before the court which is to try him, that court. Criminal Law (Jurisdiction) Act 1976, s.14(2)(b).

[109]　Criminal Law (Jurisdiction) Act 1976, s.14(2)(a).

[110]　*ibid.* s.14(3). See s.14(4) and (6) for dealing with a person who escaped from custody after such an order has been made and has since been recaptured, or a person who has been recaptured in this State after having escaped from custody imposed upon conviction in Northern Ireland for an offence within the ambit of the arrangements introduced by the 1976 Act. Such a person may also be arrested and punished in this State pursuant to ss.7 and 6(2) respectively of the Criminal Justice Act 1960; see Criminal Law (Jurisdiction) Act 1976, s.13(3).

[111]　Criminal Law (Jurisdiction) Act 1976, s.14(5).

5. Taking Evidence in this State for Trial in Northern Ireland

Letter of Request

It may happen that the proper trial of an offence in Northern Ireland depends **3–15** upon the evidence of a witness or witnesses resident in this State. This is most likely to happen in, but is by no means confined to, cases where a court in Northern Ireland is exercising its jurisdiction under the United Kingdom's Criminal Jurisdiction Act 1975 to try certain offences committed in this State. It may also prove necessary where a court in Northern Ireland is trying a person who has opted for trial in that jurisdiction under the Criminal Law (Jurisdiction) Act 1976. Whatever the reason, the 1976 Act makes provision for the taking of evidence in this State for the purposes of a criminal trial in Northern Ireland, just as it provides for the taking of evidence in Northern Ireland for use in a criminal trial in this State. These measures in question are triggered by a letter of request from a court in Northern Ireland for the taking of evidence in the State from a witness specified in the letter of request.[112] The letter of request must be produced to the Chief Justice sitting in private by or on behalf of the Attorney General. If the letter of request has been issued under provisions of the law of Northern Ireland corresponding to the reciprocal provisions in the 1976 Act, the Chief Justice must designate a judge of the High Court to take the evidence of the witness.[113] The judge so designated, known as the Commissioner, must take the evidence of the witness on oath.[114]

The Procedure

The Commissioner is generally in control of the sittings for the taking of evidence under these provisions. He or she determines the timing, location and procedure applicable.[115] The sittings will be in private unless, and to the extent that, he or she directs otherwise.[116] The Commissioner may direct any person whose evidence he or she is to take to attend and give evidence and produce any document or thing in his possession or power.[117] The members of the relevant court in Northern Ireland are entitled to be present at each sitting as are the accused and the counsel and solicitors for the accused and prosecution. The members of the court in Northern Ireland can put any question or questions to the witness.[118] Similarly, the accused (if not represented) and the counsel and solicitors for either side can question any witness and make submissions or representations to the Commissioner to the same extent as at a trial on indictment in the State.[119] The witness is entitled to the same privileges and

---

[112] *ibid.* s.12(1).
[113] *ibid.* s.12(1)(a).
[114] *ibid.* s.12(1)(b).
[115] *ibid.* s.12(2)(a) and (b).
[116] *ibid.* s.12(2)(c). The Commissioner also has the power to prohibit the publication of the name and address of any witness; s.12(2)(d).
[117] *ibid.* s.12(3). See s.12(7) for offences associated with a failure to co-operate
[118] *ibid.* s.12(4).
[119] *ibid.* s.12(5). Note also that persons entitled to practise as barristers or solicitors in Northern Ireland have a right of audience before any Commissioner taking evidence under these provisions

immunities as a witness in the Central Criminal Court.[120] By the same token if he gives false evidence he will be guilty of perjury if he would have been guilty of perjury if he had given the false evidence before a court.[121] Questions as to the exclusion of any oral evidence, or the withholding of any document or thing, on the ground of public interest are determined by the Commissioner in accordance with the law of this State.[122]

Status of the Accused

3–16 Where the accused is present in the State pursuant to the exercise of his right to be present during the taking of evidence under these provisions, he is immune from detention and any kind of suit or legal process in respect of any cause or matter, whether civil or criminal, arising before his arrival in the State.[123] However, while the accused is in the State in the exercise of his right under these provisions, he shall be kept in Garda custody or in a prison at all times when the proceedings before the Commissioner are adjourned.[124] The Commissioner may also authorise the temporary return of the accused to Northern Ireland during any adjournment of the proceedings.[125] In such a case, and at the conclusion of the proceedings, the accused must be brought by the Garda Síochána as soon as may be to some convenient point of departure from the State and delivered into the custody of the PSNI.[126]

E. Judicial Co-operation

1. Introduction

3–17 International co-operation between police and judicial authorities in criminal matters is not confined to extradition. It has already been seen that the Criminal Law (Jurisdiction) Act 1976 and the United Kingdom's Criminal Jurisdiction Act 1975 make substantive provision for the taking of evidence in one jurisdiction for use in a criminal trial in the other in certain circumstances. Although these reciprocal provisions are special to the two jurisdictions there is a growing trend towards international police and judicial co-operation in criminal matters. This trend is fuelled by public concern over certain criminal activities with an international dimension such as drug-trafficking, money-laundering, child abduction, trafficking in human beings and sex tourism. The results to date are a number of Conventions which provide for international

---

or any court in this State in which proceedings in connection with an offence under the 1976 Act arrangements are being held; s.16.

[120] Criminal Law (Jurisdiction) Act 1976, s.12(6)(a).
[121] *ibid.* s.12(8).
[122] *ibid.* s.12(6)(b).
[123] *ibid.* s.13(2).
[124] *ibid.* s.13(1). By virtue of s.13(3) a person who escapes from such custody is liable to arrest and punishment under ss.7 and 6(2) respectively of the Criminal Justice Act 1960.
[125] *ibid.* s.12(3)(d).
[126] *ibid.* s.12(9).

co-operation between police and judicial authorities in the detection of offenders and the gathering of evidence for use in a criminal trial in another jurisdiction. Although Ireland is a party to some of these Conventions their subject matter is mostly beyond the scope of this chapter and the book as a whole. Nevertheless, it is worth noting some of the main provisions which have been implemented in Irish law in order to fulfil Ireland's international obligations and to give effect to its corresponding rights in these matters.

The primary international Conventions on judicial co-operation in criminal matters to which Ireland is currently a signatory are: the Council of Europe Convention on Laundering, Search, Seizure, and Confiscation of Proceeds from Crime 1990; the UN Convention against Illicit Traffic in Narcotic Drugs and Psychotropic Substances 1988; and the European Convention on Mutual Assistance in Criminal Matters 1959 and additional Protocols 1978.[126a] Broadly speaking they provide for inter-state co-operation in: the search and seizure of criminal evidence in one state for use in another; taking criminal evidence in one state for use in another; the service of a criminal summons on witnesses and defendants in one state to appear in another; the execution in one state of confiscation orders issued in another, and the execution of forfeiture orders in one state for use in another. Each of these will be considered briefly in turn to the extent that they have been provided for in Irish law through the Criminal Justice Act 1994. There is also associated provision to enable Ireland cooperate with an international tribunal or other body established for the prosecution of persons responsible for serious violations of international humanitarian law committed outside the State.

2. Search and Seizure

A judge of the District Court has the power, in certain circumstances, to issue   **3–18** a warrant for the search and seizure of evidence[127] in this State required for the purpose of criminal proceedings in another state. This power can only be exercised pursuant to a direction from the Minister for Justice, Equality and Law Reform in response to a request which he has received from the government of a designated country.[128] Such request must be made on behalf of a prosecuting authority, or court or tribunal exercising criminal jurisdiction, in that country.[129] The Minister cannot normally give a direction unless provision is made in the law of the country concerned stipulating that any evidence furnished in response to the request will not be used, without his consent, for any purpose

---

[126a] The 1959 Convention is now supplemented by a 2000 Convention. Note also the rapid development of E.U. secondary legislation in this area, such as the Council decision establishing Eurojust; 2002/187/JHA.

[127] In this context "evidence" includes documents and other articles; Criminal Justice Act 1994, s.55(11).

[128] Criminal Justice Act 1994, s.55(4). A "designated country" for this purpose is a country which has been designated by Government Order under s.55(1). See Criminal Justice Act 1994 (section 55(1)) Order 1996 (No. 341 of 1996), Order 1997 (No. 368 of 1997), Order 1998 (No. 261 of 1998) and Order 2002 (No. 154 of 2002) for a list of the designated countries.

[129] It can also be made on behalf of any other authority in that country which appears to the Minister to be an appropriate authority for the purpose of s.55.

other than that specified in the request and that it will be returned when it is no longer required.[130]

It is not clear to whom the Minister should issue the direction under this provision. However, the warrant can only issue on the application of the DPP or a member of the Garda Síochána not below the rank of superintendent. Presumably such an application would only be made by either of these authorities pursuant to a direction from the Minister. Where such application is made the judge may issue the warrant if he is satisfied that there are reasonable grounds for believing that an offence under the law of a designated country has been committed, and that he would have the power to issue a search warrant in relation to any place if the conduct constituting the offence had been committed in Ireland.[131] In effect, therefore, the District Court judge's powers to issue a search warrant under Irish law are being extended to serve the foreign proceedings.[132] The warrant authorises entry, search and seizure in relation to the place specified in it to the extent that it would under the appropriate Irish enactment in respect of an offence committed in the State.[133] Any evidence seized must be forwarded to the Minister for transmission to the government of the country concerned or, at that government's request, the court, tribunal or authority for which it was obtained.[134] Where necessary, the evidence must be accompanied by any certificate, affidavit or other verifying document as may be specified in the direction given by the Minister.[135]

3. Taking Evidence

Nominating a judge

3–19   The Minister for Justice, Equality and Law Reform has the power, in certain circumstances, to nominate a judge of the District Court to receive evi-

---

[130]   Criminal Justice Act 1994, s.55(10).

[131]   *ibid.* s.55(3). Where a warrant has issued under this provision it is an offence to disclose information which is likely to prejudice the investigation; s.58.

[132]   Note also that under s.63 of the Criminal Justice Act 1994 a District Court judge has the power, in certain circumstances, to issue an order compelling a person to produce specified material to a member of the Garda Síochána who, in turn, may take it away or have access to it for a limited period. This power arises in connection with certain specified offences including drug trafficking and an offence in respect of which a confiscation order under s.9 of the Act may be issued. Section 55(2) of the Act stipulates that s.63 shall have effect as if references to drug trafficking or an offence in respect of which a confiscation order may be made under s.9 included any conduct which is an offence under the law of a country or territory outside the State and would constitute drug trafficking or an offence in which a confiscation order could be made if it had occurred in this State. The net effect would appear to be to permit the making of a production order under s.63 for these limited offences in the context of complying with a request from another country under s.55.

[133]   Note also that s.9 of the Criminal Law Act 1976 applies generally in relation to a search carried out under this provision (see ch.8 for a discussion of s.9). However, the reference in s.9(1) to the retention of the seized evidence for use in evidence in any criminal proceedings shall be interpreted as a reference to its retention for transmission to the country concerned; Criminal Justice Act 1994, s.55(7).

[134]   Criminal Justice Act 1994, s.55(4). If the evidence consists of a document, the original or copy shall be transmitted, and, if it consists of any other article, the article itself or a description, photograph or other representation of it shall be transmitted as may be necessary to comply with the request; s.55(6).

[135]   *ibid.* s.55(5).

dence[136] in this State for use in criminal proceedings in another country or territory. This power can arise only where the Minister receives a request for assistance from a court or tribunal exercising criminal jurisdiction (or a prosecuting authority) in another country or territory.[137] The request must be for assistance in obtaining evidence in this State in connection with criminal proceedings that have been instituted, or a criminal investigation that is being carried on, in that country or territory. If the Minister is satisfied that an offence under the law of that country or territory has been committed, or that there are reasonable grounds for suspecting that it has been committed, and that an investigation or proceedings are being carried on there with respect to the offence, he may nominate a judge of the District Court to receive such of the evidence requested as appears to the judge to be appropriate in order to give effect to the request.[138] However, the Minister cannot exercise this power unless provision is made in the law of the country or territory concerned to the effect that any evidence furnished pursuant to this provision will not, without the Minister's consent, be used for any purpose other than that specified in the request.[139]

Procedure

The procedure governing the taking of evidence under these provisions, including the attendance of witnesses, administering oaths and the privilege of witnesses broadly follows the law in this jurisdiction.[140] Evidence received by the judge must be furnished to the Minister for transmission to the court, tribunal or other authority that made the request.[141] Where necessary, the evidence must be accompanied by a certificate, affidavit or other verifying document as specified in the notice nominating the judge.[142]

Obtaining Evidence from outside the State

It is also worth noting that there are reciprocal arrangements for taking evidence[143] outside the State for use in criminal proceedings within the State. The DPP may apply to a judge of any court for the issue of a letter of request

---

[136] In this context "evidence" includes documents and other articles; Criminal Justice Act 1994, s.51(4).

[137] Criminal Justice Act 1994, s.51(1)(a). The request can also come from any other authority in such country or territory which appears to the Minister to have the function of making requests of the kind to which this section applies; s.51(1)(b).

[138] Criminal Justice Act 1994, s.51(2). For the purpose of satisfying himself as to these matters, the Minister may regard as conclusive a certificate issued by such authority in the country or territory in question as appears to him to be appropriate; s.51(3).

[139] Criminal Justice Act 1994, s.51(5).

[140] *ibid.* s.51(6) and 2nd Sched. No order shall be made for costs; 2nd Sched., para.6.

[141] Criminal Justice Act 1994, 2nd Sched., para.4(1). Where the evidence consists of a document, the original or a copy shall be transmitted and, where it consists of any other article, the article itself or a description, photograph or other representation of it shall be transmitted, as may be necessary in order to comply with the request; para.4(3).

[142] Criminal Justice Act 1994, 2nd Sched., para.4(2).

[143] In this context "evidence" includes documents and other articles; Criminal Justice Act 1994, s.52(5).

for assistance to obtain evidence outside the State for use in criminal pro-ceedings or an investigation.[144] If it appears to the judge that an offence has been committed, or that there are reasonable grounds for suspecting that it has been committed and that an investigation or proceedings have been commenced with respect to the offence, he may issue the letter specifying the evidence to be obtained. The letter must then be sent to the Minister for Justice, Equality and Law Reform for transmission either to the specified court or tribunal exercising jurisdiction in the place where the evidence is to be obtained, or to any authority recognised by the government of the country or territory concerned as the appropriate authority for receiving requests of this kind.[145]

Admissibility

3–20   A statement of evidence taken from a witness in another country or territory pursuant to a letter of request under these provisions is admissible as evidence in the associated proceedings in this State, if it is certified by or on behalf of the court, tribunal or authority by which it was taken to be a true and accurate statement of the evidence so taken.[146] Where a document is admissible under this provision, any document which purports to be a translation of it is also admissible as evidence of the translation if it is certified as correct by a person competent to do so.[147] It would appear, however, that these provisions do not oust the court's discretion to exclude evidence otherwise admissible. Indeed, it is specifically stated in the Act that in considering whether a statement obtained pursuant to these provisions should be excluded in the exercise of its discretion, the court must have regard to whether it was possible to challenge the statement by questioning the person who made it and whether the law of that country or territory concerned allowed the parties to the proceedings there to be legally represented when the evidence was being taken.[148]

The evidence obtained pursuant to a letter of request cannot be used for any purpose other than that specified in the letter, except with the consent of the appropriate authority in the country or territory concerned.[149] Where the document or other article of evidence is no longer required for that purpose, or for any other purpose for which the necessary consent has been obtained, it must normally be returned to the appropriate authority in the country or territory concerned.

---

[144] Criminal Justice Act 1994, s.52(2). Where proceedings have been instituted, the application can be made by a person charged in those proceedings.

[145] Criminal Justice Act 1994, s.52(3). In cases of urgency, a letter of request may be sent direct to a court or tribunal specified in the letter and exercising jurisdiction in the place where the evidence is to be obtained; s.52(4).

[146] Criminal Justice Act 1994, s.52(7). A document purporting to be a certificate, and signed by or on behalf, of such a court, tribunal or authority shall be deemed to be such a certificate and to be so signed unless the contrary is shown; s.52(8).

[147] Criminal Justice Act 1994, s.52(9). A document purporting to be a certificate for this purpose shall be deemed to be such a certificate and to be signed by the person purporting to have signed it, unless the contrary is shown.

[148] Criminal Justice Act 1994, s.52(10).

[149] *ibid.* s.52(6).

4. Summoning Witnesses and Defendants

Witnesses in this State

A person in this State may be summoned to appear as a witness or defendant in criminal proceedings in another country or territory. The procedure can be initiated once the Minister for Justice, Equality and Law Reform receives the necessary summons or process from the government (or other authority) of the country or territory concerned, along with a request for it to be served on a person in the State.[150] It is not clear whether the Minister is under an obligation to see that the summons or process is served on the person concerned. However, he is positively prohibited from causing it to be served where provision has not been made to protect the person affected from being proceeded against in the country or territory concerned in respect of any offence committed before his departure from this State.[151] In the case of a person summoned to appear as a defendant this is without prejudice to proceedings in respect of the offences specified in the summons.

3–21

Where the Minister causes the process to be served he shall do so by post, unless the request is for personal service in which case he shall direct the Commissioner of the Garda Síochána to cause it to be served personally on the person concerned.[152] In either case it must be accompanied by a notice explaining some of the implications to the person on whom it is served.[153] Even so, there is no obligation under Irish law to comply with any process served under these provisions.[154]

It may be that a person who can give evidence, or otherwise assist, in criminal proceedings or in the investigation of an offence in another country or territory is in prison in this State. If such a prisoner consents,[155] the Minister may issue a warrant providing for him to be transferred to another country or territory for

---

[150] *ibid.* s.49(1). There is also provision for the government of, or other authority in, the country or territory concerned to send to the Minister a document issued by a court exercising criminal jurisdiction in that country or territory and recording a decision of the court made in the exercise of that jurisdiction, along with a request for it to be served on a person in the State.

[151] Criminal Justice Act 1994, s.49(4) and (5). The provision can be made by law or by arrangement with the appropriate authority in the country or territory concerned. It must protect the person affected if he appears as a witness or defendant unless he has had a period of 15 consecutive days from the date when his presence is no longer required as a witness or defendant to leave the country or territory and has not done so, or unless he has returned to the country after having left it.

[152] Criminal Justice Act 1994, s.49(2). Where the Commissioner is directed to cause any summons, process (or document) to be served he shall, after it has been served, forthwith inform the Minister when and how it was served and (if possible) furnish him with a receipt signed by the person on whom it was served. If the Commissioner has been unable to cause it to be served, he shall forthwith inform the Minister of that fact and of the reason; s.49(7).

[153] Criminal Justice Act 1994, s.49(6). This notice must explain: that there is no obligation under Irish law to comply with the process; that the Minister cannot cause it to be served unless provision has been made to protect the person affected to the extent specified in s.49(4) and (5): that the person affected may wish to seek advice as to the possible consequences of his failing to comply with the process under the law of the country or territory where it was issued; and that under the law of that country or territory he may not, as a witness, be accorded the same rights and privileges as would be accorded to him in criminal proceedings in this State.

[154] Criminal Justice Act 1994, s.49(3).

[155] Consent may be given either by the prisoner himself or, where the Minister considers that it is inappropriate for the prisoner to act for himself by reason of his physical or mental condition or

the purpose of giving evidence in criminal proceedings there or, by his presence, assisting in the proceedings or in the investigation of an offence.[156] The warrant cannot issue unless provision is made to protect the prisoner from being proceeded against in that country or territory in respect of any offence committed before his departure from this State.[157] A warrant issued under these provisions authorises the taking of the prisoner to a point of departure from the State and his delivery from that point into the custody of a person representing the appropriate authority of the country or territory to which the prisoner is to be transferred.[158] It also authorises bringing the prisoner back to the State and his transfer in custody to the place where he is liable to be detained pursuant to his sentence. He is always deemed to be in legal custody at any time when he is being taken to and from any place under the warrant and while being kept in custody under the warrant.[159] If he escapes or is unlawfully at large he may be arrested without warrant by a member of the Garda Síochána and taken to any place to which he may be taken under a warrant issued pursuant to these provisions.[160]

Summoning Witnesses from outside the State

3–22   There are reciprocal arrangements for summoning a witness or defendant from another country or territory to appear before a court in a criminal matter in this State. A summons requiring such a person charged with an offence to appear before a court in this State may be issued and may be served outside the State in accordance with arrangements made by the Minister for Foreign Affairs. A summons or order may also be issued in this manner requiring a person to attend before a court in this State for the purpose of giving evidence in criminal proceedings. Service of a summons in either case does not impose any obligation under Irish law to comply with it. Accordingly, a failure to comply does not constitute contempt of any court, nor is it a ground for issuing a warrant to secure the attendance of the person in question.[161] Where a person is in the State in compliance with a summons issued under these provisions, he cannot normally be proceeded against in respect of any offences committed

---

his youth, by a person appearing to the Minister to be an appropriate person to act on his behalf; Criminal Justice Act 1994, s.53(2).

[156] Criminal Justice Act 1994, s.53(1). In this context a "prisoner" is a person serving a sentence in a prison or any other place for which rules or regulations may be made under the Prisons Acts 1826 to 1980, or s.13 of the Criminal Justice Act 1960. It also includes a person in custody awaiting trial or sentence and a person committed to prison for default in paying a fine or a sum due under a confiscation order (issued under s.4(4) or s.9(1) of the Act) or confiscation co-operation order (issued under s.46(2) of the Act); s.53(8).

[157] Criminal Justice Act 1994, s.53(4). The provision must be made either by the law of the country or territory concerned or by arrangement with the appropriate authority in that country or territory.

[158] Criminal Justice Act 1994, s.53(3).

[159] *ibid.* s.53(5).

[160] *ibid.* s.53(7). A person authorised by or for the purposes of a warrant issued under these provisions to take the prisoner to or from any place or to keep him in custody shall have all the powers, authority, protection and privileges of a member of the Garda Síochána; s.53(6).

[161] This is without prejudice to the service of any process on the person in question if subsequently effected in the State; Criminal Justice Act 1994, s.50(3).

before his arrival in the State.[162] Naturally this is without prejudice to proceedings in respect of offences specified in the case of a person summoned to appear before a court to answer a criminal charge.

There is also provision for the transfer of a prisoner to this State from another country or territory for the purpose of assisting a criminal investigation or criminal proceedings if a witness order or witness summons has been issued with respect to the prisoner, or if it appears to the Minister for Justice, Equality and Law Reform that it is desirable for such a prisoner to assist the investigation or proceedings by his presence.[163] In these circumstances the Minister may issue a warrant to bring the prisoner to this State, but only if he is satisfied that the appropriate authority in the country or territory where the prisoner is detained will make arrangements for him to come to the State for the required purpose.[164] Moreover, a warrant cannot be issued in respect of a prisoner unless he has consented to being brought to the State for the required purpose.[165] Where a warrant is issued it authorises the bringing of the prisoner to the State, the detention of the prisoner in custody at the place or places specified in the warrant and the returning of the prisoner to the country or territory from which he has come.[166] He is deemed to be in legal custody at any time while he is in this State pursuant to the warrant.[167] If he escapes or is unlawfully at large he can be arrested without warrant by a member of the Garda Síochána and brought to any place to which he may be taken under the warrant.[168] While the warrant is in force, he is not subject to the controls imposed by the Aliens Act 1935 and orders made under it in respect of his entry into or presence in the State.[169] Similarly, while he is in the State pursuant to the warrant he cannot be proceeded against in respect of any offence committed against the law of the State before his arrival.[170]

---

[162] Criminal Justice Act 1994, s.50(4) and (5). This protection does not apply where the person has had an opportunity to leave the State for 15 consecutive days from the date when his presence was no longer required, or where he has returned to the State after having left it.

[163] Criminal Justice Act 1994, s.54(1). In this context a "prisoner" is a person who is detained in custody in a country or territory outside the State by virtue of a sentence or order of a court or tribunal exercising criminal jurisdiction in that country or territory. It also includes a person detained in custody in a country or territory outside the State in consequence of having been transferred there under any legislative or other arrangements for the repatriation of prisoners as it applies to a person detained as in s.54(1); s.54(8).

[164] Criminal Justice Act 1994, s.54(2).

[165] *ibid.* s.54(3).

[166] *ibid.* s.54(4).

[167] *ibid.* s.54(5).

[168] A person authorised by or for the purposes of a warrant issued under these provisions to take the prisoner to or from any place or to keep him in custody shall have all the powers, authority, protection and privileges of a member of the Garda Síochána; Criminal Justice Act 1994, ss.54(5) and 53(6).

[169] Criminal Justice Act 1994, s.54(6).

[170] *ibid.* s.54(7).

5. Confiscation Co-operation Orders

Introduction

3–23 The Criminal Justice Act 1994 makes provision for the issuance of confiscation orders, in certain circumstances, in respect of property or proceeds
associated with drug-trafficking or any other criminal offence for which a
person has been convicted on indictment.[171] These measures are dealt with in
Chapter 21. For the purposes of the current chapter, however, it is necessary
to address the extent to which the Irish authorities may cooperate with foreign
judicial authorities in the enforcement in this State of comparable orders emanating from other States. The 1994 Act makes provision for the enforcement
in accordance with Irish law of such orders where the country in which they
have been made is designated for this purpose by government order.[172] This
external co-operation procedure applies in respect of property which is liable
to confiscation in accordance with orders (known as external confiscation
orders) made by a court in the country concerned for the purpose of recovering
payments or other rewards received in connection with drug-trafficking, or for
the purpose of recovering property obtained in connection with conduct which
corresponds to an offence for which a confiscation order could issue on conviction on indictment in this State.[173] These external co-operation orders are
enforced in Irish law through the medium of confiscation co-operation orders.

Initiating the Procedure

The confiscation co-operation order procedure is triggered by the making of
an external confiscation order by a court in a designated country. This must be
followed by an application to the High Court by or on behalf of that country,
with the consent of the Minister for Justice, Equality and Law Reform, for the
making of a corresponding confiscation order.[174] The High Court may make
the confiscation order requested, but only if: (i) it is satisfied that the external
confiscation order is in force and is not subject to appeal[175] at the time it is
making the order; (ii) where the person against whom the order was made did
not appear in the proceedings, it is satisfied that he received notice of the
proceedings in sufficient time to enable him to defend them; and (iii) it is of
the opinion that the making of the order would not be contrary to the interests
of justice.[176] On the hearing of the application a certificate signed by, or with
the authority of, a judge of the court which made the external confiscation

---

[171] *ibid.* ss.4(4) and 9(1).
[172] The countries currently designated for this purpose are Hungary and those listed in Criminal
Justice Act 1994 (section 46(1)) Order 1996 (No.344 of 1996), Order 1997 (No. 104 of 1997),
Order (No.2) 1997 (No. 366 of 1997), Order (No.3) 1997 (No. 463 of 1997), Order 1998 (No. 65
of 1998), Order (No. 2) 1998 (No. 259 of 1998), Order 2002 (No. 152 of 2002).
[173] Criminal Justice Act 1994, s.46(1). It also applies in respect of the value of the property obtained
and for the purpose of depriving a person of a pecuniary advantage obtained so obtained.
[174] Criminal Justice Act 1994, s.46(2).
[175] In this context "appeal" includes any proceedings by way of discharging or setting aside a judgment,
and an application for a new trial or a stay of execution; Criminal Justice Act 1994, s.46(4).
[176] Criminal Justice Act 1994, s.46(3).

order, is admissible as evidence of the making of the order or of any fact contained in the evidence or information without further proof.[177] Where a document is admissible in evidence under this provision, any document purporting to be a translation of it is also admissible as evidence of the translation, if it is certified as correct by a person competent to certify it.[178]

Enforcement of the order

Once issued, the confiscation co-operation order generally has the same effect **3–24** as a domestic confiscation order made under the 1994 Act, subject to the following qualifications.[179] If the external confiscation order was for the confiscation of specified property, other than money, the confiscation co-operation order must be confined to an order for the recovery of that property, or so much of it as is specified in the application. Similarly, if the external confiscation order was for the recovery of a sum of money, the confiscation co-operation order must be confined to the recovery of that sum, or such lesser sum as is specified in the application. The actual enforcement of the confiscation co-operation order is subject to Irish law, including the law governing the enforcement of the domestic confiscation orders which can be issued under the 1994 Act. However, the government may issue regulations to make such modifications to the Act as it considers necessary or expedient for the purpose of adapting to confiscation co-operation orders those provisions relating to domestic confiscation orders.[180] This applies in particular to the enforcement of the orders and the taking of provisional measures to prevent any dealing in, or transfer or disposal of, property that may be liable to confiscation in accordance with any confiscation co-operation order that may be made.[181]

The High Court must revoke a confiscation co-operation order if it appears to the court that the external confiscation order has been satisfied in accordance with the law of the country in which it was made.[182]

6. Forfeiture Co-operation Orders

Introduction

A forfeiture order may be issued in certain circumstances under the Criminal **3–25** Justice Act 1994 in respect of property which has been seized from a person

---

[177] Criminal Justice Act 1994, s.48(1). A document purporting to be a certificate for the purpose of this provision shall be deemed to be such and to have been signed by the person purporting to have signed it unless the contrary is shown; s.48(2).
[178] Criminal Justice Act 1994, s.48(3). A document purporting to be a certificate for the purpose of this provision shall be deemed to be such and to be signed by the person purporting to have signed it unless the contrary is shown.
[179] Criminal Justice Act 1994, s.46(5).
[180] Criminal Justice Act 1994, s.46(6). A draft of such regulations must be laid before, and approved by resolution of, each House of the Oireachtas before they can be made; s.46(8). See Criminal Justice Act 1994 (section 46(6)) Regulations 1996 (No. 343 of 1996) for the current regulations.
[181] It is worth noting that the 1994 Act itself stipulates that where property is subject to an order, any dealing with it in reliance on the law of any country or territory outside the State cannot operate so as to prevent the order taking effect; see s.60.
[182] Criminal Justice Act 1994, s.46(7).

who has since been convicted of a criminal offence.[183] The relevant provisions are considered later in Chapter 21. For the purposes of the current chapter, however, it is necessary to consider the extent to which the Irish authorities may cooperate with foreign judicial authorities in the enforcement in this State of comparable orders issued in other states. The 1994 Act makes provision for the enforcement in accordance with Irish law of such orders where the country in which they have been made is designated for this purpose by government order.[184] This external co-operation procedure applies where a forfeiture order (known as an external forfeiture order) has been made by a court in a designated country for anything in respect of which a certain offence has been committed or for anything which was used or intended to be used in connection with the commission of such an offence.[185] The offence in question must be one which corresponds to an offence under the Misuse of Drugs Act 1977, a drug-trafficking offence or an offence for which a confiscation order can be made in this State on conviction on indictment.[186] These external forfeiture orders are enforced in Irish law through the medium of forfeiture co-operation orders.

Initiating the Procedure

The forfeiture co-operation procedure is triggered by the making of an external forfeiture order by a court in a designated country. This must be followed by an application to the High Court by or on behalf of the government of that country, with the consent of the Minister for Justice, Equality and Law Reform for the making of a corresponding forfeiture co-operation order.[187] On the hearing of the application a certificate signed by, or with the authority of, a judge of the court which made the external confiscation order, is admissible as evidence of the making of the order or of any fact contained in the evidence or information without further proof.[188] Where a document is admissible in evidence under this provision, any document purporting to be a translation of it is also admissible as evidence of the translation, if it is certified as correct by a person competent to certify it.[189]

Procedure

The High Court may make the forfeiture co-operation order, but only if: (i) it is satisfied that the external forfeiture order is in force and is not subject to

---

[183] *ibid.* s.61(1).

[184] Countries currently designated for this purpose Hungary and those listed in Criminal Justice Act 1994 (section 47(1)) Order, 1996 (No. 342 of 1996), Order 1997 (No. 105 of 1997), Order (No.2) 1997 (No. 367 of 1997), Order (No.3) 1997 (No. 464 of 1997), Order 1998 (No. 66 of 1998), Order (No. 2) 1998 (No. 260 of 1998), Order 2002 (No. 153 of 2002).

[185] Criminal Justice Act 1994, s.47(1).

[186] *ibid.* s.47(5).

[187] *ibid.* s.47(2).

[188] Criminal Justice Act 1994, s.48(1). A document purporting to be a certificate for the purpose of this provision shall be deemed to be such and to have been signed by the person purporting to have signed it unless the contrary is shown; s.48(2).

[189] Criminal Justice Act 1994, s.48(3). A document purporting to be a certificate for the purpose of this provision shall be deemed to be such and to be signed by the person purporting to have signed it unless the contrary is shown.

appeal[190] at the time it is making the order; (ii) where the person against whom the order was made did not appear in the proceedings, it is satisfied that he received notice of the proceedings in sufficient time to enable him to defend them; and (iii) it is of the opinion that the making of a forfeiture co-operation order corresponding to the external forfeiture order would not be contrary to the interests of justice.[191] However, the court must not make the order if the person claiming to be the owner of the thing in question applies to be heard by the court.[192] This restriction can be avoided by giving the person the opportunity to show cause why the order should not be made. Once issued the order will operate to deprive the person concerned of his rights in the property affected, and the property shall be taken into the possession of the Garda Síochána if it is not already there.[193] It is also worth noting that the order cannot be prevented from taking effect by any dealing with the property in reliance on the law of any country or territory outside the State.[194]

7. International Criminal Tribunals

The provisions on judicial co-operation discussed in this section are confined to domestic courts and the appropriate authorities in other countries or territories. They do not extend automatically to co-operation with tribunals exercising jurisdiction solely under international law. It is worth noting, however, that the government can make regulations modifying the Criminal Justice Act 1994 for the purpose of adapting these provisions to provide co-operation for certain international tribunals.[195] Such regulations could extend to the tribunals concerned the benefits of any or all of the provisions on: search and seizure, obtaining evidence, the service of a summons or other process, the temporary transfer of a prisoner, confiscation co-operation orders and forfeiture co-operation orders as discussed above. The international tribunals in question are those established for the prosecution of persons responsible for serious violations of international humanitarian law committed outside the State.

3–26

F. Extradition

1. Legal Basis

Definition

Extradition refers generally to a legal procedure through which an individual can be detained in one jurisdiction and delivered into the custody of another

3–27

---

[190] For this purpose an "appeal" includes any proceedings by way of discharging or setting aside a judgment, and an application for a new trial or a stay of execution; Criminal Justice Act 1994, ss.47(2) and 46(4).

[191] Criminal Justice Act 1994, ss.47(2) and 46(3).

[192] *ibid.* s.47(3).

[193] Criminal Justice Act 1994, ss.47(4) and 61(4). The Police Property Act 1897 applies, with certain modifications, to such property; see ss.47(4) and 61(7) and (8) of the 1994 Act.

[194] Criminal Justice Act 1994, s.60.

[195] *ibid.* s.56(1). A draft of such regulations must be laid before, and approved by resolution of, each House of the Oireachtas before they can be made; s.56(2).

jurisdiction for the purpose of being charged and tried for a criminal offence in the latter. Walsh J. described it more comprehensively as:

> "the formal surrender, based upon reciprocating arrangements by one nation with another, of an individual accused or convicted of an offence who is within the jurisdiction of the requested country when the requesting country, being competent to try and punish him, demands his surrender. The formal arrangements by which this may be secured and the principles of reciprocity enshrined are either by way of treaties or by reciprocal legislation."[196]

Treaties

Ireland is a party to several multilateral treaties[197] on extradition and unilateral treaties with other individual jurisdictions.[198] Generally, these provide reciprocal arrangements for the extradition of a suspect in one state for the purpose of prosecution and trial in the other. Absent specific provision to the contrary it is considered that the extradition arrangements provided for by these treaties or international agreements do not pose a charge on public funds within the meaning of Article 29.5.2° of the Constitution.[199] Accordingly, they do not have to be approved by a Dáil resolution before they can come into force.[199a]

The extradition conventions or treaties can be given effect in Ireland by means of an Order issued by the government where it is satisfied that reciprocal arrangements to those it is introducing in Ireland will be afforded by the other country.[200] Indeed, it would appear that there is no prior need for a formal convention or treaty at all. The government can make an order when it is

---

[196] *Wyatt v. McLoughlin* [1974] I.R. 378 at 397.

[197] See, Extradition Act 1965 (Application Part II) Order 200 (S.I. No. 474 of 2000) and Extradition Act 1965 (Application of Part II) (Amendment) Order 2002 (S.I. No. 173 of 2002).

[198] The treaties are normally brought into effect by an Order applying Pt II of the Extradition Act 1965 to the country in question; see, e.g., Extradition Act 1965 (Part II)(No.20) Order 1984 which applies Pt II to the USA; Extradition Act 1965 (Part II)(No.19) Order 1984 which applies Pt II to Australia.

[199] In *State (Gilliland) v. Governor of Mountjoy Prison* [1987] I.L.R.M. 278 a distinction was drawn in this context between provisions which do not necessarily involve a charge upon public funds even if they might involve incidental expenses and provisions which specifically state that certain expenses or pecuniary liabilities arising from the operation of the arrangements shall be borne by the State. The former did not involve a charge on public funds (see also *Trimbole v. Governor of Mountjoy Prison* [1985] I.L.R.M. 449), but the latter did. Since the Treaty with the USA contained provisions of the latter type it followed that the State was not bound by it until such times as it was approved by resolution of Dáil Éireann. This is in turn meant that the Order purporting to put the Treaty into effect in this State was invalid. There is a suggestion in *State (McCaud) v. Governor of Mountjoy Prison* [1986] I.L.R.M. 129 that the requirements of Article 29.5.2° are satisfied generally by s.5 of the 1965 Act.

[199a] For an alternative view to the effect that such agreements do not involve a charge on public funds within the meaning of Article 29.5.2° see *Trimbole v. Governor of Mountjoy Prison* [1985] I.L.R.M. 449, *per* Egan J. at 477.

[200] Extradition Act 1965, s.8. These Orders are considered to be laws for the purposes of Article 40.4.3° of the Constitution. Accordingly, if an individual challenges his detention under such an order in the High Court and the High Court is of the opinion that he is being lawfully detained under the Order but that the Order is invalid having regard to the provisions of the Constitution, the High Court must refer the issue of the validity of the order to the Supreme Court by way of case stated. By virtue of Article 34.4.5° the decision of the Supreme Court must be delivered through one judgment. See *State (Gilliland) v. Governor of Mountjoy Prison* [1987] I.L.R.M. 278.

satisfied that reciprocal facilities will be afforded by the other country.[201] Reciprocity in this context does not mean that the extradition arrangements in both States must be identical.[202] The Orders must be laid before each House of the Oireachtas and are subject to annulment by resolution of either House within a 21-day period. Extradition arrangements with the United Kingdom are based on reciprocal legislation.

Legislation

Primary legislation governing extradition consists of the Extradition Act 1965, **3–28** the Extradition (European Convention on the Suppression of Terrorism) Act 1987, the Extradition (Amendment) Act 1987, the Extradition (Amendment) Act 1994 and the Extradition (European Union Conventions) Act 2001. These are considered as a penal statutory code involving penal sanctions on the individual. It follows that their terms must be construed strictly in the sense that a person should not be subjected to detention and extradition in the absence of clear and unambiguous provisions to that effect. Referring specifically to the 1965 Act and the statutory instrument adopted pursuant to it in order to give effect to the European Convention on Extradition, Finlay C.J., giving the judgment of the Supreme Court in *Aamand v. Smithwick* put the matter thus:

> "It is clear and of importance in this case that the Act of 1965 and the statutory instrument made pursuant to it incorporating the convention is a penal statutory code involving penal sanctions on an individual and must therefore be construed strictly as is contended in the sense that not by anything other than unambiguous provision should a person be subjected to detention and extradition."[203]

In *Byrne v. Conroy,*[204] Kelly J. reduced the correct approach to the interpretation of the Act to the following four rules:

> "1. a strict or literal construction must be applied,
> 2. words must be given their ordinary and natural meaning,
> 3. no gloss may be placed on the wording,
> 4. any reasonable doubt or ambiguity must be resolved in favour of the applicant."[205]

However, the learned judge went on to say *obiter* that in a case which raised the State's obligations under European Community law the strict literal construction would have to give way in the case of any ambiguity to an interpretation which would comply with the State's obligations in European law.

---

[201] Extradition Act 1965, s.8(1)(ii).

[202] In *Trimbole v. Governor of Mountjoy Prison* [1985] I.L.R.M. 465 it was considered that the lack of a prima facie evidence requirement in the Irish legislation did not affect the validity of the Order implementing reciprocal extradition arrangements with Australia, despite the fact that the corresponding Australian measure required the establishment of a prima facie case as a prerequisite for extradition to Ireland.

[203] [1995] 1 I.L.R.M. 61 at 67.

[204] [1997] 2 I.L.R.M. 99.

[205] *ibid.* at 108.

Reciprocity

3–29 Extradition is a specialist subject in its own right. It is not the intention of this section, therefore, to offer anything other a sketch of the main procedures and principles governing extradition from Ireland. Reference should be made to suitable specialist texts for more detailed and comprehensive treatment of the Irish extradition legislation, the extradition treaties to which Ireland is a party and general principles governing extradition.[206] Nevertheless it is worth emphasising at the outset that the making of extradition arrangements between states is a political act based on the principle of reciprocity. The law and procedure governing extradition in Ireland reflects the reciprocal nature of the arrangements with the other state or states.

The principle of reciprocity entails a presumption that the requesting state is acting in good faith in the sense that the person sought is genuinely suspected of the offence in question, will be charged with that offence and will not be pursued for another offence or purpose not specified in the extradition warrant (see further below). The Irish authorities will not normally look behind the facts stated on an extradition warrant from another state unless there is evidence suggesting that the constitutional rights of the person being sought would be denied if he or she was extradited. In *Clarke v. McMahon*,[207] for example, the applicant had escaped from prison in Northern Ireland where he was serving a sentence of imprisonment for an offence for which he had been convicted in Northern Ireland. His extradition was sought to serve out the remainder of his sentence. He challenged his extradition on the ground, *inter alia*, that his conviction was unsound as it was based on a false confession which had been extracted from him by violence and threats. He had not challenged the admissibility of his confession in the Northern Irish courts because he felt that he would not be believed. In rejecting this ground of challenge both the High Court and the Supreme Court ruled that subject to their inherent power to protect the constitutional rights of the individual they could not in an extradition case properly undertake an investigation into the validity of a conviction recorded in the requesting state. Costello J. in the High Court quoted with approval the following words of Finlay J. (as he then was) in the unreported case of *Archer v. Fleming*:[208]

> "I am clearly satisfied that under the entire provisions of the Extradition Act, and the arrangements of extradition of which it is a statutory implementation, that there cannot be any question of the courts in the requested country adjudicating upon the merits of the charge against the accused or reaching any conclusion, whether of a *prima facie* nature or otherwise, as to the guilt or innocence of the plaintiff seeking to set aside the extradition order in respect of the charge against him. To permit the court in the requested country reaching adjudication on those issues would be entirely inconsistent in my opinion with the extradition code and entirely inconsistent with the applicable provisions of

---

[206] For a text on the Irish law see Forde, M., *Extradition Law in Ireland* (2nd ed., Round Hall Sweet & Maxwell, Dublin, 1995).

[207] [1990] I.L.R.M. 648.

[208] High Court, January 21, 1980.

the Extradition Act 1965. Even, therefore, were these proceedings brought on a plenary summons and even if the plaintiff was in a position to seek from the court the declarations which are contained in paragraph one and two of the endorsement of the claim on this summons, I am satisfied that they are not declarations which could be made."

Costello J. went on to say:

"By a parity of reasoning I do not think that the courts in a requested country when the extradition of a convicted person is sought can adjudicate on the validity of a conviction by a court in a requesting state. Clearly, this cannot be done under s.50 of the 1965 Act. Equally clearly, it cannot be done by the adoption of the procedural device such as proceedings by way of plenary summons for a declaration or by way of an application for an order of *habeas corpus*.

There is in this case an added factor which militates against the applicant's claim. The court of the requesting state was not asked to adjudicate on the issue which it is now claimed invalidated its order, although it was competent to do so. In such circumstances, it would be contrary to the extradition arrangements into which our State is entered and to the principles which are to be found in the 1965 Act, that this court now can assert jurisdiction to inquire into the validity of the conviction."[209]

Order 31, r.29 of the Rules of the Supreme Courts cannot be used to order discovery of documents from a foreign sovereign State in proceedings for the extradition of a person to that State.[210]

Limits to Extradition

Normally where the government has extradition arrangements with another country and that country duly requests the extradition of a person in accordance with these arrangements then that person must be surrendered in accordance with the law and procedures governing extradition. There are, however, a number of exceptions. Unless the relevant extradition provisions or the 1965 Act state otherwise, extradition is not available against an Irish citizen.[211] Extradition is not available for certain offences,[212] where the offence is regarded by the law of the State as having being committed in the State,[213] where a prosecution is pending in the State against the person requested,[214] where final judgment has been passed in respect of the offence in question against the person requested either in the State or in a third country,[215] where by

3–30

---

[209] [1990] I.L.R.M. 648 at 651–652.
[210] *Fusco v. O'Dea* [1994] 2 I.L.R.M. 389.
[211] Extradition Act 1965, s.14 as amended by Extradition (European Union Conventions) Act 2001, s.6(a). Where an Irish citizen does an act outside the State which constitutes an offence for which he would be liable to extradition but for the fact that he is an Irish citizen he shall be guilty of the like offence and be liable on conviction to the like punishment as if the act were done within the State; see s.38 for further provisions on the prosecution of any such offence.
[212] Extradition Act 1965, ss.10–13.
[213] *ibid.* s.15.
[214] *ibid.* s.16.
[215] *ibid.* s.17(1).

reason of lapse of time the person concerned is legally immune from prosecution or punishment for the offence in question either in the State or the requesting country,[216] where the offence is punishable by the death penalty in the requesting country unless that country gives a sufficient assurance that the death penalty will not be carried out,[217] where there is no provision in the law of the requesting country respecting the rule of speciality,[218] where there is no provision in the law of the requesting country (or in the extradtion agreement with that country) protecting the person concerned against being extradited to a third country.[219] Where the extradition provisions require the production by the requesting country of evidence as to the commission of the offence, extradition shall not be granted unless sufficient evidence is produced to satisfy this requirement.[220] Also, extradition may be refused by the Minister for an offence which is also an offence under the law of the State if the DPP has decided either not to institute or to terminate proceedings against the person claimed in respect of the offence.[221]

Some of these exceptions are quite common in practice and so deserve more detailed explanation.

2. Non-Extraditable Offences

3–31   Extradition is not available for certain offences, namely: an offence which is not punishable by imprisonment for a period of at least one year or by a more severe penalty, an offence which is a political offence or an offence connected with a political offence, offences under military law which are not offences under ordinary criminal law and revenue offences.

The burden of proving that the offence in question is a political offence or an offence connected with a political offence or a revenue offence would appear to rest on the applicant making the claim.[221a]

Minimum Punishment

In order to be extraditable an offence must satisfy minimum punishment requirements under the law of both the State and the requesting country.[221b] The offence must be punishable under the laws of the State and of the requesting country by imprisonment for a period of at least one year or by a more severe

---

[216] *ibid.* s.18. See Chapter 1 and 13 for delay and time limits in Irish Criminal procedure.
[217] *ibid.* s.19.
[218] *ibid.* s.20.
[219] *ibid.* s.21 as amended by Extradition (European Union Conventions) Act 2001, s.25. This can be avoided by the consent of the Minister or a failure by the prson to leave the State concerned within a specified period of the completion of the criminal proceedings against him.
[220] *ibid.* s.22.
[221] *ibid.* s.17(2).
[221a] See, *e.g., Maguire v. Keane* [1986] I.L.R.M. 235 in the case of a political offence, but note comment of McCarthy J. in the later case of *Finucane v. McMahon* [1990] I.L.R.M. 505 at 529 to the effect that the issue had not been argued on any of the cases. See *Byrne v. Conroy* [1997] 2 I.L.R.M. 99 and [1998] 2 I.L.R.M. 113 for a revenue offence.
[221b] References to an offence punishable under the law of the State here shall be construed as including references to an act which, if it had been committed in the State, would constitute such an offence; Extradition Act 1965, s.10(3).

penalty under the laws of the State and the requesting country.[221c] If there has already been a conviction and sentence in the requesting country a period of imprisonment of at least four months or a more severe penalty must have been imposed. Extradition for offences which do not satisfy these minimum requirements can be granted, but only if they are part of an application which has been granted in respect of additional offences which do satisfy the minimum requirements.[221d] For these purposes an offence punishable under Irish law means an act which, if committed in the State on the day on which the extradition request was made, would constitute an offence under Irish law.[221e] An offence punishable under the law of the requesting country means an offence punishable on the day on which the offence was committed and the day on which the extradition was made.[221f] More relaxed definitions apply to extradition to the United Kingdom and the Member States of the European Union which have been designated Convention countries pursuant to section 10 of the Extradition (European Union Conventions) Act 2001 (see later).

Political Offence Exception

The exception which has given rise to most controversy in recent years is undoubtedly the political offence exception.

Extradition is not available for any offence which is a political offence or an offence connected with a political offence.[222] It is also not available for an ordinary criminal offence where there are substantial grounds for believing that the request was made for the purpose of prosecuting or punishing a person on account of his race, religion, nationality or political opinion or that that person's position may be prejudiced for any of these reasons.[223] The 1965 Act does not offer a definition of a political offence, apart from a stipulation that it does not include the taking or attempted taking of the life of a Head of State or a member of his or her family or an offence within the scope of Article 3 of the United Nations Convention Against Illicit Traffic in Narcotic Drugs and Psychotropic Substances 1988.[224] However, section 50 of the Extradition Act 1965 has been the source of much clarification of what does and what does not qualify as a political offence. It makes provision for the release of a person who has been arrested and detained for the purpose of extradition

---

[221c] Extradition Act 1965, s.10(1). See comments of Kelly J. with respect to the punishable available for conspiracy to defraud in *Attorney General v. Oldridge*.

[221d] Extradition Act 1965, s.10(2).

[221e] Extradition Act 1965, s.10(3)(a), as amended by Extradition (European Union Conventions) Act 2001, s.11(c). In the case of an offence under the law of the requesting State consisting of the commission of one or more acts including any act committed in the State, the definition includes such one or more acts which, if committed in Ireland on the day on which the act concerned was committed would constitute an offence; s.10(3)(b).

[221f] *ibid.* s.10(4), as inserted by *ibid.* s.11(d).

[222] *ibid.* s.11(1). To qualify as an offence "connected with a political offence" it must be shown that there is a causal or factual relationship of sufficient strength between the two offences; *Bourke v. Attorney General* [1972] I.R. 36, *Carron v. McMahon* [1990] I.L.R.M. 802. See also *Quinlivan v. Conroy* [2000] 2 I.L.R.M. 515. O'Dalaigh C.J.'s judgment in *Bourke v. Attorney General* [1972] I.R. 36 offers a substantial analysis of a "political offence" and "an offence connected with a political offence" in the context of the European Convention on Extradition and the *travaux préparatoires* for that Convention.

[223] Extradition Act 1965, s.11(2).

[224] *ibid.* s.3, as amended by Extradition (Amendment) Act 1994, s.3(a).

pursuant to the extradition arrangements with the United Kingdom. It states, in part, that the High Court (or the Minister for Justice, Equality and Law Reform) shall direct the person's release where it (or Minister) is of the opinion that the offence in question is a political offence or an offence connected with a political offence, or that there are substantial grounds for believing that the warrant was issued for the purpose of prosecuting or punishing him on account of his race, religion, nationality or political opinion or that his position would be prejudiced for any of these reasons.[225] Applications for release under section 50 have spawned a considerable body of case law on the meaning of a political offence, particularly in the context of the conflict in Northern Ireland.

At one time the Irish judges appeared to take the view that an offence committed in the course of the armed struggle to force a British withdrawal from Northern Ireland would qualify as a political offence.[226] Their assessment was based largely on English case law which broadly supported the notion that a political offence was an offence connected with an uprising, insurrection, civil war or struggle for power.[227] By the early 1980s the Irish courts had moved to a position in which they demonstrated a reluctance to accept that an offence involving the use of violence against the person could qualify as a political offence. The high water mark of this position is reflected in the following quotation from the judgment of O'Higgins C.J. in *McGlinchey v. Wren*:

> "The judicial authorities on the scope of such offences have been rendered obsolete in many respects by the fact that modern terrorist violence, whether undertaken by military or paramilitary organisations, or by individuals or groups of individuals, is often the antithesis of what could reasonably be regarded as political, either in itself or in its connections. All that can be said with authority in this case is that . . . this offence could not be said to be either a political offence or an offence connected with a political offence. Whether a contrary conclusion would be reached in different circumstances would depend on the particular circumstances and on whether those particular circumstances showed that the person charged was at the relevant time engaged, either directly or indirectly in what reasonable, civilised people would regard as political activity."[228]

In *Quinn v. Wren*[229] the Supreme Court made it clear that the political offence exception could not extend to any offence committed in pursuance of the

---

[225] Extradition Act 1965, s.50, as amended by Extradition (European Convention on the Suppression of Terrorism) Act 1987, s.9. See *Bourke v. Attorney General* [1972] I.R. 36 for the mandatory nature if this power.

[226] See *The Report of the Law Enforcement Commission to the Minister for Justice of Ireland and the Secretary of State for Northern Ireland* (Prl.3832). See also *Burns v. Attorney General* unreported, High Court, February 4, 1974; *McLoughlin v. Attorney General* unreported, High Court, December 20, 1974; *McCarry v. Attorney General* unreported, High Court, January 15, 1976; *Gilhooley v. Attorney General* (Unreported, High Court, June 4, 1976); *McManus v. Attorney General* unreported, High Court, March 23, 1977; *Swords v. Attorney General* unreported, High Court, December 22, 1977; *O'Hagan v. Attorney General* unreported, High Court, July 18, 1978; *Quigley v. Fanning* unreported, High Court, July 22, 1980.

[227] For a discussion of relevant case law, see Connolly, A., "Non-Extradition for Political Offences" (1982) 17 *Irish Jurist* 59.

[228] *McGlinchey v. Wren* [1982] I.R. 154 at 159, *per* O'Higgins C.J.. See also, *Shannon v. Fanning* [1985] I.L.R.M. 385.

[229] [1985] I.L.R.M. 410.

objectives of an organisation (in this case the INLA) whose stated aims necessarily and inevitably involved the destruction and setting aside of the Constitution of Ireland by prohibited means.[229a] Subsequently, in *Russell v. Fanning*,[229b] the Supreme by a majority of three to two extended this principle to the IRA.[230] This decision, however, has since been overturned by the Supreme Court in *Finucane v. McMahon*.[231] Delivering the leading judgment in that case Walsh J. accepted that the political offence exception could not apply to anyone charged with an offence the purpose of which was to subvert the Constitution or to usurp the functions of the organs established by the Constitution. He went on to explain that for this principle to apply it would have to be shown on the facts and circumstances of the individual case that the offence was committed for the purpose of subverting the Constitution or overthrowing the State. This could not be satisfied merely by showing that persons acting outside the State were engaged in activities which ran contrary to the Irish government's policy in relation to the unity of the country, even though the government was the proper constitutional organ for determining the methods through which the integration of the national territory was to be achieved. It follows that IRA actions outside the State would not automatically be disqualified from the political offence exception simply because they were aimed at forcing a British withdrawal from Northern Ireland or securing the reintegration of the national territory by force of arms. Also, the mere fact that an offence was committed in pursuit of the objectives of an organisation whose objectives included the subversion of the Constitution would not be sufficient to exclude the political offence exception. It would have to be shown that the actual offence was committed in circumstances which tended to subvert the Constitution.[232]

The Supreme Court decision in *Finucane v. McMahon*[233] has also gone some way to restoring the traditional definition of a political offence. Walsh J. defined political offences very bluntly as " . . . offences usually, though not necessarily, consisting of violent crime directed at securing a change in the political order".[234] The learned judge also acknowledged that the European Convention on the Suppression of Terrorism, as implemented here by the Extradition (European Convention on the Suppression of Terrorism) Act 1987, has introduced limits on the sort of violent offences which can qualify for the political offence exemption (see below). The decision in *Finucane v. McMahon* has since been applied in *Carron v. McMahon*[235] where the Supreme Court held

3–32

[229a] Some of the crimes of the INLA were considered to involve the destruction or setting aside of the Constitution. Accordingly, an offence involving raising funds for INLA could not qualify as a political offence or an offence connected with a political offence.

[229b] [1988] I.R. 505.

[230] There is also an implication in the decision of the Supreme Court in *Maguire v. Keane* [1986] I.L.R.M. 235 that the same would apply to the IRA.

[231] [1990] I.L.R.M. 505.

[232] See *Sloan v. Culligan* [1991] I.L.R.M. 641.

[233] [1990] I.L.R.M. 505.

[234] *ibid.* at 518.

[235] [1990] I.L.R.M. 802.

that the offence of possession of a firearm with intent to endanger life qualified as a political offence as it had been committed by a person for the purpose of forcing a British withdrawal from Northern Ireland so that the country could be reintegrated. In concluding that this qualified as a political offence, Finlay C.J. noted that the Convention on the Suppression of Terrorism did not apply as the warrant in this case had been issued before it came into force, and that there was no evidence that the firearm was being carried for the purpose of engaging in the sort of atrocity which had featured in *McGlinchey v. Wren*.[236]

The Extradition (European Convention on the Suppression of Terrorism) Act 1987, which gives effect to certain provisions of the European Convention on the Suppression of Terrorism, imposes restrictions on the range of offences which might otherwise have qualified for the political offence exemption in extradition arrangements with Convention countries and any countries which have adopted the European Union Convention on Extradition 1996.[237] These are: an offence within the scope of the Hague Convention for the Suppression of Unlawful Seizure of Aircraft, an offence within the scope of the Geneva Conventions,[237a] an offence within the scope of the Montreal Convention for the Suppression of Unlawful Acts against the Safety of Civil Aviation; a serious offence involving an attack against the life, physical integrity or liberty of an internationally protected person; an offence involving kidnapping, the taking of a hostage or serious false imprisonment;[238] an offence involving the use of an explosive or an automatic firearm if such use endangers persons,[239] any other serious offence involving an act of violence against the life, physical integrity or liberty of a person, or involving an act against property if the act created a collective danger for persons;[240] and any offence of attempting to commit any of the foregoing offences.[241] Also excluded in certain circumstances is any other serious offence:[242] involving an act of violence against the life, physical

---

[236] [1983] I.L.R.M. 169.

[237] Extradition (European Covention on the Suppression of Terrorism) Act 1987, s.3(2), as amended by Extradition (European Union Conventions) Act 2001, s. 12. The government may by order direct that any or all of the provisions in the Act shall apply in relation to any country which is not a Convention country and with which there is in force an extradition agreement; Extradition (European Convention on the Suppression of Terrorism) 1987, s.10.

[237a] added by Extradition (European Union Convention) Act 2001, s.27.

[238] For an example of serious false imprisonment see *Sloan v. Culligan* [1991] I.L.R.M. 641.

[239] The mere fact the automatic firearm is used only against British soldiers as part of the IRA campaign to force a British withdrawal will not affect its exclusion from the political offence exception under this provision; see *Magee v. Culligan* [1992] I.L.R.M. 186.

[240] Added by Extradition (Amendment) Act 1994, s.2(a). See Extradition (European Convention on the Suppression of Terrorism) Act 1987, s.1(1) for the definition of a serious offence.

[241] Extradition (European Convention on the Suppression of Terrorism) Act 1987, s.3(3)(a). References to an offence here include references to participation as an accomplice of a person who commits the offence. See s.3(4) and (5) for further definitions of terms used in s.3(3)(a).

[242] A serious offence is defined as an offence which, if the act constituting the offence took place in the State, would be an offence for which a person aged 21 years or over, of full capacity and not previously convicted may be punished by imprisonment for a term of five years or by a more severe penalty; Extradition (European Convention on the Suppression of Terrorism) Act 1987, s.1(1). Escaping from lawful custody was considered to be a serious offence for this purpose in *Quinlivan v. Conroy* [2000] 2 I.L.R.M. 515.

integrity or liberty of a person,[243] or involving an act against property if the act created a collective danger for persons,[244] or an attempt to commit any such act.[245] These other serious offences will be excluded if the court or the minister, as the case may be, is of the opinion that it cannot properly be regarded as a political offence (or an offence connected with a political offence) after having taken into account any particularly serious aspects of the offence, including: (1) that it created a collective danger to the life, physical integrity or liberty of persons, or (2) that it affected persons foreign to the motives behind it, or (3) that cruel or vicious means were used in the commission of the offence.[246] Also specifically excluded from the political offence exemption in the extradition arrangements with Convention countries is the whole list of offences scheduled to the Extradition (Amendment) Act 1994. The Act applies to any warrant issued after its commencement, irrespective of whether the offence in question was committed before or after the Act came into effect.[247]

In *Sloan v. Culligan*[248] the Supreme Court explained that the provisions of the 1987 Act defining those offences which were excluded from the political offence exemption would have to be construed strictly. Dealing specifically with section 3 which excludes a list of specified offences of Finlay C.J. said:

3–33

> "I am satisfied that in so far as it is a section which may impose upon an individual a liability to be delivered out of the jurisdiction for the purpose of standing trial or of serving a sentence, where, were it not for the provisions of the section such an order might not be made that it should be strictly construed."

The court went on to rule that the use of an automatic firearm "if such use endangers persons", which was one of the offences specified, would have to be interpreted as being confined to situations in which there was a present danger to persons. It could not be interpreted as extending to possession of such a weapon in circumstances where there was a future danger.

In *Ellis v. O'Dea*[249] the High Court ruled that the offences of conspiracy to cause explosions and possession of explosive substances, which were at issue in that case, were excluded from the political offence exemption, despite the fact that in the particular circumstances of the case they were linked to the IRA campaign to force a British withdrawal from Northern Ireland. The offences in question were linked to a number of indiscriminate bomb explosions in England which caused serious injuries and deaths to civilians as well as soldiers. Applying the provisions of the 1987 Act, Costello J. concluded that they could not qualify as political offences because they were serious offences which

---

243   Extradition (European Convention on the Suppression of Terrorism) Act 1987, s.4(2)(a)(i)(I).
244   *ibid.* s.4(2)(a)(i)(II).
245   *ibid.* s.4(2)(a)(ii).
246   See *Quinlivan v. Conroy* [2000] 2 I.L.R.M. 515 for an example of a situation in which cruel or vicious means were used in the commission of an offence of escaping from prison.
247   This does not infringe the constitutional prohibition on the enactment of retroactive criminal laws nor does it infringe the personal rights of the applicant under the Constitution; *Magee v. Culligan* [1992] I.L.R.M. 186.
248   [1992] I.L.R.M. 194 (SC).
249   [1991] I.L.R.M. 346 (HC).

involved acts of violence against the life and physical integrity of persons and involved an act against property which created a collective danger to persons. Interestingly he did not feel that they were automatically excluded under the heading of an explosives offence which endangered persons. The learned judge considered that this heading would not apply where the offence endangered only one person or property, as was the situation in the instant case.[250] More significant, perhaps, is the fact that Costello J. did not consider that the offences at issue in this case would have qualified as political offences even in the absence of the 1987 Act. Since they involved the use of indiscriminate violence endangering the lives of innocent civilians he considered that they could not come within the scope of a political offence as defined in *Finucane v. McMahon*.[251]

3–34   A different result might ensue where a murderous attack was carried out against a specific individual in an operation which was planned and executed in a manner which did not present a specific threat to others. In *Magee v. O'Dea*,[252] for example, the extradition of the applicant was sought for the murder of an army sergeant in Britain. The murder was claimed by the INLA as part of its campaign to force a British withdrawal from Northern Ireland. The State argued that it could not benefit from the political offence exemption as it was an act of violence against the life of a person in circumstances which created a collective danger to the life, physical integrity or liberty of persons within the meaning of the section 4 of the Extradition (European Convention on the Suppression of Terrorism) Act 1987. Flood J., however, concluded that, ". . . judged by an objective test and objective standards, the said assassination did not create a collective danger to the life, physical integrity or liberty of persons . . .".[253] Accordingly, it qualified for the political offence exemption. He based his conclusion on the following findings: (1) there was no recorded instance of a member of the public feeling endangered; (2) there was no recorded instance of a member of the public claiming to have dispersed as a result of panic induced by the shooting; (3) the operation was clearly planned and related to a specific individual who was expected to be in a particular place at a particular hour and who was to be assassinated by a shot fired at point blank range. The learned judge also found support for his conclusion in the fact that no charge had been laid against the applicant for possession of firearms with intent to endanger life.

3–35   In order to qualify as a political offence (or an offence connected with a political offence) it must be shown that the offence was committed for a political purpose against the State seeking the extradition. An offence committed in one State in pursuit of a political objective in a third State will not qualify in the event of an extradition request from the former State even though it would qualify in the event of an extradition request from the latter

---

[250] Note, however, the intimation by McCarthy J. in the Supreme Court to the effect that (at least with respect to persons) the plural would include the singular; [1991] I.L.R.M. 346 at 375–376.
[251] See also the ruling of Kelly J. in *Quinlivan v. Conroy* [2000] 2 I.L.R.M. 515.
[252] [1994] 1 I.L.R.M. 540.
[253] *ibid.* at 548.

State. The issue arose here in *Maguire v. Attorney General*[254] which concerned an extradition request from the USA. The individual whose extradition was sought was wanted in connection with offences associated with an attempt to buy arms in the USA for use in the campaign to force a British withdrawal from Northern Ireland. He claimed that his offence was covered by the political offence exception. Lynch J. rejected this claim in the High Court essentially on the ground that in order to qualify as a political offence in the context of extradition the offence must be committed in order to pursue a political objective against the State seeking his extradition. He found support for his position in the majority decision of the House of Lords in *Cheng v. Governor of Pentonville Prison*[255] which dealt with similar provisions in section 3(1) of the Extradition Act 1870. Lynch J. quoted the following passage from the speech of Lord Diplock as a correct statement of the underlying justification for the political offence exception:

> "The purpose of the restriction, as it seems to me, was twofold. First, to avoid involving the United Kingdom in the internal political conflicts of foreign states. Today's Garibaldi may well form tomorrow's government. And secondly the humanitarian purpose of preventing the offender being surrendered to a jurisdiction in which there was a risk that his trial or punishment might be unfairly influenced by political considerations. As indicated by the inclusion of the second part of the restriction, it was suspicion of the motives of requisitioning states in seeking the surrender of fugitive criminals who were political opponents of the government of that state which underlay both the requirements of s.3(1) of the Act. Such suspicion was understandable in 1870 in the light of the recent history of the struggle for the unification of Italy. But there could be no similar grounds for suspicion of the motives of a requisitioning state in seeking the surrender of a fugitive criminal who though a political opponent of the government of some other state was not a political opponent of the state demanding his surrender. Nor would there appear to be any greater risk that his trial or punishment for the offence in such a state might be unfairly influenced by political considerations than if he had committed the same offence in the United Kingdom and been tried and punished for it here. So if a purposive construction of the Act is adopted this too leads to the conclusion that an offence of a political character for the purposes of the restriction was intended to be confined to offences in which the purpose sought to be achieved by the offender was directed against the government of the state seeking his surrender."[256]

Despite the fact that a strictly literal interpretation of the relevant statutory provision does not confine the political offence exception to offences aimed at the State seeking the extradition, coupled with the fact that the decision in *Cheng* was by the slimmest of majorities, there was no appeal against Lynch J's decision.

---

[254] [1994] 2 I.L.R.M. 344.
[255] [1973] A.C. 931.
[256] [1973] A.C. 931 at 946.

The Revenue Offence Exception

3–36   Extradition cannot be granted for revenue offences, unless the relevant extradition provisions provide otherwise.[256a] The 1965 Act defines a revenue offence in relation to any country or place outside the State as:

> "an offence in connection with taxes, duties, customs or exchange control but does not include an offence involving the use or threat of force or perjury or the forging of a document issued under statutory authority or an offence alleged to have been committed by an officer of the revenue of that country or place in his capacity as such officer or an offence within the scope of Article 3 of the United Nations Convention Against Illicit Traffic in Narcotic Drugs and Psychotropic Substances 1988."[257]

The issue of what constitutes a revenue offence was dealt with by both the High Court and the Supreme Court in *Byrne v. Conroy*.[258] In that case the extradition of the applicant was sought to answer a charge of conspiring to defraud the United Kingdom's Intervention Board of monetary compensatory amounts (MCAs) applicable to grain exports. These MCAs were levies or refunds applied by the European Community to cross border trade in certain agricultural products in order to facilitate the free movement of goods throughout the Community. Although they were collected or levied by the Intervention Board in the United Kingdom in respect of imports and exports to and from the United Kingdom they were in effect charges upon or payments from the European Community. In determining whether or not they constituted a revenue offence within the meaning of the Extradition legislation, Kelly J. in the High Court declared that it was necessary to look at their true nature rather than whether they were defined as a tax. The true nature of a tax, according to Hamilton C.J. in the Supreme Court is a revenue-raising charge which is imposed in any country or place outside the State by the sovereign authority in such country or place and which is payable by the residents of such country or place and by residents of no other country or place. In applying this to the MCAs, Hamilton C.J. concluded that they could not qualify as taxes. They were imposed not for the purpose of raising revenue but to facilitate the free movement of goods. Also they are:

> " . . . payable, not in any one country or place and are not payable by virtue of the laws of any one country or place, but are payable throughout the Community by reason of the laws of the Community . . .
>
> They apply with equal force and validity within this State and the benefits therefrom do not enure for the benefit of the collecting member state but for the benefit of the Community as a whole."[259]

[256a] Extradition Act 1965, s.13, as amended by Extradition (European Union Conventions) Act 2001, s.13(b).

[257] Extradition Act 1965, s.3, as amended by Extradition (Amendment) Act 1994, s.3(a) and Extradition (European Union Conventions) Act 2001, s.13(a).

[258] [1997] 2 I.L.R.M. 99 (HC), [1998] 2 I.L.R.M. 113 (SC).

[259] [1998] 2 I.L.R.M. 113 at 128.

The Dual Criminality Requirement

The dual criminality test imposes another significant restriction on the range   **3–37**
of extraditable offences. To be extraditable under the 1965 Act the offence in
question must satisfy the dual criminality test. In effect this means that the
suspect is wanted in the requesting state for conduct which would also
constitute a criminal offence in this jurisdiction.[261] It will have to be shown
by expert evidence on the law of the requesting state that the specified offence
is an offence punishable in the requesting state.[262] Also it will have to be the
case that the alleged conduct of the fugitive in the requesting case would, if
done in this State, amount to an offence under Irish law. It will not be enough
simply to recite the offence as defined by the law of the requesting state. In
State (Furlong) v. Kelly,[263] for example, it was held that an English warrant
which stated that the fugitive did "steal" a machine contrary to the (English)
Theft Act 1968 would not necessarily correspond with larceny in Ireland. The
Supreme Court was not satisfied that, despite the use of the word "steal" there
was sufficient information in the warrant to conclude that the offence for which
the fugitive was being sought was the equivalent of larceny under Irish law.[264]
The correct approach is succinctly described as follows by Walsh J. in *Wyatt v.
McLoughlin*:

> "It is necessary that either the warrant or some other document accompanying it
> should set out sufficient information as to these acts to enable the courts of the
> State to identify the corresponding offence, if any, in our law. It cannot be
> sufficient simply to use the name by which the crime is known, or alleged to be
> known, in the requesting country even though the same name may be used in this
> country as the name of a crime, because the acts complained of, although having
> identical names, may constitute quite different criminal offences in different
> countries or, indeed, no offence at all in one of them. For example, what
> constitutes embezzlement in one country may be larceny in another, and acts
> which would constitute the offence of abortion or unlawful homosexual behav-
> iour in one country may not constitute any offence in the other."[265]

In *O'Shea v. Conroy*,[265a] however, Flood J. concluded that a warrant which   **3–38**
charged that the applicant stole a cheque book belonging to another was sufficient to correspond with the offence of simple larceny in Irish law. Similarly

---

[261] See, *e.g.*, *Wilson v. Sheehan* [1979] I.R. 423; *State (Furlong) v. Kelly* [1971] I.R. 132; *Wyatt v.
    McLoughlin* [1974] I.R. 378; *Trimbole v. Governor of Mountjoy Prison* [1985] I.L.R.M. 449;
    Ellis v. O'Dea [1991] I.L.R.M. 346; *Aamand v. Smithwick* [1995] 1 I.L.R.M. 61.
[262] *Trimbole v. Governor of Mountjoy Prison* [1985] I.L.R.M. 449.
[263] [1971] I.R. 132.
[264] See also *Trimbole v. Governor of Mountjoy Prison* [1985] I.L.R.M. 449 where it as held that
    conspiracy "to commit offences against a law of the Commonwealth namely offences of forgery
    contrary to s.67 of the Crimes Act 1914" was insufficient to satisfy the dual criminality
    requirement.
[265] *Wyatt v. McLoughlin* [1974] I.R. 378 at 398. See also *Stanton v. Governor of Arbour Hill*.
    unreported, High Court, December 7, 1999 where it was held that even through the warrant used
    the word rape there was insufficient particulars to establish correspondence with rape under s.2 of
    the Criminal Law (Rape) Act 1981. Nevertheless, there was sufficient evidence to establish
    correspondence which other sexual offences known to Irish law.
[265a] [1995] 2 I.L.R.M. 527.

he concluded that a warrant which charged the applicant with having robbed another person of a van corresponded with the offence of robbery with violence in Ireland. While acknowledging that it was not sufficient that the warrant referred to an offence which had the same name as an offence in this State, Flood J. explained that the words used to described the factual contents of the offence in the warrant must be given their ordinary meaning, unless the context suggested otherwise:

> "When it comes to the words in the warrant by which the factual content of the specified offence is identified, the correct rule is that those words should prima facie be given their ordinary or popular meaning unless they are used in a context which suggests that they have a special significance. The reason for that rule is that, when statutes or other public or formal documents directed to the public at large, or to any member of the public at large, are being interpreted, it is to be assumed, in the absence of counter indication, that the words used in such document are being used in their popular rather than any specialised sense.
>
> So also with the particulars of an offence in a formal written charge. The primary purpose of the particulars is to enable the member of the public who is being charged to identify the conduct that is being alleged against him as a criminal offence."[266]

An extradition application will not fail simply because the individual is sought for conspiracy. However, the facts disclosed in the application must satisfy conspiracy in Irish law. In *Attorney General v. Oldridge*,[267] for example, an extradition request for conspiracy to defraud from the USA was refused. The facts disclosed in the application showed that the individual concerned had not become involved with the conspirators until after all of the essential agreements and acts constituting the conspiracy had been executed. The High Court ruled that an indictment for conspiracy could not lie against the individual in such circumstances in Irish law. In *Myles v. Sreenan*,[267a] however, the High Court found that there was sufficient particulars about the offence in an extradition warrant for conspiracy to defraud in the United Kingdom to satisfy the corresponding offence of conspiracy to defraud in Irish law.

3–39 The European Convention on Terrorism, as implemented by the Extradition Act 1965 (Part II)(No.23) 1989, imposes certain restrictions on extradition for offences which are either committed on the territory of the requested State or outside the territory of the requesting State. Article 7.1 stipulates that extra-

---

[266] [1995] 2 I.L.R.M. 527 at 531, quoting Henchy J. in *Wilson v. Sheehan* [1979] I.R. 423 at 429, with respect to the words "rob", "force" and "personal violence". See also, *Trimbole v. Governor of Mountjoy Prison* [1985] I.L.R.M. 449 with respect to the words "murder" and "conspiracy to murder". In the same case it was held that there was insufficient correspondence between the Irish offence of aiding, abetting, counselling or procuring the importation of heroin and the equivalent Australian offence because of the inclusion in the latter of the additional words "or in any way knowingly concerned in the importation". The court considered that under the ordinary use of language in Ireland the words "knowingly concerned" would not be understood to be included in the meaning of aiding, abetting, counselling or procuring.
[267] [2000] 2 I.L.R.M. 233.
[267a] [1994] 4 I.R. 294.

dition may be refused if the offence has been committed either in whole or in part in a place which is regarded by the law of the requested State as its territory or in a place treated as its territory. If, however, the offence has been committed outside the territory of the requesting State, extradition may only be refused if the law of the requested party does not allow prosecution for the same category of offence when committed outside of its territory or does not allow extradition for the offence concerned. The interpretation of Article 7.2 was in issue in *Aamand v. Smithwick*[268] which concerned a request from the Danish government for the extradition of the applicant to face charges of drug smuggling on the high seas. The Supreme Court ruled that Article 7.2 was sufficient to prohibit the extradition of the applicant. Since the offence was committed outside Denmark and a person cannot be prosecuted in Ireland for smuggling drugs outside Ireland, it follows that Article 7.2 prohibits his extradition. Even though the actual wording of Article 7.2 suggests that the extraditing State has a discretion in the matter the Supreme Court ruled that it must be construed as being mandatory in effect.

The Speciality Requirement

Closely related to the dual criminality test is speciality.[269] This refers to an understanding that a suspect who has been extradited will be pursued in the requesting country only for the offence or offences for which he was extradited.[270] In the words of Walsh J. in *Ellis v. O'Dea*,[271] "All warrants sent are representations that the purpose is to bring the person charged before the court of the requesting party on the charge specified." If the requesting country subsequently wishes to institute proceedings against him for other offences he must first be given an opportunity to leave. It would appear that an Irish court will not permit evidence to be given of an undertaking from the proper authority in another State to the effect that the individual requested will not be proceeded against for offences other than those for which the individual is surrendered. If it appears to the Irish court that the circumstances are such that under the law of the requesting State the individual would be exposed to the risk of being prosecuted for an offence or offences other than that for which his surrender is ordered, then the Irish court must refuse the extradition request.[272]

3–40

It is worth noting that the High Court's duty to protect and uphold the constitutional rights of the individual can result in it quashing an extradition order where it would otherwise result in a denial of the individual's constitutional rights. This aspect is developed further below in the context of the

---

[268] [1995] 1 I.L.R.M. 61.
[269] Extradition Act 1965, ss.20 and 39. Note the relaxation of the rule in respect of countries designated for the purposes of the European Union Extradition Conventions (see later).
[270] *State (Hully) v. Hynes* 100 I.L.T.R. 145; *State (Magee) v. O'Rourke* [1971] I.R. 205; *Shannon v. Fanning* [1985] I.L.R.M. 385.
[271] [1990] I.L.R.M. 87 at 93.
[272] See O'Dalaigh C.J., obiter, in the Supreme Court in *Bourke v. Attorney General* [1972] I.R. 36 quoting with approval from the House of Lords in *R v. Governor of Brixton Prison, ex. p. Armah* [1968] A.C. 192.

extradition arrangements with the United Kingdom as the issue has arisen largely in that context. However, the principles are applicable to extradition generally.

In deciding whether the individual's constitutional rights would be infringed if extradited, or if there were circumstances in which it would be unjust, oppressive or invidious to extradite him, the court may be presented with certain undertakings as to his treatment by the requesting authorities. In *Sloan v. Culligan*,[273] for example, the applicant's extradition was sought to serve a sentence of imprisonment imposed on him by a court in Northern Ireland. The applicant had escaped from custody before the sentence could be put into effect. He was subsequently arrested in this jurisdiction, tried and convicted under the Criminal Law (Jurisdiction) Act 1976, and sentenced to a term of imprisonment. When that term of imprisonment was nearing completion his extradition was sought by the authorities in Northern Ireland to serve the sentence which had originally been imposed in Northern Ireland. In the High Court challenge to his extradition Lynch J. had to consider, *inter alia*, whether it would be unjust, oppressive or invidious to extradite the applicant if he had to serve the full sentence imposed by the court in Northern Ireland with no deduction for the time served in Ireland. The learned judge ruled that this matter was settled by undertakings from the Northern authorities Attorney General that he would only have to serve the balance of the sentence.

3–41 On appeal to the Supreme Court the applicant's extradition was quashed on other grounds. Accordingly, there was no considered analysis of the validity of undertakings given by the State when seeking extradition in an individual case. Nevertheless, there were a few observations in the Supreme Court which would call into question the extent to which an Irish court can rely on such undertakings where they might affect the rights of the individual. Finlay C.J., for example, expressly distanced himself from the High Court's acceptance of the undertakings:

> "No submissions were made to this Court as to the validity of the undertaking referred to in this part of the judgment of Lynch J. It is not clear from the papers before us by whom or upon whose authority any such undertaking was given, and no written document concerning it appears to exist. Counsel informed us that upon recollection it was simply a statement made by counsel on behalf of the respondents in these applications.
>
> I, therefore, express no view as to whether in proceedings under the Extradition Act 1965 or in judicial proceedings concerning an order for delivery of a person out of the State, pursuant to the provisions of that Act, an undertaking of this description can validly be relied upon by the courts so as adversely to affect the rights of any person sought to be delivered out of the State."[274]

McCarthy J. drew attention to *Bourke v. Attorney General*[275] where the following passage from the speech of Lord Reid in *R v. Governor of Brixton*

---

[273] [1992] I.L.R.M. 194.
[274] [1992] I.L.R.M. 194 at 201–202.
[275] [1972] I.R. 36.

Prison, ex p. Armah was quoted with approval by O'Dalaigh C.J. in the Supreme Court:

> "But I would add that in general it appears to me to be very undesirable that a foreign government should be encouraged to offer not to apply the ordinary law of its country to one of its own subjects [sic] if he is returned to that country. There may not be the same objection to the foreign government stating that it does not intend to take certain executive action with regard to the accused person and it might be proper to accept an undertaking on the lines of s.3(2) of the Extradition Act 1870. But any undertaking or statement of intention is liable to create misunderstanding and perhaps acute difficulties in the event of change of circumstances."[276]

McCarthy J. noted that the passage referred to a citizen of the State seeking extradition and opined that it had even greater force in the case of a citizen of the State from which extradition was requested.

Pardon or Amnesty

Extradition cannot be granted where the person being sought has been granted a pardon under Article 13.6 of the Constitution in respect of the offence in question.[277] Similarly, it cannot be granted where the person sought has in accordance with the law of the requesting country become immune from prosecution for the offence concerned by virtue of any amnesty or pardon.[278] The same applies where the person being sought has become immune from prosecution or punishment in respect of the offence concerned by virtue of any Act of the Oireachtas.

3-42

3. Extradition to States other than the United Kingdom and E.U. Convention Countries[279]

The Request

The procedure governing extradition to states with whom Ireland has an extradition treaty is laid down primarily in Part II of the Extradition Act 1965.[280] It differs in some respects from that applicable to the United Kingdom. The procedure commences with the Minister for Justice, Equality and Law Reform receiving a request for the suspect to be delivered to the

3-43

---

[276] [1968] A.C. 192 at 235–236.

[277] Extradition Act 1965, s.18A(1), as inserted by Extradition (European Union Conventions) Act 2001, s.14.

[278] *ibid.* s.18A(2).

[279] While the provisions outlined in this section apply generally to countries other than the United Kingdom, further simplifications have been introduced in respect of extradition to and from E.U. Member States which have been designated Convention countries for the purposes of the Extradition (European Union Conventions) Act 2001 by the Minister for Foreign Affairs. These are outlined separately later.

[280] The government may by order apply Part II to any country with which the State enters into extradition arrangements pursuant to an international agreement or convention, or where the government is satisfied that reciprocal facilities will be afforded by that country. See Extradition Act 1965, s.8, as amended by Extradition (European Union Conventions) Act 2001, s.23.

requesting state.[281] This request must be in writing and be made either by an accredited diplomat of that state or by such means as the extradition agreement in question prescribes.[282] It must be supported by:

> "(a) the original or an authenticated copy of the conviction and sentence or deten-
> tion order immediately enforceable or, as the case may be, of the warrant of
> arrest or other order having the same effect and issued in accordance with the
> procedure laid down in the law of the requesting country;
> (b) a statement of each offence for which extradition is requested specifying,
> as accurately as possible, the time and place of commission, its legal
> description and a reference to the relevant provisions of the law of the
> requesting country;[283]
> (c) a copy of the relevant enactments of the requesting country or, where this
> is not possible, a statement of the relevant law;
> (d) as accurate a description as possible of the person claimed, together with
> any other information which will help to establish his identity and
> nationality, and
> (e) any other document required under the relevant extradition provisions."[284]

A document supporting a request for extradition shall be received in evidence without further proof if it purports to be signed by a judge, magistrate or officer of the requesting country and to be certified by being sealed with the official seal of a minister of state of that country or other appropriate authority. Judicial notice shall be taken of such official seal.[285]

Warrant of Arrest

3–44   Where the Minister is of the opinion of that the documents submitted satisfy these requirements and that the extradition of the person concerned is not

---

[281]   See Extradition Act 1965, s.24 for the handling of concurrent requests from different countries.

[282]   Extradition Act 1965, s.23. Where the request is from a country designated for the purposes of the European Union Extradition Convention 1996 the request and associated documentation may be received by the Central Authority in the State by fax from the Central Authority in the requesting State. In order to guarantee the authenticity of the documents, the latter must state in its request that it certifies that the documents transmitted in support of the request correspond to the originals. To ensure confidentiality and authenticity use will be made of cryptographic devices; s.23A, as inserted by Extradition (European Union Conventions) Act 2001, s.18.

[283]   It would appear that this should contain a statement of the actual conduct of the fugitive complained of in the requesting State and not just a recitation of the offence as defined by the law of the requesting State; *Trimbole v. Governor of Mountjoy Prison* [1985] I.L.R.M. 449.

[284]   Extradition Act 1965, s.25. If the Minister is of the opinion that the information communicated to him is insufficient, he may request the requesting country to furnish such further information as he thinks proper and may fix a time limit for the receipt thereof; s.26(3). For the purposes of an extradition from a country designated for the purposes of the European Union Extradition Convention 1996 a document shall be deemed to be an authenticated copy if it has been certified as a true copy by the judicial authority that issued the original or by an officer of the Central Authority authorised to do so; s.25(2) as inserted by Extradition (European Union Conventions) Act 2001, s.17(a).

[285]   Extradition Act 1965, s.37(2), as amended by Extradition Act (European Union Conventions) Act, 2001, s. 17(b). Where the request is from a country designated a Convention country for the purposes of the European Union Extradition Convention 1996, a supporting document shall be accepted without the need for further proof where it purports to be certified by the judicial authority in the country that issued the original or by an officer of the Central Authority duly authorised to do so to be a true copy of a conviction and sentence or of a warrant of arrest. Where a seal of the relevant authority has been affixed to the document, judicial notice shall be taken of that seal; s.37(2) and (3), as inserted by *ibid.* s.17(b).

otherwise prohibited,[286] he must signify to a judge of the High Court that an extradition warrant has been made.[287] The Minister does not have to go further and satisfy himself that the offence or offences in question were extraditable offences within the meaning of the Act. Indeed, any such requirement would probably involve him in an administration of justice.[288] Nor does the Minister have to specify the equivalent offence under Irish law corresponding to that for which his extradition is sought. However, the Minister may refuse extradition if he is of the opinion that the case is one in which extradition is prohibited.[289] There is no requirement for him to transmit all of the documentation in support of the extradition request to the High Court judge, merely a communication that he has received the request. The judge must then issue a warrant for the arrest of the suspect.[290] Any member of the Garda Síochána may execute the warrant and bring the suspect on arrest before a judge of the High Court.[291] The judge has the same powers of remand and adjournment in such cases as he enjoys with respect to a suspect who is before him charged with an indictable offence.

A High Court judge also has a power to issue a provisional warrant for the arrest of a person for the purposes of extradition, without first having received a communication from the Minister. He may exercise this power where he thinks proper on the sworn information of a member of the Garda Síochána not below the rank of inspector that a request for the provisional arrest of that person has been made, on the ground of urgency, on behalf of a country to which Part II of the 1965 Act applies.[292] The judge must also be satisfied that the request complies with the relevant statutory requirements. The request for the provisional arrest must: state that one of the documents listed above exists in respect of the person concerned and that it is intended to send a request for his extradition; specify the nature of the offence and the time at which and the place where the offence is alleged to have been committed; and give a description of the person whose arrest is sought.[293] The request may be transmitted by post or telegraph or by any other means affording evidence in writing.[294] Where a judge issues a warrant for a provisional arrest under these provisions he must immediately inform the Minister. If he thinks fit the Minister may order the warrant to be cancelled and, where relevant, the person to be released.[295] A warrant issued under these provisions (and not cancelled by the Minister) may be executed by any member of the Garda Síochána in any part of the State.[296]

---

[286] This does not amount to an administration of justice on the Minister's behalf; *Trimbole v. Governor of Mountjoy Prison* [1985] I.L.R.M. 449.

[287] Extradition Act 1965, s.26(1) originally extradition proceedings were dealt with in the first instance by the District Court. Now its role has been taken over by the High Court; see Extradition (European Union Conventions) Act 2001, s.20(1).

[288] *Trimbole v. Governor of Mountjoy Prison* [1985] I.L.R.M. 449.

[289] Extradition Act 1965, s.26(4).

[290] *ibid.* s.26(1).

[291] *ibid.* s.26(2).

[292] *ibid.* s.27(1).

[293] *ibid.* s.27(2).

[294] *ibid.* s.27(3).

[295] *ibid.* s.27(5).

[296] *ibid.* s.27(4).

Executing the Warrant

3–45   A member of the Garda Síochána executing an extradition arrest warrant or provisional arrest warrant may seize and retain any property which appears to him to be reasonably required as evidence for the purpose of proving the offence alleged.[297] He may also seize and retain any property which appears to him to have been acquired as a result of the alleged offence and which is found at the time of the arrest in the possession of the person arrested or is discovered subsequently.[298] Where the Minister makes an extradition order in respect of the person concerned the property shall be handed over to any person who appears to the Minister to be duly authorised by the requesting country to receive it.[299] The property shall be handed over pursuant to such an order even if the extradition cannot be carried out by reason of the death or escape of the person in question. These provisions, however, shall not prejudice or derogate from any rights which may lawfully have been acquired by the State or any person in the State in any such property.[300] Where such rights exist the property shall not be handed over except upon condition that the requesting country shall return it as soon as may be after the trial of the person surrendered and without charge to the State or persons having such rights.

A person arrested under a provisional warrant must (unless the warrant is cancelled) be brought as soon as possible before a judge of the High Court. The judge shall then remand the person in custody or on bail pending the receipt of a certificate from the Minister stating that the extradition request has been made or (where the person is remanded in custody) pending the release by the Minister on the grounds that the extradition is prohibited.[300a] For these purposes the judge will have the same powers of remand as if the person were brought before him or her charged with an indictable offence. If no order is received within 18 days of the arrest the person must be released without prejudice to his subsequent re-arrest and extradition if a request for his extradition is received afterwards.[301]

Committal to Prison

3–46   Where a person has been brought before a High Court pursuant to a full extradition arrest warrant or a provisional warrant, the court must make an order committing him to prison, or a remand institution as the case may be, to await the order of the Minister for his extradition.[302] The court can only make this

---

[297]   *ibid.* s.36(1)(a).

[298]   *ibid.* s.36(1)(b).

[299]   Extradition Act 1965, s.36(2). If there are any criminal proceedings to which the property relates pending in the State, the property shall be retained in the State in accordance with law until the conclusion of those proceedings or may, if the Minister so directs, be handed over on condition that the requesting country shall return it; s.36(3).

[300]   Extradition Act 1965, s.36(4).

[300a] Extradition Act 1965, s.27(6), as amended by Extradition (European Union Conventions) Act 2001, s.20(d).

[301]   Extradition Act 1965, s.27(7) & (8).

[302]   Extradition Act 1965, s.29(1). The Minister may by order cause a person committed under this provision to be removed to a hospital or any other place if the Minister thinks it necessary so to

order where it is satisfied that: the extradition has been duly requested, Part II of the Act applies to the requesting country, extradition of the person is not prohibited by Part II or by the relevant extradition provisions and the documents required to support a request for extradition have been produced. If the court is of the opinion that the information communicated to it pursuant to the statutory requirements is insufficient to enable a decision to be made, it may adjourn the hearing for such period as it thinks proper to enable further information to be produced.[303] Pending consideration of the case the court shall have the same powers of adjournment and remand as if the person in question were brought before it charged with an indictable offence.

A person committed to prison to await an order from the Minister for his extradition cannot be surrendered, except with his consent given before a judge of the High Court, to the requesting country until the expiration of fifteen days from the date of his committal, or until the conclusion of any habeas corpus proceedings brought by him or on his behalf.[304] The court must inform the person of these matters where it makes an order of committal.[305] It must also inform him of the provisions of Article 40.4.2° of the Constitution which relates to the making of a complaint to the High Court alleging unlawful detention. The court must cause a certificate of committal to be sent immediately to the Minister.[306] If the court does not commit the person under these provisions it must order his discharge.[307] Either way no appeal lies to the Supreme Court against any such order of the High Court except on a point of law.[308]

Surrender

Where the statutory requirements described above have been satisfied the Minister may by order direct the person concerned to be surrendered to such other person as in his opinion is duly authorised by the requesting country to receive him.[309] The person concerned shall be surrendered pursuant to such an order. The person receiving the surrendered person may hold him in custody and convey him out of the State.[310] If the person is not surrendered and conveyed out of the State within one month after committal, or within one month after the conclusion of *habeas corpus* proceedings, the High Court may on application order his discharge.[311] Before such an order can be made there must be proof that reasonable notice of the intention to make the application was given to the Minister. If, however, the person's removal has been delayed due to his state of health or other circumstances beyond the control of the State or

3–47

---

do in the interests of his health and that person shall, while detained in that hospital or place, be in lawful custody; s.30.

[303] Extradition Act 1965, s.29(2).
[304] *ibid.* s.31.
[305] *ibid.* s.29(3)(a).
[306] *ibid.* s.29(3)(b).
[307] *ibid.* s.29(4).
[308] *ibid.* s.29(5).
[309] *ibid.* s.33(1).
[310] *ibid.* s.33(2). If the person escapes he shall be liable to be retaken in the same manner as any person who escapes from lawful custody.
[311] Extradition Act 1965, s.34(1).

requesting country, and it is likely that within a reasonable time these circumstances will not prevent his removal, the court may fix a period within which he may be surrendered.[312] He shall be released if not conveyed out of the State within that period.

There are circumstances in which the Minister either may or must refuse to make an order of surrender or postpone any such surrender order. He may postpone the surrender of a person in order that he may be proceeded against in the State or (if he has already been convicted) in order that he may serve any sentence imposed upon him in the State for an offence other than that for which his extradition is requested.[313] The Minister cannot make an order if he is of the opinion that the extradition would involve transit through any territory where there is reason to believe that the person's life or freedom may be threatened by reason of his or her race, religion, nationality or political opinion.[314] Equally, where a person is on remand or awaiting his surrender and the Minister is of the opinion that extradition is prohibited under any provision of Part II of the 1965 Act or of the relevant extradition provisions, the Minister may at any time refuse extradition and order the release of the person concerned where he is in custody.[315]

Transit through the State

There is provision for the Minister for Justice, Equality and Law Reform to grant a request for the transit of a person through the State *en route* to another State pursuant to an extradition arrangement.[315a] The Minister may arrange for the supervision of such transit by the Garda Síochána, and the person concerned shall be deemed to be in the custody of any member of the Garda Síochána accompanying him pursuant to the arrangement.[315b]

4. Extradition to the United Kingdom[315c]

Introduction

3–48   The 1965 Act makes separate provision for extradition to the United Kingdom and the Channel Islands.[316] Prior to 1965 the arrangements were based on a backing of warrants system, reflecting the fact that at one time Ireland was part of the United Kingdom. In effect a warrant for the arrest of

---

[312] *ibid.* s.34(2).
[313] *ibid.* s.32.
[314] *ibid.* s.33(3).
[315] *ibid.* s.35(1).
[315a] *ibid.* s.40(1), as amended by Extradition (European Union Conventions) Act 2001, s.19(a). There is further special provision for requests from countries designated as Convention countries for the purposes of the European Union Extradition Convention 1996; see s.40(1A), as inserted by s.19(b) and s.40(2A), as inserted by s.19(c).
[315b] *ibid.* s.40(2).
[315c] The provisions discussed under this section apply solely to the United Kingdom. However, they will be further simplified by the provisions of the Extradition (European Union Conventions) Act 2001 as and when the Minister for Foreign Affairs designates the U.K. a "Convention Country" for the purposes of the Act. These further provisions are outlined later in a separate section.
[316] Extradition Act 1965, Pt III.

the suspect would be issued in a part of the United Kingdom and then transmitted to the Garda Síochána for endorsement and execution as if it had been issued in this jurisdiction. Once the suspect had been arrested under the warrant he was simply handed over into the custody of the requesting police force in the United Kingdom without any formality.[317]

These arrangements were deemed unsatisfactory in the light of the events surrounding the case of *State (Quinn) v. Ryan*[318] in 1965. Gardaí arrested a suspect in Dublin on the basis of a warrant which had been issued by the London Metropolitan Police. The High Court, however, ordered the suspect's release when it transpired that the warrant was defective. The Gardaí concealed from the court the fact that they had secured a fresh warrant from the London Metropolitan Police. When the suspect emerged from the court they arrested him under the fresh warrant and bundled him into a car which drove him to the border where he was handed over into the custody of the Royal Ulster Constabulary (RUC) who, in turn, sent him to London. In consequence the Supreme Court ruled that the informal, backing of warrants extradition procedure was unconstitutional as it denied the suspect access to the courts to protect his constitutional rights. Accordingly the Extradition Act 1965 was enacted incorporating, *inter alia*, a judicial procedure into the extradition arrangements with the United Kingdom.

Extraditable offences

The extradition arrangements with the United Kingdom are provided for in Part III of the 1965 Act.[319] The machinery is triggered by the issue of a warrant by a judicial authority in the United Kingdom for the arrest of the suspect accused or convicted of an offence which, under the relevant U.K. law, is an indictable offence or an offence punishable on summary conviction by imprisonment for a maximum period of at least six months. It follows that to be extraditable the offence must be an indictable offence or punishable on summary conviction by at least six months under the relevant U.K. law.[319a] It must also satisfy the dual criminality test. For the purposes of extradition to the United Kingdom this test has been relaxed by an amendment effected by the Extradition (European Union Conventions) Act 2001. It stipulates that an offence under the law of that part of the United Kingdom to which the person is to be extradited corresponds to an offence under Irish law where the act constituting the offence in U.K. law would, if done in Ireland, constitute an offence under Irish law punishable on indictment or punishable on summary conviction by imprisonment for a maximum term of not less than six months

---

[317] In *Shannon v. Attorney General* [1985] I.L.R.M. 449 at 457 Finlay J. took judicial notice of the existence of reciprocal arrangements for the extradition of fugitives from the U.K. and the benefits that that affords to the administration of justice in this State.

[318] [1965] I.R. 70.

[319] The procedure must be followed scrupulously. See McCarthy J. in *McMahon v. Leahy* [1984] I.R. 525.

[319a] Extradition Act 1965, s.43(1)(a). An indictable offence for this purpose does not include an offence which is triable on indictment only at the instance or with the consent of the accused; s.42.

or by a more severe penalty.[319b] It follows that an offence can qualify even if it does not fall into the same category or description in this State to its corresponding offence in the U.K. The amendment also stipulates that to constitute an extraditable offence it will be sufficient for the offence to be criminal in Ireland at the date of the making of the extradition request and a crime in the U.K. at both the date of commission and the request.[319c] However, if any part of the act constituting the offence for which extradition is requested was committed in the State, then it has to be an offence under Irish law on the day on which it was committed.

Excluded from the extradition arrangements with the U.K. are offences of a political, military or revenue nature as defined above (paras. 2–31 *et seq*). Also excluded is any offence where there are substantial reasons for believing that the person named or described in the warrant will, if removed from the State, be prosecuted or detained for a political offence under military law which is not an offence under ordinary criminal law.

Executing the Warrant

3–49 The warrant is sent in the first instance to the Commissioner of the Garda Síochána, or a Deputy or Assistant Commissioner. If it appears to the Commissioner that the person named or described in the warrant may be found in this State he may endorse it for execution provided that it satisfies certain other requirements of Part III.[320] These stipulate that the Commissioner may accept that a document which purports to be an extradition warrant issued by a judicial authority in a place in the United Kingdom is in fact such a document where it is accompanied by an affidavit verifying the signature on the warrant and appearing to be sworn before a person duly authorised to take affidavits by the law of that place.[321] It must also be accompanied by a certificate appearing to be given by the authority or the clerk or other officer of the authority by which the warrant was issued that the offence to which it relates is, by the law of that place, an indictable offence or a summary offence punishable by a maximum period of imprisonment of at least six months.

These requirements are interpreted strictly.[322] In *McMahon v. Leahy*,[323] for example, McCarthy J. considered that a warrant was invalid because the affidavit accompanying it did not identify the signature of the Justice of the Peace who actually signed it (the name of the Justice of the Peace before whom the affidavit had been sworn was substituted in error for the name of the Justice of the Peace who had signed the warrant).

[319b] *ibid*. s.42(2), as inserted by Extradition (European Union Conventions) Act 2001, s.26.

[319c] *ibid*. s.42(3).

[320] The Commissioner's action in endorsing the warrant does not amount to an administration of justice; *Shannon v. Attorney General* [1985] I.L.R.M. 449.

[321] Extradition Act 1965, s.54(1). The affidavit is normally sworn by a constable of the police force in question.

[322] In *Ellis v. O'Dea* [1990] I.L.R.M. 87 Walsh J. intimated that he would be prepared to send back an extradition warrant on the grounds that the requesting state had failed to use the correct name of the State.

[323] [1985] I.L.R.M. 422.

When the document satisfies the statutory requirements the Commissioner may accept it as evidence that the offence for which the warrant is issued is an offence under the law of that place and that the affidavit has been duly sworn before a person authorised to take affidavits. Once endorsed by the Commissioner the warrant can be executed in the State by any member of the Garda Síochána.

Unless there is good reason to the contrary a document which appears to be a **3–50** warrant as described above may, if the signature on the warrant is verified by the accompanying affidavit, be admitted in evidence in any proceedings as a warrant duly signed and issued by a competent judicial authority without further evidence.[324] This avoids having to call the judicial authority in person in order to prove his competence and signature. Also, in any proceedings a warrant purporting to be endorsed by the Commissioner shall, unless the contrary is proved, be deemed to have been duly endorsed without proof of the signature of the person purporting to have endorsed it, or that he is such Commissioner or that, before endorsing it there was produced to him the necessary affidavit.[325] This relieves the Commissioner of the obligation to appear before the court in any such proceedings to verify his signature and the circumstances in which he signed. Indeed, unless there is good reason to the contrary the court should not require further evidence as to the statutory proofs than the legislation specifically requires.[326]

Remand

On arrest the suspect must be taken before the High Court which will inquire whether he is legally represented and whether the warrant is valid. The court enjoys the same powers of adjournment and remand in such cases as if the suspect was charged with an indictable offence. In particular, proceedings may be adjourned pending the presentation of further evidence on behalf of the party requesting extradition where it appears that there is some deficiency in the documentary materials presented.[327] Equally, if, as a result of any evidence given or legal submissions made in the court, anything arises in the nature of fatal defects appearing on the face of the documents or there are other matters sufficient to warrant the court holding that it ought not to accept the proofs presented in pursuance of the statutory requirements, then the Court may decline to make the requested order for extradition. Where the judge is satisfied that the warrant is valid and that it relates to the person before the court,[328] he can order

---

[324] Extradition Act 1965, s.55(1). If the offence is one for which a preliminary legal requirement must be satisfied under U.K. law before a warrant could have been issued, the judge must assume that that preliminary requirement has been satisfied, unless there is additional admissible evidence suggesting otherwise; *McCann and Prenty v. Clafferty* [1990] I.L.R.M. 32. See also, *Ellis v. O'Dea* [1990] I.L.R.M. 87.

[325] *ibid.* s.55(2).

[326] *Ellis v. O'Dea* [1990] I.L.R.M. 87.

[327] *ibid.*

[328] If the person before the court corresponds in name and address and former address to the person described in the warrant then the court ought to conclude that they are one and the same person; *Crowley v. McVeigh* [1990] I.L.R.M. 220.

the suspect's delivery to the police authorities in the United Kingdom. The suspect then has fifteen days in which to challenge the order of delivery in the High Court.[328a]

A Prima facie case

3–51   The establishment of a prima facie case against the suspect is not a pre-requisite for an order for his extradition to the United Kingdom.[329] Also the court can proceed on the assumption, unless there is reason to believe otherwise, that the statement of facts set out on the warrant is a truthful statement of facts. Walsh J. explained the position as follows in *Wyatt v. McLoughlin*:

> "Until there is some reason to believe the contrary, it is to be assumed that a statement of facts such as the one appearing on the warrant executed in this case, or any warrant sent here for execution, is a truthful statement of the facts of the case in respect of which the arrest is sought. If it should transpire in any case that the statements of fact set out in the charge were not supported by any evidence then, of course, a very serious situation would arise and the courts would be obliged to examine such warrants in a completely different light because to set out statements of fact on a warrant for the purpose of giving the charge the appearance of corresponding to an offence under Irish law, when those factual statements are not capable of being borne out by evidence would be to practice a fraud upon the courts of this country."[330]

The court should not normally look behind the warrant to check that it is sufficiently backed up by the information upon which it is based.[331] Since extradition is a matter of reciprocity, it requires good faith from each side.[332] All warrants sent are representations that the purpose is to bring the person charged before the court of the requesting party on the charge specified and that at the time the warrant was issued there was sufficient evidence to justify the issuing of the warrant. Also, it is no function of the court to conduct a preliminary trial of the case against the individual or investigate any defence that may be open to him before deciding whether he should be extradited.[333]

The incapacity of the courts to look behind an extradition warrant from the United Kingdom must now be seen in the context of the statutory requirement for a direction from the Attorney General before the procedures under Part III can be put into effect in an individual case. In the mid 1980s the capacity of the authorities in England and Wales to ensure a fair trial for Irish people charged with high profile terrorist offences was the subject of serious public concern in Ireland. The State responded by introducing amendments to the 1965 Act in 1987 providing for further safeguards in the extradition

---

[328a] Extradition Act 1965, s.48(2) as amended by Extradition (European Union Conventions) Act 2001, s.20(e).

[329] *Shannon v. Attorney General* [1985] I.L.R.M. 422; *Clarke v. McMahon* [1990] 1 I.R. 228; [1990] I.L.R.M. 648.

[330] [1974] I.R. 378 at 395–396.

[331] *Ellis v. O'Dea* [1990] I.L.R.M. 87.

[332] Note that RSC Ord.31.r.29 cannot be used to order discovery from a foreign sovereign State in proceedings for the extradition of a person to that State; *Fusco v. O'Dea* [1994] 2 I.L.R.M. 389.

[333] *Quinlivan v. Conroy* [2000] 2 I.L.R.M. 515.

arrangements with the United Kingdom.[334] Among the key changes is the requirement for a direction from the Attorney General before a warrant for the arrest of a person for the purposes of extradition can be endorsed or executed.[335] The Attorney General cannot give such a direction unless, having considered such information as he deems appropriate, he is of the opinion that there is a clear intention to prosecute (or continue the prosecution) of the person concerned in the place where his extradition is sought,[336] and that such intention is founded on the existence of sufficient evidence.[337]

Delay in Seeking Extradition

Where a person has been arrested for the purposes of extradition to the United Kingdom he can seek his release on the grounds of delay by the U.K. authorities in seeking his extradition. The relevant provision is to be found in section 50(1)(bbb) of the Extradition Act 1965 which reads:

3–52

> "50(1)   A person arrested under this Part shall be released if the High Court or the Minister so directs in accordance with this section.
>
> (2)   A direction under this section may be given by the High Court where the Court is of opinion that –
>
> (bbb)   by reason of the lapse of time since the commission of the offence specified in the warrant or the conviction of the person named or described therein of that offence and other exceptional circumstances, it would, having regard to all the circumstances be unjust, oppressive or invidious to deliver him up under Section 47. . . ".[337a]

This provision has been considered recently by the Supreme Court in *Fusco v. O'Dea (No.2)*,[337b] *Kwok Ming Wan v. Conroy*,[337c] *MB v. Conroy*[337d] and *McNally v. O'Toole*.[337e] In all of these cases, the Court declared that both a lapse of time and other exceptional circumstances had to be established before the Court could proceed to consider whether, by reason of such lapse of time and other exceptional circumstances, that it would in all the circumstances be unjust, oppressive or invidious to surrender the applicant. The onus rests on the applicant to establish these matters on a balance of probability. However, the Supreme Court, when reviewing the decision of the trial judge, was entitled and indeed bound to draw its own inferences from the primary facts and to form an independent opinion in the matter of injustice, oppression or invidiousness while giving due weight to the conclusion of the trial judge.

---

[334]   Extradition (Amendment) Act 1987.

[335]   Extradition Act 1965, s.44A(1). Where any such direction has been given it may subsequently be revoked in appropriate circumstances; s.44A(2).

[336]   Extradition Act 1965, s.44B(a).

[337]   *ibid.* s.44B(b).

[337a]   Inserted by Extradition (European Convention on the Suppression of Terrorism) Act 1987, s.9 and amended by Extradition (Amendment) Act 1987, s.2(1)(b).

[337b]   [1998] 3 I.R. 470.

[337c]   [1998] 3 I.R. 527.

[337d]   [2001] 2 I.L.R.M. 311.

[337e]   Unreported, Supreme Court, May 9, 2002.

It is not possible to be exact about what constitutes a sufficient lapse of time in this context. The relevant time period is that between the applicant absconding and the date of the hearing in the High Court. In *Kwok Ming Wan* a period of eight years was considered more than sufficient while in *MB* a period of a just three and a half years was considered sufficient to trigger consideration of whether there were other exceptional circumstances. At this point it would appear that the Court is concerned only with how long the period of delay is. Factors such as responsibility for the delay, and the seriousness of the offence are considered later in the context of the other criteria.[337f]

When considering the presence of "other exceptional circumstances" it would appear that the Court pays special attention to the extent to which the applicant has lived openly in this country with the full knowledge of the authorities here. If, for example, his conduct while in this country is atypical of that associated with a fugitive, that may qualify as an exceptional circumstance. In *Kwok Ming Wan*, for example, the applicant had founded a family and built up a business. He had even been in contact with the British authorities to obtain a renewal of his licence. Similarly, in *McNally* the applicant had made no effort to conceal his whereabouts. He had registered with the social welfare authorities and drawn unemployment assistance, his whereabouts were always known to the Garda and he had even visited Belfast openly to attend his mother's funeral. In both cases the failure of the British and Northern Irish authorities respectively to seek extradition in these circumstances, was considered sufficient to satisfy the "other exceptional circumstances". However, the mere fact that the applicant's family had moved to this jurisdiction while he was in prison here would not in itself be sufficient.[337g] Indeed, it would appear that it may not be enough even for the applicant to have been living openly in the State to the knowledge of the authorities for a prolonged period of time. In *O'Toole*, the Court indicated that this factor would have to be coupled with others such as family circumstances and dilatoriness on the part of the authorities in the requesting State (see below). The poor health of the applicant, on the other hand, may be sufficient in itself to constitute an "other exceptional circumstance".[337h]

There are indications that a failure by the requesting authorities over a period of time to demonstrate any serious intent to bring the applicant to justice could constitute an "other exceptional circumstance". In *MB v. Conroy*, for example, Keane C.J. said:

[337f] Note, however, that in the High Court in *Martin v. Conroy* [2002] 1 I.L.R.M. 461 Herbert J. was of the view that any period during which the applicant was attempting to evade justice could not be considered in assessing whether the lapse of time requirement was satisfied. However, a period when the applicant was in prison in the State could not be considered as a period when he seeking to evade justice.

[337g] *Fusco v. O'Dea (No.2)* [1998] 3 I.R. 470.

[337h] See *MB v. Conroy* [2001] 2 I.L.R.M. 311. See also the recent *Pinochet* case in the U.K. Also, by analogy from deportation, *D v. United Kingdom* (1997) E.H.R.R. 534 where the European Court of Human Rights held that it would be a breach of Art. 3 of the European Convention on Human Rights to deport the applicant, who was dying of aids, to St Kitts as it would result in him being deprived of humane medical treatment.

"As is clear for the authorities to which I have referred, one of the factors which may constitute an exceptional circumstance is the dilatoriness of the prosecuting authorities, if established, in applying for the extradition of the Plaintiff. It was, of course, the action of the Plaintiff in absconding to this jurisdiction which led to that delay in the first place. However, it is not in dispute that the only action taken by the Manchester police to secure the Plaintiff's return was to circulate his name on the police national computer in the United Kingdom. It is also not disputed that, had enquiries been made with the Plaintiff's estranged wife, who was the mother of the Complainant, it should have been possible to ascertain his whereabouts in Ireland. In these circumstances, I am of the view that the failure of the Manchester police to take any steps to secure his extradition until the inquiry was made by the Irish Gardai in August 1995 was an exceptional circumstance which can be taken into account in considering whether his release should have been ordered by the High Court."[337i]

Similarly, in *McNally* the failure of the RUC to check with the Garda, the Irish social welfare authorities, Interpol or police authorities or even to circulate his name in the U.K.'s national police computer suggested a degree of dilatoriness sufficient to amount to an "other exceptional circumstance".

There is authority to suggest that the lapse in time will be sufficient in itself if it is of such a length as to create a real and serious risk of an unfair trial.[337j] In effect this extends to extradition the jurisprudence on delay as a ground for prohibiting the prosecution of an accused in the domestic courts (see chapter 1).

Where the lapse of time and "other exceptional circumstances" requirements have been satisfied the court must proceed to consider whether it would in all the circumstances be unjust, oppressive or invidious to surrender the applicant. Without purporting to offer a comprehensive definition of "unjust, oppressive or invidious" in this context Denham J. offered the following definition in *Fusco v. O'Dea (No.2)*:

"... it appears to me that they suggest certain concepts. Thus 'unjust' suggests, *inter alia*, unfairness, a lack of fair treatment. 'Oppressive' indicates actions that, *inter alia*, are oppressing a person, or group of persons, treating them badly, or cruelly, keeping them in subservience. While 'invidious' raises the concept of circumstances likely to cause resentment, anger or envy, such situations may arise if there is, for example, discrimination."[337k]

In assessing whether any of these factors are present the Court will have regard to where the responsibility lies for the delay in seeking the applicant's extradition. If the authorities in the requesting State have been inexcusably dilatory in taking steps to bring him to justice then that will serve to establish justice and oppressiveness. In assessing this dilatoriness the court will take into account factors such as delay in progressing the extradition application once the process has been commenced, the complexity of the investigation

---

[337i] [2001] 2 I.L.R.M. 311 at 318–319.
[337j] *Martin v. Conroy* [2002] 1 I.L.R.M. 461.
[337k] [1998] 3 I.R. 470 at 508.

and the seriousness of the offence relative to the length of the delay.[338] The family circumstances of the applicant are also an important factor in this context. If they will be seriously prejudiced by the fact that the extradition is requested after a long delay this may be considered oppressive. In *O'Toole*, for example, if the applicant was surrendered his family would lose their home and a large part of their financial resources. Once again, the seriousness of the offence can be a factor in considering the significance of the impact on the family. That the applicant may benefit from the terms of the Good Friday Peace Agreement concerning the early release of prisoners in respect of the offence for which his extradition is sought, is not a factor which the court can take into account in assessing whether it would be unjust, oppressive or invidious to extradite him where he has not been convicted of the offence on question.[339]

Constitutional Challenges

3–53   The constitutionality of the extradition arrangements under Part III at least in so far as they pertain to Northern Ireland was challenged in *Shannon v. Attorney General*.[340] Among the grounds argued were that the constitutional rights of the individual to due process would be infringed by extraditing him to stand trial under the special emergency measures in force, and that his life and person would be endangered as a result of the political and sectarian conflict there. In upholding the constitutionality of Part III the High Court ruled that protections for the rights of the suspect in the criminal justice process in Northern Ireland did not fall below the constitutional standards applicable in this State. While it accepted the existence of the political and sectarian conflict it did not find any evidence that the applicant would suffer any victimisation or discrimination in the criminal process on account of his religion or political views.

The High Court's decision was upheld on appeal by the Supreme Court. The latter, however, made it clear that Part III would not be applied in any case where it appeared that the constitutional rights of the person being extradited would not be protected in the requesting State:

> "The presumption is that the Act will not be operated in such a manner as to violate the constitutional rights of those affected by its operation. Thus, if it were shown in a particular case that the provisions of Part III of the Act were being used for a purpose or in a manner inconsistent with such constitutional rights, the courts would be bound to refuse to give effect to Part III."[341]

The following quotation from the judgment of Walsh J. in *Ellis v. O'Dea* makes the point more fulsomely:

> "All persons appearing before the courts of Ireland are entitled to protection against all unfair or unjust procedures or practices. It goes without saying

---

[338] Note *Myles v. Sreenan* [1994] 4 I.R. where the High Court accepted that the delay could be explained by the complexity of the investigation into a conspiracy to defraud.
[339] *Quinlivan v. Conroy (No.2)* [2000] 3 I.R. 154.
[340] [1985] I.L.R.M. 449.
[341] *ibid.* at 462.

therefore that no person within this jurisdiction may be removed by order of a court or otherwise out of this jurisdiction where these rights must be protected to another jurisdiction if to do so would be to expose him to practices or procedures which if exercised within this State would amount to infringements of his constitutional right to fair and just procedures. The obligation of the State to save its citizens from such procedures extends to all acts done within this jurisdiction and that includes proceedings taken under the Extradition Act 1965. As the Extradition Act 1965 is a post-constitutional statute it must be construed as not permitting persons appearing before our courts to be by order of our courts subjected to or exposed to any judicial process or procedures inside or outside this jurisdiction, which in this jurisdiction would amount to a denial or an infringement of the constitutional right to fair procedures. Any statute which would expressly seek to do so, or by necessary implication gives rise to such a single interpretation must necessarily be unconstitutional. There is nothing in the Act of 1965 which could be construed as purporting to permit to be exposed any person, the subject of extradition proceedings, to procedures which the Constitution would not tolerate. In other words there must not be only a correspondence of offences but also a correspondence of fair procedures. No procedure to which the extradited person could be exposed must be one which if followed in this State would be condemned as being unconstitutional."[342]

An unsuccessful attempt was made in *Russell v. Fanning*[343] to persuade the High Court and, on appeal, the Supreme Court to refuse to order the extradition of individuals who had escaped from the Maze Prison in Northern Ireland. The applicants argued that if sent back to the Maze Prison they would risk reprisals from prison officers angered by the death of one of their colleagues in the course of the escape. Despite the evidence that inmates in the Prison had been victimised and subjected to violence by the Prison Officers the courts refused to accept that there was a real threat to the safety of the applicants if sent back. In the subsequent case of *Finucane v. McMahon*[344] the Supreme Court quashed orders for extradition against further applicants who had escaped from the prison during the same episode. One of the grounds for the decision was the acceptance by the court that the personal safety of the prisoners would be at risk if they were sent back.[345] Since the decision in *Russell v. Fanning* further evidence had come to light about the nature and extent of reprisals which had been inflicted on the prisoners. It also transpired that the Prison Officers involved had not been disciplined and were still serving in the Prison.

3–54

The individual's constitutional rights could also be infringed by the risk of pre-trial adverse publicity in the requesting State. If this risk was of a magnitude sufficient to deny an individual his right to a fair trial in the requesting State his extradition will be refused. In *Magee v. O'Dea*,[346] for example, the

---

[342] *Ellis v. O'Dea* [1990] I.L.R.M. 87 at 91.
[343] [1988] I.R. 505.
[344] [1990] I.L.R.M. 505.
[345] The decision in this case was applied subsequently in *Clarke v. McMahon* [1990] I.L.R.M. 648 to refuse the extradition of another prisoner who had escaped from the Maze Prison during the same break out.
[346] [1994] 1 I.L.R.M. 540.

applicant challenged his extradition to Britain to answer a murder charge on the basis that his right to a fair trial had been compromised by lurid press coverage in some British papers which included a front page photograph of him portraying him as being guilty of the murder. Although the newspaper stories had been published two years earlier Flood J. considered that there was still a very real risk that they would influence the minds of jurors:

> "I have carefully considered the weight to be given to the lurid and sensational newspaper coverage, the existence of the photograph in the said newspaper and the unvarnished assumption that the person shown in the photograph is guilty of murder, the extent of the newspaper coverage in the national newspapers, the possibility that all or a great part of the foregoing would be rekindled in the mind of a juror trying the plaintiff and I have balanced that against the fade factor, and what I accept would be a careful charge by a trial judge to the jury directing them to permit themselves to be influenced by sensational and lurid newspaper coverage at the time or anything else other than what they hear by way of evidence in the court of trial. In my judgment, on the balance of probabilities, there is a serious risk of the type of unfairness contemplated by the Chief Justice in his said judgment which I have already quoted in *D v. Director of Public Prosecutions*."[347]

Accordingly, Flood J. refused extradition on the ground, *inter alia*, that the applicant's constitutional rights to a fair trial could not be secured in the event of his extradition.[348]

3–55   An extradition request will also be refused if the accused's constitutional right to fair procedures is denied in the domestic proceedings. In *Magee v. O'Dea*[349] the accused and his solicitor had only received the extradition papers ten minutes before the judge proceeded to make an order for his extradition. In the High Court challenge to the extradition order Flood J. made it clear that a failure to adjourn or invite the solicitor to apply for an adjournment in the matter amounted to a breach of fair procedures in the circumstances:

> "Clearly, the very nature of the documents involved require some degree of checking and detailed consultation between the plaintiff and his adviser in relation to the question as to who could give evidence of identity and from what source. In the circumstances where the district judge is well aware that the solicitor consulted has only been engaged within minutes before the matter has come before the court it seems that fair procedures demand that he should invite the solicitor concerned to take an adjournment to enable him to properly investigate and prepare his defence."[350]

The judge in this case also called a witness on his own motion in order to satisfy himself as to the identity of the accused. He did not, however, advise the

---

347   *ibid*. at 550.
348   In *Quinlivan v. Conroy* [2000] 2 I.L.R.M. 515 Kelly J. felt that the "fade factor" plus the availability of procedural protections were sufficient to discount the impact of adverse publicity which was at least as strong as that in *Magee*.
349   [1994] 1 I.L.R.M. 540.
350   *ibid*. at 545.

accused's solicitor of his intention to take this course of action. With the result the accused was not afforded the opportunity to make representations in the matter. This, together with the speed with which the judge disposed of the proceedings was enough to amount to a denial of fair procedures:

> "It seems to me that the speed with which the matter was dealt with, the absence of any attempt on the judge's part to ensure that all valid considerations could be given to various aspects of the matter by the defence solicitor and his action in failing to advise (*inter alia*) the plaintiff's solicitor of his intention to recall evidence of identity, all appear to me to amount to unfair procedures in a matter where strict proof is required."[351]

Flood J. went on to conclude that "the procedure followed fell short of the constitutionally accepted standards of fairness with the result that the order made by the learned district justice on foot of those proceedings is invalid".[352]

5. Extradition to E.U. Convention Countries

Background

The European Union Conventions on Extradition 1995 and 1996 make **3–56** provision for the simplification of extradition between Member States of the Union. They have been implemented in Ireland by the Extradition (European Union Conventions) Act 2001.[353] It follows that the provisions governing extradition to countries other than the United Kingdom, as well as the separate arrangements pertaining to the United Kingdom, as described earlier (see paras. 3–43 *et seq.*) must be interpreted in the light of the following provisions in any case where extradition is being sought from or to an E.U. State which has been designated for the purposes of the 2001 Act. Essentially the 1995 Convention makes provision for the wanted person to: consent to his or her surrender and Convention extends the range of extraditable offences and makes provision to simplify the transfer and authentication of documents. It is worth noting that the Minister for Foreign Affairs must designate Convention countries separately for the purposes of each Convention.[354] It is necessary, therefore, in each case to check whether the simplified arrangements have been introduced pursuant to the 1995 or 1996 Conventions and whether the country in question has been designated for the purposes of the applicable Convention. In respect of either Convention the designation is effected by the order of the Minister for Foreign Affairs which can be amended or revoked by order at any time. Any such order must be laid before each House of the Oireachtas.[355]

---

[351] *ibid.* at 545–546.

[352] *ibid.* at 546.

[353] This has been brought into force by The Extradition (European Union Conventions) Act 2001 (Commencement) Order 2002 (S.I. No. 85 of 2002).

[354] Extradition (European Union Conventions) Act 2001, ss.4 and 10.

[355] Any order made by the government under the 2001 Act must be laid before each House of the Oireachtas as soon as may be after it is made and, if a resolution annulling the order us passed by either House within the next 21 days, the order shall be annulled accordingly, but without

Consent to Extradition

The 2001 Act amends the Extradition Act 1965 by introducing provision for a simplified procedure for the extradition of a person to a Convention country where that person consents to his or her surrender. Now where a person is brought before the High Court pursuant to an extradition request or a request for his provisional arrest, from a Convention country the person may consent to being surrendered to the Convention country concerned.[356] In this event the High Court must record the consent in writing and send a copy to the Minister for Justice, Equality and Law Reform.[357] Where the consent is made in the context of a provisional arrest the Minister must inform the country not later than 10 days after the person was arrested.[358] The person may withdraw his consent at any time up until the Minister has made an order for his surrender under the 1965 Act.[359] Where the consent is withdrawn in the case of a person who has been committed to prison on the basis of a provisional warrant (see below), the person shall be brought back before the High Court as soon as possible after a request for his extradition has been received by the Minister from the Convention country concerned. In this event the High Court shall affirm the order of committal provided that there has been compliance with the 1965 Act.[360]

The Extradition Request Procedure

3–57 The primary significance of a person's consent to surrender is that it facilitates resort to a simplified procedure for his surrender to a Convention country. The requirements of this simplified procedure differ depending on whether the person is before the High Court pursuant to an extradition request or a provisional warrant. Where a person is brought before the High Court pursuant to an extradition request from a Convention country, the Court can make an order committing the person to prison to await the order of the Minister for his extradition in certain circumstances. Before making such an order the Court must satisfy itself that: the extradition of the person has been duly requested; the request is from a Convention country which has been designated by the Minister for Foreign Affairs as having adopted the 1995 Convention; extradition of the person concerned is not prohibited by the relevant extradition provisions; the documents required to support a request for extradition under section 25 of the Extradition Act 1965 have been supplied; the person consents voluntarily to his being surrendered to the Convention country and is aware of the

---

prejudice to the validity of anything previously done thereunder; Extradition Act 1965, s.4, as amended by Extradition (European Union Conventions) Act 2001, s.21.

[356] Extradition Act 1965, s.29A(1), as inserted by Extradition (European Union Conventions) Act 2001, s.6.

[357] *ibid.* s.29A(4).

[358] *ibid.* s.29A(5)(a). Where the person does not consent the Minister must inform the country of that fact within the same time period; s.29A(5)(b).

[359] *ibid.* s.29A(6). The period between giving consent and withdrawing consent shall not be included in calculating the 18 day period for the receipt of an extradition request in respect of a person arrested pursuant to a provisional warrant.

[360] *ibid.* s.29A(7).

consequences of his consent; and where the person is an Irish citizen, the Minister for Justice, Equality and Law Reform consents to the person being surrendered to the Convention country concerned.[361]

The Provisional Warrant Procedure

Where the person is before the High Court pursuant to a provisional warrant **3–58** the Court can make an order committing the person to prison to await the order of the Minister for his extradition if it is satisfied that: there has been compliance with certain statutory requirements in the issuance of the provisional arrest warrant (see below); it is intended that a request will be made by or on behalf of the Convention country for the person's extra-dition (unless he consents to extradition); the person consents voluntarily to his or her being surrendered to the Convention country and is aware of the consequences of his or her consent; extradition of the person concerned is not prohibited by the relevant extradition provisions; and where the person is an Irish citizen, the Minister or Justice, Equality and Law Reform consents to the person being surrendered to the Convention country concerned.[362]

The requirements pertaining to the issuing of a provisional arrest warrant pursuant to a request from a Convention country are that the request must: state that one of the documents listed in paragraph (a) of section 25 of the Extradition Act 1965 exists (the original or authenticated copy of the conviction and sentence or detention order immediately enforceable or, as the case may be, the warrant of arrest or other similar order issued in accordance with the procedure laid down in the law of the requesting country);[363] be accompanied by a statement of the offences to which the request relates specifying the nature and description under the law of the requesting country of the offences concerned; specify the circumstances in which the offences were committed including the time and place of their commission or alleged commission, and the degree of involvement or alleged involvement of the person to whom the request relates in their commission or alleged commission; and specify the penalties to which that person would be liable if convicted of the offences concerned or, where he has been convicted of these offences, the penalties that have been imposed or, where he has been convicted of those offences but not yet sentenced, the penalties to which he is liable.[364]

If the High Court is of the opinion that the information communicated to it pursuant to these statutory requirements is insufficient to enable a decision to be made, it may adjourn the hearing for such periods as it thinks proper to enable further information to be produced.[365] If the Court does not adjourn or commit the person under these provisions it must order his discharge.[366]

---

[361] *ibid.* s.29A(3).
[362] *ibid.* s.29A(2).
[363] The provision refers erroneously to s.25(1)(a).
[364] Extradition Act 1965, s.27(2A), as inserted by Extradition (European Union Conventions) Act 2001, s.5.
[365] *ibid.* s.29A(8), as inserted by *ibid.* s.6.
[366] *ibid.*

Waiver of Speciality Rule

3–59   The 2001 Act amends the Extradition Act 1965 to enable a person whose extradition is sought by a Convention country to waive the speciality rule. It was seen earlier that the Minister's consent is normally required for any waiver of the speciality rule in extradition from Ireland, and that the consent can only be given in certain circumstances. Now the 1965 Act permits the Minister to consent where the extradition is being sought by a Convention country and the person in question is consenting to that request and consents to the Minister's consent to the waiver of the speciality rule.[367] To be effective the person's consent to the Minister's consent must be given voluntarily before the High Court and the person must be aware of the consequences of the Minister's consent.[368] The person may withdraw his consent at any time before the Minister has given his consent.[369] The effect will be to prevent the Minister from giving his consent. The Minister is also precluded from giving his consent on a day that is before the day on which he makes an order for the extradition of the person concerned.[370] It follows that the person will have at least up until the day that his order for extradition is made to withdraw his consent to a waiver of the speciality rule.

It is also worth noting that the application of the speciality rule to Convention countries has been relaxed by amendments effected to the Extradition Act 1965 by the 2001 Act. A person's extradition to a Convention country can no longer be refused on the grounds only that it is intended to proceed against him in the requesting country for an offence other than that for which his extradition is requested. A person extradited for one offence may be tried or prosecuted for other offences committed before his extradition if the other offences do not give rise to imprisonment or, where they do give rise to imprisonment, if he has expressly waived the benefit of speciality.[371] There are analogous provisions with respect to extradition from other Convention countries to Ireland.[372]

Surrender

Where the High Court makes an order for the surrender of a person to a Convention country pursuant to these provisions the Minister shall notify the country concerned in writing not later than 20 days after the person gave his consent to be surrendered.[373] He should normally proceed to make an extradition order in respect of the person not later than 20 days after having given notification to the country in question.[374] If, for reasons beyond the Minister's control, he is unable to comply with this requirement he must notify the

---

[367] *ibid.* s.20A(1), as inserted by *ibid.* s.7.
[368] *ibid.* s.20A(1)(b).
[369] *ibid.* s.20A(2).
[370] *ibid.* s.20A(3).
[371] *ibid.* s.20, as amended by *ibid.* s.15.
[372] *ibid.* s.39, as amended by *ibid.* s.17.
[373] *ibid.* s.33A(1), as inserted by *ibid.* s.8.
[374] *ibid.* s.33A(2).

country concerned and make an extradition order on such day as may be agreed between the Minister and that country.[375] Where such a day is agreed the person shall be surrendered not later than 20 days after that day.[376] If the person is not surrendered within that time period he must be released. These provisions are without prejudice to the Minister's power under section 32 of the 1965 Act to postpone the surrender of a person (see para. 3–47).[377]

Extraditable Offences

The 1996 Convention extends the range of extraditable offences for Convention countries. Under the 1965 Act the minimum penalty attaching to an extraditable offence is a period of imprisonment of at least one year or a more severe penalty in both Ireland and the requesting State. Where there already has been a conviction and sentence imposed in the requesting State, the sentence must have been for a period of imprisonment of not less than four months (or a more severe penalty). Now the minimum penalty required in Irish law has been reduced to a period of not less than six months' imprisonment or a more severe penalty.[378]   **3–60**

6. European Arrest Warrant

Background

Extradition within the European Union is set to undergo a further radical change once the European arrest warrant comes into effect in all Member States. At the Tampere European Council in October 1999 it was agreed that formal extradition procedures should be abolished among Member States in respect of persons convicted and sentenced and that the procedures should be speeded up in respect of persons suspected of having committed an offence. This was part of an overall objective to establish an area of freedom, security and justice in which there would be free movement of judicial decisions in criminal matters. Subsequently the European Union adopted a framework decision on a European arrest warrant. While the framework decision is legally binding on Ireland, in the manner of a Directive without direct effect, it does not automatically constitute law within Ireland. The State has until December 31, 2003 at the latest to implement the terms of the framework decision into Irish law. The following, therefore, is simply an outline of the basic contents of the framework decision as a guide to the changes that lie down the road for extradition arrangements between Ireland and all other Member States of the European Union, including the United Kingdom. With respect to arrangements with the United Kingdom, it is worth noting that the   **3–61**

---

[375] *ibid.* s.33A(3).
[376] *ibid.* s.33A(4).
[377] *ibid.* s.33A(5).
[378] *ibid.* s.10(1A), as inserted by *ibid.* s.11(a). Where a request for extradition is granted for such an offence in an individual case where extradition is also requested in respect of one or more offences which do not satisfy these standards then the request in respect of the latter offence or offences can also be granted; *ibid.* s.10(2A), as inserted by *ibid.* s.11(b).

framework decision does not preclude unilateral or multilateral arrangements between States which facilitate even simpler arrangements than those provided for in the framework decision itself.

Basic Concept

The European arrest warrant is a judicial decision by one Member State for the arrest and surrender of a person by another Member State for the purpose of prosecuting that person or executing a custodial sentence against that person in the latter State. Such warrants must be executed on the basis of mutual recognition and in accordance with the terms of the framework decision. It is a matter for national law to designate competent judicial authorities to issue and executive warrants. There may also be a Central Authority within the State to assist the judicial authorities.

Offences

3–62 The warrant may be issued for acts punishable by the law of the issuing State by a custodial sentence of at least 12 months or, where a sentence has already been imposed, for periods of imprisonment or detention of at least four months. The double criminality requirement is removed in respect of certain offences listed in the framework decision itself. Where these offences, as defined in the issuing State, can be punished by a custodial sentence of at least three years in the issuing State, surrender pursuant to a warrant is obligatory without verification of the double criminality requirement. The offences in question are: participation in a criminal organisation; terrorism; trafficking in human beings; sexual exploitation of children and child pornography; illicit trafficking in narcotic drugs and psychotropic substances; illicit trafficking in weapons, munitions and explosives; corruption; fraud (including fraud on the European Communities); laundering of the proceeds of crime; counterfeiting currency; computer-related crime; environmental crime; facilitating unauthorised entry and residence; murder and grievous bodily injury; illicit trade in human organs and tissue; kidnapping, illegal restraint and hostage taking; racism and xenophobia; organised crime or armed robbery; illicit trafficking in cultural goods; swindling; racketeering and extortion; counterfeiting and piracy of products; forgery of administrative documents and trafficking therein; forgery of means of payment; illicit trafficking in hormonal substances and other growth promoters; illicit trafficking in nuclear or radioactive materials; trafficking in stolen vehicles; rape; arson; crimes within the jurisdiction of the International Criminal Court; unlawful seizure of aircraft or ships; and sabotage. This list can be extended by the Council. For offences other than those listed, surrender subject to a warrant may be subject to the condition that the acts in respect of which the warrant was issued constitute an offence under the law of the executing State.

Obligatory Grounds for Refusal

There are certain circumstances in which a judicial authority in one State must refuse to execute a warrant issued by another State. These are: if the offence in question is covered by an amnesty in the executing Member State; where that State has jurisdiction to prosecute the offence under its own criminal law; where the person has been finally judged by a Member State in respect of the same acts and the sentence is served or is being served or is no longer executable under the law of the sentencing State; and if the person cannot be held criminally responsible due to his age under the law of the executing State for the acts on which the arrest warrant is based.

Discretionary Grounds to Refuse

There are some circumstances in which the judicial authority may refuse to execute a warrant. These are: where the act on which the warrant is based does not constitute an offence under the law of the executing State (this refers only to offences other than those listed in the framework decision as set out above); where the person is being prosecuted in the executing State for the same act; where the judicial authorities of the executing State have decided not to prosecute for the offence; where a final judgment has been passed against the person in a Member State which prevents further proceedings in respect of the same acts; where the prosecution or punishment of the person is statute barred in the executing State and the acts fall within the jurisdiction of that State; where the executing judicial authority is informed that the person has been finally dealt with in respect of the same acts by a third State; where the warrant is for a national or resident of the executing State and is in respect of a sentence and the executing State undertakes to execute the sentence; where the offence is regarded by the law of the executing State as having been committed in whole or in part in that State; and where the offence has been committed outside of the issuing State and the law of the executing State does not allow prosecution for the same offence when committed outside of its territory.

3–63

Conditions on the Execution of the Warrant

The executing State may impose conditions on the execution of the warrant in certain circumstances. If the warrant has been issued for the enforcement of a sentence imposed in the person's absence, his surrender may be made subject to the condition that the issuing judicial authority gives a guarantee that the person will be given the opportunity to apply for a retrial of the case in the issuing State and to be present at the judgment. Moreover, if the offence is punishable by a life sentence the execution of the warrant may be made subject to the condition that the issuing State makes provision for a review of sentence on request or at the latest after 20 years. Where the person is a national or resident of the executing State and the warrant is for his prosecution, his surrender may be made subject to the condition that he is returned to the executing State to serve any custodial punishment that may be imposed.

Form of Warrant

A warrant must contain the following information: the identity and nationality of the requested person; the name, address, telephone and fax numbers and e-mail address of the issuing judicial authority; evidence of an enforceable judgment, an arrest warrant or other enforceable judicial decision having the same effect within the scope of the definition of the European arrest warrant; the nature and legal classification of the offence; a description of the circumstances in which the offence was committed, including the time, place and degree of participation in the offence by the requested person; the penalty imposed, if there is a final judgment, or the prescribed scale of penalties for the offence under the law of the issuing State; and if possible, other consequences of the offence.

The warrant must be translated into the official language, or one of the official languages, of the executing State.

Transmission of the Warrant

3–64 Where the location of the requested person is known, the issuing judicial authority may transmit the warrant directly to the relevant executing judicial authority. Alternatively, or in addition, the issuing authority may issue an alert for the requested person in the Schengen Information System in accordance with the provisions of Article 95 of the 1990 Convention implementing the 1985 Schengen Agreement.

Transmission of the warrant may be effected through the secure telecommunications system of the European Judicial Network. Equally, the issuing authority may forward it by any secure means capable of producing written records under conditions allowing the executing State to establish its authenticity.

Rights of the Requested Person

When a requested person is arrested, the executing judicial authority shall inform him of the warrant and its contents and of the possibility of consenting to surrender (see below). This information must be conveyed in accordance with national law. The arrested person also has the right to the assistance of a lawyer and an interpreter in accordance with the national law of the executing State. The executing judicial authority must decide, in accordance with national law, whether the person should remain in detention. The person may be released provisionally in conformity with the national law provided that the competent authority takes all the measures it deems necessary to prevent the person absconding.

Surrender Procedure

The arrested person may consent to his or her surrender and/or waiver of the speciality rule. In either event the consent must be given before the executing judicial authority in accordance with the law of the State. The State must adopt measures to ensure that any such consent is established in such a way as to show that the person concerned expressed it voluntarily and in full awareness of the consequences. For this purpose the person has the right to legal advice. The consent must be formally recorded in accordance with the procedure laid down by the law of the executing State. Generally, consent cannot be revoked, but Member States may make provision in their law for revocation.

Where the arrested person does not consent to his surrender he is entitled to a hearing before the executing judicial authority in accordance with the law of the State. It is then a matter for the judicial authority to decide, consequent to the hearing, whether the person should be surrendered. There is provision for the judicial authority to ask for and to be supplied with further information for the purposes of reaching a decision.

Where the warrant has been issued for the purpose of conducting a criminal prosecution, the executing judicial authority must either agree that the requested person should be heard or agree to his temporary transfer. Where the authority settles on the former, the person must be heard by a judicial authority assisted by another person designated in accordance with the law of the requesting State. The requested person shall be heard in accordance with the law of the executing State.

Time Limits for Execution of Warrant

A warrant must be dealt with and executed as a matter of urgency. Where the **3–65** person consents to surrender, the final decision on execution of the warrant should be taken within 10 days of the consent. In other cases the final decision on execution should be taken within 60 days of the arrest. In either of these situations there is provision for a 30-day extension where the warrant cannot be executed within the specified time limits. In exceptional circumstances, if a State cannot observe these limits it must inform Eurojust and give reasons for the delay.

During the period prior to a final decision being taken in any case, the executing judicial authority must ensure that the material conditions necessary for effective surrender of the person remain fulfilled.

Where the person enjoys a privilege or immunity regarding jurisdiction or execution in the executing State, these time limits do not start running unless and until the executing judicial authority has been informed that the privilege or immunity has been waived.

Notification of Decision

The executing judicial authority shall notify the issuing judicial authority immediately of the decision on the action to be taken on the warrant. Where the decision is to refuse to surrender, reasons must be given.

Time Limits for Surrender

Where a decision is taken to surrender the person, he must be surrendered as soon as possible on a date agreed between the authorities concerned. This should be no later than 10 days after the final decision on the execution of the warrant. If this cannot be achieved due to circumstances beyond the control of any of the States, the judicial authorities must agree on a new surrender date and the surrender must take place within 10 days of this new date. Exceptionally the surrendered may have to be postponed for serious humanitarian reasons. In this event the judicial authorities shall agree on a new surrender date and the surrender shall taken place within 10 days of that date. If the person is still being held in the custody of the executing judicial authority after these time limits have expired, he must be released.

There is provision for the executing judicial authority either to postpone the surrender or to surrender the person temporarily. This can be done for the purpose of prosecuting the person or having him serve a sentence in the executing State.

Transit

Subject to one exception each Member State is obliged to permit the transit through its territory of a requested person pursuant to a European arrest warrant, so long as it has been given information on: the identity and nationality of the person; the existence of the warrant; the nature and classification of the offence; and the description of the circumstances of the offence. The exception is where the person is a national or resident of the State of transit and is requested for the purpose of serving a custodial sentence. Where the person is a national or resident of the transit State and is requested for the purpose of prosecution, the State may permit the transit on condition that the person is returned to the State to serve any custodial sentence that may be imposed.

Effect of Surrender

3–66   The most immediate effect of surrender is that the person is delivered into the custody of the requesting State for the purpose of prosecution for the specified offence or to serve the specified custodial sentence. The requesting State shall deduct all periods of detention arising from the execution of the warrant from the total period of detention to be served in that State consequent on any custodial sentence being imposed.

Where the surrender is effected pursuant to the European arrest warrant, there may be further consequences. There is provision for each Member State to waive the rule of speciality on a reciprocal basis with other Member States. This will permit the prosecution and/or sentencing of the person for an offence committed prior to his surrender other than that for which his surrender was requested. Even where the rule of speciality has not been waived, the person can be dealt with for other offences in certain specified circumstances. There is also provision enabling the surrender of a person to a third country after he has been surrendered to another Member State pursuant to the European arrest warrant.

Multiple Requests

If two or more Member States have issued arrest warrants for the same person, the executing judicial authority shall decide which to execute. It shall take due consideration of all the circumstances and especially the seriousness and place of the offences, the respective dates of the warrants and the purposes for which they have issued. In the event of a conflict between a European arrest warrant and a request for extradition from a third country, the decision on which takes precedence shall be taken by the executing judicial authority in a similar manner.

International Obligations **3–67**

The framework decision on the European arrest warrant does not prejudice the obligations of the executing State where the requested person has been extradited to that State from a third State and where that person is protected by provisions of the arrangement under which he was extradited concerning speciality.

Conclusion

It must be remembered that the framework decision has been drafted to accommodate the extradition procedures and concerns of all 15 Member States. It is hardly surprising, therefore, that its provisions are not exactly a model of clarity or completeness. Ultimately, the measure will have to be implemented into Irish law, presumably through an Act of the Oireachtas. The Act will lay down the principles and procedures applicable in Irish law.

CHAPTER 4

ARREST

A. Introduction

In Ireland the liberty of the individual is afforded constitutional protection. Article 40.4.1° of the Constitution states: "No citizen shall be deprived of his personal liberty save in accordance with law." It follows that a citizen's freedom of movement can be restrained only pursuant to a specific common law or statutory provision which accords with constitutional norms of due process and conforms with the other fundamental rights enshrined in the Constitution. A large number of common law and statutory powers satisfy this test. They authorise a member of the Garda Síochána to stop, search, arrest and detain an individual in a very diverse range of situations. There are also a number of powers enabling other public officials and private citizens to impose restraint on the liberty of the individual in certain circumstances relevant to the criminal process. This Chapter deals with the powers of arrest which are recognised by law. Powers to stop and search an individual are dealt with in chapter 7 while powers of detention are dealt in chapter 5.

4–01

B. The Purpose of Arrest

1. Arrest in the Criminal Process

At common law, arrest was considered as the first formal step in the judicial stage of the criminal process. It was the formal mechanism for taking a suspect into custody for the purpose of being charged and brought before a judicial authority to answer the charge. Walsh J. expressed the point succinctly

4–02

in *People v. Shaw* when he described arrest as being "simply a process of ensuring the attendance at Court of the person so arrested".[1] In particular, Walsh J. asserted that "No person may be arrested with or without warrant for the purpose of interrogation or the securing of evidence from that person".[2] In the absence of statutory provision to the contrary, the police should exercise their powers of arrest in an individual case for the purpose of charging a suspect and bringing him before a judicial authority, and not for the purpose of facilitating their investigation.[3] Arrest could be distinguished in that sense from other police powers, such as a power of entry, search and seizure, which could be used for the purpose of gathering evidence and building up a case against a suspect.

4–03   Over a period of time the police developed a practice of questioning the suspect in the period between the initial arrest and the point at which he could be brought in police custody before a judicial authority to answer the charge. Inevitably this proved very valuable in furthering police investigations in individual cases. For the most part the judges tacitly accepted this practice, even to the extent of offering guidance on procedures that should be followed when taking statements from suspects in police custody. A number of statutory provisions, most particularly, the Offences against the State Act 1939, fuelled this development by permitting the police to arrest and detain without charge for a prescribed period persons suspected of certain criminal offences. Prior to the enactment of section 4 of the Criminal Justice Act 1984 these were merely exceptions to the general rule that arrest could not be used for the purpose of furthering a police investigation.[4] With the enactment of section 4 of the 1984 Act (see chapter 5), however, the exception has now become the norm. Indeed, this development had already taken root in other common law jurisdictions. The Royal Commission on Criminal Procedure in England and Wales, for example, declared that it was well established that one of the primary purposes of arrest was to use the period of detention to dispel or confirm the reasonable suspicion against a person by questioning him or seeking further evidence with his assistance.[5]

2. Arrest in other Contexts

It is also worth noting that there are statutory powers which permit summary detention outside of the criminal process altogether.[6] Section 12 of the Mental Health Act 2001, for example, permits a member of the Garda Síochána to

---

[1] *People v. Shaw* [1982] I.R. 1 at 29.
[2] *ibid.*
[3] *Dunne v. Clinton* [1930] I.R. 366; *Attorney General v. Cox* unreported, Court of Criminal Appeal, April 5, 1929; *People v. O'Loughlin* [1979] I.R. 85; *People v. Walsh* [1980] I.R. 294; *Attorney General (McDonnell) v. Higgins* [1964] I.R. 374.
[4] *People v. Shaw* [1982] I.R. 1, *per* Walsh J.; *Re O'Laighleis* [1960] I.R. 93.
[5] *Report of the Royal Commission on Criminal Procedure in England and Wales*, cmnd. 8092 (HMSO, London, 1981), para.3.66.
[6] Powers of arrest can also be found in the civil process; *e.g.* Art.1 of the Brussels International;

detain a person suffering from a mental disorder where there is a serious likelihood of him causing harm to himself or others.[7] Equally, section 5 of the Immigration Act 1999, as amended by section 10 of the Illegal Immigrants (Trafficking) Act 2000, provides a power of arrest and detention for the purpose of facilitating the removal from the State in certain circumstances of a person who is the subject of a deportation order. The inevitable effect is to extend the concept of arrest beyond its narrow remit of making a suspect amenable to the court to answer a criminal charge.

3. Misuse of Arrest Power

The use of an arrest power to achieve a purpose extraneous to that for which the power was conferred is unlawful. Indeed, in an appropriate case it will amount to a conscious and deliberate breach of the individual's constitutional right to liberty. This, in turn, will result in the subsequent detention being unlawful and the exclusion of any evidence obtained from the suspect during the period of unlawful detention. The issue has arisen on occasion with respect to the power of arrest conferred by section 30 of the Offences against the State Act (see later at para. 4–19 *et seq.*). This power is conferred for the purpose of detaining an individual to facilitate the investigation of his or her suspected involvement in certain offences. In *Trimbole v. Governor of Mountjoy Prison*[6a] the applicant was arrested under section 30 on suspicion of unlawful possession of firearms. The High Court found that the gardaí did not entertain a genuine suspicion of possession of firearms against the applicant and were not seriously interested in investigating him for that offence. Instead, their motive in arresting him under section 30 was to ensure that he would be available to be served with an extradition warrant which was expected to arrive from the Australian authorities. The High Court had no hesitation in finding that the applicant's arrest and detention was unlawful in these circumstances. This decision was upheld on appeal to the Supreme Court.

Similarly, as will be seen later (para. 4-30), it is unlawful to arrest someone on suspicion of an offence merely as "a colourable device" to facilitate the interrogation of a suspect for a completely different offence. In *State (Bowes) v. Fitzpatrick*,[6b] for example, the High Court declared unlawful a section 30 arrest on suspicion of malicious damage to a knife which had been used in a murder. The Court found that the gardaí were not seriously interested in investigating the malicious damage offence. They were merely using it as a means of securing the arrest and detention of the suspect for the murder, an offence which was not within the scope of the section 30 power. This amounted to an unlawful use of the power. It would be very different if the

---

Convention Relating to the Arrest of Sea-Going Ships 1952 defines arrest for the purposes of the Convention as: ". . . the detention of a ship by judicial process to secure a maritime claim, but does not include the seizure of a ship in execution or satisfaction of a judgment." See Jurisdiction of Courts (Maritime Convention) Act 1989, s.4 and *In the Matter of MV "Kapitan Labunets"* [1995] 1 I.L.R.M. 430.

[6a] [1985] I.L.R.M. 465.
[6b] [1978] I.L.R.M. 195.

gardaí had a genuine interest in investigating the malicious damage charge, even though their primary interest was in the murder charge.[6c]

In *Criminal Assets Bureau v. Craft*[6d] the High Court accepted that the arrest and detention of the defendant under section 2 of the Criminal Justice (Drug Trafficking) Act 1996 (see chapter 5) on suspicion of a drug trafficking offence would constitute a conscious and deliberate violation of the defendant's constitutional rights if it was effected for the sole purpose of providing an opportunity to interrogate him in relation to arrears of tax. On the facts of the case the Court found that the gardaí were genuinely investigating the defendant for drug-trafficking offences. The mere fact that they were also investigating him for related tax evasion activities did not render the arrest unlawful.

The basic principle, therefore, is that an arrest power can be exercised only for the purpose for which it was conferred. So long as it is genuinely used for that purpose in an individual case the legality of the subsequent detention will not be affected by the mere fact that the gardaí take advantage of the suspect's presence in their custody to pursue further investigations.

C. The Concept of Arrest

4–04 Although most people are familiar with the notion of an arrest, it is a difficult concept to define precisely. Its meaning can differ depending on the context in which it is used. At its most basic it might be described as the imposition of restraint on an individual so that his freedom of movement is, at least temporarily, subject to the will of the person who has imposed the restraint. In other words, the key issue is not whether an individual has been *lawfully* arrested but whether he has been deprived of his liberty.[8] Clearly, this definition encompasses situations which are not considered to amount to arrest in the criminal process.[9] A member of the Garda Síochána, for example, has a range of powers to stop an individual for the purpose of questioning and/or searching him in certain circumstances.[10] Inevitably, the exercise of these powers involves a temporary detention of the individual concerned. However, such powers are not considered powers of arrest in the criminal process. It follows that while the deprivation of liberty is undoubtedly a prerequisite for arrest, it will not always be sufficient in itself to constitute an arrest in the

---

[6c] See, *e.g. People (DPP) v Walsh* [1988] I.L.R.M. 137.

[6d] Unreported, High Court, July 12, 2000.

[7] See also, Refugee Act 1996, s.9(8); Health Act 1947, s.38.

[8] Viscount Dilhorne, *e.g.* explained: "Whether or not a person has been arrested depends not on the legality of his arrest but on whether he has been deprived of his liberty to go where he pleases"; *Spicer v. Holt* [1977] A.C. 987 at 1000. See also, Lord Sumner in *Christie v. Leachinsky* [1947] A.C. 573 at 600; *Murray v. Ministry of Defence* [1988] 1 W.L.R. 692; *Lewis v. Chief Constable of the South Wales Constabulary* [1991] 1 All E.R. 206.

[9] For further discussion of the difficulties associated with the definition of arrest, see Zander, "When is an Arrest not an Arrest" (1977) 127 N.L.J. 352; Clarke and Feldman, "Arrest by any Other Name" [1979] Crim. L.R. 702; Telling, "Arrest and Detention – The Conceptual Maze" [1978] Crim. L.R. 320; Kidstone, "A Maze in Law!" [1987] Crim. L.R. 332; Williams, "Requisites of a Valid Arrest" [1964] Crim. L.R. 6.

[10] See Chap.7.

criminal process.[11] Something more is required. On the other hand, as will be seen later, there are circumstances in which the courts will consider an individual to be under arrest purely on the basis that he has been deprived of his liberty.

It would appear that there is no practical point in attempting to distinguish between deprivation of liberty which amounts to a *de facto* arrest and one which does not.[12] As yet there has been no case in which a court has found it necessary to define the difference.[13] In practice the courts are concerned only to determine firstly whether an individual has been deprived of his liberty, and secondly whether that deprivation is lawful. The answer to the second question frequently depends on whether the deprivation of liberty has been grounded on a recognised power of arrest, whether the specific requirements of that individual power have been satisfied, whether the formalities of arrest have been complied with and, whether, in the particular circumstances of the case, the arrest was a proper exercise of discretion. These matters are dealt with later. First, it is necessary to address the preliminary issue of whether the individual has actually been deprived of his liberty so as to constitute an arrest. Typically, this issue has been addressed by the courts in the context of an individual who has been invited to accompany the police to the police station to assist them with their inquiries.

D. Assisting the Police with their Inquiries

Introduction

The police investigation into a criminal offence will often be assisted by having the suspect or suspects available for questioning in the police station. This can be secured either by the suspect attending voluntarily at the police station to "assist the police with their enquiries," or by the police coercing his presence by arresting him. In the latter event, the police must work subject to the limitations inherent in their powers of arrest and detention. For the most part, a failure to stay within these limits will render the suspect's detention unlawful. Accordingly, gardaí regularly resort to the tactic of inviting a suspect to come to the garda station of his own free will to assist with the investigation.[14] The mere fact that an individual is being questioned in the Garda station about his knowledge of, or possible involvement in, a criminal offence does not mean that the gardaí must comply with the principles and

4–05

---

[11] *R. v. Brown* (1976) 64 Cr. App. Rep. 231.

[12] It is possible that the distinction might become relevant in the context of executive detention or internment; see *Re O'Laighleis, op. cit.*, above, n. 4 at 128.

[13] Referring to the U.K., Leigh says that there are few cases in which it is necessary to consider the distinction between a lawful detention and an arrest. The distinction was formerly important under the breathalyser provisions of the Road Traffic Act 1972 (UK) where arrest had first to be preceded by a lawful detention; see Telling [1978] Crim. L.R. 320 and Lidstone [1978] Crim. L.R. 332. Leigh, *Police Powers in England and Wales* (2nd ed., Butterworths, London, 1985) p. 53.

[14] See the judicial criticism of this practice by English police forces in *R. v. Lemsatef* [1977] 1 W.L.R. 812 and *R. v. Houghton* 68 Cr. App. Rep. 197.

procedures governing arrest and detention. These only begin to take effect once he has been arrested. Nevertheless, there may come a point where the individual's voluntary attendance at the Garda station is converted into detention. This will happen once a member of the Garda Síochána makes up his or her mind to detain the individual should he attempt to leave. Unless he is lawfully arrested at that point his continued detention will be unlawful. The matter was first seriously considered in *Dunne v. Clinton*.[15]

Detention Short of Arrest

4–06
In that case the plaintiffs had been suspected of theft. They had gone voluntarily to the Garda station around midnight to assist the police with their enquiries into the theft. At 4.30 a.m. the following morning they were still there when they were told by a Garda sergeant that they were "detained." They were not brought before a peace commissioner until the following night. In the course of their civil action for false imprisonment and trespass to the person, the defendant Garda chief superintendent testified that the plaintiffs had not been arrested on any charge, but had been detained while he sought further evidence to justify preferring charges against them. This notion of a police power to detain an individual, short of arrest, for the purpose of facilitating the police investigation into a criminal offence was firmly rebuffed by Hanna J. in the High Court in the following terms:

> "The first question that arises is whether this detention is something different from arrest or imprisonment. In law there can be no half-way house between the liberty of the subject, unfettered by restraint, and an arrest. If a person under suspicion voluntarily agrees to go to a police station to be questioned, his liberty is not interfered with, as he can change his mind at any time. If, having been examined, he is asked and voluntarily agrees to remain in the barracks until some investigation is made, he is still a free subject, and can leave at any time. But the practice has grown up of 'detention' as distinct from arrest. It is, in effect, keeping a suspect in custody . . . without making a definite charge against him . . . there [can] be no such thing as notional liberty, this so-called detention amounts to arrest, and the suspect has in law been arrested and in custody during the period of his detention."[16]

The *Dunne v. Clinton* case did not actually address the issue of how, or at what point, an individual's voluntary attendance at a Garda station could develop into his unlawful detention. Hanna J. was of the opinion that the plaintiffs had in fact been lawfully arrested.[17] Their detention became unlawful only because of the failure to bring them before a peace commissioner as soon as was reasonably possible. In other words a delay in bringing a lawfully arrested suspect before a peace commissioner could not be justified by the Garda desire for more time to gather further evidence against the suspect. There is no police power at common law to detain for such a purpose.

---

[15] [1930] I.R. 366.

[16] [1930] I.R. 366 at 372. Cited with approval by O'Higgins C.J. in *People v. Walsh* [1980] I.R. 294 at 302.

[17] It is not clear from Hanna J.'s judgment when he felt the arrest was effected. Presumably, he had in mind 4.30 a.m. of the second day.

De Facto Arrest

In *People v. O'Loughlin*[18] the Supreme Court had to consider whether the **4–07** defendant, who had gone voluntarily to the garda station, could be described as being under arrest while at the Garda station, even though he had not been formally arrested. He had gone to the Garda station to explain his possession of a muck spreader which he claimed he had bought from a dealer. He remained at the station while his story was checked out with the dealer. At 2 p.m. he was informed that the dealer denied selling him the muck-spreader. He remained at the station because gardaí from another station wished to question him about other offences. He was later taken to that other station and questioned at length. At 9.30 p.m. he agreed to tell the truth about the muck spreader. Only after he had made a statement, at about 10 p.m., was he formally arrested and charged.

At his trial the defendant argued that his statement must be excluded as it was given during a period of unlawful detention which commenced at 2 p.m.. The basis of his argument was that he was not free to leave from that point onwards and, therefore, was under *de facto* arrest. He argued further that the arrest was unlawful as the procedural formalities of a lawful arrest (see below, para 4–47 *et seq.*) had not been followed. On the basis of the evidence presented, O'Higgins C.J. found that the defendant would not have been permitted to leave the station, had he attempted to do so, after the gardaí had established that the dealer would not confirm his story. Accordingly, he should have been formally arrested and brought before a peace commissioner at that point. The Garda failure to adopt that course rendered the defendant's detention unlawful from 2 p.m. O'Higgins C.J. explained the matter thus:

> "Had what ought to have been done in this respect been done, the applicant would have been brought before a Peace Commissioner and would have been accorded his rights to bail. Instead, he was not either formally arrested or charged . . . [In the absence of specific statutory authority to the contrary], there is no procedure under our law whereby a person may be held in a Garda station without charge. In particular, our law does not contemplate or permit the holding of a person for questioning. It makes no difference whether the offence for which he is so held is an entirely separate matter to the one with which he is finally charged. 'Holding for questioning' and 'taking into custody' and 'detaining' are merely different ways of describing the act of depriving a man of his liberty. To do so without lawful authority is an open defiance of Article 40, s.4, sub-s.1 of the Constitution."[19]

It follows from the *O'Loughlin* case that where a person has come to a Garda **4–08** station voluntarily, he must be formally arrested as soon as a member of the Garda Síochána makes up his or her mind to detain him. Failure to do so will render any subsequent detention in the station unlawful. Significantly, it would appear that it is not necessary for the suspect actually to attempt to leave, nor even to be aware that he is not free to leave.

---

[18] [1979] I.R. 85.
[19] [1979] I.R. 85 at 91.

A person who goes voluntarily to the Garda station to assist the gardaí with their inquiries could also find himself being unlawfully detained even where the gardaí have not made up their minds to detain him. This could happen where the nature of the questions put to the person suggests that he might well be a suspect. In this situation an onus is placed on the gardaí to inform the suspect that he is free to leave at any time, unless of course he is actually arrested.[20] A failure to inform the suspect will render his detention unlawful if he actually believes that he is not free to leave. In *People (DPP) v. Coffey*,[21] for example, the defendant drove to a Garda station voluntarily to assist the gardaí with their inquiries about a murder. He answered questions from 3 p.m. to 6.30 p.m. at which point he was told that the gardaí did not believe his account of his movements at the critical time. In the Central Criminal Court, Hamilton J. held that the defendant became a suspect at that point and, as such, should have been reminded that he was free to leave if he so wished. This failure to inform him of his rights rendered his detention unlawful. Significantly, Hamilton J. considered it irrelevant that the defendant had not asked to leave and that the gardaí would have allowed him to leave had he so asked. The onus is on the State to prove beyond a reasonable doubt that the suspect was fully aware of his rights.

E. Powers of Arrest

1. Overview

4–09
The detention of a suspect in the course of a criminal investigation is normally preceded by a formal arrest. If, however, the "arrest" is not based on an appropriate power conferred by law, or if it is not effected in the manner prescribed by law, the ensuing detention will be unlawful. It is necessary, therefore, to identify the range of arrest powers conferred by law and the procedures governing the lawful exercise of these powers.

In Ireland powers of arrest are to be found both at common law and in a large number of diverse statutory provisions. While the bulk of the latter are laid down in Acts of the Oireachtas, there are still some significant examples to be found in pre-1922 legislation. There are even a few hidden away in statutory orders.[22] Some of these powers of arrest have a very broad scope, permitting arrest on suspicion of any one of a range of disparate offences. Some are much more narrowly circumscribed, being confined to a specific criminal offence, or a specifically defined class of offences. The remainder, few in number, are not tied to suspicion of criminal activity at all. Another general feature worth noting about these powers is that for the most part they are exercisable only

---

[20] *People v. Lynch* [1982] I.R. 64.
[21] [1987] I.L.R.M. 727.
[22] See, *e.g.* art.17 of the Aliens Order 1946; considered in *Minister for Justice (at the suit of Detective Garda Brendan Clarke) v. Wang Zhu Jie* [1991] I.L.R.M. 823. Note that the prosecution for alleged breaches of the Aliens Act 1935 and the Aliens Order 1946 ultimately failed in this case on the ground that the statutory instrument in question had not been proved.

by a member of the Garda Síochána. Having said that, there are a few very important powers which can be exercised by any citizen, and some which are exercisable by certain public officials such as customs and excise officers.[23]

Powers of arrest can be classified into those exercisable with a warrant and those exercisable without a warrant. The latter are referred to as powers of summary arrest, signifying the fact that the arresting officer can effect an instant arrest on the spot. To effect an arrest under warrant the arresting officer must have secured prior permission (a warrant) from the appropriate authority. Since most arrests are effected summarily, the following analysis is approached primarily from the viewpoint of a summary arrest. Any variations applicable to arrests under warrant are dealt with under a separate heading below.

2. Arrest at Common Law

Overview

At common law, any person had a power to arrest anyone whom he or she saw committing or attempting to commit a felony or treason in his presence.[24] A member of the Garda Síochána was probably under a duty to effect an arrest in this instance.[25] Where a felony or treason had actually been committed a citizen also had the power to arrest any person whom he or she reasonably suspected of having committed it. A member of the Garda Síochána enjoyed a wider common law power of arrest for felony and treason than that attaching to the ordinary citizen. He had the power to arrest a person where he reasonably suspected that person to have committed felony or treason. It was not necessary that the felony or treason should actually have been committed. A member could also have arrested anyone whom he reasonably suspected of being about to commit treason or felony.[26]

4–10

These powers of summary arrest have been impliedly repealed by the abolition of the distinction between felony and misdemeanour effected by the Criminal Law Act 1997.[27] Indeed, that Act has introduced some broad powers of arrest which appear very similar in definition and scope to those previously applicable in respect of felony at common law. It does not follow, however, that all powers of summary arrest are now based on statute. The common law has always recognised a power of summary arrest for breach of the peace, and this would appear to be unaffected by the 1997 Act.

---

23 Ryan and Magee provide a very useful list of statutory powers of arrest without a warrant, specifying who may exercise the power in each case; Ryan and Magee, *The Irish Criminal Process* (Mercier Press, Dublin, 1983), at Appendix G.

24 2 Hale 75; 2 Hawk. c.12 ss.1, 7. In its original formulation this power is described as a duty. Nowadays it is unlikely that an ordinary citizen would be prosecuted for a failure to effect an arrest in these circumstances.

25 See 2 Hawk., c.12, s.1. In *R. v. Dytham* [1979] 3 All E.R. 641 a constable was convicted of misconduct while acting as an officer of justice for failing to intervene when someone was badly beaten up within his view. The English Court of Appeal upheld his conviction.

26 2 Hawk. c.12, s.19; *Handcock v. Baker* 2 B&P 260. It would appear that the member could detain the person until his intent was presumed to have ceased.

27 A similar change was effected in Britain by the Criminal Law Act 1967 and in Northern Ireland by the Criminal Law Act (Northern Ireland) 1967.

Breach of the Peace

4–11   Both the citizen and a member of the Garda Síochána enjoy a common law power of arrest for breach of the peace. Either may arrest any person who has committed or who is committing a breach of the peace in his or her presence.[28] Equally, either may arrest any person whom he or she reasonably believes is going to commit a breach of the peace in the immediate future.[29] Normally, arrest will not be an option if the breach has terminated.[30] However, the citizen or the member may arrest if he or she reasonably believes that a renewal of the breach is threatened.[31] The member may even effect an arrest after termination if he or she is in hot pursuit of the offender.[32] A member may also call upon any member of the public for assistance where a breach of the peace occurs. In this event the citizen will normally be under a legal obligation to assist the member in restoring the peace.[33]

Inevitably, the scope of the power to arrest for breach of the peace is dictated largely by the range of behaviour that comes under the heading of breach of the peace. Unfortunately, there is no precise definition of this offence.[34] Broadly speaking it encompasses behaviour which occasions or threatens harm to a person or, in his presence, to his property.[35] Accordingly, it must include fighting, riot, affray and unlawful assembly. It might also include individual instances of assault or battery. While the use of threatening or abusive language may not be sufficient in itself to constitute a breach of the peace, it may amount to behaviour from which a breach is anticipated.[36] It is not entirely clear whether a breach of the peace can be committed in circumstances where the only people present are the person creating the disturbance and a member of the Garda Síochána who does not anticipate any violence from the person. The argument for saying that there can be no breach of the peace in these circumstances rests on the premise that the only person who might be provoked into violence by the disturbance is the member, and he or she is sworn to keep the peace. If, however, the member is assaulted then he or she automatically acquires the power to arrest. It is worth noting that the power to arrest for breach of the peace is now of less importance to gardaí given the powers now available to them under the Criminal Justice (Public Order) Act 1994.

---

[28]   *R. v. Howell* [1981] 3 All E.R. 383; *Timothy v. Simpson* (1835) 1 Cr.M. & R. 757; *Cook v. Nethercote* (1835) 6 C & P 741.

[29]   *R. v. Howell* [1981] 3 All E.R. 383; *Leigh v. Cole* (1853) 6 Cox CC 329.

[30]   This does not preclude a valid arrest made immediately after a breach of the peace; *Lewis v. Arnold* (1830) 4 C & P 354.

[31]   *R v. Howell* [1981] 3 All E.R. 383; *Price v. Seeley* (1843) 10 Cl & F 28; *Baynes v. Brewster* (1841) 2 Q.B. 375.

[32]   *R v. Light* (1857) Dears & B 332; *R v. Walker* (1854) Dears CC 358.

[33]   *Albert v. Lavin* [1982] A.C. 546, [1981] 3 All E.R. 878.

[34]   See Williams, "Arrest for Breach of the Peace" [1954] Crim L.R. 578.

[35]   *R v. Howell* [1982] Q.B. 416, [1981] 3 All E.R. 383.

[36]   *Simcock v. Rhodes* (1977) 66 Cr. App. Rep. 192.

3. Arrest without Warrant under Statute

Most current powers of summary arrest are either explicitly created by statute **4–12**
or defined by statute. The relevant provisions have been enacted in a
piecemeal fashion over several hundred years. Many of these powers were
introduced to deal with specific individual offences. Indeed, quite often the
enactment conferring the power of arrest will also create or define the offence
in question. Other statutory provisions introduce more general powers of
arrest covering a whole class of offences or, indeed, a range of disparate
offences. It is difficult, therefore, to identify characteristics common to all.
Most, but by no means all, are exercisable only by a member of the Garda
Síochána.[37] It is also true to say that most are triggered by a reasonable belief
that a relevant offence has been committed or is being committed. Beyond
that, however, it is not possible to generalise. Some, such as section 30 of the
Offences against the State Act 1939, are triggered by a mere suspicion.[38]
Some extend to a reasonable belief that an offence is about to be committed.[39]
Some are available where the person in question has failed to comply with a
direction issued by a member of the Garda Síochána.[40] Others are available
where a person has committed a specified offence on a public road or street
and his name and address is unknown or cannot be ascertained.[41] Ultimately,
the scope of any of these powers can be determined only by an examination
of the relevant statutory provisions.

Examples of specific offences or classes of offence which are the subject of **4–13**
associated statutory arrest powers include: road traffic,[42] misuse of drugs,[43]
organised crime,[44] official secrets,[45] offences against the State,[46] defence,[47]
aliens,[48] casual trading,[49] wildlife, fauna and flora,[49a] air transport,[50] animals,[51]

---

[37] Ryan and Magee point out that it was quite common in the nineteenth century for statutory powers
of arrest to be conferred on all citizens, while those created in the latter half of the twentieth
century are more likely to be confined to members of the Garda Síochána, with some being
conferred on specifically authorised persons or officials; Ryan and Magee, *op. cit.*, above, n.23, at
pp. 97–98. See also their table of statutory powers of arrest without warrant at Appendix G.

[38] Although the actual wording of the provision does not specifically state that the suspicion should
be based on reasonable grounds, the courts will require the presence of information upon which a
reasonable person could form a suspicion.

[39] Criminal Law (Jurisdiction) Act 1976, s.19; Official Secrets Act 1963, s.15; Offences against the
State Act 1939, s.30.

[40] Criminal Justice (Public Order) Act 1994, ss.8(1) and 24.

[41] Summary Jurisdiction (Ireland) Act 1861, s.14(2).

[42] Road Traffic Act 1961, ss.19, 40(4), 49(4), 50(6), 51(4), 53(6), 55(4), 69, 82, 107(1), 107(2),
112(6) and 113(3). Road Traffic (Amendment) Act 1968, ss.16, 56 and 59. Road Traffic
(Amendment) Act 1978, ss.12, 15(3), 16(4), and 17(3).

[43] Misuse of Drugs Act 1977, s.25.

[44] Criminal Assets Bureau Act 1996, s.16.

[45] Official Secrets Acts 1963, ss.15 and 16(4).

[46] Offences Against the State Act 1939, s.29(3) as amended by Criminal Law Act 1976, s.5. Offences
Against the State (Amendment) Act 1940, s.4.

[47] Defence Act 1954, ss.233(4), 251(1), 268(4) and 284.

[48] Aliens Order 1946.

[49] Casual Trading Act 1995, s.10(5) and 11.

[49a] Wildlife Act 1976 s.72(2A), as amended by Wildlife (Amendment) Act 2000, s.65.

[50] Air Navigation and Transport Act 1950, s.19(1). Air Navigation and Transport Act 1973, ss.7 and
11(5). Air Navigation and Transport Act 1975, s.4.

[51] Protection of Animals Act 1911, s.12(1). Diseases of Animals Act 1966, s.46(2) & (3). Control of
Horses Act 1996, s.4.

pawnbroking,[52] gaming,[53] street collections,[54] fisheries,[55] intoxicating liquor,[56] firearms,[57] electoral abuses,[58] larceny,[59] sexual offences,[60] labour,[61] children,[62] family,[63] indecency,[64] customs,[65] prisoners,[66] public order,[67] malicious damage,[68] coinage,[69] and vagrancy.[70]

Some of the more broad-based statutory powers extend to any indictable offence committed in certain circumstances. The Prevention of Offences Act 1851, for example, empowers any person to arrest anyone found committing any indictable offence by night.[71] Since not all indictable offences were felonies, this is broader than the common law power to arrest for felony. Others extend to a whole range of disparate offences listed in the Act creating the power. In some instances the offences covered by a particular power may be loosely classified under a general heading, such as improving the quality of life on the streets in urban areas. The Towns Improvement (Ireland) Act 1854, for example, permits a member of the Garda Síochána to arrest anyone engaging in any of the following in his or her view: exposing animals for sale or show in unauthorised places, permitting ferocious dogs to go unmuzzled, leading animals on the footpath, loitering for the purpose of prostitution, indecent exposure, offering for sale indecent books, etc., throwing stones, making bonfires, wantonly ringing doorbells, beating carpets before 9 a.m., throwing rubbish from houses, hanging a clothes line across a street, to mention only some.[72] In other cases the only connection binding the offences are that they are associated with terrorism. The leading examples here are to be found in the Offences Against the State Act 1939 and the Criminal Law (Jurisdiction) Act 1976.[73] The former is so important in practice that it deserves more detailed attention. First, however, it is necessary to expand upon the current statutory formulation of the former common law powers of arrest for felony and treason.

---

[52] Pawnbrokers Act 1964, ss.35–37.
[53] Street Betting Act 1906, s.1(2). Betting Act 1931, s.25(3). Gaming and Lotteries Act 1956, s.40.
[54] Street and House to House Collections Act 1962, s.24(2).
[55] Fisheries Consolidation Act 1959, s.233(1)(g). Foyle Fisheries Act 1952, s.62.
[56] Illicit Distillation (Ireland) Act 1831, ss.19, 25 and 30. Licensing Act 1872, s.12. Intoxicating Liquor Act 1927, s.22(2).
[57] Firearms Act 1925, s.22(3).
[58] Electoral Act 1923, s.32. Prevention of Electoral Abuses Act 1923, s.25.
[59] Larceny Act 1861, ss.103–104. Larceny Act 1916, s.41(1)–(3). Criminal Justice Act 1951, s.13(1).
[60] Criminal Law (Amendment) Act 1912, s.1. Criminal Law (Sexual Offences) Act 1993 and Sexual Offences (Jurisdiction) Act 1996, s.10(5).
[61] Summary Jurisdiction (Ireland) Act 1908, s.8.
[62] Summary Jurisdiction (Ireland) Act 1908, s.9. Children Act 2001, s.207(10), s.215(1) and s.254.
[63] Domestic Violence Act 1996, s.8.
[64] Indecent Advertisements Act 1889, s.6.
[65] Customs Consolidation Act 1876, s.186.
[66] Penal Servitude Act 1864, s.6. Offences Against the State Act 1939, s.32.
[67] Licensing (Ireland) Act 1836, s.12. Prohibition of Forcible Entry and Occupation Act 1971, s.9; Criminal Justice (Public Order) Act 1994, s.24.
[68] Criminal Damage Act 1861, s.12.
[69] Coinage Offences Act 1861, s.31
[70] Vagrancy Act 1847, s.4.
[71] Prevention of Offences Act 1851, s.11. Night is defined as from 9 p.m. to 6 a.m..
[72] Towns Improvement (Ireland) Act 1854, s.72, as extended to every town having Commissioners by the Local Government (Ireland) Act 1898, s.41.
[73] The Criminal Law (Jurisdiction) Act 1976, s.19 empowers a member of the Garda Síochána to

4. Criminal Law Act 1997, section 4

Arrestable Offence

4–14

Section 4 of the Criminal Law Act 1997 actually confers two distinct powers of arrest on any person and a third power on a member of the Garda Síochána alone. They all relate to the commission of an "arrestable offence" which is defined in the Act as:

> " . . . an offence for which a person of full capacity and not previously convicted may, under or by virtue of any enactment, be punished by imprisonment for a term of five years or by a more serious penalty and includes an attempt to commit any such offence."[74]

The concept of an "arrestable offence" is already known to Irish law, having first been introduced in the context of the power to detain arrested suspects in police custody under the Criminal Justice Act 1984 (see chapter 5). Clearly it is aimed at covering all serious criminal offences, whether they were classified previously as felonies or misdemeanours. The key issue is whether the offence is punishable by imprisonment for a term of five years or a more serious penalty. Where an offence can be so punished, it does not matter that the circumstances surrounding its commission in a particular case are relatively trivial to the extent that it would almost certainly not attract a sentence of imprisonment, let alone imprisonment for a term of at least five years.

It is also worth noting that there is no guidance on what may constitute a penalty more serious than imprisonment for a term of five years. Clearly, imprisonment for a term in excess of five years will qualify. Less certain, however, is a penalty which combines a lesser term of imprisonment with another primary or secondary punishment.

It follows that the powers of arrest defined by section 4 are very broad in terms of the range of offences which they cover. Nevertheless, it is important to check in each individual case that the offence for which a suspect is arrested under section 4 actually carries a possible punishment of imprisonment for a term of five years or a more serious penalty. If it does not, the arrest will be unlawful unless, of course, the person effecting it is acting under some other lawful power.

Offences in the Course of Commission

4–15

Under section 4(1) any person, including a member of the Garda Síochána, "may arrest without warrant anyone who is or whom he or she, with reasonable cause, suspects to be in the act of committing an arrestable offence."[75]

---

arrest where there is reasonable cause to suspect that the person concerned is committing, has committed or is about to commit an offence under s.2 of the Act, or has committed an offence under s.3. Section 2 refers to certain offences committed in Northern Ireland, while s.3 concerns escape from custody in Northern Ireland.

[74] Criminal Law Act 1997, s.2(1). The offence of assault contrary to s.2(1)(b) of the Non-fatal Offences against the Person Act 1997 does not satisfy this definition and there is no other power of arrest available for this offence; see *DPP v. Bradley,* unreported, High Court, December 9, 1999.

[75] Criminal Law Act 1997, s.4(1).

For this power to be available it is not essential that the person arrested was actually committing an arrestable offence. It will suffice that the person making the arrest (arrestor) suspects, with reasonable cause, that the person concerned is committing an arrestable offence. It will not be sufficient, however, that the arrestor merely suspects that an offence has been committed. In effect it is a power to arrest an offender caught in the act, or who is acting in a manner which gives reasonable cause to believe that he is actually committing an arrestable offence. If the offence has been completed then this power of arrest is not available. Less certain is the situation where the individual has embarked on a series of actions which will ultimately result in the commission of an arrestable offence. Since an arrestable offence includes an attempt, it follows that the section 4(1) power covers the arrest of someone who is reasonably suspected of attempting to commit the offence. It would be difficult to argue, however, that "being in the act of committing an arrestable offence" in the context of section 4 would be satisfied by someone who had not got beyond (or who was not suspected of having got beyond) preparatory acts which fell short of what would be necessary for an attempt.

Offences Already Committed

4–16   Section 4(2) deals with the situation where the offence has already been committed. It states:

> " . . . where an arrestable offence has been committed, any person may arrest without warrant anyone who is or whom he or she, with reasonable cause, suspects to be guilty of the offence."

In this case the power will be available when, but only when, the offence has *actually* been committed.[76] It will not be sufficient, therefore, that the arrestor reasonably suspects that an offence has been committed when in fact the offence has not been committed at all. It differs here from section 4(1) in that the latter will be available so long as there is reasonable cause to believe that the person arrested was in the act of committing the offence. The arrest under section 4(1) will not be rendered unlawful simply because the person arrested was not *actually* in the act of committing an arrestable offence. In the case of section 4(2), if an arrestable offence has actually been committed, the legality of the subsequent arrest will not be impaired solely because the wrong person is arrested, so long as the arrestor had reasonable cause to suspect that person to be guilty of the offence. If, however, the arrestable offence has not been committed, then the arrest will be unlawful even if there was reasonable cause to believe that the person arrested had committed an arrestable offence.

The combination of section 4(1) and 4(2) does not necessarily mean that a mistaken arrest will be lawful so long as there was reasonable cause to suspect the person concerned. A store detective, for example, will not necessarily be protected where he mistakenly arrests someone whom he reasonably suspects of shop lifting. If the offence has actually been committed and he merely

---

[76]   See, *Walter v. W H Smith & Son Ltd.* [1914] 1 K.B. 595; *Beckwith v. Philby* (1827) 6 B & C 635.

arrests the wrong person he will be protected so long as he has reasonable cause to suspect the person concerned. If, however, the offence has not been committed he will be protected only if he effects the arrest when he reasonably suspects that the individual is in the act of committing the offence. This, of course, will be very difficult to satisfy given that the evidence needed to satisfy a reasonable suspicion of shoplifting usually consists of actions which are synonymous with the completion of the offence itself.

Citizen's Arrest

Where either of the arrest powers in section 4(1) and (2) are exercised by a person other than a member of the Garda Síochána, two further qualifications apply. First, the power can be exercised only if the arrestor:

4–17

> " . . . with reasonable cause, suspects that the person to be arrested by him or her would otherwise attempt to avoid, or is avoiding, arrest by a member of the Garda Síochána."

This has the potential to restrict the scope of these powers in the hands of the ordinary citizen. On one interpretation, it would not be sufficient in itself that the suspect will probably have left the scene by the time the gardaí will arrive. There would actually have to be reason to believe that the suspect was either on the run from the gardaí or would actively attempt to avoid arrest by the gardaí. While this would not normally pose any difficulty in the case of a burglar, it may well lead to some uncertainty in the case of a casual shoplifter. It is at least arguable, for example, that the arrestor should first advise the shoplifter that the gardaí have been called and request him to await their arrival. Only if the shoplifter refuses to co-operate should an arrest be effected.

The second qualification is that once an arrest has been effected by the ordinary citizen he or she must transfer the person arrested into the custody of the Garda Síochána as soon as possible. This, of course, was already the position with respect to the citizen's common law power of arrest.[77]

Exclusive Garda Powers

A member of the Garda Síochána alone enjoys the third power of arrest which is defined in section 4(3) as follows:

4–18

> "Where a member of the Garda Síochána, with reasonable cause, suspects that an arrestable offence has been committed, he or she may arrest, without warrant anyone whom the member, with reasonable cause, suspects to be guilty of the offence."

In this case the offence need not actually have been committed, so long as the member suspects, with reasonable cause, that it has been committed. It is worth noting in this context that an arrestable offence includes an attempt to commit an arrestable offence. The person arrested need not actually be guilty

---

[77]   1 Hale 589.

of the offence, so long as the member suspects with reasonable cause that he is guilty. It follows that the arrest power entrusted to members of the Garda Síochána alone is broader than the other two powers which are available to gardaí and citizen alike.

Being About to Commit an Offence

None of the arrest powers in section 4 extend specifically to the situation where a person is merely suspected, with reasonable cause, of being about to commit an arrestable offence. Admittedly, the definition of an arrestable offence includes an attempt to commit that offence. In this sense, therefore, it may be possible to effect an arrest under section 4(1) even though the suspect has not quite managed to complete the commission of the substantive offence. Given the definition of an attempt in criminal law, however, this power of arrest is unlikely to extend beyond the situation of a person being on the point of committing a criminal offence. It would not, for example, cover the arrest of a suspect for the robbery of a bank when he was merely sitting in a vehicle outside the bank waiting for the appropriate opportunity.

Reasonable Cause

It is worth noting that in all of the section 4 arrest powers there must be reasonable cause for the requisite suspicion. This is a standard requirement for most powers of arrest. Accordingly, it is discussed later in the chapter (see below para 4–39 *et seq.*).

5. Section 30 of the Offences Against the State Act 1939

Overview

4–19   The power of arrest under section 30 of the Offences Against the State Act 1939 deserves detailed comment, not least because it represents a more serious infringement of the liberty of the individual than that associated with most of the other powers of arrest. It has also been the subject of considerable judicial analysis. This, in turn, is a reflection of its extensive use over the past 30 years.

Section 30(1) reads:

> "A member of the Garda Síochána (if he is not in uniform on production of his identification card if demanded) may without warrant . . . arrest any person, . . . whom he suspects of having committed or being about to commit or being or having been concerned in the commission of an offence under any section or subsection of this Act or an offence which is for the time being a scheduled offence for the purposes of Part V of this Act or whom he suspects of carrying a document relating to the commission or intended commission of any such offence as aforesaid or whom he suspects of being in possession of information relating to the commission or intended commission of any such offence as aforesaid."

4–20   In order to exercise this power a member of the Garda Síochána may stop and search, using force if necessary, any vehicle or any ship, boat or other vessel which he suspects to contain a person liable to such arrest.[78] Any person arrested under this section may be detained without charge for a period of up to 24 hours which may be extended by a further 24 hours[79] followed by a further, judicially extended, period of 24 hours.[79a] By virtue of section 30(5) of the Act, a member of the Garda Síochána may do all or any of the following things in respect of the person while detained under this provision:

"(a) demand of such person his name and address;
(b) search such person or cause him to be searched;
(c) photograph such person or cause him to be photographed; and
(d) take, or cause to be taken, the fingerprints of such person."

If the person (or any other person) obstructs or impedes a member of the Garda Síochána in the exercise of this power of arrest, or the detention or in doing of any of the things permitted by section 30(5), he shall be guilty of an offence punishable on summary conviction by imprisonment for a term not exceeding six months.[80] A similar penalty applies where, on being asked, the arrested person fails or refuses to give his name and address or gives a false or misleading name or address.

The provisions on detention and on the examination of the arrested person are considered more fully in other chapters. The discussion here is confined primarily to the actual power of arrest itself. Nevertheless, it is important to highlight two distinctive features of the section 30 power at the outset. First, a person arrested under section 30 can be detained without charge in a Garda station for up to 24 hours.[81] This period can be extended for a further 24 hours by a chief superintendent. It follows that there is no obligation to bring a person arrested under section 30 before a judicial authority as soon as is reasonably possible. It is only if the suspect is to be detained for a futher period of 24 hours or charged that he must be brought before a judicial authority. The second point, which follows from the first, is that section 30 can be used as a means of expediting the investigation of a crime. In the words of Walsh J.: **4-21**

"The object of the powers given by s.30 is not to permit the arrest of people simply for the purpose of subjecting them to questioning. Rather is it for the purpose of investigating the commission or suspected commission of a crime by the person already arrested and to enable that investigation to be carried on without the possibility of obstruction or other interference which might occur if the suspected person were not under arrest."[82]

Clearly, section 30 is a more powerful instrument for criminal detection than most other powers of arrest.

---

[78] Offences against the State Act 1939, s.30(2).
[79] *ibid.* s.30(3).
[79a] Offences against the State Act 1939, s.30(4A)–(4C), as inserted by Offences against the State (Amendment) Act 1998, s.10.
[80] *ibid*, s.30(6).
[81] *ibid.* s.30(3).
[82] *People (DPP) v. Quilligan* [1986] I.R. 495 at 509.

Offences Created by the Acts

4–22   The power of arrest conferred by section 30(1) relates generally to "an offence under any section or sub-section of [the] Act or an offence which is for the time being a scheduled offence for the purposes of Part V of [the] Act." To understand this fully it needs to be pointed out that the Act is divided into six Parts. The first four Parts are permanently in force. Part V, which deals with the establishment of special criminal courts, comes into force only when the government makes and publishes the appropriate proclamation prescribed in the Act.[83] It remains in force until such time as the Government makes and publishes a proclamation declaring that it shall cease to be in force.[84] Similar provisions apply to Part VI which deals with internment.[85]

4–23   The permanent provisions of the 1939 Act create a number of offences all of which are concerned in one way or another with the security of the State and its institutions against subversion. Broadly speaking they include: usurpation of the functions of government;[86] obstruction of the government;[87] obstruction of the President;[88] interference with military or other employees of the State;[89] the printing, distribution or possession of incriminating, treasonable or seditious documents;[90] failure to print the name and address of the printer on a document printed for reward;[91] unauthorised military exercises;[92] secret societies in the army or the Garda Síochána;[93] the administration of unlawful oaths;[94] offences associated with unlawful organisations;[95] public meetings in the vicinity of the Oireachtas;[96] the obstruction of a member of the Garda Síochána acting under the authority of a search warrant issued under section 29;[97] obstruction of a member of the Garda Síochána in the exercise of his powers to stop, search, question and arrest under section 30;[98] and aiding or abetting the escape of a person detained under the Act.[99]

The Offences against the State (Amendment) Act 1998 creates a number of additional offences, all of which are amenable to arrest under section 30 of the 1939 Act. These include: directing an unlawful organisation;[99a] possession of

---

[83]   Offences against the State Act, 1939, s.35(2).
[84]   *ibid.* s.35(3)
[85]   *ibid.* s.54.
[86]   *ibid.* s.6.
[87]   *ibid.* s.7.
[88]   *ibid.* s.8.
[89]   *ibid.* s.9.
[90]   *ibid.* ss.10, 12 and 26. Any person who is in unlawful possession of any such document and refuses to deliver it to a member of the Garda Síochána on request is also guilty of an offence.
[91]   *ibid.* ss.13 and 14.
[92]   *ibid.* s.15.
[93]   *ibid.* s.16.
[94]   *ibid.* s.17.
[95]   *ibid.* ss.18–25 and 27.
[96]   *ibid.* s.28.
[97]   *ibid.* s.29(5).
[98]   *ibid.* s.30(6).
[99]   *ibid.* s.32.
[99a] Offences against the State (Amendment) Act 1998, s.6.

articles for purposes connected with certain offences;[99b] unlawful collection of information;[99c] withholding information;[99d] and training persons in the use of firearms.[99e]

Scheduled Offences

The power of arrest under section 30(1) of the 1939 Act is always available   **4–24**
for any of these offences. In practice, however, its most common application over the past 30 years has been with respect to those offences which are scheduled for the purposes of Part V of the Act. Offences can be scheduled for the purposes of Part V only if there is in force a government proclamation bringing Part V into effect. Such a proclamation may be issued:

> "If and whenever and so often as the Government is satisfied that the ordinary courts are inadequate to secure the effective administration of justice and the preservation of public peace and order and that it is necessary that this Part of this Act should come into force . . . "[100]

The primary purpose of issuing a proclamation under this provision is to permit the establishment of a special criminal court.[101] Accordingly, it is discussed more fully in chapter 20. For present purposes the significance of the proclamation is that, while it is in force, the government may by order declare that offences of any particular class or kind or under any particular enactment shall be scheduled offences.[102] Before exercising the scheduling power the government must be satisfied that the ordinary courts are inadequate to secure the effective administration of justice and the preservation of public peace and order in relation to the offences covered by the scheduling order. A person charged with a scheduled offence will normally be tried in the special criminal court established under Part V.[103] Equally, a person suspected of committing, having committed, being about to commit or having been concerned in the commission of a scheduled offence is liable to arrest under section 30(1) of the 1939 Act. It is vital, therefore, to know precisely which offences have been scheduled under Part V.

Part V of the 1939 Act has been in force continuously since 1972, thereby   **4–25**
enabling the government to declare by order any offence to be a "scheduled offence" for the purposes of Part V.[103a] Offences currently scheduled pursuant to these provisions are: any offence under the Explosive Substances Act 1883;[103b] any offence under the Firearms Acts 1925–71;[103c] any offence

---

[99b] *ibid.* s.7.
[99c] *ibid.* s.8.
[99d] *ibid.* s.9.
[99e] *ibid.* s.12.
[100] Offences Against the State Act 1939, s.35(2).
[101] *ibid.* s.38(1).
[102] *ibid.* s.36(1).
[103] *ibid.* s.45.
[103a] Offences against the State Act 1939, s.36.
[103b] Offences against the State Act 1939 (Scheduled Offences) Order 1972.
[103c] *ibid.*

under the Offences against the State Act 1939,[103d] and any offence under sections 6-9 and section 12 of the Offences against the State (Amendment) Act 1998.[103e] Also scheduled is any offence under the Malicious Damage Act 1861.[103f] However, most of this Act has been repealed and replaced by the Criminal Damage Act 1991. A small number of relatively minor offences survive under the 1861 Act, but it is unlikely that they will feature in practice in prosecutions before the Special Criminal Court. Since no offence has been scheduled by specific reference to the Criminal Damage Act 1991 it must be assumed that offences under this Act are not scheduled for the purposes of the 1939 Act even though some of them would have been scheduled in their previous existence under the Malicious Damage Act 1861. An offence under section 7 of the Conspiracy and Protection of Property Act 1875 was also scheduled.[103g] Section 7 has since been repealed and replaced by section 31 of the Non-fatal Offences against the Person Act 1997. Since an offence under the latter provision has not been specifically scheduled it must follow that they are no longer scheduled. An attempt, conspiracy or incitement to commit any of these offences is also scheduled, as is aiding or abetting the commission of any such offence.[104]

It is worth noting that all of the offences concerned are scheduled by reference to the statutory enactments which created them. In some cases the statutory enactments in question have been amended to include additional offences after the enactments had been scheduled. It would seem reasonable to argue, therefore, that the offences which were added by amendments enacted later in time to the scheduling instruments could not be scheduled offences within the meaning of the 1939 Act. However, this argument was rejected in *State (Daly) v. Delap*[105] with respect to amendments of the Explosives Substances Act 1883 and the Firearms Act 1964 by the Criminal Law (Jurisdiction) Act 1976. Finlay P. (as he then was) explained that the intention of the legislature in inserting the new offences into the existing legislation was clearly to ensure that the new offences would attract all the features and characteristics of an offence under that legislation, including scheduling. It follows that the arrest power under section 30 of the 1939 Act extends to any offences inserted in these enactments after the scheduling order itself was issued.

Extension to Non-subversive Offences

4–26   Perhaps the most striking feature of the scheduling order is the fact that it makes no reference to the context in which the offences are committed or are suspected of having been committed. It simply lists offences by reference to

---

[103d] *ibid.*

[103e] Offences against the State (Amendment) Act 1998, s.14(2).

[103f] Offences against the State Act 1939 (Scheduled Offences) Order 1972.

[103g] Offences against the State Act 1939 (Scheduled Offences)(No.2) Order 1972.

[104]   *ibid.* s.37.

[105]   Unreported, High Court, June 30, 1980 affirmed by the Court of Criminal Appeal in *People (DPP) v. Tuite* (1983) 2 Frewen 175.

the enactments that created them. A literal interpretation of section 36(1) and the scheduling order, therefore, would suggest that the offences are scheduled irrespective of the circumstances in which they are committed or are suspected of being committed. In other words they are scheduled even where they are committed by persons who have no connections with any subversive organisation and in circumstances which have no implications for the security of the State or its institutions or officers. Equally, a literal interpretation would suggest that the offences remain scheduled even when committed in circumstances which bear no relation to the reasons why they were scheduled in the first place. This is of considerable practical significance as many of the offences scheduled under the Act are frequently committed in circumstances which pose no threat to the security of the State and which bear no relation to the factors which prompted the government to issue the proclamation.

Offences under the Firearms Acts, for example, are often committed in contexts of robberies for private gain or personal grudges between private parties. Nevertheless, a literal interpretation would suggest that persons committing a firearms offence in any of these contexts would have committed a scheduled offence. Accordingly, they would be liable to arrest under section 30, despite the fact that the firearms offences were scheduled as part of a concerted effort to combat the activities of an unlawful organisation whose objectives embraced the overthrow of the State.

An alternative interpretation would be to consider the offences under the enactments concerned to be scheduled only if they are committed or suspected of having been committed in circumstances which pose a threat to the security of the State, its institutions or its officers, or which are encompassed by the considerations which prompted the government to issue the proclamation and to schedule the offences in question. This interpretation would appear more consistent with the general contents of the 1939 Act, the background to its enactment and, indeed, the statutory pre-requisites for the exercise of the scheduling power. If this interpretation was adopted, however, it should mean that in the case of a scheduled offence the section 30 arrest power would be available for an offence in some circumstances but not in others.

4–27

This interpretative issue has been considered by the courts, and resolved decisively in favour of the literal interpretation.

The leading case on the matter is *People (DPP) v. Quilligan*.[106] In that case the two defendants had been arrested on suspicion of being involved in a robbery at the home of two elderly brothers. In the course of the robbery one of the brothers received fatal injuries. There was no subversive element to the robbery. The defendants were arrested under section 30 on suspicion of malicious damage (a scheduled offence at the time) which had been caused to a door and some furniture in the course of the robbery. While in police custody they made incriminating statements in response to questioning about

4–28

---

106   [1986] I.R. 495.

the death. Their subsequent challenge to the admissibility of these statements was upheld by the trial judge who considered that their arrest and detention was unlawful as section 30 could be used only in the context of subversive crime. This ruling was reversed on appeal to the Supreme Court which held that the availability of the section 30 power of arrest for scheduled offences was not confined to subversive activities. In the course of his judgement in the Supreme Court Walsh J. reviewed the whole of the 1939 Act and its history and concluded that there was no legislative intention to confine the operation of section 30 to subversive situations. He, and the other judges, were particularly swayed by the fact that the scheduling power in the Act related to "offences of any particular class or kind or under any particular enactment". There was no qualifying provision in the legislation restricting these offences to subversive situations. It follows that section 30 offers a general power of arrest for those offences created by the 1939 Act and those offences which are, for the time being, scheduled under the Act.[107] So long as the offence was created by the Act (or its amendments) or is scheduled pursuant to the Act, the circumstances in which the offence was committed or was suspected to have been committed are irrelevant to the availability of the arrest power.

4–29   The decision in *Quilligan* substantially extends the remit and significance of the arrest power in section 30. Nevertheless, its utility from the Garda perspective was still hampered by the fact that it was confined to a relatively narrow range of offences. Crimes such as rape and murder were excluded despite the fact that the investigation of such serious crimes might be considerably enhanced by the advantages conferred on the Garda Síochána by section 30. In practice, however, the Garda have been quite successful in circumventing this restriction, particularly in the case of murder.[108] Instead of arresting a murder suspect under section 4 of the Criminal Law Act 1997 (previously, the common law), for example, a member of the Garda Síochána might arrest him under section 30 for a scheduled offence committed in the course of the murder (*e.g.* unlawful possession of a firearm). While in detention under section 30 the suspect can be questioned both about the scheduled offence and the murder.

4–30   The legality of this practice has been considered in a number of cases. In *State (Bowes) v. Fitzpatrick*[109] the accused had been arrested under section 30 for malicious damage (a scheduled offence at the time) caused to a knife in the course of a murder. The knife had been damaged through contact with the bone of the victim. Naturally, the gardaí were primarily interested in the investigation of the murder. Finlay P., in the High Court, ruled that the arrest for malicious damage was merely a colourable device to facilitate the interrogation of the defendant on the murder charge. As such, it was not a

---

[107]   The decision in *Quilligan* was applied in *People (DPP) v. Walsh* [1988] I.L.R.M. 137.
[108]   See Walsh, "The Impact of the Antisubversive Laws on Police Powers and Practices in Ireland: The Silent Erosion of Individual Freedom" (1989) 62, 4 *Temple Law Review* 1099 at 1107–1110.
[109]   [1978] I.L.R.M. 195.

lawful exercise of the section 30 power. However, in *People (DPP) v. Walsh*[110] the accused had been arrested under section 30 for malicious damage to a window. The window had been damaged in the course of the robbery of a shop which resulted in the murder of the owner. Once again the gardaí were primarily interested in the investigation of the murder. Nevertheless, it was held by O'Hanlon J. in the Central Criminal Court, and confirmed on appeal by both the Court of Criminal Appeal and the Supreme Court, that the arrest was lawful.[111] *Bowes* was distinguished on the basis that the malicious damage offence in that case was clearly spurious and that the gardaí did not have a genuine interest in pursuing it. In *Walsh*, however, the malicious damage was distinct from the actual murder and could reasonably have been prosecuted as a separate offence. Despite the fact that the monetary value of the damage was relatively trivial, the circumstances in which it was caused were very serious. The court concluded, therefore, that the gardaí had a genuine interest in pursuing the crime and that the arrest under section 30 was lawful. Furthermore, the court ruled that there was nothing to prevent the gardaí from questioning the suspect about offences other than that for which he was arrested under section 30 so long as the arrest itself was bona fide.[112]

The latest reported case in which this issue has been considered is *People* **4–31** *(DPP) v. Howley*[113] where the defendant had been arrested on suspicion of cattle-maiming (a scheduled offence at the time) and was subsequently questioned primarily about a murder. This case differed from *Walsh* and *Bowes* to the extent that the cattle-maiming was not connected with the murder. The Supreme Court, however, ruled that that would not necessarily render the section 30 arrest unlawful. So long as a scheduled offence had been committed and the gardaí were genuinely interested in investigating it, they could arrest someone on suspicion of that offence even though they were primarily interested in questioning that person about an unrelated offence which was otherwise beyond the reach of section 30. Walsh J. took the opportunity to summarise the effect of the cases as follows:

> " . . . what the cases established is that when an arrest for a scheduled offence is effected under s.30 of the Offences Against the State Act 1939, not only must the arresting Garda have the necessary reasonable suspicion concerning the particular offence in question, but that in fact there must be a genuine desire and intent to pursue the investigation of that offence or suspected offence and that the arrest must not simply be a colourable device to enable a person to be detained in pursuit of some other alleged offence. The decisions do not provide any basis for asserting that where a person has been genuinely arrested for the purpose of investigating a scheduled offence, and when the arrest is not otherwise flawed, it must be established that there is a link

---

[110] [1988] I.L.R.M. 137.
[111] See also, *People v. Towson* [1978] I.L.R.M. 122; *People (DPP) v. Quilligan* [1986] I.R. 495.
[112] See also, *People v. Kelly* [1983] I.L.R.M. 271; *People (DPP) v. Quilligan* [1986] I.R. 495; *People (DPP) v. Howley* [1989] I.L.R.M. 629.
[113] [1989] I.L.R.M. 629. See also, *Moloney v. Member in charge of Terenure Garda Station* [2002] 2 I.L.R.M. 149, where the matter arose indirectly.

between the two offences to maintain the lawfulness of the detention if in the course of the detention the detained person is questioned in respect of the other suspected offence whether it be a scheduled offence or not."[114]

Constitutionality of Scheduling Power

There must be a doubt over the constitutionality of the government's power to schedule offences in the context of the section 30 power of arrest. By exercising the power to schedule an offence the government is effectively extending police powers of arrest and detention under section 30 to the offence in question. Given the extent to which these powers encroach upon the liberty of the individual it is at least arguable that extending them in this fashion is a legislative policy-making matter as distinct from an administrative implementation of policy laid down in legislation. Since the Constitution vests the power to make laws solely and exclusively in the Oireachtas, it would follow from this argument that the scheduling power is unconstitutional.[114a] Significantly, a majority of the Committee to Review the Offences against the State Acts considered that the section 30 arrest powers ought to be determined directly by the Oireachtas through primary legislation.[114b]

Possession of Information

4–32   The broad scope of the section 30 power is further demonstrated by the fact that it may be used even where the arresting member of the Garda Síochána does not actually suspect the person concerned to be guilty of any criminal offence. The section specifically extends the power of arrest to the situation where a garda suspects the person concerned of carrying a document relating to the commission or intended commission of an offence within the scope of the section. Similarly the power is available where the person concerned is suspected of being in possession of information relating to the commission or intended commission of any offence within the section. It follows that mere possession of a document or information relating to the commission of a section 30 offence is enough to trigger the power even though the person concerned is not actually suspected of any involvement in the commission of the offence. Gardaí consider this aspect of the power very useful in securing the assistance of persons who might have information about the commission of a relevant offence by a member of a paramilitary organisation or organised crime gang as a result of their association with such individuals. By the same token, however, it can also be used against persons who come by such information by any means.[114c]

---

[114]   *People (DPP) v. Howley* [1989] I.L.R.M. 629.

[114a]   See, for example, *McDaid v. Sheehy* [1991] 1 I.R. 1; *Laurentiu v. Minister for Justice, Equality and Law Reform* [1999] 4 I.R. 26.

[114b]   *Report of the Committee to Review the Offences against the State Acts 1939–1998 and Related Matters* (Stationery Office, Dublin, 2002), paras. 7.25 *et seq.*

[114c]   *ibid.* paras. 7.44 *et seq.*

Suspicion

The arrest power under section 30 differs from most other arrest powers in **4–33** that it is exercisable on the basis of "suspicion" as opposed to "reasonable suspicion" or "reasonable grounds to suspect". The last two standards connote an objective test. Where they apply it will not be sufficient that the arresting officer actually suspects that the person whom he or she is arresting has committed the appropriate offence. The officer must have formed his or her suspicion on the basis of information which would raise the necessary suspicion in the mind of a reasonable person. It is this additional requirement that is patently missing from the section 30 power. The officer need only have the requisite "suspicion" for the purposes of the section 30 power. It must follow that the section 30 power would be available earlier in the course of a criminal investigation than those arrest powers which are based on a reasonable suspicion. That still leaves open the question of what constitutes a "suspicion" and a "reasonable suspicion". The former is considered here in the context of the section 30 power, while the latter is considered below in the context of arrest generally.

In *Re McElduff*[115] the Northern Irish High Court had to interpret an arrest **4–34** power conferred by regulations made under the Civil Authorities (Special Powers) Act (Northern Ireland) 1922–33. Like section 30 of the 1939 Act, it permitted a police officer to arrest on the basis of "suspicion." The court concluded that this would be satisfied by an "honest" suspicion in the mind of the police officer concerned. It would not matter that another police officer would not have formed the suspicion on the basis of the same facts, so long as the arresting officer honestly held the suspicion. Unquestionably, the Irish courts also require the existence of a genuine suspicion in the mind of the arresting officer as a pre-requisite for a valid arrest under section 30. This will not be satisfied merely by a genuine reason to arrest an individual. There must be a genuine suspicion that the person is concerned in the commission of an offence within the scope of section 30. In *Trimbole v. Governor of Mountjoy Prison*,[116] for example, the applicant had been arrested under section 30 on suspicion of being in possession of firearms, an offence within the scope of section 30. However, Egan J. found in the High Court that the arresting member of the Garda Síochána did not genuinely entertain a suspicion that the applicant was in possession of firearms. Accordingly, the arrest was unlawful. The learned judge went on to find that the only rational explanation for the arrest was to ensure that the applicant would be available for arrest and detention for the purpose of facilitating his extradition to Australia. Not only was this a "gross misuse" of section 30 but it also amounted to a conscious and deliberate violation of the applicant's constitutional rights.[117]

---

[115] [1972] N.I. 1.
[116] [1985] I.L.R.M. 465.
[117] *Trimbole v. Governor of Mountjoy Prison* [1985] I.L.R.M. 465 at 479. See also, Finlay C.J. in the Supreme Court at 485–486.

4–35 In contrast to the approach of the Northern Irish court in *Re McElduff*, it is unlikely that the Irish courts would accept a mere honest or genuine suspicion as being sufficient to satisfy the suspicion required by section 30. In *People (DPP) v. Quilligan*, for example, Walsh J. intimated that the suspicion must be "*bona fide* held and not unreasonable".[118] It is not entirely clear what "not unreasonable" is meant to signify in this context. It can hardly mean that the suspicion must be an objectively reasonable one. At the same time it certainly requires something more than a mere honest suspicion in the mind of the arresting officer. Hogan and Walker suggest that it signifies the administrative law test of reasonableness that is generally applied in a judicial review of the exercise of discretionary powers.[119] In effect the judge would be looking for the existence of facts upon which a police officer could reasonably have formed a suspicion that the person to be arrested had committed the offence in question. It may be that the judge himself or even another police officer might not necessarily have formed the same suspicion. That, however, would not matter so long as the facts were such that it would not have been unreasonable for the police officer concerned to have formed the suspicion. Hogan and Walker go on to suggest that the difference between this test and that of "reasonable suspicion" which applies to most arrest powers may not be very great as the Irish courts now insist on the existence of objective evidence to justify the exercise of discretionary powers.[120]

Source of Suspicion

4–36 Although the suspicion must be bona fide and not unreasonable it would appear that it is not essential that the arresting officer personally should have formed the necessary suspicion through his or her own investigation or observations. In *People (DPP) v. McCaffrey*[121] the defendant had been arrested for possession of a firearm with intent to endanger life. The arresting officer had been directed to effect the arrest by a senior officer who had formed the necessary suspicion against the defendant. The arresting officer had not personally formed the requisite suspicion. The suspicion he entertained was based on the fact that he had been told by a senior officer that the defendant was suspected of committing an offence involving the use of firearms and ammunition. The senior officer had formed the suspicion on the basis of information received. However, it would appear that he did not actually pass on the basis of his suspicion to the arresting officer. Surprisingly, perhaps, the Court of Criminal Appeal ruled that it was not necessary for the arresting officer to have formed his own personal suspicion in

---

[118] [1986] I.R. 495 at 507.

[119] Hogan and Walker, *Political Violence and the Law in Ireland* (Manchester University Press, 1989), pp. 203–204. It is significant that Walsh J. specifically supports his statement by reference to *The State (Lynch) v. Cooney* [1982] I.R. 337 dealing with the "opinion" former by the Minister in question.

[120] See, *e.g. State (Daly) v. Minister for Agriculture* [1988] I.L.R.M. 173. See *Report of the Committee to Review the Offences against the State Acts 1939–1998 and Related Matters* (Stationery Office, Dublin, 2002), paras. 7.66 *et seq* for recommendation that the reasonable suspicion requirement should be made explicit.

[121] [1986] I.L.R.M. 687.

order to effect a valid arrest under section 30. It will be quite sufficient that he knows from his senior officer's direction that there is a section 30 suspicion against the person whom he has been directed to arrest. It is respectfully submitted, however, that this interpretation does not accord with the generally accepted principles applicable to the exercise of a discretionary power, including the power of arrest. If the statute requires that the officer effecting the arrest must entertain a "suspicion", that suspicion cannot be satisfied by the knowledge that someone else entertains the suspicion. The suspicion must be personal to the officer exercising the power. It could, of course, be derived from information given to him or her by a senior officer and which he or she believes to be true.[122] That, however, is quite a different matter from accepting the truth of a senior officer's assertion that he or she has the suspicion.

Confidential Source

Challenging whether an arresting officer had a *"bona fide . . . and not unrea-*   **4–37**
sonable"* suspicion can be difficult if the officer concerned bases it on information received from a confidential source. The courts generally have been reluctant to compel gardaí to disclose the sources of their information where its disclosure might expose that source to a risk of harm.[123] In *DPP v. Connolly,*[124] for example, the arresting officer justified the arrest of the defendant on the ground that as a result of information he received from a reliable and confidential source he formed the suspicion that the defendant was involved in an armed robbery. The defendant sought to question the nature and source of the confidential information upon which the officer had formed his suspicion. Sheridan J., however, refused to permit cross-examination on these matters beyond the assertion that the information implicated the defendant in the armed robbery. He also refused to order the arresting officer to identify the source. The learned judge considered that the source of the officer's information was protected by privilege.

Proximity of Suspicion

An interesting feature about the suspicion required under section 30 is the   **4–38**
fact that it can be satisfied by a suspicion that the person concerned is about to commit an offence within the section. This is in addition to the more familiar suspicion that the suspect has committed, is concerned in the commission, or has been concerned in the commission, of an offence within the section. Unfortunately, there is no guidance on how proximate the person's actions must be to the commission of the offence before a member of the Garda Síochána could form the suspicion that he was about to commit that offence for the purposes of a section 30 arrest. It is submitted that the actions

---

[122] *McKee v. Chief Constable for Northern Ireland* [1985] 1 All E.R. 1; *O'Hara v. Chief Constable of the Royal Ulster Constabulary* [1997] 1 All E.R. 129.
[123] See Hogan and Walker, *op. cit.,* above, n.119, at pp. 204–205.
[124] [1985] I.L.T. 83. See also, *People (DPP) v. Eccles,* unreported, Court of Criminal Appeal, February 10, 1986.

would not have to be so proximate as to satisfy an attempt, otherwise there would have been no need for the inclusion of a power to arrest on the basis of this particular suspicion. The member could simply proceed to arrest on the basis that the person concerned had committed or was in the course of committing an offence; *i.e.* an attempt.[125] It follows that mere preparatory acts could be sufficient. When this is combined with the relatively low suspicion threshold required for arrest under section 30, the effect is to permit coercive intervention by the Garda Síochána at a relatively early stage.[125a] For example, if a group of men equipped with a motorised dinghy and wetsuits are found at night acting suspiciously on a remote part of the coastline which gardaí knew from their intelligence sources was occasionally used for the unlawful importation of firearms, and the men attempted to flee on the arrival of gardaí, it is arguable that on the basis of those facts alone they could be arrested under section 30 on the basis of a suspicion that they were about to commit a scheduled offence. Certainly, it would be very difficult in practice to challenge their arrest successfully in such circumstances.

F. Reasonable Grounds for Arrest

Different Formulations

4–39   Most summary arrest powers available to gardaí are exercisable only on the basis of "reasonable grounds to suspect", "reasonable cause to suspect" or a "reasonable suspicion".[126] Indeed, one of the perplexing features about these powers is the extent to which the "reasonable" formula differs seemingly at random from one offence to another. In 1996, for example, there are three distinct statutes which specifically confer a power of arrest on a member of the Garda Síochána alone. Although all three include an objective requirement in their respective formulations, none of them actually use the same forumula. One requires the member to have "reasonable cause for believing . . . ",[127] another requires "reasonable cause to suspect . . .",[128] while the third opts for "reasonably suspects . . . ".[129]

It is unlikely that the different formulations connote any substantive differences in their interpretation. It is possible to argue of course that there is a practical difference between a test which permits a member to arrest where he or she has "reasonable grounds to suspect . . ." and one which requires him or her

---

[125]   It is worth noting in this context that attempts, etc., to commit a scheduled offence are also scheduled offences; Offences against the State Act 1939, s.37.

[125a]   See *Report of the Committee to Review the Offences against the State Acts 1939-1998 and Related Matters* (Stationery Office, Dublin, 2002), paras. 7.51 *et seq.*

[126]   The power to arrest on suspicion of "drunk-driving" conferred by Road Traffic Act 1961, s.49(6) is unusual in that it can be exercised where the member of the Garda Síochána is of the opinion that a person is committing or has committed a relevant offence. Nevertheless, the courts take the view that such an opinion must be a reasonable one and must be based on an honest belief; see *Hobbs v. Hurley* (unreported, High Court, October 6, 1980); *DPP v. Donoghue* [1987] I.L.R.M. 129.

[127]   Domestic Violence Act 1996, s.18.

[128]   Criminal Assets Bureau Act 1996, s.16.

[129]   Control of Horses Act 1996, s.4.

to "reasonably suspect . . .". The former may be considered to be satisfied simply where the member is in posession of information which would give him reasonable grounds to suspect, even though he himself did not actually harbour a suspicion against the person concerned. The latter by comparison clearly does require an actual suspicion in the mind of the member, as well as objective reasonableness for that suspicion. Significantly, some of the primary arrest powers in the police and criminal evidence legislation in England and Wales and in Northern Ireland are based on the "reasonable grounds for suspecting" formula. Nevertheless, the courts in those jurisdictions have never suggested that this terminology imports any difference from "reasonable suspicion". Indeed, they regularly use the expression "reasonable suspicion" when interpreting the statutory provisions in question. English courts have also emphatically rejected the notion that the "reasonable grounds for suspecting" formula does not require a genuine suspicion on the part of the arresting officer.[130]

Meaning of Reasonable Suspicion

Powers of summary arrest attaching to a member of the Garda Síochána at common law are based on "reasonable suspicion". This requires that a reasonable individual acting without passion or prejudice would fairly have suspected the person concerned of having committed the offence in question.[131] The test is an objective one. Lord Diplock in *Dallison v. Caffrey* put the matter thus:

4–40

> "The test whether there was reasonable and probable cause for the arrest or prosecution is an objective one, namely, whether a reasonable man, assumed to know the law and possessed of the information which in fact was possessed by the defendant, would believe that there was reasonable and probable cause."[132]

Guidance on the standard of suspicion required may be had from *Shaaban Bin Hussein v. Chong Fook Kam*.[133] In that case Lord Devlin explained that reasonable suspicion connotes a lower standard than a prima facie case. Suspicion arises at or near the starting point of an investigation of which the obtaining of prima facie proof is the end. In a typical investigation suspicion would be developed into a reasonable suspicion and from there to a prima facie case.[134] The prima facie proof would have to rest on the basis of admissible evidence, while a reasonable suspicion may take into account matters which would not be admissible at all. Accordingly, a member of the Garda Síochána may act on the basis of hearsay evidence so long as it is reasonable

---

130 *Siddiqui v. Swain* [1979] R.T.R. 454; *Chapman v. DPP* [1988] Crim L.R. 83.
131 *Allen v. Wright* (1838) 8 C&P 522. The member's reasonable suspicion must relate to the offence for which he arrested the suspect; *Chapman v. DPP* [1988] 89 Cr. App. Rep. 190.
132 *Dallison v. Caffrey* [1964] 2 All E.R. 610 at 619. See also, *Wiltshire v. Barrett* [1966] 1 Q.B. 312.
133 [1970] A.C. 9442; [1969] 3 All E.R. 1626.
134 The fact that a person may be released without charge does not signify that the suspicion upon which he was arrested was not reasonable. If information dissipating the suspicion against him comes to light after his arrest and before he is charged, he must be released immediately; *Wiltshire v. Barrett* [1966] 1 Q.B. 312.

and he or she actually believes it.[135] Similarly, he or she may have regard to the criminal record of the person concerned.[136]

Briefing from a Senior Officer

4–41 In the Northern Irish case of *O'Hara v. Chief Constable of the Royal Ulster Constabulary*[137] the House of Lords analysed in some depth how a constable might acquire a reasonable suspicion for the purpose of a power of arrest which was based on reasonable suspicion. The arresting constable in that case had attended a briefing session by a senior officer in which he was told that the plaintiff was suspected of being involved in a murder. The purpose of the briefing session was to plan the arrest and search operation in the course of which the constable was to arrest the plaintiff. The question for the House was whether the constable could have the requisite reasonable suspicion in these circumstances. The House of Lords ruled, in line with established authority, that the important issue was what was in the mind of the arresting officer.[138] Not only must he actually suspect the person to be arrested, but he must also be possessed of sufficient information to afford reasonable grounds for that suspicion. That information could not be provided simply by a direction from a senior officer to arrest an individual. However, it could be provided by information supplied by a senior officer which the arresting constable believed, irrespective of whether that information ultimately proved to be inaccurate.[139] The court did not have to look beyond what was in the officer's mind. If that information was sufficient to create a reasonable suspicion, and the constable himself had the necessary suspicion, that would be sufficient.

In *O'Hara* itself there was very little material before the court as to the information possessed by the arresting constable. He merely said in evidence that his suspicion was based on the briefing in the course of which he was told that the plaintiff was suspected of a recent murder. Although the obligation was on the chief constable to prove the existence of reasonable grounds for the suspicion, the court felt that the scant evidence given by the arresting officer about the briefing was in itself sufficient to afford reasonable grounds for the suspicion. This was upheld by the House of Lords which ruled that the existence of reasonable grounds did not have to be supported by evidence additional to that offered by the arresting officer himself. It must follow that it will be very difficult to challenge the existence of a reasonable suspicion

---

[135]   *O'Hara v. Chief Constable for Northern Ireland* [1997] 1 All E.R. 129; *Glinski v. McIver* [1962] A.C. 726; *McArdle v. Egan* (1933) 150 L.T. 412; *Moss v. Jenkins* [1975] R.T.R. 25. See *Lister v. Perryman* (1870) L.R. 4 HL for the credit to be given to informers. See also, Leigh, *Police Powers in England and Wales* (2nd ed., Butterworths, London, 1985), pp. 81–82.

[136]   *McArdle v. Egan* (1933) 150 L.T. 412. Knowledge that a warrant had been issued for the arrest of the person for felony could provide grounds for a reasonable suspicion; *Creagh v. Gamble* (1888) L.R. Ir. 458.

[137]   [1997] 1 All E.R. 129.

[138]   *Holgate-Mohammed v. Duke* [1984] 1 All E.R. 1054; *McKee v. Chief Constable for Northern Ireland* [1985] 1 All E.R. 1; *Hanna v. Chief Constable of the Royal Ulster Constabulary* [1986] N.I. 103. See also, A. Barrister, "Reasonable Suspicion and Planned Arrests" (1992) 43, 1 *Northern Ireland Legal Quarterly* 66.

[139]   See also, *Dryburgh v. Galt* (1981) J.C. 69.

where the arresting officer has been briefed for an arrest operation by a senior officer. In the case of section 30 arrests it would appear that the arresting officer can acquire the requisite suspicion simply on the basis of being told by a senior officer that he (the senior officer) has the necessary suspicion.[140] It is worth noting, however, that the section 30 provision does not specifically require the suspicion to be based on reasonable grounds.

Making Further Inquiries

The low threshold for reasonable suspicion is compounded by the likelihood that a member of the Garda Síochána is under no obligation to take all steps that may be open to him or her to check the accuracy of his information, or indeed to follow up other possible leads.[141] As soon as he is in possession of information giving rise to a reasonable suspicion he may proceed to arrest the person concerned. In *Castorina v. Chief Constable of Surrey*,[142] for example, the English Court of Appeal had to consider whether a constable had the necessary reasonable suspicion to effect an arrest under a provision of the Police and Criminal Evidence Act 1984. The constable was investigating a burglary at the plaintiff's former workplace. The burglary appeared to have been an "inside job" and the managing director told the constable that the plaintiff had been sacked recently and might therefore bear a grudge against the business. On the basis of these facts the constable visited the plaintiff at her home and arrested her, despite the fact that he had established that she was of previous good character. The trial judge concluded that the arrest was unlawful as the constable lacked a reasonable suspicion. The judge took the view that an ordinary cautious person would have sought more information from the suspect before arresting her. The English Court of Appeal, however, overturned this decision on the basis that the facts supporting a reasonable suspicion did not have to be such that they would lead an ordinary cautious man to believe that the suspect was guilty. It was sufficient if they could lead a reasonable person to suspect that he was guilty. In this case, the Court concluded, the facts were sufficient to support this belief and there was no obligation on the constable to make further inquiries before effecting the arrest.

4–42

The *Castorina* case might be considered to be at the very limits of what would be considered sufficient information to ground a reasonable suspicion.[143] Other courts have emphasised the importance of not being too hasty in effecting the arrest where further reasonable inquiries could have been made.[144] In *Shaaban Bin Hussein v. Chong Fook Kam*, for example, Lord Devlin considered that the police had acted prematurely in effecting the arrest. They

4–43

---

140 *People (DPP) v. McCaffrey* [1986] I.L.R.M. 687.
141 *McArdle v. Egan* (1933) 150 L.T. 412; *Lister v. Perryman* (1870) L.R. 4 HL 521; *McCarrick v. Oxford* [1983] R.T.R. 117.
142 (1988) N.L.J. 180.
143 See Zander, *The Police and Criminal Evidence Act 1984* (2nd ed., Butterworths, London, 1990), pp. 59–61 for criticism of this case.
144 *Kynaston v. DPP* (1988) 87 Cr. App. Rep. 200.

"made the mistake of arresting before questioning; if they had questioned first and arrested afterwards, there would have been no case against them."[145] Scott L.J. described the correct approach more fulsomely in *Dumbell v. Roberts* in the following terms:

> "[The Police] may have to act on the spur of the moment and have no time to reflect and be bound, therefore, to arrest to prevent escape; but where there is no danger of the person who has *ex hypothesi* aroused their suspicion, that he probably is an 'offender' attempting to escape, they should make all presently practicable enquiries from persons present or immediately accessible who are likely to be able to answer their enquiries forthwith. I am not suggesting a duty on the police to try to prove innocence; that is not their function; but they should act on the assumption that their prima facie suspicion may be ill-founded. That duty attaches particularly where slight delay does not matter because there is no probability, in the circumstances of the arrest or intended arrest, of the suspected person running away. The duty attaches, I think, simply because of the double-sided interest of the public in the liberty of the individual as well as in the detection of crime."[146]

It would appear, therefore, that the judicial approach to what constitutes reasonable suspicion can be influenced by the circumstances in which the arrest was effected in the individual case. If the police officer had to act swiftly in order to prevent the arrest of someone suspected of having committed a serious offence, the courts will be less demanding than they would otherwise be if, for example, the circumstances were such that there was ample opportunity to conduct further prior investigations. It is also worth bearing in mind the constitutional protection for the liberty of the individual in Ireland. It might be expected, therefore, that the Irish judges would put even more emphasis on this gloss on the holding in the *Castorina* case.

G. Discretion

4–44   Just because a member of the Garda Síochána may have reasonable grounds to suspect that an individual has committed an arrestable offence it does not follow that he or she can lawfully arrest that individual. Where all the elements of the arrest power are satisfied in a particular case, the member in question merely acquires a discretion to arrest. As with most other discretionary powers it must be exercised lawfully. It follows that when making the decision whether to effect the arrest, the member must take into account all relevant considerations and ignore all irrelevant ones.[147] If, for example, he decides to effect the arrest for a purpose alien to that for which the power was granted, he will be guilty of an unlawful exercise of discretion. This, in turn, renders the arrest unlawful. A similar result will ensue where the member is guilty of exercising the discretion to arrest in bad faith.

---

[145] [1969] 3 All E.R. 1626 at 1631.
[146] [1944] 1 All E.R. 326 at 329.
[147] See Hogan and Morgan, *Administrative Law in Ireland* (2nd ed., Sweet & Maxwell, London, 1991) chap. 10.

The role of discretion in the exercise of police powers of arrest was **4-45** considered by the House of Lords in *Holgate-Mohammed v. Duke*.[148] In that case a constable had reasonable grounds to suspect a woman of theft from her former employer. The constable called at the suspect's home to investigate the matter. Although she was willing to answer questions in her home, the constable decided to arrest her as he felt that the questioning might be more productive in the atmosphere of the police station. The suspect subsequently challenged the legality of the arrest on the basis that the constable had erred in the exercise of his discretion. Although the House of Lords accepted that a constable's decision to exercise a power of arrest could be challenged on the basis of an unlawful exercise of discretion, it went on to hold that the constable's decision in this case could not be impugned. His belief that the questioning would be more productive in the police station was a factor that he could legitimately take into account in deciding whether to exercise the power of arrest.

The Garda Síochána encourages individual members of the force to exercise **4-46** discretion when deciding whether to effect an arrest in any case where the circumstances have brought a power of arrest into play. If each member was to resort to arrest in every situation where the preconditions for the availability of a power of arrest were satisfied, police resources would be overwhelmed very quickly. Accordingly, internal force policies offer guidance on the circumstances when a member should proceed by summons or caution in cases where the power of arrest is available as an option.[149] Ultimately, however, it is a matter for the individual member to decide whether to exercise his or her power of arrest in circumstances which have brought the power into play. He or she must decide whether to exercise his or her discretion to arrest in such a case. It is likely that a failure to take a relevant force guideline into account would be a factor in determining whether the decision to arrest could be challenged successfully as an unlawful exercise of discretion. Equally, however, blind adherence to the guidance could be interpreted as a failure to exercise discretion which would also be unlawful.

H. Formalities of Lawful Arrest

Introduction

The citizen is under no obligation to submit to restraint on his or her freedom **4-47** of movement, except to the extent that the restraint is specifically permitted by law. Indeed, the common law respects the citizen's freedom to resist physically any attempt to detain him or her without specific legal authority.[150] In Ireland this is reinforced by the Constitutional protection of the right to

---

[148] [1984] A.C. 437; [1984] 1 All E.R. 1054.

[149] See, *e.g.*, the guidance on the use of summons instead of arrest in the Dublin metropolitan area.

[150] See Lord Simmonds in *Christie v. Leachinsky* [1947] A.C. 573 at 591. Note, however, that a person wrongly arrested may not use grossly excessive force in resisting arrest; *Palmer v. The Queen* [1971] A.C. 814; *R. v. Wilson* [1955] 1 W.L.R. 493; *R. v. Long* (1836) 7 C&P 314.

liberty. In order to exercise this freedom in any case where the citizen is being arrested, he will need to know that he is being placed under arrest and the reasons for his arrest. Only then can he make a reasoned decision either to submit to the restraint on his liberty or to resist it by force, if necessary.[151] Traditionally, this requirement has been satisfied by the imposition of certain formalities which should be followed in order to effect a valid arrest. A failure to follow them will normally render the arrest unlawful.

Communicating the Fact of Arrest

4–48   The first formality for a valid arrest is that the person to be arrested must be informed of the fact of his arrest.[152] This is normally achieved by using a form of words or conduct which conveys clearly to the suspect that he is not free to leave.[153] Words which are equivocal[154] or not sufficiently loud[155] for the suspect to hear will not be sufficient. Moreover, the suspect must submit to the words of arrest in order for this formality to be satisfied.[156] If he does not submit, there will have to be a seizure of the body.[157] Indeed, touching[158] or seizing the suspect, coupled with appropriate words, is the standard method of complying with the first formality. It may not even be necessary to use words or physical contact at all. There is authority for the proposition that it will be sufficient if someone, whom the suspect knows to be a police officer, acts in a manner which leads the suspect to believe on reasonable grounds that he is under arrest.[159]

Communicating Grounds for Arrest

4–49   The second formality for a valid arrest is that the suspect must be informed of the ground for his arrest.[160] The legal principles governing this formality are neatly summarised in the following quotation from Viscount Simon in *Christie v. Leachinsky*:

---

[151]   See Lord du Parcq in *Christie v. Leachinsky* [1947] A.C. 573, at 598.

[152]   See Leigh, *op. cit.*, above n.135, pp. 54–55.

[153]   *Murray v. Ministry of Defence* [1988] 1 W.L.R. 692; *Grainger v. Hill* (1834) 4 Bing NC 212; *Bird v. Jones* (1845) 7 Q.B. 742.

[154]   *Alderson v. Booth* [1969] 2 Q.B. 216, [1969] 2 All E.R. 271.

[155]   *Wheatley v. Lodge* [1971] 1 All E.R. 173, [1971] 1 W.L.R. 29.

[156]   *R v. Jones, ex parte Moore* [1965] Crim. L.R. 222; *Bird v. Jones* (1845) 7 Q.B. 742; *Police v. Thompson* [1969] N.Z.L.R. 513.

[157]   *Bird v. Jones* (1845) 7 Q.B. 742.

[158]   There is no specific requirement for the suspect to be handcuffed or otherwise seized in a manner which renders escape unlikely; *Hart v. Chief Constable of Kent* [1983] R.T.R. 484.

[159]   *Forsyth v. Goden* (1895) 32 C.L.J. 288 (Ont HC); *R v. Hoare* [1965] N.S.W.R. 1167. Leigh suggests that this reasoning helps explain those cases which treat persons detained for questioning in circumstances which appear to them to import compulsion as cases of arrest; *e.g. Campbell v. Tormey* [1969] 1 All E.R. 961. See Leigh, *op. cit.*, above, n. 135, p. 54. See also *Murray v. Ministry of Defence* [1988] 1 W.L.R. 692. *People (DPP) v. Caffrey* [1987] I.L.R.M. 727; *People v. Lynch* [1982] I.R. 64.

[160]   *Christie v. Leachinsky* [1947] A.C. 573, [1947] 1 All E.R. 567; *People (Attorney General) v. White* [1947] I.R. 247.

"(1) If a policeman arrests without warrant upon reasonable suspicion of felony, or of other crime of a sort which does not require a warrant, he must in ordinary circumstances inform the person arrested of the true ground of arrest. He is not entitled to keep the reason to himself or to give a reason which is not the true reason. In other words a citizen is entitled to know on what charge or on suspicion of what crime he is seized.

(2) If the citizen is not so informed but is nevertheless seized, the policeman, apart from certain exceptions, is liable for false imprisonment.

(3) The requirement that the person arrested should be informed of the reason why he is seized naturally does not exist if the circumstances are such that he must know the general nature of the alleged offence for which he is detained.

(4) The requirement that he should be so informed does not mean that technical or precise language need be used. The matter is a matter of substance, and turns on the elementary proposition that in this country a person is, *prima facie*, entitled to his freedom and is only required to submit to restraints on his freedom if he knows in substance the reason why it is claimed that this restraint should be imposed."[161]

These principles were approved in the following terms by the Supreme Court in *Re O'Laighléis*:

"We accept it as settled law that in the case of an arrest without the production of a warrant the arrest will not be lawful unless the person being arrested is told why he is being arrested or unless he otherwise knows: see *Christie v. Leachinsky* [1947] A.C. 573 at 587. The reason for the rule is not far to seek. Arrest must be for a lawful purpose; and since no one is obliged to submit to an unlawful arrest the citizen has a right before acquiescing in his arrest to know why he is being arrested."[162]

These requirements will easily be satisfied where the arresting member of the Garda Síochána identifies the precise offence under the criminal law as well as the victim, the time and the location of its commission.[163] What is not so clear is the minimum amount of information which must be given to satisfy the formalities. There is adequate authority for the proposition that the arresting member does not have to identify the precise offence so long as he gives sufficient factual information which corresponds broadly with an arrestable criminal offence.[164] In *DPP (Cloughley) v. Mooney*,[165] for example, Blayney J. ruled that it would be sufficient for a member of the Garda Síochána to use the commonly understood expression "drunk-driving" even though the offence in question could have been one or other of driving under the influence of an

4–50

---

[161] [1947] A.C. 573 at 587–589.
[162] *Re O'Laighléis* [1960] I.R. 93.
[163] It will not be sufficient for the arresting member to give reasons which would justify arrest for one offence when the real reasons for the arrest concern the individual's suspected involvement in a quite different offence; *Waters v. Digmore* [1981] R.T.R. 356; *Christie v. Leachinsky, op. cit.* See Leigh, *op. cit.*, above, n.135. pp. 58–59.
[164] See, *e.g. Gelberg v. Miller* [1961] 1 All E.R. 291, [1961] 1 W.L.R. 153; *R. v. Telfer* [1976] Crim. L.R. 562; *Abbassy v. Metropolitan Police Commissioner* [1990] 1 W.L.R. 385; *Christie v. Leachinsky, op. cit.*
[165] [1993] I.L.R.M. 214.

intoxicant to such an extent as to be incapable of having proper control of the vehicle, or while the concentration of alcohol in the blood exceeded a particular level within three hours after driving or attempting to drive. When the member had stopped the driver in this case he got a smell of intoxicating liquor from the driver's breath. The driver also tested positive in the breathalyser test. In such circumstances, Blayney J. felt that the expression "drunk-driving" adequately conveyed to the driver, within the meaning of the fourth point in the quotation from Viscount Simon's speech, the substance of the offence for which he was being arrested. Indeed, Blayney J. was also of the opinion that the circumstances were probably sufficient to bring the third point into play.

4–51　It is unlikely, however, that it would be sufficient for a member merely to recite the definition of a criminal offence in circumstances where it would not be obvious to the accused what it is he is suspected of doing by way of committing the offence. Merely to quote the statutory or common law source of the power being used would appear to fall very far short of what is required.[166] Nevertheless, there is authority pointing the other way. In *DPP (Cloughley) v. Mooney*[167] Blayney J. suggested *obiter* that it would have been sufficient for the member in question to have informed the motorist that he was being arrested under section 49(a) of the Road Traffic Act 1961. It is respectfully submitted, however, that the correctness of this proposition is questionable. It flies in the face of the principles enunciated by Viscount Simon in *Christie v. Leachinsky* and even runs counter to the position with respect to arrests under section 30 of the Offences Against the State Act 1939.[168] In *People (DPP) v. Quilligan* Walsh J. declared that:

> "When a person is arrested under s.30 as in any other arrest he must be informed of which of the many possible offences he is suspected unless he already has that information."[169]

4–52　There are circumstances where the obligation to inform the suspect of the reasons for the arrest are relaxed. In *Re Ó'Laighléis*,[170] for example, it was held that it is not necessary to give reasons where the suspect already knows why he is being arrested. If the suspect submits to the arrest without seeking the reasons, it would appear that a failure to state the reasons will not render the arrest unlawful.[171] Similarly, an arrest will be lawful if the reasons were not given because the suspect has created a situation which renders it impracticable to give them.[172] In this case, however, the reasons must be

---

[166]　*Re McElduff* [1972] N.I. 1.

[167]　[1993] I.L.R.M. 214.

[168]　For further discussion see Leigh, *op. cit.*, above, n.135, pp. 56–58 and Glanville Williams "Requisites of a Valid Arrest" [1954] Crim. L.R. 598.

[169]　[1986] I.R.495 at 508. See also *People v. Walsh* [1980] I.R. 294.

[170]　[1960] I.R. 93.

[171]　See *People v. Walsh* [1980] I.R. 294.

[172]　*Christie v. Leachinsky* [1947] A.C. 573. In *People (DPP) v. Kehoe* [1986] I.L.R.M. 690 the Court of Criminal Appeal upheld the legality of an arrest under s.30 of the Offences against the State

given at the first reasonable opportunity, otherwise the detention will become unlawful from that point.[173]

Consequences of Non-compliance with Formalities

If the arrest is unlawful for a failure to satisfy one or other of the formalities at the time of the arrest, the subsequent detention will be unlawful. However, if the formalities are fulfilled at some point during the suspect's detention, his custody will become lawful from that point.[174] So, for example, if the suspect was initially told that he was being arrested for criminal damage, and two hours later at the police station was told the real reason, namely that he was being detained on suspicion of murder, the initial arrest and detention would be unlawful up to the point when he was told the real reason, from which point they become lawful. It would appear that the court will treat the giving of the real reason for the detention as the beginning of a valid arrest. Moreover, it is not necessary to release the suspect from custody before the subsequent lawful arrest and detention can be effected.[175]

I. Use of Force

1. Introduction

The use of force against the person without lawful authority can result in the prosecution of the aggressor for an appropriate offence. Equally, the aggressor might be sued by the victim in a civil action for damages. Since police officers do not enjoy any immunity from these basic principles in the apprehension of suspected offenders, they will be exposed to the risk of criminal prosecution and/or a civil action in damages where they resort to the unlawful use of force in order to effect or maintain an arrest. It does not necessarily follow, however, that an arrested suspect will succeed in an application for habeas corpus, or that evidence obtained from him while in custody, will automatically be excluded where unlawful force was used in order to effect the arrest. Indeed, it would appear that the English courts are not prepared to draw such consequences from an arrest that was executed with excessive force.[176] The Irish courts, however, have adopted a much stronger exclusionary rule than their English counterparts. As a generalisation it might be said that they are predisposed to deny the State the benefit of actions which entail a conscious and deliberate infringement of the constitutional rights of the accused (see chapter 9). Since the use of excessive force in effecting an arrest is a blatant attack on the

4–53

Act 1939 where the gardaí restrained and handcuffed the suspect during a gun battle and only effected the formal arrest 50 minutes later when the shooting died down.

[173] Note, however, that a failure to give reasons at this point will not necessarily render the detention retrospectively invalid up to that point; *DPP v. Hawkins* [1988] 1 W.L.R. 1166; *Lewis v. Chief Constable of the South Wales Constabulary* [1991] 1 All E.R. 206.

[174] See *People v. Shaw* [1982] I.R. 1.

[175] *ibid.*; *R. v. Kulynycz* [1971] 1 Q.B. 367.

[176] *Simpson v. Chief Constable of South Yorkshire Police* The Times, March 7, 1991.

individual's constitutional right of bodily integrity, it is submitted that in appropriate circumstances an Irish court could be persuaded to exclude evidence obtained from a suspect whose arrest had been effected through the use of unlawful force. Also, it will be seen in chapter 6 that the courts in both Ireland and Northern Ireland are prepared to grant an order of habeas corpus where the suspect is subjected to the unlawful use of force while in police custody.

4–54   At common law a member of the Garda Síochána, and any citizen, can use such force as is reasonably necessary to effect or maintain a lawful arrest or to prevent crime.[177] It will be seen later that the use of force for such purposes is now the subject of statutory provisions.[178] It is not clear, however, whether the statutory provisions should be interpreted as a complete statement of the lawful use of force in this context or only as a limited defence to a criminal charge arising from the use of force in order to effect an arrest or to prevent crime or in self defence. Equally, it is not clear whether the provisions are confined to the use of non-lethal force or extend to the use of lethal force. From one perspective the answers to these questions are of some importance as the statutory provisions specifically abolish the common law rules governing the use of force within the meaning and scope of the statutory provisions. On the other hand, it would appear that the statutory provisions do not effect any substantive change to the common law principles as currently interpreted and applied by the courts.[179] Accordingly, the basic common law principles will be considered first before attention is drawn to the features of the statutory provisions.

2. Common Law

Handcuffing

4–55   The first question to be considered in an individual case is whether any force is necessary in order to effect or maintain the arrest. Clearly, if the suspect voluntarily submits himself to the custody of the arresting officer and the latter does not suspect that he will put up any show of resistance, any use of force would be unlawful.[180] So, for example, the officer will be acting unlawfully in such circumstances if he throws the suspect to the ground, forces his arms behind his back and handcuffs him. Equally, it would appear that handcuffing as a matter of course, even without any further show of

---

[177]   *Dowman v. Ireland* [1986] I.L.R.M. 111.

[178]   Non-fatal Offences against the Person Act 1997, ss.18–22.

[179]   If the statutory provisions extend to the use of lethal force, it is at least arguable that they have the effect of abolishing the rule that manslaughter (instead of murder) is the appropriate verdict in respect of the use of lethal force in circumstances where the use of some force was justified but the defendant used more force than was reasonably necessary in the circumstances as the defendant believed them to be.

[180]   *Allen v. Metropolitan Police Commissioner* [1980] Crim. L.R. 441; *O'Connor v. Hewitson* [1979] Crim. L.R. 46; *Marshall v. Osmond* [1982] 3 W.L.R. 120; *Truscott v. Carpenter* (1697) 1 Ld Raym 229. See Leigh, *op. cit.*, above, n. 135, p. 62.

physical force, is unlawful unless the officer genuinely suspects that the suspect will attempt to escape or will otherwise become violent if not handcuffed.[181]

Purpose of Force

Force can be used only where it is necessary in order to effect or maintain the arrest. The use of force against an arrested suspect for any other purpose will be unlawful unless it can be justified under some other rule or principle such as self defence, the prevention of crime or a member of the Garda Síochána acting in the execution of his or her duty. In *Dowman v. Ireland*,[182] for example, the plaintiff was arrested for "shop-lifting". As he was about to be placed in a Garda vehicle he resisted in order to ensure that two young children who had accompanied him and who were in his care, would not be left behind. The arresting officers used force to get the plaintiff into the car. The plaintiff succeeded in an action for damages for injury to his wrist caused by the use of force. In delivering judgment in the case Barron J. explained:

> "In the present case, the defendant Garda was not acting in the course of his duty when the injury to the plaintiff was caused. An arresting officer is entitled to use such force as is reasonably necessary to effect an arrest. Once the arrest has been effected, then he is also entitled to use such force as is necessary to ensure that the arrest is maintained. The defendant Garda was doing neither of these things. He was acting neither to effect an arrest nor to maintain one, but to deny the plaintiff the right to concern himself with the welfare of his charges. He was not therefore acting in the execution of his duty and consequently the use of force by him was an unlawful act."[183]

4–56

The issue of whether there is a risk of the suspect attempting to escape or otherwise putting up resistance is determined on the basis of what the arresting officer honestly and reasonably believed. In other words the use of force will not necessarily be unlawful just because the arresting officer mistakenly believed that the suspect was resisting or was about to use force in order to resist. If the officer genuinely holds this belief and there are reasonable grounds for his belief then he will be entitled to use no more force than is reasonably necessary in the circumstances as he mistakenly believed them to be. The fact that his belief was mistaken will not expose him to a civil action or criminal prosecution. Even if his belief was unreasonable it would appear that he will still have a defence to a criminal prosecution so long as his belief was honestly held. An honest but unreasonable mistake should offer no protection to a civil action in damages. Since these matters have been considered primarily in the case law dealing with the use of excessive force, as

4–57

---

[181] *R. v. Taylor* (1895) 59 JP 393. See also, *Reed v. Wastie* [1972] Crim. L.R. 221; *Wright v. Court* (1825) 4 B&C 596; *Leigh v. Cole* (1853) 6 Cox CC 329; *R v. Lockley* (1864) 4 F&F 155. A U.K. Home Office Circular advises that handcuffing an arrested suspect is justifiable only where it is reasonably necessary to prevent escape or to terminate a violent breach of the peace; see Home Office Consolidated Circular to the Police on Crime and Kindred Matters, 1977.
[182] [1986] I.L.R.M. 111.
[183] *ibid.* at 115.

distinct from whether the use of any force at all was justified, they are considered further in that context below.

Degree of Force

4-58   Just because the use of force is necessary to effect an arrest, it does not follow that any degree of force used to effect or maintain the arrest will be lawful. The arrestor can use only that force which is reasonably necessary in the circumstances. It is generally accepted that a proportionality test must be applied in order to determine what constitutes reasonable force in this context. So, for example, it would not be lawful for a police officer to fire a live bullet at an escaping "shop-lifter" simply because that was the only means by which the "shop-lifter" could have been apprehended in the circumstances of the case. The use of force which would cause serious injury to, and possibly the death of, the suspect is totally out of proportion to the gravity of the crime in this case.

Of course, it is not just the gravity of the crime which may be relevant to the issue of proportionality in an individual case. If the suspected offender violently resists arrest or otherwise behaves in a manner which presents a serious risk of injury to the arrestor or any other person, the arrestor will be entitled to use proportionate force in order to restrain him. This may result in the arrestor lawfully using lethal or potentially lethal force against the suspected offender even though the crime for which the arrest was originally effected or attempted was not of sufficient gravity to warrant the use of such force. In this event the lawfulness of the use of force will be assessed on the basis of whether the force used by the arrestor in arresting or restraining the suspect was proportionate to the threat posed by the suspect himself. Accordingly, the relevant principles are frequently discussed in cases dealing with self defence or police action in the prevention of crime.

Prevention of Crime

4-59   Much of the recent case law on the use of lethal force in apprehending a suspected offender has emanated from Northern Ireland. So far, neither the Northern Irish courts nor the courts in the rest of the United Kingdom or Ireland, have drawn a distinction between the lawful use of lethal force in the prevention of crime and the lawful use of lethal force in effecting an arrest. Despite the fact that the use of lethal force defeats the primary purpose of an arrest, they appear to accept that it can be justified on the same principles as pertain to the prevention of crime. In this they have the support of the European Commission on Human Rights.

4-60   In *Kelly v. United Kingdom*[183a] a military patrol had set up a road checkpoint in order to stop a stolen car the occupants of which had been seen acting suspiciously near the home of a member of the security forces. When the

---

[183a] European Commission on Human Rights Application No. 17579/90

driver of the car came upon the checkpoint he made desperate attempts to drive through it. Believing that the occupants of the car were terrorists and were getting away, members of the patrol opened fire, killing the driver and wounding two of the passengers. The injured and relatives of the deceased sued the Ministry of Defence for unlawful assault, battery and negligence. They lost at first instance in the Northern Ireland High Court which ruled that the soldiers had used reasonable force in order to prevent the suspects from escaping. An unsuccessful appeal to the Court of Appeal followed, and leave to appeal was refused by the House of Lords. An application was brought to the European Commission on Human Rights under Article 2 of the European Convention for the Protection of Human Rights and Fundamental Freedoms which protects the right to life. The Commission ruled that the soldiers had not been acting to prevent crime but in order to effect the arrest of the occupants. Nevertheless, it went on to find that the soldiers had been justified in their use of lethal force in order to effect the arrests, because the harm caused by the shooting was outweighed by the need to prevent "the freedom of the terrorists to resume their dealing in death and destruction". In actual fact the occupants of the vehicle were "joyriders".

Principles Governing Lethal Force

The broad principles which emerge from the case law are firstly that the   **4–61** arresting officer may use lethal force to arrest an offender only if such force is necessary to effect the arrest and is justified by the need to protect others from violence.[184] The justification can be supplied by a belief that the risk of harm to which others might be exposed if the suspect escaped was such that it required the use of lethal force.[185] Conversely, lethal force would not be permissible to effect an arrest for any offence where there was no immediate threat of harm to anyone if the suspect escaped.[186] Secondly, there must be some reasonable proportion between the amount of force used and the mischief sought to be averted by apprehending the suspected offender.[187] These principles would also appear to be consistent with the requirements of the European Convention for the Protection of Human Rights and Fundamental Freedoms.[188] Significantly, they would also appear to accord with the principles governing the use of force to prevent civil disorder. In *Lynch v. Fitzgerald*,[188a] for example, Hanna J. reviewed the authorities on the use of lethal force by officers of the State in the context of the fatal shooting of a young man by Garda detectives in the course of a civil disturbance. He quoted, as a correct

---

[184] In making this assessment, the court must take into account the circumstances and time available to the arresting officer for reflection; see *Attorney General's Reference for Northern Ireland* (No.1 of 1975) [1977] A.C. 105.

[185] *ibid.*

[186] See Milmo J. in *Marshall v. Osmond* [1982] Q.B. 857; *Palmer v. R.* [1971] A.C. 814; *R. v. McInnes* [1971] 3 All E.R. 295. See also, Leigh *op. cit.* above, n. 135, pp. 61–62.

[187] *R. v. Turner* (1862) VR 30.

[188] The E.C.H.R. in *Farrell v. United Kingdom* (1983) 5 E.H.R.R. 466 ruled that only moderate and proportional force may be used in effecting an arrest.

[188a] [1938] I.R. 382.

statement of the law, the following passage, among others, from the Report of the Special Commission consisting of Lord Shaw of Dunfermline, Lord Chief Justice Moloney and Mr Andrews (formerly the Right Honourable Mr Justice Andrews), upon the Bachelor's Walk shooting and the landing of guns in Howth in 1914:[188b]

> ". . . its an invariable rule that the degree of force to be used must always be moderated and proportioned to the circumstances of the case, and the end to be attained. Hence it is that arms – now at such a state of perfection that they cannot be employed without grave danger to life and limb even of distant and innocent persons – must be used with the greatest of care, and the greatest pain must be exercised to avoid the infliction of fatal injuries, but if in resisting crimes of felonious violence, all resources have been exhausted and all possible methods employed without success, then it becomes not only justifiable but it is the duty of Detective Officers, or other members authorised to carry arms to use these weapons according to the rules just enunciated, and if death should unfortunately ensue, they will, nevertheless, be justified.
>
> A gun should never be used, or used with any specified degree of force, if there is any doubt as to the necessity."[189]

3. Statutory Provisions

Scope

4–62   The use of force in order to prevent crime or effect an arrest has been placed on a statutory footing in Northern Ireland and in England and Wales since 1967. It is not thought, however, that these statutory provisions effected any change to the pre-existing common law on the subject. Statutory provisions have been introduced in Ireland thirty years later in a slightly different context. The provisions in England, Wales and Northern Ireland clearly state when it is lawful to use force in order to effect an arrest or prevent crime. The Irish provisions by contrast state that the use of force to, *inter alia*, prevent crime or effect an arrest shall not constitute an offence in certain circumstances. Given that the Act in question, namely the Non-fatal Offences against the Person Act 1997, is a criminal statute concerned primarily with a revision of the criminal law on offences against the person, it would seem reasonable to conclude that the provisions in question are concerned only with providing a defence against criminal liability. In other words they do not determine what is a lawful use of force in effecting an arrest or preventing crime for the purposes of a civil action.

4–63   It is also not clear whether the statutory provisions are meant to apply to the use of lethal force. A literal interpretation of the statutory provisions suggests that they apply irrespective of whether the force used was lethal or non-lethal.

[188b] C.D. 7631, August 5, 1914.
[189] *Lynch v. Fitzgerald* [1938] I.R. 382 at 404–405. Leigh commends Hanna J.'s judgment as offering an excellent discussion of the English authorities; see Leigh, *op. cit.*, above, n. 135, p. 60.

The Act, however, deals only with non-fatal offences against the person. It is at least arguable, therefore, that individual provisions which stipulate that it shall not be an offence to use force in certain circumstances must be interpreted to mean that it shall not be an offence under the Act. In other words they do not apply to the use of lethal force. This point is significant as the statutory provisions specifically abolish any defence available under the common law in respect of the use of force within the meaning of the pro-visions.[190] If they extend to the use of lethal force this could have the effect of abolishing the common law rule that death resulting from the intentional use of force which was excessive in the circumstances should result in murder being reduced to manslaughter.

Effecting a Lawful Arrest

The relevant provisions of the 1997 Act stipulate that the use of force by a person shall not constitute an offence in certain circumstances. The use of force to effect a lawful arrest is treated separately from the use of force for other purposes which include the prevention of crime. The relevant provisions stipulate that the use of force by a person in effecting or assisting in a lawful arrest does not constitute an offence if it is only such force as is reasonable in the circumstances as the person believes them to be.[191] For the purposes of this provision the lawfulness of the arrest shall also be determined according to the circumstances as the person using the force believed them to be. In so far as this provision is concerned with a defence to a criminal prosecution based on the use of force it is unlikely that it effects any change to the pre-existing position. The only striking feature about the provision is that it states clearly that the person using force must be treated on the basis of the circumstances as he believed them to be. It would appear, however, that the courts were already taking this approach when determining whether the force used was reasonable in the circumstances. In Northern Ireland, for example, the courts now treat police officers and soldiers on the basis of the circumstances as they believed them to be in prosecutions arising out of the use of lethal force. Accordingly, the actions of a police officer who honestly but mistakenly believes that a suspect is armed and about to fire to resist capture will be assessed as if that was the case, even though a reasonable person would not have formed the same belief in the circumstances.

Presumably, this subjective approach to mistaken beliefs does not extend to a civil action for damages arising out of the use of force in order to effect an arrest. In this context the courts treat the person using force on the basis of the facts as he honestly and reasonably believed them to be. It is submitted that the entirely subjective provisions of the 1997 Act are concerned only with the issue of criminal liability and do not affect the established position in civil actions.

4–64

---

[190] Non-fatal Offences against the Person Act 1997, s.22(2).
[191] Non-fatal Offences against the Person Act 1997, s.19(1).

Prevention of Crime, Self-defence, etc.

4–65   The use of force to prevent crime or a breach of the peace are treated together with what might be broadly defined as the use of force in self defence and the protection of property. The basic provision is the same as that for the use of force to effect an arrest. The use of force for this purpose does not constitute an offence if it is only such as is reasonable in the circumstances as the person using the force believes them to be.[192] The provision goes on to offer definitions of, *inter alia*, a crime and property in this context. Indeed, it is worth noting that the use of force to prevent crime will not constitute an offence even though the criminal act in question was being committed by a person who would be acquitted on the grounds of infancy, duress, automatism, intoxication or insanity.[193] Moreover, the question whether a crime was being committed shall be determined according to the circumstances as the person using the force believed them to be.[194] In other words if he honestly but mistakenly believed that a crime was being committed, his actions will be assessed as if his belief was true, even though a reasonable person would not have entertained the same belief. There is a limited exception, however, where the person knows that he is using force against a member of the Garda Síochána (see below para. 4–67).

Definition of Force

Although the question of what constitutes the use of force rarely presents a problem in the context of an arrest or the prevention of crime, it is worth noting that the provisions of the 1997 Act have their own definition of the use of force.[195] It covers the application of force to, as well as causing an impact on, the body of a person or property. It also covers threatening another person with the use of force, as well as detaining a person. Threatening another person with the use of force in relation to property also constitutes the use of force.

J. Resisting Arrest

1. An Offence

4–66   There is a specific offence of resisting a lawful arrest.[196] Such action is also likely to involve an assault, a battery or a related offence. However, the citizen is under no duty at common law to submit to an unlawful arrest.[197] Accordingly, he is entitled to use reasonable force to resist an unlawful arrest.[198] It would

---

[192]   *ibid.* s.18(1).
[193]   *ibid.* s.18(3).
[194]   *ibid.* s.18(5).
[195]   *ibid.* s.20.
[196]   Offences against the Person Act 1861, s.38. This provision has not been repealed by the Non-fatal Offences against the Person Act 1997.
[197]   See Glanville Williams, "Requisites of a Lawful Arrest" [1954] Crim. L.R.
[198]   *Christie v. Leachinsky* [1947] A.C. 573.

appear, however, that a balancing exercise is applied to determine what constitutes reasonable force in such cases.[199] If, for example, the only harm envisaged by the suspect was a period of unlawful detention in a Garda station it would probably be unreasonable for him to cause serious harm in order to resist an unlawful arrest. Indeed, the Non-fatal Offences against the Person Act 1997 states that the defence of self defence will not normally avail a person where he uses force against a person whom he knows to be a member of the Garda Síochána acting in the course of his duty or a person assisting such a member.[200] The situation is different if the person believes that the use of force is immediately necessary to prevent harm to himself or another.[201]

Defence

In some cases it has been accepted that the citizen may also use reasonable force to resist a lawful arrest which he honestly believes to be unlawful. The most likely example is where the suspect honestly believes that the persons seeking to arrest him are criminals who are attacking him.[202] These cases are treated as analogous to self defence cases. Accordingly, the principle should apply to any situation where the suspect's belief is based on a mistake of fact which, if true, would afford the defence of self defence. By the same token, however, the force used by the suspect must be no more than is reasonably necessary to protect himself, and it must be proportionate to the harm reasonably anticipated.

4–67

Resisting Unlawful Arrest

Now, however, as a result of the Non-fatal Offences against the Person Act 1997 a person cannot rely on this defence if he knows that the force is being used against a member of the Garda Síochána acting in the course of his duty or a person assisting such member, unless the person concerned believes the force to be immediately necessary to prevent harm to himself or another. It follows that a person should generally submit to an arrest, even though he believes that it is unlawful, where he knows that the arrest is being effected by a member of the Garda Síochána acting in the course of his or her duty or by a person assisting such member.[203] The use of force to resist can constitute an offence, unless the person concerned believes that the force is immediately necessary to prevent harm to himself or another.

4–68

---

199 *Palmer v. The Queen* [1971] A.C. 814; *R. v. Wilson* [1955] 1 W.L.R. 493; *R. v. Long* (1836) 7 C&P 314. See Leigh, *Police Powers in England and Wales* (2nd ed., Butterworths, London, 1915) p. 65.

200 Non-fatal Offences against the Person Act 1997, s.18(6).

201 *ibid.,* See also, *Kenlin v. Gardiner* [1967] 2 Q.B. 510; *Ludlow v. Burgess* (1971) 75 Cr. App. Rep. 227; *Devlin v. Armstrong* [1971] N.I. 13.

202 *Albert v. Lavin* [1982] A.C. 546; *R. v. Geen* [1982] Crim. L.R. 604; *R v. Barrett and Barrett* [1980] 72 Cr. App. Rep. 212; *R. v. Williams* [1984] 78 Cr. App. Rep. 276. Leigh suggests that where the person attempting to effect the arrest is in fact a police officer, it would still be possible to charge the suspect with the specific offence of assaulting a constable (garda) in the execution of his duty. This is based on the premise that the mistake cannot be raised with respect to the status of the officer for the purpose of this offence. See Leigh *op. cit* above, n. 199, p. 65.

203 Non-fatal Offences against the Person Act 1997, s.18(6). It would appear that the reference to a member of the Garda Síochána acting in the course of his or her duty in this context refers to a

A person may use reasonable force to rescue another from an unlawful arrest.[204] It would appear, however, that this possibility is largely confined to the situation where the arrest is in fact unlawful.[205] The Non-fatal Offences against the Person Act 1997 can be interpreted as extending the possibility to an arrest which is in fact lawful, but which the person using force honestly believes to be unlawful.[206] In any event the provisions of the Act make clear that this does not apply where the person using force knows that the arrest is being effected by a member of the Garda Síochána acting in the course of his or her duty or a person assisting such a member, unless the person concerned believes the force to be immediately necessary to prevent harm to himself or another.[207]

It is also worth noting that a person is not committing an offence merely by protesting verbally at the use of unnecessary violence in the arrest of another person.[208] Similarly, no offence is committed where a person assists another in seeking reasons for that other's arrest.[209]

K. Entry to Effect an Arrest

Introduction

4–69   At common law Garda powers of entry onto private property without a warrant and without the consent of the occupier are very restricted (see chapter 8). Where the purpose of the entry is purely to effect an arrest (as distinct from terminating an affray or protecting the right to life), it would appear that the officer must be in hot pursuit of a felon or the circumstances must be such that he could be considered to have an implied permission to enter. Powers of entry into a private dwelling are especially restricted at common law.[209a] In practice, the exact scope of such powers is likely to remain largely academic as they would appear to have been exceeded by the powers of entry to effect an arrest conferred by statute, particularly that conferred by the Criminal Law Act 1997.

Section 6 of the Criminal Law Act 1997 permits a member of the Garda Síochána in certain circumstances to enter any premises without a warrant in

---

member going about his or her normal business as a member as distinct from the lawfulness or perceived lawfulness of the member's actions in the particular situation.

[204]   *Hills v. Ellis* [1983] Q.B. 680; *Lewis v. Cox* [1984] 3 All E.R. 672.

[205]   An exception is where the person arrested appears to be in peril of life and limb so that an immediate decision is required; *R. v. Fennell* [1971] 1 Q.B. 428.

[206]   Non-fatal Offences against the Person Act 1997, s.18(1) and (5).

[207]   *ibid.* s.18(6).

[208]   *Hughes v. Casares* (1967) 111 Sol. Jo. 637; *R. v. Osmer* (1804) 5 East 304. However, if his protest includes acts of physical interference he may be guilty of obstructing a member of the Garda Síochána in the execution of his duty; see Leigh, *op. cit.,* above, n.199, p. 64.

[209]   If, however, he acts intemperately or unreasonably he may find himself guilty of obstructing a member of the Garda Síochána in the execution of his duty; *Hills v. Ellis* [1983] Q.B. 680; *Lewis v. Cox* [1984] 3 All E.R. 672; *Willmott v. Atack* [1977] Q.B. 498. Leigh, *op. cit.,* above, n. 199, p. 58.

[209a]   Note, however, that an arrest which is otherwise lawful may be effected in a dwelling where the arresting party is there with the express or implied consent of the occupier; *People (DPP) v. McCann* [1998] 4 I.R. 397.

order to effect the arrest of a person who is, or who the member with reasonable cause suspects to be, on the premises. The actual terms of the power differ depending on whether the premises are a dwelling. There is also distinct provision for entry to effect an arrest pursuant to a warrant (see below para 4–115).

Premises Other than a Dwelling

A member of the Garda Síochána may enter any premises other than a dwelling for the purpose of arresting a person without a warrant for an "arrestable offence".[210] The person to be arrested must actually be on the premises or the member must have reasonable cause to suspect that he is there. Once lawfully on the premises the member may search them for the person.

    An arrestable offence in the context of this power is defined as "an offence for which a person of full capacity and not previously convicted may, under or by virtue of any enactment, be punished by imprisonment for a term of five years or by a more severe penalty and includes an attempt to commit any such offence".[211] While this covers a very wide range of offence, it is worth emphasising that it does not cover all offences. Nor does it include behaviour likely to lead to a breach of the peace or a reasonable apprehension that a breach of the peace will be occasioned. Accordingly, the uncertainty surrounding the availability of a police power to enter onto private property to prevent a threatend breach of the peace remains (see chapter 8).

4–70

A Dwelling

A member of the Garda Síochána may also enter a dwelling for the purpose of effecting an arrest for an arrestable offence, as defined above, and where the person to be arrested is in the dwelling or where the member has reasonable cause to suspect that he is there.[212] This power will only be available, however, if the member is acting with the consent of the occupier or some other person who appears to the member to be in charge of the dwelling, or if one of the following four circumstances are present: (i) a member of the Garda Síochána has observed the person within or entering the dwelling; (ii) the member effecting the entry suspects, with reasonable cause, that before a warrant of arrest can be obtained the person will either abscond for the purpose of avoiding justice or will obstruct the course of justice; (iii) the member effecting the entry suspects, with reasonable cause, that before a warrant of arrest can be obtained the person would commit an arrestable offence;[213] or (iv) the person ordinarily resides at that dwelling. The member may search the dwelling for the person.

4–71

---

[210] Criminal Law Act 1997, s.6(2).

[211] *ibid.* s.2(1).

[212] *ibid.* s.6(2).

[213] It is not entirely clear whether the arrestable offence which the member with reasonable cause suspects the person will commit must be in addition to an arrestable offence for which the member already wants to arrest him. It is submitted that the intention was that it need not be an additional offence. However, it will take a sympathetic judicial interpretation to achieve that result.

Consequential Matters

4–72   In acting under either of these powers of entry a member of the Garda Síochána can, if need be, use reasonable force to gain entry to the premises. There is no specific requirement that he or she should always seek a consensual entry first. Presumably, it will be depend on the circumstances of each individual case whether the use of force was lawful in the absence of a prior attempt to gain a consensual entry. Once lawfully on the premises the member may search them in order to effect the arrest. It is worth emphasising, however, that none of these powers of entry and search actually confer a distinct police power of arrest. The arrest must be grounded on foot of a warrant or committal order or some other common law or statutory power of arrest (or a warrant or committal order). The elements of the particular power of arrest used in any case must be satisfied independently of the requirements of these powers of entry and search conferred by the Criminal Law Act 1997. Indeed, it would appear that the member of the Garda Síochána in question must already have made up his or her mind to effect the arrest before entering the premises. The power of entry and search is conferred solely for the purpose of effecting the arrest. It does not enable the member to enter and search for the purpose of investigating whether an arrestable offence has been or is being committed, although there are powers at common law to enter for the purpose of terminating an affray or to protect someone's right to life (see chapter 8). Once the arrest has been effected the member can rely on his common law power to search the person concerned and the immediate vicinity for any dangerous weapon or evidence relating to the offence. Moreover, if the arrest power used is conferred by statute it may be that the legislation in question confers further powers which the member may exercise with respect to the person arrested while on the premises.

L. Search and Seizure on Arrest

1. At Common Law

The Person

4–73   At common law a member of the Garda Síochána has the power to search a person whom he or she has arrested.[214] The purpose of this search would appear to be to enable the member to take into possession anything found on the person in the nature of a dangerous weapon or which may be used to facilitate an escape from custody, or any item which may be of evidentiary value. In most cases, therefore, the search will be confined to a body frisk and examination of the suspect's outer garments. In some cases, however, the circumstances may be such as to justify a strip search or an even more intimate search of the body. Although the position is still unclear at common law it is

---

[214]   *Bessell v. Wilson* 20 LT (O.S.) 233.

submitted that because a strip search or an intimate body search represents a serious infringement of the individual's right to bodily privacy, it would be lawful only if there was reasonable grounds to suspect that the individual had relevant items secreted on his person, and that they could be discovered only by the form of search used. In practice most situations in which the strip search of an individual suspect is appropriate would be covered by statutory provisions.

Immediate Area of Arrest

The police power of search and seizure consequent on arrest extends at least   **4–74**
to the immediate area in which the suspect was seized. In *Dillon v. O'Brien*,[215]
for example, police officers searched the room in which the accused was arrested and seized documents which they believed were evidence of a charge of criminal conspiracy against him. The officers did not have a warrant to search the room. Nevertheless, the police action was declared lawful. Palles C.B. explained the decision as follows:

> "[T]he interest of the State in the person charged being brought to trial in due course necessarily extends as well to the preservation of material evidence of his guilt or innocence as to his custody for the purpose of trial. His custody is of no value if the law is powerless to prevent the abstraction or destruction of this evidence, without which a trial would be no more than an empty form."[216]

It is not entirely clear from this case whether the right to search the room arises automatically on the arrest, or whether the officers must entertain a reasonable suspicion that there is relevant evidence in the room and that it may disappear or be destroyed if they have to wait for a warrant to seize it. In any event, presumably there would have to be some correlation between the nature of the search and the offence for which the suspect has been arrested. If, for example, the suspect has been arrested on suspicion of possessing stolen computer parts, it would seem unreasonable to search through his private papers. Such action can hardly be described as a search for the stolen computer parts, unless the circumstances were such that there was reason to believe that the suspect my have correspondence which throws some light on subsequent dealings with the stolen computer parts.

Areas under Suspect's Control

In *Dillon v. O'Brien* the search was carried out in the room where the suspect   **4–75**
was apprehended. The court did not specifically consider whether the search could extend beyond the room to areas which were under the suspect's control or to which he had access. In *Jennings v. Quinn*,[217] however, the Supreme Court had to consider the legality of a search of the suspect's house and the seizure of material consequent upon the search at the time of his arrest. O'Keeffe J. described the police powers of seizure consequent on a lawful arrest in the following terms:

---

[215]   20 LR (I.R.) 300.
[216]   *ibid.* at 317.
[217]   [1968] I.R. 305.

"In my opinion the public interest requires that the police, when effecting a lawful arrest, may seize, without a search warrant, property in the possession or custody of the person arrested when they believe it necessary to do so to avoid the abstraction or destruction of that property and when that property is:–
   (a) evidence in support of the criminal charge upon which the arrest is made, or
   (b) evidence in support of any other criminal charge against that person then in contemplation, or
   (c) reasonably believed to be stolen property or to be property unlawfully in the possession of that person."[217a]

4–76   The fact that the property can be seized only when the police are *"effecting"* (emphasis added) the arrest suggests that it must be found in the possession or custody of the suspect at the time of the arrest. This implies that a search may be made of the suspect's person and the immediate area under his physical control at the time of arrest. Given the decision in the case, however, it seems that a search may also be made of other rooms in the building, or parts of the property, to which the suspect had immediate access.[218] Items found there can be considered to be in the possession or custody of the suspect. It is most unlikely, however, that O'Keeffe J.'s dictum could be used to justify a search of buildings or property located elsewhere. Such a search could be effected only after the suspect had been arrested. Accordingly, it would go well beyond the ambit of what is necessary to seize property in the possession or custody of the suspect when "effecting" his arrest. It would appear, therefore, that *Jennings v. Quinn* would not afford authority for a summary search of a suspect's home where he had been arrested elsewhere.[219]

4–77   It is important to note that *Jennings v. Quinn* does not provide authority for a power of automatic search consequent on arrest. O'Keeffe J. specifically states that the police may seize property only when they believe it necessary to do so in order to avoid the abstraction or destruction of that property. The implication is that a search may only be carried out if the police believe that it may uncover relevant material which may be removed or destroyed in the time that it would take to secure a search warrant. It would appear that it will be sufficient if they honestly hold this belief. There is no specific requirement of reasonable grounds for the belief.

4–78   The material that can be seized must constitute property defined at (a) or (b) or (c) in the quotation above. Presumably, this means that a search can be carried out for evidence in support of the criminal charge upon which the arrest is made, and if evidence under (b) or (c) just happens to be uncovered, then it may also be seized.[220] It is doubtful whether O'Keeffe J. meant that a

---

[217a] *ibid.* at 309
[218] Contrast the position on the USA where such searches and seizures cannot extend to other rooms in the building even though the suspect has access to them.
[219] See the decision of the English Court of Appeal in *Jeffrey v. Black* [1978] 1 All E.R. 555.
[220] Note that section 9 of the Criminal Law Act 1976 states that a member of the Garda Síochána who is conducting a search under any power may seize anything which he believes to be evidence of any offence or suspected offence.

search could be carried out for all three categories of property. To hold otherwise would represent a significant extension of the scope of the police powers of search without a warrant as they had been understood up until the decision in *Jennings v. Quinn*. It would mean that once the police had arrested an individual in his own home on suspicion of an offence against the person, for example, they would acquire the power to carry out a general search of the home looking for stolen goods even though the individual was not under suspicion for possession of stolen goods. Such an interpretation runs contrary to common law norms of criminal justice. In the absence of any further judicial clarification, therefore, it would appear that the narrower interpretation is preferable.

2. Criminal Law Act 1976

It is also worth noting in this context that section 9 of the Criminal Law 1976   **4–79** permits a member of the Garda Síochána when conducting a search under any power to seize anything which he believes to be evidence of any offence or suspected offence. This is dealt with in chapter 8.

M. Re-Arrest

1. Arrest upon Arrest

As a general principle there is no bar on the arrest of an individual who is   **4–80** already under arrest or in custody. For example, a person may be arrested for a breach of the peace and, immediately, thereafter a member of the Garda Síochána might become aware of circumstances which justify his arrest under a statutory power which permits a period of detention for the investigation of an offence. In this situation it will generally be lawful for the member to arrest the person under the statutory power even though he is under arrest for the breach of the peace at the time.[221]

Re-arrest can also feature where the initial arrest is made by someone who is   **4–81** not a member of the Garda Síochána. This, of course, need not be an unusual situation given the fact that ordinary citizens enjoy broad powers of arrest under the Criminal Law Act 1997. Where a citizen effects an arrest under one of these powers he must transfer the person arrested into the custody of the Garda Síochána as soon as possible.[222] The Act does not specifically require the suspect to be re-arrested on transfer into Garda custody. Nevertheless, this would appear to be the proper course of action if the suspect is going to be charged and brought before a District Court judge or if he is going to be detained under one of the statutory provisions. It is also worth noting that there is no statutory prohibition on the arrest of a person by a member of the Garda Síochána at a time when he is already in custody having been arrested

---

[221] *People (DPP) v. Kehoe* [1986] I.L.R.M. 690.
[222] Criminal Law Act 1997, s.4(5).

by someone who is not a member of the Garda Síochána. Moreover, there is case law which suggests that the second arrest would be lawful.

4–82   In *Re O'Laighléis*,[222a] for example, the applicant had been arrested under section 30 of the Offences against the State Act 1939 which permitted his detention in Garda custody for up to 24 hours followed by a further period of up to 24 hours if duly authorised by an appropriate officer of the Garda Síochána. While detained under section 30 he was served with a warrant of detention issued by the Minister for Justice pursuant to the provisions of the Offences against the State (Amendment) Act 1940 which made provision for internment without trial. In his application for an order of *habeas corpus* to be made absolute he argued, *inter alia*, that his detention persuant to the ministerial warrant was unlawful as he could not be arrested at a time when he was already deprived of his liberty under section 30. In short there could not be an arrest of a person who was already in custody under arrest. In rejecting this argument in the High Court, Davitt P. explained:

> "The fallacy [in the argument] . . . lies in regarding an arrest as essentially the determination of a pre-existing liberty. This is not, in our view, an essential or necessary feature of arrest. The essence is the restraint from liberty as from the moment of arrest, that is, the subsequent or future restraint. It is irrelevant, therefore, to the true nature of an arrest whether the person arrested was then at liberty or not."[223]

4–83   This approach was applied by the Court of Criminal Appeal in *People (DPP) v. O'Shea*[224] when upholding the legality of the arrest of the appellant by gardaí at a time when he was in the custody of customs officers. In that case the appellant had been detained by customs officers under section 2 of the Customs and Excise (Miscellaneous Provisions) Act 1988 following a search of his vehicle which revealed a substantial quantity of proscribed drugs. The customs officers contacted the gardaí. When the gardaí arrived they arrested the appellant and brought him to a Garda station where he was detained under section 4 of the Criminal Justice Act 1984. Whilst in Garda custody he made an incriminating statement. It was argued on appeal that at the time he made the statement he was unlawfully detained. The basis of this argument was that the arrest by gardaí was unlawful as it was effected at a time when he was already under arrest by customs officers, and that there could not be an arrest upon an arrest. The Court of Criminal Appeal rejected this contention, preferring instead the view of Davitt P. that the hallmark of an arrest was the taking of a person into custody. It did not matter whether the transition was from freedom to custody or from one form of custody to another.

[222a] [1960] I.R. 93.
[223]   *Re O'Laighléis* [1960] I.R. 93 at 108.
[224]   [1996] 1 I.R. 557.

Arresting Person Unlawfully Detained

It would also appear that the legality of an arrest would not be vitiated solely **4–84** because the person arrested was arrested immediately after being released from unlawful detention in circumstances where he was not afforded a realistic opportunity to leave the custody of the State. In *Quinlivan v. Governor of Portlaoise Prison,*[224a] for example, the applicant had been remanded in custody by the Special Criminal Court. It transpired subsequently that the applicant's custody was unlawful because the remand had been ordered by an improperly constituted court. With a view to regularising the situation the applicant was released from the prison custody, immediately re-arrested by a member of the Garda Síochána, charged and brought before a properly constituted court which remanded him back into the custody of the prison governor. The applicant's challenge to the legality of his subsequent arrest failed in the Supreme Court essentially because the Court found that he had been released from the unlawful detention before being re-arrested. It made no difference that the subsequent arrest was effected immediately after the release and had been pre-planned. There was no conscious and deliberate plan by the authorities to deny the applicant his constitutional rights. The applicant argued that he should at least have been brought to the public street before being re-arrested. In rejecting this argument Barron J., giving the judgment of the Supreme Court, said:

> "It is significant that the challenge against this procedure is that there was no release because the applicant was not brought to the public street before he was re-arrested. The law would surely be an ass if it denied the right of the gardaí to arrest a person on private property where the person arrested had no chance of escaping arrest, in favour of permitting his arrest on the public street where he would have had the same lack of chance of escaping."[224b]

2. Restrictions on Re-arrest of Person Detained under Section 4

The primary restrictions on the re-arrest of a person who is already under **4–85** arrest or who is otherwise in custody arise in the context of the statutory powers of detention. It will be seen in chapter 5 that in some circumstances a suspect can be detained in police custody for the investigation of an offence under certain statutory provisions. Typically, the legislation creating these powers imposes limits on the extent to which a person can be re-arrested for an offence in respect of which he has already been detained.

The Statutory Provisions

The most general of these detention provisions is section 4 of the Criminal Justice Act 1984 which permits the detention of a suspect who has been

---

[224a] [1998] 1 I.R. 456. See also *Hegarty v. Governor of Limerick Prison* [1998] 1 I.R. 412; *Duncan v. Governor of Portlaoise Prison (No.2)* [1998] 1 I.R. 433; *Cully v. Governor of Portlaoise Prison* [1998] 1 I.R. 443.
[224b] *ibid.* at 462–463.

arrested on suspicion of an offence for which a person of full age and capacity and not previously convicted may be punished by imprisonment for a term of five years or by a more severe penalty. The Act imposes very clear restrictions on the nature and duration of the detention. These restrictions would be rendered nugatory if the suspect could be re-arrested and detained *ad nauseam* under section 4. Accordingly, the Act imposes restrictions on the re-arrest of a suspect who has previously been detained under section 4.

4–86   Section 10(1) of the Criminal Justice Act 1984 reads:

> "Where a person arrested on suspicion of having committed an offence is detained pursuant to *section 4* and is released without any charge having been made against him, he shall not –
> (a) be arrested for the same offence, or
> (b) be arrested for any other offence of which, at the time of the first arrest, the member of the Garda Síochána by whom he was arrested suspected him or ought reasonably to have suspected him,
> except on the authority of a judge of the District Court who is satisfied on information supplied on oath by a member of the Garda Síochána not below the rank of Superintendent that further information has come to the knowledge of the Garda Síochána since the person's release as to his suspected participation in the offence for which his arrest is sought. A person arrested under that authority shall be dealt with pursuant to section 4."

Requirement for Detention and Release without Charge

4–87   This provision clearly applies only to a suspect who has been detained under section 4 and released without charge. It is not available where the arrest did not lead on to a section 4 detention, irrespective of whether such detention was a possibility.[225] However, as will be seen later, protection against a section 4 detention is available for a suspect who has already been arrested and detained in certain circumstances under other statutory provisions.[226] It is also worth noting that the protection only applies if the suspect was released without charge from the earlier detention. A literal interpretation of the provision would suggest that if he was charged before being released or brought before a District Court judge, it may yet be possible to arrest him at some time in the future and detain him under section 4 either for the offence for which he was originally arrested or for one which the arresting officer either suspected him of at the time or ought reasonably to have suspected him. However, in *People (DPP) v. Cooney*[227] the trial judge ruled that the possibility of a re-arrest pursuant to section 10 had no application to the

---

[225]   In *People (DPP) v. Kehoe* [1985] I.R. 444 the Court of Criminal Appeal ruled that an arrest at common law would not preclude a subsequent arrest and detention under s.30 of the Offences against the State Act 1939 once the grounds for such an arrest were discovered. It would not be necessary in such circumstances to go through the colourable manouevre of an apparent release from custody before effecting the subsequent arrest.

[226]   Criminal Justice Act 1984, s.10(3) and Criminal Justice (Drug Trafficking) Act 1996, s.4(6).

[227]   [1998] 1 I.L.R.M. 321.

situation where a person had been released after having been charged for the offence for which his re-arrest was sought.

Protection against Detention under Other Statutory Powers

Where the suspect has already been detained for an offence under section 4 **4–88** and released without charge, he cannot normally be arrested again for that offence. It would appear that this protection extends to arrest under another statutory power of arrest and detention such as that provided by section 30 of the Offences against the State Act 1939.[227a] Moreover, there is provision to counter a police attempt to circumvent this protection by arresting the suspect for another offence related to the overall police investigation of him for the matter in question. The suspect cannot normally be arrested in respect of another offence where the member of the Garda Síochána who effected the original arrest either suspected, or ought reasonably to have suspected, the individual in question of the other offence at the time of the original arrest.[227b]

Protection against Related Offences

Surprisingly, perhaps, this extended protection is not specifically confined to section 4 offences. The suspect is protected against arrest for "any other offence". There is no requirement that the "other" offence should be within the ambit of section 4. It is of course arguable that the reference to "any other offence" should be interpreted as any other offence within the scope of section 4. Support for this interpretation can be derived from other features of the re-arrest provision. Should this narrower interpretation be adopted it is at least conceivable that a suspect, having been detained and released without charge under section 4, could be re-arrested and detained under section 30 of the Offences against the State Act 1939 for an offence which did not come within the scope of section 4. It will be seen below, however, that there is separate protection against this eventuality.

Potential Grounds for Arrest Sufficient

It is worth noting that the prohibition on re-arrest comes into play even if the **4–89** member of the Garda Síochána concerned was not in a position to arrest the

---

[227a] Finnegan J. adopted a contrary interpretation in *Moloney v. Member in Charge of Terenure Garda Station* [2002] 2 I.L.R.M. 149 where he concluded that the prohibition in s.10(1) on a re-arrest consequent on a section 4 detention applied only to arrests for the purposes of detaining the suspect again under s.4, and did not extend to a prohibition on re-arrest under s. 30 of the Offences against the State Act 1939. It is respectfully submitted that the learned judge fell into error by treating the section 4 power of detention as a power of arrest, as distinct from a power of detention which comes into effect consequent on arrest pursuant to another power. The decision in *Moloney* is under appeal at the time of writing.

[227b] But see *Moloney v. Member in Charge of Terenure Garda Station* [2002] 2 I.L.R.M. 149 where Finnegan J. accepted that a suspect could be arrested summarily for the investigation of a firearms charge even though he had previously been arrested for the investigation of a murder which was connected with the firearms charge. The learned judge considered that the firearms charge was a serious offence which merited investigation and was not simply a colourable device to pursue the murder investigation.

suspect for the other offence at the time he or she effected the arrest for the first offence. The statutory provision merely requires that he or she suspected or ought reasonably to have suspected the person of the other offence. Neither of these standards of "suspicion" may be sufficient to permit the member to effect an arrest in some situations. However, if the member who effected the original arrest did not suspect, and had no reasonable grounds to suspect, the individual in question for the other offence at the time of the first arrest, the prohibition will not apply even if other members of the Garda Síochána had the requisite suspicion at that time.

Application to District Court Judge

4–90   The prohibition on re-arrest is not absolute even where the circumstances for its application are present. The gardaí can avoid it by satisfying a District Court judge that further information about the suspect's participation in the offence for which his arrest is sought has come to their notice since his release from section 4 detention. This information must be supplied on oath to the judge by a member of the Garda Síochána not below the rank of superintendent. Where these requirements are satisfied, it would appear that the judge can issue an authority for the suspect's arrest. The gardaí can then deal with the suspect under section 4. This, of course, raises the issue of whether the offence would have to be an offence within the scope of section 4. The bare words of the provision do not specifically require that it should be such an offence. However, since the substantive effect of the issue of an authority by a District Court judge under this provision is that the suspect will be detained under section 4, it would seem reasonable to suppose that the power to authorise a re-arrest is confined to offences for which an arrested suspect may be detained under section 4.

4–91   Interestingly, it is only necessary for the District Court judge to be satisfied that the further information has come to the knowledge of the Garda Síochána and that this information relates to the suspect's participation in the offence for which his arrest is sought.[228] Nevertheless, the information supplied on oath must provide a basis upon which the judge can be satisfied as to the presence of the matters specified in section 10. In *Larkin v. O'Dea*,[229] for example, it was held that a District Court judge's authorisation for re-arrest was invalid as it did not satisfy these requirements. In that case the applicant had been arrested and detained under section 4 before being released without charge. In seeking authorisation for re-arrest a Garda superintendent swore an information that since "the date of that release further evidence has come into our possession and further inquiries have been made to establish the author of the alleged crime." The District Court judge's authorisation to effect the re-arrest was quashed in the High Court by Morris J. on the ground that there was no

---

[228]   It may happen that the re-arrest is sought for an offence which is different from that for which the original arrest was effected. In this event, further information about the suspect's participation in the first offence may not be sufficient.

[229]   [1994] 2 I.L.R.M. 448 and [1995] 2 I.L.R.M. 1.

evidence in the sworn information which would have enabled the judge to be satisfied that the new information related to the applicant's suspected participation in the offence. It is submitted that even if the information stated specifically that the Garda evidence related to the suspect it would not neccessarily be sufficient. There must be some evidence, apart from the mere assertion by the Garda officer, which would enable the judge to satisfy himself that further evidence relating the suspect to the offence had become available.[229a]

It is also worth noting that the further information must have "come to the knowledge of the Garda Síochána" before authorisation can issue. Given that the Garda Síochána is a body of individual members organised in ranks under the general direction and control of the Garda Commissioner, it is not entirely clear when information has come to its knowledge for the purposes of this re-arrest provision. This might happen, for example, when information comes to the knowledge of any member of the force. If this interpretation is adopted the Garda Síochána could be taken to have knowledge of the information at the time of the original arrest, even if it was not known at that time to the member or members engaged in the actual investigation of the suspect. Since the information would already be in the hands of the Garda Síochána, the mere fact that it came for the first time to the attention of those members engaged in the investigation would not be sufficient to satisfy the requirement of "further information" which has come to the knowledge of the Garda Síochána. A more likely interpretation, however, is that "further information" is any information which was not previously known to members actually engaged in the investigation. If this interpretation was adopted then the mere fact that one or more members were already aware of the information at the time of the first arrest would not in itself be sufficient to prevent the re-arrest provision coming into play if the members engaged in the investigation of the suspect were not aware of its existence at the time of the first arrest.

4–92

Section 4 Detention Consequent on Section 30 Detention

It will be seen below that there are similar restrictions on the re-arrest of a suspect who has already been detained under section 2 of the Criminal Justice (Drug Trafficking) Act 1996 or arrested under section 30 of the Offences against the State Act 1939 for the same offence or an offence of which he was suspected or ought reasonably to have been suspected at the time of the first arrest by the member of the Garda Síochána who made the first arrest. Nevertheless, it is worth noting that section 10 of the 1984 Act imposes a specific prohibition on the detention of a suspect under section 4 where he has already been arrested for a relevant offence under section 30 of the 1939 Act. It stipulates that a person who has been arrested for an offence under section 30 and released without charge cannot be detained pursuant to section 4 in

4–93

[229a] See *Larking v. O'Dea* [1994] 2 I.L.R.M. 448, by analogy, *People (DPP) v. Kenny* [1990] I.L.R.M. 569.

connection with that offence or in connection with any other offence of which, at the time of his first arrest, the member of the Garda Síochána by whom he was arrested suspected him or ought reasonably to have suspected him.[230] As will be seen below a suspect who has been arrested under section 30 cannot be re-arrested under these circumstances unless under the authority of a warrant issued by a District Court judge. Where such an authority does issue the suspect must be detained pursuant to a modified version of the provisions of section 30. In other words the possibility of detention pursuant to section 4 of the 1984 Act cannot arise.

Re-arrest for the Purpose of Being Charged

4-94   Where the requirements for a re-arrest of a suspect who has already been detained under section 4 of the 1984 Act cannot be satisfied the suspect is protected against further arrest for the offence in question. This protection is effective against any power of arrest which carries with it the possibility of a statutory period of detention in police custody. However, it does not protect the suspect from being arrested for the purpose of being charged and being brought before a District Court judge. Section 10(2) of the Act states:

> "Notwithstanding anything in *subsection (1)*, a person to whom that subsection relates may be arrested for any offence for the purpose of charging him with that offence forthwith."

This offers statutory support for the police practice of arresting a suspect detained under section 4 for the purpose of charging him with an offence. Once charged the suspect should normally be brought before a District Court judge pursuant to the provisions of section 15 of the Criminal Justice Act 1951.

3. Restrictions on Re-arrest of Person Detained under Other Powers

4-95   Just as there are restrictions on the re-arrest of suspects who have been detained under section 4 of the 1984 Act, so also are there restrictions on the re-arrest of suspects who have been detained under certain other statutory provisions. It will be seen in chapter 5 that a suspect who has been arrested under section 30 of the Offences against the State Act 1939 can be detained without charge under that provision for up to a maximum of 72 hours. Equally, it will be seen that a person who has been arrested for a drug trafficking offence can be detained for the proper investigation of the offence for up to a maximum of seven days under section 2 of the Drug Trafficking (Miscellaneous Provisions) Act 1996. The provisions governing the re-arrest of these suspects are very similar to those governing the re-arrest of a suspect who has already been detained under section 4. Each will be dealt with briefly.

---

[230]   Criminal Justice Act 1984, s.10(3).

Section 2 of the 1996 Act

Where a person has been detained pursuant to section 2 of the Criminal **4–96**
Justice (Drug Trafficking) Act 1996 and released without charge he cannot
normally be re-arrested in connection with the offence for which he was
detained or for any other offence which, at the time of the first arrest, the
member of the Garda Síochána who effected the first arrest either suspected or
ought reasonably to have suspected him of having committed.[231] The points
made above in connection with the comparable provisions of section 4 apply
equally to this prohibition on re-arrest.

Apart from the possibility of arresting the suspect for the purpose of
charging him with an offence,[232] the suspect can be re-arrested under this
provision only on the authority of a warrant issued by a Circuit Court judge or
a District Court judge.[233] There are two differences here from the provision in
section 4 of the 1984 Act. The latter refers only to an "authority" as distinct
from a warrant. Also the authority under the 1984 Act can be issued only by a
District Court judge, while in the 1996 Act the warrant can be issued either by
a judge of the Circuit Court or a judge of the District Court.

For a warrant to issue the judge must be satisfied on information supplied on **4–97**
oath by a member of the Garda Síochána not below the rank of superintendent that further information has come to the knowledge of the Garda
Síochána since the person's release as to his suspected participation in the
offence for which his arrest is sought. The points made above with respect to
the comparable provision in the 1984 Act apply here. One difference with the
1984 Act is that the judge, when issuing the warrant, may order that the
person be brought before a judge of the District or Circuit Court on arrest, or
at any specified time or times during the authorised period of detention.[234]
Where the detained person is brought before a judge pursuant to such an
order the judge must order the person's release if he is not satisfied that the
detention is justified.

A person re-arrested for a drug-trafficking offence under a warrant issued
pursuant to section 2 will be treated, with some modifications, as if he had
been arrested for a drug-trafficking offence and detained under section 2 (see
chapter 5).[235] Where the person is re-arrested for any other offence under a
warrant issued pursuant to section 2 he must be dealt with, subject to some
modification, under section 4 of the Criminal Justice Act 1984.[236]

The 1996 Act includes a specific provision prohibiting the detention of a **4–98**
suspect under section 2 where he has already been detained under section 4 of
the Criminal Justice Act 1984 or arrested under section 30 of the Offences

---

[231] Criminal Justice (Drug Trafficking) Act, s.4(1).
[232] *ibid.* s.4(5).
[233] *ibid.* s.4(1).
[234] *ibid.* s.4(2).
[235] *ibid.* s.4(3).
[236] *ibid.* s.4(4).

207

against the State Act 1939 and released without charge.[237] It is virtually identical to the comparable provision in the 1984 Act which prohibits the detention under section 4 of a suspect who has already been arrested under section 30 of the 1939 Act. It is arguable of course that the provision in section 2 is largely superfluous given the prohibitions on re-arrest to be found in the 1984 and 1939 Acts. A suspect who has already been arrested under section 30 and released without charge cannot subsequently be detained for a relevant offence except under a warrant duly issued by a District Court judge. Where such a warrant does issue the suspect can be detained only pursuant to a modified version of the provisions of section 30. Accordingly, the possibility of detention pursuant to section 2 of the 1996 Act should not arise. Similarly, where a person has been detained pursuant to section 4 of the 1984 Act he cannot be arrested again for a relevant offence except under a warrant duly issued by a District Court judge. Where such a warrant does issue the suspect can be detained only pursuant to the provisions of section 4 of the Criminal Justice Act 1984. Accordingly, the possibility of detention pursuant to section 2 of the 1996 Act should not arise.

4–99   It is worth noting, however, that the prohibition in section 2 operates in a slightly different context from the prohibitions in either the 1939 or 1984 Acts. As will be seen in chapter 5 there are two situations in which a person can be detained under section 2 of the 1996 Act. The first arises where a person is arrested for a drug trafficking offence and taken to a Garda station, and the other arises where an arrested person is taken to a place of detention. Since the first situation requires an arrest, it is highly unlikely that it would escape the prohibition on the re-arrest of a person who was first arrested under section 30 of the 1939 Act or detained under section 4 of the 1984 Act. In the second situation, however, it is at least conceivable that a person could be detained in a place of detention under section 2 of the 1996 Act, after having been first arrested and detained under section 30 of the 1939 Act or arrested under some other power followed by detention under section 4 of the 1984 Act. In this situation the specific provision prohibiting detention under section 2 consequent on an earlier detention under either of the other provisions has some practical relevance.

Section 30 of the 1939 Act

4–100   Where a person arrested on suspicion of having committed an offence is detained pursuant to section 30 of the Offences against the State Act 1939 and is subsequently released without charge, he cannot normally be arrested again for the same offence or for an offence of which, at the time of the first arrest, the member of the Garda Síochána by whom he was arrested suspected him or ought reasonably to have suspected him of having committed.[238] As with the other prohibitions on re-arrest this prohibition does not prevent the arrest

---

[237] *ibid.* s.4(6).
[238] Offences against the State Act 1939, s.30A(1), as inserted by Offences against the State (Amendment) Act 1998, s.11.

of a suspect for the purpose of charging him with an offence.[239] The primary exception to the re-arrest prohibition, however, is provided by section 30A of the Act. It permits the re-arrest of the suspect for such an offence only under the authority of a warrant issued by a judge of the District Court. Before issuing the warrant the judge must be satisfied by information supplied on oath by an officer of the Garda Síochána not below the rank of superintendent that further information has come to the knowledge of the Garda Síochána since the person's release as to his suspected participation in the offence for which his arrest is sought. This is virtually identical to the comparable provision in section 10 of the Criminal Justice Act 1984. Accordingly, the points made above with respect to that provision are applicable here.

Where a person is re-arrested under a warrant issued pursuant to section 30A   **4–101**
he can be detained in police custody for a period of 24 hours and is generally subject to the same provisions governing the detention of a person arrested under section 30, apart from those permitting extensions of the period of detention beyond 24 hours.[240]

4. Arrest of Person in Prison

There is now provision for the arrest of a person who is already in prison or a   **4–102**
place of detention pursuant to a sentence of imprisonment or detention. Section 42 of the Criminal Justice Act 1999 states that a member of the Garda Síochána may arrest a prisoner on the authority of a judge of the District Court who is satisfied on information supplied on oath by a member of the Garda Síochána not below the rank of superintendent that certain conditions are present.[241] The conditions are as follows: (i) there are reasonable grounds for suspecting that the prisoner has committed an offence other than the offence in respect of which he or she is imprisoned; (ii) the arrest of the prisoner is necessary for the proper investigation of the offence which he or she is suspected of having committed; and (iii) where the prisoner has previously been arrested for the same offence, whether prior to his or her imprisonment or under this provision, further relevant information has since come to the knowledge of the Garda Síochána.[241a]

It is important to emphasise that this power of arrest is available on the   **4–103**
authority of a judge of the District Court.[241b] In order to give the necessary authority, however, it is necessary that the judge is satisfied about the relevant conditions on the sworn information of a member of the Garda Síochána holding the appropriate rank. The first of those conditions clearly refers to

---

[239] *ibid.* s.30A(3), *ibid.* s.11.
[240] *ibid.* s.30A(2), s.11.
[241] Criminal Justice Act 1999, s.42(2).
[241a] See District Court (Criminal Justice)(No.2) Rules, 2001, Sched. 1, Form 17.8 for the relevant form.
[241b] See *ibid.* Form 17.9 for the arrest warrant.

reasonable grounds for suspecting that the offender has committed an offence. It would appear that it would not be sufficient for the member to state on oath his or her belief that there are reasonable grounds for the suspicion. He or she would have to supply information which would enable the judge to be satisfied that there are reasonable grounds. With respect to the other two conditions, however, there is no such objective requirement. It is at least arguable, therefore, that it would be sufficient for the member to state his or her belief on oath that the arrest of the prisoner is necessary for the proper investigation of the offence and, where appropriate, that further relevant information has come to the knowledge of the Garda Síochána.

It is also worth noting that an offence in this context refers to an arrestable offence as defined by the Criminal Law Act 1997. It follows that the power is available only in respect of an offence for which a person of full capacity and not previously convicted may, under or by virtue of any enactment, be punished by imprisonment for a term of five years or by a more severe penalty.

4–104 For the purposes of this power of arrest a prison is defined as a place of custody administered by the Minister for Justice, Equality and Law Reform. It follows that it covers not just prisons but also places of detention such as St Patrick's Institution. It does not, however, extend to secure accommodation administered by the Ministers for Education and/or Health. A prisoner is defined as a person who is in prison on foot of a sentence of imprisonment, on committal awaiting trial, on remand or otherwise.

4–105 A person arrested under this power shall be taken immediately to a Garda station and may be detained there for such period as is authorised under section 4 of the Criminal Justice Act 1984.[242] If at any time during the detention there are no longer reasonable grounds for suspecting that the person has committed the offence in question or for believing that his or her detention is necessary for the proper investigation of the offence, the detention must be terminated immediately.[243] Subject to a few qualifications the person must be dealt with as if he or she was detained under section 4 of the 1984 Act.[244]

On the termination or expiry of the detention under these provisions the member in charge of the Garda station where the person is detained shall transfer him or her, or cause him or her to be transferred, immediately back into the custody of the governor of the prison where the person was imprisoned at the time of the arrest.[245]

This power of arrest and detention does not prejudice any power conferred by law (apart from this section) in relation to the arrest, detention or transfer of prisoners.[246]

---

[242] Criminal Justice Act, 1999, s.42(3)(a).
[243] *ibid.* s.42(5).
[244] *ibid.* s.42(3)(b).
[245] *ibid.* s.42(6).
[246] *ibid.* s.42(7).

N. Arrest under Warrant

1. The Procedure

Police powers of summary arrest are in addition to the power of arrest which **4–106** derives from a warrant duly issued by an appropriate authority. An arrest warrant is a written authority directed to an officer authorising him or her to arrest an offender to be dealt with according to law.[247] The normal procedure for the issue of an arrest warrant is for a member of the Garda Síochána to submit a complaint by information on oath and in writing to a District Court judge or peace commissioner.[248] Typically, this information will consist of a sworn statement of the member's belief that a specified indictable offence has been committed by an identified person.[249] Having received the complaint the judge or commissioner may issue a warrant for the arrest of the person concerned if the information discloses an indictable offence which is stated to have been committed, or if the accused person resides, within the judge's or commissioner's district.[250] Equally, where a complaint is made on oath and in writing to a District Court judge that a person has committed or is believed to have committed an indictable offence outside the jurisdiction of the judge in question, and that the person concerned is or is suspected to be within the limits of the judge's jurisdiction, the judge may issue a warrant for the arrest of the person.[251]

It is not essential for the information to have been sworn before the judge **4–107** issuing the warrant. A judge may issue a warrant where the information has been sworn before another judge.[252] However, in this event the duly completed information must be produced to the judge issuing the warrant. An information can be sworn and a warrant issued on any day and at any time.[253]

An arrest warrant must be signed by the judge or commissioner who issues it.[254] The validity of the warrant is not affected by the death of the person who signed it, or by reason of his or her ceasing to hold office.[255]

2. Choice of Summons or Warrant

There is some uncertainty about the range of offences for which a warrant **4–108** may issue. Generally, a warrant may issue for any indictable offence, even where a summary power of arrest is available for the offence in question. In

---

[247] See *Garda Síochána Guide* (6th ed.,), p. 1496. Note also that a warrant can issue for the committal of a person to prison.
[248] District Court Rules 1997, Ord.16, r.1(1). See generally, Woods, *District Court Practice and Procedure in Criminal Cases* (Limerick, 1994), pp. 140–141.
[249] For the appropriate form, see District Court Rules 1997, Schedule B, Form 15.3.
[250] District Court Rules, 1997, Ord.16, r.1(2). See Schedule B, Form 16.1 for the Form in which the warrant is issued.
[251] District Court Rules, 1997, Ord.16, r.6. See Schedule B, form 16.1 for the appropriate form.
[252] *ibid.* Ord.16, r.1(3).
[253] *ibid.* Ord.16, r.1(4).
[254] *ibid.* Ord.16, r.2(1).
[255] *ibid.* Ord.16, r.2(2).

the case of summary offences, however, there is conflicting provision. Section 11(1) of the Petty Sessions (Ireland) Act 1851 states that a summons only may issue in all cases of summary jurisdiction. The District Court Rules, 1997 on the other hand, stipulates that a warrant can issue for any offence (including summary offences) where there is a power to arrest without a warrant for that offence either at common law or under statute.[256] Woods is of the opinion that the provisions of the 1851 Act must take precedence in the event of a conflict.[257]

Irrespective of what way this particular conflict is resolved, it is apparent that a judge may issue a summons in any case where he could have issued a warrant.[258] There is authority to the effect that this choice should be exercised in favour of a summons in any case where the judge believes that the summons is likely to secure the attendance of the suspect in court.[259] In any case where a judge has exercised his discretion to issue a summons instead of a warrant, he or she may still at any time issue a warrant for the arrest of the person to whom the summons was directed.[260]

3. Pre-conditions for Availability of Power

4–109   Where the information discloses a relevant offence the district judge or peace commissioner has a discretion to issue the warrant. Before his discretion can come into play, however, it is submitted that the district judge or peace commissioner must actually be satisfied that the crime in question has been committed. By analogy with *People (DPP) v. Kenny*,[261] which is discussed later in the chapter on entry, search and seizure, it would seem that a warrant may not issue on the bare statement of a member of the Garda Síochána that he or she believes that the offence has been committed. The sworn information must show some evidence on which the District Court judge or peace commissioner could be personally satisfied that the offence was committed. Only then will he be in a position to exercise his discretion to issue the warrant.

Surprisingly, in the case of an arrest warrant, there does not seem to be any general requirement for the issuing authority to be satisfied that the person identified in the information has committed the offence. However, there are a number of statutory provisions conferring a power to issue arrest warrants in certain situations. Typically, these stipulate that the issuing authority must be satisfied that there are reasonable grounds for suspicion against the person to be arrested. For example, section 10(1) of the Criminal Justice Act 1984 makes provision for the issue of a warrant to effect the re-arrest of someone who had earlier been arrested for the same offence, detained under section 4

---

[256] *ibid.* Ord.16, r.5.
[257] The District Court Rules 1948, r.34 had made provision for the issue of arrest warrants in respect of summary offences. Woods suggested that the 1851 Act took precedence over the rules.
[258] District Court Rules 1997, Ord.16, r.4 and Ord.15, r.10.
[259] *O'Brien v. Brabner* (1885) 49 JPN 227.
[260] District Court Rules 1997, Ord.16, r.4 and Ord.15, r.10.
[261] [1990] I.L.R.M. 569.

of the 1984 Act and released without charge.[262] It stipulates that a person can only be re-arrested in such circumstances:

> "... on the authority of a judge of the District Court who is satisfied on information supplied on oath by a member of the Garda Síochána not below the rank of superintendent that further information has come to the knowledge of the Garda Síochána since the person's release as to his suspected participation in the offence for which his arrest is sought."

Where the issue of an arrest warrant is governed by such provision, it is imperative that all of the statutory requirements are satisfied before the warrant is issued. In *Larkin v. O'Dea*,[263] for example, the applicant's re-arrest had been authorised by a District Court judge under section 10(1) of the 1984 Act on foot of information from a Garda superintendent which merely stated that:

4–110

> "Since the date of that release further evidence has come into our possession and further enquiries have been made to establish the author of the alleged crime."

Both the High Court and, on appeal, the Supreme Court had little difficulty in finding that the District Court judge could not have been satisfied on this information as to the requirements of section 10(1). Applying *People (DPP) v. Kenny* they concluded that the authority for the re-arrest was unlawful.

4. Contents of Warrant

Once issued the purpose of an arrest warrant is to inform the arresting officer of the identity of the person to be taken into custody and to inform the latter that he should submit to arrest.[264] Accordingly, the warrant should specify the offence charged, the authority under which the arrest is made, the person who is to execute it and the person to be arrested. Where the offence is specified in an enactment which states the offence to be the doing (or the omission to do) any one of a number of different acts in the alternative or states any part of the offence in the alternative, the acts, omissions or other matters may be stated either in the alternative or in the conjunctive in the warrant.[265] Also, where the warrant alleges an offence contrary to any statute or statutes, it is sufficient to state the substance of the offence in ordinary language with such particulars as may be necessary for giving reasonable information as to the nature of the complaint.[266] It is not necessary to negative any exception or exemption from or qualification to the operation of a statute creating the offence.

4–111

---

[262] See also, Criminal Justice (Drug Trafficking) Act 1996, s.4; Offences against the State Act 1939, s.30A.
[263] [1994] 2 I.L.R.M. 448 and [1995] 2 I.L.R.M. 1.
[264] *State (Rossi and Blythe) v. Bell* [1957] I.R. 1.
[265] District Court Rules 1997, Ord.16, r.3 and Ord.15, r.8.
[266] *ibid*. Ord.16, r.3 and Ord.15, r.9.

If the warrant is being issued under a statutory provision which does not specify to whom it shall be directed, it must be directed to a member of the Garda Síochána. If the person to be arrested cannot be identified by name, the warrant should employ the best description available. The warrant should also show the date and place of its issue.

5. Executing the Warrant

4-112   Where a warrant has issued for an indictable offence, it will remain in force until it is executed.[267] Moreover, unlike the position with respect to a summary power of arrest, a member of the Garda Síochána is normally bound to execute an arrest warrant. In *Dunne v. DPP*,[267a] for example, Carney J. described the status of a warrant as follows:

> "A warrant of apprehension is a command issued to the Gardaí by a Court established under the Constitution to bring a named person before that Court to be dealt with according to law. It is not a document which merely vests a discretion in the Guards to apprehend the person named in it; it is a command to arrest that person immediately and bring him or her before the Court which issued it. That it is a command to arrest rather than merely an authority or permission to arrest can be seen clearly from the terms of the warrant in the instant case."

When effecting the arrest the member must inform the suspect of the reason for the arrest and the fact that he is acting under the authority of a warrant.[268] Normally, he should be able to produce it on the request of the person to be arrested.[269] However, the mere fact that he does not have it in his possession at the time of the arrest will not affect the legality of the arrest itself. In such a case the warrant should be shown to the arrested person as soon as practicable.[270]

Immunity

4-113   The wide range of summary powers of arrest available to gardaí ensures that resort to the warrant procedure is more the exception than the rule. However, one of the advantages of proceeding by warrant is that the arresting officer will not be liable if it transpires that the warrant was irregular or issued in excess of jurisdiction.[271] This protection extends to anything done in compliance with the warrant, unless the person arrested has been refused the

---

[267] Petty Sessions (Ireland) Act 1851, s.11(1). Note, however, that undue delay in the execution of a warrant of committal to prison can result in an order prohibiting its execution; see *Dalton v. Governor of Training Unit* unreported, Supreme Court, February 29, 2000.

[267a] Unreported, High Court, June 6, 1996.

[268] *R v. Kulynycz* [1971] 1 Q.B. 367, [1970] 3 All E.R. 881.

[269] *Codd v. Cabe* (1875–76) L.R. 1 Ex.D. 352; *Galliard v. Laxton* (1862) 2 B. & S. 364. Ryan and Magee point out that this rule does not apply where the garda has the power to arrest the suspect without the warrant; *op. cit.*, p.99.

[270] Criminal Law Act 1997, s.5. See also, Criminal Justice Act 1984, s.13(4) and (5) for a warrant issued for a failure to answer to bail.

[271] Constabulary (Ireland) Act 1836, s.50; Protection of Constables (Ireland) Act 1802, s.6.

opportunity to inspect the warrant after having made a written request for inspection more than six days earlier.[272]

Power of Entry

For the purpose of executing a warrant of arrest or an order of committal a member of the Garda Síochána may enter any premises where the person concerned is or where the member, with reasonable cause, suspects the person to be.[273] It makes no difference that the premises is a dwelling and there is no requirement for the offence in question to be an "arrestable offence" as defined by the Criminal Law Act 1997.

4–114

Use of Force

When exercising this power of entry a member of the Garda Síochána can, if need be, use reasonable force to gain entry to the premises. There is no specific requirement that he should always seek a consensual entry first. Presumably, it will be depend on the circumstances of each individual case whether the use of force was lawful in the absence of a prior attempt to gain a consensual entry. Once lawfully on the premises the member may search them in order to effect the arrest. It is worth emphasising, however, that the power of entry and search is separate from the power of arrest. The arrest itself must be grounded on foot of a warrant or committal order.

4–115

Bringing Suspect before the Court

Unless the warrant is endorsed for bail, the person arrested must normally be brought before a District Court judge having jurisdiction to deal with the offence in question as soon as practicable.[274] It is worth noting therefore, that where an information is made on oath and in writing, the judge before whom it is made may bind the informant by recognisance to appear to give evidence in the matter of the complaint at the court where the person concerned is to be tried or the complaint is to be heard.[275]

---

[272] Public Officers Protection (Ireland) Act 1803, s.6.
[273] District Court Rules 1997, Ord.16, r.7.
[274] Criminal Law Act 1997, s.6(1).
[275] Criminal Justice Act 1951, s.15, as replaced by Criminal Justice (Miscellaneous Provisions) Act 1997, s.18.

DETENTION IN GARDA CUSTODY

A. Introduction

1. Purpose of Detention

Police powers to detain a person in their custody in certain circumstances are an **5–01** essential part of the criminal process. The most immediate justification for such powers is the need to ensure that a suspect will appear before a judicial authority to answer for a criminal offence. If there is a chance that he will not appear before a judicial authority of his own accord and it is not practicable to take him before a judicial authority immediately on apprehending him, it will be necessary to detain the suspect in police custody in the interim. Equally, it is now generally accepted that the proper investigation of some criminal offences can justify police powers to detain suspects in their custody for a limited period in certain circumstances. In the words of Walsh J. when referring to the object of the detention power under section 30 of the Offences against the State Act in *People (DPP) v. Quilligan*:

> ". . . it is for the purpose of investigating the commission or suspected com-
> mission of a crime by the person already arrested and to enable that investigation
> to be carried on without the possibility of obstructing or other interference which
> might occur if the suspected person were not under arrest."[1]

The detention, of course, must be for the proper investigation of the offence. Even section 30 does not permit detention for the purpose of interrogation *per se*. While, undoubtedly, the detained suspect can be questioned about the offence,[2] the justification for the detention must be rooted in the need to investigate the offence. Investigation in this sense will encompass not just questioning the suspect, but also matters such as the carrying out of tests on the suspect within the law and preventing him from using his liberty to interfere with the proper investigation of the offence.

---

[1] [1987] I.L.R.M. 606 at 624.
[2] *People (DPP) v. McCann* [1998] 4 I.R. 397. See, also, J White "The Confessional State – Police Interrogation in the Irish Republic: Part 1" (2000) 10 (1) I.C.L.J. 17.

5–02   It is also worth noting that police powers of detention may be necessary for purposes which are not directly connected with a criminal investigation. For example, where a person is suffering from a mental condition which renders him a danger to himself or to others if immediate action is not taken, a power of detention would enable the police to minimise the risk of serious injury or death by detaining him until the necessary medical intervention can be mobilised. Also, it may be necessary to detain persons entering the country in order to facilitate immigration and asylum procedures. Of particular note in this context is section 5 of the Immigration Act 1999, as amended by section 10 of the Illegal Immigrants (Trafficking) Act 2000. It permits an immigration officer or member of the Garda Síochána to arrest without warrant and detain in certain circumstances a person whom he, with reasonable cause, suspects is the subject of a deportation order. The circumstances are that the officer or member suspects with reasonable cause that the person has failed to comply with any provision of the order, intends to leave the state and enter another state without lawful authority, has destroyed his identity documents or is in possession of forged identity documents, or intends to avoid removal from the State. Where a person is arrested under this provision he may be detained for a period or periods not exceeding eight weeks in aggregate.

5–03   The primary purpose of this power is not to detain the person for the purpose of criminal proceedings but to facilitate arrangements for his removal from the State in accordance with the terms of the deportation order. Accordingly, the constitutional impediment to preventive detention in the criminal law, as expounded in *People (Attorney General) v. O'Callaghan*,[3] is not directly applicable.[4] Indeed, in its consideration of the constitutionality of the provision on an Article 26 reference the Supreme Court found that the purpose of the provision was not to prevent crime but to secure the implementation of a deportation order.[5] The court further explained that there are acceptable forms of detention outside of the criminal process. This particular power was one such acceptable form as it had been introduced for a legitimate purpose and was the subject of sufficient safeguards for the person detained.

In practice, most police powers of detention are provided in the context of the criminal law. This chapter focuses directly on them.

2. Based on Law

5–04   Whatever the reason for the detention, it will only be lawful in any individual case if the police action falls within the remit of a specific power. The relevant powers available to members of the Garda Síochána are discussed below.[6] It is

---

[3]   [1966] I.R. 501.
[4]   *Re Article 26 and the Illegal Immigrants (Trafficking) Bill 1999* [2000] 2 I.R. 360.
[5]   *ibid.*
[6]   For a useful summary of the laws and regulations governing police powers of arrest and detention, see Ryan, "Arrest and Detention: A Review of the Law" (2000) 10(1) I.C.L.J. 2. For a more critical account, particularly of the power of detention under s.2 of the Criminal Justice (Drug Trafficking) Act 1996, see Keane, "Detention without Charge and the Criminal Justice (Drug Trafficking) Act

worth noting at the outset that even where the initial detention is lawful, it may become unlawful because new facts have come to light which indicate that the detention is unnecessary.[7] Equally, it may become unlawful as a result of the circumstances in which the person concerned is detained or treated while in police custody. There is a body of laws which regulate, directly and indirectly, the exercise of the powers of detention and the treatment of a person while detained while in police custody. These, too, are discussed below. It is worth noting at the outset, however, that not every breach of these laws will render unlawful the continued detention of the person concerned.

B. Powers

1. Introduction

Distinguishing Detention From Stop

A member of the Garda Síochána has a wide range of powers to encroach upon the freedom of movement of the individual. It does not necessarily follow, however, that an individual has been detained in police custody when stopped under one of these powers. Detention in police custody must be distinguished from the limited restrictions imposed on the individual's freedom of movement by the exercise of police powers to stop and question or to stop and search. Typically these "stop" powers will effect only a very brief and limited interference with the freedom of movement of the individual.[8] In the vast majority of cases they are used by the police to check certain matters in relation to the stopped person. This will often take the form of questions aimed at establishing the person's identity. For example, where a member of the Garda Síochána witnesses the commission of a minor offence he or she may stop the individual concerned for the purpose of cautioning him and/or establishing his identity for the issue of a summons. Similarly, the stop may be effected to search the person for a proscribed drug or a concealed weapon.

5–05

Almost invariably, the interference with the individual's freedom of movement, consequent on the exercise of a stop power, will be very brief and confined to specific matters which can be dealt with on the spot. Accordingly, the individual stopped is not deemed to be in police custody in the sense that the formal law and procedures governing the detention of the individual in police custody come into play. Detention on the other hand connotes a situation where the individual has been taken into the custody of the police and held at a police station or other place for the purpose of facilitating further police inquiries and/or the commencement of judicial proceedings. It constitutes a much more substantial restraint on the freedom of the individual. It implies that he must

5–06

1996: Shifting the Focus of the Irish Criminal Process from Trial Court to Garda Station" (1997) 7(1) I.C.L.J. 1.

[7] *Re Article 26 and the Illegal Immigrants (Trafficking) Bill 1999* [2000] 2 I.R. 360 at 410–411.

[8] These powers are dealt with more fully in Chapter 7.

accompany the police to the police station and remain there until such time as he is released or until it is no longer lawful for the police to detain him. Moreover, while in custody he may be required to undergo a series of searches and other examinations. He may also be charged and brought before a judicial authority who may remand him in judicial custody.

Distinguishing Detention from Stop and Search

5–07 Admittedly, as police powers of stop and search independent of arrest continue to expand, it will become increasingly difficult to sustain the distinction between detention and lesser restraints on the liberty of the individual in some situations. For example, certain statutory powers of search short of arrest permit the police to take a person to a police vehicle or other secure place and to keep the person at that place for a period of time in order to conduct a body search. It is at least arguable that this amounts to detaining the person in police custody and that the normal protections for a suspect in police custody should apply.[8a] For the most part, however, detention in police custody is not lawful unless it has been commenced by a lawful arrest.

No Detention Short of Arrest

5–08 The Irish courts have consistently taken the view that, in the absence of specific statutory provision, there is no power to detain short of arrest.[9] It follows that a valid arrest is a pre-requisite for the lawful detention of an individual in police custody, and the commencement of the law and procedures governing that detention.[10] However, the nature and extent of the power to detain an arrested individual can vary with the particular power of arrest used. For some arrest powers there will be an obligation to charge the suspect and release him immediately or take him before a judicial authority as soon as practicable, while under others it may be possible to detain him for a specified maximum period before charge or release.[11] The rights and obligations of the suspect in police custody can also differ depending on the power of arrest used. For clarity of exposition, however, it is probably better to proceed by focusing on "powers" of detention such as those conferred by section 4 of the Criminal Justice Act 1984, section 30(3) of the Offences Against the State Act 1939 and section 2 of the Criminal Justice (Drug Trafficking) Act 1996. Each of these will be considered in turn.[12] First, however, it is necessary to examine

---

[8a] See, *e.g. People (DPP) v. Boylan* [1991] 1 I.R. 477, as discussed in chapter 7, para. 7–26

[9] *Dunne v. Clinton* [1930] I.R. 366; *People v. Walsh* [1980] I.R. 294; *People (DPP) v. Coffey* [1987] I.L.R.M. 727.

[10] See chapter 4 para 4–05 *et seq.* on arrest for discussion of some of the circumstances in which an unlawful detention in police custody can arise.

[11] Under the Road Traffic legislation for example a person who has been arrested on suspicion of "drunk-driving" can be detained in the Garda station for the purposes of further investigation as prescribed by the legislation.

[12] There are other statutory powers of arrest and detention designed to facilitate the investigation of criminal offences. Examples are to be found in, s.4, Air Navigation and Transport Act 1975, and, of course, in the road traffic legislation dealing with the taking of blood or urine. These are not specifically dealt with in this Chapter as they focus on very particular offences.

the common law background and the provisions of section 15 of the Criminal Justice Act 1951 which imposes a general obligation on the police to bring a suspect before a judge once he has been arrested and charged.

2. Common Law Background

Purpose of Arrest

At common law the purpose of arrest is to render a suspect amenable to the court to answer a criminal charge. Normally, the police officer would effect an arrest for the purpose of charging the suspect and bringing him before a judicial authority. The arrest and charge, therefore, were usually coincident in point of time. If the circumstances were such that the charge could not be put immediately at the time of the arrest, it would be put as soon as practicable thereafter. Once charged the suspect would have to be taken before a judge as soon as practicable. In this context arrest could be considered as the commencement of the judicial process. There was no concept of arrest and detention for the purpose of investigating the suspect or acquiring evidence which could then be sufficient to prefer a charge against him. The period spent in police custody consequent on arrest was purely incidental to the requirements of preferring a charge against the suspect and/or making the necessary arrangements to bring him before a judge on foot of the charge.

5–09

Questioning Post-arrest

In the course of the twentieth century it became common practice for the police to take advantage of having the suspect in their custody in the period between his or her arrest and the availability of a judge. They would use this period to question the suspect further about the offence and/or other offences with a view to securing evidence which could be used to support the criminal charge or charges. The Judges' Rules attempted to regulate this practice by, *inter alia*, restricting the extent to which a suspect could be questioned about an offence in police custody after having been charged with that offence.[12a] This restriction, however, was easily circumvented by the use of "holding charges" and by postponing charging until some time after the arrest. The former refers to the situation where the police arrest and charge a suspect for one offence (the "holding charge") and then proceed to question him about other offences while he or she is in their custody waiting to be brought before a judge on foot of the "holding charge". By postponing the charging of a suspect with the offence for which he was arrested the police were able to continue to question him about that offence until they had built up a stronger case against him.

5–10

Distinction between Arrest and Charge

Whatever about the strict legality of postponing the charging of an arrested suspect it began to be accepted that a valid arrest could be effected before

5–11

[12a] See chap 6 para 6–03 *et seq.*

there was sufficient evidence to justify a charge. A reasonable suspicion was generally considered sufficient to ground a valid arrest. The evidence required to raise that suspicion, however, did not have to reach the standard necessary for a charge. The latter required admissible evidence sufficient to establish a prima facie case against the suspect, while the former could be satisfied by a lower standard and by evidence which would not be admissible in court. The relationship between arrest and charge, and the implications for the use of arrest in the course of a police investigation, is explained by Lord Devlin in *Shaaban Bin Hussein v. Chong Fook Kam*:

> "Suspicion arises at or near the starting point of an investigation of which the obtaining of prima facie proof is the end. When such proof has been obtained, the police stage is complete; it is ready for trial and passes on to its next stage. It is indeed desirable as a general rule that an arrest should not be made until the case is complete. But if arrest before that were forbidden, it could seriously hamper the police . . .
>
> There is another distinction between reasonable suspicion and prima facie proof. prima facie proof consists of admissible evidence. Suspicion can take into account matters that could not be put in evidence at all . . . Suspicion can take into account also matters which, though admissible, could not form part of a prima facie case."[13]

5–12 It would appear that the Irish courts are also prepared to recognise that the charging of a suspect need not be commensurate with the arrest. As will be seen below section 4 of the Criminal Justice Act 1984 permits the detention of a suspect in Garda custody for the investigation of an offence in certain circumstances. The section as originally enacted included a provision which obliged a member of the Garda Síochána to charge a person detained under the section with an offence as soon as he or she had enough evidence to prefer the charge.[14] With reference to this obligation in *Keating v. Governor of Mountjoy Prison* O'Flaherty J. explained:

> "The section requires the garda to make a fair assessment because it has to be said that the only certainty in a criminal trial is at the moment when a jury brings in a verdict. So, provided the garda makes a fair assessment of the evidence in deciding whether it is enough to prefer charges he should not be faulted even if a court, or indeed another member of the gardaí, might have reached a different conclusion as to the sufficiency of the evidence at his disposal at any particular stage of the suspect's detention at the Garda station."[15]

It is at least implicit in this approach that there is room for the police to postpone the charging of a lawfully arrested suspect until such time as they felt that they had sufficient admissible evidence to support the charge. In other words, the evidence required to justify an arrest need not necessarily be

---

[13] [1969] 3 All E.R. 1626 at 1630–1631.
[14] Criminal Justice Act 1984, s.4(5). This section has since been amended by the Criminal Justice (Miscellaneous Provisions) Act 1997, s.2(b). The amendment had to be further amended by Criminal Justice Act 1999, s.34 in order to correct a technical drafting error. The provision is now to be found in Criminal Justice Act 1984, s.4(5) and 4(5A).
[15] [1990] I.L.R.M. 850 at 856.

of sufficient strength to support a charge. In such a case the necessary evidence may become available while the suspect is being processed in the police station.

Delaying the Charge

Today the distinction between arrest and charge is less important due to the availability of a number of statutory provisions which permit the police to detain an arrested person without charge for a prescribed period. This period can be used by the police to check their suspicion against the individual and/or to secure further evidence against him or her. Nevertheless, there are still some situations in which a suspect may be arrested under a power which does not trigger one of the statutory periods of detention. Even in these cases there will usually be a period of time between the initial arrest and the subsequent charge. This period will vary from case to case. Where the suspect is arrested in a public place, for example, it will at the very least include the time taken to bring him to the police station and to process particulars of identity. This provides the police with a limited opportunity to question the suspect about the offence. So long as the police have not delayed charging in order to build their case against the arrested suspect it would appear that this period of "detention" is not *per se* unlawful. The correct approach in assessing whether the justification for any delay in charging the suspect is set out in the following words of Lord Porter in *John Lewis and Co. Ltd. v. Tims* when he said:

> "The question throughout should be: Has the arrestor brought the arrested person to a place where his alleged offence can be dealt with as speedily as is reasonably possible? But all the circumstances in the case must be taken into consideration in deciding whether this requirement is complied with. A direct route and rapid progress are no doubt matters for consideration but they are not the only matters."[15a]

Insufficient Evidence to Charge

Where there is sufficient evidence to charge the suspect with an offence he should be charged at the first reasonable opportunity and brought before a judge as soon as practicable unless there is statutory provision permitting an alternative course of action (see below). It may happen of course that when the evidence against an arrested suspect is reviewed in the calm of the police station, it will prove insufficient to charge him with an offence. In this event the suspect should be released immediately.[16] In the absence of a statutory provision justifying his continued detention his release cannot be delayed in order to give the police an opportunity to find further evidence against him.[17]

5–13

5–14

[15a] [1952] A.C. 676 at 691.

[16] *Wiltshire v. Barrett* [1966] 1 Q.B. 312.

[17] *Dunne v. Clinton* [1930] I.R. 366; *People v. Walsh* [1980] I.R. 254.

3. Criminal Justice Act 1951

Obligation to Bring Suspect before a Judge

5–15   At common law once a suspect has been charged he must be brought before a judge as soon as reasonably practicable, unless there is a statutory provision authorising his continued detention. This obligation has now been placed on a statutory footing by section 15 of the Criminal Justice Act 1951 which distinguishes between a suspect who has been arrested without a warrant and a suspect who has been arrested on foot of a warrant.[18] Where a person is arrested on foot of a warrant he shall, on arrest, be brought as soon as practicable before a District Court judge having jurisdiction to deal with the offence.[19] Where a person is arrested without a warrant he shall, on being charged, be brought as soon as practicable before a District Court judge having jurisdiction to deal with the offence. Clearly, where the arrest is effected on foot of a warrant, the warrant functions as the charging instrument so that time begins to run from the actual arrest. In the case of an arrest without warrant on the other hand, time runs from the moment the suspect is charged which may, of course, be later in time to the actual arrest. Indeed, if the arrest is effected under a power which triggers one of the statutory periods of detention the gardaí will be generally relieved of the obligation to bring the suspect before a judge for the period authorised by the power of detention.

As Soon as Practicable

5–16   Section 15 does not define what is meant by "as soon as practicable" in relation to the obligation to bring a suspect before a judge. It is likely that what may be considered as satisfying "as soon as practicable" will differ from case to case in accordance with the particular circumstances of each case.[20] The availability of a judge is a major factor. Equally, it can be expected that some delay may result from factors such as: preparing the necessary paperwork for the appearance before the judge, permitting the suspect access to his solicitor and/or a friend, securing the services of an interpreter and/or medical advice, etc.[21]

As yet, there has been no suggestion in the case law that delay occasioned by any of these factors would be a breach of the obligation to bring the suspect before a District Court judge as soon as practicable. So long as the detention was not effected for the purpose of facilitating further investigation into the case against the suspect, there is no reason why the gardaí cannot take advantage of this opportunity to build the case against him, subject always to the rules governing the questioning of a suspect in police custody (see Chapter 6).

---

[18]   Although s.15 is framed in obligatory terms, it is submitted that the option of releasing the suspect after charge on police bail has not been abolished by implication.

[19]   Criminal Justice Act 1951, s.15(2) as substituted by Criminal Justice (Miscellaneous Provisions) Act 1997, s.18.

[20]   See Hanna J. in *Dunne v. Clinton* [1930] I.R. 366.

[21]   In *Doherty v. Liddane* [1940] Ir. Jur. Rep. 58, for example, the High Court accepted a delay occasioned by police attempts to secure bailsmen where the accused had consented.

Constitutional Rights of the Victim

Generally, delays which are occasioned by a police desire to bolster the case **5–17** against the accused by seeking further evidence against him will be considered unreasonable.[22] However, in *People v. Shaw*[22a] the Supreme Court accepted the legality of the suspect's detention where he was not brought to Galway District Court until the morning after his arrest at Galway Garda station, despite the fact that the court was sitting at the time of his arrest. In this case the accused had been arrested on suspicion of involvement in the abduction of two girls. The investigating gardaí believed that there was a possibility that at least one of the girls might still be alive. Accordingly, they delayed bringing the accused to court in the hope that he could help them find her before it was too late. The Supreme Court accepted that the delay rendered the accused's detention in Garda custody *prima facie* unlawful from the time when he could reasonably have been brought before the court. However, the court went on to find that the accused's constitutional right to liberty was outweighed in the circumstances by the girl's right to life. Accordingly, the delay in bringing the accused to court was not unlawful.

Section 15 of the 1951 Act makes provision for a general exception to the obligation to bring a suspect before a District Court judge as soon as practicable after having been arrested on foot of a warrant or after having been charged.[22b] It stipulates that where a person has been arrested pursuant to a warrant or charged after 5 p.m. and a District Court judge will be sitting in that district before noon the following day, it will be lawful for the gardaí to keep the suspect in their custody with a view to bringing him before a District Court judge at the commencement of the sitting the next day.

4. Section 4 of the Criminal Justice Act 1984

A Watershed

The Criminal Justice Act 1984 represents a watershed in Irish criminal **5–18** justice. Up until its enactment Irish law did not generally recognise the concept of detention without charge in police custody for the purpose of facilitating a police investigation. Admittedly, section 30 of the Offences against the State Act provided for a period of detention without charge consequent on an arrest under that provision. It, however, was considered an exception which had been introduced to deal with the particular threat posed by subversive activity. The Criminal Justice Act 1984 was different in that it represented an official adoption of detention without charge in police custody as an integral part of the criminal justice system. Under its provisions the police could officially detain an arrested suspect with a view to furthering their investigation against him instead of having to charge him and take him before a judge as soon as practicable.

---

[22] *Dunne v. Clinton* [1930] I.R. 366; *John Lewis and Co. Ltd. v. Tims* [1952] A.C. 676; *People v. Shaw* [1982] I.R. 1.

[22a] [1982] I.R. 1.

[22b] Criminal Justice Act 1951, s.15, as substituted by Criminal Justice (Miscellaneous Provisions) Act 1997, s.18.

The Statutory Provision

5–19   Section 4(2) of the Act, as substituted by section 2 of the Criminal Justice (Miscellaneous Provisions) Act 1997, provides the basic power of detention. It reads:

> "Where a member of the Garda Síochána arrests without warrant, or pursuant to an authority of a judge of the District Court under section 10(1), a person whom he, with reasonable cause, suspects of having committed an offence to which this section applies, that person may be taken to and detained in a Garda station for such period as is authorised by this section if the member of the Garda Síochána in charge of the station to which he is taken on arrest has at the time of that person's arrival at the station reasonable grounds for believing that his detention is necessary for the proper investigation of the offence."

This provision does not actually create a power of arrest. It comes into play only when a member of the Garda Síochána has effected an arrest in certain circumstances for an offence to which this section applies. The scope of this power of detention, therefore, is determined by the range of offences to which section 4 applies.

Range of Offences

5–20   Section 4 applies to any offence for which a person of full age and capacity and not previously convicted may, under or by virtue of any enactment, be punished by imprisonment for a term of five years or by a more severe penalty.[23] Also included is an attempt to commit any such offence. Clearly covered is any offence which carries a maximum sentence on conviction of at least five years' imprisonment and for which a member of the Garda Síochána possesses a power of summary arrest. In theory some difficulty could arise over the exact meaning of "a more severe penalty" than five years imprisonment. Could it be satisfied by a maximum period of imprisonment of less than five years coupled with the possibility of a heavy fine or some secondary punishment? Comparable legislation in the United Kingdom has always referred simply to imprisonment for five years or more, clearly implying that an offence carrying a maximum possible sentence of less than five years could not qualify. It might be reasonable to conclude that the different formula used in the 1984 Act is quite deliberate, and is meant to embrace the situation where a maximum sentence of less than five years' imprisonment coupled with some other secondary punishment could be considered a more severe penalty than a maximum sentence of five years' imprisonment standing by itself.

5–21   Given the potentially huge range of secondary punishments, it is submitted that such a strict literal interpretation would introduce substantial uncertainty over the exact scope of section 4(2). Since the provision impinges on the liberty of the individual it is unlikely that the courts would adopt such an interpretation where there were other interpretations reasonably open. For

---

[23]   Criminal Justice Act 1984, s.4(1).

example, the words "a more severe penalty" could reasonably be interpreted in the context as referring only to a longer term of imprisonment than five years. Alternatively, they could be interpreted as referring to the possibility of a harsher form of penalty than imprisonment. It may be significant in this context that the death penalty was available in Ireland for certain offences when the Criminal Justice Act was enacted.[24] This alternative interpretation has the advantage that it also accords more closely with the literal meaning of "a more severe penalty." It is submitted, therefore, that it is the correct interpretation, although it is unlikely to become a serious issue in practice since the death penalty was removed from the statute book in 1990.[25]

The Arrest

Just because a member of the Garda Síochána has arrested a suspect for an offence to which section 4 applies it does not follow that the detention power will come into play. Four further requirements must be satisfied. Firstly, the arrest must not have been effected pursuant to a warrant or to an authority of a District Court judge under section 10(1) (see Chapter 4). If the arrest is effected pursuant to a warrant, the suspect must be brought before a District Court judge in accordance with the provisions of section 15(1) of the Criminal Justice Act 1951. Secondly, when effecting the arrest, the member must have reasonable cause to suspect the individual of having committed the offence. It would appear, therefore, that the member personally must have reasonable cause to suspect. It will not be sufficient that someone else had reasonable cause and simply directed the member to effect the arrest. Equally, it would appear that the reasonable cause must be present at the time the arrest was effected. It will not be sufficient that it arose subsequent to the arrest or had existed some time before the arrest and had been dissipated by the time the arrest was actually effected. It is also worth emphasising that the member must have reasonable cause to suspect that the individual has committed the offence. Certain arrest powers enable a member of the Garda Síochána to effect an arrest when he suspects that an individual is about to commit a relevant offence. Such an arrest will not bring the section 4(2) provision into play unless the circumstances are such as to amount at least to an attempt to commit the qualifying offence.

5–22

Taken to a Garda Station

The third requirement is that the arrested person must have been taken to a Garda station for the purposes of detention under section 4. The Act, however, does not specifically oblige the arresting member of the Garda Síochána to take the suspect to a Garda station for this purpose. The measure is actually expressed in discretionary terms. If, however, the suspect is not brought to a Garda station for the purpose of detention under this provision or pursuant to

5–23

---

[24] See the Criminal Justice Act 1964, s.1.
[25] Criminal Justice Act 1990, s.1.

some other statutory provision he will have to be taken before a judge of the District Court as soon as practicable.

5–24 Section 4 of the 1984 Act does not specifically address the issue of how soon after arrest the suspect must be brought to a Garda station for the purpose of detention under that section. In *People (DPP) v. Boylan*[26] the appellant had been detained in a shed for a period of two hours while his lorry was being searched pursuant to section 23 of the Misuse of Drugs Act 1977. After the search he was formally arrested and brought to a Garda station to be detained pursuant section 4. On his appeal against conviction for drugs offences, the Court of Criminal Appeal found that the detention in the shed was not a lawful exercise of the power conferred by section 23 of the Misuse of Drugs Act and that, in effect, the accused was under arrest from the moment of his detention in the shed. The Court further ruled that in order to detain an arrested suspect under section 4 he must be brought to the Garda station as soon as reasonably possible. In this case the delay of two hours was not justifiable. The importance of arrival at the station without undue delay stems from the fact that it is only on arrival at the station that the rights and safeguards of the suspect may be set in motion. An unreasonable delay in bringing the person to the station arguably deprives him of his constitutional and legal rights and defeats the whole purpose of the regulations governing the treatment of a person in Garda custody.[27]

Grounds for Detention

5–25 The fourth requirement is that the member in charge of the Garda station to which the suspect is taken on arrest must have reasonable grounds for believing that the suspect's detention is necessary for the proper investigation of the offence.[28] It follows that he or she cannot sanction a section 4(2) detention for purposes such as to protect the suspect against himself or against harm from others. It would also appear that the member in charge cannot give the initial sanction for the detention on the grounds that it is necessary for the proper investigation of offences other than that for which the suspect has been arrested, despite the fact that it is possible to question a suspect about offences during his detention. If the detention is not necessary for the proper investigation of the actual offence for which the suspect has been arrested, detention under section 4(2) cannot arise.[29] It is submitted that

---

26 [1991] 1 I.R. 477.

27 Ryan, "Arrest and Detention: A Review of the Law" (2000) 10(1) I.C.L.J. 2 at 3.

28 "The proper investigation of the offence" is not defined. Presumably, it refers to matters such as: the questioning of the suspect, the analysis of samples taken from the suspect and/or from the scene of the crime, examining evidence, checking out alibis and the questioning of witnesses. In *People (DPP) v. Reddan* [1995] 3 I.R. 560 the Court of Criminal Appeal declined to rule on whether detention could be justified solely for the purpose of questioning.

29 It is worth noting, however, that it is not the function of the District Court judge to inquire into the legality of the detention of the accused when he is brought before him or her for remand. A challenge to the legality of the detention should be brought directly to the High Court or indirectly by way of a challenge to the admissibility of evidence; *Keating v. Governor of Mountjoy Prison* [1990] I.L.R.M. 850.

this would apply where, for example, the suspect has been arrested in circumstances which did not call for any further investigation of the nature and extent of the offence and of his guilt. In such a case it is at least arguable that the gardaí would have to proceed under section 15 of the Criminal Justice Act 1951. In appropriate circumstances there may also be the possibility of arresting the suspect under section 30 of the Offences against the State Act 1939 and proceeding under its provisions.[30]

The member in charge must suspect, and have reasonable grounds for his suspicion, at the time the suspect arrives at the station. Clearly, he or she cannot take into account any information that is acquired through the examination or questioning of the suspect after his arrival. What is not so clear, however, is whether his suspicion must be based solely on information he or she already had about the suspect immediately prior to his arrival at the station. Can the member also take into account information acquired immediately after the suspect's arrival at the station? A literal interpretation of section 4(2) would appear to rule out this possibility. However, "arrival at the station" could be given a broader meaning to embrace not just physical arrival but also the booking in. This interpretation would enable the member in charge to take into account information acquired about the suspect in the course of the booking in, including information provided by the arresting officer. This approach would seem to accord more with the legislative intention evident in the overall scheme of the 1984 Act. To adopt the strictly literal interpretation would exclude all those suspects who are arrested by gardaí responding to situations which they come across in the course of their patrol. Even though the provision is concerned with the liberty of the individual, it is difficult to imagine a court preferring the strictly literal interpretation where it would have the effect of seriously undermining the utility of section 4(2) from a police perspective and of distinguishing arbitrarily between two categories of arrested suspects.

5–26

This matter was addressed by the Court of Criminal Appeal in *People (DPP) v. O'Toole and Hickey*.[31] In that case the two appellants had been arrested on suspicion of murder and detained under section 4. On the day prior to the arrest a search warrant had been obtained in respect of the appellants. The investigating officers had informed the member in charge of the Garda station of their intention to arrest the appellants and of the information upon which they had based their decision to make the arrests. This information was conveyed to the member in charge at least one hour before the arrests were effected. The appellants challenged their detention on the ground that the member in charge had formed his belief that their detention was necessary for the proper investigation of the offence purely on the basis of the information supplied in advance by the investigating officers and, therefore, had not reached the decision based on his own independent belief. The appellants also

5–27

---

30 *People (DPP) v. Kehoe* [1985] I.R. 444.
31 Court of Criminal Appeal, July 20, 1990.

argued that the member in charge had formed his belief before they actually arrived at the station, rather than at the time of their arrival.

5-28 The trial judge rejected these arguments to the validity of their detention. In upholding his decision the Court of Criminal Appeal ruled that the member in charge must have an independent bona fide belief that the person who has arrived in custody is a person who should be detained by him. He must form this belief independently in his own mind. However, he is not precluded from basing his decision on information which has been presented to him by the person who effected the arrest.[31a] Moreover, this information may come to him either prior to the arrest or when the arrested person is brought to the station.

The member in charge of the station needs to be satisfied that the detention of the suspect is necessary at the time of the suspect's arrival at the station. There is no specific requirement for the member in charge to remain so satisfied throughout the period of the suspect's detention. It will be seen later, however, that there must actually be reasonable grounds for suspecting that the continued detention of the suspect is necessary for the proper investigation of an offence to which section 4 applies in order for that detention to remain lawful.[32]

The Proper Investigation of the Offence

5-29 It is worth emphasising that the member in charge must be satisfied that the detention is necessary for the proper *investigation* of the offence. The investigation of an offence, of course, need not be limited to the questioning of the suspect with a view to determining whether he ought to be charged or released. It can extend to conducting a search, taking samples and pursuing inquiries elsewhere which might be inhibited if the suspect was at liberty. More controversially, it would appear that it can encompass a more wide-ranging inquiry into the possible involvement of others. In *People (DPP) v. Van Onzen*,[33] for example, the appellants were arrested in possession of a large quantity of proscribed drugs on a yacht off the Irish coast. In explaining his decision to grant an extension of detention under section 4 (which must also be based on a belief that it is necessary for the proper investigation of the offence) the member in charge of the Garda station in question testified "that he thought the further investigations would centre on determining where these drugs originated; who was the person behind them and where they were destined to go and who received them and for those persons (the accused) to account for their movements." The Court of Criminal Appeal considered that this was a proper basis upon which to form the view that a further period of detention was necessary for the proper investigation of the offence.

It is worth noting that where an accused has been detained under section 4 of the 1984 Act, the fact that the member in charge of the relevant Garda

---

[31a] In *People (DPP) v. Reddan* [1995] 3 I.R. 560 the Court of Criminal Appeal accepted that the member in charge could have reasonable grounds on being told by the arresting officer that he had confidential information that the suspect had been involved in the wounding of a named individual.

[32] Criminal Justice Act 1984, s.4(4).

[33] [1996] 2 I.L.R.M. 387.

station had the necessary belief to authorise the detention will normally have to be proved. The necessary proof cannot be adduced by the member's signature on the detention record, or by hearsay evidence or by the mere fact that the detention was authorised. The member will have to appear and give evidence in person about his state of mind at the time.[33a]

Children Under 12 Years of Age

The member in charge of the Garda station to which the suspect is brought also plays a critical role in the availability of detention under section 4(2) where the suspect is under 12 years of age. The 1984 Act specifically precludes the possibility of detention under section 4(2) where the suspect in question is under 12 years of age. This prohibition does not apply where the member in charge of the Garda station in question has reasonable grounds for believing that the suspect is not below the age of 12 years old.[34] However, if the member in charge ascertains that the suspect is less than 12 years of age he must be released from custody immediately. This also applies where the member has reasonable grounds for believing that the suspect is less than 12 years old.[35] Presumably, the suspect's release under this provision would not preclude his being detained under some other statutory provision or being brought before a District Court judge.

When the relevant provisions in the Children Act 2001 are brought into force, a member of the Garda Síochána who has reasonable grounds for believing that a child under the age of 12 years of age has committed what would amount to an offence but for the child's age, must try to take the child, or arrange for the child to be taken by another member, to the child's parent or guardian.[35a] Where a child is taken to his or her parent or guardian in this situation and the member of the Garda Síochána in question has reasonable grounds for believing that the child is not receiving adequate care and protection, the member must inform the health board for the area in which the child resides of the child's name, address and age and the circumstances in which the child came to the notice of the member.[35b]

The Station to Which the Suspect is Taken on Arrest

Before proceeding to examine the provisions of section 4 which deal with the detention of a suspect who has been detained pursuant to section 4(2) it is worth pointing out that section 4(2) will only come into play at the first station to which a suspect is brought consequent on arrest. If for some reason

5–30

5–31

[33a] See, by analogy, *People (DPP) v. Byrne* [1989] I.L.R.M. 613.

[34] The provision does not specifically require the member to have an actual belief (in addition to having reasonable grounds for the belief) that the suspect is at least 12 years old.

[35] Although the provision does not specifically say so, this is probably meant to apply to the situation where, at some subsequent point during the detention, the member in charge acquires reasonable grounds for believing that the suspect is under 12 years of age.

[35a] Children Act 2001, s.53(1). Where this is not practicable the member must give the child, or arrange for the child to be given, into the custody of the health board in the area in which the child normally resides; s.53(3).

[35b] *ibid.* s.53(2).

the gardaí failed to have him booked into the first station he was taken to on arrest, there is no specific provision authorising his detention at a second or any subsequent station. Before the suspect can be detained under section 4(2) the member in charge of the station *to which he is taken on arrest* must have reasonable grounds for believing that his detention is necessary for the proper investigation of the offence. This would be the member in charge of the first station to which the suspect is taken *on arrest*. If he is taken from there to a second station it is at least arguable that he is taken *in custody* to the second station as distinct from on arrest. The member in charge of the second station, therefore, would not be a member in charge of the station to which the suspect is taken on arrest. As such he or she would not be able to satisfy the requirements of section 4(2) in respect of the suspect. Admittedly, it is unlikely that the courts would take such a restrictive approach to the interpretation of section 4(2).[36]

It would appear that once a suspect has been lawfully detained at a Garda station pursuant to section 4, the legality of his detention will not be affected by taking him from the Garda station temporarily to another location for a legitimate purpose. In *Clarke v. Member in Charge of Terenure Garda Station*,[36a] for example, the plaintiff was detained under section 4. Just as his solicitor was arriving at the station he was taken to the District Court for the purpose of being charged. At the Court the solicitor challenged the legality of his detention. There was a delay of a few hours before the matter could be heard. During that period the plaintiff was taken back to the Garda station and his period of detention was extended (see para. 5–32 *et seq*). The High Court ordered his release from custody that evening. The Supreme Court, however, ruled on appeal that his second period of detention in the Garda station was lawful. The Court considered that it was analogous to the situation in which a suspect in police custody accompanies police officers to locations to point out places or things which he had mentioned in the course of interviews. There was nothing in the legislation to prohibit such events or to confine the suspect to the Garda station for the period of his detention. So long as his removal was for a legitimate purpose and was not done for the purposes of harassing him or isolating him from assistance or access it was lawful. It would appear that the Court in the *Clarke* case did not consider whether the extended detention was necessary for the proper investigation of the offence as is required by section 4. It is difficult to see how this requirement could be satisfied on the reported facts of case as the gardaí had already taken him to the District Court for the purpose of being charged.

Period of Detention

5–32   When the requirements for detention under section 4(2) are satisfied, the suspect may be detained in a Garda station for a period not exceeding six hours from the time of the arrest.[37] It would appear, therefore, that time begins to

---

[36]   See, *e.g. People v. Kelly (No.2)* [1982] I.R. 1; *People v. Farrell* [1978] I.R. 13; and *People (Walsh) v. Maguire* [1979] I.R. 372 dealing with an analogous situation with respect to arrest and detention under s.30 of the Offences against the State Act 1939.

[36a]   [2002] 2 I.L.R.M. 11.

[37]   Criminal Justice Act 1984, s.4(3)(a).

run from the moment of arrest as distinct from the point at which the suspect was booked into the Garda station.

Grounds for Extended Detention

There are four circumstances in which the period of detention might be extended beyond six hours. The first is where an officer of the Garda Síochána, not below the rank of superintendent, exercises his or her power to direct that a person detained pursuant to section 4(2) be detained for a further period not exceeding six hours.[38] He can exercise this power when he has reasonable grounds for believing that such further detention is necessary for the proper investigation of the offence. It will be seen later that an extension is also permissible for the investigation of certain other offences (see para 5–45). However, it is not within the officer's power to sanction the extended detention for any other reason such as, for example, that it is not reasonably practicable to take the suspect before a District Court judge.

It would appear that the courts take a relaxed view of what might be considered necessary for the proper investigation of the offence in this context. As noted above in the context of the initial decision to detain the suspect (which is also premised on the belief that detention is necessary for the proper investigation of the offence) the courts accept that the investigation of an offence in this context can extend to matters which go beyond the narrow issue of the guilt or innocence of the suspect.[39] It is also worth noting that the mere fact that the gardaí have acquired sufficient evidence to warrant charging the suspect with the offence will not necessarily be sufficient. **5–33**

In *People (DPP) v. O'Toole and Hickey*[40] the Court of Criminal Appeal rejected a challenge to the validity of an extended period of detention where the appellants had argued that the extension could not be necessary for the proper investigation of the offence as they had already made inculpatory statements during the first parade of detention. During the second period of detention an identification parade was held. In upholding the validity of the second period of detention the Court of Criminal Appeal intimated that the reference to what was necessary for the proper investigation of the offence should be interpreted as what was necessary for a full and proper investigation. In other words, the mere fact that an inculpatory statement had been given or that sufficient evidence to warrant charging had been obtained would not in themselves preclude the need for further investigation. If the officer authorising the further period of detention considers that a further period of detention is necessary for the proper investigation the courts will be slow to second-guess him.[41] **5–34**

---

[38] *ibid.* s.4(3)(b).
[39] See, *e.g. People (DPP) v. Van Onzen* [1996] 2 I.L.R.M. 387.
[40] unreported, Court of Criminal Appeal, July 20, 1990.
[41] See O'Flaherty J. in *Keating v. Governor of Mountjoy Prison* [1991] 1 I.R. 61 at 68.

Direction for Extended Detention

5-35   A direction for extended detention may be given orally or in writing.[42] If given orally it must be recorded in writing as soon as practicable. Where necessary, the member issuing the direction will have to appear in person at the subsequent trial of the suspect and give evidence about his state of mind in issuing the direction.[42a] Presumably the direction must be issued prior to the expiry of the initial six hour period. It is not stated, however, whether it takes effect immediately on issue or from the expiry of the first six hour period. While, the former interpretation is more respectful of the liberty of the individual, it would appear that the legislative intention is for the extended period to run from the expiry of the first six hours. The extended period can be up to a maximum of six hours. It follows that the officer in question should not direct a full six hours extension as a matter of course. If a lesser period of time would suffice for the proper investigation of the offence, then the extension should be confined to that lesser period.

Suspending Questioning in Detention

5-36   The second situation in which the detention may be extended beyond six hours arises where the suspect is detained in the Garda station between midnight and 8 a.m. In this event, the member in charge of the station may acquire the power to suspend the questioning for a period between the hours of midnight and 8 a.m.[43] Where this power is available and is exercised any such period of suspension is excluded from the calculation of the time spent in detention. The net result is that a suspect could conceivably be detained in a Garda station for a continuous period of up to twenty hours. However, the period of detention during which he can be questioned cannot exceed a total of twelve hours.[44]

5-37   The power to suspend questioning will arise where four conditions are present. First, the suspect must be detained in a Garda station between midnight and 8 a.m. It will not matter that the initial detention has commenced prior to midnight so long as the suspect is still lawfully detained at the station under section 4, and the time is after midnight and before 8 a.m.

The second condition is that the member in charge must be of the opinion that any questioning of the suspect for the purpose of the investigation should be suspended in order to afford him reasonable time to rest.[44a] It is notable that this provision refers only to the investigation as opposed to the investigation of the offence for which the suspect was arrested. This suggests

---

[42]   Criminal Justice Act 1984, s.4(3)(c).

[42a]   See, by analogy, *People (DPP) v. Byrne* [1989] I.L.R.M. 613.

[43]   Criminal Justice Act 1984, s.4(6)(a).

[44]   To avoid any doubt about the maximum length of detention under section 4, it is specifically stated that the suspect cannot be held in detention for any longer than twelve hours from the time of his arrest, excluding any period during which the questioning is suspended under ss.4(6) or (8).

[44a]   Where a suspension is ordered the state of mind of the member in charge when issuing the suspension must be proved by him or her appearing in person to give evidence on the matter: *People (DPP) v. Byrne* [1989] I.L.R.M. 613.

that it is not confined to the investigation of the offence for which the suspect was arrested but applies also to the investigation of any other offences which the gardaí may be pursuing with the detained suspect at the time. Of greater significance perhaps, is the fact that there need not be reasonable grounds for the opinion of the member in charge. It will be sufficient merely that he or she is of the opinion that there should be a suspension.

There is no suggestion that the suspect's detention pursuant to section 4 is rendered unlawful by a failure to suspend questioning between the hours of midnight and 8 a.m. In any event, given the subjectivity of the power to suspend, it would be difficult to persuade a court, in the absence of special circumstances, that the member in charge had exceeded his powers by failing to exercise his or her discretion to suspend the questioning.

5–38 The third condition for the exercise of the suspension power is that the suspect consents to the suspension in writing.[45] It follows that it lies within the power of the suspect to keep the detention clock running into the early hours of the morning with a view to being released within the maximum six or 12 hours, whichever is applicable. If the suspect refuses to sign the consent the clock does not stop running even if the investigating officers decide to let him rest in his cell until 8 a.m. before commencing or resuming, as the case may be, his questioning. In *People (DPP) v. Cooney*,[46] for example, the appellant had been arrested on suspicion of murder at 2.35 a.m. and brought to the Garda station. He refused to answer questions and refused to sign the consent form for suspension of questioning for the purposes of rest. Nevertheless, the investigating officers decided to allow him to rest until later in the morning. His detention was extended for a further six hours at 12.45 p.m. During that second period of detention a formal identification parade was held. The identification evidence, however, was ruled inadmissible as the appellant was found to be in unlawful custody at the time. Since he had refused to sign the consent form for the suspension of questioning, the clock kept running from 2.35 a.m. in which case he should have been released at 8.35 a.m. The purported extension at 12.45 p.m., therefore, was unlawful.

5–39 The fourth condition is that the suspect has not already been served with a suspension notice. Only one suspension notice can be served on the same suspect during the same period between midnight and 8 a.m. It will be seen below that a suspension notice need not be for a period which expires at 8a.m. If it is issued for a period which expires before 8 a.m. and questioning resumes, the member of charge is precluded from issuing a subsequent suspension order even though the 8 a.m. deadline has not passed.

---

[45] The fact that a person has consented in writing must be recorded and the consent must be attached to and form part of the custody record; Criminal Justice Act 1984 (Treatment of Persons in Custody in Garda Síochána Stations) Regulations 1987, reg.12(12)(c).

[46] [1998] 1 I.L.R.M. 321.

Notice of Suspension

5–40   In order to exercise the power of suspension the member in charge must give the suspect a written notice that the questioning is suspended until the time specified in the notice.[47] The notice will also specify the time at which it is given. The suspect must be asked to sign the notice as an acknowledgement that he has received it. However, there is no suggestion that the suspect's refusal to sign will invalidate the notice or otherwise prevent the time of suspension from running so long as the suspect has signed a consent to the suspension. The period between the time stated in the notice as the time at which it was given and the time specified in the notice for suspension of questioning, is the period that cannot be taken into account for the calculation of the length of detention pursuant to section 4. In other words, the detention clock stops running at the commencement of this period of suspension and does not resume until it has expired. However, there is provision for the suspension notice to be withdrawn (see below). In this event, the period of suspension is counted as the period from the time the suspension notice was given to the time the withdrawal notice was served.[48] In other words, the detention clock begins to run again from the moment the withdrawal notice is given.

Where a notice of suspension is given, certain particulars concerning it must be entered into the records of the Garda station without delay.[49] These particulars are: the time the notice was given, the time specified in it as the time up to which the questioning is suspended, whether the suspect acknowledged that he received the notice and the time that any notice of withdrawal was given. These records must be preserved for at least twelve months.[50] If any proceedings are taken against the suspect in question for the offence in respect of which he was detained, the records must be preserved until the conclusion of the proceedings, including any appeal or retrial.

Withdrawal of Notice of Suspension

5–41   A notice of suspension may be withdrawn for serious reasons.[51] What might constitute serious reasons is not defined. Presumably, it would be satisfied where the gardaí formed the belief, after a notice of suspension had been given, that a third party was in danger of serious injury or death and that the suspect may be able to assist their efforts in averting the danger.[52] A withdrawal notice must be served in like manner to a suspension notice. Its effect is to terminate the period of suspension. It follows that the gardaí will be able to resume their questioning and examination of the suspect, and the time clock for the permitted period of detention will start up again.

---

[47] When giving the notice the member in question must give the suspect an oral explanation of its effect; Criminal Justice Act 1984, s.4(6)(c).
[48] *ibid*. s.4(6)(b).
[49] *ibid*. s.4(6)(d). See also, Criminal Justice Act 1984 (Treatment of Persons in Custody in Garda Síochána Stations) Regulations 1987, reg.12(12)(d).
[50] Criminal Justice Act 1984, s.4(6)(e).
[51] *ibid*. s.4(6)(b).
[52] This is analagous to the facts in *People v. Shaw* [1982] I.R. 1 where the Supreme Court accepted that the suspect's right to liberty could, in certain circumstances be outweighed by a third party's right to life.

Suspension for Medical Treatment

The third situation in which a period of detention might be extended beyond **5–42** six hours is where the arrested suspect is taken to a hospital or other suitable place for the purposes of medical attention.[53] This can happen either where it appears to a member of the Garda Síochána that the suspect in question is in need of medical attention, or where it comes to notice during his detention that he is in need of such attention. If the suspect is taken for medical attention before his arrival at the station, then the time between his arrest and his arrival at the station is not taken into account in the calculation of his period of detention. Similarly, if he is taken from the station for medical attention, his period of absence from the station is not taken into account in the calculation.

Suspension for Court Proceedings

The fourth situation in which the "maximum" period of detention can be **5–43** extended arises where the suspect's detention is interrupted in order to take him to court in connection with an application relating to the lawfulness of his detention. The period of time during which he is absent from the station for the purpose of the application in not included in the computation of his period of detention under section 4.[54] This suspension can only come into effect where the suspect is taken before the court to challenge the lawfulness of his detention. If he was brought before the court for some other purpose and then taken back to the Garda station time would continue to run without an interruption for the time spent at the court.[54a]

Justification for Continued Detention

Just because section 4 permits a suspect to be held in police custody for **5–44** certain maximum periods, it does not follow that every suspect who comes within its scope can always be detained for the full length of any one or more of these maximum periods. They are maximum periods. Circumstances may arise in any individual case which render it unnecessary, or even unlawful, to detain the suspect for the full period that might otherwise be available.[55] For example, if at any time during the detention there are no longer reasonable grounds for suspecting that he has committed an offence to which section 4 applies, he must be released from custody immediately unless his detention is authorised pursuant to some authority apart from the 1984 Act.[56] It is worth noting that an entirely objective test is applied to the suspicion. Even if each member of the Garda Síochána involved was acting under the honest belief that the suspect had committed a relevant offence, his continued detention

---

[53] Criminal Justice Act 1984, s.4(8).
[54] *ibid.* s.4(8A), as inserted by Criminal Justice (Miscellaneous Provisions) Act 1997, s.2(c).
[54a] See, for example, *Clarke v. Member in Charge of Terenure Garda Station* [2002] 2 I.L.R.M. 11.
[55] There must be no unnecessary delay in dealing with persons in custody; The Criminal Justice Act 1984 (Treatment of Persons in Custody in Garda Síochána Stations) Regulations 1987, Reg.3(2).
[56] Criminal Justice Act 1984, s.4(4).

will be unlawful if there are no reasonable grounds for that belief. However, a relevant offence in this context is not confined to the offence for which the suspect was arrested. It extends to any offence that comes within the scope of section 4. It follows that the continued detention may be lawful if there are reasonable grounds to suspect that the detained person has committed such an offence, even if it is not the offence for which he was arrested. Section 4 permits the detention of a suspect in certain circumstances for the investigation of an offence in addition to that for which the suspect was arrested.

5–45   The basic power of detention under section 4 is tied to the investigation of the suspect for the offence for which he or she was arrested. It may happen that an individual is arrested for one offence, but is actually suspected of having committed a number of unrelated offences. Equally, it may happen that while he is being detained for the investigation of the offence for which he was arrested grounds emerge to investigate him in respect of other offences. The 1984 Act makes provision for the continued detention of the suspect for the investigation of these further offences in certain circumstances.[57] For this provision to come into effect the suspect must be detained under section 4. At some point during the course of his detention a member of the Garda Síochána must with reasonable cause suspect the person concerned of having committed an offence within the scope of section 4 apart from the offence to which the detention relates and the member in charge of the station must have reasonable grounds for believing that the continued detention of the person is necessary for the proper investigation of that offence. Where these requirements are satisfied the person may continue to be detained in relation to that other offence as if it was the offence for which the person was originally detained. It follows, that the original time limits apply. The maximum period of detention will still be twelve hours, with due allowances for any periods of suspension, medical treatment away from the police station and time spent in court challenging the lawfulness of the detention.

5–46   Where there are no longer grounds for believing that the continued detention of a suspect under section 4 is necessary for the proper investigation of the offence for which he was arrested he must normally be released immediately or be charged with an offence.[58] The only exceptions are where his continued detention can be justified for the investigation of another offence as described above or if his detention is authorised by some other provision outside of the 1984 Act. Unless one of the exceptions applies the section 4 detention will come to an end when there are no longer reasonable grounds for believing

---

[57] Criminal Justice Act 1984, s.4(5A), as inserted by Criminal Justice (Miscellaneous Provisions) Act 1997, s.2(b). Unfortunately, due to a drafting error in the 1997 Act as originally framed s.4(5) of the Criminal Justice Act 1984 was replaced by two subsections which were designated s.4(5) and s.4(6). Since there already was a s.4(6) in the 1984 Act which had not been repealed by the 1997 Act there were then two subsections (6) of s.4. The error was remedied by Criminal Justice Act 1999, s.34 which re-designated the new s.4(6) as s.4(5A).

[58] Criminal Justice Act 1984, s.4(5), as inserted by Criminal Justice (Miscellaneous Provisions) Act 1997, s.2(b).

that his continued detention is necessary for the investigation of the offence for which he was arrested. If, however, he is charged at this point it is possible that he will remain in police custody for a further period.

Charging the Suspect

Section 4 does not make specific provision for the charging of a person who **5–47** has been detained pursuant to its provisions. It makes an indirect reference to the matter when referring to the circumstances in which the detained suspect need not be released immediately on the termination of the section 4 detention. One of these circumstances is where "he is charged or caused to be charged with an offence and is brought before a court as soon as may be in connection with such charge."[59] The section does not specifically require the suspect to be charged as soon as there is sufficient evidence to warrant a charge. Equally, it does not stipulate that the charging of the suspect will in itself terminate the section 4 detention. The provision for the continued detention of a suspect for the investigation of an offence or offences other than that for which he was arrested is not specifically predicated on the postponement of a charge for the original offence although postponement would achieve a better fit with section 15 of the Criminal Justice Act 1951. Indeed, it is not at all clear what impact, if any, section 4 of the 1984 Act has on the operation of section 15 of the 1951 Act which imposes an obligation to bring a suspect before a District Court judge as soon as practicable after being charged with an offence.

On one interpretation the section 4 detention will be terminated once the **5–48** suspect is charged with an offence and the obligation to bring him before a District Court judge comes into play. On another interpretation section 4 permits the police to detain the suspect, irrespective of whether or not they have charged him with one or more offences, until there are no reasonable grounds for believing that his continued detention is necessary for the further investigation of an offence within the scope of section 4 or until the statutory time limit has expired. What is clear is that the suspect can be detained for the maximum permissible period, irrespective of whether the police had sufficient evidence to charge him with an offence at a much earlier stage of the detention, so long as there are reasonable grounds for considering that the continued detention is necessary for the proper investigation of the offence and he has not been charged.

As originally enacted section 4 actually imposed a specific obligation on the **5–49** gardaí to charge a detainee with an offence as soon as they had enough evidence to do so, unless his continued detention was necessary for the proper investigation of another offence. In the current formulation this specific obligation has been removed. The net effect would appear to be that the

---

59 Criminal Justice Act 1984, s.4(5) as amended by Criminal Justice (Miscellaneous Provisions) Act 1997, s.2(b).

gardaí can use the full section 4 detention period to pursue the investigation of an offence against the suspect with a view to building a stronger case, even though it could be argued that they already have sufficient evidence to charge him with that offence. This interpretation would also accord with the notion, evident in the quotation cited above from the judgment of O'Flaherty J. in *Keating v. Governor of Mountjoy Prison*,[60] that the gardaí have considerable flexibility in determining when they have sufficient evidence to prefer a charge.[61]

5–50   In practice the police will normally postpone the charging of the suspect until the section 4 detention has come to an end, whether because the statutory time limit has expired or because his continued detention is not considered necessary for the further investigation of the offence. Indeed, they will actually arrest the suspect at this point and immediately charge him or her with one or more offences, thereby triggering the obligation under section 15 of the Criminal Justice Act 1951 to bring him or her before a District Court judge as soon as practicable.[62] This, of course, means that the suspect may actually spend further time in police custody if a District Court judge is not immediately available. It is arguable, of course, that this could result in the suspect being detained unlawfully if the total period in police custody from the moment of arrest to the appearance before the judge exceeds the maximum period permitted by section 4. Implicit in this argument is the notion that the gardaí must use the time available to them under section 4 to ensure that a District Court judge is available before the expiry of the permitted period of detention under that section. The counter argument is that the period in police custody after the second arrest and charge cannot be counted as part of the detention under section 4.

5. Section 30 of the Offences Against the State Act 1939

The Statutory Provision

5–51   Section 30 of the Offences against the State Act 1939 is a major statutory provision authorising the arrest and detention of a person in certain circumstances. The power of arrest is provided in section 30(1) which is dealt with in Chapter 4. The power to detain a person who has been arrested under section 30(1) was originally provided in section 30(3) and section 30(4). These have since been amended by the Offences against the State (Amendment) Act 1998 which has created new subsections (4), (4A) and 4(B). The original subsection (4) is now subsection (4C).

---

[60] [1990] I.L.R.M. 850.

[61] See also, *People (DPP) v. O'Toole and Hickey* unreported, July 20, 1990 Court of Criminal Appeal.

[62] Significantly, this will not amount to the re-arrest of a suspect for the purposes of s.10. S.10(2) specifically states that notwithstanding the restrictions on the re-arrest of a suspect who has already been detained for the offence or a related offence under s.4, he may be arrested for any offence for the purpose of charging him with that offence.

Although section 30 does not extend over as wide a range of offences as **5–52** section 4 of the 1984 Act (see Chapter 4 for the range of offences covered), it does permit a much longer period of detention. Section 30(3) reads:

> "Whenever a person is arrested under this section, he may be removed to and detained in custody in a Garda Síochána station, a prison, or some other convenient place for a period of twenty-four hours from the time of his arrest and may, if an officer of the Garda Síochána not below the rank of Chief Superintendent so directs, be so detained for a further period of twenty-four hours."

Section 30(4) permits an officer of the Garda Síochána not below the rank of superintendent to apply to a judge of the District Court for a warrant authorising the detention of the person concerned for a further period not exceeding 24 hours. The basic power of detention under section 30(3) will be considered first before examining the procedure for detention beyond 48 hours.

Purpose of Detention

The only precondition for detention under section 30(3) is that the person **5–53** must have been arrested under section 30 of the 1939 Act. There is no specific requirement that, for example, a member of the Garda Síochána should consider that the detention is reasonably necessary for the proper investigation of the offence. Nevertheless, it is highly unlikely that the courts would permit section 30 to be used to detain persons for purposes other than the proper investigation of crime. Indeed, in *People v. Quilligan* Walsh J. made it clear that:

> "[t]he object of the powers given by s.30 is not to permit the arrest of people simply for the purpose of subjecting them to questioning. Rather it is for the purpose of investigating the commission or suspected commission of crime by the person already arrested and to enable that investigation to be carried out without the possibility of obstruction or other interference which might occur if the suspected person were not under arrest."[63]

Walsh J. has probably expressed the point too narrowly in that section 30 specifically permits the arrest and detention of a person who is not personally suspected of having committed a relevant offence. Nevertheless, it is clear that he would not contemplate section 30 being used to detain someone where their continued detention was not considered reasonably necessary for the proper investigation of a section 30 offence. It is also worth noting that the provision for detention beyond the 48 hour limit specifically requires the District Court judge in question to be satisfied that further detention is necessary for the proper investigation of the offence concerned.

While a section 30 detention cannot be effected purely for the purpose of interrogation,[63a] there can be no doubt that a suspect lawfully arrested and detained under section 30 can be questioned about an offence. Indeed, it would appear that the specific use of the word "interrogate" in this section

---

[63] [1987] I.L.R.M. 606 at 624.
[63a] *People (DPP) v. Walsh* [1982] I.R. 1, *per* Walsh J. at 30.

connotes something more than a form of gentle questioning. In *People (DPP) v. McCann*,[63b] for example, the Court of Criminal Appeal made it clear that so long as there are no threats or inducements or oppressive circumstances, the gardaí are always entitled to persist with their questioning of a section 30 suspect. The section 30 detention is not meant to be a "genteel encounter".

Place of Detention

5–54   The section 30 detention must be in "a Garda Síochána station, a prison or some other convenient place." Another convenient place in this context must be interpreted *ejusdem generis* with a Garda station and a prison.[64] A car, for example, would not qualify. Nevertheless, it is permissible to take the suspect in a car journey during the detention where that is considered necessary in order to assist in the investigation. In *People v. Kelly (No.2)*,[65] for example, the accused agreed to show gardaí a dwelling where the proceeds of a robbery and guns used in the robbery had been stored. Both the High Court and the Supreme Court ruled that embarking on the car journey for this purpose did not terminate the detention under section 30. It is also worth noting that moving the detainee from one Garda station to another would not invalidate the detention under section 30 so long as it was not done mala fide for the purpose of depriving the detainee of legal assistance or communication with relatives.[66]

Calculating Period of Detention

5–55   The initial maximum period of detention is 24 hours from the moment of arrest. However, if the arrested suspect is taken to a hospital or other suitable place for medical attention after his arrest, or during his detention, then the time before his arrival at the station, or the length of his absence from the station, as the case may be, will not be taken into account in calculating the 24 hours.[67] The same applies to any period during which the second or third periods of detention are interrupted by the need to take the person away from the station or other place of detention for the purpose of medical treatment. It would appear, however, that a period of absence for the purpose of challenging the lawfulness of the detention in court will not stop time running under section 30. This contrasts with the position applicable to a detention under section 4 of the Criminal Justice Act 1984.[68]

[63b] [1998] 4 I.R. 397 at 410.

[64] *People v. Farrell* [1978] I.R. 13.

[65] [1983] I.R. 1.

[66] *People v. Kelly (No.2)* [1983] I.R. 1; *People v. Farrell* [1978] I.R. 13; *State (Walsh) v. Maguire* [1979] I.R. 372.

[67] Criminal Justice Act 1984, s.9. This provision comes into play when it appears to a member of the Garda Síochána that a person arrested under s.30 of the 1939 Act is in need of medical attention.

[68] S.2(c) of the Criminal Justice (Miscellaneous Provisions) Act 1997 added a new subsection (8A) to s.4 of the Criminal Justice Act 1984 which excludes a period spend in court challenging the lawfulness of a s.4 detention in the computation of the s.4 detention period. This particular subsection does not seem to have been extended to detentions under s.30.

Extending Detention

The initial 24-hour period can be extended by 24 hours by a simple direction **5–56** from an officer not below the rank of chief superintendent.[69] There are no specific preconditions for the exercise of this power.[70] However, it would seem that the authorising officer must entertain the same suspicion as to the commission of the offence as that necessary to effect the original arrest.[71] By the same token, it will be quite sufficient that the authorising officer believes in good faith that the detainee is suspected of being involved in the offence for which he was originally arrested. The extension will not be rendered unlawful by the mere fact that the gardaí requesting the extension wish to question the detainee about other offences and have not communicated this to the authorising officer.[72] The exclusion of time taken for medical treatment applies as much to the calculation of the second 24-hour period as it does to the first.[73]

Where a direction has issued extending the detention, it would appear that the Chief Superintendent who issued the direction would have to appear, where applicable, at the subsequent criminal trial of the person concerned to give evidence about his state of mind when deciding to issue the direction. This issue arose for decision in the case of *People (DPP) v. Byrne.*[73a] The evidence against the accused in this case included a conversation between him and a member of the Garda Síochána while he was detained in Garda custody pursuant to a direction issued by a Chief Superintendent under section 30. The Chief Superintendent could not give evidence as to his state of mind at the time of issuing the direction to extend the period of detention as he had died prior to the trial. The trial judge ruled that it could not be presumed that the Chief Superintendent had the requisite state of mind when issuing the direction. Formal proof was necessary. This proof could only be provided by evidence in person from the Chief Superintendent. It could not be provided by documentary evidence or hearsay evidence from another member of the Garda Síochána who witnessed the Chief Superintendent issuing the direction. Accordingly, the trial judge felt compelled to exclude the evidence of the conversation as it had taken place at a time when the

---

[69] An extension may be authorised by a superintendent where he is so authorised in writing by the Garda Commissioner; Offences Against the State Act 1939, s.3. However, a written extension by a superintendent which states that he has been duly authorised by the Commissioner will not be sufficient; *People v. Farrell* [1978] I.R. 13.

[70] It is a desirable practice that the direction for an extension should be in writing even though this is not a compulsory requirement; *People (DPP) v. Kehoe* [1985] I.R. 444.

[71] *People (DPP) v. Byrne* [1989] I.L.R.M. 613. In this case it was held that the authorising officer would actually have to appear and give evidence of his state of mind in order to prove the lawfulness of the extended detention. Production of the signed certificate of extension, coupled with the evidence of another garda that he witnessed the authorising officer signing the certificate, would not be sufficient.

[72] *People (DPP) v. Howley* [1989] I.L.R.M. 629.

[73] It will be sufficient that the direction simply states that the person arrested is to be detained for a further period of 24 hours commencing upon the expiry of the period of 24 hours from the time of his arrest. There is no need to state the exact commencement and termination of the further period of 24 hours; *People (DPP) v. Kehoe* [1985] I.R. 444.

[73a] *People (DPP) v. Byrne* [1989] I.L.R.M. 613.

validity of the accused's detention could not be proved. This decision was upheld by the Supreme Court. Walsh J. explained the position as follows:

> "In my view the state of mind of the chief superintendent cannot be proved simply by producing a document from which it might be inferred that he had the state of mind required by the law. If such were the case it would never have been necessary for the chief superintendent to give evidence that he did entertain the suspicion in question. In my view the learned judge was quite correct in ruling that the production of the document in question could not be offered as proof of what was the state of mind of Chief Superintendent Joy when he directed an extension of the period of arrest. Apart from the hearsay nature of the evidence it made it impossible for any examination or cross-examination to be made of the actual state of mind of the chief superintendent which is a necessary proof of fact in the case."[73b]

Cutting the Detention Short

5–57 A literal interpretation of the subsection would suggest that the extension must be for a period of 24 hours. There is no power, for example, to direct a further period of twelve hours. It would also appear that the power to extend the detention for a further period of 24 hours can be exercised only once.[74] It does not follow, however, that the suspect must be detained for the full 24- or 48-hour period before being released. The Act specifically envisages the possibility of the suspect being released before the expiry of the relevant period. An officer of the Garda Síochána may direct the release of the suspect at any time.[75] Moreover, at any time during the detention, the suspect may be charged before the District Court or the Special Criminal Court with an offence.[76] Presumably, such charging will bring the section 30(3) detention to an end. It is submitted, therefore, that the prescribed periods must be interpreted as maximum periods for the lawful detention of the suspect. They do not preclude a release short of the maximum permissible where the gardaí in question have no further need to detain the suspect in question.

5–58 Just because the detention can be cut short it does not follow that it must be cut short in any particular circumstances. The provision for the release or charging of the suspect before the expiry of the relevant maximum period is framed in purely permissive terms. There is no suggestion that either course must be adopted in any circumstances. Unlike section 4 of the Criminal Justice Act 1984, there is no specific provision in section 30 of the 1939 Act to the effect that the person must be released, at any point during the first 48 hours, where there are no longer reasonable grounds for believing that his

---

[73b] *ibid.* at 615–616.

[74] *State (Walsh) v. Maguire* [1979] I.R. 372.

[75] Offences Against the State Act 1939. s.30(4C). This clearly states that a decision to release at a time which falls short of the maximum period available must be taken by an *officer* of the Garda Síochána, *i.e.* a member of the rank of superintendent or above. However, it would appear that the lawfulness of a detainee's release and re-arrest will not be affected by the fact that the release was effected by an Inspector, *i.e.* a member as opposed to an officer. See *People (DPP) v. Kelly* [1978] I.R. 1.

[76] Offences against the State Act 1939, s.30(4C).

continued detention is necessary for the proper investigation of the offence for which he was arrested or any other offence of which he is reasonably suspected. The clear import of the relevant subsections is that once an arrest has been made under section 30 the detention is meant to continue inexorably for the relevant maximum period unless the gardaí choose to cut it short by release or charge. Nevertheless, it is at least arguable, on the basis of the dictum from Walsh J. in *Quilligan*[76a] that the person should be released or charged once there are no longer any reasonable grounds for believing that his continued detention is necessary for the proper investigation of a relevant offence. At the expiry of the permitted maximum period they must either release the suspect or charge him with an offence.

Further Extension of Detention

Where a person is already detained pursuant to a direction extending his **5–59** detention under section 30(3) for a second 24-hour period, an officer of the Garda Síochána not below the rank of superintendent may apply to a judge of the District Court under section 30(4) for a warrant authorising his detention for a further period not exceeding 24 hours.[76b] Such an application can be made only if the officer has reasonable grounds for believing that the further detention is necessary for the proper investigation of the offence concerned. It is not made clear whether this offence must be the offence for which the arrest was effected, whether it can be any offence of which the person is suspected and the gardaí are investigating or whether it can simply be any section 30 offence which the gardaí are investigating and of which they believe the person has relevant information.

On a section 30(4) application the judge must issue the warrant,[76c] but only if **5–60** he or she is satisfied that the further detention is necessary for the proper investigation of the offence concerned and that the investigation is being conducted diligently and expeditiously.[77] Although the provision is expressed in subjective terms it can be deduced from the case law on analogous provisions that there must be some objective evidence upon which the judge can be satisfied. It will not be sufficient, for example, for the officer to state on oath that he or she believes that the further detention is necessary for the proper investigation of the offence and that the investigation is being conducted diligently and expeditiously. Moreover, on any such application the person concerned must be brought before the judge and the judge shall hear any submissions made and consider any evidence adduced by or on behalf of the person and the officer making the application.[78]

Ultimately, the judge must be satisfied that the extended detention is "necessary" for the proper investigation of the offence, as well as that the

---

[76a] *op. cit.*, above, n.63.
[76b] For the form of the application, see Form 17.4 in Schedule B of the District Court Rules 1997, as set out in District Court (Offences against the State (Amendment) Act 1998) Rules 2000, Schedule 2.
[76c] For the form of the warrant see Form 17.5 *ibid.*
[77] Offence against the State Act, 1939, s.30(4A).
[78] *ibid.* s.30(4B).

investigation is being conducted diligently and expeditiously. The use of the term "necessary" suggests that an extension should not be lightly granted. Presumably, mere convenience or desirability would not be sufficient. Less certain is the relevance of evidence to the effect that the suspect had been exercising his right to silence while in police custody and would continue to do so if the extension was granted. In this situation it could be argued that it would be pointless to grant an extension if the only reason proffered by the gardaí for the extension was the desire to question the suspect.[79]

Period of Extended Detention

5-61   Where the judge issues a warrant under section 30(4) it can be for a period up to 24 hours. It does not have to be for the full period of 24 hours and it is at least arguable that it should be for a lesser period if the judge is satisfied that a lesser period will be sufficient for the proper investigation of the offence. However, there is no provision for a second application under section 4. Equally, it is not made clear whether the further period commences from the moment the warrant is issued or whether it can run from the expiry of the second 24-hour period, assuming that the latter will be due to end at a point in time later than the issue of the warrant. It is also worth noting that the legislation is silent on whether the time spent in court seeking the warrant for a further period can be excluded when calculating how long a suspect has been in detention pursuant to section 30. In the absence of a specific provision to the contrary it must be assumed that time continues to run during the hearing of an application for a warrant for a further period of detention. The gardaí must be careful, therefore, to organise the application in such a way that the period of time for which the person can be detained under section 30(3) does not expire before a warrant for a further period is granted under section 30(4).

Charging the Suspect

5-62   Section 30(4C) specifically provides that a person detained under section 30 can be charged before a District Court or a Special Criminal Court at any time during his detention. This could be interpreted as meaning that in order to charge a section 30 suspect he would have to be brought before the District Court or Special Criminal Court. Presumably, this would have to be done before the expiry of the relevant statutory maximum period of detention. In *State (Walsh) v. Maguire*,[80] however, the Supreme Court ruled that section 30(4C) (as it is now) did not preclude the possibility of the suspect being charged in the Garda station before being brought before the District Court or Special Criminal Court. According to O'Higgins C.J. in that case, the purpose of section 30(4C) (as it is now) was to ensure that a section 30 suspect who

---

[79]   See Keane, "Detention without Charge and the Criminal Justice (Drug Trafficking) Act 1996: Shifting the Focus of the Irish Criminal Process from Trial Court to Garda Station", (1997) 7(1) I.C.L.J. 1 at 18–19 referring to MacGuill "Judicial Supervision of Detention for the Purpose of Interrogation – Spectre or Safeguard?" in *Recent Criminal Legislation – Seminar Papers* (Law Society of Ireland, April 25, 1997) 31.

[80]   [1979] I.R. 372.

was charged while in Garda custody would have similar rights of appearance before a court as a suspect who was charged and dealt with under section 15 of the Criminal Justice Act 1951. The requirements of section 30(4C) would be satisfied by an explanation to the court as to why the suspect was before it. What is not so clear is the effect that charging the suspect in the Garda station will have on the detention under section 30. If it terminates the detention it presumably follows that the suspect will be dealt with under section 15 of the Criminal Justice Act 1951. This would be convenient for the gardaí since it permits them to continue holding the suspect until a District Court judge is available, even if that means that the total period spent by the suspect in police custody is in excess of the statutory maximum. If, however, charging the suspect in the Garda station does not terminate the section 30 detention, the suspect will have to be brought before a District Court or Special Criminal Court before the expiry of the applicable statutory maximum period.

In practice, the gardaí avoid this conundrum either by bringing the suspect **5–63** before a District Court or the Special Criminal Court within the prescribed maximum period, or by releasing the suspect and re-arresting him immediately outside the Garda station in order to be processed pursuant to section 15 of the Criminal Justice Act 1951. There may, of course, be a question mark over the validity of the latter practice in that it can be argued that the release is merely a colourable device designed to ensure that the gardaí are not prejudiced by their failure to bring the suspect before a District Court or Special Criminal Court within the relevant maximum period. On the other hand, as will be seen below, there is implicit statutory support for the practice of re-arresting, for the purpose of charging, a suspect who has already been arrested under section 30.[81] What is not so clear is whether the section 30 suspect must actually be released from Garda Custody, however cursorily, in order to be re-arrested for the purpose of being charged and brought before the District Court pursuant to section 15 of the 1951 Act.

It was seen in Chapter 4 that there is a broad prohibition on the extent to **5–64** which a person can be re-arrested for an offence after having been arrested previously under section 30 and released without charge. For the most part he can be re-arrested in such circumstances only under a warrant duly issued by a judge of the District Court pursuant to section 30A of the 1939 Act.[81a] Where a person is arrested under such a warrant the provisions of section 30 will apply generally to that person, subject to some modifications, as they apply to a person arrested under section 30.[82] The primary difference is that his detention cannot be extended beyond the first 24 hours by direction of an

---

[81] Offences against the State Act 1939, s.30A(3), as inserted by Offences against the State (Amendment) Act 1998, s.11.
[81a] The application for the warrant must be on oath and in writing from a member of the Garda Síochána not below the rank of superintendent; District Court Rules 1997, Ord.17, r.8. See Sched. B, Forms 17.6 and 17.7 for the information and warrant, as set out in District Court (Offences against the State (Amendment) Act 1998) Rules 2000, Sched. 2.
[82] *ibid.* s.30A(2), *ibid.* s.11.

officer of the Garda Síochána nor by an application to a judge of the District Court pursuant to section 30(4). Another important exception to the prohibition on re-arrest is the provision which permits the arrest of the suspect for the purpose of being charged with an offence.[83] It follows, that a suspect who has been arrested and detained for an offence under section 30 can be arrested and charged for the same offence without falling foul of the prohibition on re-arrest.

A final point worth noting about the detention powers under section 30(3) and section 30(4) is that their availability is not specifically limited in any way by the age of the suspect.

6. Drug Trafficking

The Offence

5–65 Section 2 of the Criminal Justice (Drug Trafficking) Act 1996 makes separate, and arguably more draconian provision, for the detention of persons suspected of a drug-trafficking offence.[84] It applies to a person who has been arrested and brought to a Garda station by a member of the Garda Síochána on reasonable suspicion of having committed a drug trafficking offence.[85] For this purpose a drug trafficking offence means any of the following:[86]

(a) an offence under any regulations made under section 5 of the Misuse of Drugs Act 1977, involving the manufacture, production, preparation, importation, exportation, supply, offering to supply, distribution or transportation of a controlled drug,[87]

(b) an offence under section 15 of that Act of possession of a controlled drug for unlawful sale or supply,

(c) an offence under section 20 of that Act (assisting in or inducing the commission outside the State of an offence punishable under a corresponding law),

(d) an offence under the Customs Acts in relation to the importation or exportation of a controlled drug or in relation to the fraudulent evasion of any prohibition, restriction or obligation in relation to such importation or exportation.

(e) an offence under section 31 of the Criminal Justice Act 1994 in relation to the proceeds of drug trafficking (moneylaundering, etc.,),

(f) an offence under section 33 or 34 of the Criminal Justice Act 1994 (drug trafficking offences involving ships), or

(g) an offence of aiding, abetting, counselling or procuring the commission of any of the offences mentioned above or of attempting or conspiring to commit any such offence or inciting another person to do so.

---

[83] *ibid.* s.30A(3), *ibid.* s.11.

[84] For commentary on certain issues raised by s.2, see Keane, "Detention Without Charge and the Criminal Justice (Drug Trafficking) Act 1996: Shifting the Focus of the Irish Criminal Process from Trial Court to garda Station" (1997) 7(1) I.C.L.J. 1; and Ryan "The Criminal Justice (Drug Trafficking) Act 1996: Decline and Fall of the Right to Silence?" (1997) 7(1) I.C.L.J. 22.

[85] Criminal Justice (Drug Trafficking) Act 1996, s.2(1)(a)

[86] *ibid.* s.1(1). The definition is taken from Criminal Justice Act 1994, s.3(1).

Detention in Garda Station

Where a member of the Garda Síochána arrests without warrant a person **5–66** whom he or she reasonably suspects of having committed a drug-trafficking offence, the member may take the person to a Garda station. He may be detained there under section 2 of the 1996 Act if the member in charge of the station has, at the time of the arrested person's arrival, reasonable grounds for believing that his detention is necessary for the proper investigation of the offence. This is almost identical to the position under section 4 of the Criminal Justice Act 1984 Act (see above).[88] It would appear, therefore, that the member in charge could form the requisite belief on the basis of what he is told by the arresting officer, whether before or after the arrest has been effected.[89] Equally, his state of mind when authorising the detention will have to be proved, where necessary, by his giving evidence in person at the trial of the person concerned.[89a]

Detention in a Place of Detention

A section 2 detention can also arise where a member of the Garda Síochána **5–67** suspects an arrested person of concealing a controlled drug on his person and brings that person to a place of detention.[90] In this case there is no specific requirement that the person should have been arrested for a drug-trafficking offence. The provision merely states that he must be "an arrested person" who is suspected of concealing a controlled drug on his or her person. It is at least arguable, therefore, that the power to bring such a person to a "place of detention" under section 2 applies even if at the relevant time the person is being detained at a Garda station under another statutory provision whether for a drug-trafficking offence or some other offence. Equally it might apply where the person has been arrested for any offence and is *en route* to the Garda station when a member of the Garda Síochána acquires the necessary suspicion. It would appear, however, from the contents of the provisions for dealing with a person at "a place of detention" that the legislative intention is to confine detentions under this provision to persons who have been arrested for a drug-trafficking offence, irrespective of whether they have been taken to a Garda station first.

Where a person is brought to a "place of detention" under this provision, he may **5–68** be detained there under section 2 if a member of the Garda Síochána not below the rank of inspector who is not investigating the drug-trafficking offence has, at the time of the person's arrival, reasonable grounds for

---

[87] A "controlled drug" has the meaning assigned to it by Misuse of Drugs Act 1977, s.2.

[88] The provisions of the 1984 Act specifically dealing with a suspect below the age of 12 years and a suspect in need of medical attention are extended to suspects detained under section 2; Criminal Justice (Drug Trafficking) Act 1996, s.5.

[89] *People (DPP) v. O'Toole and Hickey* unreported, Court of Criminal Appeal, July 20, 1990.

[89a] See, by analogy, *People (DPP) v. Byrne* [1989] I.L.R.M. 613.

[90] Criminal Justice (Drug Trafficking) Act 1996, s.2(1)(b). The Minister for Justice, Equality and Law Reform may make regulations specifying places which will qualify as places of detention for this purpose; s.2(9)(a).

believing that his detention is necessary for the proper investigation of the offence. There is no requirement that the officer in question should have any connection with or official role at the place of detention to which the person is brought. Presumably, he or she should make a record of the existence of his or her belief at the time, although the legislation does not specifically require such action. Once again, the member's state of mind when authorising the detention will have to be proved, where necessary, by his giving evidence in person at the trial of the person concerned.[90a]

Child Below the Age of 12 Years

5–69 As with detention under section 4 of the Criminal Justice Act 1984, a person below the age of 12 years cannot normally be detained under section 2 of the 1996 Act.[91] This does not apply where the member in charge of the Garda station to which the person is brought has reasonable grounds for believing that the suspect is not below the age of 12 years.[92] If, however, the member in charge ascertains or has reasonable grounds for believing that the suspect is less than 12 years of age he must be released from custody immediately.[92a] It is not clear who will perform the role of the member in charge of the Garda station in this matter where the person is brought to a place of detention. Presumably it will be the officer who had reasonable grounds for believing that his detention was necessary for the proper investigation of the offence.

Initial Periods of Detention

5–70 A person who has been brought to a garda station or a place of detention under section 2 may be detained for a period of up to six hours from the time of his arrest.[93] However, an officer not below the rank of chief superintendent may direct that the person be detained for a further period not exceeding 18 hours.[94] This power is available where the officer in question has reasonable grounds for believing that the further detention is necessary for the proper investigation of the offence. Where such a direction has been issued an officer not below the rank of chief superintendent may direct that the person concerned may be detained for a further period not exceeding 24 hours.[95] Once again, this power is available only where the officer has reasonable grounds for believing that such further detention is necessary for the proper investigation of the drug-trafficking offence. A direction for further detention under either of these provisions may be given orally or in writing.[96] If given orally, however, it must be recorded in writing as soon as practicable. Where a direction is

---

[90a] See, by analogy, *People (DPP) v. Byrne* [1989] I.L.R.M. 613.

[91] Criminal Justice (Drug Trafficking) Act 1996, s.5 applying Criminal Justice Act 1984, s.4(7)(a).

[92] *ibid.* applying Criminal Justice Act 1984, s.4(7)(b).

[92a] Note that when the relevant provisions of the Children Act 2001 come into effect there may be a requirement to bring the child to his or her parent or guardian or deliver him or her into the custody of the health board (see para. 5–30).

[93] Criminal Justice (Drug Trafficking) Act 1996, s.2(2)(a).

[94] *ibid.* s.2(2)(b).

[95] *ibid.* s.2(2)(c).

[96] *ibid.* s.2(2)(d).

given, a record must be made of the fact that it was given, the date and time when it was given and the name and rank of the officer who gave it.[97] The record must also be signed by the officer giving the direction and it must state that he or she had reasonable grounds for believing that the further detention was necessary for the proper investigation of the offence.[98] The direction is attached to and forms part of the custody record for the person concerned. The officer's state of mind when authorising the detention will have to be proved, where necessary, by his giving evidence in person at the trial of the person concerned.[98a]

It is not clear whether a direction for further detention operates from the end of the maximum period of detention for which the person can be detained in the absence of the direction, or whether it operates from the time it is issued. Either way it is possible that the person could be detained for a maximum period of 48 hours from his arrest on the directions of an appropriate officer of the Garda Síochána.

Further Detention

There is provision permitting the further detention of a person whose detention has already been extended for the second time by a period not exceeding 24 hours. An officer not below the rank of chief superintendent may apply to a Circuit Court judge or a District Court judge[99] for a warrant authorising the detention of the person for a further period not exceeding 72 hours.[100] This option will be available to the officer where he or she has reasonable grounds for believing that the further detention is necessary for the proper investigation of the offence. The judge may issue the warrant for a further period not exceeding 72 hours only if he or she is satisfied that such further detention is necessary for the proper investigation of the offence and that the investigation is being conducted diligently and expeditiously.[101] Where a warrant has issued under this provision an officer not below the rank of chief superintendent may resort to a Circuit Court judge or a District Court judge once again for a warrant authorising the continued detention of the person concerned for a further period not exceeding 48 hours.[102] The availability of this power and the requirements for the issue of the warrant are identical to those pertaining to the first warrant.

5–71

---

[97] *ibid.* s.2(2)(e).

[98] *ibid.* s.2(2)(f).

[98a] See, by analogy, *People (DPP) v. Byrne* [1989] I.L.R.M. 613.

[99] Originally, a "judge of the District Court" was defined for the purposes of the Act as the President of the District Court and any judge of the District Court standing nominated for the time being by the President of the District Court. That definition was (in s.1 of the 1996 Act) repealed by Criminal Justice Act 1999, s.35. The net effect is that any judge of the District Court is competent to discharge the functions of a District Court judge pursuant to the Act.

[100] Criminal Justice (Drug Trafficking) Act 1996, s.2(2)(g)(i).

[101] *ibid.* s.2(2)(g)(ii).

[102] *ibid.* s.2(2)(h).

Court Procedure

5–72   Where a qualified Garda officer applies for a warrant for further detention the detained person must be brought before the judge concerned. Both the detainee and the officer can make submissions and adduce evidence which will be considered by the judge.[103] From cases dealing with the judicial power to issue warrants in analogous situations it is apparent that the gardaí must present evidence which provides an objective basis upon which the judge can be satisfied that a further period of detention is necessary for the proper investigation of the offence and that the investigation is being conducted diligently and expeditiously.[104] Ultimately, the judge must be satisfied that the extended detention is "necessary" for the proper investigation of the offence, as well as that the investigation is being conducted diligently and expeditiously. The use of the term "necessary" suggests that an extension should not be lightly granted. Presumably, mere convenience or desirability would not be sufficient. Less certain is the relevance of evidence to the effect that the suspect had been exercising his right to silence while in police custody and would continue to do so if the extension was granted. In this situation it could be argued that it would be pointless to grant an extension if the only reason proffered by the gardaí for the extension was the desire to question the suspect.[105]

5–73   It is also worth noting that a hearing before a District Court judge under these provisions should be confined to the issue of whether the detention should be extended. The court should not normally address the validity of the suspect's detention. If the suspect challenges the validity of his detention the judge should remand the suspect in custody for the purposes of a *habeas corpus* application unless the time limit for his custody has expired and the judge has decided not to grant an extension. However, if the circumstances of arrest are such as to amount to an affront to the constitutional role of the courts, then the District Court judge should refuse to proceed with the matter and should discharge the person in question.[106]

5–74   When the judge issues a warrant for a further period of detention under these provisions, he may also order that the detainee must be brought before a Circuit Court judge or a District Court judge at a specified time or times during the period of detention authorised by the warrant.[107] Where a detainee is brought before a judge in compliance with such an order, the judge concerned may revoke the warrant and order the immediate release of the detainee where he is not satisfied that the detention is justified.

---

[103] *ibid.* s.2(3).
[104] See, for example, *Larkin v. O'Dea* [1995] 2 I.R. 489; *People (DPP) v. Kenney* [1990] I.L.R.M. 569.
[105] See Keane, *op. cit.* above, n. 79.
[106] *Keating v. Governor of Mountjoy Prison* [1991] 1 I.R. 61, *per* McCarthy J. at 66.
[107] Criminal Justice (Drug Trafficking) Act 1996, s.2(4).

Calculating Periods of Detention

Once again the legislation does not specify when the further period or periods   **5–75**
of detention under warrant should commence. It is clear that none of the individual periods of extension need be directed or authorised in full. Nevertheless,
if all the possible directions and warrants under section 2 are used to the full,
the person concerned could conceivably be detained in Garda custody under
section 2 for a period of seven days.[108] In calculating this seven day period no
account can be taken of any period during which the detention is interrupted
by time spent outside the Garda station or place of detention for the purpose
of providing medical attention to the person concerned. Unlike a detention
under section 4 of the Criminal Justice Act 1984, it would appear that no
account can be taken of any period during which the detention is interrupted
by the attendance of the person concerned at court to challenge the lawfulness
of his detention.[109] It is also worth noting that there is no specific provision
for the section 2 detention clock to stop running while the gardaí and the
person concerned are in court pursuant to an application for a warrant
authorising a further period of detention. It follows that the gardaí would have
to organise such an application in a manner which ensures that the current
period of detention does not expire before any further period which may be
authorised is granted.

Cutting the Detention Short

A section 2 detainee must be released if at any time during his detention there   **5–76**
are no longer reasonable grounds for suspecting that he has committed a
drug-trafficking offence.[110] He should also be released from custody or charged
if at any time there are no longer reasonable grounds for believing that his
detention is necessary for the proper investigation of the offence concerned.[111] It
does not follow, however, that a suspect must either be released or charged
once his continued investigation is no longer necessary for the investigation
of the offence which triggered his detention. If, at any time during the detention,
a member of the Garda Síochána with reasonable cause suspects the person of
having committed a drug trafficking offence other than the offence which
triggered the detention, it may be possible to continue the detention.[112] In
order for the detention to be continued in this situation the member in charge
of the Garda station or (where the person is detained in a place of detention
other than a Garda station) a member of the Garda Síochána not below the

---

[108] *ibid.* s.2(7).
[109] The Criminal Justice (Miscellaneous Provisions) Act 1997, s.2(c) inserted a new subs.(8A) into
s.4 of the Criminal Justice Act 1984 which excludes times spent in court challenging the
lawfulness of the s.4 detention from the calculation of the maximum permissible period of
detention under that provision. S.5 of the Criminal Justice (Drug Trafficking) Act 1997 applies
certain provisions of the 1984 Act (including section 4(8)) to a person detained under section 2 of
the 1996 Act. However, it would appear that there is no specific provision extending the new
s.4(8A) to a s.2 detainee.
[110] Criminal Justice (Drug Trafficking) Act 1996, s.5 applying Criminal Justice Act 1984, s.4(4).
[111] *ibid.* s.2(5).
[112] *ibid.* s.2(6).

rank of inspector who is not investigating either the original offence or the other offence must have reasonable grounds for believing that the continued detention is necessary for the proper investigation of that other offence. In this event the person concerned may continue to be detained in respect of the other offence as if it was the original offence. It is worth emphasising, however, that the other offence must be a drug trafficking offence.

A section 2 detention can also be brought to an end when a person subject to an extended period of detention by warrant is brought before a judge of the District Court or the Circuit Court in accordance with the instructions which may have been imposed by the judge of the District Court or Circuit Court when issuing the warrant (see above). In this event the judge before whom the person is brought must revoke the warrant and order the person's immediate release if he or she is not satisfied that the person's detention is justified.[113] Presumably, this would not prevent the gardaí from immediately re-arresting the person for the purpose of being charged with an offence.

Charging the Suspect

5–77 Just like section 4 of the Criminal Justice Act 1984, section 2 of the 1996 Act does not make specific provision for the charging of a person who has been detained pursuant to its provisions. It makes an indirect reference to the matter when it says that the person must be released when there are no longer reasonable grounds for believing that his continued detention is necessary for the investigation of the offence, unless "he is charged or caused to be charged with an offence and is brought before a court as soon as may be in connection with such charge."[114] The section does not specifically require the person to be charged as soon as there is sufficient evidence to warrant a charge. Equally, it does not stipulate that charging him with one offence will in itself terminate the section 2 detention if there are other drug-trafficking offences to investigate. Indeed, as with section 4 of the 1984 Act, it is not at all clear what impact, if any, section 2 of the 1996 Act has on the operation of section 15 of the Criminal Justice Act 1951 which imposes an obligation to bring a person before a District Court judge as soon as practicable after being charged with an offence.

On one interpretation the section 2 detention will be terminated once the person is charged with an offence and the obligation to bring him before a District Court judge comes into play. On another interpretation section 2 permits the police to detain the person, irrespective of whether or not they have charged him with one or more offences, until there are no reasonable grounds for believing that his continued detention is necessary for the further investigation of an offence within the scope of section 2 or until the statutory time limit has expired. What is clear is that the person can be detained for the maximum permissible period, irrespective of whether the police had sufficient evidence to charge him with an offence at a much earlier stage of the detention, so long as there are reasonable grounds for considering that the continued detention is necessary for the proper investigation of the offence.

---

[113]   *ibid.* s.2(4).
[114]   *ibid.* s.2(5).

Re-arrest

As explained in Chapter 4 there are restrictions on the extent to which a   **5–78**
person can be re-arrested for an offence for which he has already been
detained under section 2 and subsequently released without charge. By
definition this must be a drug trafficking offence. The restriction also applies
in respect of any offence of which he was suspected or ought reasonably to
have been suspected at the time of the first arrest by the member of the Garda
Síochána who effected the first arrest. It would appear that the offence here
need not necessarily be a drug trafficking offence.[115] Where the restriction
applies a person cannot be re-arrested for any such offence unless it is for the
purpose of charging him with the offence or the arrest is effected under a
warrant issued by a judge of the District Court or the Circuit Court pursuant
to section 4 of the 1996 Act.[116]

Where a person is re-arrested for a drug-trafficking offence under a section 4   **5–79**
warrant he can be treated, with some modifications, as if he had been arrested
for a drug-trafficking offence and detained under section 2.[117] The primary
modification is that the power of a Garda officer not below the rank of Chief
Superintendent to direct an extension of detention for a further maximum
period of 24 hours is replaced by a requirement to seek a warrant for such a
further period of detention from a Circuit Court or District Court judge. The
officer may apply for the warrant if he or she has reasonable grounds for
believing that the further detention is necessary for the proper investigation of
the offence concerned. On such an application the judge must issue the
warrant authorising the detention for a further period up to 24 hours if he is
satisfied that the further detention is necessary for the proper investigation of
the offence and that the investigation is being conducted diligently and
expeditiously.
     Where the person is arrested under a section 4 warrant for any other offence
he or she must be dealt with in like manner as a person arrested without a
warrant and detained under section 4 of the Criminal Justice Act 1984.[118]

When a judge issues a warrant for the arrest of a person under section 4 of the   **5–80**
1996 Act he or she may order that the person concerned be brought before a
judge of the District Court or the Circuit Court on arrest or at any specified
time or times during the period.[119] Where a person is brought before a judge
pursuant to such an order, and the judge is not satisfied that the person's
detention is justified, he or she must revoke the warrant and order the
immediate release of the person. Presumably this would not prevent the
person being re-arrested for the purpose of being charged with an offence.

---

[115] See the terms of Criminal Justice (Drug Trafficking) Act 1996, s.4(4).
[116] *ibid.* s.4(1).
[117] *ibid.* s.4(3).
[118] *ibid.* s.4(4).
[119] *ibid.* s.4(2).

5–81   It was explained in Chapter 4 that a person who has been arrested under section 30 of the Offences against the State Act 1939 or detained under section 4 of the Criminal Justice Act 1984 and released without charge, cannot be re-arrested for the same offence or for an offence of which he should have been suspected or ought reasonably to have been suspected at the time of the first arrest by the member of the Garda Síochána who effected the first arrest. These prohibitions should ensure that a suspect who has been arrested under section 30 of the 1939 Act or detained under section 4 of the 1984 Act could not be detained for the same offence etc under section 2 of the Criminal Justice (Drug Trafficking) Act 1996. Arguably, they are not sufficient to preclude the possibility of a person being detained in a place of detention under section 2 after having first been arrested under section 30 of the 1939 Act or detained under section 4 of the 1984 Act. This possibility in the case of a drug-trafficking offence is now precluded by a specific provision in the 1996 Act. It stipulates that a person arrested under section 30 of the 1939 Act or detained under section 4 of the 1984 Act in connection with an offence and released without charge cannot be detained under section 2 in connection with that offence or in connection with a drug trafficking offence of which he was suspected or ought reasonably to have been suspected at the time of the first arrest by the member of the Garda Síochána who effected the first arrest.[120]

C. Detention Procedure

1. General

The 1987 Regulations

5–82   The Criminal Justice Act 1984 requires the Minister for Justice, Equality and Law Reform to make regulations providing for the treatment of persons in custody in Garda Síochána stations.[121] A draft of any such regulations must be laid before each House of the Oireachtas and the regulations in question cannot come into force until a resolution approving the draft has been passed by each House.[122] The first and only body of regulations to be made under this power came into force on May 16, 1987 under the title, The Criminal Justice Act 1984 (Treatment of Persons in Custody in Garda Síochána Stations) Regulations 1987. Although the title of the regulations specifically refers to the Criminal Justice Act 1984, it is important to note from the start that they are generally applicable to all suspects in Garda custody irrespective of the power of arrest or detention. They are not confined to persons detained under

---

[120] Criminal Justice (Drug Trafficking) Act 1996, s.4(6).
[121] Criminal Justice Act 1984, s.7(1).
[122] *ibid.* s.7(5). This contrasts with the position for any other regulations made under the 1984 Act. Any other regulation is laid before each House of the Oireachtas after having been made and will remain in force unless a resolution annulling it is passed by either House within the next subsequent 21 days on which that House has sat after the regulation has been laid before it. Where such a resolution is passed the regulation shall be annulled, without prejudice to the validity of anything previously done under it: Criminal Justice Act 1984, s.30.

section 4 of the 1984 Act. However, the regulations are concerned exclusively with the treatment of persons in custody in Garda Síochána stations.[123] As such they do not extend to the period from arrest to arrival at the Garda station, nor the period spent in a Garda vehicle while under arrest. Similarly, they do not apply to the person who is held in Garda custody on premises other than a garda station.

General Procedure

At the outset, the regulations impose a general duty on members of the Garda Síochána to have due respect for the personal rights of the persons in their custody when carrying out their functions under the regulations. The relevant provision reads:

5–83

> "In carrying out their functions under these Regulations members shall act with due respect for the personal rights of persons in custody and their dignity as human persons, and shall have regard for the special needs of any of them who may be under a physical or mental disability, while complying with the obligation to prevent escapes from custody and continuing to act with diligence and determination in the investigation of crime and the protection and vindication of the personal rights of other persons."[124]

There is also a specific prescription against unnecessary delay in dealing with persons in custody.[125]

Consequence of Non-Compliance with Regulations

A failure to observe any of the provisions of the 1987 regulations will not of itself amount to a criminal offence or an actionable civil wrong by the member of the Garda Síochána in question.[126] Moreover, it will not of itself affect the lawfulness of the custody of the detained person, or the admissibility in evidence of any statement given by him while in detention. Nevertheless, the trial judge retains a discretion to find that a breach has rendered the suspect's detention unlawful and to exclude evidence obtained as a result. In *People (DPP) v. Spratt*, for example, O'Hanlon J. explained that:

5–84

> " . . . non-observance of the regulations is not to bring about automatically the exclusion from evidence of all that was done and said while the accused person was in custody. It appears to be left to the court of trial to adjudicate in every case as to the impact the non-compliance with the regulations should have on the case for the prosecution."[127]

---

[123] It would appear that they do apply to persons who have been brought to a Garda station for the purposes of a urine or blood test under the drink-driving laws; see *People (DPP) v. Spratt* [1995] 1 I.R. 585.

[124] The Criminal Justice Act 1984 (Treatment of Persons in Custody in Garda Síochána Stations) Regulations 1987, reg.3(1). The Children Act 2001, s.55 makes almost identical provision specifically for persons under 18 years of age.

[125] *ibid.* reg.3(2).

[126] Criminal Justice Act 1984, s.7(3).

[127] *People (DPP) v. Spratt* [1995] 1 I.R. 585 at 591.

Before excluding evidence on the basis of a reach of the regulations it seems that a court will require some evidence of prejudice to the accused which has been occasioned by a breach of the regulations.[128] Equally, persistent or multiple breaches of the Regulations may lead the Court to find that the suspect has been the victim of unfair procedures. In *People (DPP) v. Connell*,[128a] for example, the appellant had been interviewed on several occasions for periods which exceeded the mandatory four-hour limit (see later) and no mention was made in the custody record of visits by persons during his interrogation and of complaints made by or on behalf of the applicant. Referring to these matters in the Court of Criminal Appeal, Egan J. said that: "[i]t is deplorable that the Custody Regulations should in many respects have been ignored by the authorities."[128b] He proceeded to rule inadmissible the appellant's confession to murder partly because of these breaches and partly because of irregularities in dealing with the appellant's request to see a solicitor.

A breach of the regulations will also render the member in question liable to disciplinary proceedings.[129]

The following analysis of the Regulations will focus only on their application to the procedure which should be followed in respect of a person detained in Garda custody under any one of the relevant powers. The Regulations, in conjunction with the Judges' Rules, also impact directly on the questioning of a suspect in police custody.

2. The Member in Charge

Designation

5–85   The member in charge of a Garda station plays a very important role relative to the persons in custody in that station. In addition to the specific duties imposed on this member by the Act, it is provided that the regulations must include provision for assigning to him or her, or to some other member, responsibility for overseeing the application of the regulations at that station.[130] This clearly presupposes some mechanism for designating a member as the member of charge.

5–86   The regulations, rather unhelpfully, define the member in charge as the member in charge of a station at the time when the "member in charge" is required to do anything to be done pursuant to the regulations.[131] The super-

---

[128] See, *e.g. DPP (Lenihan) v. McGuire* [1996] 3 I.R. 586; *People (DPP) v. Spratt* [1995] 1 I.R. 585.

[128a] [1995] 1 I.R. 244.

[128b] *ibid.* at 252.

[129] Criminal Justice Act 1984, s.7(4). This formulation does not automatically mean that disciplinary proceedings will be instituted. It merely means there are grounds upon which the garda Commissioner could lawfully institute such proceedings.

[130] *ibid.* s.7(2). This is without prejudice to the responsibilities and duties of any other member of the Garda Síochána in these matters.

[131] The Criminal Justice Act 1984 (Treatment of Persons in Custody in Garda Síochána Stations) Regulations, 1987, reg.4(1).

intendent in charge of a district is required to issue written instructions, either generally or by reference to particular members or members of particular ranks or to particular circumstances, as to who is to be the member in charge of each station in the district.[132] It would appear, however, that the superintendent's written instructions designating the member in charge in any particular station should be interpreted as nothing more than an administrative mechanism for identifying who the member in charge is to be at any particular time. The actual designation of the member in charge at any particular time is not dependent on technical compliance with the instructions. According to Kelly J. in *DPP (Lenihan) v. McGuire*[133] the member in charge is "the person actually in charge of a station at a time when such person is required to do anything or cause to be done anything pursuant to the 1987 regulations",[134] even if he or she had not taken up the position in strict compliance with the written instructions of the superintendent in charge of the district in question. In that case the member purporting to be the member in charge had relieved another member in charge without signing the station diary at the appropriate time as required by the superintendent's written instructions. Kelly J. considered that this omission did not prevent him from being the member in charge at the relevant time if in fact he had taken up duties as the member in charge at that time. The designation of the member in charge at any given time, therefore, is as defined in the regulations namely, the member who is in charge of the station at the time when the member in charge is required to do anything or to cause anything to be done pursuant to the regulations. His status can be proved by his own testimony and the testimony of the member whom he relieved, coupled with evidence to the effect that he discharged the duties imposed upon the member in charge by the regulations.

Further support for this interpretation can be derived from the decision of the Court of Criminal Appeal in *People (DPP) v. Van Onzen*.[135] In that case the appellants had been taken to Tralee Garda station after having been arrested on a yacht off the Kerry coast containing a large quantity of proscribed drugs. They were detained under section 4 and their detention was extended for a second six hour period on the authority of the member who purported to be the member in charge of the station at the time. One of the grounds of appeal against conviction was that the member who authorised the extension was not properly the member in charge. The written instructions from the superintendent of the district stipulated that the member in charge should be the station orderly. The member who authorised an extension of detention in this case was not in fact the station orderly. However, evidence was given at trial that on occasions when the station was particularly busy, as was the situation at the time when the appellants were brought there, the function of station

5–87

---

[132] *ibid.* 1987, reg.4(2). The superintendent must ensure that a written record is maintained in each station in his or her district containing the name and rank of the member in charge at any given time; reg.4(4).
[133] [1996] 3 I.R. 586.
[134] *ibid.* at 595.
[135] [1996] 2 I.L.R.M. 387.

orderly and member in charge would be separated. Evidence was also given that that is what happened in this case and that the member who authorised the extension discharged the functions of the member in charge under the regulations in respect of this case. The trial judge accepted that this was sufficient to satisfy the court that the member in question was the member in charge for the purpose of the regulations. His decision was upheld by the Court of Criminal Appeal.

It follows from the foregoing that a member in charge need not necessarily hold a particular rank, nor is it inevitable that he or she will be the officer of most senior rank in the station at the relevant time. However, as far as practicable, he or she should not be a member who was involved in the arrest of a person for the offence in respect of which that person is in custody in the station or in the investigation of that offence.[136] This opens up the possibility that there may be more than one "member in charge" of a station at any particular time.

General Duty

5–88   The general duty of the member in charge is to oversee the application of the 1987 regulations in relation to persons in custody in the station. To that end he or she must visit them from time to time and make any necessary enquiries.[137] This duty may be delegated to another member where the member in charge is unable to carry it out adequately owing to the number of persons in custody or other circumstances.[138] If it appears to the member in charge that a direction given, or action taken, by a member of higher rank is inconsistent with the proper application of the 1987 regulations, he or she must inform that member accordingly.[139] Where the matter is not resolved he or she must report it without delay to another member not below the rank of superintendent.[140]

3. The Custody Record

Maintaining the Record

5–89   A key element in the regime for the protection of a suspect in police custody is the maintenance of a complete record of his stay in custody. Accordingly,

---

[136]   The Criminal Justice Act 1984 (Treatment of Persons in Custody in Garda Síochána Stations) Regulations 1987, reg.4(3). This restriction does not extend to having been involved in the arrest and/or investigation of the suspect for a different offence, nor, arguably, to becoming involved in the investigation while the suspect is in custody.

[137]   ibid. reg.5(1).

[138]   ibid. reg.5(4). The authorisation must be in writing and must specify the reasons for giving it. It will terminate when these reasons no longer apply. However, in the case of the Bridewell Garda station in Dublin, the member with particular responsibility for the cell area shall be deemed to have been authorised by the member in charge.

[139]   ibid. reg.5(3). On a literal interpretation of reg.5 it would appear that this duty cannot be exercised directly by a member authorised by the member in charge under reg.5(4). Of course, any member may be expected to take such action pursuant to their duty to have regard for the personal rights of persons in custody.

[140]   Presumably, where the other member is of lower rank it is implied that the member in charge will also have the option of issuing an appropriate direction to that other member.

the 1987 regulations require a "custody record" to be kept in respect of each person held in custody.[141] The member in charge must record, or cause to be recorded, in the record as soon as practicable such information as is required to be recorded by the 1987 regulations.[142] Each entry must be signed or initialled by the member making it. Nevertheless, this does not relieve the member in charge of responsibility for the accuracy and completeness of all entries made in the custody record while he or she is the member in charge.[143] Where a person in custody is transferred to another station, the member in charge of the station from which he is transferred must send with him his custody record (or a copy) to the member in charge of the other station.

Specified Details

The custody record will normally begin with details of the suspect's arrest and initial detention in the police station. Indeed, the record must include: (i) the date, time and place of arrest and the identity of the arresting member (or other person effecting the arrest); (ii) the time of arrival at the station; (iii) the nature of the offence or the matter in respect of which he was arrested, and (iv) any relevant particulars relating to his physical or mental condition.[144] Surprisingly, there is no specific obligation to record the individual power of arrest used. However, from the moment of arrival at the station to his release, many decisions and actions taken in relation to the person in custody, and anything that happens to him, must be recorded.

Initial Detention and Extension

Where the suspect is detained under section 4 of the 1984 Act the authorisation of the initial detention must be recorded.[145] Where a direction for a further period of detention not exceeding six hours was given under section 4(3)(b) of the 1984 Act, the record must show the date and time it was given and the name and rank of the officer who gave it.[146] In the case of a person detained under section 30 of the Offences against the State Act 1939, the record must include, where applicable, the fact that a direction was given to extend the detention for a period not exceeding 24 hours, the date and time

5–90

---

[141] The Criminal Justice Act 1984 (Treatment of Persons in Custody in Garda Síochána Stations) Regulations, 1987, reg.6(1). This regulation does not actually confine the duty to detention under the Act. It is apparent from other provisions in the 1987 regulations that reg.6(1) extends to custody under any power. See, *e.g.* reg.7(4) and the definitions in reg.2(1).

[142] *ibid.* 1987, reg.6(2).

[143] *ibid.* reg.6(4). This is without prejudice to the responsibility of any other member for the accuracy and completeness of any entry which he has made in a custody record.

[144] *ibid.* reg.7(1).

[145] *ibid.* reg.7(2). The member in charge of the station at the time of the suspect's arrival must enter the following statement:

"I have reasonable grounds for believing that the detention of . . . (*insert here the name of the person detained*) is necessary for the proper investigation of the offence(s) in respect of which he/she has been arrested."

[146] *ibid.* reg.7(3). The record of the extension must be signed by the officer who gave it and it must state that the officer had reasonable grounds for believing that such further detention was necessary for the proper investigation of the offence concerned. The actual direction or (if given orally) a written record of it must be attached to the custody record.

when it was given and the name and rank of the officer who gave it.[147] Where the suspect is detained under section 2 of the Criminal Justice (Drug Trafficking Act) 1996 and a direction has been issued extending his detention, the direction must be attached to (and form part of) the custody record.[148]

Treatment of the Suspect

The custody record must show the time or times at which the person in custody is given the information that he is required to be given while in police custody;[149] the fact that the person in custody requested a solicitor or a person to be notified of his custody, the time at which the request was made, the time at which it was complied with and any action taken by a member to notify the solicitor or other named person.[150]

A record must also be kept of particulars relating to the following: visits to persons in custody by the member in charge or other members, any other visits to persons in custody, telephone and other enquiries concerning them, telephone calls made or letters sent by them, any requests made by them or by persons attending at the station and seeking to visit them, meals supplied to them and the ending of their custody.[151]

Children

5–91 Where the person in custody is under 18 years of age[152] the record must show any action taken by a member to inform him of the fact of his custody and the offence or other matter for which he has been arrested. It must also show any action to inform him of his right to consult a solicitor, any action to notify the solicitor, any action to inform a parent or guardian and to request them to attend at the station without delay, any action to inform the person of his right to have notification of his custody sent to a different person and any action to notify that different person.[153] Where relevant, the record must show the fact that authority was given to a member to question an arrested person under the age of seventeen years in the absence of a parent or guardian, the name and rank of the

---

[147] *ibid.* 1987, reg.7(4).

[148] Criminal Justice (Drug Trafficking) Act 1996, s.2(2)(f)(ii).

[149] The Criminal Justice Act 1984 (Treatment of Persons in Custody in Garda Síochána Stations) Regulations 1987, reg.8(4). The member in charge must ask the arrested person, or cause him to be asked, to sign the custody record in acknowledgement of receipt of the notice specified in reg.8(2). A refusal to sign must be recorded.

[150] *ibid.* reg.9(4). The time at which any of these actions are taken must be recorded. Where an arrested person is being transferred to another station, the member in charge of the station from which he is being transferred shall inform any person who has been notified or informed under this regulation, or cause him to be informed, of the transfer as soon as practicable; reg.9(3).

[151] *ibid.* reg.23. These particulars must include the relevant time and action, if any, taken by a member in relation thereto.

[152] Any provision in the 1987 regulations which applies to a person under 18 years of age also applies to any person in custody not below that age whom the member in charge suspects or knows to be mentally handicapped; Criminal Justice Act 1984 (Treatment of Persons in Custody in Garda Síochána Stations) Regulations 1987, reg.22.

[153] Criminal Justice Act 1984 (Treatment of Persons in Custody in Garda Síochána Stations) Regulations 1987, reg.9 as extended by Children Act 2001, s.20(2).

member who gave the authority, the reasons for giving the authority and the action taken in compliance with the authority.[154]

Foreign Nationals

Where the person in custody is a foreign national the custody record must show the time when he is informed of his right to communicate with his consul, the time when any request to communicate was made, the time when the request was complied with and the time when any communication was forwarded to the consul.[155]

5–92

Deaf Persons

If the person taken into custody is deaf, the custody record must show, where relevant, his written consent to be questioned in relation to an offence without having an interpreter present.[156]

Searches etc.

Where a person in custody is searched the custody record must show: the name of the person conducting the search, the names of the other persons present and particulars of any property taken from or handed over by a person in custody.[157] Where relevant, the custody record must show: the consent of a person in custody to provide fingerprints, palm prints, photographs, swabs or samples,[158] the fact that they have been taken and, where applicable, the name and rank of the member giving the authority to take fingerprints, palm prints or photographs.[159]

Details of Interviews

The custody record must include the details of each interview conducted by a member with the arrested person.[160] It is not entirely clear whether the record of the interview actually forms part of the custody record. Presumably, it is sufficient to record a general summary of the interview noting salient points such as the outcome, the degree of co-operation from the suspect and any complaint made by the suspect.[160a] With respect to each interview there is a specific obligation to record: the times when the interview began and ended, any breaks, the place of the interview, and the names and ranks of gardaí

5–93

---

[154] The Criminal Justice Act 1984 (Treatment of Persons in Custody in Garda Síochána Stations) Regulations 1987, reg.13(4).

[155] *ibid.* reg.14(5).

[156] *ibid.* reg.12(8)(b).

[157] *ibid.* reg.17(6) and (7). The person shall be asked to sign the record of such property as being correct. If he refuses to do so, the refusal shall be recorded at the time of refusal.

[158] It is specifically provided that this consent must be signed and recorded in the custody record *or a separate document.*

[159] Criminal Justice Act 1984 (Treatment of Persons in Custody in Garda Síochána Stations) Regulations 1987, reg.18.

[160] *ibid.* reg.12(11) and (12).

[160a] See *e.g. People (DPP) v. McKeever* unreported, Court of Criminal Appeal, July 16, 1992 dealing with the duty to make a written record of an interview under the Judges' Rules.

present. It is not clear, however, whether these specifics should form part of the record of the interview or part of the custody record or both.

Suspension of Interview

Where an interview is suspended by the issue of an authority pursuant to regulation 12, the custody record must show: the name and rank of any member issuing the "authority" and the reasons for issuing the "authority".[161] An "authority" in this context refers to authorisation for the questioning of an arrested suspect between the hours of 12 midnight and 8 a.m. and to the questioning of an arrested person who is under the influence of intoxicating liquor or drugs. The record must also show, where relevant, the arrested person's written consent to the suspension of questioning between midnight and 8 a.m.,[162] the timing of a suspension notice, whether the person detained acknowledged that he received the notice and the timing of a withdrawal notice.[163]

Complaints and Medical Treatment

5–94   Where a complaint is made by a person in custody concerning the conduct of a member of the Garda Síochána this must be recorded in the custody record.[164] The complaint does not necessarily have to concern something that occurred while the person was in custody. In addition there is a specific obligation to record any complaint made by an arrested person to a member of the Garda Síochána about his treatment while in custody.[165] Equally, there is an obligation to record any action taken consequent on the duty to report the use of force or ill-treatment on a person in custody by a member of the Garda Síochána.[166] The custody record must also record the removal of a person in custody to a hospital or other suitable place, the time of removal, any instructions given by a doctor regarding his medical care, steps taken to comply with the instructions,[167] the fact that a medical examination is sought by the member in charge or the person in custody, the time the examination was sought, the time it was carried out[168] and, where relevant, the time at which a relative or other person was informed of the removal to hospital or other suitable place.[169]

---

[161]   Criminal Justice Act 1984 (Treatment of Persons in Custody in Garda Síochána Stations) Regulations 1987, reg.12(12)(b).

[162]   *ibid.* reg.12(12)(c). The consent must actually be attached to the custody record.

[163]   *ibid.* reg.12(12)(d).

[164]   *ibid.* reg. 20(7). Particulars of the complaint must be recorded in a separate document, a copy of which shall be attached to and form part of the custody record.

[165]   Criminal Justice Act 1984 (Treatment of Persons in Custody in Garda Síochána Stations) Regulations 1987, reg.12(10). The complaint must be recorded in the record of the interview.

[166]   *ibid.* reg.20(6).

[167]   *ibid.* reg.21(3).

[168]   *ibid.* reg.21(5). If it is not practicable to accede to a request by a person in custody for medical examination by the doctor of his choice at his own expense, the relevant circumstances shall also be recorded.

[169]   *ibid.* reg.21(6).

Charging

The custody record must record the time when a person in custody is charged **5–95**
with an offence and the charge sheet number.[170]

Retention of Records

A custody record must be preserved for at least 12 months.[171] However, if any
proceedings are instituted in which a custody record is relevant, the record must
be preserved until the final determination of the proceedings if that is more
than 12 months. This qualification also applies where a complaint is made
about the conduct of a member of the Garda Síochána while a person was in
custody. Where a person ceases to be in Garda custody he, or his legal representative, may seek a copy of the custody record relating to him or of such
entries in it as he may specify.[172] The record, or entries, must be supplied as
soon as practicable on a request made within twelve months of the end of the
custody.

4. Conditions of Custody

The 1987 regulations make specific provision governing the conditions in **5–96**
which a person may be kept in custody. All the basic essentials are covered.
The person must be provided with such meals as are necessary, and not less
than two light meals and one main meal in any 24-hour period.[173] He must be
allowed such reasonable time for rest as is necessary.[174] This suggests that it is
not acceptable to subject the person in custody for prolonged and continuous
periods of interrogation which leave him exhausted. Where the detention runs
for the maximum twelve hours (or longer in the case of detention under
section 30 of the Offences Against the State Act 1939 or section 2 of the
Criminal Justice (Drug Trafficking) Act 1996), breaks will normally have to
be provided in addition to the period from twelve midnight to 8 a.m. Access
to toilet facilities must also be provided for a person in custody.[175]

Unless it is decided to release the detained person almost immediately
after his arrival at the station, it will usually be necessary to accommodate
him in a cell for one or more periods of time. Where this is necessary, not
more than one person should be kept in each cell.[176] Where multiple occupancy
cannot be avoided, every effort should be made to avoid placing a violent

---

[170] *ibid.* reg.15(2). Where a copy of the charge sheet is given to a person in the station, he shall be
asked to sign the custody record in acknowledgement of its receipt. If he refuses to sign it, the
refusal shall be recorded.
[171] *ibid.* reg.24(1).
[172] *ibid.* reg.24.
[173] *ibid.* reg.19(3). He may have meals supplied at his own expense where it is practicable for the
member in charge to arrange this.
[174] *ibid.* reg.19(2). The regulations do not actually specify a set maximum period of interrogation
without a break. Moreover, the wording of reg.19(2) leaves open the possibility that what is
necessary can vary in accordance with the circumstances of each case.
[175] *ibid.* reg.19(4).
[176] *ibid.* reg.19(5).

person in a cell with other persons. As far as practicable, the member in charge should ensure that a person under the age of 18 years should not associate with a detained adult and should not be placed in a cell with an adult.[177] Persons of the opposite sex must not be placed in a cell together. Where a person is kept in a cell a member of the Garda Síochána must visit him at intervals of approximately half an hour.[178] In the case of a person under the influence of drink or drugs this should normally be done every fifteen minutes, and the person in question should be spoken to and roused, if necessary, for this purpose. Where any visit is made to a person of the opposite sex who is alone in a cell, the member making the visit must be accompanied.[179]

It is apparent from these requirements and, indeed, other provisions in the regulations that not every Garda station will be suitable for the detention of a suspect for any prolonged period. To qualify, a station must have facilities which enable the person to be treated in accordance with the requirements of the 1987 regulations for the period during which he is expected to be in custody in that station.[180]

5. Use of Force

5–97   The 1987 regulations impose a specific prohibition on the ill-treatment of a person in custody. No member of the Garda Síochána can subject the person to ill-treatment of any kind, nor can he or she permit any other person to do so.[181] This prohibition extends to the threat of ill-treatment against the person in custody or against his family or any other person connected with him. However, the regulations do recognise that a member may use force in certain limited circumstances, namely: in self-defence; to secure compliance with lawful directions; to prevent the person's escape; or to restrain the person from injuring himself or others; or damaging property or destroying or interfering with evidence.[182] When one or more of these instances apply the member concerned may use such reasonable force as is necessary.

5–98   Checks on the use of force in the Garda station are facilitated by the imposition of a duty to fill out reports in certain circumstances.[183] Where a member of the Garda Síochána uses force which causes injury to a person in custody, he or she must report the circumstances to the member in charge[184]

---

[177]   Children Act 2001, s.56. A person under the age of 17 years should not be kept in a cell unless there is no other secure accommodation available; reg. 19(8).
[178]   Criminal Justice Act 1984 (Treatment of Persons in Custody in Garda Síochána Stations) Regulations 1987, reg.19(6).
[179]   *ibid.* reg.19(7).
[180]   *ibid.* reg.19(1). The garda apply a general rule to the effect that a person should not be kept in custody for more than three hours in a station which does not have adequate facilities for rest and the provision of appropriate meals and for any necessary questioning.
[181]   *ibid.* reg.20(1).
[182]   *ibid.* reg.20(2).
[183]   A record must be made of the submission of any such reports; Criminal Justice Act 1984 (Treatment of Persons in Custody in Garda Síochána Stations) Regulations 1987, reg.20(5).
[184]   If the force is used by the member in charge he or she must report the circumstances to the superintendent.

who, in turn, must report it to the superintendent in charge of the district.[185] Similarly, any member of the force is under a duty to report, if it comes to his or her notice, that a person in custody has been subjected to ill-treatment or the threat of ill-treatment or to the use of force in contravention of the 1987 Regulations.[186] He or she must report the matter to the member in charge who, in turn, must report it to the superintendent of the district.[187] On receipt of any of these reports, the superintendent must investigate the matter without delay or cause it to be investigated.[188] The regulations do not go on to specify what, if any, action should be taken in the light of the investigation. Presumably, if it discloses evidence of a criminal offence, both criminal and internal disciplinary proceedings may be considered. The investigation report may also have an important role to play if the person in custody subsequently initiates a civil action for damages or a habeas corpus application based on alleged ill-treatment and/or the unnecessary use of force.

The issue of ill-treatment may be raised directly by a complaint from the person in custody, or by someone on his behalf. The 1987 regulations stipulate that when a complaint is made by a person in custody (or by someone on his behalf) and the complaint concerns the conduct of a member of the Garda Síochána, whether before or after the arrest, the fact that the complaint was made must be recorded.[189] If it alleges physical ill-treatment, the member in charge must arrange for the person to be medically examined as soon as practicable unless, where the allegation relates to another member, he or she considers the complaint to be frivolous or vexatious. The regulations do not make any further provision for the investigation or disposal of such complaints. Presumably they must be handled through the normal complaints and/or disciplinary procedures.[190]

5–99

6. Medical Treatment

It may happen that the condition of a person in custody, either on being brought into custody or at any point during custody, is such as to require medical treatment. The 1987 regulations make detailed provision for this eventuality. The member in charge must summon a doctor or cause him to be summoned where a person in custody: is injured, is under the influence of

5–100

---

[185] Criminal Justice Act 1984 (Treatment of Persons in Custody in Garda Síochána Stations) Regulations 1987, reg.20(3). There is no specific duty even to record the "lawful" use of force against a person in custody where it does not cause injury to that person.

[186] *ibid.* reg.20(4). A report must also be made where it comes to the notice of any member that another member has used force causing injury to a person in custody and has not filed the necessary report.

[187] If the report is about the actions of the member in charge, the member making the report must submit it directly to the superintendent.

[188] Criminal Justice Act 1984 (Treatment of Persons in Custody in Garda Síochána Stations) Regulations 1987, reg.20(6).

[189] *ibid.* 1987, reg.20(7). Particulars of the complaint shall be recorded in a separate document, a copy of which shall be attached to and form part of the custody record.

[190] For further details and analysis of the complaints and disciplinary procedures, see Walsh, *The Irish Police: a Legal and Constitutional Perspective* (Round Hall Sweet & Maxwell, Dublin, 1998), chaps. 7–9.

intoxicating liquor or drugs and cannot be roused, fails to respond normally to questions or conversation (otherwise than owing to the influence of intoxicating liquor alone), appears to the member in charge to be suffering from a mental illness, or otherwise appears to the member in charge to be in need of medical attention.[191] This duty does not apply where it appears to the member in charge that the person's condition is such as to necessitate immediate removal to a hospital or other suitable place. The clear implication is that the removal should be effected immediately.[192] In this event, an immediate relative, and any other person required under regulation 9 (see later) to be notified of the person's detention, must be informed as soon as practicable.[193]

5–101   A person in custody may ask to be examined by a doctor of his own choice at his own expense. Where this happens, the member in charge must make the necessary arrangements as soon as practicable.[194] It would appear that this duty is not confined to the situations where the member in charge is obliged to summon a doctor. However, an examination by a doctor of the person's choice does not preclude an examination by another doctor summoned by the member in charge, provided that the person in custody consents to the second examination. A record must be made of any medical examination sought by the member in charge or by the person in custody.[195] This must include the time the examination was sought and the time it was carried out.

A duty to seek medical advice will arise where the person in custody claims to need medical attention relating to a heart condition, diabetes, epilepsy or other potentially serious condition.[196] This duty will also apply if the member in charge considers it necessary because the person in custody has any such medication in his possession.

The member in charge must always ensure compliance with any instructions given by a doctor in relation to the medical care of a person in custody.[197] Any such instructions and the steps taken to comply with them must be recorded.[198]

7. Information

5–102   Knowledge of the rights attaching to a person in custody in a Garda station is an essential precondition to the effective exercise of those rights. Accordingly,

---

[191]   Criminal Justice Act 1984 (Treatment of Persons in Custody in Garda Síochána Stations) Regulations 1987, reg.21(1).

[192]   The removal of a person in custody to a hospital or other suitable place and the time of the removal shall be recorded; Criminal Justice Act 1984 (Treatment of Persons in Custody in Garda Síochána Stations) Regulations 1987, reg.21(3).

[193]   *ibid.* reg.21(6). The time at which the relative and other person were informed shall be recorded.

[194]   *ibid.* reg.21(4). If it is not practicable to accede to a request by a person in custody for medical examination by the doctor of his choice at his own expense, the relevant circumstances must be recorded; reg.21(5).

[195]   Criminal Justice Act 1984 (Treatment of Persons in Custody in Garda Síochána Stations) Regulations 1987, reg.21(5).

[196]   *ibid.* reg.21(2).

[197]   *ibid.* reg.21(1).

[198]   *ibid.* reg.21(3).

the 1987 regulations make provision for certain information about these rights and other matters to be given to a person who has been taken into custody. The member in charge[199] must inform an arrested person, or cause him to be informed, of: the offence or matter in respect of which he has been arrested,[200] his entitlement to consult a solicitor and his right to have another person informed of the fact that he is in custody.[201] This information must be given orally and without delay.[202] In addition the member in charge must give the person a notice containing the information about the right of access to a solicitor, the right of notification and such other information as directed by the Commissioner of the garda Síochána from time to time, with the approval of the Minister for Justice, Equality and Law Reform.[203] It would appear that this amounts to an obligation merely to give the relevant information to the person and to hand the notice to him. There is no obligation on the member in charge to ensure that the person understands the notice of his rights.[204]

The notice currently in use contains information under the headings of: reason for arrest; notification to other persons; legal advice; visits, telephone calls, etc.; searches; fingerprints, palmprints, photographs and tests; meals; member in charge; identification parades; bail and legal aid.[205] The times at which the oral information and notice are given must be recorded.[206]

Where the person taken into custody is less than 18 years of age the member in charge must inform him of: the offence in respect of which he has been arrested; his entitlement to consult a solicitor and how that entitlement can be exercised; and that his parent or guardian is also being informed of these matters and requested to attend at the station without delay.[207] The member must see that the child is given this information in a manner and in language appropriate to the child's age and level of understanding.

5–103

It will be seen below that a foreign national who has been arrested has the right to communicate with his consul. Accordingly, the member in charge of the station to which the arrested foreign national has been taken into custody must immediately inform him or cause him to be informed of this right.[207a]

---

[199] This refers to the member in charge of the station to which the arrested person is brought on arrest or in which he is arrested; Criminal Justice Act 1984 (Treatment of Persons in Custody in Garda Síochána Stations) Regulations 1987, reg.8(3).

[200] This information must be given in "ordinary language".

[201] Criminal Justice Act 1984 (Treatment of Persons in Custody in Garda Síochána Stations) Regulations 1987, reg.8(1).

[202] The member in charge must also explain to the arrested person that if he does not wish to exercise his right of access and/or notification immediately, he will not be precluded from doing so later.

[203] Criminal Justice Act 1984 (Treatment of Persons in Custody in Garda Síochána Stations) Regulations 1987, reg.8(2). This notice must be given without delay by the member in charge of the Garda station to which an arrested person is taken on arrest or in which he is arrested.

[204] *People (DPP) v. Ivan O'Kelly* unreported, High Court, February 10, 1999.

[205] See Form C.72(S). A larger version, Form C.72(L) is normally displayed in the Garda station.

[206] Criminal Justice Act 1984 (Treatment of Persons in Custody in Garda Síochána Stations) Regulations 1987, reg.8(4). The member in charge shall ask the arrested person, or cause him to be asked, to sign the custody record in acknowledgement of receipt of the notice. If he refuses to sign, the refusal shall be recorded.

[207] Children Act 2001, s.57.

[207a] *ibid.* reg.14(1). A record must be made of the time when a foreign national was informed or notified of this right; reg.14(5).

The foreign national must also be told that, if he so wishes, the consul will be notified of his arrest.

D. Rights of Access and Communication

1. General

5–104   Where a person will be detained in police custody for any significant length of time, there are very sound reasons why he should have a right to contact and communicate with one or more persons on the outside. It may be that he has business concerns or dependants requiring attention in the interim, family and/or friends may be alarmed at his disappearance or he may wish to secure appropriate legal advice or medical attention. Access to legal advice will often be of critical importance as the mere fact that the person has been arrested and taken into custody suggests that he will have to take decisions that may have profound implications for his future liberty and good name. The soundness of his decisions will be called into question if he takes them while being held incommunicado in Garda custody, perhaps under great strain, and without the benefit of independent professional advice. Even remaining silent may not necessarily be as sensible a course of action as it may have been at times in the past.

Affording the person in custody the right to contact and communicate with persons on the outside need not always be counterproductive from a police perspective. False information or false confessions given under stress or confusion can cause major problems for the police investigation. Accordingly, in so far as the right of access or contact enhances the reliability of any information or admission given by the accused, it should be positively welcomed from the police perspective. It must also be recognised, however, that contact with persons on the outside may be used to alert accomplices and/or to secure the destruction of evidence. A balance must, therefore, be struck between, on the one hand, protecting the rights of the individual in custody and in the criminal process as a whole and, on the other hand, facilitating the needs of the State in the prevention and prosecution of crime. Where a person is detained in police custody, the degree of access to and communication with persons on the outside plays a vital role in striking this balance.

2. Right of Access to a Solicitor

5–105   Although the right of access to legal advice might be of critical importance to a person in police custody, the full extent and status of this right in Irish law has only been clarified very recently. Writing in 1983, Ryan and Magee felt compelled to conclude that the Irish courts distinguished between the right of access in the pre-trial process and the right of access during the adjudicatory process.[208] The former appeared to be a legal, as opposed to a constitutional

---

[208]   Ryan and Magee, *The Irish Criminal Process* (Mercier Press, Dublin, 1983), p. 222.

right, and was confined to a right of reasonable access only.[209] It did not extend to a right to be informed of the right of access. This remained the position until 1987 when relevant provisions of the Criminal Justice Act 1984 and the 1987 regulations came into force.

Section 5 of the 1984 Act deals with the situation where a person is detained in a Garda station under section 4 of the 1984 Act, section 2 of the Criminal Justice (Drug Trafficking) Act 1996 or section 30 of the Offences against the State Act 1939.[210] It stipulates that the member in charge of the station must see that the detainee is informed without delay of his entitlement to consult a solicitor,[211] and, at the request of the detainee, that the solicitor is informed accordingly.[212] The 1987 regulations elaborate further on the extent of the duty of the member in charge to inform persons in garda custody of their right of access to a solicitor. Significantly, these regulations extend the duty to all persons who are arrested and held in Garda custody.[213] It would appear, however, that this right to be informed of the right of access to a solicitor does not have constitutional status.[214]

5–106

Where the person detained in custody is below the age of 18 years the member in charge must see that the person, and his parent or guardian, are informed of his entitlement to consult a solicitor.[215] Where a request is made for a solicitor the member must notify the solicitor as soon as is practicable.[216] If the solicitor requested cannot be contacted within a reasonable time or is unwilling or unable to attend at the station, the person (and his parent or guardian) must be informed and given an opportunity to ask for another solicitor.[217] The member must then notify the other solicitor as soon as is practicable. Where a solicitor, other than a named solicitor, is requested, the member shall give the person making the request the name of one or more than one solicitors whom the member in charge reasonably believes may be willing to attend at the station within a reasonable time.[217a]

---

[209] *People v. Madden* [1977] I.R. 336.

[210] Criminal Justice Act 1984, s.9 extends it to persons detained under section 30 of the 1939 Act while Criminal Justice (Drug Trafficking) Act 1996, s.5 extends it to persons detained under section 2 of the 1996 Act.

[211] Any such request made by a person and the times at which it was made and complied with and any action taken by a member pursuant to it and the time at which it was taken must be recorded; Criminal Justice Act 1984 (Treatment of Persons in Custody in Garda Síochána Stations) Regulations 1987, reg.9(4).

[212] Criminal Justice Act 1984, s.5(1). Where an arrested person is transferred to another station, the member in charge of the station from which he is being transferred shall see that the solicitor is informed as soon as possible; Criminal Justice Act 1984 (Treatment of Persons in Custody in Garda Síochána Stations) Regulations 1987, reg.9(3).

[213] The Criminal Justice Act 1984 (Treatment of Persons in Custody in Garda Síochána Stations) 1987, reg.8.

[214] *DPP v. Spratt* [1995] 2 I.L.R.M. 117. For a broader survey, see Butler, "The Right to be Informed of the Right to a Lawyer – the Constitutional Dimension" (1993) I.C.L.J. 173.

[215] Children Act 2001, ss.57(b) and 58(1)(a)(iii).

[216] *ibid.* s.60(1).

[217] *ibid.* s.60(2) and (3).

[217a] *ibid.* s.60(5).

Constitutional Status

5–107 It is important to note that section 5 of the 1984 Act does not purport to create or define a right of access to a solicitor for persons in police custody. It clearly assumes a pre-existing right of access and merely establishes a specific right to be informed of that right of access and a right to have the solicitor informed of the request to exercise the right of access. The existence of this right of access has been recognised by the courts since the 1970s.[218] It was not until the Supreme Court's decision in *DPP v. Healy*,[219] however, that it was clearly established as a constitutional right. The majority in that case considered that it played such a fundamental role in ensuring fairness in the administration of justice generally and, more particularly a measure of equality between the suspect and the State, that it had to enjoy constitutional status. Finlay C.J. explained the importance of the right in the following terms:

> " . . . I am driven to the conclusion that such an important and fundamental standard of fairness in the administration of justice as the right of access to a lawyer must be deemed to be constitutional in its origin, and that to classify it as merely legal would be to undermine its importance and the completeness of the protection of it which the courts are obliged to give."[220]

Finlay C.J. also made it clear that this constitutional right of access arises not just when the detainee requests it, but also when the solicitor arrives at the Garda station having been instructed by an appropriate person acting on behalf of the detainee. In this latter situation the detainee must be informed of the solicitor's presence.

Scope of Constitutional Right

5–108 Of course, the right of access to a solicitor is not absolute; it is merely a right of reasonable access. It follows that there will be circumstances in which it may be lawful for the gardaí to deny or postpone access to a suspect in their custody. However, given the constitutional importance attached to the right, it can be assumed that the scope for denial or postponement is strictly limited. This is confirmed by the following quotation from Finlay C.J. in *Healy*:

> "A right of reasonable access to a solicitor in a detained person . . . means in the event of the arrival of a solicitor at the garda station in which a person is detained, an immediate right to that person to be told of the arrival and, if he requests it, an immediate access. The only thing that could justify postponement of informing the detained person of the arrival of the solicitor or of immediately complying with a request made by the detained person when so informed, for access to him, would be reasons which objectively viewed from the point of view of the interest or welfare of the detained person, would be viewed by a court as being valid."[221]

---

[218] *Re Article 26 and the Emergency Powers Bill 1976* [1977] I.R. 159; *People v. Madden* [1977] I.R. 336; *People v. Farrell* [1978] I.R. 13; *DPP v. Pringle* 2 Frewen 57; *People v. Shaw* [1982] I.R. 1; *People (DPP) v. Conroy* [1986] I.R. 460.

[219] [1990] I.L.R.M. 313.

[220] [1990] I.L.R.M. 313 at 320.

[221] [1990] I.L.R.M. 313 at 320–321.

In the *Healy* case itself the Supreme Court refused to accept that the subjective belief of a superintendent, that it would be "bad manners" to interrupt an on-going interrogation in order to permit access, would be a sufficient reason. Similarly, the fact that the suspect was engaged in dictating a statement was not considered an objectively valid reason sufficient to delay access.

The absolute terms in which Finlay C.J. expresses the right of access suggests **5–109** that once the solicitor has arrived at the station access cannot be denied because gardaí fear that it might interfere unreasonably with the investigation of the offence in question, or even if they fear that it might alert accomplices. What is not so clear is whether such concerns could be used as a justification for delaying the communication of the suspect's request for access to the solicitor concerned. Equally, unclear is the extent to which the suspect is entitled to access after the first visit. If, for example, a suspect makes repeated requests to see his solicitor are the gardaí obliged to grant those requests where the solicitor is available? The regulations merely grant a right of reasonable access, while the Supreme Court in *Healy* did not address itself to what constitutes a right of reasonable access after the initial visit. It is at least arguable, therefore, that once a suspect has had an initial visit the gardaí would not be obliged to accede to every subsequent request.[222]

Where a suspect requests access to his solicitor, the gardaí are under a duty to make bona fide attempts to give effect to that request. A failure to do so will constitute a breach of the suspect's constitutional right of access and render his detention unlawful. If the gardaí are unable to make contact with the solicitor requested it is at least arguable that they are under a constitutional obligation to make every effort to ensure that the suspect has access to a solicitor while he is in their custody.[222a] Nevertheless, it would appear that there is no constitutional prohibition on the gardaí proceeding to question the suspect before a solicitor has arrived so long as they are making bona fide attempts to provide the suspect with access to a solicitor.[222b] It will be seen below that the 1987 Regulations stipulate that a suspect who has requested a solicitor should not be asked to make a written statement before a reasonable time has elapsed for the arrival of the solicitor. Not only does this not amount to a prohibition on questioning of the suspect but failure to abide by it will not automatically render the detention of the suspect unlawful nor result in the automatic exclusion of any incriminating statement obtained in the meantime.

The value of the constitutional rights of access and the statutory prohibition in taking a written statement from a suspect until a reasonable

---

[222] According to White the police practice is to confine access to one hour in a six hour period of detention; see "The Confessional State – Police Interrogation in the Irish Republic: Part 1" (2000) 10(1) I.C.L.J. 17 at 18.

[222a] If the solicitor requested cannot be contacted within a reasonable time, or if he is unable or unwilling to attend, the 1987 Regulations require the gardaí to give the suspect an opportunity to ask for another solicitor and the obligation to notify the solicitor shall then attach to that named solicitor.

[222b] *People (DPP) v. Buck* unreported, Supreme Court, April 17, 2002.

time for the attendance of the solicitor has elapsed will be undermined where the suspect is arrested at the weekend or in circumstances where it will be difficult to make contact with his solicitor or, indeed, any solicitor. In *People (DPP) v. Buck*,[222c] however, the Supreme Court held that there is no obligation on gardaí to postpone the arrest of an individual until such time as a solicitor is likely to be available or contactable. If the suspect is arrested at the weekend or at a time when it is proving difficult to secure him the services of a solicitor it will not be unconstitutional nor unlawful for gardaí to proceed to question the suspect so long as they make bona fide efforts to satisfy his request for access to a solicitor. It would be a different matter entirely if the suspect's arrest was organised as part of a conscious and deliberate attempt to defeat his constitutional right of access to a solicitor. There is anecdotal evidence to suggest that the practice of arresting suspects at the weekend may be on the increase in cases where the arrest could have been effected at other times.[222d] This does not necessarily suggest a conspiracy to deprive suspects of the benefits of their constitutional right of access to a solicitor. Nevertheless, if that proves to be the result in an increasing number of cases the Supreme Court may have to address the issue of whether giving effect to the accused's constitutional right of access requires the establishment of a duty solicitor scheme.[222e]

5–110   In *People (DPP) v. Finnegan*[223] the Court of Criminal Appeal ruled that the constitutional right of access necessarily implies, apart from the most exceptional circumstances, a right to communicate in private and out of hearing of police officers or prison wardens. Accordingly, the fact that police officers were able to overhear the suspect communicating with his solicitor on the phone due to the location of the phone in the small police station rendered his detention unlawful. It would appear, however, that a right of access does not extend to a right to have a solicitor sit in on the police questioning of the suspect. In *Lavery v. The Member in Charge, Carrickmacross Garda Station*[224] the Supreme Court ruled that a suspect's detention under section 30 of the Offences against the State Act 1939 was not rendered unlawful solely because his solicitor had been denied access to the Garda notes of interviews with the suspect. The solicitor claimed that he needed access to these notes in order to advise his client adequately on his situation with respect to the adverse inference provisions which had been introduced by the Offences against the State (Amendment) Act 1998. Giving the judgment of the Court, O'Flaherty J. stated obiter that not only is a solicitor not entitled to be present at the interview, but also that he is not entitled to the records of the interview before the suspect has been charged.

[222c] *ibid.*

[222d] See White, "The Confessional State – Police Interrogation in the Irish Republic" (2000) 10(1) I.C.L.J 17 and 10(2) I.C.L.J. 2.

[222e] The Legal Aid Review Committee came out against the establishment of a duty solicitor scheme in its *Final Report (2002).*

[223] unreported, Court of Criminal Appeal, July 15, 1997.

[224] [1999] 2 I.R. 390.

Scope of the Right under the Regulations

The 1987 regulations also specify a right of reasonable access to a solicitor   **5–111**
for an arrested person.[225] The right is to a solicitor of the person's choice[226]
and extends to an absolute right to consult privately. A consultation can be
considered private for this purpose if it takes place in the sight but out of the
sound of a member.[227] Apart from these stipulations, the regulations do not
shed any further light on the interpretation of what is meant by "reasonable"
in this context. For example, they do not address matters such as: whether the
suspect can be interviewed before his solicitor has arrived, although there is a
provision to the effect that an arrested person who has asked to see a solicitor
shall not be asked to make a written statement in relation to an offence until a
reasonable time for the attendance of the solicitor has elapsed.[228] The
practical benefit of this protection is likely to be diluted where the suspect is
arrested at the weekend.[229]

The regulations also do not specify how long a consultation can last and
whether the solicitor can sit in on the interviews of the suspect. As noted
above with respect to this latter point the Supreme Court has decided that
there is no entitlement for a solicitor to sit in on the interview.[230]

Notifying Location of Garda Station to Solicitor

It may happen that a solicitor for the person in custody will be contacted by   **5–112**
someone other than the person in custody himself.[231] The solicitor, of course,
may not know the actual garda station at which the arrested person is being
held. The question arises, therefore, whether the Garda Síochána should be
under a duty to identify the station in response to an enquiry from the
solicitor. The 1987 regulations do impose such a duty, but only if the arrested
person consents.[232] Significantly, the regulations also make provision for this
information to be disclosed in response to an enquiry from any other
person.[233] In this case, however, not only must the arrested person consent,

---

[225] Criminal Justice Act 1984 (Treatment of Persons in Custody in Garda Síochána Stations) Regulations 1987, reg.11(1).
[226] If the solicitor requested cannot be contacted within a reasonable time or if he is unable or unwilling to attend at the station, the person in custody shall be given an opportunity to ask for another solicitor, and the member in charge must see that the other solicitor is notified accordingly as soon as practicable; Criminal Justice Act 1984 (Treatment of Persons in Custody in Garda Síochána Stations) Regulations 1987, reg.9(2)(a)(ii).
[227] *ibid.* reg.11(3).
[228] *ibid.* reg.12(6). Failure to comply with this provision can result in a statement being ruled inadmissible; see, for example, *People (DPP) v. Van Onzen* [1996] 2 I.L.R.M. 387.
[229] *People (DPP) v. D'Arcy.* Unreported Court of Criminal Appeal, July 29, 1997; *People (DPP) v. Buck* unreported, Supreme Court, April 17, 2002. See also, White *op. cit.* above, n.222.
[230] *Lavery v. The Member in Charge, Carrickmacross Garda Station* [1999] 2 I.R. 390.
[231] *DPP v. Healy* [1990] I.L.R.M. 313 confirms that the constitutional right of access to a solicitor arises when the detainee requests it or when a solicitor arrives at the Garda station having been instructed by an appropriate person acting on behalf of the detainee. In the latter situation the detainee must be informed of the solicitor's presence.
[232] Criminal Justice Act 1984 (Treatment of Persons in Custody in Garda Síochána Stations) Regulations 1987, reg.10(1)(a).
[233] *ibid.* reg.10(1)(b).

but the member in charge must also be satisfied that the giving of the information will not hinder or delay the investigation of crime. The omission of this second qualification in the case of an enquiry from the solicitor suggests that the duty to disclose the identity of the station to the arrested person's solicitor is absolute once the enquiry has been made and the arrested person consents. However, the regulations do not specifically state that the information must be given without delay.

5–113   The regulations do not actually specify which member of the Garda Síochána is obliged to disclose the identity of the station when the relevant circumstances are satisfied. However, it is provided that when a person is taken on arrest to, or is arrested in, a station, the member in charge of that station must see that the district headquarters is notified accordingly.[234] A similar responsibility arises where the person is transferred to another station or is released from custody. Where the person is held in custody in a district other than that in which he resides, the member in charge of the station concerned must also notify the district headquarters for the district in which the person resides.[235] In all these cases the member in charge must act in the matter as soon as practicable. Moreover, a record must be kept in each district headquarters of persons whose whereabouts have been notified to it in accordance with these provisions.[236] The time of such notification must also be recorded.

5–114   It follows that a solicitor trying to trace the whereabouts of a client in Garda custody should contact the garda headquarters for the district in which the person resides or, if known, the headquarters for the district in which he was arrested. In the Dublin metropolitan area, however, the Commissioner may designate a station or stations for the purpose of receiving notifications under these provisions.[237] Where one or more such stations are designated, a notification from a station in any district in the metropolitan area must be made to any one of them (as opposed to the relevant district headquarters). Where the person in question resides outside the Dublin metropolitan area, a notification must also be made to the headquarters for the district in which he resides. Appropriate records must also be kept of the notifications and the times of the notifications in the station from which the notification was made and in the designated station or stations to which it was made.

Where a solicitor has been requested by, or on behalf of, a person under 18 years of age who is being transferred from one station to another, the member in charge of the former station must notify the solicitor of the transfer as soon as possible.[237a]

---

[234]   Criminal Justice Act 1984 (Treatment of Persons in Custody in Garda Síochána Stations) Regulations, 1987 reg.10(2).
[235]   *ibid.* reg.10(3).
[236]   *ibid.* reg.10(5). A record must also be kept in the station concerned of a notification to a district headquarters and the time at which it was made; reg.10(4).
[237]   *ibid.* reg.10(6).
[237a] Children Act 2001, s.60(4).

There is also authority to the effect that gardaí must not impede efforts to give effect to a detainee's right of access. In *People (DPP) v. Connell*,[237b] for example, the suspect was visited in Garda custody by a distant relative who was also a member of the force. The suspect asked the relative to contact his solicitor and to tell him that he wished to see him. The member tried unsuccessfully to contact the solicitor the following morning. He then phoned the Garda station at which the suspect was detained to convey this information. He was told by a member at that station that the suspect had already been contacted by his solicitor that morning. In delivering the judgment of the Court of Criminal Appeal, Egan J. ruled that this conveying of false information was not only highly improper but also amounted to a denial of basic fairness of procedures:

> "It was inexcusable that Garda Mulhall should have received an answer to the effect that the applicant had been contacted by his solicitor on the morning of the 22nd May, 1991. This false information dispensed with any necessity for him to continue trying to contact the solicitor for the applicant. This is a matter of great importance as the applicant might very well have avoided making the inculpatory statement had he received advice that morning from his solicitor. The identity of the person who gave the false information and the reason for so doing did not emerge in evidence, but it is immaterial whether the information was given inadvertently, carelessly or even believing it to be true. It must be held to have been the conscious and deliberate act of a member of the Garda Síochána. . . . In the foregoing circumstances the taking of statement also fell short of the requirement for fairness postulated by Griffin J. in *The People v. Shaw* [1982] I.R.1."[237c]

Egan J. proceeded to rule that the incriminating statement obtained from the suspect was inadmissible because of the impact which the false information had on his right of access to a solicitor and because of other breaches of the 1987 Regulations governing the treatment of persons in detention in Garda stations.

Consequence of Denial of Access

If a person in custody requests a right of access to his solicitor and is refused reasonable access, the refusal will render his detention unlawful.[238] It would appear that this will result in the automatic exclusion of any incriminating statement obtained from the person during the unlawful detention.[238a]

3. Rights of Communication with Others

Section 5 of the Criminal Justice Act 1984 requires the member in charge to see that a person detained in a Garda station under section 4 of the 1984 Act, section 2 of the Criminal Justice (Drug Trafficking) Act 1996 or section 30 of

5–115

[237b] [1995] 1 I.R. 244.
[237c] *ibid.* at 252.
[238] *DPP v. Healy* [1990] I.L.R.M. 313.
[238a] *People (DPP) v. Finnegan* unreported, Court of Criminal Appeal, July 15, 1997.

the Offences against the State Act 1939[239] is informed without delay that he is entitled to have notification of his detention, and of the station where he is being detained, sent to one person (in addition to his solicitor) reasonably named by him.[240] Any arrested person in custody in a Garda station may request such a person to be notified of his custody in the station concerned. Where such a request is made, the member in charge must cause the named person to be notified as soon as practicable.[241] If that person cannot be contacted within a reasonable time the person must be given an opportunity to ask for another such person to be notified.[242] A record must be made of any notification request made by a person pursuant to these provisions, the time at which it was made and complied with, and any action taken by a member on it.[243]

5–116　Unfortunately, neither the Act nor the 1987 regulations shed any light on what is meant by a "person reasonably named by him" in the context of notification. Presumably, it would be satisfied by a relative, friend or professional adviser who can be expected to be available at relatively short notice. By the same token, the Garda Síochána can hardly be required to seek to make contact with persons whose whereabouts are unknown or who cannot be expected to attend at short notice or who have no connection at all with the person detained. The position is much less certain with respect to relatives, friends or professional advisers who are available but who have a criminal record or are suspected by the Garda Síochána of being criminal associates of the person detained. A court might well deem such a person to be not "reasonably named" in this context.

5–117　As might be expected, the 1987 Regulations (as modified by the Children Act 2001)[243a] make additional provisions on notification for a person under the age of 18 years.[244] Where such a person is detained in a Garda station under section 4 of the 1984 Act, section 2 of the Criminal Justice (Drug Trafficking)

---

[239]　Criminal Justice Act 1984, s.9 extends this provision to s.30 of the 1939 Act while Criminal Justice (Drug Trafficking) Act 1996 does the same for s.2 of the 1996 Act. It is not specifically extended to arrested persons generally. It is worth noting, however, that there is a duty on the member in charge to notify a named person when requested to do so by any arrested person in garda custody; see Criminal Justice Act 1984 (Treatment of Persons in Custody in Garda Síochána Stations) Regulations 1987, reg.9(2).

[240]　Where an arrested person is being transferred to another station, the member in charge of the station from which he is being transferred shall see that the notified person is informed of the transfer as soon as possible; Criminal Justice Act 1984 (Treatment of Persons in Custody in Garda Síochána Stations) Regulations 1987, reg.9(3).

[241]　*ibid.* reg.9(2)(a)(i). This provision extends the right to any arrested person who is in custody in a garda station.

[242]　*ibid.* reg.9(2)(a)(ii).

[243]　*ibid.* reg.9(4).

[243a]　Section 70(2) of the Children Act 2001 extends regs. 9 and 13 of the 1987 Act to persons under the age of 18 in Garda custody pending the making of specific regulations under the 2001 Act.

[244]　Where a person is detained in a garda station pursuant to s.4 of the Criminal Justice Act 1984, s.2 of the Criminal Justice (Drug Trafficking) Act 1996 or s.30 of the Offences against the State Act 1939 and the member in charge of that station has reasonable grounds for believing that the person is not below the age of 18years, he shall be treated for this purpose as if he was over the age of 18 years; Criminal Justice Act 1984, s.5(3). See also s.9 of the 1984 Act and s.5 of the 1996 Act.

Act or section 30 of the Offences against the State Act 1939, the member in charge must see, as soon as practicable, that a parent or guardian (or a spouse, if relevant)[245] of the person is informed of his detention in the station, the offence or other matter in respect of which he has been arrested and of his entitlement to consult a solicitor.[246] The 1987 regulations extend this duty to all persons under the age of 18 who have been arrested and taken into Garda custody.[247] The parent, guardian or spouse, as the case may be, must also be requested to attend at the station without delay. However, if the member in charge is unable to communicate with the parent, guardian or spouse, as the case may be, or if the person contacted is unable or unwilling to attend at the station within a reasonable time, the arrested person must be informed of his entitlement to have notification of his detention in the station concerned sent to another person reasonably named by him, as if he were over the age of 18 years.[248] Where the child is transferred to another station or another place, the member in charge of the station from which the child is being transferred must alert the person contacted to the transfer.[248a] There is also provision for the member in charge to inform the local health board of the child's custody where the member has reasonable cause to believe that the child is in need of care or protection. In this event the health board must send a representative to the station as soon as possible.[248b]

The right of an arrested person to be informed of his right to have another informed of his detention, and his right to request that another named person should be informed, do not add up to a right to communicate directly with this person. However, the 1987 regulations do provide that an arrested person may receive a visit from a relative, friend or other person with an interest in his welfare where he so wishes.[249] This right is subject to the member in charge being satisfied that the visit can be adequately supervised and that it will not hinder or delay the investigation of crime. Unlike the position with respect to a visit from the arrested person's solicitor, there is no specific provision to the effect that the visit must be out of the hearing of a member of the Garda Síochána. Indeed, the regulations positively state that the person must be told in advance of the visit that anything he says during it may be given in evidence.[250] This suggests that the visit need not be in private.

5–118

---

[245] If the arrested person is married, the references to a parent or guardian shall be substituted by references to his spouse; Criminal Justice Act 1984 (Treatment of Persons in Custody in Garda Síochána Stations) Regulations 1987, reg.9(1)(c).

[246] *ibid.* reg.9(1)(a). S.9 of the 1984 Act extends this provision to s.30 of the Offences against the State Act 1939, while s.5 of Criminal Justice (Drug Trafficking) Act 1996 extends it to s.2 of the 1996 Act. See also Children Act 2001, s.58(1).

[247] The Criminal Justice Act 1984 (Treatment of Persons in Custody in Garda Síochána Stations) Regulations 1987, reg.9(1).

[248] Criminal Justice Act 1984, s.5(2)(i) and Criminal Justice Act 1984 (Treatment of Persons in Custody in Garda Síochána Stations) Regulations 1987, reg.9(1)(b). See also Children Act 2001, s.58(2).

[248a] Children Act 2001, s.58(3).

[248b] *ibid.* s.59.

[249] Criminal Justice Act 1984 (Treatment of Persons in Custody in Garda Síochána Stations) Regulations 1987 reg.11(4).

[250] *ibid.* reg.11(6).

5–119   The 1987 regulations also permit an arrested person to make a telephone call to a person reasonably named by him or to send a letter.[251] The call will be free of charge and must be of reasonable duration. For the purpose of sending a letter, writing materials and, where necessary, postage stamps must be supplied on request.[252] However, unless the call or letter is a communication with the person's solicitor, the right is subject to the member in charge being satisfied that its exercise will not hinder or delay the investigation of crime. To this end, a member may listen to any such telephone call and may terminate it if he is not so satisfied. Similarly, he may read any such letter and may decline to send it on the same grounds. Before the arrested person communicates with another person (with the exception of his solicitor) he must be told that anything he says in the communication may be given in evidence.[253]

Even if the arrested person has not exercised his right to have a person informed of his detention, it is quite possible that persons concerned for his welfare will be aware of the fact, or may suspect, that he has been arrested. They may not, of course, know at which station he is being held. Accordingly, the 1987 regulations stipulate that, in response to an enquiry by any person, information as to the station at which an arrested person is being held must be given if that person consents, and the member in charge is satisfied that giving the information will not hinder or delay the investigation of crime.[254] It is worth noting that this duty only extends to giving information as to the station at which an arrested person is held. It does not specifically require information to be given in response to a general query on whether a named person is in custody. Moreover, where the duty does arise, there is no requirement that the information should be given only to a person with an interest in the welfare of the arrested person.

4. Right of Access to Consul

5–120   Consular officers[255] are entitled to visit one of their nationals, or a national of another state for whom they offer consular assistance, where that national has been arrested.[256] The right to visit includes the right to converse and correspond with the arrested person and to arrange for his legal representation.

---

[251] *ibid.* reg.11(5).

[252] It would appear that the arrested person will have to make a choice between making one telephone call and sending one letter. It is not clear what the position is in this respect if there is no answer to the telephone call. In the case of the letter, it would appear that the addressee need not be a person reasonably named by the arrested person, *i.e.* it could be anyone.

[253] Criminal Justice Act 1984 (Treatment of Persons in Custody in Garda Síochána Stations) Regulations 1987, reg.11(6).

[254] *ibid.* reg.10(1)(b). See "Access to a Solicitor" for the internal dissemination of information on the whereabouts of an arrested person who is being held in garda custody.

[255] "Consul" means, in relation to a foreign national, the diplomatic or consular representative of that person's own country either in the State or accredited to the State on a non-residential basis, or a diplomatic or consular representative of a third country which may formally or informally offer consular assistance to a national of a country which has no resident representative in the State; The Criminal Justice Act 1984 (Treatment of Persons in Custody in Garda Síochána Stations) Regulations 1987, reg.14(6).

[256] *ibid.* reg.14(2).

However, if the member in charge has reasonable grounds to believe that the arrested person is a political refugee or is seeking political asylum, a consular officer must not be notified of his arrest nor given access to him or information about him except at the express request of the arrested person.[257] Where an arrested foreign national makes a request for his consul to be contacted, the member in charge must cause the consul to be notified as soon as practicable.[258]

These provisions are without prejudice to the provisions of a consular convention or arrangement between Ireland and the State of the foreign national concerned.[259] For example, under the Consular Convention between Ireland and the USA, an American national who is arrested must be informed that the American consulate will be notified. Unless the arrested person requests that the consulate should not be notified, the member in charge should notify the appropriate American consulate by telephone as soon as possible. An American consular officer will be permitted to visit, converse privately with, and arrange legal representation for an arrested American national. Any communication from such person to his consular officer should be forwarded without delay.

---

[257] *ibid.* reg.14(4).
[258] *ibid.* reg.14(1). A record must be made of the time when any request was made, when the request was complied with and when any communication was forwarded to a consul; reg.14(4).
[259] *ibid.* reg.14(3).

CHAPTER 6

THE INTERVIEW, EXAMINATION AND IDENTIFICATION OF THE SUSPECT IN GARDA CUSTODY

A. Introduction

When the police are in the process of investigating a crime, it will normally **6–01** be of great assistance to them to have a suspect in their custody at the police station. His presence there means, for example, that he can be questioned directly about his suspected involvement in the offence and the possible involvement of others. Of course, there will often be no compelling reason, why this cannot be done in the comfort of the suspect's own home or in some other place with which he is familiar. In practice, however, the police find it more convenient and effective to carry out the questioning in the police station. This is understandable given that the investigation will be co-ordinated from there. The necessary resources, including other officers engaged in the investigation, will be more readily available if needed to check out information given by the suspect. Moreover, there is a widespread belief that questioning a suspect in the unfamiliar and regulated environment of the police interview room will usually be more productive than questioning him in the security and comfort of his own home. The presence of the suspect at the Garda station also facilitates other investigative techniques such as: identity parades, finger and palm printing, intimate body searches and the taking of samples for forensic analysis and/or DNA testing.

The presence of the suspect in the police station and his cooperation with questioning and the other investigative processes do not have to be secured inevitably by force. The suspect can submit voluntarily. Indeed, it has long been a common and widespread practice for a member of the Garda Síochána to invite a suspect to accompany him to the Garda station to assist the Garda with their inquiries. However, it does suffer from a number of limitations. First, there is the obvious danger that the suspect might refuse to go, or that he would exercise his right to leave the station before the gardaí have had an opportunity to investigate him fully. Second, if the circumstances are such that the suspect forms the view that he is not free to leave the station voluntarily, it is likely that a court will rule that he has been unlawfully detained. A consequence of such a ruling will normally be that any evidence obtained from the suspect during the unlawful detention will be inadmissible in subsequent criminal proceedings. From the police perspective, it is likely that this outcome would defeat the whole purpose of inviting the suspect to the station in the first place.

The police can coerce a measure of cooperation from the suspect by arresting and detaining him. Formal arrest and detention places the suspect in the custody of the police at least temporarily. It also means, of course, that the police must comply with the whole body of laws and regulations governing the treatment of persons in their custody, including the strict limits on the length of time in which they can keep a person in custody. Nevertheless, the arrest will normally provide them with an opportunity to question the suspect and, perhaps, to resort to any of the other investigative techniques. This can often prove critical in providing confession or other compelling evidence of guilt in cases where the suspect has not been caught in the act. It is hardly surprising, therefore, that questioning and the other investigative opportunities provided by arrest play a prominent role in building a case against a defendant in the criminal process. The purpose of this chapter is to consider the laws and regulations governing questioning and the use of these other investigative techniques on suspects in police custody.

B. The Interview

1. Introduction

6–02   Where a suspect has been arrested summarily and taken into police custody, there will often be an expectation that he can provide information which will further the police investigation into the crime in question. The police will seek to extract as much of this information as possible by interviewing the suspect. In some cases, the primary object might be to save the victim from possible injury or death. For the most part, however, the aim will be to confirm the suspicion against the arrested person and, ultimately, to gather evidence which can be used against him in court to secure a conviction.

The police freedom to question a suspect in their custody is constrained by the general rules governing the detention of arrested persons (see chapter 5). In addition, however, there is a body of laws, regulations and administrative rules specifically aimed at controlling the interview process. These are to be found primarily, but not exclusively, in constitutional principles, the common law, the Criminal Justice Act 1984, the Criminal Justice Act 1984 (Treatment of Persons in Custody in Garda Síochána Stations) Regulations 1987, the Criminal Justice Act 1984 (Electronic Recording of Interviews) Regulations 1997 and the Judges Rules. The constitutional and common law inputs are comprised largely of the rules governing the admissibility of confession evidence and unlawfully obtained evidence. They will be covered in chapter 9 on the admissibility of evidence obtained by the police. Nevertheless, it is worth noting here that a confession will be inadmissible in evidence if it has been obtained in circumstances constituting a deliberate and conscious violation of the suspect's constitutional rights or of it is involuntary. In addition, any confession can be excluded at the discretion of the trial judge in response to the circumstances in which it has been obtained. Given that a primary object of the police interview will normally be to obtain an admissible confession or other admissible evidence implicating the suspect in the crime, these rules on admissibility must act as an indirect control on police interview practices. Accordingly, this chapter must be read in conjunction with chapters 5 and 9 in order to get a fuller picture of the legal rules governing the interview of suspects in police custody. It is also worth noting at the outset that subjecting the suspect to ill treatment, particularly where it takes the form of unlawful assaults, will render his detention unlawful.

Another constitutional point worth noting at the outset is that the suspect does not lose his right to privacy just because he has been lawfully arrested and detained in a Garda station.[1] Clearly, he must accept the restrictions on that right which are necessary to secure his presence in the station and to ensure his own safety and the safety of others in the station. This may entail keeping the suspect under regular observation.[1a] Equally, he will have to accept the restrictions on his privacy which arise necessarily from the lawful exercise of powers such as those to search and take body samples. Subject to any such lawful restrictions the suspect enjoys a right to privacy while in police custody.

2. The Judges' Rules

Origins

The Judges' Rules are a body of nine rules for the guidance of the police **6–03** when engaged in taking statements from suspects.[1b] They are unusual in our common law system in that they constitute a code drawn up by judges as opposed to a legislative or executive authority. Moreover, they were not drawn up in the course of handing down judgment in an individual case. Rather they were first formulated in 1912 by the English High Court Judges who sat together in an extra judicial capacity for the purpose of issuing guidance on the sort of interrogation practices that the courts would consider acceptable for the purposes of admitting in evidence at the subsequent trial admissions made by the suspect in the course of the interrogation. The version handed down in 1912 in response to this request was tidied up and

---

[1] *DPP v. Kenny* [1992] 2 I.R. 141.

[1a] Where relevant to an issue in the trial, evidence of the suspect's condition while in custody can be given by a person lawfully authorised to deal with him or where the suspect has consented to such observation; see *DPP v. Kenny* [1992] 2 I.R. 141; *People (DPP) v. Murray* CCA, April 12, 1999.

[1b] There is also a suggestion that a medical examination of the suspect in police custody for the purpose of seeking evidence which might connect the suspect with the offence under investigation would attract the application of the Judges' Rules; see *People (DPP) v. Murray* unreported, Court of Criminal Appeal, April 12, 2000.

published in 1918. It was subsequently replaced in 1964 by a new set of Rules. These were accompanied by a preamble setting out five general principles and an appendix of administrative directions issued by the Home Secretary.[1c] Ultimately, these Rules and administrative directions were replaced in England and Wales by the codes of practice issued pursuant to the Police and Criminal Evidence Act 1984.

The Rules

It has always been assumed that the Judges' Rules applied in Ireland and survived the enactment of the 1922 Constitution. However, the version which applies here continues to be that which was published in 1918. An attempt to have it replaced judicially by the 1964 revision was rejected by the Court of Criminal Appeal, which confirmed the applicability of the 1918 version.[2] The full text is set out in the judgment of Walsh J. in *People v. Cummins*[3] as follows:

"I.   When a police officer is endeavouring to discover the author of a crime there is no objection to his putting questions in respect thereof to any person or persons, whether suspected or not, from whom he thinks that useful information may be obtained.

II. Whenever a police officer has made up his mind to charge a person with a crime, he should first caution such a person before asking him any questions, or any further questions as the case may be.

III. Persons in custody should not be questioned without the usual caution being first administered.

IV. If the prisoner wishes to volunteer any statement, the usual caution should be administered. It is desirable that the last two words of such caution should be omitted, and that the caution should end with the words 'be given in evidence'.

V.   The caution to be administered to a prisoner when he is formally charged should therefore be in the following words:
     'Do you wish to say anything in answer to the charge? You are not obliged to say anything unless you wish to do so, but whatever you say will be taken down in writing and may be given in evidence.' Care should be taken to avoid the suggestion that his answers can only be used in evidence against him, as this may prevent an innocent person making a statement which might assist to clear him of the charge.

VI. A statement made by a prisoner before there is time to caution him is not rendered inadmissible in evidence merely because no caution has been given, but in such a case he should be cautioned as soon as possible.

VII. A prisoner making a voluntary statement must not be cross-examined, and no questions should be put to him about it except for the purpose of removing ambiguity in what he has actually said. For instance, if he has mentioned an hour without saying whether it was morning or evening, or has given a day of the week and day of the month which do not agree, or has not made it clear to what individual or what place he intended to refer in some part of his statement, he may be questioned sufficiently to clear up the point.

[1c] *Practice Note* [1964] 1 All E.R. 237; [1964] 1 W.L.R. 152.
[2] *People v. Regan* [1975] I.R. 367.
[3] [1972] I.R. 312 at 317–318.

VIII. When two or more persons are charged with the same offence and their statements are taken separately, the police should not read those statements to other persons charged, but each of such persons should be given by the police a copy of such statements and nothing should be said or done by the police to invite a reply. If the person charged desires to make a statement in reply the usual caution should be administered.

IX. Any statement made in accordance with the above rules should, whenever possible, be taken down in writing and signed by the person making it after it has been read to him and he has been invited to make any corrections he may wish."

Status

The proper interpretation of each of these Rules will be considered in the context of where it is most likely to arise in the interview process. It is worth noting at the outset, however, that they are not actually rules of law in the sense that a breach of them will automatically expose the officer concerned to a criminal prosecution or civil action. Nevertheless, a failure to observe the Rules when taking a confession statement from a suspect constitutes grounds upon which the trial judge may exercise his discretion to exclude it, even though he or she is satisfied that the confession was voluntary and had not been obtained in breach of the suspect's constitutional rights.[4] The general principle and its application in practical situations is conveyed in the following quotation from O'Higgins C.J. in *People v. Farrell*:

> "The Judges' Rules are not rules of law. They are rules for the guidance of persons taking statements. However, they have stood up to the test of time and will be departed from at peril. In very rare cases, such as *R. v. Mills and Lemon* [1947] K.B. 247 a statement taken in breach may be admitted in evidence but in very exceptional circumstances. Where, however, there is a breach of the Judges' Rules, such as a failure to make a written record of the alleged confession or a failure to invite the accused to accept or reject the statements, each of such breaches calls for an adequate explanation. The breaches and the explanation (if any) together with the entire circumstances of the case are matters to be taken into consideration by the trial judge before exercising his judicial discretion as to whether or not he will admit such statement in evidence."[5]

Chief Justice O'Higgins' guidance suggests that a statement will normally be excluded when it has been obtained in breach of the Judges' Rules. However, the extent to which that is actually reflected in judicial practice is called into question by the case law. Indeed, it must be said that there are several examples of cases where Irish judges might be accused of having adopted a cavalier approach to admitted or apparent breaches of the Judges' Rules. In *State v. Scully*,[6] for example, a police officer obtained a statement from the suspect after having read her a statement from her co-accused. The admissibility of the first statement was challenged on the basis of Rule VIII.

6–04

---

[4] This has always been the position in English law; see *R. v. Voisin* [1918] 1 K.B. 531.
[5] [1978] I.R. 13 at 21.
[6] 62 I.L.T.R. 24.

Despite appearing to accept that it was not the practice of the English courts to admit statements taken in such circumstances, the trial judge admitted it on the basis that it was the practice of the Central Criminal Court to admit such statements. Similarly, in *People v. Kelly (No.2)*,[7] the trial judge admitted a statement despite the fact that it had been taken in breach of Rule IX.[8] The accused had made two oral confessions while in police custody. The first was not taken down in writing at the time it was made. The second was taken down in writing, read over to the accused, but he refused to sign it. Later, he made and signed a written statement. The Court admitted the oral and unsigned written statements. The Court of Criminal Appeal upheld their admissibility on the ground that their accuracy was confirmed by the fact that they were substantially identical to the written signed statement.

Where the challenge is taken on the basis of a breach of Rule III, the Irish judges display a distinct reticence to exercise their discretion to exclude.[9] This is probably due in large part to their particular interpretation of Rule III. When originally formulated it would appear that it was meant to incorporate the standard judicial practice of refusing to accept statements resulting from the interrogation of suspects after they had been arrested.[10] The actual formulation, however, can be interpreted literally to mean that it is only the interrogation of an arrested suspect without the caution that is prohibited. This, in turn, can be read as implying that interrogation after arrest is not prohibited so long as the caution is administered. Whatever might be the correct interpretation of Rule III, there is no doubt that the standard police practice of questioning a suspect after arrest is now accepted. Accordingly, the argument that a trial judge should exercise his or her discretion to exclude a statement on the basis that it was obtained by questioning the suspect after he had been arrested, is likely to receive short shrift from the courts.[11] There would be more substance to the argument if the caution was not administered at the start of the questioning.[12]

Although the Judges' Rules may not have had a very dynamic impact on the admissibility of statement evidence, they do offer something which is lacking in the other admissibility rules discussed in chapter 9. Unlike the other rules, the Judges' Rules actually set out in some detail what is actually required of the police when taking a statement. In that sense it might be more appropriate to consider them primarily as part of the framework for regulating the interview process.

---

[7] [1983] I.R. 1.

[8] See also, *People v. Farrell* [[1978] I.R. 13; *People v. Pringle* (1981) 2 Frewen 57 at 98.

[9] See Ryan and Magee, *The Irish Criminal Process* (Mercier Press, Dublin, 1983) at pp. 118–119.

[10] See, *e.g.*, Home Office Circular S26059/29 which was issued in 1930 with the approval of the English judges. It reads:
   "Rule III was never intended to encourage or authorise the questioning or cross-examination of a person in custody after he has been cautioned on the subject of the crime for which he is in custody, and long before this rule was formulated and since, it has been the practice of the judges not to allow any answer to a question so improperly put to be given in evidence."

[11] See, for example, Finlay P in *People v. Kelly (No.2)* [1983] I.R. 1. See also, *People v. Madden* [1977] I.R. 336.

[12] See, for example, *People (DPP) v. Buckley* [1990] 1 I.R. 14.

3. The Interview Environment

Location of Interviews

Traditionally, the law has not prescribed any specific criteria governing the **6–05** setting in which an arrested suspect must be interviewed, apart from the general stipulation that a person must not be subjected to questioning which would be regarded as oppressive by the courts.[13] The Criminal Justice Act 1984 (Treatment of Persons in Custody in Garda Síochána Stations) Regulations 1987 have introduced a number of requirements concerning the appropriate environment for the interview of a suspect in police custody.[13a] These stipulate that as far as practicable interviews should take place in rooms set aside for that purpose.[14] Accordingly, interviewing the suspect in his cell, in the corridors or in a police car should be avoided. A further implication is that in Garda stations which are used for holding arrested suspects rooms should be set aside for interviewing.

Number of Interrogating Officers

The Regulations impose limits on the number of Garda personnel who may interview the arrested suspect at any one time and on the number who may be present in the interview room at any one time. The limit for the former is two, while that for the latter is four.[15] It would appear that exceeding these limits will not necessarily result in an inculpatory statement being declared inadmissible at the trial. In *People (DPP) v. D'Arcy*[16] a juvenile detained pursuant to section 4 of the Criminal Justice Act 1984 was interviewed in the presence of his uncle. It was accepted that three of the gardaí present participated in the questioning of the juvenile suspect on several occasions. Nevertheless, the Court of Criminal Appeal considered that this admitted breach of the Regulations did not warrant the exclusion of inculpatory statements made by the juvenile in the course of the interview. The key issue was whether the interview was oppressive or unfair. Since there was no suggestion that the interview was oppressive or unfair the Court considered that it was a matter for the trial judge to decide in the exercise of his discretion whether to admit the statements. The discretion had been properly exercised in this case.[16a]

---

[13] See Walsh J. in *People (DPP) v. Quilligan* [1987] I.L.R.M. 606. See also Criminal Justice Act 1984 (Treatment of Persons in Custody in Garda Síochána Stations) 1987, reg.12(2) which states that the interview shall be conducted in a fair and humane manner.

[13a] Breach of these regulations will not necessarily result in the exclusion of evidence obtained during the interviews; see, *e.g., People (DPP) v. O'Driscoll* unreported, Court of Criminal Appeal, May 19, 1999; *People (DPP) v. Smith* unreported, Court of Criminal Appeal, November 22, 1999; *People (DPP) v. D'Arcy* unreported, Court of Criminal Appeal, July 23, 1997.

[14] The Criminal Justice Act 1984 (Treatment of Persons in custody in Garda Síochána Stations) Regulations 1987, reg.12(5).

[15] *ibid.*, reg.12(3). It would appear that the questioning must be done by the same two gardaí throughout a single interview; see *People (DPP) v. Smith* unreported, Court of Criminal Appeal, November 22, 1999.

[16] Court of Criminal Appeal, 23 July 1997.

[16a] See also, *People (DPP) v. Smith* unreported, Court of Criminal Appeal, November 22, 1999.

"Incommunicado" Interrogation

Apart from suspects who are under 18 years of age, the Regulations have nothing to say about the presence of non-investigating personnel in the interview room or during the interview itself.[17] In particular, apart from special cases,[18] there is no specific provision permitting the suspect to be accompanied by his solicitor or a "friend" during the actual interview.[19] The standard Garda practice is to conduct the interviews incommunicado. The suspect's right of access to his solicitor is facilitated normally by suspending the interview.

The practice of conducting interviews incommunicado in the police station has obvious advantages for the police, compared with conducting the interview in, for example, the security and comfort of the suspect's own home. By the same token, however, it also creates the opportunity for over-zealous investigative practices which can result in the commission of criminal or civil offences and/or the extraction of false confessions. In the case of suspects who are unfamiliar with being detained in the police station there is also the danger that false confessions will be given in the hope that that will satisfy the demands of the police and/or secure their release. A "false" confession can, of course, result in a conviction unless it is excluded at trial. Clearly, if the defence can establish that a confession was "false" the judge will exclude it from evidence. In practice, however, it will often be very difficult to prove the falsity of a confession. Successful challenges to the admissibility of confessions usually depend not so much on proving that the substance of the confession is false but on establishing what happened in the secrecy of the interview room. More often than not this will come down to choosing between the conflicting testimony of the accused and the police officer(s) concerned. A decision in favour of the accused may result in a guilty person going unpunished, a crime unsolved, police morale being dented and a blow to the public interest in combating crime. A decision in favour of the police, on the other hand, may result in the conviction of an innocent person, a crime unsolved, police malpractice unchecked and a weakening of public confidence in and respect for the whole criminal process. It is critically important, therefore, that every effort should be made to ascertain the truth of what happened in the secrecy of the interview room.

---

[17] The Minister for Justice, Equality and Law Reform may, following consultation with the Minister for Finance, make regulations providing for the attendance of an officer of customs and excise at, and the participation of such an officer in, the questioning of a person detained under s.2 of the Criminal Justice (Drug Trafficking) Act 1996 or s.4 of the Criminal Justice Act 1984 in relation to a drug trafficking offence; Criminal Justice (Drug Trafficking) Act 1996, s.6(1).

[18] Persons under the age of 18 years and mentally handicapped persons can normally be accompanied by a parent or guardian. A deaf person might have the services of an interpreter during questioning. See later.

[19] By contrast, in England and Wales a suspect can have his solicitor present during the actual interview; "The Detention and Questioning of Persons by Police Officers (HMSO, London, 1995), para. 6.8.

4. Recording Interviews

Background

The search for an acceptable means of providing independent verification of **6–06** what occurred in the interview room has been a live issue in these islands since the late 1970s. In Northern Ireland, closed-circuit television cameras were installed in the interview rooms of the interrogation centres at Castlereagh and Holywood. This move came in response to public alarm at reports of the police beating confessions out of suspects arrested and detained under the emergency legislation.[20] However, the screens are only monitored by the police themselves at the stations concerned. They do not carry sound and the interogation is not recorded on tape so as to be available as evidence in subsequent court proceedings.[21] In Britain, the extended powers of arrest and detention conferred on the police by the Police and Criminal Evidence Act 1984 are balanced by provision for the introduction of the electronic recording of interviews of suspects in police stations.[22] Today it is standard practice for these interviews to be tape recorded. A copy of the tape is available for the suspect and his legal advisor and the original is available as evidence in court. The tapes do provide independent evidence of what happened in the interview room and may have actually resulted in a decrease in the number of challenges to the admissibility of confessions. However, they do not offer a failsafe mechanism against error or abuse.[23] One weakness is that they provide only an audio record of what happened in the interview room. It is argued that an audio-visual record of what happened both in the interview room and in the corridors might tell a different story in some cases.[24]

Ireland has not been immune to the debate on whether the police interview of arrested suspects should be conducted in complete privacy. Significantly, the Criminal Justice Act 1984 specifically empowers the Minister for Justice, Equality and Law Reform to issue regulations providing for the electronic recording of persons being questioned in Garda stations in connection with the investigation of offences.[25] In 1989 the government set up a Committee of Inquiry under the chairmanship of Judge Frank Martin to enquire into certain aspects of criminal procedure, including "whether additional safeguards are needed to ensure that such admissions are properly obtained and recorded". The Committee's Report, submitted in March 1990, recommended, *inter alia*, the introduction of audio-visual recording of the interrogation of suspects in

---

[20] See *Report of the Committee of Inquiry into Police Interrogation Procedure in Northern Ireland* (HMSO, London, 1979), "The Bennett Report".

[21] The tape-recording of interrogations has since been introduced in Northern Ireland.

[22] Police and Criminal Evidence Act 1984 (Codes of Practice) Order 1988, Code E: Code of Practice on the Tape Recording of Police Interviews. See also: Practice Direction (Crime: Tape Recording of Police Interviews) (1989) Cr. App. Rep. 132; and Home Office Circular 76/1988.

[23] For a critical assessment, see Baldwin, J and Moloney, T *Supervision of Police Investigations in Serious Criminal Cases*: RCCJ Research Study No.4 (HMSO, London, 1993).

[24] See further, Moston, S and Stephenson, G *The Questioning and Interviewing of Suspects Outside the Police Station*: RCCJ Research Study No.22 (HMSO, London, 1993).

[25] Criminal Justice Act 1984, s.27.

police custody.[26] It was not until March 1, 1997, however, that the necessary regulations came into effect under the title of the Criminal Justice Act 1984 (Electronic Recording of Interviews) Regulations 1997.

The Obligation to Record

The 1997 Regulations make provision for the electronic recording of certain interviews in certain Garda Síochána stations. The interviews in question are those conducted with persons detained under section 4 of the Criminal Justice Act 1984, section 30 of the Offences Against the State Act 1939 or section 2 of the Criminal Justice (Drug Trafficking) Act 1996.[27] The questioning of persons who have come to a Garda station voluntarily, or who are in Garda custody while being processed under section 15 of the Criminal Justice Act 1951, is not specifically covered. The Garda stations affected are those in which the electronic recording equipment has been installed.[28] Electronic recording in this context will be satisfied either by a sound recording of oral communication on tape or a video recording with or without a soundtrack.[29] It follows that there is no obligation to make a complete audio-visual recording of interviews. In practice, the equipment installed in the Garda stations concerned is designed to make a complete audio-visual recording.

It must be noted at the outset that not all Garda stations are equipped for the audio-visual recording of interviews. This is significant because the obligation to electronically record an interview only applies where the interview is being conducted at a Garda station in which the equipment has been installed. There is at least a theoretical possibility that gardaí would attempt to circumvent the recording obligations by bringing an arrested suspect to a Garda station in which the equipment had not been installed. In *People (DPP) v. Holland*,[30] for example, the accused was arrested under section 30 of the Offences against the State Act 1939 on suspicion of a firearms offence. The broader context was a Garda investigation of organised crime involvement in serious drug trafficking. He was brought to, and detained for questioning at, Lucan Garda station which did not have recording equipment installed. The accused argued that the decision to interview him in Lucan Garda station, as opposed to Tallaght or some other such station in which the equipment was installed, was a deliberate ploy to avoid the obligation to record his interviews. However, both the Special Criminal Court and the Court of Criminal Appeal accepted the Garda explanation that Lucan station was chosen because it was the centre of the investigation into what was a series of crimes in which it was believed the accused was implicated. The Court of Criminal noted that "if it had been established that the accused was brought to Lucan Garda Station deliberately to deprive him of the benefit of having an elec-

---

[26] "Report of Committee to Enquire into Certain Aspects of Criminal Procedure" (Dublin: Government Publications, 1990).
[27] Criminal Justice Act 1984 (Electronic Recording of Interviews) Regulations 1997, reg.3(2).
[28] *ibid.* reg.3(1).
[29] *ibid.* reg.2(1).
[30] CCA, June 15, 1998.

tronic recording made of his interview, then that would be a serious matter". This, however, falls well short of an obligation to take an arrested suspect to a convenient Garda station which has the necessary recording equipment installed.

Interviews which are subject to the 1997 Regulations must be electronically recorded in accordance with the Regulations.[31] There is no provision for the suspect to decline the electronic recording. It will be seen later, however, that the recording can be terminated if the suspect objects to the interview being electronically recorded. In this event the recording may be terminated, but only after the prescribed preliminaries have been recorded (see later).

6–07

The interviews must be recorded using the equipment installed for that purpose.[32] The use of other equipment is prohibited.[33] It does not follow, however, that an interview must be abandoned if, for some reason, the equipment cannot be used. An interview, or part of an interview does not have to be electronically recorded, where the equipment is unavailable due to a functional fault or where it is already in use at the time the interview is to commence.[34] In these circumstances the interview can proceed if the member in charge of the station considers on reasonable grounds that it should not be delayed until the fault is rectified or the equipment becomes available, as the case may be. Electronic recording can also be dispensed with for an interview or part of an interview where recording it is not otherwise practicable.[35] The Regulations do not offer any insight into what factors may be sufficient to render electronic recording "not practicable" in this context. Where an interview, or part of an interview, is not recorded for any of these reasons, the member in charge of the Garda station must enter or cause to be entered in the custody record of the person concerned a note setting out the fact that the interview was not electronically recorded and the reason.[36]

Recording Procedure

Before an electronically recorded interview commences the member in charge of the station must see that the person to be interviewed is informed that the interview may be electronically recorded and that he is entitled to receive a notice explaining what is to happen to the tapes of the interview.[37] The member in charge must also see that the person is given the notice. The member conducting the interview must unwrap the required number of unused blank tapes, load the equipment with the tapes and set the equipment to record. All of this must be done within the sight of the person to be interviewed.[38]

---

[31] Criminal Justice Act 1984 (Electronic Recording of Interviews) Regulations, reg.4(1).
[32] *ibid.* reg.4(1).
[33] *ibid.* reg.4(2).
[34] *ibid.* reg.4(3)(a).
[35] *ibid.* reg.4(3)(b)
[36] *ibid.* reg.4(4).
[37] *ibid.* reg.5(1). This is in addition to the information which must be provided pursuant to the Criminal Justice Act 1984 (Treatment of Persons in Custody in Garda Síochána Stations) Regulations 1987, reg.8; see chapter on Detention.
[38] Criminal Justice Act 1984 (Electronic Recording of Interviews) Regulations 1997, reg.6(1).

The Regulations do not specify how many tapes should be running independently at the same time. It can be deduced from certain provisions in the Regulations (see later) that there must be at least two. One of these is designated the "master tape".[39] It must be sealed, labelled and signed at the conclusion of each interview session or at any time when an interview is interrupted by switching off the equipment. Although the Regulations do not make specific provision on the matter it would appear that the master tape is meant to be the authoritative record of the interview to which it relates. The other tape (or tapes) which is running simultaneously with the master tape is designated the "working copy".[40]

While the equipment is recording, the member in charge must caution the person to be interviewed in the following terms:

> "You are not obliged to say anything unless you wish to do so but whatever you say will be taken down in writing and may be given in evidence. As you are aware this interview is being taped and the tape may be used in evidence."[41]

The member must also state: his name and rank, the name and rank of any other members present, the name and status of any other person present, the name of the person being interviewed, the date, the time of commencement of the recording, the location of the station and that the person being interviewed has been given a notice explaining what is to happen to the tapes of the interview.[42] Subject to these formalities, the interview should proceed as normal. Indeed, it is worth pointing out that the electronic recording of the interview does not dispense with the obligation to make a record of the interview in a notebook or other document either simultaneously with the interview or as soon as possible thereafter.[43]

At the conclusion of the interview the member conducting it must ask the person being interviewed if there is anything further he wishes to say or clarify.[44] He must also read back any notes and memoranda taken in the interview and ask the person concerned if he wishes to make any alterations or additions. There is, of course, a risk here that the notes taken by the gardaí may not fully and accurately reflect what the suspect said or meant to say. If the suspect is not fully alert to this danger his assent to the version read back to him may prove seriously prejudicial to his interests. Once the notes have been read over and any alterations and additions have been made, the member conducting the interview must record the time and switch off the equipment before removing the tapes. He must seal one of the tapes with a master tape label and give it an identification number. The same member must sign the tape label and ask the person interviewed to sign it. If the latter is either unable to sign or refuses to sign, the member in charge of the station must be called to the interview room and asked to sign the tape.[45]

---

[39] ibid. reg.2(1).
[40] ibid.
[41] ibid. reg.6(2)(a).
[42] ibid. reg.6(2)(b).
[43] ibid. reg.4(5).
[44] ibid. reg.12(1).
[45] ibid. reg.12(2).

Continuous Record

The primary purpose behind the recording of interviews is to secure an **6–08** accurate record of everything that was said and done during the interviews. The benefits of a complete audio-visual record should be realised in any context in which there is a dispute over exactly what happened in the interview room. The recording will offer independent and very persuasive evidence to support or refute allegations that a confession was concocted by gardaí, that the accused was subjected to duress or inducements to confess, that the accused was assaulted or, indeed, that the accused assaulted gardaí during the interview. This can be of vital importance where, as is sometimes the case, the accused and the gardaí offer conflicting versions of what happened in the interview room and there is no other independent evidence available. At common law tape recordings are generally admissible as evidence provided that they are shown to be both original and authentic.[46] It is also important to note that a failure to comply with a provision of the Regulations governing the electronic recording of interviews will not by itself render inadmissible as evidence anything said during the interview.[47]

Of course the value of the electronic recording, and the evidential weight to be attached to the tapes, will depend substantially on whether the tapes are a continuous and complete record of all periods during which the accused was interviewed. The 1997 Regulations leave some room for doubt on this score. It has already been noted that the electronic recording of an interview or part of an interview is not required in certain circumstances where the equipment is unavailable due to a functional fault, or is in use at the time or it is otherwise not practicable. The Regulations also permit the electronic recording to be interrupted where: (i) a tape requires to be replaced with a further unused blank tape; (ii) the equipment requires attention in order for the electronic recording of the interview to continue;[48] (iii) a break is to be taken in the interview; or (iv) the person being interviewed objects to the recording of the interview at any time after the preliminary procedures have been completed.[49]

Interruption to Replace Tape

The scope to conduct interviews or parts of interviews without electronic **6–09** recording inevitably creates the potential to undermine the value of recorded interviews. The 1997 Regulations attempt to counter this problem by prescribing a detailed procedure to be followed in each of the situations where the interview may be interrupted.

Where the electronic recording of an interview is interrupted because the tape needs to be replaced with a further unused blank tape, the member of the

---

[46] *R. v. Robson & Harris* [1972] 1 W.L.R. 691.

[47] Criminal Justice Act 1984, s.27(4). Also, a breach of the Regulations will not by itself render a person liable to civil or criminal proceedings.

[48] Where it is not practicable to recommence the electronic recording of the interview, there is provision permitting it to proceed without electronic recording; Criminal Justice Act 1984 (Electronic Recording of Interviews) Regulations 1997, reg.9(4).

[49] Criminal Justice Act 1984 (Electronic Recording of Interviews) Regulations 1997, reg.7.

Garda Síochána who is conducting the interview must normally, when the equipment indicates that a tape has only a short time left to record, inform the person being interviewed that the tape is coming to an end and record the time and reason for the interruption. He must also: switch off the equipment; remove the tapes; seal one of the tapes with a master tape label and give it an identification number; sign the master tape label and ask the person being interviewed to sign it also.[50] If the person refuses to sign the label the member in charge of the station must be called to the interview room and be asked to sign it.[51] Before recommencing the interview the member conducting the interview must unwrap the required number of unused blank tapes, load the equipment with the tapes and set the equipment to record.[52] All of this must be done within the sight of the person being interviewed. He must also remind the person that he has been cautioned. Where it is not practicable to inform the person being interviewed that the tape is coming to an end and/or to record the time and reason for the interruption at that point, the member shall do the following before recommencing the interview: unwrap the required number of unused blank tapes, load the equipment with the tapes and set the equipment to record.[53] All of this must be done in the sight of the person being interviewed. The member must also remind the person being interviewed that he has been cautioned and he must record the reason for the interruption, the duration of the interruption and the time at which the interview recommenced.

Interruption due to Equipment Fault

6–10 Where the electronic recording of an interview is interrupted because the equipment requires attention in order for the electronic recording of the interview to continue, the member must normally record on the tape the time and reason for the interruption if practicable.[54] He must then follow the exact same procedure as applies where the interview is interrupted in order to replace one of the tapes with a further unused blank tape (see above).[55] If it is not practicable to record on the tape the time and reason for the interruption before the interview is interrupted, the member must, within the sight of the person being interviewed and before recommencing the interview, unwrap the required number of unused blank tapes, load the equipment with the tapes and set the equipment to record.[56] He must also remind the person being interviewed that he has been cautioned, and record the reason for the interruption, the duration of the interruption and the time at which the interview recommenced. If it is not practicable to recommence the electronic recording of the interview in accordance with the procedure prescribed by the Regulations, the

---

[50] Criminal Justice Act 1984 (Electronic Recording of Interviews) Regulations 1997, reg.8(1).
[51] *ibid.* reg.8(2).
[52] *ibid.* reg.8(1)(f).
[53] *ibid.* reg.8(3). The Regulations give no indication of what is meant by "not practicable" in this context.
[54] Criminal Justice Act 1984 (Electronic Recording of Interviews) Regulations 1997, reg.9(1).
[55] *ibid.* reg.9(1)–(3).
[56] *ibid.* reg.9(3).

member conducting the interview must cause to be entered in the custody record of the person being interviewed a note setting out the reason for the interruption and why the prescribed procedures for recommencing are not practicable.[57] He may then proceed with the interview without the electronic recording.[58]

Interruption for a Break

Where the electronic recording of an interview is to be interrupted in order to take a break and the person being interviewed is to vacate the room, the member conducting the interview must: record that a break is to be taken and the reason for the break; record the time; switch off the equipment; remove the tapes; seal one of the tapes with a master tape label and give it an identification number; and sign the master tape label and ask the person interviewed to sign it.[59] If the person refuses to sign the member in charge of the station shall be called to the interview room and be asked to sign it.[60] Before recommencing the interview the member conducting the interview must, in the sight of the person being interviewed, unwrap the required number of unused blank tapes, load the equipment with the tapes and set the equipment to record.[61] He must also remind the person being interviewed that he has been cautioned. Where the member conducting the interview and the person being interviewed are to remain in the interview room during the break the member shall: record that a break is to be taken and the reason for the break, record the time and switch off the equipment.[62] Before recommencing the interview he must set the equipment to record, remind the person being interviewed that he has been cautioned and record the time at which the interview recommenced.

Objection to Recording

Where the electronic recording of an interview is discontinued because the person being interviewed objects to the interview being electronically recorded, the member conducting the interview must: record the time and the reason for the discontinuance; switch off the equipment if it is still recording; remove the tapes; seal one of the tapes with a master tape label and give it an identification number; and sign the master tape label and ask the person being interviewed to sign it also.[63] If the person refuses to sign, the member in charge of the station shall be called to the interview room and asked to sign it.[64] The mere fact that the person being interviewed objects to the recording is not in itself an absolute reason for discontinuing the recording. The member conducting the interview retains a discretion to continue with the recording.[65] It

---

[57] *ibid.* reg.9(4)(a).
[58] *ibid.* reg.9(4)(b).
[59] *ibid.* reg.10(1).
[60] *ibid.* reg.10(2).
[61] *ibid.* reg.10(1)(g).
[62] *ibid.* reg.10(3).
[63] *ibid.* reg.11(1).
[64] *ibid.* reg.11(2).
[65] *ibid.* reg.11(3).

is also worth noting that if the electronic recording is stopped for the reason that the person being interviewed objects to the recording, there is no provision for it to be recommenced.

Questioning without Recording

6–11 The Regulations do not impose a specific prohibition on the questioning of a suspect during any period when the electronic recording has been interrupted or discontinued. Indeed, it is clearly implicit in some of the situations where the recording can be interrupted or discontinued that the interview may continue or be recommenced without recording at a later time. There is no suggestion in the Regulations that any admission volunteered by a suspect during an interruption or after a discontinuance is inadmissible as evidence because it was not electronically recorded or was not first volunteered during a recorded interview. It can be expected, however, that the fact that a confession was allegedly made during a break in the electronic recording of an interview, in circumstances where the accused consistently denied the offence during the electronic recorded interviews, will provide indirect support for the assertion that the confession was not made at all or that it was involuntary.

The potential benefits of electronic recording will be seriously undermined, if not lost altogether, if there is scope for any party to interfere with the integrity of the tape after the recording. The 1997 Regulations include provisions which seek to minimise this risk. The member who conducted the interview must give the master tape to the member in charge of the station as soon as practicable after the conclusion of the interview.[66] The member in charge must see that a note is entered in the custody record of the person interviewed stating: that the interview has taken place; the date of the interview; that the member in charge has received the master tape; the date and time of receipt of the tape; and the identification number of the tape. It is not entirely clear where the master tape is kept, although the implication is that it remains in the custody of the member in charge of the station concerned.

Integrity of the Master Tape

The Regulations impose a specific prohibition on any person breaking the seal on the tape except: (i) at the written request of the person interviewed; (ii) pursuant to a direction given by a court; (iii) pursuant to a direction given by the Garda Síochána Complaints Board; and (iv) by a member of the Garda Síochána not below the rank of chief superintendent in the case of disciplinary proceedings.[67] If the seal is broken in any of these situations the person interviewed and/or his legal representative must be given the opportunity to be present at the time and throughout the period when the tape remains unsealed.[68] In their absence the seal can only be broken by a member of the Garda Síochána

---

[66] Criminal Justice Act 1984 (Electronic Recording of Interviews) Regulations 1997, reg.13.
[67] *ibid*. reg.15(1).
[68] *ibid*. reg.15(2).

in the presence of another member not below the rank of superintendent. The master tape must be resealed with a master tape label by the member in charge of the station, and the person interviewed and/or his legal representative must be invited to sign the tape label once it is resealed.[69] If the person interviewed or his legal representative refuse to sign, it shall be signed by a member of the Garda Síochána not below the rank of superintendent.

It is not entirely clear from these provisions how the contents of the master tape can be used during the period when the seal is broken. Presumably, they can be used as evidence in court, for the purposes of Garda complaints and disciplinary procedures and for the purposes of the person interviewed. Indeed, the only specific limitation on the use that can be made of the master tape while the seal is broken concerns the identification of the person interviewed. A tape of an interview which has been electronically recorded cannot be made available for the purposes of producing a photograph or other form of identification of the person interviewed, except with the written consent of that person.[70] Apart from that, however, it would seem that there is nothing to prevent the gardaí from making copies of the master tape and using those copies for their own purposes, so long as they comply with the requirements governing the breaking of the seal of the master tape and the resealing of that tape. In practice this should not be necessary as, presumably, the gardaí will have at least one working copy of each interview.

6–12

Custody of Tapes

The Regulations make no specific provision for the storage or handling of working copies of the tapes of interviews, apart from the provisions for the ultimate destruction of all tapes (see later). It is clearly implied that the working copies remain in the custody of the gardaí. The Regulations do not impose any restraint on their use of the working copies, apart from the prohibition on using the tapes to produce a photograph or an identification of the person interviewed without his consent. The person interviewed can also make use of the recording for his own purposes. He is specifically given a right to receive a working copy on submission of a written request from him or his legal representative to the superintendent of the District in which the interview took place.[71] However, the request can be refused where the superintendent believes on reasonable grounds that to grant it would prejudice an ongoing investigation or endanger the safety, security and well-being of another person.

Destruction of Tapes

There are limits on the Garda's power to retain the master tape and any working copies of an interview. The person interviewed can seek the destruction of the master tape and any working copies of the interview in the possession of the

---

[69] *ibid*. reg.15(3).
[70] *ibid*. reg.17.
[71] *ibid*. reg.16.

Garda Síochána. He can do this by applying to the superintendent of the District in which the interview took place after a period of six months from the date of the interview.[72] In this event the tape or tapes must normally be destroyed where criminal proceedings arising out of the interview in question have not been instituted against the person within the six months period from the date of the interview. Where proceedings have already been instituted within that period the tapes must normally be destroyed on request if the person is acquitted or discharged or if the proceedings are discontinued. However, irrespective of whether proceedings have been instituted within the six month period the superintendent of the District may authorise the preservation of the tape for a further period not exceeding six months where he or she is satisfied that it may be required for the purpose of proceedings.[73] Where civil proceedings are instituted before the tapes are destroyed there is provision for preserving the tapes until six months from the conclusion of those proceedings.[74] It is also worth emphasising that if the person interviewed does not make a request for the destruction of the master tape and working copies there is no obligation on the Garda to destroy them. Indeed, it would appear that the Garda have no power to destroy a master tape in the absence of a request from the person interviewed.

Where tapes are destroyed pursuant to a request, the person interviewed on the tapes, or his legal representative or a person authorised by him in writing to act on his behalf is entitled, on request, to witness their destruction.[75] The destruction of tapes shall be carried out by the effective removal of the electronic recording on the tapes.[76]

5. Interview Procedure

The Applicable Rules and Regulations

6–13 Rule I of the Judges' Rules confirms that there is no prohibition against a police officer putting relevant questions to any person in order to progress his or her investigation into a crime. It does not matter whether the person concerned is a suspect or whether he has been arrested. If he has been arrested, however, there are certain procedures which the police officer must follow. These procedures are laid down primarily in the Judges' Rules themselves and in the Criminal Justice Act 1984 (Treatment of Persons in Custody in Garda Síochána Stations) Regulations 1987.[76a] Certain provisions of the Criminal Justice Act 1984, the Offences Against the State Act 1939 or the

---

[72] *ibid.* reg.14(1). Where the tape(s) are being destroyed the person interviewed is entitled to witness the destruction on request; reg.14(2).

[73] *ibid.* reg.14(5).

[74] *ibid.* reg.14(4).

[75] *ibid.* reg.14(2).

[76] *ibid.* reg.14(3).

[76a] Breach of these regulations will not necessarily result in the exclusion of evidence obtained during the interviews; see, *e.g.*, *People (DPP) v. O'Driscoll* unreported, Court of Criminal Appeal, May 19, 1999; *People (DPP) v. Smith* unreported, Court of Criminal Appeal, November 22, 1999; *People (DPP) v. D'Arcy* unreported, Court of Criminal Appeal, July 23, 1997.

Criminal Justice (Drug Trafficking) Act 1996, as the case may be, may also be triggered by the circumstances of individual cases.

Preliminaries

Before commencing an interview the member of the Garda Síochána concerned must identify himself and any other person present by name and rank to the arrested person.[77] In addition, there is a general requirement that the interview should be conducted in a fair and humane manner.[78] The law on the admissibility of confessions (see chapter 9) plays an indirect role in prescribing what is fair and humane in this context. Apart from that, however, there is no prescribed list of factors which can be used to determine what is and what is not a fair and humane interview. This is hardly surprising given that the relevant circumstances can vary immensely from one interview to another. Nevertheless, the 1987 Regulations do specify a number of do's and don'ts which are explained below. Presumably, a failure to comply with any of these and/or the requirements of the Judges' Rules would be grounds for arguing that the interview was not fair and humane. Of course, the success of any such argument will depend not just on the content of the breach, but also the context in which it occurred. Moreover, it must also be pointed out that an interview which satisfies these requirements may still fall short of the fair and humane standard owing to the circumstances in which it was conducted. Where an interview is adjudged to fail the fair and humane test the officers concerned will be exposed to the risk of disciplinary proceedings. It will also enhance the argument for excluding any confession which may have been obtained during the interview. Apart from these possibilities, however, a finding that an interview was not fair and humane does not automatically trigger any legal sanction.

At the commencement of the interview the issue of a caution will arise. Rules II and III of the Judges' Rules require a police officer to administer a caution before questioning a person in two different situations. Rule II requires a caution before questions are put to a person whom the police officer has made up his or her mind to charge, while Rule III requires a caution before questions are put to a person in custody. On the face of it these two rules are very straightforward. Rule II deals with the person who has not been arrested but against whom there is sufficient evidence to charge, while Rule III deals with the person who has already been arrested. However, as Ryan and Magee point out these two Rules present immense difficulties of interpretation.[79]

The Caution

When Rules II and III were first introduced, it was not considered desirable for the police to interrogate an arrested person about his suspected involvement **6–14**

---

[77] The Criminal Justice Act 1984 (Treatment of Persons in Garda Síochána Stations) Regulations 1987, reg.12(1).
[78] *ibid.* reg.12(2).
[79] Ryan and Magee, pp. 116–119.

in the crime in question.[80] Confessions obtained by such interrogation, although prima facie admissible, were routinely declared inadmissible at trial.[81] Accordingly, it was normal police practice to postpone the arrest of the suspect for as long as possible in order to question him further about the offence. Once arrested the suspect would have to be charged with the offence and brought before a judicial authority as soon as reasonably practicable. It followed that, in some cases, there may have been scope for a gap between the moment a police officer made up his mind to charge a suspect and the moment that he actually arrested him.[82] Viewed in this light Rule II makes some sense. It requires the police officer to caution the suspect before asking him any further questions. Since the suspect had not been placed under arrest he might not have been aware of the gravity of his situation.

Rule II probably still applies in the situation where a member of the Garda Síochána is putting questions to a person in his own home or in some other such place.[83] It does not follow, of course, that a member must first caution a person before putting any questions in the course of his or her inquiries. The obligation to caution arises only when the member has made up his or her mind to charge the suspect. It is not enough that an intention to charge would be triggered if something of an incriminating nature were to emerge in response to questions being put. A conditional intention to charge is not normally sufficient to trigger the obligation. Nevertheless, the particular circumstances may be such that basic fairness of procedure will still require a caution to be administered even though the member of the Garda Síochána has not made up his mind to charge a person whom he or she is questioning. In *People (DPP) v. Breen*,[84] for example, a member of the Garda Síochána was having a general conversation with an accused whose lands were being searched at the time for hidden firearms. The accused became agitated in a manner which suggested that he was worried that firearms might be found. The member of the Garda Síochána asked him what was troubling him and if he wanted to talk about it. He did not, however, administer a caution before inviting a response. The Court of Criminal Appeal declared the resultant incriminating statements to be inadmissible. It considered that the member of the Garda Síochána ought to have appreciated in the circumstances that the accused was on the verge of admitting some involvement in the use of his property by subversives. Accordingly, basic fairness of procedure required

---

80 *R. v. Knight & Thayre* (1905) 20 Cox CC 711; *R. v. Reeson* (1872) 12 Cox CC 228; *R. v. Booth & Jones* (1910) 5 Cr. App. Rep. 177.

81 Ryan and Magee point out that there are dicta suggesting that Irish judges were adopting this line as late as the 1950s; see, *e.g.*, Judge Fawsitt in *People v. Lawlor* [1955–56] Ir. Jur. Rep. 38 at 41.

82 For a criticsm of the possible existence of such a gap, see Brownlie "Police Questioning, Custody and Caution" [1960] Crim. L.R. 298 at 307.

83 There is, nevertheless, some doubt about the admissibility of a confession obtained pursuant to such questioning even after the caution has been administered. See, for example, *R. v. Knight & Thayre* 20 Cox CC 711; *Lewis v. Harris* (1913) 110 LT 337; *R. v. Booth & Jones* 5 Cr. App. Rep. 177; and Brownlie, *op. cit.*, at 310–311. But, see judgment of the Court of Criminal Appeal in *People (DPP) v. D'Arcy* July 29, 1997 where it was accepted that the purpose of Rule II was to ensure fairness in the questioning of suspects who had not been arrested. Where such fairness was observed the Court did not envisage any difficulty over the admissibility of a resultant confession.

84 CCA, March 13, 1995.

that he should have administered a caution before inviting any admission from him.

It is unlikely that Rule II has much practical relevance today for persons being questioned in the Garda station. If a member of the Garda Síochána has made up his mind to charge such a person, then that person is considered to be in Garda custody, even if he has not been formally arrested.[85] Any further questioning of him on the offence in question, therefore, will have to be done in compliance with Rule III.

Despite appearances to the contrary, a caution under Rule III was not originally intended as a prelude to the interrogation of a person in custody.[86] Once a person had been taken into custody on reasonable suspicion of having committed an offence, the police were usually constrained in the extent to which they could question him about that offence. If they had sufficient evidence upon which to charge the person, they could not go beyond questions which were necessary to minimise harm to another person or to clear up ambiguities in any statement made by him. Moreover, by virtue of Rule III, the police would have to caution the person before putting such questions. As the twentieth century progressed, however, the police in both Britain and Ireland have resorted increasingly to the practice of arresting suspects well before they are in a position to prefer charges against them. The opportunity is then taken to build the case against an arrested suspect by questioning him in police custody. This practice has been encouraged and facilitated by the introduction of statutory powers which permit the police to detain the arrested suspect without charge in certain circumstances. The judges have also accommodated this development by quietly dropping their practice of excluding confessions obtained by questioning the suspect in custody.[87] This is vividly illustrated in an extract from Finlay P's judgment in *People v. Kelly (No.2)*[88] concerning the interrogation of the accused who had been arrested under section 30 of the Offences Against the State Act 1939. In challenging the admissibility of the accused's confession in that case it was argued that, apart from requiring an account of his movements under section 52 of the Act the gardaí in question had no power to interrogate him while he was being detained under section 30. In dismissing this proposition, Finlay P (as he then was) explained:

6–15

> "So to hold would be to create a uniquely anomalous position whereby a person arrested at common law under suspicion of having committed an ordinary offence could be questioned by the Garda Síochána and, provided due procedures and fair treatment were afforded to him, any answers he gave to such questions would be admissible in evidence against him, whereas a person arrested under section 30 of the 1939 Act (being a statute specifically enacted to deal with more serious crimes which tend to undermine the stability of the State) could not be so questioned."

---

[85] *People v. O'Loughlin* [1979] I.R. 85.
[86] See, *e.g.*, Home Office Circular 53605329.
[87] See Glanville Williams "Questioning by the Police: Some Practical Considerations" [1960] Crim. L.R. 325 at 331.
[88] [1983] I.R. 1.

The net result of these developments is that Rule III can now be given its literal interpretation. It stipulates that persons in custody should not be questioned without the usual caution being first administered. This suggests that when a suspect in Garda custody is about to be interviewed, the member conducting the interview must commence by reciting the caution to the suspect. Presumably, this will have to be done on each occasion that the suspect is interviewed while in Garda custody. It is not necessary, however, to repeat the caution parrot-like on every occasion in the course of an interview when the suspect is asked a question which may result in an incriminating answer.[89] However, any new situation which arises in the course of an interview, such as the entry of an accomplice into the interview room, should result in the suspect being cautioned anew.[90]

The Rules do not specify what form this "usual" caution should take. The clear implication, however, is that it should read;

> "Do you wish to say anything in answer to the charge? You are not obliged to say anything unless you wish to do so, but whatever you say will be taken down in writing and may be given in evidence."[91]

This formulation does not take account of the various situations in which a suspect in police custody is either obliged to answer certain questions or is at risk of having adverse inferences drawn from his silence at his subsequent trial. The Criminal Justice Act 1984, for example, makes it an offence in certain circumstances to refuse to answer questions about the unlawful possession of firearms or the possession of stolen goods,[92] and it provides for adverse inferences to be drawn at trial from the accused's failure to account for certain matters when asked to do so by a member of the Garda Síochána (see later).[93] There are similar provisions in the Criminal Justice (Drug Trafficking) Act 1996 and the Offences against the State Acts 1939–1998 (see later). Under these measure the offences can be committed or adverse inferences drawn, only if the accused persisted in his refusal or failure after he was told in ordinary language by a member of the Garda Síochána what the effect of his refusal or failure might be.

It follows that the suspect may not be wise to rely on the strict words of the caution. He may find that its content is heavily qualified, to the extent of being contradicted, by warnings given by the interviewing gardaí during the course of the interview.[94] This is hardly a very satisfactory situation.[95] Clearly, there is a very strong case for the wording of the caution to be changed to take account of the legal realities.

---

[89] *People (DPP) v. Morgan* CCA, 28 July 28, 1997.

[90] See, for example, *People (DPP) v. Buckley* [1990] 1 I.R. 14.

[91] The Garda Síochána Guide (6th ed., Incorporated Law Society of Ireland, Dublin, 1991) p. 103. Note the variation for interviews which are being electronically recorded; Criminal Justice Act 1984 (Electronic Recording of Interviews) Regulations 1997, reg.6(2)(a).

[92] Criminal Justice Act 1984, ss.15 and 16.

[93] *ibid.* ss.18 and 19.

[94] See, for example, *Quinn v. Ireland* (2001) 33 E.H.R.R. 264.

[95] In England and Wales, by contrast, the caution reads: "You do not have to say anything. But it may harm your defence if you do not mention when questioned something which you later rely on in

Charge and Caution

Where a suspect wishes to volunteer a statement while in police custody, the **6–16** combination of Rules IV and V suggests that he should be formally charged and then cautioned. The usual form of caution should be used with the last two words omitted. Care must be taken to avoid the suggestion that the suspect's statement can only be used in evidence against him. The statement need not necessarily be self-incriminating. Indeed, its contents may serve to clear him of the charge.

Once again it would appear that developments in police powers of arrest and detention sit uneasily with the strict requirements of the Judges Rules. Rules IV and V are clearly premised on the notion that the suspect will be in custody only if the police have either charged him or have sufficient evidence with which to charge him. The current reality is that such evidence will often emerge only during the questioning of the suspect in custody. If the suspect makes an incriminating statement in the course of that questioning the gardaí may stop at that point, caution the suspect and take a formal statement from him. Equally, they may continue the interview and take a formal statement after caution at the end. Either way, the value of the caution is called into question. The real substance of the incriminating statement will already have been given in the course of the question and answer session. Even if the suspect refuses to make a formal statement after caution, his incriminating answers in the course of the question and answer session will be admissible in evidence at his trial. It is arguable, of course, that Rule VI of the Judges' Rules deals with this situation. It stipulates that a suspect's statement made before there is time to caution him is not rendered inadmissible in evidence merely because it was not given under caution, so long as he is cautioned as soon as possible. This, however, was meant to deal with the situation where a suspect blurts out an incriminating statement on being arrested and before the police have had time to charge him. That is in a wholly different category from an incriminating statement which has been taken in the course of a police interview which may have lasted for hours and the object of which is to extract an incriminating statement.

Making a Written Statement

Rule IX of the Judges' Rules stipulates that, whenever possible, a volunteered **6–17** statement should be taken down in writing and signed by the person making it after it has been read to him and he has been invited to make any corrections he may wish.[96] This is interpreted as a requirement to take the statement down in writing at the time it was made. In *People v. Pringle*, O'Higgins C.J. explained that Rule IX was:

---

court. Anything you do say may be given in evidence. *The Detention and Questioning of Persons by Police Officers* (HMSO, London, 1995), para.10.4.

[96] It is also worth noting that the 1987 Regulations make provision for a record to be made of each interview. Presumably this will include details of any statement made by the suspect during an interview; The Criminal Justice Act 1984 (Treatment of Persons in Custody in Garda Síochána Stations) Regulations 1987, reg.12(11) & (12). See later.

> ". . . designed to achieve a situation in which (a) there would be accuracy in the recording of any statement made to be achieved by an early writing down of it so as to obviate errors of recollection and (b) in which an accused person would, at a time when he should have a sufficient memory of what he said, be given an opportunity of challenging the accuracy of the record made."[97]

However, if the person concerned has asked for a solicitor, the 1987 Regulations state that he must not be asked to make a written statement in relation to an offence until a reasonable time for the attendance of his solicitor has elapsed.[98] This, of course, could cause problems if the suspect is being detained under a statutory power and he indicates his wish to volunteer a confession near the end of the period for which he can be detained in custody without charge. If he asks to see a solicitor the taking of the statement will have to be delayed to give the solicitor time to attend. If the detention period runs out in the meantime the suspect will either have to be charged or released. Presumably, the police cannot take a statement from a suspect after he has been charged and while he is waiting for a District Court judge to become available, unless there is some urgent and overriding reason to take that statement, such as the situation in which the statement might enable the police to save the life of someone who is in imminent danger.

Even if the suspect's statement is not reduced to writing it does not follow that it will be automatically excluded in evidence. It will often be the case that the suspect will have made an oral statement before the expiry of the detention period. The courts have frequently rejected invitations to exercise their discretion to exclude oral statements on the basis that they were not reduced to writing and signed at the time they were made.[99] Moreover, the courts routinely admit in evidence incriminating answers made by the suspect in response to police questioning. When it is considered that the suspect will not normally have been cautioned immediately before giving such incriminating answers it becomes apparent once more just how far some of these Rules are removed from current reality.

The 1987 Regulations are clearly framed on the understanding that the suspect in police custody will be interviewed in a question and answer format before making a formal statement. To that extent they would appear to be out of step with the Judges' Rules. This apparent lack of harmony between the Rules and the Regulations was broached in *People (DPP) v. D'Arcy*.[100] However, the Court of Criminal Appeal in that case was of the view that there was no incompatibility. It considered that the Regulations were not meant in any way to deprive the suspect in police custody of any of the protections afforded by the Rules. The interviewing of the suspect under the Regulations would have to be done in accordance with the requirements of the Judges Rules. It must be said, however, that the judgment of the Court did not really

---

[97] (1981) 2 Frewen 57 at 98.

[98] The Criminal Justice Act 1984 (Treatment of Persons in Custody in Garda Síochána Stations) Regulations 1987, reg.12(6).

[99] See, *e.g.*, *People v. Farrell* [1978] I.R. 13; *People v. Pringle* (1981) 2 Frewen 57; *People v. Kelly* (No.2) [1983] I.R. 1.

[100] CCA, July 29, 1997.

address the key issue of whether the police could continue to question a suspect throughout the period of lawful detention in accordance with the Regulations so long as they postponed taking a formal statement until the end. In other words, how should the question and answer sessions be treated under the Judges Rules?

Cross-Examination on Statement

When a suspect in custody is making a voluntary statement, Rule VII protects him from being cross-examined on it. However, it is permissible to ask him questions solely for the purpose of removing any ambiguity in what he has said. An occasion for such questions would arise, for example, where the suspect mentioned an hour without specifying whether it was in the morning or the evening, or had given a day of the week and a date in the month which do not agree, or if he mentioned an individual whose identity was uncertain. In *People (DPP) v. McCann*[101] the Court of Criminal Appeal refused to accept that there was a breach of Rule VII where the accused's statement was taken by the interrogating officer asking leading questions. The Court adopted the trial judge's findings that this method had been adopted at the request of the accused and that the questions were put not for the purpose of cross-examination but for the purpose of maintaining direction and coherence.

Cross-checking Statements

Rule VIII imposes further restriction on attempts to probe the veracity of the suspect's statement. It stipulates that when two or more persons are charged with the same offence and their statements are taken separately, the police should not read one person's statement to any of the other persons charged. However, the police should give each person a copy of the statements made by the others and nothing should be said or done to invite a reply. Inviting a reply can result in any resultant statement being declared inadmissible.[102] If a person charged wishes to make a statement in reply, the usual caution must be administered.

Time Limits

The questioning of a suspect in custody will be influenced by limits on the length of time he can be held in custody and limits on the length of time he can actually be questioned. The Criminal Justice Act 1984 imposes time limits on the custody and questioning of persons detained under section 4 of that Act. More detailed restrictions applicable to all suspects who have been arrested and taken into Garda custody are laid down in the Criminal Justice Act 1984 (Treatment of Persons in Custody in Garda Síochána Stations) Regulations 1987.[103] They stipulate that an arrested person must not be

6–18

---

[101] [1998] 4 I.R. 397.
[102] See, *e.g.*, *People (DPP) v. Buckley* [1990] 1 I.R. 14.
[103] The Criminal Justice Act 1984 (Treatment of Persons in Custody in Garda Síochána Stations) Regulations 1987, reg.12(7).

questioned in relation to an offence in the period between midnight and 8 a.m., except with the authority of the member in charge of the station concerned. This authority can be given only where the suspect has been taken to the station during that period,[104] or where the member in charge has reasonable grounds for believing that to delay the questioning would involve a risk of injury to persons, serious loss of or damage to property, destruction of or interference with evidence or the escape of accomplices.[105] In the case of a suspect detained under section 4 of the 1984 Act authority can also be given if the suspect has not consented in writing to the suspension of questioning in accordance with section 4(6) of the Act.[106] The maximum period for a single interview is four hours.[107] It does not follow, of course, that an interview which lasts less than four hours cannot be challenged as oppressive. Much will depend on all the circumstances of the individual case. Any interview that has lasted the full four hours must either be adjourned or terminated for a reasonable time. The Regulations do not specify what might constitute a reasonable time in this context.[108]

It would appear that the four hour period is meant to operate as an absolute limit on the length of an interview. In *People (DPP) v. Connell*,[109] for example, the appellant had been arrested and detained under section 30 of the Offences against the State Act 1939 and was subsequently convicted of murder. On a number of occasions in the course of his detention he was interviewed for periods in excess of four hours. During one of these periods he made an inculpatory statement. He challenged the admissibility of this statement on the basis that, *inter alia*, it had been given at a time when he had been interviewed in a single interview lasting for more than four hours. The Garda evidence was to the effect that the appellant had been told on each occasion when the four hour limit had expired that he was not obliged to continue the interview and that he was offered the opportunity to rest which he declined. The Court of Criminal Appeal, however, ruled that the arrested person cannot waive the four hour time limit.[110] It is absolute. While the Court did not go so far as to rule that a breach of the time limit would in itself be sufficient to warrant the automatic exclusion of evidence obtained after the four hour limit had expired, it accepted that the breach could have that effect when taken in conjunction with other factors. In this case there were other factors including further technical breaches of the Regulations and a failure to deal properly with the applicant's request to see his solicitor. Accordingly, the Court ruled his confession inadmissible.

---

[104] This is subject to the requirement in reg.19(2) to the effect that a person in custody must be allowed such reasonable time for rest as is necessary; see The Criminal Justice Act 1984 (Treatment of Persons in Custody in Garda Síochána Stations) Regulations 1987, reg.12(7)(b).

[105] Where such authority is given, the fact that it was given, the name and rank of the member giving it and reasons for it shall be recorded; The Criminal Justice Act 1984 (Treatment of Persons in Custody in Garda Síochána Stations) Regulations 1987, reg.12(12)(b).

[106] *ibid.*

[107] *ibid.* reg.12(4).

[108] Reg.19(2) of the 1987 Regulations does specify that a person in custody must be allowed such reasonable time for rest as is necessary.

[109] [1995] 1 I.R. 244.

[110] See also, *People (DPP) v. Reddan and Hannon* [1995] 3 I.R. 560.

Provision for Deaf Persons

The conduct of an interview will have to take account of factors that affect the **6–19** suspect's capacity to understand what is being said. The most likely factors in this context concern the suspect's hearing ability, mental incapacity, age, familiarity with the English language and intoxication. The 1987 Regulations make provision for all of these impediments, apart from unfamiliarity with the English language.

Where the suspect is deaf, or there is a doubt about his hearing ability, and an interpreter is reasonably available, the suspect should not normally be questioned in relation to an offence in the absence of an interpreter without his written consent.[111] Any such consent must be signed by the suspect and be recorded in the custody record or in a separate document.[112] Even if the suspect does not consent, it would appear that questioning can proceed if an interpreter is not reasonably available. If, however, the questioning proceeds in circumstances where the suspect has requested an interpreter and one is not reasonably available, any questions must be put to him in writing.[113] The member in charge of the station can also authorise questioning in the absence of an interpreter and without the written consent of the suspect, if he has reasonable grounds for believing that to delay the questioning would involve a risk of injury to persons, serious loss of or damage to property, destruction of or interference with evidence or escape of accomplices.[114]

Provision for Children and the Mentally Handicapped

If the member in charge of the station knows or suspects that the person in custody is mentally handicapped, the provisions in the 1987 Regulations governing the questioning of persons under 17 years of age will apply, in addition to any other applicable provisions.[115] The Children Act 2001 also makes provision for the questioning of children in police custody. The provisions in question are almost, but not totally, identical to those laid down in the 1987 Regulations. The Act also makes provision for the Minister for Justice, Equality and Law Reform to makes regulations specifically for the treatment of children while in custody in Garda stations. Pending the making of such regulations it stipulates that regulations 9 and 13 of the 1987 Regulations apply to persons in Garda custody subject to the references to 17 years of age being changed to 18 years of age. The combined effect of these provisions is outlined below.

---

[111] The Criminal Justice Act 1984 (Treatment of Persons in Custody in Garda Síochána Stations) Regulations 1987, reg.12(8)(a). Where the suspect is under the age of seventeen years, the written consent of an appropriate adult is also required.

[112] *ibid.* reg.12(8)(b).

[113] *ibid.* reg.12(8)(c).

[114] Where such authority is given, the fact that it was given, the name and rank of the member giving it and reasons for it shall be recorded; The Criminal Justice Act 1984 (Treatment of Persons in Custody in Garda Síochána Stations) Regulations 1987, reg.12(12)(b).

[115] Criminal Justice Act 1984 (Treatment of Persons in Custody in Garda Síochána Stations) Regulations 1987, reg.22(1). The special provisions governing the questioning of mentally handicapped persons and persons under the age of 17 years apply without prejudice to the general provisions governing interviews; reg.13(5)(a).

Persons under 18 years of age cannot normally be questioned or asked to make a written statement in relation to an offence or be asked to make a written statement unless a parent or guardian is present.[116] Where a parent or guardian is not available, the questioning can only take place, or a written statement be taken, in the presence of another adult (not being a member of the Garda Síochána) nominated by the member in charge.[116a] Clearly, if the prohibition was absolute it could frustrate the questioning of a person under the age of 18 years where a parent or guardian was not reasonably available, or where the parent or guardian chose not to cooperate. Accordingly, the member in charge may authorise the questioning or the taking of a written statement in the absence of a parent or guardian where the member has reasonable grounds for believing that to delay the questioning would involve a risk of death or injury to persons, serious loss of or damage to property, destruction of or interference with evidence or escape of accomplices.[117] The 1987 Regulations stipulate that the prohibition on the questioning of a person under 17 years of age can also be overridden on the authority of the member in charge[118] where one of the following requirements are satisfied: (i) it has not been possible to inform a parent or guardian that the person is in custody, of the circumstances pertaining to the custody and that the parent or guardian should attend without delay;[119] (ii) no parent or guardian has attended at the station concerned within a reasonable time of being informed of the matters specified in (i) or (iii) it is not practicable for a parent or guardian to attend within a reasonable time. The current status of this provision in the Regulations is not clear. Section 61(1) of the 2001 Act imposes a prohibition on the questioning of a child in the absence of a parent or guardian. The only qualification to this prohibition is provided in section 61(2) which permits questioning in the absence of a parent or guardian where delay might involve

---

[116] Children Act 2001, s. 61(1). The Criminal Justice Act 1984 (Treatment of Persons in Custody in Garda Síochána Stations) Regulations 1987, reg.13(1). If the person is married, the references to a parent or guardian are deemed to be references to the spouse. If the spouse is either unavailable or is excluded from the questioning, the person concerned will be treated as an unmarried individual under the age of 17 years; reg.13(5)(b).

[116a] Children Act 2001, s.61(1)(b). It is also worth noting that a parent or guardian, at least for the purposes of the Children Act provisions can include an adult relative of the child, an adult reasonably named by the child (where the parent or guardian cannot be contacted or is refusing to attend at the Garda station) or an adult nominated by the member in charge; s.61(7).

[117] Children Act 2001, s.61(2). Since references to a parent or guardian in these provisions include references to an adult relative of the child, an adult reasonably named by the child and an adult nominated by the member in charge, it must follow that the child can be questioned alone when these circumstances arise. The Regulations, however, suggest that the member in charge is under a duty to ensure that a responsible adult, other than a member of the Garda Síochána, is present during the questioning where the parent or guardian etc is not present; see Criminal Justice Act 1984 (Treatment of Persons in Custody in Garda Siochana Stations) Regulations 1987, regs.13(2) and 22(2).

[118] Where such authority is given, the fact that it was given, the name and rank of the member giving it, the reasons for doing so and the action taken to secure an alternative parent, guardian or adult must be recorded; The Criminal Justice Act 1984 (Treatment of Persons in Custody in Garda Síochána Stations) Regulations 1987, reg.13(4).

[119] The circumstances pertaining to the custody refer to the fact that the child is in custody, the offence or other matter in respect of which the child has been arrested and his entitlement to consult a solicitor.

a risk of death or injury etc. It must follow that the additional circumstances in which questioning without a parent or guardian can proceed as provided for in the 1987 Regulations (at least with respect to a person under 17 years of age) are now defunct.

Even where the parent or guardian has attended at the station as requested there are circumstances where they may be excluded from the questioning with the authority of the member in charge.[120] This can only happen (i) where the parent or guardian concerned is the victim of the offence in question or has been arrested in respect of it; or (ii) where the member in charge has reasonable grounds for suspecting him or her of complicity in the offence or for believing that he or she would be likely to obstruct the course of justice if present during the questioning or that his or her conduct during the questioning has been such as to amount to an obstruction of the course of justice. It is uncertain in this context what actions on the part of the parent or guardian would be sufficient to give rise to a reasonable suspicion that his or her presence during the questioning would be likely to obstruct the course of justice. It is possible that advising the person concerned not to say anything would be sufficient.

The role of the parent or guardian etc in the interview is not specifically **6–20** defined in the Children Act or in the 1987 Regulations. Presumably, the purpose of his or her presence is to observe whether the interview is being conducted properly and fairly, and perhaps to help interpret anything said by the person in custody. Excessive intervention might result in his or her exclusion from the interview on the ground that he or she is obstructing justice. Nevertheless, at any point during the questioning he or she or the client can request the attendance of a solicitor.[121] Where he makes such a request, the child cannot be asked to make an oral or written statement in relation to an offence until a reasonable time for the attendance of the solicitor has elapsed.

Where the person being questioned in custody is under 18 years of age and is from a Gaeltacht area, or Irish is their first language, they are entitled to be questioned and to make a written statement in Irish. Any other child is entitled to make a written statement in Irish but can be questioned in English. There is no positive right for a person of whatever age to be questioned or to make a written statement in their first language where that language is not Irish.

Under the Influence of Alcohol or Drugs

A suspect who is under the influence of alcohol or drugs presents special problems for interviewers. Any incriminating statement obtained from such a

---

[120] Children Act, 2001 s.61(3) and (4). The Criminal Justice Act 1984 (Treatment of Persons in Custody in Garda Síochána Stations) Regulations 1987, reg.13(1). A record must be made of the fact that authority was given to exclude a parent, etc., from questioning, the name and rank of the member giving it, the reasons for doing so and the action taken to secure an alternative adult; reg.13(4).

[121] The Criminal Justice Act 1984 (Treatment of Persons in Custody in Garda Síochána Stations) Regulations 1987, reg.13(3).

suspect is liable to be challenged on the grounds of fairness or on the basis that it is unreliable. Accordingly, the 1987 Regulations stipulate that an arrested person who is under the influence of intoxicating liquor or drugs to the extent that he is unable to appreciate the significance of questions put to him or his answers should not normally be questioned in relation to an offence.[122] However, the member in charge may authorise questioning where he or she has reasonable grounds for believing that any delay would involve a risk of injury to persons, serious loss of or damage to property, destruction of or interference with evidence or escape of accomplices.[123] Moreover, it is worth noting that questioning is not prohibited merely because alcohol has been taken or drugs consumed. The acid test is whether the suspect is so affected that he is unable to appreciate the significance of questions put to him or his answers. It may be that a suspect brought into custody in such a state will have recovered sufficiently to be questioned before he must be charged or released (see Chapter 9, para. 9–53).

Written Record of Interview

The issue of making a written record of an interview with a suspect in Garda custody arises under both the Judges' Rules and the 1987 Regulations. It was seen above that where a suspect volunteers a formal statement after caution Rule IX of the Judges' Rules require that it should be taken down in writing and signed by the person taking it. Also when a caution must be given it is in terms that the person need not say anything but anything he does say will be taken down in writing and may be given in evidence. It does not follow, however, that the Judges' Rules require a complete written record to be made of everything said in the course of an interview. It is only necessary to record anything of consequence.[124]

The 1987 Regulations are more specific. They make provision for the keeping of records of each interview by the member conducting it or by another member who is present. A record must include particulars of the time the interview began and ended, any breaks in it, the place of the interview and the names and ranks of the members present.[125] Also, if the suspect makes a complaint during interview about his treatment in custody, the member concerned must include it in the record of the interview and bring it to the attention of the member in charge of the station.[126] Where the interview is not recorded by electronic or other similar means, the record must be made in the notebook of the member concerned or in a separate document.[127] There is no specific requirement for this written record to be a verbatim account of the interview. However, it must be as complete as practicable. Moreover, it

---

[122] *ibid.* reg.12(9).
[123] Where such authority is given, a record must be kept of the fact that it was given, the name and rank of the member giving the authority and the reasons for doing so; The Criminal Justice Act 1984 (Treatment of Persons in Custody in Garda Síochána Stations) Regulations 1987, reg.12(12)(b).
[124] *People (DPP) v. McKeever*, CCA, July 16, 1992.
[125] The Criminal Justice Act 1984 (Treatment of Persons in Custody in Garda Síochána Stations) Regulations 1987, reg.12(11) & (12)(a).
[126] *ibid.* reg.12(10).
[127] *ibid.* reg.12(11)(b).

should be made while the interview is in progress if it is practicable to do so and if the member concerned is of the opinion that it will not interfere with the conduct of the interview. In most cases this should result in a statement by the suspect being recorded at the time it was made. Where the record is not made during the interview, it must be made as soon as practicable afterwards. In any event, it must be signed by the member making it and include the date and time of signature.

C. Right to Silence in Police Custody

1. Constitutional Status

The interrogation of a suspect in police custody inevitably raises the issue of the extent to which the suspect is under an obligation to answer police questions. At common law it is firmly established that persons suspected of committing an offence enjoy an immunity from being compelled to answer questions while being interviewed by the police or others in a similar position of authority.[128] It would also appear that this immunity carries with it a correlative right to be informed of the general right to remain silent in the face of police questioning.[129] Although the immunity is commonly referred to as "the right to silence" it is in fact merely one of a range of immunities "which differ in nature, origin, incidence and importance" and which share the general designation of "the right to silence".[130] In *Heaney v. Ireland*, Costello J., referring to it as the suspect's immunity, explained its origins and nature thus:

6–21

> "The *suspect's immunity* was developed in order to avoid the risk of untrue confessions being obtained from a person while in police custody. The law does not prohibit a suspect from confessing to a crime – nor does it prohibit the questioning of a suspect in custody. It provides, however, that a suspect should not be required to answer questions on pain of punishment should he not wish to do so, and that he is free to remain silent should he so choose and that he should be informed of his right to do so."[131]

Indeed, the learned judge went further and declared that this particular immunity enjoyed constitutional protection by virtue of Article 38.1 of the Constitution which provides that "no person shall be tried on any criminal charge save in due course of law".

Costello J. found support for his decision in the immunity from being compelled to give evidence against oneself in a criminal trial:

> "This is an immunity long established in the common law world and has been a basic concept of criminal trials in this country for many years. It was enacted as the 5th Amendment to the American Constitution. It was declared in article

---

128 *R. v. Director of Serious Fraud Office, ex p. Smith* [1993] A.C. 1.
129 See Finlay C.J. in *People (DPP) v. Quilligan* (No.3) [1993] 2 I.R. 305 at 322.
130 *R. v. Director of Serious Fraud Office, ex p. Smith* [1993] A.C. 1. See also, *People (DPP) v. Finnerty* [2000] 1 I.L.R.M. 191.
131 [1994] 2 I.L.R.M. 420. See also, Lord Templeman in *A.T.and T. Istel Ltd v. Tully* [1992] 3 All E.R. 523 at 530.

14(8)(3)(g) of the UN International Covenant on Civil and Political Rights that in the determination of any criminal charge against him everyone shall be entitled not to be compelled to testify against himself or to confess guilt. It was provided in article 6(1) of the European Convention on Human Rights that in the determination of a criminal charge against him everyone has the right to a fair hearing and the European Court of Human Rights has construed that article as conferring on an accused person the right to remain silent and not to incriminate himself (see *Funke v. France* (1993) 16 E.H.R.R. 297). I am of the opinion that the concept is such a long-standing one and so widely accepted as basic to the rules under which criminal trials are conducted that it should properly be regarded as one of those which comes within the terms of the guarantee of a fair trial contained in Article 38.1."

The learned judge took the view that the fairness of a criminal trial can be compromised by what has happened prior to it. For this reason he considered that the suspect's right to silence in police custody could not properly be distinguished from the immunity against being compelled to give evidence at his criminal trial. Accordingly, the right to remain silent in police custody was a necessary incident of his right to a fair trial on a criminal charge as protected by Article 38.1 of the Constitution.

Costello J.'s decision in *Heaney* and his ruling that the right to silence in police custody has constitutional status was upheld on appeal by the Supreme Court.[132] However, the Supreme Court preferred to rest the constitutional foundation of the right to silence on Article 40 and the freedom of expression, as distinct from Article 38.1, as it considered that the right to silence was a corollary of the freedom of expression. It is also worth noting that the Supreme Court seemed to take a more restrictive approach to the right to silence, interpreting it as a right not to have to say anything that might afford evidence that is self-incriminating. In other words there could be no such thing as a constitutional right not to answer police questions which would not involve self-incrimination. Costello J., by comparison, seemed to be more favourably predisposed towards the argument that the right to silence was applicable to both the innocent and the guilty.

6–22   The European Court of Human Rights has also addressed the right to silence in police custody in the specific context of section 52 of the Offences against the State Act 1939 (see below), the very same provision which was at issue before the High Court and the Supreme Court in *Heaney*. The European Court of Human Rights was asked in *Quinn v. Ireland*[133] to rule on the compatibility of section 52 of the 1939 Act with Article 6 (right to a fair trial) and Article 10 (freedom of expression) of the European Convention for the Protection of Human Rights and Fundamental Freedoms. It dealt with the matter on the basis of Article 6 which guarantees to everyone charged with a criminal offence, *inter alia*, the right to a fair hearing and the right to be presumed innocent until proved guilty according to law. On the facts the Court felt that the

---

[132]   [1996] 1 I.R. 580.
[133]   (2001) 33 E.H.R.R. 264. This case arose from the same police investigation at issue in *Heaney*.

essential issues raised by the applicant's complaints could be considered under Article 6 and that Article 10 did not give rise to any separate issue.

Although it is not specifically mentioned in Article 6 the Court had no difficulty in finding that the right to silence and the right not to incriminate oneself "are generally recognised international standards which lie at the heart of the notion of a fair procedure under Article 6".[134] It also felt that they were directly applicable to the questioning of a suspect by the police:

> "Their rationale lies, *inter alia*, in the protection of the accused against improper compulsion by the authorities, thereby contributing to the avoidance of miscarriages of justice and to the fulfilment of the aims of Article 6. The right not to incriminate oneself, in particular, presupposes that the prosecution in a criminal case seek to prove their case against the accused without resort to evidence obtained through methods of coercion or oppression in defiance of the will of the accused. In this sense the right in question is closely linked to the presumption of innocence contained in Article 6 § 2 of the Convention. The right not to incriminate oneself is primarily concerned, however, with respecting the will of an accused person to remain silent."[135]

The Court emphasised that it was dealing with the situation where the suspect was being questioned by the police as distinct from the situation where the suspect was being compelled to provide material, such as documents or blood samples, which had an existence independent of the will of the suspect.

The European Court of Human Rights in *Quinn* acknowledged that the right to silence and the right not to incriminate oneself under the Convention were not absolute.[136] Similarly, both the High Court and the Supreme Court in *Heaney* were agreed that the constitutional right to silence, howsoever framed, was not absolute. Indeed, O'Flaherty J., giving the judgment of the Supreme Court, offered a selection of diverse legislative provisions which encroach in different ways on the right to silence. He went on to say:

> "This short analysis indicates the *ad hoc* and varied manner in which the legislation impinges on the right to silence. These statutes are as diverse as they are many. In light of the inconsistencies between each, it would be idle to engage in summarising or parsing the various statutes any further; however, they each serve to illustrate that in certain circumstances a person may be required to disclose information under threat of penal sanction. They evoke a legislative intent to abrogate, to various extents, the right to silence, in a myriad of contrasting circumstances."[136a]

Some of the encroachments are so important that it is necessary to examine them in a little more detail below, after first considering the scope and application of the general right itself.

---

[134] *ibid.*
[135] *ibid.*
[136] See also, *Murray v. United Kingdom* (1996) 23 E.H.R.R. 29.
[136a] [1996] 1 I.R. 580 at 588.

2. Scope and Application

6–23   The scope and application of the right to silence during questioning in police custody was addressed in some detail by the Supreme Court in *People (DPP) v. Finnerty*.[137] In that case the accused was convicted of rape. In the course of his evidence he gave an account of what had transpired on the night of the rape which totally contradicted the version given by the complainant. Counsel for the prosecution obtained leave from the trial judge to put it to the accused that he had not given this version of events to gardaí when he was held for questioning for a period of twelve hours pursuant to section 4 of the Criminal Justice Act 1984. It was also put to him that he had not made any statement at all to the gardaí during this period. In his charge to the jury the trial judge made no reference to whether the jury were entitled to take into account, when assessing the credibility of the accused's evidence, the unchallenged evidence of the gardaí that the accused had made no statement during the course of his detention.

Counsel for the accused applied to the trial judge to discharge the jury on the ground that the accused's silence while in detention had been brought to the attention of the jury in an adverse way. This application was refused and the accused was convicted. He appealed to the Court of Criminal Appeal primarily on the basis that the trial judge had erred in permitting evidence of his silence during police questioning to be put to the jury and in permitting him to be cross-examined as to why he had refused to answer questions during his period in police detention. The Court of Criminal appeal rejected his appeal but acceded to his application for a certificate of leave to appeal to the Supreme Court on a point of law of exceptional public importance. The questions to be determined on appeal by the Supreme Court were defined as follows: Given that the accused had put to the complainant on cross-examination a totally different account of what had transpired on the night of the alleged rape than the account given by the complainant, (i) was it permissible for the prosecution to elicit from members of the Garda Síochána who had interviewed the accused during his 12 hours' detention in the Garda station in the hours after the rape was alleged to have occurred that he declined to say anything during such interviews in relation to the complainant's accusations; and (ii) was it permissible for the prosecution to cross-examine the accused when he gave detailed evidence as to alleged consent by the complainant to everything that happened on the night in question as to why he had not given that account of events when interviewed by members of the Garda Síochána during his twelve hours' detention in the Garda station?

In answering these questions in the negative the Supreme Court surveyed the law on the right to silence in its application to the questioning of a suspect in police custody under section 4 of the Criminal Justice Act 1984. The Court drew attention to the tension between two competing principles which was evident in the history of the criminal law prior to the enactment of the 1984 Act.

---

[137]   [2000] 1 I.L.R.M. 191.

The first is the right and duty of the police to investigate crime of every sort in the interests of the community as a whole, and the corresponding obligation on citizens to assist them in that task. The second is the right of a suspect at a defined stage in the investigation to refuse to answer any questions, and the obligation on the police to inform him of that right through the means of the caution. This second principle was underpinned by the contents of the Judges Rules, the law governing the admissibility of confessions and the common law prohibition on the detention of a person for questioning. Prior to the Criminal Justice Act 1984, the police managed to circumvent the restrictions associated with the second principle by inviting suspects to accompany them to the police station to assist them with their inquiries and by creative use of the statutory power of arrest and detention provided by section 30 of the Offences against the State Act.

The Supreme Court perceived the Criminal Justice Act 1984 as something of a watershed. The policy behind the Act was to end the dubious police practice of inviting persons to the police station for the purpose of assisting them with their inquiries and the creative use of section 30. To this end the Act provided a power to detain persons who had been arrested for an offence which carried a possible punishment on conviction of a term of imprisonment for at least five years or a more severe penalty. The period of detention could then be used to facilitate the investigation of the suspect for the crime in question. This, of course, would include, questioning him. The Supreme Court also pointed out that the new power of detention and the consequent encroachment on the suspect's pre-existing rights at common law were balanced by the provision of express safeguards such as those set out in the 1987 Regulations on the treatment of persons in detention in Garda stations.

The Supreme Court went on to find that the 1984 Act did not modify in any **6–24** way the right of a person whom the gardaí suspect of having committed a crime to refuse to answer questions put to him by the gardaí and his entitlement under the Judges Rules to be reminded of that right before any questioning begins. The Court considered that this right would be significantly eroded if at the subsequent trial of the person concerned the jury could be invited to draw inferences adverse to him from his failure to reply to those questions and, in particular, his failure to give the investigating gardaí an account similar to that subsequently given by him in evidence. It would also render virtually meaningless the caution required to be given under the Judges Rules. The Court acknowledged that there are a number of statutory provisions, including some in the 1984 Act itself, which encroach upon the right to silence (see later). It found, however, that in the absence of any express statutory provision entitling a court or jury to draw inferences from silence during questioning in police custody, the right to silence prevails and must be upheld by the courts. Accordingly, evidence should not be adduced, nor should the accused be cross-examined, in a manner which brings to the attention of the jury that the accused remained silent under questioning in the police station. The Court summed up the relevant principles applicable where a suspect has exercised his right to silence while in police custody as follows:

"(1) Where nothing of probative value has emerged as a result of such a detention but it is thought desirable that the court should be aware that the defendant was so detained, the court should be simply informed that he was so detained but that nothing of probative value emerged.

(2) Under no circumstances should any cross-examination by the prosecution as to the refusal of the defendant during the course of his detention to answer any questions be permitted.

(3) In the case of a trial before a jury, the trial judge in his charge should, in general, make no reference to the fact that the defendant refused to answer questions during the course of his detention."[138]

It is worth noting that the Supreme Court offered this analysis of the law purely in the context of a suspect's right to refuse to answer questions put to him by gardaí during the course of his detention in police custody. It was careful to emphasise at the outset that it was not concerned with matters such as: the suspect's right not to give evidence at his trial; the admissibility in evidence of a statement made in the presence of a defendant accusing him of a crime upon an occasion which may be expected reasonably to call for some explanation or denial from him; the considerations which may arise where the accused denies the charge; and the admissibility of the response of an accused person following his being formally charged.

3. Statutory Encroachments

Introduction

6–25   There are many statutory provisions which encroach directly or indirectly upon the scope of the suspect's immunity against self incrimination.[139] Some of these have very little relevance in practice for the police questioning of a person who is in custody suspected of having committed a criminal offence. Accordingly, there is no need to deal comprehensively here with all powers concerned. The most important for the suspect in police custody are to be found in: the Offences Against the State Act 1939, the Criminal Justice Act 1984 and the Criminal Justice (Drug Trafficking) Act 1996. Broadly, they fall into two categories: those which make it a criminal offence to fail to answer certain questions or give certain information; and those which permit inferences to be drawn at the trial from the accused's failure to answer certain questions or to provide certain information. Many of the provisions in question are operative irrespective of whether the accused was in police custody at the time when he was asked the questions. In practice they are particularly relevant to the exercise of the suspect's right to silence when being interviewed in police custody. Accordingly, they are dealt with here, even though several of them are also particularly relevant to chapter 7 which deals with police powers of investigation apart from those associated with arrest, detention and entry, search and seizure.

---

138   [2000] 1 I.L.R.M. 191 at 208.
139   For an illustrative list, see O'Flaherty J. in *Heaney v. Ireland* [1996] 1 I.R. 580 at 587–588.

Section 52 of the Offences against the State Act 1939

Section 52 of the Offences Against the State Act 1939 imposes an obligation on persons detained under section 30 of the Act to answer certain questions concerning their movements and actions and their knowledge concerning the commission of any offence under the Act or of any scheduled offence. The full section reads:

> "(1) Whenever a person is detained in custody under the provisions in that behalf contained in Part IV of this Act, any member of the Garda Síochána may demand of such person, at any time while he is so detained, a full account of such person's movements and actions during any specified period and all information in his possession in relation to the commission or intended commission by another person of any offence under any section or sub-section of this Act or any scheduled offence.
>
> (2) If any person, of whom any such account or information as is mentioned in the foregoing sub-section of this section is demanded under that sub-section by a member of the Garda Síochána, fails or refuses to give to such member such account or any such information or gives to such member any account or information which is false or misleading, he shall be guilty of an offence under this section and shall be liable on summary conviction thereof to imprisonment for a term not exceeding six months."

The provisions have been qualified by section 13 of the Offences against the State (Amendment) Act 1998 which stipulates that a member of the Garda Síochána can demand from a person detained under section 30 a full account of that person's movements etc only if, immediately before the demand is made, a member of the Garda Síochána informs the person in ordinary language of the fact that the demand is being made under section 52 and the consequences provided by that section of a failure or refusal to comply with such a demand or the giving of any account or information in purported compliance with a demand which is false or misleading.

It is worth noting that the obligation to answer only arises when a person has been detained under section 30. It would not be sufficient that a person had merely been stopped or arrested under section 30. Moreover, unlike the powers to stop, arrest and detain under section 30 the power to demand answers under section 52 is only available to gardaí when Part V of the 1939 Act has been brought into play. For this to happen there must be in force a government proclamation declaring that the government is satisfied that the ordinary courts are inadequate to secure the effective administration of justice and the preservation of peace and order and that it is therefore necessary that Part V of the Act should be brought into force.[140]

In *Heaney v. Ireland*[141] section 52 was challenged on the ground that it breached the individual's constitutional immunity against self-incrimination which was implicit in Article 38.1 of the Constitution. Although Costello J., in the High Court accepted that the immunity against self-incrimination was covered by Article 38.1, he upheld the constitutionality of section 52.

---

[140] Offences against the State Act 1939, s.35.
[141] [1994] 2 I.L.R.M. 420.

Applying the proportionality test,[142] the learned judge noted that the primary object of the section was to assist the police in their investigation into serious crimes of a subversive nature involving the security of the State. Obviously this was an object for which parliament was entitled to legislate in a democratic State. Accordingly he concluded that the provisions of section 52 were neither arbitrary nor based on irrational considerations. Taking into account the other protections afforded a suspect in police custody under section 30, Costello J. went on to find that the restrictions imposed by section 52 impaired the suspect's rights as little as possible and, as such, their effects were proportional to the objectives which they sought to achieve.

6–26   Since the Supreme Court in *Heaney* based the constitutional status of the right to silence on Article 40 and the freedom of expression, as distinct from Article 38.1 and the right to a fair trial which found favour with the High Court, it is not surprising that the Supreme Court took a slightly different approach to upholding the constitutionality of section 52. Although it ultimately applied a proportionality test, the Supreme Court first considered whether the obligation to answer the relevant questions on pain of penalty could be justified on the grounds maintaining public order. It asked itself the question: "[i]s the restriction on the right to silence any greater than is necessary having regard to the disorder against which the State is attempting to protect the public."[143] It answered by finding that:

> "the State is entitled to encroach on the right of the citizen to remain silent in pursuit of its entitlement to maintain public peace and order. Of course in this pursuit the constitutional rights of the citizen must be affected as little as possible. As already stated, the innocent person has nothing to fear from giving an account of his or her movements, even though on grounds of principle, or in the assertion of constitutional rights, such a person may wish to take a stand. However, the Court holds that a prima facie entitlement of citizens to take such a stand must yield to the right of the State to protect itself. A *fortiori*, the entitlement of those with something relevant to disclose concerning the commission of a crime to remain mute must be regarded as of a lesser order."[144]

The Court concluded that there was proper proportionality in section 52 between the infringement of the citizen's rights and the entitlement of the State to protect itself.

In its decision in *Heaney* the Supreme Court expressly reserved its position on whether information obtained pursuant to a demand under section 52

---

[142] This is the test typically used to determine whether restrictions on the exercise of rights are permitted by the Constitution. Under this test, the objective of the impugned provision must be of sufficient importance to warrant overriding a constitutionally protected right. It must relate to concerns pressing and substantial in a free and democratic society. The means chosen must be rationally connected to the objective and not be arbitrary, unfair or based on irrational considerations. They must impair the right as little as possible and be such that their effects on rights are proportional to the objective. See *The Sunday Times v. United Kingdom* (1979) 2 E.H.R.R. 25; *Chaulk v. R* (1990) 3 SCR 1303, 1335–1336.
[143] *Heaney v. Ireland* [1996] 1 I.R. 580 at 590.
[144] *ibid.*

would be admissible as evidence in the criminal trial of the person who had given the information. The Court of Criminal Appeal in the earlier case of *People (DPP) v. McGowan*[145] had suggested that statements would not be inadmissible in evidence against a person simply because they had been obtained from him under a provision which made it a criminal offence to refuse to answer. More recently, however, the Supreme Court in *Re National Irish Bank Ltd and the Companies Act 1990*[146] ruled that a confession obtained from a bank official pursuant to a statutory demand by inspectors under section 10 of the Companies Act 1990 would not generally be admissible as evidence against the bank official in his criminal trial, unless the trial judge was satisfied that the confession was voluntary. Failure to comply with the statutory demand is a criminal offence. The Supreme Court considered that compelling a person to confess and then convicting that person on the basis of the compelled confession would be contrary to Article 38.1 of the Constitution. In the light of the decision in *National Irish Banks* it is difficult to see how information obtained from a person pursuant to a demand under section 52 would be admissible against him in a criminal trial for an offence other than that created by section 52 itself. The issue would seem to have been put beyond doubt by the decision of the European Court of Human Rights in *Quinn v. Ireland*.[147]

In *Quinn* the European Court of Human Rights held that section 52 of the Offences against the State Act infringed the right to silence and the right not to incriminate oneself as protected by Article 6 of the European Convention for the Protection of Human Rights and Fundamental Freedoms (see earlier). While the Court accepted that these rights were not absolute it felt that the terms of section 52 imposed restrictions on them which went further than was necessary to meet the legitimate interests of the state. In effect, section 52 left the individual with the stark choice of providing the police with what may be incriminating information about his movements or suffer a possible penalty of six months imprisonment. The Court took particular note of the fact that at the time the applicant was required to give an account of his movements there was considerable uncertainty in Irish law on the admissibility of any such account in evidence against him in a trial for an offence other than that created by section 52 itself. The Court of Criminal Appeal's views on the matter in *McGowan* had not been expressly overruled, the Supreme Court decision in *Heaney* in which it refrained from making any judgment on the matter was handed down a few days after the applicant's interrogation and the decision in *National Irish Bank* was not handed down until some years later. At the very least, therefore, the applicant could have harboured the fear that any answer he gave pursuant to the section 52 demand could be used as evidence against him on a criminal charge arising out of the investigation.

The Court also took account of the fact that the applicant was provided with conflicting information by the police in respect of his position. At the

6–27

---

145 [1979] I.R. 45.
146 [1999] 1 I.L.R.M. 321.
147 (2001) 33 E.H.R.R. 264.

beginning of each interview he was told that he had the right to remain silent. However, when the section 52 requests were made he was told that if he did not answer he risked six months' imprisonment. He was not told that any answers he gave pursuant to the section 52 demands could not be used in evidence against him. Indeed, the only information he was given on this matter was the general caution that anything he said would be written down and might be used in evidence. Moreover, it would have been difficult for the applicant to determine which questions related to the section 52 demands. Even the presence of the applicant's solicitor would not have remedied the situation:

> ". . . the position remained that the applicant had to choose between on the one hand, remaining silent, a criminal conviction and potentially a six-month prison sentence and, on the other, forfeiting his right to remain silent and providing information to police officers investigating serious offences at a time when the applicant was considered to have been "charged" with those offences and when it was unclear whether, in domestic law, any section 52 statements made by him would have been later admissible or not in evidence against him."[147a]

Given the uncertainty in which the applicant was placed with respect to the admissibility of any statement he might make under section 52, the Court concluded that degree of compulsion imposed upon him by section 52 was sufficient to destroy the very essence of his privilege against self-incrimination and his right to remain silent. Presumably the government will move to amend section 52 in order to remedy the infringement. One possibility, of course, is the addition of a provision, common to several other measures which compel persons to answer police questions in certain circumstances, but prevent answers being used as evidence against the individual in a prosecution for an offence other than that created by section 52 itself.[147b] There is no guarantee, of course, that such a minimalist amendment will be sufficient to satisfy the requirements of the European Convention for the Protection of Human Rights and Fundamental Freedoms. The Court in *Quinn* did not really address the issue of whether section 52 would still be flawed even if evidence obtained pursuant to it was inadmissible as evidence against the person concerned in a subsequent prosecution for an offence other than that created by section 52 itself.

Section 2 of the Offences against the State (Amendment) Act 1972

6–28   Closely related to section 52 is the provision in section 2 of the Offences against the State (Amendment) Act 1972 which makes it a criminal offence to fail or refuse to answer certain questions put by a member of the Garda Síochána who is investigating an offence scheduled for the purposes of Part V of the 1939 Act (scheduled offence). The requirements for this offence are

---

[147a] *ibid.*

[147b] For discussion on the *Quinn* case and its implications, see *Report of the Committee to Review the Offences Against the State Acts 1939–1998 and Related Matters* (Dublin, Stationery Office, Dublin, 2002), at para. 8–42 *et seq.*

that: a member of the Garda Síochána has reasonable grounds for believing that a scheduled offence is being or has been committed at any place; the member has reasonable grounds for believing that a person whom he found at or near the place at the time of the commission of the offence or soon afterwards knew of its commission; the member informed the person of his belief; demanded of the person his name and address and an account of his movements; and the person failed or refused to give the information or gave information which was false or misleading. Where these requirements are satisfied the person shall be guilty of an offence and shall be liable on conviction to a fine not exceeding £200 or to imprisonment for a term not exceeding twelve months or to both.

There can be little doubt that section 2 falls foul of the decision of the European Court of Human Rights in *Quinn* in so far as it seeks to penalise the suspect's failure to give an account of his movements at the time of the commission of the offence under investigation. Equally, in the light of the Supreme Court's decision in *Re National Irish Bank* it would appear that any information obtained from an accused pursuant to section 2 would be inadmissible in evidence against him in a prosecution for an offence other than that actually created by section 2 itself.

Section 30 of the Offences against the State Act 1939

Neither section 52 of the 1939 Act, nor section 2 of the 1972 Act, imposes an obligation on the suspect to give his name and address. That, however, is provided for in section 30 itself by giving a member of the Garda Síochána the power to require a person detained under the section to give his name and address.[148] Any person who fails to give his name and address in response to such a demand or who gives a false or misleading name or address is guilty of an offence which is punishable on summary conviction by a term of imprisonment not exceeding six months.[149] As with section 52, this power is only available with respect to a person who has been detained, as distinct from stopped or arrested, under the section.[150] Its constitutionality was challenged in *People (DPP) v. Quilligan (No.3)*[151] primarily on the ground that it infringed the individual's right to silence. The challenge was dismissed by the Supreme Court in a decision which was handed down prior to the High

---

[148] Offences against the State Act 1939, s.30(5).

[149] *ibid.* s.30(6).

[150] Note also that s. 7(1)(a) of the Criminal Law Act 1976 (as amended by Criminal Justice Act 1984, s.6(5)) permits a member of the Garda Síochána to require a person "in custody" under section 30 of the 1939 Act to give his name and address. Any person who obstructs or attempts to obstruct any member of the Garda Síochána in this matter or who fails or refuses to give his name and address when so demanded or who gives a name and address which is false or misleading shall be guilty of an offence and shall be liable on summary conviction to a fine not exceeding €1,270 or to imprisonment for a term of 12 months or to both. Since the maximum term of imprisonment under the comparable provision in section 30(5) of the 1939 Act is only six months, it is at least arguable that the member of the Garda Síochána requiring the person's name and address under either of these provisions would have to make it clear to the person under which power he was acting; see *Re McElduff* [1971] NI 1.

[151] [1993] 2 I.R. 305.

Court's decision in *Heaney*. The basis of the Supreme Court's decision was that the right to silence of the suspect detained under section 30 was protected to such an extent by law that the interrogation authorised by section 30 did not constitute an invasion of or failure to protect that right. The Court further held that there was no need to determine whether the right to silence or the protection against self-incrimination was an unenumerated right pursuant to the Constitution.

Name and Address under the Criminal Justice Act 1984

6–29   A person detained under section 4 of the Criminal Justice Act 1984 is under an obligation to give his name and address when demanded by a member of the Garda Síochána.[152] A failure to comply, or the giving of a false or misleading name or address, is an offence punishable upon summary conviction by a fine not exceeding €1,270 or imprisonment for a term not exceeding 12 months or both.[153]

Information about Firearms under the 1984 Act

The Criminal Justice Act 1984 makes it a criminal offence for a person to withhold information concerning the possession of firearms in certain circumstances. The offence can arise where a member of the Garda Síochána finds a person in possession of a firearm or ammunition. If the member has reasonable grounds for believing that the possession is contrary to the criminal law and informs the person of his belief, he may require that person to give him any information as to how he came by the firearm or ammunition.[154] This requirement can extend to any information as to previous dealings with the firearm or ammunition whether by the person concerned or any other person. Moreover, it can cover not only information in the possession of the person concerned but also information which he can obtain by taking reasonable steps.

If the person concerned fails or refuses, without reasonable excuse, to give the information or gives information that he knows to be false or misleading, he is guilty of an offence punishable on summary conviction by a fine not exceeding €1,270 or to imprisonment for up to twelve months or both.[155] Criminal liability can attach under this provision only if the person concerned was told in ordinary language by a member of the Garda Síochána at the time he was asked for the information what the effect of the failure or refusal might be.[156]

The obligation to give the information required under this provision is not confined to persons detained under section 4 of the Criminal Justice Act 1984. It can be used against persons detained under any police power. Indeed, it is not necessary that the person concerned should be in police custody at all. So long as the basic preconditions are satisfied a member of the Garda

---

[152] Criminal Justice Act 1984, s.6(1)(a).
[153] *ibid.* s.6(4).
[154] *ibid.* s.15(1).
[155] *ibid.* s.15(2).
[156] *ibid.* s.15(3).

Síochána can require the person to give the information whether or not the person has been arrested. Significantly, however, information given by a person pursuant to a demand under this provision is statutorily inadmissible in evidence against that person or his spouse in any civil or criminal proceedings, apart from a prosecution for the actual offence created by the provision itself.[157] It is less likely, therefore, that this provision would fall foul of the decision of the European Court of Human Rights decision in *Quinn*.

Information about Stolen Propery under the 1984 Act

A member of the Garda Síochána enjoys a similar power to demand information in respect of stolen property.[158] For this power to become available the member concerned must have reasonable grounds for believing that an offence consisting of the stealing, fraudulent conversion, embezzlement or unlawful obtaining or receiving of property has been committed. The member must also find a person in possession of property and have reasonable grounds for believing that it is or may include such property or the proceeds of such property or any part of the property or its proceeds. If he then informs the person of his belief, he may require that person to give him an account of how he came by the property.

6–30

Where the person concerned fails or refuses to comply with a request under this provision without a reasonable excuse, or if he gives information which he knows to be false or misleading, he will be guilty of an offence punishable on conviction by a fine not exceeding €1,270 or to imprisonment for a term not exceeding twelve months or both.[159] However, criminal liability can attach only if, at the time the information was demanded, the member of the Garda Síochána told the person concerned what the effect of a failure or refusal to comply might be.[160]

As is the case with firearms, this power to demand information is applicable whether or not the suspect is under arrest or is in detention at the time. Also, any information given by a person in compliance with a demand under this provision is not admissible in evidence against him or his spouse in any civil or criminal proceedings, apart from proceedings for an offence under these provisions.[161] Presumably this is sufficient to protect it against the fate which befell section 52 of the Offences against the State Act 1939 in *Quinn*.

Penalising Withholding Information about Others

A different type of provision which penalises a failure to give certain information is to be found in section 9 of the Offences against the State (Amendment) Act 1998 which creates an offence of withholding information. The offence can arise where a person has information which he knows or believes might be of material assistance in preventing the commission of a

---

[157] *ibid.* s.15(4).
[158] *ibid.* s.16(1).
[159] *ibid.* s.16(2).
[160] *ibid.* s.16(3).
[161] *ibid.* s.16(4).

serious offence by any other person, or in securing the apprehension, prosecution or conviction of any other person for a serious offence.[162] A person will be guilty of the offence of withholding information if he fails without reasonable excuse to disclose the information as soon as practicable to a member of the Garda Síochána.[163] He shall be liable on conviction on indictment to a fine or imprisonment for a term not exceeding five years or both.[164]

Clearly, this offence does not constitute a direct limitation on the suspect's right to silence during police questioning. It does not actually penalise the failure of a person to volunteer information about his own criminal activities. Also, it is not confined in its operation to persons who are detained in police custody. In practice, however, it is often used to force the co-operation of persons who are being detained in police custody; particularly those who are detained under section 30 of the Offences against the State Act 1939.

Adverse Inference from Object, Substance or Mark

6–31 Statutory provisions which permit inferences to be drawn from an accused's failure to answer certain questions put by the police in specified circumstances can have a significant impact on the suspect's right to silence in police custody. Such provisions are to be found in the Criminal Justice Act 1984, the Criminal Justice (Drug Trafficking) Act 1996 and the Offences against the State (Amendment) Act 1998.

Where a person is arrested without warrant[165] by a member of the Garda Síochána and there is on his person, clothing,[166] possession, or in the place where he has been arrested, any object, substance or mark or any mark on any such object, he may find himself under an obligation to account for that object, substance or mark.[167] This obligation will arise where the member reasonably believes that the presence of the object, substance or mark may be attributable to that person's participation in the commission of the offence for which he was arrested, and requests that person to account for the presence of the object, substance or mark after informing the person of his belief.[168] The obligation applies irrespective of which statutory power has been used to detain the suspect. Indeed, it is not even necessary for the suspect to be in detention at

---

[162] A serious offence in this context is defined as an offence for which a person of full age and capacity and not previously convicted may, under or by virtue of any enactment, be punished by imprisonment for a term of five years or by a more severe penalty. As well as satisfying these requirements it must also be an offence which involves loss of human life, serious personal injury (other than injury that constitutes an offence of a sexual nature), false imprisonment or serious loss of or damage to property or a serious risk of any such loss or injury, imprisonment or damage. Offences against the State (Amendment) Act 1998, ss.9(3) and 8.

[163] Offences against the State (Amendment) Act 1998, s.9(1).

[164] *ibid.* s.9(2).

[165] This provision applies to any power of arrest without warrant.

[166] The provision also applies to the condition of clothing or footwear; Criminal Justice Act 1984, s.18(3).

[167] Criminal Justice Act 1984, s.18(1).

[168] It would appear that it must be the same officer who affects the arrest, harbours the reasonable suspicion, requests the account and informs the person of the consequences of a refusal or failure to comply. However, there is no specific requirement that this same officer must actually discover the object, substance or mark.

all when the member requests the account. It is only necessary for him to have been arrested without a warrant for the offence which is connected with the object, substance or mark.

If the person concerned fails or refuses to comply with a request for an explanation of the object, substance or mark, and evidence of such matters is given in subsequent proceedings in respect of the offence,[169] such inferences may be drawn from the failure or refusal as appear proper in those proceedings.[170] In particular, the failure or refusal may be treated as corroboration of any other evidence in relation to which it is material, although a person cannot be convicted of an offence solely on the basis of an inference drawn from the failure or the refusal. Any such inference can be drawn only in cases where the accused had been told in ordinary language by the member of the Garda Síochána when making the request what the effect of a failure or refusal to comply might be.[171] It is worth emphasising that a failure or refusal to comply is not an offence in itself. Accordingly, the provision does not compel the individual to speak or to incriminate himself. Nevertheless, it does mean that a suspect in police custody may find himself in a situation where he has to make a difficult choice between remaining silent and offering an explanation for the object, substance or mark which has been found on his person, clothing or in the place where he was arrested. The option of remaining silent may not always be in his best interest.

Adverse Inferences from Presence at a Place

A person may find himself in a similar situation where he has been arrested **6–32** without warrant after having been found by the member of the Garda Síochána who effected the arrest at a particular place around the time when the offence concerned was alleged to have been committed.[172] If the member who effected the arrest reasonably believes that the person's presence there at that time may be attributable to his participation in the commission of the offence, the member may require the person to account for his presence after informing the person of his belief.[173] If the person refuses or fails to comply with the request and evidence of these matters is given in subsequent proceedings in respect of the offence,[174] then such inferences from the failure or refusal may be drawn as appear proper in those proceedings in respect of the

---

[169] In the context of an application for dismissal under Pt 1A of the Criminal Procedure Act 1967, evidence shall be taken to include a statement of the evidence to be given by a witness at the trial; Criminal Justice Act 1984, s.18(2).

[170] The inferences can be drawn where the court is deciding whether a charge should be dismissed under Part 1A of the Criminal Procedure Act 1967, or where it is determining whether the accused is guilty of the offence charged or of any other offence of which he could be lawfully convicted on that charge.

[171] Criminal Justice Act 1984, s.18(4).

[172] The offence for which the person was arrested and the "offence concerned" must be the same.

[173] Criminal Justice Act 1984, s.19(1). It would appear that the same officer must effect the arrest, harbour the reasonable suspicion, inform the person of his belief and request the account.

[174] In the context of an application for dismissal under Pt 1A of the Criminal Procedure Act 1967, evidence, for this purpose, shall be taken to include a statement of the evidence to be given in court by a witness at the trial; Criminal Justice Act 1984, s.19(2).

offence.[175] Once again, the failure or refusal may be treated as corroboration of any other evidence in relation to the offence, subject to the caveat that a person cannot be convicted solely on an inference drawn from the failure or refusal.

An inference can be drawn under this provision only where the accused had been told in ordinary language by the member of the Garda Síochána when making the request what the effect of a failure or refusal might be.[176] It would appear that the request for an explanation does not necessarily have to be made at the time of the arrest. It could be made subsequently during an interview of the suspect in detention, or at a later date. Indeed, there is no pre-requisite for the suspect to be detained when the request is made. It is only necessary that he should have been arrested without a warrant in the relevant circumstances.

Adverse Inferences under 1984 Act Not Obligatory

Just because the basic requirements for the drawing of inferences under section 18 or 19 are satisfied on the facts of a case, it does not follow that the court is obliged to draw inferences. It is merely entitled to draw such inferences as appear proper. Moreover, in deciding what inferences may properly be drawn from an accused's failure or refusal to give an account of the matter in question, the court is obliged to act in accordance with the principles of constitutional justice and having regard to an accused person's right to a fair trial.[177] It follows that the court is under an obligation to ensure that no improper or unfair inferences are drawn or are permitted to be drawn from a failure or refusal. So, for example, a court could refuse to allow an inference in circumstances where its prejudicial effect would wholly outweigh its probative value as evidence.[178]

Constitutionality of Adverse Inferences under the 1984 Act

6–33   The constitutionality of sections 18 and 19 of the Criminal Justice Act 1984 were challenged unsuccessfully in *Rock v. Ireland*[179] as an infringement of the individual's constitutional right to silence. The Supreme Court accepted that sections 18 and 19 constituted, in some respects, a more serious intrusion into the individual's right to silence than that posed by section 52 of the Offences against the State Act 1939. Nevertheless, applying the principle of proportionality in *Heaney*, it went on to hold that the restrictions on the right to silence imposed by sections 18 and 19 were no greater than was necessary to enable the State fulfil its constitutional obligations to protect citizens from attacks on their person or property:

---

[175] The inferences can be drawn where the court is deciding whether to dismiss a charge under Pt 1A of the Criminal Procedure Act 1967, or where it is determining whether the accused is guilty of the offence charged or of any other offence of which he could be lawfully convicted on that charge.
[176] Criminal Justice Act 1984, s.19(3).
[177] *Rock v. Ireland* [1998] 2 I.L.R.M. 35, *per* Hamilton C.J. at 47.
[178] *ibid* at 50.
[179] [1998] 2 I.L.R.M. 35.

"It is the opinion of this Court that, in enacting sections 18 and 19 of the 1984 Act, the legislature was seeking to balance the individual's right to avoid self-incrimination with the right and duty of the State to defend and protect the life, person and property of all its citizens. In this situation, the function of the court is not to decide whether a perfect balance has been achieved, but merely to decide whether, in restricting individual constitutional rights, the legislature have acted within the range of what is permissible. In this instance the Court finds that they have done so, and must accordingly uphold the constitutional validity of the impugned statutory provisions."[180]

In reaching this decision the Court was particularly influenced by the fact that a court was not obliged to draw any inference from the failure of the accused to co-operate with the police investigation in the manner required by the sections. Moreover, in deciding what inferences, if any, may properly be drawn, the court is obliged to act in accordance with the principles of constitutional justice. Equally, it must have regard to an accused person's entitlement to a fair trial and ensure that no improper or unfair inferences are drawn or permitted to be drawn from an accused's failure or refusal to co-operate with the police in the manner envisaged. Even where inferences are drawn, they amount to evidence only. They cannot be taken as proof of the guilt of the accused:

"If inferences are properly drawn, such inferences amount to evidence only; they are not to be taken as proof. A person may not be convicted of an offence solely on the basis of inferences that may properly be drawn from his failure to account; such inferences may only be used as corroboration of any other evidence in relation to which the failure or refusal is material. The inferences drawn may be shaken in many ways, by cross-examination, by submission, by evidence or by the circumstances of the case."[181]

It is worth noting, however, that the manner in which they are applied in any individual case could infringe the individual's right to silence and the right not to incriminate oneself as protected by Article 6 of the European Convention for the Protection of Human Rights and Fundamental Freedoms (see *Quinn* case discussed above and the cases discussed below at paras. 6–39 *et seq.*).

Adverse Inferences under the Drug Trafficking Act 1996

The Criminal Justice (Drug Trafficking) Act 1996 contains a more loosely framed inference drawing provision. It permits inferences to be drawn from the failure of an accused person to mention facts in certain circumstances where he subsequently relies on those facts in his defence in proceedings for a drug trafficking offence.[182] The failure to mention the fact must have occurred when the person was being questioned by a member of the Garda Síochána or a customs officer before being charged with the offence, or when he was charged or informed by a member or customs officer that he might be

---

[180] *ibid. per* Hamilton C.J. at 50.
[181] *ibid.* at 47.
[182] Criminal Justice (Drug Trafficking) Act 1996, s.7.

prosecuted for it.[183] There is no requirement that the person should be detained or be in police custody at the time when he failed to mention the fact. It is quite sufficient that the person was questioned about, charged with or informed that he might be prosecuted for a drug trafficking offence and failed to mention the fact in question at the time.[184] Where the failure arose during questioning by a member of the Garda Síochána or a customs officer at any time before being charged, the provision will apply only if the member or officer were questioning him with a view to ascertaining whether a drug trafficking offence had been committed or by whom it had been committed.[185]

An inference can be drawn under this provision only if the fact in question is one on which the accused relies in his defence and which, in the circumstances existing at the time, he could reasonably have been expected to mention when being questioned, charged or informed, as the case may be. Equally, it is a precondition for the drawing of the inference that the member of the Garda Síochána or the customs officer in question must have told the accused in ordinary language when being questioned, charged or informed as the case may be, what the effect of a failure to mention a fact might be.[186]

Where these conditions are satisfied and evidence is given of the accused's failure to mention the fact or facts in question, the court may draw such inferences from the accused's failure as appear proper when determining whether to send him forward for trial, whether there is a case to answer or whether he is guilty of the offence charged or of any other offence of which he could lawfully be convicted on the charge.[187] The failure may also be treated as corroboration of any evidence in relation to which the failure is material, although a person cannot be convicted of an offence solely on the basis of an inference drawn from the failure.

6–34   The impact of the drug-trafficking provision on the immunity against self-incrimination is clearly more substantial than the corresponding provisions in the Criminal Justice Act 1984.[188] The latter are confined to inferences which can be drawn from the accused's failure to answer specific questions put in specific circumstances by a member of the Garda Síochána. The former by comparison are much more open-ended. The accused himself will have to forecast what fact or facts he is likely to rely on in the event of being charged with a drug-trafficking offence, and then he will have to make a decision on whether it is in his best interests to volunteer those facts to the member or customs officer as the case may be. Given that this difficult mental exercise

---

[183] *ibid*. s.7(1). The provision applies to a customs officer only where the officer is participating in the investigation pursuant to regulations made by the Minister for Justice, Equality and Law Reform pursuant to s.6 of the Act.

[184] The provision does not apply in respect of a failure to mention a fact if the failure occurred before the commencement of the section on September 9, 1996; Criminal Justice (Drug Trafficking) Act 1996, s.7(4).

[185] Criminal Justice (Drug Trafficking) Act 1996, s.7(1)(a).

[186] *ibid*. s.7(2).

[187] *ibid*. s.7(1).

[188] It is important to remember that the provisions of the Criminal Justice Act 1984 also apply to investigations under the 1996 Act which lead to charges for drug-trafficking offences.

may have to be done in the pressurised environment of police custody it is not unlikely that the accused will be prone to errors of omission or commission. In other words he may simply forget to mention facts that he subsequently wishes to rely on in his defence, or he may end up giving much more information about his activities than is relevant to his defence against the drug-trafficking offence. This superfluous information may provide a basis for charging him with other offences which had not been under consideration by the police.

Although the inference drawing provision in the 1996 Act is expressly **6–35** triggered by a failure to mention, when asked, the facts which the accused subsequently relies on in his defence at the trial, it does not follow that an adverse inference cannot be drawn where he made some mention of the facts in question during the earlier police investigation.

In the Northern Irish case of *R. v. Averill*[189] the accused had been stopped by a police patrol about eight miles from the spot where a car which was used in a double murder one hour earlier had been set on fire. When asked to give an account of his movements at the time of the murders the accused stated that he had been helping two brothers with sheep on their farm in the vicinity. The two brothers corroborated this account. He was arrested and questioned further about the murders in police custody. He was specifically questioned about his movements at the time of the murders and the presence on his clothing and hair of fibres from balaclavas and gloves which were found in the car which had been used in the murders. He refused to answer these questions. At his subsequent trial he repeated in evidence his explanation that he was helping the two brothers with sheep at the time of the murders and added, for the first time, that he had been wearing a balaclava and gloves as protective clothing during this work.

In giving judgment following his conviction in Northern Ireland's no-jury "Diplock" court the trial judge explained that he had drawn strong adverse inferences from the accused's failure to answer police questions in custody. One of the inference drawing provisions which the judge relied on in the Criminal Evidence (Northern Ireland) Order 1988 is very similar to that in the Criminal Justice (Drug Trafficking) Act, apart from the fact that it is not confined to drug trafficking offences. The accused appealed on the grounds, *inter alia*, that the judge should not have drawn an adverse inference from his evidence as to his movements at the time of the murder as he had already given this account when stopped at the police checkpoint. Since he did not give it for the first time at his trial he argued that the requirements of the inference drawing provision had not been made out. In rejecting this argument, the Court of Appeal explained that the inference drawing provision was intended to enhance the police investigation and, as such, its invocation at the trial in response to a detailed defence could not be precluded solely by virtue of the fact that a broad outline of that defence had been given to the police at an early stage of the investigation. A persistent failure to elaborate on that

---

[189] Unreported, Northern Ireland Court of Appeal, January 3, 1997.

defence during police questioning could be sufficient to justify adverse inferences where the accused offers a much more detailed version for the first time in the witness box, and does not present a cogent explanation for his failure to provide this version under police questioning:

> ". . . [the inference drawing provision] is not designed solely to prevent a line of defence being produced for the first time at trial. It cannot have been the intention of the legislature that [the provision's] requirements would necessarily be satisfied by the bare recital of the bones of a defence. It is to be recalled that the purpose of the [provision] is to assist an officer "trying to discover whether or by whom the offence has been committed." Very often interviews of suspects provide the best setting in which to probe and test the authenticity of an exculpatory account. In our view it is inconceivable that [the provision] should not extend to the interview of a suspect who had given no more than an outline of a defence without any elaboration."[190]

It would appear, therefore, that an individual cannot necessarily escape the adverse inference provision simply by giving to the police a general outline of the defence which he subsequently relies on at his trial. If he refuses to respond to police questioning of his account and subsequently provides details at his trial which were missing from the version he gave to the police, the adverse inference provision may still be invoked. It will be a matter for the trial judge or the jury, as the case may be, to assess whether a sufficient account of the defence had been given during the police investigation. By the same token, however, the weight to be attached to any such inference will be affected by the quality of information given during the police investigation. The position is neatly summarised in the following quotation from the decision of the Northern Ireland Court of Appeal in *R. v. Massey*, another appeal from a decision of the no-jury "Diplock" Court:

> "Where a suspect says something at arrest or at interview it will be for the trial judge to assess whether or not it is a satisfactory early mention of the facts upon which he subsequently relies – if it is not satisfactory the trial judge may draw such an inference or inferences as may appear proper to him and the nature of such an inference may be governed by the quality of the information which was given at interview."[191]

6–36   A considerable body of case law has been built up on the interpretation of a very similar inference drawing provision in the British Criminal Justice and Public Order Act 1994.[192] Like the equivalent provision in the Criminal Evidence (Northern Ireland) Order 1988 it differs from the provision in the Criminal Justice (Drug Trafficking) Act essentially on the basis that it extends to other offences besides drug trafficking. Nevertheless, the case law might be considered a very useful aid to the interpretation of the provision in the

---

190   *ibid. per* MacDermott L.J.
191   Unreported, Northern Ireland Court of Appeal, January 17, 1995.
192   See, for example, *R. v. Cowan* (1996) 1 Cr. App. Rep. 1; *R. v. Argent* (1997) Cr. App. Rep. 27; *R. v. Roble* (1997) Criminal Law Review 449; *R. v. Daniel* (1998)2 Cr. App. Rep. 373; *R. v. Bowden* (1999) 1 W.L.R. 823; and *R. v. McGarry*(1999) 1 Cr. App. Rep. 377. See also the specimen jury charge drawn up by the Judicial Studies Board, 1999.

Criminal Justice (Drug Trafficking) Act. These cases establish that in a case where it might be appropriate to draw an adverse inference the trial judge should direct the jury that they should only draw an adverse inference from the defendant's failure to mention some fact or facts during police questioning if they are satisfied that the prosecution case against him is already sufficiently compelling to call for an answer by him. A defendant cannot be convicted solely or mainly on the basis of an adverse inference. Where this condition is satisfied the jury should consider the nature of the fact which the defendant has failed or refused to mention and the circumstances in which that failure or refusal arose before deciding whether to draw an adverse inference:

> "[Before drawing an inference the jury must be satisfied] that the appellant failed to mention a fact which in the circumstances existing at the time the accused could be reasonably have been expected to mention when questioned. The time referred to is the time of questioning, and account must be taken of all the relevant circumstances existing at the time. The courts should not construe the expression 'in the circumstances' restrictively: matters such as the time of day, the defendant's age, experience, mental capacity, state of health, sobriety, tiredness, knowledge, personality and legal advice are all part of the relevant circumstances; and those are only examples of things which may be relevant . . ."[193]

In making this determination the jury should apply their common-sense and experience:

> "Like so many other questions in criminal trials this is a question to be resolved by the jury in the exercise of their collective common-sense, experience and understanding of human nature. Sometimes they may conclude that it was reasonable for the defendant to have held his peace for a host of reasons, such as he was . . . worried at committing himself without legal advice, acting on legal advice, or some other reason accepted by the jury."[194]

Once again, it is worth noting that the manner in which these adverse inference provisions are applied in any individual case could infringe the individual's right to silence and the right not to incriminate oneself as protected by Article 6 of the European Convention for the Protection of Human Rights and Fundamental Freedoms (see the case law discussed below).

Inference Drawing under the Offences against the State (Amendment) Act 1998

6–37

The Offences against the State (Amendment) Act 1998 contains a very similar inference drawing provision to that in the Criminal Justice (Drug Trafficking) Act 1996. It permits inferences to be drawn from the failure of an accused person to mention a fact or facts in certain circumstances where he subsequently relies on that fact or those facts in his defence in proceedings for an offence within the scope of the provision.[195] The offences covered by the provision must come within one of the following three categories: an

---

[193] *R. v. Argent* (1997) 2 Cr. App. Rep. 27, *per* Lord Bingham C.J..
[194] *ibid.*
[195] Offences against the State (Amendment) Act 1998, s.5.

offence under the Offences against the State Act 1939–1998; an offence which is scheduled for the purposes of Part V of the Offences against the State Act 1939 and an offence which arises out of the same set of facts as an offence which would come within the first two categories.[196] Not all offences which come within one or other of these categories are covered. The inference drawing provision only applies to any of these offences for which a person of full age and capacity and not previously convicted could, under or by virtue of any enactment, be punished by imprisonment for a term of five years or by a more severe penalty.

For the inference drawing provision to apply, the failure to mention the fact must have occurred when the person was being questioned by a member of the Garda Síochána in relation to the offence at any time before being charged or when he was charged with the offence or informed by a member that he might be prosecuted for it.[197] There is no requirement that the person should be detained or be in police custody at the time when he failed to mention the fact. It is quite sufficient that the person was questioned about, charged with or informed that he might be prosecuted for the offence and failed to mention the fact in question at the time.[198] Where the failure arose during questioning by a member of the Garda Síochána at any time before being charged, the provision will apply only if the member was questioning him about the offence.

An inference can be drawn under this provision only if the fact in question is one on which the accused relies in his defence and which, in the circumstances existing at the time, he could reasonably have been expected to mention when being questioned, charged or informed, as the case may be. Equally, it is a precondition for the drawing of the inference that the accused was told in ordinary language when being questioned, charged or informed as the case may be, what the effect of a failure to mention a fact might be.[199]

Where these conditions are satisfied and evidence is given of the accused's failure to mention the fact or facts in question, the court may draw such inferences from the accused's failure as appear proper when determining whether there is a case to answer or whether he is guilty of the offence charged or of any other offence of which he could lawfully be convicted on the charge.[200] The failure may also be treated as corroboration of any evidence in relation to which the failure is material, although a person cannot be convicted of an offence solely on the basis of an inference drawn from the failure.

Given the basic similarity between this inference drawing provision and that in the Criminal Justice (Drug Trafficking) Act 1996 the issues discussed above with respect to the latter will also prove useful with respect to the interpretation and application of the former. Indeed, the Northern Irish case

---

[196] *ibid.* s.5(1).

[197] *ibid.* s.5(2).

[198] The provision does not apply in respect of a failure to mention a fact which occurred before the passing of the 1998 Act (September 3, 1998); Offences against the State (Amendment) Act 1998, s.5(5).

[199] Offences against the State (Amendment) Act 1998, s.5(3).

[200] *ibid.* s.5(2).

law on the Criminal Evidence (Northern Ireland) Order 1988 is particularly relevant here given the fact that it consists primarily of decisions of the no-jury "Diplock" Court. Likewise, the general inference drawing provision in the Offences against the State (Amendment) Act 1998, arises mostly in the no-jury Special Criminal Court.

Inference Drawing with Respect to Membership

The Offences against the State (Amendment) Act 1998 contains an additional **6–38** inference drawing provision which is confined specifically to the offence of membership of an unlawful organisation as created by section 21 of the Offences against the State Act 1939. It is framed in even stronger terms than any of the provisions described above. It permits inferences to be drawn from the failure of a person to answer any question material to the investigation of the offence when being questioned by a member of the Garda Síochána in relation to the offence at any time before the accused was charged with the offence of membership.[201]

The Act gives partial definitions of what constitutes a question material to the investigation and what constitutes a failure for the purpose of this provision. The former, at least potentially, covers much more than questions directed specifically at the accused's interactions with an unlawful organisation. It includes any question requesting the accused to give a full account of his or her movements, actions, activities or associations during any specified period.[202] The partial definition of a failure to answer is also quite broad in that it is not confined to maintaining silence in the face of questioning. It includes the giving of an answer or other reaction (or silence) which is false or misleading.[203]

The inference drawing provision clearly differs from the others in that its focus is not on the failure of the accused to mention a fact which he subsequently relies on in his defence, but on his failure to answer a question material to the investigation of the offence. Before deciding whether to refuse to answer any question the accused must make a judgement on whether a court will subsequently deem that question to have been material to the investigation. A wrong judgement call may result in the court drawing an adverse inference from his failure to answer. It is apparent, therefore, that this provision places a heavier onus on the person to answer questions relevant to the alleged offence during police questioning.

The accused need not be in police custody at the time of a failure to answer a question in order for this inference drawing provision to apply. It is sufficient that the failure arose when he was being questioned by a member of the Garda Síochána at some time before being charged with the offence.[204] The questioning must actually have been in relation to the offence of mem-

---

[201] *ibid.* s.2.
[202] *ibid.* s.2(4)(a).
[203] *ibid.* s.2(4)(b).
[204] The provision does not apply in respect of any failure to answer a question which occurred before the passing of the Act (September 3, 1998); Offences against the State (Amendment) Act 1998, s.2(5).

bership. Also, the accused must have been told at the time in ordinary language what the effect of his failure might be.[205]

Where these preconditions have been satisfied and evidence is given in any proceedings against the accused of his failure to answer a relevant question, the court may draw such inferences as appear proper when determining whether there is a case to answer or whether the accused is guilty of the offence.[206] On the basis of such inferences, the failure may be treated as, or as capable of amounting to, corroboration of any evidence in relation to the offence. However, a person cannot be convicted of the offence solely on the basis of an inference drawn under this provision.

4. The European Court of Human Rights and Adverse Inferences

The Murray *Case*

6–39 It is unlikely that any of these inference drawing provisions are *per se* incompatible with the European Convention for the Protection of Human Rights and Fundamental Freedoms. Circumstances may arise, however, in which they would infringe the individual's right to a fair trial. In *John Murray v. United Kingdom*[207] the European Court of Human Rights was called upon to consider the compatibility with the Convention of inference drawing provisions in the Criminal Evidence (Northern Ireland) Order 1988. The Court accepted that it would be incompatible with the right to silence to base a conviction solely or mainly on the accused's failure or refusal to answer police questions. However, it also accepted that there could be circumstances where it would be permissible to take the accused's silence into account in assessing the persuasiveness of the evidence adduced by the prosecution. Particularly important in this context is if the weight of evidence against the accused is such that an explanation might reasonably be expected:

> "The national court cannot conclude that the accused is guilty merely because he chooses to remain silent. It is only if the evidence against the accused 'calls' for an explanation which the accused ought to be in a position to give that a failure to give that explanation 'may as a matter of common sense' allow the drawing of an inference that there is no explanation and that the accused is guilty. Conversely, if the case presented by the prosecution had so little evidential value that it called for no answer, a failure to provide one could not justify an inference of guilt. In sum, it is only common sense inferences which the judge considers proper, in the light of the evidence against the accused, that can be drawn under the Order."[208]

Other relevant factors are: whether appropriate warnings have been given as to the effect of remaining silent; whether the accused understood the warnings; access to legal advice; and the fairness and reasonableness of the inferences which were actually drawn.

---

[205] *ibid.* s.2(3).
[206] *ibid.* s.2(2).
[207] (1996) 22 E.H.R.R. 29.
[208] *ibid.* at 62.

In the *Murray* case, the Court was satisfied that the circumstances were such that an explanation of his movements could reasonably have been expected from the applicant. He had been found by the police coming down the stairs of a house in which a person was being falsely imprisoned in a paramilitary type operation. However, the Court went on to find that it would be contrary to Article 6 to draw adverse inferences in this case as the accused had been denied the right to legal advice when deciding whether or how to respond to the police questions about his presence in the house:

> "The Court is of the opinion that the scheme contained in the [1988] Order is such that it is of paramount importance for the rights of the defence that an accused has access to a lawyer at the initial stages of police interrogation. It observes in this context that, under the Order, at the beginning of police interrogation, an accused is confronted with a fundamental dilemma relating to his defence. If he chooses to remain silent, adverse inferences may be drawn against him in accordance with the provisions of the Order. On the other hand, if the accused opts to break his silence during the course of interrogation, he runs the risk of prejudicing his defence without necessarily removing the possibility of inferences being drawn against him. Under such conditions the concept of fairness enshrined in Article 6 requires that the accused has the benefit of the assistance of a lawyer already at the initial stages of police interrogation. To deny access to a lawyer for the first 48 hours of police questioning in a situation where the rights of the defence may well be irretrievably prejudiced is – whatever the justification for such denial – incompatible with the rights of the accused under Article 6."[209]

It would appear, therefore, that permitting adverse inferences from silence in police custody will infringe the right to a fair trial under Article 6 if the individual was denied access to legal advice prior to his failure or refusal to answer the questions in issue.

The Averill Case

In *Averill v. United Kingdom*,[210] another case concerning the adverse **6–40** inference provisions of the Criminal Evidence (Northern Ireland) Order, the applicant had been denied access to a solicitor for the first 24 hours of his detention in police custody. During that period he refused to answer police questions about his movements at the time of a double murder and how fibres from his hair and clothes came to be found on a balaclava and gloves found in a car used by the gang who carried out the murder. After 24 hours he was granted access to his solicitor but he persisted in his refusal to answer the police questions about his movements and the fibres. In convicting him of the murders the trial judge made it clear that he drew strong adverse inferences from his refusal to answer the police questions. The European Court of Human Rights ruled that the adverse inferences were properly drawn in this case on account of the nature of the evidence which demanded an explanation from the accused, the fact that the accused did have the benefit of legal

---

[209] *ibid.* at 67.
[210] See also *Averill v. United Kingdom*, E.C.H.R. Application no. 36408/97 (June 6, 2000).

advice, albeit after 24 hours in police custody, and the lack of any cogent explanation for his failure to answer the police questions. Nevertheless, the Court continued to emphasise the importance to be attached to the right to silence and the need for adequate safeguards before adverse inferences can be drawn in a manner compatible with the requirements of Article 6:

> ". . . the Court considers that the extent to which adverse inferences can be drawn from an accused's failure to respond to police questioning must be necessarily limited. While it may no doubt be expected in most cases that innocent persons would be willing to co-operate with the police in explaining that they were not involved in any suspected crime, there may be reasons why in a specific case an innocent person would not be prepared to do so. In particular, an innocent person may not wish to make any statement before he has had the opportunity to consult a lawyer. For the Court, considerable caution is required when attaching weight to the fact that a person, arrested, as in this case, in connection with a serious offence and having been denied access to a lawyer during the first 24 hours of his interrogation, does not provide detailed responses when confronted with incriminating evidence against him. Nor is the need for caution removed simply because an accused is eventually allowed to see his solicitor but continues to refuse to answer questions. It cannot be excluded that the accused's continued silence is based on, for example, *bona fide* advice received from his lawyer. Due regard must be given to such considerations by the fact-finding tribunal when confronted with the possible application of Articles 3 and 5 of the 1988 Order."

The Condron Case

As indicated in the above quotation from the judgment in *Averill* prior access to a solicitor will not always be sufficient to protect the drawing of adverse inferences from silence falling foul of Article 6. The accused's explanation for his silence will also be relevant. In *Condron v. United Kingdom*[211] two drug addicts were convicted of supplying heroin after sachets of the drug were found in their flat. In accordance with the relevant British legislation they were warned during police questioning that it might harm their defence if they failed to mention anything which they subsequently relied on in court. Both accused replied "no comment". At their trial they claimed that the drugs were for their own personal use. They also stated for the first time that a packet which one of them was observed receiving and then returning to the occupant of a neighbouring flat contained either cigarettes or money. When asked why they had not given this information when being questioned in police custody, they explained that they had acted upon their solicitor's advice which was to the effect that they were suffering from heroin withdrawal symptoms and as such were not in a fit state to respond to police questioning.

In his direction to the jury the judge did not make it clear that they should not draw an adverse inference from the accuseds' silence unless they were satisfied that it could only be attributed to their having no tenable answer to the charge. The judge should have instructed the jury that if they were

---

[211] E.C.H.R. Application no. 35718/97 (May 2, 2000).

satisfied that the accuseds' explanation for their silence was plausible they should not proceed to draw an adverse inference from their silence. The judge's failure to make this clear to the jury fell short of the balance which must be struck between the right to silence and the circumstances in which an adverse inference may be drawn from silence. Accordingly, the applicants' convictions were in reach of Article 6.

5. Other Statutory Encroachments

In addition to the statutory encroachments on the right to silence as described above there are a large number of disparate statutory provisions which oblige **6–41** a person to co-operate with the police in certain circumstances. For the most part each of these measures have been introduced to deal with very specific situations. It is difficult, therefore, to generalise about them. Referring to them when delivering the judgment of the Supreme Court in *Heaney v. Ireland* Keane J. (as he then was) quoted with approval the following passage from the speech of Lord Mustill in *R. v. Director of Serious Fraud Office, ex p. Smith*:

> "These statutes differ widely in their aims and methods. In the first place, the ways in which the overriding of the immunity is conveyed are not the same. Sometimes it is made explicit. More commonly, it is left to be inferred from general language which contains no qualification in favour of the immunity. Secondly, there are variations in the effect on the admissibility of information obtained as a result of the investigation. The statute occasionally provides in so many terms that the information may be used in evidence; sometimes that it may not be used for certain purposes, inferentially permitting its use for others; or it may be expressly prescribed that the evidence is not to be admitted; or again, the statute may be silent. Finally, the legislation differs as to the mode of enforcing compliance with the questioner's demands. In some instances failure to comply becomes a separate offence with prescribed penalties; in others, the court is given a discretion to treat silence as if it were a contempt of court."[212]

While most of these powers can be exercised by the police in the course of questioning a suspect in police custody in the course of a criminal investigation, very few of them are confined to that situation. Most of them can be used by the police in the course of their inquiries. Accordingly, they are dealt with primarily in chapter 7. Apart from those which are discussed above other powers which are intended to be used primarily against persons detained in police custody are discussed below under the headings: Prints and Photographs, Forensic Samples and Testing for Alcohol and Drugs. It is also worth noting the obligation on a defendant to provide advance notice of an alibi in certain circumstances. This is dealt with in chapter 18.

---

[212] *Heaney v. Ireland* [2000] 1 I.L.R.M. 191, *per* Keane J. at 586–587, quoting Lord Mustill in *R. v. Director of Serious Fraud Office, ex p. Smith* [1993] A.C. 1 at 40.

D. Prints and Photographs

1. Introduction

The Statutory Provisions

6–42   Techniques for gathering incriminating evidence from a suspect have developed in recent years in line with scientific advances. Nevertheless, the long established techniques of fingerprinting, measuring and photographing still play a central role in the gathering of evidence. Fingerprinting a suspect without his consent is of course an unlawful trespass against the person at common law. In the absence of appropriate statutory authority, evidence obtained as a result would risk being excluded on the grounds that it was obtained in violation of the person's constitutional rights. While the measuring and photographing of a person without his consent is not *per se* unlawful, it could entail an unlawful trespass against the person if physical restraint was applied to facilitate it. It follows that specific statutory powers are required to realise the investigative and evidentiary potential of photographing, fingerprinting and measuring a suspect in police custody.

Distinct legislative provisions conferring powers to take photographs, fingerprints and palmprints are contained in the Criminal Justice Act 1984 (extended to the Criminal Justice (Drug Trafficking Act 1996) and the Criminal Law Act 1976 (applicable to persons detained under section 30 of the Offences against the State Act 1939). Which power applies in any given situation will depend on the power under which the person in question has been detained. It is also worth taking note of the Measuring and Photography of Prisoners Regulations 1955 which are aimed at persons who have been remanded in custody or imprisoned pursuant to a judicial order.

Proving Prints, etc., by Certificate

It is worth noting at the outset that where an enactment confers a power to take the fingerprints or palmprints of any person, it includes the power to record an image of that person's fingerprints or palmprints by electronic means or in any other manner.[213] Also, a photograph of a person or an image of any fingerprint or palmprint of a person which is attached to or contained in a certificate stating that it is the photograph or image of the fingerprint or palmprint, as the case may be, of the person specified in the certificate can be accepted as evidence of the fact stated.[214] For this to happen the photograph or image must be attached to or contained in the certificate, and the certificate must purport to be signed by the member who took the photograph or recorded the image, as the case may be, and it must state that it was taken or recorded by the member in question. Where these requirements are satisfied the certificate shall, unless the contrary is proved, be evidence of the matters stated in it. Given the wording of the statutory provision it would appear that

---

[213]   Criminal Justice (Miscellaneous Provisions) Act 1997, s.11(1).
[214]   *ibid.* s.11(2).

so long as the certificate purports to be signed by the person who took the photograph and/or recorded the image it is not necessary for the signature to be proved, unless evidence is given to the effect that it is not the signature of that person or that the signature is not that of the person who took the photograph or recorded the image.

2. General Statutory Authority

Power to Take Prints, etc.

Where the suspect in police custody has been detained pursuant to section 4 **6–43** of the Criminal Justice Act 1984 or section 2 of the Criminal Justice (Drug Trafficking) Act 1996, he may be photographed, fingerprinted and palm-printed, but only on the authority of a member of the Garda Síochána not below the rank of Superintendent.[215] There is no requirement to secure the prior consent of the suspect. Any person who obstructs or attempts to obstruct any member of the Garda Síochána or any other person acting under this power shall be guilty of an offence and shall be liable on conviction to a fine not exceeding €1,270 or to imprisonment for a term not exceeding 12 months or to both.[216]

Destruction of Prints, etc.

The infringement of privacy and civil liberties inherent in this power is **6–44** softened by provision for the destruction of the records in certain circumstances. All photographs, fingerprints and palm-prints taken from a suspect in police custody pursuant to this power (including all copies, records and negatives) must be destroyed where proceedings for an offence within the scope of section 4 of the 1984 Act (this includes a drug trafficking offence) are not instituted within a period of six months from the date of taking the photograph or print.[217] This does not apply if the failure to institute proceedings is due to the fact that the suspect has absconded or cannot be found. Where proceedings have been instituted for a relevant offence and the accused is acquitted or discharged, or the proceedings are discontinued, the destruction must be carried out on the acquittal, discharge or discontinuance.[218] The person concerned has the right to witness the actual destruction on request.[219] The destruction can be witnessed in person, or by his solicitor or by some person authorised by him in writing to act on his behalf.

---

[215] Criminal Justice Act 1984, s.6(1)(c), 6(1)(d) and 6(2) and Criminal Justice (Drug Trafficking) Act 1996, s.5.

[216] Criminal Justice Act 1984, s.6(4) and Criminal Justice (Drug Trafficking) Act 1996, s.5.

[217] Criminal Justice Act 1984, s.8(2) and Criminal Justice (Drug Trafficking) Act 1996, s.5. It is worth noting that the institution of proceedings for an offence which is not within the scope of section 4 of the 1984 Act will not stop time running for this purpose.

[218] Criminal Justice Act 1984, s. 8(3) and Criminal Justice (Drug Trafficking) Act 1996, s.5. Where the person in question is the subject of an order under s.1(1) or 1(2) of the Probation of Offenders Act 1907, the destruction shall be carried out at the expiration of three years from the making of the order provided that he or she has not been charged with an offence during that period; s.8(4)(a). This does not apply where the order is discharged on appeal against conviction where the conviction itself is affirmed; s.8(4)(b) of the 1984 Act and s.5 of the 1996 Act.

[219] Criminal Justice Act 1984, s.8(5) and Criminal Justice (Drug Trafficking) Act 1996, s.5.

There are two situations in which the destruction may be delayed. First, before the expiry of the six month period a party to civil proceedings may serve notice on the Commissioner that the photograph or print may be required in connection with the proceedings. In this event the photograph or print must be preserved until six months after the conclusion of the civil proceedings or until the conclusion of any proceedings on appeal, whichever is later.[220] Second, a District Court judge has an overriding power, exercisable on the application of the DPP, to authorise the preservation of a photograph or print for a period not exceeding six months on being satisfied that it may be required for the purpose of further proceedings in relation to the offence.[221] It is worth noting that this provision does not envisage the preservation of the photograph or print for use against the accused for any other offence.

Measurement

There are no specific provisions in the 1984 Act or the 1996 Act for the measurement of suspects in police custody.

3. Section 30 of the Offences Against the State Act 1939

6–45   The police powers to photograph, fingerprint and palm-print a suspect in their custody pursuant to section 30 of the Offences Against the State Act 1939 are identical to those for suspects detained under section 4 of the 1984 Act or section 2 of the 1996 Act.[222] In the case of section 30 suspects, however, there is no provision for the destruction of the photographs or prints. The clear implication is that they can be retained even if the suspect is released without charge, or if he is acquitted or discharged in related criminal proceedings. This may raise an issue of privacy under the Constitution and the European Convention for the Protection of Human Rights and Fundamental Freedoms. As with persons detained under section 4 of the 1984 Act and section 2 of the 1996 Act, there is no specific statutory provision for taking measurements of persons detained under section 30 of the 1939 Act.

4. Taking Prints, etc., from Prisoners and Offenders

Introduction

6–46   A suspect cannot be fingerprinted or palmprinted without his consent, except in accordance with those provisions of the Criminal Justice Act 1984 and the Criminal Law Act 1976 which deal with the photographing, fingerprinting and palmprinting of suspects detained under section 4 of the Criminal Justice Act 1984, section 2 of the Criminal Justice (Drug Trafficking) Act 1996 or section 30 of the Offences against the State Act 1939. There are, however, provisions for photographing, fingerprinting and palmprinting persons without their

---

[220]   *ibid.* s.8(6) and *ibid.* s.5.
[221]   *ibid.* s.8(7) and *ibid.* s.5.
[222]   See Criminal Law Act 1976, s.7 as amended by Criminal Justice Act 1984, ss.6(5) and 9.

consent in certain circumstances where they have been charged and remanded in custody and where they have been convicted of an offence or made the subject of a probation order.

Remand Prisoners

The Measuring and Photography of Prisoners Regulations 1955 stipulate that a person who has been charged and remanded in custody can be photographed, fingerprinted, palmprinted and his height measured on the written application of a member of the Garda Síochána not below the rank of inspector, so long as the person does not object.[223] The person must be informed of his right to object, but it seems that there is no obligation to administer a caution.[224] If the person does object, he can still be photographed, fingerprinted and palm-printed on the authority of the Minister for Justice, Equality and Law Reform, or upon the written application of a member of the Garda Síochána not below the rank of inspector approved by a District Court judge.[225] The application must make out a case for taking the photograph or prints. It must state that from the character of the offence or for other specified reasons there are grounds for suspecting that the person has been convicted previously or has been engaged in crime, or that for other specified reasons the photograph or prints are required for the purpose of justice.[226] If the charges are dropped against the prisoner, or he is acquitted, the prints, etc., are handed over to him on discharge.

Persons Convicted, etc., of an Indictable Offence

The Criminal Justice Act 1984 makes further provision for the taking of the fingerprints, palmprints and photograph of a person who has been processed through the criminal justice system.[227] It applies to a person who has been prosecuted for an indictable offence and made the subject of a probation order under section 1(1) or 1(2) of the Probation of Offenders Act 1907 or is convicted of such an offence and is dealt with in some other way. The offence must be an indictable offence, although it could be dealt with summarily. Where these requirements are satisfied a member of the Garda Síochána may, at any convenient place, take the fingerprints, palmprints or photograph of the person within seven days of the making of the probation order or the conviction, as the case may be.[228] Equally, he may require the person to attend, within seven days of the making of the order or the conviction, at a named

6–47

---

[223] Measuring and Photography of Prisoners Regulations 1955, reg.4. *People (Attorney General) v. Mc Grath* (1965) 99 I.L.T.R. 59.

[224] *People v. Walsh* [1980] I.R. 294 (SC); but see *People v. Lawlor* [1955–56] Ir. Jur. Rep. 38.

[225] Measuring and Photography of Prisoners Regulations 1955, r.4(1). In the Dublin Metropolitan district, the approval can be given by a Commissioner or Deputy Commissioner of the Garda Síochána.

[226] Measuring and Photography of Prisoners Regulations 1955, r.4(2).

[227] Criminal Justice Act 1984, s.28, as substituted by Criminal Justice (Miscellaneous Provisions) Act 1997, s.12.

[228] *ibid.* s.28(1)(a). There is no definition of what constitutes a convenient place for this purpose. The original version specified the precincts of the court or any other convenient place. Presumably, it would include a Garda station and a prison.

Garda station for the purpose of having his fingerprints, palmprints or photograph taken.[229] Such a requirement must be made in writing. Where a person attends a Garda station pursuant to a requirement under this provision a member of the Garda Síochána may take his fingerprints, palmprints or photograph.[230] Any person who refuses to comply with a requirement under these provisions, or who refuses to allow his fingerprints, palmprints or photograph to be taken pursuant to them shall be guilty of an offence and shall be liable on summary conviction to a fine not exceeding €1,905 or to imprisonment for a term not exceeding 12 months or both.[231]

Where a person has made it impracticable for his fingerprints, palmprints or photograph to be taken within this period of seven days, a member of the Garda Síochána may require that person to attend at a named Garda station on a specified day for the purpose of having his fingerprints, palmprints or photograph taken.[232] Such a requirement must be made in writing. The wording of these provisions would suggest that if the fingerprints, palmprints or photograph have not been taken within the seven day period, and nothing that the accused has done has rendered it impracticable to take them within the seven day period, they cannot be taken pursuant to these provisions.

There is provision for the subsequent destruction of the fingerprints, plamprints and photographs taken under these provisions in respect of a person by reason of the fact that he was the subject of a probation order. In this event they must be destroyed at the expiration of three years from the making of the order, provided that he has not been charged with an offence during that period.[233] It would appear that the fingerprints, palmprints or photograph do not have to be destroyed in accordance with this provision if, on appeal against a probation order made under section 1(2) of the Probation of Offenders Act 1907, the order was discharged and the conviction affirmed.[234] There is provision for a stay on destruction in certain circumstances. Where civil proceedings are instituted before the photograph or print is required to be destroyed and a party to the proceedings serves notice on the Garda Commissioner that it may be required in connection with the proceedings, the photograph or print shall be preserved until six months from the conclusion of the proceedings or until the conclusion of any proceedings on appeal, whichever is the later.[235] Also, a District Court judge may, on the application of the DPP, authorise the preservation of a photograph or print for a period not exceeding six months where he is satisfied that it may be required for the purpose of further proceedings for the offence.[236]

Where fingerprints, palmprints or photographs are being destroyed under these provisions, the person concerned, his solicitor or some other person

---

[229]   *ibid.* s.28(1)(b).
[230]   *ibid.* s.28(2).
[231]   *ibid.* s.28(4).
[232]   *ibid.* s.28(1).
[233]   *ibid.* s.8(4)(a), as applied by s.28(3).
[234]   *ibid.* s.8(4)(b), as applied by s.28(3).
[235]   *ibid.* s.8(6), as applied by s.28(3).
[236]   *ibid.* s.8(7), as applied by s.28(3).

authorised in writing to act on his behalf is entitled, on request, to witness the destruction.[237]

There is no provision for the destruction of the prints taken from the accused who has been convicted and dealt with in some other way.

Convicted Prisoners

The 1955 Regulations stipulate that where an individual has been convicted and sentenced to a term of imprisonment, he can be photographed, finger-printed, palm-printed and measured at any time during his subsequent imprisonment.[238] No distinction is drawn between persons who have been convicted on indictment and persons who have been convicted in summary proceedings. Although it is not explicitly clear from the Regulations, the implication is that the fingerprints are taken by, and retained for the benefit of the prison authorities. They do not form part of the Garda criminal intel-ligence database. Moreover, the power does not extend to persons who have not been sentenced to a term of imprisonment on conviction.

E. Forensic Samples

1. Introduction

The police investigation of many serious crimes is greatly enhanced by the capacity to take minute samples from the clothes or body of the suspect, and to match them with equally minute samples taken from the victim, from items used in the course of the crime or from the scene of the crime itself. Scientific advances in this area are such that the contribution of these techniques in criminal investigation can only increase. DNA testing, in particular, has a potentially huge contribution to make in the investigation of sexual offences and homicide. The material evidence taken by such scientific methods is often highly probative of guilt. However, in the absence of the consent of the person concerned, their application will normally involve an unlawful trespass against the person or property. Accordingly, specific statutory powers are required. Powers for the taking of bodily samples are laid down substantially in the Criminal Justice (Forensic Evidence) Act 1990, while the Criminal Justice Act 1984 makes further provision for the taking of external samples for forensic testing.

6–48

2. Bodily Samples

The Power

The Criminal Justice (Forensic Evidence) Act 1990 confers a power on certain members of the Garda Síochána to authorise the taking of bodily

6–49

---

[237] *ibid.* s.8(5), as applied by s.28(3).
[238] Measuring and Photography of Prisoners Regulations 1955, r.3.

samples for forensic testing from persons suspected of certain criminal offences. The samples in question are: blood, pubic hair, other body hair, urine, saliva, a nail, any material found under a nail, a swab from any part of the body including a body orifice and genital region, a dental impression and an impression of any part of the person's body other than a part of his hand.[239] The power applies in respect of any person who is in police custody pursuant to the provisions of section 4 of the Criminal Justice Act 1984, section 30 of the Offences Against the State Act 1939 or section 2 of the Criminal Justice (Drug Trafficking) Act 1996.

The power also extends to a person in prison, but only if the sample is required in connection with an investigation into the commission of an offence within the ambit of the 1939 Act (including offences scheduled pursuant to the Act), the 1984 Act or the 1996 Act and is not the offence for which the person is in prison or for which he could be convicted on an indictment alleging that offence.[240] On a literal interpretation of this provision it would appear that the power cannot be used against a person in prison in respect of any offence in respect of which he could be convicted on indictment. It is submitted, however, that any such interpretation would substantially defeat the whole purpose of the provision in respect of persons in prison, and would be inconsistent with other provisions of the Act. A more reasonable interpretation is that it is meant to preclude the possibility of using the power in respect of an offence of which the prisoner is actually charged or of which he could be convicted on an indictment charging the offence for which he is in prison. In other words the offence was one in respect of which the jury could return a verdict of guilt on the indictment even though the indictment did not specifically charge that offence. This leaves open the possibility of using the power against persons in prison in respect of certain other qualifying offences arising out of the same matter or offences arising out of an entirely different matter, so long as they satisfy the basic criteria for the use of the power.

Preconditions

6–50   The taking of any of these bodily samples clearly involves a gross infringement of the right to bodily integrity and the privacy of the person. It is hardly surprising, therefore, that a sample cannot be taken simply because it might be deemed helpful to a Garda investigation. Certain preconditions must be satisfied. The general precondition is that a member of the Garda Síochána not below the rank of superintendent must authorise a sample to be taken.[241] Such authorisation can be given only if the member concerned has reasonable grounds for suspecting the involvement of the person in a certain offence.[242] Where the person is in custody it must be the offence for which he is in custody, whereas if

---

[239]   Criminal Justice (Forensic Evidence) Act 1990, s.2(1). Fingerprints and palmprints are covered by the Criminal Justice Act 1984.

[240]   *ibid.* s.2(2) & (3).

[241]   *ibid.* s.2(4) (a). The authorisation may be given orally, but it must be confirmed in writing as soon as possible; s.2(7).

[242]   *ibid.* s.2(5).

he is in prison it must be an offence under the 1939 Act, an offence which is scheduled pursuant to Part V of the 1939 Act or an offence which is within the detention provisions of the 1984 or 1996 Acts. The member must also have reasonable grounds for believing that the sample will tend to confirm or disprove the involvement of the person concerned in the offence.

Consent for Intimate Samples

In the case of the more intimate and intrusive samples a further safeguard applies. An appropriate written consent is required before a sample of blood, pubic hair, urine, saliva, a swab from a body orifice or genital region or a dental impression can be taken.[243] An appropriate consent can be made by a person who has attained the age of 17 years. If the person is below the age of 14 the consent can only be given by a parent or guardian, while the consents of both the person concerned and a parent or guardian are required for a person who has attained the age of 14 years but has not attained the age of 17 years.[244] Before seeking the consent of the person concerned the member of the Garda Síochána concerned must inform the person of the nature of the offence in question, that the necessary authorisation has been given, the grounds on which the authorisation was given and that the results of any tests on the sample may be given in evidence in any proceedings.[245]

Consent is not required under these provisions for the taking of hair (other than pubic hair), a nail, any material found under a nail, a swab from any part of the body (other than a body orifice or a genital region) or a footprint or similar impression of any part of a person's body other than a part of his hand or mouth. The necessary authorisation from a member of the Garda Síochána not below the rank of superintendent is sufficient so long as the other prerequisites are satisfied.

The protection inherent in the requirement for a written consent is undermined to some extent by the possible consequences of a refusal to consent without good cause. When determining whether a charge should be dismissed under Part 1A of the Criminal Procedure Act 1967,[246] or whether there is a case to answer, the court may draw such inferences, if any, from the refusal as appear proper.[247] The same applies to the determination of whether the person is guilty of the offence charged or of any other offence of which he could lawfully be convicted on that charge. In any of these situations this may result in the refusal being treated as corroboration of any evidence in relation to which the refusal is material. This is qualified by the stipulation that a person cannot be convicted of an offence solely on an inference drawn from the refusal. It is worth noting that inferences may not be drawn from a refusal unless the person concerned had been told by a member of the Garda

---

243 *ibid.* s.2(4)(b).
244 *ibid.* s.2(10).
245 *ibid.* s.2(6).
246 Criminal Justice (Forensic Evidence) Act 1990, s. 3(1)(a)(i), as amended by Criminal Justice Act 1959, s.17(1).
247 *ibid.* s.3(1).

Síochána when seeking his consent that the sample was required for the purpose of forensic testing, that his consent was necessary and, if his consent was not given, what effect the refusal might have.[248] No inferences can be drawn from a refusal where the person in question is below the age of 14 years of age or where the consent has been withheld by a parent or guardian.[249]

Taking the Sample

6–51   Before proceeding to exercise the power to take a bodily sample the member of the Garda Síochána concerned must give the person from whom the sample is to be taken the same information that must be given, where necessary, in order to obtain a valid consent (see above).[250] Moreover, if the sample is blood, pubic hair or a swab from a body orifice or genital region, it may be taken only by a registered medical practitioner.[251] A dental impression may be taken only by a registered dental or medical practitioner. Anyone who obstructs or attempts to obstruct any member of the Garda Síochána, or any other person, exercising the power to take a sample is guilty of an offence punishable on summary conviction by a fine not exceeding €1,270 and/or imprisonment for a term not exceeding 12 months.[252]

Destruction of Samples

The availability of a police power to take bodily samples in the course of criminal investigations could result in the establishment of a databank of the most personal information on people who have come to the notice of the police. While this might appear attractive to those engaged in the prevention and detection of crime, it clearly has the potential to inflict enormous damage on the extent to which the personal rights of the citizen are protected. The 1990 Act has struck a balance between these competing interests by making provision for the destruction of bodily samples, and the results obtained from those samples, in a wide range of situations. They must be destroyed where proceedings for an offence for which a person could be detained under the 1984, 1939 or 1996 Acts have not been instituted against the person concerned within six months from the taking of the sample.[253] Where proceedings have been instituted, they must be destroyed if the person concerned is acquitted or discharged or the proceedings are discontinued.[254] Also in the case of a convicted person who is the subject of an order under section 1(1) or 1(2) of the Probation of Offenders Act 1907 there is provision for the destruction of the

---

[248]   *ibid.* s.3(3).
[249]   *ibid.* s.3(4).
[250]   *ibid.* s.2(6).
[251]   *ibid.* s.2(8).
[252]   *ibid.* s.2(9).
[253]   *ibid.* s.4(1) & (2). This obligation to destroy will not arise where the failure to institute proceedings is due to the fact that the person concerned has absconded or cannot be found.
[254]   *ibid.* s.4(3).

sample and every record identifying it.[255] The destruction must be carried out after the expiration of three years from the making of the order, providing that the person has not been convicted of an offence to which section 4 of the Criminal Justice Act 1984 applies.[256]

The obligation to destroy samples and associated records is not absolute even when the necessary preconditions have been satisfied. If an application is made to the court by, or on behalf of, the DPP or the person from whom the sample was taken, and the court is satisfied that there is good reason why the samples and records in question should not be destroyed, it may make an order authorising their retention for such purpose or period as it may direct.[257]

Further Powers under Offences against the State Act

Although the provisions of the Criminal Justice (Forensic Evidence) Act 1990 apply to persons detained under section 30 of the Offences against the State Act 1939 there is further provision for these persons. The Criminal Law Act 1976 permits a member of the Garda Síochána to make or cause to be made any test designed for the purpose of ascertaining whether a person in custody under section 30 of the 1939 Act has been in contact with any firearm or explosive substance. To this end the member may take swabs from the person's skin or samples of his hair.[258]

3. External Samples

The 1990 Act does not address the issue of taking samples from anything in a person's possession or under his control. Taking such external samples without the consent of the person concerned could amount to an unlawful trespass on the property concerned. However, the Criminal Justice Act 1984 does make some provision on the matter. Where a person is detained under section 4 of the 1984 Act or section 2 of the Criminal Justice (Drug Trafficking) Act 1996, a member of the Garda Síochána may seize and retain for testing anything that he has in his possession.[259] Presumably, this includes the actual clothes that the person is wearing at the time of arrest. What is not so clear is whether it is confined to seizing items which the person actually has in his physical possession or which are immediately accessible to him at the time of arrest. Could it, for example, be used to seize and test items that are found only after a search of the person's property either at the time of the arrest or at some point in time thereafter? The general sense of the section,

6–52

---

[255] *ibid.* s.4(4). This does not apply to an order under section 1(2) of the 1907 Act which has been discharged on appeal against conviction if on appeal the conviction is confirmed.

[256] A literal interpretation of this provision suggests that the probation order need not necessarily relate to the same offence or proceedings as the bodily sample. It seems likely, however, that the legislative intention was that there should be a direct relationship between the bodily sample, conviction and probation order.

[257] Criminal Justice (Forensic Evidence) Act 1990, s.4(5).

[258] Criminal Law Act 1976, s.7(1)(c).

[259] Criminal Justice Act 1984, s.6(1)(f). See s.6(4) for the offence of obstructing or attempting to obstruct the exercise of this power.

coupled with the principle that statutory provisions intruding on the rights of the citizen should be interpreted strictly, suggest that the narrow interpretation should be preferred. In practice the courts have demonstrated a willingness to interpret powers of search and seizure in favour of the gardaí. It is perhaps more likely, therefore, that this provision will be interpreted in its broader sense.

The Criminal Law 1976 makes identical provision in respect of persons in custody under section 30 of the Offences Against the State Act 1939.[260]

F. Testing for Excess Alcohol or Drugs

6–53 Under the Road Traffic legislation[261] there is provision for certain samples to be taken from a person who is suspected of "drunken-driving" or of being in charge of a vehicle having consumed intoxicating liquor or while under the influence of drugs. These provisions are analysed fully in other specialist texts.[262] Accordingly, it will suffice here to outline briefly the most relevant provisions.

A specimen of breath may be required of a person in charge of a vehicle where a member of the Garda Síochána is of the opinion that he has consumed intoxicating liquor.[263] A failure or a refusal to comply is an offence.[264] Where a person has been arrested under certain provisions of the Road Traffic legislation and brought to a Garda station he may be required to provide a specimen of breath.[265] Alternatively, he may be required to permit a designated doctor to take a specimen of his blood or he may opt to provide a specimen of urine for the doctor.[266] Once again a failure or a refusal to comply amounts to an offence.[267] A similar requirement to provide a specimen of blood or urine arises where a person has accompanied a member of the Garda Síochána to a Garda station where the member is of the opinion that the person was in charge of a vehicle while under the influence of a drug or drugs.[268] A blood or urine specimen may also be required of a person who has been admitted or who is attending a hospital on account of having been injured in a road traffic accident. This requirement may arise where a member of the Garda Síochána is of the opinion that at the time of the accident the person concerned had consumed an intoxicant.[269]

---

[260] Criminal Law Act 1976, s.7(1)(f).

[261] Road Traffic Acts 1961–1995.

[262] See M. de Blacam, *Drunken Driving and the Law* (2nd ed., Round Hall Sweet and Maxwell, Dublin, 1995); Pierse, *Road Traffic Law in Ireland* (2nd ed., Butterworths, Dublin, 1995)

[263] Road Traffic Act 1994, s.12(1).

[264] *ibid.* s.12(2).

[265] *ibid.* s.13(1)(a).

[266] *ibid.* s.13(1)(b).

[267] *ibid.* s.13(2) & (3). It is at least arguable in the light of *Quinn v. Ireland* (2001) 33 E.H.R.R. 264 that this provision is in breach of Art. 6 of the European Convention on Human Rights.

[268] *ibid.* s.14(1).

[269] *ibid.* s.15(1).

[270] *ibid.* s.18.

A specimen of blood or urine is forwarded for analysis to the Medical Bureau of Road Safety.[270] The Bureau, in turn, will send a certificate of the results back to the Garda station and the person concerned.[271] The certificate and the form completed by the doctor who took the specimen are evidence of the facts stated therein, until the contrary is shown.[272]

A breath specimen taken in the Garda station is exhaled into an apparatus for determining the concentration of alcohol in the breath. A member of the Garda Síochána must present a statement of the results automatically produced for the signature of the person concerned.[273] A signed statement is evidence of the facts stated therein, until the contrary is shown.[274] A refusal or failure to sign is an offence.[275]

G. Visual Identification

1. Parades

Status

The evidence against the accused may include an identification by the victim, **6–54** a member of the Garda Síochána or a civilian witness. Where there is no other material evidence implicating the accused in the offence, and the accused denies that he was the perpetrator, such identification evidence will be critical. The courts, however, adopt a cautious approach to the weight to be attached to such evidence. Although there is no rule of law requiring an identification parade to be held in any case,[276] the courts will normally look for a satisfactory explanation as to why a parade was not held in a case where identification was in issue. Where one is not held in such circumstances, the trial judge must put all the implications of it not being held to the jury.[277] The mere fact that the suspect did not live at home and was not always readily available would not be a sufficient excuse.[278] Similarly, it would not be sufficient for gardaí to make a subjective decision that it would be more beneficial to the accused not to have a formal identification parade.[279] The accused should be permitted to make the choice himself.

---

[271] *ibid.* s.19(3).
[272] *ibid.* s.21(2) & (3).
[273] *ibid.* s.17(1).
[274] *ibid.* s.21(1).
[275] *ibid.* s.17(4).
[276] See, for example, *People v. Martin* [1956] I.R. 22 (CCA) where the accused refused to take part in an identification parade and was identified by a garda witness.
[277] See dictum of Haugh J. in *People v. Hughes* 92 I.L.T.R. 179 at 181 (CCA). Ryan and Magee suggest that this dictum should be construed in the specific context of the witness being a member of the Garda Síochána, *op. cit.*, p. 138.
[278] *People (Attorney General) v. Fagan* 1 Frewen 375.
[279] *People (DPP) v. O'Reilly* [1991] I.L.R.M. 10.

Procedure

In Ireland there are no published rules governing the procedure to be followed in the conduct of an identity parade.[280] However, the Garda Síochána Manual of Criminal Investigation Techniques sets out in some detail how a parade should be conducted. It stipulates that the parade should be conducted by a member of the force other than the member who is in charge of the investigation in which identity is in issue. The conducting member should explain the arrangements for the parade in advance to the suspect and inform him that he may have a solicitor or friend present at the parade. If the suspect objects to participating in the parade, it should not be held. Where a parade is held the conducting member must have the names, addresses and descriptions of the volunteers. He must also be familiar with the facts of the case and have the names of the witnesses. The suspect will be placed among at least eight volunteers who are, as far as possible, roughly of the same age, height, general appearance, dress and socio-economic status as the suspect. In the event of the suspect having some distinguishing characteristic steps should be taken to ensure that its effect is neutralised. Where there are two suspects of roughly similar appearance, they may be paraded together with at least twelve other persons. If the suspects are not similar in appearance, or if there are more than two suspects, separate parades should be held using different volunteers on each parade. Where all members of a particular group are possible suspects there is no objection to having a parade made up entirely of suspects. This would only apply where there are not more than two culprits sought and all the suspects are of roughly similar appearance. Two suspects of obviously dissimilar appearance should not be included in the same parade.

6–55   The parade can be held either indoors or outdoors. However, it is desirable to hold it outdoors if it is a case where a witness has seen the person to be identified outdoors in daylight on the occasion of the crime under investigation. Where it is held outdoors the parade ground should not be overlooked by windows, and similar facilities to those required for an indoors parade should also be available. In an indoors parade, a well-lighted room is essential and, if possible, it should have entry and exit doors to facilitate witnesses. In either case, the witnesses should be isolated in a room as far as possible away from the room or place where the parade is being held. A member of the Garda Síochána should be available to ensure that there is no communication between them and any witness who has viewed the parade. None of the witnesses should be given an opportunity to see the suspect (or a photograph or description of him) before he is paraded. Similarly, volunteers taking part in the parade must not be known to any of the witnesses and no witness should be given an opportunity to see the volunteers (or a photograph or

---

[280] See *People (DPP) v. O'Reilly* [1990] 2 I.R. 415 and *People (Attorney General) v. O'Driscoll* (1972) 1 Frewen 351 for an outline of the basic elements. The English rules are set out in Annex A to Code D: Code of Practice for the Identification of Persons by Police Officers, Police and Criminal Evidence Act 1984 (Codes of Practice)(No.2) Order 1990.

description of them) before the parade. All unauthorised persons, including members of the Garda Síochána, should be excluded from the parade.

The parade should be formed in line and those present should remain in front of the parade. Once the parade has been formed everything done thereafter in respect of it should take place in the presence and hearing of the suspect. Before proceeding he must be asked if he has any objection to any of the volunteers. If he does make an objection he should be asked to give reasons and any reasonable objection should be met. The suspect should be told that he may select his own position in the parade and that he may change his position between witnesses.

The conducting member should address each witness in the presence and hearing of the suspect as follows:

> "This is an identification parade. I want you to look very carefully at this line of men and see if you can recognise the person you have come to identify (or the person who assaulted you, or the person you saw at _____ (place) at _____ (time) on _____ (date), etc). Do not say anything until I ask you a question."

Any reasonable request made by a witness should be granted, including: seeing the parade walk, removing headgear from a volunteer; hearing a volunteer speak; seeing the parade from the rear. When the witness has scrutinised the parade the conducting member should ask him if he has identified the person. If the witness indicates that he has, the member should ask him to place his hand on the identified person's shoulder. Identification by pointing may be permitted where the witness is reluctant to touch the person identified. If the person in question is the suspect he should be cautioned and a note made of his reply, if any. When all of the witnesses have been called, the suspect should be asked whether he has any comments to make concerning the manner in which the parade has been conducted. The conducting member should record every circumstance connected with the parade, including any statement or request made by the suspect. Full particulars of the parade should be entered on a prescribed form, although the original record should also be preserved for production in court and should be supported by a statement of evidence.

2. Informal Identification

Street Identification

A witness may identify a suspect in more informal circumstances such as in the street, in the court surroundings or from a photograph. Evidence of such identification is generally admissible. In *People v. Galvin*,[281] for example, the accused had been identified by a witness on the street and he was subsequently picked out at an identification parade. The trial judge directed the jury that the important identification was the one made on the street. Indeed, in some cases the circumstances may be such that a street identification may be

6–56

---

[281] [1962] I.R. 325.

more acceptable.[282] Referring to the Supreme Court decision in *People (Attorney General) v. Martin*[282a] the Court of Criminal Appeal in *People (Attorney General) v. Fagan* explained:

> " . . . there is no rule of law or practice that requires visual identification of a person to be proved by means of an identification parade; each case must be considered on its own facts. It is readily understandable that other types of identification may in certain circumstances be fairer and more dependable than a formal identification parade which, because of its surroundings, atmosphere, range of choice and limited opportunity for observation may be a less than satisfactory means of achieving a reliable identification. But the acceptability of an alternative method must always depend on the circumstances of the case."[282b]

Nevertheless, the courts display a preference for formal identification parades to the extent that they will look for a satisfactory explanation of a decision not to hold one in any case where identity is in issue.[283] In *People (DPP) v. Reilly*,[283a] for example, the accused was convicted of the larceny of a sum of money from an elderly woman living on her own. The circumstances were that two strangers called to her house in the middle of the day and created a diversion during which the money went missing. The victim was severely traumatised by the incident. Nevertheless, she accompanied a member of the Garda Síochána in the patrol car along the main street of Edgeworthstown to see if she could identify the strangers, one of whom she had described as having "a most notorious face, an awful face". While in the patrol car, the victim identified the accused as being this person. However, the member driving the car was unable to give details of the other persons who were in the immediate vicinity at the time of the identification. In quashing the conviction the Court explained that this was a case in which there should have been a formal identification parade. The witness was in a state of shock and her opportunity to observe the features of the strangers when they called to her house were limited. Moreover, there were no reasons which would have rendered it impractical or desirable to hold a formal identification parade. The Court also took the opportunity to highlight key differences between a formal and an informal identification as follows:

> ". . . in the former the accused (and his legal adviser if one is present) has full knowledge about the composition of the parade and may object if it is perceived to be unfair. Furthermore, the court of trial will have the benefit of a detailed account of the parade and a description of those who participated in it. By contrast, an accused has no input when there is an informal identification and is unlikely even to have knowledge that it is happening. Therefore, he may be seriously inhibited in challenging its fairness at the trial."[283b]

---

[282] *People (Attorney General) v. Martin* [1956] I.R. 22.
[282a] [1956] I.R. 22.
[282b] (1974) 1 Frewen 375 at 377.
[283] *People (DPP) v. Reilly* [1991] I.L.R.M. 10; *People (Attorney General) v. Fagan* 1 Frewen 375.
[283a] [1990] 2 I.R. 415.
[283b] *ibid.* at 421, *per* O'Flaherty J.

Procedure

Irish law does not prescribe any formal requirements which must be followed for a street identification. However, the Garda Síochána Manual of Criminal Investigation Techniques sets out guidelines for the benefit of the gardaí concerned. These guidelines stipulate that the witness should be brought to a suitable place for making observation. The only requirement is that there should be a reasonable number of people congregated there and the suspect should be allowed to mingle freely with them. The conducting member should explain to the witness that he should watch out carefully to see if he can recognise the person who assaulted him or whom he saw at _____ (place) at _____ (time) on _____ (date), as the case may be. It should be arranged that if the witness makes an identification he should either give a signal or place his hand on the person he identifies. Apart from this pre-arranged signal, there should be no communication between the conducting member and the witness once observation has commenced. The witness should normally be left on his own, with the conducting member remaining in the vicinity in sight of the witness but out of speaking distance with him.

The conducting member should record all the details in relation to the observation and identification, including the approximate number of persons of the same sex as the identified person in the vicinity at the time.

It may happen that a member of the Garda Síochána is approached on the street or elsewhere by someone who has just witnessed a crime or who has just been the victim of a crime. In this event it would be quite normal for the member to make a tour of the area with the witness to see if the witness will be able to point out the person responsible. According to the Garda Manual this situation should be treated akin to an informal identification. However, the courts have on occasion displayed a reluctance to accept such an identification when it would have been feasible to conduct a formal identification parade.

Alternative Procedure

The Garda Síochána Manual makes provision for an alternative identification procedure where neither an informal identification nor a formal identification parade is feasible. Under the alternative procedure, the suspect may be placed in a room with at least eight other persons of similar build and appearance. The witnesses should be invited one at a time to view those present and asked if they could recognise the person responsible. It is not entirely clear how this procedure would be feasible in circumstances when the others are not. Indeed, the Manual states that this method of identification should only be adopted as a last resort.

6–57

Photographs

In many cases where any form of formal or informal identification procedures are impractical, a standard police practice is to show a witness a number of photographs in the hope that the witness will be able to pick out the offender. Where they suspect that they know the identity of the individual, they should present the witness with at least 12 photographs including the one of the suspected offender.[284] The photographs must not bear any names, dates or distinguishing marks. The witness should then be asked if he recognises the offender from any of the photographs.

There are, however, limits on the extent to which the police can seek a positive identification from the use of photographs. A witness should not be shown photographs before a formal or informal identification.[285] If a suspect has already been arrested for the offence, the police should not show the witness a photograph of that suspect.[286] Furthermore, if one witness has already identified a suspect from a photograph, other witnesses should not be shown photographs. Instead, a formal identification parade should be held in which all the witnesses should participate, including the one who has already made a photograph identification.[287] Where witnesses have been shown photographs, neither they nor the police ought to reveal this fact in their examination-in-chief. Ryan and Magee explain that this is in order to avoid the risk of the jury drawing an adverse inference from the fact that the police had a photograph of the accused.[288] Nevertheless, the defence ought to be informed if photographs have been shown to a witness.[289] The Garda Síochána Manual of Criminal Investigation Techniques lays down further detailed guidance which gardaí should follow when seeking an identification through the use of photographs.

---

[284] *People v. Mills* [1957] I.R. 106, applying *R. v. Dwyer* [1925] 2 K.B. 799.
[285] See, *e.g. People (DPP) v. O'Reilly* [1990] 2 I.R. 415; *People (DPP) v. Meleady and Grogan* [1995] 2 I.R. 517; [1999] 2 I.R. 249.
[286] *R. v. Haslam* 19 Cr. App. Rep. 59.
[286] Ryan and Magee, *op. cit.*, p. 138.
[288] *ibid.*
[289] See the controversy that arose over the apparent use of photographs in *People (DPP) v. Meleady and Grogan* [1995] 2 I.R,. 517 and [1995] 2 I.R. 249 (see chapter 22)

CHAPTER 7

GARDA POWERS OF STOP AND SURVEILLANCE

A. Introduction

Each member of the Garda Síochána may investigate and detect crime. To   **7–01**
that end he or she may observe and record the actions of any other person,
and seek the cooperation of any person, whether or not he or she suspects that
person of committing a criminal offence. Of course, these matters are also
within the competence of the ordinary citizen. Prior to the advent of organised
police forces, law enforcement depended very heavily on the voluntary
exertions of private citizens. In fact, the original peace officers and constables
were considered to be nothing more than ordinary citizens who were burdened
with the special duty to discharge the policing responsibilities that attached
generally to all citizens.[1] Today, ordinary citizens can still be found investigating and detecting certain criminal offences; the most obvious examples
being private investigators and security guards in shops.

Police officers can be distinguished from ordinary citizens in their law
enforcement role by the fact that they are public officers charged with a specific
duty to enforce the law.[2] A wilful neglect to perform this duty can constitute a
criminal offence in certain circumstances.[3] In *R. v. Dytham*,[4] for example, the
English Court of Appeal upheld the conviction of a constable for the common
law offence of misconduct in a public office. The substance of the offence
was that the constable deliberately failed to take steps to enforce the law in a
fracas in which a man was beaten to death. The incident happened within
sight and sound of where the constable was standing. Although this duty was
considered, at one time, to extend to the private citizen,[5] it is unlikely that it

---

[1] See DPJ Walsh *The Irish Police: A Legal and Constitutional Perspective* (Round Hall Sweet & Maxwell, Dublin, 1998) Ch.3.

[2] *ibid.*

[3] *Stephen's Digest of the Criminal Law* (9th ed., 1950), p. 114 , art.145.

[4] [1979] Q.B. 722.

[5] See, *e.g.*, 2 Hale 75; 2 Hawk. c.12, ss.1 & 7.

would apply to him or her today.[6] However, there is authority for the proposition that a citizen, when called upon to do so, must assist a police officer in restraining an arrested suspect or in restoring public order.[7] Equally, it is a criminal offence in certain circumstances to withhold information about the commission or intended commission of a serious criminal offence by another person.[8]

7–02   The law enforcement role of police officers can easily be distinguished from that of ordinary citizens in the sense that the former are officially established, maintained, resourced and authorised by the State to provide a public police service, which includes general law enforcement. The distinction is also reflected in the respective legal capacities of the ordinary citizen and the police officer in matters of law enforcement. For example, while the private citizen may choose to spend his or her time investigating the criminal activities of others, he or she cannot compel their cooperation. Apart from a limited power of arrest, the common law does not confer the ordinary citizen with any coercive powers of criminal investigation. While there are a number of statutory police powers which do extend to the ordinary citizen, these pale into insignificance when compared with those available to a member of the Garda Síochána. Each member of the force is invested with powers to stop, search, question, arrest and detain an individual in certain circumstances. They also enjoy powers of entry, search and seizure with respect to property.

In order to exercise any one of his or her law enforcement powers lawfully a member of the Garda Síochána must stay within the confines of the power he or she is purporting to exercise in the individual case. A failure to stay within the limits of the power in question can result in the victim succeeding in a civil action for damages.[9] Also, evidence obtained as a result of the unlawful exercise of the power might be excluded from the subsequent criminal prosecution on account of the illegality. It is essential, therefore, to have a clear understanding of the scope and limitations of these powers. The arrest powers are dealt with in chapter 4, detention and questioning consequent on arrest are covered in chapters 5 and 6, while powers of entry, search and seizure are described in chapter 8. This chapter will focus on those disparate powers of criminal investigation and surveillance which a member of the Garda Síochána can use at the earliest stages of an investigation from the moment when he first forms the vaguest suspicion that some criminal activity might be afoot, up to the point where he might reasonably contemplate an arrest or an entry, search and seizure.

B. Seeking Information

7–03   At common law a member of the Garda Síochána enjoys the same freedom as any private citizen to ask questions of another. If he or she is investigating a

---

[6] Ryan and Magee point out that there are no reported Irish cases where a person has been prosecuted for breach of this duty. Ryan and Magee, *The Irish Criminal Process* (Mercier Press, Dublin, 1983), p. 95.

[7] *R. v. Pinney* (1832) 3 B & Ad 947.

[8] Offences against the State (Amendment) Act 1998, s.8.

[9] See further, DPJ Walsh, *op. cit.*, chap.10.

criminal offence there is no legal obstacle to his or her seeking the cooperation of others by asking questions about their movements at the relevant time, what they saw and heard etc.[10] This is confirmed by Rule I of the Judges Rules which reads:

> "When a police officer is endeavouring to discover the author of a crime there is no objection to his putting questions in respect thereof to any person or persons, whether suspected or not, from whom he thinks that useful information may be obtained."

The catch, of course, is that at common law the citizen is under no obligation to answer such questions or otherwise co-operate with the police officer's investigation.[11]

Increasingly, however, this right to be left alone is being encroached upon by statute. There are now many situations in which individuals engaged in defined activities must provide specific information when required to do so by a member of the Garda Síochána in certain circumstances. For the most part, however, the primary objective of these powers is the police regulation of certain social and economic activities, as opposed to the investigation of specific criminal offences. There are, however, a number of statutory provisions, primarily in the Criminal Justice Act 1984 and the Offences against the State (Amendment) Act 1998, which penalise the failure to provide information when demanded by a member of the Garda Síochána in certain circumstances. Although these provisions are not confined to the questioning of a suspect in police custody they are covered under the subheading of the right to silence in chapter 6 which deals with the interview, examination and identification of the suspect in Garda custody as, in practice, they often feature in that context.

C. Stop and Question

1. Common Law

Stopping Pedestrians on Suspicion

At common law it had always been considered that a member of the Garda Síochána has no power to restrain the liberty of the citizen short of arrest. Up until very recently, the Irish authorities on this point have all related to the situation where a citizen was detained in a Garda station with a view to assisting the Garda with their investigation into a criminal offence.[12] The English courts, however, have been confronted with situations where a constable tried to stop an individual on the street in order to check his possible involvement in criminal activity.

In *Kenlin v. Gardiner*,[13] for example, two plain-clothed detectives observed two boys calling at houses in the middle of the day. Suspecting that they might be engaged in some criminal enterprise, the detectives stopped the boys

7–04

---

[10] *DPP v. Cowman* [1993] 1 I.R. 335.
[11] *Kenlin v. Gardiner* [1967] 2 Q.B. 510; *Rice v. Connolly* [1966] 2 Q.B. 414.
[12] See, for example, *Dunne v. Clinton* [1930] I.R. 366; *People v. O'Loughlin* [1979] I.R. 85.
[13] [1967] 2 Q.B. 510.

to ask them what they were doing. Not realising that the detectives were in fact police officers the boys tried to run away, fearing that they were being abducted. The detectives attempted to restrain one of the boys who kicked him in order to make good his escape. In upholding the boys appeal against a conviction for assaulting a police officer in the execution of his duty, Winn L.J. acknowledged that the police officers had no power, short of arrest, to restrain the boys for the purpose of obtaining answers to their questions.

7–05   The point is more directly illustrated in the case of *Rice v. Connolly*[14] where uniformed police officers spotted the accused behaving suspiciously late at night in an area where there had been a number of burglaries. They stopped him and asked for his name and address. The accused refused to cooperate unless he was arrested. He was promptly arrested and charged with obstructing a police constable in the execution of his duty. The subsequent conviction was quashed on appeal on the ground that a citizen was under no legal duty to assist the police, either by answering their reasonable questions or by accompanying them to a police box for the purpose of checking his or her identity. Lord Parker C.J. explained that:

> ". . . though every citizen has a moral duty or, if you like, a social duty to assist the police, there is no legal duty to that effect and indeed the whole basis of the common law is the right of the individual to refuse to answer questions put to him by persons in authority, and to refuse to accompany those in authority to any particular place; short, of course, of arrest."[15]

It does not follow that a police officer must operate through the medium of arrest powers every time he or she wishes to check out whether an individual has been, or is, engaged in criminal activity. He does not act unlawfully simply by putting questions to a possible suspect, even where that suspect does not want to answer. Indeed, the English courts have accepted that the constable is acting lawfully even when he or she seeks to attract someone's attention by tapping them on the shoulder.[16] It is only where he goes further and actually uses force to restrain an individual's freedom of movement, short of arrest, that the constable risks exceeding his or her powers at common law. The mere fact that he suspects the individual of involvement in criminal activity, and wishes to talk briefly to that individual to check out his suspicion will not afford him a defence.

The USA Approach

The English common law authorities are in marked contrast to their counterparts in the USA. It is now firmly established that a police officer in the USA has a common law power to stop and frisk-search a suspect in certain circumstances short of actual arrest. In *Terry v. Ohio*,[17] for example, it was accepted that a police officer has a power to stop and frisk a suspect in public where the officer had reasonable grounds to justify his action. In *Terry* the officer observed three

---

[14]   [1966] 2 Q.B. 414.
[15]   *Rice v. Connolly* [1966] 2 Q.B. 414 at 419.
[16]   See, *e.g. Donnelly v. Jackman* [1970] 1 All E.R. 987; *Collins v. Wilcock* [1984] 3 All E.R. 374.
[17]   392 US 1; 88 S.Ct 1868, 20 L.Ed.2d 889 (1968).

men acting as if they were contemplating the robbery of a store. When he asked them what they were doing he received an unsatisfactory response. The movements of one of the men led him to believe, on the basis of his experience, that he might be armed. Fearing for his personal safety the officer conducted a quick frisk search of the men and found a firearm. The Court concluded that his actions were lawful in the circumstances.

Stopping Motorists at Random

The American authorities on this point have not received any serious consideration by the Irish or British courts. Nevertheless, there are clear signs that they are prepared to countenance a limited common law police power to stop a citizen temporarily, short of actual arrest, in order to check out that citizen's possible involvement in criminal activity. The Irish authority is to be found in the majority decision of the Supreme Court in *DPP (Stratford) v. Fagan*.[18] In that case a member of the Garda Síochána watched the accused come out of a pub late at night, get into his car and drive away. Although there was nothing in the manner of the accused's driving to create a reasonable suspicion that he was driving with excess alcohol in his blood or was committing any other driving offence, the member stopped the car. In his brief conversation with the accused the member detected a smell of alcohol on the accused's breath whereupon the member proceeded to breathylise him. The breathyliser test proved positive and the member arrested the accused on suspicion of driving with excess alcohol in the blood.

7–06

In the subsequent appeals to the High Court and the Supreme Court against the conviction for drunk-driving one of the primary issues was whether the member of the Garda Síochána had acted lawfully in stopping the accused in the first place. Was there a police power to stop motorists temporarily for the purpose of checking whether they were engaged in criminal activity? It is possible, for example, that section 109(1) of the Road Traffic Act 1961, which obliges a motorist to bring his vehicle to a stop when required to do so by a member of the Garda Síochána, would have provided sufficient authority to cover the situation in *Fagan*.[19] The Supreme Court, however, preferred to base its decision in that case on the premise that gardaí have a common law power to stop motorists at random in order to detect and prevent crime. This might be used, for example, in the vicinity of licensed premises at night to identify drunk-drivers, or to check traffic using a particular route where a serious crime had been committed and it was possible that a car carrying the perpetrators would use that route. In the High Court Carney J. also envisaged the power being used to stop "a strange car being driven by two men after midnight through a good class residential area" in order to check that it was "there for an innocent purpose." The learned judge also acknowledged that

---

[18] [1994] 2 I.L.R.M. 349. For English authority see *Steel v. Goacher* [1983] RTR 98.

[19] Although Carney J. accepted this point in the High Court it did not stop him finding that the member also had the power to stop the vehicle at common law. Significantly, both Blayney and Denham JJ. in the Supreme Court felt that s.109(1) would not permit gardaí to stop motorists in the absence of suspicion.

there was no legal obligation on the driver or passengers to answer questions about their movements.

7–07   The *Fagan* case is clearly limited to the stopping of motorists. There is no suggestion in the judgments in either the Supreme Court or the High Court that it could have a broader application. As such it might be explained as a reaction to the particular law enforcement and crime prevention problems posed by the motor car. Nevertheless, it must also be said that the nature of the power upheld in *Fagan* is at odds with the traditional Irish concept of police powers.[20] In particular, it conflicts with the firmly established principle that there is no police power at common law to curtail the liberty of the individual short of arrest.[21] Indeed, it is significant that no Irish authority was cited in support of the decision in either the Supreme Court or the High Court, nor was any attempt made to distinguish the Irish authorities which might be considered to be at odds with the ruling in *Fagan*.[22] It is possible, therefore, that the scope, and perhaps even the very existence, of the police power recognised in *Fagan* could be re-examined at some time in the future. The cogently argued dissenting judgement of Denham J. in the Supreme Court is worth noting in this respect.

2. Statutory Powers

Introduction

7–08   There are a considerable number of statutory provisions which allow a member of the Garda Síochána to stop a citizen for certain purposes. Some of these powers are very specific in that they are available only in narrowly defined circumstances, while others are much more general in their scope. It must also be said that some are conferred solely for the purpose of putting certain questions to, or making certain demands of, the citizen who has been stopped, while others permit the searching of the citizen and/or the vehicle in which he or she is found. It is beyond the scope of this chapter to offer a full analysis of all the statutory provisions that permit a member of the Garda Síochána to stop a citizen. In this sub-section attention will focus on those powers of stop and question which prove most important in practice. Significant powers of stop and search are covered in the following sub-section.

Scope of the Section 30 Power

There is only one statutory power which specifically permits a member of the Garda Síochána to stop and question an individual short of arrest. It is found in section 30 of the Offences Against the State Act 1939 which stipulates that a

---

[20]   See criticism of the High Court decision in this case see D Walsh "*Steel v. Goacher* Takes Root in Ireland" [1994] Crim.LR. 187.

[21]   *Dunne v. Clinton* [1930] I.R. 336; *People v. Walsh* [1980] I.R. 294; *People v. O'Loughlin* [1979] I.R. 85.

[22]   In the High Court, Carney J. based his decision largely on the authority of the English case of *Steel v. Goacher* [1983] RTR 98 which, in turn, is notable for the fact that it made no attempt to distinguish the English authorities against such a police power at common law; see D Walsh, *op. cit.*

member of the Garda Síochána may "stop . . . [and] . . . interrogate . . . any person whom he suspects of having committed or being about to commit or being or having been concerned in the commission of . . ." any offence in the 1939 Act or any offence scheduled for the purposes of the Act. The power also extends to persons who are suspected of conduct which falls short of actually committing a criminal offence. It can be used against any person whom a member of the Garda Síochána "suspects of carrying a document relating to the commission or intended commission of [a relevant offence] . . . or whom he suspects of being in possession of information relating to the commission or intended commission of any such offence." Equally, it can be used against any person whom the member suspects to be about to commit a relevant criminal offence.

This power to stop and question is identical to the arrest power under section 30(1), apart from the fact that "arrest" is substituted by "stop" and "interrogate". Accordingly, the analysis of elements of the section 30 arrest power in chapter 4 is also relevant here.

Clearly, the power can be used to stop a suspect on foot in a public place. Equally, however, it can be used to stop any vehicle or any ship, boat or other vessel with a view to interrogating (and/or searching and/or arresting) a suspect within the scope of section 30.[23] A member of the Garda Síochána can stop a vehicle etc for this purpose where he or she suspects that it contains a person whom he or she is empowered to arrest under section 30. Presumably, this power to stop a vehicle carries with it an implicit power to require the driver of the vehicle to bring it to a halt even if the requisite suspicion relates to a passenger in the vehicle as distinct from the driver.

Although this power to stop and interrogate is most likely to be used to stop an individual in a public place, it would appear that it can be used, in appropriate circumstances, to stop a suspected person found on private property.

A member of the Garda Síochána must entertain a suspicion that the person he wishes to stop under section 30 is involved in, or has been involved in, the commission of a relevant offence, or has a document or other information relating to the commission of such an offence. In chapter 3 it was explained that the courts have taken the view that for the purpose of a valid arrest under section 30 there must be circumstances upon which the member could reasonably form the requisite suspicion. Presumably this also applies to the power to stop.

Obligation to Answer Questions under Section 30

A member of the Garda Síochána may "interrogate" a person whom he or she **7–09** stops under section 30. This term is not actually defined in the Act. There must be a presumption, however, that the purpose of the stop is to check out the suspicion which the member harbours against the person stopped. It follows that the member can use the power to ask that person questions pertinent to his suspicion. That, of course, does not mean that a person who is

---

[23] Offences against the State Act 1939, s.30(2).

stopped, as opposed to arrested, under section 30 is under an obligation to answer the questions. Certainly, there is no general obligation to answer questions put by a member of the Garda Síochána. However, sections 30(5) and 52 of the Offences Against the State Act 1939 impose an obligation on persons "detained" under section 30 to answer certain questions.[24] The latter applies only to persons "detained in custody". It would be reasonable to argue, therefore, that it applies only to persons who have actually been arrested under section 30 and, as such, has no application to persons who have merely been stopped under the section. It is considered more fully in the chapter on arrest which also describes how the power in section 52 was found to be in breach of Article 6 of the European Convention for the Protection of Human Rights and Fundamental Freedom.

The scope of section 30(5) is more ambiguous. It applies to persons "detained" under section 30. Undoubtedly, that covers persons who have been arrested. The more difficult question is whether it also covers persons who have merely been stopped under section 30. The more likely interpretation is that it is confined to persons arrested. Certainly, where the word "detained" is used in the context of the police having put someone under restraint, it normally connotes an arrest situation. Moreover, the only other occasions on which the word "detained" is used in section 30 relate to an arrest situation. Section 30(3), for example, reads in part: "A person detained under the next preceding subsection of this section may, at any time during such detention, be charged before the District Court . . .". It is also worth noting that the only questions the person is obliged to answer when "detained" under section 30 concerns his name and address. Significantly, section 30(5) also requires him to submit to being searched, photographed and fingerprinted. This is much more consistent with detention preceded by arrest than a temporary stop and "detention" on the street. It must follow, therefore, that a member of the Garda Síochána may "interrogate" a person whom he has stopped under section 30, but the person is not under any legal obligation to answer the questions put unless he is actually arrested.

There is nothing in the legislation to suggest that someone stopped under section 30 can be compelled to accompany a member of the Garda Síochána to a Garda station, or to a Garda car or to any other location for the purpose of being questioned. The clear implication is that the stop and questioning should be brief and should not entail any prolonged detention of the suspect.

Other Provisions

7–10   There are a number of disparate statutory provisions which permit a member of the Garda Síochána to stop a person in defined circumstances and demand answers to certain specific questions. For example, the National Monuments (Amendment) Act 1987 states that where a member of the Garda Síochána finds a person in possession of an archaeological object, and the member reasonably

---

[24]   S.52(2) makes it a summary offence to fail or refuse to answer the questions put under s.52(1), or to give answers which are false or misleading. S.30(6) does likewise for questions put under s.30(5).

suspects that an offence has been committed under the Act, he or she may require the person concerned to give an account of how he came to have the object.[25] If the member suspects that the person concerned has committed an offence he or she can demand his name and address. In both situations the person concerned is under an obligation to cooperate. Similarly, the Street and House to House Collections Act 1962 empowers a member of the Garda Síochána to demand the name and address of a person taking up a collection in public.[26] The person concerned is under an obligation to cooperate and, if required, to produce his authorisation for taking up the collection. Under the Litter Pollution Act 1997 a member of the Garda Síochána may demand the name and address of a person where the member has reasonable grounds for believing that the person in question has committed or is committing a litter offence.[27] If the member is not satisfied with the person's response he may require the person to accompany him to the Garda station for the purpose of verifying the name and address. A failure or refusal to comply with either of the member's requests is a criminal offence. Powers to demand the name and address of a person stopped can also be found in the Wildlife Act 1976[28] and the Diseases of Animals Act 1966.[29]

Questioning Persons Stopped under Other Powers

It is arguable that Garda powers to stop persons for other purposes can also be   **7–11**
used for the questioning of the persons stopped. Certainly, there is nothing to prevent a member of the Garda Síochána from taking the opportunity presented by a stop to put questions to the person whom he or she has stopped. However, in the absence of explicit statutory provisions to the contrary it would appear that the person stopped is not under any obligation to answer the questions. The Licensing (Combating Drug Abuse) Act 1997, for example, empowers a member of the Garda Síochána to stop a person whom he or she reasonably believes is on his way to an unlicensed dance in respect of which a direction has been issued under section 12 of the Act.[30] This power can normally be exercised only within two miles of the place where the dance is being held or is due to be held. Although the Act does not oblige the person stopped to answer any questions, it does permit the member to direct him not to proceed in the direction of the dance. Inevitably, this will create at least the opportunity for the member to put questions to the person stopped. A failure to comply with a direction not to proceed is a criminal offence.

It is also worth noting that the exercise of police powers to demand the production of a licence or certificate from persons engaged in certain defined

---

[25] National Monuments (Amendment) Act 1987, s.20.
[26] Street and House to House Collection Act 1962, ss.19 and 20.
[27] Litter Act 1997, s.23.
[28] Wildlife Act 1976, s.72(2) and s.72(2A), as amended by Wildlife (Amendment) Act 2000, s.65.
[29] Diseases of Animals Act 1966, s.17A, as inserted by Diseases of Animals (Amendment) Act 2001, s.2.
[30] Licensing (Combating Drug Abuse) Act 1997, s.13(1). S.12 of the Act gives an officer not below the rank of superintendent the power to give directions to a person preparing etc for an unlicensed dance to leave the place in question and remove any sound equipment etc which they have with them at that place.

activities can create a situation in which a person might find himself being questioned by a member of the Garda Síochána. Examples include: driving licence,[31] insurance certificate,[32] firearms licence[33] and a casual trading licence.[34] None of the statutory provisions concerned specifically empower gardaí to stop the person concerned, nor do they oblige the person concerned to answer questions. Nevertheless, there is an obligation to comply with the demand and this will normally involve stopping and communicating with the member of the Garda Síochána who demands the production of the licence etc.[35]

Stopping and Questioning Motorists

7-12 A very broad police power of stop which affects a wide section of the population is the power to compel a motorist to bring his or her vehicle to a halt. Although it does not specifically impose an obligation on the motorist to answer questions it can provide an opportunity for a member of the Garda Síochána to question motorists on a range of matters. For this reason and the fact that it is framed in such broad terms it is worth considering it in a little more detail here. The power itself is found in section 109(1) of the Road Traffic Act 1961 which reads:

> "A person driving a vehicle in a public place shall stop the vehicle on being so required by a member of the Garda Síochána and shall keep it stationary for such period as is reasonably necessary to enable the member to discharge his duties."

A failure to stop or remain stationary when required is an offence. The full ambit of this provision has yet to be tested in the Irish courts. A literal interpretation would suggest that it permits a member of the Garda Síochána to stop motorists at random simply where he or she is acting in the course of his or her duty. Since a member's duties can be defined in very broad terms, this interpretation would give the power a very broad ambit. The likelihood, however, is that the lawful exercise of the power is confined to the discharge of a member's road traffic duties. When discussing the provision in *DPP (Stratford) v. Fagan*[36] both Denham and Blayney JJ. distinguished between a Garda power to stop a motorist and a motorist's obligation to bring his or her vehicle to a halt when required to do so by a member of the Garda Síochána. Both agreed that section 109(1) did not go beyond the latter. In other words it was available only to assist the member in the discharge of his or her traffic duties. It did not afford the member an independent power to stop motorists.

---

[31] Road Traffic Act 1961, s.40.
[32] *ibid.*, s.69.
[33] Firearms Act 1925, s.22.
[34] Casual Trading Act 1995, s.10(2).
[35] A member of the Garda Síochána is also possessed of a range of powers permitting him to enter onto certain business premises to check things such as licences, registers equipment, etc, (see chapter 8 on entry, search and seizure). Although the exercise of these powers do require a certain level of cooperation from the persons concerned they are not classed here as powers of stop and question because they are exercised on the business premises as opposed to the street.
[36] [1994] 2 I.L.R.M. 349.

Such statutory powers of stop are available only on suspicion. Of course, the practical relevance of this interpretation has been greatly diminished by the decision in *Fagan* itself which recognised the existence of a common law power to stop motorists at random. Nevertheless, it is worth noting that while a motorist is keeping his or her vehicle stationary pursuant to a direction under section 109(1) there is nothing to prevent a member of the Garda Síochána putting questions to him or her. Moreover, if the member forms a suspicion which would permit him or her to stop the motorist for a certain purpose he may proceed to exercise that power.[37]

D. Stop and Search

1. Common Law

Since the common law did not traditionally recognise any power to restrain the liberty of the individual short of arrest, it follows that it did not recognise a power of stop and search short of arrest. Although a common law power to stop and frisk-search is now firmly established in American jurisprudence, there is no suggestion that the courts on this side of the Atlantic are likely to follow suit. The decision in *DPP (Stratford) v. Fagan*[38] was concerned only with an actual stop and subsequent conversation with a motorist. No question of a search of the motorist arose and there is nothing in the *obiter* remarks of Carney J. in the High Court or the judgments in the Supreme Court to suggest that a member of the Garda Síochána could frisk-search anyone whom he or she had stopped for the purpose of checking that person's movements. These comments are also pertinent to the English decision in *Steel v. Goacher*[39] which formed the basis for Carney J.'s recognition of a common law power to stop in *Fagan*.

7–13

It must be said, however, that the decisions in *Fagan* and *Steel v. Goacher* provide a basis on which the courts in Britain and Ireland might develop more intrusive police powers to carry out checks on possible criminal activity. If a member of the Garda Síochána has a power to stop and question strangers about their movements late at night in a "good-class residential area" to satisfy himself that they are not engaged in criminal activity, why should he not also have the power to frisk them down for weapons or contraband if he is not satisfied with their answers? Presumably, the answer in Ireland would be that a personal search, even one confined to outer clothing, represents a more serious infringement of the individual's personal rights than a mere stop. As such it would require stronger justification in order to avoid falling foul of the Constitution. It does not inevitably follow, however, that this justification can be provided only by a suspicion that the person concerned has committed or is committing a specific criminal offence. The common law power to stop and

---

[37] *Sanders v. DPP* [1988] Crim. LR. 605.
[38] [1994] 2 I.L.R.M. 349.
[39] [1983] RTR 88.

question recognised in *Fagan* was based on nothing more than the mere possibility than a person's presence in a particular area at a particular time might be for the purpose of pursuing an undefined criminal enterprise. If that possibility was not discounted by the answers given by the person stopped, might that not provide sufficient justification for a frisk-search for contraband, offensive weapons or tools that could be used for burglary? In the light of the decision in *Fagan* the likelihood of such a development cannot be dismissed lightly.

2. Statutory Provisions

7-14   *Stop and Search Formalities*

There are a number of significant statutory provisions permitting a member of the Garda Síochána to stop and search a person in certain defined circumstances. It is worth noting at the outset that a member of the Garda Síochána who intends to subject a person to a stop and search under one of these powers should, as a general rule, inform the person that it is intended to subject him or her to such a search and the basis upon which the search is justified. The issue has been considered by the High Court in *DPP v. Rooney*[40] in respect of section 29 of the Dublin Police Act 1842.[41] This provision empowers a member of the Garda Síochána to, *inter alia*, stop and search any person reasonably suspected of having or conveying any thing stolen or unlawfully obtained. A member of the Garda Síochána had stopped a person on the street and asked him if he had any money on him apart from the notes he was carrying in his hand. On receiving a negative reply the member put his hand into the person's pocket and found what he believed to be a forged £20 note. On a consultative case stated from the District Court where the person was being tried for being in possession of two forged £20 notes O'Hanlon J. ruled that, as a general rule, it was incumbent on a member exercising this power to inform the person concerned of his suspicion and of the power in section 29 of the 1842 Act before effecting the search. The learned judge considered that the power of stop and search constituted such a serious encroachment upon the liberty of the individual that it should be subject to formalities analogous to those pertaining to an arrest:

> "Although less drastic in its effect than a power of arrest, such action on the part of the police authorities does nevertheless amount to a substantial and significant interference with the liberty of the subject, and it appears to me that the same principles which underlie the decisions in *Christie v. Leachinsky* [1947] A.C. 573 and *People (Attorney General) v. White* [1947] I.R. 247 must apply with equal force in this situation also, if the constitutional guarantees of liberty of the person are to be adequately defended and vindicated. Consequently I would hold that before the power of search given by s.29 of the Dublin Police Act 1842, already referred to, can now be lawfully exercised, the suspect is

---

[40]   [1992] 2 I.R. 7.
[41]   See also, *Farrelly v. Devally* [1998] 4 I.R. 76.

entitled to be informed of the nature and description of the statutory power which is being invoked."[42]

Stop and Search under Section 30

Undoubtedly one of the broadest powers of stop and search is that found in section 30 of the Offences against the State Act 1939. It is worded in identical terms to the power to "stop and interrogate" discussed above, apart from the fact that "search" is substituted for "interrogate." Accordingly, the points discussed above with respect to the power to stop and interrogate are also applicable to the power to stop and search. In addition, it is also worth noting that there is no definition of a search in the Act. It is unlikely, however, that the power could be used to effect a strip search or any form of search that would require the suspect to remove an indecent amount of clothing. Since it is a power to stop and search the implication is that the search should take place at the spot where the suspect is stopped and that it should be cursory. Presumably, there must also be some correlation between the search and the suspicion upon which the search is grounded.

7–15

Section 30 also provides a power to "stop and search (if necessary by force) any vehicle or any ship, boat or other vessel" which the member of the Garda Síochána concerned "suspects to contain a person whom he is empowered" to arrest under section 30.[43] It is arguable that this power to search is confined to a search of the vehicle etc for the person who is liable to arrest under section 30. Once found, the person could then be searched, interrogated or arrested under section 30. On this interpretation a search of the car for evidence of the offence of which the person is suspected could be carried out only if the person is actually arrested. As noted above under "stop and question", it is arguable that this power to stop a vehicle etc carries with it an implicit power to require the driver of the vehicle etc to bring it to a halt, even where the requisite suspicion relates to a passenger as distinct from the driver.

Stop and Search under Criminal Law Act 1976

Closely related to the search powers under section 30 is that found in section 8 of the Criminal Law Act 1976. Section 8 of the 1976 Act confers a power of search in respect of a vehicle which has been stopped in certain circumstances. A member of the Garda Síochána may exercise the power where he or she with reasonable cause suspects that an offence within the scope of the section has been, is being or is about to be committed. The offences in question are:

7–16

"(a) an offence under the Act of 1939 or an offence that is for the time being a scheduled offence for the purposes of Part V of that Act;

(b) an offence under section 2 or 3 of the Criminal Law (Jurisdiction) Act 1976;

---

[42] [1992] 2 I.R. 7 at 10.
[43] Offences against the State Act 1939, s.30(2).

    (c) murder, manslaughter [or an offence under section 18 of the Offences against the Person Act 1861];[44]

    (d) an offence under section 23, 23A or 23B of the Larceny Act 1916;

    (e) an offence of malicious damage to property involving the use of fire or of any explosive substance (within the meaning of section 7(1)(e) of this Act;

    (f) an offence under the Firearms Acts, 1925 to 1971;

    (g) escape from lawful custody;

    (h) an offence under section 11 of the Air Navigation and Transport Act 1973, or under section 10 of the Criminal Law (Jurisdiction) Act 1976;

    (i) an offence under this Act;[45]

    (j) an offence under section 12(1) of the Firearms and Offensive Weapons Act 1990;

    (k) an offence under section 112(2) of the Road Traffic Act 1961 (substituted by section 3(7) of the Road Traffic (Amendment) Act 1984;[46]

    (l) an offence under section 2 of the Illegal Immigrants (Trafficking) Act 2000".[47]

7–17 There is no requirement for the member to harbour the suspicion against any occupant of a vehicle to be stopped and/or searched. It is quite sufficient that he or she reasonably suspects that a relevant offence has been committed, is being committed or is about to be committed. The purpose of the search of the vehicle, however, must be to ascertain whether:

> "(a) any person in or accompanying the vehicle has committed, is committing or is about to commit the offence, or
>
> (b) evidence relating to the commission or intended commission of the offence by any person is in the vehicle or on any person in or accompanying it."[48]

It would appear, therefore, that the provision is intended to confer a power on gardaí to stop and, if necessary, search cars at random as a means of preventing or detecting a relevant offence which they believe with reasonable cause has been committed, is being committed or is about to be committed. The wording of the provision, however, is problematic. While it purports to confer a power of search in respect of a vehicle which the member has required a person to stop, it does not specifically confer a power on the member to require the person to stop the vehicle. It seems to proceed on the assumption that a member of the Garda Síochána has an inherent power to require a person to stop a vehicle with a view to enabling the member ascertain any of the matters in (a) or (b) above. It is submitted, however, that a member of the Garda Síochána does not have any such power at common law in the absence of a prior suspicion against the driver or occupants of the vehicle. A general suspicion that a relevant offence has been committed, is

---

[44] The section 18 offence has been abolished by the Non-fatal Offences against the Person Act 1997. Surprisingly, it would appear that none of the offences created by the 1997 Act have been specifically added to this list.

[45] Criminal Law Act 1976, s.8(1). An attempt or conspiracy to commit any one of these offences is also included; s.8(4).

[46] Inserted by Criminal Justice (Miscellaneous Provisions) Act 1997, s.13.

[47] As inserted by Illegal Immigrants (Trafficking) Act 2000, s.6.

[48] Criminal Law Act 1976, s.8(2).

being committed or is about to be committed would not be sufficient. If such a power exists it must be conferred by statute. Section 109 of the Road Traffic Act 1961, which empowers a member of the Garda Síochána to require a person to being a vehicle to a halt, can hardly be sufficient for this purpose as it has been provided as a means of enforcing the Road Traffic code.

It is arguable, of course, that section 8 of the 1976 Act can be interpreted as implicitly conferring the necessary power on a member of the Garda Síochána to require a person to stop a vehicle where the member entertains only the general suspicion required for a search under the section. Indeed, there can be little doubt that the intention behind the section was that it should enable gardaí to stop vehicles with a view to checking whether they contained persons or evidence connected with a relevant offence which had been committed or which was in the course of commission. Section 8(3), for example, specifically permits a member of the Garda Síochána to compel a person to comply with a requirement to stop a vehicle. Such force may include the placing of a barrier or other device in the path of vehicles. While there is no provision which specifically requires a person to stop a vehicle when required by a member of the Garda Síochána who wishes to exercise his or her powers under section 8, it is likely but by no means certain that the courts will find such an obligation implicit in section 8.

    Where the power of search is available it is exercisable, in the first instance, only in respect of the vehicle. If, however, the member of the Garda Síochána concerned suspects with reasonable cause that any one of the facts mentioned in (a) or (b) above exists, he or she may also search any person in or accompanying the vehicle. This suspicion may arise as a result of the search of the vehicle or it may have been in existence prior to the vehicle being stopped.

7–18

Section 8 does not specify precisely how the initial general suspicion should be followed up with respect to the occupants of a vehicle which has been stopped. Presumably, the member of the Garda Síochána exercising the power can ask the driver and occupants for details of their identity, movements and what, if anything they know, about the offence(s) in question. However, section 8 does not impose any specific obligation on the occupants to answer these questions. It is submitted that in the absence of any such specific obligation in the section the member is confined to relying on the voluntary cooperation of the occupants, backed up by his power under the Road Traffic Acts to demand the production of the driver's driving licence.[49] The coercive provisions of sections 30(5), 30(6) and 52 of the Offences Against the State Act 1939 would seem to have no application here. Nevertheless, it may happen that as a result of things said, or of other matters which come to the member's notice in the course of the stop or search of the vehicle, that he or she forms the requisite reasonable suspicion with respect to the vehicle or any person in it. In this event he may proceed to search the occupants. Equally, he

7–19

---

[49] See Road Traffic Act 1961, s.40.

or she may already have formed the requisite suspicion prior to stopping the car, in which case he or she can proceed to search the occupants.

The wording of section 8 does not specifically address the issue of how long the vehicle and occupants should remain at the spot where they are stopped. Clearly, they must remain until the search, if any, of the vehicle has been completed. Equally, where relevant, they must wait until any search of the occupants is completed. However, the section does not confer a specific power to detain for questioning. In the absence of a search, therefore, it would appear that the occupants would be justified in leaving once the member of the Garda Síochána exercising the power has had a reasonable opportunity to ascertain the matters specified in the section. The member, however, is not precluded from acting on other criminal matters that come to his or her notice as a result of the stop, so long as the stop was not effected for the purpose of checking matters which were beyond the scope of section 8. If these matters are sufficient to justify the arrest of one or more of the occupants, an arrest may be effected and the normal arrest procedure will apply.

Stop and Search at Borders and Ports

7–20   Other police powers of stop and search which are relatively broad-based arise largely in the context of the enforcement of the customs laws or of persons entering or leaving the State. A member of the Garda Síochána does not actually enjoy a general power to stop and search travellers entering or leaving the State. However, there are a number of disparate powers which, collectively, might be considered to produce much the same result. Under the Customs Consolidation Act 1876 a member of the Garda Síochána may, upon reasonable suspicion, stop and examine any cart, wagon or other conveyance to ascertain whether any smuggled goods are contained in it.[50] The driver of such a vehicle commits an offence if he refuses to stop or allow such an examination when required to do so. Persons reasonably suspected of carrying goods the export of which is prohibited may also be stopped and searched.[51] Clearly, these powers of stop and search can be exercised anywhere within the jurisdiction. They are not confined to points of entry and exit to and from the State.

Additional powers are available in, or in the vicinity of, points of entry and departure to and from the State. For example, any ship or boat within the limits of any Irish port may be searched for uncustomed goods.[52] No suspicion is required. Persons on such boats, or who have landed from such boats, may also be searched, but only if the member of the Garda Síochána in

---

[50]   Customs Consolidation Act 1876, s.203.

[51]   Customs (Amendment) Act 1942, s.1. A member of the Garda Síochána has a power to question and demand relevant information from a person in control of goods whose export is prohibited; Customs Act 1956, s.4.

[52]   Customs Consolidation Act 1876, s.184. This provision confers the power on "any customs officer or person duly employed for the prevention of smuggling". However, s.5 of the Illicit Distillation Act 1857 confers a member of the Garda Síochána with all the powers of customs officers as regards seizure, detention or prosecution in the enforcement of the Customs Acts. Although it is by no means certain, it would appear that this would extend to a member the powers contained in provisions such as that in s.184 of the 1876 Act.

question has good reason to suspect that the person to be searched has in his possession uncustomed or prohibited goods.[53] Furthermore, a member may search any alien landing in the State in order to ascertain if he is carrying any letters, written messages or memoranda, or any written or printed matter including plans, photographs and other pictorial representations.[54] No suspicion is required, although any such search will normally be preceded by the alien being requested to make a declaration as to whether he is carrying any such material.

The problem of uncontrolled drugs attracts specific powers of search exercisable against any person found at, or in the vicinity of, any port or airport or the land frontier with Northern Ireland. A member of the Garda Síochána may search any such person whom he or she reasonably suspects is in possession of a controlled drug which was imported, or is being or is intended to be exported, unlawfully.[55] If the member considers it necessary he or she may detain the person for such time as is reasonably necessary for carrying out the search which may involve the removal of the person's clothing. The member may also search any vehicle, vessel or aircraft in which he or she suspects that a controlled drug may be found and for that purpose he or she may require the vehicle to stop and to be kept stationary.

A member of the Garda Síochána enjoys broad powers of stop and search in an aerodrome which he or she may exercise in the interests of the proper operation, or the security or safety, of the aerodrome or the security or safety of persons, aircraft or other property.[56] These powers are not confined to travellers but extend to any persons on the aerodrome. The member may stop and search any person or vehicle on the aerodrome. He or she may require any person to give his name and address, produce other evidence of identity, state the purpose of his presence on the aerodrome and account for any baggage or other property which may be in his possession. The member may detain the person for such time as is reasonably necessary for the exercise of any of these powers. Where a person does not cooperate fully with these requirements, or if the member reasonably suspects that he does not have a lawful reason for being on the aerodrome, the member may order him to leave the aerodrome or any part of it. There is no directly equivalent body of powers exercisable in any sea port.

Other more limited powers of stop and search have been developed ad hoc and in a piecemeal manner throughout the past two centuries, and the practice continues to this day.[57] For the most part each of these powers have been created separately to deal with a specific type of criminal offence or criminal activity. Typically, a member of the Garda Síochána, or other authorised official, will be permitted to stop and search a person and/or a vehicle where the member has reason to believe that the relevant criminal offence has been

7–21

---

[53] Customs Consolidation Act 1876, s.182.
[54] The Aliens Order 1946, art.7(10).
[55] Customs and Excise (Miscellaneous Provisions) Act 1988, s.2.
[56] Air Navigation and Transport Act 1988, s.33(1).
[57] For a discussion of features common to some of these powers, see Williams "Statutory Powers of Search and Arrest on the Ground of Unlawful Possession" [1960] Crim LR 598.

committed or is being committed. Examples of such statutory powers are to be found in the: Wildlife Act 1976,[58] Road Traffic Act 1961,[59] Misuse of Drugs Act 1977,[60] the Explosive Substances Act 1875,[61] the Diseases of Animals Act 1966[62] and liquor legislation.[63] Section 29 of the Dublin Police Act 1842 would appear to be the only measure which provides a power to stop and search for stolen goods or goods unlawfully obtained. It permits a member of the Garda Síochána to, *inter alia,* stop, search and detain any person who may be reasonably suspected of having or conveying in any manner any thing stolen or unlawfully obtained. However, it can be used only within the Dublin Metropolitan area.

Scope of a Search

7–22 None of the relevant statutory provisions actually define what is meant by a "search" pursuant to the powers which they create.[64] Presumably, the scope and nature of any individual search must be commensurate with the suspicion on which it is grounded. It does not necessarily follow, however, that a strip search will be lawful in a particular case simply because the authorised officer is looking for an item that is small enough to be secreted away in a body crevice. Most of these search powers can be exercised only on the basis of a "stop." This suggests a situation where it is considered necessary to subject the person stopped to a search on the spot, as opposed to the situation where it is possible to arrest the suspect and subject him to a search later in the police station. Since most stops will be effected in public, it must be presumed, in the absence of any clear indication to the contrary in the relevant statute, that the legislative intention is that the search cannot extend beyond a person's outer clothing.[65] Anything approaching a strip search, or intimate body search, would require the person to be taken to a room or cubicle where the search can be carried out in circumstances of privacy and decency. It can be argued that to compel a person to enter such a room or cubicle goes beyond a requirement to "stop" and submit to a search on the spot. Certainly, if the room or cubicle is located some distance away from where the stop was effected, it would seem that a mere power to "stop" and search would not be sufficient to impose a legal obligation on the person stopped to go to that room or cubicle for the purpose of being searched. This

---

[58] S.72, as amended by the Wildlife (Amendment) Act 2000, s.65.

[59] S.20

[60] S.23.

[61] S.75.

[62] S.17A, as inserted by Diseases of Animals (Amendment) Act 2001, s.2. This provision expires after 12 months unless it is continued in force from time to time by a resolution of each House of the Oireachtas.

[63] Illicit Distillation (Ireland) Act 1831, s.25; Intoxicating Liquor Act 1960, s.22(3).

[64] The power to breathalyse persons under the drink-driving legislation might be considered to be in a category of its own; see Road Traffic Act 1994, s.12 and R Pierse *Road Traffic Legislation in the Republic of Ireland* (Butterworths, Dublin 1995), pp. 363–401.

[65] The common law power to stop and frisk-search suspects in public in the USA is confined to a search of the outer clothing; see *Terry v. Ohio, op. cit.*

conclusion could be avoided, of course, by the expression of a clear intention to the contrary in the statutory provision conferring the power.

Stop and Search under the Misuse of Drugs Act

One power that has given rise to particular difficulty in this context is that provided by section 23 of the Misuse of Drugs Act 1977. It enables a member of the Garda Síochána to search any person whom he or she has reasonable cause to suspect is in possession of a controlled drug in breach of the Act.[66] A prior arrest is not made a precondition for the exercise of this power.[67] Where the member entertains a reasonable suspicion with respect to a person he or she may also stop and search any vehicle, vessel or aircraft in which he or she suspects that such a drug may be found.[68] The member who intends to search a person under this provision may require the person to accompany him to a Garda station for the purpose of being searched at the station.[69] There is no specific precondition to the effect that the member should be satisfied that it is necessary to bring the person to the Garda station in order to carry out the search. Where a member intends to carry out a search of a vehicle etc under section 23 he or she may require the person who appears to him to be the owner or in control or charge of the vehicle at the time not to move anything from the vehicle etc pending the commencement of the search.[70] The member may also require the person to remain in or accompany the vehicle etc for the purpose of the search.[71] Moreover, where the member considers reasonably that the place in which he or she finds the vehicle is unsuitable for the search he or she may require the person concerned to take the vehicle or cause it to be taken to a specified place which the member considers suitable for the search.[72]

It is worth noting that the power to stop and search the vehicle requires only a suspicion, as distinct from a reasonable suspicion, with respect to the vehicle. While a reasonable suspicion against any person is a precondition for a search of the vehicle, there is no specific requirement that the suspicion should relate to the driver or any person within the vehicle. The power to search the vehicle, however, does not carry with it an automatic power to search the occupants of the vehicle. An individual can be searched under this power only if the member entertains a reasonable suspicion with respect to that person.

Another point to note about the search power under section 23 is that it is not predicated on a prior stop. It is available irrespective of whether the person to be searched is stopped in public, is in a Garda station, is in his own home or is on property belonging to another. It follows that the scope and

---

[66] Misuse of Drugs Act 1977, s.23(1)(a).
[67] A person being searched and detained under this power should be informed of the reason; *Pedro v. Diss* [1981] 2 All E.R. 59; *Farrelly v. Devally* [1998] 4 I.R. 76.
[68] Misuse of Drugs Act 1977, s.23((1)(b). For the purposes of the search he may require the person in control of the vehicle to bring it to a halt and to keep it stationary and/or to take it to a place more suitable for conducting the search.
[69] Misuse of Drugs Act 1977, s.23(1A), as inserted by Misuse of Drugs Act 1984, s.12.
[70] *ibid.* s.23(1B)(a).
[71] *ibid.* s.23(1B)(c).
[72] *ibid.* s.23(1B)(b).

nature of a search under this power is not intended to be limited by the environment in which it is likely to be effected. Where the relevant suspicion is present the member of the Garda Síochána in question is empowered simply to search the person concerned.

Given the nature of controlled drugs it can often happen that a personal search will have to be very intimate and, as such, will represent a gross invasion of the individual's personal rights of privacy and bodily integrity. Nevertheless, it is clear from the terms of the section that that will not operate as a constraint on the exercise of the power. A member of the Garda Síochána who has the requisite suspicion is specifically empowered both to detain the person for such time as is necessary to make the search, and/or to require the person to accompany him or her to a Garda station for the purpose of being searched at the station. Where a person fails to comply with the member's request under these provisions the member may arrest him without a warrant. However, the option of carrying out the search at the Garda station is not predicated on a prior arrest. A person can be taken into Garda custody and subjected to a strip search under this power without actually being arrested. Given that the Irish courts have been emphatic in discounting the notion of a police power to detain short of arrest this represents a very significant development in police powers. Nevertheless, a challenge to its constitutionality has been upheld by both the High Court and the Supreme Court.

7–24   In *O'Callaghan v. Ireland*[73] the plaintiff had resisted the attempt by a member of the Garda Síochána to search him for possession of controlled drugs under the section 23 power. He was subsequently charged with assault on the member and resisting the search. The plaintiff challenged the constitutionality of the search power primarily on the basis that it amounted to a police power of detention independent of arrest. In rejecting the challenge the Supreme Court considered that this power to search on the basis of a reasonable suspicion is an extension of the power to arrest on reasonable suspicion. Any assessment of its constitutionality must be based on a balancing of the personal rights of the individual on the one hand and the interests of the common good on the other. The correct test to apply in this regard is that laid down by Kenny J. in *Ryan and Attorney General* as follows:

> "The Oireachtas has to reconcile the exercise of personal rights with the claims of the common good, and its decision on the reconciliation should prevail unless it was oppressive to all or some of the citizens, or unless there is no reasonable proportion between the benefits which the legislation will confer on the citizens or a substantial body of them and the interference with the personal rights of the citizen."[74]

In applying this test the Supreme Court was swayed by the nature and extent of the threat posed to society by the possession, use and distribution of controlled drugs. It considered that this threat was so great that the legislature

---

73   [1994] 1 I.R. 555.
74   [1965] I.R. 294 at 312.

had acted reasonably and properly in conferring a power to search in circumstances where a power of arrest was available. Indeed, it was of the opinion that the availability of such a search power could actually protect the rights of the suspect against greater police intrusion. Since arrest would be an option in every case where the search power is available the use of the latter could actually avoid the need to bring the suspect into custody in many cases.

One of the potential problems with the power to bring the suspect to a Garda station for the purpose of a search under section 23 is the fact that there are no statutory provisions or regulations governing the rights of the suspect and his treatment while in the station. Since this contrasts with the position where the suspect has been brought to the station under arrest, there is the danger that the search power will be used as a means of circumventing the statutory requirements applicable to arrest and detention. The Supreme Court countered this argument by ruling, without referring to any authority, that a suspect lawfully in Garda custody for the purpose of a search is entitled to all the appropriate rights concerning access to legal advice, freedom from harassment, interrogation or assault and all the other rights that are appropriate to an arrested person. Moreover, the court also indicated that it must proceed on the assumption that discretionary powers will be exercised in a constitutional manner. The victim would have a remedy in any case where he or she was exposed to unnecessary harassment, distress, or embarrassment as a result of the improper exercise of the search power.

    It does not follow from the decision in *O'Callaghan* that all police powers of search which entail a period of custodial detention in the absence of arrest are beyond constitutional challenge. The Court in *O'Callaghan* was strongly influenced by the fact that the power of search under section 23 was aimed at the major social danger posed by the unlawful use and supply of controlled drugs, and by the fact that the power was exercisable only on the basis of reasonable suspicion. The outcome might well be different in the case of a power which permitted an intimate body search for stolen or uncustomed goods in the absence of a reasonable suspicion.

7–25

Even though the Supreme Court in *O'Callaghan* considered that the section 23 power was an extension of the power to arrest on reasonable suspicion, it does not follow that gardaí can use it as a substitute for arrest. If a person is purportedly detained under section 23 in circumstances which amount to arrest it is likely that his or her detention will be unlawful and any evidence obtained from him or her during that period of unlawful detention will be inadmissible against him in his subsequent trial. In *People (DPP) v. Boylan*[75] the appellant had been stopped by gardaí at Dublin Port under section 23. A subsequent search of his lorry quickly revealed a package containing a quantity of cannabis. The appellant was taken to a shed at the Port to meet with two gardaí. He was kept there for a further period of two hours even

7–26

---

[75] [1991] 1 I.R. 477.

though his lorry was not subjected to anything more than a minimal search during that period. He was then taken to a Garda station and detained under section 4 of the Criminal Justice Act 1984. Section 4 requires a person to be brought to a Garda station after having been arrested. In this case the Court of Criminal Appeal found that the appellant had effectively been placed under arrest when he was brought to the shed. His detention there could not be justified under section 23 as being necessary to conduct a proper search of the vehicle as no such search was carried out. Since he had been effectively arrested at that point he should have been brought immediately to a Garda station for the purpose of being detained under section 4 of the Criminal Justice Act 1984. Since this did not happen until two hours later the Court ruled his purported detention under section 4 unlawful. It follows that a person can be detained under section 23 strictly for the purpose of facilitating a search under that provision. Detention in excess of what is required for that purpose may amount to an arrest, If the correct formalities and procedures for such arrest are not followed it is likely that any further detention of the person concerned beyond that point will be unlawful.

Where a member of the Garda Síochána intends to exercise his or her powers of stop and search under section 23 it would appear that he or she should follow the formalities appropriate to an arrest, as applied by analogy to the situation of a stop and search. Accordingly, he or she should advise the person concerned that he (and/or his vehicle, etc.,) is suspected of being in possession of controlled drugs and that a search will be carried out under section 23. Equally, if it is intended that the person and or vehicle will be brought to a Garda station or a suitable place (in the case of the vehicle) for the purpose of the search, the person should be asked to cooperate. It would appear, however, that simply telling the person that he (and/or his vehicle) will be brought to a Garda station for the purpose of a search under section 23 may not in itself be sufficient to impose an obligation on the person to comply.[76] The member of the Garda Síochána exercising the power must actually require him to accompany him or her to the Garda Station for the purpose of search and/or to bring his vehicle to a suitable place and/or to accompany the vehicle for the duration of the search.

E. Surveillance

1. Introduction

7–27   It is quite common for a police investigation into suspected criminal activity to include the surveillance of persons believed to be involved. Evidence gathered during the course of such an investigation may prove sufficient subsequently to justify a stop and search of such persons, or even to effect one or more arrests. Equally, where the police have received information that a crime is going to be committed at a particular location, such as a bank, they

---

[76] *Farrelly v. Devally* [1998] 4 I.R. 76.

may keep that location under surveillance. A successful outcome to such surveillance will be the arrest of the persons involved without injury to the person or damage to property.

The importance of surveillance in the police detection of crime and the apprehension of offenders suggests that the police enjoy certain powers to engage in surveillance. It is necessary, therefore, to consider the nature and extent of these powers.

2. Common Law

At common law, a member of the Garda Síochána has the same freedom as every citizen to observe the movements of another person or to keep another person's property under observation. In short, this means that he or she can follow another person around in public, and can keep watch outside a building for a particular person to emerge. Equally, he or she may photograph and take audio and visual recordings of any person, and he may keep any building or property under observation. The only limitations on such freedom at common law are found in the law of trespass and possibly nuisance.[77] For example, if the observer trespasses on property in order to carry out the observation, he or she is liable to be sued by the owner or occupier of that property. The person under observation, however, will have no cause of action unless he is the actual owner or occupier. Similarly, if the observer commits a trespass against the person or a trespass to goods in the pursuit of his or her observation, the victim of the trespass will be able to sue. The person under observation will not be able to maintain an action against the observer solely on the ground of the observation unless, of course, the manner in which the observation is conducted satisfies a statutory offence created by measures such as the Non-fatal Offences against the Person Act 1997,[78] or the Postal and Telecommunications Services Act 1983.[79]

7–28

3. Constitutional Protection

The victim of surveillance may find more protection in the Constitution than at common law. It is possible that the nature of the observation or the manner in which it is conducted could amount to a breach of the individual's constitutional right to privacy. Although privacy as such is not specifically mentioned as one of the fundamental rights of the individual in the Constitution,

7–29

---

[77] See Law Reform Commission *Privacy: Surveillance and the Interception of Communications* (Law Reform Commission, Dublin, 1996), pp. 54–60.

[78] See, for example, the offence of harassment in Non-fatal Offences Against the Person Act 1997, s.10.

[79] Section 84(1) makes it an offence to interfere with any postal packet addressed to another person, while s.98(1) makes it a criminal offence to intercept telecommunications messages. However, it is worth noting that the Minister for Justice, Equality and Law Reform and the Minister for Communications have a power to issue directions for the interception of phone calls and the opening of mail. See Interception of Postal Packets and Telecommunications Messages (Regulation) Act 1993 for the circumstances in which this power can be exercised and the procedure that must be followed.

the Supreme Court has recognised that it does attract constitutional protection.[80] It follows that a victim of surveillance could maintain an action for breach of the right to privacy against the person or persons who have been keeping him under surveillance. This possibility has already been tested in the context of police surveillance of a suspect, but without very promising results from the perspective of the suspect.

In *Kane v. Governor of Mountjoy Prison*[81] the applicant had been arrested and detained under section 30 of the Offences against the State Act 1939 on suspicion of being a member of the IRA. The arrest was effected at a time of heightened security tension when a nationwide search for IRA arms was being conducted. By the time of his release from custody the Garda were aware that a warrant for his extradition to Northern Ireland would be arriving shortly. Accordingly, they attempted to keep him under observation so that the warrant could be served on him when it did arrive. A bizarre "cat and mouse" chase ensued. This entailed several gardaí openly walking behind and in front of the applicant at close quarters along public streets backed up by two Garda cars, the spectacle of several gardaí waiting on the stairs leading to the office of a solicitor while the applicant was in the office seeking legal advice, several gardaí keeping watch around the house of a friend of the applicant while he and others were in the house, a high speed car chase in which several Garda cars kept track of a car in which the applicant was travelling and, finally, the spectacle of a member of the Garda Síochána following the applicant through a hedge and into a ditch. The applicant was arrested in the ditch for allegedly assaulting the member in question. While he was still in custody the extradition warrant arrived and was served on him.

The applicant unsuccessfully challenged the lawfulness of his detention in the High Court. On appeal to the Supreme Court he argued that: (i) the nature of the overt surveillance applied to him was such that he was never truly released from the original section 30 detention or, alternatively, the nature of the surveillance was such that it had the effect of bringing him back into custody; and (ii) the extent and nature of the surveillance amounted to an unlawful harassment of him within the terms of section 7 of the Conspiracy and Protection of Property Act 1875. Although dismissing the appeal the Supreme Court was willing to accept that an individual may enjoy a right of privacy even while travelling on the public streets and roads. It also accepted that the sort of overt surveillance applied in this case would be "objectionable" and "clearly unlawful" in the absence of a basis to justify it. In the words of Finlay C.J.:

> "Overt surveillance including a number of Garda on foot, closely following a pedestrian, and a number of Garda cars, marked as well as unmarked, tailing a driver or passenger in a motor car would, it seems to me, require a specific justification arising from all of the circumstances of a particular case and the nature and importance of the particular police duty being discharged.

---

[80] *McGee v. Attorney General*; [1974] I.R. 284; *Norris v. Attorney General* [1984] I.R. 36; *Kennedy v. Ireland* [1987] I.R. 587. See also, Law Reform Commission, *op. cit.*, pp. 38–53.
[81] [1988] I.L.R.M. 724.

Such surveillance is capable of gravely affecting the peace of mind and public reputation of any individual and the courts could not, in my view, accept any general application of such a procedure by the police, but should require where it is put into operation and challenged, a specific adequate justification for it."[82]

In determining whether there is a sufficient justification for the surveillance in any individual case a key issue is the nature of the duty which the gardaí were attempting to discharge. In *Kane* the Supreme Court refused to draw any distinction between the duty of investigating or detecting crime and the execution of an extradition warrant in this context.[83] It was satisfied that the State had a very clear interest in the efficient discharge of the reciprocal obligations undertaken between it and other States for the apprehension of fugitive offenders. This, according to the court, translates into a duty on a member of the Garda Síochána to take reasonable steps to ensure that the warrant is executed once it is issued. The court did not feel that the intensive overt surveillance applied in this case was unreasonable. While this would suggest that it would be very difficult to challenge the legality of overt police surveillance, it must be remembered that the actual facts of *Kane* were exceptional. The court was influenced particularly by the applicant's status as an IRA suspect who had been in hiding and who was likely to go back into hiding at the first opportunity. Also relevant was the fact that the applicant was suspected of being associated with a subversive arms cache which was uncovered in the course of the ongoing nationwide search for arms.

7–30

4. Statutory Provisions

Police surveillance tactics are not confined to keeping a suspect in view. The range of technological devices available for keeping people under visual observation, eavesdropping on their conversations and intercepting their communications is immense and the devices themselves are steadily advancing in sophistication. It would, of course, be remiss of the police if they did not seek to avail of these devices in order to tackle crime more effectively. By the same token, however, the uncontrolled resort to such devices by a national police force poses major difficulties not just for the individual's right to privacy but also for society's interest in the maintenance of a pluralist democracy based on civil and political liberties. As yet Ireland has not attempted to strike a balance between these conflicting interests through general legislation governing surveillance and privacy.[84] In the meantime the police enjoy at least the same freedom as any other citizen to resort to these devices for the

7–31

---

[82] [1988] I.L.R.M. 724 at 735–736.

[83] It is worth noting that McCarthy and Hederman JJ. were prepared to rank the enforcement of extradition obligations as generally less important than the investigation and detection of crime in this context. Nevertheless, they joined the other three judges in dismissing the appeal because in this case the arrival of the warrant was imminent.

[84] For an excellent discussion of the issues, the current law and proposals for reform, see Law Reform Commission, *op. cit.*

purposes of keeping a check on the activities of other persons. Of course, this freedom must be exercised within the constraints of the law.[84a]

The common law and constitutional principles identified above are just as relevant to the use of technological surveillance devices as they are to the more basic forms of surveillance. In addition, there are a number of statutory criminal offences affecting the interception of communications which would be particularly relevant to the use of some technological devices. These offences include: telephone-tapping,[85] the possession of certain listening devices without a licence;[86] the interception of telecommunications messages;[87] and using a computer to gain unauthorised access to data.[88] Although these offences apply generally to the police as much as the ordinary citizen, there are certain limited provisos in favour of the former. For example, it is not an offence for a member of the Garda Síochána to intercept a telecommunication's message for the purpose of investigating telephone calls which constitute a criminal offence under section 13(1) of the Post Office (Amendment) Act 1951.[89] A member may also be authorised to intercept telecommunications messages by a direction issued by the Minister for Justice, Equality and Law Reform[90] under section 110 of the Postal and Telecommunications Services Act 1983.[91] Indeed, the interception of postal and telecommunications messages deserves more detailed examination as it is now the subject of specific statutory provision.

F. Police Interception of Postal and Telecommunications

Criminal Offences

7–32   The Postal and Telecommunications Services Act 1983 protects mail and telecommunications messages from interception. It is generally a criminal offence to open, delay or detain a postal packet addressed to another person.[92] It is also a criminal offence to permit another person to do any of these things. Similarly, it is generally a criminal offence to intercept, attempt to intercept, permit another person to intercept, or do anything which would enable another person to intercept any telecommunications message being trans-mitted by Telecom Éireann.[93] Normally, where a person is charged with any one of these offences no further proceedings can be taken in the matter (other

---

84a See *Walsh and McCutcheon op. cit.*

85 Malicious Damage Act 1861, s.37 (as amended by the Criminal Damage Act 1991, s.14(2)(a); Post Office Act 1908, s.51 (as amended by s.8(1) of the Postal and Telecommunications Services Act 1983); Larceny Act 1916, s.10

86 Wireless Telegraphy Acts 1926 to 1988; Wireless Telegraphy (Control of Sale, Letting on Hire or Manufacture, and Importation of Radio Transceivers) Order, 1981.

87 Postal and Telecommunications Services Act 1983, s.98(1).

88 Criminal Damage Act 1991, s.5.

89 Postal and Telecommunications Services Act 1983, s.98(2).

90 A direction may also be issued by the Minister for Communications.

91 For a useful discussion of the scope of this power see Law Reform Commission *op. cit.* at ch.6.

92 Postal and Telecommunications Services Act 1983, s.84(1).

93 Postal and Telecommunications Services Act 1983, s.98(1).

than a remand in custody or on bail) except by or with the consent of the DPP.[94]

Defences

Of course, the capacity to open mail or tap telephone calls is potentially a very effective device for combating crime and political subversion. Accordingly, the 1983 Act excludes from criminal liability the interception of postal packets or telecommunications messages in certain circumstances. For example, opening a postal packet pursuant to a direction issued by the Minister for Communications under section 110 of the Act would not constitute a criminal offence (see below).[95] Similarly, it would not be a criminal offence to intercept a telecommunications message pursuant to a direction issued by the Minister for Communications under section 110 (see below).[96] Nor would it be an offence for a member of the Garda Síochána to intercept a message for the purpose of an investigation of a suspected offence under section 13 of the Post Office (Amendment) Act 1951 (telecommunications messages of an obscene, menacing or similar character) on the complaint of a person claiming to have received such a message.[97]

Section 110 of the Postal and Telecommunications Services Act 1983 permits the Minister for Communications to issue written directions to An Post or Telecom Éireann requiring them, *inter alia*, to do or refrain from doing anything which he may specify from time to time as necessary in the national interest.[98] This is clearly broad enough to encompass the interception of postal packets and telecommunications messages in appropriate circumstances.[99] As seen above it will not be a criminal offence for any person to intercept a postal packet or telecommunications message pursuant to such a direction issued by the Minister. It does not follow, however, that interceptions pursuant to such a direction will be lawful for all purposes. Indeed, the State's obligations under the European Convention for the Protection of Human Rights and Fundamental Freedoms requires the interception of postal and telecommunications messages to be placed on a structured and transparent basis which offers protection to the privacy rights of the individual without unduly compromising the capacity of the State to combat terrorism and serious crime. In Ireland these require-ments have been satisfied by the Interception of Postal Packets and Telecommunications Messages (Regulation) Act 1993.[100]

---

[94] Interception of Postal Packets and Telecommunications Messages (Regulation) Act 1993, s.10(1). The same applies where a person is charged under s.45 of the Telegraph Act 1863 or the second paragraph of s.11 of the Post Office (Protection) Act 1884.

[95] Postal and Telecommunications Services Act 1983, s.84(2)(b).

[96] *ibid.* s.98(2)(b).

[97] *ibid.* s.98(2)(a).

[98] *ibid.* s.110(1)(b).

[99] A direction requiring such interceptions will only be effective where there is also in force a suitable authorisation issued by the Minister for Justice, Equality and Law Reform under the Interception of Postal Packets and Telecommunications Messages (Regulation) Act 1993; see below.

[100] For more detailed analysis, see Law Reform Commission *Privacy: Surveillance and the Interception of Communications* (Law Reform Commission, Dublin, 1996).

Authorising Interception

7–33 The 1993 Act empowers the Minister for Justice, Equality and Law Reform to authorise the interception of postal packets and telecommunications messages in certain circumstances.[101] For this purpose the interception of a postal packet means an act which consists of the opening or attempted opening of a postal packet addressed to any person or the delaying or detaining of any such packet or the doing of anything to prevent its due delivery.[102] Also covered is the authorising, suffering or permitting of another person (apart from the person to whom the packet is addressed) to do any of these things. The interception of telecommunications messages in this context is defined as an act which consists of the listening or attempted listening to, or the recording or attempted recording, by any means, in the course of its transmission, of a telecommunications message, except where the person on whose behalf the message is transmitted or the person intended to receive the message has consented to the listening or recording.[103]

In the case of both telecommunications messages and postal packets a Ministerial authorisation under the 1993 Act is confined to those situations in which an interception would constitute a criminal offence if not done pursuant to an authorisation or a direction issued by the Minister for Communications under section 110 of the 1983 Act.[104] It has no application, therefore, to those situations which would not normally attract criminal liability, or to those which are specifically excluded from criminal liability without the need for a ministerial direction.

7–34 Interceptions may be authorised under the 1993 Act only for the purpose of criminal investigation and for the protection of state security.[105] In the case of criminal investigation the offence must be serious and other means of investigation must be unlikely to produce evidence of its commission.[106] If it has already been committed there must be a reasonable prospect that the interception would be of material assistance in providing evidence. In the case of an apprehended offence there must be a reasonable prospect that the interception would be of material assistance in preventing or detecting the crime. The importance of obtaining the information or evidence in a criminal investigation must be sufficient to justify the interception having regard to the importance of preserving the privacy of postal packets and telecommunications messages.

Before an authorisation can be given on the grounds of state security, there must be reasonable grounds for believing that the particular activities being

---

[101] Interception of Postal Packets and Telecommunications Messages (Regulation) Act 1993, s.2.

[102] *ibid*. s.1. While it is by no means certain, it would appear that a postal packet in this context relates only to those entrusted to An Post.

[103] Interception of Postal Packets and Telecommunications Messages (Regulation) Act 1993, s.1. Although it is by no means certain it would appear that telecommunications messages in this context are confined to those transmitted through Telecom Éireann. It definitely covers telegrams.

[104] Interception of Postal Packets and Telecommunications Messages (Regulation) Act 1993, s.1.

[105] s.2(1).

[106] *ibid*. ss.2(3) and 4.

investigated are endangering, or are likely to endanger, the security of the state.[107] Equally, other forms of investigation must be unlikely to produce the information necessary to assess the threat posed by the activities. There must also be a reasonable prospect that the interception will be of material assistance in providing that information, and the importance of obtaining it must be sufficient to justify the interception having regard to the importance of preserving the privacy of postal packets and telecommunications.

Only the Garda Commissioner can apply for an authorisation in the case of a **7–35** criminal investigation, while both he and the Chief of Staff of the Defence Forces can apply in the case of state security.[108] All applications must be made in writing to an officer nominated for the purpose by the Minister. They must contain sufficient information to enable the Minister determine whether the relevant detailed considerations have been satisfied. Each application is examined in the first instance by the nominated officer who, in turn, makes a submission and recommendation to the Minister.[109] Where authorisation is granted it is given in the form of a warrant signed by the Minister, who must be satisfied that all the relevant requirements have been satisfied.[110] The warrant must show the date on which the authorisation was given and state whether the interception relates to a postal packet or telecommunications message or both.[111] It must also specify the postal address (and/or telecommunications address) to which the interception relates. In the case of the former it must also specify the person or persons to whom the interception relates, unless the Minister considers that to restrict the authorisation to a specified person or persons would be prejudicial to the purposes of the proposed interception. The warrant may also require the person to whom it is addressed to disclose the intercepted material to such persons as are specified in the warrant. An authorisation normally remains in force for three months unless the Commissioner or Chief of Staff considers that interceptions to which it relates are no longer required or the judge appointed to review the operation of the Act thinks it should be cancelled.[112] An authorisation can also be extended beyond three months in certain circumstances.[113]

Independent Scrutiny

The extent to which the operation of the scheme is amenable to independent **7–36** scrutiny is a key factor in determining whether it satisfies Ireland's obligations under the European Convention on Human Rights. In this regard the Act provides for the designation of a High Court judge who will report to the Taoiseach on the operation of the Act and compliance with its provisions.[114]

---

[107] *ibid.* ss.2(3) and 5.
[108] *ibid.* s.6(1).
[109] *ibid.* s.6(2).
[110] *ibid.* s.2(2) and (3). There is provision for an oral authorisation in cases of exceptional urgency.
[111] *ibid.* s.2(4).
[112] *ibid.* s.2(5).
[113] *ibid.* s.2(6).
[114] *ibid.* s.8.

A copy of his report must normally be laid before each House of the Oireachtas.[115]

The designated judge has a specific role to play at the level of individual authorisations. He or she has the power to investigate any case in which an authorisation has been given and, for this purpose, has access to any official documents relating to an authorisation or an application for authorisation.[116] If the judge informs the Minister that he or she considers a particular authorisation should not have been given or that it should be cancelled, the Minister must cancel the authorisation.[117] The judge is fully independent in the performance of these functions and continues to serve as a judge of the High Court while doing so.

Another form of independent scrutiny is provided in the form of a "Complaints Referee" who must be a judge of the Circuit Court or District Court or a practising barrister or solicitor of not less than ten years standing.[118] Where a person believes that a communication sent to or by him has been intercepted in the course of its transmission by An Post or Telecom Éireann he may apply to the Referee for an investigation into the matter.[119] The referee will investigate whether there has been any contravention of a number of the statutory provisions relating to the authorisation.[120] If he or she concludes that there has been a contravention of any of these provisions, the Referee must notify the applicant in writing to that effect and make a report to the Taoiseach.[121] He or she may also quash the authorisation, direct the destruction of any copy of the intercepted communication and make a recommendation for compensation. If the Referee makes a recommendation for compensation the Minister for Justice, Equality and Law Reform is legally obliged to implement it.[122] Where the Referee concludes that there has been no contravention of the relevant provisions but that the offence in question was not serious, he must refer the matter to the designated judge.[123] If the latter agrees that the offence was not serious then the Referee is under the same duty in the matter with respect to the applicant that he or she would have been under if he or she had concluded that there had been a contravention of the relevant provisions. Where the Referee comes to a conclusion other than that there has been a contravention or that the offence in question was not serious, he or she must notify the applicant in writing that there has been no contravention of specified provisions of the Act in relation to a relevant authorisation.[124] In the discharge of his or her functions the Referee has the same powers of access to official documents as the designated judge.[125]

---

[115] *ibid.* s.8(7).
[116] *ibid.* s.8(3).
[117] *ibid.* s.8(6).
[118] *ibid.* s.9(2).
[119] *ibid.* s.9(3).
[120] *ibid.* s.9(4).
[121] *ibid.* s.9(5).
[122] *ibid.* s.9(12).
[123] *ibid.* s.9(6).
[124] *ibid.* s.9(8)
[125] *ibid.* s.9(10) & (11).

Limiting Disclosure of Interceptions

The Minister for Justice, Equality and Law Reform is under an obligation to **7–37** ensure that such arrangements as he considers necessary exist to limit to the minimum necessary the disclosure of the fact that an authorisation has been given and the contents of any communication which has been intercepted pursuant to an authorisation.[126] This obligation extends to arrangements to ensure that copies of any such communication are not made to any extent greater than is necessary and are destroyed as soon as their retention is no longer necessary. All official documents relating to an authorisation and an application for an authorisation must be retained for a period of at least three years from the date on which the authorisation ceases to be in force.[127]

The 1993 Act specifically states that a contravention of the provisions governing the application and authorisation procedure for a warrant, or the provisions governing the format of the warrant, or the conditions necessary for the issuance of a warrant will not in itself render the authorisation invalid or constitute a cause of action at the suit of a person affected by the authorisation.[128] This, however, does not affect a cause of action for the infringement of a constitutional right.

Special procedural provisions apply to any action in respect of any alleged act **7–38** or omission which could amount to an offence of intercepting a postal packet or telecommunication's message (or which would constitute such an offence had the act or omission not been covered by an authorisation or other lawful authority).[129] These provisions clearly cover any civil action, but it is not clear whether they also extend to any criminal action. It is stated, however, that they do not apply if a person has been convicted of an offence in respect of the act or omission.[130]

Limiting Disclosure in Legal Proceedings

Under these special procedural provisions the question whether the alleged act or omission was done or made shall be determined before the determination of any question whether an authorisation was given.[131] Unless and until it is established that the act or omission was done or made no "person" shall give evidence, or be asked any question, and nothing shall be made the subject of discovery, or be disclosed, produced or alleged by or on behalf of the defendant that would show or tend to show that an authorisation was or was not given, or that an application for an authorisation was or was not made, or that proposals for or steps towards the making of such an application were or were not made or taken. A "person" in this context refers to any

---

[126] *ibid.* s.12(1). "Necessary" in this context means necessary for the purpose of the prevention or detection of serious offences or in the interests of the security of the State; s.12(2).
[127] *ibid.* s.11.
[128] *ibid.* s.9(1).
[129] *ibid.* s.10(2)(a).
[130] *ibid.* s.10(2)(e).
[131] *ibid.* s.10(2)(b).

member of the civil service, the Defence Forces or the Garda Síochána, any person in the employment of An Post or Telecom Éireann or any other person on whom a function is conferred by the 1993 Act.[132] Where it is determined that the act or omission was done or made the court shall, on the application of any party to the proceedings, and on such terms as the court may determine, allow any amendment to any pleading that may be necessary for the determination of the question whether an authorisation was given.[133]

The Act also protects a person from being compelled in any proceedings, other than proceedings for an offence relating to the interception of postal packets and telecommunications, to make discovery of any document, to produce or disclose any document or thing, or to give evidence or information, to a court or tribunal or to any person (other than a designated judge or Referee under the 1993 Act) that shows or tends to show that an authorisation was given or was not given, or that an application for an authorisation was or was not made, or that proposals for or steps towards the making of such an application were or were not made or taken.[134] This provision does not apply in relation to evidence of a conviction for an offence related to the interception of postal packets or telecommunications messages.[135] Also, where a person is convicted of such an offence evidence of the conviction shall be admissible in any proceedings for the purpose of proving, where relevant, that he committed the offence.[136]

A certificate signed by a person authorised for the purpose by the Minister for Justice, Equality and Law Reform and stating that an authorisation was or was not given, or that an application for an authorisation was or was not made, or that proposals for or steps towards the making of such an application were or were not made or taken shall be admissible as evidence of the facts stated in the certificate in any legal proceedings in which evidence of those facts is admissible.[137] This clearly covers criminal, as well as civil proceedings. A document purporting to be a certificate under this provision of an authorised person and to be signed by him or her, shall be deemed for the purpose of this provision to be such a certificate and to be so signed unless the contrary is shown.[138]

Disclosing Telephone Records

7–39   It is worth noting that it is an offence for an employee of Telecom Éireann to disclose to any person any information concerning the use made of telecommunications services provided for any other person by the company. However, section 98(2A) of the Postal and Telecommunications Services Act 1983 which

---

[132]   *ibid.* s.10(2)(d).
[133]   *ibid.* s.10(2)(c).
[134]   *ibid.* s.10(3).
[135]   *ibid.* s.10(4)(b).
[136]   *ibid.* s.10(4)(a).
[137]   *ibid.* s.10(5)(a).
[138]   *ibid.* s.10(5)(b).

creates the offence,[139] also makes provision for a number of specific exceptions concerning disclosures made: at the request or with the consent of the other person; for the prevention or detection of crime or for the purpose of any criminal proceedings; in the interests of the security of the State; in pursuance of the order of a court; for the purpose of civil proceedings in any court; and to another person to whom he is required, in the course of his duty as such employee to make such disclosure. It follows that it is not a criminal offence for Telecom Éireann or an employee of Telecom Éireann to disclose the record of a person's telephone calls over a period of time to gardaí who are carrying out a criminal investigation against the person. It does not follow, of course, that a member of the Garda Síochána has a power to demand the records. Any such power would have to arise from another source, such as an appropriate direction from the Minister for Communications. Having said that, section 98(2B) of the Postal and Telecommunications Services Act 1983 states that any request by a member of the Garda Síochána to a person employed by the company to make disclosure in accordance with the provisions of subsection 2A must be in writing and signed by a member of the Garda Síochána not below the rank of chief superintendent.[140] There appears to be an assumption here that subsection 2A confers a power on a member of the Garda Síochána to require an appropriate disclosure from an employee of Telecom Éireann for the prevention of crime etc. It is submitted, however, that the bare words of subsection 2A and 2B cannot have this effect. A more likely interpretation is that in order to gain protection from criminal liability under section 2A the employee would have to be acting in response to an appropriate written and signed request from a member of the Garda Síochána. That is quite a different matter from obliging an employee to comply with any such a request.

Private Operators

Although the 1993 Act represents a very substantial attempt to regulate the   **7–40**
state interception of communications, it does suffer from some fairly major omissions. It does not specifically extend to the postal and telecommunications services provided to the public by bodies other than An Post and Telecom Éireann. Given the range and extent of such services currently available and the rate at which they are expanding this omission must be considered a serious weakness. Even more significant from the perspective of the individual's right to privacy is the fact that the regulatory scheme does not extend to the use of forms of state surveillance other than the interception of postal packets and telecommunications messages.

---

[139] Inserted by Interception of Postal and Telecommunications Messages (Regulation) Act 1993, s.13(2).
[140] There is a similar provision in s.98(2c) with respect to a member of the Defence Forces.

ENTRY, SEARCH AND SEIZURE

A. Introduction

1. Private Property Rights

The police will often find it necessary in the course of a criminal investigation   **8–01**
to enter onto private property to arrest a suspect and/or to conduct a search for
evidence of a criminal offence. They may also wish to enter premises in hot
pursuit of a suspect or to terminate a breach of the peace. If the police lack
the power to effect an entry onto private property in any of these situations,
their capacity to enforce the criminal law and to protect individuals from
violence will be severely hampered. Equally, however, the individual's
fundamental rights of ownership and privacy in his or her own property must
be respected. Where the property in question is a dwelling the common law is
particularly jealous in the protection of these rights against forcible entry. In
the seminal case of *Entick v. Carrington*[1] the King's messengers executed a
warrant from the Secretary of State which authorised them to enter and search
the plaintiff's house and to seize all of his papers and books found there and
to bring them and the plaintiff before the Secretary of State for examination
on suspicion of publishing seditious libels. In finding that there was no
authority under law for the issue of such a warrant, Lord Camden C.J. in the
Court of Common Pleas declared the importance of the right to private
property in the following terms:

> "The great end, for which men entered into society, was to secure their
> property. That right is preserved sacred and incommunicable in all instances,
> where it has not been taken away or abridged by some public law for the good
> of the whole. . . . By the laws of England, every invasion of private property,
> be it ever so minute, is a trespass. No man can set his foot upon my ground

---

[1] (1765) 19 State Trials 1030. See also, *Leach v. Money* (1765) 19 State Trials 1001.

without my licence, but he is liable to an action, though the damage be nothing; which is proved by every declaration in trespass, where the defendant is called upon to answer for bruising the grass and even treading upon the soil. If he admits the fact, he is bound to show by way of justification, that some positive law has empowered or excused him."[2]

The special protection afforded the dwelling had been recognised more than one hundred and fifty years earlier in the following colourful passage from the judgment of the Earl of Chatham in *Semayne's* case:

"The poorest man may in his cottage bid defiance to all the forces of the Crown. It may be frail – its roof may shake – the wind may blow through it – the storm may enter – the rain may enter – but the King of England cannot enter – all his force dare not cross the threshold of the ruined tenement."[3]

In Ireland the private dwelling also attracts specific Constitutional protection over and above that afforded to private property generally. Article 40.5 of Bunreacht na hEireann states:

"The dwelling of every citizen is inviolable and shall not be forcibly entered save in accordance with law."

The Supreme Court has made it clear that protection against unjustified searches and seizures is not confined to the citizen's dwelling; it extends to every person's private property.[4]

2. Range of Police Powers

8–02   The need to balance the conflicting interests between the rights of private property and the requirements of a criminal investigation is reflected in the nature and scope of the police powers of entry, search and seizure. A member of the Garda Síochána is not possessed of a general power of entry onto private property to facilitate the discharge of his or her duty to enforce the criminal law. The member does, however, have a wide range of individual common law and statutory powers of entry, search and seizure. Each of these differs with respect to the circumstances and purpose for which they can be exercised. Accordingly, the member must be careful that his actions come within the scope of the power under which he is purporting to act when he effects an entry and search on private property without the consent of the occupier. A mistake on this issue might result in evidence found in the course of the unlawful search and seizure being excluded from subsequent criminal proceedings. The State might also be sued in trespass by the occupier.

The position of a member of the Garda Síochána wishing to enter property in the course of his or her duties without the consent of the occupier is not made any easier by the fact that the diverse powers have not been laid down as part of a coherently designed code. Some are of common law origin while others have been created statutorily in an ad hoc and piecemeal fashion over

---

[2] *Entick v. Carrington* (1765) 19 State Trials 1030 at 1066.
[3] (1604) 5 Co Rep 91a.
[4] *Simple Imports Ltd v. Revenue Commissioners* [2000] 2 I.R. 243 at 250.

the last few centuries. Some can be exercised summarily while others require a warrant. Some are exercisable in a wide range of situations while others are very narrow in their remit. Most, but not all, are exercisable only on the basis of a reasonable suspicion with respect to some defined matter. Some are confined to a power of entry only, while others extend to various combinations of entry, search and seizure. Some apply to private property generally, while others do not extend to dwellings. Inevitably, therefore, the following treatment of these powers is selective in the issues and powers that it covers and recognises that there is a considerable degree of overlap and interaction among them.

B. Powers of Entry

1. Common Law

Implied Powers

A member of the Garda Síochána does not enjoy any general authority at common law to enter onto or remain upon private property for the purpose of investigating a criminal offence without the consent of the owner or occupier.[5] However, it is not always necessary for a member to secure the express consent of the owner or occupier before entering for this purpose. Like any member of the public he or she has an implied licence to enter onto private property to communicate with the owner or occupier in the course of his or her lawful business.[6] Equally, the Supreme Court is of the view that a member of the Garda Síochána has the implied authority of any householder to enter onto the forecourt of his premises to enforce the law or prevent a breach of the law. In *DPP v. Forbes*,[7] for example, the Supreme Court upheld the legality of the arrest where the arresting officer pursued a motorist suspected of drunk-driving, eventually apprehending him in the driveway of a third party's house. The implied authority to enter is even more extensive in the case of business premises which are open to the public. In *Minister for Justice v. Wang Zhu Jie*,[8] it was held that gardaí are entitled to assume that they can enter business premises which are open to the public to make inquiries in the ordinary course of their duties as law enforcement officers.

8–03

In all of these situations the implied authority of a member of the Garda Síochána to enter onto private property is subject to the expression of a contrary wish by the owner or occupier. A refusal does not always have to be conveyed expressly. It may be apparent from the circumstances of the case that the owner or occupier is not consenting to the member's presence. If, for

---

[5] *Davis v. Lisle* [1936] 2 K.B. 434; *Morris v. Beardmore* [1981] A.C. 446; *DPP v. Gaffney* [1988] I.L.R.M. 39. Note that where there is more than one occupier the consent of one will be sufficient to authorise entry; *DPP v. McCloskey* unreported, High Court, February, 6, 1984; *DPP v. Delaney* [1996] 1 I.L.R.M. 536.

[6] *Bailey v. Wilson* [1968] Crim. L.R. 617; *Robson v. Hallett* [1967] 2 Q.B. 979; *Minister for Justice v. Wang Zhu Jie* [1991] I.L.R.M. 823.

[7] [1993] I.L.R.M. 817.

[8] [1991] I.L.R.M. 823.

example, gardaí are covertly investigating the owner with a view to charging him with criminal offences committed on his business premises, they will not normally benefit from an implied licence to enter.[9] The same applies if the owner or occupier is attempting to evade gardaí.[10] If the property in question is a dwelling it is especially difficult, but not impossible,[11] to assert an implied permission to enter. In *DPP v. Gaffney*,[12] for example, gardaí sought entry to the defendant's house in the course of their investigation into certain road traffic offences. They were ordered to leave on two occasions by another occupier whom they arrested and took into custody. Later they knocked on the open door for a third time and asked if there was anyone in. The defendant responded, "yes, in here" whereupon the gardaí entered and arrested him. The Supreme Court concluded that the defendant's words, viewed in the context of the circumstances as a whole, were not sufficient to amount to a permission to enter.

Common Law Powers

8–04   It is also important to note that the common law recognises a number of police powers to enter onto private property without a warrant and without the consent of the owner. Controversially, in the case of *Thomas v. Sawkins*[13] the English Court of King's Bench ruled that a constable could enter premises without a warrant to prevent a breach of the peace and to prevent the commission of a criminal offence for which he had reasonable grounds to believe was likely to occur. The facts were that the police forced their way into a meeting that was being held on private premises in circumstances where they had reason to believe that inflammatory and seditious speeches would be made and that the meeting would become the scene of an unlawful assembly, riot and/or breaches of the peace. The Court accepted that they had acted lawfully in the circumstances. However, the broad and vague terms in which the Court formulated the police power of entry in this case have been the subject of incisive criticism.[14] Moreover, in *DPP v. Delaney*[15] Morris J. expressed the view, *obiter*, that an Irish court would not have decided *Thomas v. Sawkins* in favour of the police on account of the constitutional implications.

A more firmly established power of entry without warrant at common law is that which permits a member of the Garda Síochána to enter onto private property, including a dwelling house, in order to terminate an actual affray,[16]

---

[9]   *DPP v. McMahon* [1986] I.R. 393.
[10] *DPP v. McCreesh* [1992] 2 I.R. 239; *DPP v. Gaffney* [1988] I.L.R.M. 39; *DPP v. Corrigan* [1986] I.L.R.M. 575.
[11] *DPP v. Delaney* [1996] 1 I.L.R.M. 536.
[12] [1988] I.L.R.M. 39. *DPP McCloskey* High Court, February 6, 1984 was distinguished.
[13] [1935] 2 K.B. 249. Although the decision in this case has yet to be specifically approved in a reported decision of an Irish Court, Hewart L.C.J., giving the leading judgment in the case, specifically cited the decisions of the Irish Courts in *Humphries v. O'Connor* 17 I.C.L.R. 1 and *O'Kelly v. Harvey* 14 LR Ir 105 as authorities for his formulation of the law.
[14] See LH Leigh *Police Powers in England and Wales* (Butterworths, London, 1975) p. 173; and A L Goodhart "*Thomas v. Sawkins*: A Constitutional Innovation" (1936–38) 6 Camb L J 22.
[15] [1996] 1 I.L.R.M. 536.
[16] *R. v. Walker* (1854) Dears CC 358; *Timothy v. Simpson* (1835) 1 Cr M & R 757; *Robson v. Hallett* [1967] 2 Q.B. 939; *R. v. Marsden* (1925) 88 JP Jo 369.

or to prevent an occupant from causing serious injury to someone else on the premises.[17] This will cover many domestic violence situations and instances of serious disorder at a private party. In *DPP v. Delaney*[18] the High Court was prepared to countenance a police duty to enter a dwelling in order to protect the constitutional right to life of a person within it. The fact that the threat came from persons outside the house, as was the case in *Delaney*, did not affect this duty. A member of the Garda Síochána also has a summary power of entry at common law in order to arrest a felon.[19] Surprisingly, it would appear that it is not yet settled whether there must actually be a felon on the premises or whether it will be sufficient that the member entertains a reasonable suspicion to that effect.[20] In practice the point is likely to remain academic as the Criminal Law Act 1997 provides a statutory power to enter onto private property without a warrant in order to effect an arrest (see later).

Use of Force

Reasonable force may be employed to effect an entry under all of these powers. At common law, however, it would appear that an entry for the purpose of effecting an arrest must be preceded by a demand to enter.[21] Only where the demand is refused can a member of the Garda Síochána use force. Again, the significance of this constraint is largely academic in the light of the Criminal Law Act 1997 (see later).

Consequences of Unlawful Entry

If a member of the Garda Síochána enters or remains on private property without the consent of the owner and in the absence of some other lawful authority, he or she can be sued for damages in an action for trespass. The purported exercise of any powers of arrest, detention or examination while on the property as a trespasser will also be unlawful.[22] Insofar as the decision in *DPP v. Corrigan*[23] would appear to suggest the contrary it must be considered unsafe. In practice, however, many of the difficulties that this might pose for law enforcement are offset by the provision of statutory powers to enter private property without the consent of the owner in order to effect an arrest in certain circumstances[24] (see later).

---

[17] *Handcock v. Baker* (1800) 2 Bos & P 260; *Bailey v. Wilson* [1968] Crim. L.R. 617.

[18] [1996] 1 I.L.R.M. 536.

[19] *Smith v. Shirley* (1846) 3 CB 142; *Maleverer v. Spinke* (1537) 1 Dyer 35b; *Monrey v. Johnson* (1607) 1 Brownl. 211; *Smith v. Smith* (1600) Cro Eliz 741; *Seyman v. Gresham* (1605) Cro Eliz 908. It seems that this power does not extend to the private citizen; see, The Criminal Law Revision Committee, 7th Report, *Felonies and Misdemeanours* 1965 (HMSO, London, Cmnd 2659).

[20] Leigh, *op. cit.*, p. 172.

[21] *Launock v. Brown* (1819) 2 B & Ald 592; *Burdett v. Abbott* (1811) 14 East 1; *DPP v. Corrigan* [1986] I.R. 291.

[22] *DPP v. McCreesh* [1992] 2 I.R. 239; *Morris v. Broadmore* [1981] A.C. 446; *DPP v. Gaffney* [1988] I.L.R.M. 39.

[23] [1986] I.R. 291.

[24] The decision in *McCreesh, op. cit.* can now be avoided by the exercise of the power conferred by s.39 of the Road Traffic Act 1994, while that in *Gaffney, op. cit.* can be avoided by the power conferred by s.6 of the Criminal Law Act 1997.

2. Statutory Powers

8–05   There are several statutory powers enabling a member of the Garda Síochána
to enter onto private property in certain circumstances without the consent of the
owner and without a warrant. Some of these are primarily aimed at facilitating a
search of specified premises for the purpose of ensuring that nothing unlawful or
improper is being carried on there or for the purpose of securing evidence
related to a suspected offence. These powers are considered below under the
heading of entry and search. With the notable exception of the statutory
power to enter for the purpose of effecting an arrest,[25] most of the others are
concerned essentially with the superficial inspection of the conduct of a
business on the premises. The sort of premises that might be affected by these
powers are those which are used for businesses which are a potential source of
anti-social behaviour, criminal or subversive activity, danger to customers or
employees and public health risks.[26] Examples include: premises used for:
trading,[27] betting,[28] gaming,[29] pawnbroking,[30] the sale and consumption of
liquor,[31] public dancing,[32] accommodation,[33] air transport,[34] mining and
quarrying;[35] the slaughter of animals;[36] farming;[37] the manufacture and sale
of controlled drugs;[38] fisheries;[39] shipping;[40] road transport;[41] and insurance.[42] Usually the power in question will permit a member of the Garda
Síochána to enter onto the premises during normal business hours and to
check some or all (depending upon the particular power) of the following: the
premises; relevant licences, registers and records; relevant goods; and the
identity of persons on the premises. Prior suspicion is not normally required.
Failure to cooperate constitutes a criminal offence. A member of the Garda
Síochána also has a summary power to enter onto property for the purpose of
extinguishing fire or protecting persons or property threatened by fire.[43]

---

[25]   See Criminal Law Act 1997, s.6, discussed later.
[26]   Some powers extend to a range of premises; see, for example, Equal Status Act 2000, s.33;
       Planning and Development Act 2000, ss.235 and 253.
[27]   Shops (Hours of Trading) Act 1938, s.9; Casual Trading Act 1995, s.10(2); Occasional Trading
       Act 1979, s.8(2); Turf (Use and Development) Act 1936, s.28; Firearms Act 1925, ss.13 and 21.
[28]   Betting Act 1931, s.26.
[29]   Gaming and Lotteries Act 1956, s.38.
[30]   Pawnbrokers Act 1964, s.46(1).
[31]   Spirits (Ireland) Act 1845, s.2; Refreshment Houses (Ireland) Act 1860, s.20; Beer Houses
       (Ireland) Act 1864, s.6; Licensing (Ireland) Act 1874, s.23.
[32]   Public Dance Halls Act 1935, s.13(1).
[33]   Aliens Order, 1946, art.12.
[34]   Air Transport and Navigation Act 1988, s.18(1); Aviation Act 2001, s.42(3).
[35]   Mines and Quarries Act 1965, s.131.
[36]   Slaughter of Animals Act 1935, s.9; Abattoirs Act 1988, s.54(1).
[37]   Control of Bulls for Breeding Act 1985, s.5; Noxious Weeds Act 1936, s.4; Diseases of Animals
       Act 1966, s.17A(8) as inserted by Diseases of Animals (Amendment) Act 2001, s.2(1).
[38]   Misuse of Drugs Act 1977, s.24.
[39]   Fisheries (Consolidation) Act 1959, ss.163 and 296.
[40]   Merchant Shipping Act 1992, s.25.
[41]   Road Transport Act 1933, s.35.
[42]   Insurance Act 1989, s.60(2), as amended by Insurance Act 2000, s.10.
[43]   Fire Services Act 1981, s.28.

C. Power of Entry to Effect an Arrest

It was noted above that there is a limited common law power of entry to effect **8–06** an arrest. In practice this has been surpassed by the provision of a statutory power of entry and search to effect an arrest conferred by the Criminal Law Act 1997. Broadly speaking, it permits a member of the Garda Síochána to enter any premises without a warrant in order to effect the arrest of a person who is, or who the member with reasonable cause suspects to be, on the premises. The actual terms of the power differ depending on whether the member is acting pursuant to an arrest warrant or committal order and on whether the premises are a dwelling. In fact, it might be more accurate to say that there are three distinct powers. First, the member may enter any premises for the purpose of arresting a person on foot of a warrant or pursuant to an order of committal.[44] The primary requirement is that the person to be arrested is actually on the premises or that the member, with reasonable cause, suspects him to be on the premises. It makes no difference that the premises is a dwelling. Second, a member enjoys an identical power to enter premises (other than a dwelling) for the purpose of effecting an arrest without a warrant, so long as the offence in question is an arrestable offence.[45] An arrestable offence in this context is defined as "an offence for which a person of full capacity and not previously convicted may, under or by virtue of any enactment, be punished by imprisonment for a term of five years or by a more severe penalty and includes an attempt to commit any such offence".[46]

The third power enables a member of the Garda Síochána to enter a dwelling for the purpose of effecting an arrest for an arrestable offence as defined above. This power will only be available, however, if the member is acting with the consent of the occupier or some other person who appears to the member to be in charge of the dwelling, or if one of the following four circumstances are present: (i) a member has observed the person within or entering the dwelling;[47] (ii) the member suspects, with reasonable cause, that before a warrant of arrest can be obtained the person will either abscond for the purpose of avoiding justice or will obstruct the course of justice; (iii) the member suspects, with reasonable cause, that before a warrant of arrest can be obtained the person would commit an arrestable offence;[48] or (iv) the person ordinarily resides at that dwelling.[49] It is worth noting that while the first requirement can be satisfied by any member of the Garda Síochána, the second and third requirements must be satisfied specifically by the member effecting the entry and arrest.

---

[44] Criminal Law Act 1997, s.6(1).
[45] *ibid.* s.6(2).
[46] *ibid.* s.2(1).
[47] The observation can be made by any member of the Garda Síochána. It does not have to be the member who effects the entry to make the arrest.
[48] It is not entirely clear whether the arrestable offence which the member with reasonable cause suspects the person will commit must be in addition to an arrestable offence for which the member already wants to arrest him. It is submitted that the intention was that it need not be an additional offence. However, it will take a sympathetic judicial interpretation to achieve that result.
[49] Criminal Law Act 1997, s.6(2).

Use of Force

When acting under any of the powers of entry a member of the Garda Síochána can, if need be, use reasonable force to gain entry to the premises.[50] There is no specific requirement that he or she should always seek a consensual entry first. Presumably, it will be depend on the circumstances of each individual case whether the use of force was lawful in the absence of a prior attempt to gain a consensual entry. Once on the premises the member may search them in order to effect the arrest.

The Arrest

It is worth emphasising that none of these three powers of entry and search actually confer a distinct power of arrest on the member concerned. The arrest must be grounded on foot of a warrant or committal order or some other common law or statutory power of arrest. The elements of the particular power of arrest used in any case must be satisfied independently of the requirements of these powers of entry and search conferred by the Criminal Law Act 1997. Indeed, it would appear that the member in question must already have made up his or her mind to effect the arrest before entering the premises. The power of entry and search is conferred solely for the purpose of effecting the arrest. It does not enable the member to enter and search for the purpose of investigating whether an arrestable offence has been or is being committed. Once the arrest has been effected, however, the member can rely on his or her common law power to search the person concerned and the immediate vicinity for any dangerous weapon or evidence relating to the offence. Moreover, if the arrest power used is conferred by statute it may be that the legislation in question confers further powers which the member may exercise with respect to the person arrested while on the premises.

The introduction of the statutory power of entry without a warrant to effect a summary arrest has effected a substantial change in the law in this area, particularly where the entry is to a dwelling. The limitations and uncertainties surrounding the common law power to enter a dwelling for the purpose of arrest are now largely academic, at least as far as arrestable offences are concerned. Similarly, the significance of the typical requirement to secure a search warrant to enter private property and/or a dwelling for the purpose of effecting an arrest under a wide range of statutory provisions is now greatly diminished where the offence in question is an arrestable offence. Indeed, the definition of an arrestable offence in this context is such that many offences will come within the scope of the entry and arrest powers conferred by the Criminal Law Act 1997. Included are: murder, manslaughter, rape, other serious offences against the person, abduction, false imprisonment, larceny and certain other offences concerning fraud, criminal damage, certain offences concerning road traffic, certain offences concerning controlled drugs, possession of offensive weapons, firearms and explosives offences, certain offences

---

[50] *ibid.* s.6(1).

against the State, offences under the Official Secrets Act and certain environmental and wildlife offences, to mention only some.

It is worth noting that where a member of the Garda Siochána calls to a
dwelling house armed with a search warrant and is invited into the house
without having to resort to the warrant, he or she can arrest a person in the
dwelling premises where the preconditions for the exercise of a summary
power of arrest are satisfied.[50a]

D. Summary Powers of Entry and Search

1. Common Law

There are very few common law powers to enter and search private property **8–07**
without a warrant, as distinct from summary powers to enter *per se* or to enter
in order to effect an arrest. However, the power to search property can arise
incidentally if a member of the Garda Síochána is already on private property
either with the consent of the occupier or pursuant to the exercise of a power
of entry. The major example at common law arises in the context of an arrest
on private property. It would appear that the member can search those parts of
the premises which are in the possession of, or under the control of, the
suspect at the time of the arrest. The purpose of the search is to look for and
seize evidence relevant to the charge upon which the arrest is made, or which
is relevant to any other contemplated charge against the suspect, or which is
reasonably believed to be stolen property or to be property unlawfully in the
possession of the suspect. A member of the Garda Síochána can also search
the arrested person for any dangerous weapon or evidence relevant to the
offence in question. These powers are dealt with in greater detail in chapter 4
on Arrest.

The common law has also displayed a distaste for powers of entry and
search pursuant to a warrant. Indeed, it seems that such a power was available
only in respect of stolen goods.[51] Even that, however, was supplanted for all
intents and purposes by a statutory provision, namely section 42(1) of the
Larceny Act 1916 which has now been replaced by an even broader provision
in section 48(2) of the Criminal Justice (Theft and Fraud) Offences Act 2001,
which reads:

> "A judge of the District Court, on hearing evidence on oath given by a member
> of the Garda Síochána, may if he or she is satisfied that there are reasonable
> grounds for suspecting that evidence of, or relating to, the commission of an
> offence to which this section applies is to be found in any place, issue a warrant
> for the search of that place and any persons found there."

[50a] *DPP v Buck* Unreported, Court of Criminal Appeal 6 December 1999.
[51] Ryan and Magee *The Irish Criminal Process* (Mercier Press, Dublin, 1983) at p. 147.

2. Statutory Powers

Where Suspicion Not Necessary

8–08   A mere power of entry and inspection will not always be sufficient to check that premises are not being used for an unlawful, harmful or improper purpose. In some situations the nature of the premises or activity being carried on there may require an actual search to ensure that everything is in order. Accordingly, the legislature has provided the police with a number of specific powers of entry and search without a warrant. Once again these mostly concern premises which are being used for purposes which present the potential for anti-social behaviour, criminal or subversive activity, public health and environmental risks and danger to the person or property of customers and employees. Examples include premises used for: gaming;[52] production of illicit liquor;[53] rearing and slaughtering of animals;[54] fisheries;[55] manufacturing and retailing of goods;[56] public dancing;[57] pawnbroking;[58] and air travel.[59]

The exercise of these powers is not predicated on a prior suspicion of wrongdoing or an unlawful state of affairs. The relevant statutory provisions permit a member of the Garda Síochána to enter and search or inspect the premises without a warrant and do one or more of the following (depending on the particular power): inspect and take samples of relevant goods, equipment and animals; inspect and take copies of records; take the names and addresses of persons on the premises; and make inquiries. In some cases the entry and search of a dwelling is specifically excluded.

On Reasonable Suspicion

A member of the Garda Síochána also enjoys a range of powers to enter and search premises without a warrant where there are reasonable grounds to believe that a relevant offence is being committed. Traditionally, such powers have been exercisable only on foot of a warrant. Increasingly, however, the legislature has been introducing summary powers for this purpose. These include powers of entry and search relating to offences connected with: the sale of liquor;[60] cruelty to horses;[61] unlawful occupation of a dwelling;[62] the possession of explosives and chemical weapons;[63] the health or welfare of a

---

[52]   Betting Act 1931, s.26.
[53]   Illicit Distillation (Ireland) Act 1831, s.18.
[54]   Protection of Animals Kept for Farming Purposes Act 1984, s.8; Abattoirs Act 1988, s.54(1); National Beef Assurance Scheme Act 2000, s.23.
[55]   Fisheries (Consolidation) Act 1959, s.296.
[56]   Metrology Act 1996, s.10.
[57]   Licensing (Combatting Drug Abuse) Act 1997, s.14. A unusual feature about this power is that it is confined to any place in which a public dancing licence is not in force.
[58]   Pawnbrokers Act 1964, s.46.
[59]   Air Navigation and Transport Act 1988, s.18(1).
[60]   Intoxicating Liquor Act 1988, s.43; Irish Horseracing Industry Act 1994, s.67.
[61]   Control of Horses Act 1996, s.34.
[62]   Housing (Miscellaneous Provisions) Act 1997, s.12.
[63]   Explosives Act 1875, s.33; Chemical Weapons Act 1997, s.8.

child;[64] the manufacture, distribution or use of animal remedies;[65] drug trafficking;[66] and moneylending.[67] For the most part these provisions confer more extensive and coercive powers on gardaí with respect to search and seizure, although the search of dwellings is excluded in some cases. Some of the powers specifically permit the use of force to effect an entry where that is necessary.

Others

It is also worth noting that some powers of entry and search are not related to any particular kind of premises or the commission of any criminal offence. They permit an entry and search of premises by reference to a specified public nuisance, health or environmental risk. These include: diseases of farm animals;[68] the protection of wildlife;[69] the protection of the marine environment;[70] aviation regulation;[71] and the enforcement of a court order to examine premises which are the subject of a public nuisance complaint.[72] A member of the Garda Síochána also has a power to enter premises for the purpose of taking a person into custody for the purposes of receiving mental health treatment.[73]

E. Search Warrants

1. Introduction

Despite the current tendency to introduce summary powers of entry and search where there are reasonable grounds to suspect that a criminal offence has been, or is being, committed, most statutory powers of entry, search and seizure are still exercisable only on foot of a warrant. Where the property to be searched is, or includes, a dwelling a warrant is a standard pre-requisite. There are very few powers to search a dwelling without a warrant. Those that do exist are normally exercisable only where there are reasonable grounds to believe that the harm would be done or the evidence disappear by the time a warrant was procured.[74] Indeed, it is worth emphasising that search warrants generally are issued not just for the purpose of furthering a Garda investigation but also to secure evidence for the prosecution. The point is made succinctly in the following quotation from Kinlen J. in *Hanahoe v. Hussey*:

8–09

---

[64]   Child Care Act 1991, s.12.
[65]   Animal Remedies Act 1993, s.11.
[66]   Criminal Justice Act 1996, First Schedule.
[67]   Consumer Credit Act 1995, s.105.
[68]   Diseases of Animals Act 1966, s.17A(8), as inserted by Diseases of Animals (Amendment) Act 2001, s.2.
[69]   Wildlife Act 1976, s.72 as amended by Wildlife (Amendment) Act 2000, s.65.
[70]   Dumping at Sea Act 1996, s.6(2).
[71]   Aviation Regulation Act 2001, s.42(3).
[72]   Public Health (Ireland) Act 1878, s.121.
[73]   Mental Health Act 2001, s.13(4).
[74]   See, *e.g.*, Child Care Act 1991, s.12; Animal Remedies Act 1993, s.11.

"A warrant might be issued for the purpose of obtaining information which would assist the gardaí but it may also be used for the gathering of evidence necessary to pursue prosecution. While the gardaí may have significant information they may still require documentary evidence which would be an essential part of the prosecution. Evidence gathering is as important as information gathering and is the necessary work of a Garda investigation.[75]

It does not follow that a search warrant can be issued in any case where a member of the Garda Síochána has reasonable grounds to believe that a criminal offence is being committed, or that evidence of its having been committed is to be found on a particular property. Unfortunately, the current statutory powers to issue warrants constitute an unwieldy collection of disparate provisions which have been developed in a piecemeal fashion over the past two centuries. Each authorises the issue of a search warrant only when its own peculiar requirements have been satisfied. Inevitably, these requirements can differ widely from one provision to another. For example, some statutory provisions permit the issue of a warrant to search premises for items, property or purposes which are defined in very broad terms. Others confine the scope of the search to a very narrowly defined type of property or purpose. Some provisions are limited to a search of premises alone, while others can extend to persons found on those premises. This haphazard arrangement means that the applicant for a search warrant must be careful to proceed on foot of a statutory provision which meets his or her specific needs. Because a warrant of entry, search and seizure constitutes a serious encroachment on the property rights of the citizen the courts will enforce the statutory requirements for their issue strictly:

"Search warrants . . . entitle police and other officers to enter the dwelling-house or other property of a citizen, carry out searches and remove material which they find on the premises and, in the course of so doing, use such force as is necessary to gain admission and carry out the search and seizure authorised by the warrant. These are powers which the police and other authorities must enjoy in defined circumstances for the protection of society, but since they authorise the forcible invasion of a person's property, the courts must always be concerned to ensure that the conditions imposed by the legislature before such powers can be validly exercised are strictly met."[76]

2. The Statutory Provisions

Range of Powers

8–10   There will not inevitably be a statutory provision authorising the issue of a search warrant in every case where the legitimate interests of law enforcement might best be served by a warrant.[77] The most that can sensibly be done here

---

[75] [1998] 3 I.R. 69 at 97.
[76] *Simple Imports Ltd v. Revenue Commissioners* [2000] 2 I.R. 243. In delivering a dissenting judgment in this case Barron J. took the view that a warrant was merely a document through which the exercise of a power to authorise entry and search was expressed. The majority by contrast seemed to take the view that the warrant itself constituted the authority to enter.
[77] Ryan and Magee point out that there is no statutory authority which the police can use to seek a warrant to search specifically for the body of a murder victim or for a murder weapon; at p. 148.

with respect to all of these statutory provisions is to attempt to give an idea of the situations in which a search warrant can issue, followed by a consideration of some features which apply generally to most search warrant provisions.

Warrants of entry, search and seizure may be issued in a wide range of circumstances including: the unlawful presence of aliens;[78] trafficking in illegal immigrants;[79] customs offences;[79a] wireless telegraphy (including unlicensed TV sets);[80] broadcasting;[81] breach of censorship laws;[82] ill-treatment or neglect of children;[83] breach of copyright and patents;[84] planning and development;[85] immorality;[86] domesticated animals;[87] animal health;[88] food processing in the beef industry;[89] firearms, explosives and chemical weapons;[90] fisheries;[91] fraud and forgery;[92] gaming;[93] manufacture, consumption and sale of liquor;[94] stolen goods;[95] controlled drugs and substances;[96] damage to property;[97] offences against the State;[98] official secrets;[99] court records;[100] incitement to hatred;[101] road traffic;[102] public collections;[103] videos;[104] wildlife;[105] seizure of criminal assets;[106] sexual offences;[107] business books and records;[108] salvage and

---

This omission has now been remedied, see Criminal Justice (Miscellaneous Provisions) Act 1997, s.10.

[78] Aliens Act 1935, s.7.
[79] Illegal Immigrants (Trafficking) Act 2000, s.7.
[79a] Customs and Excise (Miscellaneous Provisions) Act 1998, s.5(1).
[80] Wireless Telegraphy Act 1926, s.8.
[81] Broadcasting Act 1990, s.14.
[82] Censorship of Publications Act 1929, s.19(1); Censorship of Publications Act 1946, s.17.
[83] Children Act 1908, s.24, Children Act 2001, s. 254(5).
[84] Copyright Act 1963, s.27; Merchandise Marks Act 1887, s.12; Trade Marks Act 1996, s.25.
[85] Planning and Development Act 2000, s.253(4).
[86] Criminal Law Amendment Act 1885, s.10; Criminal Law Amendment Act 1935, s.19.
[87] Control of Dogs Act 1986, s.26; Control of Horses Act 1996, s.35.
[88] Disease of Animals Act 1966, s.17A(8)(17)–(18), as inserted by Diseases of Animals (Amendment) Act 2001, s.2(1).
[89] National Beef Assurance Scheme Act 2000, s.23(3)–(5).
[90] Explosives Act 1875, s.73; Firearms and Offensive Weapons Act 1990, s.15; Chemical Weapons Act 1997, s.7(7).
[91] Fisheries (Consolidation) Act 1959, s.297.
[92] Forgery Act 1913, s.16.
[93] Gaming and Lotteries Act 1956, s.39.
[94] Illicit Distillation (Ireland) Act 1831, s.17; Spirits (Ireland) Act 1854, ss.2 & 4; Beer Houses (Ireland) Act 1864, s.6; Licensing (Ireland) Act 1874, s.24; Registration of Clubs (Ireland) Act 1904, s.7.
[95] Criminal Justice (Theft and Fraud Offences) Act 2001, s.48; Summary Jurisdiction (Ireland) Act 1862, s.6.
[96] Misuse of Drugs Act 1977, s.26; Animal Remedies Act 1993, s.12; Criminal Justice (Drug Trafficking) Act 1996, s.8.
[97] National Monuments (Amendment) Act 1987, s.22; Criminal Damage Act 1991, s.13.
[98] Offences Against the State Act 1939, s.29 as substituted by Criminal Law Act 1976, s.5.
[99] Official Secrets Act 1963, s.16.
[100] Petty Sessions (Ireland) Act 1851, s.6.
[101] Prohibition of Incitement to Hatred Act 1989, s.9.
[102] Road Traffic Act 1961, s.106(6).
[103] Street and House to House Collections Act 1962, s.23.
[104] Video Recordings Act 1989, s.25.
[105] Wildlife Act 1976, ss.73, as amended by Wildlife (Amendment) Act 2000, s.67.
[106] Criminal Assets Bureau Act 1996, s.14.
[107] Criminal Law (Sexual Offences) Act 1993, s.10(2); Sexual Offences (Jurisdiction) Act 1996, s.10.
[108] Companies Act 1995, s.20; Investment Intermediaries Act 1990, s.75; Stock Exchange Act 1995, s.66.

wreck;[109] aviation regulation;[110] assisting a foreign court;[111] money-laundering;[112] moneylending;[113] regulation of electronic commerce;[114] insurance;[115] enforcement of the Equal Status Act 2000;[116] information on abortion services;[117] and certain serious offences against the person.[118]

Garda Authorisation

Although the nature and scope of the relevant statutory provisions differ immensely, it is still possible to identify some general features. For example, most of them confine the authority to issue warrants to District Court judges and peace commissioners. Many authorise District Court Judges alone. There are also a few significant provisions which authorise a member of the Garda Síochána to issue a warrant in certain circumstances. For example, a member not below the rank of superintendent can issue a search warrant where he or she is satisfied that there are reasonable grounds for believing that evidence relating to an offence (whether committed or intended) under the Offences against the State Act 1939 (or an offence scheduled under that Act or created by the Criminal Law Act 1976) is to be found in any building, property or vehicle.[119] The warrant authorises a named member of the Garda Síochána not below the rank of sergeant to enter and search the specified property, and any person found in it, within one week of the issuance of the warrant. The member in question can be accompanied by other members of the force and/or by members of the Defence Forces. If necessary, he or she may use force to gain entry. The member may "seize anything found there" or found on any person there.[120]

Other situations where a senior member of the Garda Síochána may issue a search warrant are associated with the necessity for immediate action. For example, under the Misuse of Drugs Act 1977 a warrant may be issued by a superintendent where the offence in question is a drug trafficking offence and the circumstances are such that it would be impracticable to apply to a District Court judge or peace commissioner.[121] Before issuing the warrant he

---

[109] Merchant Shipping (Salvage and Wreck) Act 1993, s.57.
[110] Aviation Regulation Act 2001, s.43.
[111] Criminal Justice Act 1994, s.55.
[112] Criminal Justice Act 1994, s.64.
[113] Consumer Credit Act 1995, s.106.
[114] Electronic Commerce Act 2000, s.27.
[115] Insurance Act 1989, s.60(9), as amended by Insurance Act 2000, s.10.
[116] Equal Status Act 2000, s.33(4)-(5).
[117] Regulation of Information (Services Outside the State for Termination of Pregnancies) Act 1995, s.9.
[118] Criminal Justice (Miscellaneous Provisions) Act 1997, s.10.
[119] Offences Against the State Act 1939, s.29, as substituted by Criminal Law Act 1976, s.5.
[120] Under s.24 of the Firearms Act 1925 a superintendent may issue a "search order" to a member of the Garda Síochána authorising him to enter and search the specified premises within 24 hours of the warrant being issued. If the premises belong to a firearms dealer he may also inspect relevant books and records. Although the member may arrest any person found on the premises where he has reason to believe that the person is guilty of an offence under the Act the order does not specifically authorise him to seize anything.
[121] Misuse of Drugs Act 1977, s.26(1) and Criminal Justice (Drug Trafficking) Act 1996, s.8.

or she must be satisfied by information submitted on oath by a member of the Garda Síochána that there are reasonable grounds for believing that evidence of unlawful possession of controlled drugs is to be found on the premises. The warrant expires after 24 hours of issue. By contrast, where it is issued by a District Court judge or peace commissioner it remains in force for one month. A similar power to issue a warrant is conferred upon a Garda officer of the Criminal Assets Bureau not below the rank of superintendent.[122] In this instance the warrant relates to criminal assets.[123] It is also worth noting that under the Larceny Act 1916 a senior officer[124] has the power to authorise a member of the Garda Síochána to enter and search property where he or she reasonably believed stolen goods were being harboured.[125] The property in question must in the previous 12 months have been in the possession of someone convicted of receiving stolen goods or of harbouring thieves or it must have been in the occupation of a person who had been convicted of an offence of fraud or dishonesty punishable with imprisonment. This power does not appear to have been carried over into the Criminal Justice (Theft and Fraud) Offences Act 2001.

Constitutionality of Warrants Issued by Authorities other than Judges

The constitutionality of a statutory provision empowering a peace commissioner to issue a search warrant was challenged in *Ryan v. O'Callaghan*.[126] In this case a peace commissioner exercised his power under section 42(1) of the Larceny Act 1916 to issue a warrant to search for stolen goods in the defendant's home. The defendant argued that the power amounted to an invasion of the constitutional right of the citizen to privacy in his own home and a judicial act in a criminal prosecution. As such, he argued that it could only be exercised by a judge appointed in accordance with the Constitution. These arguments were rejected by the High Court, where Barr J. ruled that it was in the interests of the common good to have a procedure whereby the police could readily obtain a warrant to facilitate their investigation of larceny and allied offences in appropriate cases. The learned judge was further of the opinion that the prosecution of offences commences with the issue of a summons or the preferring of a charge. The issue of a search warrant, and the search itself, were merely steps in the investigative process. As such, they were of an executive, as distinct from a judicial, nature. Although Barr J. was dealing specifically with the power of a peace commissioner to issue a search warrant under section 42(1) of the Larceny Act 1916, it is submitted that his comments have general application to statutory provisions conferring the power to issue a search warrant.[127]

8–11

---

122 Criminal Assets Bureau Act 1996, s.14.
123 For a slightly different power conferred upon a member not below the rank of chief superintendent, see Official Secrets Act 1963, s.16.
124 An Assistant Commissioner in the Dublin Metropolitan Area and a superintendent in charge of a District outside the DMA.
125 Larceny Act 1916, s.42(2). The 1916 Act is set to be repealed by the Criminal Justice (Theft and Fraud Offences) Act 2001.
126 High Court, 22 July, 1987. See also *Berkeley v. Edwards* [1988] I.R. 217; *Byrne v. Grey* [1988] I.R. 31.
127 See *Byrne v. Grey* [1988] I.R. 31.

The fact that a warrant issued by a peace commissioner is not in any statutorily prescribed form will not, of itself, render the warrant invalid. This issue was considered by the Supreme Court in *DPP v. Edgeworth*.[128] The defendant had appeared for trial on drugs charges before the Circuit Court. The primary evidence against him consisted of proscribed drugs which had been found in the course of a search of his home under a search warrant issued pursuant to section 26(2) of the Misuse of Drugs Act 1977. Although the warrant was issued by a peace commissioner it was expressed in a form which was headed "the District Court" and did not specify the county for which the peace commissioner acted. The Court declared the warrant unlawful and found the defendant not guilty.

On a reference under section 34 of the Criminal Procedure Act 1967, the Supreme Court upheld the validity of the warrant. It found that a special form had been prescribed for the issue of a warrant by a judge of the District Court pursuant to section 26(2) of the Misuse of Drugs Act 1977, but that no such form had been prescribed for a warrant issued by a peace commissioner. While that was a regrettable omission, the Court went on to hold that it did not necessarily invalidate the usage of the District Court form. Despite the fact that the form used in this case conveyed on its face an association with the District Court when in fact there had been no application to a judicial personage at all, there was no intention to mislead and there was no evidence before the trial judge to suggest that anyone was misled. The misdescription involved in the use of the heading "The District Court" was not a breach of any condition or criterion imposed by the legislature for the issue of the warrant. It would be a different matter altogether if a condition or pre-requisite for the issue of the warrant in question had been omitted from or struck off the warrant, even inadvertently.[129] Moreover, there was no requirement that a search warrant issued under section 26 should carry on its face a statement of the counties to which a peace commissioner's warrant of appointment lies. So long as his or her warrant of appointment extends to the area in which the premises to be searched were situated that is sufficient. Accordingly, the use of the District Court form did not invalidate the warrant in this case.

3. Grounds for Issuing a Warrant

Sworn Information

8–12　Normally a warrant can be issued only on the basis of information which has been sworn before the appropriate authority.[130] In a few instances, however,

---

[128] [2001] 2 I.R. 131.

[129] See, *DPP v. Dunne* [1994[2 I.R. 537.

[130] See Sched. B to the District Court Rules 1997 for standard *pro forma* applications in respect of the following: misuse of drugs (Form 32.1); stolen goods (Form 34.1); national monuments (Form 34.3); incitement to hatred (Form 34.5 or 34.6); video-recordings (Form 34.9); firearms or offensive weapons (Form 34.11); broadcasting (Form 34.13); companies (Form 34.15); criminal damage (Form 34.17); sexual offences (Form 34.20); and using a premises as a brothel (Form 34.22).

this is not necessary. For example, information on oath is not required for the issuance of a search warrant under the Offences Against the State Act 1939 by a member not below the rank of superintendent.[131] The same applies to the power conferred upon a member not below the rank of superintendent by the Misuse of Drugs Act 1977,[132] and to that conferred on a District Court judge by the Official Secrets Act 1963.[133] Further examples are to be found in some offences with an extra-territoriality element.[134] In many cases, but by no means all, it is a specific requirement that the information should be in writing. Another standard feature is the requirement that the information should be sworn by a member of the Garda Síochána. Occasionally, he or she must be a member not below a designated rank. Equally, however, there are examples where the information can be sworn by other designated officials, or even by a "credible witness".

Reasonable Grounds

Typically, the warrant can be granted only if the issuing authority is satisfied that there are reasonable grounds for the suspicion.[135] Accordingly, it will not be sufficient if the applicant swears that on the basis of information which has come to his attention he has reasonable grounds to believe that relevant items are to be found in a specified place. The applicant must also present evidence to satisfy the issuing authority that his belief is based on reasonable grounds. In *Byrne v. Grey*,[136] for example, a peace commissioner issued a search warrant under section 26(1) of the Misuse of Drugs Act 1977 on the basis of sworn information from a member of the Garda Síochána that he was a member of the Garda Síochána and had reasonable grounds for believing that cannabis plants were being cultivated at a specified address. No further information was offered. On an application for leave to seek an order of certiorari quashing the warrant Hamilton P. (as he then was) explained the correct approach to the interpretation of section 26(1) as follows:

> "These powers encroach on the liberty of the citizen and the inviolability of his dwelling as guaranteed by the Constitution, and the courts should construe a statute which authorises such encroachment so that it encroaches on such rights no more than the statute allows, expressly or by necessary implication."[137]

Accordingly before a warrant could issue under this provision:

> " . . . the District Justice or Peace Commissioner should himself be satisfied by information on oath that facts exist which constitute reasonable grounds for suspecting that an offence has been or is being committed."[138]

---

[131] Offences Against the State Act 1939, s.29.
[132] Misuse of Drugs Act 1977, s.26(1) and Criminal Justice (Drug Trafficking) Act 1996, s.8.
[133] Official Secrets Act 1963, s.16.
[134] Sexual Offences (Jurisdiction) Act 1996, s.10; Criminal Justice Act 1994, ss.55 and 64.
[135] A major exception is found in the Offences Against the State Act 1939, s.29.
[136] [1988] I.R. 31.
[137] *Byrne v. Grey* [1988] I.R. 31 at 38.
[138] *ibid.* at 39.

He was not entitled to rely on the oath of a member of the Garda Síochána that the member had reasonable grounds for the suspicion. The member would actually have to be in a position to satisfy the District Court judge or peace commissioner that there were reasonable grounds for his suspicion. Since there was no basis on which he could have been satisfied in this case the warrant was issued unlawfully. This decision was applied by the Supreme Court in *People (DPP) v. Kenny*,[139] another case concerning the issue of a warrant under section 26(1).

It does not follow from these cases that a member of the Garda Síochána seeking a search warrant must submit compelling evidence of the matters in question in order to satisfy the issuing authority. In *Berkeley v. Edwards*,[140] for example, Hamilton P. upheld the validity of a search warrant in a decision handed down on the same day he handed down his judgment in *Byrne v. Grey*. In the former case the search warrant was issued by a peace commissioner under section 42(1) of the Larceny Act 1916 which required the commissioner to be satisfied by information on oath from a member of the Garda Síochána that there were reasonable grounds to suspect that stolen goods were to be found on the premises in question. In this case the member of the Garda Síochána had submitted an affidavit on oath which stated that he was making enquiries concerning the larceny of certain electrical items and, as a result of information which he had received and which he believed to be true, he had reasonable cause to suspect that all or some of the property would be found at a specified premises. The learned judge ruled that this was sufficient to enable the peace commissioner to be satisfied that there was reasonable cause to believe that the stolen property would be found on the premises. The only significant difference between the evidence before the peace commissioner in this case and that in *Byrne v. Grey* would appear to be the inclusion in the member's sworn information of the words "from information which I have received and which I believe to be true".

Discretion

8–13   Where the issuing authority is satisfied on the basis of the evidence presented to it that there are reasonable grounds for the requisite suspicion, the warrant may issue. However, the issuing authority will not normally be obliged to issue the warrant in such circumstances. Most of the relevant statutory provisions confer a power to issue the warrant where the necessary preconditions have been satisfied. Accordingly, the issuing authority retains a discretion to refuse it, although examples of this actually happening in practice are rare.

4. Contents of the Warrant

The Basics

8–14   When a search warrant has issued lawfully, it will state on its face, *inter alia,* the statutory power under which it has issued, the statutory preconditions for

---

[139]   [1990] I.L.R.M. 569.
[140]   [1988] I.R. 217.

its issue and the fact that those statutory preconditions have been satisfied. The validity of the warrant is dependant on strict compliance with these requirements. The warrant must show unequivocally on its face authority for the search in question. In *DPP v. Dunne*,[141] for example, a search warrant had been issued in respect of a dwelling by a peace commissioner pursuant to section 26(2) of the Misuse of Drugs Act 1977. The occupier of the dwelling was subsequently prosecuted for resisting the search. It transpired that that part which referred to the peace commissioner being satisfied that the controlled drug "is on the premises" was inadvertently crossed out from the *pro forma* warrant. The wording of the statutory provision requires the peace commissioner to be satisfied that the controlled drug is on the premises. On a case stated from the District Court to the High Court Carney J. declared the warrant invalid. He stressed the importance of full compliance with the statutory requirements when issuing a warrant in the following terms:

> "The constitutional protection given in Article 20, s.5 of the Constitution in relation to the inviolability of the dwellinghouse is one of the most important, clear and unqualified protections given by the Constitution to the citizen. If it is to be set aside by a printed form issued by a non-judicial personage it would appear to me to be essential that that form should be in clear, complete, accurate and unambiguous terms. It does not seem to me to be acceptable that the prosecuting authority can place reliance on words crossed out by asserting that that was an inadvertence or slip. Such an approach would facilitate the warrant becoming an empty formula."[142]

While Carney J. refers specifically to the fact that the warrant in this case was issued by a non-judicial personage it is unlikely that a different approach would have been taken had it been issued by a District Court judge. The fact that one of the statutory criterion for the issuance of the warrant was omitted from the warrant meant that the peace commissioner had exceeded his jurisdiction and the warrant was fatally flawed. As has been seen above in the case of *DPP v. Edgeworth*[143] not every error on the face of the warrant will render it void. Only those defects which go to the heart of the jurisdiction to grant the warrant will have this effect. Errors or omissions related to technical matters which did not mislead anyone will not necessarily have this result. Further examples are given below.

Jurisdiction on its Face

Even where a warrant has issued within jurisdiction, it will be declared invalid if it does not show jurisdiction on its face. This is illustrated by the majority decision of the Supreme Court in *Simple Imports Ltd v. Revenue Commissioners*.[144] In that case warrants had issued authorising the entry and search of commercial premises in Dublin, Cork and Limerick for the purpose

8–15

---

[141] [1994] 2 I.R. 537.
[142] *DPP v. Dunne* [1994] 2 I.R. 537 at 540–541.
[143] [2001] 2 I.R. 131.
[144] [2000] 2 I.R. 243. The House of Lords decision in *Reg. v. IRC, ex p. Rossminster* [1980] A.C. 952 was distinguished

of finding and seizing pornographic materials which were believed to be on the premises. The warrants were issued under section 205 of the Customs Laws Consolidation Act 1876 and section 5(1) of the Customs and Excise (Miscellaneous Provisions) Act 1988. Both provisions require the District Court judge issuing the warrants to be satisfied by information on oath that the applicant customs officer has reasonable grounds to suspect that the relevant goods are on the premises. When issuing the warrants in this case the judges used the standard *pro forma* for the warrants in question, filling in the blank space with handwritten entries. In each case the critical section of the *pro forma* stated that the District Court judge was satisfied on the basis of information submitted on oath that the customs officer in question ". . . hath cause to suspect and doth suspect" that the contraband goods were on the premises. On the face of it this recital did not ground jurisdiction for the issue of the warrants. The relevant statutory provisions clearly require that the District Court judge must be satisfied that there is reasonable grounds for the customs officer's suspicion. It is not sufficient that the officer merely suspects or has cause to suspect.

Despite the fact that the Supreme Court was satisfied that there was sufficient evidence before the District Court judges to establish reasonable grounds for the officers' suspicion, the Court quashed the warrants. The mere fact that the District Court judges had acted within jurisdiction could not save the warrants where they purported on their face to have issued without jurisdiction. In delivering the judgment for the majority Keane J. (as he then was) declared:

> "I am satisfied that the submission on behalf of the respondents that, in a case where the warrant itself states that it is being issued by the district judge on a basis which is not justified by the statute creating the power, the invalidity of the warrant can be cured by evidence that there was in fact before the district judge evidence which entitled him to issue the warrant within the terms of the statute is not well founded. The proposition seems to me contrary to principle and unsupported by authority. Given the necessarily draconian nature of the powers conferred by the statute, a warrant cannot be regarded as valid which carries on its face a statement that it has been issued on the basis which is not authorised by the statute. It follows that the warrants were invalid and must be quashed."[145]

It might be a different matter if the warrant merely stated on its face that the applicant officer had submitted information on oath to the effect that there was reasonable grounds for believing the relevant matters, without specifically stating that the judge was satisfied that there was reasonable grounds for the belief. So long as there was evidence upon which the judge could be satisfied that there was reasonable grounds for the belief it would appear that the validity of the warrant would not necessarily be vitiated by a failure to state the judge's belief on the face of the warrant. That, however, is quite a different situation from a warrant which states explicitly an erroneous ground for its issue.

---

[145] [2000] 2 I.R. 243 at 255.

Addressee

Once duly issued a warrant confers legal authority on the person concerned to **8–16** enter and search the relevant premises for the items or property in question. The warrant will normally state on its face the person who is authorised to search the premises, the premises to be searched and the items or property which are the object of the search. Presumably, the search must be carried out by the member named in the warrant. In some, but not all, cases the relevant statutory provision conferring the power stipulates that he or she may be accompanied by such other members as he or she considers necessary, or even that any member of the Garda Síochána may enter and search the premises. It is also worth noting that some statutory provisions specifically require that the member to whom the warrant is issued must be above a particular rank. Typically, a warrant will be addressed to the superintendent of the Garda Síochána station for the area in which it is to be executed. This will be made clear at the bottom of the warrant.[146] There is no suggestion, however, that this confers on the superintendent the authority to execute the warrant. In the absence of any specific provision to the contrary it is submitted that a warrant can be executed only by the member who is named on the warrant as the applicant and person to whom it was issued.

Description of Property

Errors in the description of the premises to be searched, the identity of the occupier of the premises and the items or property which are the object of the search will not in themselves automatically render void a warrant which has otherwise been issued within jurisdiction. In *People (DPP) v. Balfe*,[147] for example, the information upon which a search warrant for stolen goods was based stated the wrong address of the premises to be searched, the name of the person who was allegedly in possession of the goods and the date on which the goods were alleged to have been stolen. These errors were repeated in the draft warrant which was before the District Court judge. Although the judge corrected these particular errors by making the necessary amendments to the warrant, other defects remained, including the name of the applicant for the warrant and the failure to describe the goods in respect of which the warrant was issued. The accused appealed her conviction for handling stolen goods on the ground, *inter alia*, that these defects rendered the search warrant invalid and, as such, the goods seized on foot of the warrant should have been excluded from evidence.

In delivering the judgment of the Court of Criminal Appeal Murphy J. distinguished between errors made within jurisdiction in the issue of a search warrant and errors which go to the authority to issue the warrant in question.

---

[146] See, for example, the standard *pro formas* set out in Sched. B to the District Court Rules 1997 for: drugs (Form 32.2), stolen goods (Form 34.2); national monuments (Form 34.4); incitement to hatred (Form 34.7 or 34.8); video-recordings (Form 34.10); firearms and offensive weapons (Form 34.12); broadcasting (Form 34.14); companies (Form 34.16); criminal damage (Form 34.18 or 34.19); sexual offences (Form 34.21); and premises used as a brothel (Form 34.23).

[147] [1998] 4 I.R. 50.

The latter renders the warrant void and of no effect. Accordingly, evidence obtained pursuant to such a warrant is automatically inadmissible in a criminal trial. The former may relieve the occupier of the premises in question of the obligation to submit to the warrant. If, however, he does submit then the goods obtained as a result of the search may be admitted in evidence at his subsequent trial:

> " . . . where a judge of the District Court acting within his jurisdiction agrees to issue a search warrant, a mistake, however gross, in the recording of his order will not necessarily render the warrant invalid for all purposes though it might justify persons to whom it is addressed, or intended to be addressed, declining to co-operate with it. Where, however, the search warrant is made without authority then it has no value in law, however innocent the mistake in granting the same or however apparently plausible the document issued."[148]

8–17   The key issue, therefore, is the distinction between errors within jurisdiction and errors which take the District Court judge or peace commissioner outside his or her jurisdiction in issuing a search warrant. As explained above the latter arise generally where the basic statutory preconditions for the issue of the warrant in question have not been satisfied or where the warrant on its face does not accurately state the basis upon which the warrant has been issued. Broadly, the former might be described as technical errors on the face of the warrant which are not so great as to mislead anyone affected by the warrant. An innocent mistake with respect to the address to be searched, for example, would be an error within jurisdiction. In the seminal case of *People (Attorney-General) v. O'Brien*[149] where the Supreme Court first formulated the exclusionary rule for evidence which has been obtained by a conscious and deliberate breach of constitutional rights, the address on the warrant was mistakenly stated to be "118 Cashel Road, Crumlin" instead of 118 Captains Road, Crumlin". The error was entirely innocent and went unnoticed at the time. The Supreme Court acknowledged that the occupants of 118 Captains Road would have been entitled to refuse entry on the basis of the defective warrant. Since they acquiesced the evidence obtained as a result of the search was admissible. Similarly, in *Balfe* Murphy J. said that:

> ". . . it is clear that a search warrant which innocently but wholly misdescribes premises which may be searched on foot thereof is not without operative effect. Property seized in innocent reliance thereon may be admissible in evidence on a subsequent criminal charge."[150]

Even omitting a description of the items in respect of which the warrant has issued will not necessarily be sufficient to render the warrant void and of no effect. In *Balfe*, for example, the information upon which the search warrant for stolen goods was based specified the stolen items which were believed to be on the premises in question. For some unexplained reason this list of items

---

[148] *People (DPP) v. Balfe* [1998] 4 I.R. 50 at 60.
[149] [1965] I.R. 142.
[150] [1998] 4 I.R. 50 at 59.

was not transposed onto the search warrant. Despite the fact that the printed form version of a warrant issued pursuant to section 42(1) of the Larceny Act 1916 calls for a specification of the stolen items, the warrant in this case contained no description of them. While Murphy J. accepted that the terms of section 9 of the Criminal Law Act 1976 (see later) rendered it less important to specify the particular items on the search warrant, he still considered that there should be some description of the goods which were the subject matter of the search. Nevertheless, he proceeded to rule that a failure to describe the goods would not necessarily render the warrant void and of no effect:

> "It is, however, the opinion of this Court, notwithstanding the paucity of authority, that the very concept of an application for and the granting of a warrant to search for stolen goods involves the provision of some description of the goods stolen and the goods for which it is intended to search. We are satisfied that the description provided of the goods in the present case in the information was adequate but the failure to transpose that description in the warrant involved a serious error with a resultant defect in the warrant. However, the Court is satisfied that the patent defect, serious though it was, is similar to and falls within *People (Attorney General) v. O'Brien* [1965] I.R. 142 type of patent defect rather than *People (Director of Public Prosecutions) v. Kenny* [1990] 2 I.R. 110 type of inherent or fundamental defect and, accordingly, the goods seized in pursuance of the warrant were properly admitted in evidence by the learned trial judge."[151]

Coincidence between Warrant and Information

The lack of coincidence between a warrant as issued and the information upon **8–18** which it was based was also addressed generally by Murphy J. delivering the judgment of the Court of Criminal Appeal in *Balfe*. The learned judge was of the view that factual differences between the information and the warrant cannot be considered a fatal defect in the warrant. Indeed, such differences might be expected to result from the District Court judge or peace commissioner probing the facts sworn in the information in order to satisfy himself or herself that the statutory preconditions for the issue of the warrant have been fulfilled. Sometimes, as a result of such probing it may be necessary to amend or insert material into the warrant which does not correspond exactly with what was originally stated in the information. Ultimately, it is more important that the citizen's constitutional rights are protected by such scrutiny than that there should be complete correspondence between the information and subsequent warrant:

> "The fact that the information and warrant do not coincide cannot be a fatal defect. A judge or commissioner issuing a warrant may, and usually will, be required by the decision of *People (DPP) v. Kenny* [1990] 2 I.R. 110 (and perhaps, more particularly, the decision of Hamilton P. (as he then was) in *Byrne v. Grey* [1988] I.R. 31) to make such inquiries as are necessary to form his own opinion as to the existence of an appropriate cause or suspicion. A hearing of that nature may lead to a discrepancy between the original

---

[151] *ibid.* at 62.

information and any warrant actually granted. There is no prohibition on amendments being made and no stipulation that where made they must be initiated or verified by any particular means. Clarity is desirable but most of all it is critical that a person exercising authority which could result in an interference with the constitutional right of the citizen should direct his or her mind and satisfy himself or herself as to the existence of facts justifying the action sought of him or her. However urgent or important the application, those exercising important functions of this nature must never permit themselves to endorse automatically the decisions or actions of others. The protection and vindication of constitutional rights in this area is achieved by the introduction of a competent, detached authority exercising an independent jurisdiction and not by the manner in which such decisions are recorded."[152]

5. Effect of warrant

8–19 A primary function of a search warrant is to provide legal authority to enter and search private property in the absence of the consent of the owner. It follows that the right to use force, where necessary, in order to gain access to the property is an integral element of the authority conferred by the warrant. In most cases the legislation creating the power to issue the warrant will specifically permit the use of force where necessary in its execution. In some cases the legislation goes further and confers a power to take the names and addresses of persons found on the property and, increasingly, to search such persons.[153] The latter power is particularly significant as persons found on the property may have a perfectly innocent reason for being there and may not be the subject of any suspicion. Nevertheless, they may conceivably find themselves being subjected to a strip search where, for example, the warrant has been issued under the Misuse of Drugs Act 1977. Some of the statutory provisions also include a specific power to stop and detain persons found on the premises for the purpose of searching them.[154] None of them, however, confer a specific power to detain persons on the premises, or on a particular part of the premises, in order to facilitate a search of the actual premises.

The statute creating a power to issue a search warrant will normally specify a time limit for the execution of the warrant. When this time limit has expired the warrant will be spent irrespective of whether it has actually been used. Periods of one week and one month from the date of issue are most typical. The legislation will usually stipulate that the search may be effected at any time during this period. As soon as the warrant has been used, however, it is spent even if the relevant time limit has not expired. There are a few significant exceptions to this rule. A warrant issued under section 26(2) of the Misuse of Drugs Act 1977, for example, may be executed at "any time or

---

[152] *ibid.* at 61.
[153] See, for example, Misuse of Drugs Act 1977, s.26(2); Offences Against the State Act 1939, s.29; Consumer Credit Act 1995, s.106; Criminal Damage Act 1991, s.13; Animal Remedies Act 1993, s.12; Merchant Shipping (Salvage and Wreck) Act 1993, s.57; Criminal Assets Bureau Act 1996, s.14; National Monuments (Amendment) Act 1987, s.22; Official Secrets Act 1963, s.16.
[154] See, for example, Animal Remedies Act 1993, s.12(3)(a); Merchant Shipping (Salvage and Wreck) Act 1993, s.16.

times" within one month from the date of issue. It follows that it can be used to search the specified premises for the specified items on several occasions within the one month period. The legislature appears to be resorting to this formulation more frequently.[155]

6. Criminal Justice (Miscellaneous Provisions) Act 1997

Before leaving the subject of entry and search under a warrant it is worth drawing particular attention, for different reasons, to the search warrant provisions introduced by the Criminal Justice (Miscellaneous Provisions) Act 1997 and the production and access order provisions of the Criminal Justice Act 1994 and the Criminal Justice (Theft and Fraud Offences) Act 2001. The former are unusual in the sense that they cover a range of disparate criminal offences,[156] namely: an indictable offence involving the death of or serious bodily injury to any person, false imprisonment, rape, incest, offences under sections 1 and 2 of the Criminal Law Amendment Act 1935, sections 3 and 4 of the Criminal Law (Rape) (Amendment) Act 1990 and sections 3 and 5 of the Criminal Law (Sexual Offences) Act 1993. A judge of the District Court may issue a search warrant for any place where he or she is satisfied, after hearing evidence on oath from a member of the Garda Síochána not below the rank of inspector, that there are reasonable grounds for suspecting that evidence relating to the commission of one of these offences is to be found at that place.[157] The place in question may be a dwelling.[158] The warrant will authorise a named member of the Garda Síochána to enter and search the place named on the warrant within one week of its issue. The member may be accompanied by other gardaí and, if necessary, they may use reasonable force to gain entry. The gardaí may also search and demand the names and addresses of any persons found on the premises. The obstruction or attempted obstruction of a member acting under the authority of the warrant is made a criminal offence as is the failure to give a correct name and address when demanded.[159] A member of the Garda Síochána may arrest summarily any person committing such an offence.[160]

Anything found at the place named in the warrant, or on a person at that place, may be seized at the time of the search where the member concerned reasonably believes it to be evidence relating to an offence for which a warrant could be issued under this provision. It is worth noting here that the power of seizure is probably not confined to evidence relating to the actual offence for which the warrant was issued. Although it is not entirely clear

8–20

---

[155] Other examples are to be found in: Consumer Credit Act 1995, s.106; Investment Intermediaries Act 1995, s.75; Regulation of Information (Services Outside the State for Termination of Pregnancies) Act 1995, s.9; Stock Exchange Act 1995, s.66; Criminal Damage Act 1991, s.13; Animal Remedies Act 1993, s.12; Merchant Shipping (Salvage and Wreck) Act 1993, s.57; Control of Horses Act 1996, s.35; Chemical Weapons Act 1997, s.7.

[156] The only other provision which does anything similar is s.29 of the Offences Against the State Act 1939.

[157] Criminal Justice (Miscellaneous Provisions) Act 1997, s.10(1).

[158] *ibid.* s.10(6).

[159] *ibid.* s.10(4).

[160] *ibid.* s.10(3).

from the wording of the statutory provision, it would appear that the power of seizure extends to evidence relating to any of the offences for which a warrant could be issued under the provision. In practice, of course, the significance of this point of statutory interpretation is rendered largely academic in the light of the excessively broad power of seizure conferred on gardaí by section 9 of the Criminal Law Act 1976 (see later).

7. Criminal Justice Act 1994

Introduction

8–21   The search warrant provisions in section 64 of the Criminal Justice Act 1994 are distinctive in that they can be used in order to search for and seize documentary evidence of a relevant offence in the custody of an innocent legal or financial advisor to the person suspected of the offence. The provisions were introduced as part of a package of measures in the 1994 Act designed to combat drug trafficking and moneylaundering. They interact in particular with provisions for the grant of a production or access order in section 63 of the Act.

Application for Production of Access Order

Section 63 of the Criminal Justice Act 1994 enables a member of the Garda Síochána to apply to a judge of the District Court for a production or access order in respect of any particular material or material of a particular description for the purpose of an investigation into a drug trafficking offence, a moneylaundering offence or whether a person has benefited from drug trafficking or an offence in respect of which a confiscation order can be issued under section 9 of the Act.[161] An essential precondition for the order is that the judge is satisfied that there are reasonable grounds for suspecting that a specified person (not necessarily the person who is in possession of the materials which are the subject of the production order application) has carried on drug trafficking or has committed a money-laundering offence or has benefited from drug trafficking or an offence in respect of which a confiscation order can be issued under section 9 of the Act.[162] The judge must also be satisfied that there are reasonable grounds for suspecting that the material to which the application relates is likely to be of substantial value to the investigation and does not consist of or include items subject to legal privilege,[163] and that there are reasonable grounds for believing that it is in the public interest that the material should be produced or that access to it should be given.[164] In assessing the public interest the judge must have regard to the benefit likely to accrue to the investigation if the material is obtained and to the likely circumstances under which the person in possession of the material holds it.[165]

---

[161] Criminal Justice Act 1994, s.63(1).
[162] *ibid.* s.63(4)(a).
[163] *ibid.* s.63(4)(b).
[164] *ibid.* s.63(4)(c).
[165] *ibid.* s.63(4)(c)(i) and (ii).

Effect of Order

Where these preconditions are satisfied the judge may order the person who appears to him to be in possession of the material in question to produce it to a member of the Garda Síochána for him or her to take away,[166] or to give the member access to it within such period as the order may specify.[167] It is worth noting that the obligations are expressed in the alternative and that the time period is expressed to apply to the access option only. The period to be specified in an access order shall be seven days unless it appears to the judge that a longer or shorter period would be appropriate in the particular circumstances of the application.[168] In *Hanahoe v. Hussey*[169] Kinlen J. was of the view that if the order was made in respect of client material held in a solicitor's office the solicitor would need time to contact his or her client for instructions on whether to comply with the order or to seek to have it discharged or varied. Even if there were exceptional circumstances which rendered it undesirable to give the solicitor time to contact the client, he or she would still need reasonable time to comply with the order. Accordingly, the statutory provision could not be interpreted to permit immediate access.

Where a judge makes an access (as distinct from a production) order under these provisions in respect of material on any premises he or she may, on the application of a member of the Garda Síochána, order any person who appears to him to be entitled to grant entry to the premises to allow a member to enter the premises to obtain access to the material.[170]

Overriding Obligations of Secrecy or Confidentiality

It would appear that, subject to two exceptions, an order issued under these provisions overrides any obligation of secrecy or confidentiality under which the material is held, even if such obligation or restriction upon disclosure is imposed by statute.[171] Medical records, financial records, solicitors files etc are not beyond the reach of an order issued under these provisions. Indeed, one of the primary objects of the measures is to trace dealings in property and finance through records held in the offices of solicitors and accountants. The primary exception provided for in the legislation is legal privilege.[172] Presumably this is confined to correspondence between solicitor and client and between solicitor and counsel in respect of litigation or prospective litigation involving the client. There is also a partial exception for material which has been supplied to a government department or other authority by or

8–22

---

[166] *ibid.* s.63(2)(a). If the material consists of information in a computer, the order shall have effect as if it was an order to produce the material in a form in which it can be taken away and in which it is visible and legible; s.63(7)(a).

[167] *ibid.* s.63(2)(b). If the material consists of information contained in a computer the order shall have effect as if it was an order to give access to the material in a form in which it is visible and legible; s.63(7)(b).

[168] *ibid.* s.63(3).

[169] [1998] 3 I.R. 69.

[170] Criminal Justice Act 1994, s.63(5).

[171] *ibid.* s.63(8).

[172] *ibid.* s.63(8)((b).

on behalf of the government of another State in accordance with an under-taking on the department or authority that the material will be used only for a particular purpose or purposes.[173] In this event an order under these provisions cannot require or permit the production of, or access to, the material for a purpose other than the one permitted in accordance with the undertaking. The material shall not, without the consent of the other State, be further disclosed or used otherwise than in accordance with the undertaking.

Variation or Discharge

A judge of the District Court may vary or discharge an order made under these provisions.[174] Any person who fails or refuses without reasonable excuse to comply with an order under these provisions shall be guilty of an offence.[175]

Comparison with Search Warrant

A production or access order differs in several respects from a search warrant. Typically, the order will be narrower and more specific with respect to the materials affected. The person in possession of the materials will be required to produce them or permit access to them. A production or access order does not permit the police to search premises or to trawl through other records in order to find what they are looking for. There is also a delay factor in the production and access orders which is missing from a search warrant. Although the order will have been granted in an *ex parte* hearing the delay factor will enable the person affected to mount a challenge to the order and/or to consider how to manage his affairs in order to comply with it in a manner which minimises its impact on his privacy and property rights. With a search warrant it is the police who are in the driving seat. They decide, within the limits of the warrant, when they are going to exercise it and they do not normally give the person concerned advance notice. The search warrant, therefore, is a very valuable option in any situation where the police have reason to believe that the production or access order may prove counter-productive by giving the person or persons concerned the opportunity to destroy the material or simply by alerting them to the fact that their affairs are being investigated. It is also important to note that a search warrant can also be much more damaging to fundamental property and privacy rights than a production or access order where it is issued in respect of documents or records that are held in the offices of an innocent solicitor or accountant. The adverse publicity that can be attracted by a high profile search of a solicitors office, for example, can prove damaging to the solicitor's reputation and business.[176]

---

[173] *ibid.* s.63(9).
[174] *ibid.* s.63(6).
[175] *ibid.* s.63(10).
[176] See, for example, *Hanahoe v. Hussey* [1998] 3 I.R. 69 where damages were awarded to a firm of solicitors as a result of gardaí tipping off the media about an imminent search of the offices of a major firm of solicitors who were acting for a high profile figure in the organised crime world.

Search Warrant

Section 64 of the Criminal Justice Act 1994 enables a member of the Garda   **8–23**
Síochána to apply to a judge of the District Court for a search warrant in
relation to specified premises in exactly the same circumstances in which he
or she can seek a production or access order for material under section 63.[177]
There are three separate situations in which the judge may grant the
application.[178] The first is where the statutory preconditions for the issue of a
production or access order are satisfied (see above) and the judge is also
satisfied: that it would not be appropriate to make a production or access
order for the material in question because it is not practicable to communicate
with any person entitled to produce the material, or that it is not practicable to
communicate with any person entitled to grant access to the material or
entitled to grant entry to the premises on which the material is situated, or that
the investigation in question might be seriously prejudiced unless a member
of the Garda Síochána could secure immediate access to the material.[179] The
second situation arises where the judge is satisfied that there are reasonable
grounds for suspecting that a specified person (not necessarily the person
occupying the premises) has carried on drug trafficking or moneylaundering
or has benefited from drug trafficking or from an offence in respect of which
a confiscation order might be made under section 9 of the 1994 Act.[180] The
judge must also be satisfied that there are reasonable grounds for suspecting
that there is on the premises material relating to the person or the offence
which is likely to be of substantial value to the investigation in question but
which cannot be particularised at the time of the application.[181] In addition
the judge must be satisfied: that it is not practicable to communicate with any
person entitled to grant entry to the premises, or that entry to the premises
will not be granted unless a warrant is produced, or that the investigation in
question might be seriously prejudiced unless a member of the Garda
Síochána arriving at the premises could secure immediate entry to them.[182]
The third situation arises where a production or access order has already been
granted and the judge is satisfied that it has not been complied with.[183]

Where these preconditions are satisfied in any one of the three situations the   **8–24**
judge may issue a warrant authorising a specified member of the Garda
Síochána, accompanied by such other members as the member thinks
necessary, to enter and search the premises.[184] Force may be used if necessary. A member who has entered premises under such a warrant may seize
and retain any material which is likely to be of substantial value to the
investigation for the purpose of which the warrant was issued. Items which

---

[177] Criminal Justice Act 1994, s.64(1).
[178] *ibid.* s.64(2).
[179] *ibid.* s.64(3).
[180] *ibid.* s.64(4)(a).
[181] *ibid.* s.64(4)(b).
[182] *ibid.* s.64(4)(c).
[183] *ibid.* s.64(2)(a).
[184] *ibid.* s.64(2).

are subject to legal privilege are specifically exempted from seizure. Apart from them, however, items are not protected by virtue of the fact that they are held pursuant to an obligation of secrecy or confidentiality. So, for example, gardaí acting under a warrant issued pursuant to these provisions can seize and take away client files from a solicitor's office where they are likely to be of substantial value to the investigation.

Clearly the execution of a search warrant under section 64 of the Criminal Justice Act 1994 is a more draconian intrusion into the privacy and property rights of an innocent third party than a production or access order issued under section 63. Indeed, it seems to be implicit in the wording of section 64 that the police should seek a warrant only where there is reason to believe that a production or access order would not serve the purposes of the investigation. In *Hanahoe v. Hussey*[185] Kinlen J. considered that the decision to seek a search warrant instead of a production or access order is an operational policing matter and as such is not appropriate for judicial review. However, the learned judge also noted that it was a matter for the court to decide whether to give effect to the police choice in any individual case by issuing a warrant. In making this decision: "[t]he court must be ever conscious of the fact that this is a new and serious invasion of constitutional rights including the invasion of privacy and possibly the invasion of confidential relationships."[186]

8. Criminal Justice (Theft and Fraud Offences) Act 2001

The Criminal Justice (Theft and Fraud Offences) Act 2001 makes provision for the issue of production and access orders to gardaí in respect of material in the possession of a third party.[186a] The measure applies in respect of any offence under the Act which is punishable by imprisonment for a term of five years or by a more severe penalty.[186b] These cover a very wide range of theft-related offences, including fraud affecting the financial interests of the European Communities.

An order can be issued under these provisions by a District Court judge if he or she is satisfied on the basis of having heard evidence on oath by a member of the Garda Síochána that: the Gardaí are investigating a relevant offence; a person has possession or control of particular material or material of a particular description; and there are reasonable grounds for suspecting that the material constitutes evidence of or relating to the commission of the offence.[186c] Where these conditions are satisfied the judge can issue an order for the person in question to produce the material to a member of the Garda Síochána or to give a member access to it, either immediately or within such period as the order may specify. If the material is contained in a computer, the order entails a requirement to produce it or give the member access to it in a

---

185 [1998] 3 I.R. 69.
186 *Ibid.* at 94.
186a Most of the Act came into force on August 1, 2002.
186b Criminal Justice (Theft and Fraud Offences) Act, 2001, s.52(1).
186c *ibid.* s.52(2).

form which is visible and legible and in which it can be taken away.[186d] The order confers a power on the member to take a copy of the document.[186e] Any material taken away may be retained by the member for use as evidence in any criminal proceedings.[186f]

Information contained in a document produced pursuant to these provisions shall be admissible in any criminal proceedings as evidence of any fact in it of which direct oral evidence would be admissible.[186g] This does not apply where the information is privileged from disclosure; was supplied by a person who would not be compellable to give evidence at the instance of the prosecution; was compiled for the purposes of any criminal investigation or other proceedings or inquiry; or where certain specified provisions of the Criminal Evidence Act 1992 are not complied with.[186h]

An order issued pursuant to these provisions shall not confer any right to production of, or access to, any document subject to legal privilege.[186i] This restriction does not extend to documents held under other obligations of secrecy or other restriction on the disclosure of information imposed by statute or otherwise.[186j] A judge of the District Court may vary or discharge an order on the application of any person to whom an order relates or a member of the Garda Síochána.[186k]

A person who without reasonable cause fails or refuses to comply with an order under these provisions is guilty of an offence.[186l]

F. Seizure

1. Introduction

Where a member of the Garda Síochána is conferred with a power to search   **8–25**
for certain items, it must be implicit that he or she also has the power to seize those items if he or she finds them.[187] Where the search is conducted pursuant to a warrant, the warrant will normally specify the object of the search and, by implication, the items that may be seized. Some warrants can be framed in such broad terms that a very wide range of items may be seized in the course of the search. For example, section 29 of the Offences against the State Act 1939 provides for the issue of a search warrant which enables a member of

---

[186d] *ibid.* s.52(3).
[186e] *ibid.* s.52(4)(a).
[186f] *ibid.* s.52(5).
[186g] *ibid.* s.52(6).
[186h] *ibid.* s.52(6)(a). The relevant provisions in the 1992 Act are: s.7 (notice of documentary evidence to be served on the accused); s.8 (admission and weight of documentary evidence) and s.9 (admissibility of evidence as to credibility of supplier of information); see s.52(6)(b) of the 2001 Act.
[186i] *ibid.* s.52(4)(b).
[186j] *ibid.* s.52(4)(c).
[186k] *ibid.* s.52(7).
[186l] *ibid.* s.52(8).
[187] A member of the Garda Síochána also enjoys a few statutory powers of seizure unconnected with search. See, *e.g.*, Casual Trading Act 1995, s.12; Street Trading Act 1926, s.10.

the Garda Síochána to seize anything found on the premises in question or on any person found on those premises which the member reasonably believes to be evidence of or to relate to directly or indirectly the commission or intended commission of an offence under the Offences against the State Acts or treason. Most, however, are much more specific about the matter which may be seized. This can give rise to problems in practice where a member of the Garda Síochána is searching property pursuant to a warrant and discovers items which he or she believes are evidence of a criminal offence, but which are not covered by the warrant. If the member has to go off to obtain a warrant in order to seize the goods, it is highly likely that they will have disappeared by the time he or she returns to execute the new warrant. The common law, as developed by the English Court of Appeal, comes to the rescue of the police officer in this situation by extending the power of seizure.[188]

2. Common Law

In *Chic Fashions (West Wales) Ltd v. Jones*[189] the police searched premises under a warrant for clothing made by a particular manufacturer. In the course of the search they discovered clothing made by manufacturers other than the one named on the warrant. Nevertheless, they seized the clothing as they reasonably believed that it had been stolen. In subsequent civil proceedings the question arose whether the seizure of the clothing was unlawful on account of the fact that it did not come within the description in the search warrant. Upholding the legality of the seizure in the Court of Appeal, Lord Denning formulated the law in the following terms:

> "[W]hen a constable enters a house by virtue of a search warrant for stolen goods, he may seize not only the goods which he reasonably believes to be covered by the warrant, but also any other goods which he believes on reasonable grounds to have been stolen and to be material evidence on a charge of stealing or receiving against the person in possession of them or anyone associated with him."[190]

Taken at face value it would seem quite reasonable to extend this power to the gardaí. It is confined to the situation where the police are searching premises under a warrant for stolen goods of a specified description. To deny them the power to seize other goods which they come across in the course of the search, and which they reasonably believe to be stolen, seems an excessive concession to the rights of private property. If the police had to go off and secure another warrant before seizing the goods, there is a serious risk that they would have disappeared by the time the warrant could be executed. A pertinent analogy might be found in the police common law power of search and seizure associated with arrest.[191] If they can search the immediate area in

---

[188] For cogent criticism of this development see Leigh *op. cit.* at pp. 189–196.
[189] [1968] 2 Q.B. 299.
[190] *Chic Fashions (West Wales) Ltd v. Jones* [1968] 2 Q.B. 299, at p. 313.
[191] Both Lord Denning and Lord Diplock cited the Irish case of *Dillon v. O'Brien and Davis* (1887) 16 Cox CC 245 in their judgments. The learned judges found support for their formulation of the

which the arrest is effected and seize any material which they reasonably believe to be evidence of the offence in question, it would seem reasonable to allow them to seize goods believed to be stolen when they are searching premises under a warrant for other stolen goods. A different view might be taken should the power extend to search warrants granted for other purposes, or if the material seized was not reasonably suspected to be stolen.

3. Criminal Law Act 1976

Section 9

As yet, *Chic Fashions* has not been cited in a reported Irish decision. Presumably, that is due in no small measure to the sweeping provisions of section 9 of the Criminal Law 1976 which reads:

8–26

> "(1) Where in the course of exercising any powers under this Act or in the course *of a search carried out under any other power*, a member of the Garda Síochána, a prison officer or a member of the Defence Forces finds or comes into possession of anything which he believes to be evidence of any offence or suspected offence, it may be seized and retained for use as evidence in any criminal proceedings, or in any proceedings in relation to a breach of prison discipline, for such period from the date of seizure as is reasonable or, if proceedings are commenced in which the thing so seized is required for use in evidence, until the conclusion of the proceedings, and thereafter the Police (Property) Act 1897, shall apply to the thing so seized in the same manner as that Act applies to property which has come into the possession of the Garda Síochána in the circumstances mentioned in that Act. (*emphasis added*)
>
> (2) If it is represented or appears to a person proposing to seize or retain a document under this section that the document was, or may have been, made for the purpose of obtaining, giving or communicating legal advice from or by a barrister or solicitor, that person shall not seize or retain the document unless he suspects with reasonable cause that the document was not made, or is not intended, solely for any of the purposes aforesaid."

Scope of the Power

Where section 9 applies, a member of the Garda Síochána[192] may seize anything which he or she believes to be evidence of any offence. This effectively drives a coach and horses through the pre-existing law. It means that when a member of the Garda Síochána is carrying out a search under any power, whether conferred by statute or at common law, he or she may seize anything which he or she believes to be evidence of an offence. It does not matter that the power of search was confined to an offence which is totally unrelated to that associated with the suspected offence for which the goods

---

law in the fact that the common law admitted a seizure of material evidence which was found at the place where the suspect was arrested and which was relevant to the charge against him.

[192] The power also extends to a prison officer and a member of the Defence Forces; Criminal Law Act 1976, s.9(1).

were seized. Moreover, it does not matter that the search was being carried out under a warrant which specifically prescribed the goods to be seized. A member acting under this warrant will still be able to seize anything which he or she suspects to be evidence of any offence, even though it might have no connection at all with the goods or offence mentioned in the warrant. The fact that the member in question need only suspect, as opposed to reasonably suspect, that the goods seized are evidence of an offence (or any suspected offence) emphasises its exceptional scope. The combination of these elements goes much further in favouring the interests of the police over private property than anything contemplated in the judgments of the English Court of Appeal in *Chic Fashions*.

8–27 It is also worth noting that section 9 refers to a search carried out under any power. Presumably, this extends to any common law power of search available to a member of the Garda Síochána. It follows that when a member is exercising his or her very broad common law power to search the area where a suspect has been arrested, he or she will enjoy an even broader power of seizure under section 9 than that recognised in *Jennings v. Quinn*.[193] Indeed, the section does not even require the search to be effected in connection with a suspected offence. It will be sufficient that the member is acting under a "power." Gardaí do, of course, have certain powers of stop and search which are not dependant on suspicion that the person actually stopped and searched has committed or is committing an offence. Where a person is stopped and searched under such a power it would appear that section 9 permits the member of the Garda Síochána concerned to seize anything found in the person's possession which he or she believes is evidence of any offence.

Ryan and Magee point out that section 9 would appear to put into reverse the whole restrictive approach of the pre-existing law and, *de facto*, erodes the liberties which *Leach v. Money* and *Entick v. Carrington* sought to secure. In their view the scope of the power to seize property under the provision is so wide that it could face constitutional challenge.[194] It is important, however, to remember that section 9 is only a power of seizure. It does not carry with it the power to search. Before the seizure power will arise the member of the Garda Síochána in question must be acting under a lawful power of search. Given the reasoning of the English Court of Appeal and the current Irish judicial approach to the scope of police powers, as reflected in *DPP (Stratford) v. Fagan*,[195] it is submitted that the prospects for a successful challenge to section 9 on this ground are weak. It would require the Court to conclude that the individual's fundamental rights to privacy and private property would preclude a member of the Garda Síochána from seizing material which he or she comes across in the lawful exercise of his or her powers and which he or she believes is evidence of a criminal offence. It is more likely that the Court would conclude that it was the member's duty to seize the material in such circumstances. The

---

[193] [1968] I.R. 305.
[194] Ryan and Magee, *op. cit.*, p. 153.
[195] [1994] I.L.R.M. 349.

arguments based on the state of the pre-existing law and judicial practice are likely to be met with the response that they are rooted in the very different circumstances of the last century, and that the crime challenge facing society and the police today are much greater than anything that prevailed then. Support for the need to allow the police greater freedom in this context will be found in the English case law and in the view of the legislature as reflected in the enactment of section 9 itself.

Limits to the Power

It might be a wholly different matter, of course, if a member of the Garda   **8–28**
Síochána attempted to rely on section 9 to seize material which he or she came across in the course of a search which was conducted in a manner which bore no relationship to the power of search in question. For example, if a member was acting under a warrant to search for a stolen piano and proceeded to look under cushions and mattresses in a dwelling house, it can be argued that he has gone beyond the scope of his power. In this event, if the member seizes material which he or she believes is evidence of an offence, quite separate from the theft of the piano, the prospects of a successful challenge to the admissibility of the material in evidence must be quite high. This, however, is based on the premise that section 9 would not have been triggered in such a case as the member in question would not have been exercising a lawful power of search. It is submitted that a similar result would ensue if the member's power of search had expired before he or she seized material under section 9. This would apply if the material was seized in the course of a search which continued after the piano had been found.

As yet the scope and application of section 9 of the Criminal Law Act 1976 has not been the subject of an authoritative judicial ruling. In *People (DPP) v. Balfe*[196] Murphy J. opined that the existence of section 9 may render it less important to identify the particular items to be seized under a search warrant for stolen goods. He considered, nevertheless, that the concept of the application for and the granting of a warrant to search for stolen goods must involve the provision of some description of the goods in question. In other words the existence of section 9 would not necessarily set at nought the effect of the specific words of a statute conferring a power to issue a search warrant in particular circumstances.

3. Other Statutory Powers

It is also worth noting that there are several statutory provisions which permit a member of the Garda Síochána to seize summarily certain items without reference to any prior stop, entry or search. The Criminal Justice Act 1994, for example, permits a member of the Garda Síochána to seize any cash being imported into or exported out of the State in excess of a prescribed amount, if he or she has reasonable grounds for suspecting that it represents the proceeds

---

[196] [1998] 4 I.R. 50.

of any drug trafficking or is for use in any drug trafficking.[197] Cash so seized can be detained for no longer than 48 hours, unless its further detention is authorised by a District Court judge. A similar power to seize property in order to prevent it from being removed from the State is provided by the Proceeds of Crime Act 1996,[198] while the National Monuments (Amendment) Act 1994 provides powers of seizure designed to protect archaeological sites and artefacts.[199] These powers are all preventative in nature. They are clearly aimed at preserving the status quo until a perceived threat to an important public interest is checked out.

4. Powers of Retention

Introduction

8–29 It may happen that the police come into possession of property quite innocently, and subsequently decide to retain temporary custody of it on the ground that it is reasonably believed to be evidence of a criminal offence. They may wish to carry out forensic tests on the property and/or use it as evidence in criminal proceedings. If the owner demands the immediate return of the property before these objectives have been satisfied, the question arises whether the police have any legal power to resist those demands. Undoubtedly, there will be many situations in which the necessary power will be present. For example, if the police happen to come across the property while acting under a warrant to search for other goods, there can be little doubt now that they can lawfully seize the property. A similar result will ensue if they happen to find it while searching the immediate area where an arrest has been effected. There are other circumstances, however, where the availability of the necessary power is less certain. If, for example, bank robbers used an innocent person's car in the course of the robbery and subsequently abandoned it, a member of the Garda Síochána could not secure a warrant to seize the vehicle.[200] This is because there is no statutory authority permitting the issue of a warrant in such circumstances. Moreover, there is no statutory provision which would enable the member to seize the vehicle without a warrant. Even the wide-ranging power of seizure provided in section 9 of the Criminal Law Act 1976 would not be sufficient as it will come into play only when the member is acting under a power of search or any other power conferred by the Act.

The Police (Property) Act 1897 does not appear to deal directly with this situation. It prescribes a procedure whereby a person can reclaim an item or items of his property which has come into the possession of the police. The assumption behind the Act however, is that the police have recovered the property for the benefit of the true owner, either through it being handed in by

---

[197] Criminal Justice Act 1994, s.38.
[198] Proceeds of Crime Act 1996, s.15.
[199] National Monuments (Amendment) Act 1994, s.7.
[200] This is the example offered by Lord Denning MR (as he then was) in the leading English case of *Ghani v. Jones* [1970] 1 Q.B. 693.

a third party who has found it or by the police recovering it from a third party who was in unlawful possession of it. It does not specifically address the situation whereby the police would wish to seize property directly from an innocent owner and retain it in order to use it as evidence in a criminal prosecution. Surprisingly, perhaps, it would appear that the common law may provide the necessary authority. The leading case is a decision of the English Court of Appeal in *Ghani v. Jones*.[201]

English Common Law

Ghani v. Jones concerned a murder investigation in the course of which the police entered and searched a dwelling house with the consent of the owner. While in the house they asked for and received the passports of the occupier and two of his relatives. The police took the passports away and the owners subsequently sought their return. The police resisted their claim on the basis that a person would ultimately be charged with murder and the passports would be relevant evidence in the prosecution. Although the Court of Appeal decided in favour of the owners on the facts, it purported to lay down sweeping new rules concerning the police power to seize and detain property. Lord Denning MR, delivering the judgment of the Court, proceeded on the basis that it was open to the police to seize property as evidence for use in subsequent criminal proceedings where the owner has not been arrested or charged. He defined the following requirements that must be satisfied before the power would come into play:

> "*First*: The police officers must have reasonable grounds for believing that a serious offence has been committed – so serious that it is of the first importance that the offenders should be caught and brought to justice.
> *Second:* The police officers must have reasonable grounds for believing that the article in question is either the fruit of the crime (as in the case of stolen goods) or is the instrument by which the crime was committed (as in the case of the axe used by the murderer) or is material evidence to prove the commission of the crime (as in the case of the car used by a bank raider)...
> *Third*: The police officers must have reasonable grounds to believe that the person in possession of it has himself committed the crime, or is implicated in it, or is an accessory to it, or at any rate his refusal must be quite unreasonable.
> *Fourth:* The police must not keep the article, nor prevent its removal, for any longer than is reasonably necessary to complete their investigations or preserve it for evidence. If a copy will suffice, it should be made and the original returned. As soon as the case is over, or it is decided not to go on with it, the article should be returned.
> *Finally*: The lawfulness of the conduct of the police must be judged at the time, and not by what happens afterwards."[202]

8–30

8–31

The central feature of these requirements is the implication that the police can seize and keep goods from their lawful owner even if he is not implicated in

---

[201] [1970] 1 Q.B. 693.
[202] *ibid.* at 708–709.

the crime to which they relate. However, this power will arise only where the offence in question is very serious, the article in question is directly associated with the commission of the crime and the owner's refusal to cooperate is quite unreasonable. Clearly, in defining the scope of this power Lord Denning MR is attempting to balance the public interest in effective criminal investigation with private property rights. The lack of binding precedent from the House of Lords in the matter enabled him to proceed to a straightforward policy decision on what he deems to be an acceptable balance between the interests of the State in this area and the rights of the private citizen.[203]

Transposition into Irish Law

Ghani v. Jones has been accepted as a correct statement of the law in the English courts.[204] It does not follow, however, that it will be successfully imported into Irish law. The primary difficulty is, of course, the specific constitutional protection for the rights of private property against unjust attack. If the police were to seize evidence in the *Ghani v. Jones* type situation there is a very real risk that an Irish Court would feel compelled to exclude it at trial on the grounds that it was seized in violation of the constitutional rights of the citizen. Given the absence of a clearly established legal power to seize property in such circumstances it is difficult to see how an Irish court could circumvent the constitutional impediment.[205] Indeed, in a succession of recent cases the Irish courts have demonstrated a marked reluctance to extend common law police powers at the expense of the rights of private property.[206] That is not to say that a legislative provision which attempted to balance the interests of private property against those of criminal prosecution would be equally unconstitutional. As yet, however, the legislature has not conferred a general power on the police to seize and retain property for use in evidence in criminal proceedings where the owner is neither the defendant in those proceedings nor consents to the retention of his property by the police. There are, however, a number of specific powers which gardaí can use to seize and retain property without the consent of the owner and in circumstances where the owner is not necessarily the subject of a criminal investigation.[207]

---

[203] Lord Denning chose not to follow a previous decision of the English Court of Criminal Appeal (as it then was) in *R. v. Waterfield* [1964] 1 Q.B. 164 which would have decided the issue without having to embark on a novel formulation of the law.

[204] See, *e.g.*, *Garfinkel v. Metropolitan Police Commissioner* [1972] Crim. L.R. 44; *Frank Truman Ltd v. Police Commissioner* [1977] Q.B. 952. But see implied doubts expressed by Lord Donaldson in *McLorie v. Oxford* [1982] 3 All E.R. 480. The formulation of the law in *Ghani v. Jones* has also been the subject of incisive criticism; see Leigh, *op. cit.*, pp. 194–196.

[205] In *Rogers v. DPP* [1992] I.L.R.M. O'Hanlon J. impliedly acknowledged the right of an owner to secure the expeditious return of his property which may have evidential value in a criminal prosecution.

[206] *DPP v. McCreesh* [1992] 2 I.R. 239; *DPP v. Gaffney* [1988] I.L.R.M. 39; *DPP v. Delaney* [1996] 1 I.L.R.M. 536; *DPP v. McMahon* [1986] I.R. 393. Interestingly, the courts have not demonstrated a similar restraint in respect of police powers to stop motorists temporarily for the purposes of checking whether they are engaged in criminal activity; see *DPP (Stratford) v. Fagan* [1994] 2 I.L.R.M. 349.

[207] See, *e.g.*, Criminal Justice Act 1994, s.38; Proceeds of Crime Act, 1996, s.15; National Monuments (Amendment) Act 1994, s.7.

G. Procedural Matters

1. Admissible Evidence when Applying for a Warrant

The determination of an application for a search warrant is a ministerial act as **8–32** distinct from an exercise of judicial power. The District Court judge or peace commissioner does not adjudicate on any *lis* between the parties when deciding whether to issue the warrant. Accordingly, he or she is not bound by the strict rules of evidence which apply to a criminal trial. He or she is entitled to rely on material, such as hearsay, when deciding whether the statutory preconditions for the issue of a warrant have been satisfied and whether he or she should exercise his or her discretion to issue the warrant.[208]

2. Proving a Search Warrant Issued by a Peace Commissioner

In *DPP v. Owens*[209] the Supreme Court was asked to rule on whether a search **8–33** warrant issued by a peace commissioner must be proved by the peace commissioner appearing in person to give evidence about his or her state of mind. In that case a peace commissioner had issued a search warrant for the proceeds of a robbery which were believed to be stored in the defendant's house. At his trial the defence indicated that they were challenging the validity of the warrant and putting the prosecution to formal proof it. The trial judge ruled that the peace commissioner's signature on the warrant was not sufficient to prove the validity of the warrant and that the peace commissioner must be present in person to prove his state of mind and to be available, if necessary, for cross-examination. The peace commissioner, however, was too ill to come to court to give evidence about his state of mind when issuing the warrant. Accordingly, the trial judge ruled the search warrant invalid.

The Supreme Court upheld the trial judge's ruling. Since the peace commissioner was not a court of record he was in the same position in this matter as a chief superintendent who authorises the extension of a person's detention in police custody under section 30 of the Offences against the State Act 1939. In *People (DPP) v. Byrne*[210] the Supreme Court had ruled that it would have to be positively proved that a chief superintendent had the requisite suspicion when authorising the extension of detention under section 30. This could be done only by the chief superintendent appearing in person to give evidence about his state of mind at the time. It could not be presumed by virtue of the fact that he granted the extension, nor by his signature on the document authorising the extension, nor by hearsay evidence. In *Owens* the Supreme Court ruled that exactly the same principle applies to a search warrant issued by a peace commissioner. It must be proved by the peace commissioner giving evidence in person. The search warrant is a document which may affect constitutional rights and it does not speak for itself in a criminal trial.

---

[208] *Simple Imports Ltd v. Revenue Commissioners* [2000] 2 I.R. 243.
[209] [1999] 2 I.L.R.M. 421.
[210] [1989] I.L.R.M. 613.

It is submitted that the *Owens* ruling does not extend directly to search warrants issued by a judge of the District Court. Since the District Court is a court of record, it can be expected that, where the warrant shows jurisdiction on its face, the judge will benefit from the presumption that he acted lawfully and properly in issuing the warrant.[211]

3. Challenging the Validity of a Search Warrant

8–34   The validity of a search warrant may be challenged in several different contexts. The first practicable opportunity to challenge it is at the point of execution. The occupier of the premises may refuse to submit to the entry and search on the basis that the warrant is void or defective. Clearly, if the warrant is void the occupier will be justified in refusing entry. His refusal will be lawful even where he had no personal knowledge at the time of the flaw which rendered the warrant void. It would also appear that he is justified in refusing entry if there is a technical defect on the face of the warrant which in itself is not sufficient to render the warrant void and of no effect. Examples include: the wrong address, a failure to specify the items for which the warrant has been granted or a failure to sign it. If the entry and search is executed in the face of his objection it is at least arguable that any material seized in the course of the search should be ruled inadmissible in evidence even though the defect in the warrant was not sufficient to render it void.

Where a warrant has been executed and it subsequently transpires that the warrant was defective the occupier may have a cause of action for trespass and/or breach of constitutional rights against the State. However, a complication may arise here by virtue of the fact that a member of the Garda Síochána enjoys a statutory immunity from being sued in respect of an entry and search pursuant to a search warrant which was defective due to error on the part of the District Court judge or peace commissioner issuing the warrant.[212]

8–35   In practice the validity of a warrant is most likely to be challenged in the course of a criminal trial where the accused seeks to have evidence obtained pursuant to the search warrant excluded on the ground that the warrant was void and of no effect. Such a challenge should normally be taken at the trial itself.

In *DPP v. Judge Windle*[213] the High Court was called upon to rule on the validity of the respondent's decision to declare a search warrant invalid in the course of a preliminary examination. McCracken J., delivering the judgment of the High Court in the matter, acknowledged that a search warrant has serious implications for the constitutional rights of the individual and that the District Court, in common with all other courts, is under an obligation to

---

[211]   See, *e.g.*, *Simple Imports Ltd v. Revenue Commissioners* [2000] 2 I.R. 243 *per* Keane J. at 253.
[212]   This issue was raised but not pursued in *Hanahoe v. Hussey,* unreported, High Court, November 14, 1997.
[213]   High Court, July 23, 1999.

protect the constitutional rights of the individual. However, he went on to rule that the preliminary examination is not a suitable occasion for the District Court to rule on the validity of a search warrant. The learned judge explained that the preliminary examination is not a trial of the accused. Its sole purpose is to determine whether there is a sufficient case to put the accused on trial. Further evidence, in addition to that which is called at the preliminary examination, may be called at the trial. It would be premature, therefore, to rule on the validity of a search warrant at the preliminary examination:

> "I am quite satisfied that it is not for a Judge conducting a preliminary examination to determine the validity or otherwise of a search warrant. This is a matter purely for the Trial Judge, to be determined by him on the evidence before him. If there had been no search warrant in the present case, then certainly the District Judge would have been justified in refusing to send the second named Respondent forward for trial, as there would have been no evidence to justify the search of his premises, but once a search warrant existed, in my view the question of its validity was one for the trial and not one for a preliminary investigation."[214]

Although McCracken J. was referring specifically to a preliminary examination, it is arguable that his ruling applies by analogy to an application to dismiss a charge or charges under Part 1A of the Criminal Procedure Act 1967. Just like the preliminary examination the application to dismiss is not a full trial of the charge or charges in question. The task for the court is merely to determine whether there is a sufficient case to put the accused on trial for the charge or charges. Equally, however, it can be argued that there are fundamental differences between the preliminary examination and the application to dismiss. In particular the latter is heard before the trial court, as distinct from the District Court, and the outcome of a successful application is an order to "dismiss the charge". While it is not specifically stated in the legislation, it is at least arguable that such an order will prevent the DPP from proceeding against the accused in respect of the same charge at a future date, unless the order is quashed on appeal (see chapter 14, at para 14–17). On this interpretation there would appear to be no reason in principle why the accused could not challenge the admissibility of evidence on an application to dismiss.

Certiorari will not normally issue to quash a search warrant where the primary object is to have the results of the search excluded as evidence in the forthcoming criminal trial. In *Byrne v. Grey*,[215] for example, the High Court refused to grant an order of *certiorari* to quash a search warrant despite its finding that the warrant was null and void. It took the view that the warrant was spent, having been exercised, and that the only objective in seeking to have it quashed at this stage was to have the results of the search excluded as evidence in the forthcoming criminal trial. This was a matter which should be determined by the trial judge. Since *certiorari* should only issue where it is necessary to achieve a just resolution of the matter with minimal inconvenience consistent with the regularity of judicial procedures, this was not an

---

[214] *ibid.*
[215] [1988] I.R. 31. See also *Berkeley v. Edwards* [1988] I.R. 217.

appropriate case for its exercise. If, however, criminal proceedings have not been initiated or are not certain to follow upon an entry, search and seizure the Courts will entertain an application for *certiorari* where the objective is to secure the return of the seized goods. This is most likely to arise in the context of seizures on foot of warrants issued under the Customs legislation.[216]

H. Search and Seizure on Arrest

8–36   See Chapter 4 on Arrest.

---

[216] See, *e.g.*, *Simple Imports Ltd v. Revenue Commissioners* [2000] 2 I.R. 243.

CHAPTER 9

ADMISSIBILITY OF IMPROPERLY OBTAINED EVIDENCE

A. Introduction

The success of every criminal prosecution depends upon the presentation of **9–01** admissible evidence in court. The evidence in question may come in a wide range of forms including: a confession from the accused; statements from victims, witnesses and experts; sound and video recordings; and other material evidence such as an instrument used in the commission of the crime and forensic evidence which has been analysed in laboratories. Where such evidence is relevant and cogent, and has been obtained through the voluntary cooperation of the persons concerned, there usually will be no difficulty in having it admitted at the trial. Where voluntary cooperation is not forthcoming the police will often have to resort to their coercive powers to obtain the evidence. Typical examples include: the arrest, detention and questioning of a suspect; a stop and search of a suspect; the taking of samples from a suspect; and an entry onto private property for the purpose of search and seizure.

The manner in which the police exercise their coercive powers to obtain evidence will have a critical bearing on the admissibility of that evidence at trial. Evidence may be excluded if the police act beyond their powers in an individual case. Exclusion can result even where the police transgression does not amount to a criminal offence or a tortious infraction in itself. Moreover, there are circumstances where the police conduct will result in the exclusion of evidence despite the fact that they did not rely on their coercive powers to obtain it. For a full treatment of these and the other detailed rules on the admissibility of evidence in a criminal trial, reference should be made to specialised works on the law of evidence.[1] However, in order to appreciate fully the ambit and significance of

---

[1] See, for example, *Phipson on Evidence* (15th ed., Sweet & Maxwell, London, 1999); *Wigmore on Evidence*; C Fennell *The Law of Evidence* (2nd ed., Butterworths, Dublin, 2001); C Tapper *Cross on Evidence* (9th ed, Butterworths, London, 1999); R May *Criminal Evidence* (4th ed, Sweet & Maxwell, London, 1998); P Mirfield, *Silence, Confessions and Improperly Obtained Evidence* (Clarendon Press, Oxford, 1998).

many of the police powers of investigation described in this text, it is necessary to deal at some length with the principles governing the admissibility of improperly obtained evidence in Ireland. For ease of exposition, the common law rules on the admissibility of statement evidence will be treated separately from the rules governing the admissibility of unconstitutionally obtained evidence and those on unlawfully obtained evidence.

B. Inculpatory Statements

1. Exception to the Hearsay Rule

9–02   Where the prosecution alleges that the accused has made a statement implicating himself in the crime charged, it may wish to call as a witness the person to whom the statement was allegedly made. This course of action will often be vital to a successful prosecution where the accused pleads not guilty. By calling the witness in question the prosecution will hope to prove that the accused has already confessed to the crime. To get the accused's alleged statement admitted in evidence in this manner, however, the prosecution will have to overcome the hearsay obstacle.

The rule against hearsay states that: "an assertion other than one made by a person while giving oral evidence in the proceedings is inadmissible as evidence of any fact asserted."[2] Without further qualification this would mean that a member of the Garda Síochána could not give evidence to the effect that the accused had made a statement to him admitting his guilt. This situation is avoided, however, by the fact that several substantial exceptions have been grafted onto the hearsay rule both at common law and by statute. One of the most important exceptions at common law is that which admits in evidence at the criminal trial an inculpatory statement made by the accused, so long as the prosecution can prove beyond a reasonable doubt that the statement was voluntary. In this context an inculpatory statement generally refers to a statement by the accused the contents of which implicate him in the offence with which he is charged or for which he is under investigation. It can take the form of a full confession or an account of events which, when taken in conjunction with other evidence, is sufficient to implicate him in the crime.[3] In *Attorney General v. McCabe*,[4] for example, Kennedy C.J. explained that:

> "[S]ome statements, without being actually confessions, would be of so incriminating a character as to have the effect of implicating the accused like a confession or admission, and so to come for practical purposes under the latter category, and to require the like strict rules governing their admission in evidence."[5]

---

[2] *Cross on Evidence* at p. 42. This definition of hearsay was approved by the House of Lords in *R. v. Sharp* [1988] 1 All E.R. 65 at 68.

[3] In *Customs and Excise v. Harz* [1967] 1 A.C. 760 the House of Lords rejected the notion that a different admissibility rule could apply depending on whether the statement was a confession or an admission which fell short of a full confession.

[4] [1927] I.R. 129.

[5] *ibid.* at p. 133.

The classic form of inculpatory statement is that which is dictated to and **9–03** recorded in writing by the police and which is then signed by the person making it. Equally, however, it can take the form of a question and answer session between the person and the police which is recorded in writing by the police and then signed by the person. In either case the written record and the signature of the person making the statement are not essential prerequisites for the admissibility of such a statement in evidence. An unsigned written statement may be admitted in evidence as may an oral statement. Indeed, it is not even necessary that the person should say or write anything. Conduct may be sufficient to constitute the equivalent of an inculpatory statement. Where a person is required to undergo a test in police custody, for example, the results of that test can amount to an inculpatory statement which, in order to be admissible in evidence, will have to comply with the normal rules governing the admissibility of such evidence.[6] In *Sullivan v. Robinson*,[7] for example, Davitt P. explained the implications for tests carried out on persons in police custody to determine whether they had been driving with excess alcohol in their blood:

> "Admission or confession may be by conduct as well as by words. A person charged with driving a car while drunk may in words admit he was drunk at the time. He may also by his conduct, shortly after the time at which it is alleged he was drunk, make such an admission. For instance, he may undertake a test, which a sober man can perform adequately, and by failure to do so confess his incompetence. That seems to me to be as much a confession as if he used words to confess his incompetence.
>
> For these reasons it seems to me that when a doctor is called in by the police to examine a person, who is suspected of being drunk, with a view to preferring a charge such as that in the present case, and the doctor converses with him, or conducts an examination involving question and answer, or submits him to certain tests, evidence as to what he said, or the result of the test, should not be received by any Court trying the person upon the criminal charge unless the prosecution affirmatively establishes to the satisfaction of the Court that any statement in the nature of the confession made by the accused was voluntarily made, and any test the result of which tends to incriminate him was voluntarily undergone. In my opinion, the principles as to admissibility of confessions apply to the question whether evidence of the result of such tests is admissible."[8]

Even the results of the observation of a person in police custody can be **9–04** considered as an inculpatory statement by the person for these purposes where the observation is carried out as part of a criminal investigation.[9]

The rules governing the admissibility of inculpatory statements are considered below. The point being made here simply is that they apply not just to oral and written statements but also conduct which is the equivalent of an admission or confession. The position with respect to exculpatory statements

---

[6] *People (DPP) v. Murray* CCA, April 12, 1999.
[7] [1954] I.R. 161.
[8] *ibid.* at 168.
[9] *DPP v. Kenny* [1992] 2 I.R. 141. It does not follow that persons who are lawfully authorised to deal with a suspect in police custody cannot give evidence about the conduct or condition of the accused while in custody without first having cautioned the suspect that such evidence may be given.

(*i.e.* statements which are neither confessions nor admissions) is less certain. Kennedy C.J. intimated, without deciding the point, in the *McCabe* case that exculpatory statements could be admitted in evidence without satisfying the strict requirements pertaining to confessions and admissions.[10]

2. Voluntary Confessions in Police Custody

9–05   In practice the inculpatory statements most frequently proffered in evidence by the prosecution are those allegedly made by the suspect under questioning by the police.[11] Typically, but not invariably, the questioning will take place in the police station while the suspect is detained consequent upon arrest. In most contested cases there are no independent witnesses to the fact that the confession was made nor as to the circumstances in which it was made. This scenario must be qualified in Britain where the tape recording of interviews and the presence of solicitors during questioning of suspects is now a common practice. In Ireland, while progress is being made on the introduction of audio-visual recording of interviews in some police stations, it is still the case that most interviews are conducted in the absence of any independent witnesses. This created a situation favourable to accusations from the accused that he did not make the statement attributed to him, or that the police pressurised him into making the statement which is in fact false. Equally, of course, it also affords rogue police officers the opportunity to extract confessions from suspects by foul means. The question arises, therefore, whether and, if so, in what circumstances should confessions obtained from suspects in police custody be admitted in evidence. Traditionally, it has been left primarily to the courts in Ireland and Britain to chart a path through the conflicting interests involved.

The development of organised professional policing in the nineteenth century led to an increasing number of contested confession cases coming before the courts in that era. For the most part, the judges adopted a healthy scepticism towards the reliability of confessions obtained in police custody, particularly when there was no corroborating evidence.[12] This attitude is vividly captured in the following quotation from Cave J. in *R. v. Thompson*[13]:

> "I always suspect these confessions, which are supposed to be the offspring of penitence and remorse, and which nevertheless are repudiated by the prisoner at the trial. It is remarkable that it is of very rare occurrence for evidence of a

---

[10]   [1927] I.R. 129 at 133–134. See also, *Attorney General v. O'Leary* [1926] I.R. 445 at 42. In *McCabe* the court refused to extend to exculpatory statements the principles applicable to confessions. It justified the distinction on the ground that the exculpatory statements in question did not contain anything incriminating the accused. See also *Wigmore on Evidence* (3rd ed.,) Vol.111, 243.

[11]   Note, that there is authority to suggest that the prosecution should not take the view that the existence of a the confession relieves them of the obligation to seek or retain further material evidence; see *Braddish v. DPP* [2001] 3 I.R. 127, per Hardiman J. at 133. Note also that where uncorroborated evidence is given of a confession on trial on indictment, the judge must advise the jury to have due regard to the absence of corroboration; see Criminal Procedure Act 1993, s.10(1).

[12]   There are those, however, who decried the extent to which the admissibility rules were seen to favour the accused; see, for example, Erle J. in *R. v. Baldry* 5 Cox CC 523.

[13]   [1893] 2 Q.B. 12.

confession to be given when the proof of the prisoner's guilt is otherwise clear and satisfactory; but, when it is not clear and satisfactory, the prisoner is not infrequently alleged to have been seized with the desire born of penitence and remorse to supplement it with a confession; – a desire which vanishes as soon as he appears in a court of justice."[14]

Accordingly, the admissibility rules developed at that time reflected a distinct bias in favour of the accused.[15] This has been associated in some quarters with a more general judicial drive to counter the harshness evident in other aspects of the criminal process at that time. The severity of criminal penalties and the inability of the accused to testify on his own behalf are frequently cited examples in this context. Although these features of the criminal justice process have long since disappeared, the basic rules on the admissibility of confession evidence have survived and continue to apply in Ireland today. Moreover, they are not confined to confessions obtained from the questioning of a suspect in police custody. They apply to inculpatory statements generally. As explained above, statements in this context must be interpreted to include the results of tests or observations carried out on a suspect at the behest of the police or other law enforcement authorities.

3. Voluntariness

The general common law rule on the admissibility of inculpatory statements can be summed up in the word voluntariness. For a confession to be admissible in evidence the prosecution must prove beyond a reasonable doubt that it was voluntarily made.[15a] If the prosecution fails to satisfy this voluntariness test the trial judge has no option but to exclude the confession. The classic statement of the law is still to be found in the following words of Lord Sumner in *Ibrahim v. R*:

> "[I]t is a positive rule of law that such a statement shall not be admitted in evidence against a prisoner unless it is a voluntary statement, in the sense that it has not been obtained from him either by fear of prejudice or hope of advantage exercised or held out by a person in authority, and the onus is on the prosecution tendering the statement to show that it is voluntary in that sense . . ."[16]

This was adopted as a correct statement of the law in Ireland by Kennedy C.J. in *Attorney General v. McCabe*[17] and has been followed by the courts ever since.[18] In *Re National Irish Bank Ltd*[19] Barrington J., giving the judgment of

9–06

---

[14] *ibid.* at 18.

[15] See, generally, Cross *op. cit* at 598–604.

[15a] *People (DPP) v. Buck*, unreported, Supreme Court, April 17, 2002.

[16] [1914] A.C. 599 at 609. It will be seen later that confessions which have been obtained by oppression are considered to be involuntary confessions. For the most part the conditions which amount to oppression will come within the scope of a "fear of prejudice" or "hope of advantage". Nevertheless, it is common to see the words "or by oppression" added on to the standard definition of voluntariness immediately after the words "a person in authority".

[17] [1927] I.R. 129 at 134.

[18] See, *e.g.*, *People (Attorney General) v. Cummins* [1972] I.R. 312; *People (Attorney General) v. Gilbert* [1973] I.R. 383; *Re National Irish Bank Ltd* (No.1) [1999] 3 I.R. 145.

[19] [1999] 3 I.R. 145.

the Supreme Court, declared that "any trial at which an alleged confession other than a voluntary confession were admitted in evidence against the accused person would not be a trial in due course of law within the meaning of Article 38 of the Constitution . . .".[20]

It can be deduced from Lord Sumner's formulation that the judicial concept of a "voluntary" confession may not always equate with the layman's understanding of the term voluntary. This is, indeed, borne out by judicial practice. The accused may have made a conscious and deliberate choice to make a full confession and yet it could be deemed involuntary. In *People v. Moriarty (No.2)*,[21] for example, the accused was charged with the murder of a new-born illegitimate child. He was the only person present with the mother when she gave birth. Initially, he made a statement in the police station to the effect that the child was born dead. A Garda inspector informed the accused that a post mortem would be carried out to determine whether the child was born alive or dead. If it was born alive, the post mortem would reveal the cause of death. The inspector also advised the accused that the baby's mother had told a maternity nurse that the baby was born alive. The inspector then invited the accused to reconsider his initial statement. The accused responded, "According to that, I might as well tell the truth". The trial judge, however, refused to admit the full confession on the ground that it was involuntary.

Clearly, the judge in *Moriarty* was not using the term "voluntary" in its ordinary sense. There can be no doubt that the accused made a fully-informed, conscious and deliberate decision to tell the truth. The real question for the court, however, is whether the accused's freedom of choice in the matter might have been overborne by a factor which the law deems to be unfair. If the accused's decision to incriminate himself might have been affected by a fear of prejudice or hope of advantage exercised or held out by a person in authority or by oppression then his resultant confession is involuntary.

4. Fear of Prejudice

Threats of Violence

9–07   In practice "fear of prejudice" is often used interchangeably with the word "threat".[22] That, however, does not resolve the problem of what will satisfy it in the context of police interrogation. It would seem appropriate, therefore, to look to the facts of previous cases in order to construct an accurate picture of what might constitute a "fear of prejudice" in this context. Admittedly, the results of any such survey would have to be interpreted against the background of Lord Salmon's warning that "it is useless . . . to search for another case in which the facts seem to be similar and treat it as binding".[23] Griffin J. in *Shaw v. DPP* also cautioned that: "[t]he circumstances which will make a statement inadmissible for lack of voluntariness are so varied that it would be impossible to

---

[20]   *ibid.* at 186–187.
[21]   [1947] Ir. Jur. Rep. 30.
[22]   See Ryan and Magee, *The Irish Criminal Process* (Mercier Press, Dublin 1983) at p. 126.
[23]   *DPP v. Ping Lin* [1976] A.C. 574, at 606.

enumerate or categorise them fully."[24] Nevertheless, it is possible to offer some general guidance on what an Irish court is likely to consider amounts to a "fear of prejudice". Griffin J. himself, said that:

> ". . . the decided cases show that a statement will be excluded as being involuntary if it was wrung from its maker by physical or psychological pressures, by threats or promises made by persons in authority, by the use of drugs, hypnosis, intoxicating drink, by prolonged interrogation or excessive questioning, or by any one of a diversity of methods which have in common the result or the risk that what is tendered as a voluntary statement is not the natural emanation of a rational intellect and a free will."[25]

Broadly speaking, the Irish Courts will look to see if anything said or done is capable of persuading the accused to confess when otherwise he would have remained silent or persisted in his denial. It follows that a fear of prejudice would be satisfied in any case where the accused is subjected to physical violence, or the threat of physical violence, while he is being questioned or while he is being held in police custody. A similar result would ensue in response to threats that the accused would be exposed to violence from his accomplices or others who would wish to do him harm. Threats of violence or harm to members of the accused's family, including threats to charge another member of the family or to have children taken into care, would also produce a fear of prejudice. Even a suggestion that members of the accused's family would be interrogated about the offence may be sufficient.[26]

Harassment

The fear of prejudice does not have to result from physical violence or the threat of it. Harassment, or the threat of harassment, which wears the accused down mentally will also be sufficient. So, for example, if the accused has confessed in response to the police keeping him under constant surveillance, stopping and arresting him at every opportunity, it is likely that the confession will be found to have been extracted under a fear of prejudice. The threat to inflict material injury on the suspect will also qualify. Examples, would be threats to pass on information about the accused that would result in him losing his employment, or losing customers or, perhaps, just losing face in the social circles in which he moves. Indeed, in *R. v. Smith*[27] Lord Parker C.J. suggested that even the most gentle threats (or slight inducement) will taint a confession.

9–08

Borderline Cases

More controversially, it seems that a fear of prejudice would also arise where the police do or say something which leads the accused to believe that his guilt will ultimately be established by objective evidence. That, at least,

---

[24] [1982] I.R. 1 at 60. See also, Henchy J. in People *(DPP) v. Hoey* [1988] I.L.R.M. 666 at 673–674.
[25] *ibid.* at 60–61.
[26] *People (DPP) v. Hoey* [1987] I.L.R.M. 666.
[27] [1959] 2 Q.B. 35 at 39.

would appear to be the result of the decisions in *People v. Moriarty (No.2)*[28] and *Attorney General v. Cleary.*[29] In the latter case, the accused was charged with the killing of her child shortly after its birth. She was questioned about the matter by a Garda sergeant who cautioned her and told her that he intended to take a statement from her. In the course of conversation the sergeant raised the suggestion of a medical examination, whereupon the accused made a confession. The trial judge found that the woman was not frightened in any way by anything in the demeanour or authority of the sergeant. He also found, however, that she was frightened by the realisation that her guilt might be found out by the medical examination. The Court of Criminal Appeal concluded that the accused had confessed only because she believed that her guilt would be discovered. Accordingly, it ruled that her confession was involuntary and, as such, should have been excluded by the trial judge.

9–09 The decisions in *Moriarty (No.2)* and *Cleary* represent the high point of the "fear of prejudice" test. They establish that an accused may be labouring under a fear of prejudice (or hope of advantage) as a result of something said or done by a police officer, even though no impropriety can be attributed to the actions of the officer in the matter.[30] Indeed, it will not matter that the officer was not attempting to procure a confession from the accused. It may be that he was merely explaining what further investigations would necessarily follow if the suspect did not admit full and sole responsibility for the offence under investigation. If such explanation is calculated to induce the suspect to confess to the offence then the confession will be inadmissible even if the officer did not intend to induce a confession by giving the explanation. In *People (DPP) v. Hoey*[31] for example, the accused made a statement admitting unlawful possession of firearms after one of the officers questioning him suggested that if he did not accept responsibility for the firearms it would be necessary to question other members of the family to see if they would accept responsibility. The Supreme Court ruled that the confession had to be excluded on the grounds that it was involuntary. In reaching this conclusion the Court focused on the effect that the suggestion had on the accused. It was particularly influenced by the fact that the accused had refused to cooperate for a lengthy period right up until the suggestion was made.[32] Whether the officer had intended, or ought to have realised, that his suggestion would operate as a threat was irrelevant. In the words of Henchy J.:

---

[28] [1947] Ir. Jur. Rep. 30.
[29] 72 I.L.T.R. 84; [1934] LJ Ir 153.
[30] See also the House of Lords in *DPP v. Ping Lin* [1975] 3 All E.R. 175.
[31] [1988] I.L.R.M. 666.
[32] The importance of looking at the surrounding circumstances in order to determine whether a citizen might have been improperly induced is also present in *People (Attorney General) v. Flynn* [1963] I.R. 255.
[33] [1988] I.L.R.M. 666 at 673.

"It is no part of the test to consider the intention or the motive of the person whose conduct is alleged to have led to the statement. It is entirely a question as to whether that conduct could be said to have vitiated the free will of the person making the statement."[33]

The interpretation given to a "fear of prejudice" does not create a situation in which the police cannot actively seek to extract a confession from a suspect in their custody.[34] There is no reported case in which an Irish court has found a fear of prejudice emanating solely from the questioning of a suspect in police custody about his alleged involvement in an offence.[35] This is despite the fact that there is now ample evidence to suggest that, for some individuals, the mere fact of being questioned while in police custody can be sufficient in itself to make them confess, sometimes falsely, when otherwise they would have remained silent.[36] Moreover, it would seem that the fear of prejudice must relate to something material that might happen. Threats of a religious nature might not be sufficient.[37]

9–10

The position is less clearcut, perhaps, when the content and circumstances of the questioning is taken into account. In *R. v. Johnston*[38] it was said that a confession will be rejected if it has been extracted by "pestering interrogatories," or if it has been made by an unwilling accused who has been taken at a disadvantage by "subtle and ensnaring questions, such as those which are framed so as to conceal their drift and object".[39] Similarly, in *People (AG) v. Murphy*[40] O'Byrne J. intimated that well established rules of evidence show that "questioning may be of such a character and carried on to such an extent that the statements thereby evoked cease to be free and voluntary."[41] It must be said, however, that these sentiments were expressed at a time when the law permitted much less scope for the questioning of suspects in police custody compared with the position today. When suspects are arrested and detained under section 30 of the Offences Against the State Act 1939 or detained under section 4 of the Criminal Justice Act 1984 or section 2 of the Criminal Justice (Drug Trafficking) Act 1996, it is normal practice to subject them to prolonged interrogation designed to probe their suspected involvement in criminal activity. These developments have been

---

[34] *R. v. Johnston* 15 Ir CLR 60; *People (Attorney General) v. Galvin* [1964] I.R. 325.
[35] But note that in *R. v. Flynn & Leonard* Belfast City Commission, May 24, 1972, the Lord Chief Justice for Northern Ireland refused to admit a confession on the ground that the interrogation set-up was officially organised and operated in order to obtain information from persons who would otherwise have been less willing to give it. See also, *R. v. Gargan* Northern Ireland Court of Appeal, October 10, 1972.
[36] See, *e.g.*, G H Gudjonsson *The Psychology of Interrogation, Confession and Testimony* (Wiley, Chichester, 1992); G H Gudjonsson, I Clare, S Rutter and J Pearse *Persons at Risk During Interviews in Police Custody: The Identification of Vulnerabilities* (HMSO, Royal Commission on Criminal Justice Research Study No.12, London, 1993); *Report of the Tribunal of Inquiry into "The Kerry Babies Case"* (Stationery Office, Dublin, 1985).
[37] See *R. v. Sleeman* Dears 29; *R. v. Gibney* Jebb 15.
[38] (1864) 15 Ir CLR 60.
[39] *ibid. per* Hayes J. at 83–84.
[40] [1947] I.R. 236.
[41] *ibid.* at 241.

accompanied by a greater judicial willingness to accept the fruits of prolonged interrogation, particularly in cases where the interrogation occurs in the context of arrest and detention under section 30 of the Offences against the State Act 1939.[42] Nevertheless, confessions obtained in such interrogations will still be excluded if they are not voluntary or have been obtained in breach of the constitutional rights of the accused. In *People v. Ward*,[43] for example, the Special Criminal Court excluded confessions allegedly made by the accused in the course of his interrogation in the investigation of the murder of Veronica Guerin. The court accepted that gardaí had sought to extract a confession from him by exerting grievous psychological pressure on him, by subjecting him to unrequested visits from his aged mother and partner both of whom were in custody and in a distressed state. The court concluded that any confession he may have made in such circumstances would have to be excluded as having been obtained "by a deliberate denial of fundamental fairness in the interrogation . . . ".

Statements Given Under Threat of Penal Sanction

Resort to statutory powers to demand information can render statements obtained as a result inadmissible. There are a number of statutory provisions which compel a person to answer certain questions put by a member of the Garda Síochána in specified circumstances. Failure to answer fully and truthfully is a criminal offence. When these powers are used against a suspect in a criminal investigation the question arises whether a resultant incriminating statement is admissible even though it was made in order to avoid the criminal penalty which would otherwise have ensued had the suspect refused to answer. It might be considered that a statement given under such circumstances is clearly given under a fear of prejudice. Indeed, the decision of the Supreme Court in *Re National Irish Bank* (No.1)[44] suggests that a statement obtained pursuant to the exercise of a statutory power to demand information upon pain of penalty will be inadmissible in criminal proceedings. However, when the issue first came before the Supreme Court in *State (McCarthy) v. Lennon*[45] the Court took a different view.

9–11   The *McCarthy* case concerned the amendment of the 1922 Constitution by the Constitution (Amendment No.17) Act 1931 which inserted a new Article 2A. This provision compelled persons to answer certain questions when detained by gardai. Failure to comply with the requirement under Article 2A was a criminal offence punishable by the death penalty. In the event of a clash between the terms of Article 2A and the subsequent Articles of the Constitution the former were to prevail. McCarthy had been arrested and detained under Article 2A and had initially refused to answer questions.

---

[42]   See, *e.g.*, *People (DPP) v. Madden* [1977] I.R. 336; *People (DPP) v. McGowan* [1979] I.R. 445; *People (DPP) v. Kelly* [1983] I.R. 1; *People (DPP) v. Pringle* 2 Frewen 57.

[43]   Unreported, Special Criminal Court, November 27, 1998.

[44]   [1999] 3 I.R. 145.

[45]   [1936] I.R. 485.

When the full implications of his refusal had been explained to him he relented and made a statement which proved the only substantial evidence against him at his trial. By a majority of two to one the Supreme Court held that the statement had been properly admitted against him. The majority based their decision essentially on the ground that since the statement was lawfully obtained under Article 2A it was automatically admissible as evidence in any legal proceedings.[46] The Court was clearly of the opinion that it was obliged to give effect to the bare words of Article 2A.

The decision in *McCarthy* has been followed in cases concerning section 52 of the Offences against the State Act 1939. Section 52 penalises a failure to answer certain questions or to answer such questions fully and truthfully when put by a member of the Garda Síochána to a person detained in Garda custody under section 30 of the Act. In *People v. McGowan*,[47] for example, the Court of Criminal Appeal stated *obiter*:

"Section 52 of the Act of 1939 is almost identical in terms with section 15, sub-section 1, of Article 2A of the Constitution of the Irish Free State. In *State (McCarthy) v. Lennon* the former Supreme Court held that a statement taken in pursuance of the provisions of section 15 of Article 2 was lawfully taken and was admissible in evidence. Counsel on behalf of McCarthy had objected at the trial to the admission of the statement in evidence on the ground that it was not voluntary, being made under compulsion by reason of the punishment to which persons declining to answer questions put to them pursuant to section 15 of Article 2A rendered themselves liable. In the course of his judgment, Fitzgibbon J. said at p.500 of the report:– 'The plain and obvious effect of Article 2A section 15, is to empower the Garda Síochána to interrogate persons detained on suspicion under the Article, and section 16 makes it a criminal offence to refuse to answer, or to answer untruthfully. Therefore statements so obtained are obtained lawfully, and I know of no law which makes statements or confessions lawfully obtained or made, inadmissible as evidence in any legal proceedings.' At p.506 Murnaghan J. said that he could not see how relevant evidence which had been obtained in a lawful manner could be declared inadmissible. This Court respectfully agrees with those opinions. In the opinion of this Court, the law applicable is succinctly summarised at p.248 of the 4th edition of Cross on Evidence where it is stated:– 'It seems that, if information has been lawfully obtained pursuant to statutory provisions and there is no express restriction on the use which can be made of the information, the person giving it cannot object to its being used in evidence against him either on the ground that such use would infringe his privilege against self-incrimination or because the information would not have been given voluntarily.'"[48]

---

[47] The strong dissentient judgment of Kennedy C.J. took the view that just because a person loses the privilege against self-incrimination in one circumstance, it does not follow that he automatically loses it for all circumstances. In other words just because a person was legally compellable to answer a police question it did not automatically follow that his answer would be admissible against him at a subsequent criminal trial.

[47] [1979] I.R. 45. See also, *People v. Madden* [1977] I.R. 336.

[48] *ibid.* at 52–53.

9–12   In *People v. Madden*[49] the Court of Criminal Appeal accepted that evidence obtained as a result of repeated requests for an account of a suspect's movements (backed up by the threat of a criminal sanction for a refusal or failure to answer) would be inadmissible if the suspect has already given an account of his movements.

The courts, however, have not always applied the *McCarthy* approach in non-section 52 cases. In *People (Attorney General) v. Gilbert*,[50] for example, the Court of Criminal Appeal ruled inadmissible an inculpatory statement which had been given in response to a demand made by a member of the Garda Síochána in circumstances where a failure to answer or a failure to answer truthfully would be a criminal offence. The accused was tried and convicted on a charge of receiving a motor vehicle knowing it to have been stolen. In the course of the investigation a member of the Garda Síochána had asked him who had been driving the car at a particular time. The member made it clear to the accused that a failure to answer or a failure to answer truthfully would amount to a criminal offence under section 107 of the Road Traffic Act 1961. The accused responded that he had been driving the car at the relevant time. The Court of Criminal Appeal ruled that this statement was not voluntary and therefore could not be admitted. Referring to the judgment of Walsh J. in *People (Attorney General) v. Cummins* the Court explained:

> "As in the present case the statement in question was made after the sergeant had stated that a failure or refusal to answer would constitute an offence involving serious penalties, in our opinion it could not be said in any case to be a voluntary statement and so the trial judge should not have admitted it in evidence on the trial of the offences with which the appellant was charged under the Larceny Act 1916."[51]

9–13   The decision of the Supreme Court in *Re National Irish Bank (No.1)*[52] would appear to spell the end of the road for the approach in *McCarthy* which suggested that statements are admissible even though they have been extracted by resort to a statutory demand for information in circumstances where a failure to comply with the statutory demand will incur a criminal penalty. In *National Irish Bank* inspectors were appointed by the High Court pursuant to section 8(1) of the Companies Act 1990 to investigate and report on certain matters concerning the operations of the Bank. Section 10 of the Act obliges persons under investigation to assist the inspectors by, *inter alia*, answering their questions in certain circumstances. Section 18 states that any statements taken in such circumstances may be used in evidence against the person making them. The inspectors sought directions from the High Court on whether, *inter alia*, persons from whom information, documents or evidence was sought in the course of the investigation were entitled to refuse to answer questions etc on the ground that the answers might tend to incriminate them. The High

---

[49]   [1977] I.R. 336.
[50]   [1973] I.R. 383.
[51]   *ibid.* at 387.
[52]   [1999] 3 I.R. 145.

Court ruled that section 10 impliedly abrogated the privilege against self-incrimination and as such a person could not refuse to answer questions on the grounds that the answers might incriminate him. The High Court also found that the abrogation was constitutional but did not go on specifically to address the admissibility of statements obtained pursuant to section 10.

The Supreme Court accepted that section 10 was a constitutionally permissible restriction on the right to silence. However, it also directly addressed as a separate and distinct issue the question whether statements obtained pursuant to section 10 were admissible in the criminal trial of the person who made them. Delivering the judgment of the Court Barrington J. distinguished *McCarthy* on the ground that the Court in that case was dealing with a constitutional amendment which took precedence over any provision of the Constitution conflicting with it. Section 10, on the other hand, was subject to the provisions of the Constitution including, in particular, Article 38 which guarantees due process in a criminal trial. The learned judge went on to hold that any trial at which an alleged confession other than a voluntary confession was admitted in evidence against the accused would not be a trial in due course of law. Accordingly, if section 10 was used to extract a confession from a person who was otherwise unwilling to give it, the confession would not be admissible in evidence against the person at his criminal trial. It would appear that this also holds good for confessions obtained pursuant to section 52 of the Offences against the State Act 1939 or, indeed, pursuant to any statutory provision which compels a person to answer questions or provide information upon pain of penalty. If the answer or information is self-incriminating then it cannot be used in criminal proceedings against the person providing it. This, of course, applies only where the statutory demand and associated penalty were instrumental in obtaining the statement. If the statement was in fact voluntary then it will not be rendered inadmissible automatically simply because the circumstances were such that a statutory demand could have been used had the person been unwilling to cooperate.

The ruling in *National Irish Bank* only affects the admissibility of confessions. In the words of Barrington J.: **9–14**

> ". . . what is objectionable under Article 38 of the Constitution is compelling a person to confess and then convicting him on the basis of the compelled confession."[53]

It would appear that evidence obtained as a result of the compelled confession would remain unaffected. Since the power to demand the information upon pain of penalty was found to be both lawful and constitutional, the learned judge was of the view that it would operate in the same manner as a lawful search warrant. Information or material which the inspectors may obtain consequent on the answers compelled under section 10 would generally be admissible, even though self-incriminating answers would not.

---

[53] *ibid.* at 188.

In reaching its decision in *National Irish Bank* the Supreme Court was influenced by the decision of the European Court of Human Rights in *Saunders v. United Kingdom.*[54] That case concerned similar powers vested in company inspectors in the United Kingdom. The European Court of Human Rights accepted that such powers were necessary for the investigation of fraud. However, it went on to rule that self-incriminating answers obtained pursuant to the exercise of such powers could not be used in evidence in criminal proceedings against the person making them. The use of such compulsorily obtained answers would infringe the right to a fair trial under Article 6(1) of the European Convention for the Protection of Human Rights and Fundamental Freedoms. Significantly, in *Quinn v. Ireland,*[55] a decision handed down after *National Irish Bank*, the European Court of Human Rights declared section 52 of the Offences against the State Act 1939 to be in breach of Article 6(1) of the Convention. In reaching this decision the Court was heavily influenced by the position, as it was then understood to be, that incriminating answers compelled by section 52 could be used in evidence in criminal proceedings against the person making them.

Statements Given to Avoid Adverse Inferences

9–15   The decision in *National Irish Bank* raises a question mark over the admissibility of self-incriminating statements made by a suspect in police custody in response to being told that a failure to answer or to provide certain information may result in an adverse inference being drawn at his subsequent criminal trial. There are a number of statutory provisions which encroach on the privilege against self-incrimination by permitting adverse inferences to be drawn at the criminal trial from the suspect's silence when questioned by gardaí. Even though these provisions may withstand constitutional scrutiny,[56] it is at least arguable that a self-incriminating statement is not a voluntary statement if it was obtained from a suspect as a result of him being told that his failure to answer questions will invite adverse inferences at his trial.

The key issue is whether the threat of an adverse inference being drawn at the subsequent trial from a failure or refusal to answer certain police questions would be sufficiently strong to render a resultant confession involuntary. There can be no doubt that the nature of such a threat is of a much lower order than the threat at issue in *National Irish Bank*. Although the ultimate penalty for remaining silent is not expressly spelled out in section 10 of the Companies Act it is clear that it may involve a breach of a High Court order which can be punished as a criminal offence. In section 52 of the Offences against the State Act 1939 the threat is that of criminal punishment. Clearly, these consequences are more severe than those associated with the adverse inference. By remaining silent in the face of an adverse inference provision the suspect is merely exposing himself to an enhanced risk that he will be

---

[54]   [1997] 23 E.H.R.R. 313.
[55]   European Court of Human Rights *Application No.36887/97* (December 21, 2000).
[56]   See, *e.g.*, *Rock v. Ireland* [1998] 2 I.L.R.M. 35.

found guilty of the substantive offence for which he is being investigated. Indeed, this may prove a lesser and more attractive risk than that associated with answering the questions fully and truthfully. It is unikely, therefore, that an inculpatory statement will be involuntary where it was made only because the accused was told that if he did not answer the questions it would be open to the court to draw inferences about his guilt from his refusal or failure? Nevertheless, circumstances may arise where a suspect who would not otherwise have made a statement, gives an incriminating statement only because he was told that his failure to cooperate by answering fully and truthfully may result in the court drawing inferences about his guilt. In such circumstances, it is submitted, that the statement would be involuntary and, therefore, inadmissible. In the light of *National Irish Bank* the mere fact that adverse inferences could be drawn lawfully in the circumstances, and that the member of the Garda Síochána questioning the suspect was under an obligation to advise the suspect about the adverse inference provisions, would not be sufficient to render admissible a confession which had been made involuntarily under the influence of the adverse inference provisions.

5. Hope of Advantage

In practice a "hope of advantage" is often referred to as an inducement. If the accused confessed in response to an inducement held out by a person in authority, his confession will be inadmissible. The judicial approach to inducements in this context is similar to that for threats. The key issue is whether the confession was given as an act of free will on the part of the accused, or whether the inducement encouraged him to confess when otherwise he would have persisted in his silence or denials. Typical examples of inducements are the promise of being released early from police custody, the prospect of getting bail,[57] the promise of police intercession to avoid a prison sentence or a severe punishment or the dropping of charges against other members of the family or a friend.[58]

9–16

Once again it must be emphasised that there is no requirement for impropriety on the part of the police. In *DPP v. Ping Lin*[59] the House of Lords made it clear that impropriety on the part of the person in authority is not a pre-requisite for involuntariness. It is not even necessary that the person in authority should have a subjective intent to induce a confession. Something innocently said or done which excites fear of prejudice or hope of advantage in the suspect can render a confession involuntary. It is evident that the Irish courts adopt a similar approach. In *People v. Murphy*,[60] for example, a member of the Garda Síochána in an effort to restrain the accused who was attempting to run away said "[c]ome along with me, Stephen – you are all right." The accused responded by making an inculpatory statement to the member. The court

---

[57] *R. v. Zaveckas* [1970] 1 All E.R. 13.
[58] *People v. Pringle* 2 Frewen 57.
[59] [1976] A.C. 574.
[60] [1947] I.R. 236.

concluded that the member's words amounted to an improper inducement in that they led the accused to believe that he would be "all right."

6. Persons in Authority

9–17   Threats or inducements are not sufficient in themselves to render a confession inadmissible. They must emanate from a "person in authority".[61] It is essential, therefore, to have a clear understanding of what is meant by a person in authority. Cross defines it as "anyone whom the prisoner might reasonably suppose to be capable of influencing the course of the prosecution."[62] A fuller version was offered by Bain J. in the Canadian case of *R. v. Todd* as follows:

> "A person in authority means, generally speaking, anyone who has authority or control over the accused or over the proceedings or the prosecution against him. And the reason that it is a rule of law that confessions made as a result of inducements held out by persons in authority are inadmissible is clearly this, that the authority that the accused knows such persons to possess may well be supposed in the majority of instances both to animate his hopes of favour on the one hand and on the other to inspire him with awe."[63]

Police officers invariably qualify as persons in authority when interacting with accused persons. In practice, of course, the author of the alleged threat or inducement is usually a police officer. The prosecutor is another obvious candidate. However, many other relationships have been held to satisfy the "authority" requirement in certain circumstances. Less likely examples which have been accepted on their particular facts are: an employer and his wife where the offence was committed against the employer,[64] the owner of the goods that were stolen,[65] a customs officer enquiring into offences involving the importation of drugs,[66] a regimental sergeant major enquiring into a barrack room stabbing[67] and a school mistress where the offence was allegedly committed by one of the pupils in the school.[68] Even persons who assist in the apprehension or investigation of a suspect might qualify. In *Sullivan v. Robinson*[69] Davitt P was prepared to accept that a doctor called in by the police to examine a person suspected of drunk-driving was a person in authority. A more unusual example occurred in *People v. Murphy*[70] where a member of the Garda Síochána enlisted the assistance of a citizen in his

---

[61]   This is no longer a requirement in the U.K. The statutory test introduced by s.76 of the Police and Criminal Evidence Act 1984 replaces the common law test with a test based on oppression and reliability. See also Police and Criminal Evidence (NI) Order 1989, art.74.

[62]   *Cross on Evidence* (5th ed., Butterworths, London, 1979), p. 541.

[63]   (1901) 13 Man LR 364, quoted with approval in *Deokinanan v. R* [1969] 1 A.C. 20 where it was held that a friend of the accused who had been deliberately placed in a cell close to the accused and was co-operating with the police did not qualify as a person in authority.

[64]   *R. v. Moore* (1852) 2 Den 522.

[65]   *R. v. Wilson* [1967] 2 Q.B. 406.

[66]   *R. v. Grewal* [1975] Crim. L.R. 159.

[67]   *R. v. Smith* [1959] 2 Q.B. 35.

[68]   *R. v. McLintock* [1962] Crim. L.R. 549.

[69]   [1954] I.R. 161.

[70]   [1947] I.R. 236.

efforts to keep the accused under covert surveillance. The citizen, Mr Cadden, engaged the accused in conversation in order to give the member the opportunity of seizing him. In response to the accused's reluctance to submit to the member, Mr Cadden said, "Go with the guard – the guard is only for your good." The accused then began to make an inculpatory statement, the admissibility of which was challenged subsequently at his trial on the basis that it had been induced by a person in authority. O'Byrne J. ruled:

> "In view of the fact that Cadden was acting in concert with the guard and on the instructions of the latter and that Cadden's statement to the accused man was uttered in the presence of the guard and without any demur by him, we are of opinion that Cadden's statement to the accused should be treated as a statement by a person in authority."[71]

These examples suggest that it will not always be a straightforward matter to identify who may qualify as a "person in authority" in this context. This apparent vagueness is unfortunate. Any person who does qualify must tread with care in their dealings with a person suspected of having committed a criminal offence. They must avoid saying or doing anything which could constitute a threat or inducement to the suspect to confess. Police officers, of course, will be aware of this danger. The same cannot be said of others who are not engaged professionally in the investigation of crime.

7. Involuntary Tests

Although the voluntariness issue arises typically in the context of the admissibility of a written or oral statement it also has application to the results of any test, examination or observation carried out on the suspect by or on behalf of the police. As noted earlier such tests etc are considered the equivalent of a statement by the suspect for admissibility purposes. It follows that if they are not carried out pursuant to lawful authority the results will be inadmissible in evidence against the suspect.[72] Lawful authority in this context might be found at common law or in a statutory provision or by the suspect himself submitting voluntarily.

9–18

8. Oppression

Background

It is now firmly established in Irish and British jurisprudence that a confession will be involuntary and, therefore, inadmissible if it has been obtained by subjecting the accused to oppression. Relative to the "fear of prejudice or hope of advantage" test, oppression is a recent innovation. It made its first reported appearance in the context of the admissibility of statement evidence in the 1964 English case of *Callis v. Gunn*[73] where Lord Parker said:

9–19

---

[71] *ibid.* at 244.
[72] *People (DPP) v. Murray* CCA, April 12, 1999; *Sullivan v. Robinson* [1954] I.R. 161; *DPP v. Kenny* [1992] 2 I.R. 141.
[73] [1964] 1 Q.B. 495. Ryan and Magee (*op. cit.* at p.132) suggest that Kenny J. in the 1964 Irish case

"There is a fundamental principle of law that no answer to a question and no statement is admissible unless it is shown by the prosecution not to have been obtained in an oppressive manner and to have been voluntary in the sense that it has not been obtained by threats or inducements."[74]

In this statement Lord Parker clearly states that a confession is inadmissible if obtained in an oppressive manner. However, he also implies that this rule is in addition to that which excludes confessions automatically on the ground of involuntariness. The more conventional view is that a confession obtained in an oppressive manner is inadmissible because it is involuntary. This conventional position is expounded by Sachs J. in *R. v. Priestly*[75] where he said:

"[T]his word [oppression] in the context of the principles under consideration imports something which tends to sap, and has sapped, that free will which must exist before a confession is voluntary . . .".

Definition

Unfortunately, it is not possible to present a neat and comprehensive statement of what amounts to oppression in this context. The standard approach is to offer a list of factors that a court will consider relevant in any individual case. This is reflected in the following, regularly quoted, extract from the judgement of Sachs J. in *R. v. Priestly*:

"Whether or not there is oppression in an individual case depends upon many elements. I am not going into all of them. They include such things as the length of time of any individual period of questioning, the length of time intervening between periods of questioning, whether the accused has been given proper refreshment or not, and the characteristics of the person who makes the statement. What may be oppressive as regards a child, an invalid or an old man or somebody inexperienced in the ways of the world may turn out not to be oppressive when one finds that the accused person is of a tough character and an experienced man of the world."[76]

Speaking extra-judicially in an address to the Bentham Club in 1968, Lord MacDermott described oppressive questioning as:

"questioning which by its nature, duration or other attendant circumstances (including the fact of custody) excites hopes (such as the hope of release) or fears, or so affects the mind of the suspect that his will crumbles and he speaks when otherwise he would have stayed silent."[77]

---

of *People v. Galvin* [1964] I.R. 325 also recognised that a confession could be excluded on the ground of oppression. It is submitted, however, that the learned judge was merely referring to circumstances in which a confession might be excluded at the discretion of the trial judge.

[74] *ibid.* at p. 501. Adopted by Finlay J. in the Court of Criminal Appeal in *People (DPP) v. McNally and Breathnach* 2 Frewen 43 at 53–54.

[75] See *Note to Martin Priestly* 51 Cr App R 1 for a report of relevant extracts from Sachs J.'s judgement; and see 50 Cr App R 183 for a report of the facts of the case.

[76] *op. cit.*, quoted with approval by Edmund Davies L.J. in *R. v. Prager* [1972] 1 All E.R. 1114 at 1119.

[77] Also quoted with approval by Edmund Davies L.J. in *R. v. Prager* [1972] 1 All E.R. 1114 at 1119, and by Finlay P. in the Court of Criminal Appeal in *People (DPP) v. McNally and Breathnach* 2 Frewen 43 at 53.

It is worth noting that these definitions or descriptions were handed down at a time when a suspect's custodial and interrogation environments were only very loosely regulated. Since then, in both Britain and Ireland, the treatment of a suspect in custody and during interrogation is governed by detailed and complex bodies of regulations. Indeed, all of the factors specifically mentioned by Sachs J. are now the subject of regulation. These are discussed in the chapter on detention.

Breaking the Will of the Suspect

Compliance with the regulations undoubtedly is a factor which courts today will take into consideration in any individual case when deciding whether a confession must be excluded on the ground of oppression. It should not be assumed, however, that full compliance will preclude exclusion on the ground of oppression. The court is primarily concerned with the effect that the treatment and conditions had on the individual suspect. The free will of a particularly weak and vulnerable individual may be overborne by treatment and conditions in custody which do not breach the regulations and which would not have any serious adverse effect on a reasonable person. Nevertheless, it would be open to a court to find oppression in such circumstances. The converse, of course, is that treatment and conditions which do breach the regulations and which would have serious adverse effects on a reasonable person, might not constitute oppression in a case where the accused concerned was of a particularly strong mental and physical disposition. **9–20**

The subjectivity inherent in the judicial approach to oppression suggests that there is little to be gained from looking to past cases as precedents for what does and what does not amount to oppression. However, it is not entirely a pointless task. They can be used to build up a fuller picture of the factors that the courts are prepared to take into account in finding oppression.

It is arguable that the courts apply a higher threshold for oppression in respect of persons being questioned in police custody while detained under section 30 of the Offences against the State Act 1939 as compared with persons detained under section 4 of the Criminal Justice Act 1984. This may result from a judicial perception that persons arrested under section 30 on suspicion of involvement in terrorist activities are generally more able to withstand rigorous interrogation techniques than may be the case with persons arrested on suspicion of involvement in ordinary criminal cases.

In *People (DPP) v. Madden*,[78] one of the first cases in which oppression was an issue in the courts of this jurisdiction, the accused had been arrested under section 30 of the Offences Against the State Act 1939 and detained in custody for a continuous period of 36 hours. He argued that this coupled with the fact that he was interviewed for lengthy periods by a total of 12 to 14 gardai amounted to oppression. This was rejected by O'Higgins C.J. in the following terms: **9–21**

---

[78] [1977] I.R. 336.

"Obviously it would be possible for a protracted period of detention, coupled with persistent interviewing or interrogation, to constitute oppression even without physical violence or threats of violence. It would be possible also for such treatment or circumstances so to reduce the will of a suspect that the statement made by him during the course of it or at its conclusion would not be a voluntary statement. However, there was in this case clear direct evidence as to the condition, morale and mental capacity of the accused at the time when he made the statement; the evidence is that his condition was good, and that he was alert and normal."[79]

The clear message is that the court will have to be satisfied that the will of the individual suspect was overborne before it will find oppression. It will not be sufficient in itself that the treatment or conditions might be oppressive to the average individual.

9–22   In *People (DPP) v. McGowan*,[80] the accused was arrested under section 30 at 9.15 a.m. on October 18, and questioned intermittently into the early hours of the 19th about his alleged involvement in the kidnapping of Dr Tiede Herrema. He was then allowed to sleep until 11am before being questioned for the rest of the day and into the early hours of the morning of the 20th. He dozed for four to five hours in the interrogation room and was subsequently released at 9 a.m. on the morning of the 20th. While hitching a lift to his home at Tullamore he was picked up by two of the officers who had interrogated him. In the course of the journey towards Tullamore the accused admitted his involvement in the kidnapping. He was arrested again under section 30 and brought back to the Garda station where he was questioned at 5.30 p.m. The accused made a full confession that evening. The Court of Criminal Appeal rejected the argument that the length and number of interrogation sessions coupled with lack of sleep were sufficient in themselves to create oppression. It considered that the actions of the accused were not consistent with someone who had been subjected to oppressive treatment.

Similarly, in *People (DPP) v. Kelly*[81] the Court of Criminal Appeal and the Supreme Court failed to find oppression despite the fact that the accused had been arrested under section 30 at 9.55 a.m. on April 5, questioned from: 12 midday to 12 midnight, from 9.30 a.m. to 1 p.m. and from 3 p.m. to 6.30 p.m. on April 6, and from 9 p.m. on April 6, through to 5.30 a.m. on April 7. He made an oral admission at 11.30 p.m. on the 6th and commenced a full written statement at 4.30am on the 7th. These interrogation sessions were accompanied by admitted breaches of the Judges Rules. Nevertheless, both the Court of Criminal Appeal and the Supreme Court refused to exclude the statement on the ground of oppression.

In *People (DPP) v. Pringle*[82] the Court of Criminal Appeal was not satisfied that oppression had been established on the basis of lengthy interrogation sessions. In that case the accused had been questioned extensively

---

[79]   *ibid.* at 354–355.
[80]   [1979] I.R. 45.
[81]   [1983] I.R. 1.
[82]   2 Frewen 57.

into the early hours of the morning on two successive days and at intervals throughout these days. Nevertheless, the Court of Criminal Appeal ruled that the lengthy duration of the interrogation sessions combined with the shortness of the time allowed for sleep did not in themselves establish oppression. The physical, mental and emotional characteristics of the accused must also be thrown into the balance. In this case the accused was 42 years old, in good health, was accustomed to conditions of physical hardship on account of his occupation as a fisherman in Galway and was an experienced man of the world. Accordingly, it ruled that it was open to the trial court to conclude that his will would not have been overborne by the conditions of his custody and interrogation. It is also worth noting, however, that in reaching this decision the Court was influenced by the fact that the accused had the benefit of five visits from his solicitor and that his admission was not made at the end of a lengthy period of continuous interrogation.

Objective Element

It does not follow from *Pringle* that the measure of what constitutes oppression **9–23** varies widely in response to the mental and physical condition of the suspect in police custody. Where all of the circumstances of the detention and interrogation taken as a whole are sufficiently harsh in themselves, the courts have demonstrated a willingness to conclude that the will of the suspect must have been overborne. In *People (DPP) v. McNally and Breathnach*,[83] for example, the Court of Criminal Appeal ruled that Breathnach's statement given after forty hours in police custody was not voluntary. It reached this conclusion primarily on the basis that it could not be satisfied that the circumstances in which the confession was given did not amount to oppression. Finlay P. summarised these circumstances as follows:

> ". . . the previous forty hours in custody during which the applicant obdurately refused to make a statement, the strange fact that the statement was made after questioning not in an interview room, but in an underground passage in the early hours of the morning, after the applicant had suffered an untimely awakening from what must have been a much-needed sleep and of his being brought to what may have been the menacing environment of an underground passage in the Bridewell Garda Station, and the unexcused and seemingly inexcusable fact that, since the previous day, he had been denied the access to his solicitor which he had clearly asked for."[84]

Similarly, in *People (DPP) v. Lynch*[85] the Supreme Court ruled that the accused's confession should have been excluded on the grounds of oppression. O'Higgins C.J. summarised the operative circumstances very succinctly as follows:

> "The fact that for almost 22 hours the appellant was subjected to sustained questioning, that he never had the opportunity of communicating with his

---

[83] 2 Frewen 43.
[84] *ibid.* at p. 56.
[85] [1982] I.R. 64.

family or friends, and that he never was permitted to rest or sleep until he made an admission of guilt, all amount to such circumstances of harassment and oppression as to make it unjust and unfair to admit in evidence anything he said."[86]

It is worth noting, however, that the accused in this case had not been arrested and detained under section 30 and the case itself did not have any associations with terrorism or organised crime.

In *People v. Ward*[86a] the application of grievous psychological pressure was found to be sufficient to warrant the exclusion of a confession. The suspect had been arrested and detained under section 30 on suspicion of involvement in the murder of Veronica Guerin. He maintained silence over many interrogation sessions until meetings with his partner and his aged mother who had also been arrested and detained under section 30. The court accepted that both meetings had been set up by the gardaí for the deliberate purpose of breaking the will of the suspect:

> "The court is satisfied beyond all reasonable doubt that the visit from Mrs Ward was a deliberate ploy devised and orchestrated by the police in a final effort to prevail on the accused to disclose what he had done with the gun. It is obvious that if it had been possible to trace the weapon it might have yielded valuable forensic information which could have been helpful in establishing the guilt of others in addition to the accused. The court is satisfied that the visit was not arranged for any humanitarian purposes but was a cynical ploy which it was hoped might break down the accused and cause him to make what was perceived to be a crucial admission regarding what had happened to the weapon.
>
> As to the visit of Ms Vanessa Meehan to the accused; the court accepts her evidence that she was successfully subjected to grievous psychological pressure by Detective Sergeant Hanley and perhaps other officers also to assist the police in breaking down the accused who up until then had maintained consistent silence over many interrogation sessions. Both meetings amounted to a conscious and deliberate disregard of the accused's basic constitutional right to fair procedures and treatment while in custody. They constituted deliberate gross violations of the fundamental obligation which the interrogators and their superiors had of conducting their dealings with the accused in accordance with the principles of basic fairness and justice."

The court proceeded to exclude the alleged confessions. The court concluded that as a result of the meetings the accused was subjected to grievous psychological pressure which had affected his free will to such a degree that it undermined the voluntary nature of the alleged confessions.

9–24 There have been at least two cases in Northern Ireland where the courts have been prepared to exclude confessions automatically on account of the fact that they had been obtained in a custodial and interrogation regime which is designed to produce confessions by oppression. In *R. v. Flynn*,[87] for example the issue was the admissibility of confessions obtained from suspects who had

---

[86] *ibid.* at 74.
[86a] Unreported, Special Criminal Court, November 27, 1998.
[87] Belfast City Commission, May 24, 1972.

been arrested and detained in Holywood Interrogation Centre under emergency powers. Lowry L.C.J. found that the interrogation regime in place at the interrogation centre had been designed and implemented specifically for the purpose of extracting information from persons who were unwilling to give it. He concluded that the regime amounted to oppressive circumstances and that any confession obtained through it must, *per se*, be inadmissible.

An important feature of the Irish case law is what it reveals about the limitations in the judicial approach. The factors which predominate are the material conditions of custody, particularly food and rest, the length and frequency of interrogation sessions and the extent to which a suspect may have been verbally and/or physically abused. There is no evidence in any of the reported cases of the judges being willing to address the suspect's psychological reaction to being detained in police custody or to the standard investigative techniques used upon him or her by the police. The extent to which the judges can continue to ignore this psychological dimension must come under increasingly closer scrutiny as it becomes more widely acknowledged that the mere fact of being questioned in police custody can cause some persons to make false confessions.[88] So long as police interrogations in Ireland are conducted in the absence of any independent person or adviser to help preserve some semblance of a balance between the police and the suspect, the case for a more intrusive judicial scrutiny will continue to grow.

Discretion

It will be seen later that just because a confession is voluntary, or has not been obtained by oppression, it does not follow that it will automatically be admissible in evidence against the person who made it. The trial judge retains a discretion to exclude evidence where its admission would be unfair to the accused and/or where there has been a breach of the Judges Rules. It can happen that circumstances which fall short of establishing that a confession has been obtained by oppression are nevertheless sufficient to persuade the judge that he or she should exercise the discretion to exclude the confession in the interests of fairness to the accused. Indeed, it can be difficult on occasions to determine with certainty whether a judge has excluded a confession automatically because oppression has been made out or whether he or she has excluded it in the exercise of the discretion because of the unfair circumstances in which it was obtained. Since the judicial discretion to exclude is not confined to confession evidence it is considered later in the chapter.

9–25

---

[88] See, *e.g.*, G H Gudjonsson, *The Psychology of Interrogation, Confession and Testimony* (Wiley, Chichester, 1992); G H Gudjonsson, I Clare, S Rutter and J Pearse, *Persons at Risk During Interviews in Police Custody: The Identification of Vulnerabilities* (HMSO, Royal Commission on Criminal Justice Research Study No.12, London, 1993); *Report of the Tribunal of Inquiry into "The Kerry Babies Case"* (Stationery Office, Dublin, 1985).

9. Dissipation of Threats and Inducements

Causal Connection

9–26   The mere fact that an accused has been subjected to treatment which would render a confession involuntary does not automatically mean that any confession he does give must be excluded. There must be a causal connection between the threat or inducement and the impugned statement. As explained above, it is not necessary for the author of the threat or inducement to have intended to make a threat or inducement with a view to extracting an admission of guilt. It will be quite sufficient that his actions and/or words were calculated to have such an effect on the accused in the circumstances.[89] However, they must actually operate on the mind of the accused so that he confessed when otherwise he would have remained silent.

Breaking the Causal Connection

It can happen that the causal connection between a threat or inducement and a subsequent admission is broken as a result of the effects of the threat or inducement having dissipated by the time that the admission is made. The mere passage of time between the threat or inducement and the admission will not in itself be sufficient to have this effect. The court will have to be satisfied that the effect of the threat or inducement is no longer affecting the suspect when he makes the confession.[90] In *R. v. Doherty*,[91] for example, a constable told the suspect in the morning that it would be better to tell the truth. Although the confession, made to another constable, was not forthcoming until that evening it was still ruled inadmissible. It is likely, however, that this case is over-generous in the interests of the accused. Irish courts today will look closely at whether a threat or inducement is still operative after a passage of time. In *People v. Galvin*,[92] the accused was being questioned in police custody about a murder. At 12.10 a.m. the inspector told the accused that he "should not be keeping us here all night and to tell the truth and be finished with it." Without deciding whether this statement actually amounted to a threat or inducement, the Court of Criminal Appeal concluded that its effect had dissipated by the time he spoke to his parents at 2.40 a.m. the same morning. In the interval he had been told that he was being detained in connection with the murder investigation, cautioned twice and the police questioning had ceased some hours earlier.

Effect of Legal Advice

Access to legal advice would also appear to be a relevant factor in assessing whether a threat or inducement had dissipated. In *People (DPP) v. Pringle*[93]

---

[89]   See *People (DPP) v. Hoey* [1987] I.L.R.M. 666.
[90]   *People (DPP) v. Lynch* [1982] I.R. 64; *R. v. Meynell* (1834) 2 Lew CC 122; *R. v. Rue* (1876) 13 Cox CC 209; *R. v. Smith* [1959] 2 Q.B. 35.
[91]   13 Cox CC 23.
[92]   [1964] I.R. 325.
[93]   2 Frewen 57.

gardai told the accused that his girlfriend would not be charged if he made a statement. Nevertheless, the Court of Criminal Appeal ruled that the effect of this inducement had dissipated by the time the accused made a statement the following morning. In reaching this decision the Court was clearly influenced by the fact that the accused had a visit from his solicitor after the inducement and before the statement. In the opinion of the Court the effect of the solicitor's advice was to remove the effect of the inducement.

Dissipating Breach of Judges' Rules

It would appear that the courts are more inclined to find that the effects of any   **9–27** impropriety have dissipated where the nature of the impropriety is insufficient to render a confession inadmissible as a matter of law. In *People (DPP) v. Buckley*,[94] for example, the trial court exercised its discretion to exclude confessions obtained in successive interviews of the accused in police custody. In each interview the confession was tainted by a breach of the Judges' Rules.[95] However, a confession obtained in the third interview was admitted. The Court of Criminal Appeal rejected the argument that this confession was inevitably tainted by the breaches of the Judges' Rules in the first two interview sessions. The Court accepted that where a confession is rendered inadmissible as a result of a threat, inducement or oppression the trial court must, in respect of a later incriminating statement obtained in the absence of any such impropriety, have regard to the possibility that the earlier threat, inducement or oppression was still operating to affect the free will of the person concerned thereby rendering the later statement inadmissible. Equally, however, the Court was of the view that different considerations apply where a previous admission of guilt is ruled inadmissible not by virtue of any threat, inducement or oppressive circumstances, but by the exercise by the trial court of a discretion concerning a breach of the Judges' Rules. On the facts of *Buckley* the Court of Criminal Appeal found that on account of the lapse of time between the earlier infringements of the Judges' Rules, coupled with the fact that the Judges' Rules had been observed, the confession could be safely admitted.

10. Corroboration

A conviction can be based solely on a contested confession allegedly made by the accused to the police. If the jury (or court) is satisfied that the accused made the confession voluntarily and it is probative of guilt, they can convict even in the absence of any other corroborating evidence. Nevertheless, it has long been recognised that confession evidence can be the source of a miscarriage of justice. It may be that the accused, for whatever reason, confesses to a crime that he or she did not commit. Equally, the circumstances in which confession evidence typically is obtained often leave scope for the

---

[94] [1990] 1 I.R. 14.
[95] It will be seen later that a breach of the Judges Rules does not automatically result in the exclusion of a confession but is a ground upon which the trial judge may exercise his discretion to exclude it.

use of improper police methods which can result in involuntary or unreliable confessions. By the same token they facilitate allegations of such improper police methods. It was to counter these risks that the Martin Committee recommended the audio-visual recording of the interrogation of suspects in police custody (see chapter 6). The Committee also recommended that consideration be given to the possibility of the judge warning the jury of the dangers of convicting on the basis of confession evidence alone.[95a] This recommendation has been implemented by the Criminal Procedure Act 1993 by way of a requirement on the judge to warn the jury of the absence of corroboration on appropriate cases.

Section 10 of the Criminal Procedure Act 1993 reads:

> "(1) Where at a trial of a person on indictment evidence is given of a confession made by that person and that evidence is not corroborated, the judge shall advise the jury to have due regard to the absence of corroboration.
> (2) It shall not be necessary for a judge to use any particular form of words under this section."

Since the requirement to advise the jury to have due regard to the absence of corroboration is framed in mandatory terms, it would seem to follow that a failure to so advise the jury in any case where there was no corroboration would provide grounds for appeal. It must also be said, however, that the provision clearly falls short of a requirement to give a clear warning to the jury of the dangers of convicting on the basis of an uncorroborated confession. The judge is merely required to advise the jury to have due regard to the absence of corroboration, where that is applicable. Nevertheless, the judge is not bound to any particular form of words. It follows that he or she can tailor the warning to suit the particular circumstances of the case. So, for example, if the manner in which the confession was obtained is such that there may be some doubt over its reliability, or the fact that it was given at all, it might be expected that the judge will give the jury a strong warning about the dangers of convicting in the absence of corroboration for the confession.

It is not clear how this statutory warning will apply in trials on indictment before the Special Criminal Court. Presumably, in an appropriate case, the judges will have to advise themselves to have due regard to the absence of corroboration.

C. Unconstitutionally Obtained Evidence

1. Introduction

9–28   Where the police have engaged in improper or unfair practices in the gathering of evidence, the admissibility of that evidence will be called into question in the criminal trial. If the method used results in an involuntary statement, that statement must be excluded in accordance with the rules described above. However, a statement is not rendered involuntary simply

---

[95a] Report of Committee to Enquire into Certain Aspects of Criminal Procedure (Stationery Office, Dublin, 1990), p.39.

because it has been obtained by what might be described as improper or unfair means. The question arises, therefore, whether an inculpatory statement should be excluded because, for example, it has been obtained by a trick, or in breach of the rules governing the detention of a suspect in police custody, or from a suspect who was being detained in custody unlawfully. Furthermore, not all evidence against the accused in a criminal trial takes the form of a statement. The admissibility of material evidence, such as a firearm, stolen goods, or forensic evidence will also be called into question if it has been obtained by improper or unfair means, such as a trick or an unlawful search.

The admissibility of evidence obtained by improper or unfair means presents an acute dilemma. Quite often such evidence will be reliable and highly probative of the accused's guilt. In many cases a refusal to admit it will result in persons guilty of very serious crimes walking free. Clearly this is not conducive to the common good. To admit such evidence, however, raises the spectacle of the courts condoning wrongs inflicted on the accused by agents of the criminal process in order to secure a conviction against the accused. Not only does this represent an injustice to the individual accused, but it also threatens to undermine the integrity of the whole criminal process. This latter danger is particularly apparent where the police wrongdoing itself takes the form of a criminal offence. It conveys the appearance of the courts being willing to accept and act upon evidence which has been obtained by the criminality of those who are sworn, empowered and paid to enforce the law. Furthermore, the courts passivity in the face of such improper or unfair police practices creates the danger that they will become more prevalent. This, in turn, is not conducive to the common good.

Common Law Approach

Although Irish and English positions on the exclusion of involuntary statement evidence historically have been based on common principles, the same cannot be said for the admissibility of improperly or unfairly obtained evidence. At common law the English courts adopted the relatively extreme position of admitting such evidence so long as it was relevant, subject to a discretion to exclude where its prejudicial effect outweighed its probative value.[96] Under this test evidence would not be excluded in an English criminal trial simply because a police officer had committed a criminal offence in order to obtain it.[97] If, however, the admission of such evidence would be unfair to the accused in the sense that its prejudicial effect outweighed its probative value, the English courts had a discretion to exclude it. Beyond that they were not prepared to go at common law. They did not consider it to be part of their function in a criminal trial to exclude evidence in order to punish the police for the use of improper or unfair methods in the gathering of the evidence. This position has been ameliorated in favour of the accused by section 78 of the Police and Criminal Evidence Act 1984 which gives the court a discretion

---

[96] *R. v. Sang* [1980] A.C. 402.
[97] *R. v. Leathem* 8 Cox CC 498; *Kuruma v. R* [1955] A.C. 197.

to exclude where the circumstances in which the evidence was obtained "would have such an adverse effect on the fairness of the proceedings that the court ought not to admit it."[98]

Primacy of Constitution

9–29 The Irish approach to the admissibility of evidence obtained by improper or unfair police practice is dominated by the impact of the Constitution. Unlike the English courts, the Irish courts are constrained by the constitutional imperative of protecting the fundamental rights of the individual. It is hardly surprising, therefore, that Irish jurisprudence in this area bears closer similarities to other jurisdictions, such as the USA, where relevant fundamental rights are protected by a written constitution.[99] This constitutional dimension compels the Irish courts to give more weight to the rights of the individual where evidence against him has been obtained by police practices which infringe his constitutional rights. O'Higgins C.J. explained the basis of the Irish approach as follows:

> "In countries governed by a written constitution one may expect the judges, by their oath of office, to be bound to uphold the Constitution and its provisions and to do so on all occasions in the courts in which they preside."[100]

The Chief Justice went on to quote approvingly the following passage from Warren C.J. in the landmark United States case of *Terry v. Ohio*:[101]

> "Courts which sit under our Constitution cannot and will not be made party to lawless invasions of the constitutional rights of citizens by permitting unhindered governmental use of the fruits of such invasions. Thus in our system evidentiary rulings provide the context in which the judicial process of inclusion and exclusion approves some conduct as comporting with constitutional guarantees and disapproves other actions by state agents. A ruling admitting evidence in a criminal trial, we recognise, has the necessary effect of legitimising the conduct which produced the evidence, while an application of the exclusionary rule withholds the constitutional imprimatur."

Indeed, it would appear that the Irish courts may be even more fastidious in the protection of the constitutional rights of the accused than their American counterparts. The approach of the latter is heavily influenced by the deterrence principle. They apply the exclusionary rule to deter law enforcement officers from violating the constitutional rights of the accused. If the facts of the case are such that the application of the rule can have no deterrent effect it will not normally be applied. The Irish courts, by contrast, are motivated solely by the imperative of protecting the constitutional rights of the accused.

---

[98] See C Tapper, *Cross on Evidence* (7th ed), pp. 481–485.

[99] Ryan and Magee distinguish the approach of the Scottish courts from that of their English counterparts at common law by suggesting that the former were prepared to exclude evidence obtained by irregular or illegal means, subject to a discretion to admit it. They proceed to classify the Irish approach as an amalgam drawn from different legal traditions, particularly, those of Scotland and the USA. See Ryan and Magee, *op. cit.*, pp 156–176.

[100] *People (DPP) v. Lynch* [1982] I.R. 64 at 76.

[101] (1968) 392 US 1.

According to Finlay C.J. in *People (DPP) v. Kenny*[102] this requires an absolute rule which will exclude evidence purely on the basis of the violation itself rather than on the basis that exclusion will be effective in deterring future violations.

2. The Basic Principle

It follows that Irish law imposes an automatic exclusion on evidence obtained through a deliberate and conscious violation of the accused's constitutional rights. The leading authority is the Supreme Court's decision in *People (Attorney General) v. O'Brien*.[103] In that case the accused were charged with stealing and receiving stolen goods. The primary evidence against them was stolen articles which had been found in the course of a police search of their home at 118 Captain's Road. The search was effected on the basis of a warrant which, due to an oversight, was issued in respect of 118 Cashel Road. The accused sought to have the evidence excluded on the basis that it had been obtained in violation of their constitutional right to the inviolability of the dwelling. The evidence was admitted at first instance and the accused were convicted. They appealed unsuccessfully to the Court of Criminal Appeal which certified that a point of law of general public importance was involved, and that it was desirable in the public interest that an appeal should be taken to the Supreme Court. The point of law in issue was summarised as follows by Kingsmill-Moore J.:

> "Is evidence procured by the guards in the course of and as a result of a domiciliary search, unauthorised by a search warrant, admissible in subsequent criminal proceedings"[104]

Although the Supreme Court's decision in the case revolved around the exercise of the judicial discretion to exclude evidence which has been obtained by improper means, its primary importance lies in Walsh J.'s analysis of the scope of the exclusionary rule applicable to evidence obtained through a conscious and deliberate violation of the accused's constitutional rights. The scope of, and justification for, this exclusionary rule, from Walsh J.'s perspective, is summed up in the following extract from his judgement:

> "When the illegality amounts to infringement of a constitutional right the matter assumes a far greater importance than is the case where the illegality does not amount to such infringement. The vindication and the protection of constitutional rights is a fundamental matter for all courts established under the Constitution. That duty cannot yield place to any other competing interest. In Article 40 of the Constitution, the State has undertaken to defend and vindicate the inviolability of the dwelling of every citizen. The defence and vindication of the constitutional rights of the citizen is a duty superior to that

9–30

9–31

---

[102] [1990] I.L.R.M. 569.
[103] [1965] I.R. 142.
[104] *ibid.* at 150.
[105] *ibid.* at 170.

of trying such citizen for a criminal offence. The Courts in exercising the judicial powers of government of the State must recognise the paramount position of constitutional rights and must uphold the objection of an accused person to the admissibility at his trial of evidence obtained or procured by the State or its servants or agents as a result of a deliberate and conscious violation of any constitutional rights of the accused person where no extraordinary excusing circumstances exist, such as the imminent destruction of vital evidence or the need to rescue a victim in peril. A suspect has no constitutional right to destroy or dispose of evidence or to imperil the victim. I would also place in the excusable category evidence obtained by a search incidental to and contemporaneous with a lawful arrest although made without a valid search warrant.

In my view evidence obtained in deliberate conscious breach of the constitutional rights of an accused person should, save in the excusable circumstances outlined above, be absolutely inadmissible. It follows therefore that evidence obtained without a deliberate and conscious violation of the accused's constitutional rights is not excludable by reason only of the violation of his constitutional right."[105]

This statement of basic principle has been adopted repeatedly in subsequent decisions of both the Court of Criminal Appeal and the Supreme Court.[106] Nevertheless, it has not always received unambiguous support in all its aspects. Commencing with his judgement in *People (DPP) v. Shaw*[107] Griffin J. has consistently promoted a more restrictive interpretation of two fundamental elements of Walsh J.'s formulation. The first of these concerns the actual scope of the rule itself.

3. Application to Statement Evidence

9–32   In *Shaw* Griffin J. opined that the decision in *O'Brien* applied only to the exclusion of real evidence. The learned judge pointed out that the *O'Brien* case was concerned only with the admissibility of real evidence in the form of items of clothing and that the *ratio* of the case did not extend to confession or statement evidence. He contended that the rules governing the admissibility of the latter were firmly established. Accordingly, a confession or statement must be excluded only if the prosecution failed to establish beyond a reasonable doubt that it was voluntary. In addition, the trial judge has a discretion to exclude a statement if the circumstances in which it was obtained fell below basic standards of fairness. In assessing what was required by basic standards of fairness the trial judge would take into account, but would not be confined to, the postulates of the Constitution. Moreover, there would have to be a balancing of the rights of the accused with the requirements of the prosecution in the interests of the common good. It would appear, therefore, that Griffin J. did not countenance the automatic exclusion of statement evidence

---

[106]   See, *e.g.*: *People (DPP) v. Madden* [1977] I.R. 336; *People (DPP) v. Farrell* [1978] I.R. 13; *People (DPP) v. O'Loughlin* [1979] I.R. 85; *People (DPP) v. Walsh; People (DPP) v. Healy* [1990] 2 I.R. 73 and *People (DPP) v. Kenny* [1990] 2 I.R. 110. A notable exception is to be found in *People (DPP) v. Shaw* [1982] I.R. 73. For further discussion, see "The Admissibility of Unconstitutionally Obtained Evidence in Irish Law" (1982) Irish Jurist 257.

[107]   [1982] I.R. 1.

on the ground that it was obtained by virtue of a conscious and deliberate breach of the accused's constitutional rights. The most he was prepared to accept was a discretion to exclude where the statement, which was otherwise voluntary, had been obtained in circumstances which fell below basic standards of fairness.

Although Griffin J. was supported by three of his Supreme Court colleagues, his formulation of the rule has not been accepted without criticism.[108] Indeed, it is unlikely to be followed as the weight of judicial opinion now seems to follow the approach advocated by O'Higgins C.J. in *People (DPP) v. Lynch*.[109] In that case the accused appealed his conviction directly from the Central Criminal Court to the Supreme Court on the ground that his statements should have been excluded. The Supreme Court agreed after finding that the accused had made the statements in circumstances which amounted to harassment and oppression. O'Higgins C.J. took the opportunity, albeit obiter, to re-iterate that, absent extraordinary excusing circumstances, confession or statement evidence must automatically be excluded when it is obtained in violation of the accused's constitutional rights. It is not a matter for discretion. The Chief Justice expressed his disagreement with Griffin J.'s approach in *Shaw* in the following emphatic terms:

> "[E]ven if the *O'Brien* case did not effectively decide that statements obtained as a consequence of a deliberate and conscious violation of the constitutional rights of an accused should be excluded except in the circumstances mentioned, it seems to me that such a proposition must be accepted. It does not seem to me possible for any judge, except in such special circumstances as occurred in the *Shaw* case, to countenance or endorse a deliberate violation of the Constitution by the admission of a statement obtained as a consequence of the violation. It is probable that the vast majority of such statements would in any event be excluded on other grounds, but this is not the point. I do not see that any discretion is possible.
>
> Once the Constitution has been violated for the purpose of securing a confession the fruits of the violation must be excluded from evidence on that ground alone. Nor can it be said that the matter can safely be left to a decision on fairness or the voluntary nature of the statement.[110]

9–33

In practice, it is likely that the different tests propounded respectively by Griffin J. and O'Higgins C.J. will often give the same result when applied to the facts.[111] Equally, however, it is quite possible to envisage factual situations which result in a confession being admitted under Griffin J.'s test and excluded under O'Higgins C.J.'s formulation. Typical examples would be confessions obtained from suspects who had been detained unlawfully or who had been denied access to a solicitor while in police custody. It is significant, therefore, that the authorities since *Lynch* appear to endorse O'Higgins C.J.'s formulation.[112]

---

[108] See, for example, McAuley and McCutcheon "Shaw and the Admissibility of Unconstitutionally Obtained Statements (1982) 4 D.U.L.J. 386.

[109] [1982] I.R. 64. See also *People (DPP) v. Buck*, unreported, Supreme Court, April 17, 2002.

[110] [1982] I.R. 64 at 78–79.

[111] See, *e.g.*, *People (DPP) v. Healy* [1990] I.L.R.M. 313.

[112] *ibid.* 73.

4. "Conscious and Deliberate"

The second element of Walsh J.'s formulation which has been attacked trenchantly by Griffin J. concerns the meaning of a "conscious and deliberate" violation of constitutional rights. *People (DPP) v. Madden*[113] presented the first real opportunity since *O'Brien* to consider the meaning of "conscious and deliberate" in this context. In that case the accused had been arrested under section 30 of the Offences Against the State Act 1939. He began to make an inculpatory statement at 6.40 a.m. on the second day of his detention. He did not finish the statement until 9.00 a.m., one hour and forty five minutes beyond the maximum period for which he could have been lawfully detained. This extra period of detention amounted to an infringement of the accused's constitutional right to liberty. Although the Court of Criminal Appeal accepted that the statement was voluntary and that the gardai had not acted in bad faith in detaining the accused until he had finished the statement, it ruled nevertheless that the constitutional infringement was conscious and deliberate. The court's reasoning is neatly summed up in the following quotation from O'Higgins C.J.:

> "[T]he onus on the prosecution of showing that there has been some factor such as inadvertence which might excuse the failure to observe the end of the period of lawful detention, or some other extraordinary circumstance such as envisaged in *O'Brien's* case, has not been discharged. As matters stand, this statement was taken by a senior Garda officer who must have been aware of the lawful period of detention which applied in this defendant's case; it was taken in circumstances which suggest that he deliberately and consciously regarded the taking and completion of the statement as being of more importance than according to the defendant his right to liberty, should he desire to exercise such right. This Court cannot regard the taking and completion of a statement in these circumstances as any justification or excuse for the continued detention of a person in the position of the defendant."[114]

9–34   It follows from *Madden* that the failure to address one's mind to whether the constitutional rights of the suspect are being infringed will not prevent an infringement from being conscious and deliberate. This reflects Walsh J.'s position that it is not necessary for the member of the Garda Síochána in question to be aware that he was acting unlawfully or unconstitutionally in his actions in obtaining the evidence. In the learned judge's view culpability or blameworthiness on the part of the member are not prerequisites for a finding that the violation of the accused's constitutional rights was "conscious and deliberate". All that is necessary is that the member concerned is aware of the circumstances which amount to the violation. Walsh J. explains the position as follows in *People (DPP) v. Walsh*:

> "If a man is consciously and deliberately kept in a garda station or anywhere else without a charge being preferred against him and without being brought

---

[113] [1977] I.R. 336.
[114] *ibid*. at 346–347.

before a court as soon as reasonably possible, he is in unlawful custody and there has been a deliberate and conscious violation of his constitutional right to be at liberty. That this was the position in the present case is abundantly clear from the evidence given by the police officer at the trial. The fact that the officer or officers concerned may not have been conscious that what they were doing was illegal or even that if they did know it was illegal, that they did not think it was a breach of the Constitution does not affect the matter. They were conscious of the actual circumstances which existed."[115]

It follows that it is not necessary for the member of the Garda Síochána concerned to be aware specifically that he is breaching the constitutional rights of the accused. It will be sufficient that he is aware of the circumstances which gave rise to the constitutional infirmity. If, however, the member is not aware of the circumstances which gave rise to the infirmity his act or omission will not amount to a conscious and deliberate breach of the accused's constitutional rights. In *O'Brien*, for example, the discrepancy between the address on the warrant and the address of the premises searched was an innocent error of which the gardai concerned were unaware. Accordingly, while the Court accepted that there was a breach of the constitutional rights of the defendant, it found that it was not a conscious and deliberate breach.

Griffin J.'s interpretation, by contrast, is neatly summed up in the following extract from his judgement in *Shaw*:

> "Nor do I find myself able to support the opinion that a person's statement is to be ruled out as evidence obtained in deliberate and conscious violation of his constitutional rights, even though the taker of the statement may not have known that what he was doing was either illegal or unconstitutional. I consider the authorities to be to the contrary effect. For example, in *People (Attorney General) v. O'Brien* Kingsmill Moore J. (who gave the majority judgment) having held that evidence obtained in deliberate and conscious violation of constitutional rights should be excluded except in 'extraordinary excusing circumstances' (which he preferred to leave unspecified) excused as 'purely accidental and unintentional infringement of the Constitution' the violation complained of in that case: see p.162 of the report. See also *People v. Madden* at p.36 where a 'factor such as inadvertence' was recognised as being capable of being one of the 'extraordinary excusing circumstances' envisaged in *O'Brien's* case. In my opinion, it is the violation of the person's constitutional rights, and not the particular act complained of, that has to be deliberate and conscious for the purpose of ruling out a statement."[116]

Although Griffin J.'s interpretation on this point attracted majority support in the Supreme Court in *Shaw*, the balance would appear to have shifted in favour of Walsh J. since.[117] In *People (DPP) v. Kenny*,[118] for example, the Supreme Court had to decide whether controlled drugs found during a search of the accused's flat must be excluded as evidence on account of the fact that the search was conducted on foot of a defective warrant. When seeking the

---

[115] [1980] I.R. 294 at 317.
[116] [1982] I.R. 1 at 55–56.
[117] See *People (DPP) v. Healy* [1990] I.L.R.M. 313; *People (DPP) v. Kenny* [1990] I.L.R.M. 56.
[118] [1990] I.L.R.M. 569.

search warrant the member of the Garda Síochána in question had not sworn sufficient information to give the peace commissioner reasonable grounds to suspect that the controlled drugs were in the flat in contravention of the Misuse of Drugs Act 1977 and 1984. Nevertheless, the peace commissioner issued the warrant. By a three to two majority, led by Finlay C.J., the Supreme Court decided that the drugs had to be excluded on account of the fact that they had been found pursuant to a conscious and deliberate violation of the accused's constitutional right to the inviolability of his dwelling.

9–35   Finlay C.J. directly addressed the conflict between Walsh J. and Griffin J.'s respective interpretations of what was required for a breach of constitutional rights to qualify as a "conscious and deliberate" breach.[119] The Chief Justice came down emphatically in favour of Walsh J.'s interpretation:

> "After careful consideration I conclude that I must differ from the majority of this Court expressed in the judgment of Griffin J. in *Shaw's* case. I am satisfied that the correct principle is that evidence obtained by invasion of the constitutional rights of a citizen must be excluded unless a court is satisfied that either the act constituting the breach of constitutional rights was committed unintentionally or accidentally, or is satisfied that there are extraordinary excusing circumstances which justify the admission of the evidence in its (the court's) discretion."[120]

Applying this test to the facts in *Kenny,* Finlay C.J. concluded that the drugs must be excluded. This was despite the fact that in seeking the warrant the member of the Garda Síochána had followed a practice that had been standard in such cases for several decades, albeit an unlawful practice. There was no suggestion that it occurred or ought to have occurred to the member that the warrant might be unlawful. The majority in the Supreme Court considered it sufficient that the member's acts in seeking the warrant and, subsequently in acting upon it, were neither unintentional nor accidental. This approach considerably restricts the circumstances in which evidence obtained in violation of an accused's constitutional rights might be admitted on the basis that the violation was not conscious and deliberate.

    Griffin J., one of the two minority judges in *Kenny,* maintained his position that the member of the Garda Síochána must be aware that his actions are illegal or unconstitutional before they can amount to a conscious and deliberate violation of the accused's constitutional rights. He was strongly supported in this view by Lynch J. It is unlikely, therefore, that the issue can be considered to have been settled finally.

5. Causation

9–36   One aspect of a conscious and deliberate breach of constitutional rights which has not received detailed attention in the case law is causation. Presumably,

---

[119] Finlay C.J. had already indicated his position in *People (DPP) v. Healy* [1990] I.L.R.M. 313 where he ruled that it was irrelevant that a member of the Garda Síochána had not actually addressed his mind to the issue of whether the suspect's constitutional rights were being infringed.

[120] [1990] I.L.R.M. 569 at 579.

there must actually be a causal connection between the constitutional breach and the obtaining of the evidence. In most cases a causal connection can be assumed. For example, if the accused confesses while he is detained unlawfully in police custody, it can usually be assumed that the accused would not have made the confession had he not been detained unlawfully in the Garda station. Nevertheless, it is possible to envisage circumstances where the connection between the unlawfulness of the detention and the resultant confession is very tenuous. Will the courts examine the sufficiency of the causal connection in such cases, or will they simply assume such a connection in any case where the accused has been unlawfully arrested and detained in the course of a criminal investigation? In none of the reported cases to date have the courts shown any inclination to investigate whether the unlawfulness of the custody was instrumental in extracting the confession from the accused.[121]

The issue has received some, albeit scant, attention in the context of access to a solicitor for a suspect held in police custody. In *People (DPP) v. Healy*,[122] the accused was in the course of making a statement in Garda custody when, unknown to him, his solicitor arrived at the Garda station having been sent by the accused's family. The gardai delayed the solicitor's access to the accused until the accused had finished making the statement. The trial judge ruled that the incriminating statement must be excluded as he could not be satisfied that it had been completed before the solicitor arrived at the station. This decision was upheld by the Supreme Court on appeal. It seems as though the temporal correlation between the denial of access and the giving of the statement were deemed sufficient to satisfy the causal connection. If the accused had access to his solicitor he might not have made the statement. Presumably, that was the real reason why access was delayed. There was at least a basis, therefore, on which the Court could have found a causal connection between the breach of the constitutional right of access to a solicitor and the confession. If, however, the denial of access to a solicitor can have no effect on the course of events which result in the evidence being secured, the causal connection will be broken.

In *Walsh v. O'Buachalla*,[123] for example, the accused had been arrested on suspicion of drunk driving. Shortly before he was required to give a specimen of blood he requested access to his solicitor, but his request was denied. The accused subsequently sought to have his conviction quashed on the basis that the specimen had been obtained in breach of his constitutional right of access to his solicitor. In refusing the application Blayney J. ruled that there was no causative link between the refusal of access and the obtaining of the specimen. In *People (DPP) v. Spratt*[124] O'Hanlon J. explained this decision

---

[121] Note the interesting position adopted by Walsh J. in *People (DPP) v. Shaw* [1982] I.R. 1 to the effect that a confession obtained from a suspect while unlawfully detained in police custody could nevertheless be rendered admissible by virtue of extraordinary excusing circumstances. Also his ruling that material evidence found with the assistance of the suspect while unlawfully detained was admissible where the suspect voluntarily accompanied the gardai in the search which unearthed the evidence.

[122] [1990] I.L.R.M. 313.

[123] [1991] I.R. 56.

[124] [1995] 2 I.L.R.M. 117.

on the basis that, given the requirements of the Road Traffic legislation in drunk-driving cases, there was no advice that the solicitor could give to the accused which would materially change his circumstances. Accordingly, the specimen may have been obtained after a breach of his constitutional rights but not as a result of that breach. The learned judge distinguished the questioning of an individual who was suspected of having committed an offence. In that situation the advice which a solicitor might give the individual could materially affect his situation. That in itself, it would seem, is sufficient to satisfy the causal connection between the breach of the constitutional right of access to the solicitor and any incriminating statement that the individual makes while that breach is subsisting.

The decision in *Spratt* must have implications for any case in which the constitutional rights of a suspect have been infringed in the course of the police investigation. If the nature of the infringement is such that the suspect's position in respect of the case against him is not materially affected, it would appear that he cannot rely on the infringement to have the prosecution quashed. So, for example, if gardai enter a person's dwelling in circumstances which infringe Article 40.5 of the Constitution to arrest him for dangerous driving, the arrest and subsequent detention will clearly be unlawful. However, unless the prosecution case rests on evidence obtained from the investigation of the person while he was detained unlawfully, it would appear that the breach of his constitutional rights in this case should not automatically result in the quashing of the charges against him.

It is important not to focus too heavily on causation, particularly in the context of denial of a suspect's right of access to a solicitor while in police custody. It may be that access is denied in circumstances which render the suspect's detention in custody unlawful. Some of the authorities are to the effect that the illegality of the detention is sufficient in itself to render any evidence obtained from the suspect during the unlawful detention inadmissible.[124a]

6. Range of Constitutional Rights

9–37   Another factor which has not been the subject of any considered analysis in the case law is the range of constitutional rights which are capable of triggering the exclusionary rule. The task of identifying what the rights of the accused are in the specific context of a criminal investigation is not helped by the fact that there is no exclusive list of the fundamental rights of the individual in Irish law. The sensible place to start, of course, is the statement of fundamental rights in Articles 40 to 44 of the Constitution. Of these, the most likely to be directly relevant to the suspect being investigated by the police are: the personal rights in Article 40.3, the right to liberty in Article 40.4, the inviolability of the dwelling in Article 40.5 and the freedom of expression, assembly and association in Article 40.6. The right to a criminal

---

[124a] See, for example, *People (DPP) v. Finnegan* unreported, Court of Criminal Appeal, July 15, 1997. See further Chap. 5, paras. on access to a solicitor.

trial in due course of law, which is protected in Article 38.1 has also proved an important source of restraint on police freedom of action.

In addition, there are the unspecified personal rights, so called because they enjoy constitutional protection even though they are not expressly defined in the Constitution. Since 1965, however, the Irish courts have been prepared to recognise the existence of such unspecified fundamental rights as being implicit in the Christian and democratic nature of the State.[125] It is now firmly established that the Constitution confirms the existence of such rights which are identified by the courts on a case by case basis. For the suspect in the pre-trial criminal process the most relevant rights to have been identified so far are: the right to bodily integrity,[126] the right to privacy,[127] the right of access to a solicitor,[128] the privilege against self-incrimination[129] and the right to be informed of the right to legal aid in the case of serious criminal charges.[130] By contrast, attempts to establish the constitutional status of the right to be informed of the right of access to a solicitor have been rebuffed by the courts.[131]

The existence of unspecified constitutional rights ensures that there will always be potential to extend the reach of the exclusionary rule by the recognition of "new" fundamental rights. Similarly, the broad terms in which the fundamental rights, whether specified or unspecified, are framed, permit a flexibility of interpretation which, in turn, impacts upon the scope of the exclusionary rule.[132] This is particularly apparent in the case of the right to bodily integrity. In *Ryan v. Attorney General*,[133] where the right was first recognised, the Supreme Court declined the invitation to define the scope of the right or the circumstances in which the State could justifiably encroach upon it.[134] There can be little doubt that the unlawful infliction of actual bodily harm upon an individual would be an unconstitutional interference with his right to bodily integrity. Such action, however, is unlikely to give rise to any difficulty in the context of the admissibility of evidence. Where it does arise in this context, it is almost invariably associated with the admissibility of a confession which has been obtained from a suspect who alleges that he

9–38

---

[125] *Ryan v. Attorney General* [1965] I.R. 294. See generally, J Casey, *Constitutional Law in Ireland* (2nd ed)(Sweet and Maxwell, London, 2000) pp. 394–433.

[126] *Ryan v. Attorney General* [1965] I.R. 294.

[127] *McGee v. Attorney General* [1974] I.R. 284; *Kennedy v. Ireland* [1987] I.R. 581; and *Kane v. Governor of Mountjoy Prison* [1988] I.R. 257.

[128] *People (DPP) v. Healy* [1990] 2 I.R. 73. This includes the right to consult the solicitor in private; *People (DPP) v. Finnegan* unreported, Court of Criminal Appeal, July 15, 1997.

[129] *Heaney v. Ireland* [1997] 1 I.L.R.M. 117.

[130] *State (Healy) v. Donoghue* [1976] I.R. 325. In *McSorley v. Governor of Mountjoy Prison* [1996] 2 I.L.R.M. the High Court quashed the applicants convictions because the District Court judge had not advised them of their right to legal aid before proceeding to impose a custodial sentence for taking a motor vehicle without the consent of the owner.

[131] *People (DPP) v. Madden* [1977] I.R. 336; *People (DPP) v. Spratt* [1995] 2 I.L.R.M. 117

[132] See, in particular, the comments of O'Higgins C.J. in *State (Healy) v. Donoghue, op. cit.*, p 347.

[133] *op. cit.*

[134] Note that in the High Court Kenny J. proceeded on the basis that an infringement of the right would entail something that was " . . . dangerous or harmful to the life or health of the citizens . . ."; [1965] I.R. 294 at 313.

has been subjected to an unlawful assault. If the court is not satisfied that the accused was not assaulted, the confession will almost inevitably be excluded on the grounds of involuntariness. Accordingly, there will be no need to consider the constitutional issue.

The real problems arise where the alleged interference with the right to bodily integrity is not such as to render a confession involuntary or, more likely, has resulted in the procurement of material evidence. Unfortunately, there is very little guidance to be had from Irish case law on this subject. Ryan and Magee suggest that the unlawful extraction of intimate body fluids, such as blood or semen, would be an infringement of the individual's constitutional right to bodily integrity.[135] This is almost certainly correct, especially if the method of extraction involves the insertion of a needle or some other form of surgical interference with the human body. Presumably the same would apply to the forceful extraction of human hair from the body. It does not follow, of course, that gardai are precluded from using, or benefiting from, such methods in the investigation of crime. On the contrary there are statutory provisions making these methods available in certain circumstances. If, however, they are used in circumstances, or by persons, not covered by the legislation, or if the prescribed procedure is not followed, it is likely that the subject will be the victim of an unlawful assault. In this eventuality the court may conclude that the unlawful assault also amounted to an unconstitutional interference with the subject's right to bodily integrity. Where the statutory requirements have been respected absolutely in an individual case, the only possibility is to attack the statutory power itself as an unconstitutional attack on the citizen's right to bodily integrity. The prospects of success in such a venture are slight as the court will have to balance the individual's right against the collective interest in making such powers available to the police in certain limited circumstances.[136]

9–39 The position with respect to evidence obtained through fingerprinting, palm-printing, the taking of swabs from the body or the scraping of fingernails is less certain. Once again there is legislative provision authorising the use of these methods in certain circumstances. If, however, these are used in circumstances not covered by the legislation and without the consent of the accused, they will constitute an unlawful assault. Nevertheless, they need not entail the application of any significant force, pain or harm on the subject. The admissibility of evidence obtained unlawfully by such means, therefore, depends on whether the courts will view any unlawful interference with the individual's autonomy over his or her body as an infringement of the constitutional right to bodily integrity *per se*, or whether they will require that interference to

---

[135] Ryan and Magee, *op. cit.*, at 172.

[136] Ryan and Magee suggest that s.26(2) of the Misuse of Drugs Act 1977 may be unconstitutional in that it permits gardai to search persons on premises being searched in pursuance of a warrant even though the gardai may not entertain any reasonable suspicion in relation to the person searched. They refer to the American case of *Henderson v. United States* 390 F.2d 805 (1967) where the search of a person's vagina was held to be unconstitutional for lack of clear indication that evidence would be found. See Ryan and Magee, *op. cit.*, p 172.

involve the infliction of some degree of harm or pain. The decision in *Ryan v. Attorney General* suggests that Irish courts may require at least some degree of discomfiture, harm or pain on the part of the accused. Significantly, American courts have been prepared to recognise that some parts of the body are more private than others, and that a non-consensual internal search of these parts by someone who is not medically qualified would be unconstitutional. In *Huguez v. United States*,[137] for example, a forced search of the rectum was held to be unconstitutional, while a search of the anal cavity by a doctor was held to be constitutional in *Blackford v. United States*.[138] This, in turn, gives grounds for arguing that an unlawful strip search would constitute an infringement of the individual's right to bodily integrity. There is no obvious reason why an Irish court would not follow these American authorities.

7. Extraordinary Excusing Circumstances

A conscious and deliberate violation of the accused's constitutional rights will not always result in the automatic exclusion of evidence obtained consequent to the violation. In *O'Brien* Walsh J. accepted that the exclusionary rule might not operate where there were "extraordinary excusing circumstances". Where such circumstances exist he accepted that the trial judge would have a discretion to admit the evidence in question. The learned judge offered examples of what might constitute extraordinary excusing circumstances: the imminent destruction of vital evidence,[139] the need to rescue a victim in peril and evidence obtained without a valid search warrant where the search is incidental to and contemporaneous with a lawful arrest. While the other judges in the court also accepted the existence of a discretion they preferred not to predict concrete examples. Kingsmill-Moore J. explained that: "[t]he facts of individual cases vary so widely that any hard and fast rules of a general nature seem to me to be dangerous and I would leave the exclusion or non-exclusion to the discretion of the trial judge."[140]

9–40

People (DPP) v. Shaw[141] is the leading case since *O'Brien* in which the exercise of this discretion has been considered. The accused was arrested at night on September 26, 1976 on suspicion of being in possession of a stolen car. Although he could have been brought before a District Court at 10.30 a.m. on the following morning he was kept in Garda custody for further questioning as he was suspected of involvement in the abduction and possible murder of two young women. The gardai believed that one of the women might still be alive and that the accused could give information which could establish her whereabouts in time to save her life. In the event, the accused

---

[137] 406 F.2d 366 (1968).
[138] 247 F.2d 745 (1957).
[139] See, *e.g.*, the Garda power to seize property in the context of a lawful arrest; discussed in chapter 8.
[140] [1965] I.R. 142 at 162.
[141] [1982] I.R. 1. For a detailed analysis of this case see F McAuley and P McCutcheon "*People v. Shaw*: An Analysis" (1981) D.U.L.J. 63 and "*Shaw* and the Admission of Unconstitutionally Obtained Evidence" (1982) D.U.L.J. 86.

made a statement at 6.50 p.m. on September 28, admitting the rape and murder of the young woman. He also took gardai to places in Connemara to show them where the body had been disposed of and certain items concealed. He was not brought before a District Court judge until the evening of September 29. In his appeal against the convictions for rape and murder the accused argued that both his confession and the evidence found on the trip to Connemara should have been excluded as having been obtained pursuant to a deliberate and conscious breach of his constitutional right to liberty. The basis of his argument was that he had been detained unlawfully in police custody from 10.30 a.m. on September 27.

9–41   The Supreme rejected the appeal broadly on the ground that the accused's constitutional right to liberty had to give way to the right to life of the victim. It was agreed unanimously that concern for the victim's life qualifies as an "extraordinary excusing circumstance" which justified the curtailment of the accused's constitutional right to liberty. However, there was a material difference in approach to the issue between Walsh J. and the other members of the Court lead by Griffin J. The latter felt that the need to protect the victim's right to life rendered the accused's detention lawful; despite the fact that he had not been charged and brought before a District Court judge as soon as practicable. Walsh J., by contrast, considered that the detention was both unlawful and a conscious and deliberate violation of the accused's constitutional right to liberty. However, the need to protect the victim's superior right to life amounted to an extraordinary excusing circumstance which had the effect of justifying the admission of the accused's confession. From Walsh J.'s perspective the extraordinary excusing circumstance which was present did not actually render the detention itself lawful. The material evidence found on the trip to Connemara was admissible, according to Walsh J., because the accused had went there voluntarily.

D. Discretion

1. Introduction

9–42   In addition to the absolute exclusionary rule, Irish courts recognise a discretion to exclude evidence in three situations. The first concerns the situation where there are extraordinary circumstances excusing a conscious and deliberate breach of the accused's constitutional rights. This might more properly be described as a discretion to admit evidence. In any event it has already been considered above and no more need be said about it here. The second situation arises when a voluntary statement has been taken in breach of the Judges Rules. The third concerns a residual discretion to exclude evidence which has been obtained by unlawful or unfair means. These two discretions will now be considered in turn.

2. The Judges' Rules

The General Principle

It was explained earlier that the Judges' Rules are not actually rules of law in **9–43** the sense that a breach of them will automatically expose the officer concerned to a criminal prosecution or civil action. Nevertheless, a failure to observe the Rules when taking a confession statement from a suspect constitutes grounds upon which the trial judge may exercise his discretion to exclude the confession, even though he is satisfied that it was voluntary and had not been obtained in breach of the suspect's constitutional rights.[142] Equally, it would appear that a failure to abide by the rules could result in the exclusion of evidence obtained by tests carried out on the suspect or by examining or observing the suspect in the course of the criminal investigation against him.[143] The general principle and its application in practical situations are conveyed in the following quotation from O'Higgins C.J. in *People v. Farrell*:

> "The Judges' Rules are not rules of law. They are rules for the guidance of persons taking statements. However, they have stood up to the test of time and will be departed from at peril. In very rare cases, such as *R. v. Mills and Lemon* [1947] KB 247 a statement taken in breach may be admitted in evidence but in very exceptional circumstances. Where, however, there is a breach of the Judges' Rules, such as a failure to make a written record of the alleged confession or a failure to invite the accused to accept or reject the statements, each of such breaches calls for an adequate explanation. The breaches and the explanation (if any) together with the entire circumstances of the case are matters to be taken into consideration by the trial judge before exercising his judicial discretion as to whether or not he will admit such statement in evidence."[144]

In *People (DPP) v. Buck*[144a] Keane C.J., giving the judgment of the Supreme Court, explained that the underlying reason for the discretion to exclude was fairness to the accused and the public interest that the law should be observed in the investigation of crime.

Application in Practice

Chief Justice O'Higgins' guidance in *Farrell* suggests that a statement will **9–44** normally be excluded when it has been obtained in breach of the Judges' Rules. However, the extent to which that is actually reflected in judicial practice is called into question by the case law. Indeed, it must be said that there are several examples of cases where Irish judges might be accused of having adopted a cavalier approach to admitted or apparent breaches of the

---

[142] *People (DPP) v. Buck* unreported, Supreme Court, April 17, 2002. This has always been the position in English law; see *R. v. Voisin* [1918] 1 K.B. 531.

[143] *People (DPP) v. Murray* CCA, April 12, 1999. See also, *Sullivan v. Robinson* [1954] I.R. 161; *DPP v. Kenny* [1992] 2 I.R. 141.

[144] [1978] I.R. 13 at 21.

Judges' Rules. In *State v. Scully,*[145] for example, a police officer obtained a statement from the suspect after having read her a statement from her co-accused. The admissibility of the first statement was challenged on the basis of Rule VIII. Despite appearing to accept that it was not the practice of the English courts to admit statements taken in such circumstances, the trial judge admitted it on the basis that it was the practice of the Central Criminal Court to admit such statements. Similarly, in *People v. Kelly (No.2),*[146] the trial judge admitted a statement despite the fact that it had been taken in breach of Rule IX.[147] The accused had made two oral confessions while in police custody. The first was not taken down in writing at the time it was made. The second was taken down in writing, read over to the accused, but he refused to sign it. Later, he made and signed a written statement. The Court admitted the oral and unsigned written statements. The Court of Criminal Appeal upheld their admissibility on the ground that their accuracy was confirmed by the fact that they were substantially identical to the written signed statement.

Where the challenge is taken on the basis of a breach of Rule III, the Irish judges display a distinct reticence to exercise their discretion to exclude.[148] This is probably due in large part to their particular interpretation of Rule III. When originally formulated it would appear that it was meant to incorporate the standard judicial practice of refusing to accept statements resulting from the interrogation of suspects after they had been arrested.[149] The actual formulation, however, can be interpreted literally to mean that it is only the interrogation of an arrested suspect without the caution that is prohibited. This, in turn, can be read as implying that interrogation after arrest is not prohibited so long as the caution is administered. Whatever might be the correct interpretation of Rule III, there is no doubt that the standard police practice of questioning a suspect after arrest is now accepted. Accordingly, the argument that a trial judge should exercise his or her discretion to exclude a statement on the basis that it was obtained by questioning the suspect after he had been arrested, is likely to receive short shrift from the courts.[150] There would be more substance to the argument if the caution was not administered at the start of the questioning. However, there are no reported Irish cases where an appeal court has overturned a trial judge's exercise of discretion to admit a confession solely on the basis that the caution had not been administered.[151]

[144a] Unreported, Supreme Court, April 17, 2002.

[145] 62 I.L.T.R. 24.

[146] [1983] I.R. 1.

[147] See also, *People v. Farrell* [[1978] I.R. 13; *People v. Pringle* Frewen 1979–83, 57 at 98.

[148] See Ryan and Magee, pp. 118–119.

[149] See, *e.g.*, Home Office Circular S26059/29 which was issued in 1930 with the approval of the English judges. It reads:
"Rule III was never intended to encourage or authorise the questioning or cross-examination of a person in custody after he has been cautioned on the subject of the crime for which he is in custody, and long before this rule was formulated and since, it has been the practice of the judges not to allow any answer to a question so improperly put to be given in evidence."

[150] See, for example, Finlay P in *People v. Kelly (No.2)* [1983] I.R. 1. See also, *People v. Madden* [1977] I.R. 336.

[151] Note also that in *People (DPP) v. Murray* (April 12, 1999) the Court of Criminal Appeal refused

Dissipation

Even where an incriminating statement has been ruled inadmissible on **9–45** account of a breach of the Judges Rules a similar statement, obtained later from the suspect at a time when the effects of the breach have dissipated, may be admitted in evidence. In *People (DPP) v. Buckley*[152] incriminating statements made by the accused in police custody were ruled inadmissible on account of a breach of Rule VIII and a failure to caution. Similar incriminating statements made at a further interview commenced ninety minutes later were admitted. The Court of Criminal Appeal accepted that where a statement is excluded on the basis of inducements, threats or oppression which subsequently ceased, the court should be alive to the risk that a later statement could still be tainted by the earlier circumstances of inducement, threat or oppression. However, where the earlier statement was excluded as a result of a breach of the Judges' Rules which did not involve inducements, threats or oppression a later statement taken in full compliance with the Rules would not be tainted by the earlier breach and so would be properly admissible.[153]

3. Breach of the 1987 Regulations

The practical significance of the Judges' Rules in regulating the questioning **9–46** of suspects in police custody is now rivalled by the provisions of the Criminal Justice Act 1984 and the Regulations made pursuant to it, namely the Criminal Justice Act 1984 (Treatment of Persons in Custody in Garda Síochána Stations) Regulations 1987. The Act specifically states that a breach of these provisions will not affect the lawfulness of the detention of the suspect nor the admissibility of any statement made by him.[154] Nevertheless, in *People (DPP) v. Spratt*[155] Gannon J. in the High Court ruled that it would be a matter for judicial discretion to decide whether non-compliance with the provisions or a failure by the prosecution to adduce evidence of compliance was of such a character that it should result in dismissal of the charge.

> ". . . non-observance of the regulations is not to bring about automatically the exclusion from evidence of all that was done and said while the accused person was in custody. It appears to be left to the court of trial to adjudicate in every case as to the impact the non-compliance with the regulations should have on the case for the prosecution."[156]

---

to upset the trial judge's exercise of discretion to admit the evidence of a doctor who, at the request of the investigating gardai and with the consent of the suspect, carried out an examination of a cut on the accused's lip with a view to determining whether it might connect the suspect with the offence under investigation. Although it was accepted that the Judges Rules would be applicable to such an investigation the caution had not been administered to the suspect before the investigation was carried out.

[152] [1990] 1 I.R. 14.
[153] See also, *People (DPP) v. Reddan* [1995] 3 I.R. 560.
[154] Criminal Justice Act 1984, s.7(3).
[155] [1995] 2 I.L.R.M. 117.
[156] *People (DPP) v. Spratt* [1995] 1 I.R. 585 at 591.

The clear implication is that the trial judge will have a discretion to exclude evidence obtained from a suspect in police custody where the treatment of the suspect was not in accordance with the provisions of the 1984 Act and the 1987 Regulations. Unfortunately the learned judge did not elaborate on when the discretion ought to be exercised. In that case the suspect had been arrested on suspicion of drunk driving. He submitted a sample of urine as required by law. He challenged the admissibility of this sample on the ground, *inter alia*, that the prosecution had failed to prove compliance with the requirement in the 1987 Regulations that he should be informed of his right of access to a solicitor when he was taken into Garda custody. Gannon J., on a case stated, intimated that this would not be a sufficient ground upon which to exercise the discretion. Even if the suspect had consulted with a solicitor it would not have had any material effect on his situation as he was required by law to submit the sample.

9–47   A mere breach of the 1987 Regulations was also considered insufficient by the Court of Criminal Appeal to warrant the exercise of the discretion to exclude a confession in *People (DPP) v. Murphy*.[157] In that case it was admitted that gardai interrogating the accused had failed to make a record of parts of the interview with the suspect as required by Regulation 12(11). This omission related to the period when the applicant engaged in a "general chat" with the interviewing officers immediately before deciding to make a full confession. While the Court accepted that there was a breach it did not consider that that alone was sufficient to warrant the exercise of the discretion to exclude the confession:

> "The mere absence of a record, without any other matter being raised, whilst a breach of the regulations, was a matter for consideration and determination within the judicial discretion of the trial judge. Non compliance with the regulations per se does not render the custody unlawful or the statement inadmissible."[158]

In refusing to interfere with the trial judge's exercise of discretion the Court drew particular attention to the fact that no case was made to the effect that the accused was prejudiced by the breach in any way. It went on to rule that:

> "The appropriate test, therefore, is (a) whether a breach of regulations has taken place, and, (b) whether the accused has suffered prejudice as a consequence of the breach. This test is subject to the constitutional duty of the trial judge to ensure that the trial is fair and just."[159]

Even a breach of the regulation which limits the length of any single interrogation session to four hours will not necessarily be sufficient in itself to warrant the exclusion of a confession given after more than four hours questioning. In *People (DPP) v. Reddan*,[160] for example, the accused had

---

[157] CCA, July 12, 2001. See also, *DPP (Lenihan) v. McGuire* [1996] 3 I.R. 586.
[158] *ibid.* at 7.
[159] *ibid.* at 10.
[160] [1995] 3 I.R. 560.

waived her right to have a rest after four hours of questioning. Despite declaring that the rest period could not be waived the Court of Criminal Appeal ruled that breach of the regulation did not render the subsequent confession inadmissible. Similarly, a breach of the regulation limiting to two the number of gardai who may ask questions of the suspect during an interview was considered insufficient in itself to warrant the exercise of the discretion to exclude in *People (DPP) v. Smith*.[161]

Evidence of a causal connection between the breach and prejudice to the applicant was present in *People (DPP) v. Connell*.[162] In that case the appellant had been interviewed on several occasions for periods which exceeded the mandatory four hour limit (see later) and no mention was made in the custody record of visits by persons during his interrogation and of complaints made by or on behalf of the appellant. In holding that the appellant's confession should have been excluded the Court of Criminal Appeal noted that not only had there been persistent breaches of the Regulations but that the accused had been prejudiced by the Garda failure to contact his solicitor and his lack of sleep. If, however, there is no prejudice to the accused and the interviews are conducted in a fair and humane manner it is unlikely that the Court of Criminal Appeal will waive a trial judge's exercise of discretion to admit a confession, even though there had been repeated technical breaches of the Regulations governing the treatment of the suspect in police custody.[163]

9–48

4. The Residual Discretion

Introduction

Situations will arise where incriminating evidence has been obtained by unlawful or improper methods which do not amount to a deliberate and conscious violation of the accused's constitutional rights or, in the case of statement evidence, do not amount to oppression or render the statement involuntary. Will the evidence nevertheless be ruled inadmissible on account of the illegality or impropriety? At common law English courts have treated such evidence as admissible, subject to the exercise of the trial judge's general discretion to exclude it on the grounds that its prejudicial effect outweighs its probative value. In effect the trial judge had to consider whether the admission of the evidence would result in an unfair trial for the accused. If its admission would not result in an unfair trial, it could not be excluded simply because it had been obtained in an unlawful or unfair manner.[164] The discretion has since been put on a statutory footing in the United Kingdom,[165] and it would appear that the English courts are now prepared to exercise it not just

9–49

---

[161] CCA, November 22, 1999.
[162] [1995] 1 I.R. 244.
[163] See, *e.g.*, *People (DPP) v. O'Driscoll* CCA July 19, 1999.
[164] *R. v. Sang* [1980] A.C. 402.
[165] See Police and Criminal Evidence Act 1984, s.78 and Police and Criminal Evidence (NI) Order 1989, art.76.

to ensure a fair trial for the accused but also to uphold the public interest in the integrity of the criminal justice system.[166] This is much closer to the approach of the Irish courts which have always attempted to balance the public interest in the detection and prosecution of crime with the public interest in ensuring that the State does not resort to unlawful or unfair methods of investigation.[166a] Having said that, it must be acknowledged that the existence and exercise of the residual discretion has been considered on such few occasions by the Irish courts that it is difficult to make any firm statements about it.

The Basic Principle

People (Attorney General) v. O'Brien[167] is the first reported case in which the existence of the residual discretion was acknowledged. In that case Kingsmill-Moore J. was of the opinion that where evidence had been obtained by unlawful means which fell short of constitutional infraction the court would have a discretion to exclude it. Walsh J., on the other hand, felt that evidence could not be excluded in such circumstances if it was relevant. Although it was not entirely clear from the other judgements in that case which of these two conflicting statements of the law enjoyed majority support, it would appear that Kingsmill-Moore J.'s approach has since been preferred.[168]

9–50 Kingsmill-Moore J., in *O'Brien*, positively refrained from laying down any absolute rules on the circumstances in which the discretion will be exercised, beyond saying that the decision would have to be taken by balancing the public interests for and against exclusion on a case by case basis. This is neatly summed up in the following extract from his judgment:

> "It would not be in accordance with our system of jurisprudence for this court to attempt to lay down rules to govern future hypothetical cases. We can do no more than decide the case now before us, and to lay down that, in future cases, the presiding judge has a discretion to exclude evidence of facts ascertained by illegal means where it appears to him that public policy, based on a balancing of public interests, requires such exclusion. If he decides to admit the evidence an appeal against his decision should lie to a superior Court which will decide the question according to its own views and will not be bound to affirm the decision of the trial judge if it disagrees with the manner in which the discretion has been exercised, even if it does not appear that such discretion was exercised on wrong principles. The result of such decisions, based on the facts of individual cases, may in time give rise to more precise rules."[169]

The learned judge also indicated the factors that would have to be taken into account in balancing the public interests involved:

---

[166] See the House of Lords decision in *R v. Loosely* [2001] 4 All E.R. 897.

[166a] Note, however, that Gannon J. sitting in the High Court in *People (DPP) v. McCutcheon* [1986] I.L.R.M. 433 was of the opinion that the Irish and English courts were ad idem on the exercise of the discretion in the light of the House of Lords decision in *Sang*. Gannon J. proceeded on the basis that the vital issue in the exercise of the discretion was ensuring a fair trial for the accused.

[167] [1965] I.R. 142.

[168] *People (DPP) v. McMahon* [1987] I.L.R.M. 87.

[169] [1965] I.R. 142 at 161.

"It is desirable in the public interest that crime should be detected and punished, It is desirable that individuals should not be subjected to illegal or inquisitorial methods of investigation and that the State should not attempt to advance its ends by utilising the fruit of such methods. It appears to me that in every case the determination has to be made by the trial judge as to whether the public interest is best served by the admission or by the exclusion of evidence of facts ascertained as a result of, and by means of, illegal actions, and that the answer to the question depends on a consideration of all the circumstances. On the one hand, the nature and extent of the illegality have to be taken into account. Was the illegal action intentional or unintentional, and if intentional, was it the result of an *ad hoc* decision or does it represent a settled or deliberate policy? Was the illegality one of a trivial and technical nature or was it a serious invasion of important rights, the recurrence of which would involve a real danger to the necessary freedoms? Were there circumstances of urgency or emergency which provide some excuse for the action? The nature of the crime which is being investigated may also have to be taken into account."[170]

These statements were specifically approved by the Supreme Court in *People (DPP) v. McMahon*[171] subject to the qualification that the factors listed in the second extract should not be considered as exclusive or complete.

Application in Practice

Clearly this approach leaves the Irish courts the scope to punish police infractions which are deemed a sufficiently serious threat to the rights and freedoms of the individual. At the same time it avoids the spectacle of reliable and critical evidence being excluded simply because the manner in which it was obtained involved some minor or technical infringement of the law or procedure. Indeed, in the *O'Brien* case itself the evidence in question was admitted even though it had been obtained as a result of a search which was technically unlawful.[172] The judicial reluctance to exercise the discretion to exclude on the basis of some minor infringement of the law is also reflected in *People (DPP) v. McMahon*.[173] In that case the gardai concerned entered a publican's premises with a view to getting evidence of a possible breach of the gaming laws. Technically speaking they were trespassers and as such the evidence they acquired had been obtained unlawfully (although no breach of constitutional rights was involved). At the conclusion of argument on the admissibility of the evidence the Circuit Court postponed judgment on the admissibility issue and stated a case for the opinion of the Supreme Court. The Supreme Court found that the gardai in question had acted unlawfully in obtaining the evidence and, therefore, the trial judge would have to decide whether to exercise his discretion to exclude the evidence. In balancing the public interest that crime should be detected against the undesirability of using improper methods, the Court considered that "particular importance

9–51

---

[170] *ibid.* at 160.
[171] [1987] I.L.R.M. 87.
[172] See also *People (DPP) v. Lawless* unreported, CCA November 28, 1985.
[173] [1986] I.R. 393.

may attach to the fact that the Gardai in entering the public house to view the machines were trespassers only, not involved in any criminal or opprobrious conduct and that the offence of permitting gaming on licensed premises may be considered as one with grave social consequences."[174]

Entrapment

9–52 Evidence obtained by entrapment or by a member of the Garda Síochána acting as an *agent provocateur* may raise issues of fairness pertinent to the exercise of the judicial discretion to exclude.[174a] As yet, however, the question of entrapment has not received substantial judicial scrutiny in the Irish Courts. It has, however, been the subject of recent decisions of the European Court of Human Rights and the House of Lords. In *Texeira de Castro v. Portugal*[175] two undercover police officers applied pressure to a drug user to act as an informer and introduce them to his supplier. Failing to locate his supplier, the user identified the plaintiff as a possible supplier. The informer set up a meeting between the police officers and the plaintiff at which the officers offered to buy a quantity of heroin. The plaintiff supplied the heroin and was subsequently arrested, prosecuted and convicted for supplying drugs. The plaintiff complained that the police action breached his right to a fair trial under Article 6.1 of the European Convention on Human Rights. The court ruled that the guarantee of fairness under Article 6.1 was not confined to the trial but extended to the proceedings as a whole, including the police investigation. With respect to the police methods of investigation, the court drew a distinction between undercover investigative activity, which is not *per se* a breach of Article 6.1, and investigative activity which amounts to incitement to commit the offence in question. In this case the police officers had gone beyond passive involvement in the commission of the crime to actively encouraging its commission. They did so in circumstances where the plaintiff was not otherwise predisposed to commit the offence and they had acted on their own initiative without judicial supervision or good reason to suspect that the plaintiff was a drug trafficker. The court concluded that these factors amounted to unfairness in the administration of justice sufficient to constitute a breach of Article 6.1. On the specific use of incitement as a method of detection it had this to say:

> "The use of undercover agents must be restricted and safeguards put in place even in cases concerning the fight against drug trafficking. While the rise in organised crime undoubtedly requires that appropriate measures be taken, the right to a fair administration of justice nevertheless holds such a prominent

---

[174] *ibid.* at 93. McCarthy J. added a rider to the effect that if the trial judge found that there was a policy to conduct searches without a warrant the discretion ought to be exercised to exclude; at 94.

[174a] There is voluminous literature on entrapment in the journals. For some notable examples see: S Bronitt, *Entrapment, Human Rights and Criminal Justice: A Licence to Deviate* (1999) 29(2) Hong Kong Law Journal 216; G Dworkin, *The Serpent Beguiled Me and I Did Eat: Entrapment and the Creation of Crime* (1985) 4 Law and Philosophy 17; A Ashworth, "Should the Police Be Allowed to Use Deceptive Practices?" (1998) 114 Law Quarterly Review 108 G Robertson *Entrapment Evidence: Manna from Heaven or Fruit of the Poisoned Tree* [1994] Criminal Law Review 805; S Sharpe, *Covert Policing: a Comparative View* (1996) 25(2) Anglo-American Law Review 163.

[175] (1998) 28 E.H.R.R. 101.

place that it cannot be sacrificed for the sake of expedience. The general requirements of fairness embodied in Article 6 apply to proceedings concerning all types of criminal offence, from the most straightforward to the most complex. The public interest cannot justify the use of evidence obtained as a result of police incitement."

Significantly, the court considered that the use of evidence obtained as a result of police incitement would not be in the public interest.

In *R v. Loosely*[176] the House of Lords had to consider the implications of the decision in *Teixeira* for the remedies for entrapment in English law, namely a stay of proceedings on the ground of abuse of process and the exercise of judicial discretion to exclude evidence obtained by entrapment. While the latter had traditionally been exercised solely in the interests of securing a fair trial for the accused,[177] there were some indications that proceedings could be stayed in the exercise of the judge's discretion in order to protect the public interest in the integrity of the criminal justice system.[178] The House of Lords concluded that English law was compatible with the principles enunciated in *Teixeira*. In particular, it accepted that the exercise of judicial discretion to exclude evidence or stay proceedings was concerned not just with securing a fair trial for the accused but also to protect the public interest in preserving the integrity of the judicial process. In the context of entrapment this meant that evidence which had been obtained by police officers actively encouraging or causing the commission of crime, as distinct from providing an unexceptional opportunity for the accused to commit the crime, should be excluded. The focus, in other words, is on the actions of the police, as distinct from the propensity of the accused to commit the crime in question:

> " . . . the judicial response to entrapment is based on the need to uphold the rule of law. A defendant is excused, not because he is less culpable, although he may be, but because the police have behaved improperly. Police conduct which brings about, to use the catch-phrase, state-created crime is unacceptable and improper. To prosecute in such circumstances would be an affront to the public conscience, to borrow the language of Lord Steyn in *R v. Latif* [1996] 1 W.L.R. 104 at 112. In a very broad sense of the word, such a prosecution would not be fair."[179]

In determining whether the police had crossed the line on the facts of an individual case the court would look at factors such as whether they were acting on a reasonable suspicion and under proper supervision, as well as the nature of the offence. Undercover operations should be employed only where the offences were consensual or for the purpose of infiltrating conspiracies. The seriousness of the offence, however, would not be an operative factor. In one of the cases at issue in *Loosely* the House of Lords decided that the police officer did not incite the offence of supplying drugs. He was acting in the

---

[176] [2001] 4 All E.R. 897.
[177] *R v. Sang* [1980] A.C. 402.
[178] See, for example, *R v. Latif* [1996] 1 All E.R. 353.
[179] [2001] 4 All E.R. 897, *per* Lord Nicholls at 904.

course of an authorised undercover operation and the pub where the deal was made was reasonably suspected to be a focal point of the trade. Although the officer made the initial approach there was reasonable cause to suspect subsequently that the defendant was a dealer, and the willingness of the defendant to deal was neutral. In the other case the police action was considered to have crossed the line. The officers in question had set out to gain the defendant's confidence by selling him cheap "contraband" cigarettes. When approached for heroin he was initially reluctant to deal and only succumbed after he was supplied with more cheap cigarettes. In one case, therefore, the police merely presented themselves as customers but did little more by way of encouraging the defendant to deal, while in the other they had to persist in their efforts to get an otherwise reluctant defendant to commit the offence.

As yet the Irish courts have not been called upon to address the admissibility of evidence obtained by gardaí engaged in an entrapment operation. In *Dental Board v. O'Callaghan*[179a] the High Court distinguished between an *agent provocateur* and an accomplice for the purpose of the rule on corroboration, holding that no warning was required in respect of the evidence of an *agent provocateur*. This, however, should not be interpreted as an indication that the Irish courts would be any less hostile than the European Court of Human Rights or the House of Lords to the admissibility of evidence obtained by undercover police officers inciting a person to commit a crime. Given the readiness of the Irish courts to exercise the discretion to exclude evidence in order to uphold the integrity of the judicial process, it might be expected that they would treat the approach in *Loosely* as a minimum standard.[179b]

Application to Police Custody

9–53   Where the impugned evidence is an admission by the accused given while he was in police custody the focus will be on whether the circumstances in which it was obtained are so unfair as to justify the exercise of the discretion to exclude it, even though it was a voluntary statement. Once again it is impossible to be prescriptive about what constitutes unfairness in these circumstances. Undoubtedly, any attempt to question a suspect while he is labouring under the effects of alcohol, drugs or lack of sleep would suffice. It must be said, however, that if a trial judge admits a confession which has been taken while the suspect is allegedly suffering from alcohol or drug withdrawal symptoms the appellate courts will be most reluctant to overturn his decision. So long as there is evidence upon which the trial judge could have concluded that the suspect was physically and mentally fit for ques-

---

[179a] [1969] I.R. 181.
[179b] In *R v. Shannon* [2001] 1 W.L.R. 51 the English Court of Appeal refused to quash a conviction for supplying drugs where the accused, a celebrity entertainer with a past history of drug abuse, had been tricked into supplying drugs for a party by an investigative reporter from the News of the World. The reporter, posing as a wealthy Arab Sheikh, had arranged a meeting with the accused to supposedly to discuss employment opportunities in Dubai. In the course of the meeting the reported asked the accused if he could supply the drugs.

tioning they will not interfere.[180] In *People (DPP) v. Murphy*,[181] for example, the Court of Criminal Appeal had to consider whether the trial judge had erred in exercising his discretion to admit a confession given by a suspect who had spent the previous day drinking, had slept for three hours on the floor of a Garda cell for three hours during the night and had actually vomited from the effects of the alcohol during the interrogation the following morning. Nevertheless, the Court of Criminal Appeal felt that there was sufficient evidence before the trial judge to support his decision that the suspect was under no distress during the questioning. This evidence consisted mainly of the opinions of the Garda officers dealing with the suspect and the opinion of the doctor who examined him and concluded that his condition did not require postponement of the interview. It would be quite a different matter if the suspect was deliberately denied the opportunity to sleep by the gardaí. In that event a statement taken would normally be excluded even it was voluntary.[182]

There is also the possibility of the judge exercising his or her discretion on public policy grounds to exclude a statement. In *People (DPP) v. Buck*[182a] the Supreme Court addressed *obiter* the admissibility of an incriminating statement taken from a suspect in Garda custody before the arrival of his solicitor in a case where the suspect had requested his solicitor. The regulations governing the treatment of suspects in Garda custody stipulate that when an arrested person asks for a solicitor he shall not be asked to make a written statement in relation to an offence until a reasonable time for the attendance of the solicitor has elapsed (see chapter 6).[182b] The court in *Buck* accepted that the gardaí involved were not to blame for the delay in the suspect securing access to the solicitor. Delivering the judgment of the court Keane C.J. explained that the admissibility of a statement taken in such circumstances where the detention was lawful and there was no deliberate and conscious breach of the suspect's constitutional rights came within the discretion of the trial judge:

> "It would also seem to me that, where a person being detained under a statutory provision asks for a solicitor to be present and the garda make *bona fide* attempts to comply with that request, the admissibility of any incriminating statement made by the person concerned before the arrival of the solicitor should be decided by the trial judge as a matter of discretion in the light of the common law principles to which I have referred, based on considerations of fairness to the accused and public policy. Such an approach would seem preferable to a rigid exclusionary rule that would treat such statements as inadmissible without any regard to the circumstances prevailing in the particular case."

---

[180]   See, for example, *People (DPP) v. C*, Court of Criminal Appeal, July 31, 2001.

[181]   CCA, November 22, 1999.

[182]   *ibid*. See also *People v. Breathnach* [1982] I.R. 64.

[182a] Supreme Court, April 17, 2002.

[182b] Criminal Justice Act 1984 (Treatment of Persons in Custody in Garda Síochána Stations) Regulations 1987, reg.12(6)

People (DPP) v. Lynch,[183] is a rare example of the Supreme Court ruling that the trial judge had erred in refusing to exercise his discretion to exclude a confession. In the opinion of the Supreme Court the circumstances in which the suspect had been subjected to lengthy and exhausting interrogation sessions in that case before he ultimately confessed were so oppressive that it would have been unjust and unfair to admit the confession.

E. Procedure

1. Matter for the Judge

9–54   The admissibility of evidence in a criminal trial is a matter for the trial judge to determine in accordance with the law. This applies irrespective of the designation of the trial court, the grounds upon which the evidence is being challenged and whether the challenge involves determinations of law and fact. In *Blanchfield v. Judge Hartnett*,[184] for example, the question arose whether the trial judge in the Circuit Court could rule on the admissibility of evidence which had been obtained pursuant to an order issued by a District Court pursuant to the Bankers Books Evidence Act 1879. The defence in this case had challenged both the legality and the constitutionality of the District Court order. The prosecution contended that the legality or constitutionality of a court order was a matter for the High Court only on a judicial review. In upholding the jurisdiction of the trial judge in the matter, O'Neill J. in the High Court explained:

> "In the course of [criminal] proceedings issues arise as to the admissibility of evidence and the resolution of such issues rests solely with the trial judge. Where it is alleged that evidence has been obtained illegally the question of whether or not such is the case i.e. whether an illegality has occurred is one solely for the trial judge and following upon that whether or not the evidence should be admitted is again one solely for the discretion of the trial judge, a discretion to be exercised in accordance with law. In my view the regularity of judicial proceedings requires that all questions relevant to the determination of such issues rest with the trial judge."[185]

Later in the same judgment the learned judge went on to say:

> "It seems to me therefore, that it would necessarily follow that a trial judge asked to adjudicate on an issue as to the admissibility of evidence has a jurisdiction to hear and determine all questions of fact and law relevant to the determination of the issue of admissibility, including questions relating to allegations of breaches of constitutional rights, allegations of non-compliance with statutory provisions, and all other illegalities."[186]

---

[183]   [1982] I.R. 64.
[184]   HC, June 30, 2000.
[185]   *ibid.* p. 17.
[186]   *ibid.* pp. 18–19.

2. Voir Dire

Where the trial is by judge and jury the traditional practice is to exclude the jury from the proceedings when an admissibility issue is being determined.[187] This is considered necessary in the interests of the accused as it ensures that the jury does not become aware of prejudicial evidence against the accused which is legally inadmissible. Reporting of proceedings is normally suspended until the admissibility issue is determined.[188] The admissibility hearing in the absence of the jury is termed a trial within a trial or the *voir dire*.[189]

    9–55

Where, as is often the case, the admissibility of the evidence is being challenged on the basis of the circumstances in which it was obtained, the prosecution will lead evidence of those circumstances in the *voir dire*. There is no pre-requisite for the defence to raise a prima facie case that the evidence is or might be inadmissible. It is quite sufficient for counsel for the defence to alert the judge that he or she is contesting the admissibility of the evidence on one or more specified grounds. That is usually sufficient for the judge to enter into a *voir dire* in which the onus is on the prosecution to establish that the evidence was obtained properly and in accordance with the defendant's legal and constitutional rights.[190] Once the prosecution has led its evidence to this end the defence can test it by way of cross-examination and by leading evidence in rebuttal.[191] At the conclusion of argument the judge must decide whether the evidence is admissible.

Where the judge rules at the conclusion of the *voir dire* that the evidence is inadmissible the jury is recalled and the trial proceeds without the jury being informed of the existence or nature of the evidence. To this end counsel for the prosecution is precluded from cross-examining the accused or adducing evidence about the truth of the matters which have been ruled inadmissible in evidence. So, for example, where a confession has been ruled inadmissible counsel cannot ask the accused if he confessed, nor can he call the court clerk to testify as to what the accused had said during the *voir dire*.[192] During the *voir dire* itself counsel for the prosecution should not cross-examine the accused about the truth of his contested confession.

Where the evidence is ruled admissible the prosecution will present it to the jury as if it was being introduced for the first time. Equally, the defence will be entitled to test it by cross-examination and to lead evidence in rebuttal as if these matters had not already been rehearsed in the *voir dire*.[193] This time, however, the purpose is not to persuade the jury that the evidence is

---

[187] *Bartlett v. Smith* (1843) 11 M&W 483; *State v. Treanor* [1924] 2 I.R. 193; *Attorney General v. McCabe* [1927] I.R. 129; *Minter v. Priest* [1930] A.C. 558; *R. v. Sparks* [1964] A.C. 964; *R. v. Chan Wei Keung* [1967] 2 A.C. 160.

[188] *Irish Times Ltd. v. Ireland* [1998] 1 I.R. 359 at 393–394, *per* O'Flaherty J.

[189] Note the broader definition given to *voir dire* by Walsh J. in *People (DPP) v. Conroy* [1986] I.R. 460 at 475 where he says that it extends to the judicial examination of the competence of a witness even in the presence of a jury.

[190] *People (DPP) v. Conroy* [1986] I.R. 460.

[191] *R. v. Wong Kam-Ming* [1980] A.C. 247; *R. v. Ng Chun-Kwan* [1974] H.K.L.R. 319.

[192] *Wong Kam-ming v. R* [1980] A.C. 247.

[193] *People v. Ainscough* [1960] I.R. 136; *R. v. Chan Wei-Keung* [1967] 2 A.C. 160.

inadmissible, as the jury has no function in that regard. Rather the purpose, from the perspective of the defence, is to persuade the jury not to attach any weight or credibility to the statement. This is particularly important where the evidence is an inculpatory statement which has been obtained in disputed circumstances. Equally, the defence may seek to persuade the jury that the defendant did not make the alleged inculpatory statement at all.

9–56   Where the trial judge has ruled a confession voluntary and admissible in the course of the *voir dire* he should avoid conveying information to the jury that he has formed the opinion or has given a ruling to the effect that the confession was made voluntarily.[194] There is a risk that the statement of any such opinion or ruling will be interpreted by the jury as a direction from the judge on how they should view the circumstances in which the confession was made and the weight which they should give it. These are matters which must be determined by the jury as matters of fact.

The traditional approach to the admissibility issue has been determined largely in the context of the common law rules on the admissibility of confessions. Its greatest advantage from the perspective of the defence is felt in those cases where the judge has had to make findings on disputed facts before going on to rule a statement voluntary and, therefore admissible. In these cases the last word on the disputed facts is left to the jury. If the jury takes a different view of the facts from the judge, the result might well be that it will attach little weight or credibility to the statement, or that the statement was not made at all. If, however, the disputed facts have little relevance to the existence or credibility of the statement, the possibility of the jury taking a different view of the facts loses much of its importance. For example, the accused might challenge the admissibility of a statement on the grounds that it was obtained while he was in police custody in circumstances which amounted to a conscious and deliberate violation of his constitutional rights. If the facts pertaining to the accused's presence in the police station are disputed and the judge decides them in favour of the prosecution in a manner which discounts a constitutional violation, that will be an effective end of the matter. Even if the jury would take a different view of the facts, this is unlikely to have any relevance for the weight or credibility which it would attach to the statement. Nor can it result in the statement being declared inadmissible. In effect, therefore, the judge's finding of fact will have determined the admissibility issue and the jury's role will have been sidelined.

3. Alternative Approaches

Fact-Finding by the Jury

9–57   In *People (DPP) v. Lynch*[195] O'Higgins C.J. proceeded, obiter, to reformulate the traditional admissibility procedure in a manner which would allocate the

---

[194]   *People (DPP) v. Donnelly* CCA, February 22, 1999.
[195]   [1982] I.R. 64.

fact finding role exclusively to the jury, at least in matters concerning the liberty of the individual:

> "In this case, apart from the defence that the incriminating statements were involuntary or obtained unfairly, it was also part of the defence that these had been secured in breach of the appellant's constitutional rights. The latter issue seemed to depend on whether, as the gardai swore, the appellant had remained in the garda station of his own free will and had never asked to go home or to be put in touch with his wife, or whether (as he swore) he was detained against his will and, although requesting to be allowed to leave, was not permitted to go. The trial judge disbelieved the appellant and, therefore, did not consider any question of illegal detention or breach of constitutional rights. In my view, this fact alone rendered this trial unsatisfactory. The conflict of evidence, and the true facts, ought to have been decided by the jury. On the jury's finding as to where the truth lay, the trial judge could decide whether or not there has been an illegal detention. In my view, the jury, either by a specific question or by an appropriate direction ought to have been asked to decide, as a question of fact material to the defence, whether the appellant's evidence that he had been held against his wishes was or was not true."[196]

In practice, this would mean that the circumstances in which the evidence had been obtained would be examined in the presence of both judge and jury. When disputed matters of fact had to be resolved they would be left to the jury as a separate issue during the trial. On the basis of the jury's findings the judge would rule as a matter of law on the admissibility of the evidence. Walsh J, in the same case, considered that this approach would be more in keeping with the constitutional function of the jury to determine questions of fact.[197]

A major problem with the approach adopted in *Lynch* is the risk that the jury **9–58** will become aware of evidence that is legally inadmissible and that this will influence its ultimate decision on guilt. This is compounded by the fact that the Supreme Court in that case did not offer a detailed blueprint on how the new procedure was meant to work. The sparse comments offered *obiter* by O'Higgins C.J. and Walsh J. were hardly sufficient in themselves to deal with all the problems that would ensue from an attempt to rewrite procedure that had been settled for many years. It is hardly surprising, therefore, that the Supreme Court had to return to the issue only a few years later. In *People (DPP) v. Conroy*[198] the Court of Criminal Appeal certified the following point of law of exceptional public importance for the opinion of the Supreme Court:

> "Where in the course of the trial the admissibility of an inculpatory statement is challenged on the grounds that
> (a) it was obtained in conscious and deliberate breach of constitutional rights
> (b) it was unfairly obtained
> (c) it was not voluntary
>   1. In what circumstances are the relevant issues of fact to be determined by the jury?
>   2. At what stage of the trial is such determination to be made?"[199]

---

[196] *ibid.* at 79.
[197] See *People (DPP) v. Conroy* [1988] I.L.R.M. 4 at 22.
[198] [1988] I.L.R.M. 4.
[199] *ibid.* at 11.

The Supreme Court, by a four to one majority (Walsh J. being the dissenting judge on this particular issue) restored the orthodox *voir dire* approach that issues of both fact and law necessary to determine the admissibility of any evidence should be tried by a judge in the absence of the jury. This should be done at the point in the trial where the evidence in question was about to be introduced.

Pre-Trial Proceedings

Traditionally a *voir dire* will be held at that point in the trial where the impugned evidence is about to be introduced. Typically, the defence will have signalled before the trial their intention to challenge the evidence in question. The case will be opened by the prosecution without reference to the existence of the impugned evidence. At the appropriate point in the trial counsel for the prosecution will alert the judge of the need to initiate the *voir dire*. It has long been recognised that this particular form of procedure can be very disruptive of the criminal trial, and onerous on the jury. Accordingly, it has been suggested from time to time that a more appropriate form of procedure would be to conduct the *voir dire* at the outset before the jury has been sworn in.[200] There have been examples of this in practice in both Britain and Northern Ireland in cases where virtually the sole evidence against the accused was a confession the admissibility of which was challenged.[201]

Trial Without a Jury

9–59 Where the trial is by a judge (or judges) sitting without a jury the question of a *voir dire* does not arise. The judge (or judges) will hear argument about the admissibility of evidence when it arises in the course of the trial. Where the issue concerns the exercise of the discretion to exclude evidence, the judge (or judges) must be sufficiently informed of the nature and substance of the evidence to assess whether it is necessary to proceed to argument over the exercise of the discretion.[202] In other words, the evidence should normally be introduced by the prosecution and tested by the defence before argument over its admissibility commences. Where the evidence is excluded the judge (or judges) will proceed with the trial, being careful to leave the inadmissible evidence out of account when reaching the verdict. Unlike the position with respect to the non-jury 'Diplock' Courts in Northern Ireland there is no specific statutory provision which enables a trial to resume before a differently constituted court after evidence has been ruled inadmissible in a *voir dire*.[203] Indeed, in *DPP v. Special Criminal Court*[204] Carney J. intimated that it would not be appropriate for the

---

[200] For a fuller discussion of the issues see D. Goldberg "Voir Dire: Disrupting the Jury" *Practice and Procedure 2(2) [2000] 10.*

[201] See *Wong Kam-ming v. R.* [1980] A.C. 247; *R. v. Brophy* [1982] A.C. 410.

[202] *People (DPP) v. McCutcheon* [1986] I.L.R.M. 433.

[203] The sitting members of the Special Criminal Court have a discretion to disqualify themselves in a case where inadmissible evidence highly prejudicial to the accused is given in the course of the trial. It would appear, however, that this discretion will not be exercised lightly; see *DPP v. McMahon* [1984] I.L.R.M. 431.

[204] [1999] 1 I.R. 60.

admissibility of evidence to be considered by a chamber other than that hearing the trial itself, even where the trial was being conducted without a jury:

> "It is the function of every professional judge to adjudicate on the admissibility of evidence prejudicial to an accused person and to exclude it from his mind if it is not admissible according to the rules of evidence. I would not see it as necessary for another chamber of the court to deal with the matter."[205]

Where evidence is ruled admissible after a challenge in a trial without a jury the issue arises whether it is necessary to re-introduce the evidence as well as evidence about the circumstances in which it was obtained. In a jury trial this is necessary as the jury will be hearing the evidence for the first time. In a trial without a jury the judge (or judges) will already have heard the evidence, including evidence about the circumstances in which it was obtained, in the course of the challenge to its admissibility. It would seem pointless, therefore, to repeat the exercise. In respect of trials before the (juryless) Special Criminal Court, however, section 41(4) of the Offences against the State Act 1939 stipulates that the practice and procedure applicable to the trial of a person on indictment in the Central Criminal Court shall apply so far as practicable. In *People v. McGowan*[206] it was argued that this meant that once the Special Criminal Court had decided on the admissibility of statement evidence which was at issue in that case, the evidence should be re-introduced so that counsel for the accused could have the opportunity to cross examine the Garda witnesses on the accuracy of the matters contained in their testimony about the circumstances in which the statements were obtained. The purpose of such cross-examination, it was claimed, would have a bearing on the weight which the Court might attach to the Garda testimony. In response to this contention, and at the suggestion of the Court the prosecution recalled each witness who had previously given evidence in regard to the taking of the statements. Each witness duly re-affirmed the written record of their testimony. Defence counsel was then given an opportunity to cross-examine each of the witnesses on their testimony. The Court of Criminal Appeal ruled that this was sufficient to comply with the requirements of section 41(4). It was not necessary for each witness to repeat the testimony which they had already given to the Court.

9–60

---

[205] *ibid.* at 76.
[206] [1979] I.R. 45.

CHAPTER 10

BAIL

A. Introduction

Bail can be defined as the release of a person from custody subject to an **10–01** undertaking to surrender to custody at a court or garda station at an appointed time in the future. Before being released on bail the individual will normally be required to enter into a recognisance to surrender to custody at the appointed time and place. This will usually take the form of a legally binding commitment to pay a specified sum of money to the court if he fails to surrender in accordance with the terms of his bail. In addition, he may be required to provide one or more independent sureties. A surety is a person who undertakes to pay a specified sum of money to the court in the event of the accused failing to surrender in accordance with the terms of his bail. This obligation to submit to the jurisdiction of the court distinguishes bail from those situations where the individual is simply released from the custody of the State because the State no longer has an interest in restricting his or her freedom. A lawful refusal to grant bail in an individual case means that the person affected can be detained for a further period while criminal proceedings are advanced.

B. Jurisdiction to Grant Bail

1. Introduction

The jurisdiction to grant bail vests in certain members of the Garda Síochána, **10–02** trial judges, the District Court, the Special Criminal Court, the Court of Criminal Appeal and the Supreme Court. The scope of the jurisdiction and the procedure applicable differ from one authority to another. Accordingly, each will be dealt with in turn. It is worth noting at the outset, however, that the bail jurisdiction formerly exercised by peace commissioners[1] was declared unconstitutional by the Supreme Court in *O'Mahony v. Melia*.[2] In that case the Supreme Court found that the decision to remand a person in custody or on bail amounted to an administration of justice within the meaning of Article 34 of the Constitution. Since a peace commissioner was not a judge appointed in accordance with the Constitution, his power to remand in custody or on bail was deemed unconstitutional. Accordingly, the option of bringing an arrested suspect before a peace commissioner to be remanded in custody or on bail is no longer available.

2. Garda Síochána

The Power

10–03   Whenever a person is brought in custody to a Garda station by a member of the Garda Síochána, the sergeant or other member in charge of the station has jurisdiction to release the person on bail where he or she considers it prudent to do so and no warrant requiring the person's detention is in force.[3] This is referred to generally as police bail or station bail. Before releasing the person on bail the member may take from him a recognisance with or without sureties for his due appearance before the District Court at the next sitting of the court in the District Court area in which the person was arrested or at any subsequent sitting of the Court in that area during the thirty days immediately following that sitting.[4] Although the wording of the statutory provision is ambiguous it would appear that the taking of a recognisance, with or without sureties, is not mandatory. Where a recognisance is taken, a sum of money equivalent to the amount of bail may be accepted *in lieu* of a surety or sureties.[5] In this event the recognisance and the money must be deposited by the member of the Garda Síochána taking it with the clerk of the court before which the person is bound by the recognisance to appear.[6]

The relevant provision does not expressly impose any limitation on the range of offences which can benefit from police bail. However, an earlier

---

[1] Although the office of Peace Commissioner was first given a statutory role in this matter by s.4 of the District Justices (Temporary Provisions) Act 1923 it is likely that it also enjoyed a common law jurisdiction in this regard by virtue of the fact that it inherited many of the powers and authorities previously vested in the office of Justice of the Peace. The statutory authority for the duty of a member of the Garda Síochána to bring an arrested suspect before a Peace Commissioner was found in Criminal Justice Act 1951, s.15 as substituted by Criminal Justice Act 1984, s.26 (prior to the changes effected by the Supreme Court's decision in *O'Mahony v. Melia* [1990] I.L.R.M. 14).

[2] [1990] I.L.R.M. 14.

[3] The police were first given the power to release an arrested suspect on bail by s.24 of the Justices (Dublin Metropolis) Act 1824. It is now to be found in the Criminal Procedure Act 1967, s.31(1) as substituted by Criminal Justice (Miscellaneous Provisions) Act 1997, s.3. See also, District Court Rules 1997, Ord.17, r.4(1); see Schedule B, Form 17.2. This facility does not extend to a person arrested under s.251 of the Defence Act 1954 on suspicion of being a deserter or an absentee without leave from the Defence Forces; District Court Rules, 1997, Ord.17, r.4(4).

[4] In the case of the District Court in the Dublin Metropolitan District, it is the next sitting of that court or any subsequent sitting thereof during the period of 30 days immediately following that sitting.

[5] District Court Rules 1997, Ord.17, r.4(2).

[6] See District Court Rules 1997, Schedule B, Form 17.3 for the recognisance in this event.

provision in the 1967 Act stipulates that a person charged with one of a specified list of offences cannot be admitted to bail except by order of the High Court (see below para 10–07).[7] While the provision in question is primarily concerned with a person who has been brought before a court charged with one of the listed offences, it would seem by implication that it also extends to a person released on police bail. It is possible, of course, that a suspect might not be charged in police custody, but released on police bail to appear before a later sitting of the District Court for the purpose of being charged. Since the statutory provision which reserves certain offences to the bail jurisdiction of the High Court specifically refers to a person charged, it is arguable that it does not apply to a person who is released on police bail to appear before the District Court without being charged in the first instance in the police station. In practice such a situation is most unlikely to arise. Even if it did arise it is likely that the courts would interpret the relevant provisions to mean that the Garda Síochána could not release on bail a suspect who could not be released on bail by any other court apart from the High Court.

Period of Bail

The 30-day period within which the person can be remanded to appear **10–04** is significant. It was introduced by the Criminal Justice (Miscellaneous Provisions) Act 1997. Prior to that the legislation stipulated that the suspect could be bailed from a Garda station to appear before a District Court at "an appropriate time and place." In *State (Lynch) v. Ballagh*[8] the Supreme Court interpreted this to mean the next sitting of the District Court in the area in which the Garda station is situated. In the case of a summary offence rule 39(1) of the District Court Rules 1948,[9] issued by the District Court Rules Committee, had provided that it should be either the next sitting of the court in the area in which the suspect was arrested, or any subsequent sitting of that court not later than thirty days after the next sitting. This rule was struck down as *ultra vires* by the Supreme Court on the ground that the jurisdiction of the District Court Rules Committee did not extend to matters which took place prior to the lodging of a complaint with the District Court.[10] Accordingly, it had no jurisdiction to make rules governing police bail. Now, however, the thirty day rule has effectively been reinstated by statute, thereby making a substantial contribution to Garda flexibility in the matter.

Formalities

While there is no statutory limit to the amount of bail which can be set by a member there is authority for saying that it must represent a sum which is

---

[7] Criminal Procedure Act 1967, s.29.
[8] [1987] I.L.R.M. 65.
[9] As substituted by the District Court (Criminal Procedure Act 1967) Rules 1985.
[10] The jurisdiction of the District Court Rules Committee is conferred by s.91 of the Courts of Justice Act 1924 which reads in part:
    ". . . rules may be made for . . . the practice and procedure of the District Court generally including . . . the adaptation or modification of any statute that may be necessary for the purposes aforesaid and all subsidiary matters."

reasonable in all the circumstances.[11] Moreover, the acceptability of any sureties offered by the accused is a matter for the member in charge of the station.[12] However, a sum of money equivalent to the amount of bail may be accepted instead of a surety.[13] Alternatively, the suspect can apply for bail when he is brought before the District Court. In this event the suitability of the suspect's sureties will be a matter for the judge. Any recognisance taken, or money accepted in lieu of a surety or sureties, must be given by the member receiving it to the District Court clerk for the District Court area in which the sitting of the court to which the person has been remanded is situated.[14] Where a person fails to comply with the terms of his bail his recognisance may be estreated in the same manner as the estreatment of a recognisance entered into before a District Court judge (see below para 10–63 *et seq.*).[15]

Where a person is being released on bail from a Garda station the normal practice is for him to be given a copy of the charge sheet together with a copy of his recognisance after he has signed it. The originals are sent to the relevant District Court clerk and copies are retained in the Garda station.[16]

Status of Garda in Bail Matters

10–05   It might be considered that the Supreme Court's decision in *Melia v. O'Mahony* declaring a peace commissioner's bail jurisdiction unconstitutional would have implications for the role of the Garda Síochána in bail matters. While Garda bail jurisdiction has yet to be the subject of a direct judicial ruling, Walsh J. has expressed a clear view to the effect that the Garda's role in bail matters is purely ministerial as opposed to judicial.[17] Accordingly, it can be distinguished from the jurisdiction formerly vested in the peace commissioner and, as such, does not fall foul of Article 34 of the Constitution. It must be said, however, that the distinction between the former role of the peace commissioner and the current role of a member of the garda Síochána in bail matters is a very fine one. In making his or her determination in any individual case the member will consider, as a matter of practice, all aspects of the case including the gravity of the charge, the surrounding circumstances, the character and the sex of the accused and whether it would be inconvenient, unreasonable or impracticable to bring the accused before a District Court judge.[18]

---

[11] *People (Attorney General) v. O'Callaghan* [1966] I.L.R.M. 501.
[12] In practice gardaí will not normally accept vehicles, documents or any article as a surety.
[13] Criminal Procedure Act 1967, s.31(3); District Court Rules 1997, Ord.17, r.4(2) and Schedule B, Form 17.3.
[14] Criminal Procedure Act 1967, s.3A, inserted by Criminal Justice (Miscellaneous Provisions) Act 1997, s.3.
[15] *ibid.* s.31(2); District Court Rule 1997, Ord.17, r.4(3).
[16] District Court Rules 1997, Ord.17, r.4(5).
[17] *State (Lynch) v. Ballagh* [1987] I.L.R.M. 65, *per* Walsh J. at pp. 70 and 72.
[18] If the suspect has been arrested under s.251 of the Defence Act 1954 on suspicion of being a deserter or an absentee without leave from the Defence Forces it would appear that he cannot be admitted to bail by a member of the Garda Síochána; Criminal Procedure Act 1967, s.31(4).

Children

There is separate provision for the release of child suspects (suspects under the age of 18 years) on police bail. Up until the enactment of the Children Act 2001 this was to be found in a combination of the Children Act 1908 and the Criminal Procedure Act 1967 as amended.[19] These stipulated that where a person who appeared to be under the age of 17 years had been arrested and it was not practicable to take him or her before a court immediately the officer in charge of the station had to enquire into the case. The officer was obliged to release the young person as soon as he or she, or the parents or guardian, had entered into a recognisance with or without sureties. However, the officer had a discretion to detain the suspect in custody where the charge was one of homicide or other grave crime, or if it was necessary in the interest of the young person to remove him or her from association with any reputed criminal or prostitute or where the officer had reason to believe that release would defeat the ends of justice.

These provisions have now been superseded by the Children Act 2001 which makes new provision for the release on police bail of persons who are under 18 years of age. It stipulates that the member in charge of the station may, if he or she considers it prudent to do so and no warrant directing the detention of the child is in force, release the child on bail.[19a] For that purpose he or she may take, or arrange to have taken, from the child a recognisance with or without sureties for the child's due appearance before the next sitting of the Children Court in the District Court area in which the child has been arrested or at any subsequent sitting in the 30 days immediately following that next sitting.[19b] In the case of the Children Court in the Dublin Metropolitan District this requirement applies to the relevant sitting of that Court.[19c]

The recognisance may be taken from the child's parent or guardian and may be for the due appearance of the parent of guardian, as well as the child, before the Children Court.[19d] If the child is married the role of the parents or guardians in this matter shall be taken by the child's spouse.[19e] The recognisance may be estreated in the same manner as a recognisance entered into before a judge of the District Court.[19f] A sum of money equivalent to the amount of bail may be accepted in place of the surety or sureties.[19g] Where money is lodged pursuant to these provisions the person receiving it must transmit it to the District Court clerk for the District Court area in which the relevant sitting of the Children Court is being held.[19h]

---

[19]   Children Act 2001, s.68(1). This does not apply in the case of the arrest of a child under section 251 of the Defence Act 1954 (deserters and absentees); s.68(6).

[19a] *ibid.* s.68(1)(a).

[19b] *ibid.* s.68(1)(b).

[19c] *ibid.* s.68(2). Where the child is married the reference to a parent or guardian shall be construed as a reference to his or her spouse; s.69(a).

[19d] *ibid.* s.69(a).

[19e] *ibid.* s.68(3).

[19f] *ibid.* s.68(4).

[19g] *ibid.* s.68(5).

[19h] Despite the incongruity of a decision to grant bail being described as a "consequential order" when granted pending an application for leave to appeal, the Courts have given effect to the clear

Warrant Endorsed for Bail

10–06   The Bail Act 1997 makes provision for the release on station bail of persons who have been brought into custody on foot of a warrant. It stipulates that the court, when issuing a warrant of arrest, may direct that the person named on the warrant should be released on bail on his entering into a recognisance, with or without sureties.[20] The recognisance will require the person concerned to appear before a court on such date and at such time and place as specified in the endorsement. The endorsement will also fix the amounts in which the person and his surety or sureties are to be bound and will specify any other conditions of the recognisance. When the accused is brought on arrest to the Garda station the member in charge of the station must discharge him once he has entered into a recognisance approved by the member and payment has been made in an amount equal to one third (or such greater amount as the court may determine) of any recognisance entered into by the person.[21] Any money paid to a member of the Garda Síochána pursuant to this requirement must be deposited by him with the District Court clerk for the District Court area in which the Garda station is situated.[22]

The provision requiring payment of at least one third of the amount of bail before the individual can be discharged is new. Under the provision which it replaces in the Criminal Procedure Act 1967 the individual could be released once he, and any sureties, had entered into a recognisance in accordance with the endorsement on the arrest warrant.[23] Undoubtedly many individuals arrested pursuant to a warrant endorsed for bail will not immediately be able to secure payment of one third of the amount of the recognisance (or such greater amount as required by the court). It follows that they will have to be brought in custody before the court.

Comparison with English Provisions

It is worth noting that, contrary to the position in the United Kingdom,[24] there is no scope for the possibility of releasing a suspect on police bail to report back to the police station at a specified time in the future. The clear implication of all the relevant provisions is that police bail is available only for suspects who have already been charged in the Garda station. Either they must be released on bail or they must be detained in Garda custody until they can be brought before a District Court judge.

---

intention of the legislature in the matter; *People (DPP) v. Corbally* [2001] 2 I.L.R.M. 102; *People (DPP) v. Sweetman* [1997] 3 I.R. 448.

20   Bail Act 1997, s.8(1). See District Court Rules 1997, Schedule B, Form 26.1
21   *ibid.* s.8(2); District Court Rules 1997, Ord.17, r.5.
22   Bail Act 1997, s.8(3).
23   Criminal Procedure Act 1967, s.30 (now repealed by Bail Act 1997, s.12).
24   J. Sprack, *Emmins on Criminal Procedure* (6th ed., London: Blackstones Press, 1955) at Chap. 22.

3. District Court

Overview

More bail applications are made to the District Court than to any other **10–07**
authority. Where the District Court remands a person or sends him forward
for trial or sentence, it may commit him to prison or other lawful custody, or
it may release him conditionally on his entering into a recognisance with or
without sureties.[25] In practice the regular occasions on which a bail application is made are: where the court remands the accused to a later sitting;
where it sends the accused forward for trial or sentence; where it remands the
accused to a sitting of the court in another district for the purpose of taking
further evidence of an indictable offence charged against him; where it
adjourns the trial of the accused; and where it remands the accused for the
preparation of reports relevant to sentencing. The District Court may also
consider a bail application from an accused who exercises his statutory right of
appeal against conviction to the Circuit Court.[26] Indeed, it would appear that
the District Court judge is obliged to accede to such an application.[27]

Jurisdiction

Where a bail application is submitted the District Court judge must admit the
applicant to bail if it appears to him or her to be a case in which bail ought to
be allowed.[28] The relevant principles governing the bail decision are discussed later.[28a] There are, however, some offences for which the judge lacks
jurisdiction to grant bail. For the most part these are set out in section 29 of
the Criminal Procedure Act 1967 as follows:[29] murder, attempted murder,
conspiracy to murder, piracy, treason, genocide,[30] certain offences under the
Treason Act 1939,[31] certain offences under the Offences against the State Act,
1939,[32] a grave breach of the Geneva Convention Act 1962,[33] and certain
offences under the Official Secrets Act 1963.[34] Only the High Court has jurisdiction to admit to bail an accused charged with any of these offences. A further
restriction on the District Court judge's bail jurisdiction arises when Part V of the
Offences Against the State Act 1939 has been activated resulting in the setting up
of a Special Criminal Court. When a District Court judge returns an accused for

---

[25] Criminal Procedure Act 1967, ss.21 and 22 and Part III generally.
[26] Courts of Justice Act 1928, s.18, as amended by Courts of Justice Act 1936, s.58.
[27] *People v. McCormack*, unreported, High Court, 1972, *per* Griffin J. See Ryan and Magee, *The Irish Criminal Process* (Mercier Press, Dublin, 1983), p. 199.
[28] Criminal Procedure Act 1967, s.28(1).
[28a] See below para. 10–25 *et seq.*
[29] Also included is an accessory before or after the fact to any of these offences.
[30] Added by Genocide Act 1973, s.7.
[31] Ss. 2–3.
[32] Ss. 6–8.
[33] Such as that referred to in s.3(1)(i).
[34] S.9, or an offence under Part II committed in a manner prejudicial to the safety or preservation of the State.

trial to the Special Criminal Court on an indictable offence the accused may not be admitted to bail without the consent of the DPP.[35]

Recognisance and Sureties

10–08 A person can be released on bail only on condition that he enters into a recognisance, with or without sureties. A recognisance in this context takes the form of a binding obligation on the individual to appear at a sitting of the court at a specified time and place in the future and to comply with any ancillary conditions imposed by the court.[36] It is normally secured by payment of a sum of money which will be forfeited if the accused fails to comply with the terms of his bail. The amount of bail is a matter within the discretion of the judge.[37] If the judge requires a surety or sureties to guarantee compliance with the bail conditions, the amount or amounts in which each surety shall be bound is also a matter within the discretion of the judge.

Money in lieu of Sureties

Where a District Court judge decides to admit to bail a person charged with an offence, he or she may direct that a sum of money equivalent to the amount of bail shall be accepted in lieu of a surety or sureties.[38] In this event, so long as the accused is not in custody for any other matter he must be released once he has entered into the recognisance, and the money has been lodged with the clerk of the court area in which the order admitting the accused to bail was made or with the governor of the prison in which he is held in custody.[39] The clerk or the governor receiving the money, as the case may be, must issue a receipt for it and complete the certificate of lodgment on the recognisance.[40] Where the recognisance is conditioned for the appearance of the accused before a court other than a sitting of the District Court, the clerk or governor receiving the money must deposit it with the appropriate County Registrar or the appropriate officer of the Central Criminal Court or the Special Criminal Court as the case may be.[41] Once the condition or

---

[35] Offences against the State Act 1939 ss.45(2) and 46(2), as amended by the Prosecution of Offences Act 1974, s.3.

[36] Criminal Procedure Act 1967, s.23. See District Court Rules 1997, Schedule B, Form No.18.1 for a recognisance on remand (this also covers the situation where the accused is remanded to a sitting of the court in another district for the purpose of taking further evidence of an indictable offence), and Form No.18.2 for a recognisance on sending forward for trial or sentence.

[37] District Court Rules 1997, Ord.18, r.1. Note, however, Walsh J.'s advice on the level of bail in *People (AG) v. O'Callaghan* [1966] I.R. 501 (see para. 10–51).

[38] Criminal Procedure Act 1967, s.26. For the appropriate forms, see District Court Rules, 1997, Schedule B, Forms Nos. 18.3 and 18.4. It would appear that an instrument which is evidence of the title of a person to property (other than land or any estates or interest in land can be accepted *in lieu* of money. Such instruments include bank, building society, credit union or post office deposit books. See Bail Act 1997, s.5(2).

[39] District Court Rules 1997, Ord.18, r.6; see Schedule B, Forms 18.3 (recognisance to appear at later sitting) and 18.4 (recognisance on sending forward for trial or sentence).

[40] Any such money received by the governor shall be deposited with the clerk of the court area of the court in which the accused is to appear; District Court Rules 1997, Ord.18, r.7. The surety can request that the money be paid into a deposit account; see Schedule B, Form 18.5.

[41] District Court Rules 1997, Ord.18, r.8.

conditions of the recognisance have been fulfilled the judge shall give to the person by whom the sum of money was lodged a certificate to the effect that the condition or conditions have been fulfilled.[42] The money will then be repaid to that person.

Consent to Bail

Where the court consents to bail it may take the recognisance from the accused and sureties, as appropriate, and release him immediately unless he is in custody for another matter.[43] If it happens that the accused and/or his sureties are not in a position to enter into the recognisance, the court may fix the amount of the recognisance which can be taken subsequently by a District Court judge or a peace commissioner.[44] The consent to bail and the amount of bail required will normally be certified on the committal warrant.[45]

10–09

Even if the committal warrant is not endorsed with consent to bail, the accused can always submit an application for bail from custody.[46] On such an application the judge in question may admit him to bail at any time prior to the day of the adjourned hearing or at any time prior to the first day of the sitting of the court to which he has been sent forward for trial, as the case may be.[47] For this purpose the judge may order that the accused be brought before him or, alternatively, he may notify the prison governor of his consent to bail and the amount of bail required.[48]

Where a certificate of consent to bail is granted a peace commissioner at the prison or other place where the person is held in custody must, on production of the certificate, admit the person to bail as directed by the certificate.[49] This can be done at any tine before the day of the adjourned hearing if the person in question is on remand or before the first day of the sitting of the court before which the person is to be tried or sentenced if he or she has been sent forward for trial or sentence. If a surety is required to join in the recognisance and it is not convenient for the surety to attend at the prison, the peace commissioner, or judge having jurisdiction in the place where the surety resides, may take the recognisance from the surety and forward it to the clerk of the court area where the committal order was made.[50] The clerk must then transmit the

---

42 *ibid.* Ord.18, r.10; see Schedule B, Form 18.6.
43 *ibid.* Ord.18, r.5; see Schedule B, Form Nos.18.1 and 18.2.
44 Criminal Procedure Act 1967, s.22(2) and (3). A recognisance taken by a peace commissioner must be transmitted to the clerk of the court before which the person is bound by the recognisance to appear; District Court Rules 1997, Ord.18, r.16.
45 District Court Rules 1997 Ord.18, r.11; for the relevant forms see Schedule B, Forms No.19.1 (remand to later sitting), 19.2 (remand in the absence of the accused through illness or accident), 20.3 (remand on being about to abscond), 20.4 (remand on being about to abscond while awaiting trial), 20.5 (remand on being about to abscond having been charged), 24.2 (sending forward on a plea of guilty), 24.3 (sending forward without a preliminary examination), 24.4 (child or young person sent forward without a preliminary examination), 24.15 (sending forward for trial of offence charged), 24.17 (sending forward for trial of offence other than that charged), 24.35 (sending forward for trial or sentence), 24.36 (remand to another district).
46 Criminal Procedure Act 1967, s.28(2).
47 District Court Rules 1997, Ord.18, r.12.
48 See District Court Rules 1997, Schedule B, Forms 18.7 and 18.8 for the appropriate forms.
49 District Court Rules, 1997, Ord.18, r.13.
50 *ibid.* Ord.18, r.14.

recognisance to the governor of the prison concerned. On production of the recognisance of the surety the peace commissioner attending at the prison may proceed to take the recognisance of the person in custody and admit him to bail, in which case the governor of the prison must release him unless he is in custody for a cause other than the offence in respect of which bail is granted.[51]

A recognisance of an accused and of any surety for the purpose of admitting the accused to bail may be taken on any day and at any time.[52]

Obligation to Appear

10-10　Where the accused is remanded on bail the recognisance binds him to appear before the District Court at the end of the period of remand, and at every place and time to which the hearing may be adjourned during the proceedings.[53] In practice this is interpreted as extending right up to the point of trial in the District Court or until the accused is returned for trial on indictment. The effect is that the accused will not have to enter into fresh recognisances after each intervening District Court appearance. This is particularly significant in the case of an indictable offence where the accused can expect to be remanded on several successive occasions while awaiting the completion of the book of evidence. If, however, the accused has been returned for trial after the committal proceedings he, and his bailsmen, will have to enter into fresh recognisances for his appearance before the court to which he has been returned.[54]

Further Applications

10-11　An accused whose bail application has been refused can make further applications at any subsequent appearance before the District Court judge or while he is in custody awaiting trial.[55] Equally he can appeal to the High Court against a refusal.[56] It is worth noting that the appeal against a refusal of bail by the District Court is to the High Court, as distinct from the Circuit Court.

Even if an applicant is granted bail it may be that he is dissatisfied with some or all of the conditions attached. In this event, he may appeal to the High Court against the imposition of the conditions in question.[57] Equally, however, there would appear to be no reason why he could not submit a further application to the District Court seeking to have the terms of his bail varied.[58] Under this option, presumably, he would have to show that new

---

[51]　*ibid.* Ord.18, r.15.

[52]　*ibid.* Ord.18, r.18.

[53]　Criminal Procedure Act 1967, ss.22 and 23. For this purpose a period or periods of adjournment will be treated as part of the period of remand.

[54]　See District Court Rules 1997, Schedule B, Forms Nos.18.2 (recognisance on sending forward for trial or sentence) and 24.35 (committal warrant sending forward for trial or sentence).

[55]　Criminal Procedure Act 1967, s.28(2).

[56]　Criminal Procedure Act 1967, s.28(3). There is an argument for saying that an appeal is in effect a new application as the High Court will treat the hearing as an application *de novo*. See Ryan and Magee, *The Irish Criminal Process* (Mercier Press, Dublin, 1983), at pp. 194 and 197–199.

[57]　*ibid.* s.28(3).

[58]　Admittedly, a literal interpretation of Criminal Procedure Act 1967, s.28 suggests that a variation can be granted only by the High Court. However, the District Court Rules 1948, r.60(1) stated that

relevant considerations had arisen. On an appeal to the High Court by comparison he could argue in the alternative that the District Court was wrong to impose the conditions. Since there is no specific provision enabling the prosecution to appeal a District Court Judge's decision admitting a defendant to bail it is unlikely that the prosecution would have the power to seek a variation in the terms of bail in any case.[59] However, the prosecutor must be given notice of any application to vary the bail terms, and is entitled to be heard on any such application: Bail Act, 1997, s.6(4).

Clearly, these options raise the possibility of successive bail applications being made to a District Court judge by a defendant in custody, particularly on remand hearings. It is unlikely, however, that the judge is obliged to entertain a fully argued application at every hearing. The English courts acknowledge that a defendant's application for bail will have been considered by the Magistrate's Court which remanded him in custody on his first appearance. This should be borne in mind by magistrates at subsequent hearings where further bail applications are made. Accordingly, the magistrates need not entertain a full bail application at any subsequent hearing unless relevant considerations are present which were not before the court at the first appearance.[60] Although there is no specific Irish authority on the point it seems reasonable to expect that the Irish courts would adopt a similar approach in any case in which the defence persisted with repetitive bail applications in the absence of any significant change in circumstances.

Procedure

The procedure followed on a bail application to the District Court may vary depending upon the particular context in which the application is made. The following account is based on what normally happens on the occasion of the accused's first appearance at a sitting of the District Court consequent on his arrest.

Typically, the judge will raise the issue of bail by asking the prosecution whether they have any objections to bail. The mere fact that they may have no objections will not ensure that the accused will be granted bail but it will

10–12

---

the bail conditions imposed by a District Court judge may be varied by that judge at any subsequent hearing. This has not been repeated in the 1997 Rules. In England and Wales the defendant can seek a variation in either the Magistrates' Court or the Crown Court where he has been committed to the Crown Court for trial or sentence; Bail Act 1976, s.3(8)

[59] The prosecution can appeal to the Supreme Court against a High Court's decision to release an accused on bail. However, this possibility is available only where the prosecution is alleging that the High Court erred in law. See, *e.g. DPP v. Ryan* [1989] I.L.R.M. 333; *People (Attorney General) v. Gilliland* [1986] I.L.R.M. 357. By contrast, in England and Wales the Bail Act 1976 permits the prosecution to apply for the imposition of, or a variation in, the conditions of bail; see s.3(8).

[60] *R v. Nottingham Justices, ex p. Davies* [1981] Q.B. 38. The strictness of this rule is relaxed in the case of a defendant who is arrested without warrant and brought straight to court from the police station. In such cases the defence will have had little opportunity to prepare their case for bail. Accordingly, the Divisional Court in *ex p. Davies* accepted that a full bail application should be heard on the occasion of the second appearance in these cases. Note also that even at committal proceedings the English courts do not recognise an automatic right to re-open the arguments for bail; *R v. Slough Justices, ex p. Duncan* (1982) 75 Cr. App R. 384. In most cases, however, the defence will be able to point to new considerations sufficient to justify a full application at the committal proceedings; see Emmins (6th ed., at 22.5.1.).

render that outcome more likely. If there are no objections the judge will go on to consider what conditions if any to attach to the bail order. If there are objections the defence will be asked if they are applying for bail. Normally[61] this will elicit a positive response in which case the prosecution will proceed to present their objections. These are usually offered by a member of the Garda Síochána giving evidence on oath. Where this includes a reference to the defendant's previous convictions the preferred practice is to hand a list of those convictions to the judge rather than referring to them orally in open court.[62] The member will be subject to cross-examination by the defence. The scope for effective cross examination, however, is limited owing to the fact that much of the member's evidence will be based on speculation and opinion. This is followed by a defence submission in which the defence counsel or solicitor (if the defendant is legally represented) will emphasise the factors in favour of granting bail.

At the conclusion of these submissions the judge will announce his decision. Where the decision is in favour of granting bail and is subject to the provision of sureties it is always possible that the prosecution will challenge the suitability of the bailsmen presented by the defendant. In this event it is for the judge to satisfy himself as to the substance, reliability and independence of any bailsman (see below para 10–57 *et seq.*).[63] He will normally do this on the basis of questions put to the bailsman in person and submissions from both the prosecution and the defence. Ultimately the decision on the suitability of a bailsman is a matter for the judge. Additionally, the judge may direct that a sum of money equivalent to the amount of bail be accepted in lieu of a surety or sureties.[64]

Reasons

10–13 There is no specific provision obliging a District Court judge (or any other tribunal) to give reasons for allowing or refusing bail.[65] This omission can be significant in cases where the defendant must decide whether to appeal a refusal or submit a further application. Clearly, he will be in a much better position to make this decision if he knows the grounds upon which his initial application was refused. A statement of reasons will also assist the court which must adjudicate on the appeal or further application. There is no apparent barrier to a defendant requesting a statement of reasons from the judge who has exercised his discretion to refuse bail. Indeed, there is a growing acceptance that a tribunal adjudicating on a dispute may be under a legal duty to give

---

[61] It is always possible that a defendant may prefer to be remanded in custody as, for example, in a situation where the publicity surrounding his alleged offence has generated considerable public hostility towards him.

[62] *R v. Dyson* (1943) 29 Cr. App. R. 104.

[63] Bail Act 1997, s.7(1); District Court Rules 1997, Ord.18, r.3.

[64] Criminal Procedure Act 1967, s.26.

[65] This contrasts with the position in England and Wales where the Bail Act 1976, s.5 obliges the Magistrate's Court and the Crown Court to give reasons in any case where they withhold bail from a defendant who has a right to bail.

reasons for its determination in certain circumstances. This is particularly so in matters affecting the liberty of the individual.[66]

4. Trial Judge

Jurisdiction

Where the accused is being tried on indictment before the Circuit Court or the **10–14** Central Criminal Court the trial judge has jurisdiction over bail from the time of arraignment to the end of the trial. In this context it would appear that the end of trial means the commencement of sentence. The fact that the defendant has been convicted does not of itself deprive the court of jurisdiction to admit him to bail pending determination of sentence. Even where the court may be contemplating a custodial sentence it would appear that it can release him on bail until sentence has actually been imposed. There have also been cases of defendants sentenced to a term of imprisonment being released on bail for a short period to make arrangements for the management of their private affairs before the term of imprisonment commences.

It would also appear that the trial judge has jurisdiction to grant bail pending an appeal against conviction and/or sentence. The point was considered by the Court of Criminal Appeal in *People (Attorney General) v. Kirwan*[67] where the defendants had been convicted and sentenced to twelve months imprisonment with hard labour. The trial judge issued a certificate of leave to appeal to the Court of Criminal Appeal but refused to grant bail pending the appeal. Although the Court of Criminal Appeal also refused to grant bail it acknowledged that bail could be granted in appropriate circumstances pending an appeal even where the defendants had been sentenced to custodial terms.[68] Nevertheless, it would appear that neither the trial court nor the Court of Criminal Appeal should admit an appellant to bail pending a decision on his application for leave to appeal (or an appeal against that decision) unless it considers that an arguable case can be presented for a reconsideration of his case on appeal.[69]

Just like the District Court, however, the trial judge in the Circuit Court has no jurisdiction to admit to bail a person charged with an offence listed in section 29 of the Criminal Procedure Act 1967. Since the Central Criminal Court is the High Court exercising its criminal jurisdiction it can be assumed that it has jurisdiction to grant bail to a person charged with one of these offences.

Procedure

Apart from the fact that the bail issue will normally be initiated by an application from the defence, the relevant procedure in the Circuit Court or Central Criminal Court does not differ significantly from that in the District

---

[66] *Doody v. Secretary of State for the Home Department* [1993] 3 All E.R. 92; *R v. Harrow Crown Court, ex p. Dave* [1994] W.L.R. 98. See also Cragg, "A Duty to Give Reasons?" (1994) 144, 6637 *New Law Journal* 291.

[67] (1950) 1 Frewen 111.

[68] See also, *People (Attorney General) v. O'Callaghan* [1966] I.R. 501, *per* Walsh J. at 513.

[69] *People (Attorney General) v. Hayden* 1970 Vol. 1 Frewen 347.

Court. Where a defendant has been refused bail in the Circuit Court it is at least arguable that he can apply to the High Court *de novo*. In *People (Attorney General) v. O'Callaghan*[70] Walsh J. explained that "the High Court's jurisdiction to grant bail is an original jurisdiction and is in no sense a form of appeal *from any other court* which may have dealt with the question of the bail of the applicant"[71] (emphasis added). Having said that, it would appear that the High Court will be very slow to interfere with the exercise of a District Court judge's (and by extension a Circuit Court judge's) discretion to refuse bail in any individual case (see below para 10–16).

5. Special Criminal Court

Jurisdiction

10–15   The Special Criminal Court has jurisdiction to admit a defendant to bail where he has been charged before the court or sent there for trial by a District Court or has been transferred there for trial by any ordinary court.[72] This jurisdiction applies from the time of the relevant charging, returning or transferring decision right up to conviction or acquittal. Like most other courts, apart from the High Court, the Special Criminal Court has no jurisdiction to admit to bail a person charged with an offence listed in section 29 of the Criminal Procedure Act 1967. Moreover, it would appear that the Special Criminal Court may also lack jurisdiction to grant bail after conviction.[73] The relevant statutory provision states that the Special Criminal Court may admit the accused person to bail up until "conviction or acquittal".[74] A literal interpretation would suggest that this refers to a conviction or acquittal by the court itself rather than any appellate decision by the Court of Criminal Appeal or the Supreme Court upholding or overturning the conviction. However, the Special Criminal Court Rules state that where a trial before the court has been adjourned or where the verdict *or sentence* has been postponed the court *may* order the detention of the accused in custody.[75] This suggests that the court has a discretion in the matter which could be exercised to release the accused on bail.

Procedure

There is no prescribed procedure for a bail application in the Special Criminal Court. In practice it is dealt with in similar fashion to an application in the District Court. It is worth noting that the Special Criminal Court can grant bail with or without sureties.

---

[70]   [1966] I.R. 501
[71]   *ibid* at p. 511.
[72]   Offences Against the State Act 1939, s.43(1)(c) and Offences Against the State Act 1939 Special Criminal Court Rules 1972, rr.16(3) and 18(1).
[73]   Ryan and Magee suggest that the Special Criminal Court does not have jurisdiction to admit the defendant to bail after conviction; *op. cit.*, p. 195. Presumably, they are basing this view on a literal interpretation of the Offences Against the State Act 1939, s.43(1)(c).
[74]   Offences Against the State Act 1939, s.43(1)(c).
[75]   *ibid.* Special Criminal Court Rules 1972, r.19.

Role of High Court

It is arguable that the High Court has jurisdiction to grant bail to a defendant who has been refused bail by the Special Criminal Court. Its full original jurisdiction to determine all questions of law or fact whether civil or criminal should be broad enough to encompass a bail jurisdiction in cases where bail has been refused by an inferior court such as the Special Criminal Court. Moreover, the Offences against the State Act 1939 specifically empowers the High Court to grant bail to a defendant who has been sent or sent forward in custody by the District Court for trial by the Special Criminal Court.[76] In practice, of course, it is unlikely that the High Court would grant bail in a case where bail had been refused by the Special Criminal Court.

6. High Court

Jurisdiction

The High Court has an original jurisdiction to grant bail to persons at various **10–16** stages of the criminal process.[77] The High Court's jurisdiction in this matter is discretionary. It used to be the case that it was obliged to grant bail in respect of an application during the court vacation from a person charged with a misdemeanour.[78] This requirement has been removed by the Criminal Law Act 1997 in the context of the abolition of the distinction between felonies and misdemeanours.[79]

There are at least six situations in which the High Court's jurisdiction to grant bail can arise. First, it has an appellate jurisdiction where a person appearing before the District Court has been refused bail or is dissatisfied with any bail order made by that court.[80] Although there is no uncertainty over the existence of the High Court's jurisdiction to grant bail in cases where it has been refused by the District Court,[81] there has been some confusion over how that jurisdiction should be exercised. Speaking in the Supreme Court in *People v. O'Callaghan*[82] Walsh J. explained that:

> "The jurisdiction of the High Court to grant bail is an original jurisdiction and is in no sense a form of appeal from the District Court or from any other Court which may have dealt with the question of the bail of the applicant."[83]

Speaking in the High Court in the same case, however, Murnaghan J. expressed the view that "it was not the function of this Court to substitute its

---

[76] Offences against the State Act 1939, ss.45(3) and 46(3).
[77] *People v. O'Callaghan* [1966] I.R. 501, *per* Walsh J. at 511.
[78] *ibid.* 512. See also *Re Frost* 4 T.L.R. which relates to the Habeas Corpus Act 1679, s.3 which is identical to s.2 of the 1781 Act.
[79] Criminal Law Act 1997, s.3 and s.16 and Third Schedule.
[80] Criminal Procedure Act 1967, s.28.
[81] *People (Attorney General) v. Duffy* [1942] I.R. 529; *People (Attorney General) v. McCabe* (1944) Ir. Jur. Rep. 41; *People (Cadden) v. O'Grady* (1939) Ir. Jur. Rep. 35; *People (Attorney General) v. Ball* [1958] I.R. 280; *People (Attorney General) v. O'Callaghan* [1966] I.R. 501.
[82] [1966] I.R. 501.
[83] *ibid.* at 511.

opinion for that of the District [Court judge]" on the bail decision.[84] Before the High Court could intervene in this matter it would have to be satisfied that the District Court judge had erred in the exercise of his discretion. The learned judge found support for this view in his own judgment in the earlier case of *Attorney General v. Ball*.[85] The standing of this authority is undermined, however, by the gloss put on it by Maguire C.J. when *Ball* reached the Supreme Court. He did not interpret Murnaghan J's remarks as a denial of the High Court's jurisdiction to overturn a District Court judge's exercise of discretion in a bail decision. Instead he perceived them as a reference to the fact that the District Court judge has the case before him and, by virtue of his legal training and experience in such matters, is the appropriate authority to determine these applications. Accordingly, the High Court should interfere with the exercise of the District Court judge's discretion in these cases only in very exceptional circumstances.[86] The only reported case in which this has happened actually pre-dated the *Ball* decision. In *People v. Duffy*[87] Hanna J. admitted the applicant to bail despite accepting that the discretion of the District Court judge in refusing bail had not been wrongly exercised.

Since the decision was handed down in *People (Attorney General) v. O'Callaghan* the Criminal Procedure Act 1967 has specifically provided a right of appeal to the High Court against a denial of bail in the District Court or against the nature of the bail granted in the District Court.[88] It would appear that this is intended to operate as a re-hearing of the matter rather than a review of the District Court's exercise of discretion.

10–17   The second example of the High Court's bail jurisdiction arises where the District Court has sent or sent forward a defendant in custody for trial by a Special Criminal Court (see para. 10–15).[89] The third example is where a person has served notice of appeal to the Circuit Court from a conviction in the District Court[90] and the District Court judge has refused to admit him to bail, or has failed to fix recognisances or has fixed recognisances which he cannot satisfy.[91] In any of these situations the prospective appellant can apply to the High Court for bail. If this option was not available there would be a grave risk that persons convicted and sentenced to short terms of imprisonment in the District Court would already have served their sentences, or a major part of them, before their appeal against conviction could be heard in the Circuit Court. Given that the maximum sentences which may be imposed by the District Court are relatively low this need not be an exceptional occurrence.

---

[84]   *ibid.* at 502–503.
[85]   [1958] I.R. 280.
[86]   *ibid.* at 286–287.
[87]   [1942] Ir. Jur. Rep. 63.
[88]   Criminal Procedure Act 1967, s.28(3).
[89]   Offences Against the State Act 1939, ss.45(3) and 46(3).
[90]   A person tried and convicted in the District Court has an automatic right of appeal to the Circuit Court; Courts of Justice Act 1928, s.18 as amended by the Courts of Justice Act 1936, s.58.
[91]   The District Court has a discretion to fix recognisances in the event of an appeal to the Circuit Court; District Court Rules 1997, Ord.101, r.4.

The fourth example of the High Court's bail jurisdiction is where a person seeks an order of certiorari to quash a conviction handed down in the District, Circuit or Special Criminal Courts. This jurisdiction can be exercised to grant bail pending the making absolute of such an order. Similarly, the High Court may entertain a bail application from a person in custody pending an application for the making absolute of an order of prohibition or habeas corpus.[92] The importance of this jurisdiction is illustrated by the facts of *State (McKenna) v. Durkan*.[93] The applicant was convicted by the District Court and sentenced to three months imprisonment. Consequent on an appeal to the Circuit Court the sentence was reduced to two months. On the same day that the applicant began to serve his sentence of imprisonment conditional orders of certiorari and habeas corpus were obtained on his behalf. Four weeks later he applied for bail pending the hearing of an application to have the conditional orders made absolute. In granting the application for bail Kingsmill Moore J. explained that if bail was refused the applicant would have served his sentence before the application to have the conditional orders made absolute could be heard. Accordingly, if the orders were made absolute an injustice would have been done to the applicant. This reasoning also supports the jurisdiction of the High Court to grant bail to a person who is appealing a conviction from the District Court to the Circuit Court.

The fifth example of the High Court's bail jurisdiction arises where a person **10–18** has been convicted following a trial on indictment and has sought leave to appeal or where the Court of Criminal Appeal has granted a certificate that a case is fit for appeal to the Supreme Court. Unfortunately, the High Court's jurisdiction in this matter has not been the subject of a definitive decision in the Irish courts.[94] However, the fact that the Constitution invests the High Court with full jurisdiction on all matters whether of law or fact, civil or criminal suggests that it would not be beyond its power to grant bail in such circumstances. Indeed, in *People v. O'Callaghan*[95] Walsh J. intimated that:

> "Apart . . . from any question of bail arising on a habeas corpus application the High Court has a jurisdiction to grant bail to a person who has been convicted as the jurisdiction of the High Court in bail matters as in other matters is considerably wider than that of the Court of Criminal Appeal."[96]

The Court of Criminal Appeal has jurisdiction to grant bail only after leave to appeal has been granted.

Finally, it is worth emphasising that only the High Court has jurisdiction to admit to bail a person charged with any of the offences listed in section 29 of

---

[92] Presumably, this jurisdiction would extend to situations where the custody or imprisonment is not based on the sentence of a court handed down in consequence of a conviction.

[93] 87 I.L.T.R. 62.

[94] In *People (Attorney General) v. Cashell* 62 I.L.T.R. 31, when dealing with an application for bail pending leave to appeal, the Court of Criminal Appeal expressly left open the question whether there was any other method of obtaining bail besides applying to the Court of Criminal Appeal.

[95] [1966] I.R. 501.

[96] *ibid.* at 513.

the Criminal Procedure Act 1967 (see para. 10–07). Also, it probably has jurisdiction where bail has been refused by the Circuit Court or the Special Criminal Court (see paras. 10–14 and 10–15)

Procedure

10–19   The Rules of the Superior Courts stipulate that a bail application from a person in custody shall be made by motion on notice to the Chief Prosecution Solicitor.[97] The application must be supported by an affidavit from the applicant setting out the grounds for his application. Where the applicant is not represented by a solicitor the Court may dispense with the notice of motion and affidavit and proceed instead by issuing appropriate directions.[98] In this event the court may hear the applicant before issuing directions. The content of these directions may differ in accordance with the circumstances of the individual case, but they would normally include a direction that the applicant should be brought before the Court on a date and time specified. Notice of the date and time shall be communicated to the Chief Prosecution Solicitor.

In the bail hearing proper the procedure is virtually identical to that applicable in the District Court. However, when the High Court grants bail subject to the provision of sureties it will set the amount of bail required but the actual recognisances will be entered into before a District Court judge. Accordingly, it will normally be left to the District Court judge, as opposed to the High Court, to determine the substance, reliability and independence of the bailsmen in any individual case. Once recognisances have been acknowledged they must be transmitted to the Central Office of the High Court and filed there.[99] No recognisance can be forfeited or estreated without an order of the High Court.[100] Notice of application for any such order must be served on the parties from whom the recognisance in question was taken.

Where the person seeking bail, whether on an original application or on appeal, is charged with one or more of certain offences listed in section 29 of the Criminal Procedure Act 1967 there is provision for part of the proceedings to be held *in camera*.[101] The offences in question are: treason; an offence under sections 2 or 3 of the Treason Act 1939; an offence under sections 6, 7 or 8 of the Offences against the State Act 1939; and an offence under section 9 of the Official Secrets Act 1963, or an offence under Part II of that Act committed in a manner prejudicial to the safety or preservation of the State. Where the person seeking bail is charged with one or more of these offences and the prosecutor submits an application to the effect that the publication of any evidence or statement to be given or made during any part of the bail proceedings would be prejudicial to the safety or preservation of the State and

---

[97]   R.S.C. Ord.84, r.15(1). See r.15(2) for the appropriate form. Although the Rules of the Superior Courts (No.4)(Chief Prosecution Solicitor) 2001 (S.I. No. 535 of 2001) do not deal specifically with the matter, it would appear that the Chief State Solicitor's role in this matter is now taken over by the Chief Prosecution Solicitor.

[98]   Ord.84, r.15(3).

[99]   Ord.84, r.16.

[100]   Ord.84, r.17.

[101]   Criminal Procedure Act 1967, s.29(3).

that that part of the proceedings should be held *in camera*, the court must make a order directing that the part of the proceedings in question should be held *in camera*. Nevertheless, the decision of the court on the bail matter must be announced in public.

Where the High Court has refused a bail application the unsuccessful applicant can, in principle, apply again and again until successful. In practice, however, a renewed application is unlikely to be successful unless the applicant can point to new grounds or changed circumstances. Alternatively, there is always the possibility of an appeal to the Supreme Court against a refusal of bail, the amount at which bail is set or the conditions attaching to bail.

7. Court of Criminal Appeal

Jurisdiction

Section 32 of the Criminal Justice Act 1924, as amended by section 3(6) of the Criminal Procedure Act 1993 reads:

10–20

> "Leave to appeal shall be granted by the Court of Criminal Appeal in cases where the court is of the opinion that a question of law is involved, or where the trial appears to the court to have been unsatisfactory, or there appears to the court to be any other sufficient ground of appeal, and the court shall have power to make all consequential orders it may think fit, including an order admitting the appellant to bail pending the determination of his appeal or application for leave to appeal."

This clearly confers on the Court of Criminal Appeal a jurisdiction to grant bail not just pending the hearing of an appeal against conviction and/or sentence but also pending the hearing of an application for leave to appeal.[102] The extension to applications for leave to appeal is a consequence of the court's practice either to refuse an application for leave to appeal or to treat the application as the hearing of the appeal itself which it then allows. Accordingly, if the court was unable to grant bail pending the hearing of the application for leave to appeal, there would be a real danger that an accused whose conviction was eventually quashed (or custodial sentence reduced) would secure no benefit as he would already have served his sentence by the time the decision was handed down.[103]

In addition to the power conferred by section 32 of the 1914 Act, it would appear that the court can also admit a person to bail pending a re-trial in a case where the court has quashed a conviction and ordered a re-trial. However, it has declined jurisdiction to grant bail in a case where it has granted a certificate of leave to appeal to the Supreme Court. In *People v. Boggan* the appellant had been convicted on indictment. He sought leave to appeal against conviction to the Court of Criminal Appeal on the basis, *inter alia*, that the trial judge had no

---

[102] Prior to the extension of the Court's bail jurisdiction by the Criminal Procedure Act 1993 the Court lacked jurisdiction to grant bail on an application for leave to appeal; see *People (Attorney General) v. O'Callaghan* [1966] I.R. 501, per Walsh J. at 513.

[103] [2001] 2 I.L.R.M. 102.

jurisdiction to hear the case as the District Court judge who had conducted the preliminary examination had refused to return the appellant for trial. The Court of Criminal Appeal dismissed the application but certified that the case involved a point of law of exceptional public importance for the purposes of an appeal to the Supreme Court. Nevertheless, it refused to admit the appellant to bail pending the appeal to the Supreme Court on the grounds that it had no inherent jurisdiction to grant bail and that there was no provision in the 1924 Act specifically giving it jurisdiction to admit an appellant to bail where it has issued a certificate for leave to appeal to the Supreme Court. Even if it had jurisdiction the Court intimated that it would be reluctant to exercise it in favour of the appellant in this case. Presumably, an applicant who has been refused bail by the Court of Criminal Appeal pending an appeal to the Supreme Court can still apply to the Supreme Court for bail (see below para 10–24). Indeed, it should also be possible to submit an application to the High Court.

10–21   Even where the Court of Criminal Appeal clearly has jurisdiction to admit a defendant to bail it would appear from the reported cases that it exercises that jurisdiction sparingly in certain circumstances. In considering the Circuit Court's refusal to grant bail to the defendants in *People v. Kirwan*,[104] for example, Maguire C.J. said in the Court of Criminal Appeal that: "[t]he fact that the applicants have been convicted by a jury weighs down the scales heavily against them."[105]

In *People (DPP) v. Corbally*,[106] the Supreme Court was called upon to declare the appropriate principles which the Court of Criminal Appeal should apply in granting bail to a convicted person who has sought leave to appeal or who has been granted leave to appeal. Giving the judgment of the court Geoghegan J. made it clear that the fact that the applicant comes before the court as a convicted person would not in itself preclude a decision to grant bail. However, a decision in favour of bail would have to be supported by special factors such as the strength of the applicant's case on the appeal or the possibility that his sentence of imprisonment would expire before the hearing of his application or appeal:

> "I do not think it desirable that the Court of Criminal Appeal should have to go so far as to make a definite determination as to whether 'the appeal is likely to be successful' but I think that there should be enough materials before the court to enable it to hold that there was at least a strong chance of success before it grants bail. I would also agree that the possibility of a sentence of imprisonment expiring before the hearing of an application for leave to appeal or the hearing of an appeal may be a ground for the granting of bail. As far as the certified question is concerned, I think that this Court should simply state that bail should be granted where notwithstanding that the applicant comes before the court as a convicted person, the interests of justice requires it, either because of the apparent strength of the applicant's appeal or the impending

---

[104]   89 I.L.T.R. 120.
[105]   *ibid.* at 123. See also *People v. Sigal* [1946] Ir. Jur. Rep. 21.
[106]   *ibid.* at 107–108.

expiry of the sentence or some other special circumstances. It must always be borne in mind that the applicant for bail in this situation is a convicted person and the Court of Criminal Appeal should therefore exercise its discretion to grant bail sparingly."[107]

Delivering the judgment of the Court of Criminal Appeal in the subsequent case of *People (DPP) v. Quinn*,[108] Denham J. rejected the argument that *Corbally* was an authority for the proposition that bail should be granted simply on the ground that a sentence would be served by the time an appeal would be heard. She considered that there would also have to be at least a reasonable prospect of the sentence being reduced on appeal. It is respectfully submitted that this is an unnecessarily narrow interpretation of the decision in *Corbally* which appears to leave open the prospect of bail being granted solely on the grounds of the sentence being served by the time the appeal is heard, or because of the strength of the case on appeal or even because of some other special circumstances.

Procedure

The procedure for a bail application in the Court of Criminal Appeal is laid down in the Rules of the Superior Courts.[109] Where the appellant wishes to be admitted to bail pending the determination of his appeal or any re-trial he must, unless the court dispenses with this requirement, serve notice to that effect on the registrar.[110] The registrar, in turn, will notify the State Solicitor. As soon as the court has fixed a date for the hearing of the bail application the Registrar shall notify the applicant and the Chief Prosecution Solicitor. The hearing itself follows a similar pattern to that in a District Court application.

10–22

When admitting the applicant to bail the court shall specify the amount in which he and his surety (if any) shall be bound by recognisance.[111] The registrar will notify the governor of the relevant prison of the terms and conditions upon which the appellant has been admitted to bail.[112] Unless the court orders otherwise the recognisances of the applicant and his surety shall be taken before a judge of the District Court.[113] When the recognisances and sureties have been perfected the clerk of the District Court area of the judge before whom the recognisances have been taken shall notify the governor of the prison of that fact and send the perfected recognisances to the registrar of the court.[114] Once the recognisances have been perfected the governor of the prison is obliged to release the appellant without further order.[115]

---

[107] Unreported, Court of Criminal Appeal, February 15, 2001.
[108] *ibid.* s.90(1).
[109] RSC O.86, r.19.
[110] *ibid.* r.19(1). Notice is served using Forms Nos.9 or 11 as appropriate.
[111] *ibid.* r.19(2).
[112] *ibid.* r.19(3).
[113] *ibid.* r.19(4). The recognisances shall be in the Forms Nos. 10 or 12 as appropriate The clerk of the District Court area in which the recognisance of a surety is taken shall give to the surety a certificate in Form No.14 which the surety shall sign and retain; Ord.86, r.19(5).
[114] Ord.86, r.19(6). Notification to the governor is in Form No.13.
[115] *ibid.* r.19(7).

Bail Obligations

The order admitting the appellant to bail shall require the appellant to be present in person at each and every hearing of his appeal up to and including its final determination.[116] Whenever his case is called on before the court he must surrender himself to such persons as the court shall from time to time direct. He may be searched by them and shall be deemed to be in their lawful custody until further released on bail or otherwise dealt with as the court shall direct. If the appeal is adjourned from time to time presumably the court has jurisdiction to release the appellant on bail during the adjournments. Where the appellant fails to surrender himself at any hearing of his appeal the court may dismiss the appeal and issue a warrant for his apprehension.[117] Alternatively the court may consider the appeal in his absence, or make any such other order as it thinks fit.

Revocation and Variation

10–23   Where the appellant has been released on bail the court may revoke or vary the bail order or enlarge the recognisance of the appellant or of his sureties or substitute any other surety for a surety previously bound.[118] It follows that either the prosecution or the appellant can return to the court for a variation or revocation of the bail order, as the case may be, in the light of changed circumstances from the time that the bail order was first granted. A literal interpretation of the rules suggests that the court's jurisdiction in this matter extends to bail orders issued by other courts pending an appeal. In addition, at any time after the appellant has been released on bail the court may revoke the order admitting him to bail and issue a warrant for his apprehension and order him to be committed to prison.[119] Although the rules express this jurisdiction in absolute terms it can be assumed that it will be exercised only on the basis of just cause.

Where the surety upon whose recognisance an appellant has been released on bail suspects that the appellant is about to depart from the jurisdiction of the court or fail in any manner to observe the conditions of his recognisance, the surety may lay an information before a judge of the District Court acting in and for the district in which the appellant is or is believed to be or in which the surety is at the time.[120] In this event the judge shall issue a warrant for the apprehension of the appellant.[121] When apprehended the appellant must be taken before the District Court specified in the warrant. Having verified the information by oath of the informant the judge shall commit the appellant to the prison in which persons charged with indictable offences before that District Court are ordinarily committed.[122] The clerk of the District Court

---

[116] *ibid.* r.19(8).
[117] Form No.15 is used for this purpose.
[118] Ord.86, r.19(9).
[119] *ibid.* r.19(14). The warrant is issued in the Form No.15.
[120] *ibid.* r.19(10). The information is laid in the Form No.16.
[121] The warrant is issued in the Form No.17.
[122] Ord.86, r.19(11). The warrant of committal is issued in Form No.18.

concerned shall notify the registrar of the appellant's committal and forward to him the relevant information, deposition and a copy of the warrant of committal.[123] Once the appellant is actually in prison pursuant to these provisions, the governor of the prison shall notify the registrar who, in turn, shall inform the court. The court may then give such directions as to the appeal or otherwise as it thinks fit.[124] It is also worth noting that, with a view to discharging himself of his suretyship, a surety can always exercise his right to apprehend and surrender into custody the person for whose appearance he has become bound.[125]

On breach of the recognisance of an appellant who has been admitted to bail, the court may order the estreatment of his recognisance, and may also, on notice to the surety, order the estreatment of the surety's recognisance.[126]

It would appear that there is no provision to appeal a refusal of bail by the Court of Criminal Appeal to the Supreme Court.

8. Supreme Court

Jurisdiction

Article 34 Bunreacht na hÉireann confers the Supreme Court with appellate jurisdiction from all decisions of the High Court with such exceptions and subject to such regulations as may be prescribed by law. Since there is no statute, regulation or judicial decision excluding a bail application from this jurisdiction it must follow that an appeal will lie to the Supreme Court against any bail decision of the High Court or the Central Criminal Court. **10–24**

Procedure

The procedure applicable to the exercise of the Supreme Court's jurisdiction to grant bail on appeal from a refusal in the High Court is the same as that applicable to any other High Court appeal before the court. This is because the Supreme Court's appellate jurisdiction in bail matters, as in all other matters, is concerned with points of law only.

The Rules of the Superior Courts make specific provision for an individual who is appealing against conviction and/or sentence in the Central Criminal Court. He can apply to the Supreme Court for bail pending the determination of his appeal or of any retrial. The procedure applicable is the same as that for an application for bail to the Court of Criminal Appeal pending the determination of the appeal or of any re-trial (see above paras 10–22 and 10–23), subject to the substitution of the Supreme Court for the Court of Criminal Appeal.[127] The rules do not make specific provision for an appeal to the Supreme Court against a decision of the Court of Criminal Appeal to refuse

---

[123] *ibid.* r.19(12).
[124] *ibid.* r.19(13).
[125] *ibid.* r.19(15).
[126] Ord.86, r.19(16). The warrant for estreatment is issued in Form No.19.
[127] *ibid.* r.16.

bail pending its determination of an application for leave to appeal against conviction or sentence or pending an appeal against its decision to deny leave to appeal. Equally, the rules do not make specific provision for an application to the Supreme Court where the Court of Criminal Appeal has granted leave to appeal to the Supreme Court. In *People (Attorney General) v. Boggan*[128] the Court of Criminal Appeal ruled that it had no jurisdiction to grant bail in this case. It would be reasonable to suppose, however, that the Supreme Court has jurisdiction to consider a bail application in both these situations and that the procedure applicable is similar to that for an application to the Court of Criminal Appeal.

C. Principles Governing the Bail Decision

1. Presumption in Favour of Bail

10–25 Detention in custody pending trial can be a source of great hardship. Imprisonment can have severe economic consequences for both the accused and his or her family, in addition to the other strains which it inevitably imposes on their private lives. It also runs counter to the presumption of innocence insofar as an accused is being punished and being seen to be punished even though he has yet to be tried, convicted and sentenced. The very fact that he has been imprisoned prior to the commencement of trial can convey an appearance of guilt. The prejudice that may result is compounded by the fact that imprisonment before trial makes it more difficult for the accused to prepare his defence. It would be reasonable to expect, therefore, that a criminal justice system based on due process would reflect a presumption in favour of bail. In England and Wales, for example, an accused person enjoys a statutory right to bail unless the circumstances of his case satisfy one of a number of criteria set out in Schedule 1 to the Bail Act 1976.[129]

The principles governing the exercise of the discretion to grant bail in Ireland are laid down in a mixture of the common law, the Bail Act 1997 and the Constitution. Traditionally, the common law has always taken the view that an accused person should not be kept unnecessarily in custody, and that therefore there was a presumption in favour of bail. Indeed, the sole purpose of bail is to secure the appearance of the accused person at his trial.[130] In *People (Attorney General) v. Gilliland*, for example, the Supreme Court was of the view that a prisoner should be admitted to bail unless:

> ". . . the party resisting the application for bail has satisfied the court that there is a likelihood that if the prisoner is granted bail he will defeat the ultimate purpose of the imprisonment by absconding."[131]

---

128 [1958] I.R. 67.
129 Bail Act 1976, s.4. This right does not apply where the applicant has been convicted summarily and committed to the Crown Court for sentence, or where the applicant is appealing against conviction or sentence. Of course a court retains the power to grant bail in these circumstances if it otherwise has jurisdiction in the matter.
130 *Per* Walsh J. in *People (at the suit of the Attorney General) v. O'Callaghan* [1966] I.R. 501 at 513.
131 [1986] I.L.R.M. 357 at 360. The court ruled that this is the appropriate test to use in both domestic criminal matters and in bail applications in the context of extradition proceedings.

Punishment or prevention have never been recognised as legitimate grounds for a denial of bail.[132] These basic principles have been modified in part as a result of the 1996 constitutional referendum on bail which resulted in the insertion of Article 40.4.7° into the Constitution and the subsequent enactment of the Bail Act 1997.

2. The Constitutional Background

Background

The overriding constitutional principles governing bail were addressed most famously by Walsh J. in *People (Attorney General) v. O'Callaghan*.[133] In that case the defendant had been returned for trial on charges of larceny, breaking and entering, malicious damage, receiving, resisting arrest and assault. All these offences were alleged to have been committed while he was on bail in respect of other charges. The Attorney General contested the defendant's application for bail in the High Court on the ground that he would endeavour to evade justice by interfering with the witnesses. In the course of his judgment refusing bail Murnaghan J. declared that the fundamental matter which the court must consider on a bail application is the likelihood of the prisoner attempting to evade justice. He proceeded to list the factors which should, where appropriate, be taken into account when assessing whether it was likely that the prisoner would attempt to evade justice. One of these concerned the likelihood of the accused committing further offences if released on bail. The defendant appealed successfully to the Supreme Court against the High Court's refusal to grant bail. In delivering the judgment of the Supreme Court Walsh J. took the opportunity to review the principles governing bail in Ireland and, in particular, the notion that bail could be refused in order to prevent the defendant from committing further offences pending his trial.

10–26

Preventative Detention

Although there were English precedents which appeared to accept the relevance of this factor Walsh J. declared emphatically that "it is a form of preventative justice which has no place in our legal system and is quite alien to the true purposes of bail."[134] To accept the admissibility of this factor would be to accept that an individual could be imprisoned to prevent him from committing an offence, that he could be punished for an offence of which he has not been convicted and that he could be punished on the basis of a mere likelihood that he might commit an offence in the future.[135] In Walsh J.'s view none of these

---

[132] *People (Attorney General) v. O'Callaghan op. cit*, above n.133; *DPP v. Ryan* [1989] I.L.R.M. 333. See also, *R v. Rose* 67 L.J.Q.B. 289; *Re Frost* 4 T.L.R. 757.

[133] [1966] I.R. 501.

[134] *op. cit.* at 516, also, Finlay C.J. in *DPP v. Ryan* [1989] I.L.R.M. 333 was of the opinion that there is no basis in the common law for saying that a likelihood of committing crime while on bail is a permissible ground for refusing bail; at 337.

[135] In *People (Attorney General) v. Gilliland* [1986] I.L.R.M. 357 the Supreme Court was of the view that the State's duty in making the prisoner available for extradition or trial must operate in a way

objectives had any place in the Irish legal system. Indeed, he considered that a refusal of bail on the ground of a defendant's propensity to commit offences if released would raise an issue of constitutionality:

> "In this country it would be quite contrary to the concept of personal liberty enshrined in the Constitution that any person should be punished in respect of any matter upon which he has not been convicted or that in any circumstances he should be deprived of his liberty upon only the belief that he will commit further offences if left at liberty, save in the most extraordinary circumstances carefully spelled out by the Oireachtas and then only to secure the preservation of public peace and order or the public safety and the preservation of the State in a time of national emergency or in some situation akin to that."[136]

10–27 Of course, Walsh J.'s treatment of this individual factor in *O'Callaghan* was *obiter*. However, the matter was raised directly before the Supreme Court in *DPP v. Ryan*.[137] In this case the accused was refused bail in the District Court on the ground that he was likely to commit further offences if released on bail. On appeal, the President of the High Court considered himself bound by *O'Callaghan* to admit the accused to bail as the only objection was the belief that the accused would commit further offences if released. The DPP challenged the authority of *O'Callaghan* on this point on appeal to the Supreme Court. Once again, however, the Supreme Court emphatically rejected the possibility of refusing bail on the ground that the accused may commit further offences if released. It was decided that to hold otherwise would be to accept a form of preventive detention and an invasion of the presumption of innocence, both of which would be unconstitutional. Moreover, Finlay C.J. asserted that:

> " . . . if the discretion vested in the courts in relation to granting bail were to be exercised in an attempt to prevent the apprehended commission of a crime, it would, in my view, constitute an abuse of a power, namely, the exercise of it for a purpose which was outside its scope."[138]

Interestingly, the prosecution had argued that in making the bail decision the court should balance the accused's constitutional right to liberty against other constitutional rights such as the right to life. Accordingly, if it was established that there was a likelihood that an accused would commit a serious offence against the person if released, the court would have a discretion to refuse bail. The Supreme Court rejected this proposition partly on the basis that it would amount to the criminalisation of intention. Not only was this something that the court had no power to do, but the prosecution of such a novel offence would create immense practical problems which would be beyond the jurisdiction of the court to resolve.

---

that will not conflict with the fundamental right to personal liberty of a person who stands unconvicted of an offence under the law of the State; at 359.

[136] *People (Attorney General) v. O'Callaghan* at 516–7.
[137] [1989] I.L.R.M. 333. See also, *People (DPP) v. Doherty*, Supreme Court, February 26, 1993; *People (DPP) v. Brophy*, Supreme Court, April 2, 1993.
[138] *ibid.* l at 337.

Campaign for Constitutional Amendment

One consequence of the decisions in *O'Callaghan* and *Ryan* was the **10–28** imposition of a severe restraint on the capacity of the Oireachtas to enact legislation, equivalent to that in England and Wales, permitting a tribunal to refuse bail on the ground that there is a likelihood that the defendant will commit further offences if released on bail. The Garda authorities were particularly vocal in their objections to the constraint, claiming that the commission of further offences while on bail was a standard practice for an increasing number of defendants. The attraction was that since they were going to be convicted and sentenced anyway they might as well take the opportunity for further criminal gain while it was available. Moreover, the likelihood was that the sentence, if any, for these further offences would run concurrently with that imposed on the current charge. Not everyone concurred with this analysis, nor indeed with Garda claims as to the prevalence of offending while on bail. Nevertheless, a specific provision was included in the Criminal Justice Act 1984 for mandatory consecutive sentences for offences committed while on bail.[139] That, however, proved insufficient to mollify the growing public concern over crime during the 1990s.

The Amendment and Bail Act

Eventually the government acceded to the demands for a constitutional referendum aimed at undoing the effects of the Supreme Court's interpretation of the constitutional right to bail in *O'Callaghan* and *Ryan*. The referendum resulted in the addition of the following Article 40.4.7° to the Constitution:

> "Provision may be made by law for the refusal of bail by a court to a person charged with a serious offence where it is reasonably considered necessary to prevent the commission of a serious offence by that person."

This amendment paved the way for the enactment of the Bail Act 1997 which, *inter alia*, permits the court to refuse bail in certain circumstances in order to prevent the commission of further offences by the applicant. This measure came fully into effect on May 15, 2000.[140] The relevant provisions are considered further below. It is worth emphasising, however, that they do not exist in isolation. They merely amend one aspect of the basic common law and constitutional principles governing bail. Accordingly, these principles will be explained first before proceeding to the relevant provisions of the 1997 Act. It is also worth noting that the 1997 Act does much more than make provision for a refusal of bail in order to prevent a defendant charged with a serious offence from committing further serious offences if released on bail. It also makes piecemeal provisions on: the payment of bail money into court, the imposition of bail conditions, the sufficiency of bail persons and various amendments and repeals of provisions in the Criminal Procedure Act 1967. These are considered later in context under relevant headings.

---

[139] Criminal Justice Act 1984, s.11. See also, further amendment effected by s.10 of the Bail Act 1997.

[140] Bail Act 1997, s.13(2) and Bail Act 1997 (Commencement) Order 2000.

3. Surrendering to Trial

10–29 In *O'Callaghan* the Supreme Court confirmed the established common law position that the fundamental test to be applied in deciding whether to grant bail was the likelihood of the accused appearing for his trial if released on bail. Walsh J., in particular, acknowledged that the common law offered a number of guidelines which all courts must respect in applying this fundamental test to the facts of an individual case and that these guidelines had been the subject of elaboration over the years. The learned judge then proceeded to review the extent to which the factors identified by Murnaghan J. in the High Court were consistent with these guidelines. While due allowance must now be made for the change effected by the Bail Act 1997 the result is an authoritative statement of factors that can be taken into account and factors that must not be taken into account by an Irish court when determining a bail application.

Three of the factors that can be taken into account are the seriousness of the charge, the nature of the evidence supporting the charge and the likely sentence on conviction. All of these concern aspects of the case against the accused which could influence his decision whether to appear for the trial. If, for example, the accused was facing a very serious charge which would carry a long prison sentence and the evidence against him was compelling it might reasonably be considered that he had little to lose by absconding before the trial. A court might reasonably exercise its discretion to refuse bail in such a case.[141] If, on the other hand, the charge was relatively minor, the risk of a lengthy prison sentence was remote and the evidence was purely circumstantial the presumption would have to be in favour of releasing the defendant on bail in the absence of other relevant factors.

10–30 Consideration of the likely sentence that would be imposed in the event of conviction raises the issue of the accused's prior criminal record. Walsh J. recognised that the record is relevant and that it may be proper to introduce it as evidence in a bail hearing in some cases, particularly where the accused has a bad criminal record. At the same time, however, the learned judge acknowledged that it would be most undesirable if a defendant's criminal record was referred to in a manner which could prejudice the pending trial. Accordingly, he laid down some qualifications on its use. First, the tribunal which hears evidence of the defendant's previous record should not be the tribunal of trial. This precludes resort to the record where the bail application is made during the course of the trial. Second, the learned judge was of the opinion that such evidence should be adduced only where the nature of the previous convictions would probably cause the trial judge to add substantially to the penalty he might otherwise have imposed in the event of conviction. This suggests the need for some degree of similarity between the substance of the current charge and the contents of the previous record. Third, the record would have to be properly proved and be open to the same examination and

---

[141] See, *e.g. State v. Purcell* [1926] I.R. 207 where bail was refused to an accused on a capital murder charge.

comment on the part of the defendant as it would have been if produced after conviction. Fourth, there should also be weighed in the balance in favour of bail the fact that the defendant appeared for trial on previous occasions. By the same token, however, a defendant's failure to answer to bail on a previous occasion suggests a risk that he may do the same again and fail to appear for trial on the current charges if released on bail. Accordingly, it is a factor that the court could legitimately take into account in deciding to refuse bail.[142]

It will be seen later that a defendant's criminal record is one of the factors which a court must take into account when deciding whether to exercise its discretion to refuse bail under the Bail Act 1997. That Act includes a number of provisions designed to protect the defendant against prejudice arising from the contents of his previous criminal record being disclosed in court in advance of his trial. While these particular provisions relate specifically to the exercise of the judge's statutory discretion to refuse bail in certain circumstances, it is reasonable to expect that they will also inform the judicial approach when an accused's criminal record is raised in the context of bail applications generally.

4. Evading Justice

Even before the constitutional amendment and the enactment of the Bail Act 1997 it was evident that the prospects of the defendant appearing for trial was not the sole basis upon which a decision to refuse bail could be justified. Indeed, there was no doubt that the likelihood of the defendant committing certain offences while on bail awaiting trial would be a legitimate ground upon which to deny bail, if those offences were aimed at evading justice by means other than failing to surrender for trial. In *O'Callaghan*, for example, the possibility that the defendant may interfere with prospective witnesses or jurors, and the likelihood that he may destroy or conceal evidence were accepted by Walsh J. as factors that the tribunal could legitimately take into account in deciding whether to grant bail. The learned judge went on to say that these factors should be used as grounds to refuse bail only where it is reasonably probable that the events in question will occur if bail is granted.

The inclusion of these factors certainly appear to call into question the notion that the key issue is whether the defendant will surrender to trial. Walsh J. was alive to this apparent anomaly in *O'Callaghan*. Nevertheless, he felt that factors such as interfering with witnesses or jurors or destroying or concealing evidence were relevant as indicating a desire to evade justice. The evasion of justice, however, would appear to be broad enough to encompass a failure to surrender to trial. It is submitted, therefore, that the former is the true fundamental principle and that the latter is merely an important aspect of it.[143] Support for this broader interpretation of the fundamental principle is

10–31

---

[142] See, *e.g.*, *DPP v. Desmond* unreported, High Court, April 25, 2001.

[143] See also *People v. Crosbie* [1966] I.R. 426. In *Attorney General v. Kervick* unreported, Supreme Court, July 29, 1971, Walsh J. used the expression "evading justice" to mean that the accused "would probably destroy evidence, interfere with witnesses or fail to appear for his trial"; at 7.

forthcoming from the Supreme Court's decision in *DPP v. Ryan*.[144] Referring specifically to the *O'Callaghan* case and other authorities, Finlay C.J. stated that:

> "the established reasons for the refusal of bail all come within the broad category of preventing the evasion of justice, either by the accused absconding; by the accused interfering with witnesses; or by the accused destroying, concealing or otherwise interfering with physical evidence."[145]

Since the decisions in *O'Callaghan* and *Ryan* the Constitution has been amended and the Bail Act 1997 enacted. These make it clear that the fundamental principle or principles governing bail must now incorporate the notion that bail can be refused in certain circumstances in order to prevent the defendant from committing further offences while on bail, even if those offences are not concerned with an attempt to evade justice.

5. Committing Further Offences

The Statutory Provision

10–32   The Bail Act 1997 enables a court to refuse bail in certain circumstances in order to prevent the commission of further offences by the person seeking bail. The key provision reads:

> "Where an application for bail is made by a person charged with a serious offence, a court may refuse the application if the court is satisfied that such refusal is reasonably considered necessary to prevent the commission of a serious offence by that person."[146]

The individual elements of this provision require further analysis.

A Serious Offence

10–33   Before the provision can come into play the person concerned must actually be charged with a serious offence which is defined as:

> " . . . an offence specified in the *schedule* for which a person of full capacity and not previously convicted may be punished by a term of imprisonment for a term of five years or by a more severe penalty."[147]

This definition is rather clumsy compared with the Criminal Law Act 1997 which uses similar, although not identical, terms for the definition of an arrestable offence.[148] It is also worth emphasising that if an offence is not listed in the Schedule bail cannot be refused to a defendant charged with that offence solely to prevent him from committing further offences while free on

---

144   [1989] I.L.R.M. 333.
145   *ibid.* at 337.
146   Bail Act 1997, s.2(1).
147   *ibid.* s.1(1).
148   The inclusion of the words "a term of" immediately prior to "imprisonment" is rather cumbersome given the inclusion of the words "for a term" immediately after "imprisonment". Presumably, nothing would be lost in the intended sense of the definition if the words "a term of" were omitted.

bail. Presumably, the Schedule will have to be amended from time to time to incorporate new offences where it is intended that bail can be denied to defendants charged with such offences in order to prevent them committing further offences if released on bail.

The first requirement is that the offence must be specified in the Schedule to the Act. These are:[149]

- Murder,
- Manslaughter,
- Rape,
- Any offence under the following provisions of the Non-Fatal Offences against the Person Act 1997
  - section 3 (assault causing harm)
  - section 4 (causing serious harm)[150]
  - section 5 (threats to kill or cause serious harm)
  - section 6 (syringe, etc., attacks)
  - section 7(1) (possession of syringe, etc., in certain circumstances)
  - section 8 (placing or abandoning syringe)
  - section 9 (coercion)
  - section 10 (harassment)
  - section 13 (endangerment)
  - section 14 (endangering traffic)
  - section 15 (false imprisonment)
  - section 16 (abduction of child by parent, etc.,)
  - section 17 (abduction of child by other persons)
- Assault with intent to cause bodily harm or commit an indictable offence (Criminal Justice (Public Order) Act 1994, s.18)
- Assault or obstruction of peace officer (Criminal Justice (Public Order) Act 1994, s.19)
- Incest by males (Punishment of Incest Act 1908, s.1)
- Incest by female of or over 17 years (Punishment of Incest Act 1908)
- Defilement of girl under 15 years of age (Criminal Law Amendment Act 1935, s.1)
- Defilement of girl between the ages of 15 and 17 (Criminal Law Amendment Act 1935, s.2)
- Sexual assault (Criminal Law (Rape) Amendment Act 1990, s.2)
- Aggravated sexual assault (Criminal Law (Rape) Amendment Act 1990, s.3)
- Section 4 rape (Criminal Law (Rape) Amendment Act 1990, s.4)

---

[149] Schedule to the Bail Act 1997, as amended by the Non-Fatal Offences against the Person Act 1997, s.30.

[150] The legislative text actually says "causing harm" but the offence it refers to in s.4 is causing serious harm.

- Buggery of persons under 17 years of age (Criminal Law (Sexual Offences) Act 1993, s.3)
- Protection of mentally impaired persons (Criminal Law (Sexual Offences) Act 1993, s.5)
- Organisation, etc., of prostitution (Criminal Law (Sexual Offences) Act 1993, ss.9 and 11)
- Causing explosion likely to endanger life or damage property (Explosive Substances Act 1883, s.2)
- Possession, etc., of explosive substances (Explosive Substances Act 1883, s.3)
- Making or possessing explosives in suspicious circumstances (Explosives Substances Act 1883, s.4)
- Possessing firearm or ammunition with intent to endanger life or cause serious injury to property (Firearms Act 1925, s.15)
- Possession of firearm while taking vehicle without authority (Firearms Act 1964, s.26)
- Use of firearm to resist arrest or aid escape (Firearms Act 1964, s.27)
- Possession of firearm or ammunition in suspicious circumstances (Firearms Act 1964, s.27A)
- Carrying firearm with criminal intent (Firearms Act 1964, s.27B)
- Reckless discharge of firearm (Firearms and Offensive Weapons Act 1990, s.8)
- Possession of other knives and other articles (Firearms and Offensive Weapons Act 1990, s.9)
- Trespassing with a knife, weapon of offence or other article (Firearms and Offensive Weapons Act 1990, s.10)
- Production of article capable of inflicting serious injury (Firearms and Offensive Weapons Act 1990, s.11)
- Any offence under the Larceny Acts, 1916–1990
- Damaging property (Criminal Damage Act 1991, s.2)
- Threat to damage property (Criminal Damage Act 1991, s.3)
- Possessing any thing with intent to damage property (Criminal Damage Act 1991, s.4)
- Dangerous driving causing death or serious bodily harm (Road Traffic Act 1961, s.53)
- Taking vehicle without authority (Road Traffic Act 1961, s.112)
- Unlawful seizure of aircraft (Air Navigation and Transport Act 1973, s.11)
- Unlawful acts against safety of aviation (Air Navigation and Transport Act 1975, s.3)
- Unlawful seizure of vehicles (Criminal Law (Jurisdiction) Act 1976, s.10)

- Personating the owner of certain stock and transferring or receiving or endeavouring to transfer or receive stock or dividends (Forgery Act 1861, s.3)
- Forgery of certain documents with intent to defraud (Forgery Act 1913, s.2)
- Forgery of certain documents with intent to defraud or deceive (Forgery Act 1913, s.3)
- Forgery of seals and dies (Forgery Act 1913, s.5)
- Demanding property on forged documents (Forgery Act 1913, s.7)
- Possession of forged documents, seals and dies (Forgery Act 1913, s.8)
- Making or having in possession paper or implements for forgery (Forgery Act 1913, s.9)
- Any offence under the Offences Against the State Act 1939
- Treason
- A drug trafficking offence under the meaning of s.3(1) of the Criminal Justice Act 1994
- Riot (Criminal Justice (Public Order) Act 1994, s.14)
- Violent disorder (Criminal Justice (Public Order) Act 1994, s.15)
- Affray (Criminal Justice (Public Order) Act 1994, s.16)
- Being an accomplice to any of the offences listed above
- An attempt or conspiracy to commit any of the offences listed above

Just because an offence is specified in the Schedule it does not follow that it will automatically qualify as a serious offence for the purposes of the Bail Act. It must also be punishable by imprisonment for a term of five years or a more severe penalty. While most of the offences included in the Schedule satisfy this requirement, some do not. Examples can be found among those offences which are designated by reference to the statutory enactments creating them. Some of these enactments create more than one criminal offence. In some of these cases the maximum punishment applicable can be greater or lesser than a term of imprisonment for a term of five years, depending on the presence or absence of one or more prescribed factors. Section 9 of the Firearms and Offensive Weapons Act 1990, for example, creates the offence of possessing knives or any other article with a blade or sharp point in a public place. The maximum sentence which can be imposed on conviction for this basic offence is a fine not exceeding €1,270 or imprisonment for a term not exceeding twelve months or both. Section 9, however, also creates more serious offences. If, for example, the article in question is a flick-knife or is specially made or adapted to cause injury or to incapacitate, or if the person has the knife or other article in a public place intending to cause injury, or to incapacitate or to intimidate any person, then the maximum sentence on conviction on indictment is a fine or imprisonment for a term not exceeding five years or both.

10–34

523

Since the power to refuse bail in order to prevent the commission of a serious offence is available only in respect of offences which are specified in the Schedule and which carry a possible punishment of five years imprisonment or a more severe penalty, it is vitally important to look closely at the particular offence charged. In the example above, the basic offence under section 9 does not qualify as a serious offence for the purposes of the Bail Act. However, the other offences under section 9 clearly do qualify.

10–35 The inclusion of the words "or a more severe penalty" at the end of the statutory definition of a serious offence in this context gives rise to some uncertainty over the exact scope of the definition. Undoubtedly, any offence specified in the Schedule and for which an individual can be punished by a sentence of imprisonment for a term in excess of five years is covered. What is less certain is whether an offence which carries a maximum sentence less than five years imprisonment can also qualify if it also carries an ancillary penalty which, together with the maximum term of imprisonment, might be deemed to be a more severe penalty than a straight term of five years imprisonment.

It is also not entirely clear whether it is sufficient in order to qualify as a serious offence that the offence in question is simply listed in the Schedule and carries a possible sentence of five years imprisonment or a more severe penalty. Many individuals charged with such an offence will apply for bail before a court in circumstances where it is highly likely or even certain that they will not be exposed to a possible sentence on conviction of five years imprisonment or a more severe penalty. These will include not just many juvenile offenders but also adult offenders who will be tried summarily for the offence in question. In such cases the court of trial would not have jurisdiction to sentence them to imprisonment for a term of five years or a more severe penalty. If such facts are known at the time to the court dealing with the bail application the question arises whether the offence in question can be treated as a serious offence for the purposes of the bail application.

The general sense of the definition suggests that an offence will be treated as a serious offence simply if it is listed in the Schedule and carries a possible prison sentence of five years or a more severe penalty. It will not matter that the defendant is a juvenile as the definition applies a test of the sentence which can be imposed on a person of full capacity and not previously convicted. The position with respect to an offence which is to be tried summarily is less clear. If, for example, the court before whom the bail application is brought knows at the time that the offence is to be tried summarily and, as such, cannot be punished by imprisonment for a term of five years or a more severe penalty, it is at least arguable that it cannot treat the offence as a serious offence for the purposes of the Bail Act. This, however, would result in tremendous uncertainty over the definition of a serious offence in this context. A more likely interpretation is that all offences which are specified in the Schedule and which carry a possible sentence of five years imprisonment or a more severe penalty qualify as serious offences, even though there will be cases in which the facts are such that a penalty of this nature cannot be imposed. It is also worth noting that when the court is deciding whether to exercise its jurisdiction to refuse bail under the Act in the case of a person charged with a serious offence, it can take into account the individual circumstances of the case (see below para 10–37). Nevertheless, it is worth remembering that Article 40.4.7° specifically limits the provision for a denial of bail to prevent the commission of a further offence to, *inter alia*, the situation where a person is charged with a serious offence. There is always the possibility that an offence which qualifies as serious under the Bail Act will not qualify as serious for the purposes of Article 40.4.7°.

The Discretion and Statutory Criteria

It is important to note that bail cannot be refused automatically under the Act simply because the accused is likely to commit further offences if released on bail. The court must be satisfied that a remand in custody is reasonably considered necessary to prevent the accused from committing a serious offence within the scope of the Act.[151] Where the court is satisfied that the basic condition is met it has a discretion to refuse bail. In exercising this discretion the court is obliged to take into account the following statutory criteria:[152] **10–36**

1. the nature and degree of seriousness of the offence charged and the sentence likely to be imposed on conviction;

2. the nature and degree of seriousness of the offence apprehended and the sentence likely to be imposed on conviction;

3. the nature and strength of the evidence in support of the charge;

4. any conviction of the accused person for an offence committed while he or she was on bail;

5. any previous convictions of the accused person including any conviction the subject of an appeal (which has neither been determined nor withdrawn) to a court;

6. any other offence in respect of which the accused person is charged and is awaiting bail.

Then there is an unusual provision which stipulates that where the court has taken into account one or more of these factors, it may also take into account the fact that the accused person is addicted to a controlled drug within the meaning of the Misuse of Drugs Act 1977. **10–37**

This last provision is particularly difficult to interpret. It only arises where the court has taken one or more of the six prescribed criteria into account, despite the fact that the basic provision in section 2(1) clearly states that the court must take them into account. Perhaps, the intention is that the drugs angle can be taken into account only when the court has specifically based its

---

[151] The commission of a road traffic offence while on bail would not normally have been sufficient for this purpose in the past; *DPP v. Desmond*, unreported, High Court, April 25, 2001.
[152] Bail Act 1997, s.2(2).

decision to refuse bail on one or more of the six criteria. In this context it is worth noting that the court is not actually compelled to base a refusal of bail on one or more of the six criteria. It is simply required to take them into account in deciding whether a refusal is reasonably considered necessary to prevent the accused from committing a serious offence. The corollary would appear to be that if the court does not base its bail decision on at least one of these criteria, it should not take into account the fact that the accused person is addicted to a controlled drug within the meaning of the Misuse of Drugs Act 1977. Indeed, it is difficult to determine the purpose behind the inclusion of this provision relating to the accused's addiction. It is possible that the legislative intention was to ensure that the judge will take into account the impact that a denial of bail would have on an individual who was addicted to a controlled drug. Equally, it could be that the intent was to make it more difficult for a drug addict to secure bail, on the assumption that he might continue to commit serious offences to feed his drug habit while free on bail. Unfortunately, it is not clear from the words used in the statutory provision what the legislative intention is in this matter.

Another problem that will arise here is how the court can determine the "fact" that the accused person is addicted to a controlled drug within the meaning of the Misuse of Drugs Act 1977. The 1977 Act permits the court to order a report to be compiled on the circumstances of an individual who has been convicted of a drugs offences. On submission of such a report the court has a wider range of sentencing options than otherwise would be the case. These can be used, for example, to address the individual's addiction as disclosed by the report. The Bail Act, however, does not contain any comparable provisions nor does it specify how addiction can be established. It also does not address the issues of where the burden of proof lies nor the standard of proof applicable in this matter.

10–38   It is apparent that of all the statutory criteria which the judge must take into account in exercising his or her discretion to refuse bail under this provision only one relates directly to the offence which it is apprehended the accused might commit if he is let out on bail. Also, the legislation states that in determining whether the refusal of an application for bail is reasonably considered necessary to prevent the commission of a serious offence by the defendant, it shall not be necessary for the court to be satisfied that the commission of a specific offence by the defendant is apprehended.[153] It would appear, therefore, that it would be quite sufficient if the court having considered the statutory criteria was satisfied that the defendant was the type of person who was likely to commit any serious offence within the scope of the legislation if freed on bail.

Three of the other criteria might be considered indirectly relevant to the defendant's propensity to commit further offences if released on bail. Two of these relate to his past criminal record while the third concerns any other offence or offences for which he is awaiting trial. If the accused has a record

---

[153]   *ibid.* s.2(3).

of repetitive offending it could be argued that there is a greater likelihood that he would continue to offend if released on bail. That, however, does not necessarily explain the inclusion of "any other offence in respect of which he is charged and is awaiting trial". It is difficult to see how the fact that the accused has been charged with or is awaiting trial for one or more other offences should be relevant to his propensity to commit further offences. Since he has not been convicted of the offence or offences with which he has been charged or is awaiting trial they cannot be used as a reliable indicator of his propensity to commit further charges.[154]

It is even more difficult to see how the remaining two criteria, namely the seriousness of the offence with which he is currently charged and the strength of the evidence, could be relevant to his propensity to commit further offences while on bail. The only remote possibility is that an individual charged with a very serious offence who is virtually certain to be convicted and sentenced to a long term of imprisonment might be considered to have an incentive to commit further offences if released on bail as he had nothing to lose.

10–39 It may be, of course, that these five criteria could be very relevant to a decision not to refuse bail. It could be, for example, that the offence with which the defendant is charged is a serious offence within the scope of the definition laid down in the legislation. The particular circumstances of the offence and the offender, however, may be such that it is highly unlikely that a custodial sentence would be handed down or even that a conviction would be returned. The judge would be alerted to these circumstances by having to address the issues raised in the criteria which are not directly concerned with any specific offence which it is considered that the defendant might commit if released on bail. In other words the collective effect of these five criteria would be to personalise or individualise the otherwise abstract definition of a serious offence in the legislation. Accordingly, in appropriate cases the judge could justifiably decline to exercise his or her discretion to refuse bail under the legislation, even though the defendant was charged with a serious offence (as defined by the legislation) even if a refusal of bail might be reasonably considered necessary to prevent the defendant from committing another such serious offence if freed on bail.

Ultimately, the statutory criteria are only factors which the judge is required to take into account when exercising his or her jurisdiction to refuse bail where it is reasonably considered necessary to prevent the defendant from committing serious offences while free on bail. Their presence or absence in any individual case do not compel the judge to exercise his or her discretion in any particular way.

Proving the Statutory Criteria

10–40 The Act is vague on how the prosecution should prove the criteria which the judge must take into consideration in satisfying himself or herself that a

---

[154] O'Higgins, "Bail – A Privilege or a Right?" (1998) 3 *Bar Review* 318 at 319.

refusal of bail is reasonably considered necessary to prevent the commission of a serious offence by the person concerned. The difficulties that may arise here were touched on above with respect to drug addiction. However, they apply with equal force to some of the other criteria including, in particular, the nature and degree of seriousness of the offence apprehended and the sentence likely to be imposed on conviction, and the nature and strength of the evidence in support of the charge. The most that the legislation does in this regard is state that the court may, where necessary, receive evidence or submissions on these matters. It is not clear whether concrete proof is required before the court can be satisfied, nor is it clear what standard of proof applies. Indeed, some of the matters are really not capable of proof, given that they relate to something that may or may not happen in the future.[155] Addressing a comparable issue in *Ryan v. DPP*, Finlay C.J. queried whether a bail hearing on this matter might not take on all the trappings of a criminal trial:

> "How can such an intention [to commit a serious offence in the future] be proved and by what standard of proof must it be established? Could there be any grounds on which an accused person suspected of such an intention would be afforded less comprehensive notice of the evidence to be offered against him of the grounds for such suspicion and less opportunity to prepare and be represented to contest such allegations than he is afforded in relation to the presenting of a criminal charge against him? Would every application for bail, accordingly, in which this ground was advanced as the substantial ground of opposition, take on the nature and necessary requisites of a criminal trial?"[156]

10–41   It is also worth noting that the legislation does not address the obligation, if any, on the prosecution to supply the applicant for bail with advance notice of the grounds of opposition. If, for example, the prosecution was opposing bail on the grounds that the applicant was likely to commit a serious offence if released on bail, it is at least arguable that they should supply the applicant with advance notice of their case. This applies not just in respect of opposition under section 2 of the Bail Act but also where it is alleged that the applicant will attempt to evade justice by, for example, intimidating a witness. If the prosecution intends to rely on a witness statement in support of such a criminal allegation, then it is arguable that they should supply the applicant with a copy of that statement in advance.[157]

Prejudicial Publicity

10–42   There is also an issue of how information relevant to the statutory criteria is brought to the attention of the court. Presumably prosecution evidence adverse to the interests of the defendant is open to cross-examination. Nevertheless, there is an obvious danger that the defendant's right to a fair trial could be prejudiced by the publication of details about his criminal record or the

---

[155] *ibid.* and see *Ryan v. DPP* [1989] I.R. 399.
[156] *Ryan v. DPP* [1989] I.R. 399 at 407.
[157] O'Higgins *loc. cit.* at p. 320.

offence itself. To protect against this danger the legislation stipulates that the defendant's previous criminal record must not be referred to in the course of the bail hearing in a manner which may prejudice his right to a fair trial.[158] The court may also direct that the proceedings may be heard otherwise than in public. Alternatively, it may exclude from the court during the hearing all persons, apart from officers of the court, persons directly concerned in the proceedings, bona fide representatives of the press and such other persons if any as the court may permit to remain.[159] It is specifically made a criminal offence to publish information relating to the defendant's criminal record in a report of the bail proceedings in a written publication available to the public.[160] It is also an offence to broadcast such information.[161]

The person or persons who may be criminally liable for the publication of information relating to the defendant's criminal record in this context are defined in quite broad terms. Where the information is published in a newspaper or periodical the persons guilty of the offence are any proprietor, editor and publisher of the newspaper or periodical in question.[162] In the case of any other publication it is the person who publishes it.[163] In the case of a broadcast it is any person who transmits or provides the programme in which the broadcast is made and any person having functions in relation to the programme corresponding to those of the editor of a newspaper.[164] Where the offence is committed by a body corporate criminal liability extends not just to the body corporate but also to any director, manager, secretary or other officer of the body, or a person purporting to act in any such capacity, where the offence is proved to have been committed with the consent or connivance of, or be attributable to any neglect on the part of, any such person.[165] Where the affairs of a body corporate are managed by its members this criminal liability shall apply in relation to the acts and defaults of a member in connection with his or her functions of management as if he or she were a director or manager of the body corporate.[166]

It was seen earlier that Walsh J. in *O'Callaghan* stressed the importance of protecting the defendant against possible prejudice arising from details of his criminal record being disclosed in open court in the course of a bail hearing. Walsh J. was considering the matter in the different context of the prospects of the defendant surrendering to trial. Nevertheless, it is submitted that the

---

[158] Bail Act 1997, s.4(1).

[159] *ibid.* s.4(2).

[160] *ibid.* s.4(3). A written publication in this context includes a film, sound track and any other record in permanent form (including a record that is not in a legible form but which is capable of being reproduced in a legible form) but does not include an indictment or other document prepared for use in particular legal proceedings; s.4(5).

[161] A broadcast in this context is defined as the transmission, relaying or distribution by wireless telegraphy of communications, sounds, signs, visual images or signals intended for direct reception by the general public whether such communications, sounds, signs, visual images or signals are actually received or not; Bail Act 1997, s.4(5).

[162] Bail Act 1997, s.4(3)(a).

[163] *ibid.* s.4(3)(b).

[164] *ibid.* s.4(3)(c).

[165] *ibid.* s.4(6).

[166] *ibid.* s.4(7).

qualifications which the learned judge sought to impose upon the use of a past criminal record in a bail hearing have some relevance to the exercise of judicial discretion under the Bail Act. In particular the tribunal hearing the evidence of past criminal record should not be the tribunal of trial, and the record would have to be properly proved and fully subject to examination and comment on the part of the defendant. By analogy with one of the qualifications cited by Walsh J. it can also be argued that the criminal record should only be introduced where it shows a substantial likelihood of the defendant committing further offences if released on bail.

Appeal

10–43   The Bail Act does not make specific provision for an appeal against a refusal of bail on the ground that the court is satisfied that such refusal is reasonably considered necessary to prevent the commission of a serious offence by the defendant. Presumably the usual appeal provisions apply. Equally, it can be assumed that a disappointed applicant can still apply *ab initio* to the High Court. In either case, however, the court in question will still have to consider and apply the provisions of the Bail Act 1997.

Another possibility for a defendant who has been refused bail on the ground that he might commit a serious offence if released on bail is to submit a renewed application if his trial has not commenced within four months of the refusal. This is dealt with further below under the subheading of *res judicata*.

Consequences of Committing an Offence on Bail

10–44   It is worth noting that section 2(1) of the Bail Act 1997 is not the only provision of the Act concerning the relationship between the grant of bail and the commission of further offences while on bail. It will be seen later that the Act addresses other matters such as the conditions which may be imposed on the grant of bail. In particular it stipulates that when a person is admitted to bail on entering into a recognisance, the recognisance shall be subject to the conditions that the person shall not commit any offence and shall otherwise be of good behaviour.[167] These are mandatory conditions and are in addition to the condition requiring the person's appearance before the court at the end of the period of remand. Critically, this provision is not confined to cases in which the person is charged with a serious offence as defined by section 1 and the Schedule to the Act. It applies to any case in which a person is released on bail, irrespective of the offence with which he is charged. Moreover, this mandatory condition relates to the commission of any offence. It is not confined to the commission of a serious offence as defined by the Act.

It follows that if a person is admitted to bail and commits any offence (or fails to be of good behaviour) while released on bail he is automatically in breach of one of the conditions of his bail. It will be seen later that a warrant of arrest may be issued in respect of such a person. When he is brought on arrest before the court that fixed the recognisances, that court, on being satisfied that

---

[167]   *ibid.* s.6(1)(a).

the person has committed an offence or failed to be of good behaviour, must order the estreatment of the recognisances entered into by the person and by any surety or sureties. Although the legislation does not specifically preclude the possibility of the defendant being admitted to bail again on fresh recognisances, it will clearly be more difficult for him to succeed in any such application.

The commission of an offence while on bail carries the prospect of a harsher sentence than might otherwise have been imposed had the offence in question not been committed while the offender was on bail. Section 11 of the Criminal Justice Act 1984 stipulates that any sentence of imprisonment passed on a person for an offence committed after the commencement of the section (March 1, 1985) and while the person was on bail shall be consecutive on any sentence passed on him for a previous offence.[168] If he is sentenced for two or more previous offences then the sentence of imprisonment for the offence committed while on bail will be consecutive on the sentence last due to expire.

It would appear that the sentencing court is compelled to impose consecutive sentences when the requirements of section 11 are present. However, it cannot impose consecutive sentences under this provision where one or more of the sentences is imprisonment for life or a sentence of detention under section 103 of the Children Act 1908.[169] Moreover, where two or more consecutive sentences are passed under this provision by the District Court their aggregate term of imprisonment cannot exceed two years.[170]

As a result of an amendment inserted by the Bail Act 1997 section 11 of the Criminal Justice Act 1984 impinges upon judicial discretion in determining the appropriate sentence for an offence committed while on bail. It stipulates that in a case where the consecutive sentence provisions of section 11 apply and the court in question is determining the appropriate sentence to impose for an offence committed while on bail, the fact that the offence was committed while on bail must be treated as an aggravating factor. Accordingly, the court must impose a sentence that is greater than that which would have been imposed in the absence of such an aggravating factor.[171] The only exceptions are where the sentence for the previous offence is one of imprisonment for life, and where the court considers that there are exceptional circumstances justifying its not imposing a sentence greater than it would otherwise have imposed had the offence not been committed while on bail.

Presumably this provision applies only in respect of offences which were committed after it came into effect on June 2, 1998.[172]

---

[168] Criminal Justice Act 1984, s.11(1).
[169] *ibid.* s.11(2).
[170] *ibid.* s.11(1).
[171] *ibid.* s.11(4), inserted by Bail Act 1997, s.10.
[172] Bail Act 1997 (Section 10)(Commencement) Order 1998.

6. Other Factors

Prospect of a Speedy Trial

10–45   It is worth mentioning four other factors which were touched upon in the *O'Callaghan* case in the context of matters which might be relevant to a decision to grant or refuse bail. The first is the prospect of a speedy trial. In the High Court Murnaghan J. had suggested that this could be a ground for refusing bail. In the Supreme Court, Walsh J. accepted that if there was no prospect of a speedy trial a court could legitimately decide to grant bail in a case where it was otherwise inclined towards a refusal. The corollary, however, does not hold true:

> "It cannot be too strongly emphasised . . . that the prospect of a speedy trial is not a ground for refusing bail where it ought otherwise be granted."[173]

It is also worth noting in this context that, as explained above, where bail has been refused under the Bail Act and a renewed application is submitted on the ground of delay the court must accede to the application where it is satisfied that the interests of justice so require.[174]

Protective Custody

The second factor concerns protective custody. In the High Court, Murnaghan J. had suggested that bail could be refused in certain cases in order to protect the defendant from the likelihood of personal danger from persons injured or incensed by his offence. Walsh J. repudiated this paternalistic suggestion in cursory fashion:

> "If an accused wants protective custody he need not ask for bail or accept it. A bail motion cannot be used as a vehicle to import into the law the concept of protective custody for an unwilling recipient. An accused person is entitled to as much protection from the law as may be required."[175]

Police objections

The third factor concerns objections from the police or the prosecution. In the Supreme Court Walsh J. acknowledged that the court must pay attention to the objections of the prosecuting authority or the police authorities when considering a bail application. However, he also made it clear that a decision to refuse bail solely because either of these authorities objected would be a violation of the constitutional guarantees of personal liberty.[176] Furthermore, when the objections do relate to the grounds upon which bail may be validly refused they must be supported by evidence[177] and be open to questioning by

---

[173]   *op. cit.* at 518.
[174]   Bail Act 1997, s.3(1).
[175]   *op. cit.* at 517. See, however, *Re Dolan* unreported, High Court, November 5, 1973 where bail was refused on the ground that if the accused was released he would be subject to such threats of violence that, contrary to his present intentions, it was unlikely that he would surrender to his trial.
[176]   *State v. Purcell* [1926] I.R. 207.
[177]   The hearsay evidence of an accomplice has been held to be of scant evidentiary value in this context; *Attorney General v. Kervick.* unreported, High Court, July 29, 1971.

the defendant. The court cannot act simply on the unsupported belief voiced by the objecting authority. It must be satisfied that the objection is sufficient to enable the court to arrive at the necessary conclusion of probability.[178]

Reliability of Bailsmen

Finally, where the court is disposed to grant bail subject to satisfactory sureties, the court must always have regard to the substance, reliability and independence of the prospective bailsmen. Walsh J. elaborated upon this by pointing out that the question whether a prospective bailsman owned his own house was relevant in considering his financial ability to meet the demands of the bail. However, there was no requirement in law that the bailsmen should be householders or own their own houses. To hold otherwise would rule out as prospective bailsmen the large sectors of the population who live in public sector housing mostly in urban areas.

7. Res Judicata

General Approach

It was seen earlier that a refusal of bail in a lower court does not prevent a **10–46** subsequent bail application to the same court or an application to the High Court. Equally, an applicant can submit repeated applications to the High Court. If, however, an applicant has been refused bail after a full hearing a subsequent application to the same court is likely to be met by a plea of *res judicata*. In other words the prosecution will argue that the matter has already been adjudicated upon and should be struck out. In order for an applicant to defeat a plea of *res judicata* he must be able to show that there has been such a sufficient change of cirumstances in his case to warrant a court revisiting the question of bail.

It would appear that there is no reported case setting out the criteria which an applicant must meet before a court will re-open a previously heard bail application. O'Higgins, in an article in the *Bar Review*, identifies the following sample of "change of circumstances" which have been presented from time to time in this context in the High Court, some with greater success than others:

- "The fact that an applicant will not get a trial for an appreciable length of time;

- The fact that there has been a delay in serving the book of evidence;

---

[178] In *Re Dolan loc. cit.*, however, the prosecution objection was based on the evidence of a Garda Inspector who testified that, on the basis of information in his possession and which he believed to be true, the accused would be subject to such threats of violence if released that he would not surrender for his trial. Although the Inspector refused to reveal his source on the ground that it would endanger the accused, Finlay P. was prepared to refuse bail on the basis of this evidence. For the learned judge the fundamental issue was whether the court believed, as a matter of probability on the evidence before it, that the accused would stand his trial. See Ryan and Magee *op. cit.*, p. 190.

- The fact that an anticipated trial date has been lost;

- The fact that new and relevant evidence has emerged (although some judges regard this factor as more appropriately a matter relevant to an appeal to the Supreme Court);

- The fact that an applicant has been unable, despite efforts, to raise or find independent sureties to meet bail conditions previously set;

- The fact that an appreciable length of time has elapsed since the previous bail application."[179]

O'Higgins identifies other circumstances which might arise and which might be relied upon to defeat a plea of *res judicata* in this context. For example, a previously relied upon ground of opposition may have been removed or rendered less significant. Another possibility is a deterioration in the applicant's health or in the health of a family member who has no-one to care for them.

The court's approach to these applications is to treat each case on its own merits and to weigh up the various competing factors so as to achieve a just and reasonable balance.

The Bail Act and Renewed Applications

10–47 The Bail Act 1997 does not address the issue of *res judicata* directly or generally. It does, however, make provision for delay in a situation where bail has been refused under the Act on the ground that the defendant might commit a serious offence if released on bail. The Act stipulates that if his trial has not commenced within four months of the refusal then the person may renew the bail application on the ground of delay by the prosecutor in proceeding with the trial. The renewed application is made to the court which refused bail under the Act. The court may receive evidence or submissions concerning the delay in proceeding with the trial.[180]

On a renewed application under these provisions the court must grant bail if satisfied that the interests of justice so require it.[181] The wording of this provision is unusual in that the application must be brought on the basis of delay, while the court is required to release the person on bail if satisfied that the interests of justice so require. There is at least an implication that the court would be obliged to release the defendant on bail if satisfied that that was in the interests of justice, even though it was not satisfied that there had been delay on the part of the prosecutor. It is also worth noting that the provision is mandatory. The court must grant bail where it is satisfied that the interests of justice so require.

This procedure for a renewed bail application applies only where a person has originally been refused bail in order to prevent the commission of a serious offence. It does not apply where bail has been refused on some other ground. Moreover, it would appear that this provision would not preclude a renewed

---

[179] O'Higgins "Bail – A Privilege of a Right?" (1998) 3 *Bar Review* 318 at 320.
[180] Bail Act 1997, s.3(2).
[181] *ibid.*, s.3(1).

application for bail on some other ground. In the case of the District Court, for example, it has already been seen that a refusal of bail shall not prevent a renewed application at a subsequent appearance or while the accused is in custody awaiting trial.[182] Realistically, however, there would have to be new evidence or circumstances which persuaded the court that the likelihood of the defendant committing further offences if released on bail had diminished, or on the changed facts of the case that the court no longer had jurisdiction to refuse bail in order to prevent the commission of further offences, or that the interests of justice were such that the defendant should now be released on bail.

8. Admission of Hearsay Evidence

Before a court can refuse a bail application it must be satisfied that the defendant will fail to surrender to the terms of his bail, attempt to evade justice or commit a serious offence if released on bail. It follows that evidence on such of these matters as are relevant in a individual case must be laid before the court. Frequently, the prosecution will rely heavily on the evidence of a member of the Garda Síochána that the defendant will not answer to his bail, will attempt to evade justice or will commit a serious offence, as the case may be. The member will have to lay a basis for this belief by, for example, referring to situations in the past where the defendant failed to answer to his bail, the fact that the defendant does not have a permanent address in the country, and so on. It will also happen from time to time that the member will refer to allegations made against the defendant by third parties in order to lay a basis for his belief. This raises the issue of the admissibility of hearsay evidence in a bail application. The matter was considered directly by the Supreme Court in *People (DPP) v. McGinley*.[183]

10–48

In the *McGinley* case the defendant was charged with having unlawful carnal knowledge of a girl under the age of 15 years. The prosecution had objected to his application for bail in the High Court. A detective sergeant gave evidence that he believed that the defendant would attempt to intimidate witnesses if released on bail. In support of this belief he referred to, *inter alia*, threats that the defendant's family were purported to have made to the victim's family not to report the incident to gardai. He also referred to inducements which the former were purported to have made to the latter to drop the complaint. These allegations were denied by the defendant in evidence. Basing himself on an earlier decision of the Supreme Court in *McKeon v. DPP*,[184] the High Court judge considered that hearsay may be admissible on a bail application, and that the judge must attribute to it only such weight as it deserves. He proceeded to deny bail.

The Supreme Court, on appeal, felt that a bail application could not be treated as analogous to an interlocutory application in a civil matter, in which

10–49

---

182 Criminal Procedure Act 1967, s.28(2).
183 [1998] 2 I.L.R.M. 233.
184 unreported, Supreme Court, October 12, 1995.

hearsay evidence is frequently admitted. Given the implications for the liberty of an individual who is presumed innocent the court felt that, at least in general terms, a bail applicant was entitled to expect that evidence upon which the court was going to rely would be given *viva voce* on oath and tested by cross-examination. It does not follow, however, that hearsay evidence can never be admitted in a bail application. In any case where a bail application is contested, the individual's constitutional right to liberty must be balanced against the public interest in the integrity of the trial process. Where there is evidence which indicates as a matter of probability that the applicant would not stand trial or would interfere with witnesses if granted bail, the right to liberty must yield to the public interest in the administration of justice. It is in that context, according to the court, that hearsay evidence may become admissible. However, before admitting it the court would have to be satisfied that there are sufficient grounds for not requiring the witness to give *viva voce* evidence. Where it does admit hearsay evidence the court would have to consider what weight should be given to the evidence, having regard to the fact that the author of the statement had not been produced and to any other relevant circumstances which arose in the particular case.

On the facts of *McGinley* the Supreme Court felt that the High Court had erred in admitting the hearsay evidence. Although counsel for the defendant had objected to the admission of the hearsay evidence no reason had been given why those concerned should not give *viva voce* evidence. In any case where there was a positive conflict between the evidence given by the bail applicant on an issue crucial to the application and the opinion of a member of the Garda Síochána based on evidence derived from other sources, the appropriate course would be to take *viva voce* testimony on oath from the witnesses concerned and submit them to cross-examination. It would be different, however, if there was a legitimate reason why the witness or witnesses should not be called. In *McKeon v. DPP*,[185] the Supreme Court upheld the admissibility of hearsay evidence to support the opinion of a member of the Garda Síochána that bail should be revoked because the defendant was preparing to leave the country with assistance from an illegal organisation. The information upon which the member's opinion was based came from a confidential informant. The police privilege in relation to confidential information was considered to be a sufficient reason to justify admitting the hearsay evidence. Of course, the weight to be given to such evidence would be a matter for the court.

9. Standard of Proof

10–50   It would appear that the standard of proof required on a bail application has not been the subject of a reported case in this jurisdiction. There are, however, a number of dicta which suggest that the civil standard applies, at least for the prosecution when objecting to bail. In *People (Attorney General) v. O'Callaghan*, for

---

[185]   *ibid.*

example, Walsh J., when addressing how the court should approach objections to bail said:

"... they cannot simply be made *in vacuo* but when made must be supported by sufficient evidence to enable the court to arrive at a conclusion of probability and the objections made must be open to questioning on the part of the accused or his counsel. It is not sufficient for the objecting authority or witness to have a belief, nor can the court act simply upon the belief of someone else. It must itself be satisfied that the objection made is sufficient to enable the court to arrive at the necessary conclusion of probability".[186]

Similarly, in *People (DPP) v. McGinley* Keane J. when dealing with the issue of the admissibility of hearsay evidence to support an objection to bail said:

"Where there is evidence which indicates as a matter of probability that the applicant, if granted bail, will not stand his trial or will interfere with witnesses, the right to liberty must yield to the public interest in the administration of justice."[187]

The issue of the standard of proof probably arises most acutely in the context of an objection to bail on the ground that the applicant was likely to commit a serious offence if released on bail. Section 2 of the Bail Act 1997 states that the court may refuse bail if it is satisfied that such refusal is reasonably considered necessary to prevent the commission of a serious offence. It goes on to list a number of factors that the court must take into account when making this assessment. As noted, above, however, the Act does not specify what standard of proof applies to the primary issue and/or the factors which the court must take into account. It is clear, however, that the court does not have to be satisfied (whether beyond a reasonable doubt or on a balance of probabilities) that the applicant will commit a serious offence if released on bail. It merely has to be satisfied that a refusal of bail is reasonably considered necessary (presumably by the police) to prevent the commission of a serious offence.

D. Bail Conditions

1. Amount of Bail

Introduction

Where a defendant is admitted to bail it will be on condition that he surrender   **10–51**
to custody at an appointed time and place. This is normally secured by the defendant entering into a recognisance to pay a specified amount of money which will be forfeited if he fails to surrender to custody at the appointed time and place. The defendant can be admitted to bail on his own recognisance. It is also quite normal, however, for the court to impose a requirement for recognisances to be entered into on the defendant's behalf by one or more sureties. A surety in this context is a person who undertakes to pay to the

---

[186] *People (Attorney General) v. O'Callaghan* [1966] I.R. 501 at 517.
[187] [1998] 2 I.L.R.M. 233 at 238.

court a specified sum of money in the event of the accused failing to surrender in accordance with the terms of his bail. A typical example of bail, therefore, would be a recognisance of €500 from the accused and two independent sureties of €500 each. Where a District Court judge decides to admit a person to bail, he or she may direct that a sum of money equivalent to the amount of bail should be accepted *in lieu* of a surety or sureties.[188]

Common Law

Clearly, the level at which bail is set will have a critical bearing on the prospects of the defendant securing his release prior to trial. When setting the amount of bail the court will have in mind the probability of the accused failing to surrender to custody. It can be expected, therefore, that the greater the likelihood of the defendant absconding the higher will be the amount of bail required. Similarly, the greater the risk the more likely it is that the court will require one or more independent sureties. However, the court is not free to set bail at any figure it chooses. That the common law[189] imposes some restraint is reflected in the following passage from Walsh J. in *O'Callaghan*:

> "Bail must not be fixed at a figure so large as would in effect amount to a denial of bail and in consequence lead to inevitable imprisonment. As I indicated earlier in this judgment both Bracton and Hawkins testify that at common law the Court in fixing the amount of the bail is to be guided by the ability to give bail and the condition or quality of the prisoner, in addition, of course to the other factors, such as the nature of the offence and the gravity of the evidence. If persons come from a humble walk in life or are of little means it is most likely that their friends or those of them who are prepared to go as surety for them are of the same condition and the amount of bail required must be just and reasonable in all the circumstances having regard to the condition and ability of the accused, bearing in mind all the time the overriding test of the probability of the accused failing to appear for trial. Needless to say, any bail which a party can in fact procure cannot be considered excessive."[190]

10–52   It is apparent, therefore, that the court must consider the individual circumstances of the case before it, including the financial circumstances of the defendant and his immediate social circle. Two defendants with similar records facing similar charges in similar circumstances could be set very different amounts of bail and surety requirements, reflecting their different social and financial circumstances. Nevertheless, it is not a requirement that bail must be set at a level which the defendant can satisfy. The nature of the offence, or the defendant's previous record, may be such that the tribunal may

---

[188]   Criminal Procedure Act 1967, s.26. It would appear that an instrument which is evidence of the title of a person to property (other than land or any estate, right or interest in or over land) can be accepted *in lieu* of money. Such instruments include bank, building society, credit union or post office deposit books. See Bail Act 1997, s.5(2).

[189]   "The Bill of Rights, 1688, which provided that excessive bail should not be required did not apply to Ireland and there was no Irish statute corresponding to it, but the enactment was itself declaratory of the common law which did apply to Ireland", *per* Walsh J. in *People (Attorney General) v. O'Callaghan* [1966] I.R. 501 at 518.

[190]   *People (Attorney General) v. O'Callaghan* [1966] I.R. 501 at 518.

reasonably consider that it is necessary to set bail at an amount beyond the personal means of the defendant in order to ensure that he appears for his trial. On a murder charge, for example, the court will have to take into account the increased temptation on the accused to flee from justice in order to avoid the mandatory sentence of life imprisonment on conviction. In such a case if the court does not actually refuse bail it may feel justified in imposing very exacting requirements.[191] The defendant will only be able to secure his release, therefore, if he can persuade others to risk what may be a substantial amount of money to them on him appearing at his trial. The only limitation on the court in such circumstances is that where it decides to admit the accused to bail it must not set the amount at a figure so high as to constitute an effective denial of bail.[192]

Impact of Bail Act

The Bail Act 1997 does not deal directly with the level at which bail should be set in particular circumstances. It is possible, however, that its provisions enabling the court to deny bail in order to prevent the commission of a serious offence by the defendant will impact on the judicial approach to the level at which bail is set in certain cases. Prior to the relevant provisions of the Act coming into effect courts could not deny bail solely in order to prevent the commission of further offences, even in those cases where the defendant's criminal record suggested a strong likelihood that he would commit further offences if released on bail. However, the judges could respond to this situation by imposing stiff bail conditions on the pretext that the defendant's past criminal record increased the likelihood of a long prison sentence on conviction and that this in turn increased the likelihood of the defendant fleeing from justice. Now, however, the judges can deal with many such cases under the Act by refusing bail.

2. Other Conditions

General

Where a person is admitted to bail on his or her entering into a recognisance, the recognisance is subject to the conditions that the accused person shall not commit any offence, and will otherwise be of good behaviour.[193] These are mandatory conditions which apply automatically in every case. The Bail Act also recognises that in any individual case the court may impose such further conditions as it considers appropriate having regard to the circumstances of the case, including any one or more of the following:[194]

10–53

---

[191] In *People v. Crosbie* [1966] I.R. 426 the Supreme Court granted bail on a non-capital murder charge. The terms for each accused were a personal recognisance of £1,000 and two independent sureties of £1,000 each (or four of £500 each) and the surrender of their passports.
[192] Where the District Court has fixed bail at an amount which the High Court considers excessive the latter will reduce it; *Attorney General v. Coleman* 67 I.L.T.R. 183; (1933) L.J. Ir. 138.
[193] Bail Act 1997, s.6(1)(a).
[194] *ibid.* s.6(1)(b).

- that the accused person resides or remains in a particular district or place in the State
- that the accused person reports to a specified Garda Síochána station at specified intervals
- that the accused person surrenders any passport or travel document in his or her possession or refrains from applying for either
- that the accused person refrains from attending at such premises or other place as the court may specify
- that the accused person refrains from having any contact with such person or persons as the court may specify.

The court's jurisdiction to impose these discretionary conditions did not originate with the Bail Act 1997.[195] Indeed, it is clear from the wording of the statutory provision that the list is not meant to be interpreted as an exclusive statement of the conditions which the court can impose. The court may impose such other conditions as it considers appropriate having regard to the circumstances of the case.

Children

Where the person in question is under 18 years of age and is being released on bail by the Children Court, the court may, in the interests of the child, make the release subject to one of the following conditions:

- that the child resides with his or her parents or guardian or such other specified adult as the court considers appropriate;

- that the child receives education or undergoes training as appropriate;

- that the child reports to a specified Garda station at a specified time at such intervals as the court considers appropriate;

- that the child does not associate with a specified individual or individuals;

- that the child stays away from a specified building, place or locality except in such circumstances and at such times as the court may specify;

- such other conditions as the court considers appropriate.[196]

Where a child who is released on bail does not comply with any condition to which the release is subject and is subsequently found guilty of an offence, the court when dealing with the child for the offence may take into account the child's failure to comply with the conditions and the circumstances in

---

[195] In *People (Attorney General) v. Gilliland* [1986] I.L.R.M. 357, for example, the accused was granted bail on terms that he lodge £80,000 in court and report every morning and afternoon at the local Garda Síochána station. Also, in *People v. McCabe* [1944] Ir. Jur. Rep. 41 (conspiracy to commit an abortion) the High Court granted bail subject to the accused surrendering all passports and travel permits.

[196] Children Act 2001, s.90(1).

which that occurred.[196a] This may well result in a stiffer sentence than would otherwise have been imposed. Moreover, this does not affect the court's power under any other enactment to deal with offences committed by a person while on bail.[196b]

Variation of Discretionary Conditions

Where one or more discretionary conditions have been imposed, the court may, on application at any time by the accused person, vary a condition as it considers appropriate.[197] This could entail the alteration, addition or revocation of a condition.[198] The prosecutor will be given notice of the application by the accused and will be entitled to be heard.[199] It would appear from the wording of the statutory provision that on such an application the court could take the opportunity to add a new condition, or vary or revoke a condition apart from that which was the subject of the application, irrespective of whether it accedes to the accused's request for a revocation or alteration of one or more of the original conditions. It follows that the prosecutor might take advantage of any such application to argue for more stringent bail conditions. It is also worth noting that this power to alter, add or revoke a condition applies only to discretionary conditions. It has no application to the mandatory conditions.

Where a person is admitted to bail on his or her entering into a recognisance (with or without a surety or sureties) the court will direct that a copy of the recognisance containing the conditions be given to the accused person and, where relevant, to the surety or sureties.[200]

3. Payment of Moneys into Court

The Bail Act Provision

Prior to the relevant provision of the Bail Act 1997 coming into force, where **10–54** a District Court judge granted bail to a person in custody that person would be released as soon as he and his surety or sureties, if any, had entered into the recognisance(s) required by the court.[201] Now, by virtue of section 5 of the Bail Act it would appear that entering into the recognisance(s) is not sufficient. Section 5 stipulates that where a court admits a person in custody to bail he cannot be released until an amount equal to one-third (or such

---

[196a] *ibid.* s.90(2).
[196b] *ibid.* s.90(3).
[197] In the English case *R. v. Marquess of Blandford*, unreported, where one of the charges was making off without paying a taxi fare, the accused was released on bail on condition that, *inter alia*, he did not use taxis. This condition was relaxed subsequently to permit him to travel in taxis only when accompanied by his solicitor.
[198] Bail Act 1997, s.6(3).
[199] *ibid.* s.6(4).
[200] *ibid.* s.6(2).
[201] Criminal Procedure Act 1967, s.28(4).

greater amount as the court may determine) of a recognisance entered into by the person and by any surety or sureties has been paid into court.[202]

Meaning of "in custody"

10–55   There is a very real danger that this requirement to pay at least one third of the bail up front will at least delay, if not preclude, the release of persons who would otherwise have been released automatically on bail. The matter has arisen before the High Court in respect of an accused whose application for bail was not contested but who was not in a position to pay one third of the bail money up front. Giving judgment in *People (DPP) v. Russell*[202a] Kearns J. explained that in such cases a judge must satisfy himself that the defendant had sufficient funds to cover one third of the bail. If the defendant lacked the necessary funds then bail should be fixed in a purely nominal sum so as not to frustrate the intentions of the court in granting bail. The sum fixed in respect of the defendant's own bail and in respect of a surety should not be so much as to preclude the defendant from securing his release in an uncontested case.

Nevertheless there is still a likelihood that the requirements of section 5 will result in a delay in a defendant securing his release after having been granted bail by a court. Indeed, there may even be some confusion over the scope of section 5. Undoubtedly, it applies to any person who is granted bail at a time when he is in custody on foot of a committal order. What is not clear is whether it also extends to any person who has been brought before a court consequent on arrest. The provision refers to a person who "is in custody". Custody is not defined. It is at least arguable, therefore, that it extends to a person who has been arrested and charged by the Garda Síochána and brought in Garda custody before the District Court for the purpose of being formally charged and remanded. Significantly, the Criminal Procedure Act 1967 also makes distinct provision for the grant of bail to an accused person who is in custody.[203] It, however, specifically defines "custody" to mean a District Court committal to prison or other lawful custody.[204] It is clear, therefore, that the provision in the 1967 Act does not apply to a person who has been admitted to bail on being brought before a court after having been arrested and charged in a Garda Síochána station.

If "custody" in section 5 of the Bail Act 1997 is to be given its literal meaning then that provision has undoubtedly effected a major change to the pre-existing situation. Not only will it require a significant portion of the bail money to be lodged in court before the accused can be released, but it will also apply to virtually every individual who is remanded on bail by the District

---

[202]   Bail Act 1997, s.5(1). This does not apply where the person is under 18 years of age; Bail Act, 1997, s.5(4), as inserted by Children Act 2001, s. 89.

[202a]   Unreported, High Court, May 15, 2000.

[203]   Criminal Procedure Act 1967, s.28(4).

[204]   *ibid.* s.22(1).

Court. Inevitably, this will result in many individuals, who have been arrested and charged and brought before the District Court, being remanded in custody until such time as they can arrange for the required sum or sums of money to be lodged in court. It might seem reasonable to suppose, therefore, that "custody" in section 5 of the Bail Act 1997 is meant to bear the same interpretation which it is given in the comparable provisions of the Criminal Procedure Act 1967. This would ensure that those individuals who are required to lodge in court the equivalent of at least one third of their recognisances before they can be released, are limited to those who are admitted to bail at a time when they are already in custody on foot of a committal order.

It must be said, however, that there are indications that section 5 is meant to **10–56** apply to any person who is granted bail by a court at a time when he is in custody, irrespective of whether the custody is on foot of a committal order or on foot of arrest. For example, subsection (3) of section 5 makes provision for the repayment of moneys paid into court (or release of any security accepted by the court) on foot of recognisances entered into by or on behalf of a person "charged with an offence". The person "charged with an offence" in section 5(3) is the same individual as the person "in custody" in section 5(1). The former, however, clearly encompasses an individual who has been brought before the court for the first time after having been arrested and charged in the Garda Síochána station. This suggests that the expression "in custody" in section 5(1) is not confined to persons in custody pursuant to a committal order. Further support for this interpretation can be found in section 8 of the Bail Act 1997 which makes provision for a warrant of arrest to be endorsed with consent to bail.

Significantly, where a person has been arrested on foot of such a warrant he can be released on bail only upon payment of an amount equivalent to one third (or such greater amount as the court may determine) of the bail in question. This is a significant departure from the pre-existing provision in the Criminal Procedure Act 1967.[205] It is highly unlikely that the legislature would have intended to treat differently in this matter persons arrested under warrant and persons arrested summarily. Accordingly, it seems likely that the requirement to pay at least one third of the recognisances into court before a person admitted to bail can be released applies not just to persons in custody on foot of a committal order but also to persons who have been brought before the court in Garda custody.

Mode of Payment

Where section 5 applies each person who has entered into a recognisance must pay one third (or the greater amount as the case may be) of his own recognisance. The wording of the provision suggests that it is the individual who has entered into the recognisance who must pay the required sum. There is no scope for cross-subsidisation, although, as will be seen below, the

---

[205] *ibid.* s.30 (repealed by Bail Act 1997, s.12).

position is less certain where a security instrument is accepted *in lieu* of money. It is also worth noting that the provision does not specify how the money should be paid into court. Presumably, a payment in Irish bank notes is acceptable. It is less certain whether payment in foreign currency, by cheque or by credit card can suffice.

Despite the uncertainty over the form in which a money payment may be made there is specific provision permitting the court to accept certain security instruments *in lieu* of money. Section 5(2) stipulates that the court may accept as security an instrument which is evidence of the title of a person to property as the court considers adequate. It would appear that this can relate to title to any property, apart from land or any estate, right or interest in or over land.[206] If, however, the security takes the form of a bank, building society, credit union or post office deposit book, the court must make an order directing the bank, building society, credit union or post office concerned, as the case may be, not to permit the moneys on deposit to be reduced below an amount equal to the amount required to be paid into court or the amount then on deposit, whichever is the lesser.[207]

The wording of section 5(2) would appear to leave open the possibility of a single person depositing certain property title instruments *in lieu* of the payment of moneys by any or all of the parties who had entered into recognisances in any individual case. While a literal interpretation of the provision would suggest that the person depositing the title instrument does not even have to be one of the parties who had entered into a recognisance, it is submitted that the deposit would have to come from a person subject to a recognisance.

E. Sureties

1. Sufficiency and Suitability

10–57   In some jurisdictions the accused can purchase a bail surety in the same manner as he might purchase insurance against certain eventualities. In this situation the relationship between the accused and his surety is based on a commercial contract.[208] In Ireland, by comparison, the usual practice is for an accused to seek sureties among his friends and relations. This is implicitly acknowledged by Walsh J. in *O'Callaghan* when considering guidelines on the amount at which bail should be set in an individual case. He said that:

> "If persons come from a humble walk in life or are of little means it is most likely that their friends or those of them who are prepared to go as surety for them are of the same condition"[209]

---

[206]   Bail Act 1997, s.5(2)(a).
[207]   *ibid.* s.5(2)(b).
[208]   Ryan and Magee cite the example of the USA where it is common practice for insurance companies and individuals to act as bailsmen in return for the payment of insurance premiums related to the amount of the bail bond. Ryan and Magee, *The Irish Criminal Process* (Mercier Press, Dublin, 1983), p. 182.
[209]   [1966] I.R. 501 at p. 518.

The relationship is more likely to be personal as distinct from commercial.[210] This in turn means that the court must examine the circumstances of a surety in each individual case in order to determine his suitability. Indeed, the Bail Act 1997 states specifically that a court, when considering whether to admit a defendant to bail, must satisfy itself as to the sufficiency and suitability of any person proposed to be accepted as a surety.[211] In determining the suitability and sufficiency of the proposed surety the court is required to have regard to the following:[212]

- the financial resources of the person;
- the character and antecedents of the person;
- any previous convictions of the person; and
- the relationship of the person to the accused person.

The significance of the financial resources of the proposed surety is obvious. **10–58** The court will want to be satisfied that the surety has the financial resources to cover the amount of his commitment under the recognisance in the event of estreatment. It does not follow, however, that a surety must be a householder or own his own house.[213] The issue under this heading is whether the surety has sufficient resources to meet his obligations in the matter. At the other extreme, presumably the court will also want to be satisfied that the financial resources of the surety are not so extensive that the estreatment of the amount of his commitment under the recognisance would be of little consequence to him. It will defeat the whole purpose of having a surety if the surety in question has little material interest in ensuring that the defendant complies with the bail conditions.

The significance of the relationship of the surety to the defendant is equally clear. It is reasonable to assume that a defendant is less likely to expose a family relation or close acquaintance to the risk of estreatment as compared to a stranger or someone towards whom he felt no sense of obligation. Similarly, it is more likely that a family relation or close acquaintance will be able to encourage the defendant to comply with the terms of his bail. On the other hand the court will want to be assured that a family relation or close acquaintance is exercising a freewill in the matter. A person who is being pressurised by threats into acting as a surety is unlikely to be in a position to discharge the obligations of a surety. A conflict of interest between the obligations of a surety to the court and his obligations to the defendant could also prove fatal. There is authority, for example, that the defendant's solicitor ought not to be accepted as a surety.[214]

---

[210] There is authority for saying that it is an offence at common law to enter into a contract to indemnify a surety against liability for breach of a bail condition; *R v. Porter* [1910] 1 K.B. 369.

[211] Bail Act 1997, s.7(1).

[212] *ibid.* s.7(2).

[213] In *O'Callaghan op. cit.* at 518 Walsh J. observes that when exercising its discretion over the sufficiency of a surety the court should bear in mind that "there is no requirement in law that the bailsmen should be householders or own their own houses."

[214] *R v. Scott-Jarvis, The Times,* November 20, 1976 (Q.B.D.); cited in Ryan and Magee, *op. cit.,* p. 183.

The significance of the surety's character, antecedents and previous convictions are more problematic. It is easy to see how they might be relevant to an assessment of the reliability of the surety and the extent to which he can be trusted to fulfil his obligations as a surety. It would surely be objectionable, however, if a court was to declare a surety unsuitable solely because he had previous convictions or because of some aspect of his character or antecedents unrelated to his capacity to discharge his obligations as a surety. There is common law authority, for example, to suggest that a court cannot reject a surety merely because of his moral character or political opinions.[215]

Ultimately, of course, the decision on the sufficiency and suitability of a person to act as a surety in any individual case is a matter for the court. The 1997 Act merely requires the court to have regard to the matters listed above when making that determination. It is also worth noting that the Act does not attempt to tie the court's hands in this matter by excluding any particular class of person from acting as a surety. Prior to the enactment of the 1997 Act it was well settled that certain persons were ineligible to act as sureties. These included persons under the age of 18 years, persons in custody, persons who have been convicted of infamous crimes and recently discharged insolvents.[216] It is not clear in the light of the 1997 Act whether these persons are still ineligible *per se*, or whether their eligibility is now a matter for the discretion of the court having regard to the statutory criteria listed above.

2. Procedure

10–59   In determining the sufficiency and suitability of a surety the court may, where necessary, receive evidence or submissions concerning the statutory criteria which it is obliged to take into account when making its determination.[217] Before an individual agrees to be a surety it is the practice to explain to him the nature of the obligations involved and the consequences for him if the accused absconds while on bail. The surety will be asked if he has net assets sufficient to cover the amount of the recognisance. If he answers in the affirmative the court will normally accept him as a surety unless the prosecution objects. In the event of an objection the court will consider submissions and, where necessary, evidence from both the prosecution and the defence before making its determination.

Recognisances are normally taken from the accused and his sureties by a District Court judge. This is true not only where the bail has been fixed by the District Court but also where it has been fixed by the Circuit Court, the High Court and the Court of Criminal Appeal.[218] The exception is the Special Criminal Court where the accused and the sureties must appear personally and acknowledge themselves to be bound in the required sums.[219] It may happen

---

[215]   *R v. Badger* (1843) 4 Q.B. 468.
[216]   *The Garda Síochána Guide* (5th ed.), p. 39.
[217]   Bail Act 1997, s.7(2).
[218]   See RSC Ord.86, r.20(4) to this effect for the Court of Criminal Appeal.
[219]   Special Criminal Court Rules 1972, Ord.25.

that a court will fix the amount of a recognisance in which the accused and his sureties, if any, are to be bound, with a view to the recognisance being taken later. In this event the recognisance may be taken later by a District Court judge or a peace commissioner.[220] Until they are so taken, the accused will be committed to custody.[221]

F. Failure to Comply With Bail Terms

1. Absconding

Section 13 of the Criminal Justice Act 1984 provides for a summary offence of failing to surrender to bail. It stipulates that if a person who has been released on bail fails to appear before a court in accordance with his recognisance he shall be guilty of an offence and shall be liable on summary conviction to a fine not exceeding €1,270 or to imprisonment for a term not exceeding twelve months or to both.[222] Such an offence is treated as an offence committed while on bail for the purposes of the provisions on sentencing for offences committed while on bail.[223] In any proceedings for this offence it shall be a defence for the accused to show that he had a reasonable cause for not so appearing.[224] It would appear that the onus of proof for the existence of such reasonable cause lies on the accused. Presumably it can be discharged on a balance of probabilities.

10–60

2. Arrest

Power to Issue Warrant

Where a person charged with an offence has been admitted to bail on entering into a recognisance, the court may issue a warrant for his or her arrest on the application of a member of the Garda Síochána or a surety of the accused.[225] The court can issue the warrant only if the application is supported by information in writing and on oath by or on behalf of the member or the surety to the effect that the accused is about to contravene any of the conditions of the recognisance.[226] It is worth noting that this power can be triggered by an imminent breach of any of the conditions of bail. It is not confined to the situation where the accused is about to abscond. Accordingly, a surety or a member of the Garda Síochána could apply to the court where the surety or member believes that the accused is about to commit any offence, as it is one of the conditions of being admitted to bail that the accused must not commit any offence while free on bail.

10–61

---

[220] Criminal Procedure Act 1967, s.22(3); District Court Rules 1997, Ord.18, rr.12–14.
[221] *ibid.* 1967, s.22(2).
[222] Criminal Justice Act 1984, s.13(1).
[223] *ibid.* s.13(3).
[224] *ibid.* s.13(2).
[225] See District Court Rules 1997, Schedule B, Form 20.2 for the warrant.
[226] Bail Act 1997, s.6(5). See District Court Rules 1997, Schedule B, Form 20.1 for the information.

Police Power under Warrant

Where the warrant has been issued a member of the Garda Síochána may arrest the accused notwithstanding that he does not have the warrant in his possession at the time.[227] In this event, however, the member must produce and serve it on the accused as soon as practicable after the arrest.[228] Once arrested the accused must be brought as soon as practicable before the court that fixed the recognisance.[229] The court may then commit the accused to prison to await trial or until he enters into a fresh recognisance or, if the accused is on remand, the court may further remand him.[230]

Arrest Warrant for Failing to Answer to Bail

10–62   There would not appear to be a statutory power of arrest in respect of an accused person who has actually failed to appear before a court in answer to his bail. Nevertheless, the existence of a power to issue a warrant for the arrest of such a person cannot be doubted. Section 13 of the Criminal Justice Act 1984 clearly assumes the existence of such a power. It stipulates that where a court has issued a warrant for the arrest of a person who has failed to appear before the court in answer to his bail, a member of the Garda Síochána may arrest that person even though he does not have the warrant in his possession at the time of the arrest.[231] In this event the member must produce and serve the warrant on the person as soon as practicable after the arrest.[232]

Certainly, a court order releasing an individual on bail subject to him entering into a recognisance which binds him to appear before that court at a specified time and place in the future would have little practical meaning if the court had no means of enforcing that order. The problem is identifying the source of the power. The failure to appear before a court in answer to bail has been made a summary offence by section 13 of the Criminal Justice Act 1984, and there is authority to the effect that an arrest warrant cannot issue in respect of a summary offence.[233] It would appear, nevertheless, that the District Court Rules 1997 provide authority for the issue of a warrant for the arrest of an individual who fails to appear before a court in answer to his bail.[234] This applies both to a person who was released on bail subject to a recognisance

---

227   Bail Act 1997, s.6(6).
228   *ibid.* s.6(7).
229   *ibid.* s.6(8). If the accused is brought before a judge otherwise than at a sitting of the court for the district in which the order sending him forward for trial was made or of the court before which he was remanded to appear, the judge shall remand him to appear before the sitting at which the relevant order was made; see District Court Rules 1997, Schedule B, Form 20.3.
230   Bail Act 1997, s.6(9). See District Court Rules 1997, Schedule B, Forms 20.4 and 20.5.
231   Criminal Justice Act 1984, s.13(4). See also Bail Act 1997, s.9(1) which refers to a situation where a court has issued a warrant for the arrest of a person who has failed to appear before the court in answer to his bail.
232   Criminal Justice Act 1984, s.13(5).
233   Petty Sessions (Ireland) Act 1851, s.11(1). Woods suggests that this provision takes precedence over any provision in the District Court Rules which purports to authorise the issue of a warrant of arrest for a summary offence. See J. Woods, *District Court: Practice and Procedure in Criminal Cases* (Limerick, 1994) at pp. 141–142.
234   District Court Rules, 1997, Ord.22, r.2.

by a member of the Garda Síochána and a person who was released on bail subject to a recognisance after appearing before a court on connection with an offence. Where the person fails to appear in accordance with his recognisance the judge sitting at the time may, on production of the recognisance, issue a warrant for the arrest of the person in question.[235] No further formalities are required.

Arrest Warrant for Failure to Comply with Bail Conditions

The Bail Act 1997 does make provision for the issue of a warrant of arrest in respect of a person who is believed to have contravened one or more conditions of his recognisance, apart from the fundamental obligation to appear before the court at the time and place specified in the recognisance. The court may issue such a warrant on the application of a member of the Garda Síochána where that application is supported by information in writing and on oath by or on behalf of the member that the accused person has contravened a condition of his recognisance, apart from the requirement to appear before the court at the time and date specified in the recognisance.[236] Where a warrant is issued under this provision it does not affect the recognisances or moneys paid into court. The accused and any surety remain bound by their recognisances, and any money paid into court in connection with those recognisances cannot be released until the conclusion of the proceedings commenced on foot of the warrant.[237]

Once the warrant has been issued, any member of the Garda Síochána may arrest the accused even if he or she does not have possession of the warrant at the time of arrest.[238] In this event, however, he or she must produce and serve the warrant on the accused as soon as practicable after the arrest.[239] A person arrested under such a warrant must be brought as soon as practicable before the court that fixed the recognisance.[240] Apart from the estreatment of the recognisances and forfeiture of moneys paid into court (see below para 10–63 *et seq.*) the Act is silent about the powers of the court to deal with an accused brought before it on foot of a warrant issued under this provision. Presumably, the court can either remand the accused in custody or fix new recognisances for releasing him on bail.

3. Estreating a Recognisance

Overview

The Bail Act 1997 makes separate provision for the estreatment of a recognisance or forfeiture of a sum of money lodged *in lieu* of a surety or sureties in two situations; firstly where a court issues a warrant for the arrest

10–63

---

235 See Form 22.3 in Schedule B to the District Court Rules 1997.
236 Bail Act 1997, s.9(2).
237 *ibid.* s.9(5).
238 *ibid.* s.9(3).
239 *ibid.* s.9(4).
240 *ibid.* s.9(6).

of a person who has failed to appear before the court in answer to his bail, and secondly where a person has been brought before a court on foot of a warrant commanding his appearance to answer the charge that he has failed to comply with one of the secondary conditions of his bail. Both situations will be explained below. It must be pointed out at the outset, however, that the Bail Act obliges the court to estreat or forfeit when issuing the warrant in the first situation or, in the second situation, on being satisfied that the person brought before it has breached one of the secondary conditions of his bail. The court has no discretion in the matter, although it must give notice to the individual and any surety concerned that an application to vary or discharge the order to estreat or forfeit can be made to the court within 21 days of the making of the order. These provisions do not conform easily with the relevant District Court Rules and the provisions of the Petty Sessions (Ireland) Act 1851 and The Fines Act (Ireland) 1851 on the estreatment of recognisances and the forfeiture of money lodged. These confer a discretion on the court to estreat or forfeit and lay down a detailed application and enforcement procedures.

Unfortunately, the Bail Act 1997 does not make any reference to the rules or the 1851 legislation. The best that can be done here, therefore, is to set out the relevant provisions of the Bail Act followed by those of the rules and the 1851 legislation. Since the former go more to the jurisdiction of the court to estreat or forfeit and the latter are concerned primarily with the procedure applicable to estreatment and forfeiture, there is no reason why the latter cannot apply substantially to the exercise of the former. The difficulty arises over the issue of whether an order of estreatment or forfeiture is mandatory in certain circumstances or whether it is always within the discretion of the court. There is also the problem of the relationship between the Bail Act provisions on an application to vary or discharge an estreatment or forfeiture order and the provisions of the rules and the 1851 legislation in the application for and enforcement of these orders.

Estreatment for Failure to Appear

10–64 The first situation in which a recognisance can be estreated or sum of money forfeited under the Bail Act arises where a court issues a warrant for the arrest of an accused person who has failed to appear before the specified court at the specified time and place in accordance with the terms of the recognisance which he entered into on being released on bail. In this event the court shall order the recognisance of the accused person and the recognisance of any surety or sureties to be estreated.[241] The court must also order the forfeiture of the amount paid into court by the accused person and any surety or sureties.

There are a few points worth emphasising about this provision. First, it arises only in respect of a warrant of arrest which issues when the accused person fails to appear before the court at the time and date specified in the recognisance which he entered into on being released on bail. It is not triggered simply by a warrant of arrest which is issued on foot of information

---

[241] Bail Act 1997, s.9(1).

submitted in writing and on oath to the effect that the accused is about to contravene any of the conditions of his recognisance. The warrant must issue for the arrest of an accused person who has already failed to comply with the fundamental obligation to appear before the court at the time and date specified in the recognisance. It is also worth noting that a warrant for the arrest of a person who has already failed to comply with other conditions of the recognisance is not sufficient to trigger the estreatment provision, although (as will be seen below) there is provision for estreatment where a court is satisfied that a person arrested and brought before it has contravened any of the conditions of his recognisance.

Secondly, the estreatment requirement is mandatory. Once the court issues the warrant for the arrest of the accused person who has failed to appear in court in accordance with the terms of his recognisance, it must order the estreatment of his recognisance and the recognisances of any sureties, and the forfeiture of the amount paid into court by the accused and any surety. It has no discretion in the matter. It is also worth noting in this context that the statutory provision is silent about the forfeiture of any property in respect of which instruments of title may have been accepted by the court *in lieu* of the payment of moneys into court. It would appear, therefore that the court cannot automatically order the forfeiture of such property. That of course would not preclude the institution of proceedings to estreat the amount of moneys for which the instruments of title were accepted *in lieu*.   **10–65**

Thirdly, when an estreatment or forfeiture order is made under this provision the court must give notice to the accused person and any surety stating that an application to vary or discharge the order can be made to the court within 21 days from the date of the making of the order.[242] Where an application is made, the applicant may make representations in relation to the order and the court may vary or discharge it if satisfied that the interests of justice so require.[243]

Estreatment for Breach of Condition

The second situation in which the Bail Act 1997 makes provision for the estreatment of a recognisance arises where a person has been brought before the court on foot of a warrant which it issued on being satisfied that the accused had contravened a condition of his recognisance (other than the fundamental condition to appear before the court in accordance with the terms of the recognisance). In this event, if the court is satisfied that the accused person has contravened a condition of the recognisance, it must order his recognisance and that of any surety or sureties to be estreated. It must also order the forfeiture of any moneys paid into court by the accused or any surety.[244] Once again, the Act is silent about the forfeiture of property in respect of which instruments of title were accepted *in lieu* of moneys being   **10–66**

---

[242] Bail Act 1997, s.9(8).
[243] *ibid.* s.9(9).
[244] *ibid.* s.9(7).

paid into court. It is also worth noting that the requirement to issue an order of estreatment and, where relevant, forfeiture is mandatory once the court is satisfied that the accused has contravened a condition of his recognisance.

The same requirements with respect to notice and an application to vary or discharge the order which apply to the first situation in which an order can be made apply also to the second situation in which it can be made.

The District Court Rules 1997 and the Petty Sessions (Ireland) Act 1851 set out the procedure which should be followed on an application to estreat a recognisance or to forfeit a sum of money lodged in *lieu* of a recognisance. The rules do not specifically refer to the forfeiture of moneys lodged in pursuance of the obligation to pay into court a sum equal to at least one third of the recognisance, nor to the forfeiture of instruments of title to property which have been accepted *in lieu* of the payment of moneys. This may be because the payment of such sums or the lodgment of the title instruments are really part of the recognisance. Accordingly they are covered by the provisions dealing with the estreatment of the recognisance.

Procedure

10–67   Where it is intended to apply to the court for an order to estreat a recognisance, or to forfeit a sum of money lodged *in lieu* of a surety or sureties, for non-performance of a condition, the recognisance must first be produced to a judge assigned to the Court district in which it is deposited.[245] The judge may, on the basis of such proof as he shall think fit, endorse the recognisance with a certificate in the form set out in 27.1 of Schedule B of the District Court Rules 1997. Such certificate shall be evidence of the non-performance of any certified condition of the recognisance.

An application to estreat the recognisance or to forfeit the sum of money shall be made by a Garda superintendent.[246] The application may be made at any subsequent sitting of the court at which it was ordered that the recognisance should be entered into or before which the principal party was bound by the recognisance to appear. The application must be preceded by the issue and service of the appropriate notice upon the principal bound by the recognisance and/or the surety or sureties as the case may be.[247] Such notice must be served on each person to whom it is directed by a summons server or by ordinary post at least seven days before the date fixed for the hearing.[248] Where the intended recipient of the notice has no fixed address within the State, service may be effected in such manner as the judge shall direct.[249] If the notice relates to an application to forfeit a sum of money lodged *in lieu* of a surety or sureties, the judge may dispense with service in a case where he or

---

[245]   District Court Rules 1997, Ord.27, r.1.
[246]   *ibid.* Ord.27, r.2.
[247]   *ibid.* Ord.27, r.3(1) and (2). See Schedule B, Form 27.2 in the case of an application to estreat a recognisance and Schedule B, Form 27.3 in the case of an application to forfeit a sum of money lodged *in lieu* of a surety or sureties.
[248]   *ibid.* 1997, Ord.27, r.3(3).
[249]   *ibid.* 1997, Ord.27, r.3(4).

she is satisfied, upon application made in that behalf, that the intended recipient has no fixed address in the State and that his whereabouts cannot be ascertained by reasonable enquiries.[250] When service of a notice has been effected, the original notice together with a statutory declaration of service shall be lodged with the court clerk at least four days before the date fixed for the hearing.[251]

On the hearing of an application for an order to estreat a recognisance the court may make an order to estreat the recognisance in such amount or amounts and against the principal party or the surety or sureties or against all or any of them as it thinks fit.[252] The court can issue such an order upon production of the recognisance duly endorsed with the certificate of non-performance, and after hearing such further evidence (if any) tendered in support of the application. Both the District Court Rules and the Petty Sessions (Ireland) Act 1851 state that a recognisance cannot be estreated against any person who has not been served with notice of application to estreat.[253] Where the application is for an order to forfeit a sum of money lodged *in lieu* of a surety or sureties, the court may make an order, which may be by way of an endorsement on the recognisance, directing the forfeiture of the sum of money lodged or any part of it.[254] As with the issue of an order to estreat a recognisance, the court can issue an order to forfeit a sum of money upon production of the recognisance duly endorsed with the certificate of non-performance and after hearing such further evidence (if any) tendered in support of the application.

Whenever the court makes an order to estreat a recognisance the court clerk will send a notice in the appropriate form to each person against whom the order was made.[255] The notice will inform the person that the order has been made, of the amount in which the recognisance has been estreated against that person and of the time (if any) allowed for payment of the sum due. In the case of an order directing the forfeiture of a sum lodged *in lieu* of a surety or sureties the court clerk shall inform the person who lodged the money, if his whereabouts is known, that the order has been made and of the amount of money which was directed to be forfeited.[256] Any balance between the amount lodged and the amount forfeited shall be repayable to the person concerned.

Enforcing an Order of Estreatment

Where an order to estreat a recognisance has not been complied with, the court may, on the application of a Garda superintendent, issue a warrant in the appropriate form to levy the amount due by any person under the order by

10–68

---

[250] *ibid.* 1997, Ord.27, r.3(5).
[251] *ibid.* 1997, Ord.27, r.3(6).
[252] *ibid.* 1997, Ord.27, r.4(a); see Schedule B, Form 27.4.
[253] Petty Sessions (Ireland) Act 1851, s.34; District Court Rules 1997, Ord.27, r.4(a).
[254] District Court Rules 1997, Ord.27, r.4(b); see Schedule B, Form 27.5.
[255] *ibid.* Ord.27, r.5(1); see Schedule B, Form 23.1.
[256] *ibid.* Ord.27, r.5(2).

distress and sale of the goods of such person.[257] Such an order may issue at any time after the expiration of the time allowed for payment or, if no time was allowed, at any time after the making of the order to estreat. Once the warrant for distress has issued the superintendent may apply to the court for a warrant to commit the respondent to prison, after having first given the respondent at least seven days' notice of the application and having lodged the original of the notice of application with the court clerk.[258] On such an application the court may issue a warrant to commit the respondent to prison for a term not exceeding the appropriate period specified in the scale set out in Order 23, rule 7 of the District Court Rules 1997.[259] In this event the superintendent shall return the warrant of distress to the court for cancellation.

Where the court estreats a recognisance to keep the peace and/or to be of good behaviour against the principal party, it may also order the principal party to enter into a fresh recognisance with or without sureties to perform the obligation of the original recognisance during the period for which it would have remained in force but for the order to estreat.[260]

G. Legal Aid

10–69   Bail proceedings are not specifically provided for in the legal aid legislation. For the most part this will not give rise to a problem in practice. If an accused has been granted legal aid for the preparation and conduct of his defence or for his appeal against conviction or for a case stated that will normally be interpreted as extending to a relevant bail application. If the accused has been refused bail in the District Court, or in the court of trial, and submits a further application to the High Court legal aid may be available for the High Court application under the Attorney General's scheme (see Chapter 11, para 11–16). This will extend to an appeal to the Supreme Court against the High Court's determination. Similarly, where an accused launches a collateral attack against conviction or custody through an application for a state side order, the Attorney General's scheme will cover an associated bail application.

H. Legislative Drafting

10–70   The enactment of the Bail Act 1997 has rendered the bail laws more complex not just because of the substantive additions it has effected, but also because of an amount of loose drafting in the Act itself. Several examples have been

---

[257] *ibid.* Ord.27, r.6(1); see Schedule B, Form 27.6.
[258] The Fines Act (Ireland) 1851, s.3; District Court Rules 1997, Ord.27, r.6(2); see Schedule B, Form 27.7 for the form of notice of application to the Court for a warrant of committal.
[259] *ibid.*, see District Court Rules 1997, Schedule B, Form 27.8 for the warrant of committal. The scale is: 5 days for not more than €63.49; 15 days for more than €63.49 and not more than €317.43; 45 days for more than €317.43 and not more than €634.87; and 90 days for more than €500. Any such period shall be terminated upon payment of the full amount, or reduced on part payment; see Criminal Justice Administration Act 1914.
[260] District Court Rules 1997, Ord.27, r.7.

noted at relevant points throughout this Chapter. Nevertheless, it is worth drawing attention to one further example of a very specific and technical nature. The latter is to be found in section 11(c) which deletes "or a peace commissioner" from section 33(1) of the Criminal Procedure Act 1967 despite the fact that the immediately preceding section (section 12) repeals section 33. This relatively minor drafting error is symptomatic of a more general failure to achieve a better fit between the provisions of the pre-existing legislation and rules and the provisions of the 1997 Act itself. The inevitable result is a degree of uncertainty in the law on some aspects of bail. Indeed, it is unfortunate that the opportunity was not taken to produce a single comprehensive statute dealing with all aspects of bail.

CHAPTER 11

LEGAL REPRESENTATION

A. Introduction

The criminal law and trial procedure, particularly the procedure on indictment, **11–01** are now so complicated that professional legal representation is virtually indispensable for the defendant. Even in respect of the summary trial of minor offences the issues can be sufficiently complex and the consequences of conviction so severe as to render legal representation essential in the interests of the defendant. It might seem strange, therefore, that the law has not always recognised the defendant's basic right to legal representation in felony cases. Langbein asserts that it was only from about the 1730s that defence lawyers began to make their presence felt in criminal trials at the Old Bailey.[1] Statutory authority for their role, however, was not forthcoming until the Trial of Felonies Act 1836. Today, of course, it is taken for granted that a person accused of a criminal offence has a right to avail of legal advice for the purpose of preparing for the trial and for the conduct of his defence at the trial, including the examination and cross examination of witnesses, the presentation of evidence, submissions on points of law, addresses to the judge and the jury and answering questions on behalf of the defendant. In recent years the right of access to legal advice has been extended to the suspect in police custody.

     The issue, therefore, is not so much whether the defendant in the criminal process has a right to avail of legal advice and representation. Rather, it concerns what that right means in practice. There are effectively two issues here. First, there is the whole question of legal aid for impecunious defendants. Does an impecunious defendant have a right to be provided with legal advice and representation by the State and, if so, what is the extent of that right? Second, to what extent can a defendant, whether impecunious or not, challenge his conviction on the ground that he did not receive adequate legal advice and representation from the lawyers acting for him? Each of these issues will be dealt with in turn.

---

[1] Langbein, "The Criminal Trial before the Lawyers" (1978) 45 U Chic Law Review 263.

It is useful from the outset to distinguish the right to legal representation from the right to legal advice in the criminal process. Traditionally the former is confined to the preparation of the defence case for trial and representation at the trial. The latter, by contrast, is normally taken to refer to the right of access to a solicitor for a suspect in police custody. In *People (DPP) v. Healy*[2] the Supreme Court declared for the first time that a suspect's right of access to a solicitor while in police custody is a constitutional right. Surprisingly, perhaps, it stopped short of finding that the suspect also enjoyed a constitutional, as distinct from a legal, right to be informed of his right of access. These matters are dealt with fully in Chapter 5 on detention and will not be pursued further here. The focus in this chapter will be on the nature and extent of the right to legal representation for the preparation of the defence case for trial and for the actual conduct of the trial. The constitutional status of the right to legal representation and its full ramifications will be considered first. This will be followed by an examination of how the right is put into effect through the statutory scheme introduced by the Criminal Justice (Legal Aid) Act 1962. It will conclude with an assessment of the relevance, if any, of the quality of legal representation afforded to an accused in a criminal trial.

B. The Constitutional Right to Legal Representation

11–02 The constitutional dimension of the right to legal representation has been considered by the courts primarily in the context of the right to free legal aid. The seminal case is *State (Healy) v. Donoghue*.[3] In that case two youths, Healy and Foran, were charged with stealing and causing malicious damage to two cars on two separate occasions. They appeared at the District Court without legal representation and elected to have the charges dealt with summarily. They pleaded guilty to both charges of stealing and to one of the charges of malicious damage. They were found guilty of the other charge of malicious damage after a trial. The matter was then adjourned for sentencing to a later sitting of the court and both were remanded in custody. When they were eventually brought back before the court for sentencing they applied for free legal aid under the Criminal Justice (Legal Aid) Act 1962. Their application was granted, a solicitor was assigned to them from the legal aid panel and the matter was adjourned to a future date. When the case finally came on for hearing the applicant's solicitor did not appear as solicitors had withdrawn from the legal aid scheme in the course of a dispute with the Department of Justice over the operation of the scheme. The District Court judge was faced with the choice of continuing to remand the defendants in custody until such time as the dispute was over or proceeding with the sentencing. The judge, against the wishes of the defendants, opted for the latter course and sentenced each to two consecutive, six-month terms of detention. In separate proceedings Healy, again without the benefit of legal representation, pleaded guilty in the

---

[2] [1990] 2 I.R. 73.
[3] [1976] I.R. 325.

District Court to a charge of breaking and entering and a charge of stealing. He was sentenced subsequently to a term of three months in detention.

On the application of the defendants the High Court granted conditional orders of certiorari quashing all the sentences and convictions. These were later made absolute, with the exception of Healy's conviction and sentence handed down in the separate proceedings for the breaking and entering and stealing offences. Gannon J. explained this exception on the ground that Healy had not applied for legal aid as specifically required by the terms of the 1962 Act. While the learned judge accepted that there would be cases where the right to legal representation would be an essential pre-requisite for the satisfaction of the accused's basic right to a trial "in due course of law" as prescribed by the Constitution, he stopped short from defining it as a distinct constitutional right. Moreover, he could find nothing in the Constitution or the 1962 Act which gave the accused the right to be informed of the free legal aid scheme.

On appeal, the Supreme Court adopted a more expansive approach to the status and scope of the right to legal representation. O'Higgins C.J. based his approach on Article 38.1 of the Constitution which reads: **11–03**

> "No person shall be tried on any criminal charge save in due course of law."

According to the Chief Justice this entails that the accused must be afforded the opportunity to defend himself. If this requirement was not satisfied not only would the accused be denied a fair trial as mandated by the Constitution, but the State would have failed to vindicate his personal rights contrary to Article 40.3.1°–2° of the Constitution. That, of course, is not quite the same thing as a constitutional right to be legally represented in all circumstances in criminal proceedings. O'Higgins C.J. defined the right to legal representation as follows:

> "The requirements of fairness and of justice must be considered in relation to the seriousness of the charge brought against the person and the consequences involved for him. Where a man's liberty is at stake, or where he faces a very severe penalty which may affect his welfare or his livelihood, justice may require more than the application of normal and fair procedures in relation to his trial. Facing, as he does, the power of the State which is his accuser, the person charged may be unable to defend himself adequately because of ignorance, lack of education, youth or other incapacity. In such circumstances his plight may require, if justice is to be done, that he should have legal assistance. In such circumstances, if he cannot provide such assistance by reason of lack of means, does justice under the Constitution also require that he be aided in his defence? In my view it does."[4]

Clearly O'Higgins C.J. associates the right to legal representation with the adversarial nature of the criminal process and the need to put the defendant on an equal footing with the State. Without legal representation the ordinary

---

[4]   *State (Healy) v. Donoghue* [1976] I.R. 325.

layperson with no experience or knowledge of the technicalities of the criminal law and criminal procedure will always be at a disadvantage, even in the most simple and straightforward of criminal cases, when confronted with the full resources of the State. This disadvantage will be magnified substantially where the defendant suffers from social or intellectual inadequacy, youth or some other incapacity which reduces even further his ability to defend himself adequately in the courtroom. These factors alone, however, do not confer on the defendant an absolute constitutional right to legal representation.

11–04   O'Higgins C.J. specifically links the constitutional requirements of fairness and justice in the criminal trial to the seriousness of the charges against the defendant and the consequences involved for him. It is only when the defendant's liberty is at stake or where he faces a very severe penalty which may affect his welfare or his livelihood that the right to legal representation may be triggered.[5] Accordingly, if conviction is likely to lead to a term of imprisonment or a criminal record which will seriously damage the employment prospects of the defendant or result in the defendant losing custody of his or her children, it can be expected that the right to legal representation will be brought into play. By the same token, of course, if the charge is likely to result in a relatively small fine with no long term adverse consequences for the defendant the right will not arise. It is worth emphasising, therefore, that the critical issue is not so much the nature of the charge or whether it is being tried summarily or on indictment, but the likely sentence that will be imposed on the individual defendant and the personal circumstances of that defendant.

In *Byrne v. Judge McDonnell*,[5a] for example, the accused's conviction for failing to pay the correct bus fare was quashed by the High Court on the ground that he had not been afforded legal aid from the commencement of his trial as distinct from the commencement of the sentencing stage. In this case the defendant had pleaded guilty. On hearing an outline of the facts of the case for the purpose of sentence the judge formed the view that a custodial sentence might be appropriate. Accordingly, he granted the defendant legal aid for the purposes of a plea in mitigation. The High Court held that once the seriousness of the case became apparent the judge should have permitted the defendant to change his plea from guilty to not guilty and afforded him legal aid for the whole of the trial.

There has been some uncertainty over the extent to which a prison sentence must be imminent to trigger the defendant's right to be told of his entitlement to legal aid. In *Cahill v. Reilly*,[5b] for example, Denham J. considered that it would not be sufficient merely that a sentence of imprisonment was possible. In her view the circumstances of the case would have to be such that a custodial sentence was probable or likely. In *Clarke v. Kirby*,[5c] however,

---

[5]   Note that the right only applies to criminal proceedings proper and does not extend to proceedings aimed at determining whether criminal proceedings should be commenced; *State (O) v. Daly* [1977] I.R. 312.

[5a]   [1997] 1 I.R. 392.

[5b]   [1994] 3 I.R. 547.

[5c]   [1998] 2 I.L.R.M. 30.

Shanley J. preferred a lower threshold. In his view it would be sufficient that the judge is empowered to impose a custodial sentence in the case and that there is a possibility that such a sentence might in fact be imposed. In that case the accused was faced with a choice between a prison sentence and a community service order. Shanley J. held that in those circumstances he was entitled to be told of his right to legal aid.

It may seem surprising that our law does not afford the defendant an absolute right to legal representation in a criminal trial, even where he is willing and able to obtain it through his own private means. In practice, of course, it is highly unlikely that a defendant in a criminal trial would ever be denied the option of conducting his defence through an appropriately quali-fied lawyer hired at his own expense. Nevertheless, particular circumstances could arise in which the court may feel that the defendant's freedom in the matter is being exercised in a manner which was not conducive to the fair and efficient disposal of the case. Before refusing legal representation, however, the court would have to consider whether the circumstances were such as to trigger the defendant's right to legal representation.

The most likely setting in which the issue of the defendant's constitutional right **11–05** to legal representation will arise concerns free legal aid. In any case where the constitutional right to legal representation applies, the State has a positive duty to provide the defendant with the opportunity to secure appropriate professional legal representation where he does not have the means to secure it himself. O'Higgins C.J., in his leading judgment in *Healy*, said that only by recognising and discharging this duty can the State be said to vindicate the personal rights of the individual as required by Article 40.3.1°–2° of the Constitution. Unfortunately, none of the judges in the Supreme Court elaborated on what might be required in practice in order to satisfy this duty. O'Higgins C.J. merely intimated that in so far as the Criminal Justice (Legal Aid) Act 1962 provides for legal aid it discharges the duty imposed on the State. It follows that there is no absolute constitutional duty on the State to provide legal representation for impecunious defendants in the criminal process through, for example, the appointment of salaried, public defenders.[6] Putting the defendant in the position whereby he can purchase appropriate representation is sufficient. If, however, circumstances arise in which the legal aid scheme under the 1962 Act proves inadequate for a qualifying defendant to secure legal representation, the State would risk being in breach of its duty to vindicate his personal right to a trial in due course of law if it did not act to secure him legal representation.

The facts and outcome of the *Healy* case demonstrate that the free legal aid scheme established by the 1962 Act will not always be sufficient in itself to satisfy a defendant's constitutional right to legal representation.[7] Although

---

[6] The establishment of a public defender system has been considered and rejected twice in Ireland; see Criminal Legal Aid Review Committee *First Report: An Examination of the Feasibility of Introducing a Public Defender System for Ireland* (Stationery Office, Dublin, 2000); and *The Tormey Committee* (1975–1981).

[7] The provision of legal aid in criminal cases has been under review recently by the Criminal Legal

Healy had not actually applied for free legal aid for the separate breaking and entering case, as required by the 1962 Act, the Supreme Court found that his constitutional right to a trial "in due course of law" had still been infringed. Overturning the decision of Gannon J. on the point in the High Court, the Supreme Court ruled that if the defendant is ignorant of his right to free legal aid and for that reason does not apply for it, his constitutional right is violated. O'Higgins C.J. reasoned that:

> ". . . if a person who is ignorant of his right fails to apply and on that account is not given legal aid then, in my view, his constitutional right is violated. For this reason it seems to me that when a person faces a possible prison sentence and has no lawyer, and cannot provide for one, he ought to be informed of his right to legal aid. If the person charged does not know of his right, he cannot exercise it; if he cannot exercise it, his right is violated."[8]

Accordingly, although not specifically required by the 1962 Act, there is a duty on the trial judge to inform the defendant of his right to legal aid. A failure to discharge that duty will be sufficient in itself to deny the defendant his right to a trial in due course of law. A resultant conviction will be null and void, necessitating, where appropriate, the immediate release of the person affected.[8a] Henchy J. explained the inter-relationship between the terms of the 1962 Act and fulfilment of the constitutional imperative as follows:

> "As the Act is designed to give practical implementation to a constitutional guarantee, the judicial function in respect of the Act would be incompletely exercised if a bare or perfunctory application of it left the constitutional guarantee unfulfilled."[9]

It is also worth noting that all of the judges, including O'Higgins C.J., discussed the right to be informed of the existence and purport of the legal aid scheme by reference to defendants who were facing a possible prison sentence. Only O'Higgins C.J. actually elaborated upon the scope of the substantive right to free legal aid itself. In doing so he included within the ambit of the substantive right defendants facing a very severe penalty which may affect their welfare or livelihoods. There is some doubt, therefore, over whether the right to free legal aid, and the concomitant right to be informed of the existence and purport of the legal aid scheme, are confined to defendants facing likely prison sentences or whether they also extend more broadly to those facing a severe penalty as indicated at one point by O'Higgins C.J.

11–06 The constitutional aspect of the right to legal representation also raises the question of whether a criminal trial can proceed when the defendant is not legally represented. It has never been seriously asserted that a defendant, whether impecunious or not, must be legally represented in criminal proceedings. There seems little doubt that a defendant can make an informed decision

---

Aid Review Committee. It has made several recommendations for improvement, many of which have already been implemented.

[8] [1976] I.R. 325 at 352.

[8a] *McSorley v. Governor of Mountjoy Prison* [1996] 2 I.L.R.M. 331.

[9] *Op. cit.* at 354.

to waive his right to legal representation, even where the charges in question are serious. In *Healy*, for example, Griffin J. admitted the possibility of a defendant waiving his right to free legal aid. The only qualification imposed by the learned judge was that the trial judge should satisfy himself that the defendant was waiving his right "intelligently and understandingly". If, however, the defendant asserts his right to legal representation it would appear that the judge should not proceed to trial and/or sentence where that right has not been satisfied, even if that means having to remand the defendant in custody for a longer period than would otherwise have been necessary. Both the High Court and the Supreme Court agreed that the District Court judge in *Healy* had breached the constitutional rights of the defendants to a fair trial by proceeding without their consent in the absence of their solicitor. The District Court judge's actions were not excused by the fact that he was motivated by the prospects of the defendants facing further lengthy remands in custody before legal representation under the legal aid scheme became available.

The State, of course, could be faced with a serious dilemma in any case where a defendant who had been properly granted free legal aid could not obtain appropriate representation. This might happen where, for example, solicitors and counsel withdrew their services from the legal aid scheme. In such circumstances the fulfilment of the State's duty to vindicate the constitutional right of the defendant to a trial in due course of law may require the State to appoint representation directly to the defendant. Certainly, it would appear that the State has the power to assign legal representation to a defendant who has failed to make an appropriate nomination despite having been granted legal aid.[10]

C. The Free Legal Aid Scheme

1. Introduction

It is clear from *Healy* that in any case where the defendant's constitutional **11–07** right to legal representation applies and the defendant does not have the financial means to secure that representation for himself, the State is under a positive obligation to provide for his legal representation. The *Healy* decision does not prescribe any particular scheme which the State must adopt in order to satisfy this obligation, although O'Higgins C.J. acknowledged that the Criminal Justice (Legal Aid) Act 1962 was sufficient to discharge the State's obligation in the matter in so far as it provides for free legal aid.[11] It must also be said, however, that the court went on to hold that there is an obligation to inform the defendant of the existence and purport of the scheme, even though that is not strictly required by the provisions of the Act.

The scheme adopted by the 1962 Act is based on the principle of enabling the defendant to use public funds to engage the services of a professional

---

[10] *State (Royle) v. Kelly* [1974] I.R. 259.
[11] *State (Healy) v. Donoghue* [1976] I.R. 325 at 352.

lawyer to conduct his defence and represent his interests in the criminal proceedings against him. The implementing legislation, the Criminal Justice (Legal Aid) Regulations 1965, lay down conditions for the operation of the scheme. These set out the fees and expenses (including reasonable disbursements) payable to solicitors and counsel for work under the scheme. The Regulations also make provision for the payment of certain expenses of defence witnesses.

The legal aid scheme established by the 1962 Act covers certain District Court proceedings, proceedings in the trial court, appeals and a case stated.[11a] In order to benefit from any of these the defendant must obtain the appropriate legal aid certificate. There are 5 in all, each corresponding to the relevant stage in the criminal process:

- Legal aid (District Court) certificate;

- Legal aid (trial on indictment) certificate;

- Legal aid (appeal) certificate;

- Legal aid (case stated) certificate; and

- Legal aid (Supreme Court) certificate.

11–08 Clearly there are a range of vitally important professional legal services which are not covered by the 1962 Act, including: legal advice to a suspect while in police custody, bail applications to the High Court and applications for *habeas corpus*. It is at least arguable that the State would be in breach of its constitutional duty to protect and vindicate the individual's right to liberty if it did not make some provision for legal aid in these situations. Equally, a defendant might argue that his constitutional right to a criminal trial in accordance with due process had been denied as a result of his inability to obtain the services of a solicitor when he was being interviewed in police custody. Some of these shortcomings have been addressed administratively by the Attorney General's Scheme. Initially this made provision for legal aid, on a non-statutory basis, for habeas corpus applications. It was subsequently extended to bail motions, judicial review proceedings and applications under section 50 of the Extradition Act 1965. In February 2001 an additional non-statutory scheme was introduced, pursuant to the recommendations of the Criminal Legal Aid Review Committee.[12] Designated the Garda Station Legal Advice Scheme, it makes provision for legal aid for the services of a solicitor to a suspect detained in police custody.

Not only do these certificates and schemes differ from each other in terms of what they cover, but the criteria applicable in granting them also differ slightly from one to the other. Accordingly, each will be considered in turn.

[11a] There was provision for legal aid in certain circumstances for the preliminary examination of certain offences but this was abolished along with the abolition of the preliminary examination; Criminal Justice Act 1999, s.12(1), repealing s.2A of the Criminal Justice (Legal Aid) Act 1962 as inserted by section 15(4) of the Criminal Evidence Act 1992.

[12] See Criminal Legal Aid Review Committee *Interim Report*; and Press Release from Department of Justice, Equality and Law Reform, February 13, 2001.

This will followed by the procedure which must be followed in applying for legal aid and the range of benefits covered.

2. District Court Certificate

When the defendant is first charged before the District Court he can apply for a legal aid (District Court) certificate.[13] In order to qualify he must satisfy four criteria. First, he must be charged with an offence before the District Court. Second, the Court must be satisfied that his means are insufficient to enable him to obtain legal aid. Third, the Court must be satisfied that, by reason of the gravity of the charge or of exceptional circumstances, it is essential in the interests of justice that he should have legal aid in the preparation and conduct of his defence before the Court. Clearly, this third factor will render it difficult to secure legal aid for offences which will be tried summarily unless the circumstances are such that the defendant can expect a term of imprisonment or the consequences of a conviction will be seriously damaging to his character. Fourth, the defendant must actually apply for legal aid. As was seen in the *Healy* case, a failure to satisfy this fourth requirement will not be fatal if the defendant was not aware of the existence and purport of the free legal aid scheme. The court has an exceptionally broad discretion in interpreting and applying the qualifying criteria. If it appears to the court that the criteria are satisfied in a case, it must grant the applicant a legal aid (District Court) certificate. The court's decision is final and cannot be appealed.[14]

11–09

3. Preliminary Examination Certificate

Legal aid under the District Court certificate is also available for certain pre-trial proceedings in the District Court which were introduced consequent on the abolition of the preliminary examination.[15] The proceedings in question are applications by the prosecutor to extend the period for service of the book of evidence, and the taking of evidence from a person by way of sworn deposition or though a live television link (see chapter 14).

11–10

4. Trial on Indictment Certificate

When a person is returned for trial on indictment he can apply for a legal aid (trial on indictment) certificate.[16] Such application can be made to the District Court once the person has been sent for trial on indictment. Equally, it can be made to the court before which the person will be, or is being, tried. The applicant must satisfy four criteria. First, he must be sent for trial for an indictable offence. Second, he must satisfy the court that his means are insufficient to enable him to obtain legal aid. Third, the defendant must be

11–11

---

[13] Criminal Justice (Legal Aid) Act 1962, s.2(1).
[14] *ibid.* s.2(2).
[15] Criminal Procedure Act 1967, s.4H(1), as inserted by Criminal Justice Act 1999, s.9.
[16] Criminal Justice (Legal Aid) Act 1962, s.3(2).
[17] See Courts of Justice Act 1924, s.34 and Courts of Justice Act 1928, s.5.

charged whith murder, or it must appear to the court, having regard to all the circumstances of the case, that it is in the interests of justice that the defendant should have legal aid in the preparation and conduct of his defence at the trial. When considering all the circumstances in the interests of justice (in a case where the charge is not one of murder), the court must take into account the defence, if any, relied upon by the defendant. Fourth, the defendant must actually apply for a legal aid (trial on indictment) certificate. It is worth emphasising that on a charge of murder the defendant's application for legal aid must be granted in any case where it appears to the court that his means are insufficient to enable him to obtain legal aid. Unlike the legal aid (District Court) certificate, there is no specific provision rendering the court's decision final and unappealable. Where a legal aid (trial on indictment) certificate is granted in respect of a person the Court of Criminal Appeal loses its jurisdiction to award costs[17] to the person in respect of court proceedings in relation to which the certificate applies.[18]

Legal aid under the trial on indictment certificate is also available for certain pre-trial proceedings in the trial court (and for appeals from those proceedings) which were introduced consequent on the abolition of the preliminary examination.[18a] The proceedings in question concern an application by the defendant for dismissal of one or more charges at any time after he has been sent forward for trial, or an appeal to the Court of Criminal Appeal from the dismissal of any such application (see chapter 14).

5. Appeal Certificate

11–12   A person who has been convicted of a criminal offence and wishes to appeal from the conviction or penalty can apply for a legal aid (appeal) certificate.[19] The application must normally be made to the District Court or to the judge of the court before which he was tried.[20] Four criteria must be satisfied before an appeal certificate can be granted. First, the applicant must have been convicted of an offence. Second, the court hearing the application must be satisfied that the applicant's means are insufficient to enable him to obtain legal aid. Third, the conviction must be for murder, or it must appear to the court hearing the application that, by reason of the serious nature of the offence or of exceptional circumstances, it is essential in the interests of justice that the person should have legal aid in the preparation and conduct of the appeal. Fourth, the person must actually apply for the legal aid (appeal) certificate. Even if the applicant is refused a legal aid appeal certificate by the District Court or court before which he was tried, he may still obtain a certificate by applying to the court to which an appeal against his conviction lies.[21] He can do this either by sending a letter to the registrar of the court setting out the facts

---

[18]   Criminal Justice (Legal Aid) Act 1962, s.8(1).
[18a]   Criminal Procedure Act 1967, s.4H(2), as inserted by Criminal Justice Act 1999, s.9.
[19]   Criminal Justice (Legal Aid) Act 1962, s.4(2).
[20]   The applicant can also apply to the court to which the appeal against conviction lies if his first application for an appeal certificate is refused.
[21]   Criminal Justice (Legal Aid) Act 1962, s.4(3).

of the case and the grounds of the application. Alternatively, he can apply directly to the court itself. In either event it is the court which will take the decision. The criteria for granting the certificate are identical to those governing the application to the District Court or the court before which the person was tried. Where a legal aid (appeal certificate) is granted in respect of a person appealing to the Court of Criminal Appeal, the court loses its jurisdiction to award costs[22] to that person in respect of court proceedings in relation to which the certificate applies.[23]

6. Case Stated Certificate

A legal aid (case stated) certificate can be sought where a person is charged **11–13**
with an offence before the District Court or Circuit Court, or is appealing to the Circuit Court against a conviction by the District Court, and the judge before whom the charge or appeal is being heard refers a question of law arising in the proceedings to the High Court or the Supreme Court by way of case stated.[24] Equally, the certificate can be sought where a judge of the District Court states a case in relation to the proceedings before him for the opinion of the High Court. Three further criteria must be satisfied before a case stated certificate can be granted by the District Court or Circuit Court. First, the court before which the charge or appeal is heard must be satisfied that the means of the applicant are insufficient to enable him to obtain legal aid. Second, the court before which the charge or appeal is heard must be satisfied that, by reason of the serious nature of the offence with which the person is charged or by reason of exceptional circumstances, it is essential in the interests of justice that a legal aid (case stated) certificate should be granted. Third, the defendant in the proceedings before the District Court or Circuit Court must actually apply for the certificate. If the legal aid application is refused by the District Court or Circuit Court, he may apply for a certificate to the court before which the case stated will be heard.[25] He can do this by a letter addressed to the registrar of that court setting out the facts of the case and the grounds of the application. Alternatively, he can apply directly to the court itself. In either case it is the court which will take the decision. The criteria for granting the certificate are identical to those governing the application to the District Court or Circuit Court.

7. Supreme Court Certificate

A legal aid (Supreme Court) certificate can be sought by a person in a **11–14**
criminal case where an appeal is brought to the Supreme Court from a determination of the Court of Criminal Appeal in relation to the offence or penalty in question.[26] Equally it can be sought in a criminal case where an

---

[22] See Courts of Justice Act 1924, s.34 and Courts of Justice Act 1928, s.5.
[23] Criminal Justice (Legal Aid) Act 1962, s.8(2).
[24] *ibid.* s.5(2).
[25] *ibid.* s.5(3).
[26] *ibid.* s.6(2).

appeal is brought from a determination of the High Court on a case stated by a District Court judge in regard to the offence or in relation to a question of law arising out of the proceedings in the District Court. Three further criteria must be granted before the certificate can be granted by the Court of Criminal Appeal or the High Court. First, the court must be satisfied that the means of the person charged with the offence are insufficient to enable him to obtain legal aid. Second, in the case of an appeal from a determination of the High Court on a case stated by a District Court judge, the High Court must be satisfied that, by reason of the serious nature of the offence with which the person is charged or by reason of exceptional circumstances, it is essential in the interests of justice that a legal aid (Supreme Court) certificate should be granted. Third, the defendant must actually apply for the certificate. If the application is refused he may apply to the Supreme Court for a certificate.[27] He can do this by a letter addressed to the registrar of the Supreme Court setting out the facts of the case and the grounds of the application. Alternatively, he may apply directly to the Supreme Court itself. The criteria for granting the certificate are identical to those governing the application to the Court of Criminal Appeal or High Court.

8. Special Criminal Court Certificate

11–15 The Special Criminal Court may grant certificates for free legal aid as if the court was the Central Criminal Court.[28] It follows that the conditions appropriate to a trial on indictment certificate apply.

9. The Attorney General's Scheme

11–16 Towards the end of 1967 an undertaking was given in the Supreme Court on behalf of the Attorney General and the Minister for Finance to the effect that the State would defray the fees payable to the solicitor and counsel for *habeas corpus* applications where the applicant was not in a financial position to engage such professional representation.[29] The undertaking was given in respect of the application in hand and in respect of future applications.[30] Since then the scheme has been extended to: bail motions, judicial review proceedings which consist of or include certiorari, mandamus or prohibition and which are concerned with criminal matters or matters where the liberty of the applicant is at issue; applications under section 50 of the Extradition Act 1965 and extradition applications before the District Court.[31] Judicial notice has been taken of the scheme since its inception.[32]

Legal aid is available under the Attorney General's scheme whenever the applicant's means are insufficient to obtain the necessary legal representation

---

27 Criminal Justice (Legal Aid) Act 1962, s.6(3).
28 Special Criminal Court Rules, 1972, r.28.
29 See Criminal Legal Aid Review Committee *First Report: An Examination of the Feasibility of Introducing a Public Defender System for Ireland, op. cit.* at 14.
30 The case in question was *In re Woods* [1970] I.R. 154.
31 See Attorney General's website for position as from May 1, 2000; http://www.irlgov.ie/ag/ago/agscheme.htm.

and the court in question considers that it is proper that a solicitor and counsel should be assigned to make submissions in support of an application. To enable the court assess his or her financial circumstances, the applicant must provide such information about his or her means as the court deems appropriate. Before it will recommend a grant of legal aid under the scheme the court must also be satisfied that the case warrants the assignment of a solicitor and/or counsel. If it considers that the complexity or importance of the case requires it the recommendation for counsel may also include one senior counsel. Where there is more than one applicant, but only one matter is at issue before the court, the solicitor and counsel assigned under the Scheme shall represent all the applicants.

The Scheme does not function as an alternative to costs. The application must be **11–17** made at the commencement of the proceedings to which they relate. The commencement of proceedings in this context refers to proceedings in a particular court. It follows that an application before the Supreme Court would not be prejudiced simply because an application had not been made in the earlier High Court proceedings. Equally, however, if the application was granted for the Supreme Court proceedings it would not operate retrospectively to cover the High Court proceedings.

It is worth emphasising that the Scheme is non-statutory.[32a] It is purely an administrative arrangement operated by the Attorney General and may be expanded or contracted as he sees fit. Nevertheless when counsel instructed by the Attorney General gives an assurance to the court that the fees of solicitor and counsel will be paid under the scheme the court ought to accept that assurance without question, save in truly exceptional cases.[33] If the court in question is satisfied that legal aid should be granted under the Scheme, it will make a recommendation to that effect and the Attorney General will act upon it. Indeed, it would appear that the court is under an obligation to embark on an inquiry as to the applicant's means in appropriate cases to see if it should make a recommendation.[34] Where aid is recommended costs payable to the solicitor and the fees payable to counsel under the Scheme will not exceed the rates payable in cases governed by the Criminal Justice (Legal Aid) Regulations current at the time.

10. Garda Station Legal Advice Scheme

In February 2000 the Minister for Justice, Equality and Law Reform **11–18** requested the Criminal Legal Aid Review Committee to review the situation whereby legal aid was not available for consultations between detained persons and solicitors in Garda Stations. The Committee reported with a

---

[32] *Byrne v. Governor of Mountjoy Prison* [1999] 1 I.L.R.M. 386.
[32a] The *Criminal Legal Aid Review Committee: Final Report* (Stationery Office, Dublin, 2002) recommends that the Attorney General's Scheme should be put on a statutory footing and brought within the scope of the Criminal Legal Aid Scheme.
[33] *ibid.*
[34] *ibid.*

recommendation to the effect that consultations should be paid for in certain circumstances.[35] After consultations with the Law Society the Minister gave effect to the Committee's recommendation by announcing the establishment of the Garda Station Legal Advice Scheme in February 2001. The Scheme has been established initially on a non-statutory basis with a view to being reviewed after one year.

The Scheme applies to persons detained in a Garda station for the purpose of the investigation of an offence under the Offences against the State Act 1939, the Criminal Justice Act 1984 or the Criminal Justice (Drug Trafficking) Act 1996. Where such a detained person has a legal entitlement to consult with a solicitor and his or her means are insufficient to enable him or her pay for such consultation, the consultations with the solicitor will be paid for by the State under the scheme. It would appear that the Schemes operates a strict test for qualification on the ground of insufficient means. Eligibility is confined to persons who are in receipt of social welfare payments or persons whose earnings are less than €20,315.81 per annum. Fees payable to the solicitor differ depending on whether there is an actual visit and the time of the visit. Visits between 9am and 7pm from Monday to Friday are currently valued at €100.70 plus VAT. Visits outside those hours (and weekends and bank holidays) are currently valued at €136.94. Telephone conversations are valued at €40.99 VAT. Travelling expenses are currently paid at €.76 per mile.

It is not entirely clear why the scheme refers to a legal entitlement to consult with a solicitor as a specific condition to qualification under the Scheme. All persons arrested and detained under the specified Acts have both a legal and constitutional right of access to a solicitor. It is true that circumstances may arise from time to time with respect to an individual case whereby access can lawfully be denied. It is unlikely that an individual would be granted access to a solicitor where these circumstances arise. However, if he or she was granted access in such circumstances it is inconceivable that the State would attempt to deny legal aid for the consultation on the ground that access could lawfully have been denied.

11. The Application

11–19   With the exception of the Garda Station Legal Advice Scheme an application for legal aid must be made to the court before which the relevant proceedings are being or will be conducted. The application may be made orally or in writing by the applicant or his or her legal representative. The first issue which the court must consider is whether the applicant lacks sufficient means to pay for his or her own legal representation. In making this assessment the court may require the applicant to furnish a written statement of his means. The court is not obliged to take this course and can decide the matter on the spot simply on the basis of oral representations.

In practice the statement of means is rarely required, although practice varies from court to court. Typically, if the accused asserts that he or she is in

---

[35]   Criminal Legal Aid Review Committee *Interim Report, op. cit.*

receipt of unemployment benefit or assistance that is accepted as sufficient evidence of a lack of means. While it is a criminal offence to make a false statement or representation for the purposes of a legal aid application,[35a] there is little or no verification of claims and prosecutions for false claims are rarely if ever brought.[35b]

Where a written statement of means is demanded it should be presented in the form set out in the Second Schedule to the Criminal Justice (Legal Aid) Regulations 1965. This requires information about the applicant's financial income and outgoings, including average weekly income, rent and mortgage payments, as well as dependants and any sources of finance or assets that might be available to cover his legal expenses. The Criminal Legal Aid Committee has recommended the updating of this statement of means to bring it more into line with current indications of income and liabilities.[35c]

When assessing an applicant's means for the purposes of a legal aid application the courts are not bound by prescribed eligibility ceilings. It is within their discretion to determine whether an applicant's means are sufficient to afford his own legal costs. In making this assessment the court will not confine itself purely to the applicant's income and liabilities. It will also take into account the likely duration, complexity and cost of the trial.[35d]

Once satisfied that the applicant has insufficient means to pay for his own legal representation the court will go on to consider whether the case is one in which by reason of "the gravity of the charge" or "exceptional circumstances" it is essential in the interests of justice that the applicant should have legal aid in the preparation and conduct of his or her case. This requirement does not arise where the charge is one of murder or where the appeal is one from the Court of Criminal Appeal to the Supreme Court. In such cases legal aid must be granted where the applicant satisfies the means test. With respect to the other cases it is not possible to offer a comprehensive statement on what does or does not qualify as a sufficiently grave charge or exceptional circumstances. From *State (Healy) v. Donoghue*[36] it can be deduced that a charge will be considered sufficiently grave in this context if it is likely to lead to a term of imprisonment for the defendant or a criminal record which will seriously damage his or her employment prospects or result in him or her losing custody of his or her children. Even cases which are not considered to involve sufficiently grave charges may qualify as a result of exceptional circumstances which, of course, will depend on the peculiar facts of each individual case. In practice it would appear that the courts are generous in the their interpretation of the criteria. So far there is no reported case in which the

---

[35a] Criminal Justice (Legal Aid) Act 1962, s.11(1). Persons convicted under this provision can be ordered to repay the legal aid in whole or in part; s.11(2).

[35b] *Criminal Legal Aid Review Committee: Final Report* (Stationery Office, Dublin, 2002) para.7.4. The Committee recommends random testing of applications; para.7.10.5.

[35c] *ibid.* at para.7.10.6. See Appendix 1 to its Final Report loc. cit. for its proposal on a revised statement of means.

[35d] The *Criminal Legal Aid Review Committee: Final Report* recommends the retention of this discretionary approach; loc. cit. at paras.7.10.2–7.10.4.

[36] [1976] I.R. 325.

appellate courts have had to interpret the qualifying criteria on an appeal from a lower court's refusal to grant legal aid.

In some Districts there is a practice of granting one legal aid certificate in a case involving several qualifying defendants. In such cases the one certificate covers all of the qualifying defendants.

The direct role of the courts in the operation of the statutory and the Attorney General's legal aid schemes avoids the need for a separate agency to administer legal aid.[37] The overall administrative, policy and financial responsibility for the schemes rests with the Courts Division of the Department of Justice, Equality and Law Reform.

There is no appeal against a refusal to grant legal aid. However, there is a form of appeal in that an accused can apply to each court jurisdiction for a legal aid certificate for that court. This is not available to a person accused of a summary offence in the District Court. Nevertheless the Criminal Legal Aid Review Committee recommended against provision for a formal appeal structure in legal aid applications.[37a]

12. Free Legal Aid Benefits

11–20   Where a legal aid certificate is granted for court proceedings it entitles the defendant to free legal aid for the fees, costs or other expenses properly incurred in preparing or conducting the defence, appeal or case stated in question. The primary expense is usually the fees of the defendant's solicitor and/or counsel. In all cases where the defendant qualifies for legal aid, he or she is entitled to the services of a solicitor. Entitlement to counsel arises where he is returned for trial, on appeal to the Court of Criminal Appeal or the Supreme Court, on a case stated. He is also entitled to the services of counsel for the District Court proceedings where he is charged with murder or in certain circumstances where evidence is being taken from a witness through a live television link for use in a subsequent trial on indictment. In any case in which he is entitled to have counsel assigned, the court can authorise the assignment of one or even two senior counsel where it seems that that is necessary for the adequate preparation and conduct of the defendant's case. In all of these cases the legal aid will cover the lawyers fees with respect to the conduct of the trial itself, the remand hearings, bail applications, adjournments, sentencing hearings, general preparation and essential prison visits by the solicitor.

For cases heard in the District Court (and appeals to the Circuit Court) the solicitor's fees are paid on a fixed scale in accordance with rates laid down from time to time by the Minister for Justice, Equality and Law Reform.[38] The

---

[37]   The Criminal Justice Legal Aid Committee recommends leaving responsibility with the courts; *Final Report, loc. cit.,* para.7.10.4.

[37a]   *Final Report, loc. cit.* at para.7.10.9.

[38]   See Criminal Justice (Legal Aid)(Amendment)(No.2) Regulation 2001 (S.I. 429 of 2001). These regulations also set out the fees payable to solicitors and counsel for bail application to the Circuit Court and Special Criminal Court and visits to a prison or other custodial centre (apart from a Garda station).

solicitors are paid an initial brief fee for the first appearance in court and a refresher fee for each subsequent day in court. The system is "competitive" as a number of solicitors have tended to specialise in legal aid work, particularly in Dublin, Cork and Limerick, in recent years. These solicitors compete on quality and reputation.[39] The question of counsel fees do not normally arise in respect of the District Court proceedings, unless the accused is charged with murder or it is a case in which evidence is being taken through a live television link with a view to having the accused sent for trial on indictment for one or more prescribed offences.

For indictable cases in the Circuit Court and higher the accused will be assigned a solicitor and counsel. Legal aid certificates for most of the cases which are heard in the Central and Special Criminal Courts generally provide for the engagement of two counsel; one senior and one junior. It is also normal for two counsel to be assigned for the most serious cases heard in the Circuit Court.[40] The fees paid to counsel in the Circuit and higher courts in respect of indictable offences are determined entirely by the fees which the DPP pays to the prosecution counsel, through parity agreements introduced by Regulations made in 1976 and 1978 under the Criminal Justice (Legal Aid) Act 1962. The fees paid to solicitors in respect of their services in the higher courts are related to the fees payable to the defence counsel which are in turn based on the fees paid to the prosecution counsel as determined by the DPP.[41]

11–21

It will often happen, particularly in the more serious cases, that the adequate preparation and conduct of the defence will require the services of experts in disciplines and professions other than law. The usual subjects are: medicine, psychiatry, psychology, forensic science, chemistry, biology, engineering, language and foreign law. Where the defence lawyers deem the services of such experts necessary for the defence, their expenses will normally be covered by free legal aid. The same applies to the reasonable expenses incurred by witnesses in attending the trial to give evidence.

13. Choice of Solicitor

The constitutional right to free legal aid for impecunious defendants does not extend to a right to choose a particular solicitor or counsel. Moreover, neither the 1965 Act nor the regulations made pursuant to it purport to confer such a right on the defendant.[42] Indeed, there is no specific legal obligation on either

11–22

---

[39] Criminal Legal Aid Review Committee *First Report: An Examination of the Feasibility of Introducing a Public Defender System for Ireland op. cit* at 12. In its *Final Report* (Stationery Office, Dublin 2002) the Committee recommend against a replacement of the current method of delivery of legal aid services by a "contracting-out" arrangement.

[40] *ibid.*

[41] *ibid.* The *Criminal Legal Aid Review Committee; Final Report* recommends the retention of the parity framework but also recommends that the Department of Justice, Equality and Law Reform renegotiate with the Law Society the terms of the existing relationship between solicitors and counsel under the current scheme so that the former can be paid fully for their work; *loc. cit.*, para.8.6.

[42] The regulations are the Criminal Justice (Legal Aid) Regulations 1965.

solicitors or barristers to participate in the free legal scheme. They are free to opt in and, subsequently, to opt out. Each county registrar is under a duty to compile and maintain a register of those solicitors who have notified him of their wish to participate in the scheme in respect of the court or courts within his or her area.[43] Similarly the Minister for Justice, Equality and Law Reform is under a duty to compile and maintain such a register with respect to barristers notified to him by the Bar Council as being willing to participate in the scheme.[44] These lists are circulated to the registrars of the Supreme Court, the Court of Criminal Appeal, the High Court, the Central Criminal Court and the Special Criminal Court. They are also sent to each District Court clerk.[45] Registrars of the various courts, the county registrars and the District Court clerks must keep a register of all legal aid applications specifying: date of application; name of applicant; in general terms, the charge or charges involved and the nature of the proceedings; and, if the application is granted, the names of the solicitor and counsel (if any) assigned.[46]

Where a defendant is granted free legal aid, the court in question will assign a solicitor from the list of those registered as willing to act under the scheme for sittings of the court in that area. In making the assignment the court must take into consideration the representations, if any, of the defendant concerned.[47] In practice this usually results in the assignment of the particular solicitor chosen by the defendant.[47a] This, however, should not be interpreted as an absolute right to the assignment of the solicitor of one's own choice. The court retains a discretion in the matter, particularly if, for some reason, the defendant's choice of solicitor is not readily available. In *State (Freeman) v. Connellan*[48] Barr J. confirmed that the court has a discretion to decide what solicitor will be assigned to a successful applicant for legal aid. Before making the assignment the court must take into account any representations made by the accused as to why he or she wants to have a particular solicitor assigned. Indeed, there would have to be good and sufficient reason not to assign the solicitor of choice in a any individual case:

> "I am also of the opinion that the court should be very slow indeed to refuse to nominate the applicant's choice of solicitor if the person nominated is duly qualified for assignment and should do so only if in the view of the judge there is good and sufficient reason why the applicant should be deprived of the services of the solicitor nominated by him."[48a]

If, however, the court is satisfied that there is a strong compelling reason for refusing to assign the solicitor of the accused's choice, the court should state

---

43 Criminal Justice (Legal Aid) Regulations 1965, reg.4.
44 *ibid*. reg.5.
45 The list of solicitors is also sent to the Secretary of the Law Society.
46 Criminal Justice (Legal Aid) Regulations 1965, reg.6.
47 Criminal Justice (Legal Aid) Regulations 1965, reg.7.
47a The *Criminal Legal Aid Review Committee: Final Report* (Stationey Office, Dublin, 2002) recommends against the adoption of a "Duty-solicitor" scheme for defendants on their first appearance before the District Court.
48 [1986] I.R. 433.
48a *ibid*. per Barr J. at 440.

the reason, and should enquire whether the accused wishes to nominate any other particular solicitor. The reason would have to relate to some quality in the solicitor as distinct from the particular circumstances of the case. In *Mulhall v. O'Donnell*,[48b] for example, the High Court quashed the applicant's conviction because he had been denied the solicitor of his choice. The District Court judge had refused to nominate his solicitor of choice because his three co-accused had all nominated another solicitor. Murphy J. explained that that was not a sufficient reason to deny the applicant his choice of solicitor.

The limits to freedom of choice are illustrated by *State (Royle) v. Kelly*.[49] In **11–23** that case the applicant was granted free legal aid by the Special Criminal Court and the solicitor of his choice was assigned. On the day fixed for the commencement of the trial the solicitor notified the court that he was not in a position to proceed with the case as he had just received the book of evidence. He also submitted that he would have to withdraw from the case if compelled to proceed. Even though his application for an adjournment was refused the case did not proceed that day as it was adjourned on the application of a co-accused. The registrar of the court subsequently invited the applicant to nominate another solicitor after informing him that his solicitor of choice had withdrawn from the case. However, the applicant refused to be represented by anyone other than his original choice, and was duly tried and convicted without legal representation. The Supreme Court ruled that the Special Criminal Court was acting within its powers when it refused to assign the solicitor originally selected by the applicant. It was acting within its discretion in holding the applicant's choice of solicitor to his withdrawal from the case. While this is a clear acknowledgement of the court's discretion in the matter, the Supreme Court specifically declined to define the limits of that discretion.

D. Quality of Legal Representation

In *State (Healy) v. O'Donoghue*[50] the Supreme Court specifically linked the **11–24** right to free legal aid to the accused's constitutional right to a fair trial. According to the Supreme Court there are circumstances in which the accused's right to a fair trial depend on the availability of professional legal representation. Without the benefit of such legal representation the accused might be denied the equality of arms with the prosecution which was essential to vindicate his right to a fair trial. Where the accused could not afford such representation, therefore, the state was under a duty to make it available to him. In most cases this duty would be satisfied simply by the state paying for the accused's legal representation. If, however, that representation was so defective that the accused was denied equality of arms with the prosecution, the mere fact that the state paid or was willing to pay for it could

---

[48b] [1989] I.L.R.M. 367.
[49] [1974] I.R. 259.
[50] [1976] I.R. 325.

not avert the fact that the accused had been denied a fair trial. Moreover, this argument is not confined to cases in which the accused has depended on the free legal aid scheme. If professional legal representation for the accused is a necessary component of a fair trial in certain circumstances, it must follow that he is denied a fair trial in those cases where the quality of representation has been so poor as to deny him equality of arms with the prosecution. The question of who paid for the representation can hardly be the sole determinant. If, however, the state seeks to take advantage of it by standing on the conviction, it is arguable that the state has failed in its duty to vindicate the right of the accused to a fair trial. This raises the awkward question of whether the accused can challenge his conviction on the basis of the inadequacy of his legal representation.

A conviction has never been quashed in Ireland on the basis of the poor performance of the defendant's legal representatives. This might be partly explained by the impact of the House of Lords decision in *Rondell v. Worsley*[51] which afforded an advocate immunity for negligence in the conduct of litigation. It has been assumed in some quarters that the public policy reasons underpinning this decision would apply equally to an attempt to upset a conviction on the basis of poor advocacy. While the issue in *Worsley* has not been the subject of a direct judicial decision in Ireland it was cited with approval by the High Court in *W v. Ireland (No.2)*[52] in support of its decision that on public policy grounds the Attorney General was immune from a civil action for negligence in the handling of an extradition matter. Since then the House of Lords has resiled from its decision in *Worsley* and declared that advocates no longer enjoy immunity from suit in respect of their conduct of civil and criminal proceedings.[53] These decisions, however, do not determine the central issue which is whether poor legal representation can afford a basis for quashing a conviction and/or sentence. It is at least arguable that the constitutional right to a fair trial implicit in Article 38.1 provides a sound basis for such a claim.[54]

The Court of Criminal Appeal has accepted that a person's right to a criminal trial in due course of law, as protected by Article 38.1 of the Constitution, can be vitiated by the manner in which his defence is conducted by his legal advisers. It would only be in exceptional circumstances, however, that the conduct of the defence during the trial and/or in matters preliminary to the trial would afford grounds for appeal against conviction. An example would be a decision not to call the accused to give evidence on his own behalf where such decision was taken either in defiance of or without proper instructions or when all the "promptings of reason and good sense" pointed the other way.[55] In *People (DPP) v. McDonagh*[56] the Court of Criminal

---

[51] [1969] 1 A.C. 191.

[52] [1997] 2 I.R. 141.

[53] *Arthur J S Hall v. Simons* [2000] 3 All E.R. 673. The immunity with respect to advocacy in criminal proceedings was by a majority of four to three.

[54] See Ryan and Magee *The Irish Criminal Process* (Mercier Press, Dublin, 1983), pp.218–221.

[55] *People (DPP) v. McDonagh* [2001] 3 I.R. 411, *per* Keane C.J. at 426, quoting with approval from Rougier J. in the English Court of Appeal in *R v. Clinton* [1993] 1 W.L.R. 1181 at 1188.

[56] *ibid.*

Appeal considered that while it would not be necessary for the appellant to go so far as to show that counsel's conduct of the case could be described as "flagrantly incompetent advocacy", it would equally not be sufficient merely to show that counsel may have made a mistaken decision in the course of the trial or one which, in retrospect, is shown to have been mistaken.

In the *McDonagh* case counsel made a professional decision not to call the defendant to give evidence on his own behalf and not to interview certain witnesses who had given statements in support of the defendant's claim that he was not present at the scene of the crime. On the particular facts of the case counsel considered that the better option would be to pursue an acquittal primarily by attacking weaknesses in the prosecution case. He concluded that the defendant would be an unimpressive witness and that the other witnesses would be unlikely to assist in the conduct of the defence. The Court of Criminal Appeal concluded that even if this could be described as a mistaken decision (and the court was very far from saying that it could be described thus) it fell very far short of what would be required to warrant upsetting the conviction.

The court in *McDonagh* also drew attention to the fact that senior counsel who had originally been engaged by the defence had to withdraw at a very late stage due to commitments in another trial. The result was that the senior counsel who actually conducted the defence in court was briefed the weekend before the trial commenced and did not have a consultation with the defendant until one hour before the trial was listed for hearing. This was in clear breach of the Code of Conduct of the Bar of Ireland. The court described these circumstances as "a highly regrettable state of affairs" and felt compelled to draw the attention of the Bar Council to the situation. However, there was no suggestion that it would be sufficient in itself to constitute a ground of appeal against conviction.

CHAPTER 12

PROSECUTORS AND THE DECISION TO PROSECUTE

A. Introduction

Once sufficient incriminating evidence has been compiled against a criminal suspect a decision must be taken on whether he or she is to be prosecuted. The suspect will be tried in court on a specific criminal charge only if a positive decision is taken to initiate and proceed with the prosecution. This immediately raises the issue of who has the responsibility for initiating these steps in any individual case. The first person to spring to mind is, of course, the victim, assuming that there is an identifiable victim. Indeed, in the not too distant past it was quite normal in Britain for victims to initiate and conduct criminal prosecutions in much the same way that they pursue civil actions today. Prosecutions were also brought regularly by private individuals and societies who were committed to the prevention and detection of crime and the improvement of the morals of the community. Towards the end of the seventeenth century numerous societies for the reformation of manners sprang up in England with the object of increasing the rate of prosecution for offences associated with anti-social behaviour and immorality. Radzinowicz states that these spread throughout the British Isles.[1] No doubt many were also motivated by financial gain in that fixed sums were often payable to those responsible for securing convictions in a whole range of offences.[2]

    By the end of the eighteenth century it was generally accepted in both Britain and Ireland that the heavy reliance on private initiative in the detection

12–01

---

[1] L Radzinowicz, *A History of the English Criminal Law vols.1–4* (Stevens and Sons, London, 1956); see generally, vol.2 "The Enforcement of the Law" chap.1, and vol.3 "The Reform of the Police" chaps. 6 and 7.

[2] *ibid.* at vol.1 chaps. 3, 4 and 5.

and prosecution of crime had proved inadequate. From then on the strategy moved very definitely in favour of the establishment of public professional police forces and prosecution agencies.[3] The Dublin Metropolitan Police was established initially in 1786, the London Metropolitan Police followed in 1829 and, by the middle of the nineteenth century virtually the whole of Britain and Ireland was policed by public professional police forces. Also, the office of Director of Public Prosecutions was established in Britain in 1879, while the Attorney-General for Ireland, in conjunction with Crown Solicitors, provided a similar service in Ireland. Prosecutions by private citizens and societies were not abolished, but as the century progressed they diminished in relative importance to those taken by the police and public prosecutors.

This chapter addresses the status, powers and functions of the prosecutors in the initiation of prosecutions only. Treatment of how prosecutions are progressed through the criminal process is left to the chapters dealing with the relevant parts of that process. One feature which can be deduced from the following survey of the primary prosecutors in the Ireland is the fact that they have developed in a haphazard manner and without the benefit of any clear and coherent system.[4] In its fifteenth report the Select Committee on Crime, Lawlessness and Vandalism had this to say on the matter:

> "A fundamental question in examining the prosecution system and making recommendations for the future is to consider whether, if, assuming the total absence of any existing prosecution system, anyone would recommend the establishing of a system on the lines of the present one. In the view of the Select Committee, the answer to any such hypothetical question is a resounding 'No!'"[5]

The haphazard development of the authorities has resulted in serious gaps in transparency and accountability.[6] These matters are not addressed directly in the following account which focuses primarily on the status, composition, function and modus operandi of each of the primary prosecuting authorities recognised by Irish law.

B. Attorney General

12–02   The current office of Attorney General was established by Article 30.1 of the 1937 Constitution which reads:

---

[3] *ibid.* at vol.3, chs.1, 2, 5, 9, 10, 14 & 15. See also S. Palmer, *Police and Protest in England and Ireland 1780–1850* (Cambridge University Press, Cambridge 1988).

[4] A private member's bill providing for, *inter alia*, the introduction of a unified prosecution system was introduced in the Dáil in February 1996, but was defeated by 73 votes to 58. The first incumbent in the Office of DPP, Eamonn Barnes, was a strong advocate of a unified prosecution system; see, for example, "The Role of the Office of the Director of Public Prosecutions" *Communique 1993*. The arguments for and against a unified prosecution system are set out very succinctly in *Report of the Review Group on the Law Offices of the State* (Stationery Office, Dublin, 1997) at paras.3.16–3.27.

[5] *Fifteenth Report of the Select Committee on Crime, Lawlessness and Vandalism: the Prosecution of Offences* (Stationery Office, Dublin, PL4703) para.8.6.

[6] For further discussion see J. Casey, *The Irish Law Officers* (Round Hall Sweet & Maxwell, Dublin, 1996) at 261–276.

"There shall be an Attorney General who shall be the adviser of the Government in matters of law and legal opinion, and shall exercise and perform all such powers, functions and duties as are conferred or imposed on him by the Constitution or by law."

As far as the Attorney General's "powers, functions and duties" pertaining to the criminal law are concerned the Constitution specifically states in Article 30.3:

"All crimes and offences prosecuted in any court constituted under Article 34 of this Constitution other than a court of summary jurisdiction shall be prosecuted in the name of the People and at the suit of the Attorney General or some other person authorised in accordance with law for that purpose."

However, the antecedents of the office in Ireland stretch far back beyond the 1937 Constitution. Although not mentioned in the 1922 Constitution there was an office of Attorney General in the Irish Free State. Prior to 1922 it existed in the form of the Attorney General for Ireland, which in turn was rooted in the common law.[7]

These antecedents are significant because Article 30.1 of the 1937 Constitution stipulates that the Attorney General shall exercise and perform those powers, functions and duties "as are conferred or imposed on him by the Constitution *or by law*" (emphasis added). It follows that the statement of the Attorney General's prosecutorial powers, functions and duties specified in Article 30.3 can be supplemented by statutory and common law provisions. The most important of these are to be found in section 9 of the Criminal Justice (Administration) Act 1924 which reads:

"(1) All criminal charges prosecuted upon indictment in any court shall be prosecuted at the suit of the Attorney General of Saorstát Éireann.
(2) Save where a criminal prosecution in a court of summary jurisdiction is prosecuted by a Minister, Department of State, or person (official or unofficial) authorised in that behalf by the law for the time being in force, all prosecutions in any court of summary jurisdiction shall be prosecuted at the suit of the Attorney General of Saorstát Éireann."

This provision confirms what had already been the position at common law **12–03** namely that the Attorney General is competent to prosecute all offences on indictment and is a competent prosecutor of summary offences. However, there are two features which require further comment. First, section 9(1) purports to confer on the Attorney General an exclusive power to prosecute offences upon indictment. Prior to its enactment private citizens were competent to prosecute on indictment at common law (see later). It would appear, therefore, that section 9(1) has abolished this common law competence of the private citizen to pursue a prosecution beyond the committal stage.[8] Indeed,

---

7 See J Casey *The Office of the Attorney General in Ireland* (Institute of Public Administration, Dublin, 1980) at chaps 1 and 2.
8 Ryan and Magee cite s.9(1) as authority for the proposition that the right of private prosecution has been abolished except in courts of summary jurisdiction; Ryan and Magee *The Irish Criminal Process* (Mercier Press, Dublin, 1983) at p. 71. However, Casey suggests that this may be a misinterpretation of the original legislative intention; *op. cit.* at p. 94.

this is confirmed by the Supreme Court in *State (Ennis) v. Farrell*[9] where O'Dalaigh C.J. explained that:

> "The only limitation on the right of a private prosecutor is that a prosecution on *indictment* must be conducted by the Attorney General; s.9 sub–s.1, of the Act of 1924. As a consequence, the private prosecutor may conduct the prosecution thus far, i.e. up to the receiving of informations and the order for return for trial. Thereafter the Attorney General becomes *dominus litus*"[10]

Second, the terms of section 9(2) raise some doubt over the competence of the Attorney General to prosecute in courts of summary jurisdiction in cases where "a Minister, Department of State or person (official or unofficial)" is authorised by law to prosecute. This issue was addressed in *Attorney General v. Healy*.[11] In that case the Attorney General had initiated a summary prosecution in a matter where a statutory provision specifically empowered an officer of the Customs and Excise to prosecute. In rejecting a challenge to the Attorney General's competence to prosecute in the case, Sullivan P. explained that the Attorney General is competent to prosecute in all cases where a prosecution has not been instituted by the appropriate "Minister, Department of State, or authorised person."[12] In this context an "authorised person" would include a private citizen at common law. At the very least, therefore, the Attorney (now his successor the DPP) is a prosecutor of last resort in such cases. What is not so clear, however, is whether the Attorney General (or his successor the DPP) can prosecute in a court of summary jurisdiction where there is another competent prosecutor who has yet to decide on prosecution.[13] In *People (DPP) v. Roddy*,[14] O'Higgins C.J. intimated that the DPP would not be competent to prosecute in such a case unless the other competent prosecutor decided against prosecution.[15] In contrast, however, Parke J. felt that the DPP was something more than a prosecutor of last resort in courts of summary jurisdiction, although he did not elaborate upon the point.[16]

12–04 Article 30.3 of the Constitution clearly envisages the possibility of persons other than the Attorney General having the right to prosecute on indictment. That much is evident from the inclusion of the words "or some person authorised in accordance with law for that purpose". Since the common law right of private citizens to prosecute upon indictment had been abolished by the Criminal Justice (Administration) Act 1924, the competence of these other

---

9   [1966] I.R. 107.
10 *State (Ennis) v. Farrell* [1966] I.R. 107 at 121.
11 [1928] I.R. 460. See also *Attorney–General v. Dillon* [1959] Ir. Jur. Rep. 53.
12 *Attorney General v. Healy* [1928] I.R. 460 at 478.
13 Ryan and Magee take the view that the DPP is a prosecutor of last resort in such cases; *op. cit.* at p. 73.
14 [1977] I.R. 177.
15 *ibid.* at pp. 183–184. Interestingly, at p. 185, O'Higgins C.J. opined that the DPP could instruct the member of the Garda Síochána concerned not to prosecute in an individual case and thereby take over the prosecution of the case himself. It is respectfully submitted that the member would be under no legal obligation to comply with such a request; see *State (DPP) v. District Justice Ruane* [1985] I.L.R.M. 349.
16 *ibid.* at p. 191.

persons would have to be based on statutory authority enacted after that Act. Such legislation has been enacted in the form of the Prosecution of Offences Act 1974. It creates the office of the Director of Public Prosecutions (DPP) and confers on that office most of the Attorney General's functions in criminal matters. The nature, powers and functions of the DPP's office will be considered in some detail below, along with the impact that the creation of the office has had on the scope of the Attorney General's powers of prosecution.

C. Director of Public Prosecutions

The Office of Director of Public Prosecutions was established by the **12–05** Prosecution of Offences Act 1974.[17] The official reason given at the time was the need to reduce the demands on the Attorney General's office.[18] Ireland's accession to the European Communities had greatly increased the demands on the Attorney. It was considered, therefore, that his prosecutorial functions should be hived off in order to permit the more effective discharge of his primary functions as legal adviser to the government. The DPP's office was established to undertake these prosecutorial functions.

Although it did not form part of the official explanation, there can be little doubt that the establishment of the office of DPP was also motivated by the need to secure the appearance of independence in prosecutions.[19] Given that the Attorney General was effectively a political appointee and functioned as legal adviser to the government, there was always the danger that the appearance of independence would be compromised in prosecutions which had domestic political implications. The integrity of prosecutions and the judicial process in criminal matters required not only that prosecutions were handled impartially, but that they also had the appearance of being handled impartially. Accordingly, the 1974 Act specifically provides that the DPP shall have the status of a civil servant "in the Civil Service of the State (as distinct from a civil servant of the government),[20] and that he "shall be independent in the performance of his functions".[21] He is not answerable either to the government or to the Attorney General for the performance of his functions.[22] In his annual report for 1998 the DPP explains that the nature of the office is such that it necessitates the same requirement for totally independent judgement and action as constitutionally attributed to the Attorney General.[23] In stipulating that the DPP shall be

---

[17] Prosecution of Offences Act 1974, s.2(1).
[18] Dáil Debates Vol.273, Col.803.
[19] The office of DPP for Northern Ireland was established in 1972 to subsume the Attorney General for Northern Ireland's prosecutorial functions (see Prosecution of Offences Act (Northern Ireland) Act 1972). Interestingly, the explanation given for this development in Northern Ireland was to remove prosecutions from any hint of political influence.
[20] Prosecution of Offences Act 1974, s.2(4). See *McLoughlin v. Minister for Social Welfare* [1958[I.R. 1 for development of the notion that a civil servant of the State enjoys an independence from political direction which is lacking in a civil servant of the government.
[21] Prosecution of Offences Act 1974, s.2(5).
[22] See J Casey *The Irish Law Officers* (Round Hall Sweet & Maxwell, Dublin, 1996), p. 255.
[23] Office of the DPP *1998 Annual Report* (DPP, Dublin, 1999), p. 13.

independent in the performance of his functions, therefore, the 1974 Act was merely underlining the constitutional position. In the DPP's view the independence of his office is essential as a safeguard for the citizen against arbitrary, unjust or improperly motivated prosecution.[24] This point is developed further below in the context of the exercise of the discretion to prosecute. It is important to emphasise, however, that it is an independence from improper interference or influence, and not independence from the rule of law. Ultimately he is subject to, and is obliged to act in accordance with, the Constitution and the law.

The DPP's independence from improper political interference receives further support from section 6 of the Prosecution of Offences Act 1974 which renders unlawful certain communications aimed at securing a decision not to initiate criminal proceedings (this includes a decision to seek a sentence review as well as a decision to initiate a prosecution), the withdrawal of criminal proceedings which have already been initiated, a decision not to prefer a particular charge or the withdrawal of a particular charge which has already been preferred. The prohibited communication covers any such communication with the Attorney General or an officer of the Attorney General, the DPP or an officer of the DPP, the Acting DPP, a member of the Garda Síochána or a solicitor who acts on behalf of the Attorney General in his official capacity or on behalf of the DPP in his official capacity.[25] It does not specifically extend to any other person competent to initiate a prosecution in an individual case. The section specifically precludes from the prohibition communications made by a person who is a defendant or a complainant in a criminal proceedings or who believes that he is likely to be a defendant in such proceedings.[26] Equally it does not extend to communications made by a person involved in the matter either personally or as a legal or medical adviser to a person involved in the matter or as a social worker or a member of the family of a person involved in the matter.[27] A prosecutor within the scope of section 6 is under a duty not to entertain any communication rendered unlawful by the section.[28]

Section 6 clearly outlaws attempts by politicians acting on behalf of constituents to persuade the DPP (or other prosecutors within the scope of the section) to drop a prosecution or individual charges. It also places the DPP under a duty not to entertain such unlawful communications. In his 1998 Annual Report the DPP describes the provision as constituting valuable assistance in

---

[24] *ibid*. In describing the Mission of the Office, the DPP's Strategy Statement 2001–2003 states that Independence is a core value of the Office. It goes on to say that: "The need for the prosecution service both to be and to be seen to be independent was a key reason for its establishment. Subject to the Courts, the Director is independent of all other bodies and institutions, including both the Government and the Garda Síochána, and decisions are taken free from political or other influence." At para.5.3.

[25] Prosecution of Offences Act 1974, s.6(1)(a).

[26] *ibid*. s.6(2)(a)(i).

[27] *ibid*. s.6(2)(a)(ii). For this purpose, "member of the family" means: wife, husband, father, mother, grandfather, grandmother, stepfather, stepmother, son, daughter, grandson, granddaughter, stepson, stepdaughter, brother, sister, half-brother, half-sister, and a person who is the subject of, or in whose favour there is made, an adoption order under the Adoption Acts 1952 and 1964; Prosecution of Offences Act 1974, s.6(2)(b).

[28] *ibid*. s.6(1)(b).

withstanding any such attempts to influence him not to initiate or continue a prosecution.[29] However, there is no counterpart specifically outlawing communications aimed at influencing a decision to initiate a prosecution.

The DPP's independence is not compromised by the fact that he is appointed by the government,[30] he can be removed by the government[31] and his office comes under the general remit of the Department of Justice, Equality and Law Reform. It is also worth noting that the Deputy DPP is the Accounting Officer for the Office and appears before the Dáil Committee of Public Accounts to answer questions on the expenditure, general administration and effectiveness of the Office.[32] There is no suggestion that any of these powers or authorities can be used as an improper means of influencing the DPP's prosecutorial policies or decisions in individual cases. Indeed, the qualifications for appointment and the procedures which must be followed for appointment and removal severely limit the scope for improper interference in the independence of the office.

The qualifications for appointment to the office are laid down by statute as are the procedures for appointment and removal. Eligibility is confined to a person who, at the date of appointment, is a practising barrister or a practising solicitor and has practised as a barrister or a solicitor for at least ten years.[33] Service in the Civil Service in a position for which practice as a solicitor or a barrister was a pre-requisite qualifies as practice for this purpose.[34] When making an appointment the government must choose from a list of candidates selected by a committee composed of: the Chief Justice, the Chairman of the Bar Council, the President of the Law Society, the Secretary to the Government and the senior legal assistant in the office of the Attorney General.[35] Before removing the incumbent from the office of DPP the government must request a committee composed of the Chief Justice, a judge of the High Court and the Attorney General to investigate the health of the Director or inquire into his conduct either generally or in an individual case.[36] This committee must carry out the investigation or inquiry into the matters mentioned in the request and report to the government. For the purpose of its investigation the committee has all the powers, rights and privileges of the High Court. The government may remove the DPP after consideration of the report. These procedures severely limit the scope for any political interference in the independence of the office. Similarly, the Minister for Justice, Equality and Law Reform is not answerable to the Dáil for the actual prosecutorial policies or decisions applied or taken by the DPP.

---

[29] *1998 Annual Report of the DPP op. cit.* at 13.
[30] Prosecution of Offences Act 1974, s.2(2).
[31] *ibid.* s.2(9).
[32] *1998 Annual Report op. cit.* at 23.
[33] Prosecution of Offences Act 1974, s.2(3)(a).
[34] *ibid.* s.2(9)(b).
[35] *ibid.* s.2(7).
[36] *ibid.* s.2(9). The DPP describes this committee as in effect a standing tribunal of enquiry available to examine the performance of the DPP and his fitness for office; see *1998 Annual Report, op. cit.* at 23.

12–06 The functions of the DPP are set out in section 3 of the 1974 Act. Broadly speaking he has replaced the Attorney General in criminal matters. The relevant subsection reads as follows:

> "Subject to the provisions of this Act, the Director shall perform all the functions capable of being performed in relation to criminal matters and in relation to election petitions and referendum petitions by the Attorney General immediately before the commencement of this section and references to the Attorney General in any statute or statutory instrument in force immediately before such commencement shall be construed accordingly."[37]

Clearly section 3 transfers to the DPP all of the functions of the Attorney General in relation to the initiation and conduct of criminal prosecutions, as well as some other matters pertaining to election and referendum petitions.[38] In practice this has been interpreted to mean that, subject to some clearly defined exceptions, all of the functions of the Attorney General in criminal matters, including the power to initiate prosecutions on indictment, have been transferred completely to the DPP.[39] The Attorney General is no longer competent in these matters, although there is provision for the Government to clawback transferred matters to the Attorney General in certain limited circumstances. Generally, legislation would be required before the Attorney General could initiate a prosecution in any of the transferred matters.[40] Furthermore, the independence of the office of DPP precludes the Attorney General from exercising control over any of the DPP's decisions with respect to prosecutions. Although there is provision for them to consult from time to time,[41] this does not mean that the DPP is under any obligation to seek or to act upon the advice of the Attorney General.[42]

The 1974 Act also extends to prosecutions in courts of summary jurisdiction. It follows that the DPP can prosecute in courts of summary jurisdiction where "a Minister, Department of State, or person (official or unofficial) authorised in

---

[37] Prosecution of Offences Act 1974, s.3(1).

[38] This includes the power to enter a *nolle prosequi*; see *State (O'Callaghan) v. O'hUadaigh* [1977] I.R. 42. However, it does not affect the functions of the Attorney General in relation to any question as to the constitutional validity of any law; Prosecution of Offences Act 1974, s.3(3). Moreover, the DPP has not stepped into the shoes of the Attorney General for the purposes of the requirement that the consent of the Attorney General must be forthcoming before prosecutions can proceed for offences under s.3 of the Geneva Conventions Act 1962, the Official Secrets Act 1963 and the Genocide Act 1973.

[39] There is an *obiter dictum* from Walsh J. in *State (Collins) v. District Justice Ruane* [1984] I.R. 105 at 118–119 which suggests that the DPP shares these functions with the Attorney General, but that view would appear to be exceptional. See J Casey *The Irish Law Officers op. cit.* at 255–256 and J Casey "Criminal Procedure-Prévert's General? The Supreme Court on the DPP" (1984) 6 D.U.L.J. 171.

[40] Prosecution of Offences Act 1974, s.5(1). Note also that legislation has been enacted to confer on the Attorney General exclusive powers of prosecution on indictment in relation to certain criminal offences (see later).

[41] Prosecution of Offences Act 1974, s.2(6) reads:
"The Attorney General and the Director shall consult together from time to time in relation to matters pertaining to the functions of the Director."

[42] Paragraph 4 of the Explanatory Memorandum issued by the Taoiseach's Department states: "The provision (for consultation) would not confer on the Attorney General any right to give directions to the Director as to how he will perform his functions in relation either to particular cases or generally." Quoted in Casey *op. cit* at p. 227 fn.12

that behalf by the law for the time being in force" has declined to prosecute (see above under 'The Attorney General').[43] He has replaced the Attorney General in these matters. Just as the DPP has acquired the prosecutorial competence of the Attorney General in most summary matters, so also is he subject to the limitations that applied to the Attorney General's competence in such matters. Accordingly, if a duly authorised person or body has the power to prosecute in an individual case before a court of summary jurisdiction, it is unlikely that the DPP can prosecute in that case unless the "duly authorised person or body" has declined to prosecute. Moreover, where a person has exercised the right to prosecute as a common informer the DPP cannot intervene to have the prosecution withdrawn.[44]

It would be a mistake to conclude that the 1974 Act has completely divested the Attorney General of his prosecutorial authority. In fact, the Act specifically retains some functions for the Attorney General. For example, the functions of the Attorney General in relation to the question of the constitutional validity of any law remain unaffected.[45] More particularly, the Act preserves the requirement for his consent before prosecutions can be taken for certain offences.[46] In addition, he retains his power (also enjoyed by the DPP) to certify cases to the Supreme Court under the Courts of Justice Act 1924 and the Criminal Procedure Act 1967.[47] The Government has also retained a limited power to transfer back to the Attorney General any of the powers over criminal matters which the 1974 Act purports to transfer to the DPP. It reads:

12–07

> "Whenever the Government are of the opinion that it is expedient in the interests of national security to do so, they may from time to time declare by order that, in relation to criminal matters of such kind or kinds as are specified in the order, the functions conferred on the Director by this Act may be performed only by the Attorney General, and where any criminal matters stand for the time being so specified, the functions conferred on the Director by this Act in relation thereto shall be performed by the Attorney General and not by the Director."[48]

Clearly, the reference to national security limits the circumstances in which this power may be used. Moreover, where the power is exercised it can be expected that the transfer effected by it will be for a limited period of time. The wording of the provision also suggests that the power can be used only with respect to specified types of offences or criminal proceedings. It is submitted that it could not be used to transfer from the DPP to the Attorney General the power to decide for or against prosecution in a single individual case.

Although the government has yet to exercise the power to effect a temporary transfer back to the Attorney General any of the functions conferred on the DPP by the 1974 Act, legislation has been enacted which vests exclusively in the

---

43 Criminal Justice (Administration) Act 1924, s.9(2) and *Attorney General v. Healy* [1928] I.R. 460.
44 *State (DPP) v. District Justice Ruane* [1985] I.L.R.M. 349.
45 Prosecution of Offences Act 1974, s.3(3).
46 *ibid.* s.3(5). The offences in question arise under the Geneva Conventions Act 1962, the Official Secrets Act 1963 and the Genocide Act 1973.
47 Prosecution of Offences Act 1974, s.3(4).
48 *ibid.* s.5(1).

Attorney General the power to prosecute on indictment for certain specified offences. Such measures, of course, represent an intrusion into the territory of the DPP. Examples include offences created by: section 11(1) of the Dumping at Sea Act 1996; the Sea Pollution Act 1991; and the Fisheries (Amendment) Act 1978. This action has been explained on the basis that the offences in question may involve sensitive political and diplomatic considerations which are more suitable for the Attorney General than the DPP.[49]

Apart from the general stipulation that the DPP shall perform all the functions previously performed by the Attorney General in criminal matters the Prosecution of Offences Act does not define the functions of the DPP in criminal cases. It will be seen later that the DPP's prosecutorial function consists largely of taking the decision on whether or not to prosecute on indictment and, subsequently, the direction or supervision of any such prosecution. He has no investigative function in criminal offences. Whether or not a criminal investigation is warranted on foot of a complaint is a matter primarily for the Garda Síochána, or other appropriate specialist agency, acting in accordance with the law. While the advice and guidance of the Director may be sought from time to time in the conduct of investigations, he has no role in the decision whether to initiate or terminate an investigation.[50] Even in respect of the decision to prosecute it is important to note that the Director's role is confined to a relatively small number of cases.[51] For the most part his office will only be involved directly in the more serious cases. If a case is to be tried on indictment, or before the Special Criminal Court, the decision to prosecute must either be taken or confirmed by the DPP. In purely numerical terms, however, the vast majority of criminal prosecutions are disposed of summarily in the District Court. Most of these are initiated by members of the Garda Síochána without any direct involvement by the DPP.

12–08   It will also be seen later that the DPP, or staff from his office, do not appear in person to present the prosecution case. Cases prosecuted on indictment are normally presented by counsel in private practice instructed on a case by case basis by a State Solicitor outside of Dublin and the Chief State Solicitor within the Dublin Metropolitan Area. As will be seen later, however, the Chief State Solicitor's function in this matter has been transferred to a newly created position of Chief Prosecution Solicitor established within the Office of DPP. Similarly, it is expected that the State Solicitors will provide a solicitor service to the DPP pursuant to a direct contractual relationship with the DPP, rather than, as is the case at the moment, pursuant to a contract with the Attorney General. Most summary prosecutions are presented by an officer of the Garda Síochána.

---

[49]   Dáil Debates Vol.461, Col.377. See also, J Casey *The Irish Law Officers op. cit* at 256–257 for specific discussion on the Fisheries (Amendment) Act 1978.

[50]   Although there is no strict lawyer-client relationship between the DPP and these investigation authorities, the DPP aims to provide a service to them of a standard which a good law firm would provide for its clients; *Strategic Statement 2001–2003* (DPP, Dublin, 2001) at 4.10.

[51]   *1998 Annual Report of the Office of the Director of Public Prosecutions* (DPP, Dublin, 1999), pp. 9–10.

Many of the functions of the DPP in criminal matters are neatly summarised in the following list as set out in the DPP's Annual Report for 1998:[52]

(i) The consideration of Garda criminal investigation files submitted to the Office

(ii) the decision as to whether or not a prosecution should be initiated or as to whether a prosecution already initiated by the Garda Síochána should be maintained and the advising of any further investigations necessary for the commencement or continuation of a prosecution

(iii) the determination of the charges to be preferred and the consideration of any charges already preferred

(iv) the determination of the proofs and other materials to be tendered to the court and to the accused, including issues regarding the disclosure to the defence of unused material

(v) the issuing of decisions regarding the many questions of law and of public policy which can arise in the course of criminal proceedings

(vi) conferring as necessary with counsel, state solicitors, members of the Garda Síochána and persons giving scientific or technical evidence

(vii) deciding whether appeals, including appeals by way of case stated, should be brought or contested and the prosecution or defence of proceedings for judicial review and habeas corpus arising out of criminal proceedings

(viii) the consideration of complaints and allegations of the commission of criminal offences received from members of the public and where appropriate their transmission to the Garda Commissioner

(ix) the consideration of files submitted by the Garda Complaints Board

(x) the drafting or settling of documents necessary for the prosecution of requests for extradition into the State

(xi) the drafting of requests for international mutual assistance in criminal matters

(xii) serving on committees and attending meetings relating to prosecutions and criminal law and procedure; identifying operational problems arising in the administration of the criminal law and assisting on request on matters relevant to proposed criminal legislation; lecturing at the Garda Síochána Training College.

The DPP's functions also include: deciding whether certain cases should be sent for trial in the Special Criminal Court, giving consents for certain indictable offences to be tried summarily, electing between summary and indictable procedures for certain statutory offences, directing the initiation of certain types of prosecution which by law require his consent, the granting of certificates for appeal from the Court of Criminal Appeal to the Supreme Court on points of law of exceptional public importance, considering whether to seek a review of a sentence on grounds of leniency and giving his views to the trial court on whether a custodial sentence would be appropriate.[53] To these must be added his functions under the Criminal Justice Act 1994 in

12–09

---

[52] *ibid.* at pp. 11–12.

[53] In *People v. Furlong* (CCA July 3, 2000) the Court of Criminal Appeal said that if called upon to do so by the court the prosecutor should indicate whether a custodial sentence was or was not appropriate in the circumstances of a particular case. Following consultations with the Bar Council procedures have been put in place to permit the DPP to assist a court on this issue if called upon to do so; *2000 Annual Report of the DPP* (DPP, Dublin, 2001) at para.3.1.

relation to: orders of restraint and confiscation in respect of criminal assets, money-laundering and international mutual assistance in criminal matters. Each of these are dealt with in more detail at the appropriate place in this chapter and elsewhere in the book. The DPP also has certain functions which extend beyond the criminal process. For example, the Attorney General's functions in relation to election petitions and referendum petitions are now performed by the DPP.[54] The DPP also has powers under the Companies Acts to seek the disqualification of persons from holding office as auditor or director in a company or managing a company.[54a]

Despite its central role in the criminal process the Office of the DPP is relatively small. At the end of 2001 it comprised 17 professional officers (barristers and solicitors) and a total of 50 staff.[55] The professional officers were hierarchically structured into a deputy director and professional officer grades II, III and IV.[56] The administrative support services comprised the following units: registry, word processing, personnel and finance, fees, information technology and library. Of these, the registry provides the core essential clerical support required on a daily basis to facilitate the discharge of the primary function of the Office, namely the processing of directions in an efficient and effective manner. According to the DPP's 1998 Annual Report the registry provides a very high level of support through the operation of a centralised file registration and tracking system which facilitates and monitors the movement of all criminal case files and related correspondence within the Office.[57] It also serves to generate a range of information on the status of workload obtaining at any given time. The unit liaises with the State Solicitor Service and the Garda Síochána in the routing and direction of inquiries to the appropriate professional officers in the Office.

12–10   The official establishment and organisation of the Office is undergoing significant change as a result of the implementation of the recommendations of the Public Prosecution System Study Group (see below). The establishment will be increased by the creation of the new post of Chief Prosecution Solicitor, the transfer of solicitors and staff from the Chief State Solicitor's Office and the assignment of the contracts with State Solicitors from the Attorney General's Office to the DPP's Office. A new policy development unit has been created and there has been some organisational changes within the existing units.

The 1974 Act permits the DPP to delegate any of his functions to any of the professional officers in his office.[58] This delegation can relate to a particular case, category of cases or cases generally.[59] The delegatee will be acting

---

[54]   The DPP has suggested that he should be relieved of this function; *Strategy Statement 2001–2003* (Dublin: DPP, 2001) at 3.
[54a] Companies Act 1990, s.160 as amended by Company Law Enforcement Act, 2001, s.42.
[55]   *Strategy Statement 2001–2003* (DPP, Dublin, 2001) at para.2.6.
[56]   *ibid.* at Appendix 3.
[57]   *ibid.* at 26.
[58]   Prosecution of Offences Act 1974, s.4(1). The terms of section 4 also apply to the Attorney General. However, solicitors or barristers appointed by the DPP or the Attorney General to conduct the prosecution in a case are not considered "professional officers" for the purposes of this provision; *Flynn v. DPP* [1986] I.L.R.M. 290.
[59]   The delegation can also be revoked; Prosecution of Offences Act 1974, s.4(2).

on behalf of the DPP and subject to his instructions. The sort of matters that might be delegated under this provision include the making of decisions, issuing of specific directions to lawyers acting on behalf of the DPP and the issuing of certificates where they arise under various statutes of decisions and consents required from the DPP.[60] This power of delegation is a power of internal delegation only. It does not govern, nor does it preclude, the practice of engaging a solicitor or barrister to conduct the actual prosecution.[61] The fact that a function of the DPP has been performed, whether by him personally or by his delegatee, may be established by a statement of that fact in writing and signed by the DPP, or orally to the court concerned by a person appearing on behalf of, or prosecuting in the name of, the DPP.[62]

Up until very recently the DPP had to rely on the services of separate agencies, namely the Chief State Solicitor and State Solicitors (see below) to handle prosecutions on his behalf. The former acted as solicitor for the DPP in prosecutions on indictment and in summary cases in the Dublin Metropolitan Area where directions had been sought from the DPP by members of the Garda Síochána. Outside the Dublin Metropolitan Area these functions are discharged by the State Solicitors. Even though he was heavily dependant on these Solicitors for the discharge of his prosecutorial duties, the DPP had no function in their appointment or management. In effect he had statutory responsibilities with respect to criminal prosecutions without the commensurate control over the means and resources necessary to carry them out fully.[63] This situation has now changed as a result of the implementation of the recommendations of the Public Prosecutions System Study Group (PPSSG).

Pursuant to the PPSSG recommendations a new position of Chief Prosecution **12–11** Solicitor has been created in the DPP's Office.[64] The responsibility for providing a solicitor service to the DPP, which had previously been delivered by the Chief State Solicitor's Office, is now discharged by the Chief Prosecution Solicitor. This development has also entailed the transfer of solicitors and staff involved in providing the service from the criminal division of the Chief State Solicitor's Office to the DPP's Office. The critical difference is that these solicitors and the Chief Prosecution Solicitor are professional officers within the DPP's Office and, as such, are subject to his direct management. In particular this will enable the DPP to delegate the handling of individual prosecutions to them.[65] In addition it is expected that the State Solicitors throughout the country will provide a solicitor's service to the DPP on a contract basis directly with DPP. Initially, this will be achieved

---

[60] *Flynn v. DPP* [1986] I.L.R.M. 290 at 294.
[61] *ibid.*
[62] Prosecution of Offences Act 1974, s.4(3).
[63] *Report of the Public Prosecution System Study Group op. cit.* at para.4.4.
[64] *ibid.* at 5.7; *2000 Annual Report of the DPP* (DPP, Dublin, 2001) 9; and *Strategy Statement 2001–2003* (DPP, Dublin, 2001) at 4.1–4.4.
[65] The *Report of the Public Prosecution System Study Group* also recommended that the DPP should consider delegating to the Chief Prosecution Solicitor the power to take decisions on whether to prosecute in certain categories of case; *op. cit.* at para.5.7.9.

by the assignment of their current contracts from the Attorney General to the DPP. Presumably, legislative action would be required to establish the State Solicitors as professional officers of the DPP, thereby enabling him to delegate prosecutorial functions to them.[66]

D. The Common Informer

12–12 A common informer is the technical name given at common law to an individual who is capable of giving information about the commission of an offence. He or she is most likely to be the victim of the offence, a witness to the offence or someone who has received reliable information about the offence.[67] It follows that a common informer in any individual case will often be a member of the Garda Síochána. Indeed, in *People (DPP) v. Roddy*[68] O'Higgins C.J. confirmed that it was normal practice for policemen to prosecute as common informers in both summary and indictable offences in pre-1922 Ireland.

It would appear, however, that a corporation does not have the status of a common informer. In *Cumann Luthchleas Gael Teoranta v. District Justice Windle*[69] the Supreme Court rejected the argument that a Fire Authority (in effect Dublin Corporation) could bring a prosecution under the Fire Services Act 1981 in the capacity of a common informer. Finlay C.J. giving the judgment of the Court explained that the common law right of prosecution by common informer arose from the status of the person complaining or instituting the proceedings as a member of the public. Members of the public have an interest, attributed to them by legal principle, in the conviction and punishment of offenders against public law. Since a body corporate could not be seen as a member of the public it could not have the status of a common informer at common law.

The common law has always recognised the right of a common informer to prosecute in courts of summary jurisdiction and on indictment.[70] This right was abolished in the case of charges prosecuted on indictment by section 9(1) of the Criminal Justice (Administration) Act 1924. Its survival in the case of summary charges has been confirmed in a number of cases.[71] In *Wedick v. Osmond and Son (Dublin) Ltd,*[72] for example, the prosecutor was an inspector

---

[66] The *Report of the Public Prosecution System Study Group* recommended that in the interests of objectivity and impartiality the Civil Service Commission should be mandated to recommend candidates for appointment as State Solicitors; *op. cit.* at para.5.7.2. This recommendation was not accepted by the government.

[67] See *McCormack v. Carroll* 45 I.L.T.R. 7; and *R (Wilbond) v. Armagh JJ* [1918] 2 I.R. 347 for authority for the proposition that a common informer does not need to be an eye witness of the offence which he prosecutes.

[68] [1977] I.R. 177 at 182–183.

[69] [1994] 1 I.R. 525.

[70] *People (DPP) v. Roddy* [1977] I.R. 177; *Attorney General v. Thompson* 7 I.L.T.R. 161; *Murphy v. Cryan* [1952] I.R. 225; *Kenealy v. O'Keeffe* [1901] 2 I.R. 39; *Lawler v. Egan* [1901] 2 I.R. 589.

[71] The point is now regarded as settled by the Supreme Court in *State (Ennis) v. District Justice Farrell* [1966] I.R. 107.

[72] [1935] I.R. 820.

of the Pharmaceutical Society of Ireland acting in the capacity of a common informer. It was contended in the District Court that he was not a competent prosecutor as the right of a common informer to prosecute in summary matters had been abolished by section 9(2) of the Criminal Justice (Administration) Act 1924. In rejecting this argument Sullivan P said:

> "[I]t seems to me that the sub-section in question is not inconsistent with the pre-existing right of a common informer to prosecute in certain cases. If the Legislature had intended to abolish such a right there would be no difficulty in expressing such intention in plain and unambiguous terms. A common informer prosecuting may well be described as a 'person (unofficial) authorised in that behalf by the law for the time being in force', and, if that be so, his right to prosecute is expressly preserved by the sub-section."[73]

Not only has the citizen's right to prosecute as a common informer survived the establishment of the office of the DPP, but the DPP has no power to intervene in the District Court to effect the withdrawal of a prosecution brought by a common informer.[74]

Although a common informer is not competent to prosecute charges on indictment, it does not follow that he is dependant on the DPP to initiate and proceed with a prosecution on such charges. In *State (Ennis) v. Farrell*[75] the Supreme Court had to consider whether, and to what extent, a common informer could proceed with a private prosecution for the offence of fraudulent conversion which could not be tried summarily. In delivering the judgment of the Court, O'Dalaigh C.J. referred to section 9(1) of the Criminal Justice (Administration) Act 1924 and explained that a prosecution on indictment must be conducted by the Attorney General (now the DPP). However, the common informer remained competent to direct the prosecution up to the receiving of informations and the order for return for trial. Accordingly:

12–13

> "The duty of the District Justice in the case of a private prosecution in respect of an indictable offence is therefore clear. He must permit the private prosecutor to direct and conduct the entire of the preliminary investigation – and at the conclusion of the evidence and including any evidence offered by the defendant must consider whether he should refuse informations or return the accused for trial."[76]

If the District Court judge receives informations in such a case, the common informer is entitled to assume that the DPP will proceed with the prosecution to trial on indictment. A decision to enter a *nolle prosequi* could be taken only after the fullest consideration and for very good reason.[77]

It cannot be assumed that a common informer can prosecute any offence up to the decision to refuse informations or return for trial. His or her competence may be restricted in two situations, irrespective of whether the offence in

---

73 *Wedick v. Osmond and Son (Dublin) Limited* [1935] I.R. 820 at 842–843.
74 *State (DPP) v. District Justice Ruane* [1985] I.L.R.M. 349.
75 [1966] I.R. 107.
76 *State (Ennis) v. Farrell* [1966] I.R. 107 at 121–122.
77 *ibid. per* at 122 O'Dalaigh C.J..

question is summary or indictable.[77a] Firstly, legislation may specifically preclude or restrict the prosecutorial competence of the common informer in respect of specified offences. The second situation arises where the offence in question is designed to protect the interests of identifiable persons, as distinct from the public generally.[78] In this situation, it can be assumed that, in the absence of compelling countervailing considerations, only a person aggrieved or a specifically designated authority can prosecute. An example of a prosecution by a person aggrieved is afforded by *Meath County Council v. Smith*[79] where the County Council had instituted proceedings against the defendant for a failure to maintain her illegitimate child so that he became eligible for general assistance from the County under the Public Assistance Act 1939. The Court ruled that the Council was not prosecuting as a common informer but as a person aggrieved. It is unlikely, therefore, that a member of the general public would have been competent to prosecute in this case unless he or she could show that he was a person aggrieved.

E. An Garda Síochána

12–14   Although the office of DPP has been established in Ireland now for about a quarter of a century, it is still the case that most prosecutions are in fact taken by members of the Garda Síochána. This practice has its roots in the centuries old office of constable, the common law attributes of which have been inherited by each member of the Garda Síochána.[80] Just as it was the normal practice for the constable to prosecute as a common informer in respect of criminal offences which came to his notice, so also have members of the Garda Síochána brought such prosecutions since the establishment of the State. Indeed, in *State (McCormack) v. Curran*[81] Walsh J. intimated that not only was it the common law duty of a member of the Garda Síochána to bring criminals to justice, but a refusal to pursue a criminal who came to his or her attention would in itself be a criminal offence.[82]

The competence of a member of the Garda Síochána to prosecute as a common informer has been considered directly and indirectly by the courts. In *State (Cronin) v. The Circuit Court Judge of the Western Circuit*,[83] for example, the High Court was called upon to consider whether a sergeant in

---

[77a] Note also the impact of the abolition of the preliminary examination by the Criminal Justice Act 1999.

[78] *Kenealy v. O'Keeffe* [1901] 2 I.R. 39.

[79] (1946) 80 I.L.T.R. 122.

[80] See D.P.J. Walsh, *The Irish Police: a Legal and Constitutional Perspective* (Round Hall Sweet & Maxwell, Dublin, 1998) ch.3; and D.P.J. Walsh, "The Legal Status of a Member of the Garda Síochána: New Clothes for the Ancient Office of Constable" *Anglo-American Law Review* 23, 1 (1994) 63–99.

[81] [1987] I.L.R.M. 225 at 239.

[82] Finlay C.J. also adverted to the general duty of a member of the Garda Síochána to pursue persons whom he suspects of committing serious crimes, although he recognised that the member enjoys an element of discretion in deciding whether or not to arrest in an individual case; *op. cit* at p. 236. See *R. v. Dytham* [1979] Q.B. 722; [1979] 3 All E.R. 641.

[83] [1937] I.R. 34.

the Garda Síochána was a competent prosecutor in the District Court on a charge of being drunk in charge of a motor vehicle. The Court upheld his competence to prosecute as a common informer. Kennedy C.J., in delivering the judgment of the Court, stated the law in the following terms:

"Where no statute debars an officer of the Garda Síochána, or any other person, in the guise of a common informer, such person is entitled to lay a charge before the District Justice in the first instance. It was *prima facie* within the authority of Sergeant Cronin to institute the present proceedings."[84]

In *State (DPP) v. District Justice Ruane*[85] the Supreme Court had to consider whether the DPP could intervene in the District Court to effect the withdrawal of a prosecution which had been taken as a member of the Garda Síochána in his capacity as a common informer. The case originated with a member of the Garda Síochána laying a complaint of disorderly behaviour while drunk against Michael Collins who, in turn, laid a complaint of assault and assault occasioning actual bodily harm against the member. Although the member was acting in the course of his duty, his complaint was laid in his own name as a common informer. Collins' complaint against the member was taken by the DPP who also sought to take over and enter a nolle prosequi on the member's complaint against Collins. The question for the Supreme Court was whether the DPP was competent to intervene and withdraw the member's complaint without the member's consent.

The Supreme Court ruled that the DPP had no power to intervene in this manner. Walsh J. explained that a member of the Garda Síochána retains his right to prosecute in his own name as a common informer. Surprisingly, perhaps, the learned judge maintained that this is not altered by the fact that the member may be bringing the prosecution at the expense of public funds and is not liable to have an order for costs awarded against him. While he accepted that a member of the Garda Síochána can be distinguished from other common informers on the basis of his or her function, he concluded that the difference is not so great as to deprive a member of the status as a common informer. Since there is no statutory or common law authority empowering the DPP (or the Attorney General as his predecessor) to have a summons instituted by a common informer withdrawn, it must follow that the DPP has no such power with respect to a member of the Garda Síochána who has instituted a complaint in his capacity as a common informer. If, however, a member institutes a complaint in the name of the DPP (as is often the case) he will be deemed to be bringing it on behalf of the DPP. In this event Walsh J. was of the opinion that the DPP could exercise control over the prosecution.

12–15 The District Court Rules specifically state that any member of the Garda Síochána (or any other person appearing on behalf of the DPP) is entitled to appear and address the Court and conduct proceedings at the suit of the DPP in respect of an offence.[86] In 1975 the DPP issued a general authorisation for

---

84 *State (Cronin) v. Circuit Court Judge, Western Circuit* [1937] I.R. 34 at 51.
85 [1985] I.L.R.M. 349.
86 District Court Rules 1997, Ord.6, r.1(e).

members of the Garda Síochána to institute summary proceedings, and proceedings up to a return for trial, in the name of the DPP. In effect this was carrying on a practice which had prevailed with respect to the Attorney General before the office of DPP had been established (see below under 'Title of Prosecutions'). The net effect was that a member of the Garda Síochána could prosecute in the name of the DPP without having to secure the prior consent of the DPP or even bringing the case to his attention. It also meant, however, that the DPP could exercise control over the prosecution, a power which would be absent if the member prosecuted in his own name as a common informer. This includes the power to stop a prosecution which has been initiated in his name by the Garda Síochána, and the power to prosecute in a case where the Garda Síochána has decided against prosecution.

In practice, it would appear that most Garda prosecutions are taken in the name of the DPP. Casey explains this practice as a result of the position governing the award of costs in the event of a failed prosecution.[87] A member of the Garda Síochána prosecuting as a common informer is not liable to have costs awarded against him in the event of an acquittal in the District Court or withdrawal of the summons.[88] If, however, a conviction is appealed successfully to the Circuit Court, that Court will have jurisdiction to award costs against a member acting in the capacity of a common informer.[89] The member will be personally liable for these costs and he or she cannot assume that they will be discharged out of public funds. Where a Garda prosecutor acts in the name of the DPP there is no danger of him or her having personal liability for an award of costs arising out of the prosecution. There is a clear financial incentive, therefore, to prosecute in the name of the DPP.

12–16   Most summary prosecutions are taken by a member of the Garda Síochána, whether acting in the name of the DPP or as a common informer.[90] Within the Dublin Metropolitan District as many as eighty percent of summary cases are prosecuted by a member of the Garda Síochána, usually the member who investigated the matter.[91] The remainder are prosecuted directly by solicitors from the Chief State Solicitor's Office (now the Chief Prosecution Solicitor), or by counsel retained by the Office. Outside of the Dublin Metropolitan District summary prosecutions initiated as a result of police action are normally presented by a Garda superintendent or inspector. In some cases the prosecution may be taken by the relevant State Solicitor or counsel retained by him. This will happen where, for example, the cases involves a novel legal point, is complex, is of special importance or where the identity or occupation of the defendant may make it desirable in the public interest.

---

[87]   *loc. cit.* at 282–283.
[88]   District Court Rules 1997, Ord.36, r.1. The constitutionality of this rule was upheld in *Dillane v. Ireland* [1980] I.L.R.M. 167.
[89]   *State (DPP) v. Kennedy* High Court, July 11, 1985.
[90]   The Select Committee on Crime Lawlessness and Vandalism felt that this was undesirable. It recommended the establishment of a comprehensive prosecutorial system centred on the DPP; see *Fifteenth Report of the Select Committee on Crime, Lawlessness and Vandalism: the Prosecution of Offences* (Dublin: Stationery Office, PL4703).
[91]   *1998 Annual Report of the Director of Public Prosecutions* (Office of the DPP, Dublin, 1999) p. 10.

In very minor cases the prosecution is sometimes taken by the investigating member of the force without seeking higher authority, although normally the sergeant in charge will have looked at the case and allotted a member to prosecute it. Where civilian witnesses are involved the decision is normally taken by an inspector or sergeant, while outside of Dublin it will be the relevant superintendent or inspector.[92]

It is not unusual for a member of the Garda Síochána to consult with or seek the guidance of the DPP on any aspect of a prosecution, including: what criminal charges are open, whether there is sufficient evidence to support a charge, the admissibility of evidence, the most appropriate charge in the circumstances, the present state of the law, whether a matter should be disposed of summarily or on indictment, advice in relation to cases stated or judicial review and advice in relation to the disclosure of evidence.[93] As a general rule such requests should be made in writing. It must be borne in mind, however, that the DPP's advice in response does not have the status of binding directions.[94]

Generally, the decision whether to seek advice or directions from the DPP before charging is primarily one for the investigator. However, there are a number of offences in respect of which directions on prosecution must be sought from the DPP. These include: homicide, certain sexual offences, fatal road traffic offences, offences under the Official Secrets Act, offences in which it is proposed to ask the DPP to direct a trial in the Special Criminal Court, offences involving explosive substances and offences involving corruption.[95]

In principle, a file should be sent to the DPP's Office in respect of any indictable offence where a decision has to be taken whether to prosecute summarily or on indictment. In order to avoid excessive submission of files the DPP has given gardaí a general election or consent for summary trial in many cases, subject to the right of the presiding judge to refuse jurisdiction.[96] Where it is intended that a case will be prosecuted on indictment the file must be forwarded by the Garda Síochána to the DPP (*via* the relevant State Solicitor or Chief Prosecution Solicitor) for directions on prosecution. It can happen, of course, that an individual will be charged by a member of the Garda Síochána in such a case without the file having first been forwarded to the DPP. Where this happens and the case is proceeding on indictment directions should be sought from the DPP prior to any sending forward for trial.[97] Also,

12–17

---

[92] *Report of the Public Prosecution System Study Group* (Dublin: Stationery Office, 1999) para. 2.2.7.

[93] The Public Prosecution System Study Group recommended that the guidance issued from time to time in response to ad hoc requests should be codified and consolidated to form a constantly updated set of guidelines which should remain confidential within the prosecution system to the extent that that was necessary; see *Report of the Public Prosecution System Study Group* (Dublin: Stationery Office, 1999) para.5.9.3.

[94] See, for example, *State (McCormack) v. Curran* [1987] I.L.R.M. 225.

[95] *Statement of General Guidelines for Prosecutors* (DPP, Dublin, 2001) 19 and 43.

[96] *Report of the Public Prosecution System Study Group* (Stationery Office, Dublin, 1999) para.2.2.5. If, in any such case, the gardaí feel that trial on indictment is warranted and they wish the DPP to revoke his election or consent for summary trial, they must refer the file to his Office.

[97] *ibid.* at 20.

detailed instructions from the Garda Commissioner's Office requires members of the force to seek advice, and where appropriate, instructions from the DPP in the following matters, irrespective of whether they relate to proceedings on indictment:[98]

(a) any case in which it is proposed to seek the accused's extradition;
(b) whether or not an accomplice should be granted immunity;
(c) whether a case should be stated or a judicial review sought;
(d) certain cases involving allegations against members of the Garda Síochána
(e) any case in which the Director's sanction or approval is required for the commencement of proceedings;
(f) any case involving a novel or important point of law or involving a question of law where there is no recent Irish precedent;
(g) matters of particular sensitivity or unusual public interest, such as allegations of corruption or misconduct by public officials.

Arrangements are in place to ensure that a member of the DPP's staff is available outside office hours to deal with urgent cases.

The Report of the Public Prosecutions System Study Group recommends retention of the practice whereby minor offences are prosecuted by the Garda Síochána.[99] In the interests of transparency, however, it suggested that there should be some standardisation of the safeguards within Garda stations against any possible abuse of the process. In particular, it recommended an administrative restriction on the freedom of gardaí to bring criminal prosecutions in their own name as common informers, and the early introduction of the recording of interviews of suspects in Garda stations.

F. Other Prosecutors

12–18   It is quite common for specific statutory bodies or Government Ministers to be given a statutory power to prosecute for specified criminal offences. Typically, this will occur where the body or Minister in question has been given enforcement responsibilities in the context of a regulatory scheme. Where enforcement includes resort to the criminal law it will normally involve conferring the body or Minister with a power to prosecute for statutory offences which have been created as part of the scheme. In the year 2000 alone no less than ten statutes out of a total of 42 confer a power of summary prosecution on bodies such as the Minister for Public Enterprise; the Minister for Enterprise, Trade and Employment; Minister for Social, Community and Family Affairs; Minister for Agriculture, Food and Rural Development; Minister for Justice, Equality and Law Reform; local Planning Authorities; the Collector General; the Equality Authority; the Marine Casualty Investigation Board and the National Education Welfare Board.[100] In each case the power relates to offences created under the

---

[98]   *ibid.*
[99]   *Report of the Public Prosecution System Study Group, op. cit.*, para.5.5.14.
[100] The statutory provisions in question are: Electronic Commerce Act 2000, s.6(1); Copyright and Related Rights Act 2000, s.11; Planning and Development Act 2000, s.157(1); National Training

Act in question. It is worth repeating that the conferral of such a power on a specific body is normally in addition to, instead of in substitution for, that inherent in the common informer. Moreover, the DPP still retains his residual power to prosecute for any of these offences where a competent prosecutor has declined to prosecute.[101]

A feature common to all of these statutory powers is that they relate to prosecutions in a court of summary jurisdiction. Where the offence in question is a summary offence no difficulty arises as the prosecution will be initiated and completed summarily before the District Court. If, however, the offence is indictable the defendant will be returned for trial unless the preconditions for summary trial are satisfied or a decision is taken not to send the defendant forward for trial. Where the defendant is returned for trial on indictment, the statutory body will not be able to sustain the prosecution beyond the return for trial in the absence of specific statutory provision to the contrary. There is also a question over whether a statutory power to prosecute summarily is sufficient to enable a statutory body (other than the DPP) to sustain a prosecution for an indictable offence which is triable summarily up until the point at which the District Court sends the defendant forward for trial. Since a statutory body established as a body corporate does not have the capacity of a common informer for this purpose,[102] its competence in the matter will depend entirely on the correct interpretation of the statutory provision conferring its power to prosecute.

In *TDI Metro Ltd (No.2) v. Judge Delap*[102a] the Supreme Court had to decide whether a statutory body which was empowered to "prosecute summarily" could initiate a prosecution for an indictable offence in the District Court where the offence was triable either way. The issue arose in the context of the Planning legislation which made it a criminal offence to carry out development works without planing permission. Originally this was designated a summary offence. The Planning Act specifically empowered a local Planning Authority to prosecute this offence. As a result of amendments to the legislation the offence was re-designated as an indictable offence which could be tried summarily if the relevant conditions were satisfied. The Authority's power to prosecute offences under the Act was also amended to read that it could "prosecute summarily". Since the offence in question was now an indictable offence and it would not be determined in any individual case whether it would be tried summarily until after the prosecution had been initiated, the question arose whether the Authority had lost its power to prosecute the offence. Geoghegan J., giving judgment for the majority in the Supreme Court, accepted that the words "prosecute summarily" do not make it to crystal clear whether the Planning Authority may only prosecute for summary

12–19

Fund Act 2000, s.8(4); Insurance Act 2000, s.4; National Beef Assurance Scheme Act 2000, 26(1); National Minimum Wage Act 2000, s.37(4); Equal Status Act 2000, s.44(1); Merchant Shipping (Investigation of Marine Casualties) Act 2000, s.41; and Education (Welfare) Act 2000, s.7(1).

[101] *Attorney General v. Healy* [1928] I.R. 460.
[102] *Cumann Luthchleas Gael Teo v. Windle* [1994] 1 I.R. 525.
[102a] [2000] 4 I.R. 337 and 520.

offences or whether they can also prosecute for indictable offences so long as they are being tried summarily. He went on to find that the legislative intention must have been to preserve the Authority's power to prosecute the offence in summary proceedings at least up until such point, if any, that the District Court declines jurisdiction.[103]

TDI Metro highlights the importance of careful drafting when seeking to empower regulatory bodies to prosecute offences created by the regulatory code in question. This is particularly relevant where the code creates offences which are triable either way as well as summary offences. If the legislative intention is to enable a regulatory body to initiate and sustain the prosecution of the indictable offences up until the point when they are either disposed of summarily or the defendant is returned for trial, this should be clearly reflected in the form of wording used. Formulae which enable the body to "prosecute summarily" or to take "summary proceedings" leave too much room for argument either way.

It is worth noting that no single formula is used consistently in conferring a power of summary prosecution. In the year 2000 alone three different formulae are used. The most common (and most ambiguous) is that "Summary proceedings for an offence under this Act may be brought and prosecuted by . . .". In all cases where this formula is used the Act creates offences which are triable either way. In the light of the Supreme Court decision in *TDI Metro* this is sufficient to enable the body in question to prosecute all such offences in the District Court to a conclusion or up until the point where the District Court refuses jurisdiction in the matter. It would appear, however, that the other two formulae empower the bodies in question to prosecute only for summary offences. They read: " Proceedings in relation to a summary offence under this Act may be prosecuted by . . .", and "A summary offence under this Act may be prosecuted by . . .". In all such cases the Act in question creates offences which are triable either way as well as at least one summary offence. It is submitted that the prosecutorial competence of the bodies concerned is confined to the summary offences only and does not extend to the summary trial of the offences which are triable either way.

12–20   *Cumann Luthchleas Gael Teo v. District Judge Windle*[104] provides another salutary illustration of the need for care in the drafting of prosecution powers with respect to indictable offences which are triable summarily. In that case the applicants were prosecuted by a Fire Authority for alleged breaches of the fire regulations in Croke Park contrary to the Fire Services Act 1981. Section 5(1) of the Act effectively classifies all offences under the Act, apart from those to which section 5(2) applies, as summary offences. Section 5(2) classifies certain offences as indictable offences but goes on to stipulate that they can be disposed of summarily in certain specified circumstances. The Fire Authority for the functional area in which the offence is alleged to have been committed is given a power of prosecution in the following terms:

---

[103] For a more literal approach to the interpretation of these words and its consequences see the dissenting judgment of Hardiman J.
[104] [1994] 1 I.R. 525.

"Summary proceedings for an offence to which section 5(1) applies may be brought and prosecuted by the fire authority . . ."[105]

The fact that the power of prosecution was defined by reference to section 5(1) alone meant that the Fire Authority was not competent to pursue summary proceedings for an offence under section 5(2), even though such offences could be disposed of summarily in certain circumstances. Since the offences at issue in *Cumann Luthchleas Gael Teo* were subject to section 5(2) it followed that the local Fire Authority was not competent to initiate and pursue the prosecution in the District Court. An attempt to circumvent the lacuna in the Act by treating the Fire Authority as a common informer was rebuffed by the Supreme Court on the ground that a corporation does not have the status of a common informer.

G. State Solicitors and Chief State Solicitor

The DPP does not conduct the actual prosecution in any case. Nor does he have a staff of prosecutors along the lines of the Criminal Prosecution Service in England and Wales. Outside of the Dublin Metropolitan Area he relies primarily on the State Solicitors to proceed with cases on indictment and, for the most part, the gardaí and other persons authorised by law to do likewise in summary cases. Within the Dublin Metropolitan Area he has relied on the Office of Chief State Solicitor for this purpose.

12–21

Surprising as it may seem, the State solicitors do not come under the direct control of the DPP. They trace their origins back to 1801 when Crown Solicitors were appointed on a part-time basis by the Lord Lieutenant for each of the court circuits in Ireland.[106] Prior to independence, a Crown Solicitor would present to the Attorney General all charges on indictment taken by magistrates within his circuit. In those cases where the Attorney General directed a prosecution the Crown Solicitor would do the necessary preparatory work and brief counsel for the prosecution. At some point in the 1830's Sessional Crown Solicitors were appointed on a part-time basis to perform a similar role in summary cases.[107] Indeed, they would normally present the case at Quarter Sessions and occasionally in courts of summary jurisdiction.

The functions of the Crown Solicitors and Sessional Crown Solicitors were taken over by State Solicitors in 1922. These consisted of a Chief State Solicitor whose responsibility in criminal matters was confined to criminal cases in Dublin, and local State Solicitors who continue to deal with criminal cases within their localities outside of Dublin.

The Chief State Solicitor's office is a constituent part of the Attorney General's Office and he is answerable to the Attorney General for the performance of his functions. He is a civil servant of the government with the rank of secretary general and is appointed by the Attorney General. Up until

---

[105] Fire Services Act 1981, s.6.
[106] Casey, *op. cit* at pp. 22–25.
[107] See Casey, *op. cit.* Also Ryan and Magee, *op. cit.*, p. 69.

2001 the Chief State Solicitor's functions included acting as a solicitor for the DPP and gardaí in the prosecution of cases requiring a solicitor in the Dublin Metropolitan Area. These functions included: preparing the book of evidence, attending to pre-trial matters such as the disclosure of documents, preparing pre-trial applications to the court, conveying the DPP's instructions to counsel retained to present the prosecution case, ensuring that the case is ready to go ahead on the date fixed for trial and attending counsel at the trial. He also served as the formal line of communication between the Garda Síochána and the DPP where the later were seeking advice or directions. Solicitors from the Chief State Solicitor's Office prosecuted, or instructed counsel to prosecute, summary cases in the District Court where, for any reason, it was not considered appropriate for members of the Garda Síochána to conduct the prosecution. In all of these matters the Chief State Solicitor's decisions were based on instructions received from the DPP and material submitted by the Garda Síochána or other investigating authority. It is also worth noting that pursuant to the *Victims Charter* he was required to work with the Garda Síochána to ensure that victims of crime were kept fully informed of developments in the prosecution of offenders, especially where the offence was of a violent or sexual nature. At the victim's request his Office would facilitate a pre-trial meeting with a representative from his Office (or the State Solicitor as the case may be) and counsel to discuss the case (but not for the purpose of discussing evidence with a witness).[108]

Following the recommendations of the Public Prosecution System Study Group the Chief State Solicitor's functions in criminal prosecutions have been transferred to the newly created office of Chief Prosecution Solicitor.[109] This office functions as the DPP's solicitor and discharges all of the functions in criminal matters for the DPP which had previously been discharged by the Chief State Solicitor.[110] The office has been established within the Office of DPP. The solicitors and staff who had previously worked on criminal matters for the DPP within the Chief State Solicitor's Office have been transferred to the DPP's Office and work to the Chief Prosecution Solicitor. The Study Group has also raised the possibility of the appointment of regional offices of the Chief Prosecution Solicitor.[111]

12–22 Outside of Dublin there are 32 State Solicitors.[112] They are appointed primarily on a county basis by the Attorney General from a list drawn up following a competitive interview of suitable applicants by a board consisting of the Secretary General of the Attorney General's Office, the Chief State

---

[108] *Victims Charter* (Dublin: Department of Justice, Equality and Law Reform).

[109] *Report of the Public Prosecution System Study Group, op. cit.,* 5.7, and *2000 Annual Report of the DPP, op. cit.,* at 9.

[110] *The Report of the Public Prosecution System Study Group* also recommended that the DPP should consider delegating to the Chief Prosecution Solicitor the power to take decisions whether to prosecute in specific categories of case; *op. cit.,* 5.7.9.

[111] *Report of the Public Prosecution System Study Group, op. cit.,* para.5.7.10.

[112] There is one in each county, apart from Galway, Limerick, Kildare and Tipperary which have two each and Cork which has four.

Solicitor and the Deputy Director of Public Prosecutions.[113] For the most part, however, they differ little from their predecessors in terms of status and function. They continue to function on a part-time basis while retaining their own private practice. They undertake by contract with the Attorney General to perform certain services within their areas, which include providing a solicitor service to the DPP in criminal prosecutions outside of Dublin. Although technically servants of the State when discharging their functions as State Solicitors, they do not form part of the staff of the DPP,[114] nor can he exercise any managerial control over them.[115] The difficulties that this situation can give rise to have been recognised by the Public Prosecution System Study Group. It recommended that the provision of a solicitor service to the DPP in criminal prosecutions outside of Dublin by the State Solicitors should be done on the basis of a direct contractual relationship between the DPP and the State Solicitors.[116] In effect the contracts should be assigned from the Attorney General to the DPP. This recommendation has been accepted and is in the course of being implemented.[117]

Before proceeding to the practice it is worth noting that the DPP is not bound to rely on the services of a State Solicitor to conduct a prosecution. In *Flynn v. DPP*[118] the Supreme Court had to consider the legality of the DPP's decision to appoint a solicitor employed by the Post Office to conduct a prosecution on indictment for an offence under the Post Office Act 1908. Delivering the judgement of the full Court, Finlay C.J. explained that the practice of the Attorney General to engage solicitors in the public service to conduct prosecutions was nothing more than a convenient administrative practice. There had never been any legal restriction on the Attorney General's choice of solicitor to conduct a prosecution. In any event, the DPP's power to appoint a solicitor for this purpose derived directly from statute and was not inherited from the Attorney General. By vesting the DPP with the power and duty to prosecute offences, the 1974 Act was necessarily implying that the DPP had the power to engage solicitor and counsel for the purpose of conducting the prosecution. Furthermore, the DPP was as free in his choice of solicitor or counsel as the Attorney General had been before him. The practice, of course, is to rely primarily on the State Solicitors. The *Flynn* case was somewhat exceptional in that the prosecution was initiated by a large semi-state body whose interest in the prosecution of the offence was specifically recognised in statute. Since that body had its own solicitors there was some practical sense in appointing them, as opposed to a State Solicitor, to conduct the prosecution.

---

113 *Report of the Public Prosecution System Study Group, op. cit.*, 2.2.15.
114 *McLoughlin v. Minister for Social Welfare* [1958] I.R. 1.
115 The DPP is of the opinion that the State Solicitors are not answerable to him nor subject to his day to day to day control for the implementation of his prosecutorial decisions; see E Barnes "The Role of the Office of the Director of Public Prosecutions" *Communique (September, 1995) 3 at 10*. In *Flynn v. DPP* [1986] I.L.R.M. 290, however, the Supreme Court proceeded on the basis that a solicitor appointed by the DPP to conduct a prosecution would remain entirely within the control and subject to the detailed instructions of the DPP; at p. 295.
116 *Report of the Public Prosecution System Study Group, op. cit.*, at 5.7.
117 *2000 Annual Report of the DPP, op. cit.*, at 9.
118 [1986] I.L.R.M. 290.

12–23   Most of a State Solicitor's work is confined to prosecutions for indictable offences. However, they also handle a significant number of summary prosecutions. In the Dublin Metropolitan District, for example, about 20 percent of summary prosecutions have been presented by a solicitor from the Chief State Solicitor's office.[119] Outside of the Dublin District summary cases are presented by the State Solicitor (or counsel retained by the State Solicitor) where, for example, the case is unusually complex, involves a novel point of law or where the identity or occupation of the defendant is such as to make it desirable for the case to be presented by the State Solicitor (or counsel retained by the State Solicitor).

In a prosecution on indictment the standard practice is for the Garda Síochána to send the file to the State Solicitor of the relevant county. Where the case arises in the Dublin Metropolitan Area it used to be sent to the Chief State Solicitor.[120] Now presumably, it is sent to the Chief Prosecution Solicitor. The State Solicitor (or Prosecution Solicitor, as the case may be) will send the file on to the DPP for a direction on prosecution. At this stage the file will normally contain the results of the Garda investigation, including witness statements, records of interviews with the suspect, statements (if any) by the suspect, a list of material exhibits and any observations by the investigating gardaí and/or the State Solicitor. Subsequent communications between the DPP and the Garda Síochána with respect to the case will normally be conducted through the State Solicitor. In the event of a direction to prosecute, it is the State Solicitor who will prepare the book of evidence, undertake other preparatory work necessary to prepare the case for trial and conduct any preliminary proceedings. In serious cases counsel might be engaged to assist in the preparation of the book of evidence and/or in the conduct of preliminary proceedings. Where the accused is sent forward for trial, the State Solicitor transmits the files to the DPP for further directions. Where the DPP directs a prosecution on indictment, the file normally goes back down to the State Solicitor to advance it accordingly. The trial itself will normally be conducted by counsel briefed by the State Solicitor.[121] If the matter is to be disposed of summarily, the State Solicitor might handle it himself or herself. Summary charges are normally left to the Garda Síochána and other persons duly authorised by law to prosecute. Occasionally, the gardaí will seek directions or advice from the State Solicitor in individual cases.

Prosecutions in the Special Criminal Court are in a class of their own (see Chapter 20). They arise either where the offence in question is scheduled under the Offences Against the State Act 1939 or where it is considered that an ordinary offence, even one triable summarily, might come within the remit

---

[119] *1998 Annual Report of the Office of the Director of Public Prosecutions* (Office of the DPP, Dublin, 1999), p. 10.

[120] If the case concerns an offence which is scheduled pursuant to the Offences against the State legislation, or otherwise is one which the Garda Síochána feel should be tried in the Special Criminal Court, it will be sent to the Chief State Solicitor (now the Chief Prosecution Solicitor) irrespective of which county it comes from.

[121] The DPP is under a duty to ensure that such briefs are distributed on the basis of inclination and ability; Prosecution of Offences Act 1974, s.7(2). In practice, the counsel for any individual case are chosen from a panel drawn up by the DPP. They are paid fees only for each case they undertake.

of the Special Criminal Court. The DPP has complete control over all of these cases. The practice is for the Garda Síochána to refer them to the Chief Prosecution Solicitor who, in turn, seeks the directions of the DPP.

H. Revenue Solicitor

The Office of Revenue Solicitor provides legal services to the Revenue Commissioners.[122] The Office also acts as solicitor to the DPP in revenue matters in the Dublin Metropolitan District. The Revenue Solicitor is a civil servant, with the rank of assistant secretary, who is appointed by the Minister for Finance following a recommendation from the Top Level Appointments Committee and is accountable to the Revenue Commissioners. About 25 percent of the work of the Revenue Solicitor's Office is attributable to prosecution work.

12–24

Revenue offences are investigated by staff of the Revenue Commissioners, as distinct from the Garda Síochána.[122a] The files on offences which have been fully investigated and detected are referred directly to the DPP for a decision on prosecution. Revenue prosecutions in the Dublin Metropolitan District are presented by a solicitor from the Office of Revenue Solicitor. Cases outside Dublin are referred by the Revenue to the appropriate State Solicitor for prosecution. The Public Prosecution System Study Group recommended no change in these arrangements.[123]

I. Title of Prosecutions

The range of possible prosecutors has implications for the correct title of a prosecution in any individual case. Prosecutions on indictment are relatively straightforward. Article 30.3 of the Constitution stipulates that they must be "prosecuted in the name of the People and at the suit of the Attorney General or some other person authorised in accordance with law to act for that purpose." In practice this means that the correct title for a prosecution on indictment is "*People (at the suit of the Attorney General) v. Defendant*" or, more likely, "*People (at the suit of the DPP) v. Defendant*". Applying this by analogy to charges tried summarily it might be assumed that the correct title would always be "*People (name of individual, person or body bringing the prosecution) v. Defendant*". While that is an appropriate and acceptable formula, the practice has arisen whereby individual gardaí often bring "public" prosecutions in the name of the DPP even though they are really acting in their capacity as common informers. This has given rise to some difficulty, particularly where it is evident that the prosecutor has not sought specific instructions from the DPP in the case at hand.

12–25

---

[122] The following account is taken primarily from the *Report of the Public Prosecution System Study Group op. cit.* at paras.2.2.16–2.2.18.

[122a] Not the Criminal Assets Bureau where they work together.

[123] *ibid.* at para.5.7.11.

The problem seems to have arisen largely from the fact that since 1924 there has been no settled policy on the title of "public" prosecutions (those paid for out of public funds).[124] In some cases they were taken in the name of the DPP (previously the Attorney General), in others they were taken in the name of the DPP and at the suit of the superintendent of the Garda Síochána for the relevant area, and in others still they were taken solely in the name of the member of the Garda Síochána who investigated the case. To complicate matters further, it often happened that the real prosecutor in all three situations was an individual member acting on his or her own initiative.

The correctness of a member of the Garda Síochána proceeding under the name of the DPP to bring a public prosecution without obtaining the prior authorisation of the DPP was considered by the Supreme Court in *People (DPP) v. Roddy*.[125] In that case three charges triable summarily were brought against the defendant William Roddy by a member of the Garda Síochána. One was brought on foot of a charge sheet where the complainant was stated to be "the People at the prosecution of the Director of Public Prosecutions". The other two were brought on foot of summonses where the complainant was stated to be "the People at the suit of the DPP". The member in question had not sought the permission of the DPP to proceed with the prosecution in respect of any of these three offences. In the High Court McMahon J. ruled that these descriptions of the complainant are "not a mere formal title which may be adopted by the real initiator of a prosecution, but bear their ordinary meaning which is that the Director of Public Prosecutions has authorised the proceedings to be brought."[126] Since the permission of the DPP had not been obtained in this case McMahon J. felt that the charges were invalid. However, he was overruled on this point by a majority in the Supreme Court (Griffin and Parke JJ.; O'Higgins C.J. dissenting).

Griffin J., for the majority in the Supreme Court, explained that before the passing of the Criminal Justice (Administration) Act 1924 all prosecutions were brought in the name of the King, unless they were brought by persons duly authorised by law. For the purposes of bringing a prosecution in the name of the King it was not necessary to obtain the prior consent or permission of the King. The effect of the 1924 Act, in this context, was merely to substitute the Attorney General for the King in respect of prosecutions brought in courts of summary jurisdiction. Apart from that, existing rights were preserved and continued. Accordingly prosecutions since 1924 have been brought in the name of the Attorney General. Equally, of course, it was quite usual for prosecutions to be brought at the suit of the Garda superintendent of the area in question or in the name of the investigating member as a common informer. There was no settled practice in the matter. Between 1924 and 1974 many summary cases had gone from the District Court to the Supreme Court on points of law. Nevertheless, the learned judge could find no reported case in which a challenge had been taken to the practice of prosecuting summary

---

[124] *People (DPP) v. Roddy* [1977] I.R. 177.
[125] [1977] I.R. 177.
[126] *ibid.* at 180.

offences in the name of the Attorney General in cases where his prior consent had not been sought and given. Accordingly, he concluded that the practice must be accepted as having been perfectly proper up to 1974. Since the Prosecution of Offences Act 1974 has put the DPP in the shoes of the Attorney General as far as criminal matters are concerned. The learned judge reasoned that in the absence of clear words to the contrary gardaí can also bring summary prosecutions in the name of the DPP without having to secure his prior permission in each individual case.[127] The only qualification is that summary prosecutions should not be brought using the Article 30.3 formula "The People at the suit of the [DPP]" as that applied only to prosecutions on indictment. In Griffin J.'s view, the correct title for summary prosecutions is "'the Director of Public Prosecutions' simpliciter".

The proposition that all summary prosecutions should be brought in the name of the DPP will give rise to certain problems if it is followed. First, it is evident from the decision of the Supreme Court in *State (DPP) v. District Justice Ruane*,[128] and indeed from the majority decision in *Roddy*, that a member of the Garda Síochána who prosecutes in his own name does so as a common informer and, as such, is beyond the control of the DPP. On the other hand where he prosecutes in the name of the DPP the prosecution is subject to the control of the DPP. It follows that if all summary prosecutions must be brought in the name of the DPP, the effect in practice will be to deprive members of the Garda Síochána of their capacity to sustain prosecutions as common informers. In *Ruane*, however, not only did the Supreme Court hold that the DPP had no power to intervene in a summary prosecution brought by a common informer, but it explicitly acknowledged that a member of the Garda Síochána still retained his capacity to prosecute in his own name as a common informer. Clearly, Griffin J.'s advice that all summary prosecutions are to be taken in the name of the DPP has not settled the issue.

    Two further loose ends remain. The first is whether any other prosecutor who is not a member of the Garda Síochána can launch a summary prosecution in the name of the DPP without obtaining his prior authorisation. It has been argued that there is no inherent reason why the *ratio* of *Roddy* should not extend to other common informers generally.[129] Certainly, there is nothing specific in the majority judgement in *Roddy* to suggest that the option is confined to members of the Garda Síochána, and there is nothing in principle which would preclude its extension to other common informers. In practice, however, it must be recognised that the ruling in *Roddy* was based heavily on the unchallenged practice which had prevailed prior to 1974. Griffin J. did not specifically suggest that persons other than members of the Garda Síochána

12–26

---

[127] The legislation creating some statutory offences specifically require that prosecutions must be brought at the suit and in the name of the DPP. Presumably, this can be satisfied by a member of the Garda Síochána bringing the prosecution in the name of the DPP.

[128] [1985] I.L.R.M. 349.

[129] See *Casey op. cit.* at 100. In *Attorney General v. Thompson* (1936) 70 I.L.T.R. 161 Judge Comyn ruled that any person could use the Attorney General's name in District Court proceedings where the District Court judge thought it fit and proper to allow this to be done.

regularly prosecuted in the District Court under the name of the Attorney General. Moreover, it must be accepted that gardaí are full-time, paid, public servants who have a specific legal duty to enforce the law. Although they are not the servants of the DPP they invariably operate in such a close relationship with his office on matters of public prosecutions that it would be unreal not to distinguish between them and other common informers in the prosecution of summary offences. Having said that, the fact is that the point has not been settled one way or the other in *Roddy*.

The second loose end is indirectly related to the first, but more problematic. It concerns the capacity of a prosecutor, other than the DPP, to sustain a prosecution on indictment through the simple expedient of proceeding in the name of the DPP.[130] Certainly, in principle this would appear to be a viable option. It is clearly implicit in both the *Ruane* and *Roddy* cases that the effect of proceeding under the name of the DPP is to change the status of the prosecution from a prosecution by a common informer to a prosecution by the DPP. This is reflected in the fact that the DPP can intervene in a prosecution brought by a member of the Garda Síochána acting in his name, whereas he cannot intervene where the member acts in his own name as a common informer. There is a qualitative difference between a prosecution brought in the name of the DPP and one brought in the name of a common informer. The former is treated as a prosecution brought by the DPP even if his prior authorisation has not been sought and given. It would seem logical to assume, therefore, that a prosecution on indictment brought in the name of the DPP would satisfy the requirements of section 9(2) of the Criminal Justice (Administration) Act 1924, even if the DPP had not specifically authorised the prosecution. The only obstacle seemingly is the decision of the Supreme Court in *State (Ennis) v. Farrell*[131] to the effect that the 1924 Act has abolished the right of private prosecution on indictment. However, that decision concerned a prosecutor who was attempting to proceed in his own name and as a common informer. It did not specifically address the issue of whether it would have been feasible for him to proceed by donning the mantle of the DPP. In the light of the reasoning of the majority in *Roddy* it would appear that this is a realistic prospect, at least in theory. In practice, it can be expected that the DPP would assert his authority to exercise control over any such prosecution.

12–27   Before leaving the *Roddy* case it is worth adverting to a letter sent by the DPP to the Garda Commissioner dated January 9, 1975. The final paragraph of this letter read:

> "All prosecutions commenced on or after the 19th of January, 1975, which, but for the [Prosecution of Offences] Act would have been taken in the name of the Attorney General should be taken in the name of the DPP".

In the appeal in *Roddy* the DPP argued that this letter gave a general authorisation for prosecutions to be taken in the name of the DPP by members of the

---

130   See Casey, *op. cit.*, pp. 98–100.
131   [1966] I.R. 107.

Garda Síochána. This argument, of course, was rendered superfluous as a result of the decision of the majority in the Supreme Court. Accordingly, they did not consider the status of the letter any further. Interestingly, O'Higgins C.J. did address the status and effect of this letter in his dissenting judgement. Basing himself on the premise that the DPP was a prosecutor of last resort in summary matters, O'Higgins C.J. concluded that he would have to consider prosecutions on a case by basis. Accordingly, it was not possible to give a general permission for prosecutions to be brought in his name. It follows that both the majority and minority felt, albeit for different reasons, that the letter had no legal effect.

J. The Decision to Prosecute

The decision whether or not to prosecute on indictment is a matter solely for the DPP, subject to one or two clearly defined exceptions where the power is vested in the Attorney General. The DPP will be called upon to make this decision (usually referred to as giving directions on prosecution) on each occasion a file is submitted to him by the Garda Síochána or other investigating authority.[132] Typically, the file will consist of witness statements, records of interview (if any) with the suspect, statements (if any) by the suspect, a list of material exhibits and observations (if any) from the investigating gardaí and/or the State Solicitor in question. Where the case originates outside the Dublin Metropolitan area, the file will normally be submitted *via* the State Solicitor for the relevant county. Where he considers it necessary the DPP can request the Garda Síochána or relevant investigating authority to carry out further investigations and/or supply further information. In the exceptional cases where the DPP feels that it is necessary to seek information about the government's position on public policy matters raised by an individual case, the information would normally be sought through a consultation with the Attorney General.

12–28

The decision to prosecute or not to prosecute in an individual case is at the very centre of the prosecutorial function. How that decision is taken in any individual case can have immense consequences at the very least for the accused, the victim and the wider community. Its importance is very neatly summed up in the following extract from the DPP's Annual Report for 1998:

> "It has long been recognised that the decision to prosecute or not to prosecute is of fundamental importance in a criminal justice system and particularly in an accusatorial system such as exists in Ireland. Many observers regard it as by far the most important stage in the criminal process, involving as it does serious and far reaching consequences for those affected by it. The consequences for a defendant can and frequently do include irretrievable loss of

---

[132] While most files are submitted by the Garda Síochána, the DPP is expecting an increasing volume to be submitted by other investigation authorities such as the Revenue Commissioners, the Competition Authority and the Corporate Enforcement Agency; *Strategy Statement 2001–2003* (DPP, Dublin, 2001) at 4.5.

reputation or of employment, disruption of family relations and very substantial expense. If in fact the person charged is innocent, the resulting injustice is obvious. The consequences for the victim of a crime or for a victim's family when an incorrect decision not to prosecute is taken can be equally damaging. It is essential that every effort humanly possible be made to get this decision right. . . . Obviously, the more serious the accusation the more important it is to try to ensure that the initial prosecutorial decision is right. It cannot be sufficiently emphasised however that in one sense there is no such thing as a minor offence because an accusation which is trivial in the hierarchy of criminal offences can often be, for various reasons, of great significance to the person accused. In all cases, irrespective of gravity or otherwise, the greatest care must be taken to ensure that all who should be prosecuted are prosecuted and that those who should not be prosecuted are not."[133]

12–29   Surprisingly, perhaps there is no legal provision in Ireland specifically governing when a decision to prosecute may be taken in any individual case. In theory, a prosecution can be initiated on every occasion a criminal complaint is made against an identifiable individual. In practice, of course, it would be grossly improper for the judicial process to be invoked in any case where there was insufficient admissible evidence against the defendant to justify it. Indeed, it is likely that the courts would view any attempt to initiate a prosecution in such a case as an abuse of process.[134]

According to the DPP the decision whether or not to prosecute in an individual case is taken in two stages, although it often happens that both stages are run into one. The first is the determination of whether or not the evidence submitted establishes a prima facie case of guilt of a criminal offence in relation to an identified person.[135] A prima facie case in this context means a body of admissible evidence on which a jury (or a judge sitting alone as the case may be), properly instructed on the relevant law, could conclude beyond a reasonable doubt that the suspected person was guilty of the offence charged. The prosecutor at this stage is not concerned with the question whether the jury would find the accused guilty, merely whether they could find him guilty. According to the DPP this is a relatively easy question to settle in most cases. Difficulties can arise from time to time in assessing the admissibility of particular types of evidence, and it may be necessary in any individual case to request further investigations to clarify some evidential matters. Ultimately, however, if the DPP is not satisfied that there is sufficient admissible evidence upon which the accused could be found guilty beyond a reasonable doubt, he must decide against prosecution.

---

[133] *1998 Annual Report of the Office of the DPP, op. cit.,* at 14.

[134] In *Eviston v. DPP* (High Court, January 26, 2001) the High Court prevented a prosecution from going ahead where, after an internal review of the case, the DPP had reversed his original decision not to prosecute. One of the reasons for the Court's decision was the absence of any new facts or objective basis upon which the DPP could justify the reversal of his original decision not to prosecute.

[135] 1998 *Annual Report of the DPP, op. cit.,* at 15; E Barnes "The Role of the Director of Public Prosecutions" *Communique September 1995, 3 at 6.*

Where the DPP considers that there is a prima facie case he must go on to consider whether or not the evidence in question is credible and reliable. This presents a much more difficult challenge for the prosecutor as it involves him in making a judgment on matters of fact without having had the benefit of seeing the evidence tested in the manner in which it would be tested in a trial. There is no prescribed set of principles or guidelines which he can rely upon in order to make his judgment in any individual case. However, in his 1998 Annual Report the DPP identifies a number of relevant factors which the careful prosecutor will bear in mind:

> "A careful prosecutor obviously will always have regard to any inherent improbability attaching to particular evidence. The fact that it is improbable however does not mean that it will be automatically rejected. Other factors will be examined, notably whether or not there is any independent corroboration for the improbable assertion. Possible motives for particular assertions will be considered in particular types of cases. The question of the ability of particular witnesses such as children of tender years and persons suffering from certain disabilities to give cogent and reliable evidence cannot be ignored, nor can issues relating to the circumstances in which a person first makes an accusation or statement."[136]

These are only some of the many factors which the prosecutor will address when making his judgement. The following non-exclusive list is set out in the *Statement of General Guidelines for Prosecutors* issued by the DPP in 2001:[137] **12–30**

  a. Are there grounds for believing that evidence may be excluded, bearing in mind the principles of admissibility under the Constitution of Ireland, at common law and under statute? For example, has confession evidence been properly obtained? Has evidence obtained as a result of search or seizure been properly obtained?
  b. If the case depends in whole or in part on admissions by the suspected person, are there grounds for believing that the admissions may not be reliable considering all the circumstances of the case including the age, intelligence, mental state and apparent understanding of the suspect? Are the admissions consistent with what can be objectively proved? Is there any reason why the suspect would make a false confession?
  c. Does it appear that a witness is exaggerating, or has a faulty memory, or is either hostile or friendly to the accused. or may be unreliable in some other way? Did a witness have the opportunity to observe what he or she claims to have seen?
  d. Has a witness been consistent in his or her evidence? Does the evidence tally with the behaviour of the witness?
  e. Does a witness have a motive for telling an untruth or less than the whole truth?
  f. Could the reliability of evidence be affected by physical or mental illness or infirmity?

---

[136] *1998 Annual Report of the DPP, op. cit.,* at 16.
[137] *Statement of General Guidelines for Prosecutors* (DPP, Dublin, 2001) at 11–13.

g. What sort of impression is a witness likely to make? How is the witness likely to stand up to cross-examination?

h. If there is conflict between witnesses, does it go beyond what might be considered normal and hence materially weaken the case?

i. If, on the other hand, there is a lack of conflict between witnesses, is there anything which causes suspicion that a false story may have been concocted?

j. Are all necessary witnesses available to give evidence, including any who may be abroad? In the case of witnesses who may be abroad, the possibility of obtaining the evidence through a live television link, pursuant to section 28 of the Criminal Evidence Act 1992, or by means of the issue of a letter of request, under the Criminal Justice Act 1994 should be considered.

k. Are all the necessary witnesses competent to give evidence? If so, are they compellable? If competent but not compellable, have they indicated their willingness to testify?

l. Where child witnesses are involved, are they likely to be able to give sworn evidence or evidence in accordance with the criteria in section 27 of the Criminal Evidence Act 1992? How is the experience of a trial likely to affect them? In cases of sexual offences or offences involving violence, should children's evidence be presented by way of television link in accordance with section 13 of the Act?

m. In relation to mentally handicapped witnesses, are they capable of giving an intelligible account of events which are relevant to the proceedings so as to enable their evidence to be given pursuant to section 27 of the Criminal Evidence At, 1992?

n. If identification is likely to be an issue, how cogent and reliable is the evidence of those who claim to identify the accused?

o. Where there might otherwise be doubts concerning a particular piece of evidence, is there any independent evidence to support it?

In assessing the evidence the prosecutor must also have regard to any defences which are plainly open to, or have been indicated by, the accused.

Each case must be considered on its own merits, and the factors which may be relevant in one case will not necessarily be relevant in another. It is also worth bearing in mind that when assessing the credibility and reliability of the evidence supporting a prima facie case the prosecutor can take into account matters which may not be admissible as evidence. Both the investigator (usually members of the Garda Síochána) and the solicitor dealing with the case are expected to express views on the evidence when referring the case to the DPP.[138] It is worth noting, however, that when taking his decision on prosecution the DPP is under a duty not to entertain communications aimed at influencing him not to prosecute, where the communications come from a person or persons who are not directly involved in the criminal proceedings. Section 6 of the Prosecution of Offences Act 1974 renders such communications unlawful (see above). The DPP will have regard in any individual case to views expressed by the crime victim. These communications can come direct from the victim or be relayed through a legal or medical advisor or through a social worker or through a member of the family.[139]

---

[138] *ibid.* at 13.

Ultimately, the question for the prosecutor is whether the available admissible **12–31** evidence is sufficiently credible and reliable to warrant charging the suspect with the particular offence. In deciding this question the prosecutor must be careful not to cross the line of demarcation between his role and that of the court. It is the court which must decide whether the defendant is guilty in fact. While the prosecutor will aim to prosecute all who are guilty and decide against prosecution in the case of all who are innocent, he is not concerned with making a judgment on the guilt or innocence of the suspect in any individual case. It is also worth noting that a decision not to prosecute due to insufficiency of evidence will not preclude a prosecution at a later stage when further evidence becomes available. In difficult cases, therefore, postponement of prosecution may be preferable to a premature prosecution which ultimately fails due to an insufficiency of evidence.[140] Where the prosecutor decides in favour of prosecution he should keep the credibility and reliability of the evidence against the defendant under review as the case progresses and further information becomes available.

Even if the DPP is satisfied that there is a prima facie case against a suspect and that the evidence is credible and reliable, the circumstances of an individual case may be such that he will feel obliged not to prosecute. It is submitted that a distinction can be drawn here between a situation where the DPP exercises his discretion not to prosecute (see below) and that where he feels obliged not to prosecute. The former refers to the situation where the DPP's discretion has come into play and the only question is whether he has exercised it correctly. The latter refers to the situation where the DPP never really had a discretion in the matter; *i.e.* he was obliged not to prosecute. Such situations can arise where there is a prima facie case based on credible and reliable evidence but, as a result of the actions of the prosecutor or other circumstances, the defendant cannot be guaranteed a fair trial. Attempts by the DPP to prosecute in such circumstances are liable to be restrained by the High Court exercising its jurisdiction to grant an order of prohibition.[141] There have been several such cases in recent years concerning excessive delay between the date of the alleged offence and the date upon which the criminal complaint was first made.[142] In some of these cases, which are dealt with more fully in Chapter 1, the High Court (or the Supreme Court on appeal) made absolute an order of prohibition restraining the DPP from proceeding with prosecutions for sexual offences against children because the excessive delay between the date of the alleged offences and the date of the complaints were such that the defendants would be unduly prejudiced in

---

[139] *1999 Annual Report of the DPP, op. cit.*, at 12. See also *Victims Charter* (Department of Justice, Equality and Law Reform, 1999).

[140] *ibid.*

[141] In *State (O'Callaghan) v. O'hUadhaigh* [1977] I.R. 42 it was held that any act done by the DPP in the course of a criminal prosecution which contributed to or was likely to contribute to an unfair or unjust proceeding is restrainable by the courts on that ground alone. In this case a fresh prosecution following the entry of a *nolle prosequi* was held to be unfair in the particular circumstances of the case and the District Court was prohibited from hearing the fresh prosecution.

[142] See, for example, *P.M. v. District-Judge Malone*, unreported, June 7, 2002; *P. O'C v. DPP* [2000] 3 I.R. 87; *J.L. v. DP.* [2000] 3 I.R. 122; *P.P. v. DPP* [2000] 1 I.R. 403.

meeting the allegations, and as such could not be guaranteed a fair trial. As a result of these decisions the DPP decided against prosecution in several similar cases where excessive delay was a material issue.

12–32   The unavailability of material evidence for inspection by the accused can also undermine the prospects of a fair trial to the extent that a prosecution will be prohibited. In *Murphy v. DPP*,[143] for example, the High Court granted an order restraining the DPP from proceeding with charges relating to the unlawful taking of a motor vehicle and dangerous driving. The circumstances were that the Garda Síochána had returned the vehicle in question to its owner without notice to the accused despite the fact that they knew that the accused wanted to have the vehicle subjected to forensic examination. The Court considered that the actions of the Garda amounted to a breach of the rules of fair procedures and on that basis issued an order preventing the DPP from proceeding with the prosecution despite the existence of a prima facie case.[144]

Prejudicial publicity can also damage the prospects for a fair trial.[145] It is only in the most exceptional of circumstances, however, that the courts have been persuaded to prohibit a prosecution on the ground of prejudicial publicity.[146]

1. Discretion to Prosecute

12–33   Despite the mandatory nature of the words used in section 9 of the Criminal Justice (Administration) Act 1924 and Article 30.3 of the Constitution, it has never been seriously contended that the DPP and/or the Attorney General are obliged to prosecute in every case where the option of prosecution is open to them.[147] The practical reality is that absolute prosecution in all such cases is not feasible. The police, the Attorney General's office, the DPP's office, the State Solicitors, the legal profession, the courts and the prisons simply could not cope with the results of a policy of absolute enforcement. There will also be cases where a decision in favour of prosecution might be inimical to the interests of the common good. It is generally accepted, therefore, that the competent prosecutor must enjoy a discretion to prosecute in those cases where prosecution is a valid option.[148] More difficult questions concern when the discretion comes into play, how it is exercised and the extent, if any, to which it is subject to judicial review. It is admitted that some of the factors which are considered below as pertinent to the proper exercise of prosecutorial

---

[143]   [1989] I.L.R.M. 71.

[144]   For a similar case which was distinguished on its facts see *Rogers v. DPP* [1992] I.L.R.M. 695. See also *Nolan v. DPP* [1994] 3 I.R. 626.

[145]   See, *e.g. D. v. DPP* [1994] 2 I.R. 465; *Z. v. DPP* [1994] 2 I.R. 476.

[146]   See, *e.g. People (DPP) v. Haugh (No.2)* [2001] 1 I.R. 162.

[147]   In *State (McCormack) v. Curran* [1987] I.L.R.M. 225 at 237 the Supreme Court, *per* Finlay C.J., acknowledged that the discretion to prosecute is not related solely to the sufficiency of evidence. He indicated that there are many other factors which can appropriately and properly be taken into account. However, he considered that it would not be wise or helpful to seek to list them in any exclusive way.

[148]   The DPP has publicly acknowledged that he does enjoy a discretion in the decision to prosecute in any individual case. Indeed, he has indicated that the exercise of that discretion is one of the more difficult aspects of his role. See Barnes *Communique, op. cit.*, at p. 8.

discretion might be considered as equally relevant to the chronologically pre-ceding issue of whether the discretion has become available in an individual case. The distinction between the circumstances which must be satisfied before a discretionary power becomes available and the circumstances relevant to the proper exercise of the discretion, readily recognisable in other areas of public administration, has yet to be fully developed in the prosecutorial function.

One of the issues which appears to straddle the borderline between the existence of prosecutorial discretion and its exercise concerns the prospects of a conviction. Just because there is a prima facie case against the accused based on credible and reliable evidence, it does not follow that the prosecutor will be satisfied that a conviction is more likely than not. There may be circumstances in any individual case which render a conviction less likely or even doubtful. For example, the character of the defendant may be such that a jury would be most unlikely to convict for the offence in question, or there may be certain facets of the case guaranteed to produce a jury reaction against the prosecution. In Northern Ireland and Britain a 51 percent rule has traditionally been applied; *i.e.* the DPP will not prosecute in any case where he is not satisfied that a conviction is more likely than not. In Ireland the DPP eschews any such rule. So long as he is satisfied that there is a prima facie case based on credible and reliable evidence he is prepared to prosecute.[149] However, it would appear that the prospects of a conviction can influence the DPP in the exercise of his discretion to prosecute. The DPP has acknowledged that he will rarely prosecute if there are no prospects of securing a conviction.[150] The most recent *Guidelines* issued by the DPP (see below) positively state that a prosecution should not be taken where there is no reasonable prospects of a conviction.[151] To prosecute in such a case would constitute an irresponsible waste of public money and scarce resources. In some cases, however, he has considered a prosecution to be in the public interest even though the prospects of a conviction were low.[152] In these cases factors such as the seriousness of the offence will be particularly important.[153]

Once it is accepted that the prosecutor enjoys a measure of discretion over the prosecutorial decision in each case, the question of policy to govern the exercise of this discretion comes into play. Unfortunately, there is no statutory provision in Ireland compelling the DPP (or any other public prosecutor) to publish a code giving guidance on the policy.[154] However, basic principles of legality require that there should actually be a policy and that the prosecutor should apply that policy in order to ensure that like cases are treated alike. Nevertheless, it has not been the practice in Ireland to spell out precisely the terms of prosecutorial policy. Up until very recently the most that the DPP

12–34

---

[149] Barnes *Communique op. cit* at p. 7.
[150] *ibid*. See also, *Statement of General Guidelines for Prosecutors* (DPP, Dublin, 2001) at 10–11.
[151] *Statement of General Guidelines for Prosecutors op. cit.* at 10–11.
[152] 1998 Annual Report of the DPP, *op. cit.*, at 17.
[153] *Statement of General Guidelines for Prosecutors op. cit.* at 11.
[154] The U.K.'s Prosecution of Offences Act 1985, s.10 obliges the DPP in the U.K. to issue a code of practice for Crown Prosecutors giving guidance on, *inter alia*, when a prosecution should be

has done is identify the sort of issues which necessitate the availability of discretion. These include: personal responsibility, youth, age, health, special mitigating circumstances, the public interest (particularly the likelihood that the suspect will never re-offend) and "a wide range of other factors which can properly influence prosecutorial decisions but to which no legal measuring tape can readily be applied."[155] In his Annual Report for 1998 he also draws attention to the granting of immunity for a law enforcement or other public interest reason, before going on to say that the prosecutorial discretion has been used for this purpose very infrequently since the office of DPP was established.[156] Prior to the issuing of a *Statement of General Guidelines to Prosecutors* in 2001 the DPP had not gone further to specify how, and the extent to which, these factors impinge upon his prosecutorial discretion.[157] While the Guidelines do not constitute the promulgation of a comprehensive code of prosecutorial policy, they do set out general principles which should guide the initiation and conduct of prosecutions.[158] They aim to give general guidance to prosecutors so that a fair, reasoned and consistent policy underlies the prosecution process. For this purpose the *Guidelines* identify a prosecutor as: the DPP, officers of the DPP, the solicitors and legal technical staff who provide a solicitor service to the DPP, the local State Solicitors who do likewise in the areas outside Dublin, counsel who act for the DPP on a case-to-case basis and members of the Garda Síochána prosecuting on the DPP's behalf.[159]

The *Guidelines* describe the general duty of the prosecutor as follows:[160]

- The prosecutor has a duty to act honestly, fairly, impartially and objectively.
- The prosecutor should at all times respect the fundamental right of all human persons to be held equal before the law, and should abstain from any wrongful discrimination.
- The prosecutor has a duty to respect, protect and uphold the universal concept of human dignity and human rights.
- The prosecutor should at all times uphold the rule of law, the integrity of the criminal justice system and the right to a fair trial.
- The prosecutor should remain unaffected by individual or sectional interests and public or media pressures having regard only to the public interest.
- These fundamental duties should inform all aspects of the prosecutor's work, including decisions whether to prosecute or withdraw charges, bring appeals, decisions concerning the choice of charge and the conduct of the prosecutor in court.

12–35 On the more specific issue of the discretion to prosecute in an individual case, the *Guidelines* start from the premise that there is a clear public interest in

---

discontinued and charging policy in general. The initial Code was issued in 1985; see *Crown Prosecution Service: Code for Prosecutors.*
[155] Barnes, *op. cit.,* p. 8.
[156] *1998 Annual Report of the DPP, op. cit.,* at 16.
[157] *Statement of General Guidelines for Prosecutors* (Dublin: DPP, 2001)
[158] For comparative purposes see the U.K.'s Code and the Australian Federal Code as discussed in J Casey *The Irish Law Officers op. cit.* at 270-273.
[159] *Statement of General Guidelines for Prosecutors, op.cit.,* at 2.
[160] *ibid.* at 7.

ensuring that crime is prosecuted and that the wrongdoer is convicted and punished.[161] Accordingly, it will generally be in the public interest to prosecute a crime where there is sufficient evidence to justify doing so, unless there is a countervailing public interest reason not to prosecute. The factors which may properly be taken into account in deciding whether the public interest requires a prosecution may vary from case to case. According to the *Guidelines* the more serious the offence and the stronger the evidence to support it, the less likely it is that that public interest in seeing crime punished will be outweighed by some other factors. The first factor to be considered is the seriousness of the alleged offence and whether there are any aggravating or mitigating factors. The *Guidelines* go on to identify the following aggravating factors which tend to increase the seriousness of the offence and, where present, will increase the likelihood that the public interest requires a prosecution (these are not meant to be exhaustive):[162]

    a. where a conviction is likely to result in a significant penalty;

    b. if the accused was in a position of authority or trust and the offence is an abuse of that position;

    c. where the accused was a ringleader or an organiser of the offence;

    d. where the offence was premeditated;

    e. where the offence was carried out by a group;

    f. where the offence was carried out pursuant to a plan in pursuit of organised crime;

    g. where the victim of the offence has been put in fear, or suffered personal attack, damage or disturbance. The more vulnerable the victim the greater the aggravation;

    h. where there is a marked difference between the actual or mental ages of the accused and the victim and the accused took advantage of this;

    i. if there is any element of corruption;

    j. where the accused has previous convictions or cautions which are relevant to the present offence;

    k. if the accused is alleged to have committed the offence whilst on bail, on probation, or subject to a suspended sentence or an order binding the accused to keep the peace and be of good behaviour, or released on licence from prison or a place of detention;

    l. where there are grounds for believing that the offence is likely to be continued or repeated, for example, where there is a history of recurring conduct.

On the other hand, the following factors are presented as mitigating factors which tend to reduce the seriousness of the offence and hence the likelihood of a prosecution being required in the public interest:[163]

    a. if a court is likely to impose a very small or nominal penalty;

    b. where the loss or harm can be described as minor and was the result of a single incident, particularly if it was caused by an error of judgement;

    c. where the offence is a first offence, if it is not of a serious nature and is unlikely to be repeated.

---

[161] *ibid.* at 10.
[162] *ibid.* at 14.
[163] *ibid.* at 14–15.

12–36 The *Guidelines* also identify factors, apart from those affecting the seriousness of the offence, which may arise when considering whether the public interest requires a prosecution. Some of these militate in favour of a decision to prosecute while others are mitigating factors which might justify a decision not to prosecute. They are listed non-exclusively as follows:[164]

(a) where the offender is either very young or elderly or suffering from significant mental or physical ill health or disability. In such cases, however, other factors tending to indicate that the offence is serious or that there is a risk of the offence being repeated must be taken into account. In the case of young offenders the use of the Juvenile Diversion Programme should be considered;

(b) the availability and efficacy of any alternatives to prosecution;

(c) the prevalence of offences of the nature of that alleged and the need for deterrence, both generally and in relation to the particular circumstances of the offender;

(d) whether the consequences of a prosecution or a conviction would be disproportionately harsh or oppressive in the particular circumstances of the offender;

(e) the attitude of the victim or the family of a victim of the alleged offence to a prosecution;[164a]

(f) the likely effect on the victim or the family of a victim of a decision to prosecute, or not to prosecute;

(g) whether the likely length and expense of a trial would be disproportionate having regard to the seriousness of the alleged offence and the strength of the evidence;

(h) whether the offender is willing to cooperate in the investigation or prosecution of other offenders, or has already done so;

(i) if a sentence has already been imposed on the offender in relation to another matter whether it is likely that an additional penalty would be imposed;

(j) whether an offender who has admitted the offence has shown genuine remorse and a willingness to make amends.

Where there are mitigating factors in a case the prosecutor should consider whether these should be taken into account by a sentencing court in the event of a conviction, instead of being used as the basis for a decision not to prosecute.[165] If, however, the offence is not so serious as to plainly warrant prosecution then the prosecutor should consider whether the public interest really requires a prosecution.

---

[164] *ibid.* at 15.

[164a] Note that in *BF v. DPP* [2001] 1 I.R. 656 at 659, Geoghegan J., giving the judgment of the Supreme Court, said *obiter* that: "while it may be perfectly reasonable for the gardaí or the respondent [DPP] to regard as a relevant factor the consent of the parents of a victim to the alleged culprit being let off with a caution, the converse is not the case. It would not be a proper exercise of the powers of the prosecution authorities to proceed with a prosecution against a child or young person where other more suitable courses of action might be open, merely because the parents of the victims were insisting upon it." Geoghegan J. at 659. See also *Eviston v. DPP* [2002 1 I.L.R.M. 134 (para. 12–43).

[165] *ibid.* at 16.

The *Guidelines* also address the issue of delay in the decision to prosecute. **12–37** Although they do not specifically say so, the *Guidelines* at least imply that delay is a factor which should be taken into account by the prosecutor when exercising the discretion to prosecute. As explained above there are at least some circumstances in which delay will actually preclude a decision to prosecute. If the delay in question is not in this category then presumably there is always the possibility if it being considered as a factor which the prosecutor would take into account in deciding whether a prosecution was in the public interest. It is submitted that that is the context in which the *Guidelines* on delay should be interpreted. They stipulate that the prosecutor should bear in mind the following:[166]

(a) whether any delay was caused or contributed to by the alleged offender;
(b) whether the fact of the offence or of the alleged offender's responsibility for it has recently come to light;
(c) where any delay was caused or contributed to by a long investigation, whether the length of the investigation was reasonable in the circumstances;
(d) where the victim has delayed in reporting the offence, the age of the victim both when the offence was committed and when it was reported;
(e) whether the alleged offender exercised a dominant position over the victim;
(f) whether there is actual prejudice caused to the alleged offender by reason of any delay or lapse of time.

The status of the DPP's *Statement of General Guidelines for Prosecutors* is nothing more than what it purports to be on its face. It is a statement of general guidelines. The guidelines are not law and they are not binding. A decision to prosecute or not to prosecute will not be unlawful simply because it appears to be at odds with one or more of the guidelines. Similarly, the *Guidelines* do not fetter the DPP, his officers, agents or counsel in the proper exercise of any discretion conferred upon them to consider any particular case or set of circumstances on its own merits.[167] Nevertheless, they are a statement of policy and basic principles of legality in these matters would require that there should be objective justification to depart from them in an individual case. It remains to be seen whether their existence will encourage the courts to be more active in reviewing the legality of prosecutorial decisions.[168]

Before addressing the judicial review of the decision on prosecution it is **12–38** worth noting that the ultimate task for the prosecutor, having considered all relevant factors, is to decide whether a prosecution is warranted. In the case of the DPP he will issue a direction to prosecute or not to prosecute as the case may be. Where he issues a direction for prosecution he will also specify

---

[166] *ibid.*
[167] *ibid.* at 2.
[168] In *Eviston v. DPP*, High Court, January 26, 2001, the High Court prohibited a prosecution which had been initiated by the DPP after he reversed his original decision against prosecution. One of the grounds for the Court's decision was that the DPP had not complied with his own published guidelines on when he would conduct an internal review of the original decision on prosecution in any case.

the appropriate charge or charges.[169] Before issuing any such direction the DPP will have to be satisfied not just that there is a *prima facie* case based on credible and reliable evidence and that it is in the public interest to prosecute, but also that the necessary evidence is either in his possession or will be available and forthcoming at the trial. He cannot embark upon a speculative prosecution.[170] Equally, the DPP must approach all prosecutorial decisions with absolute impartiality.[171] All persons must be accorded the same measure of justice. Persons should not be immune from prosecution because of who they are or what they do. Similarly, no-one should be prosecuted because of any anticipated public reaction to a decision not to prosecute, nor should a decision be made not to prosecute because of any anticipated negative reaction to a decision to prosecute.[172]

2. Judicial Review of the Decision on Prosecution

12–39   The courts have always displayed a marked reluctance to interfere with the exercise of the DPP's decision to prosecute or not to prosecute in any individual case. The judicial treatment of his decision on this specific issue cannot be considered in isolation from the treatment of the powers he exercises at certain other stages of a prosecution such as the transfer of a trial to the Special Criminal Court and the entry of a *nolle prosequi*, both of which are dealt with more fully in later chapters. Indeed, by the time the Irish courts came to deal directly with the DPP's decision to prosecute in an individual case, a distinct bias in favour of judicial reticence had already been set by decisions concerning these other two stages of the prosecutorial process. This is reflected in the cases of *State (Killian) v. Attorney General*;[173] *Judge v. DPP*[174]; and *Savage v. DPP*[175] which are discussed in a later chapter.

There are very few reported Irish cases in which the court has had to consider directly the extent to which the DPP's decision to prosecute or not to prosecute is subject to judicial review. The leading case must be *State (McCormack) v. Curran*.[176] It presents the rare spectacle of an individual seeking an order of mandamus to secure his prosecution for a criminal offence. The prosecutor, McCormack, had been charged in Northern Ireland with offences which had allegedly been committed in Ireland. The offences in question were extra-territorial offences, *i.e.* they came within the scope of Criminal Law Jurisdiction legislation which had been enacted in both Ireland and Northern Ireland. Under

---

[169] The DPP's policy on the selection of the appropriate charge is dealt with in the chapter on the Indictment.

[170] *1998 Annual Report of the DPP op. cit.* at 20.

[171] *1999 Annual Report of the DPP* (DPP, Dublin, 2000) at para.5.9.

[172] The DPP's Mission statement includes fairness as an essential component of a prosecution service in a democratic society. It goes on to state: "The Director's Office aims to operate to the highest professional standards and to treat all those with whom it has dealings fairly, equally, and consistently without any wrongful discrimination." *Strategy Statement 2001–2003* (DPP, Dublin, 2001) at para.5.4.

[173] (1957) 92 I.L.T.R. 182.

[174] [1984] I.L.R.M. 224.

[175] [1982] I.L.R.M. 385.

[176] [1987] I.L.R.M. 225.

the Northern version McCormack could be tried in Northern Ireland. However, he could opt instead for trial in Ireland if a warrant for his arrest had been issued for the same offence in Ireland. McCormack preferred to be tried in Ireland, but the appropriate chief superintendent in the Garda Síochána failed to apply for the necessary arrest warrant. It appeared that the chief superintendent had been informed by the DPP in Ireland that the DPP would not prefer an indictment against McCormack if he was brought back to Ireland. McCormack sought an order of mandamus to compel the DPP to prosecute him for the offences in question and an order of mandamus to compel the chief superintendent to seek the requisite arrest warrant.

The application failed in the High Court. McCormack's appeal to the Supreme Court was dismissed essentially on the basis that the chief superintendent's decision not to seek a warrant was reasonable given that he had grounds for believing that it would not result in the applicant being prosecuted for the offences in question in this jurisdiction. Nevertheless, both courts addressed the extent to which the DPP's discretion to prosecute could be the subject of judicial review. In the High Court, Barr J. adopted the line taken in *Killian*, *Judge* and *Savage* namely that the exercise of this discretion was unreviewable. The Supreme Court, however, appears to have moved from this absolutist position to one where there is at least some scope for judicial review. This is clearly reflected in the following passage from the judgment of Finlay C.J.:

> "In regard to the DPP I reject also the submission that he has only got a discretion as to whether to prosecute or not to prosecute in any particular case related exclusively to the probative value of the evidence laid before him. Again I am satisfied that there are many other factors which may be appropriate and proper for him to take into consideration. I do not consider that it would be wise or helpful to list them in any exclusive way. If, of course, it can be demonstrated that he reaches a decision *mala fides* or influenced by an improper motive or improper policy then his decision would be reviewable by a court. To that extent I reject the contention made on behalf of this respondent that his decisions were not as a matter of public policy ever reviewable by a court."[177]

The Supreme Court's approach accords with a general judicial trend, evident in both this jurisdiction and in Britain, in favour of restricting the range of executive powers which are immune to review by the courts. It is a more difficult matter, however, to deduce from the judgments the grounds upon which the exercise of the DPP's decision on prosecution might be challenged. Finlay C.J. proceeds on the assumption that a decision to prosecute can be challenged on the basis of the probative value of the evidence available to the DPP. The clear implication is that a decision to prosecute can be quashed if the DPP, applying his mind to the value of the probative evidence before him, could not reasonably have reached a decision to prosecute. This, of course, still leaves open the question of how strong the value of the probative

---

[177] [1987] I.L.R.M. 237. Finlay C.J. also rejected the contention that a decision of a member of the Garda Síochána not to proceed to arrest or initiate a prosecution can never be reviewable.

evidence must be in order to support a reasonable decision to prosecute. Presumably, evidence which rendered a conviction more likely than not would be sufficient, but what about evidence which afforded only a prima facie case or less. The Supreme Court's decision does not shed any further light on this issue. Admittedly, Walsh J. intimates that a decision to prosecute could be struck down on the basis that it was perverse.[178] Undoubtedly, this would encompass a situation where the value of the probative evidence was insufficient to support prosecution, but it sheds little light on what is meant by "insufficient" in this context.

Finlay C.J. entertains no doubt that a decision to prosecute which had been taken mala fides or which had been influenced by improper motives or an improper policy would be invalid. Walsh J. also accepts that a decision influenced by improper motives can be struck down. The mala fides or bad faith option holds no surprises. It has long been accepted that the exercise of most discretionary powers can be challenged on this basis. Realistically, however, it would be a most exceptional case in which a court would find that the DPP had been guilty of bad faith in taking a decision to prosecute. In effect the court would be deciding that the DPP's decision was motivated by malice against the accused.

12–40 Challenging the DPP's decision on the basis of improper motives or an improper policy is more problematical. These are firmly established concepts in the law of judicial review of administrative action. In essence they entail a claim that the decision maker has taken an extraneous matter or policy into account when exercising his or her discretion or has failed to take a relevant matter into account or has failed to follow the appropriate policy.[178a] Arguably, in the case of the DPP's decision to prosecute in an individual case, factors such as the accused's wealth, the victim's social status and a policy in favour of absolute prosecution in all complaints of a particular crime would be improper matters or policy. If that is the import of Finlay C.J.'s and Walsh J.'s judgments they represent a distinct change in the law governing the scope of the DPP's discretion as previously understood. In practice, however, it is unlikely that the learned judges meant to go so far. Indeed, the tenor of their judgments suggests that they intended the expressions "improper motive or improper policy" to be given a very narrow interpretation in the prosecutorial context.[179] Accordingly, a decision to prosecute could be challenged under these headings only if it was akin to mala fides or was otherwise so improper as to be perverse.[180] This limitation is critically important as it leaves intact the practice of the DPP to take

---

[178] [1987] I.L.R.M. 225 at 239.

[178a] See Hogan and Morgan, *Administrative Law in Ireland*, (3rd ed., Round Hall, Dublin, 1998), at Chap. 13.

[179] See further, *ibid.* at 688 *et seq.*

[180] Lynch J. in *Foley v. Director of Public Prosecutions* (High Court, 19.6.89) opined that *McCormack* should be interpreted in the light of *Savage*. Accordingly, when the DPP was exercising his discretion to transfer a trial to the Special Criminal Court, his decision could not be impugned unless the applicant had established a prima facie case of "some irregularity of a serious nature such as to amount to some impropriety of some sort or other. It is submitted that this is also applicable to the DPP's decision to prosecute.

a range of factors into account when exercising his discretion not to prosecute in an individual case.

Support for the narrow interpretation of the grounds upon which the DPP's decision on prosecution can be challenged can be found in the Supreme Court's decision in *H v. DPP*.[181] In that case the applicant was seeking, *inter alia*, an order of mandamus to compel the DPP to take a prosecution against her husband and brother for sexual offences allegedly committed against her son. In refusing her application the Court explained that:

> "If the Director of Public Prosecutions were to be subjected to frequent applications for *mandamus* compelling him to bring prosecutions by discomfited persons I apprehend that his office would be stretched beyond endurance in seeking to justify that which should not require to be justified."[182]

The Court went on to hold, in line with its decision in *State (McCormack) v. Curran*, that the Director's decision not to prosecute could only be impugned on the basis of evidence from which it could reasonably be inferred that his decision was perverse or inspired by improper motives or that he had abdicated his functions. Unsubstantiated allegations of impropriety, whether or not denied by the DPP, were not sufficient in themselves to give rise to an adverse inference about the DPP's decision.

The conclusion, therefore, is that the DPP's decision to prosecute or not in an individual case is subject to judicial review. If the circumstances are such that the accused, for whatever reason, cannot get a fair trial then the courts will block the prosecution. Apart from that it will be very difficult to challenge the DPP's decision successfully as the court will require prima facie evidence that there was something so seriously irregular about the DPP's decision as to render it perverse or bordering on mala fides. Nevertheless, it is clear that a decision by the DPP not to prosecute in all crimes of a particular nature would be unlawful.[183]

3. Reasons for the Decision to Prosecute

Closely related to the question of the judicial review of the DPP's prose-   **12–41**
cutorial decision is the issue of whether he is obliged to give reasons for a decision not to prosecute in any individual case. The DPP follows a clear policy of not giving reasons.[184] He justifies this reticence on the basis of natural justice to the parties affected. Moreover, he feels that if he gives reasons in one case he will have to give reasons in all cases, with consequent unfairness to the individuals concerned in many such cases.[185] However, the DPP has issued a standing instruction to the effect that the State Solicitor and the Garda Síochána should be informed of the reasons why a decision is taken not to proceed with a

---

[181] [1994] 2 I.L.R.M. 285.
[182] *H v. DPP* [1994] 2 I.L.R.M. 285 at 290.
[183] See *Norris v. Attorney General* [1984] I.R. 36 at 81. See also *Duggan v. An Taoiseach* [1989] I.L.R.M. 710.
[184] Barnes *Communique, op. cit*, p. 9.
[185] For further detail on this see, 'Statement to Press Issued by Director of Public Prosecutions on 22/7/83' to be found in Appendix 7 to *1998 Annual Report of the DPP op. cit.*

prosecution in any case submitted by them.[186] If there is a failure to give reasons in any case, or if the reasons given are inadequate, they are encouraged to seek a full statement of reasons from the DPP's office.[187] The DPP has also stated that reasons would always be given without question to the Attorney General should he request them, and to any other public agency (such as a relevant government department) having a functional interest in them.[188]

The question of whether the DPP is under any legal obligation to give reasons for a refusal to prosecute was considered in *H v. DPP*.[189] In that case Barron J. had ruled that where a decision of the DPP is challenged by a person with *locus standi*, the DPP is in the same position as any other person acting under statutory powers and, as such, is obliged to give reasons. Barron J. based his decision on the ruling in *International Fishing Vessels Ltd v. Minister for the Marine*[190] to the effect that a person exercising a statutory power is under a duty to act fairly and judicially and the provision of reasons was an essential prerequisite to ensure the necessary fairness of procedures. On the DPP's appeal, however, the Supreme Court distinguished *International Fishing Vessels* partly on the basis that it concerned the exercise of a ministerial power which was fully subject to judicial review while the DPP's power was subject to judicial review to a limited extent only, and partly because the DPP's decision on prosecution does not settle or decide any question, dispute, rights or liabilities. The Supreme Court went on to hold that the DPP was not under an obligation to give reasons in any case because if he gave reasons in one he would have to give reasons in all and that could be unfair to individuals affected. In other words, the DPP's justification for refusing to give reasons has received judicial sanction. It is worth noting, however, that this does not exonerate the DPP from the responsibility to act reasonably in reaching a decision.[191] If, after conducting an internal review (see below), he reverses an initial decision not to prosecute, he must have good and sufficient reasons for changing his mind.[192]

In *Deeley v. The Information Commissioner and DPP*[193] the High Court confirmed that the Freedom of Information Act 1997 does not apply to a record held by the DPP, other than one concerning the general administration of the Office.[194] It also ruled that section 18 of the Act could not be used to compel the DPP to give to the person being prosecuted reasons why he had taken the decision to prosecute.[195]

---

[186] Barnes *Communique* at p. 9. It would appear that this also extends to other public bodies which have carried out investigations; for example, the inspectorate in a government department or a body such as the Health and Safety Authority, the Revenue Commissioners, the Competition Authority and the Corporate Enforcement Agency. See *1999 Annual Report of the DPP, op. cit.,* para.6.2.

[187] *1998 Annual Report of the DPP, op. cit.,* at 22.

[188] *ibid.*

[189] [1994] 2 I.L.R.M. 285.

[190] [1989] I.R. 149.

[191] *Eviston v. DPP*, HC, January 26, 2001.

[192] *ibid.*

[193] HC, May 11, 2001.

[194] *2001 Annual Report of the DPP, op. cit.,* at 25.

[195] The court also decided that an accused did not enjoy a common law right to be told why the prosecution was being brought.

4. Internal Review of the Decision to Prosecute

The DPP is conscious of the potential problems posed by the limited scope **12–42**
for a judicial review of his decision on prosecution in any individual case.
Accordingly, he has put in place a system of internal review.[196] In effect it
enables an interested party to seek an internal review of a decision on
prosecution in any individual case. It is anticipated that most such requests
will emanate from the Garda Síochána. Indeed, it would appear that the
Garda Síochána has been reminded on many occasions by personnel in the
DPP's office of the availability on request of the internal review procedure.

Where a request for review is issued through the office of the Garda
Commissioner it will be granted. Requests by another official reporting
agency are given similar consideration. Requests from other persons having a
legitimate interest in the decision, such as a victim or a suspect or accused,
are sympathetically received. Several reviews have been conducted as a result
of such requests. Nevertheless, the DPP states that his Office cannot automatically grant all requests from these other sources. To do so would divert
already scarce resources from its urgent ongoing business. However, if the
person seeking the review advances a reasonable basis for the request, it
would be granted unless the particular factor had already been exhaustively
considered.

A request for review need not point to any new fact not included in the file **12–43**
already submitted. However, it should provide at least general reasons why
the original decision was considered to be erroneous or required fresh
consideration. This is particularly important in the case of requests from
persons other than the Garda Síochána or other reporting agencies. The
procedure followed is set out as follows in the DPP's 1998 Annual Report:

> "Where a request is granted it is conducted thoroughly and by way of
> complete re-examination of the case unless the request itself is confined to a
> specific point or points. The procedure adopted will vary according to the
> circumstances of the case. It will usually be conducted by a professional
> officer other than the officer who took the original decision. In difficult cases
> several opinions including that of the Director may be sought. The important
> point is that it is a real review and neither the professional officers individually
> nor the Office itself would experience any problem in altering its original
> decision where that is considered to be the correct course. Apart from cases
> where new facts are brought to attention, alternations of the original decision
> would be the exception rather than the rule but there have been examples of
> alterations where either the officer originally concerned or another officer
> came to the conclusion that the decision given had been incorrect. It should be
> emphasised that in the small number of cases in which decisions have been
> either reversed or modified without new facts having been brought to
> attention, the judgement call involved has usually been a very fine one."[197]

---

[196] See (1998) *Annual Report of the DPP op. cit.* at 24. See also, V*ictims Charter* (Department of
Justice and Law Reform, Dublin, 1999).
[197] *ibid.*

A cloud currently hangs over the operation of the internal review procedure as a result of the High Court decision in *Eviston v. DPP.*[198] In that case the DPP initially decided against prosecution in a case of causing death by dangerous driving. This decision was conveyed to the suspect and the family of the deceased, whereupon the father of the deceased sought an internal review. Following that review a decision was taken to charge the suspect who then applied to the High Court for a order of prohibition to prevent the prosecution. The Court quashed the prosecution on the ground that it would be unfair and oppressive to the suspect to allow it to continue. In reaching this conclusion the Court considered that the DPP's reversal of his original decision was arbitrary and perverse. There were no new facts to justify it, no contradiction of the facts upon which the original decision was based, no suggestion that anything had been overlooked and no suggestion that some other undisclosed fact might explain the reversal. The Court also considered that the DPP did not comply with his own published guidelines on the exercise of his decision to conduct the review. According to these guidelines a review would be conducted only if the applicant raised matters which had not been exhaustively considered in the original application. In this case the reason proffered for conducting the review was the extreme distress suffered by the victim's family. In the Court's view it was considered that this matter had been exhaustively considered when taking the original decision not to prosecute.

It is not yet clear how this ruling will affect the DPP's policy on the conduct of internal reviews. At the very least it would appear that the DPP cannot reverse an original decision not to prosecute unless the application raises some material fact or facts which had not been fully considered in the original decision. In other words the original decision cannot be reversed solely because another professional officer within the Office takes a different view on whether there should be a prosecution. The Court also intimated that before reversing an initial decision not to prosecute the DPP would have to take into account the fact that, as a matter of policy, citizens who had been told in unqualified terms that no prosecution would be brought should not thereafter be exposed to prosecution without good and sufficient cause.

K. Consent to Prosecute

12–44   For some offences prosecutions can proceed only with the express consent of the DPP (previously the Attorney General). These must be distinguished at the outset from those indictable offences which can be disposed of summarily, but only where the DPP consents.[199] Similarly they are quite distinct from those indictable offences which can be disposed of by the District Court on a guilty plea, but only if the DPP consents.[200] What is being considered in this section are those offences which cannot be prosecuted at all unless the

---

[198] [2002] 1 I.L.R.M. 134.
[199] See Criminal Justice Act 1951, s.2 (as amended by Criminal Procedure Act 1967, s.19).
[200] Criminal Procedure Act 1967, s.13.

consent of the DPP or, where applicable, the Attorney General is forth-coming.

The origins of the consent requirement can be traced back to a time when the private prosecutor was much more active than he is today. It was useful then to have some device whereby the State could exercise some control in individual cases where a decision to prosecute might raise issues of public policy. Examples of offences which require the prior consent of the DPP before a prosecution can proceed include: offences under the Explosives Substances Act 1883; marital rape;[201] certain offences created by the Criminal Assets Bureau Act 1996;[202] offences under the Criminal Justice (United Nations Convention against Torture) Act 2000; and offences under the Criminal Justice (Safety of United Nations Workers) Act 2000. There are also a number of offences for which the consent of the Attorney General only will suffice. For the most part, these have been created by legislation which has been enacted during the second half of the twentieth century. Not surprisingly, they concern matters affecting either the security of the State or the State's international obligations. Examples include offences under: Official Secrets Act 1963, s.14(1); the Geneva Conventions Act 1962, s.3(3); the Genocide Act 1973, s.2(3); and the Criminal Law (Jurisdiction) Act 1976, s.20(2).

Although the formula used to insert the consent requirement does not differ significantly from one offence to another the same cannot be said for the actual contents of a valid consent. The contents are conditioned by the underlying purpose of the consent requirement which can, of course, differ significantly from one offence to another. What these details should include in the case of offences under the Explosive Substances Act 1883, for example, is evident from the following quotation from the judgment of Lord MacDermott L.C.J. in the Northern Irish case of *R. v. Downey*:

> "The details which a consent should contain depend on its underlying purpose, which is to ensure for the individual in danger of being charged with one or more of the grave offences created by the Act of 1883, the protection that his prosecution may only proceed, if a law officer of the Crown, after such investigation as is requisite, consents thereto. The consent should, therefore, describe the offence or offences with reasonable particularity, and this means that the indictment and the trial thereof cannot rove outside the material particulars stated in the consent."[203]

This quotation also highlights an important consequence of the consent requirement, namely that the prosecution case cannot stray beyond the material particulars set out in the consent. It follows that the consent actually has a substantive impact upon the trial.

Since the Attorney General or the DPP would not normally be acting in person at the trial, their consent would have to be conveyed through another

12–45

---

201 Criminal Law (Rape)(Amendment) Act 1990, s.5(2).
202 Intimidation of Bureau personnel (s.13) and assault on Bureau personnel (s.15); see Criminal Assets Bureau Act 1996, s.17.
203 [1971] NI 224 at 228.

medium. The most appropriate, of course, would be a written consent form duly signed by the Attorney General or the DPP as the case may be. Any possible problem[204] over proof that the person signing the form held the appropriate office is avoided by the terms of section 8 of the Prosecution of Offences Act 1974. These stipulate that every document purporting to be issued by the Attorney General or the DPP, as the case may be, and to be signed by him shall be received in evidence and be deemed to be such document unless the contrary is shown. However, the Act also stipulates that where the consent of the DPP or the Attorney General is required by statute, counsel acting for them may inform the court orally that the appropriate consent has been given.[205] This provision applies to the requirement of consents generally and is not confined to consents to prosecution. It is submitted, however, that it is unsatisfactory for the oral communication to be used in respect of the latter consents. Bearing in mind what Lord MacDermott L.C.J. said about the role of consents in *Downey* it would seem that an oral communication would hardly be sufficient to fulfil the legislative intention in inserting the requirement for consent in the first place.

L. Challenging a Refusal to Consent

12–46   The requirement to secure the consent of the DPP or the Attorney General, as the case may be, in order to prosecute raises the question of what happens when the necessary consent is not forthcoming. The immediate result, of course, is that that prosecution cannot proceed. It may be possible, however, to challenge the refusal. There are two possibilities here. The first is to launch a full frontal constitutional challenge to the consent requirement, while the second would involve seeking an order of mandamus to compel the DPP (or the Attorney General) to exercise his discretion in the matter "properly". Each will be considered briefly in turn.

As yet there is no reported case in which the consent requirement has been challenged on constitutional grounds. Significantly, however, the statutory requirement for a plaintiff to secure the fiat of the Attorney General before suing the Minister for Posts and Telegraphs (as he then was) was successfully challenged in *Macauley v. Minister for Posts and Telegraphs.*[206] In that case Kenny J. in the High Court ruled that the fiat requirement amounted to an unwarranted interference with the citizen's constitutionally guaranteed right of access to the courts. This holds out the prospect of a successful challenge to the consent requirement in criminal cases. It is worth cautioning, however, that the consent requirement in the criminal statutes will raise policy issues which were not present in *Macauley*. Unlike civil actions in tort, criminal prosecutions are recognised as having a major public interest dimension

---

[204]   See, for example, In re *McCurtain* [1941] I.R. 83.

[205]   Prosecution of Offences Act 1974, s.4(3)(b). See also, *Attorney General v. Downes* [1958] I.R. 228.

[206]   [1966] I.R. 345.

which will normally supersede the interest of any private victim or complainant. This is reflected in the fact that prosecutions on indictment can be taken only by the DPP and in the extreme reluctance of the courts to question the exercise of the DPP's discretion in such matters. It follows that the law already recognises a serious limitation on the citizen's right of access to the courts in criminal matters. Moreover, it is a limitation which has never been challenged successfully as being unconstitutional.

Given the additional special policy issues that can arise in the particular offences subject to the consent requirement, it is difficult to foresee a court concluding that the restriction is not justified in the interests of the common good. This is especially so for those offences which require the consent of the Attorney General. Most of them impact upon the conduct of the government's external relations. The Constitution vests the executive power in external relations in the government. It is unlikely, therefore, that the High Court or the Supreme Court would rule unconstitutional a statutory provision which gives the Attorney General a discretionary power to exercise control over decisions to prosecute in certain cases which could have serious implications for the conduct of the government's external relations. Admittedly, the policy arguments will differ from one offence to another, particularly, for those which are subject to the consent of the DPP. It follows that each will have to be considered on its merits. As a general proposition, however, it should not be assumed that just because the fiat requirement was declared unconstitutional in a particular civil case that the consent requirement must be constitutionally suspect in criminal cases. The particular issues raised in the criminal context present a much greater obstacle to a successful constitutional challenge.

Even if the consent requirement in some of the offences is amenable to constitutional challenge, the question of *locus standi* will arise. Will the courts accept that an individual has the *locus standi* necessary to challenge the consent requirement imposed in a statute creating a criminal offence? Given the extent to which the traditional *locus standi* requirements have been relaxed in recent years it is unlikely that this will prove a significant obstacle.[207] If the applicant can show a legitimate interest in seeking a prosecution for the offence in question it is highly unlikely that he or she will fail on the *locus standi* issue. A victim, a parent or guardian of the victim, or even a member of an organisation with a direct interest in the victim or victims of the crime in question would have a legitimate interest.

A less drastic option to a constitutional challenge to the consent requirement is to seek an order of mandamus where the DPP or the Attorney General has refused his consent to the prosecution. In effect the prosecutor would be seeking an order from the court compelling the DPP or the Attorney General to exercise his discretion on the consent issue properly. The first matter that will arise in this context is whether the DPP's (or the Attorney General's) decision to refuse consent is subject to judicial review at all. In *Macauley* Kenny J. was

12–47

---

[207] See, *e.g. PUC v. Coogan* [1990] I.L.R.M. 70; *Iarnród Éireann v. Ireland* [1995] 2 I.L.R.M. 161.

of the opinion that the Attorney General's decision to withhold his consent was not reviewable. Of course, the "consent" in this case related to civil proceedings against the Minister. Its relevance to the consent requirement in prosecutions therefore is by analogy only, with due allowance being made for the policy differences between the two situations. Moreover, the weight that can be attached to Kenny J.'s observation on reviewability must be tempered by the fact that he did not examine the issue in any detail.

Since the decision in *Macauley,* the Irish courts have charted a much more activist role in subjecting executive discretion to judicial review.[208] This is reflected in areas which might be considered pertinent to the issue of the consent requirement in prosecutions. For example, on the question of reviewing the DPP's decision to enter a *nolle prosequi* the courts have moved from an absolute position of immunity from review, to one where they have jurisdiction to intervene on the grounds of basic concepts of fairness and justice.[209] Indeed, the courts are prepared to restrain the DPP from taking any decision in the course of a prosecution which is likely to contribute to an unfair or an unjust proceeding.[210] There is no obvious reason to assume that this does not extend to a decision by the DPP (or the Attorney General, as the case may be) to refuse his consent to a prosecution where such consent is required by statute.

12–48 Recent developments in the area of relator actions also strengthen the case for asserting the reviewability of "consent" decisions. The relator action is a device which enables members of the public to use the Attorney General's name to commence civil proceedings where the individual litigant personally lacks the necessary *locus standi.*[211] This is most likely to arise where the individual is seeking to enforce a public, as opposed to a private right. The Attorney General, in his capacity as *parens patriae*, is considered to enjoy an exclusive role in the enforcement of public rights. If he has not acted to enforce a public right in an individual case, a private individual may request his consent to the use of his name to enforce the right by way of a relator action. Where the Attorney General grants a request to use his name for this purpose the litigation will be taken in his name and he will be able to exercise control over it. In practice, however, the litigation is normally conducted and paid for by the private litigant. Although relator actions are confined to civil proceedings they can, and do, impinge upon criminal matters. For example, the private litigant may be seeking an injunction to prevent another from committing a criminal offence. Since the enforcement of the criminal law is

---

[208] See, for example, Hogan and Morgan *op. cit.* at pp. 678–690.

[209] In *State (Killian) v. Attorney General* (1958) 92 I.L.T.R. 182 the Supreme Court ruled that a decision by the Attorney General to enter a *nolle prosequi* was not open to review in the courts. See Casey *op. cit* at pp. 102–104 for a critique of this decision and, in particular, for an analysis of how its reasoning has now been overtaken by related judicial developments. See State *(O'Callaghan) v. O'hUadhaigh* [1977] I.R. 42 for an example of a High Court ruling to the effect that the power to enter a *nolle prosequi* must be construed in accordance with basic concepts of justice and fairness.

[210] See, for example, *State (O'Callaghan) v. O'hUadhaigh* [1977]I.R. 42; *Flynn v. DPP* [1986] I.L.R.M. 290 at 295.

[211] See Hogan and Morgan, *op. cit,* pp. 758–764; also, Casey, *op. cit,* pp. 1448–157.

normally considered a matter of public concern, the private litigant may be considered to lack the necessary *locus standi* to seek the injunction; thus the relator action.

The reviewability of the Attorney General's decision to grant or withhold his consent to a relator action has not been the subject of judicial decision in Ireland. In England, it was ruled by the House of Lords in the seminal case of *Gouriet v. Union of Post Office Workers*[211a] that the Attorney General's decision is not reviewable. Casey is of the opinion that that decision would not be followed in Ireland today.[212] In the light of the development of the law of judicial review in this State in recent years, he considers that it would be open to an Irish court to hold that the Attorney General may be compelled to grant his consent to a relator action in any case where he is found to have withheld it unreasonably. If this view is correct, it offers strong support for the notion that the DPP's (or the Attorney General's) decision to grant or withhold consent to a prosecution, where such consent is required by statute, is at least subject to judicial review.

Interestingly, the courts have begun to relax the requirements of *locus standi* to enable certain private litigants to enforce public rights in certain circumstances without bothering to secure the consent of the Attorney General to a relator action.[213] So far this development is restricted to situations which involved a possible infringement of the constitutional rights of the litigants.[214] However, it does extend to seeking an injunction to restrain the commission of statutory criminal offences, where the commission of such offences will entail an infringement of the constitutional rights of the litigant.[215] This development suggests that the courts are likely to be more critical of attempts by the Attorney General (and the DPP) to block efforts by private citizens to enforce the criminal law. It might be thought that this lends indirect support to the argument that the Irish courts would not be sympathetic to the proposition that the DPP's (and the Attorney General's) power to grant or withhold his consent to prosecutions for certain statutory criminal offences is beyond the reach of judicial review.

[211a] [1978] A.C. 435.

[212] Casey, *op. cit*, pp. 155–156.

[213] *SPUC v. Coogan* [1990] I.L.R.M. 70.

[214] In *Incorporated Law Society of Ireland v. Carroll* [1996] 2 I.L.R.M. 95, the Supreme Court refused to accept that the plaintiff would have locus standi to seek an injunction to restrain the commission of a statutory offence. The Court ruled that only the Attorney General has *locus standi* to seek a civil remedy to enforce such a public right. Significantly, no obvious constitutional right of the plaintiff was at stake.

[215] See, *e.g. Parsons v. Kavanagh* [1990] I.L.R.M. 560; *Lovett v. Gogan* [1995] 1 I.L.R.M. 12.

CHAPTER 13

THE DISTRICT COURT AND THE INITIATION OF CRIMINAL PROCEEDINGS

A. Introduction

The District Court plays a vital role in the criminal process.[1] In virtually   **13–01**
every case a person arrested and charged with a criminal offence will be
brought in the first instance before a judge of the District Court. Indeed, the
court often has an input at an earlier stage. An application for a warrant may
be made to a judge of the District Court for the arrest of a suspect or for the
search and seizure of evidence. Similarly, a person detained under section 2
of the Criminal Justice (Drug Trafficking) Act 1996 or section 30 of the
Offences against the State Act 1939 might be brought before the a judge of
the District Court for the purpose of having his or her detention extended.

Where a person is brought before a judge of the District Court on foot of a
criminal charge he may be dealt with in one of a number of ways depending
on the particular circumstances of the case. On the first occasion he will
normally be remanded to a sitting of the court at some date in the future. Indeed,
there may be a whole series of such remand appearances before the accused is
either tried or sent forward for trial or sentence. If the charge relates to a
summary offence the accused must be tried in the District Court, unless it is a
scheduled offence for the purposes of Part V of the Offences against the State
Act 1939 or the DPP has issued the necessary certificate under the 1939 Act to
have the case tried in the Special Criminal Court. Some indictable offences
can also be tried in the District Court in certain circumstances.

---

[1] For a detailed exposition of the jurisdiction, practice and procedure of the District Court, see J
Woods *District Court: Practice and Procedure in Criminal Cases* (Woods, Limerick 1994).

The focus of this chapter is on District Court proceedings in respect of a person who has been charged with a criminal offence. It will cover the jurisdiction of the District Court in criminal matters and the power of the District Court Rules Committee to make rules for the court. Under the heading of initiating the prosecution it will examine how a person can be brought before the District Court to answer a criminal charge. This is followed by an account of the procedure on first appearance before the District Court, an overview of the course of the summary trial and the court's jurisdiction to send an accused forward for sentence on a plea of guilty. The following chapter will address how the accused is sent forward for trial and related matters.

B. Jurisdiction

1. Introduction

13–02   Before a judge of the District Court can deal with a criminal charge in any individual case he must have jurisdiction in the matter. The two key factors here are where the alleged offence is supposed to have been committed, and the classification of the alleged offence. The former will be dealt with here, while the latter has already been dealt with in chapter 1.

2. Territorial Jurisdiction

Districts and areas

The territorial jurisdiction of a District Court judge is limited to the district to which he or she is assigned.[1a] As a general rule the judge has jurisdiction in any criminal case where the alleged offence has been committed within his or her *district* or if the alleged offender resides or has been arrested within that *district*.[2] However, each district is also divided up into areas (see chapter 2). The District Court Rules state that criminal proceedings shall be brought, heard and determined in the court area where the offence is alleged to have been committed, the court area in which the accused has been arrested or the court area in which the accused resides.[3] This focus on the court area, as distinct from the court district, is also reflected in the District Court (Areas) Order 1961 which requires the judge to deal with any particular case in the appropriate District Court area.[4] It follows that the proceedings must actually be held in the relevant court area, but they can be heard by a judge having jurisdiction in the relevant district.

In *State (Reilly) v. Circuit Court Judge of Midland Circuit and District Justice for Port-Laoighise*,[4a] Hanna J. had to determine in a civil case whether

---

[1a] See Chap. 2.
[2] Courts of Justice Act 1924, s.79.
[3] District Court Rules 1997, Ord.13, r.1. If more than one offence has been committed within a judge's district it may be dealt with in a court area where any one of them has been committed.
[4] See Chap. 2.
[4a] [1936] I.R. 372.

a District Court judge had jurisdiction to deal with a defendant at a sitting of the Court in an area other than that in which the defendant resided. It is submitted that his decision is applicable by analogy to the situation where a defendant is being tried at a sitting of the Court in an area other than that in which the offence was committed or in which the defendant resides or has been arrested. Hanna J. explained that the limitation of jurisdiction to the District Court area in question is not simply a matter of procedure. It is intended to confer rights on the defendant with respect to the forum and territorial area of the forum in which he is to be tried. A failure to respect these rights will provide grounds for quashing a conviction in the case in question.

This reasoning was applied in criminal proceedings in *O'Brien v. O'Halloran*.[4b] In that case, the applicant had been convicted of summary offences in Abbeyfeale on foot of summonses which had been issued in Listowel. The proceedings were held in Abbeyfeale as the premises in Listowel were unfit for the conduct of business. While Abbeyfeale was in the same District Court district as Listowel, it lay in a different court area and was not within one mile of the border of the Listowel District Court area. Accordingly, the Minister issued a statutory order which effectively merged the two court areas. While this order was in force at the time of the substantive hearing of the case, it was not in force when the matter first arose before the District Court judge. Nevertheless, the District Court judge rejected the applicant's objections to her lack of jurisdiction in the matter and proceeded to adjourn the case. At the resumed hearing, at a time when the statutory instrument was in force, the applicant renewed his objection to jurisdiction, but without success.

On the application for certiorari to quash the convictions, Kearns J. explained that a District Court judge can lawfully embark on the hearing of a criminal matter only if she has jurisdiction in the matter. This applies even for the purpose of granting an adjournment. Accordingly, the mere fact that the statutory instrument had come into effect by the time that the District Court judge embarked upon the substantive hearing of the case was not enough to give her jurisdiction in the matter if she had no jurisdiction at the time she granted the adjournment. Applying the reasoning of Hanna J. in *Reilly*, the learned judge found that a District Court judge's jurisdiction in a criminal matter was confined generally by the territorial limit of the area. Since Abbeyfeale and Listowel were two separate District Court areas at the relevant time, proceedings on foot of the summonses in this case could not be commenced in Abbeyfeale. There was a provision in the statutory instrument which stated that business which is initiated and not completed before the commencement of the instrument shall be continued and completed as if the order had been in force at the time at which the business had been initiated. Kearns J. ruled that this was not sufficient to give jurisdiction in the instant case as it could relate only to business which had been properly initiated and outstanding prior to the commencement of the instrument. In this case there

---

[4b]   High Court, November 16, 1999.

was a complete lack of jurisdiction as the proceedings had not been commenced in the proper court area.

Where the proceedings are in respect of an indictable offence they may be dealt with in any court area within the judge's district.[5] Similarly, where the proceedings are in respect of a summary offence and the accused is in custody and is unable to give bail for his or her appearance at a sitting of the court, such proceedings may be heard and determined in any court area within the judge's district.[6]

In practice prosecutions are normally taken in the court area where the offence was committed.[7] Where the accused is charged with several offences which have been committed at different locations within a judge's district, the proceedings in respect of all of the offences may be taken at a sitting of the court in a court area where any one of the offences was committed.[8] Offences committed outside a judge's district may be heard at a sitting in a court area within his or her district only if the accused was arrested or resides in that area, or if there is statutory provision specifically conferring jurisdiction on the judge.[9]

13–03 The choice of area in which to bring proceedings can be critical. If proceedings are brought in the wrong area the judge cannot cure the matter by adjourning the proceedings to the proper area. He has no jurisdiction in the matter as the proceedings are not properly before him.[10] Indeed, the proceedings themselves are void *ab initio*.

It does not follow that an error in naming the place where the offence is alleged to have been committed will necessarily be fatal to the prosecution. It may happen, for example, that the place specified in the complaint as the place of commission does not correlate with the evidence adduced in support of the complaint. The District Court Rules stipulate that no such variation between the complaint and the supporting evidence shall be deemed material provided that the offence was committed within the jurisdiction of the judge hearing the case.[11] The judge may amend the summons and proceed to hear and determine the case. If, however, he or she is of the opinion that the variation is one which has misled the accused or which might affect the merits of the case, he or she may refuse to make the amendment and dismiss the case either on its merits or without prejudice to it being made again.[12] If the judge proceeds to make the amendment in this situation he or she may adjourn the proceedings to any future day at the same or any other place upon such terms as he or she thinks fit (see paras. 13–14 *et-seq.*).[13]

---

[5] District Court Rules 1997, Ord.13, r.2.

[6] *ibid.* Ord.13, r.3.

[7] J Woods, *District Court Practice and Procedure in Criminal Cases* (Limerick, 1994), p.28.

[8] District Court Rules 1997, Ord.13, r.1(a).

[9] The most likely examples concern offences committed outside the State in circumstances where Irish courts have jurisdiction. See Chap. 3.

[10] *State (Reilly) v. Circuit Court Judge of the Midland Circuit* [1936] I.R. 372.

[11] District Court Rules 1997, Ord.38, r.1.

[12] *ibid.* Ord.38, r.1(3).

Proving Location

If a dispute arises as to the geographical location of the place where the offence **13–04** is alleged to have been committed, it would appear that it should be settled by reference to appropriate maps. In *People v. McGeough*,[14] for example, the appellant had been convicted in the Central Criminal Court of an attempt to export goods the exportation of which had been prohibited by statute. The prosecution case depended upon proof that the forecourt and sheds attached to a dwelling lay in County Louth while the dwelling itself was situated across the border in County Armagh. The prosecution attempted to provide the necessary proof by calling two customs officials to give evidence of where the border with Northern Ireland lay with respect to the dwelling and the forecourt and sheds. The Court of Criminal Appeal, however, ruled this form of proof "inadmissible and inadequate" as being based solely on the "expressed opinions or satisfaction" of the two witnesses. Walsh J. explained as follows:

> "The Courts have judicial knowledge of the extent of the State and, for example, of the administrative counties which are comprised in the State and of the cities and towns which are in the State. The Courts have not judicial knowledge that any particular farmhouse or yard, as such, is within or without the State. Where it is necessary to prove the geographical situation of any such place, it should be done with the assistance of maps drawn to scale where the point in question may be identified in relation to other points in the area and where the whole area in the map may be identified. This is particularly important in a case such as this where the measurement has to be so fine because the total distance involved is to be counted in yards. It requires no great effort to identify a particular place as being in the county of Louth, as is alleged here, and to identify another place as being in the county of Armagh."[15]

C. The District Court Rules

1. The Rules Committee

In matters of pleading, practice and procedure generally, the jurisdiction of the **13–05** District Court must be exercised in the manner provided by rules of court made under section 91 of the Courts of Justice Act 1924.[16] The rule making authority for the purposes of section 91 is the District Court Rules Committee with the concurrence of the Minister for Justice, Equality and Law Reform.[17] Its competence extends to making rules and orders regulating the practice and procedure of the District Court in the exercise of any new jurisdiction conferred on the Court by an Act of the Oireachtas or any extension or variation of an existing jurisdiction.[18] The Committee is composed of two *ex officio*

---

[13] *D.P.P. v. William Winston*, unreported, High Court, May 25, 1992.
[14] [1978] I.R. 384.
[15] *ibid.* at 385–386.
[16] Courts (Supplemental Provisions) Act 1961, s.34.
[17] Courts of Justice Act 1936, s.72.
[18] Interpretation Act 1937, s.17.

members and seven nominated members.[19] The former are the President of the District Court (Chairman) and one of the District Court clerks for the Dublin Metropolitan district. The seven nominated members comprise four District Court judges nominated by the Minister for Justice, Equality and Law Reform, one practising barrister nominated by the Bar Council and two practising solicitors nominated by the Council of the Law Society. Meetings must be held at least once a year. After each meeting the Committee must report to the Minister on whether any, and if so what, amendments or alterations should be made in the practice, procedure or administration of the District Court, or in the law affecting or administered by the court, with a view to the improvement of the administration of justice.[20]

2. Scope of the Rule-making Power

13–06   The scope of the Committee's rule making authority is set out in section 91 of the Courts of Justice Act 1924 which reads in part:

> ". . . In particular rules may be made for all or any of the following matters, viz., for regulating the sittings and the vacations and the districts of the Justices and the places where proceedings are to be brought and the forms of process, summons, case stated, appeal or otherwise, and the conditions which a party who requires a case stated or an appellant must comply with in civil cases or in criminal cases or in licensing cases as the case may be and the practice and procedure of the District Court generally including questions of costs and the times for taking any step in the District Court, the entering-up of judgment and granting of summary judgment in appropriate cases and the use of the national language of Saorstat Eireann therein. . . . . . . and the adaptation or modification of any statute that may be necessary for any of the purposes aforesaid and all subsidiary matters."[21]

The scope of the Committee's rule making power under this provision is heavily dependant on the interpretation of the "practice and procedure of the District Court generally."[22] A very broad interpretation would empower the Committee to make rules which could have a substantive impact on the jurisdiction of the District Court and on the powers of officers, including members of the Garda Síochána. This prospect is enhanced by the fact that Rules made by the Committee may adapt or modify the provisions of any statute. The courts, however, have preferred a narrower interpretation.

In *State (O'Flaherty) v. O'Floinn*,[23] for example, a District Court rule purporting to extend the statutory period for which an accused could be remanded in custody was held to be ultra vires. Both the High Court and the

---

[19] Courts of Justice Act 1936, s.71, as amended by the Courts (Supplemental Provisions) Act 1961, s.44. Members hold office for a term of five years and are eligible for renomination.

[20] Courts of Justice Act 1936, s.75.

[21] The fixing of courts fees, which previously had been within the competence of the Committee, is now a function of the Minister for Justice, Equality and Law Reform acting with the consent of the Minister for Finance; see the Courts of Justice Act 1936, s.65.

[22] For interpretation of this provision see: *Woolf v. O Griobhta* [1953] I.R. 276; *State (O'Flaherty) v. O'Floinn* [1954] I.R. 295; *Attorney General v. Healy* [1928] I.R. 460; *Attorney General v. Bruen* [1935] I.R. 615; *Attorney General v. Burke* [1955] I.R. 30; *State (Lynch) v. Ballagh* [1986] I.R. 203.

[23] [1954] I.R. 295.

Supreme Court rejected the argument that the rule was merely a modification or adaptation of a statutory enactment affecting the practice and procedure of the court. The power to remand in custody was considered to be a matter of jurisdiction. Any extension of the period of remand went beyond a matter of practice and procedure and amounted to an amendment of the Act in question. Similarly, in *Rainey v. Delap*[24] the Supreme Court found that District Court Rules which purported to give a District Court clerk the power to receive a complaint with a view to issuing a summons went far beyond the modification of a statute. Prior to the Rules in question the authority to receive a complaint for the purpose of issuing a summons had been conferred by statute on a District Court judge.[25] By way of comparison it was held in *Attorney General v. Healy*[26] that a Rule permitting a summons to be grounded on a verbal complaint was merely a modification or adaptation of a provision in the Customs and Inland Revenue Act 1879 which had required the complaint to be in writing. The court was of the opinion that the change was procedural in character and did not impact upon the substantive jurisdiction of the District Court.

District Court Rules which are not directly concerned with the practice and **13–07** procedure of the District Court will be *ultra vires*. In *State (Lynch) v. Ballagh*,[27] for example, a majority of the Supreme Court considered *ultra vires* a Rule which empowered a member of the Garda Síochána to release a person on station bail subject to a recognisance conditioned for his appearance at the next sitting of the District Court in the area in which he had been arrested or at any subsequent sitting to be held not later than 30 days after the next sitting. The relevant statutory provision by contrast permits release on station bail subject to a recognisance for the person's appearance before the District Court at the appropriate time and place, which in practice means the next sitting in the area. In effect, the Rule was purporting to regulate how a member of the Garda Síochána should exercise the statutory power to release a person on station bail. The majority in the Supreme Court was of the view that the District Court Rules Committee had no power to regulate the performance of the functions of the Garda Síochána or matters preliminary to or consequential on what might take place in court. The exercise of police discretion prior to a complaint being made to a judge of the District Court could not, anymore than the arrest itself, be regarded in any sense as falling under the heading of pleading, practice and procedure of the District Court. The majority favoured a narrow interpretation of the scope of the rule-making power:

> "Section 91 of the Courts of Justice Act, 1924, provides that the '. . . rule-making authority may at any time and from time to time . . . make District Court Rules . . . for . . . the practice and procedure of the District Court generally . . . including . . . the adaptation or modification of any statute that may be necessary for any of the purposes aforesaid and all subsidiary matters.' The words 'pleading, practice and procedure generally' refer to the jurisdiction

---

[24] [1988] I.R. 470.
[25] Petty Sessions (Ireland) Act 1851, s.10, as amended by the Courts of Justice Act 1924.
[26] [1928] I.R. 460.
[27] [1986] I.R. 203.

conferred upon the District Court or transferred to it and are matters strictly procedural in the narrow sense – see the judgements in *State (O'Flaherty) v. O Floinn* [1954] IR 295: *per* Davitt P. at p.296, Kingsmill Moore J. at pp. 304 and 305 and O'Dalaigh J. at p. 313. The same judgments also make clear that the 'adaptation or modification of any statute' has an application so narrow as to exclude any possibility of achieving what was sought to be achieved by Statutory Instrument No.23 of 1985 in relation to section 31 of the Criminal Procedure Act, 1967, or s.26 of the Criminal Justice Act, 1984. The power of adaptation or modification of any statute is expressly confined by s.91 to what 'may be necessary for any of the purposes aforesaid and all subsidiary matters.'[28]

D. Initiating the Criminal Prosecution

1. Introduction

13–08 Before the District Court can validly enter upon the hearing of a criminal charge its jurisdiction must be triggered in the appropriate manner. Basically, there are three procedures through which this can be done. The first and traditional method is by laying a complaint or information before a District Court judge for the issue of process. The issue of process in this context refers to the issue of a summons or an arrest warrant to secure the attendance before the court of the person against whom the information is made. It is a judicial procedure. The second method involves the issue of a summons through an administrative process introduced by the Courts (No.3) Act 1986. The third possibility arises where a suspect has been arrested without warrant by the police and taken in custody to be charged before a District Court judge, or charged in police custody and then released on bail to appear before the District Court. Each procedure will be considered in turn. From the outset, however, it should be noted that the judicial procedure can be further broken down into a summons procedure and a warrant procedure.

2. The Summons Procedure

Laying an Information

13–09 Traditionally the District Court's jurisdiction to enter on the hearing of a criminal charge has been triggered where a valid complaint or information alleging a criminal offence is made to a person or body duly authorised to receive it. A complaint or information in this context is simply a statement of facts constituting an offence.[29] Under the Petty Sessions (Ireland) Act 1851 an information can be laid before a District Court judge (formerly a Justice of the Peace) who may issue process on foot of it in any case in which he or she has jurisdiction in the district to which he or she is assigned:

---

[28] *per* Walsh J. at pp. 208–209.
[29] *per* O'Dalaigh C.J. in *Attorney General (McDonnell) v. Higgins* [1964] I.R. 374 at 385. For a summary of the law on the commencement of summary proceedings see the judgement of Gannon J. in *D.P.P. v. Sheeran* [1986] I.L.R.M. 579 at 587.

"Whenever information shall be given to any justice that any person has committed or is suspected to have committed any treason, felony, misdemeanour, or
other offence within the limits of the jurisdiction of such justice, for which such
person shall be punishable either by indictment or upon summary conviction . . .
or whenever a complaint shall be made to any justice as to any other matter
arising within the limits of his jurisdiction upon which he shall have power to
make a summary order, it shall be lawful for such justice to receive such
information or complaint, and to proceed in respect to the same."[30]

The information can be made either orally or in writing and with or without
oath as the judge may direct.[31] If it is made on oath it shall be made by way
of a sworn information.[32] Either way it can be laid by any person, although in
practice the vast majority are laid by members of the Garda Síochána in
respect of criminal offences which they have witnessed. The person laying the
information is referred to as the prosecutor or the complainant. Normally,
they are laid *ex parte* but the judge has a discretion to allow the alleged
offender to appear and argue against the issue of process.[33]

The information should set out brief particulars of: the date of the information, the name and address of the alleged offender, the name and address
of the complainant and the basic facts of the offence alleged including when it
was supposed to have been committed. If the offence alleged is a statutory
offence it is desirable, but not essential that the complaint should conclude
with the words "contrary to [the relevant section of the statute concerned]".[34]
It is also worth noting that for some offences certain statutory preconditions
must be satisfied before a summons can issue.[35]

Time Limits

Generally a complaint alleging a summary offence must be laid within six   **13–10**
months of the commission of the alleged offence, otherwise it lapses.[36] This
rule is subject to specific provision to the contrary in legislation relating to
particular offences. Increasingly, it is becoming common for the time limit to
be extended statutorily to twelve months for specified offences.[37] In some

---

[30] Petty Sessions (Ireland) Act 1851, s.10. See also the District Court Rules 1997, Ord.15, r.1(3).
[31] District Court Rules 1997, Ord.15, r.(1)1.
[32] *ibid.* Ord.15, r.1(2). For the standard form used for a sworn information see District Court Rules
1997, Sched. B, Form No.15.3.
[33] *R v. West London Metropolitan Stipendiary Magistrate, ex p. Klahn* [1979] 1 W.L.R. 933. Note also
that the complainant need not attend in person unless requested to do so; see *Irish Insurance
Commissioners v. Trench* (1913) 47 I.L.T.R. 115; *Foster v. Fyfe* (1896) 60 J.P. 423. See Woods at
p. 125.
[34] *Attorney General (McDonnell) v. Higgins* [1964] I.R. 374 *per* O'Dalaigh C.J. at 385.
[35] For *e.gs.*, see Woods at pp.129–130.
[36] Petty Sessions (Ireland) Act 1851, s.10(4) as amended by Statute of Limitations Act 1957, s.9. It
would appear that this rule does not extend to indictable offences which can be tried summarily as
minor offences; see *State (Kiernan) v. Governor of Mountjoy Prison* unreported, High Court,
February 2, 1973.
[37] See, *e.g.*, Trading Stamps Act 1980, s.14; Postal and Telecommunications Services Act 1983, s.5;
Child Care Act 1991, s.71; Payment of Wages Act 1991, s.10(2); Package Holidays and Travel
Trade Act 1995, s.7(3); Qualifications (Education and Training) Act 1999, s.64(2); National
Minimum Wage Act 2000, s.37(5); Equal Status Act 2000, s.44(4); Electronic Commerce Act

cases the limit is even longer.[38] The general six months time limit for sum-mary offences does not apply to indictable offences, even if they are being tried summarily.[39] Generally there is no time limit for the institution of criminal proceedings with respect to such offences. In respect of certain individual offences, however, a time limit is imposed by statute.[40] It is also worth noting that excessive delay in bringing a prosecution in any individual case can amount to a breach of the accused's constitutional right to a fair trial (see chapter 1).

If the complaint is not lodged within the requisite time period the defendant is entitled to raise that issue as a matter of defence. While it would appear that breach of the time limit does not affect the jurisdiction of the District Court to proceed to a hearing,[40a] it can be expected that it will amount to an absolute defence for the complainant. A court does not have the power to extend or abridge a time limit fixed by statute.[41] However, where the time limit has been fixed by the District Court Rules and relates to the service or lodgment for entry of any summons, it would appear that the judge does have a discretion to abridge or extend the time provided by the Rules.[42] Where the judge exercises this power a note of abridgement or extension of the time for service shall be endorsed on the original summons and on the copy issued for service and shall be signed by the judge. Moreover, if the substance of the complaint can constitute an indictable offence it is open to the DPP to circumvent the invalidity of summonses which were issued outside the time limit by instituting proceedings on indictment. In *Kelly v. DPP*,[43] for example, the accused had been charged with a number of summary offences arising out of a fatal road traffic accident. The application for the summonses was lodged outside of the six months time limit and, as such, would have been struck out had the case gone to summary trial. The DPP, however, withdrew the summonses and the applicant was subsequently charged on indictment with

---

2000, s.6(2); Copyright and Related Rights Act 2000, s.11(2); Valuation Act 2001, s.64(2); Teaching Council Act 2001, s.61(2); Industrial Designs Act 2001, s.5; Local Government Act, s.235; Mental Health Act 2001, s.74(2). See also, Wireless Telegraphy Acts; and Customs and Excise Acts.

[38] See, *e.g.*, Consumer Information Act 1878, s.18 as amended by Restrictive Practices (Amendment) Act 1987, s.30(1); Finance Act 1983, s.94; Sea Pollution Act 1991, s.30(3); Housing (Miscellaneous Provisions) Act 1992, s.34; European Communities (Amendment) Act 1993, s.5; Animal Remedies Act 1993, s.22(2); Consumer Credit Act 1995, s.14(3); Investment Intermediaries Act 1995, s.79(3); Stock Exchange Act 1995, s.70(3); National Beef Assurance Scheme Act 2000, s.26(2); Planning and Development Act 2000, s.157(2); National Training Fund Act 2000, s.8(5); Asset Covered Securities Act 2001, s.97. See also Customs and Excise Acts.

[39] Criminal Justice Act 1951, s.7. *State (Kieran) v. Governor of Mountjoy Prison* unreported, High Court, February 19, 1973); *McGrail v. Ruane* [1989] I.L.R.M. 498; *DPP v. William Logan* unreported, High Court, February 26, 1993.

[40] See Woods, at pp.75–76.

[40a] See *The Minister for Agriculture v. Norgro Ltd* [1980] I.R. 155; *Murray v. McArdle* unreported High Court, November 5, 1999.

[41] *Ganly v. Minister for Agriculture* [1950] I.R. 191.

[42] District Court Rules 1997, Ord.12, r.1. Note also that the Rules confer a general power on the judge to enlarge or abridge time limits which have been appointed by the Rules or fixed by the judge. This does not extend to time limits fixed by statute; Ord.12, r.3. See also, *Attorney General v. Shivnan* [1970] I.R. 66; *DPP (Murphy) v. Regan* [1993] I.L.R.M. 335; and Woods at p.78.

[43] [1997] 1 I.L.R.M. 69.

causing death by dangerous driving. The Supreme Court rejected the applicant's challenge to the validity of the proceedings holding that no issue of estoppel arose, there had been no adjudication on any issue and the applicant had not secured any gain which he would stand to lose if the proceedings on indictment were to continue. Accordingly, the applicant was never in jeopardy by virtue of the summary proceedings and there could be no injustice to him by virtue of the withdrawal of the summonses and the institution of proceedings by way of indictment.

For the most part the time limit begins to run from the date of the commission **13–11** of the offence. In the case of continuing offences this is taken to be the latest day on which the offence is alleged to have been committed.[44] Where the offence consists of failing to do something within a time period specified by statute, the time will begin to run from the end of that time period. If no period is specified in the statute creating the offence time will begin to run from the expiry of a reasonable time after it became possible to do the matter in question.[45] The time limit for some offences can also be affected by a stipulation that time can begin to run from a date later than the actual commission of the offence; such as, for example, the time that the offence first comes to the notice of the relevant prosecuting authority.[46]

For the purposes of determining whether the applicable time limit has expired in any case the critical date is the date on which the complaint was made to the District Court judge. Where the time limit is six months from the date of the offence, the complaint must be made to a District Court judge within six months of the date when the offence was committed. In computing this period of six months the day the offence was committed counts as a full day and the day the complaint was made counts as a full day. A month in this context refers to a calendar month. It follows that if the offence was committed on January 1, proceedings must be instituted by a complaint made on or before the June 30, the same year. So long as the complaint is made within the six months period it will not matter that the summons was issued outside that period. Even if the summons lapses as a result of not being dealt with on the return day, a fresh summons may be issued providing that the original complaint was made within the applicable period.[47] It may be, of course, that undue delay in issuing the summons will unfairly prejudice the defendant in making his defence. In such circumstances natural justice will require that the summons should be dismissed.[48]

---

[44] See Woods at p.77.

[45] *Minister for Finance v. Denvir* (1950) 84 I.L.T.R. 189.

[46] See, *e.g.*, Planning and Development Act 2000, s.157(2); National Monuments Act 1954, s.19.

[47] *Ex p. Fielding* (1861) 25 J.P. 759; *D.P.P. v. Gill* [1980] I.R. 263; *DPP v. McKillen* [1991] 2 I.R. 506.

[48] *DPP v. Gill* [1980] I.R. 263, *per* Henchy J. at 267.

Judicial Discretion

13–12   The issue of a summons is a judicial act.[49] Where a complaint has been laid with a view to the issue of a summons under the 1851 Act the judge must consider the information before him or her and decide whether it justifies a summons.[50] It follows that if, for example, the complaint is frivolous or vexatious, or the evidence is clearly inadequate, the judge could exercise his or her discretion to refuse to issue a summons.[51] The High Court will refuse to interfere with the exercise of the judge's discretion in such matters if he or she exercises it judicially. If, however, the judge refuses to entertain the application for a summons, decides mistakenly that he or she has no jurisdiction in the matter or is influenced in his or her decision by irrelevant or extra-judicial matters the High Court may intervene. It is also worth noting that a summons cannot be issued by a peace commissioner or a District Court clerk as neither has the status of a judge appointed in accordance with the terms of the Constitution (see later under "Administrative Procedure").

Form of Summons

A summons issued under the 1851 Act procedure will contain a brief statement in ordinary language of particulars of the complaint or offence alleged and the name and address of the person against whom the complaint is made.[52] In the case of an offence based on an enactment which prescribes several alternative modes of committing the offence, the summons may state these modes in the alternative or the conjunctive.[53] Moreover, two or more complaints or offences may be alleged in a single summons.[54] The summons must be signed by the judge,[55] although it will not be invalidated solely because the signature is illegible[56] or has been affixed by a rubber stamp.[57]

Effect of Summons

Technically, a summons is "a written command issued to a defendant for the purpose of getting him to attend court on a specified date to answer a specified complaint".[58] Accordingly, the summons will require the person concerned to appear at a sitting of the Court having jurisdiction to deal with the complaint or the offence alleged.[59] The Court in question must be within

---

[49] *State (Clarke) v. Roche* [1986] I.R. 619; *Rainey v. Delap* [1988] I.R. 470.

[50] *R. v. Gateshead Justices, ex p. Tesco Stores* [1981] Q.B. 470.

[51] *R. v. Bros* (1901) 66 J.P. 54; *R. v. Mead* (1916) 80 J.P. 382.

[52] District Court Rules 1997, Ord.15, rr.3(1) and 9. For a copy of the form see Form 15.1, Sched. B.

[53] District Court Rules 1997, Ord.15, r.8.

[54] *ibid.* Ord.15, r.4.

[55] *ibid.* Ord.15, r.5(1). The validity of the summons will not be affected by the subsequent death of the judge who signed it; Ord. 15, r.5(3)(a).

[56] *DPP v. Collins* [1981] I.L.R.M. 447.

[57] *State (Bruce) v. Judge Shannon* (1948) 82 I.L.T.; (1948) S.J. 180. The affixing of a rubber stamp must be proved if it is questioned by a party entitled to call for proof; *State (Attorney General) v. Judge Roe* [1951] I.R. 172. See Wood at p.126.

[58] *DPP v. Clein* [1983] I.L.R.M. 76, *per* Henchy J. at 77; *Attorney General (McDonnell) v. Higgins* [1964] I.R. 374; *Finnegan v. Clifford* [1992] I.L.R.M. 674..

[59] District Court Rules 1997, Ord. 15, r.3(3).

the area of jurisdiction of the judge who issues the summons.[60] The date to which the summons is made returnable is usually a matter of administrative convenience.[61] In some cases the statute creating the offence will specify a minimum period from the date of issue. While there is no statutory maximum there is a risk that the fixing of a return date far in the future could vitiate the proceedings on account of unconscionable delay.[62] As a general rule summonses should not normally be issued for August sittings.

Fees

The issue of a summons attracts a court fee under the District Court (Fees) Order, Part 1, unless the complainant is exempt or the judge remits the fee in whole or in part.[63] The question of whether this amounts to an unconstitutional restriction on the citizen's right of access to the courts was raised but not determined in *MacGairbhith v. Attorney General.*[64] In any event prosecutions at the suit of the Attorney General, the DPP, a member of the Garda Síochána, a Government Minister or the Revenue Commissioners are exempt. Also exempt are prosecutions at the suit of a local authority under the Local Authorities (Traffic Wardens) Act 1975 and proceedings instituted by a probation and welfare officer under the Probation of Offenders Act 1907 or the Criminal Justice (Community Service) Act 1983.

Service

The summons may be served anywhere in the State,[65] and a copy must be served on each person to whom it is directed.[66] Service can be effected by personal delivery to the individual concerned[67] or by leaving it for him at his last, or most usual, place of abode or at his place of business or employment.[68] Where this method is adopted the service is normally effected by a member of the Garda Síochána.[69] In cases of summary jurisdiction the summons can

13–13

---

[60] *ibid.* Ord. 15, r.3(3)(a).

[61] Woods at p.133.

[62] In *DPP v. Corbett* [1992] I.L.R.M. 674 Lynch J. ruled there was no question of a return date of seven and a half months after the commission of the alleged offences amounting to unconscionable delay as laid down in the authorities. See also, *State (Cuddy) v. Mangan* [1988] I.L.R.M. 720; *DPP v. Carlton* unreported, June 24, 1991, High Court.

[63] The judge may remit the fees in whole or in part where he is satisfied that the party liable is unable to pay them.

[64] [1991] 2 I.R. 412 (HC); unreported, Supreme Court, March 29, 1995.

[65] District Court Rules 1997, Ord.15, r.7.

[66] *ibid.* Ord.15, r.6. See r.6 for service on a company; r.7 for a local authority; r.8 for a firm; r.9 for a minor; r.10 for a lunatic or person of unsound mind; r.11 for a prisoner and r.12 for service via a solicitor.

[67] Courts Act 1991, s.22(1)(b) and the District Court Rules 1997, Ord.10, r.5.

[68] District Court Rules 1997, Ord.10, r.5. It seems that there would have to be a domestic relationship between the accused and the third party on whom the summons is served. Service on a company secretary, for example, may be sufficient for service on the company but it is not sufficient for service on a director of the company; see *O'Shea v. DPP* unreported, High Court, November 30, 2000.

[69] District Court Rules 1997, Ord.10, r.3. Where the prosecutor is a private citizen the summons will normally be served by a summons-server assigned to the particular court area; r.2(1). See r.13 for service by registered post where no summons-server is assigned – only applies to proceedings to which s.7(1) of the Courts Act 1964 as amended by s.22 of the Courts Act 1971 applies.

be served by registered post in an envelope addressed to the person concerned at his last known residence or most usual place of abode or at his place of business.[70] In practice the vast majority are served in this manner, although the option of service by hand remains.[71] Where service is effected by hand the summons must be served at least seven days before the date fixed for the hearing. In the case of service by registered post the period is 21 days.[72] Documents intended for entry at the District Court hearing must normally be lodged with the District Court clerk at least four days before the date fixed for the hearing.[73]

So long as a valid complaint has been made within the requisite time period it will not be fatal to the proceedings that the summons issued on foot of that complaint was not served until after the expiry of that time period or, indeed, that a fresh summons was issued outside that period.

3. Defects in the Summons

Technical Defects

13–14   The scope for securing a dismissal on the basis of errors or omissions in the summons is severely limited. Order 38, r.1(1) and (2) of the District Court Rules 1997 reads:

> "(1) Subject to the provisions of paragraph (3) hereof [see below], in cases of summary jurisdiction no variance between the complaint and the evidence adduced in support thereof, as to the time at which the offence or cause of complaint is stated to have been committed or to have arisen, shall be deemed material, provided that such information or complaint was in fact made within the time limited by law for making the same; nor shall any variance between the complaint and the evidence adduced in support thereof, as to the place in which the offence or cause of complaint is stated to have been committed or to have arisen, be deemed material, provided that the said offence or cause of complaint was committed or arose within the jurisdiction of the Judge by whom the case is being heard, or that, the accused resides or in the case of an offence was arrested within such jurisdiction. In any such case the court may amend the summons, warrant or other document by which the proceedings were originated and proceed to hear and determine the matter.
>
> (2) Subject to the provisions of paragraph (3) hereof [see below], no objection shall be taken or allowed on the ground of a defect in substance or in form or an omission in the summons, warrant or other document by which the proceedings were originated, or of any variance between any such document and the evidence adduced on the part of the prosecutor at the hearing

---

[70] Courts Act 1991, s.22(1) and the District Court Rules 1997, Ord.10, r.13(2). See s.22(2) and Ord.10, rr.16–19.

[71] Courts Act 1991, s.22(1)(c) and the District Court Rules 1997, Ord.10, r.13(2)(b). See also Ord.10, r.14 for other possible modes of service.

[72] District Court Rules 1997, Ord.10, r.20. The summons is deemed to be served at the time at which the envelope containing a copy of the summons would be delivered in the ordinary course of post; Courts Act 1991, s.22(3).

[73] District Court Rules 1997, Ord.10, rr.21 and 22.

of the case in summary proceedings or at the examination of the witnesses during the preliminary examination of an indictable offence, but the Court may amend any such summons, warrant or other document, or proceed in the matter as though no such defect, omission or variance had existed."[73a]

Accordingly, discrepancies between the facts alleged on the summons and the facts as presented in evidence with respect to the time and place of commission of the offence, will not normally be fatal. In *DPP v. Winston*,[74] for example, the summons charging the accused with a road traffic offence stated that the offence had occurred at Tawnaghmore, Cummer in the County of Galway. At his trial the accused argued that the evidence established that the place where the offence had been committed was situated in the townland of Cummer and not in Tawnaghmore. The District Court judge acceded to his application to dismiss the charge. This decision was overturned on a case stated to the High Court. Referring to the equivalent rules in the District Court Rules 1948, O'Hanlon J. said:

> "It appears to me that these provisions in the District Court Rules were designed to discourage the taking of purely technical objections based on variations between the written detail of the complaint and the facts established in evidence and to leave scope for the District Judge to resolve such matters of objection by amendment, if necessary on his or her own motion without awaiting a formal application for an amendment on the part of the prosecution. I am also of the opinion that the Rules envisage that this course will be taken by the Judge except where it appears to him or her that the variance, defect or omission is one which has misled or prejudiced the Defendant or which might affect the merits of the case.
>
> Even if he or she does form such opinion, the position of the accused person can be protected either by making the amendment subject to adjourning the proceedings to a later date, or by dismissing without prejudice to the complaint being again made, and it appears to me that a dismiss on the merits based on a purely technical objection to the form of the complaint should be very much the exception rather than the rule."

Technical Defects Cured by Appearance

Technical defects in the form of the summons are equally unlikely to form the basis for a successful defence. They do not automatically render the proceedings void or relieve the respondent of the obligation to answer the summons, so long as the form used is otherwise sufficient to express the intention of the person who issued it.[75] It is the making of a valid complaint, and not the issue of a summons, which gives the court jurisdiction in the matter. The summons is merely a device to secure the attendance of the defendant in court to answer the complaint.[76] If it has not been validly issued or the defect on its face is fundamental, the defendant will be relieved of the obligation to appear in

13–15

[73a] The reference to the preliminary examination is now defunct.

[74] Unreported, High Court, May 25, 1992.

[75] For an unusual application of this see *Finnegan v. Clifford* [1996] 1 I.L.R.M. 446.

[76] *DPP v. Clein* [1983] I.L.R.M. 76, *per* Henchy J. at 77; *Attorney General (McDonnell) v. Higgins* [1964] I.R. 374, *per* Kingsmill Moore J. at 391.

response to it. If, however, he is present in the court (for a purpose other than to challenge the validity of the summons) there is no reason why proceedings cannot be instituted against him on the basis of the complaint being read out in court.[77] So long as the complaint is a valid complaint it can be dealt with if the defendant is present in court to answer it. It will not normally matter how or why the defendant has come to be present in court.

In *DPP v. Clein*,[78] for example, the defendant argued that a summons was invalid because the original dates of issue and hearing specified on the summons had been altered before the summons was served. In holding that even if there was a defect in the summons it was not such as to affect the validity of the proceedings as the defendant had appeared in court in response to the summons, Henchy J. explained:

> "The amended summonses were clearly served within six months of the making of the complaints, and it has not been shown that they were in breach of any essential requirement of the District Court Rules. But even if they had breached any procedural requirement, the breach would have been cured when the defendant appeared in the District Court on the day specified in the summonses for the hearing. A summons, after all, is only a written command issued to a defendant for the purpose of getting him to attend court on a specified date to answer a specified complaint. If he responds to that command by appearing in court on the specified date and by answering the summons when it is called in court, he cannot be heard to say that he was not properly summoned if the complaint set out in the summons is a valid one."[79]

It is quite a different matter, of course, if the requisite time limit has expired by the time a valid complaint is made. Equally, the District Court does not have jurisdiction to hear charges against a defendant where the defendant's appearance before the court has been procured by a deliberate and conscious violation of his constitutional rights.[80] Where the accused asserts that the summons, or facts stated in the summons, have been obtained by a conscious and deliberate breach of his constitutional rights, the District Court should investigate the assertion in order to establish whether it could lawfully proceed to hear the charges.[81]

It would appear, however, that there would have to be a gross violation before the District Court would be justified in refusing to proceed where the defendant had appeared. The mere fact that the defendant had been brought before the Court pursuant to an illegal process would not be sufficient in itself even if it entailed an infringement of constitutional rights. Keane J. (as he then was) put the matter as follows in *DPP (Ivers) v. Murphy*:

13–16
> "It has been repeatedly pointed out that, as a general rule, the jurisdiction of the District Court to embark on any criminal proceeding is not affected by the fact, if it be the fact, that the accused person has been brought before the Court

---

[77] *DPP v. Clein* [1981] I.L.R.M. 465, [1983] I.L.R.M. 76; *Attorney General v. Burke* [1955] I.R. 30.
[78] [1983] I.L.R.M. 76.
[79] *ibid*. at 77.
[80] *State (Lynch) v. Ballagh* [1986] I.R. 203, *per* Henchy J. at 218.
[81] *Coughlan v. Judge Pattwell* [1991] 1 I.R. 31.

by an illegal process. If I refer to a judgment which I delivered in *Killeen v. Director of Public Prosecutions* [1997] 3 I.R. 218, it is simply because, so far as I am aware, it is the latest re-statement of that well settled principle. I said (pp. 228/229–210): 'It can, in general, be said that the jurisdiction of the District Court to embark on any criminal proceeding, including the holding of a preliminary examination, is unaffected by the fact, if it be the fact, that the accused person has been brought before the court by an illegal process'. This was so held by Davitt P in *State (Attorney General) v. Fawcitt* [1955] I.R. 39 at 43 where he said:

> 'The usual methods of securing the attendance of an accused person before the District Court, so that it may investigate a charge of an indictable offence made against him, is by way of arrest or by way of formal summons, but neither of these methods is essential. He could, of course, attend voluntarily, it is perfectly immaterial in what way his attendance is secured, so long as he is present before the District Justice in Court at the material time. Even if he is brought there by an illegal process, the Court's jurisdiction is nonetheless effective.'

Some qualifications to that general principle may be noted in passing. Firstly evidence obtained from the accused person during the course of a detention which proves to be unlawful, whether because of a defective warrant or for some other reason, may subsequently be excluded as inadmissible by the Court of trial. Secondly, where the process by which the person is brought before the Court involves a deliberate and conscious violation of his constitutional rights, of which the most graphic example is *State (Trimbole) v. Governor of Mountjoy Prison* [1985] I.R. 550, the Court may be justified in refusing to embark upon the hearing. There may be cases in which a question is raised as to the validity of the detention in Garda custody of a person brought before the District Court, in which case the approiprate course is to remand the person concerned, enabling him, if he wishes so to do, to apply to the High Court for an order of habeas corpus. (See the observations of McCarthy J. in *Keating v. Governor of Mountjoy Prison* [1991] 1 I.R. 61. None of these considerations arise in the present case."[81a]

13–17

Applying these principles in *DPP (Tiernan) v. Bradley*,[81b] the High Court ruled that the District Court judge had erred by refusing to proceed with a summary prosecution because the accused had been brought before the Court pursuant to the exercise of a power of arrest which was not available for the offence in question. While the unlawful arrest and detention clearly involved an infringement of the defendant's constitutional rights it was not of such a nature as to justify the District Court judge in halting the prosecution. Other remedies were available.

Discretion to Amend

The District Court's discretion to amend a defective summons, evident from Order 38, r1(1) and (2) above, is also expressed in Order 12, r.2 as follows:

13–18

[81a] [1999] 1 I.L.R.M. 46 at 61.
[81b] Unreported, High Court, December 9, 1999.

"A Judge may amend any summons . . . by adding or striking out parties or by amending such other defects or errors in any such document as may be necessary for the purpose of determining the real question at issue between the parties. Such amendments may be made in such manner as the Judge directs and upon such terms as the Judge thinks fit. If in the opinion of the Judge, the amendment is one which might prejudice any party to the proceedings in the merits of that party's case, he or she may make the amendment and, if necessary, adjourn the case or may refuse to make any such amendment and, if necessary, dismiss the proceedings."

The manner in which the discretion should be exercised is also stated in paragraph (3) of Order 38, r.1:

"(3) Provided, however, that if in the opinion of the Court the variance, defect or omission is one which had misled or prejudiced the accused or which might affect the merits of the case, it may refuse to make any such amendment and may dismiss the complaint either without prejudice to its being again made, or on the merits, as the Court thinks fit; or if it makes such amendment, it may upon such terms as it thinks fit adjourn the proceedings to any future day at the same time or at any other place."

So long as the amended summons alleges an offence which is grounded in the substance of the complaint, it will not matter that the amendment is effected outside the relevant time limit for the making of the complaint.[82]

This discretion to amend should be exercised judicially and in favour of amending a summons where such an amendment is necessary to allow the real issues to be tried and can be made without prejudice to the other party. If necessary an adjournment should be granted in order to overcome any possible prejudice. In *DPP v. Corbett*,[83] for example, the prosecution sought to have summonses relating to a drink-driving offence amended by changing the number of the respondent's address from 27 to 25 and the date of the offence from September 19, 1989 to September 18, 1989. Lynch J. noted that the respondent was represented in the District Court by counsel and solicitor and, accordingly, could not have been prejudiced in any way by the amendment of his address, This amendment, therefore, should have been granted by the District Court judge as a matter of course. The amendment of the date of commission of the alleged offence was slightly more problematic. The respondent claimed that he had alibis for the original date on the summons and would be prejudiced as a result of the change of date. Lynch J. ruled, however, that the mere fact that he had alibi witnesses for the wrong date did not mean that he would be prejudiced in meeting the allegation of the offence on the right date. Moreover, the learned judge noted that the respondent now had sufficient notice of the changed date so that an adjournment was not necessary to give him an opportunity of preparing his defence in the light of the altered summons.

---

[82] *Attorney General (McDonnell) v. Higgins* [1964] I.R. 374; *DPP v. Corbett* [1992] I.L.R.M. 674.
[83] [1992] I.L.R.M. 674.

In *State (Duggan) v. Evans*[84] Finlay P. (as he then was) explained the correct approach for a District Court judge when deciding what action to take when presented with a defective summons. Although he was dealing with the 1948 version of the District Court Rules, the difference between them and the current version is not material in this instance:

> "1. He must first ascertain as to whether the variance, defect or omission has in his opinion misled or prejudiced the defendant or might in his opinion affect the merits of the case.
>
> 2. If he is of the opinion that none of these consequences has occurred he must either amend the document or proceed as if no such defect, variance, or omission had existed.

> The Rule contains no express guidance in the event of [the frailty not being fatal] as to whether the justice should proceed by amendment or by ignoring the frailty in the document. It appears to me, however, that this choice should be made by reference to the effect of such frailty on an eventual conviction if such were recorded. Where, as would appear to be the position in this case, amendment is necessary to make a conviction on the charge valid, the amendment should be made; where it is not it may be omitted. Furthermore, this jurisdiction and obligation of the Justice in an appropriate case to make an amendment is not in my view dependent on an application by the prosecution but can and should be exercised, as is the power of a Court to amend an Indictment, on his own initiative.

> 3. If on the other hand the justice is of the opinion that the frailty in the document has misled or prejudiced the defendant or if of the opinion that it might affect the merits of the case three alternative courses are open to him:
> (a) He may dismiss the case without prejudice,
> (b) He may dismiss the case on the merits,
> (c) He may amend the document and adjourn the case upon terms.

> Again the Rule contains no express guidance as to the grounds on which the choice between these three alternatives must be made and it is not possible to define them with particularity save that the decision must presumably rest on the extent and nature of the misleading, prejudice, or possible affect on the merits of the case set against the requirements of justice between the prosecution and the defendant.

> It would appear to me that a dismiss on the merits would not be justified unless the opinion of the justice was that there was a possibility that the defect would affect the merits in a manner not certain to be cured by adjournment or that an adjournment was necessary but would be an injustice."[85]

In this case the District Court judge had dismissed charges of burglary contrary to section 23A of the Larceny Act 1916 owing to a defect in the charge. Although the offence charged (and the penalty) was created by the Criminal Law (Jurisdiction) Act 1976 there was no mention of the 1976 Act in the charge. Finlay P. accepted that the omission rendered the charge insuffi-

---

[84] (1978) 112 I.L.T.R. 61.
[85] *ibid.* at 63.

cient in that a conviction based upon it would be bad. However, he also found that the judge had erred in dismissing the charges on the merits as he had not first formed the opinion that the defect was such that it could not be cured by adjournment or that any such adjournment would be an injustice.

4. The Warrant Procedure

Information on Oath

13–19   A summons may not always be the most appropriate means of securing the appearance of a person to answer a charge at a sitting of the District Court. Where, for example, the offence in question is very serious it might be deemed more appropriate that the person concerned should be brought before the District Court as soon as practicable after he has been located. Accordingly, in the case of indictable offences, process might issue in the form of an arrest warrant.[86] For this to happen an information must be submitted on oath and in writing to a judge of the District Court charging the person concerned with having committed an indictable offence.[87] There are no restrictions on who may submit such an information. In practice, most are submitted by a member of the Garda Síochána.[88] Jurisdiction to receive the information, however, is probably confined to a judge of the District Court. In the light of the Supreme Court's decision in *State (Clarke) v. Roche*[89] and the High Court's decision in *O'Mahony v. Melia*[90] it would appear that the former jurisdiction of the peace commissioner to issue a warrant for arrest is no longer available.

Judicial Power

13–20   The judge may issue the warrant if the offence concerned was committed, or if the person to be arrested resides, within his or her district.[91] It does not matter that there is a power to arrest without warrant for the offence concerned.[92] As with the issue of a summons, however, the decision to issue the arrest warrant is a judicial act. Accordingly, the judge must satisfy himself or herself as to the matters sworn in the information and decide in the exercise of his or her discretion whether a warrant should issue. The judge

---

[86] Petty Sessions (Ireland) Act 1851, s.11(1).

[87] District Court Rules 1997, Ord.16, r.1(1). See Form 15.3, Sched. B. It will not matter that the information has been sworn before another judge, so long as the duly completed information is produced to the judge issuing the warrant; r.1(3). The information should be signed by the informant and the judge.

[88] The judge before whom a sworn information is made may, if he or she thinks fit, bind the informant by recognisance to appear at the Court where the complaint is to be heard; District Court Rules 1997, Ord.16, r.7.

[89] [1987] I.L.R.M. 309.

[90] [1990] I.L.R.M. 14.

[91] District Court Rules 1997, Ord.16, r.1(2). Where the complaint alleges an offence has been committed outside the jurisdiction of the judge, the judge may still issue a warrant if the person concerned is, or is believed to be, within the limits of the judge's jurisdiction; r.6. See Form 16.1, Sched. B.

[92] District Court Rules 1997, Ord.16, r.5.

cannot simply act as a ministerial officer of the person submitting the information (see chapter 4 on Arrest). If he or she is satisfied that the matters sworn in the information amount to an offence he can issue a warrant.[93] The mere fact that the matters sworn in the information turn out to be false will not invalidate the warrant.[94] However, the warrant will be bad if it fails to state that an information charging a criminal offence has been made on oath and in writing.[95] Equally, the warrant will be bad if it is based on an information which fails to disclose an offenced.[96]

Form of Warrant

Even though the complaint has been submitted by sworn information, the judge retains the option of issuing a summons instead of a warrant.[97] Indeed, it would appear that he should not issue a warrant where a summons would prove equally effective in securing the appearance of the alleged offender.[98] There are no time restrictions on when an information can be laid charging a person with an indictable offence. Furthermore the information may be sworn and the warrant may be issued on any day and at any time.[99]

Where a warrant does issue it must be signed by the judge who issues it.[100] In substance the warrant is very similar to the summons. As well as specifying the name and address of the person at whom it is directed,[101] it will state brief particulars of the complaint against the person and the alleged offence.[102] Where the offence is based on an enactment which prescribes several alternative modes of committing the offence, the warrant may charge these modes in the alternative or conjunctive.[103]

Endorsed for Bail

The warrant may be endorsed for bail.[104] When issuing the warrant the court may direct that the person named in it should be released after having been

13–21

---

93 A warrant based on an information which fails to disclose an offence will be invalid; *McDonald v. Bulwer* (1862) 13 I.C.L.R. 549.

94 *Cave v. Mountain* 9 L.J.M.C. 90.

95 *Caudle v. Seymour* (1841) 1 Q.B. 889.

96 *McDonald v. Bulwer* (1862) 13 I.C.L.R. 549.

97 District Court Rules 1997, Ord.15, r.10 and Ord.16, r.4. Where a summons is issued in lieu of a warrant, the judge may at any time issue a warrant for the arrest of the person to whom the summons was directed.

98 *O'Brien v. Brabner* (1885) 49 J.P.N. 227.

99 District Court Rules 1997, Ord.16, r.1(4).

100 *ibid.* Ord.16, r.2(1). The validity of a warrant is not affected by the death of the judge who signed it or by his ceasing to hold office; r.2(2).

101 *Hodgens v. Poe* (1866) 17 I.C.L.R. 383. If the name is unknown that fact must be stated and the person identified by such description as to leave no reasonable doubt as to his identity; *State (Rossi and Blythe) v. Bell* [1957] I.R. 281.

102 District Court Rules 1997, Ord.16, r.3 and Ord.15, r.9.

103 *ibid.* Ord.16, r.3 and Ord.15, r.8.

104 The relevant provisions in s.30 of the Criminal Procedure Act 1967 have now been replaced by the Bail Act 1997, s.8 which was brought into force on May 15, 2000 by the Bail Act (Commencement) Order 2000. Note, however, that the current provisions do not apply to a person arrested under s.251 of the Defence Act 1954 on suspicion of his or her being a deserter or absentee without leave from the Defence Forces; Bail Act 1997, s.8(4).

arrested and after having entered into a recognisance, with or without a surety or sureties, conditioned for his appearance before a court on such date and at such time and place as may be specified in the endorsement.[105] The endorsement shall fix the amounts in which the person and his or her surety or sureties (if any) are to be bound, and shall specify any other conditions of the recognisance. Where the warrant is endorsed for bail the member in charge of the Garda Station to which the person is brought on arrest shall discharge him once he has entered into a recognisance, with or without sureties, approved by the member and upon payment of an amount equal to one third, or such greater amount as the court may determine, of any recognisance entered into by the person.[106] There is at least an implication here that the member in charge of the Garda Station may accept a recognisance which differs in some respects from that endorsed on the warrant. Any moneys paid to the member pursuant to these provisions must be deposited by him or her with the District Court clerk for the District Court area in which the Garda Station is situated.[107]

Where the warrant is not endorsed for bail the arresting officer must bring the person concerned before a judge of the District Court having jurisdiction to deal with the offence concerned as soon as practicable.[108] A warrant for the arrest of a person charged with an indictable offence remains in force until executed.[109]

5. The Administrative Procedure

Background

13–22   The jurisdiction of a District Court judge to issue a summons under section 10 of the Petty Sessions (Ireland) Act 1851 was extended to peace commissioners by the Courts of Justice Act 1924 and, in the case of summary offences only, to District Court clerks by the District Court Rules 1948. In *State (Clarke) v. Roche*,[110] however, the Supreme Court intimated that the issue of a summons on foot of a complaint is a judicial, as opposed to an administrative, act when done under section 10 of the 1851 Act. Accordingly, it would be constitutionally improper for a peace commissioner or a District Court clerk to issue a summons under this procedure, as neither has the status of a judge appointed in accordance with the terms of the constitution. Since the Supreme Court's decision in *Roche* the High Court has confirmed that the peace commis-

---

[105] Bail Act 1997, s.8(1); District Court Rules 1997, Ord.17, r.5(1), as amended by the District Court (Criminal Justice) Rules 2001, r.4(a).

[106] Bail Act 1997, s.8(2); District Court Rules 1997, Ord.17, r.5(2), as amended by the District Court (Criminal Justice) Rules 2001, r.4(a). See Form 17.10, Sched. B.

[107] Bail Act 1997, s.8(3); District Court Rules 1997, Ord.17, r.5(3), as amended by the District Court (Criminal Justice) Rules 2001, r.4(a).

[108] Criminal Justice Act 1951, s.15, as substituted by the Criminal Justice (Miscellaneous Provisions) Act 1997, s.18. Where the person is arrested later than 5 p.m. and a judge of the District Court is due to sit in the District Court district in which the person was arrested not later than noon on the following day, it will be sufficient if the arrested person is brought before a judge of the District Court sitting in that district at the commencement of that sitting; s.15(3).

[109] Woods, p.142.

[110] [1987] I.L.R.M. 309. See also, *Rainey v. Delap* [1988] I.R. 470.

sioner's power to grant bail is unconstitutional as it amounts to an exercise of judicial power.[111] The clear implication is that peace commissioners and District Court clerks have no power to issue process under the 1851 Act.[112]

The precise issue at stake in *State (Clarke) v. Roche*[113] was whether, under the 1851 Act the complaint actually had to be considered by the person issuing the summons. In practice the huge volume of complaints was such that it simply was not feasible for each to be considered personally by a District Court judge, District Court clerk or peace commissioner, even if the last two did have jurisdiction in the matter. Accordingly, it had been standard practice for many years, particularly in the Dublin Metropolitan district, for the vast bulk of complaints to be processed by staff in the office of the District Court clerk, with the resulting summonses being issued in the name of the District Court clerk. The Supreme Court ruled that this administrative practice was contrary to the specific requirements of the 1851 Act which demanded that each complaint should be considered personally by the person authorised to receive it.[114]

The Supreme Court's decision in *State (Clarke) v. Roche*[115] threatened to throw the whole procedure for the initiation of prosecutions into disarray. In the Dublin Metropolitan district alone more than 100,000 complaints were being laid annually with a view to the issue of summonses. It simply would not be practicable for each of these to be considered individually by a judge of the District Court before a summons could issue. Cognisant of the scale of the problem the Supreme Court charted a way forward in the case of complaints laid by members of the Garda Síochána, at least in respect of summary offences. Finlay C.J. offered the following advice on behalf of the court:

13–23

> "Consideration . . . should be given to replacing sections 10 and 11 of the Act of 1851, with statutory provisions more suitable to the modern District Court which could include the procedure for the issuing of summonses, in criminal cases at least, as being an administrative procedure only and which could then, without any question of constitutional challenge, provide that the complaint should be made to the District Court and that the summons should be issued by the officers of that court upon the making of the complaint."[116]

The government acted swiftly on this advice by introducing an administrative procedure for the initiation of criminal prosecutions. The necessary legislation was enacted in the form of the Courts (No.3) Act 1986.

---

[111] *O'Mahony v. Melia* [1990] I.L.R.M. 14. See also, *State (Lynch) v. Ballagh* [1987] I.L.R.M. 65.

[112] The District Court Rules 1997 refer only to a judge receiving a complaint and issuing a summons under the 1851 Act; see Ord.15, r.1(1) and (3).

[113] [1987] I.L.R.M. 309.

[114] Finlay C.J. at 314–315 accepted that the following cases provide support for the contention that a complaint in order to be made within the meaning of the 1851 Act must be brought to the attention of the person authorised to receive it: *Minister for Agriculture v. Norgro Ltd* [1980] I.R. 155; *State (O'Leary) v. Neylon* [1984] I.L.R.M. 35; *Attorney General (McDonnell) v. Higgins* [1964] I.R. 374; *Irish Insurance Commissioners v. Trench* [1914] 2 I.R. 172; *R. (Futter) v. Justices of County Cork* [1917] 2 I.R. 430.

[115] [1987] I.L.R.M. 309.

[116] *State (Clarke) v. Roche* [1987] I.L.R.M. 309 at 315.

The Procedure

Under the 1986 Act, a criminal prosecution may be commenced in the District Court by the issue of a summons as a matter of administrative procedure by the appropriate office of the District Court.[117] In effect the Act introduces an administrative procedure for the issue of a summons, in addition to the judicial procedure under the 1851 Act. The administrative procedure is initiated by an "application" to the appropriate office of the District Court, as opposed to a "complaint" to a judge of the District Court.[118] In practice, the application looks just like the information or complaint which must be laid for the issue of a summons under the 1851 Act. Applications can be made by, or on behalf of, the Attorney General, the DPP, a member of the Garda Síochána or any person statutorily authorised to prosecute the offence. The resultant summonses are issued under the general superintendence of an appropriate District Court clerk and the name of an appropriate District Court clerk will appear on each summons.[119] In effect this means that applications can be processed by staff in the office of the District Court clerk, using computerised systems, in accordance with procedures laid down by the District Court clerk. Indeed, it seems that there is no discretion in the matter. So long as the application is in order and the issuing clerk is assigned to any court area in the district in which a judge has jurisdiction in relation to the offence concerned, the summons must issue.[120] However, the time limits which apply to making complaints for a summons under the 1851 Act (see paras. 13–10 *et seq.*) also apply to the making of an application for a summons under the administrative procedure.[121] In any proceedings a document purporting to be a summons will be deemed to be a summons duly applied for and issued.[122]

Form of Summons

13–24 A summons issued pursuant to the administrative procedure is very similar, but not identical, to a summons issued under the judicial procedure of the 1851 Act. It will give brief particulars of the cause of the complaint or offence alleged and it will state the name and address of the person against whom the complaint is made or who is alleged to have committed the offence.[123] Two or more complaints or offences may be alleged in the one summons,[124] and where the summons relates to an offence which can be committed by any one of a number

---

[117] Courts (No.3) Act 1986, s.1(1). "Appropriate office of the District Court" in this context is defined as the office of any District Court clerk assigned to any District Court area in the District Court district in which a judge of the District Court has jurisdiction in relation to the offence to which the summons relates; s.1(9).

[118] Courts (No.3) Act 1986, s.1(4).

[119] *ibid.* s.1(2). "Appropriate District Court clerk" in this context means a District Court clerk assigned to any District Court area in the District Court district in which a judge of the District Court has jurisdiction in relation to the offence to which the summons relates; s.1(9).

[120] District Court Rules 1997, Ord.15, r.2(2). This contrasts with the judicial procedure in which the District Court judge has a discretion; see r.1(3).

[121] Courts (No.3) Act 1986, s.1(7)(a).

[122] Courts (No.3) Act 1986, s.1(5).

[123] District Court Rules 1997, Ord.15, rr.3(1) and 9. See Form 15.2, Sched. B.

[124] *ibid.* Ord.15, r.4.

of different acts in the alternative, those acts may be stated in the alternative or conjunctive in the summons.[125] The summons will require the appearance of the person before a sitting of the court having jurisdiction to deal with the complaint or offence.[126] That court must be within the district in which a judge has jurisdiction in relation to the actual offence stated in the summons.[127]

Status of Summons

Where the wording of the summons issued under the 1986 Act differs from that under the 1851 Act is that the former states that the person named in the summons will be accused of the offence outlined in the summons at the specified sitting of the court.[128] This has given rise to some argument about the exact status of a summons issued under the 1986 Act. Indeed, the validity of District Court proceedings instituted on the basis of a summons issued pursuant to the administrative procedure provided for by the 1986 Act was challenged in the High Court, and on appeal to the Supreme Court, in the joined cases of *DPP v. Roche; DPP v. Nolan*.[129] At the time of the Supreme Court's decision there were a number of other cases pending in which similar issues had been raised. Finlay C.J. in giving the judgment of the Supreme Court, took the opportunity to summarise the position with respect to summonses issued under the administrative procedure in the interests of removing all possible doubt. It is worth quoting the summary in full:

"(1) The 1986 Act duly authorises the issue of summonses for the trial of offences by the District Court.

(2) The time limit applicable to such summonses issued pursuant to the 1986 Act is a limit of six months from the date of the alleged offence to the date of the application pursuant to s.1(4) for the issue of a summons. No other time limit arises except in the case of certain statutory offences where shorter time limits may apply.[130]

(3) The form of the summons provided for by the District Court Rules, S.I. No.23 of 1987 is adequate and proper for the purposes of the procedure provided by the 1986 Act.

(4) A District Justice before whom a person has been summoned pursuant to the provisions of the 1986 Act is entitled, according to his or her discretion, upon it being satisfactorily established that such person was duly served with the summons but has not appeared, either to proceed to hear and determine the charge contained in the summons in the absence of the accused or if he or she shall so decide, to adjourn the hearing of the

---

[125] *ibid.* Ord.15, r.8.

[126] *ibid.* Ord.15, r.3(3).

[127] *ibid.* Ord.15, r.3(3)(b).

[128] District Court Rules 1997, Ord.15, r.3(2).

[129] [1989] 1 I.L.R.M. 39.

[130] This should not be interpreted as precluding a time limit of longer than 6 months where such longer time limit is prescribed by statute. In *DPP v. Howard* unreported, High Court, November 27, 1989, *e.g.*, Barron J. held that the 12 month time limit applicable to revenue offences extended to an application for a summons under the 1986 Act. Similarly, in *DPP v. Fox* [1997] 1 I.L.R.M. 440 McGuinness J. ruled that the two year time limit applicable to offences under the Diseases of Animals Act 1966 also applied to such cases.

summons to a later date and to secure the attendance of the accused by warrant or otherwise."[131]

It is not necessary for the summons to be issued on foot of a complaint. It can be issued on foot of an application pursuant to the administrative procedure provided for by the 1986 Act. The complaint, which is necessary to ground the jurisdiction of the District Court, is not actually made until the defendant appears before the District Court in answer to the summons.[131a] Moreover, if the summons is struck out by the Court on that date without proceeding to a hearing of the complaint it would appear that it can be re-instituted by the complainant at a later date. So long as the initial summons was issued pursuant to an application having been made within the requisite time limit the subsequent proceedings will not be statute barred.[131b] The time limit applicable to the making of a complaint under the 1851 Act, however, applies to an application for a summons under the 1986 Act, subject to the fact that the relevant time period for the latter is from the date of the offence to the date on which the application for a summons was lodged.[132] The argument that the period appropriate to the administrative procedure runs from the date of the offence to the date when the case is first brought before a District Court judge was specifically rejected in *DPP v. Nolan*.[133]

The rules governing the service of the summons are the same as for summonses issued under the 1851 Act.[134]

Survival of Judicial Summons

13–25   In practice the vast majority of summonses are now issued on foot of a complaint laid in accordance with the administrative procedure introduced by the 1986 Act. It is important to note, however, that the judicial procedure under sections 10 and 11 of the Petty Sessions (Ireland) Act 1851 has not been abolished.[135] It is still available to be used even by those who can avail of the administrative procedure under the 1986 Act. Indeed, in some cases a summons can only issue pursuant to the 1851 Act procedure. An application for a summons under the 1986 Act procedure can be made only by, or on behalf of, the Attorney General, the DPP, a member of the Garda Síochána and any person statutorily authorised to prosecute the offence. Clearly this does not extend to citizen complainants exercising their common law authority as common informers. It follows that a complaint laid by a citizen as a common informer will have to be processed through the 1851 Act procedure in accordance with the strictures of the Supreme Court in *State (Clarke) v. Roche*.[136] It is likely,

---

[131]   *DPP v. Nolan* [1989] 1 I.L.R.M. 39 at 45.
[131a] See also, *National Authority for Safety and Health v. O'Brien* [1997] I.R. 543.
[131b] *DPP v. Gill* [1980] I.R. 263; *Murray v. McArdle* unreported, High Court, February 19, 1999.
[132]   It would appear that the date when an application is lodged is the date on which it is received in the office of the District Court clerk; *R. v. Manchester Stipendiary Magistrate, ex p. Hill* [1983] A.C. 328.
[133]   [1989] 1 I.L.R.M. 39 *Murray v. McArdle* unreported High Court November 5, 1999.
[134]   District Court Rules 1997, Ord.10.
[135]   Courts (No.3) Act 1986, s.1(8).
[136]   [1986] I.R. 619.

therefore, that such complaints would have to be laid before a judge of the District Court who would have to consider them personally. Similarly, it would appear that a summons on foot of a complaint against a member of the Garda Síochána cannot be issued pursuant to the administrative procedure. A summons against a member of the Garda Síochána must be signed by a District Court judge and, as such, can issue only through the judicial procedure.[137]

6. Charging in Custody

The final method for initiating a criminal prosecution is the formal charging of a person before a District Court after he has been arrested without warrant and charged by a member of the Garda Síochána. Not every arrest without a warrant results in the person concerned being brought before the District Court to be formally charged with an offence. Many individuals will simply be released without any further action being taken against them. Some will be released and subsequently summonsed to appear before the District Court. The remainder will be charged in the Garda station and either released on bail to appear before a specified sitting of the District Court[138] or brought before the court in the custody of the Garda Síochána.[139] Where a person is charged in the Garda station particulars of the offence alleged must be set out on a charge sheet and a copy furnished to the person concerned.[140]

13–26

The charge sheet is lodged as soon as possible with the District Court clerk for the court area in which the case is to be heard.[141] The entry of a charge on a charge sheet, however, does not amount to the making of a complaint for the purpose of conferring jurisdiction on the court. Initially, the charge sheet is merely an internal police document. The court is not actually seised with the case until the complaint is made to the court. The following quotation from the judgment of Kingsmill Moore J. in *Attorney General (McDonnell) v. Higgins*[142] sets out the status of a charge on a charge sheet very clearly:

13–27

> "This charge cannot be a complaint or information for it is not made before a District Justice, a Peace Commissioner or a Clerk. The charge sheet on which it is entered initiates as a purely police document and the entry of the offences charged is necessary for the protection of the Garda to show that such offences justify arrest and detention in the barracks without warrant. Subsequently,

---

137 Courts of Justice Act 1924, s.88(3). See *Finnegan v. Clifford* [1996] 1 I.L.R.M. 446.
138 Criminal Procedure Act 1967, s.31. See also, District Court Rules 1997, Ord.17, r.4 and Forms 17.2 and 17.3, Sched. B.
139 A person arrested without warrant shall, on being charged with an offence, be brought as soon as practicable before a judge of the District Court having jurisdiction to deal with the offence concerned; Criminal Justice Act 1951, s.15(2) as substituted by s.18 of the Criminal Justice (Miscellaneous Provisions) Act 1997, s.18. If the person is charged in the Garda station after 5 p.m. and a judge of the District Court is due to sit in the district in which the person was arrested not later than noon on the following day, it will be sufficient if the person is brought before a judge of the District Court sitting in that district at the commencement of that sitting; s.15(3).
140 District Court Rules 1997, Ord.17, r.1(1) and (2). See Form 17.1, Sched. B.
141 District Court Rules 1997, Ord.17, r.1(3).
142 [1964] I.R. 374.

when the charge sheet is put before the District Justice and the final two columns are utilised by him to record his decisions, it becomes a document of the Court, but before the District Justice enters on the case it seems to me that there must be a complaint to him by some person, preferably but not necessarily, the Superintendent, alleging the commission of the offences by the defendant with such particularity and details as are required by the authorities for a legal complaint. Only when this has been done is jurisdiction conferred to enter on the hearing of the case."[143]

There is also authority for the proposition that the complaint can be made by the District Court judge reading out the charge or charges from the charge sheet to the accused in court.[144]

If the charge or charges are tried summarily, the charge sheet is normally treated as the information against the accused.

7. Failure to Appear

13–28   Where a person fails to appear at the appropriate sitting of the District Court in answer to a summons the judge may issue a warrant for his arrest if satisfied that the person concerned has been served with the summons.[145] A warrant may also issue in respect of a person who fails to appear after having been arrested, charged and released on bail by a member of the Garda Síochána to appear before a specified sitting of the court.[146] The same applies to a person who fails to appear after having been accused of an offence before the court and remanded on bail to appear before the court at the date, time and place specified in the recognisance.[147]

An appearance in all of these situations means a personal appearance. It will not inevitably be satisfied by a solicitor appearing on behalf of the person concerned to seek an adjournment. Accordingly, if the accused does not appear in person to answer the charge the court may proceed in his absence or issue a warrant for his arrest. Equally, the court may exercise its discretion to grant an adjournment on the application of the solicitor for the accused.

13–29   Where a summons has been issued and an information is laid to the effect that the person concerned is evading service or is about to abscond or has absconded the judge may issue a warrant for his arrest.[148] The information can be made either before or after the date on which the person was required to appear in answer to the summons.[149] There was also provision in section 33 of the Criminal Procedure Act 1967 for the arrest of a person on bail who was about to abscond. It stipulated that where a person has been charged with an offence and been admitted to bail the court could issue a warrant for his

---

143   *ibid.* at 393. See also, *State (Lynch) v. Ballagh* [1984] I.R. 203, *per* Walsh J. at 212.
144   *State (Lynch) v. O hUadhaigh* [1975] I.R. 98.
145   District Court Rules 1997, Ord.22, r.1. This also applies where the person fails to appear at any adjourned hearing of the matter.
146   District Court Rules 1997, Ord.22, r.2(a). See Form 22.3, Sched. B for the issue of the warrant.
147   *ibid.* 1997, Ord.22, r.2(b).
148   *ibid.* Ord.22, r.1. See Form 22.2, Sched. B.
149   See Form 22.1, Sched. B of the District Court Rules 1997 for the information.

arrest on the application of the surety or any of the sureties or a member of the Garda Síochána.[150] The application must be made in writing and on oath to the effect that the accused was about to abscond for the purpose of evading justice.[151] When the person was arrested he had to be brought before a judge of the District Court who could further remand him.[152] However, section 33 was specifically repealed by the Bail Act 1997 without provision for a replacement.[153] Indeed, it would appear that the repeal was an unintentional error as section 11(c) of the Bail Act actually purports to amend section 33 of the 1967 Act (the provision which was purportedly repealed by section 12 of the 1997 Act) by formally removing the power of a peace commissioner to issue a warrant of arrest in these circumstances. Perhaps the anomaly can be cured by the fact that Order 20 of the District Court Rules 1997 effectively repeats the terms of section 33 of the 1967 Act. Order 20 has not been specifically repealed by the 1997 Act. Nevertheless, there must be a doubt about whether a court would give effect to a provision in a rule where identical wording on an associated statutory provision had been repealed.

8. Witness Summons

Witnesses may be summonsed to attend and give evidence or produce docu-   **13–30**
ments or things to the District Court. Any party seeking the issue of a witness summons must apply to the judge, clerk or a peace commissioner.[154] Where a summons is issued it must be signed by the person issuing it and served at least three days before the date fixed for the hearing of the associated complaint.[155] The summons may be served anywhere in the State.[156] If the witness concerned fails to attend at the specified time and place without just excuse the judge before whom the complaint is due to be heard may issue a warrant for his arrest.[157] An arrest warrant may also issue where an information is made that the witness is able to give evidence in the case and is evading service of the summons.[158] Moreover, if the judge is satisfied by an information made on oath and in writing that a witness who is able to give evidence in the case will probably not attend without being compelled to do so, he or she may issue a warrant for the arrest of the witness.[159] Once arrested the witness must

---

[150] Criminal Procedure Act 1967, s.33.
[151] See District Court Rules 1997, Ord.20, r.1(1). See Form 20.1, Sched. B for the information, and Form 20.2, Sched. B for the warrant.
[152] Criminal Procedure Act 1967, s.33(2)–(4) and District Court Rules 1997, Ord.20.
[153] Bail Act 1997, s.12 (brought into force on May 15, 2000 by the Bail Act 1997 (Commencement) Order.2000).
[154] District Court Rules 1997, Ord.21, r.1(1). In case of difficulty application may be made to the court which may issue the summons or otherwise deal with the matter in such manner as to it shall seem just; r.1(2).
[155] District Court Rules 1997, Ord.21, r.1(3). See Form 21.1, Sched. B for the summons.
[156] *ibid.* Ord.21, r.1(4).
[157] *ibid.* Ord.21, r.1(5). See Form 21.3 or 21.4, Sched. B for the warrant.
[158] See District Court Rules 1997, Form 21.2, Sched. B for the information.
[159] District Court Rules 1997, Ord.21, r.1(6). See Form 21.5, Sched.e B for the information and Form 21.6, Sched. B for the warrant.

be brought before the judge who will remand him in custody or on bail until the hearing of the complaint.[160]

E. Procedure on First Appearance

1. Summary Offence

Putting the Complaint to the person

13–31   Where a person makes his first appearance before the District Court in response to a complaint or a charge, the procedure can differ depending on the nature of the offence and the mode of appearance. In the case of a summary offence the complaint will be put to the person concerned. If he pleads guilty it is likely that a conviction will be entered and sentence imposed there and then.[161] Nothing turns on the issue of how the defendant came to be before the court. The court's jurisdiction depends on the complaint being put to the person in court or by the charge being laid before the court.[162] Defects in the summons or warrant for arrest will not deprive the court of jurisdiction so long as the person is actually present in court to be charged on foot of a valid complaint.[163] Indeed, the Supreme Court has ruled that the District Court has no jurisdiction to enquire into the lawfulness of the detention of a person before it for the purpose of ordering that person's release.[164] It would be a different matter where proof of a valid arrest was an essential ingredient to ground the charge.[164a]

Adjournment

If the defendant pleads not guilty it is possible that the court will proceed immediately to try the case.[165] The more likely approach, however, is that the case will be adjourned until a future sitting and the defendant will be remanded to appear again at that sitting. Indeed, there may be a succession of such remands before the defendant is actually tried.[166] The same may happen even

---

[160] District Court Rules 1997, Ord.21, r.1(7). If remanded on bail it may be a condition of the recognisance that the witness shall bring with him and produce all such accounts, papers, documents or things as required.

[161] District Court Rules 1997, Ord.23, r.1.

[162] *Attorney General (McDonnell) v. Higgins* [1964] I.R. 374.

[163] *DPP v. Clein* [1983] I.L.R.M. 76: *Attorney General v. Burke* [1955] I.R. 30, for discussion see para. 13–15.

[164] *Keating v. Governor of Mountjoy Prison* [1990] I.L.R.M. 850 See also, *DPP (Ivers) v. Murphy* [1988] I.L.R.M. 46. This does not effect the jurisdiction of the Court to take whatever steps it considers proper where the defendant alleges that his constitutional rights have been infringed in the procedures adopted in bringing him before the Court; *DPP v. Delaney* [1997] 3 I.R. 453. But see *DPP (McTiernan) v. Bradley* unreported, High Court, December 9, 1999, and para. 13–15 *infra.* for limits to this jurisdiction. See also chap. 2.

[164a] See, *e.g., DPP v. Forbes* [1993] I.L.R.M. 817

[165] District Court Rules 1997, Ord.23, r.1.

[166] S. 21 of the Criminal Procedure Act 1967 states that:
"Where an accused person is before the District Court in connection with an offence the Court may, subject to the provisions of this Part, remand the accused from time to time as occasion requires."
Section 22 goes on to that that the court may remand the accused in custody or on bail.

in cases where the defendant has pleaded guilty and the only issue is sentence. The judge may wish to adjourn the case for the receipt of further information about the accused and/or the victim before deciding on an appropriate sentence.

The judge may adjourn the hearing of proceedings at any time upon such terms as he or she thinks fit.[166a] The discretion is framed in very broad terms and the higher courts will be very slow to quash the order of a District Court judge in relation to the grant or refusal of an adjournment.[166b] Nevertheless, the High Court has jurisdiction to intervene where a refusal to grant an adjournment results in a lack of due process for a defendant in a criminal matter. Such a situation arose in *O'Callaghan v. Clifford*,[166c] where the applicant defendant was charged before the District Court on several counts of failing to make tax returns. The prosecution case was based on certificates issued by a tax inspector declaring a failure by the defendant to make the returns. Pursuant to the relevant statutory provisions a conviction could be based on such certificates. At the first appearance before the District Court counsel for the applicant sought an adjournment as the applicant could not make it to the Court until 4.30 p.m. and counsel had not had an opportunity of taking instructions from the applicant who wished to contest the charges. The judge refused the request as there were witnesses for the prosecution who were present in Court to give evidence on the matter of sentence. The refusal was upheld by the High Court as being within the discretion of the judge.

In quashing the High Court decision, the Supreme Court emphasised the importance of constitutional justice and in particular the right to have one's case presented by instructed counsel. Giving the judgment of the Court, Denham J. pointed to the following six factors which the Court must consider in protecting the accused's right to constitutional justice in this case:

> "1. This was a criminal trial with the consequent possibility of a penalty of imprisonment (which in fact happened).
>
> 2. This was the first time this case had come before the court.
>
> 3. Counsel had not had an opportunity of obtaining instructions from the applicant.
>
> 4. Because of the nature of the prosecution, by certificate, matters could arise on trial (such as to how the notice was served) which even if the applicant had had an opportunity to instruct counsel prior to the trial (which was not the case here) he would not have been able to instruct fully in advance.
>
> 5. The applicant was to be in court at 4.30 p.m.
>
> 6. The witnesses which the State indicated were in court were for sentencing purposes only."[166d]

By failing to give sufficient weight to these six factors and the associated requirements of the fair administration of justice, the District Court judge had exceeded his jurisdiction in failing to grant an adjournment when requested.

[166a] See, generally, Criminal Justice Act 1953, s.27(3) and District Court Rules 1997, Ord.2.
[166b] *O'Callaghan v. Clifford* [1993] 3 I.R. 611; *Carey v. Hussey* unreported, High Court, December 21, 1999.
[166c] [1993] 3 I.R. 603.
[166d] *ibid.* at 611-612.

While the facts of this case were special in some respects, particularly the fact that the prosecution was based on certificate evidence from which *mens rea* would have to be inferred, it does nevertheless confirm that the trial judge does not have an open-ended discretion to refuse a defence application for an adjournment in a criminal matter. If an adjournment is necessary to protect the accused's right to a fair trial on the facts of the case then it must be granted.

Legal Aid

If the charge carries a possible prison sentence and the defendant is not legally represented the District Court judge is required to inform him that he may be entitled to legal aid.[167] If the defendant wishes to be legally represented and claims that he cannot afford it, the judge must consider whether he qualifies for free legal aid.[168]

2. Indictable Offence and Certificate Evidence

13–32   Where a person appears before the District Court charged with an indictable offence after having been arrested without warrant and charged in the Garda station, the prosecutor (usually a member of the Garda Síochána) will submit evidence of the person's identity, arrest, charge and caution in the Garda station. The immediate purpose of this hearing is to formally charge the person concerned and have him remanded in custody or on bail to a later sitting of the court.[169] Nevertheless, it usually requires the presence of the relevant Garda personnel to give evidence of arrest and charge. In practice, of course, this is a mere formality as rarely, if ever, is issue taken with these matters at this stage.[170] It has meant, however, that many members of the Garda Síochána spent a significant period of time in court in order to facilitate these formalities. In Garda and political circles this has long been considered an extravagant use of valuable police time and resources. The Criminal Justice (Miscellaneous Provisions) Act 1997 addresses this problem by permitting evidence of these formalities to be submitted by certificate.

Where a person arrested without a warrant is charged for the first time before the District Court a certificate stating that a member of the Garda Síochána arrested or charged that person at a specified time and place with a specified offence may be admissible as evidence of the matters stated.[171] Similarly, a certificate stating that the person was cautioned at a specified time and place after having been arrested for, or charged with, a specified offence may be admissible as evidence of the matters stated. To be admissible

---

[167]   *State (Healy) v. O'Donoghue* [1976] I.R. 325 *Byrne v. Judge McDonnell* [1997] 1 I.R. 392.

[168]   Criminal Justice (Legal Aid) Act 1962, s.2(1); as substituted by the Criminal Justice (Miscellaneous Provisions) Act 1997, s.5(6).

[169]   The court can remand the accused in custody or on bail from time to time as the occasion requires; Criminal Procedure Act 1967, ss.21 and 22.

[170]   In *Keating v. Governor of Mountjoy Prison* [1990] I.L.R.M. 850 the Supreme Court ruled that the District Court should not embark upon an inquiry into the legality of the detention of an accused who has been brought before it consequent on arrest.

[171]   Criminal Justice (Miscellaneous Provisions) Act 1997, s.6(1).

the certificate must be signed by the member concerned and must be tendered in evidence by a member not below the rank of sergeant.[172] In practice this means that a prosecuting Garda officer can appear in court with a bundle of these certificates covering all or most of the cases in which an accused will be charged that day before the court for the first time. The actual gardai who effected the arrests, preferred the charges or administered the cautions are relieved of the obligation to appear. Nevertheless, problems may still arise. It is not clear, for example, how it will be established that the person being charged before the court is the same person named in the associated certificate. The Act does stipulate that where a charge sheet and recognisance are laid before the District Court:

> " . . . the court shall require the person (if any) present and to whom the charge sheet and recognisance relate, to identify himself or herself, and accordingly, on being so required, the person shall identify himself or herself, as the case may be, to the court."[173]

It is not certain that this provision applies to persons arrested without warrant and brought in Garda custody before the court. Even if it does apply, the Act does not impose any specific penalty for a failure to comply. Ultimately, the court may direct that oral evidence be submitted of the matters stated in a certificate if it considers that that is required in the interests of justice.[174]

3. Summary Trial of Indictable Offence

Mode of trial is likely to be an issue when the accused appears before the District Court charged with an indictable offence. Where the offence charged is one which the court has jurisdiction to try summarily the judge must inform the defendant of his right to be tried by a jury.[175] If the accused stands on his right to be tried by jury the judge will remand him in custody or on bail to a future sitting of the court. This is likely to be followed by a whole series of remands until the accused is sent forward for trial (see chapter 14). However, if the judge is satisfied that the person does not object to being tried summarily, and that the DPP does not object to summary trial,[176] he or she can proceed to try the case immediately or put it back for consideration at a later sitting of the court.[177] Before the judge can take this decision he or she must hear the facts alleged in support of the charge and form the opinion that

13–33

---

172 *ibid.* s.6(5).
173 *ibid.* s.6(6).
174 *ibid.* s.6(4). The court may adjourn the proceedings to a later date for the purpose of receiving the oral evidence.
175 Criminal Justice Act 1951, s.2 and District Court Rules 1997, Ord.24, r.1, as amended by the District Court (Criminal Justice) Rules 2001, r.8, Sched. 11. The offences concerned are laid out in the Schedule to the Criminal Justice Act 1951; see Chap. 1.
176 This consent may be conveyed in writing and signed by the DPP or orally by a person prosecuting at the suit of the DPP or appearing on his behalf; Criminal Procedure Act 1967, s.20; District Court Rules 1997, Ord.24, r.4, as amended by the District Court (Criminal Justice) Rules 2001, r.8(a) and Sched. 11.
177 Criminal Justice Act 1951, s.2(2) as substituted by s.8 of the Criminal Justice (Miscellaneous Provisions) Act 1997.

they constitute a minor offence fit to be tried summarily.[178] In *State (Nevin) v. Tormey*,[179] for example, the accused was charged with three indictable assault offences and one summary offence of malicious damage. The indictable offences were triable summarily. Although he was informed of his right to a jury trial the accused did not request that option. The judge proceeded to try all charges summarily without knowing any of the facts, apart from the statement of the charges on the charge sheet. Subsequently, the judge averred that had he known in advance of the facts which were proved he would not have dealt with the matter summarily. The High Court ruled that the proceedings were a nullity as a necessary preliminary to the court's jurisdiction in respect of the indictable offences is that the judge should first form the opinion that they were of a minor nature. Butler J. explained the appropriate procedure to be followed by the District Court in this matter as follows:

> " . . . the prosecution first gives a general statement of the facts of the case. On this statement the court may form an opinion whether the offence is fit to be tried summarily and, if it so decides, the court may go on to fulfil the second condition by informing the accused of his rights and ascertaining that he has no objection to being tried summarily. If this course is followed it is of course desirable that the order should correctly recite that the court was satisfied as to the nature of the offence on the facts *alleged*. Even though these may be subsequently proved before the court makes its adjudication upon the guilt or innocence of the accused, its jurisdiction so to adjudicate will have arisen from the facts alleged by the prosecution before the trial commenced."[180]

If the judge deals with such a case summarily his sentencing powers are restricted. It is worth noting, however, that the normal time limit of six months for making a complaint in respect of summary offences does not apply where an indictable offence is disposed of summarily.[181]

Where the person before the court is a young person (under 17 years of age) charged with an indictable offence, other than homicide, the court will have jurisdiction to deal with it summarily if the young person consents and the court thinks it expedient to do so having regard to the character and antecedents of the person charged, the nature of the offence and all the circumstances of the case.[181a] This provision was considered by the High Court in *DPP (Stratford) v. O'Neill*[181b] where Smyth J. explained that the reference to the "character and antecedents" of the young person referred not to his moral character and criminal record but to his degree of maturity and appreciation of the correctness of choosing summary trial over trial by jury.

---

[178] District Court Rules 1997, Ord.24, r.1, as amended by the District Court (Criminal Justice) Rules 2001, r.8(a) and Sched. 11.

[179] [1976] I.R. 1.

[180] *ibid.* at 6.

[181] Criminal Justice Act 1951, s.7; *State (Kiernan) v. Governor of Mountjoy Prison* unreported, High Court, February 19, 1973.

[181a] Summary Jurisdiction Over Children (Ireland) Act 1884, as amended by Children Act 1908, s.133(6). Note that this provision is set to be replaced by Children Act 2001, s.75 which does much the same thing but refers to the age and level of maturity of the child rather than his character and antecedents.

[181b] [1998] 1 I.L.R.M. 221.

The burden on the District Court judge is to ensure that a young person who opts for summary trial is making an informed decision. To this end it may be necessary for the judge to embark upon a preliminary investigation of the young person's level of understanding in the matter. The High Court rejected the notion that any such investigation creates a risk of the judge subsequently embarking upon the trial in a prejudiced position. Apart from the fact that the preliminary investigation should not concern the young person's criminal record the judge's oath of office should be sufficient protection against this risk.

4. Pleading Guilty to Indictable Offence

An accused person charged with an indictable offence may also have the option **13–34** of pleading guilty in the District Court. This option applies to all indictable offences apart from: an offence under the Treason Act 1939, murder, attempt to murder, piracy, genocide or a grave breach of the Geneva Conventions Act 1962, including an offence by an accessory before or after the fact.[182] Where the accused is charged with a qualifying offence and the District Court ascertains, at any time, that he wishes to plead guilty, the court may proceed to deal with the case summarily providing that the DPP does not object and the court is satisfied that the accused understands the nature of the offence and the facts alleged.[183] In this event, the maximum penalty that may be imposed is a term of imprisonment for a period of 12 months and/or a fine of €1,270.[184] Alternatively, the District Court may send him forward on the plea of guilty to the appropriate higher court for sentence in certain circumstances. This is dealt with below.

5. Bail and Other Matters

Although there is little room for argument about the facts or the law at the **13–35** initial remand hearing in the case of an indictable offence, it can happen that the accused's solicitor will put some questions to the prosecutor designed to draw attention to evidential weaknesses in the case against his or her client or to allegations of impropriety on the part of gardai who investigated the case. The focus of the hearing, however, is more likely to be bail, legal aid and the mode of trial. Indeed, the only contentious issue likely to arise at this point is whether the accused should be remanded in custody or on bail.[185] In those cases where this is an issue the judge will hear representations from the accused, usually through his solicitor, and from the prosecutor before making his or her decision. A decision in favour of bail will not automatically result in the accused being released. Before this can happen he will have to enter into a recognisance requiring his appearance before the court at the end of the

---

[182] Criminal Procedure Act 1967, s.13(1).
[183] Criminal Procedure Act 1967, s.13(2)(a); District Court Rules 1997, Ord.24, r.2, as amended by the District Court (Criminal Justice) Rules 2001, r.8(a) and Sched. 11.
[184] Criminal Procedure Act 1967, s.13(3). As amended by the Criminal Justice Act 1984, s.17.
[185] *Keating v. Governor of Mountjoy Prison* [1990] I.L.R.M. 850.

period of remand. Independent sureties may also be required. These matters are dealt with in chapter 10 on bail. Where the accused is remanded in custody he will be committed to prison or detention to await his appearance before the court at the end of the period of remand.[186]

6. Remands

The Power

13–36   Where the accused is pleading not guilty on his first appearance before the District Court, or if the judge requires reports to be prepared before deciding on sentence, the case will usually be put back to a later sitting of the court. In this event the accused may be remanded in custody or on bail.[187] If released on bail his recognisance will be conditioned for his appearance before the court at the end of the period of remand and at every place and time to which the hearing may be adjourned during the course of the proceedings.[188] If his case is not dealt with at that sitting he will be remanded again, whether in custody or on bail, to a later sitting; and so the process may continue until the court is in a position to deal with it.[189] Where the accused is granted bail throughout he will remain at liberty so long as he enters into the necessary recognisance and provides the required sureties, if any. Where he is remanded in custody he will normally be committed to prison or a place of detention.[190] If the period of remand does not exceed four days, the court may remand him into the custody of a member of the Garda Síochána.[191] However, before making such an order outside the Dublin Metropolitan district the court must satisfy itself that suitable facilities are available for the custody of the person.[192] In any case where the accused has been remanded in custody the judge may, if it is expedient in the interests of fair procedure, order that he be brought before him or her at any time before the expiration of the period of remand for the further hearing of the charge.[193] There is analogous provision for persons on bail.[194]

Maximum and Minimum Periods

13–37   The maximum period for which the District Court can remand the accused on his first appearance varies depending on whether he is remanded in custody or on bail. The limits originally set by the Criminal Procedure Act 1967 have

---

[186] S.22(1)(a) of the Criminal Procedure Act 1967 stipulates that where the court remands a person in custody it may commit him to prison. If the person concerned is not less than 16 and not more than 21 years of age the power to remand in custody includes a power to remand him to a remand institution (detention in St Patrick's Institution); Criminal Justice Act 1960, s.9(1).

[187] Criminal Procedure Act 1967, s.21.

[188] *ibid.* s.23(1).

[189] *ibid.* s.22(4)

[190] *ibid.* s.22(1)(a). See District Court Rules 1977, Form 19.1, Sched. B, as amended by the District Court (Criminal Justice) Rules 2001, r.6(b) and Sched. 8, for the warrant of committal.

[191] Criminal Procedure Act 1967, s.25(1). See the District Court Rules 1997, Form 19.4, Sched. B.

[192] *ibid.* s.25(2).

[193] District Court Rules 1997, Ord.19, r.4. See Form 18.7, Sched. B for the form of the warrant.

[194] *ibid.* Ord.19, r.5.

been relaxed by the Criminal Justice (Miscellaneous Provisions) Act 1997 in order to facilitate a policy of releasing gardai from the burden of routine court appearances. If the accused is remanded in custody on his first appearance the maximum period of remand is eight days.[195] If he is remanded on bail the period of remand may be longer than eight days, but only if he and the prosecutor consent.[196] This applies to any remand on bail, irrespective of whether it is a first appearance. At each subsequent sitting the accused may be remanded in custody for a period not exceeding 15 days, unless the court is of the opinion that in all the circumstances of the case it would be unreasonable to remand him for the full 15 days.[197] Where the court is of this opinion it can remand the accused for such lesser period than 15 days that it considers reasonable. In any case, apart from the initial remand hearing, the court may remand the accused in custody for a period exceeding 15 days but not exceeding 30 days if both the accused and the prosecutor consent.[198]

Where a person has been remanded in custody and there is no sitting of the court on the day to which he has been remanded, he is automatically remanded to the next sitting of the court in the same District Court district.[199] If the same happens with respect to an accused who has been remanded on bail he is automatically remanded to the next sitting of the court in the same District Court area.[200] The court may also remand a person in his absence if, due to illness or accident, he cannot appear or be brought before the sitting to which he has been remanded. In this event an accused who is remanded in custody may be further remanded in his absence for such further period as the court considers reasonable, subject to a maximum period of 15 days.[201] If the accused has been remanded on bail he may be further remanded in his absence for such further period, which may exceed eight days, as the court considers reasonable.[202]

It is worth noting that these provisions do not specifically preclude a District Court judge from remanding a person in custody when he appears before the Court charged with a criminal offence which is not punishable by a custodial sentence. Nevertheless, it can be expected that there would have to be very exceptional circumstances in which it would be lawful for the Court to exercise its powers of remand to deprive a person of his right to liberty in a

---

[195] Criminal Procedure Act 1967, s.24(1), as substituted by the Criminal Justice (Miscellaneous Provisions) Act 1997, s.4.

[196] *ibid.* s.24(2).

[197] Criminal Procedure Act 1967, s.24(3).

[198] *ibid.* s.24(4), as substituted by Criminal Justice (Miscellaneous Provisions) Act 1997, s.4.

[199] Criminal Procedure Act 1967, s.24(6)(a), as substituted by the Criminal Justice (Miscellaneous Provisions) Act 1997, s.4. In this event the clerk must transmit to the governor of the prison or the person in charge of the remand institution where such person is detained a certificate informing him of the time, date and place of the next sitting; District Court Rules 1997, Ord.19, r.2(6)(a). See Form 19.3, Sched. B for the form of certificate.

[200] Criminal Procedure Act 1967, s.24(6)(b); as substituted by the Criminal Justice (Miscellaneous Provisions) Act 1997, s.4.

[201] *ibid.* s.24(5)(a). See the District Court Rules 1997, Form 19.2, Sched. B, as amended by the District Court (Criminal Justice) Rules 2001, Sched. 8.

[202] Criminal Procedure Act 1967, s.24(5)(b); as substituted by the Criminal Justice (Miscellaneous Provisions) Act 1997, s.4.

case where the person, if convicted, could not be sentenced to a term of imprisonment or detention.[202a]

Remand to a Sitting if in another District

13–38 Normally where a person is remanded in custody he is remanded to a sitting of the court in the same District Court district. This, however, creates logistical problems for the Garda Síochána and the Prison Service where the prison or place of detention in which the person is committed is a considerable distance from the District Court to which he is remanded. At regular intervals the accused will have to be brought in custody on a return journey from the prison or place of detention to the court in question for remand hearings. The Criminal Justice (Miscellaneous Provisions) Act 1997 responds to this problem. It stipulates that the District Court before which the person charged with an offence first appears may remand him in custody to appear before a District Court in the District Court district in which the relevant prison or place of detention is situated.[203] Alternatively he may be remanded to appear before a District Court in a District Court district adjoining that district in which the prison or place of detention is located. Where this power is exercised the District Court to which the accused has been remanded in custody can further remand him, either in custody or on bail, to appear before it or a sitting of the court in the same district or in a district adjoining the prison or place of detention.[204] It also has the same jurisdiction with respect to legal aid as the District Court before which the accused was originally charged.[205] If, however, the accused is being remanded for the purpose of the trial the court must remand him back to a sitting of the District Court in the District Court District where the offence was committed or in which he resides or was arrested.[206] It has no jurisdiction to conduct the trial itself.

Where a person is charged before a District Court with an indictable offence the court may remand him to appear before the court in another District where it appears to the court that evidence will be available before the court in that other district.[206a] The remand may be in custody or on bail. Where a remand in custody is for a period not exceeding four days the court may commit the accused to the custody of a member of the Garda Síochána.

[202a] See *Howard v. Early* unreported, Supreme Court, July 4, 2000.

[203] Criminal Justice (Miscellaneous Provisions) Act 1997, s.5(1).

[204] Criminal Justice (Miscellaneous Provisions) Act 1997, s.5(2). It does not have the power to transfer the case to a sitting of the District Court in the District Court district in which the offence was committed or where the accused was arrested or resides, unless the accused is being remanded for trial; see Criminal Justice Act, 1924, s.79, as amended by Criminal Justice (Miscellaneous Provisions) Act 1997, s.5(4) and (5), and Criminal Justice Act 1999, s.22(a).

[205] Criminal Justice (Legal Aid) Act 1962, s.2(1), as substituted by the Criminal Justice (Miscellaneous Provisions) Act 1997, s.5(6).

[206] Criminal Justice (Miscellaneous Provisions) Act 1997, s.5(3), as amended by the Criminal Justice Act 1999, s.21. See the District Court Rules 1997, Ord.19, r.6(3), as amended by the District Court (Criminal Justice) Rules 2001, r.6(a). See Form 19.1 Sched. B, as amended by Sched. 8 to the 2001 Rules.

[206a] District Court Rules 1997, Ord.24, r.19(1), as amended by District Court (Criminal Justice) Rules 2001, r.8(a) and Sched. 11. The warrant of committal shall be in accordance with Form 24.19 or 24.20, Sched. B to the 1997 Rules as amended by Sched. 12 to the 2001 Rules. In the case of a

Transfer to a mental Institution

The Minister for Justice, Equality and Law Reform can order the transfer of an **13–39** accused person, who has been remanded in custody, to a mental institution where the person concerned has been duly certified by two physicians or surgeons or by one of each.[207] Such detention in the mental institution cannot extend beyond the date to which the court remanded the accused.[208] Also, where a person has been sent forward for trial or sentence in custody the Minister can order his removal to a mental institution where he is certified to be insane.[209] In this case he must be detained in the mental institution until the sitting of the court to which he has been sent forward.

Temporary Detention in a Lock-up

There is provision for a prisoner to be detained temporarily in a lock-up provided in a Garda Síochána station or in any other place designated for the purpose by the Minister for Justice, Equality and Law Reform.[210] This possibility is available where the prisoner is in transit from a prison to a court for trial, or on adjournment or remand or while a case in which he is involved is at hearing, or for a period of not more than 48 hours while awaiting removal to a prison on conviction or remand.

F. Summary Trial

Initial Formalities

The summary trial of offences in the District Court is characterised by speed **13–40** and informality, compared with trial on indictment.[211] The proceedings commence with the clerk calling out the name of the accused. If the accused is neither present nor represented to answer the complaint the court may adjourn the proceedings, issue a warrant for his arrest or proceed to deal with the case. The last two options can be exercised only if the court is satisfied that the summons (if applicable) was duly served.[212] Moreover, if a summons has been served and the court considers that it would be undesirable in the interests of justice, because of the gravity of the offence or otherwise, to proceed with the hearing in the absence of the accused, it must adjourn the pro-

---

remand on bail the recognisance shall be in accordance with Form 18.1 or 18.3, Sched. B to the 1997 Rules as amended by Sched. 12 to the 2001 Rules.

[207] Lunatic Asylums (Ireland) Act 1875, s.13.

[208] *State (C) v. Minister for Justice* [1967] I.R. 106.

[209] Criminal Lunatics (Ireland) Act 1838, s.3.

[210] Prisons Act 1956, s.1.

[211] It does not follow that the accused can be convicted and sentenced in a peremptory fashion. There is a positive obligation on the District Court judge to ensure that the accused's constitutional right to a fair hearing is observed; see, *e.g.*, *Nevin v. Crowley* [2001] 1 I.R. 113. See also chap. 2 for obligation on District Court to protect the constitutional rights of the accused.

[212] District Court Rules 1997, Ord.23, r.2.

ceedings to enable the accused to be notified of the adjourned hearing.[213] The issue of legal aid may also arise (see chapter 11).

Where the accused is present, or represented, before the court and the prosecutor or his representative fails to appear, the court may strike out, dismiss without prejudice or adjourn the hearing of the complaint.[214]

Guilty Plea

At the commencement of the trial of a summary offence, the clerk will read out the complaint against the accused.[215] If the accused appears, whether personally or through his solicitor or counsel, he will be asked whether he admits the complaint. Where he admits the truth of the complaint the court may convict unless it sees sufficient reason to the contrary.[216] The prosecutor will then normally outline the gist of the offence to the court and the accused will be asked if he wishes to make a plea in mitigation of sentence. In the vast majority of these summary cases the accused pleads guilty and the proceedings are over in the space of a couple of minutes. Indeed, it is not unusual for the plea in mitigation to be the primary focus, particularly if the accused is at risk of being sentenced to a term of imprisonment. In this event he may even consider it necessary to call character witnesses to testify on oath to his good character. Once the plea in mitigation has been taken the judge will proceed to impose sentence on, or impose an order against, the accused. Much the same applies where the court is disposing of an indictable offence on a guilty plea.[217]

Trial

13–41   Where the accused appears, either personally or through his solicitor or counsel, and does not admit the truth of the complaint, the court must proceed to hear and determine the complaint or charge.[218] Similarly, where an indictable offence is being tried summarily, the court must take the accused's plea and proceed to trial.[219] The court has a discretion to proceed to deal with a complaint if the accused is not present and is not represented to answer the complaint.[220] This is one of the features distinguishing summary trial and trial on indictment. In the latter the accused must be present to plead to the indictment and must normally be present throughout his trial.

Although there are some differences between a summary trial and a trial on indictment the basic procedure and rules of evidence are common to both.

---

[213] Courts Act 1991, s.22(4); District Court Rules 1997, Ord.22, r.3.

[214] District Court Rules 1997, Ord.23, r.3.

[215] See earlier [para 13–34] for the preliminaries associated with the summary trial of an indictable offence.

[216] District Court Rules 1997, Ord.23, r.1.

[217] See earlier [para 13–34] for the preliminaries associated with the disposal of an indictable offence on a guilty plea.

[218] District Court Rules 1997, Ord.23, r.1.

[219] Criminal Justice Act 1951, s.2(2)(a); District Court Rules 1997, Ord.24, r.1, as amended by the District Court (Criminal Justice) Rules 2001, r.8(a) and Sched. 11.

[220] District Court Rules 1997, Ord.23, r.2.

These are dealt with in greater detail in chapters 18 and 19 on Trial on Indictment, so the briefest of outlines will suffice here. The prosecution presents its case by calling and examining its witnesses and presenting any exhibits. The witnesses can be cross-examined by the defence and re-examined by the prosecution if need be. Once the prosecution has concluded its case the defence can present its case by calling and examining its witnesses and presenting any exhibits. These witnesses can be cross-examined by the prosecution and re-examined by the defence if need be. Additionally, or alternatively, the defence might challenge the prosecution case on the basis of legal arguments. For example, they could argue that the prosecution evidence was not sufficient to prove the case against the accused beyond a reasonable doubt, or that some essential ingredient of the offence had not been proved. Both sides then have the opportunity of making closing submissions in the order of the prosecution followed by the defence.

Comparison with Trial on Indictment

Although the formal rules governing trial procedure may not differ radically, it must be said that the perception and experience of summary trial and trial on indictment are quite different. The former, almost invariably, is much quicker and conducted in a less formal atmosphere than the latter. The predominance of counsel in their wigs and gowns and, of course, the presence of the jury, in the Circuit Court and the Central Criminal Court give the proceedings on indictment an air of formality that is noticeably missing from the District Court. This is compounded by the fact that the charges being tried on indictment are likely to be much more serious than those dealt with summarily. The fact that there is normally a jury in trials on indictment also means that questions of admissibility of evidence are often dealt with on a *voir dire*. The summary trial is spared the inevitable delay which this causes as evidential matters can be dealt with by the judge as they arise. Since the judge is the tribunal of fact in the District Court, he or she will decide whether the accused is guilty or not guilty of the charges. This decision is normally handed down on completion of the case for both sides. Equally, of course, the judge may take time before reaching a decision and may adjourn the proceedings for this purpose. In the event of a finding of guilt the judge will proceed to hear a plea in mitigation of sentence.

G. Sending Forward on a Plea of Guilty

Where the accused appears before a District Court charged with an indictable **13–42** offence and pleads guilty the court may be able to sent him forward for sentence on that plea to the court to which he would have been sent forward for trial had it not been for the plea of guilty. This option is not available in respect of: murder, attempt to murder, conspiracy to murder, piracy, an offence under the Treason Act 1939 or a grave breach such as is referred to in section 3(1)(i) of the Geneva Conventions Act 1962.[221] Where the accused signs a plea of guilty to a qualifying offence, the District Court may send him forward for sentence, provided that the DPP does not object and the court is satisfied that the accused understands the nature of the offence and the facts alleged.[222] In this event he will be sent forward for sentence to the court to which he would have been sent forward for trial had it not been for his plea of guilty.[223]

Where an accused is sent forward for sentence under these provisions, the full range of sentencing options available to the court to which the accused has been sent forward apply. However, further charges may not be added after the accused has been sent forward. In *State (Brien) v. Kelly*[224] the accused pleaded guilty before the District Court to a number of indictable offences. After he was sent forward for sentence to the Circuit Court for sentence an alteration was made to the charges to which he had pleaded guilty. The effect of this alteration was to add a new count to which he had not pleaded guilty in the District Court. In holding that the Circuit Court had no jurisdiction to sentence him on this additional count even though he pleaded guilty to all the counts as put in the Circuit Court, O'Dalaigh C.J. explained that:

> " . . . Count 3 in respect of which the prosecutor pleaded guilty in the Circuit Court and for which he was there sentenced was not an offence to which he pleaded guilty in the District Court. There was therefore no jurisdiction to add the charge. The procedure under section 3 of the Act of 1951 [the relevant statutory authority at the time] is different from a return for trial without a plea of guilty after depositions have been taken. The practice of adding to the charges, on which the return was made, such other charges of which there is evidence in the depositions was approved in *State (Cannon) v. Kavanagh* but that practice cannot be applied where the accused is returned on a plea under section 3. The court of trial, in pronouncing sentence, is there confined to the offences to which the accused pleaded in the District Court. Therefore, the acceptance of the plea in respect of Count 3 was not warranted in law and, accordingly, no basis was laid for a sentence in respect of this count."[225]

It is open to the accused to withdraw his guilty plea after having been sent forward.[226] Where this happens, the court must enter a plea of not guilty and the case will proceed as if the accused had been sent forward for trial in accordance with the provisions of Part 1A of the Criminal Procedure Act 1967 (see chapter 14).[227] Any documents which must be served on the accused and

---

[221] Criminal Procedure Act 1967, s.13(1). Also excluded are offences of being an accessory before or after the fact to any of these offences.

[222] Criminal Procedure Act 1967, s.13(2)(b) and s.13(2A), as amended by the Criminal Justice Act 1999, s.10(3). See the District Court Rules 1997, Form 24.1, Sched. B (plea of guilty) and Form 24.2 Sched. B (judge's order). The amended versions are to be found in the District Court (Criminal Justice) Rules 2001, Sched. 12. The requirement for the DPP's consent was added by Criminal Justice Act 1999, s.10(3).

[223] Criminal Procedure Act 1967, s.13(2)(b).

[224] *State (Brien) v. Kelly* [1970] I.R. 69. Any defect in the charge may be corrected by the sentencing court where it is of the opinion that the correction will not result in injustice. The plea will then be treated as a plea of guilty to the corrected charge. Criminal Procedure (Amendment) Act 1973, s.2

[225] *ibid.* at 80.

[226] Criminal Procedure Act 1967, s.13(4)(a).

[227] *ibid.* s.13(4)(b)(i), as amended by the Criminal Justice Act 1999, s.10(4).

which have not already be supplied must be served on him.[228] The time requirements for service run from the date on which the guilty plea was entered.[229]

There are no specific provisions governing the remand in custody or on bail of a person sent forward for sentence on a plea of guilty. Presumably, it is dealt with by analogy to a person being sent forward for trial (see chapter 14).

H. Sending the Accused Forward for Trial on Indictment

The jurisdiction of the District Court to send an accused forward for trial on indictment is considered in the following chapter, together with a number of related pre-trial procedures.

13–43

---

[228] *ibid.* s.13(4)(b)(ii).
[229] *ibid.* s.13(4)(b)(iii).

CHAPTER 14

SENDING THE ACCUSED FORWARD FOR TRIAL ON INDICTMENT AND RELATED PRE-TRIAL APPLICATIONS

A. Sending the Accused Forward for Trial on Indictment

1. Abolition of Preliminary Examination

14–01

Until recently an accused could not normally be sent forward for trial on indictment without at least being given the option of having a preliminary examination of the case against him in the District Court.[1] Indeed, the preliminary examination had been a feature of criminal procedure in these islands for several centuries.[2] In the days before professional police forces and public prosecution agencies it served as a very necessary device to ensure that serious criminal charges were pursued all the way to trial on indictment only in those cases where there was some prospects of conviction. As such, the preliminary examination was identified as an important safeguard protecting the liberty of the individual against intrusion from the State.[2a] It enabled the

---

[1] For a history of the procedure for putting an accused on trial on indictment see judgment of Davitt P. in *State (Attorney General) v. Judge Fawsitt* [1953] I.R. 39, and the judgment of Lavery J. in *People (Attorney General) v. Boggan* [1958] I.R. 67

[2] E Ryan and P Magee *The Irish Criminal Process* (Mercier Press, Dublin, 1983) pp. 229–230.

[2a] *People (Attorney General) v. Boggan* [1958] I.R. 67; *Glavin v. Governor of Mountjoy Prison* [1991] 2 I.R. 421. However, the courts have stopped short of recognising a constitutional right to a preliminary examination; see, *e.g.*, *O'Shea v. DPP* [1988] I.R. 655. See also, J. Casey *The Irish Law Officers* (Round Hall Sweet & Maxwell, 1996), p.300.

accused to demand that the prosecution justify its decision to proceed to a full trial by establishing that there was a *prima facie* case against the accused. A *prima facie* case in this context meant that there was evidence upon which a jury could reasonably convict the accused. The prosecution sought to establish a prima facie case by presenting its case and calling its witnesses before a District Court judge. The accused could cross-examine these witness and call evidence on his own behalf in order to undermine the prosecution case. If a *prima facie* case was made out the accused would be returned for trial; if not, he would be discharged.

It is also worth noting that section 62 of the Courts of Justice Act 1936 purported to confer a power on the DPP to direct that an accused be sent forward for trial on indictment where a judge of the District Court has refused to send him forward. In effect it gave the DPP a power to reverse the judge's refusal to send the accused forward. This is discussed further below where it will be seen that the power has since been declared unconstitutional.

For many years the preliminary examination was criticised, primarily by the prosecution, as an unnecessary and burdensome aspect of criminal procedure. They pointed to the fact that most defendants waived their right to a preliminary examination. More controversially, they asserted that it was used primarily by experienced criminals as a means of delaying the process of justice in their cases, and even as a means of bringing pressure to bear on State witnesses to retract their evidence. These arguments eventually proved successful as the preliminary examination has now been abolished in both Britain and Ireland. In Ireland the legislation which governed the preliminary examination (the Criminal Procedure Act 1967) has now been heavily amended by Part III of the Criminal Justice Act 1999 which inserts a new Part 1A into the Criminal Procedure Act 1967 and makes further piecemeal amendments to the 1967 Act and other relevant enactments. These provisions abolish the preliminary examination and make provision for the District Court to send the accused forward for trial directly.[3] They came into force on October 1, 2001.[4] Consequential changes in the District Court Rules 1997 are effected by the District Court (Criminal Justice) Rules 2001.

2. Obligation to Send Forward

The General Rule

14–02   Where an accused is before the District Court charged with an indictable offence, the court must send him or her forward for trial to the court before which he or she is to stand trial.[5] There are three situations where this obligation does not apply: where the case is to be tried summarily; where the case is being dealt with under section 13 of the 1967 Act (plea of guilty); and where the accused is unfit to plead.

---

[3] S.9 of the Criminal Justice Act 1999 inserts a new s.4A into the Criminal Procedure Act 1967. This replaces ss.5–12 of the 1967 Act.

[4] Criminal Justice Act 1999 (Part III) (Commencement) Order 2001.

[5] Criminal Procedure Act 1967, s.4A(1).

DPP's Consent

There are also two preconditions which must be satisfied before the accused can be sent forward for trial under this provision. First the DPP must consent.[6] If the DPP refuses to give a consent in relation to an indictable offence, the District Court must strike out the proceedings against the accused in relation to that offence.[7] This shall not shall prejudice the institution of proceedings against the accused by the DPP.[8] It is not immediately clear whether this means that the DPP can re-institute proceedings for the same offence before the District Court at a later stage or whether he can institute proceedings directly before the court of trial or both.

As will be seen later (para. 14-14) there was a time when the DPP had the power to send the accused directly for trial on indictment where the District Court judge had refused informations. The statutory provision conferring this power was declared unconstitutional in *Costello v. DPP*.[8a] Since the 1999 Act has not introduced a new provision which clearly and unequivocally confers such a power on the DPP it must be assumed that the reference to the institution of proceedings by the DPP refers to the re-institution of proceedings before a District Court judge, as distinct from the institution of proceedings on indictment directly before the trial court.

A literal interpretation of the provisions suggests that in order to avoid the proceedings being struck out the DPP will have to consent to the accused being sent forward for trial on the first occasion on which he appears before the District Court charged with an indictable offence. As will be seen below, the accused cannot actually be sent forward for trial until the book of evidence has been served (the second precondition), and that will not normally occur until many months later. In the meantime, if the DPP consents to the accused being sent forward for trial on indictment, the judge can remand the accused to a further sitting of the court to allow service of the book of evidence.[9]

Time Limits for Book of Evidence

The second precondition is that certain documents (generally known as the **14–03** book of evidence) must be served on the accused or his solicitor. He or she cannot be sent forward for trial by the District Court until these documents have been served.[10] Where the DPP consents to the accused being sent forward for trial he must serve the book of evidence on the accused or his solicitor within 42 days after the accused first appears in the District Court charged with the indictable offence.[11] This compares with a period of thirty days which had prevailed prior to October 2001. Despite the increase it is

---

[6] *ibid.* s.4A(2).
[7] *ibid.* s.4A(3).
[8] *ibid.* s.4A(4).
[8a] [1984] I.R. 436.
[9] District Court Rules 1997, Ord. 24, r.6, as amended by the District Court (Criminal Justice) Rules 2001, r.8(a) and Sched. 11.
[10] Criminal Procedure Act 1967, s.4A(5).
[11] As soon as the documents are served on the accused the prosecutor must furnish copies of them to the District Court; the Criminal Procedure Act 1967, s.4B(2).

likely that 42 days will still prove too short in many cases for the preparation of the book of evidence. Indeed, the thirty day period was normally extended by leave of the court almost as a matter of practice. The current provisions also permit extensions. On an application by the DPP the District Court may extend the 42-day period if it is satisfied that there is good reason for doing so and that it would be in the interests of justice to do so.[12] This application may be made (and an extension granted) before or after the expiry of the 42-day period.[13] The legislation does not prescribe any limit on the length of an extension. Moreover, further applications for extensions can be made before or after the expiry of any extension granted.[14] Where the court refuses to grant an extension it must strike out the proceedings against the accused in relation to the offence in question.[15] This is without prejudice to the institution of any proceedings against the accused by the DPP.[16] Once again it is not absolutely clear whether this is meant to refer to proceedings being instituted again in the District Court or directly before the court of trial, or to both. Presumably both are intended. Indeed, the specific reference to "any proceedings" suggests that both are intended.

As soon as the documents listed below (book of evidence) have been served on the accused or his solicitor the DPP must furnish copies to the District Court.[17] The copies must be lodged, together with a statutory declaration of service on the accused, with the clerk within eight days of service on the accused.[18]

Contents of Book of Evidence

14–04   The documents which must be served on the accused or his solicitor before he or she can be sent forward for trial are listed in the Criminal Procedure Act 1967, as amended by the Criminal Justice Act 1999. They are: a statement of the charges against the accused; a copy of any sworn information in writing upon which the proceedings were initiated; a list of the witnesses whom the DPP proposes to call at the trial; a statement of the evidence that is expected to be given by each of them;[19] a copy of any document containing information which it is proposed to give in evidence by virtue of Part II of the Criminal Evidence Act 1992 (broadly speaking records compiled in the course of a business or by or on behalf of certain public bodies);[20] where appropriate, a copy of a certificate under section 6(1) of the 1992 Act (a certificate relating

---

[12] Criminal Procedure Act 1967, s.4B(3)
[13] *ibid.* s.4B(4).
[14] *ibid.* s.4B(4)(b).
[15] *ibid.* s.4B(5).
[16] *ibid.* s.4B(6).
[17] *ibid.* s.4B(2).
[18] District Court Rules 1997, Ord.24, r.7(2), as amended by District Court (Criminal Justice) Rules 2001, r.8(a) and Sched. 11.
[19] See District Court Rules 1997, O.24, r.7 and Sched. B, Forms 24.3 to 24.7 for the relevant forms, as amended by District Court (Criminal Justice) Rules 2001, r.8 Schedules 11 and 12.
[20] For further detail see Chap.18 (Trial Evidence).

to the information contained in a record compiled in the course of a business);[21] and a list of the exhibits (if any).[22]

It is also worth noting that there is specific provision in the Criminal Evidence Act 1992 permitting an accused to see a video-recording of a statement which is to be given in evidence against him by the alleged victim where the statement was given during an interview with a member of the Garda Siochana or other competent person.[23] This provision applies where: the DPP consents to the accused being sent forward for trial, the offence in question is a sexual offence or an offence involving violence or the threat of violence, the alleged victim was under 14 years of age at the time of making the statement and is under 17 years of age on the date consent is given to the accused being sent forward for trial.[24] Where these conditions are satisfied the DPP must notify the accused that it is proposed to give the statement in evidence and give the accused an opportunity of seeing the video-recording of the interview. It is important to emphasise that the accused must be given the opportunity to see the video-recording of the whole interview, as distinct from the video-recording of the statement itself. It may happen of course that the statement was given during a series of interviews. In this event it is at least arguable that the accused should be given an opportunity of viewing the whole series of interviews instead of being confined to the single interview in which the statement was given.

Additional Materials

The serving of the book of evidence does not preclude the prosecutor from serving further documents on the accused or his solicitor. There was always statutory authority for the DPP to serve further statements of evidence from witnesses who had already supplied statements for the book of evidence. The amendment effected by the Criminal Justice Act 1999 affords much greater latitude to the DPP.[25] It enables him to serve statements from new witnesses as well as new sources of documentary evidence and exhibits. There is no specific requirement for the additional sources of evidence to have been available or known at the time the book of evidence was served. Nor are there any specific time limits on the DPP's freedom to serve these documents. Presumably the court would postpone the commencement of the trial on the application of the accused if new documents were served too close to the scheduled commencement date. The relevant provision states that at any time after the service of the book of evidence the DPP must cause the following documents, if any, to be served: a list of any further witnesses the DPP proposes to call at the trial; a statement of the evidence that is expected to be

14–05

---

21 *Ibid.*
22 Criminal Procedure Act 1967, s.4B(1).
23 See Criminal Evidence Act 1992, ss.15(1) and 16(1)(b), as amended by the Criminal Justice Act 1999, ss.19 and 20.
24 Criminal Evidence Act s.15(1), as amended by the Criminal Justice Act 1999, s.19. This also applies where the alleged victim is over the prescribed age but is suffering from a mental handicap; Criminal Justice Act 1999, s.19.
25 Criminal Procedure Act 1967, s.4C(1).

given by each witness whose name appears on the list of further witnesses; a statement of any further evidence that is expected to be given by any witness whose name appears on the list already served;[26] any notice of intention to give information contained in a document in evidence under section 7(1)(b) of the Criminal Evidence Act 1992 (notice of intention to give evidence of information in a document), together with a copy of the document; where appropriate, a copy of a certificate under section 6(1) of the Criminal Evidence Act 1992 (see above); a copy of any deposition taken under section 4F of the Criminal Justice Act 1999 (see below);[27] and a list of any further exhibits.[28] As soon as these documents are served the DPP must furnish copies to the trial court.[29]

It is also worth noting that there is provision for the DPP (and the accused) to apply to the trial court for an order permitting evidence to be taken by way of a sworn deposition or through a live television link in pre-trial proceedings in certain circumstances. This is dealt with below.

Compiling the Book of Evidence

14–06   Compiling the book of evidence can be a lengthy task, particularly if the case is complex and there are a large number of witnesses. Inevitably, the witness statements are the dominant element in terms of bulk. In a typical case they will include the statements of police officers who were involved in the case in a material fashion. So, for example, it will include statements from officers who arrested, interrogated, charged and cautioned the accused, as well as statements from officers who claim to have seen the accused committing the offence or who retrieved material evidence of the commission of the offence. These will detail what the officer did and said, what he observed and what he heard or was told, as the case may be. Statements concerning the interrogation of the accused can be particularly important. They will normally contain a detailed account of the question and answer sessions between the officers concerned and the accused. If the accused made an incriminating statement during the course of an interrogation it will be included in the officers' statements. It may equally appear as a statement in its own right if the accused made and signed a formal statement of admission while in police custody. Where the prosecution case includes forensic evidence, there will be statements from the scientists who carried out the tests. Similarly, the existence of fingerprint, handwriting etc evidence will be reflected in the inclusion of statements from the relevant expert witnesses. Where the case involves

---

[26]   District Court Rules 1997, Ord.24, r.8, as amended by the District Court (Criminal Justice) Rules 2001, r.8(a) and Sched. 11. Any such statement must be served in accordance with the District Court Rules 1997, Form 24.8, Sched. B, as amended by Sched. 12 to the 2001 Rules.

[27]   District Court Rules 1997, Ord.24, r.18, as amended by the District Court (Criminal Justice) Rules 2001, r.8(a) and Sched. 11. See Form 24.18, Sched. B, as amended by Sched.12 to 2001 Rules.

[28]   Criminal Procedure Act 1967, s.4C(1). Any further statement served on the accused pursuant to this provision must be in accordance with Form 24.8 Sched. B of the District Court Rules 1997; see District Court Rules 1997, Ord.24, r.8, as amended by the District Court (Criminal Justice) Rules 2001, r.8(a) and Sched.11. See Sched. 12 of the 2001 Rules for the amended Form.

[29]   Criminal Procedure Act 1967, s.4C(2).

personal injury to a victim the book will contain statements from the medical practitioners who examined the victim. The statements of a victim or victims and eyewitnesses will also be a regular feature.

Another critical component of the book of evidence is the list of exhibits. The **14–07** evidence in support of the prosecution case will not always include material objects. Where it does, however, the book of evidence must include a list of these objects or exhibits. In a case of robbery, for example, this might include a weapon, banknotes, a sketch of the internal layout of the premises robbed, an item of clothing left behind by the robbers etc. The requirement to list such exhibits in the book of evidence puts the accused on notice that they exist and that the prosecution intends to rely on them at the trial. The accused has the right to inspect all of the exhibits mentioned in the list of exhibits served on him or his solicitor in the book of evidence or subsequently.[30]

An important feature of the book of evidence is the fact that it must include a list of the witnesses whom it proposes to call at the trial, as well as a statement of the evidence that they will give. The actual identity of the witnesses can be important to the accused for several reasons. It may be, for example, that a witness bears a personal grudge against the accused, was a former accomplice in crime, had a criminal record, has a record of dishonesty and unreliability, has a record of mental illness or is a paid police informer. Any of these factors can be important to the defence in deciding whether and how best to contest the charge. By the same token, however, there may be circumstances where the prosecution has a strong interest in protecting one or more of its witnesses, at least until the trial. In terrorist cases, for example, or in cases involving organised crime where there may be a threat to the life of the witness or his or her family the prosecution will be keen to protect information about the location of a witness. Indeed, the willingness of the witness to cooperate and give evidence may depend on the capacity of the prosecution to keep his or her location secret. There is no requirement in the legislation to disclose the location of witnesses against the accused. Indeed, it is now a criminal offence to disclose information about the location of a "relocated witness" without lawful authority.[31]

The book of evidence is meant to be a statement of the evidence that the prosecution intends to use against the accused at the trial. It does not necessarily represent all of the evidence that the police have amassed in the course of their investigation. As a general rule it is a matter for the DPP to decide in the exercise of his discretion what evidence to use and what not to use in the case against the accused. If, however, the prosecution is in possession of evidence which is relevant and beneficial to the accused, it is under an obligation to disclose it to the accused. This can give rise to difficulties where, for example, the evidence in question includes statements from informers in cases involving terrorism or organised crime. Revealing the

---

[30] Criminal Procedure Act 1967, s.4D. District Court Rules 1997, Ord.24, r.9, as amended by the District Court (Criminal Justice) Rules 2001, r.8(a) and Sched. 11.
[31] Criminal Justice Act 1999, s.40.

statements to the defence may expose the identity of an informer and thereby compromise the future value of that informer or even place him or his family at risk. Accordingly, the DPP may claim privilege with respect to the identity of an informer in the interests of the effective investigation and detection of crime. This is dealt with later.

14–08   Work on the compilation of the book of evidence will normally commence immediately after the accused has been remanded on his first appearance before the District Court. It usually takes months, and occasionally more than a year, before the book is ready to be served. In the meantime the accused is remanded at periodic intervals by the District Court. There is no absolute time limit beyond which service of the book of evidence becomes time-barred. However, if the prosecution delays too long in serving the book of evidence the accused can apply to the court at one of the periodic remand hearings to have the proceedings thrown out. The court is unlikely to accede to such an application at the first attempt. Nevertheless, if the delay is exceptional it will normally seek a commitment from, or impose a requirement on, the prosecution to serve the book of evidence within a specified time frame. If the prosecution fail to comply it is more likely that the court will accede to an application to have the pro-ceedings thrown out. This does not prevent the prosecution from re-instating the case against the accused at some time in the future. It must be remembered, however, that excessive delay can result in an order preventing the DPP proceeding with the prosecution (see chapter 1).

3. Decision to Send Forward

14–09   Once the statutory preconditions have been satisfied the District Court must send the accused forward for trial. It would appear that the judge's order sending the accused forward for trial must be in writing and signed by the judge.[32] The clerk for the court area where the order sending the accused forward for trial was made must transmit the following documents to the appropriate County Registrar[33]:

- the book of evidence;
- the order of the judge sending the accused forward for trial;
- any recognisance taken in relation to the case, or money lodged in lieu of surety or sureties; and
- a plea of guilty (if any).

These documents must be transmitted within ten days of the making of the order, or immediately if the trial is imminent.

It is also worth noting that before sending him forward for trial the District Court must inform the accused of the requirements of section 20 of the

---

[32] District Court Rules 1997, Ord.24, r.10, as amended by the District Court (Criminal Justice) Rules 2001, r.8(a) and Sched. 11. See Form 24.9, Sched. B, as amended by Sched. 12 of the 2001 Rules.
[33] District Court Rules 1997, Ord.24, r.11, as amended by the District Court (Criminal Justice) Rules 2001, r.8(a) and Sched. 11.

Criminal Justice Act 1984 with respect to giving notice of alibi evidence.[34] If the accused intends to rely on the evidence of an alibi at his trial he must normally give notice of the alibi within 14 days of being served with the book of evidence.

Where the court makes an order sending the accused forward for trial, it may by warrant commit him to prison to await trial.[35] Alternatively, it may release the accused conditionally on his entering into a recognisance.[36] In this event the general rules governing bail apply.[37]

B. Application to Dismiss

1. Introduction

The preliminary examination afforded the accused the opportunity of chal- **14–10**
lenging the case against him before it actually went to trial. If successful he would be discharged by the District Court. With the abolition of the preliminary examination, the District Court no longer has a role in considering whether there is a sufficient case to put the accused on trial for the offence with which he has been charged. Under the new procedure, however, the accused has the option of applying to the court of trial to have one or more of the charges dismissed before the actual trial.

2. Procedure

At any time after he has been sent forward for trial the accused may apply to the trial court to dismiss one or more of the charges against him.[38] Notice of any such application must be given to the DPP not less than fourteen days before the date on which it is due to be heard.[39] The trial court may determine that in the interests of justice less than 14 days notice of an application may be given.[40] Although it is not specified it can be presumed that the notice must be served by the accused.

---

[34] See the Criminal Justice Act 1984, s.20(3)(a) and 20(6); and the District Court Rules 1997, Ord.24, r.10, as amended by the District Court (Criminal Justice) Rules 2001, r.8(a) and Sched. 11.

[35] Criminal Procedure Act 1967, s.22(1)(a); District Court Rules 1997, Ord.24, r.12, as amended by the District Court (Criminal Justice) Rules r.8 and Sched. 11. See Form 24.10, Sched. B, as amended by Sched. 12 of the 2001 Rules.

[36] Criminal Procedure Act 1967, s.22(1)(b); District Court Rules 1997, Ord.24, r.12, as amended by the District Court (Criminal Justice) Rules 2001, r.8 and Sched. 11. See Forms 18.2 or 18.4, Sched. B, as amended by Sched. 12 of the 2001 Rules. Where the accused is sent forward for trial on a scheduled offence, he can be released on bail by the District Court only with the consent of the DPP; Offences against the State Act 1939, s.45(2). If that consent is not forthcoming the accused will have to apply to the High Court for bail.

[37] District Court Rules 1997, Ord.24, r.13, as amended by the District Court (Criminal Justice) Rules 2001, r.8(a). See Ord.18 for the provisions regarding bail.

[38] Criminal Procedure Act 1967, s.4E(1).

[39] *ibid.* s.4E(2).

[40] *ibid.* s.4E(3).

The legislation does not prescribe the procedure which must be followed on any such application. It would appear, however, that the onus is on the accused to present arguments to persuade the court that there is not a sufficient case to justify putting him on trial for any charge. There is no suggestion in the legislation that an application *per se* is sufficient to trigger an inquiry by the court into the sufficiency of the case. Equally, there is no suggestion that it would be sufficient to place the onus on the prosecution to establish that there is a sufficient case. This is a very significant departure from the preliminary examination in which the onus was on the prosecution to persuade the court that there was a sufficient case against the accused to warrant putting him on trial.

3. Evidence

Overview

14–11 A challenge might take the form of pure legal argument directed to matters such as: the soundness of the indictment, the sufficiency of the evidence as disclosed in the book of evidence,[40a] the capacity of the accused, *res judicata*, the jurisdiction of the court, or whatever. It is also apparent that oral evidence may be called and that documents (those making up the book of evidence or any such additional documents) may be served on the accused or his solicitor, but only if it appears to the court that such evidence is required in the interests of justice.[41]

Evidence through TV Link

Oral evidence in this context includes any evidence given through a live television link pursuant to the provisions of Part III of the Criminal Evidence Act 1992 or section 39 of the Criminal Justice Act 1999, or a video-recording of any such evidence taken in the District Court pursuant to an order of the trial court (see below). Part III of the 1992 Act refers to sexual offences or offences involving violence or the threat of violence (including aiding, abetting, etc., such offences). Evidence from the victim may be given through a live television link in respect of such offences where he or she was under 17 years of age at the date on which the accused was sent forward for trial, or in any other case with the leave of the court.[42] Where such evidence has been taken in the District Court pursuant to an order of the trial court (paras 14–21 *et seq.*) then a video-recording of the evidence may be given.[43] A video-recording of a statement made by the victim during an interview with a member of the Garda Siochana or other competent person may also be considered by the judge hearing the application where the victim was under

---

[40a] It is not clear whether this can extend to consideration of the the the admissibility of evidence; see chap.8 at para. 8–35.
[41] Criminal Procedure Act 1967, s.4E(5) & (6).
[42] Criminal Evidence Act 1992, s.13(1)(b).
[43] Criminal Procedure Act 1967, s.4E(5)(ii).

14 years of age at the time, but only if the victim is available for cross-examination.[44] If the accused person consents an edited version of the video-recording may be shown at the hearing with the leave of the judge.[45] In this event, the edited version shall be admissible as evidence of any fact stated therein of which direct oral evidence by the witness would be admissible. However, the edited version (or part thereof) shall not be admitted in evidence if the court is of the opinion that in the interests of justice it ought not to be admitted.[46] There is no express provision for the court to consider an unedited video-recording of the interview, whether with or without the consent of the accused. It is submitted, however, that the court could consider an unedited version at the request of the accused if it appears to the court that such evidence is required in the interests of justice.

Section 39 of the 1999 Act permits evidence to be given at the hearing through a **14–12** live television link where the court is satisfied that the witness is likely to be in fear or subject to intimidation in giving evidence. Where evidence is given through a live television link under this provision and evidence is given that the accused was known to the witness before the offence was alleged to have been committed, the witness shall not be required to identify the accused unless the court in the interests of justice directs otherwise.[47] In any other case (where evidence is given through a live television link under section 39), evidence by a person other than the witness that the witness identified the accused as being the offender at an identification parade or by other means shall be admissible as evidence that the accused was so identified.[48] These provisions are designed primarily to protect the victim against the trauma of having to identify his or her alleged attacker in a case involving a sexual offence or violence against the person.

Where evidence is to be given through a live television link under the provisions described above and the necessary facilities are not available in the circuit in which the application to dismiss is being heard, the court may by order transfer the proceedings to a circuit where such facilities are available.[49] Where such an order is made the jurisdiction of the court to which the proceedings have been transferred may be exercised by the judge of the circuit concerned.

Calling Witnesses

Interestingly, the legislation does not specifically state who may call the oral evidence. It simply states that oral evidence may be given on an application, so long as it appears to the trial court that such evidence is required in the

---

[44] Criminal Evidence Act 1992, s.15(2), as amended by the Criminal Justice Act 1999, s.19.

[45] *ibid.* s.15(3).

[46] In considering whether in the interests of justice such edited version, or any part thereof, ought to be admitted in evidence, the court shall have regard to all the circumstances, including any risk that its admission will result in unfairness to the accused.

[47] Criminal Justice Act 1999, s.39(5)(a).

[48] *ibid.* s.39(5)(b).

[49] *ibid.* s.39(4) and the Criminal Evidence Act 1992, s.17.

interests of justice.[50] It would appear, therefore, that if the accused wished to call one or more witnesses to give evidence on his behalf he would have to apply to the court for permission to do so. Similarly, if the prosecution wished to call one or more of its witnesses it would have to apply to the court. Presumably, the accused can also seek to have one or more prosecution witnesses called to give evidence. Unlike the situation in the old preliminary examination, however, he does not have the right to demand the appearance of such witnesses. He will have to persuade the court that oral evidence from the witness or witnesses in question is required in the interests of justice. Equally, there is nothing in the legislation to prevent the prosecution seeking to have oral evidence given by one or more of the defence witnesses on the same basis.

Previous Sexual History

14–14 Where the application to dismiss relates to a sexual assault offence evidence cannot be adduced, nor can a witness be asked, about the previous sexual history of the victim with a person other than the accused without the leave of the judge.[51] The judge must refuse an application for leave unless he or she is satisfied that leave would be likely to be given at the trial.[52] If the judge is satisfied that leave would be granted at the trial then he or she must grant an application for leave.[53]

Depositions

It is also worth noting that a deposition taken from a witness by the District Court may be considered by the trial judge on an application for dismissal.[54] The procedure applicable to the taking of such depositions is considered more fully below. Where it applies it can be used either by the accused or the prosecution to compel the appearance of a person before a judge of a District Court so that his evidence may be taken either by sworn deposition or, where applicable, through a live television link. Either party may use this power to seek the appearance of one or more of its own witnesses and/or a witness or witnesses for the other side. It follows that there is scope for the accused to use this procedure in order to achieve a close equivalent of what was possible at a preliminary examination. He can seek to have one or more prosecution witnesses called to give evidence and submit to cross-examination before a judge of the District Court. The record of the examination and cross-examination may then be considered by the trial court in an application to dismiss. The big difference from

---

[50] Criminal Procedure Act 1967, s.4E(5)(a). Oral evidence in this context includes evidence given through a live television link pursuant to Pt III of the Criminal Evidence Act 1992 or s.39 of the Criminal Justice Act 1999, or a video-recording of any evidence given through a live television link pursuant to Pt III or s.39 in proceedings under s.4 of the Criminal Procedure Act 1967; Criminal Procedure Act 1967, s.4E(5)(b).

[51] Criminal Law (Rape) Act 1981, s.4(1), as amended by the Criminal Justice Act 1999, s.15.

[52] *ibid.* s.4(2)(a).

[53] *ibid.* s.4(2)(b).

[54] Criminal Procedure Act 1967, s.4G(1).

the preliminary examination is that a person may only be required to give evidence under this procedure if the trial court is satisfied that it is in the interests of justice to do so. Equally, the procedure can also be used by the prosecution to call witnesses.

Documents

14–15

The legislation is more specific about the procedure to be followed where the court is satisfied that it is in the interests of justice that any relevant document should be served on the accused or his solicitor at the hearing of an application to dismiss. In this event the DPP must serve the document on the accused or his solicitor at the hearing, and the court may, if it considers it appropriate to do so, adjourn the hearing for that purpose.[55]

The legislation is silent on the production of material evidence at an application to dismiss. However, the accused's statutory right to inspect exhibits mentioned in the list of exhibits served on him or his solicitor is not time restricted. Accordingly, there would appear to be no reason why the accused could not present arguments based on the exhibits at the application to dismiss, providing of course that the list of exhibits has already been served on him or his solicitor. If the list has not been served, the accused could apply to the court to have the document served and, if necessary, seek an adjournment for that purpose.

Adverse Inferences

It is worth noting that the adverse inference provisions of sections 18 and 19 of the Criminal Justice Act 1984 can be taken into account on an application to dismiss. Accordingly, in deciding whether or not to grant an application to dismiss the court may draw such inferences as appear proper from the accused's failure or refusal to provide an explanation for relevant marks or objects on his person etc, or his presence at a particular place, when asked to do so by a member of the Garda Siochana in the course of the investigation of a offence (see Chapter 6 for further detail on these provisions).[56] Similarly, in deciding whether a charge should be dismissed on an application to dismiss, the court may draw such inferences as appear proper from an accused's failure or refusal to consent to the taking of a bodily sample under the provisions of the Criminal Justice (Forensic Evidence) Act 1990.[57] He refusal may also be treated as, or as being capable of amounting to, corroboration of any evidence in relation to which the refusal is material.[58]

---

[55] Criminal Procedure Act 1967, s.4E(6).
[56] Criminal Justice Act 1984, ss.18 and 19, as amended by the Criminal Justice Act 1999, s.16(1) & (2).
[57] Criminal Justice (Forensic Evidence) Act 1990, s.3(1)(a)(i), as amended by the Criminal Justice Act 1999, s.17(1).
[58] *ibid.* s.3(1) as amended by s.17(2).

Advance Notice

Where the accused is charged with the offence of membership of an unlawful organisation contrary to section 21 of the Offences against the State Act 1939 he must normally give advance notice of his intention to call any person on his behalf at the trial.[59] Although it is by no means certain, it would appear that this obligation extends to the situation where the accused intends to call any person to give evidence on his behalf on an application to dismiss. The notice must be given in writing to the solicitor for the prosecution within a period of 14 days after the date on which the accused was served with the book of evidence.[60]

4. The Decision

The Issue

14–16   Where an application for dismissal is brought under these provisions the task for the court of trial is to decide whether the application has established that there is not a sufficient case to put the accused on trial for one or more of the charges. If it decides that there is not a sufficient case then it must dismiss the charge or charges in question.[61] This differs from the situation under the old preliminary examination where the District Court had to decide whether the prosecution had established that there was sufficient case to put the accused on trial. Under the current procedure it would appear that the onus rests on the accused to establish that there is not a sufficient case. Nevertheless, the standard is the same. In order to establish that there is not a sufficient case the accused will have to show that a reasonable jury properly charged could not convict the accused of the charges on the evidence presented.

Amending the Indictment

Significantly, the current provisions do not specifically give the trial court the power to amend a charge or charges in the indictment on an application for dismissal. Either it must reject the application or grant it. In the latter event it must dismiss the charge or charges in question. By contrast, under the preliminary examination procedure the District Court had the power to have the accused charged and sent forward for trial for an offence other than that specified on the indictment. It can be argued, of course, that the trial court can amend the indictment pursuant to its general power under the Criminal Justice (Administration) Act 1924 (see chapter 15 on indictment), and the very similar power conferred by the Criminal Procedure Act 1967 (see below).[62] These provisions enable the trial court to amend a defective indictment. The

---

[59]   Offences against the State (Amendment) Act 1998, s.3.
[60]   *ibid.* s.3(5) & (7).
[61]   Criminal Procedure Act 1967, s.4E(4).
[62]   Criminal Justice (Administration) Act 1924, s.6; and the Criminal Procedure Act 1967, s.4O, as amended by the Criminal Justice Act 1999, s.9.

provision in the 1924 Act has been interpreted to enable the trial court to amend the indictment by the addition (or substitution) of new counts in certain circumstances (see chapter on indictment). It is possible, therefore, that the trial court could use this power to amend an indictment and reject an application for dismissal, in circumstances where it might otherwise have felt compelled to dismiss the charges due to weaknesses in the indictment. There is also provision for the addition or substitution of charges in the indictment after the accused has been sent forward for trial. This is considered further below.

Result

Where the trial court grants an application to dismiss the charge or charges it **14–17** would appear that this operates as a complete dismissal. Any further attempt by the prosecutor to charge the accused with offences arising out of the same matter could be met with the defence of double jeopardy. However, the DPP can appeal a decision by the trial court to dismiss the charges on an application to dismiss under these provisions. The DPP can appeal against the dismissal to the Court of Criminal Appeal within 21 days after the date of the dismissal decision.[63] On such an appeal the Court of Criminal Appeal may either affirm or quash the decision of the trial court.[64] Where it quashes the decision the trial of the accused may proceed as if the charge had never been dismissed.[65]

Appeal

The legislation does not specifically confer a right of appeal on an accused **14–18** against a rejection of his application to dismiss. There may be scope, however, to bring several applications to dismiss. It is not at all clear whether the accused can bring more than one application to have a charge or charges dismissed. A literal interpretation of the relevant provisions would suggest that there is nothing to prevent multiple applications. In practice, of course, the trial court is unlikely to entertain subsequent applications in the absence of new evidence or changed circumstances.

5. Other matters

Timing

It is worth noting that the statutory provisions do not impose a specific time limit on when an application for dismissal can be taken. They merely stipulate that an application can be taken at any time after the accused is sent forward for trial. It is arguable, therefore, that an application could be brought after the trial has commenced. In other words the accused could make an application for dismissal at the close of the prosecution case, in much the same fashion as a submission of no case to answer. It would appear, however,

---

[63] Criminal Procedure Act 1967, s.4E(7).
[64] *ibid.* s.4E(8).
[65] *ibid.* s.4(8)(b).

that the legislative intention is to confine an application for dismissal to the period between the date on which the accused is sent forward for trial and the date on which the trial commences. This can be deduced from the wording of the court's power to dismiss any charge which is the subject of an application. The relevant provision stipulates that the court may dismiss such charge or charges "[i]f it appears . . . that there is not a sufficient case to put the accused on trial for any charge to which the application relates . . . ".[66] The implication is that the application should be brought before the accused is actually put on trial.

No Case to Answer

Presumably, it is still possible to make a submission of no case to answer at the close of the prosecution case, even where an unsuccessful application for dismissal had been brought earlier. The legislation does not specifically address the relationship between the application for dismissal and the submission of no case to answer.

New Evidence

14–19 The fact that an accused can bring an application under these provisions at any point after he or she has been sent forward for trial sits uneasily with the fact that the DPP enjoys a broad freedom to add to the book of evidence throughout the same period. It is not difficult to imagine the DPP responding to some applications for dismissal by relying on sources of evidence which have not been disclosed or detailed in the documents already served on the accused. Clearly, this has the potential to operate unfairly against the accused. The statutory provisions in question grant only partial protection. They stipulate that where the trial court is satisfied that it is in the interests of justice for a document to be served on the accused at the hearing of an application for dismissal, the DPP must serve the document on the accused at the hearing.[67] If the court considers it appropriate to do so, it may adjourn the hearing for that purpose. The document in question must be one which the DPP is under an obligation to serve on the accused by virtue of the Act. This, of course, helps to protect the accused against having to argue in favour of a dismissal while being kept in the dark about evidentiary sources relied on by the DPP. It does not, however, protect the accused against the risk of mounting a challenge to the DPP's case as presented in the book of evidence, only to find that the weaknesses in the case are remedied by documentation produced at the hearing of the application itself.

C. Taking Evidence in the District Court

1. Introduction

14–20 Under the preliminary examination procedure evidence could be taken by way of sworn deposition. Such depositions could be considered by the District Court

---

[66] *ibid.* s.4E(4).
[67] *ibid.* s.4E(6).

judge in deciding whether to send the accused forward for trial. Equally, in certain circumstances, they could be admitted and read as evidence at the actual trial of the accused. The abolition of the preliminary examination has required some consequential changes in the legislation governing the taking and application of depositions from witnesses. While the procedure for taking pre-trial depositions from witnesses has changed the basic facility still exists. Moreover, as indicated above such depositions may be considered by the trial court in an application to dismiss.

2. The Power

At any time after the accused is sent forward for trial the DPP or the accused may apply to the trial court for an order requiring a person to appear before a judge of the District Court so that the person's evidence may be taken either by way of sworn deposition, or through a live television link in the case of a person whose evidence is to be given through a live television link pursuant to Part III of the Criminal Evidence Act 1992 or section 39 of the Criminal Justice Act 1999.[68] If the trial court thinks that it would be in the interests of justice to do so, it may order the person in question to attend before a judge of the District Court in the District Court district in which the offence was committed, or in which the accused was arrested or resides, so that the judge may take the person's evidence accordingly.[69] A judge of the District Court has the same powers for enforcing compliance by a prospective witness with these provisions, and any order made under them, as the District Court enjoys in relation to witnesses in criminal proceedings (see below).[70] The same applies to securing the attendance of the accused.[71] However, a judge of the District Court cannot exercise these powers to require the attendance of a person before that court for the purpose of taking a sworn deposition if it appears to the judge that the person is outside the State, or that it is not reasonably practicable to secure his attendance before the court.[72]

14–21

---

[68] *ibid.* s.4F(1). Pt III of the Criminal Evidence Act 1992 permits evidence to be given through a live television link in certain circumstances in respect of sexual offences or offences involving violence or the threat of violence, while s.39 of the Criminal Justice Act 1999 permits evidence to be given through a live television link in certain circumstances where the court is satisfied that the witness is likely to be in fear or subject to intimidation in giving evidence.

[69] Criminal Procedure Act 1967, s.4F(2). District Court Rules 1997, Ord.24, r.14, as amended by District Court (Criminal Justice) Rules 2001, r.8 and Sched. 11. See Forms 24.11 and 24.12, Sched. B, as amended by Sched. 12 of the 2001 Rules.

[70] Criminal Procedure Act 1967, s.4F(4)(a). District Court Rules 1997, Ord.24, r.15, as amended by the District Court (Criminal Justice) Rules 2001, r.8 and Sched. 11. A warrant for the arrest of a person who fails to attend in answer to a summons shall be in accordance with Form 24.13, Sched. B, as amended by Sched. 12 to the 2001 Rules.

[71] Criminal Procedure Act 1967, s.4F(4)(b). District Court Rules 1997, Ord.24, rr.16 and 17, as amended by the District Court (Criminal Justice) Rules 2001, r.8 and Sched. 11. A summons or warrant for securing the attendance of the accused shall be in accordance with Form 24.14 or 24.15, Sched. B as the case may be, as amended by Sched. 12 to the 2001 Rules. A warrant for the arrest of an accused who fails to attend in answer to a summons shall be in accordance with Form 24.17, as amended by Sched. 12 to the 2001 Rules . If he is already in custody it shall be in accordance with Form 24.16, as amended.

[72] Criminal Law (Jurisdiction) Act 1976, s.18, as amended by the Criminal Justice Act 1999, s.14.

An application can be made under these provisions either by the DPP or the accused, and it can be made in respect of a person whether or not that person's name appears on the list of witnesses served on the accused by the DPP in the book of evidence (or in additions thereto).

3. The Procedure

14–22   Where the trial court grants an application under these provisions, the person in question will be required to attend before a judge of the District Court in the relevant District Court district so that the judge may take his evidence. Presumably, this does not require a physical presence where the evidence is to be given through a live television link. When his or her evidence is being taken both the accused and a judge of the District Court must be present. The wording suggests that evidence cannot be taken through this procedure unless the accused is actually present.[73] Indeed, before the evidence can be taken the judge must inform the accused of the circumstances in which the evidence may be admitted in evidence at his or her trial (see below).[74]

The legislation stipulates that the witness may be cross-examined and re-examined.[75] However, it does not expressly state who shall examine the witness. Presumably, the examination will be carried out by the party for whom the person is a witness, and not necessarily by the party who lodged the application for the witness to be called. Where the evidence is taken by way of sworn deposition (as distinct from a live television link) the deposition and any cross-examination and re-examination shall be recorded, read to the deponent and signed by the deponent and the judge.[76] Where a deposition is taken under these provisions after the accused has been sent forward for trial, the clerk shall transmit the deposition to the appropriate County Registrar.[77]

Where the offence in question is a sexual offence, evidence cannot be adduced, nor can a witness be asked, about the previous sexual history of the victim with a person other than the accused without the leave of the judge.[78] The judge must refuse an application for leave unless he or she is satisfied it would be likely to be given at the trial.[79] If the judge is satisfied that leave would be granted at the trial then he or she must grant an application for leave.[80]

---

[73] The judge in question has the same powers to secure his or her attendance as the District Court enjoys in relation to witnesses in criminal proceedings; Criminal Procedure Act 1967, s.4F(4)(b).

[74] Criminal Procedure Act 1967, s.4F(3)(b).

[75] *ibid.* s.4F(3)(c).

[76] *ibid.* s.4F(3)(d). District Court Rules 1997, Ord.24, r.18, as amended by the District Court (Criminal Justice) Rules 2001, r.8 and Sched. 11 states that the deposition shall be in accordance with Form 24.18 Sched. B, as amended by Sched. 12 to the 2001 Rules.

[77] District Court Rules 1997, Ord.24, r.18, as amended by the District Court (Criminal Justice) Rules 2001, r.8(a) and Sched. 11.

[78] Criminal Law (Rape) Act 1981, s.4(1), as amended by the Criminal Justice Act 1999, s.15.

[79] *Ibid.* s.4(2)(a).

[80] *Ibid.* s.4(2)(b).

4. Admissibility of Deposition on an Application to Dismiss

As will be seen below, the DPP might avail of this procedure to take evidence **14–23** from a witness who is not expected to live long enough to give evidence at the trial or who, for some other reason, will be unavailable or unwilling to give evidence at the trial. However, there is no fundamental reason, of course, why the accused cannot also seek to use these provisions for the same reasons as the DPP. Equally it is always possible that the accused could use the procedure for the purpose of testing the evidence of one or more witnesses for the prosecution for the purposes of an application for dismissal. A deposition taken under these provisions can be considered by the trial court on an application for the dismissal of one or more charges.[81] In other words the deposition and application for dismissal provisions might be used together to go some way towards achieving one of the primary advantages of the former preliminary examination procedure. It is worth noting, however, that there is no specific provision permitting the trial court to consider a video-recording of the evidence of a witness taken by way of a live television link (as distinct from a deposition) pursuant to these provisions on an application for dismissal. The clear implication is that the video-recording cannot be considered on such an application.

It is also worth emphasising that the trial court can issue an order under these provisions only if it is satisfied that it would be in the interests of justice to do so. Even then the trial court retains a discretion as to whether or not a deposition will be considered in an application to dismiss one or more charges.

5. Admissibility of Depositions and Video-Recordings at the Trial

Unless the trial court is of the opinion that it would not be in the interests of **14–24** justice to do so, a sworn deposition taken from a witness under the provisions described above can be admitted in evidence in certain circumstances at the trial of the accused.[82] The deposition may be admitted in evidence if it is proved that the witness in question: (i) is dead[82a]; (ii) is unable to attend to give evidence at the trial; (iii) is prevented from so attending; or (iv) does not give evidence at the trial through fear or intimidation. It must also be proved that the accused was present at the taking of the evidence and that an opportunity was given to cross-examine and re-examine the witness.

There is separate provision for the admission of a person's evidence which has been taken through a live television link pursuant to an order of the trial court. A video recording of the evidence can be admitted in certain circumstances as evidence of any fact stated therein of which direct oral evidence by the witness would be admissible.[83] The preconditions are that the accused must have been present at the taking of the evidence by live television link;

---

[81] Criminal Procedure Act 1967, s.4G(1).

[82] *ibid.* s.4G(2).

[82a] It would appear that death can be proved for this purpose by circumstantial evidence; see *Mulligan v. Judges of the Circuit Criminal Court*, unreported, Supreme Court, May 19, 1999.

[83] Criminal Procedure Act 1967, s.4G(3).

and there must have been an opportunity to cross-examine and re-examine the witness. Where these conditions are satisfied the video-recording of the evidence will be admissible as evidence of any fact stated therein unless the trial court is of the opinion that in the interests of justice the video-recording ought not to be so admitted.[84]

6. Broader Implications

14–25   These provisions represent a significant development on the pre-existing law. Whereas before only the DPP could make an application for evidence to be taken by way of deposition or a live television link after the accused had been sent forward for trial, now an application can also be made by the accused. Previously, the application was made to a judge of the District Court who could only make an order if he or she was of the opinion that the witness was dead, or would be unable to attend or would be prevented from attending to give evidence at the trial. In the last two eventualities the order could be made only if the accused consented. Now the requirement for the accused's consent has been dropped, and an order can also be made if the person will not give evidence at the trial through fear or intimidation. Equally, an order can now be made in certain circumstances in respect of giving evidence given through a live television link pursuant to the provisions of Part III of the Criminal Evidence Act 1992, or section 39 of the Criminal Justice Act 1999.[85] A video-recording of such evidence may be admitted at the trial in certain circumstances.

The greater ease with which evidence can be taken before a judge of the District Court and subsequently admitted into evidence at the trial without the need to call the witness or witnesses in question has serious implications for the conduct of the criminal trial. Where the necessary prerequisites have been satisfied, a significant part of the criminal trial on indictment, perhaps the most significant part, can be held before a District Court judge. If, for example, the prosecution case against the accused is heavily dependant on the evidence of a former accomplice who has "done a deal" with the prosecution to give evidence against the accused, it is possible that the prosecution would seek to have this evidence taken by way of sworn deposition in the District Court on the ground that the witness would not give evidence at the trial due to fear or intimidation. If the trial court grants such an the application the former accomplice will not have to give his evidence at the actual trial. Instead the deposition of his evidence plus the cross-examination and re-examination can be read out and admitted into evidence, unless the court is of the opinion that

---

[84] In considering whether in the interests of justice such video-recording or part thereof ought not to be admitted in evidence, the court shall have regard to all the circumstances, including any risk that its admission will result in unfairness to the accused or, if there is more than one, to any of them; Criminal Procedure Act 1967, s.4G(3) and Criminal Evidence Act 1992, s.16(2)(b).

[85] Pt III of the Criminal Evidence Act 1992 permits evidence to be given through a live television link in certain circumstances in respect of sexual offences or offences involving violence or the threat of violence against the person, while s.39 of the Criminal Justice Act 1999 permits evidence to be given through a live television link in certain circumstances where the court is satisfied that the witness is likely to be in fear or subject to intimidation in giving evidence.

it would not be in the interests of justice to do so. While the accused will have the opportunity to cross examine the witness on his or her evidence in the District Court, the fact remains that the examination and cross-examination will have been conducted in the absence of the jury. It follows that the jury will not have witnessed the examination and cross-examination of the witness whose evidence is absolutely critical to their determination on guilt.

D. Legal Aid

1. District Court

The legal aid (District Court) certificate provisions apply to District Court proceedings under these provisions.[86] It follows that if the defendant satisfies the current requirements for legal aid in the District Court he or she also qualifies for legal aid for the purposes of: contesting an application by the prosecutor for an extension of time for the service of the book of evidence; the proceedings in which he is before the court for the purpose of being sent forward for trial; and the taking of evidence from a witness pursuant to an order of the trial court. See chapter 11 for further detail on legal aid qualifications and entitlements in the District Court.

14–26

2. Trial Court and Appeals

The legal aid (trial on indictment) certificate provisions extend to the accused in relation to all proceedings under these provisions before the trial court, the Court of Criminal Appeal or an alternative court (see later).[87] It follows that if the defendant satisfies the current requirements for legal aid under a trial on indictment certificate he or she qualifies for legal aid for: an application to the trial court for dismissal of a charge or charges; an appeal by the prosecutor to the Court of Criminal Appeal against the trial court's dismissal of a charge or charges under the provisions described above; and an application to the trial court for an order requiring a person to appear before a judge of the District Court so that his or her evidence may be taken by way of sworn deposition or live television link. See chapter 11 for further detail on legal aid qualifications and entitlements in these courts.

E. Publicity

1. Introduction

The place in which the District Court sits to hear proceedings under Part 1A of the Criminal Procedure Act 1967 is generally deemed an open court to

14–27

---

86 Criminal Procedure Act 1967, s.4H(1).
87 *ibid.* s.4H(2).

which the public generally may have access so far as they can be accommodated.[88] There is always the danger, of course, that the accused's right to a fair trial could be prejudiced by such open access or by excessive publicity being given to the evidence presented against him in pre-trial proceedings, such as an application to dismiss the charges. Potential jurors who read about or hear the evidence may form an opinion about the case which could affect their judgement if and when they are selected to serve on the jury. Accordingly, there are limitations on who may be present during these proceedings and on what can be published about them.

2. Power to Exclude the Public

14–28   As a general rule, a proceeding under the provisions described above must be conducted in open court.[89] As was the case with the preliminary examination, however, there is provision for the public, a section of the public or individuals to be excluded. Where the court conducting the proceeding is satisfied, because of the nature or circumstances of the case or otherwise in the interests of justice, that it is desirable to do so, it may exclude from the court during the proceeding the public or any portion of the public or any particular person or persons.[90] Bona fide representatives of the press cannot be excluded under this provision. Equally, this power to exclude does not override the right of a parent, relative or friend of the accused or of an injured party to remain in court in certain cases.[91] The cases in question are: where the accused is under 18 years of age; where the offence in question is of an indecent or obscene nature and the person with or against whom it is alleged to have been committed is under that age or is a female[92]; and a rape or aggravated sexual assault.[93]

These provisions are generally in line with the pre-existing law applicable to a preliminary examination. The primary difference is that they extend beyond the District Court to include relevant proceedings in the trial court and the Court of Criminal Appeal. It is also worth emphasising that the power to exclude (and the limitations thereto) under these provisions is exercisable only where the nature or circumstances of the case or the interests of justice make it desirable that it should be exercised. This does not affect other powers which the court may have to exclude one or more individuals from the proceedings.

---

[88] District Court Rules 1997, Ord.14, r.1, as amended by the District Court (Criminal Justice) Rules 2001, r.3(a).
[89] Criminal Procedure Act 1967, s.4I(1).
[90] Criminal Procedure Act 1967, s.4I(2); District Court Rules 1997, Ord.14, r.3, as amended by the District Court (Criminal Justice) Rules 2001, r.3(b).
[91] Criminal Procedure Act 1967, s.4I(3). There is no definition of an "injured party". Presumably it refers to the alleged victim.
[92] Criminal Justice Act 1951, s.20(4).
[93] Criminal Law (Rape) Act 1981, s.6, as amended by the Criminal Law (Rape) (Amendment) Act 1990, s.11.

3. Publication of Proceedings

There are severe restrictions on what can be published or broadcast about pro-   **14–29**
ceedings taken under the provisions described above.[94] For the most part
these restrictions are identical to those previously applicable to the preliminary examination. The publication or broadcast of any information about a
proceeding under these provisions is prohibited, apart from a statement of the
fact that the proceeding was brought by a named person in relation to a
specified charge against a specified person and the decision resulting from the
proceeding.[95] The judge hearing an application for dismissal may also permit
the publication or broadcast of information at the request of the accused.[96]

Where, on the application of the DPP, it appears to a judge of the District
Court that a person has published or broadcast material in breach of this
prohibition, he or she may certify to that effect to the High Court.[97] After
inquiring into the matter and hearing any witnesses and any statement offered
in defence of the person alleged to have contravened the prohibition, the High
Court may punish, or take steps for the punishment of, that person as if he
had been guilty of contempt of the High Court.[98]

It is worth noting that these provisions do not affect the operation of any
enactment which imposes further restrictions on the extent to which information relating to court proceedings may be published or broadcast.[99] Nor do
they affect any power conferred on a court by such enactment to make an
order authorising the publication or broadcast of such information.[100]

F. Witness Order and Summons

1. Introduction

There is provision for the trial court to issue witness orders and witness sum-   **14–30**
mons to compel the attendance of witnesses at the trial to give evidence and to
produce relevant documents or things. These provisions relate specifically to the
trial. There is no express provision for the court to compel the attendance of
witnesses at an application to dismiss, while there is separate provision for the
appearance of persons to give evidence by way of deposition or through a live
television link before a judge of the District Court.[101]

---

[94] For this purpose "publish" means publish to the public or a portion of the public, and "broadcast"
means the transmission, relaying or distribution by wireless telegraphy of communications,
sounds, signs, visual images or signals, intended for direct reception by the general public whether
or not such communications, sounds, signs, visual images or signals are actually received;
Criminal Procedure Act 1967, s.4J(5).

[95] Criminal Procedure Act 1967, s.4J(1)(a); District Court Rules 1997, Ord.14, r.5(1). As amended
by the District Court (Criminal Justice) Rules 2001, r.3(c) .

[96] Criminal Procedure Act 1967, s.4J(1)(b).

[97] *ibid.* s.4J(2). The certificate shall be in accordance with Form 14.1, Sched. B, see the District
Court Rules 1997, Ord.14, r.6, as amended by the District Court (Criminal Justice) Rules 2001,
r.3(d) and (e) and Sched. 2 to the 1997 Rules for the amended form.

[98] Criminal Procedure Act 1967, s.4J(3).

[99] *ibid.* s.4J(4)(a).

[100] *ibid.* s.4J(4)(b).

[101] *ibid.* s.4F(4)(a).

2. Witness Order

Where an accused has been sent forward for trial, the trial court may, in relation to the trial, make a witness order requiring a person whose statement was served on the accused or whose deposition was taken to attend before the trial court and give evidence at the trial of the accused.[102] The order may also require the person to produce to the court any document or thing specified in the order.[103] Any person who, without just excuse, disobeys such an order is guilty of contempt of the trial court.[104]

If, on the application of the DPP or the accused, the trial court is satisfied by evidence on oath that a particular person is unlikely to comply with a witness order, the court may bind the person by recognisance to appear at the trial.[105] If the person concerned refuses to be so bound the court may issue a warrant committing him to custody until the trial or until he enters into the recognisance.[106] For the purpose of exercising these powers the trial court has the same powers to enforce the attendance of witnesses before it as it has to enforce the attendance of witnesses in criminal proceedings.[107] The provisions are virtually identical to the current position with respect to witness orders, subject to the fact that the trial court replaces the District Court.

3. Witness Summons

A witness order is issued by the court on its own initiative with respect to persons whose evidence has been served on the accused or whose deposition was taken before a judge of the District Court. There is also provision for the DPP and the accused to have persons summonsed to give evidence before the trial court. Indeed, for the accused the witness summons is a very necessary device to ensure that witnesses whom he or she wishes to call actually come to court and give evidence.

On the application of the DPP or the accused a witness summons may issue out of the trial court requiring the person to whom it is directed to attend before the trial court and give evidence at the trial of the accused.[108] It may also direct him or her to produce to the court any document or thing specified in the summons.[109] The summons cannot issue if the court is satisfied that the person in question cannot give any material evidence or, as the case may be, produce any document or thing likely to be material evidence. A person who disobeys a witness summons without just excuse shall be guilty of contempt of the court out of which the summons was issued.[110]

---

[102] *ibid.* s.4K(1)(a).
[103] *ibid.* s.4K(1)(b).
[104] *ibid.* s.4K(2).
[105] *ibid.* s.4K(3)(a).
[106] *ibid.* s.4K(3)(b).
[107] *ibid.* s.4K(3)(c).
[108] *ibid.* s.4L(1)(a).
[109] *ibid.* s.4L(1)(b).
[110] *ibid.* s.4L(2).

It is worth noting that the power to issue a witness summons under these provisions is a discretionary power. The court will exercise this discretion to ensure that the power is not used oppressively or for purposes which would amount to an abuse of the judicial process. If, for example, the court is satisfied that the person who is the subject of a witness summons application cannot give any material evidence or produce any document or thing likely to be material evidence, it will not issue the summons.

These provisions empowering the trial court to issue a witness summons are without prejudice to any other powers for enforcing the attendance of witnesses at the trial.[111]

G. Amendment, etc., of Charges

1. The Power

The Criminal Justice (Administration) Act 1924 empowers the trial court to amend a defective indictment.[112] This power has been virtually duplicated in the Criminal Procedure Act 1967 as a result of amendments effected by the Criminal Justice Act 1999. The latter stipulates that where the accused has been sent forward for trial under Part 1A of the 1967 Act the trial court may correct any defect in a charge against the accused unless it considers that the correction would result in injustice.[113] As explained in the chapter on indictment the power in the 1924 Act has been interpreted to mean that the trial court can add counts to an indictment and substitute counts for counts on the indictment in certain circumstances. Now, however, the 1967 Act (as amended) makes specific provision for the addition or substitution of counts on an indictment.

14–31

2. New Counts Founded on Existing Documents

Where the accused has been sent forward for trial under Part 1A of the 1967 Act the indictment may include, either in substitution for or in addition to counts charging the offence for which he has been sent forward, counts which are founded on any of the documents served on the accused and which may lawfully be joined in the same indictment.[114] Although it does not specifically say so, the clear implication is that the indictment may be amended to add (or substitute) the new counts. What is less clear is who can effect the amendment and at what point? The legislation is silent on these matters. Presumably, the additions or substitutions can be made by the DPP. The only express restrictions are that the new counts must be founded on the documents already served on the accused, and they must be counts which can lawfully be joined in the same indictment (see chapter on indictment for the rules on joinder). There is at least an implication here that this power cannot be used to replace all of the counts on

---

[111] *ibid.* s.4L(3).
[112] Criminal Justice (Administration) Act 1924, s.6. See chap.15 on indictment.
[113] Criminal Procedure Act 1967, s.4Ord.
[114] *ibid.* s.4M.

the original indictment with new counts. It is also worth noting that the legislation does not provide an express power to serve a new indictment on the accused after he or she has been sent forward for trial under these provisions.

3. Completely New Counts

The 1967 Act as amended, also makes provision for the indictment to include counts which are not founded on the documents served on the accused, apart from those for which the accused was sent forward for trial.[115] The counts must charge an offence justiciable within the State. The inclusion of such counts is possible only after the accused has been sent forward for trial and has consented to their inclusion. Once again there is no indication as to who can add the new counts to the indictment. Presumably the power rests with the DPP, although it can be exercised only with the consent of the accused.

H. Remand to Alternative Court

14–32   When the accused has been sent forward for trial to the Circuit Court there may be a considerable delay before the trial commences. It is likely, there-fore, that the accused will appear from time to time before the Circuit Court to be further remanded. Where the accused is in custody and the prison or place of detention is located a considerable distance from the circuit of the Circuit Court which remanded him in custody, this will present considerable inconvenience for all concerned. Accordingly, there is provision for the Circuit Court to which the accused has been sent forward for trial to remand him in custody to appear at a sitting of the Circuit Court in the circuit in which is situated the relevant prison or place of detention.[116] For the purposes of these provisions this court is known as the alternative court.

Where the accused has been remanded to an alternative court it may from time to time as the occasion requires further remand him in custody or on bail to that court or to another alternative court.[117] This court shall be treated as the trial court for the purposes of an application from the DPP for an extension of time to serve the book of evidence on the accused, for an application to dismiss a charge or the charges and for the purposes of a transfer to the Central Criminal Court, where relevant.[118] The alternative court also has the same power as the trial court to correct any defect in the charge against the accused.[119]

---

[115] *ibid.* s.4N.

[116] *ibid.* s.4Q(1).

[117] *ibid.* s.4Q(2)(a).

[118] *ibid.* s.4Q(2)(b). It is not clear how the issue of an extension of time in which to serve the book of evidence could arise before an alternative court since an accused cannot be remanded to an alternative court until he has been sent forward for trial, and he cannot be sent forward for trial until the book of evidence has been served.

[119] Criminal Procedure Act 1967, s.4Q(2)(c).

The alternative court cannot actually try the accused for the offence. For this purpose it must remand the accused to a sitting of the Circuit Court in the circuit of the Circuit Court in which the offence was committed or in which the accused was arrested or resides.[120]

I. Transfer of Jurisdiction

1. Introduction

It was seen in chapter two that the country is divided up into seven circuits for the purposes of exercising the jurisdiction of the Circuit Court. As a general rule, the criminal jurisdiction of the court is exercised by the judge or judges of the circuit in which the offence in question was committed or in which the accused resides or has been arrested.[121] This can give rise to difficulty in certain circumstances, particularly where there is a risk that a local jury might be unduly prejudiced for or against the defendant. It may be, for example, that the defendant has earned such a notorious reputation in the locality that a local jury would find it difficult to approach the question of his innocence or guilt with an open mind. Equally, it may be that the nature of the offence charged has attracted such notoriety locally that it would be difficult for any jury drawn from the local community to bring an impartial and dispassionate judgement to bear on the case. On the other hand there may be a risk that a local jury would be unduly sympathetic towards the defendant and/or prejudiced against his victim. Equally, there may be a risk that the jury would be intimidated by the accused or his associates.

14–33

Whatever the reason, it is necessary to have some mechanism for the transfer of the trial of a case to another circuit or to another part of the circuit where that is deemed necessary in order for justice to be done and to be seen to be done in the case. At one time either the accused or the prosecution could apply to have a trial transferred to the Central Criminal Court in any case where the accused had been returned for trial to the Circuit Court, including the Dublin Circuit Court.[122] The Courts Act 1981 changed this to the effect that the accused or the prosecution could apply to have the case transferred from any sitting of the Circuit Court outside Dublin to the Dublin Circuit Court.[123] The current provisions are to be found in the Courts and Court Officers Act 1995.

2. Transfer to Dublin Circuit

Where an accused person has been sent forward for trial to the Circuit Court, sitting outside of the Dublin Circuit, either the prosecution or the accused can

14–34

---

[120] Criminal Procedure Act 1967, s.4Q(3).
[121] Courts (Supplemental Provisions) Act 1961, s.25(3).
[122] Courts Act 1964, s.6.
[123] Courts Act 1981, s.31.

apply to have the trial of the case transferred to the Dublin Circuit.[124] The application is made to the Circuit Court judge before whom the case is triable.[125] If the judge is satisfied that it would be manifestly unjust not to do so, he or she may transfer the trial to the Circuit sitting within the Dublin Circuit. The judge's decision is final and unappealable. It should be noted, however, that the power only extends to the transfer of a trial from the sitting of the Circuit Court outside Dublin to the sitting within the Dublin Circuit. There is no power to transfer a trial from the Circuit Court to the Central Criminal Court.

Complications can arise where two or more accused are sent forward for trial together and not all of them applies to have the trial transferred. In this event if the judge grants the application for transfer the prosecution may apply to the judge who granted the application to have the trial of one or more of the remaining accused transferred to the sitting of the Dublin Circuit Court. The judge must grant such an application.[126]

3. Transfer within the Circuit

14–35   There is provision for the transfer of the trial of a case from one place to another within a circuit. Either the prosecution or the accused may apply to a judge of the Circuit Court to transfer the trial of the case, or any criminal issue, from the place in his or her circuit where it is required by law to be held to any other place within that circuit.[127] The judge may order the transfer if he or she thinks fit, and he or she may provide for matters ancillary or incidental to the transfer.[128] The judge's decision is final and unappealable.[129] Where a judge makes an order under this provision the trial will be held at the place to which it has been transferred with a jury drawn from the jury district or other area prescribed for trials by the Circuit Court sitting in that place.

4. Transfer to Central Criminal Court

14–36   Where the accused has been sent forward for trial to the Circuit Court for one offence and is then sent forward for trial to the Central Criminal Court for another offence connected with or arising from the circumstances which gave rise to the first offence, the Circuit may transfer the first offence to the Central Criminal Court.[130] This option is not available where the Circuit Court considers that it would not be in the interests of justice to make the transfer.

---

[124] Courts and Court Officers Act 1995, s.32(1).
[125] Provision may be made by rules of court for the giving of notice of intention to make an application and the grounds upon which the application will be based; Courts and Court Officers Act 1995, s.32(2).
[126] Courts and Court Officers Act 1995, s.32(3).
[127] Courts (Supplemental Provisions) Act 1961, s.26(1).
[128] *ibid.* s.26(2)(b).
[129] *ibid.* s.26(2)(c).
[130] Criminal Procedure Act 1967, s.4P.

5. Transfer to Special Criminal Court

There is provision enabling the DPP to transfer a trial to the Special Criminal   **14–37**
Court. This is dealt with fully in chapter 20.

J. Applications for Separate Trials

1. Separate Trials for Different Counts

The Power

In the chapter on Indictment it was seen that the prosecution could join   **14–38**
several counts in a single indictment so long as they are founded on the same
facts or form part of a series of offences of the same or a similar character.
This can result in a number of distinct offences being joined together in a
single indictment. If this is likely to cause inconvenience for the prosecution
it can elect to proceed for the time being on one or more of the counts,
leaving open the possibility of proceeding with the others at a later time. The
more likely consequence of joining several separate offences in the same
indictment is that the accused will be prejudiced or embarrassed in the
conduct of his defence to one or more of the counts. The Criminal Justice
(Administration) Act 1924 offers protection against this risk. It stipulates:

> "Where before trial or at any stage of a trial, the court is of opinion that a
> person accused may be prejudiced or embarrassed in his defence by reason of
> being charged with more than one offence in the same indictment, or that for
> any other reason it is desirable to direct that the person should be tried
> separately for any one or more offences charged in an indictment, the court
> may order a separate trial of any count or counts of such indictment."[131]

This provision is expressed in directory rather than mandatory terms.
Accordingly, the judge is not under a duty to direct separate trials on the
application of the accused. He must exercise his discretion judicially to protect the accused against prejudice or embarrassment.

The inclusion of a number of several sexual offences is often problematic,
particularly if there is a danger that the jury's acceptance of corroboration in
relation to one charge might be accepted as corroboration of the other charges.
In *Attorney General v. Duffy*,[131a] for example, it was held that the accused had
been prejudiced by the joint trial of a number of charges of gross indecency
owing to the risk of cross-corroboration. It has also been held that several
counts alleging offences of a sexual nature against different victims should be
tried separately, unless the circumstances of their commission are sufficiently
similar to bring them within the scope of the similar fact rule in evidence.[131b]

---

[131] Criminal Justice (Administration) Act 1924, s.6(3).
[131a] [1931] I.R. 144.
[131b] *DPP v. Boardman, op. cit.; R. v. Scarrott* [1978] Q.B. 1016.

The principles governing the severing of an indictment in the context of "similar fact" evidence was considered by the Court of Criminal Appeal in *DPP v. Kelly*.[131c] In that case, the accused was convicted on several counts of attempted buggery and indecent assault on young boys in his care. His application to have the counts tried separately was refused by the trial judge. He appealed on the ground, *inter alia*, that each of the counts should have been tried separately. Giving the judgment of the court, Barron J. explained that in most cases the real test with respect to whether several counts should be tried together is whether the evidence in respect of each of them would be admissible on each of the other counts. For the evidence to be admissible its probative value would have to outweigh its prejudicial effect. In practice, that means applying a "similar fact" test. For this purpose Barron J. helpfully distinguished between "system evidence" which would be admissible and "similar fact" evidence which would not be admissible. The latter refers to the situation where evidence that the accused acted in a certain way on one occasion is proffered as proof that he acted in the same way on another occasion. Such evidence is not admissible *per se* for that purpose. There would have to be some further nexus between the two occasions to permit evidence of one to be admitted as proof on the other. That further nexus can be satisfied by "system evidence". This refers to the situation where the manner in which a particular act was done on one occasion suggests that it was also done on another occasion by the same person and with the same intent. The difficulty, of course, is establishing when the requirements of "system evidence" have been satisfied on the facts of any individual case.

In *Kelly*, Barron J. reviewed some of the leading authorities in the English Court of Criminal Appeal, the House of Lords and the Judicial Committee of the Privy Council. He emphasised the two distinct situations identified in the judgment of Lord Herschell LC in *Makin v. Attorney General for New South Wales*.[131d] The first concerns the situation where the prosecution presents evidence of previous criminal acts of the accused for the purpose of establishing that the accused is guilty of the offence charged because he is a person likely from his criminal conduct or character to have committed the offence in question. If the evidence goes no further than that it is inadmissible. Where there is nothing to connect the accused with the offence except bad character or similar crimes committed in the past it must be excluded as its prejudicial effect would outweigh its probative value. The second situation is where such evidence is relevant to an issue before the jury because it bears upon the question whether the acts alleged to constitute the crime charged in the indictment were designed or accidental, or to rebut a defence which would otherwise be open to the accused. In this event the evidence will be admissible. In *Boardman v. DPP* Lord Hailsham, with respect to this second situation, explained:

> "The truth is that a mere succession of facts is not normally enough whether the cases are many or limited to two . . . there must be something more than

---

[131c] Unreported, Court of Criminal Appeal, December 13, 1999.
[131d] [1894] A.C. 57 at 65.

mere repetition. But they must be as variously described as 'underlying unity', 'system', 'nexus', 'unity of intent, project, campaign or adventure', part of the same criminal conduct', 'striking resemblance'."[131e]

Similarly, Lord Cross, in the same case, said:

"A Viscount Simon said in *Harris v. Director of Public Prosecutions* [1952] A.C. 694, 705, it is not possible to compile an exhaustive list of the sort of cases in which 'similar facts' evidence – to use a compendious phrase – is admissible. The question must always be whether the similar fact evidence taken together with the other evidence would do no more than raise or strengthen a suspicion that the accused committed the offence with which he is charged or would point so strongly to his guilt that only an ultra cautious jury, if they accepted it as true, would acquit in the face of it. In the end, although the admissibility of such evidence is a question of law, not of discretion – the question as I see it must be one of degree."[131f]

These passages were specifically approved by Barron J. in Kelly as showing the test to be applied when deciding whether evidence comes within the category of system evidence or similar fact evidence. He proceeded to quote from the judgment of Lord Mackay in *DPP v. P*[132] to the effect that system evidence was not confined to situations where there was a striking similarity in the manner of the commission of separate offences. Equally, he referred to the judgment of *Budd J. in B v. DPP*[133] to the effect that the probative value of multiple accusations may depend in part on their similarity but also on the unlikelihood that the same person would find himself falsely accused on various occasions by different and independent individuals. Barron J. attempted to summarise the principles emerging from all of these cases as follows:

"(1) The rules of evidence should not be allowed to offend common sense.
(2) So, where the probative value of the evidence outweighs its prejudicial effect, it may be admitted.
(3) The categories of cases in which the evidence which can be so admitted is not closed.
(4) Such evidence is admitted in two main types of cases:
  (a) to establish that the same person committed each offence because of the particular feature common to each; or
  (b) where the charges are against one person only, to establish that offences were committed.
In the latter case the evidence is admissible because:
  (a) there is the inherent improbability of several persons making up exactly similar stories;
  (b) it shows a practice which would rebut accident, innocent explanation or denial."

Applying these principles to the facts of the case in *Kelly*, Barron J. concluded that there was no system evidence simply on the basis that the

---

[131e] [1975] A.C. 421 at 452, approved by Barron J. in *Kelly, op. cit.*
[131f] *ibid.* at 457, approved by Barron J. in *Kelly, op. cit.*
[132] [1991] 2 A.C. 447.
[133] [1997] 3 I.R. 140.

accused was charged with attempted buggery and/or indecent assault against boys who were under his care as inmates of a residential institution for boys. At this level the evidence went no further than saying that because the accused was charged with the offences against one boy he is more likely to have committed the offences alleged against the other boys. Accordingly, the judge should have acceded to the defence request for separate trials in respect of these offences. A direction to the jury to treat them separately would not be sufficient to protect the accused against the prejudice which would be occasioned by them being tried together. For two of the offences, however, there was a sufficient connection. The evidence as to the manner of commission of these offences was sufficiently different to establish a "system". Each of these was alleged to have been committed in unusual but identical circumstances, namely; on a visit to a caravan; while the parties were sleeping in a double bed; in the same furtive manner; and by broadly similar actions. Barron J. concluded that these factors were sufficient to establish a system and to justify the trial judge's decision not to grant separate trials in respect of them.

For further discussion of "similar fact" evidence see chapter 19, paras. 19–35 et seq.

It does not follow that an indictment must be severed simply because it contains counts charging similar offences which have been committed in circumstances which do not satisfy the "system evidence" standard. Ultimately, the task for the judge is to exercise his or her discretion judicially to protect the accused against prejudice or embarrassment. While it might be considered there is always a higher risk of prejudice or embarrassment in such circumstances in the context of sexual offences, the same does not necessarily apply for all types of offence. So, for example, in R v. McGlinchey[134] the English Court of Appeal refused to quash the trial judge's exercise of discretion to refuse separate trials for a count of receiving stolen photographic equipment and a count of receiving a stolen credit card. The mere fact that separate trials may be appropriate for counts of sexual offences committed against different victims where there was no striking similarity between the crimes[135] did not mean that separate trials would be appropriate for non-sexual offences in similar circumstances. The key issue was whether, in the opinion of the judge, the accused would be embarrassed or prejudiced by a joint trial.[136] There was nothing in the McGlinchey case to suggest that the judge had not exercised his discretion judicially. Similarly, the mere fact that an indictment contains a large number of counts will not be sufficient in itself to require severance.[137]

---

[134] (1984) 74 Cr. App. Rep. 282.

[135] See DPP v. Boardman [1975] A.C. 421.

[136] R. v. Lockett [1914] 2 K.B. 720.

[137] See, e.g., Attorney General v. Reilly [1937] I.R. 118 where the indictment contained a large number of counts of obtaining by false pretences or fraudulent conversion of different sums of money. Also, People v. O'Connor (1943, vol 1) Frewen 42 where the indictment contained 44 counts relating to offences infringing an Order on the sale of tea, flour and other commodities.

If, however, the judge is of the opinion that there is some special feature in the case which would make a joint trial of the several counts prejudicial or embarrassing to the accused and that separate trials are required, it would appear that he or she is under a duty to order separate trials.[138] For example, it may be that there are so many distinct offences charged in the indictment that there is a real risk of the jury simply assuming that the accused must be guilty of something. Equally, the number and complexity of the charges may be such as to cause confusion in the minds of the jurors[139] or render it difficult for them to disentangle the evidence pertaining to one offence from the evidence pertaining to another.[140] Alternatively, it may be that the indictment contains a count which is so scandalous in nature and likely to arouse such hostility in the minds of the jurors that the trial of the accused for the other offences in the indictment will almost certainly be prejudiced by its inclusion.[141]

Discretion

The judge can sever the indictment where he or she is of the opinion that "for any other reason it is desirable to direct that the person should be tried separately for any one or more offences charged in an indictment."[142] As yet, however, it would appear that the circumstances in which this broader discretion might properly be exercised has not featured in the case law.

14–39

Procedure

An application to sever the indictment is normally taken immediately after the accused has pleaded to the indictment. If, however, the application is made and granted during the trial the court may order that the jury is to be discharged from giving a verdict on the count or counts the trial of which is postponed on the indictment.[143] The procedure on the separate trial of a count shall be the same in all respects as if the count had been preferred in a separate indictment.[144] It is also worth noting that the court has a power to postpone the trial where an order for severance is made whether before the trial or at any stage of the trial.[145] In this event it will have a similar power to discharge the jury as it has on an order for severance during the trial. Where an order for severance or postponement is made the court may make such order as to costs and as to admitting the accused to bail as it thinks fit.[146]

---

[138] *Ludlow v. Metropolitan Police Commissioner* [1971] A.C. 29; *People v. Wallace* unreported, Court of Criminal Appeals, November 22, 1982.
[139] *R. v. King* [1897] 1 QB 214; *R. v. Bailey* [1924] 2 K.B. 300.
[140] *R. v. Norman* [1915] 1 K.B. 341.
[141] *R. v. Southern* (1930) 22 Cr. App. Rep. 6; *R. v. Muir* [1938] 2 All E.R. 516; *R. v. Fitzpatrick* [1963] 1 WLR 7.
[142] Criminal Justice (Administration) Act 1924, s.6(3)
[143] Criminal Justice (Administration) Act 1924, s.6(5)(a).
[144] *ibid.* s.6(5)(b).
[145] *ibid.* s.6(4).
[146] *ibid.* s.6(5)(c).

2. Separate Trials of Different Accused

The Context

14–40 As a general rule it is desirable that two or more persons charged with the same offences, or separate offences arising out of the same incident, should be tried together. Not only does this save time and expense but it enables the jury to get a more complete picture of the crime or crimes in question.[147] Equally, however, the joint trial of several offences can present difficulties for both the prosecution and the defence. The most likely problems concern matters of evidence. For example, the prosecution may wish to secure a conviction against one accused for larceny and then call him as a witness against another accused on the same indictment for a count of receiving the goods in question. This would not be possible if both were tried together. Similarly, one accused may be prejudiced by an inculpatory statement made by another accused which implicates the former. Technically the statement is admissible only against the accused who made it. If the two accused are tried together, however, there is clearly a risk that the jury will be influenced by the statement when considering the case against the accused who was merely implicated by it. This risk would not arise if the two accused were tried separately by two different juries. It follows, therefore, that there are circumstances in which the interests of the prosecution or the defence will be prejudiced by the joint trial of two or more accused on a single indictment charging separate counts against each.

The Power

14–41 Accordingly, the trial judge has a power to order separate trials in the interests of justice. Unlike the power to sever an indictment it does not find expression in statute. Nevertheless, the exercise of the discretion in any individual case can be reviewed on appeal to the Court of Criminal Appeal. The nature and extent of the discretion is summed up in the following extract from the judgment of Sullivan P in the Court of Criminal Appeal in *Attorney General v. Joyce*:[148]

> "Where . . . persons jointly indicted plead not guilty, the trial Judge may direct that they be separately tried if, in his opinion, separate trials are desirable in the interests of justice. The trial Judge has a discretion in the matter which must be exercised judicially. The exercise of such discretion may be reviewed by this Court, and a retrial directed, if we are satisfied that a refusal to direct separate trials has resulted in a miscarriage of justice."[149]

---

[147] In upholding the trial judge's refusal to order separate trials in *People (Attorney General) v. Ryan* 1 Frewen 308, the Court of Criminal Appeal noted that the joint trial actually favoured the appellant's defence as it enabled the jury to contrast his involvement with that of other defendants including the principal.
[148] [1929] I.R. 526. See also *People v. Carney* [1955] I.R. 324; *People v. Mulcahy* 87 I.L.T.R. 137.
[149] *Ibid.* at 537.

Presumably, the discretion will be exercised to protect either the prosecution or the defence against the risk of prejudice resulting from the joint trial of two or more accused. In order to succeed, however, the applicant counsel will have to do more than merely state that he will be seriously embarrassed by a joint trial without indicating the nature or cause of that embarrassment.[150] Moreover, in deciding whether to exercise the discretion the judge will weigh in the balance the interests of justice in having the accused tried together. Even if the prosecution evidence includes a statement from one accused implicating another, that may not always be sufficient in itself to outweigh the arguments in favour of a joint trial.[151] According to Kenny J:

". . . the fact that one of the accused has made a statement which incriminates another of the accused is not by itself a matter which compels the trial Judge to grant separate trials: this is always a matter for the discretion of the trial Judge. When two or more accused are charged in connection with one trans-action, the interests of justice may require that they should be tried together even if a statement made by one of them incriminates another of them. When two or more persons are charged with a single transaction, it is possible for each of the accused to cast the entire blame for the transaction on the other if they are tried separately and this may result in the acquittal of both."[152]

The weight of evidence against the accused may also be relevant in considering a defence application for separate trials. If the case against the accused is so overwhelming it might be considered that no injustice was done in refusing an order for separate trials in a case where an order might otherwise have issued.

K. Postponement or Adjournment

1. Distinction

The postponement of a trial refers to the fact that it has been put back to a later date. Adjournment on the other hand signifies the fact that the further hearing of a trial which has already commenced has been suspended to some date in the future. In practice it seems that the terms are often used inter-changeably without regard to their strict meanings.

14–42

2. Power

There is no fixed body of rules governing when a trial can or cannot be postponed or adjourned. For the most part it is left to the trial judge to deal with applications from the prosecution or the defence as he or she sees fit. However, the Criminal Justice (Administration) Act 1924 does make specific

---

[150] See *People v. Carney, op. cit.*
[151] The statements of two accused which are incompatible, but not inculpatory, would not provide a basis for the exercise of the discretion; *People v. Sykes* [1958] I.R. 355.
[152] *People v. Murtagh* [1966] I.R. 361 at 363. See also *Attorney General v. Corcoran* 63 I.L.T.R. 145.

provision for the postponement or adjournment of a trial where the court has made an order for the amendment of the indictment, or for the separate trial of offences charged in the indictment. Where the court is of the opinion that the postponement or adjournment of the trial is expedient as a consequence of any such order it may make whatever order for the postponement or adjournment of the trial as appears necessary.[153] Where it makes an order for the adjournment of the trial under this provision, the court may further order that the jury is to be discharged from giving a verdict.[154] Once the trial resumes in a case where the jury had been discharged the procedure shall be the same in all respects as if the trial had not previously been commenced.[155] The court may also make such order as to costs, bail and recognisances as it thinks fit.[156] This power to postpone or adjourn a trial under the 1924 Act is in addition to any other power of adjournment or postponement that the court may have.[157]

3. Delay

Where the trial is postponed or adjourned and the accused is remanded in custody it is imperative that the delay should be kept to a minimum. The fundamental rights of the accused to liberty and to a presumption of innocence requires nothing less. This is reflected in the fact that if the trial is postponed or adjourned to the next sitting of the Circuit Court and the accused is remanded in custody, he must be indicted either at the current or the next sitting. A failure to do so will result in the warrant of committal lapsing.[158] Nevertheless, the validity of the original return for trial remains unaffected. Accordingly, the accused may be re-arrested and arraigned before a subsequent sitting.[159] Equally, if the accused is arraigned before the next sitting and then remanded in custody by the court until the following sitting the remand is good.[160]

L. Sending the Accused Forward for Trial on Indictment on the Direction of the DPP

14–43 In *Attorney General v. Colleary*[161] the Attorney General presented an indictment against the accused in a case where a District Court judge had conducted a preliminary examination and refused to send the accused forward for trial. The trial judge ruled that he had no jurisdiction to try the case as the Attorney General had no power to present an indictment where the judge had refused to send the accused forward for trial after conducting the preliminary

---

[153] Criminal Justice (Administration) Act 1924, s.6(4).
[154] *ibid.* s.6(5)(a).
[155] *ibid.* s.6(5)(b).
[156] *ibid.* s.6(5)(c).
[157] *ibid.* s.6(6).
[158] *Re Singer* 97 I.L.T.R. 130.
[159] *Re Singer (No.2)* 98 I.L.T.R. 112.
[160] *Re Francis* 97 I.L.T.R. 151.
[161] 69 I.L.T.R. 233.

investigation. The following year the legislature responded to this decision by the enactment of section 62 of the Courts of Justice Act 1936, subsection (1) of which reads:[162]

> "Where a person is brought before a justice of the District Court charged with an indictable crime, and such charge either cannot lawfully be or is not disposed of summarily by such justice, and such justice refuses to send such person forward for trial on such charge, then and in every such case it shall be lawful for the [DPP] to direct that such person be sent forward for trial to a specified Court to which such justice could lawfully have sent such person."

This provision was interpreted by the Supreme Court in *People (Attorney General) v. Boggan*.[163]

In *Boggan* the accused was charged with a number of indictable offences involving embezzlement, falsification of accounts, forgery and uttering of forged documents. Having been returned for trial after a preliminary investigation he was found guilty on several counts. His appeal to the Court of Criminal Appeal was unsuccessful. The Supreme Court granted a certificate that the decision involved a point of law of exceptional public importance and that it was desirable in the public interest that an appeal should be taken to the Supreme Court. For the purpose of this appeal it was accepted that the proceedings in the preliminary investigation in the District Court were irregular to the extent that the order returning him for trial was not sufficient in itself to confer jurisdiction. The essential question for the court, therefore, was whether the Attorney General (DPP) has the right to prefer an indictment against any person in the Circuit Criminal Court or Central Criminal Court without any preliminary investigation or order returning the accused for trial.

In delivering the leading judgment in the Supreme Court Lavery J. traced the development of the trial of offences on indictment from early times up to the enactment of section 62(1) of the 1936 Act. He found that prior to the enactment of section 62(1) the Attorney General did not have the power to prefer an indictment independent of the order of a District Court judge receiving informations or sending the accused forward for trial.[164] Section 62(1) changed that by conferring such a power specifically on the Attorney General. However, Lavery J proceeded to explain that section 62(1) did not confer on the Attorney a general power to put the accused on trial on indictment. The net effect of the power when exercised was to reverse the order of the District Court refusing to send the accused forward for trial. It could be exercised only where a judge of the District Court had refused to send the accused forward for trial:

> "The provision seems to emphasise that a preliminary investigation and the taking of depositions in accordance with the Rules of the District Court is a condition precedent to the placing of a person on trial on indictment."[165]

---

[162] As amended by Criminal Procedure Act 1967, Schedule.
[163] [1958] I.R. 67.
[164] For a contrary view see the judgment of Davitt P. in *State (Attorney General) v. Judge Fawsitt* [1955] I.R. 39.
[165] [1958] I.R. 67.

14–44 Inevitably this interpretation of section 62(1) raises the issue of whether an exercise of the power conferred by the subsection would amount to an unconstitutional intervention by the executive in the administration of justice. In *State (Shanahan) v. The Attorney General*,[166] the Supreme Court rejected the argument that section 62(1) involved an unconstitutional exercise of the judicial power by the executive. Giving the judgment of the Court, Walsh J. explained that a decision by the Attorney General (now the DPP) under section 62(1) to send an accused forward for trial after a District Court judge had refused informations did not amount to an interference in the justiciable controversy before the District Court judge. In effect, there were two separate justiciable controversies. The first, which concerned whether there was a sufficient case to send the accused forward for trial, was brought to an end by the decision of the judge to refuse informations. The second, which was concerned with the determination of the guilt of the accused, was initiated by the decision of the Attorney General (now the DPP) to send the accused forward for trial. The two were quite separate and, as such, did not involve an intervention by the Attorney General in the justiciable controversy before the District Court.

The matter came before the Supreme Court again in *Costello v. DPP*[167] where the Court, finding Walsh J.'s reasoning unconvincing, overruled its previous decision in *Shanahan*. In giving the judgment of the Court, O'Higgins C.J. first identified the essential ingredients of the preliminary examination in order to establish that they involved an administration of justice within the meaning of Article 34 of the Constitution, a matter which had been left hanging in *Shanahan*. He proceeded to explain that the actions of the Attorney General (now the DPP) in sending the accused forward for trial was a direct and impermissible interference in the justiciable controversy before the District Court judge. That issue had already been decided by the judge and the actions of the Attorney General had the effect of rendering his determination nugatory. In the words of O'Higgins CJ:

> "The Court is satisfied that, in conducting a preliminary examination and in determining these questions, the Justice was exercising the judicial power of the State as conferred by law on the District Court in accordance with the Constitution: see Articles 6 and 34 of the Constitution and The *State (C) v. The Minister for Justice* [1967] I.R. 106. When, in the exercise of such judicial power, there is a determination of these justiciable issues, that determination cannot be set aside or reversed by any other authority. Such action would constitute an invasion of the judicial power and an attempt to exercise the judicial power of government otherwise than by the organ of the State established for this purpose by the Constitution."

The combined effect of the decisions in *Costello* and *Boggan* deprives the DPP of any power to send an accused forward for trial on indictment directly. It does not follow that any such power would inevitably be unconstitutional.

---

[166] [1964] I.R. 239.
[167] [1984] I.R. 436.

Nevertheless, when the preliminary examination was abolished by the Criminal Justice Act 1999 no provision was introduced enabling the DPP to send the accused forward for trial directly. However, the Act does make the consent of the DPP a precondition for an order of a District Court judge sending the accused forward for trial. If the DPP refuses to give his consent the judge is obliged to strike out the proceedings. Intriguingly, the legislation goes on to say that any such striking out is without prejudice to the institution of proceedings against the accused by the DPP. Since the DPP no longer enjoys a power to send the accused for trial directly, this must refer to the re-institution of proceedings before a District Court judge. In any event, the fact that the District Court judge must send the accused forward for trial where the statutory requirements have been satisfied should render superfluous any need for the DPP to retain a power to send the accused forward for trial directly.

M. Disclosure

1. Introduction

General Duty to Disclose

Although the Irish criminal process trial is based on an adversarial, as distinct **14–45** from an inquisitorial, model, there are many aspects which are inconsistent with a pure adversarial contest. A primary example is the duty of disclosure. The prosecution is subject to an extensive duty to disclose material in its possession to the defence in advance of the trial where that material may be of assistance to the defence case. While the defence is not subject to a reciprocal duty, it may be obliged to make advance disclosure of some aspects of its case to the prosecution in certain circumstances. It will be seen later that the disclosure obligations on the defence are prescribed by statute and are quite narrowly circumscribed. The prosecution's duty of disclosure on the other hand is based partly on statute and partly on common law precepts which have yet to evolve to the point where they offer a comprehensive and detailed blueprint for the nature and extent of the duty.[168]

Book of Evidence

As discussed earlier, the Criminal Procedure Act 1967 (as amended by the Criminal Justice Act 1999) imposes an obligation on the prosecution to serve what is commonly referred to as the book of evidence on the defence in proceedings on indictment. This book of evidence will consist of all the evidence which the prosecution intends to rely on against the accused at the trial. As such it will include: a statement of the charges against the accused; a copy of any sworn information in writing upon which the proceedings were initiated; a list of the witnesses whom the DPP proposes to call at the trial; a

---

[168] For a discussion of the common law developments in the context of trials on indictment, see Mullan "The Duty to Disclose in Criminal Prosecutions" *Bar Review* 5 4 (2000) 174.

statement of the evidence that is expected to be given by each of them;[169] a copy of any document containing information which it is proposed to give in evidence by virtue of Part II of the Criminal Evidence Act 1992 (broadly speaking records compiled in the course of a business or by or on behalf of certain public bodies);[170] where appropriate, a copy of a certificate under section 6(1) of the 1992 Act (a certificate relating to the information contained in a record compiled in the course of a business);[171] and a list of the exhibits (if any).[172] There is also provision for the serving of a videotape of evidence which has been video-recorded pursuant to the provisions of the Criminal Evidence Act 1992. These materials must be served on the accused before he or she can be sent for trial on indictment.

Other Material Relevant to Defence

In the normal course of events the prosecution will have gathered much more evidence in its investigation of the accused than it intends to use at the trial. Much of this evidence will be innocuous in that it does not add to nor detract from the case against the accused. Some of it, however, may be of potential use to the defence because, for example, it undermines some aspects of the prosecution case, or because it supports an aspect of the defence or because it opens up a new line of defence which the accused had not considered because he was unaware of the material in question.

A simple illustration can be provided by a case which rests on disputed identification evidence. The prosecution will call a witness who has identified the accused in a line up. They may not reveal the existence of witnesses who failed to pick out the accused. Equally they may not reveal the fact that the witness was shown a book of photographs before picking out the accused in a line-up or in a public place. It may also happen that, unknown to the defence, the witness in question has a reputation for making false complaints to the police. None of these matters would necessarily be disclosed in the book of evidence, but they are all matters which would be in the possession of the prosecution and which could be of use to the defence. The question arises, therefore, to what extent if any is the prosecution under an obligation to reveal these matters to the defence?

Third Party Material

It may also happen that a third party is in possession of information which might be helpful to the defence. This raises the question of whether the third party is under any obligation to make that information available on request to the defence. Related to this is the issue whether the prosecution is under any duty to secure material from a third party for the benefit of the defence.

---

[169] See District Court Rules, 1997, Ord.24, r.7 and Sched. B Forms 24.3 to 24.7 for the relevant forms, as amended by District Court (Criminal Justice) Rules 2001, r.8 Schedules 11 and 12.
[170] For further detail see Chap.18 – Trial Evidence.
[171] *ibid.*
[172] Criminal Procedure Act 1967, s.4B(1).

2. The General Principle

The fundamental importance of the prosecution's duty of disclosure is reflected **14–46**
by the fact that the European Court of Human Rights has held that disclosure
of all material evidence to an accused is a requirement of a fair trial under
Article 6 of the European Convention on Human Rights.[173] Similarly, the Irish
courts see the disclosure obligation as being firmly rooted in the individual's
constitutional right to fair procedures in a criminal trial. McCarthy J. stated
the basic principle as follows in *People (DPP) v. Tuite*:

> "The constitutional right to fair procedures demands that the prosecution be
> conducted fairly; it is the duty of the prosecution, whether adducing such
> evidence or not, where possible, to make available all relevant evidence, parol
> or otherwise, in its possession, so that if the prosecution does not adduce such
> evidence, the defence may, if it wishes, do so."[174]

Just what this general principle entails in particular cases will depend heavily
on the meaning of the key elements such as, "relevant evidence" and "in its
possession". Each will be considered briefly in turn. Because of its importance,
privilege will also be addressed briefly. For a fuller treatment of these issues
reference should be made to specialist texts.[175] It is also important to emphasise at the outset the overriding principle that the accused is entitled to fair
procedures. It may be, therefore, that the facts of an individual case are such
that the prosecution will be required to provide certain information even
though one or other of these elements for the duty of disclosure may not be
fully satisfied.

3. Relevant Evidence

The obligation on the prosecution is to disclose "relevant evidence". Relevant **14–47**
in this context refers to anything which is relevant to the defence case in the
sense that it tends to undermine the prosecution case or assists the defence
case. It follows that the prosecution is not bound to disclose everything just
because it has been gathered in the course of the investigation which led to
the charge being preferred. Beyond that, however, it is very difficult to offer a
definition which clearly distinguishes between that which must be revealed
from that which need not be revealed. In some of the Irish cases the judges
use the term "material" evidence, but this hardly carries the matter much
further, apart from the fact that it suggests that the disclosure obligation may
reach beyond material considered to be relevant in the strict sense of that term
in the law of evidence.

It is well established that where the prosecution has a statement of a person
who may be in a position to give material evidence, whom they do not want
to call as a witness, they are under a duty to make that person available as a

---

[173] *Edwards v. UK* (1992) 15 E.H.H.R. 417.
[174] 2 Frewen 175 at 180–181.
[175] See, *e.g.*, Cahill *Discovery in Ireland* (Round Hall Sweet & Maxwell, Dublin, 1996).

witness for the defence, and any statements that he may have given.[176] Equally, when the prosecution intend to rely on witness statement it is submitted that they are under a duty to supply the accused with any information in their possession about the circumstances or factors in which the statement was taken and which may affect the reliability of the statement. In *People (DPP) v. Meleady and Grogan*,[177] for example, the Court of Criminal Appeal quashed a conviction which had been based on identification evidence, at least partly because the defence was not made aware of the possibility that the key prosecution witness had been shown a book of photographs of suspects before making the identification.

4. In its Possession

Prosecution Duty to Retain Possession

14–48   The obligation to disclose relates to evidence in the possession of the prosecution. Presumably, for this purpose, no issue turns on how the evidence came into the possession of the prosecution so long as it is there. Once evidence is in the possession of the prosecution they are under an obligation to retain it where it may be relevant to the defence, even if the prosecution does not intend to rely on it at the trial.

In *Murphy v. DPP*[178] the accused was charged with a number of offences alleged to have been committed while driving a motor vehicle which had been crashed and seriously damaged. The wreck was in the possession of the Garda Síochána who advised that they would not be subjecting it to forensic examination as they would be relying entirely on identification evidence. The defence request to examine the wreck was granted, but before they managed to carry out the examination it was removed from Garda custody by the insurance company which was interested in its salvage value. Accordingly, the defence sought an injunction restraining any further prosecution of the charges, essentially on the ground that the removal of the car had prevented them from adducing possible scientific evidence which might have served to refute the visual identification evidence. The defence also claimed that the actions of the gardai in failing to preserve evidence which might have been helpful in preparing the defence amounted to a breach of natural justice. Lynch J., having reviewed the authorities, concluded:

> "The authorities establish that evidence relevant to guilt or innocence must so far as is necessary and practicable be kept until the conclusion of the trial. These authorities also apply to the preservation of articles which may give rise to the reasonable possibility of securing relevant evidence."[179]

Applying that principle to the facts of this case the learned judge took into account that an examination of the car could possibly produce evidence that

---

[176] *DPP v. Special Criminal Court* [1999] 1 I.R. 60.
[177] [1995] 2 I.R. 517.
[178] [1989] 1 I.L.R.M. 71.
[179] *ibid.* at 76.

would rebut the identification evidence against the accused, and corroboration of his denial that he was the driver of the car. In other words the examination related to material evidence in the case. The learned judge also noted that the gardai were made aware at an early stage that the defence wished to examine the wrecked car. Moreover, the evidence in question was in their possession and there was no urgent need to return the wreck to its owner or the insurance company. Lynch J. concluded, therefore, that the Garda failure to retain the wreck has materially affected the preparation of the accused's defence to his detriment. This was sufficient to amount to a breach of fair procedures. Accordingly the learned judge granted the injunction restraining the prosecution of the driving offences, but emphasised that this did not necessarily affect the prosecution of other offences arising out of the same incident.

Lynch J's analysis was approved by the Supreme Court in *Braddish v. DPP*[180] In that case the accused was charged with the robbery of a shop which had been caught on video-tape. He was arrested on the basis of being identified on the video by a member of the Garda Síochána. While in detention he allegedly made and signed a confession. However, he was not formally charged until 9 months later. On his first appearance in the District Court his solicitor requested any signed statements, any video footage and any stills of video footage. The request was repeated five months later. One month after that his solicitor was informed that the video-tapes were no longer available as they had been returned to the owner after the accused had admitted the crime. The accused sought an injunction restraining any further prosecution. This was refused in the High Court, but granted on appeal to the Supreme Court.

In giving the judgment of the Supreme Court Hardiman J. noted that the prosecution was not relying on any evidence from the videotape. Instead they were content to rely on the alleged confession. Nevertheless, the learned judge considered that this did not relieve the prosecution of their obligation to retain the video evidence. The only real basis upon which the accused could challenge the admissibility of his confession was on the basis that the video had not afforded a sufficient basis to ground a reasonable suspicion for his arrest and subsequent detention. If the arrest and detention were unlawful then the confession would have been rendered inadmissible. To pursue this possible line of defence, however, the accused would need access to the video-tape as the stills taken from the tape were totally useless for the purposes of identification. By returning the video-tapes to their owner the gardai had effectively frustrated the accused from pursuing this line of defence.

Hardiman J. also took the opportunity to address directly and forcefully the issue of whether the prosecution can dispose of evidence which they do not intend to rely on at the trial simply because they feel that they have much stronger and better evidence. In doing so he couches his remarks specifically in the context of the facts of the case in which the gardai dispensed with evidence which actually showed the crime in progress in favour of confession evidence:

---

[180] [2001] 3 I.R. 127.

"More fundamentally, this is a video tape which purports actually to show the robbery in progress. It is not acceptable, in my view, to excuse the absence of so vital and direct a piece of evidence simply by saying that the prosecution are not relying on it, but prefer to rely on an alleged confession. Firstly, the confession is hotly disputed. Secondly, a confession should if possible be corroborated and relatively recent history both here and in the neighbouring jurisdiction has unfortunate examples of the risks of excessive reliance on confession evidence. Thirdly the video tape has a clear potential to exculpate as well as to inculpate.

This video tape was real evidence and the Gardai were not entitled to dispose of it before the trial. It is now admitted that they should not have done so. Lest however the sentence already quoted from the State Solicitor's letter (and which can only have been based on his instructions from the Gardai) can be read to suggest that because the prosecution was based wholly on an alleged confession, other items of evidence can be destroyed or rendered unavailable, I wish to state emphatically that this is not so. It is the duty of the Garda, arising from their unique investigative role, to seek out and preserve all evidence having a bearing or potential bearing on the issue of guilt or innocence. This is so whether the prosecution proposes to rely on the evidence or not, and regardless of whether it assists the case the prosecution is advancing or not.

The evidence leading to the identification of a suspect often differs greatly from the evidence in the ensuing prosecution. This may be because the former would be quite inadmissible, such as anonymous information, or because the evidence is cogent enough to suggest a suspect or a course of investigation, but not nearly cogent enough to prove the guilt of any particular person. There are other possible explanations for the prosecution's unwillingness to deploy in evidence material which was used in the investigation. But the fact that such material is not used can never justify its destruction or unavailability, or the destruction of notes or records about it. This is because a particular fact or piece of real evidence which it would be irrelevant or counter productive for the prosecution to deploy may (perhaps for that very reason) be very useful to the defence. It must therefore be preserved and disclosed. The prosecution are not entitled to take the view that once they have better evidence, or evidence more convenient to them to deploy, they are entitled to destroy the evidence which came first to hand. They are not entitled to say, for instance, 'This is a confession case: we will stand or fall on the confession and are therefore entitled to ignore the video tape'."[181]

The missing evidence in *Braddish* was clearly of very special significance. The fact that it purported to show the crime in operation meant that it was virtually certain to be of primary interest to the defence. Nevertheless, Hardiman J. emphasised that the duty on the prosecution to retain evidence was not confined to such matters. It extended to items which may give rise to the reasonable possibility of securing relevant evidence. It was not necessary, therefore to show that the items in question must contain evidence relevant to the defence. A mere possibility that they will contain such evidence should be sufficient. On the other hand if it is highly unlikely that the video-evidence would have captured scenes relating to the commission of the offence, the

---

[181] *ibid.* at 132–133.

obligation to retain the video or inform the defence of its existence would be much weaker and, perhaps, non-existent.[182]

Video Evidence

There is a growing acceptance that where evidence of a crime may have been caught on street or shop video cameras the Garda should take and keep possession of it for a reasonable time, even if the prosecution does not intend to rely on it as part of its case. The defence may wish to examine it and make use of it for the purposes of preparing its case. Accordingly, there may be circumstances in which the prosecution would be under a duty to notify the defence of the existence of the video-tape and even to give advance notice of their intention to destroy it unless the defence requested its retention. Geoghegan J. put the matter thus in the following *obiter dictum* in *Mitchell v. DPP*:

14–49

> ". . . as a general proposition, there would be cases where the gardai, in the interests of justice and fair procedures, would quite definitely be obliged to inform an accused person of the existence of video evidence and notify him of an intention to destroy that video evidence. An example is where the gardai fully intended in the first instance to use video evidence in the investigation or prosecution of the offence and then subsequently decided not to do so. But I think the duty goes beyond such a situation. For example, where gardai take away tapes (say from a shop) and retain them for a period on the basis that they may arguably be of evidential value but subsequently decide that the tapes would not be used by them, a requirement to inform the accused person before the tapes were destroyed or erased arises."[183]

It does not follow that gardai are under a duty to collect all video evidence that there may be relating to a crime and retain it until any proceedings in the case have been exhausted, even though the prosecution will not be relying on the video evidence. Much will depend on the facts of each case. Clearly the duty will be more onerous in a case where it was genuinely considered that the tapes could be of relevance or where the defence had specifically requested access to such tapes. However, gross delay on the part of the defence in seeking the tapes, particularly in a case where the accused has made and not retracted a full admission and the prosecution are not relying on any element of identification, is likely to defeat any attempt to stop a prosecution on the grounds that the tapes have not been retained by the prosecution.[184] Equally, gardai do not have to go to extraordinary lengths to retain items which may contain relevant evidence. Their duty is to preserve evidence in so far as it is "necessary and practicable" to do so. What this requires cannot be defined exhaustively or precisely in advance. Much will depend on the particular facts of individual cases.

---

[182] *Mitchell v. DPP* [2000] 2 I.L.R.M. 396.
[183] *ibid.* at 398.
[184] *Dunne v. DPP* unreported, High Court, March 23, 2001.

Third Party Property

14–50   Further complications can arise where property belonging to an innocent third party has been seized in the course of preventing or detecting crime. If the prosecution do not require it as part of their case they should return it to its owner unless the defence seeks an opportunity to subject it to analysis. A failure to give the defence an opportunity to inspect it before returning it, as in *Murphy v. DPP*,[185] may result in the prosecution having to be abandoned where the material in question could provide evidence relevant to the defence. It would appear, however, that the courts will be slower to stop a prosecution in these circumstances where the gardai merely returned the material to its rightful owner instead of destroying it. In *Rogers v. DPP*,[186] for example, the High Court refused to stop a prosecution where the gardai had returned a stolen vehicle to its owner. Their action denied the defence the opportunity of subjecting the car to forensic analysis. The facts were very similar to those in *Murphy* where the prosecution was stopped because of unfairness to the accused. In *Rogers*, however, the High Court refused the defence application to stop the prosecution, partly because it felt able to distinguish *Murphy* on the facts. In particular it pointed out that there was some delay on the part of the defence in advising the prosecution that they wished to inspect the vehicle and, unlike the situation in *Murphy*, the vehicle had already been subjected to forensic analysis with negative results. However, the court also laid emphasis on the significance of the need to return the vehicle to its rightful owner at the earliest opportunity:

> "I think that some consideration has to be given to the owner of a motor car which has been stolen or unlawfully taken; similarly in relation to other property the subject of criminal charges where deprivation of possession thereof will seriously prejudice or inconvenience the innocent owner thereof. In relation to such property I would hold that any forensic examination, whether by the gardai or on behalf of an accused person, should be sought and should take place within a reasonable time, having regard to all the circumstances of the case, so that the property can then be returned as expeditiously as possible to its true owner."[187]

5. Impossibility

14–51   The prosecution may not be in a position to hand over evidence because it no longer exists in any tangible or useful form. This will not necessarily relieve them of their obligations to the accused. As noted above, they are under a duty to retain evidence which may be relevant to the accused. If they fail to fulfil this obligation and the accused's defence is prejudiced as a result then a case may be withdrawn from the jury or a conviction quashed on appeal. It does not follow, however, that the prosecution are obliged to retain possession of the evidence indefinitely until all proceedings, including any appeal, have

---

[185] 1989] 1 I.L.R.M. 71.
[186] [1992] 2 I.L.R.M. 695. See also, *Dutton DPP* unreported, High Court, July 14, 1998.
[187] *Rogers v. DPP* [1992] 2 I.L.R.M. 695 at 698.

been exhausted. If the prosecution have no reason to believe that the evidence is relevant to the defence and have not been put on notice by the defence that they wish to inspect the evidence and the evidence has since been dissipated or destroyed, the prosecution may be able to claim successfully that it is not possible to hand it over to the defence.[188] The success of such a claim will depend on the circumstances of the case and, in particular, the length of delay on the part of the defence in expressing an interest in examining the evidence.[189]

6. Third Party Disclosure

In the course of a criminal investigation the prosecution may be given or may seize material belonging to third parties but which is believed to be evidence relating to the offence. It has been seen above that the prosecution will be under an obligation in certain circumstances to retain possession of this material for the benefit of the defence even though the prosecution does not intend to rely on it as evidence against the accused. As yet there is no suggestion in the case law that the prosecution is also under an obligation to seek or secure material belonging to a third party, and which is not already in the possession of the prosecution, simply because it may be relevant to the defence. It would appear that it is a matter for the defence to secure access to this material through an order for third party discovery.

14–52

The jurisdiction to grant an order for third party discovery, and the applicable procedure, in a criminal trial are not at all clear. Nevertheless, it would appear that such applications are becoming more frequent in the Circuit Court.[190] The practice seems to be that the defendant seeks voluntary disclosure in the first instance. Where that does not produce the desired result he applies to the trial court for an order of discovery directed to the third party. It seems that the Circuit Court has been prepared to grant such orders at least where it is satisfied that the material may be relevant to an issue to be decided in the trial.[191] Where a trial (or appeal) court declines to exercise this jurisdiction it is worth considering an application to the High Court. Order 31, rule 29 of the Rules of the Superior Courts make provision for non-party discovery. There is nothing in this order which confines the exercise of the jurisdiction to civil cases. The availability of this jurisdiction would now seem to have been closed off as a result of the Supreme Court's decision in *People (DPP) v. Sweeney*.[191a]

In *Sweeney* the accused made an application for non-party party discovery under RSC Ord.29, r.31 against the Rape Crisis centre. On appeal against the High Court's decision to grant discovery the Supreme Court reviewed the jurisdiction of the High Court to order discovery in criminal proceedings.

[188] *Mitchell v. DPP* [2000] 2 I.L.R.M. 396.
[189] *Dunne v. DPP* unreported, High Court, March 23, 2001.
[190] See, *e.g.*, *People (DPP) v. Flynn* [1986] 1 I.L.R.M. 317; *DPP v. SK* unreported, Circuit Court, December 14, 1999. Mullan "The Duty to Disclose in Criminal Prosecutions" *Bar Review* 5, 4 (2000) 174.
[191] *Ibid.*
[191a] [2002] 1 I.L.R.M. 532.

Giving the judgment of the Court, Geoghegan J. explained that there was no history of the current High Court, or its predecessors, exercising jurisdiction to order discovery of documents in criminal cases. The learned judge acknowledged that the Rules of the Supreme Court made provision for discovery in any 'cause' which is defined in the Rules generally as including any criminal proceedings. However, the Rules also state that the definition is not to apply if "there is anything in the subject or context repugnant thereto". Geoghegan J. considered that the nature of criminal proceedings was such that discovery was wholly inappropriate and, therefore, outside the discovery jurisdiction conferred on the High Court. Not only was there no history of the High Court exercising a discovery jurisdiction in criminal matters, but criminal proceedings were particularly unsuited to the exercise of such a jurisdiction. There was both a legal and constitutional obligation on the prosecution to serve all relevant documents in their possession on the defence, but no correlative obligation on the defence. Indeed, apart from a few statutory exceptions, the defence are entitled to conceal their case and evidence from the prosecution. It would be wholly inappropriate in this context to issue an order for discovery. The point is well made in the following passage from the judgment of Moriarty J. in *People (DPP) v. Flynn* and quoted with approval by Geoghegan J. in *Sweeney*:

> "2. The principle that each party should be entitled to know from the other in advance any information that would enhance his own case or destroy his adversary's case was less applicable in criminal proceedings where the entire burden of proof rested on the prosecution.
>
> Discovery was intended to be mutual between the parties and it could not be mutual in a criminal case because it would not be ordered against the accused. It followed that a non-party should not be subjected to a greater obligation than could be imposed on the accused."[191b]

It could be argued, of course, that this reasoning would not necessarily preclude a jurisdiction to order non-party discovery in a criminal case at the instance of the accused. Geoghegan J. explained that the jurisdiction to order discovery is normally exercised in civil cases only after the close of pleadings at which point the issues have been clarified with some precision. Where an order was being made against a non-party that party was entitled to know the issues raised by the pleadings with the same degree of precision as a party. Accordingly, the order for discovery should identify the issues. That, however, would not be possible in criminal proceedings given that the accused is not generally obliged to reveal his or her hand in advance of the trial. Geoghegan J. concluded, therefore, that discovery was not available against a non-party in criminal proceedings.

The judgment in *Sweeney* suggests that discovery is not available at all in criminal cases, although Geoghegan J. did specifically state that nothing in his judgment should be construed as expressing any view on the jurisdiction

---

[191b] *ibid.* at 539.

to make orders for discovery (including orders for non-party discovery) in applications to the Court of Criminal Appeal under section 2(1) of the Criminal Procedure Act 1993 (miscarriage of justice applications). It follows that if an accused wishes to gain access to material which is in the hands of a non-party he or she will have to be content with calling that party as a witness.

7. Privilege

Introduction

It will happen from time to time that the prosecution will be in possession of **14–53** evidence which might be useful to the defence case but which the prosecution does not want to hand over to the defence because of the risk that it might present to others, the efficacy of criminal investigations or the security of the State. This situation can arise typically in relation to the sources of evidence which the prosecution intends to rely on at the trial. It may be, for example, that the life of an informer would be in jeopardy if it became known that he had supplied information to the police which led to the detection of the accused. Equally, if it was known that an informer's identity could be disclosed in the course of a trial individuals would be much less likely to give information in confidence to the police, thereby rendering the successful detection and prosecution of crime much more difficult. It may also happen that revealing how evidence was acquired in a particular case would expose police methods to the detriment of ongoing or future investigations or even to the security of the State. In any of these situations the police may calculate that the damage likely to be caused by revealing how they acquired the evidence, or even that they have the evidence at all, would be greater than the damage caused by failing to secure a conviction in the case at hand. The public interest in the detection of crime, therefore, would be defeated at least in the instant case.

From the perspective of the accused it can be vitally important to know the manner in which the police acquired the evidence in order to prepare his defence properly. If, for example, the evidence had come from a paid police informer, the accused would have a very clear interest in attacking the credibility of this informer. In order to do that effectively, he would need to know the identity of the informer, how he was recruited, how much he was being paid by the police and so on. Equally, it may happen that the police have resorted to unlawful or unconstitutional methods to obtain evidence against the accused. Again it would be vital for obvious reasons that the accused should be able to access documents or material evidence relating to these methods and their results. In short, the accused's right to have the opportunity to prepare his defence, and the public interest in the fairness and transparency of the criminal process, would be defeated if the prosecution was permitted to keep secret the existence or to deny access to, evidence that may be useful to the defence.

Demise of Class Privilege

14–54   The courts have developed a number of legal principles governing the resolution of these conflicting interests in an individual case. Previously these principles could have been discussed under the general heading of privilege. While Irish law still recognises the informer privilege and legal professional privilege it no longer recognises the notion of executive privilege for documents simply because they belong to a certain class.[192] Instead it is the responsibility of the court in the exercise of the administration of justice to resolve the conflicting public interests by inspecting the documents in question and determining whether, and if so to that extent, they should not be made available to the defence.

   The prosecution cannot evade this general prohibition on privilege for certain classes of documents simply by asserting in respect of documents in an individual case that they consist of confidential communications by one police officer to another,[193] or between the police and the DPP's office, in connection with the initiation of a prosecution. In *Breathnach v. Ireland (No. 3)*,[194] for example, the prosecution made such a claim in respect of information which had been submitted to the DPP's office in respect of the plaintiff's alleged involvement in an armed robbery. The High Court considered that to permit such a claim for privilege in respect of these documents would effectively confer privilege on such documents as a class. Instead it would be necessary for the court to inspect the individual documents in order to determine whether the public interest favoured disclosure or non-disclosure.

   Where the evidence in question is in any way relevant to the issues to be determined in the case the onus is on the prosecution to establish that the evidence in question should not be disclosed.[195] The court will normally conduct an inspection of the documents in order to decide the issue, although in very exceptional circumstances it may feel able to hold that the public interest must be decided in favour of non-disclosure without the need to inspect the documents. It is submitted that, at least in respect of material which may contain relevant evidence, this possibility would have to be confined to cases of legal professional privilege or informer privilege, otherwise it will result indirectly in the creation of executive privilege for certain classes of document.

Current Approach

14–55   Most of the case law on how the conflicting public interests at stake should be resolved concern civil matters. Nevertheless, the guidance they offer can be accepted as relevant to a criminal trial in the sense that they lay down the

---

[192] *Murphy v. Dublin Corporation* [1972] I.R. 215; *Geraghty v. Minister for Local Government* [1975] I.R. 3000; *Ambiorix Ltd. v. Minister for the Environment (No.1)* [1992] 1 I.R. 277; *DPP (Hanly) v. Holly* [1984] I.L.R.M. 149; *Breathnach v. Ireland (No.3)* [1993] 2 I.R. 458.
[193] *DPP (Hanly) v. Holly* [1984] I.L.R.M. 149, effectively overruling *Attorney General v. Simpson* [1959] I.R. 105.
[194] [1993] 2 I.R. 458.
[195] *Murphy v. Dublin Corporation* [1972] I.R. 215; *Breathnach v. Ireland (No.3)* [1993] 2 I.R. 458.

absolute minimum entitlements of the accused in the criminal trial. Some of the civil cases actually arise out of criminal matters as, for example, where an individual sues for damages in respect of the methods employed by the police in the course of a criminal investigation. A few cases concern the accused seeking access to documents for the purpose of his defence in a criminal trial.

In *Breathnach*, Keane J., as he then was, proceeded to offer the following guidance on how the court should balance the conflicting public interests when deciding whether to order disclosure in an individual case:

> ". . . the court, as I understand the law, is required to balance the public interest reflected in the grounds put forward for non-disclosure in the present case. The public interest in the prevention and prosecution of crime must be put in the scales on the one side. It is only where the first public interest outweighs the second public interest that an inspection should be undertaken or disclosure should be ordered. In considering the first public interest, it is necessary to determine to what extent, if any, the relevant documents may advance the plaintiff's case or damage the defendant's case or fairly lead to an enquiry which may have either of those consequences. In the case of the second public interest, the various factors set out by Mr. Liddy [the prosecutor] must be given due weight. Again, as has been pointed out in the earlier decisions, there may be documents the very nature of which is such that inspection is not necessary to determine on which side the scales come down. Thus, information supplied in confidence to the gardai should not in general be disclosed, or at least not in cases like the present where the innocence of an accused person is not in issue, and the authorities to that effect, notably *Marks v. Beyfus* (1890) 25 Q.B.D. 494, remain unaffected by the more recent decisions, as was made clear by Costello J. in *Director of Consumer Affairs v. Sugar Distributors Ltd* [1991] 1 I.R. 225. Again, there may be material the disclosure of which may be of assistance to criminals by revealing methods of detection or combating crime, a consideration of particular importance today when criminal activity tends to be highly organised and professional. There may be cases involving the security of the State, where even disclosure of the existence of the document should not be allowed. None of these factors – and there may, of course, be others which have not occurred to me – which would remove the necessity of even inspecting the documents is present in this case."[196]

This guidance was handed down in the context of a civil case arising out of a criminal matter. While the general approach is equally applicable to a criminal prosecution it must be borne in mind that a very strong case would have to be made out for non-disclosure. The interest at stake in the criminal prosecution is the opportunity for the accused to establish his innocence as distinct from the opportunity to pursue a civil claim for compensation or to enforce a related civil right.

Informer Privilege

The mere fact that information has been given in confidence to the police is not in itself a ground for refusing disclosure of that information.[197] Informer

14–56

---

[196] *op.cit.* at 469.
[197] *Skeffington v. Rooney* [1997] 1 I.R. 22; *DPP v. Special Criminal Court* [1999] 1 I.R. 60.

privilege, however, has acquired particular recognition by the courts. This refers to the situation where information about criminal activities is fed to the police by an informant whose usefulness for such purposes is dependant upon his identity not being revealed publicly. The classic formulation of the rule aimed at protecting the identity of the informant from being revealed through disclosure is that given by Pollock CB in *Attorney General v. Briant*:

> ". . . the rule clearly established and acted on is this, that in a public prosecution a witness cannot be asked such questions as will disclose the informer, if he be a third person. This has been a settled rule for fifty years, and although it may seem hard in a particular case, private mischief must give way to public convenience . . . and we think the principle of the rule applies to the case where a witness is asked if he himself is the informer."[198]

Pollock CB was clearly referring to what questions could not be asked of a witness in the course of the criminal trial. The rule, however, has equal application to the non-disclosure of the existence of an informer and/or any information or statement he may have supplied to the prosecution. The rule could, of course, prove seriously unfair to an accused in a criminal trial. Accordingly, there is an "innocence at stake exception" as described by Esher M.R. in *Marks v. Beyfus*:

> ". . . if upon the trial of a prisoner the judge should be of the opinion that the disclosure of the name of the informant is necessary or right in order to shew the prisoner's innocence, then one public policy is in conflict with another public policy, and that which says that an innocent man is not to be condemned when his innocence can be proved is the policy that must prevail."[199]

The Irish courts have endorsed this statement of informer privilege and the related "innocence at stake" exception.[200] In *Director of Consumer Affairs v. Sugar Distributors Ltd*,[201] for example Costello J. held that a complaint of a breach of a Restrictive Practices Order (a criminal matter) attracted the privilege. If the Director relies on the privilege in response to a claim for disclosure by the defendant the court should examine the documents in question. If the court finds that they form part of the complaint to the Director it should refuse disclosure, unless it concludes that the documents might tend to show that the defendant had not committed the wrongful acts alleged against him.

It is not certain whether a court must always order disclosure where the material in question might tend to show that the accused was innocent. It may be that a court could refuse disclosure where to do otherwise would present a real risk to the life of an informant. In *Burke v. Central Independent Television plc*,[202] where the plaintiff sought discovery of the defendant's sources in an action for defamation, the Supreme Court held that the right to life and bodily must take precedence over a citizen's right to protection or vindication of his

---

[198] (1846) 15 M. & W. 169 at 185.
[199] (1890) 25 Q.B.D. 494 at 498.
[200] *Director of Consumer Affairs v. Sugar Distributors Ltd* [1991] 1 I.R. 225; *Skeffington v. Rooney* [1997] 2 I.L.R.M. 56; *DPP v. Special Criminal Court* [199] 1 I.R. 60.
[201] [1991] 1 I.R. 225.
[202] [1994] 2 I.R. 61.

name. While the right not to be wrongly convicted would weigh more heavily than the right to one's good name, particularly where one's liberty is at stake, it can nevertheless be argued by analogy that there may be circumstances in which the degree of risk to the life of the informant is such that disclosure ought to be refused even if that renders it more difficult for the accused to mount his defence.

In *DPP v. Special Criminal Court*[203] an attempt was made by defence counsel to gain access to statements from informers which the prosecution admitted were relevant to issues raised on the trial but which the prosecution did not intend to use. The prosecution sought privilege for these documents on the ground that they did not undermine the prosecution case, would not be helpful to the defence case and would put the lives of the informants at risk if they were disclosed. The defence argued that since the documents were relevant to issues raised in the trial the accused would be prejudiced in the preparation of his defence if he did not have access to them. It would not be sufficient for the court to inspect the documents as the court would not be able to assess the significance of information in the documents with the benefit of the information known to the accused. Moreover, inspection by the court would expose it to material prejudicial to the accused. Since the court sat without a jury this could result in the trial being tainted by inadmissible material.

The Special Criminal Court sought to balance the conflicting interests by ordering that the documents could be released for inspection by defence counsel and solicitor on the basis that the accused would waive any personal inspection and briefing on the contents of the documents. Equally, the defence counsel and solicitor would have to agree not to divulge the contents of the documents to any party. If counsel identified material in the documents in respect of which he felt he needed to get instructions from his client he could return to the court with a suitable application. This order was quashed by the High Court on the application of the DPP and the High Court's ruling was upheld on appeal by the Supreme Court.[204] Both the High Court and the Supreme Court considered that the order could give rise to serious problems in practice. Not only would it interfere with the special nature of the relationship between lawyer and client, but it would also discriminate between those who were and those who were not legally represented. The solution, in the view of the Supreme Court, begins with counsel for the prosecution. His task in a criminal trial is not just to secure a conviction. He must also function as a minister for justice. In this role he must bear a responsibility to disclose all relevant material to the defence and to accommodate both informer privilege and the innocence at stake exception. In cases of doubt it is a matter for the trial court to make a ruling on the matter. For this purpose it can inspect the documents in question, although there is no absolute need for it to do so in every case. This applies as much in respect of the Special Criminal Court as for a court sitting with a jury. Judges are well experienced in ignoring inadmissible matters when reaching a verdict on the evidence.

---

[203] [1999] 1 I.R. 60.
[204] *Ambiorix Ltd v. Minister for the Environment (No.1)* [1992] 1 I.R. 277 distinguished.

Legal Professional Privilege

14–57   It is unlikely that legal professional privilege will arise as a live issue in a criminal prosecution. It protects from disclosure communications between a lawyer and client for the purpose of giving or receiving advice for the purpose of litigation. It also protects such communications between the litigant and/or his lawyer and a third party. Although the DPP does not stand in the relationship of a client to any other lawyer it would appear that communications between him and his professional officers, solicitors and counsel for the purpose of individual prosecutions would be protected by legal professional privilege. It is highly unlikely, however, that the defence would be seeking disclosure of such communications. Their interest is more likely to lie in those parts, if any, of the file and other communications submitted to the DPP by the Garda Síochána consequent on a criminal investigation and which have not already been supplied to the defence. Since there is no lawyer client relationship between the Garda Síochána and the DPP in respect of individual prosecutions such communications would not normally benefit from legal professional privilege. Nevertheless, circumstances may arise in which such material could be covered by legal professional privilege.

In *People (DPP) v. Nevin*,[205] for example, information came to the attention of the DPP which could possibly provide support for an important aspect of the defence which the accused had relied on unsuccessfully at her trial. The information was that a pub which had featured centrally in the case had been under surveillance for IRA-related activity. The accused in her defence to a charge of murdering her husband and owner of the pub had attempted to present the murder as being IRA related. The DPP directed the Garda to carry out an investigation into the information which would of course be relevant. Geoghegan J, in giving the judgment of the Court of Criminal Appeal on an application for disclosure of the investigation report was of the view that the report would benefit from legal professional privilege as a report furnished to him by a member of the Garda Síochána for the purpose of seeking his legal advice and the advice of counsel thereto. It is respectfully submitted that the claim would be sounder if it was presented as a report commissioned and received by the DPP with a view to preparing his defence in the appeal.

It is also worth noting that a court will be slow to order disclosure of material which consists of material submitted by gardaí to the DPP in the course of criminal investigations unless it could be of practical value to the defence. In *Nevin*, for example, the Court of Criminal Appeal, having inspected the investigation report, considered that there was nothing in it of practical relevance to the accused, while disclosure would reveal the methodology of the Garda Síochána in anti-racketeering investigations. Accordingly, the State interest in non-disclosure outweighed any potential interest that the accused may have in the report. It does not follow, of course, that there is a presumption in favour of non-disclosure in such matters. The prosecution will still

---

[205] Unreported, Court of Criminal Appeal, December 13, 2001.

have to establish clear reasons why particular materials which could be relevant to the defence should not be disclosed in any individual case. The position is explained very well in the following extract from the judgment of Keane J, as he then was, in *Breathnach v. Ireland (No.3)*:

> "It is obvious that in every case where the commission of a crime, whether trivial or serious, is suspected, documentary material will be assembled by the gardai irrespective of whether a prosecution is ever initiated. The fact that the documents in question may, as in the present case, be submitted by the investigating gardai to the Director of Public Prosecutions in order to obtain his decision as to whether a prosecution should be instituted could not possibly give that material the same status as, to take an obvious example, a medical report obtained by a plaintiff in a personal injuries action solely for the purpose of his claim. If privilege exists in relation to such documents, it can only be because of the other factors referred to by Mr. Liddy, of which undoubtedly the most important is the desirability of freedom of communication between the gardai and the Director Public Prosecutions. The extent to which that freedom might be inhibited by the knowledge that the documents furnished to the Director of Public Prosecutions may subsequently be disclosed in court proceedings is clearly a matter which has to be taken into consideration in determining whether the public interest in the particular case requires its production."[206]

8. Disclosure in Summary Proceedings

The General Principles

14–58 There is no statutory obligation to prepare and serve a book of evidence on the accused in advance of a summary criminal trial, even if the offence to be tried summarily is an indictable offence. The question arises, therefore, whether there is any obligation on the prosecution to supply the defence with any material which may be useful in preparing the defence or meeting the prosecution case, apart from the summons itself.[207]

The matter was considered by the Supreme Court in *DPP v. Doyle*.[208] In that case the accused was tried summarily for indictable offences. Prior to the trial he sought copies of all statements which had been taken by gardai from prosecution witnesses. It transpired that no such formal statements had been taken. The prosecution case depended solely on the written admission of the accused. When the trial commenced the accused objected to it proceeding further until the prosecution had served on him all statements from all witnesses whose evidence was crucial to the prosecution case. The judge stated a case for the opinion of the High Court on: (1) whether, in the summary trial of an indictable offence, there was a general obligation on the prosecution to furnish on request statements of the proposed witnesses for the prosecution; and (2), if the answer to (1) was in the affirmative, does the obligation extend

---

[206] *op. cit.* at 472.
[207] For further discussion of the law and practice in this area, see Dwyer "The Duty of Disclosure in Criminal Proceedings" (1993) 3 I.C.L.J. 66.
[208] [1994] 2 I.R. 286.

to a case where no such statements had been taken by the Garda Síochána in the course of their investigation of the offence. Barr J., in the High Court, ruled that there was no general obligation on the prosecution to serve such statements, but that it was a matter for the judge to determine in the circumstances of each individual case whether the requirements of justice required such statements to be served.[209] If no statements had been taken, and the requirements of justice required that statements should be served, a summary of the crucial evidence for the prosecution should be served on the defence prior to the trial.

The High Court ruling was upheld on appeal to the Supreme Court. In giving the judgment of the Supreme Court Denham J. explained that there was a clear distinction between procedure and entitlements in a trial on indictment and summary trial. The statutory requirements governing production of the book of evidence in a trial on indictment do not carry over even in a modified form to a summary trial for an indictable offence. Moreover, there is no general obligation on the prosecution to serve statements of prosecution witnesses on the defence in respect of either a summary or indictable offence. Nevertheless, the circumstances may be such in an individual case that in order for the accused to receive a fair trial there should be advance disclosure. This was a matter for the judge to decide in each individual case in the course of his or her duty to ensure justice and fair procedures for the accused. Many very minor cases would not require such statements to be furnished. In others, where the charges were serious or involved more complex issues, it may be necessary to provide the accused with copies of statements and other relevant documents in advance of his trial so that he may properly prepare his defence. Denham J. specifically identified the following as factors which the judge may find relevant when making his or her determination:

"(a) the seriousness of the charge;
(b) the importance of the statements or documents;
(c) the fact that the accused has already been adequately informed of the nature and substance of the accusation;
(d) the likelihood that there is no risk of injustice in failing to furnish the statements or documents in issue to the accused."[210]

Denham J. also indicated that the presence or absence of a request for the documents to be served was a factor which the judge should take into account when making his or her determination.

On the facts of the case both the High Court and the Supreme Court ruled that there was no need for advance disclosure of witness statements or a summary of the crucial evidence for the prosecution. The central issue in the case would be the admissibility of the accused's confession. It could be distinguished from the facts in *Cowzer v. Judge Kirby*[211] where a re-trial

---

[209] Preferring *Clune v. DPP* [1981] I.L.R.M. 17 to *Cowzer v. Judge Kirby* unreported, High Court, February 11, 1991.
[210] [1994] 2 I.R. 286 at 302.
[211] Unreported, High Court, February 11, 1991.

application was made to substitute the original charge with another charge and to change the date of the alleged offence. These factors indicated that there might be an issue over the chief prosecution witness's veracity and credibility in which case it would be necessary for the defence to have advance notice of the statement of his evidence.

Garda Notebooks

The issue of whether the accused could get access in advance of the trial to relevant entries in Garda notebooks arose in *McHugh v. Brennan and the DPP*[212] In that case the District Court judge had ordered production of all relevant evidence in the possession of the prosecution. Pursuant to this order the prosecution served on the accused all witness statements taken, the custody record and a memorandum of an interview with the applicant. The applicant sought further disclosure of, *inter alia*, copies of all relevant entries in Garda notebooks in which the statements were taken. The judge ruled that the prosecution had complied with his order and refused to make a further order with respect to the notebooks. His decision on this matter seems to have been influenced by the fact that the defence solicitor would have an opportunity to inspect the notebooks on the morning of the trial. The judge's ruling was upheld by the High Court which considered that the material disclosed to the accused was sufficient to apprise him of the nature and substance of the allegations against him and the evidence in support of those allegations. Accordingly, the court felt that it was entirely reasonable that the notebook entries should be withheld until the day of the trial. While it is accepted that these rulings are entirely consistent with the principles laid down in *Doyle*, it is not immediately obvious why copies of the notebook entries should not be made available almost as a matter of course if they will be available for inspection anyway at the trial.

14–59

Procedure

Where the defence wish to secure advance disclosure of prosecution evidence they should seek it in the first instance directly from the prosecution. If the relevant materials are not furnished they should have the matter listed before the District Court judge or raise the matter on appearance before the District Court. The very nature of the summary trial means that proceedings can be adjourned from time to time to deal with any such application in the course of a trial.

9. Duty to Call Witnesses

Closely associated with the subject of disclosure is the issue of the extent to which the prosecution is under a duty to procure the attendance of witnesses at the trial of the accused. It can be expected that the prosecution will call all

14–60

---

[212] Unreported, High Court, April 14, 2000.

witnesses who are in a position to give evidence relevant to the charge against the accused. Equally, it can be expected that the defence will call any witnesses which it considers will advance its case. Circumstances may arise, however, where the defence wish to see a witness called but are reluctant to call that witness as a defence witness, preferring instead to have the witness called by the prosecution. There may be a tactical advantage in having the prosecution examine the witness in chief rather than exposing the witness to cross-examination. In this event, the defence might rely on the prosecution calling the witness pursuant to its general duty to make all relevant evidence available to the court, even if parts of that evidence are damaging to the prosecution. The question arises, therefore, to what extent is the prosecution under a duty to identify, locate and secure the attendance of witnesses at the trial.

This issue arose before the Supreme Court in *O'Regan v. DPP*.[213] This case concerned a prosecution for drunk-driving in which a Dr Prendiville had taken a blood sample from the accused and supplied the necessary form as part of the prosecution case. However, Dr Prendiville was not actually called as a witness for the prosecution. Although the defence could have called the doctor as a witness it preferred to have him called by the prosecution so that it could subject him to cross-examination. The question that was presented to the Supreme Court on these facts was:

> "Whether in a criminal prosecution the Director of Public Prosecutions is under a duty to call as a witness or tender for cross-examination all available witnesses who can give evidence directly material to the issues in the prosecution; and, in particular, to call Dr Prendiville as a witness, or tender him for cross-examination, in the instant prosecution; and whether the Director of Public Prosecutions having failed to do so, the learned District Court judge should have called the doctor as a witness to allow him to be cross-examined on behalf of the applicant."

Although the Court answered these questions in the negative as far as summary proceedings were concerned, it referred with approval to English authority which highlights the heavy duty on the prosecution to secure the attendance of all relevant witnesses:

> "In *Joseph Francis Oliva* [1965] 49 Cr. App. Rep. 298 the Court of Criminal Appeal in England reviewed at some length the historical development of the duty imposed upon the prosecution to call or tender for cross-examination witnesses who gave evidence at the committal proceedings and whose names appeared on the back of the indictment. That Court held that the prosecution was bound to procure, in so far as possible, the attendance in Court of all such witnesses and certainly emphasised the obligation on the prosecution to exercise '*the utmost candour and fairness*' but did not conclude that there is not an obligation on the prosecution to call all such witnesses. In practice I think it would be recognised – and for the purposes of this appeal I would be prepared to accept – that the general and well-accepted practice in this country is for the prosecution to call or tender for cross-examination all witnesses

---

[213] Unreported, Supreme Court, July 20, 1999.

whose names are included in the Book of Evidence. However, that is the high
water mark of the practice to be adopted in proceedings heard on indictment."

It must follow that there is at least a heavy duty on the prosecution to call all
witnesses whose statements have been included in the book of evidence.
There would have to be very exceptional circumstances not to do so in the
face of opposition from the defence. It is not yet clear whether the same
heavy duty extends to the identification and location of witnesses whose
statements have not been included. Presumably, the duty to exercise the
"utmost candour and fairness" would involve a duty to make all reasonable
efforts to identify and locate witnesses for the purpose of taking witness
statements and subsequently to secure the attendance of the witnesses at the
trial. However, there is some authority to the effect that the prosecution
cannot be expected to go to extraordinary lengths for this purpose.[214]

10. Defence Disclosure

There is no general duty on the defence to disclose aspects of its case in
advance to the prosecution. However, there are piecemeal statutory provisions
which impose a limited duty in defined circumstances. The primary examples
are evidence of alibi and the duty to give advance notice of an intention to
call a witness on a charge of membership of an unlawful organisation (see
Chapter 19, paras 19–32 *et seq.*)   **14–61**

It is also worth noting the various adverse inference provisions in this
context. These are dealt with in Chapters 6 and 7.

---

[214] *Geaney v. DPP* unreported, High Court, December 8, 1999.

THE INDICTMENT

A. Introduction

The indictment is the formal document setting out the charge or charges **15–01** against an accused who has been sent forward for trial on indictment. A valid indictment is an essential pre-requisite for the commencement of a valid trial. If the indictment upon which an accused is tried suffers from a defect which renders it invalid, the whole of the subsequent trial proceedings are null and void.

The indictment is drafted initially as a bill of indictment by counsel for the prosecution after the accused has been sent forward for trial. The bill of indictment is delivered to the court registrar to be signed. This is known as the preferment of the bill of indictment. It would appear that this requirement for the indictment to be duly signed is not a mere formality. In *R. v. Morais*[1] the English Court of Appeal ruled that the requirement of a proper signature was a necessary precondition for the existence of a valid indictment.[2] The conviction in that case was quashed and a re-trial ordered on the ground that the indictment had not been duly signed.

B. The Indictment Rules

The form of the indictment is prescribed by the Criminal Justice **15–02** (Administration) Act 1924 and the rules contained in the First Schedule to the Act.[3] This Act is quite peculiar in that it has a First Schedule containing a

---

[1] (1988) 87 Cr. App. Rep. 29.
[2] It is unlikely that this requirement is affected by s.4 of the Criminal Justice (Administration) Act 1924 (see below para 15–02)
[3] These rules include specifications for the paper, margins, writing etc. However, a failure to comply

body of rules which give more detailed effect to the general provisions laid out in the main body of the Act itself. The Schedule also has an appendix setting out examples of forms of indictment. The Act states that the rules shall have effect as if they were enacted in the Act.[4] They can also be extended, varied or annulled by further rules made under the Act.[5] The rules are made by the Minister for Justice, Equality and Law Reform[6] and do not come into force until they have been approved by a resolution of each House of the Oireachtas.[7]

Section 4(2) of the Act stipulates that:

> "Notwithstanding any rule of law or practice, an indictment shall, subject to the provisions of this Act, not be open to objection in respect of its form or contents if it is framed in accordance with the rules under this Act."

It is submitted that this does not affect the requirement for an indictment to be signed by an officer of the court. An indictment only qualifies as an indictment once it is duly signed by an officer of the court. Up until that point it is no more than a bill of indictment and as such cannot benefit from the protection offered by section 4(2).

C. The Prosecutor

15–03   The rules scheduled to the Criminal Justice (Administration) Act 1924 stipulate that the indictment shall be headed: "The Attorney General of Eire v. A.B.".[8] Since the establishment of the office of DPP the practice has been to use "The People of Ireland (at the suit of the Director of Public Prosecutions) v. A.B." unless, of course, the charge or charges relate to one of those few offences which can be prosecuted only by the Attorney General. The heading is followed immediately below with the name of the court at which the indictment is to be preferred. In practice this is likely to be the Central Criminal Court, the Circuit Court Limerick (or whatever the Circuit Court area in question) or the Special Criminal Court, as the case may be.

D. Choice of Offences

15–04   The indictment is drawn up by counsel for the prosecution. Typically it will charge that offence, or those offences, for which the accused has been sent for trial. Equally, however, other offences may be included by way of addition or substitution.[9] The prosecution may include any count which is found on any

---

fully with the specifications is not a ground for objection to the indictment; Criminal Justice (Administration) Act 1924, Sched. 1, r.1.
[4] Criminal Justice (Administration) Act 1924, s.1.
[5] *ibid.* ss.1 and 3.
[6] *ibid.* s.2(1) and Courts of Justice Act 1924, s.36.
[7] *ibid.* s.2(2) and s.101.
[8] *ibid.*, Sched. 1, r.2.
[9] Criminal Procedure Act 1967, s.4M, as inserted by Criminal Justice Act 1999, s.9. See also the provisions on the joinder of unrelated charges discussed below.

of the documents (book of evidence) served on the accused pursuant to the requirements of section 4M of the Criminal Procedure Act 1967 (see chapter 14), subject to the rules governing the joinder of counts which are discussed below.[10] So, for example, if the accused was sent forward for trial solely on a charge of simple larceny, the prosecution might add a charge of handling stolen goods if the evidence shows that the accused was found in possession of the goods in circumstances which might be consistent with either simple larceny or handling. Similarly, if the accused has been sent forward for trial on a charge of manslaughter, the prosecution might decide to replace the charge with one for murder if it considers that the material served on the accused provided sufficient evidence of malice aforethought.

As will be seen below under the heading of "Joinder of Counts" (paras. 15–28 *et seq*) there is provision enabling the prosecution to add to the indictment one or more counts which are not founded on the documents (book of evidence) served on the accused after he has been sent forward for trial.[11] This option will be available only with the consent of the accused and if the additional counts charge an offence justiciable within the State.

Instead of adding or substituting new charges in an indictment the prosecution may opt to serve a completely new indictment. It would appear that this is possible even after the High Court has fixed a date for trial in the Central Criminal Court pursuant to an application based on the original indictment.[12]

E. Statement of Offence

General Layout

Section 4(1) of the Criminal Justice (Administration) Act 1924 stipulates that: **15–05**

> "Every indictment shall contain, and shall be sufficient if it contains, a statement of the specific offence or offences with which the accused person is charged, together with such particulars as may be necessary for giving reasonable information as to the nature of the charges."

Accordingly, the indictment will set out immediately below the name of the court the offence or offences with which the accused is charged. A description of each offence charged must be set out in a separate paragraph called a count.[13] Where more than one offence is charged in the same indictment each must be charged in a separate count, and the counts must be numbered consecutively.[14] Each count will commence with the words: "A.B. is charged

---

[10] See *State (Conor) v. Kavanagh* [1937] I.R. 428 for an example under the old preliminary examination procedure. There is English authority to the effect that the indictment cannot consist of counts composed entirely of charges in respect of which the accused was not committed; *R v. Lombardi* [1989] 1 W.L.R. 73.

[11] Criminal Procedure Act 1967, s.4N, as inserted by Criminal Justice Act 1999, s.9.

[12] *People (Attorney General) v. Singer* 1 Frewen 214. Note, however, that the Attorney General's competence to serve a new indictment in such circumstances was not argued in this case.

[13] Criminal Justice (Administration) Act 1924, Sched. 1, r.4(1).

[14] *ibid.* r.4(6).

with the following offence (offences):".[15] There then follows a statement of the offence using non-technical language and without necessarily stating all the elements of the offence.[16] The essential feature is that the basic substance of the offence should be clear. In a murder case, for example, it will read quite simply, murder. If the statement leaves any doubt about what is being charged that doubt may be resolved by looking at the particulars of the offence which follow immediately below. In *Attorney General v. Cunningham*,[17] for example, the statement of the offence read "firing into a dwelling house". Although there was no such offence known at common law the judge was prepared to consider whether, read in the light of the particulars, the offence of breach of the peace was disclosed.

Statutory Offence

15–06   Where the offence in question is a common law offence there is no need to include the words "contrary to common law" after the statement of the offence.[18] If, however, the offence has been created by statute the statement of the offence must refer to the section of the statute creating the offence.[19] So, for example, the statement of offence in a case of obtaining by false pretences will read: "Obtaining goods by false pretences, contrary to section 32(1) of the Larceny Act 1916". If the statutory provision in question has been amended, the amending provisions should also be included.[20] Nevertheless, it would appear that there are occasions where a reference to a statute is considered unnecessary and even unhelpful. For example, if the statute does no more than merely state the established common law definition of the offence it is probably better not to refer to it at all. In *State (Quinn) v. Mangan*,[21] for example, it was held that it was not necessary to refer to section 42 of the Offences against the Person Act 1861 for a charge of assault which existed independently of the statute at common law. Gavan Duffy J. explained that:

> "Sect.42 may be viewed as a procedural enactment and as a penal enactment; viewed as a procedural enactment, its mention was unnecessary and, viewed as prescribing the penalty . . ., its mention was unnecessary, unless there be any conflicting enactment applicable, to cause uncertainty, and none has been produced."[22]

If, however, the name of a pre-existing common law offence has been changed by statute, then it is probably best to include a reference to the relevant statutory provision. In the case of a charge of sexual assault, for example, it is

---

[15]   *ibid.* r.2.
[16]   *ibid.* r.4(2) and (3).
[17]   [1932] I.R. 28.
[18]   *Attorney General v. Sullivan* [1964] I.R. 169.
[19]   Criminal Justice (Administration) Act 1924, Sched. 1, r.4(3). See also, *State (Cunningham) v. O'Floinn (District Justice)* (1960) 95 I.L.T.R. 24; *Attorney General v. Sullivan* [1964] I.R. 169.
[20]   In *State (Duggan) v. Evans* (1978) 112 I.L.T.R. 61 Finlay P. ruled that a count for burglary which merely cited s.23A of the Larceny Act 1916 was bad in so far as it did not cite the Criminal Law (Jurisdiction) Act 1976 which inserted the s.23A into the Larceny Act 1916.
[21]   [1945] I.R. 532.
[22]   *ibid.*

probably best to include a reference to section 10 of the Criminal Law (Rape)(Amendment) Act 1990, that being the statutory provision which changed the name of the common law offence of indecent assault.[23]

Statutory Penalty

Difficulties can arise where the statute prescribes the penalty for a pre-existing offence. If the statute does no more than specify the penalty applicable to the offence it is not necessary to include a reference to it in the indictment. Nevertheless, the Supreme Court has suggested that a reference to the statutory provision might be helpful in pointing out where the punishment is to be found.[24] Moreover, if the penalty differs depending on some particular aspect of the offence, reference to the statutory provision would appear to be appropriate.[25] Even then, a failure to do so would not appear to be fatal.[26] If, however, the statute goes further and creates a distinct offence it is necessary to include it in the indictment. In *People (DPP) v. Murray*,[27] for example, it was held that the Criminal Justice Act 1964 created capital murder as a distinct offence from murder at common law. As such the indictment should charge the offence by reference to section 3 of the Criminal Justice Act 1964.[28] In the case of an attempt to commit a statutory offence the attempt is usually charged as a common law offence and, as such, should not cite the statutory provision creating the complete offence.[29]

Common Law and Statutory Offence

If the same offence is to be found both at common law and in statute, an indictment should not charge the accused with both. In *People (Attorney General) v. Dermody*,[30] for example, the Court of Criminal Appeal cited section 14 of the Interpretation Act 1937 as authority for the proposition that an accused should not be charged in the one indictment with rape and unlawful carnal knowledge contrary to section 1 of the Criminal Law Amendment Act 1935. Section 14 of the 1937 Act protects the individual against being punished twice for the same offence. The ruling in *Dermody* was followed by the Court of Criminal Appeal in *People (Attorney General) v. Coughlan*[31] even though Haugh J., in delivering the judgment of the court, acknowledged that there was room for argument over whether rape and unlawful carnal knowledge contrary to section 1 of the Criminal Law Amendment Act 1935 were the same offence within the meaning of section 14 of the 1937 Act. The former requires lack of consent by the victim while the latter does not.

15–07

---

[23] *DPP v. F.* unreported, Supreme Court, February 2, 1994.
[24] *ibid.*
[25] See, *e.g. State (O) v. O'Brien* [1971] I.R. 42.
[26] See, *e.g. State (Foley) v. DPP* unreported, High Court, July 23, 1979; *State (Scott) v. Clifford* High Court, July 14, 1980, both cited in Ryan and Magee, *The Irish Criminal Process* (Mercier Press, Dublin, 1983), p. 246.
[27] [1977] I.R. 360.
[28] See now Criminal Justice Act 1990, s.3.
[29] *Attorney General v. Sullivan* [1964] I.R. 169.
[30] [1956] I.R. 307.
[31] (1968) 1 Frewen 325.

Extra-territorial Offence

Care should be taken in the wording of an indictment which charges an extra-territorial offence. If a statutory provision creates an offence which happens to have an extra-territorial element then it will normally be sufficient to charge the offence by reference to the statutory provision.[32] It may be, however, that the statutory provision merely extends the reach of the criminal law to matters done abroad, without actually creating a separate offence consisting of such matters done abroad. In this event the indictment should charge the accused specifically by reference to the statutory provision creating the offence in domestic law as applied by the statutory provision giving it extra-territorial effect.[33]

F. Particulars of Offence

1. General Requirements

15–08 The statement of offence in each individual count is followed by the particulars of the offence.[34] Once again these must be set out in ordinary language, avoiding the use of technical terms where they are not necessary. The rules scheduled to the 1924 Act offer some practical guidance on the drafting of particulars. These are supplemented by a collection of illustrative forms appended to the rules. It is stipulated that these illustrative forms should be used in cases to which they are directly applicable.[35] In other cases forms which conform as closely as possible to the illustrations should be adopted. It can be deduced from these examples that the key ingredients in the particulars are: the name of the accused; the date on which the offence was committed; the place where the offence was committed; and the key acts or omissions giving rise to the offence; in that order. As a general rule:

> ". . . it shall be sufficient to describe any place, time, thing, matter, act, or omission whatsoever to which it is necessary to refer in any indictment, in ordinary language in such a manner as to indicate with reasonable clearness the place, time, thing, matter, act or omission referred to."[36]

This, of course, is subject to more specific provisions laid down in the rules.

The key issue is whether the particulars stated in the indictment or elsewhere make clear to the defence the nature of the case it has to meet. Even errors of fact will not be fatal so long as the defence is not prejudiced by

---

[32] *People (DPP) v. Campbell* (1983) 2 Frewen 131 dealing with s.2(1) of the Criminal Law (Jurisdiction) Act 1976.

[33] See *Hatchell v. DPP* High Court, April 6, 2001 dealing with s.2 of the Sexual Offences (Jurisdiction) Act 1996.

[34] Criminal Justice (Administration) Act 1924, Sched. 1, r.4(4). This is subject to the proviso that "where any rule of law or any statute limits the particulars of an offence which are required to be given in an indictment, nothing in this rule shall require any more particulars to be given than those required".

[35] Criminal Justice (Administration) Act 1924, Sched. 1, r.4(5).

[36] *ibid.* r.9

the erroneous description of the offence. The particulars of the offence are not to be treated like the words of a statute.[37] It is also worth noting that the particulars will be important in identifying what it is that the accused is admitting to for the purpose of sentence on a guilty plea.[38]

2. The Accused

The description of the accused in the particulars should be reasonably sufficient to identify him. Typically, this will be achieved simply by naming him, although an error in stating his name will not be fatal so long as he can reasonably be identified from the particulars.[39] There is no need to state his address or occupation, unless these are essential to establish his identity.

15–09

3. The Victim

Generally, it is not necessary to identify or describe the victim of the offence. For some offences, particularly offences against the person, the indictment will almost inevitably name the victim. Even so it is possible to have particulars which, for example, charge the accused with the murder of a person or persons unknown. On the other hand, there are some offences where it is essential to describe certain characteristics of the victim. For example, in a prosecution for unlawful carnal knowledge of a girl under the age of 15 years, the indictment would have to state that the victim was a girl under the age of fifteen years.[40] Failure to specify the age element will result in the case being treated as a prosecution for unlawful carnal knowledge *per se*.[41] Similarly, if the domestic or contractual relationship between the accused and the victim was an essential element of the offence it would be necessary to specify the status of the victim relative to the accused.

15–10

4. Date and Location

The date and location of the offence do not normally have to be specified with detailed precision. If the exact date of commission is unknown it is usually acceptable to state "at a date unknown" between two specified dates. This practice is often followed in child sexual abuse cases where the abuse is alleged to have been carried out over a period of time. In such cases the indictment will normally consist of a number of counts, each of which will charge a single sexual assault on a date unknown between two specified dates which are twelve months apart. The reality often is that several assaults will have been committed during this period, but the rule against duplicity (see below para 15–15 *et seq.*) prevents the indictment from charging the commission of two or more identical offences during the same period. The

15–11

---

[37] *R. v. Moses* [1991] Crim. L.R. 617.
[38] *People (DPP) v. Naughton*, unreported, Court of Criminal Appeal, February 22, 1999.
[39] Criminal Justice (Administration) Act 1924, Sched. 1, r.7.
[40] *R. v. Martin* (1840) 9 C. & P. 213.
[41] *R. v. Stephenson* [1912] 3 K.B. 341.

Supreme Court has strongly criticised this practice. In *DPP v. F*,[42] for example, the substance of the allegations were that the accused had subjected the victims to sexual abuse several times a week every week over a period of years. Each count in the indictment, however, charged one incident of sexual abuse in each year. Egan J. described the indictment as unreal in its failure to conform more closely with the allegations. In the absence of legislation to deal with the problem of duplicity he suggested that each count should refer to a month rather than a year. In *D O'R v. DPP*,[43] on similar facts, the High Court approved of an indictment in which each count referred to a sexual assault on a date unknown within a specified quarter of a specified year.

15–12 An error concerning the date specified in the indictment will not necessarily be fatal to a conviction, unless the accused has been prejudiced by the error.[44] Clearly if the timing of the alleged offence is relevant to the offender's liability as, for example, where the age of the victim is a factor, an error may prove fatal.[45]

The time of day at which the offence is alleged to have been committed is not usually specified in the indictment. If, however, it is relevant to one of the elements of the offence then it must be specified. For example, an indictment for larceny under section 13 of the Larceny Act 1916 should specifically state that the breaking and entering with intent to steal occurred at night on the specified date.

The location of the offence is normally satisfied in an indictment by stating the county in which it is alleged to have been committed. In *People (Attorney General) v. Melody*,[46] however, the Court of Criminal Appeal suggested that the inclusion of the words "in the county of Galway" in a count for receiving stolen goods was surplusage and that it would have been better if they had been omitted. Their inclusion would only be essential where it was necessary to establish jurisdiction to try the offence or if a failure to establish the precise place of receiving might prejudice the accused.

It may be that the nature of the offence will require specificity as to the location of its alleged commission. Since burglary, for example, can only be committed in a building, an indictment for burglary should identify the building in which the offence is supposed to have occurred. Similarly, a road traffic offence will normally require a reference to the road on which the offence is alleged to have been committed.

5. Substance of Acts or Omissions

15–13 *General Layout*

Most difficulty arises in connection with the substance of the acts or omissions at the heart of the offence in question. It is not generally necessary

---

[42] Unreported, Supreme Court, February 24, 1994.
[43] Unreported, High Court, February 27, 1997.
[44] *R. v. Dossi* (1918) 13 Cr. App. Rep. 158.
[45] *R. v. Radcliffe* [1990] Crim. LR. 524.
[46] 1967 1 Frewen 319

to state what the accused is alleged to have done in fulfillment of each of the individual elements of the offence. An extreme example of this is the offence of murder where the practice is simply to state that "A.B. on the – day of – in the County of – murdered J.S.". The particulars need not specify how the murder was committed nor even that the accused acted with malice afore-thought. For the most part, however, it is necessary to state the acts or omissions which establish the key ingredients of the offence, particularly where they are instrumental in defining the accused's conduct as criminal or in distinguishing the offence alleged from a related offence. Similarly, the prosecution in a rape case would have to state that the accused acted without the consent of the victim,[47] unless the offence in question was one of the statutory varieties in which the consent of the victim was not required. In that event the statement of the offence would have to refer to the statutory provision in question and the particulars would have to specify the factor or factors which brought the case within the scope of the provision.[48]

Guidance in the Rules

The rules scheduled to the 1924 Act offer some general guidance which is applicable to the description of the acts or omissions at the heart of the offence in question. Where the indictment refers to property, for example, it will be sufficient to describe it in ordinary language which identifies the property with reasonable clarity.[49] Generally, it is not necessary to name the owner of the property or its value unless the offence in question depends on some special ownership or value as the case may be. Larceny under section 17(1)(e) of the Larceny Act 1916 is an example of an offence where the status of the owner is relevant. A count charging this offence would have to state that the accused was a clerk or servant of the owner of the goods at the time of the alleged offence. In the case of an offence under the Criminal Damage Act 1991 the value of the property may be relevant. In any case where the indictment refers to the owner of property which is owned by more than one person, it will be sufficient to state that the property is owned by one of those persons by name with others.[50] Where the property is owned by a body with a collective name, such as "Inhabitants", "Trustees", "Commissioners", "Club", etc., it is sufficient to use the collective name. If it is necessary to refer to any document or instrument in the indictment it will be sufficient to describe it by any name or designation by which it is usually known or by its contents.[51] It is not necessary to set out a copy of the document.

Statutory Offences

Further rules apply to statutory offences. If the offence involves the doing, or **15–14**
the omission to do, any one of a number of different acts in the alternative,

---

[47] In *Re Extradition; Stanton v. Governor of Arbour Hill*, unreported, High Court, December 7, 1999.
[48] *R. v. Martin* (1840) 9 C. & P. 213; *R. v. Stephenson* [1912] 3 K.B. 341.
[49] Criminal Justice (Administration) Act 1924, Sched. 1, r.6(1).
[50] *ibid.* r.6(2).
[51] *ibid.* r.8.

the acts may be stated in the alternative in the count charging that offence.[52] The same applies where the act or omission can be done in any one of a number of different capacities or with any one of a number of different intentions. Equally, if the statute creating the offence specifies any exception or exemption from, or qualification to, the offence it is not necessary to negative that exception, exemption or qualification in the count charging the offence.[53] In any statutory offence involving an intent to defraud, deceive or injure a person, it is not necessary to state the intent with respect to any particular person, unless the statute creating the offence makes it an essential ingredient to have the intent with respect to a particular person.[54] Offences which can be committed in one of a number of different ways or with any one of a number of different intents can give rise to problems of duplicity. This issue is pursued further under the heading of duplicity (see below para. 15–15 *et seq.*).

Relevance of Previous Conviction

Some offences are rendered more serious by the fact that the accused has been convicted of a certain offence in the past. In such cases a reference to the previous conviction or convictions should be charged at the end of the count by a statement to the effect that the accused has previously been convicted of the relevant offence at a certain time and place.[55] It is not necessary to state the particulars of the previous offence.

G. Duplicity

1. Introduction

15–15 Although it is perfectly proper for a single indictment to contain several counts, no single count should charge more than one offence.[56] Where two or more offences are alleged in a single count that count is said to be bad for duplicity. The same applies to counts specified in the disjunctive.[57] Where a count is affected by duplicity the defence should bring a motion to have the count quashed. If the judge accedes to the motion the accused is relieved of the obligation to plead to that count. Where the motion is rejected and the accused is subsequently convicted on that count there may be grounds for appeal. However, a failure to object to the inclusion of a duplicitous count before the jury retires will not operate as a bar to a subsequent appeal against conviction on the grounds of duplicity.[58]

In order to determine whether a count charges more than one offence, the court should look at the wording of the count itself and any further particulars

---

[52] *ibid.* r.5(1).
[53] *ibid.* r.5(2).
[54] *ibid.* r.10.
[55] *ibid.* r.11.
[56] *R. v. Morley* (1827) 1 Y. & J. 221; *Reg. v. Meath Justices* (1841) 2 Leg. Rep. 8 (Q.B.).
[57] *R. v. Stocker* (1695) 5 Mod. 137; *Attorney General (Mahony) v. Hourigan* [1945] I.R. 266.
[58] *People (Attorney General) v. Blogh* [1958] I.R. 91.

supplied by the prosecution. If they disclose only one offence then the count does not offend against duplicity. It will not matter that the evidence called subsequently by the prosecution discloses more than one example of the offence charged. In *R. v. Greenfield*,[59] for example, a count charged conspiracy to commit by use of an explosive substance an explosion in the United Kingdom of a nature to endanger life or to cause serious injury to property. The evidence called by the prosecution disclosed the existence of several conspiracies to cause explosions. Nevertheless, the English Court of Appeal rejected the defence argument that the count was bad for duplicity.

While it is easy to state that a single count must not charge more than one offence, it is not always easy in practice to establish whether more than one offence is being charged. The problem can arise either with respect to the legal definition of the offence or with respect to the circumstances in which it is alleged to have been committed. A simple example of the former is a count which alleges that "A.B . . . raped or sexually assaulted C.D." Although rape may involve a sexual assault they are clearly two distinct offences and as such should be charged as separate counts. If, however, the offence is a combined offence it will be necessary to include its constituent parts in the count even though each may constitute a distinct offence in its own right. Robbery, for example, consists of stealing involving an assault. A count charging robbery, therefore, cannot be challenged merely on the ground that it includes two distinct offences namely stealing and assault.

15–16

Particular care must be taken when framing a count for burglary. The offence can be committed where a person enters a building as a trespasser with intent to steal anything therein, do unlawful damage to the building or anything therein, inflict grievous bodily harm or rape.[60] Equally it can be committed where a person steals or inflicts grievous bodily harm after having entered the building as a trespasser.[61] It follows that it would be perfectly proper to include the completed offences of stealing or grievous bodily harm in the burglary count where the accused is alleged to have entered a building as a trespasser and stole or inflicted grievous bodily harm therein. If, however, the accused entered the building as a trespasser and raped or did unlawful damage, the completed rape or unlawful damage offence would have to be charged in a separate count. It does not form part of the burglary offence.

2. Alternative Modes of Commission

Examples

Further problems arise when a statute creates an offence and stipulates that it can be committed through any one of a number of different acts or omissions, or with any one of a number of different intents.[62] An example of the former

15–17

---

[59] [1973] 1 W.L.R. 1151.
[60] Larceny Act 1916, s.23A(1)(a), as inserted by Criminal Law (Jurisdiction) Act 1976, s.6.
[61] *ibid.* s.23A(1)(b), s.6.
[62] See *State (Hardy) v. District Justice O'Floinn* 83 I.L.T.R. 58 where it was held that s.7 of the

is section 10(1) of the Non-fatal Offences against the Person Act 1997 which makes it an offence for any person who, without lawful authority or reasonable excuse, by any means including by use of the telephone, harasses another by persistently following, watching, pestering, besetting or communicating with him or her. An example of an offence which can be committed with any one of a number of different intents is section 27B(1) of the Firearms Act 1964 which makes it an offence to have a firearm with intent to commit an indictable offence, or to resist or prevent arrest. In such cases the question arises whether the statute is creating a single offence which can be charged in a single count alleging the alternatives, or a number of distinct offences which would have to be charged individually in separate counts.

The Rules

The indictment rules make specific provision enabling an offence to be charged in the alternative where the statute in question defines it in the alternative. The relevant provision reads:

> "Where an enactment constituting an offence states the offence to be the doing or the omission to do any one of any different acts in the alternative, or the doing or the omission to do any act in any one of any different capacities, or with any one of any different intentions, or states any part of the offence in the alternative, the acts, omissions, capacities, or intentions, or other matters stated in the alternative in the enactment, may be stated in the alternative in the count charging the offence."[63]

While this clearly permits a count to charge an offence in the alternative it does not follow that several distinct offences can be included in a single count simply because they have been created by a single statutory provision. In other words the indictment rules do not resolve the basic problem of determining in each individual case whether a statutory provision is creating several distinct offences or a single offence which can be committed in a number of different ways. Unfortunately, the drafting of criminal statutes does not always make it clear whether a given provision is creating several distinct offences or a single offence which can be committed in several different ways.

Single Act or Several Acts

15–18   The standard approach is to consider whether the prohibited conduct is defined as a single act or omission or several acts or omissions. If the conduct is defined as a single act or omission then the enactment is likely to be interpreted as creating a single offence, even if the *mens rea* or other elements can be satisfied in the alternative. In *R v. Naismith*,[64] for example, it was held that section 18 of the Offences against the Person Act 1861 created three separate offences of wounding, shooting or causing grievous bodily harm to a

---

Conspiracy and Protection of Property Act 1875 and s.14(13) of the Dublin Police Act 1842 each created only one offence but specified various methods of committing it.

[63]   Criminal Justice (Administration) Act 1924, Sched. 1, r.5(1).
[64]   [1961] 1 W.L.R. 952.

person, each of which could be committed with any one of several specified intents. The count in that case charged the accused with "caus[ing] grievous bodily harm to H with intent to do him grievous bodily harm or to maim, disfigure or disable him". Since it charged only a single act which could be committed with one of several different intents it did not offend the rule against duplicity. If, however, the count had repeated the full words of the enactment it would have been bad for duplicity as it would have charged several prohibited acts.

In *Thompson v. Knights*[65] the accused was charged with being in charge of a motor vehicle when unfit through drink or drugs contrary to the appropriate statutory enactment. On a case stated to a Divisional Court it was held that the count was not bad for duplicity simply because it included the alternatives of being unfit though drink or drugs. The court explained that the enactment created three offences of driving, attempting to drive and being in charge of a motor vehicle. Each of these offences could be committed when the accused was under the influence of either drink or drugs. Being under the influence of drink or drugs were the circumstances in which the specified acts would be criminal. It did not constitute separate modes of commission. This decision was cited with approval by the majority in the Supreme Court in *State (Roddy) v. Carr*[66] where a similar issue arose in the interpretation of section 49 of the Road Traffic Act 1961.[67]

Circumstances in Which the Act Occurs

It can be difficult to determine whether the statutory words in question are part of the conduct or the circumstances in which the conduct occurs. In *Thompson v. Knights*,[68] for example, the reference to being unfit through drink or drugs was interpreted as a description of the condition or state of the accused as distinct from his actual conduct. In *State (McLoughlin) v. Judge Shannon*,[69] by comparison, the prosecutor had been convicted of dangerous driving contrary to section 51 of the Road Traffic Act 1933. The particulars of the offence, following the statutory provision, charged him with driving the vehicle at a speed or in a manner which having regard to all the circumstances of the case . . . was dangerous to the public.[70] Following the precedent of *R (Burrowes) v. Justices of Cavan*,[71] the High Court ruled that the statutory provision created two distinct offences as the alternatives related to the conduct of the accused as distinct from his state or the circumstances in which the conduct occurred. Accordingly, the offences could not be charged

---

[65] [1947] K.B. 336.
[66] [1975] I.R. 275.
[67] The offence has now been replaced by s.10 of the Road Traffic Act 1994 in a manner which disposes of the points raised in the dissenting judgment of Walsh J.
[68] [1947] K.B. 336.
[69] [1948] I.R. 439.
[70] See now s.53(1) of the Road Traffic Act 1961 (as amended by s.51 of the Road Traffic Act 1968). It creates only one offence of dangerous driving.
[71] [1914] 2 I.R. 150.

in the alternative in a single count. This decision was approved by the Court of Criminal Appeal in *People (Attorney General) v. Blogh.*[72]

Conjunctive Acts

15–19   Further difficulties can arise where a count charges the accused with more than one act or omission conjunctively. In *R. v. Clow,*[73] for example, the accused was charged with "driving at a speed *and* in a manner dangerous to the public" (emphasis added) contrary to the appropriate enactment. Nevertheless the English Court of Criminal Appeal ruled that it was permissible to charge these separate modes of commission in a single count as they related to a single act of driving. The decision, however, has come in for considerable criticism and in practice is not generally followed.[74] In *Mallon v. Allen,*[75] by contrast, a Divisional Court quashed a conviction based on an information for "admitting and allowing to remain" in a licensed betting office a person under 18 years of age contrary to the appropriate enactment. Distinguishing *R. v. Clow* the court found that "admitting" and "allowing to remain" were two separate acts. Accordingly, the enactment created two separate offences. Charging them in a single information, whether conjunctively or disjunctively offended the rule against duplicity.

Two or More Types of Intention

Although the intention of the accused strictly speaking is not a part of his conduct, it would appear that the rule against duplicity can be offended by the inclusion of two or more types of intention. This can happen where the effect of their inclusion is to create uncertainty as to the precise offence with which the accused has been charged.[76] In *People v. Ruttledge,*[77] for example, the accused was charged with an offence under section 33(4) of the Larceny Act 1916. Secion 33(4) created two offences, one being a felony the other a misdemeanour. The difference between the two offences concerned the particular intention with which the prohibited act was done. Since one created a felony and the other a misdemeanour the Supreme Court ruled that they could not be included in the same count either conjunctively or disjunctively.

Of course, the distinction between felonies and misdemeanours has now been abolished. Nevertheless, there have been suggestions that the rule against duplicity could be offended by the inclusion of two different mens reas where one was of a considerably higher standard than the other. In *Hanlon v.*

---

[72]   [1958] I.R. 91.
[73]   [1965] 1 Q.B. 598.
[74]   See *Blackstone's Criminal Practice* (1997), D9.22.
[75]   [1964] 1 Q.B. 385.
[76]   In *People v. Ruttledge* [1978] I.R. 376 O'Byrne J. in the Supreme Court said that the Criminal Justice (Administration) Act 1924 was intended to simplify procedure in criminal proceedings and that it undoubtedly allows great latitude in the drawing up of indictments. However, he went on to say that it does not permit an indictment to be drawn up in such a form that a conviction based upon it is uncertain as to the precise offence of which the accused has been convicted.
[77]   [1978] I.R. 376.

Fleming,[78] Henchy J. in the Supreme Court said that a conviction for handing stolen goods knowing or believing them to be stolen (instead of just knowing as was required by section 33(1) of the Larceny Act 1916 at the time) could be bad for duplicity. His suggestion was heavily influenced by his view that knowing is a considerably higher standard of *mens rea* than believing.

3. Commission on Separate Occasions

The General Rule

A count may suffer from duplicity if it alleges that the offence was committed on several different occasions. In *R. v. Thompson*,[79] for example, the accused was charged in a single count of committing incest with his daughter "on divers days between the month of January, 1909, and the 4th day of October, 1910". It was accepted that the count was "irregular" as it clearly charged the accused with more than one offence of incest. Nevertheless, the accused's appeal against conviction was dismissed as he had ample notice of the precise dates on which the acts of incest were alleged to have occurred and, as such, was not prejudiced in his defence by the wording of the count. In *People (Attorney General) v. Singer*[80] a count charging fraudulent conversion on two different months as part of an ongoing activity was held bad for duplicity, as was a count charging fraudulent conversion in respect of the distribution of a sum of profits among several investors over a period of time.

15–20

Even if the offences are committed on the same day as part of a single enterprise it does not follow that they can be charged in the same count. For example, if a person is accused of stealing goods from several different shops while on a shopping trip it would not be proper to include each incident in the same count simply because they all involved simple larceny. Since each theft constituted a separate offence each would have to be charged in a separate count. It does not follow, however, that there has to be a separate count for each item stolen from each shop. In *R. v. Wilson*,[81] for example, the accused paid a visit to a department store during which he stole items from several different departments. He then moved on to another department store where he repeated the exercise. He was subsequently charged on two counts of theft from each store. Each count covered all of the items stolen in the relevant store. The accused appealed his conviction on the ground that there should have been separate counts for each department in the stores. The English Court of Appeal rejected this argument on the basis that the accused's acts in each store were not separated by his movement from one department to another. They constituted part of the same criminal act.

---

[78] [1981] I.R. 489.
[79] [1914] 2 K.B. 99.
[80] 1 Frewen 214.
[81] (1979) 69 Cr. App. Rep. 83.

Connection in Time and Place

15–21   It is not always easy to determine whether individual acts are sufficiently connected in time and place to be charged as a single offence in one count rather than as similar offences in separate counts In *DPP v. Merriman* the House of Lords advocated a practical common sense approach to this problem:

> "The rule against duplicity, viz. that only one offence should be charged in any count of an indictment . . . has always been applied in a practical, rather than in a strictly analytical, way for the purpose of determining what constituted one offence. Where a number of acts of a similar nature committed by one or more defendants were connected with one another, in the time and place of their commission or by common purpose, in such a way that they could fairly be regarded as forming part of the same transaction or criminal practice, it was the practice, as early as the eighteenth century, to charge them in a single count of an indictment."[82]

Although the House of Lords in this case was concerned with a situation where the accused had participated in the multiple stabbing of the victim in the course of an attack which lasted only a few seconds, the principle enunciated applies more generally. In *Jemmison v. Priddle*,[83] for example, it was held that a single count was appropriate in a case where two deer were shot separately within seconds at the same place. Widgery L.C.J. explained:

> "One looks at this case and asks oneself what was the activity with which the appellant was being charged. It was the activity of shooting red deer without a game licence, and although as a nice debating point it might well be contended that each shot was a separate offence, I find that all these matters, occurring as they must have done within a very few seconds of time and all in the same geographical location, are fairly to be described as components of a single activity, and that made it proper for the prosecution in this instance to join them in a single charge."[84]

McCarthy J. quoted this passage with approval in the Court of Criminal Appeal in a case where the appellant had been convicted of a single count of indecent assault.[85] The prosecution evidence was that the appellant had attacked the victim and subjected her to an ordeal which included a number of assaults, some relatively minor, others horrendous. Since they were all part of the same chain of events the court rejected the appellant's argument that the prosecution should have been required to charge each individual assault separately.

Similarly, in *R. v. Giddins*,[86] it was held that a count of robbing A of one shilling and B of two shillings was valid since the robberies were virtually simultaneous. Interestingly, in this case the robberies were from two different

---

[82] [1973] A.C. 584, *per* Lord Diplock at 607.
[83] [1972] 1 Q.B. 489.
[84] *ibid.* at 495.
[85] *People (DPP) v. Barr* unreported, Court of Criminal Appeal, July 21, 1992.
[86] (1842) Car & M 634.

victims.[87] A sufficient connection has also been established on the basis that the individual offences are identical in all respects apart from the fact that they were committed at different times.[88]

Offences Committed over Period of Time

Circumstances may dictate that a single count charging the commission of an offence on a single date is acceptable, or even desirable, where several individual criminal acts have been committed over a long period of time. In *R. v. Tomlin*,[89] for example, the accused was charged with embezzling an aggregate of £420 from his employers on a date unknown between two specified dates. The circumstances were such that it was impossible to identify which particular sums were embezzled at which particular time. Accordingly, the English Court of Criminal Appeal held that it was proper to include the total in a single count which alleged the embezzlement of the aggregate sum. To do otherwise would defeat the interests of justice.[90]

Similarly in *R. v. Firth*[91] a single count for stealing gas on a certain date was upheld even though it had been taken over a number of years. Since the stealing took the form of a continuous act it could be treated as one act of stealing. Accordingly, the prosecution could adduce evidence of the stealing over the whole period despite the fact that the indictment charged the accused with stealing on a specific date. By the same token, a conviction for stealing on that date would preclude the subsequent prosecution of the accused for stealing the gas or any quantity of the gas on any other day or days within the period of the continuous act.

In *DPP v. McCabe*[92] a count charging the accused with stealing 76 library books between two specified dates from a public library was upheld. The English Court of Appeal ruled that where a number of articles are stolen and there is no evidence of when the individual appropriations occurred, it is appropriate to charge the theft of the aggregate number over a specified period.

It does not follow from these authorities that cases involving larceny or fraudulent conversion of similar items over a period of time can always be charged as a single offence. In *People (Attorney General) v. Singer* the Court of Criminal Appeal ruled that where it is possible to charge individual takings as separate offences, it is not generally acceptable to lump them together into an "omnibus" count.[93]

15–22

---

[87] See also, *R. v. Bleasdale* (1848) 2 Car & Kir 765 where the accused was convicted on a single count of stealing coal from the same mineshaft belonging to a number of owners.

[88] *R. v. Shepherd* (1868) 11 Cox CC 119.

[89] [1954] 2 Q.B. 274 approving *R. v. Lawson* (1952) 36 Cr.App.Rep. 30. *R. v. Chapman* (1843) 1 C & K 119; *R. v. Morris* (1933) 24 Cr. App. Rep. 105. See also, *Attorney General v. Gleeson* 64 I.L.T.R. 225.

[90] See also *R. v. Lambert* (1847) 2 Cox CC 309; *R. v. Balls* (1871) LR 1 CCR 328; *R. v. Henwood* (1870) 11 Cox CC 526; *R. v. Bleasdale* (1848) 2 Car & Kir 765. However, this will not be permitted where it would be unfair to the accused; see *People (Attorney General) v. Singer* (1961) 1 Frewen 214.

[91] (1869) LR 1 CCR 172.

[92] [1992] Crim. L.R. 885.

[93] See *People (Attorney General) v. Singer* (1961) 1 Frewen 214; *R. v. Robertson* (1936) 25 Cr. App. Rep. 208; *R. v. Tomlin* [1954] 2 Q.B. 274.

Continuous offences

15–23   Some statutory offences can, on their proper construction, be treated as continuous offences. In *Hodgetts v. Chiltern District Council*,[94] for example, the House of Lords accepted that an offence which consisted of using land in contravention of a planning notice is an offence which can be committed over a period of time. Accordingly, it was quite proper to charge the defendant with permitting certain land and buildings to be used in contravention of a planning enforcement notice "on and since May 27, 1980". It was not necessary to charge the defendant with a separate offence for each day on which he used the land in contravention of the notice. Lord Roskill explained that:

> "It is not an essential characteristic of a criminal offence that any prohibited act or omission, in order to constitute a single offence, should take place once and for all on a single day. It may take place whether continuously or intermittently, over a period of time."[95]

4. Separate Victims

15–24   Given what has been said already it might be assumed that a single act causing injury or death to more than one person could be charged in a single count. In practice, however, it would appear to be the norm to frame a separate count for each victim. In *R. v. Mansfield*,[96] for example, the accused set fire to an hotel as a result of which seven people died. The prosecution opted for a separate count of murder for each victim. It would appear that this practice does not extend to a single act which causes property damage or loss to more than one person.[97]

5. Location

15–25   An indictment will not generally be bad for duplicity if it alleges that the defendant committed the offence at a specified place "or elsewhere". Since the actual location need not be specified at all, the inclusion of the words "or elsewhere" is mere surplusage.[98] It would be different if the definition of the offence was such that location was an operative factor in establishing liability.

6. Money

15–26   Where the offence charged relates to a number of bank notes or coins a count will not be bad for duplicity if it simply refers to the notes and/or coins collectively as money. That would appear to be the effect of section 18 of the Criminal Procedure Act 1851 which reads:

---

[94]   [1983] 2 A.C. 120.
[95]   *ibid.* at 128.
[96]   [1977] 1 W.L.R. 1102.
[97]   *R. v. Bleasdale* (1848) 2 Car & Kir 765; *R. v. Giddins* (1842) Car & M 634.
[98]   *R. v. Wallwork* (1958) 42 Cr. App. R. 153.

"In every indictment in which it shall be necessary to make any averment as to money or any note of the Bank of England or any other bank, it shall be sufficient to describe such money or bank note simply as money, without specifying any particular coin or bank note; and such allegation, so far as regards the description of the property, shall be sustained by proof of any amount of coin or of any bank note, although the particular nature of the bank note shall not be proved."

7. Procedure

Where a count is bad for duplicity the defence should move to quash it before the accused is arraigned. While objection can be taken at a later stage the courts generally disapprove of postponement for tactical advantage.[99] If, however, the circumstances are such that the true nature of the duplicity does not become apparent until the prosecution evidence is called the defence cannot be prejudiced by a failure to object earlier. Rejection of a motion to quash a count for duplicity will provide grounds for appeal against conviction.

15–27

H. Joinder of Counts

1. Introduction

An indictment may contain several counts.[100] Typically these will be included in the indictment when it is first drawn up. It would appear, however, that new counts can be added at a later stage. Indeed, in *Conlon v. His Honour Judge Cyril Kelly*[101] the High Court accepted that new counts could be joined to an indictment after an order for a re-trial on the charges initially specified in the indictment. The re-trial could then proceed on the basis of the expanded indictment.

15–28

The indictment rules specify the criteria which must be satisfied before counts may be joined together in a single indictment:

"Charges for any offences . . . may be joined in the same indictment if those charges are founded on the same facts, or form or are part of a series of offences of the same or similar character."[102]

There are two situations, therefore, where charges may be joined in the same indictment: (i) where they are founded on the same facts; and (ii) where they are part of a series of offences of the same or similar character. Before dealing with each of these in turn it is worth noting that the Criminal Justice Act 1999 makes provision for the joinder of unrelated charges subject to the consent of the accused (see below para 15–42).[103]

---

[99] *R. v. Asif* (1982) 82 Cr. App. Rep. 123.
[100] Criminal Justice (Administration) Act 1924, s.5.
[101] unreported, High Court, December 14, 1999. See also, *People (DPP) v. Moylan*, unreported, Court of Criminal Appeal, May 19, 1999.
[102] Criminal Justice (Administration) Act 1924, Sched. 1, r.3.
[103] Criminal Procedure Act 1967, s.4N, as inserted by Criminal Justice Act 1999, s.9.

2. Founded on the Same Facts

Basic Requirements

15–29
The simplest illustration of several charges being founded on the same set of facts is a single act which incorporates a number of distinct offences. For example, if a person throws a petrol bomb into a dwelling which ignites and causes the death of some occupants and serious injury to others he might be charged with murder, causing serious harm to another, arson, possession of an explosive substance with intent to endanger life and possession of an explosive substance. These are all distinct offences arising out of the same facts and, as such, can be joined as separate counts in the same indictment. Indeed, there can also be separate counts of murder for each fatality and separate counts of causing serious harm to another for each person seriously injured. Although there was a time when it was considered improper to join any other count with a count of murder on an indictment, this is no longer the case.[104]

It is not always easy to determine whether incidents or events are sufficiently connected to justify joining counts arising from them in a single indictment. Charges can be considered to arise out of the same set of facts for the purpose of joinder even though they bear only an incidental relationship to each other. For example, if a motorist causes an accident through dangerous driving and it transpires that at the time of the accident he was driving the vehicle without the consent of the owner and was not insured to drive the vehicle, he could be charged on the same indictment with separate counts for dangerous driving contrary to section 51 of the Road Traffic Act 1961, taking a motor vehicle without the consent of the owner contrary to section 112 of the Road Traffic Act 1961 and driving without insurance contrary to section 56 of the Road Traffic Act 1961. If, however, a search of the accused at the scene of the accident revealed that he was in possession of stolen credit cards, it is submitted that it would not be proper to include counts of larceny or handling stolen goods in the indictment. The fact that evidence of these other offences fortuitously came to light as a result of the accident is hardly sufficient in itself to qualify them as arising out of the same set of facts.

Lapse of Time

15–30
A considerable time lapse between two or more offences will not necessarily be fatal to their joinder in a single indictment if there is a connection between them. In *R. v. Barrell and Wilson*,[105] for example, the two accused were charged with affray and assault arising out of an incident at a discotheque. After the committal proceedings one of them attempted to bribe a prosecution witness. He was charged on the same indictment with an additional count of attempting to pervert the course of justice. Although this offence was allegedly committed at a time and place far removed from the other offences it was considered proper to include it in the same indictment. Since it would

---

[104] *People v. Murray* [1977] I.R. 360; *Connolly v. DPP* [1964] A.C. 1254.
[105] (1979) 69 Cr. App. Rep. 250.

not have been committed had the incident at the discotheque not occurred it could be said to arise out of the same set of facts. In giving the judgment of the court Shaw L.J. offered a "but for" test to explain the meaning of "founded on the same set of facts":

> "The phrase 'founded on the same set of facts' does not mean that for charges properly to be joined in the same indictment, the facts in relation to the respective charges must be identical in substance or virtually contemporaneous. The test is whether the charges have a common factual origin. If the charge described by counsel as the subsidiary charge is one that could not have been alleged but for the facts which give rise to what he called the primary charge, then it is true to say for the purposes of [rule 3] that those charges are founded, that is to say have their origin, in the same set of facts and can legitimately be joined in the same indictment."[106]

Alternative Counts

Sometimes it may be necessary to charge several offences in an indictment arising out of the same set of facts because it is not possible in advance of the trial to determine which one of several possible offences the accused has committed. The typical example is where the accused has been found in possession of stolen goods shortly after they have been stolen. Depending on which view the jury takes of the evidence it may be possible to convict of simply larceny or receiving stolen goods. The solution is simply to include a separate count for each in the indictment on the understanding that a conviction can be entered for only one of them. It is worth noting, however, that the indictment will not state on its face that the counts are being charged in the alternative. Nevertheless, prosecuting counsel and the judge will explain to the jury that they should either acquit of all three offences or enter a conviction for only one of them.[107]

15–31

A slight variation on this practice is where the indictment contains counts which are "mutually destructive" of each other.[108] In *R. v. Bellman*,[109] for example, the accused was charged with counts of obtaining by deception and conspiracy to evade the prohibition on the importation of controlled drugs. He had obtained large sums of money from other individuals on the understanding that it would be used to import controlled drugs into the United Kingdom in a manner which would produce large profits for all concerned. If his representations to the others were false he would be guilty of obtaining by deception. If, on the other hand, the representations were true he would be guilty of conspiracy to evade the prohibition on the importation of controlled drugs; thus the inclusion of "mutually destructive" counts in the indictment. The judge directed the jury that they should consider first whether the plan to import drugs was genuine. If they found that it was genuine then they should

---

[106] *ibid.* at 252–253.
[107] See, *e.g.*, *R. v. Shelton* (1986) 83 Cr. App. R. 379.
[108] See *Blackstone's Criminal Practice* (1997) D9.25.
[109] [1989] A.C. 836.

convict of conspiracy. Only if they acquitted of conspiracy should they go on to consider the deception count. In the event the jury found the accused guilty of deception. On appeal the House of Lords rejected the argument that the prosecution cannot include two mutually contradictory counts in the one indictment. So long as the evidence was capable of sustaining a conviction for either of the counts there was no rule of law or practice which precludes their inclusion in the one indictment.[110] The accused, of course, could not be convicted of both counts. Moreover, if the jury are satisfied that the accused committed one of the offences but are not sure which, they must acquit of both. The matter has yet to come up for decision in Ireland. It may be that the constitutional protection of the individual's right to a fair trial would limit the scope for the inclusion of mutually contradictory counts in such circumstances.

Conspiracy

15–32   The option of including alternative counts should not be used as a device to include a count of conspiracy along with a separate count for the substantive offence where the evidence discloses the commission of the substantive offence. By the same token the indictment should not include a conspiracy count and a count for the substantive offence where the evidence for the former is the same as the evidence for the latter. In *People (Attorney General) v. Singer*,[111] for example, the accused was charged with three counts of conspiracy to obtain by false pretences, 16 counts of fraudulent conversion and two counts of obtaining money by false pretences. Counsel for the prosecution conceded that the evidence for the conspiracy counts was to be inferred from the evidence of the substantive offences. In condemning this practice O'Dalaigh J. in the Court of Criminal Appeal said:

> "Moreover, it has been said on more than one occasion in this Court that conspiracy should not be charged when the evidence relied upon to establish it is the evidence of substantive offences also laid in the same indictment. This course is not merely undesirable but is one fraught with danger in a case such as this where the type of fraud alleged in the conspiracy differs fundamentally from the type of fraud alleged in the substantive offences charged."[112]

Similarly, in *Ellis v. O'Dea* Walsh J. said, *obiter*:

> "For many years judicial authorities have condemned the joinder of a conspiracy charge when there is a charge for the substantive offence. Whatever justification may exist for preferring this charge of an inchoate crime such as that it may prevent a substantive crime from being committed it is difficult to see what, if any, justification can exist in justice for adding it to the substantive offence if charged."[113]

---

[110]   See *R. v. Barnes* (1985) 83 Cr. App. R. 38 for an example of a case where the inclusion of mutually contradictory counts in the one indictment can be considered necessary in the interests of justice.

[111]   (1961) 1 Frewen 214.

[112]   *ibid.* at 229.

[113]   [1990] I.L.R.M. 87 at 91.

In Britain the Lord Chief Justice has issued a practice direction on the use of conspiracy as an alternative count. It states that the judge should require the prosecution to justify such a course of action.[114] Joinder can be justified if the evidence may prove too weak to support a conviction on the substantive charge but is sufficient for the conspiracy charge. Alternatively, it may be justified where a number of counts for relatively minor substantive offences do not reflect the true gravity of the conduct of the accused. If the prosecution cannot justify joinder on either ground it must elect to proceed on either the conspiracy count or the substantive count.

15–33

Summary Offences

Where offences do qualify for joinder on account of arising out of the same set of facts it will not matter that some of them are summary offences. Section 6 of the Criminal Justice Act 1951 stipulates that the indictment may include a count in respect of a summary offence, provided that the accused has been charged with it and it arises out of the same set of facts as the indictable offence or offences on the indictment. Although the accused may be sentenced on conviction only to a punishment which could be inflicted on a person summarily convicted of the offence, the offence will be treated for all other purposes as an indictable offence. In *State (Harkin) v. O'Malley*,[115] for example, the accused had been charged on indictment with manslaughter, dangerous driving causing death and drunken driving. He was acquitted by direction of the trial judge on the count of manslaughter. The jury found him not guilty of dangerous driving causing death but guilty of careless driving and could not agree on the drunk driving count. Although drunk driving was a summary offence which was only included in the indictment pursuant to the provisions of section 6 of the Criminal Justice Act 1951 the Supreme Court ruled that the accused could be re-tried on indictment for that offence alone.[116]

Section 6 of the Criminal Justice Act 1951 was introduced to relieve the accused of the burden of facing a trial on indictment followed by a sumary trial for offences arising out of the same matter. Its interpretation, however, has given rise to some difficulty. In *State (Cahill) v. President of the Circuit Court*[117] the accused was charged before the District Court with manslaughter, dangerous driving contrary to section 51 of the Road Traffic Act 1933 and driving without exercising reasonable consideration for other road users contrary to section 50 of the Act. The last two offences were triable summarily. The accused was sent forward for trial on indictment on the manslaughter charge while the two summary charges were adjourned. When the indictment was lodged it also contained counts for the two summary

15–34

---

114 Practice Direction (*Crime: Conspiracy*) [1977] 1 W.L.R. 537.
115 [1978] I.R. 269; overruling *People v. Doyle* (1964) 101 I.L.T.R. 136.
116 This does not apply if the summary offence was not properly included in the indictment because, for example, it was not charged in the District Court; *R. v. Hall* [1891] 1 Q.B. 747; *People v. O'Brien* [1963] I.R. 92
117 [1954] I.R. 128.

charges pursuant to section 6 of the Criminal Justice Act 1951. Meanwhile the two summary charges were also adjourned in the District Court. The trial on indictment commenced on the same day that the summary charges came up before the District Court. The District Court proceeded with the charges and when the prosecution called no evidence the District Court judge dismissed the charges. The Circuit Court felt that it could not try the accused for summary charges after they had been dismissed by the District Court. Equally, it felt that the dismissal of the summary charges would preclude a trial for the indictable offence as the former were so closely connected to the latter. Accordingly, the prosecution sought to quash the orders of the District Court dismissing the summary charges.

The High Court refused to make absolute a conditional order of certiorari to quash the District Court orders dismissing the summary charges. However, the District Court orders were subsequently quashed on appeal to the Supreme Court where Murnaghan J. explained that section 6 comes into effect once the accused has been sent forward for trial on the indictable charge. It enables the Attorney General (now the DPP) to add the summary charges to the indictment after the accused has been sent forward for trial. The exercise of this power is not dependant on the District Court having first returned the accused for trial on the summary charges. Indeed, the District Court judge should adjourn the summary charges until it has been ascertained what action has been taken by the DPP in the matter.[118] If the DPP decides not to include the summary charges in the indictment then it would appear that the District Court can proceed with the trial of these charges in the event of the accused being acquitted of the indictable offence, as was the case prior to the enactment of section 6. If, however, the DPP includes the summary charges in the indictment then the jurisdiction of the District Court in the matter is at an end.

15–35 Ryan and Magee suggest that the section 6 power should not be used to add summary counts to an indictment if they are merely incidental to the principal charge or charges which the jury is being asked to consider.[119] For example, an indictment for causing death by reckless driving should not include counts of driving without a licence or insurance. The evidence for such charges would be irrelevant to the primary charge which the jury has to consider.

Overlapping Counts

The joinder of counts based on the same facts can result in an unacceptable overlapping among counts. This is a particular danger where the offences arise out of fraudulent activities which have been carried on over a period of time. In *People (Attorney General) v. Singer*,[120] for example, the accused was charged, *inter alia*, with 16 counts of fraudulent conversions and obtaining

---

[118] Murnaghan J. left open the point whether the District Judge could proceed immediately to try the summary offence. However, he did suggest that this would deprive the DPP of his statutory rights under s.6 and would continue the inconvenience which the section was designed to avert.

[119] Ryan and Magee, *The Irish Criminal Process* (Mercier Press, Dublin, 1983), p. 255.

[120] (1961) 1 Frewen 214.

money by false pretences. One of the counts covered the general deficiency which showed up in the company's accounts, while others charged separate sums which were part of that general deficiency. The result was a serious overlap in the charges which the Court of Criminal Appeal deemed unacceptable. The court also struck o ut a count of conspiracy to obtain money by false pretences as it referred to a period of time which overlapped with periods covered separately by two other counts. While the court accepted that there may be circumstances in which a general deficiency count would be permitted,[121] they did not apply on the facts of this case where the charge effectively consisted of the results of a balance sheet for ten and a half months trading.

3. Series of Offences of a Same or Similar Character

Charges can also be joined on the same indictment even if they arise out of **15–36** totally separate incidents. The pre-requisite for this is that they are of a same or similar character and constitute a series of offences. For this purpose even two offences can constitute a series.

Obviously if the offences are the same and are committed in the context of a pre-planned enterprise they will qualify for joinder. The mere fact that each occurred at a different time and place and involved a different victim will be irrelevant. The difficulty arises with respect to offences which differ in terms of definition, are not committed in the course of a pre-planned enterprise but bear some similarity in the manner of commission. English case law suggests that relatively innocuous similarities may be sufficient. In *Ludlow v. Metropolitan Police Commissioner*,[122] for example, the accused was charged with one count of attempted theft and a separate count of robbery. The facts of the former were that he was seen exiting through a window from the private part of a public house in Acton. The prosecution case on this count was that he was disturbed while attempting to steal. The facts behind the second count were that the accused went in to another public house in Acton sixteen days later, paid for a drink and then punched the barman as he snatched back the payment. The common elements in the counts were that they involved theft or attempted theft in public houses in the same town within a period of just over two weeks. It could equally be said, of course, that there was a number of substantial differences between the offences, not least being the fact that one charged robbery and the other attempted theft. Nevertheless, the House of Lords rejected a challenge on the ground that the counts should not have been joined on the indictment.

Lord Pearson, delivering the judgment of the House, explained that to be of a same or a similar character the offences would have to display similarities in both legal and factual characteristics. In order to qualify as a series there must be a "nexus" between them.[123] While a connection sufficient to satisfy the "similar fact" evidence rule would undoubtedly satisfy the

---

[121] *R. v. Ball* LR 1 CCR 328.
[122] [1971] A.C. 29.
[123] Two offences can qualify as a series for this purpose; *R. v. Kray* [1970] 1 Q.B. 125.

requirements of a nexus for this purpose, it is clear that a lesser connection could also qualify. Unfortunately, Lord Pearson did not offer any more concrete guidance on what would be sufficient. However, he was satisfied that there was a sufficient nexus between the offences in *Ludlow*. Both involved theft or attempted theft from neighbouring public houses in the space of 16 days. While these similarities would hardly be sufficient to satisfy the "similar fact" evidence rule, they were considered to warrant joinder of the counts in the one indictment.[124]

It is unlikely that an Irish court would accept that there was a sufficient nexus between separate offences on the basis of the facts in *Ludlow*. Delivering the judgment of the Court of Criminal Appeal in *DPP v. Kelly*,[124a] Barron J. reviewed the leading English authorities on what is generally referred to as "similar fact" evidence. He considered it significant that the decision in *Ludlow* was neither referred to in argument or in the judgments in two subsequent House of Lords decisions on the subject. Barron J. concluded from his review of the authorities that what is necessary in order to avoid prejudice to the accused in the joinder of counts relating to separate offences "is a series of facts relating to alleged criminal activity which are such that a jury properly charged may hold that offences were committed in each case; that they were committed by the same person and, where necesssary to prove a specific intent, with the same intent. On the facts of *Kelly*, Barron J. concluded that separate counts for attempted buggery should not have been included on the same indictment simply because they alleged buggery of male inmates of a home for children by a carer in that home. However, he did accept that joinder was acceptable in respect of some counts which alleged that the offences were committed in a dormitory at night following lewd suggestions having been made during the day. Similarly, a separate joinder was acceptable where the alleged offences took place in a caravan where the accused was alleged to have made sleeping arrangements which facilitated the commission of the offences.

15–37 Another illustration of two offences which would not qualify as a series of offences of a same or similar character is provided by *R. v. Harward*.[125] In that case the accused was charged on the same indictment with one count of conspiring to use cheque cards to obtain money fraudulently from banks and a second count of handling stereo equipment which had been found in his possession shortly after it had been stolen. He was acquitted on the first count and convicted on the second count. However, the English Court of Appeal quashed the conviction on the ground that the two counts should not have been joined together in the one indictment. The only similarity between them was that both involved an element of dishonesty. In the case of the conspiracy count the dishonesty related to his involvement in fraudulent practices, while

---

[124] See *Blackstone's Criminal Practice* (1997) at D9.26 for a summary of relevant decisions from the Court of Appeal for England and Wales.

[124a] Court of Criminal Appeal, December 13, 1999.

[125] (1981) 73 Cr. App. Rep. 168.

in the handling count it related to his state of mind when he handled the stolen goods. There being no other points of similarity the court concluded that there was not a sufficient nexus between the offences to qualify them as a series of the same or similar character.

4. Proliferation of Counts

Just because offences can be joined on a single indictment under the joinder rules it does not necessarily follow that they should be included. Indeed, the Court of Criminal Appeal has specifically discouraged the undue proliferation of counts on an indictment in a case where the accused was charged with rape and unlawful carnal knowledge contrary to section 1 of the Criminal Law Amendment Act 1935 arising out of the same incident:

15–38

> "The Court feels called upon to add that it has noticed a tendency towards unnecessary proliferation of counts in the drawing up of indictments. It may be necessary to have a number of counts in relation to a particular event where each count is in the alternative. It is difficult to understand why it is considered necessary to have more than one count in relation to one event except in such circumstances. In this case two counts were laid each of which attracted the same maximum punishment. The adoption of this course led, in the first place, to a disregard of section 14 of the Interpretation Act 1937. In the second place, because the first count was laid, the prosecution took on the onus of establishing that the carnal knowledge of the prosecutrix by the accused was had by force and without her consent. This involved calling the prosecutrix as a witness. This Court is of the opinion that prosecutors in cases involving the carnal knowledge of young girls should seriously consider the possibility of being able to sustain a conviction without the necessity of calling such young girls as witnesses and thereby exposing them to the ordeal of having to recount in court what must have been for them a terrifying experience."[126]

It follows that section 14 of the Interpretation Act 1937, which prohibits the punishment of an offender twice for the same offence, and the undesirability of exposing young children to the ordeal of giving evidence at trial in sexual assault cases should militate against the undue proliferation of counts in an indictment in such cases.

McGuinness J. in *Conlon v. Judge Cyril Kelly*[127] identified a number of problems which may ensue for both the prosecution and defence as a result of the inclusion of too many counts in a single indictment:

15–39

> "The joinder of counts may be unsatisfactory from the point of view of the prosecution or from that of the defence. Too many counts, e.g. relating to a series of elaborate frauds, may tend to confuse the jury, and the prosecution may elect to proceed for the time being on some one or more of the counts, probably those which are the most serious, or in respect of which the evidence is the strongest. Conversely, the presentation of a number of counts before the

---

[126] *People (Attorney General) v. Coughlan* (1908) 1 Frewen 325, *per* Haugh J. at 331–332.
[127] unreported, High Court, December 14, 1999.

same jury may prejudice the accused. He is presumed to be innocent until his guilt is established, and evidence of his previous bad character is usually inadmissible. A jury having to try an accused person for a number of quite distinctive offences may well be tempted to think that there cannot be smoke without fire, that the accused would hardly be facing such a variety of charges unless he was guilty of some at least."

Generally, however, there is little judicial guidance on when it would be improper to include counts on a single indictment where the technical rules for joinder are satisfied. One obvious example, perhaps, is the impropriety of joining separate counts for lesser offences which are subsumed within a more serious offence on the indictment. A count of manslaughter, for example, should not be joined on the one indictment with a count of murder where both offences relate to the same victim. Since it would be open to the jury to return a verdict of guilty of manslaughter where only murder had been charged, the separate count of manslaughter would clearly be superfluous. There are many statutory offences where a similar result may ensue. Care must be taken in each case, however, to check that the lesser offence is subsumed within the more serious offence and that it is open to the jury to return a verdict of guilty of the lesser offence even though it is not specifically included in the indictment. In case of doubt the prosecution should err on the side of caution and join separate counts for the more serious and the lesser offences, particularly where the evidence may not be sufficient to establish the more serious offence.

5. Consequences of Improper Joinder

15–40   Where charges against the accused relate to entirely separate and unconnected matters they should not be included in the same indictment. In *R. v. Newland*,[128] for example, the accused was charged with counts of possession of proscribed drugs with intent to supply and counts of assault. The former arose out of a police search of his home on November 28, 1986 while the latter occurred on December 18, 1986 when the police were called to a disturbance in which the accused was involved. Clearly, the events and the counts arising from them were unconnected. At the trial it was accepted that the counts should not have been joined together in a single indictment. The judge, however, accepted the prosecution submission to sever the indictment whereupon the accused pleaded guilty to all of the counts on two separate indictments. On appeal it was held that the joinder of the unconnected counts in a single indictment rendered the indictment invalid (as distinct from void).[129] The invalidity could have been remedied by deleting either the drugs counts or the assault count in which case the trial could properly have proceeded on the amended indictment.[130] By contrast the power of severance was not available as that power was available only in respect of a valid indictment. Since the indictment was invalid the consequent proceedings,

---

[128]   [1988] Q.B. 402.
[129]   See *R. v. Bell* (1984) 78 Cr. App. Rep. 305.
[130]   See also, *R. v. Follett* [1989] Q.B. 338.

including the plea of guilty and conviction, were null and void. Accordingly, the court quashed the conviction and decided against ordering a re-trial.

6. Separate Trial of Different Counts

Just because several counts are joined on the same indictment it does not necessarily follow that they will be tried together. Indeed, there is provision for a court to order a separate trial for one or more offences in an indictment which contains more than one count. Section 6(3) of the Criminal Justice (Administration) Act 1924 reads:

> "Where, before trial, or at any stage of a trial, the court is of opinion that a person accused may be prejudiced or embarrassed in his defence by reason of being charged with more than one offence in the same indictment, or that for any other reason it is desirable to direct that the person should be tried separately for any one or more offences charged in an indictment, the court may order a separate trial of any count or counts of such indictment."

The principles governing the separate trial of different counts on a single indictment are considered in Chapter 14.

7. Joinder of Unrelated Counts

Section 4N of the Criminal Procedure Act 1967 as inserted by the Criminal Justice Act 1999 permits the joinder of unrelated charges in an indictment subject to the consent of the accused. It stipulates that where the accused is sent forward for trial in accordance with Part 1A of the Criminal Procedure Act 1967 (as inserted by the 1999 Act) the indictment may be amended to include counts charging an offence justiciable in the State and which is additional to the offence(s) for which the accused was sent forward for trial. This option is available only with the consent of the accused. The additional count or counts do not have to be founded on the documents (book of evidence) served on the accused under the provisions of Part 1A of the 1967 Act.[131] It would appear that the purpose of this provision is to enable the joinder of unrelated charges in the same indictment. In other words it short-circuits the requirements of the Criminal Justice (Administration) Act 1924 concerning counts being founded on the same facts or being part of a series of offences of the same or a similar character.

15–41

15–42

---

[131] Arguably, the option is not available if the additional charges are founded on the book of evidence. In this event the prosecution would be thrown back on s.4M of the 1967 Act (as inserted by s.9 of the Criminal Justice Act 1999) which is subject to the pre-existing laws governing joinder.

J. Joinder of Defendants

1. Introduction

15–43   Two or more defendants may be charged in the same indictment. They could be charged in one count with respect to the same offence or they could be charged in separate counts with separate offences.

2. The Same Count

Joint Participation

15–44   Where two or more persons are charged with being parties to the same offence it would be normal to charge all of them in the same count with respect to that offence. So, for example, in *Attorney General v. O'Leary*[132] a brother and a sister were charged together in a single count with the murder of another brother. Equally, however, it is acceptable to charge defendants together in the same count where they have participated in the same offence in different capacities. A and B, for example, may have burgled a bank using equipment supplied to them for that purpose by C who did not actually participate in the substantive burglary. Even though C is only a secondary party to the crime he is liable to be tried as a principal offender. Accordingly, it is perfectly proper to charge him along with A and B in a single count of burglary. The fact that his contribution to the substantive offence was materially different from that of A and B will be brought out in court.

15–45   When including a secondary party to an offence there is no need to identify him as such. Section 8 of the Accessories and Abettors Act 1861 states:

> "Whosoever shall aid, abet, counsel or procure the commission of any indictable offence at common law or by virtue of any Act passed or to be passed, shall be liable to be tried, indicted and punished as a principal offender."

Accordingly, it is permissible to use the same form of words for indicting a secondary party as for a principal.[133] There are, of course, some situations in which the defendant can be guilty only as a secondary party. In these cases it is appropriate to describe him as such. It is also worth noting that where the prosecution is unsure of the precise role played by the defendant it is permissible to charge aiding, abetting, counselling or procuring in the alternative in one count.[134]

Independent Contributions

15–46   Surprisingly, perhaps, it would appear that several defendants may be charged in the same count even though they may have contributed to the offence independently of each other. If their individual acts are of a similar nature and

---

[132] [1926] I.R. 445.
[133] For criticism of this practice, see *DPP v. Maxwell* [1978] 1 W.L.R. 1350.
[134] *Ferguson v. Weaving* [1951] 1 K.B. 814.

sufficiently connected in time and place it is acceptable to charge them in the same count. A simple example would be a situation where several individuals are caught on camera taking advantage of a broken window to enter and steal goods from a shop. Presumably they could all be charged on a single count of burglary, even though they were acting independently of each other.

In *DPP v. Merriman*[135] two brothers were charged together on a single count of wounding with intent. One pleaded guilty and the other not guilty. The trial judge directed the jury to ignore the possibility that they had acted in concert when considering the latter's guilt. In upholding the conviction Lord Diplock explained that where two or more persons have been charged together on the same count, the jury may convict all or any of them on the basis that they committed the offence independently of the others. The mere fact that they have been charged together on the same count does not necessarily mean that they must have acted in concert. A conviction will be warranted where the prosecution has established that the individual in question did a physical act which was an essential ingredient of the offence charged (or helped the another to do it) and had the appropriate *mens rea* at the time.

Special Statutory Provisions

For some offences there are specific statutory provisions permitting several defendants to be charged together with the same offence even though they may have committed it separately and at different times. In the case of receiving stolen goods, for example, it is provided that two or more persons may be charged and tried together for receiving the same property even though each of them received it at a different time from the others.[136] Presumably, the defendants can be charged in the same count or joined in separate counts in the same indictment.

3. Separate Counts on the Same Indictment

The circumstances in which defendants can be charged on separate counts in the same indictment would appear to be broader than those in which they can be charged together in the same count. In *R. v. Assim*,[137] the two defendants were charged in a single indictment arising out of an incident in a nightclub in which two individuals suffered injuries. One of the defendants was charged with wounding one of the victims and the other defendant was charged with occasioning actual bodily harm to the other victim. Clearly each defendant was being charged with a separate offence with respect to separate victims. Nevertheless, the defence said that they had no objection to a joint trial. On appeal against conviction it was argued that two individuals should not be charged in the one indictment with two different offences.

15–47

---

[135] [1973] A.C. 584.
[136] Larceny Act 1916, s.40(3). See also, *R. v. Tizard* [1962] 2 Q.B. 608 where it was held that two defendants may be charged in the same indictment for receiving, at different times, parts of the same stolen property.
[137] [1966] 2 Q.B. 249.

Sachs L.J. giving the judgment of a five-judge Court of Appeal found that joinder of offences or offenders are matters of practice over which the court has inherent power to formulate its own rules, except to the extent that it is restrained by statute or statutory rules.[138] After an extensive review of the authorities on the correct practice with respect to the joinder of offenders charged with separate offences in separate counts, Sachs J. (as he then was) concluded that joinder is appropriate if the offences alleged separately are so closely related by time or other factors that the interests of justice are best served by a single trial:

> "As a general rule it is, of course, no more proper to have tried by the same jury several offenders on charges of committing individual offences that have nothing to do with each other than it is to try before the same jury offences committed by the same person that have nothing to do with each other. Where, however, the matters which constitute the individual offences of the several offenders are upon the available evidence so related, whether in time or by other factors, that the interests of justice are best served by their being tried together, then they can properly be the subject of counts in one indictment and can subject always to the discretion of the court, be tried together. Such a rule, of course, includes cases where there is evidence that several offenders acted in concert but it is not limited to such cases."[138a]

The learned judge went on to give some examples of situations in which there would be a sufficient connection between separate offences to warrant the joinder of the charges against the defendants in a single indictment. These include: offences committed contemporaneously such as in an affray; offences committed in succession such as in a protection racket; and two or more persons committing perjury in relation to the same or a similar matter in the course of the same trial.

Sachs L.J. had little difficulty in concluding that the facts of *Assim* easily satisfied the requirements of joinder. Indeed, he was of the opinion that the offences were so closely related in the circumstances that it would have been justifiable to charge the offenders together in the same count. Where an indictment contains a joint count against the two defendants it was accepted that the joint count could be followed by a separate count or counts against one or more of the defendants, even in respect of a distinct matter, so long as it did not involve a breach of the indictment rules.[139]

15–48 It is also worth noting that since the rules governing the joinder of offenders on a single indictment are a matter of judicial practice as opposed to statutory authority, errors in the application of the rules amount to an irregularity in the proceedings but do not deprive the court of jurisdiction. Accordingly, if such an irregularity is raised as a ground of appeal against conviction the court will be able to apply the proviso and dismiss the appeal so long as that does not

---

[138] See also, *R. v. Camberwell Green Stipendiary Magistrate, ex p. Christie* [1978] Q.B. 602.
[138a] [1966] 2 Q.B. 249 at 261.
[139] See also *R. v. Cox* [1898] 1 Q.B. 179; *R. v. Barrell* (1979) 69 Cr. App. Rep. 250.

occasion a miscarriage of justice. A failure by the defence to object to the joinder at trial will militate in favour of the proviso.

4. Proliferation of Defendants on a Single Indictment

Just as the courts discourage the proliferation of counts on a single indict-ment, so also do they discourage the practice of charging too many defen-dants together on the same indictment. Even though the circumstances are such that several defendants can be charged together for a number of offences on a single indictment, it does not follow that the prosecution should opt for a single trial instead of several shorter and simpler trials. Emmins cites *R. v. Thorne*[140] as an excellent example of what might happen when an indictment jointly charges too many defendants.[141] In that case 14 defendants were tried together on a single indictment containing three counts of robbery and numerous related offences such as conspiracy to rob, handling the proceeds of the robberies and attempting to pervert the course of justice in respect of the robbery prosecutions. The trial involved 27 counsel and 10 firms of solicitors, lasted 111 working days and included a 12 day summing up from the judge. Although it declined to allow an appeal on the ground that the trial had been too long, the English Court of Appeal did suggest that two or three shorter trials would have been preferable. The burden placed on the judge and jury by the strategy adopted in *Thorne* is immense and should be avoided where possible.[142]

15–49

5. Different Verdicts on the Same Count

Where two defendants are charged on the one count it is open to the jury to convict one and acquit the other.[143]

15–50

6. Separate Trials on the Same Indictment

The mere fact that several persons have been joined together on the one indictment does not mean that they will necessarily be tried together. The judge retains a discretion to order the separate trial of defendants in such cases. The principles governing the exercise of this discretion are considered in Chapter 14.

15–51

---

[140] (1978) 66 Cr. App. Rep. 6.
[141] Emmins, *A Practical Approach to Criminal Procedure* (6th ed., Blackstone Press, London, 1995), 6.6.3.
[142] See also *R. v. Novac* (1976) 65 Cr. App. R. 107, where Bridge L.J. in the English Court of Appeal heavily criticised the prosecution for opting for a single trial of four defendants on 19 counts instead of four separate trials.
[143] *DPP v. Merriman* [1973] A.C. 584.

J. Amending the Indictment

1. Introduction

15–52   If a defect is discovered in an indictment after the accused has been sent forward for trial it will not necessarily be fatal to the success of the prosecution. The trial court has a broad power to amend an indictment in order to cure any defect in it. This power is found in section 6(1) of the Criminal Justice (Administration) Act 1924 which reads:

> "Where, before trial, or at any stage of a trial, it appears to the court that the indictment is defective, the court shall make such order for the amendment of the indictment as the court thinks necessary to meet the circumstances of the case, unless the required amendments cannot in the opinion of the court be made without injustice, and may make such order as to payment of any costs incurred owing to the necessity for an amendment as the court thinks fit."[144]

It would appear that the court is actually under a duty to amend the indictment, unless it is of the opinion that the necessary amendment could not be made without resulting in injustice.[145]

Once the verdict has been delivered and the jury discharged no amendment can be made even if it would be in the interests of the defendant to have the indictment amended. In *State (McGinley) v. Durkin*,[146] the accused was charged with dealing in uncustomed goods to the value of £500. He was found guilty in respect of some, but not all, of the goods. Nevertheless, it was held that the trial judge could not amend the indictment by substituting £482 for £500, even though that would be to the benefit of the accused.

2. Scope

15–53   The power of amendment may be exercised in respect of formal or technical defects in the wording of a count such as a failure to specify the relevant statutory enactment which has been breached, or a misdescription of an offence known to the law.[147] Equally, however, it may be used to effect more substantial changes such as the addition of a new count or the substitution of a new count for an existing count.[148] In *R. v. Fyffe*,[149] for example, the prosecution was permitted to amend an 11 count indictment to contain 27 counts. The English Court of Appeal rejected the defence argument that the amendments were so extensive as to amount to a fresh indictment. In substance the 27 counts merely reproduced the 11 counts. No new allegations had been added.

---

[144]   Criminal Justice (Administration) Act 1924, s.6(1). See also, Criminal Procedure Act 1967, s.40 (inserted by Criminal Justice Act 1999, s.9) which reads:
"Where the accused has been sent forward for trial in accordance with this Part, the trial court may correct any defect in a charge against the accused unless it considers that the correction would result in injustice."

[145]   *R. v. Fraser* (1923) 27 Cox CC 579.

[146]   unreported, High Court, May 5, 1975. See Ryan and Magee *op. cit.*, p. 244.

[147]   *R. v. McVitie* [1960] 1 Q.B. 483.

[148]   *R. v. Johal* [1973] Q.B. 475.

[149]   [1992] Crim. L.R. 442.

Prior to the abolition of the preliminary examination it was accepted that an indictment which failed to allege an offence disclosed in the committal statements could be amended to include that offence.[150] It was not clear, however, whether an indictment could be amended to include an offence not founded on the evidence disclosed at committal.[151]

Alterations may also be made to times, dates, places or descriptions in an existing count. In *R. v. Pople*,[152] for example, the prosecution was permitted to amend a count charging obtaining by deception so that it referred to the cheque in question rather than the sum of money for which the cheque was drawn.

The scope of the power of amendment in any individual case will always be tempered by the fact that an amendment cannot be made where the judge is of the opinion that it would cause an injustice to the accused. Obviously, whether any particular amendment will cause an injustice to the accused will depend on the circumstances of the individual case. Timing will often be a critical factor. The later the amendment is made the more likely it is that the accused will be prejudiced. This is considered further below.

If an indictment is so defective as to be a nullity then the power of amendment cannot be exercised to remedy the defect.

3. Timing

So long as it will not cause injustice to the accused an amendment may be made at any stage of a trial, whether before or after arraignment.[153] In this context the trial is deemed to continue until the verdict has been delivered and the jury discharged. In *R. v. Dossi*,[154] for example, the accused was charged on indictment with indecent assault on a child on March 19. The jury returned a verdict of "with regard to the date March 19 not guilty, if the indictment covers other dates guilty". The trial judge then amended the indictment by substituting "on someday in March" for "on March 19" and referred it back to the jury who found the accused guilty on the amended charge. The English Court of Criminal Appeal refused to quash the conviction on the ground of the amendment. It is unlikely, however, that a more substantial amendment would be permissible so late in the trial.

Generally, the longer the interval between arraignment and the application to amend the more likely it is that the amendment would cause injustice, in which case it will be refused. In *R. v. Johal*, Ashworth J. accepted that there was no rule of law which precluded the amendment of an indictment after arraignment. However, he went on to say:

15–54

---

[150] *R. v. Radley* (1973) 58 Cr. App. Rep. 394.
[151] See *R. v. Dixon* (1991) 92 Cr. App. Rep. 43 and *R. v. Hall* [1968] 2 Q.B. 788 for dicta precluding this possibility, and *R. v. Osieh* [1996] 1 W.L.R. 1260 for dicta going the other way. See further, J. Smith "Adding Counts to an Indictment" *Criminal Law Review* [1996] 889.
[152] [1951] 1 K.B. 53.
[153] *R. v. Johal* [1973] Q.B. 475.
[154] (1918) 13 Cr. App. Rep. 158.

". . . this court shares the view expressed in some of the earlier cases that amendment of an indictment during the course of a trial is likely to prejudice an accused person. The longer the interval between arraignment and amendment, the more likely it is that injustice will be caused, and in every case in which amendment is sought, it is essential to consider with great care whether the accused person will be prejudiced thereby."[155]

Much will depend on the facts of each individual case. In *Johal* itself, for example, the amendment was made immediately after arraignment. The court concluded that there had been no injustice to the accused as the material situation was the same as if it had been made before arraignment.

15–55   In *R. v. Gregory*,[156] the trial judge deleted the name of the owner of stolen goods from the particulars of a count for handling stolen goods. This amendment was made after all the evidence had been given despite the fact that much of the case was concerned with whether the goods found in the defendant's possession were the same goods that had been stolen from the owner named in the count. The English Court of Appeal quashed the conviction on the ground that the amendment had altered the whole basis of the prosecution case and, as such, it would be unfair to the defendant to permit it to be made at such a late stage of the proceedings. However, if the amendment is necessary to cure a technical problem which has arisen it may be possible to make it at a very late stage. In *R. v. Collison*,[157] for example, a new count was added after the jury had retired to consider their verdict. The amendment was considered necessary to resolve a difficulty over whether the jury could return a verdict of guilty of a lesser offence. It did not alter the nature of the prosecution case. Accordingly, the English Court of Appeal upheld the amendment.[158]

4. Procedure

15–56   An application to amend an indictment will normally be made by the prosecution. However, the judge may raise the matter on his or her own initiative and then seek the views of prosecution and defence. It is unlikely that the defence would have much to gain by an application to quash the indictment on account of a defect in it. The normal outcome of any such application would simply be an amendment to cure the defect.[159] Even if the application succeeds and the indictment is quashed there is nothing to prevent the prosecution from starting again with a new indictment which omits the defect.

Where an indictment is amended a note of the order for amendment is endorsed on the indictment and the indictment is then treated for the purposes

---

[155] [1973] Q.B. 475 at 481.
[156] [1972] 1 W.L.R. 991.
[157] (1980) 71 Cr. App. Rep. 249.
[158] See also, *R. v. Johal* [1973] Q.B. 475.
[159] It may be worth noting that if it appears to the court that an indictment contains unnecessary matter, or is of unnecessary length, or is materially defective in any respect, the court may make such order as to the payment of that part of the costs of the indictment which contain the unnecessary matter, or which is of unnecessary length, or which is materially defective, as the court thinks fit; Criminal Justice (Administration) Act 1924 s.7.

of the trial, and all associated proceedings, as having been preferred to the jury in the amended form.[160] The court can make such order as it thinks fit as to the payment of any costs incurred owing to the necessity to make the amendment.[161]

Where a significant amendment is made to the indictment during the course of the trial it will usually be necessary to adjourn the proceedings in order to give the defence an opportunity to assess how their position has been affected. Moreover, if it is desired to make a substantial amendment after arraignment, the interests of justice normally dictate that the accused should be re-arraigned on the amended indictment.[162] Indeed, the court may postpone the trial if it considers that that is expedient as a consequence of an amendment to the indictment.[163] In this event the jury may be discharged and the trial may proceed at a later date as if it was being commenced for the first time.[164]

See Chapter 16 on Pleas for motion to quash indictment.

5. Defects in the Indictment as a Ground of Appeal

If defects in an indictment are not cured at the time of the trial they may afford grounds for appeal against conviction. In practice, however, appellate courts display a marked reluctance to quash convictions on the grounds of defects in the indictment. Unless the defect renders the indictment a nullity or has caused serious prejudice or injustice to the accused it is likely that the appellate court will apply the proviso (see Chapter 22 on Appeals) and uphold the conviction. Fundamental defects such as the joinder of counts which cannot lawfully be joined together in a single indictment will be sufficient to render the indictment and the subsequent proceedings a nullity.[165]

15–57

Distinguishing between defects which are sufficient to quash a conviction and those which are not can be difficult. Much depends on the facts of each individual case. A useful guide is offered in the following extract from the judgment of Lord Bridge in *R. v. Ayres*:

"In a number of cases where an irregularity in the form of the indictment has been discussed in relation to the application of the proviso a distinction, treated as of critical importance, has been drawn between an indictment which is 'a nullity' and one which is merely 'defective'. For my part, I doubt if this classification provides much assistance in answering the question which the proviso poses. If the statement and particulars of the offence in an indictment disclose no criminal offence whatever or charge some offence which has been abolished, in which case the indictment could fairly be described as a nullity, it is obvious that a conviction under that indictment cannot stand. But if the statement and particulars of offence can be seen fairly to relate to and be intended to charge a known and subsisting criminal offence but plead it in

---

[160] Criminal Justice (Administration) Act 1924, s.6(2).
[161] *ibid.* s.6(1).
[162] *R. v. Radley* (1974) 58 Cr. App. Rep. 394.
[163] Criminal Justice (Administration) Act 1924, s.6(4).
[164] *ibid.* s.6(5).
[165] *R. v. Newland* [1988] Q.B. 402, distinguishing *R. v. Bell* (1984) 78 Cr. App. Rep. 305.

terms which are inaccurate, incomplete or otherwise imperfect, then the question whether a conviction on that indictment can properly be affirmed under the proviso must depend on whether, in all the circumstances, it can be said with confidence that the particular error in the pleading cannot in any way have prejudiced or embarrassed the defendant."[166]

The House of Lords in this case refused to quash the conviction despite the fact that the indictment had charged the accused with common law conspiracy to defraud when it should have charged him with the statutory conspiracy to obtain by deception contrary to section 1 of the Criminal Law Act 1977 (UK). The particulars of the offence clearly showed that the crime alleged was a conspiracy to obtain money by deception, the judge gave the jury appropriate directions in relation to that offence and the judge passed a modest sentence comfortably below the maximum for that offence. Accordingly, the House of Lords concluded that the misdescription of the offence in the indictment had no practical significance and that no actual miscarriage of justice had ensued.

It would appear to follow from Ayres that so long as the indictment charges an offence known to the law, a conviction will not be quashed simply because the offence is described inaccurately.

6. District Court

15–58   A summons, complaint or other document can also be amended in the District Court on a summary trial. Indeed, under the District Court Rules a District judge enjoys even broader powers to deal with a defect in any such document. Not only can he effect an appropriate amendment to cure the defect, but he can also proceed as if there was no such defect. In both cases, however, the judge has a discretion to dismiss the case if he or she is of the opinion that the defect misled or prejudiced the accused or otherwise affected the merits of the case. The relevant provisions read:[167]

> "(2) Subject to the provisions of paragraph (3) hereof, no objection shall be taken or allowed on the ground of a defect in substance or in form or an omission in the summons, warrant or other document by which the proceedings were originated, or of any variance between any such document and the evidence adduced on the part of the prosecutor at the hearing of the case in summary proceedings but the Court may amend any such summons, warrant or other document, or proceed in the matter as though no such defect, omission or variance had existed.
>
> (3) Provided, however, that if in the opinion of the Court the variance, defect or omission is one which had misled or prejudiced the accused or which might affect the merits of the case, it may refuse to make any such amendment and may dismiss the complaint either without prejudice to its being again made, or on the merits, as the Court thinks fit; or if it makes any such amendment, it may upon such terms as it thinks fit adjourn the proceedings to any future day at the same or at any other place."

---

[166] [1984] A.C. 447 at 460–461.
[167] District Court Rules 1997, Ord.38.

In *State (Duggan) v. Evans*[168] the District Court dismissed a charge of burglary on the ground that the count referred only to section 23A of the Larceny Act 1916 and did not refer to the Criminal Law (Jurisdiction) Act 1976 which inserted section 23A in the 1916 Act. On a case stated Finlay P. (as he then was) in the High Court ruled that the correct course of action for the judge was to ascertain whether the defect misled or prejudiced the defendant or otherwise affected the merits of his case. If he is of the opinion that none of these consequences have occurred he must either amend the document or proceed as if no such defect had existed. He cannot, as in this case, simply dismiss the summons on the basis of the defect without considering whether it has prejudiced or misled the defendant or affected the merits of his case.

---

[168] (1978) 112 I.L.T.R. 61.

CHAPTER 16

ARRAIGNMENT AND PLEAS

A. Arraignment

Procedure

Where the accused has been sent forward for trial on indictment the next **16–01**
stage in the procedure is normally the arraignment. At the arraignment the
accused is called before the court of trial where his identity is established, the
indictment is read out to him by the clerk of the court and he is asked whether
he pleads guilty or not guilty. The appearance must be made in person. In the
case of a company the appearance is made by a representative duly appointed
by the company to represent it in the proceedings. Where the accused pleads
guilty the plea must be made in person by the accused.[1] It cannot be offered
on his behalf by counsel.

If there is more than one count on the indictment, a plea must be taken on
each one separately after it is read out.[2] Where the counts are in the alternative and the accused pleads guilty to one of them it is not necessary to take
a plea on the other. Where there is a joint indictment against several accused
the practice is to arraign them together. Separate pleas must be taken from
each accused.

Formality and Substance

It would appear that the formality of an arraignment is less important than the **16–02**
actual substance where the accused is contesting the charge. In *R v. Williams*[3]
the appellant appeared before the English Crown Court to answer charges to
which he intended pleading not guilty. In the event the proceedings were

---

[1] *R. v. Ellis* (1973) 57 Cr. App. Rep. 571; *R. v. Williams* [1984] 1 All E.R. 874.
[2] *R. v. Boyle* [1954] 2 Q.B. 292.
[3] [1977] 1 All E.R. 874.

postponed before he was formally arraigned. The court clerk erroneously endorsed the record with a plea of not guilty and a note that the proceedings were adjourned to a date to be fixed. When the proceedings re-commenced at a later date, before a differently constituted court, court clerk and counsel, it was assumed that the appellant had been arraigned and had pleaded not guilty at the previous proceedings. The only person present who was aware of the error was the appellant, and he remained silent. Accordingly, the prosecution proceeded on the basis of a not guilty plea even though the appellant had never been formally arraigned and given the opportunity formally to plead not guilty. He was convicted and appealed on the basis that the trial was a nullity as he had not been formally arraigned, had not been called on to plead, and had not pleaded, to the indictment. In dismissing the appeal Shaw L.J. in the English Court of Appeal cited with approval the following passage of the Corpus Juris Secundum[3a] summarising the position in the United States with respect to the waiver of arraignment in a case where the accused intends to plead not guilty:

> "The modern trend is that arraignment, and even the plea, may be waived in criminal cases . . . Waiver may be express or by conduct, as where the accused, without objection proceeds to trial as if he had been duly arraigned. Irregularities in connection with arraignment and plea may be similarly waived . . . Waiver may be effected not only by express waiver, which may even be made by counsel, but it may also be implied from acts equivalent thereto, which show an intent to waive. Thus accused may waive arraignment where he appears in court and pleads to the indictment or information without objection; and, even though accused has not pleaded, waiver will be implied, where he and his counsel were present, were aware of the charge, and proceeded to trial as if he had been duly arraigned, without objecting or in any manner calling to the attention of the court the fact that he had not been arraigned. Accordingly, rights to be arraigned and to make a plea may be waived by failing to call to the attention of the court the defect in the proceedings at the proper time, by announcing readiness for trial, by selecting a jury, by allowing a jury to be struck and sworn . . . "[4]

It is worth noting that the accused in *Williams* was always aware that he had not been properly arraigned and had remained silent on the matter. If he had objected to the failure to arraign him properly and the trial court had refused to act on his objection it is submitted that the Court of Appeal would have quashed his conviction.

B. Failure to Plead

1. Introduction

16–03 When the charge or charges are put to the accused on arraignment it may happen that he makes no response or fails to make a rational response. This may result from a deliberate refusal to co-operate on the part of the accused in which case he is said to be "mute of malice". Equally it may result from

---

[3a] (ed., 1961), Vol. 22.
[4] [1977] 1 All E.R. 874 at 879.

the accused being unable to understand the charge or charges being put to him because he is deaf or dumb or because he is a foreigner who does not understand the language. In this case he is said to be "mute by visitation of God". Yet another possibility is that he is unfit to plead due to some mental incapacity. This third possibility is considered below under unfitness to plead.

2. Standing Mute

Where the accused fails to answer the charge on arraignment the judge must decide whether his failure is due to mute of malice or by visitation of God.[5] To this end the judge must consider such relevant evidence as is adduced before him or her. Where the prosecution asserts that the accused is mute of malice the onus is on it to prove the matter beyond a reasonable doubt.[6] Where the accused is found to be mute by visitation of God the trial can still proceed unless the accused is found unfit to plead (see below). If the disability can be overcome satisfactorily, it will usually be possible to proceed with the trial. In the case of a foreigner who cannot understand the language the solution is to rely on the services of an interpreter.[7] This can include translating the book of evidence.[8] In the case of an accused who is deaf or dumb another form of communication, such as sign language, may be used so long as it is sufficient for him to understand and follow the proceedings.[9]

    Where the accused stands mute before the court and the judge finds that he is not mute by visitation of God, the judge must direct a plea of not guilty to be entered on behalf of the accused and the trial will proceed accordingly (unless, of course, the accused is unfit to plead).[10] The same applies if the accused refuses to plead on the ground that he does not recognise the authority of the court to try him.[11]

16–04

3. Unfitness to Plead[11a]

Relevant Factors

Even if the accused is willing and able to speak he may be suffering from a mental incapacity which renders him unfit to plead. The appropriate test

16–05

---

[5] Juries Act 1976, s.28. In England the issue is determined by a jury sworn in for the purpose; *Archbold* (Sweet & Maxwell, London, 1997) 4–164.

[6] *R. v. Sharp* [1960] 1 Q.B. 357.

[7] Article 6(3) of the European Convention for the Protection of Human Rights and Fundamental Freedoms stipulates that anyone charged with a criminal offence has the right to be informed promptly, in a language which he understands, and in detail, of the nature and cause of the accusation against him and to have the free assistance of an interpreter if he cannot understand or speak the language used in court. If the accused relies on his constitutional right to present his case in Irish (see Art.5 of the Constitution and *O'Monachain. v. An Taoiseach*, unreported, High Court, February 27, 1990) it may be necessary to employ the services of an interpreter for the benefit of the jury; see Ryan and Magee, *The Irish Criminal Process* (Mercier Press, Dublin, 1983) at p. 268.

[8] *R. v. Lee Kun* [1916] 1 K.B. 337; *Kunnath v. State* 98 Cr. App. Rep. 455.

[9] *R. v. Jones* (1773) 1 Leach 102; *R. v. Steel* (1787) 1 Leach 451; *R. v. M'Entyre* (1840) 1 Craw & D 402.

[10] Juries Act 1976, s.28. See also *R. v. Schleter* (1886) 10 Cox CC 409; *R. v. Sharp* [1960] 1 Q.B. 357.

[11] *R. v. Davis* (1820) Gow 219.

[11a] For detailed treatment, see P. Casey and C. Craven, *Psychiatry and the Law* (Dublin: Oak Tree Press, 1999) at Ch. 17; and F. McAuley, *Insanity, Psychiatry and Criminal Responsibility* (Round Hall, Dublin, 1993).

is whether he is of sufficient intellect to understand the course of the proceedings to the extent that he can make a proper defence. Relevant factors would be whether he has the mental capacity to instruct counsel to act on his behalf, whether he is capable of challenging a juror to whom he might wish to object and whether he would be able to follow the evidence.[12] It is not sufficient that the accused is highly abnormal[13] or even that he might act against his own best interests.[14] The key issue is whether these or associated conditions render him incapable of following the trial and making his defence.[14a] Moreover, the issue is the accused's mental state at the time of the trial and not whether he was suffering from any mental deficiency at the time of commission of the alleged offence. Indeed, the mere fact that the accused cannot remember the alleged offence will not be sufficient in itself to render him unfit to plead.[15]

An accused who is mute by visitation of God may also be found unfit to plead if his incapacity is such as to prevent him from understanding the course of the proceedings and making a proper defence.[16] Although a jury determining the issue of the accused's fitness to plead will be asked to inquire "whether the prisoner at the bar, be insane or not",[17] it would appear that mental illness as defined in the McNaghten rules is not a pre-requiste to unfitness to plead.

Procedure

16–06   Where the accused's fitness to plead is put in issue either by the prosecution, the defence or the court itself it must be dealt with immediately. Usually, where the accused is being tried on indictment, this will happen at arraignment, but it could also happen at any time during the course of the trial. When the issue does arise it is normally determined by a jury specially empannelled for that purpose[18] although there is authority for it to be tried by the trial jury.[18a] The oath taken by each juror is: "I will well and diligently inquire whether [name of the accused] the prisoner at the bar be insane or not and a true verdict give according to the best of my understanding."[19] Presumably the jury's

---

12   See Alderson B. in *R. v. Pritchard* (1836) 7 C&P 303 at 304–305. See also McAuley, *Insanity, Psychiatry and Criminal Responsibility* (Round Hall, Dublin, 1993), pp. 139–144 for discussion on the interpretation and application of the test. Also, *State (Coughlan) v. Minister for Justice* (1968) I.L.T.R. 177.

13   *R. v. Berry* (1977) 66 Cr. App. Rep. 157.

14   *R. v. Robertson* [1968] 1 W.L.R. 1767.

14a   *State (C) v. Minister for Justice* [1967] I.R. 106; *State (Caseley) v. Daly* unreported High Court, February 19, 1979.

15   *R. v. Podola* [1960] 1 Q.B. 325; *Russell v. HM Advocate* [1946] J.C. 37.

16   *R. v. Pritchard* (1836) 7 C&P 303; *R. v. Governor of Stafford Prison, ex. p. Emery* [1968] 1 W.L.R. 1767.

17   Juries Act 1976, s.19(2).

18   This is implicit in the wording of s.2 of the Criminal Lunatics Act 1800 (as adapted by the Lunacy (Ireland) Act 1821). Where the case is before the District Court, the issue of fitness to plead is dealt with by the judge applying the same criteria as would be applied by the jury; *State (C) v. Minister for Justice* [1967] I.R. 106; *O'Connor v. Judges of the Metropolitan District* [1994] 3 I.R. 246.

18a   See Casey and Craven, *op.cit.*, at p. 432.

19   Juries Act 1976, s.19(2).

determination will be based on the weight of the medical evidence called, although it can take into account the demeanour of the accused in court.[20] If the issue of unfitness is raised by the prosecution, it must prove the matter beyond a reasonable doubt.[21] By contrast, if the accused's fitness to plead is put in issue by the defence it will only have to prove the matter on a balance of probabilities.[22] If the jury finds the accused unfit to plead he has no right of appeal against the decision to the Court of Criminal Appeal.

Where an accused is found unfit to plead the judge will issue an order that he be detained in the Central Mental Hospital at the pleasure of the government.[23] In practice this means until such time as he is fit to be released, at which point he might be re-arraigned and tried for the offence. It follows that an accused has little to gain and, perhaps, much to lose in being found unfit to plead at the arraignment. It may be, for example, that if the case went to full trial he would have been acquitted. Equally, it might be that a submission of no case to answer would have succeeded at the close of the case for the prosecution.

Constitutional Considerations

There must surely be some doubt about the constitutionality of a judicial **16–07** power to direct the indefinite detention of an individual in the Central Mental Hospital solely on the basis that he has been accused of a criminal offence and is found mentally incapable of pleading to the offence and presenting his defence. Equally, it is possible that the power is not compatible with provisions of the European Convention for the Protection of Human Rights and Fundamental Freedoms. At the very least it would appear that the individual's fundamental right to liberty and right to a fair trial on a criminal charge would require that he should not be locked up in the Central Mental Hospital without a determination that he did the acts charged against him and/or that he posed a threat to himself or other persons on account of his mental illness.

Where an accused is found unfit to plead in England and Wales the court must proceed to make a determination on whether the accused actually did the acts in the offence charged against him. If the jury find that he did not, they must acquit him. If they find that he did they must enter a finding accordingly. In this event the court has four options. It can make an order admitting the accused to hospital, a guardianship order, a professional treatment order or an order of absolute discharge.[24]

Another statutory option available to the judge in England and Wales is to postpone consideration of the accused's fitness to plead until any time up to

---

[20] *R. v. Goode* 1837 7 A & E 536.

[21] *R. v. Robertson.*

[22] *R. v. Podola* [1960] 1 Q.B. 325.

[23] Criminal Lunatics Act 1800, s.2; Lunacy (Ireland) Act 1821, s.17; Central Criminal Lunatic Asylum (Ireland) Act 1845, s.8; Mental Treatment Act 1961, s.39. McAuley points out that s.2 of the Criminal Lunatics Act 1800 states that "it shall be lawful" for the court to make such an order. This would suggest that the judge is not actually bound to make a committal order if the defendant is found unfit to plead; McAuley, *loc. cit.*

[24] Criminal Procedure (Insanity) Act 1964, s.4A (U.K.).

the opening of the defence case.[25] In exercising this discretion the judge will assess the strength of the prosecution case from the admissible evidence against the accused contained on the book of evidence and will look at the medical reports on the accused. The weaker the prosecution case and the less severe the mental incapacity of the accused, the more likely it is that the judge will exercise his or her discretion to postpone consideration of the fitness issue.[26]

There is no statutory equivalent to either of these provisions in Irish law. It may be, of course, that the judge has an inherent discretion to postpone consideration of the accused's fitness to plead in the interests of justice.

Unfit during the Course of Proceedings

16–08   There is no clear Irish authority on what should be done if the accused becomes unfit to follow the proceedings during the course of the trial. In *People (Attorney General) v. Messit*[27] the accused had become violent and unruly in the course of his trial. There was evidence to the effect that his behaviour might be the result of physical and/or mental illness. The trial judge ordered him to be removed from the court and proceeded with the trial in his absence. The Court of Criminal Appeal ruled that before taking this action the judge should have determined whether the accused's behaviour was the result of a medical condition which prevented him from conducting his defence. The judge's failure to do this, coupled with the fact that it resulted in the hearing of a substantial part of the prosecution case in the absence of the accused, vitiated the trial. The implication is that the proper course for the judge to take when an accused becomes unfit to follow proceedings in the course of his trial is to discharge the jury and have the accused re-arraigned before a jury specially empannelled for the purpose of determining his fitness to plead.[28]

Offence Committed when Detained in a Mental Hospital

It may happen that a person is already detained in a mental hospital when charged with an indictable offence before a District judge. If evidence is presented which, in the opinion of the judge, constitutes prima facie evidence that the person concerned has committed the offence and would, if placed on trial, be unfit to plead the judge must certify that he is suitable for transfer to the Central Mental Hospital.[29] In this event the accused will not actually be arraigned on the charge and so the question of empanelling a jury to determine his fitness to plead will not arise. Although the District judge would be exercising the criminal jurisdiction of the court when considering the matter it is not necessary for the accused to be present in person.

---

[25]   *ibid.* 1964, s.4 (U.K.).

[26]   *R. v. Burles* [1970] 2 Q.B. 191.

[27]   [1972] I.R. 204.

[28]   Ryan and Magee, *op. cit.*, p. 270. *R. v. Streek* (1826) 2 C & P 413; *People v. Messitt* [1972] I.R. 204.

[29]   Mental Treatment Act 1945, s.207 as adapted by the Mental Treatment Act 1961 and the Mental Treatment Acts (Adaptation) Order 1971. It would appear that this provision is set to be repealed once s.6 of the Mental Health Act 2001 is bought into force.

Consequence of Being Found Fit to Plead

In any case where the accused's fitness to plead has been put in issue and he is found to be fit to plead, he will be arraigned in the usual manner and a fresh jury will be empannelled to try the case.

C. Motion to Quash

At common law either the prosecution or the defence may seek to quash the **16–09** indictment on the ground that it is bad on its face or that it is so insufficient as to make any judgment given on it erroneous.[30] It may be, for example, that the indictment does not disclose on its face an offence known to the law,[31] or that the offence charged is not within the jurisdiction of the court, or that the accused has not been properly sent forward for trial.[32]

In practice, the defence will rarely have much to gain from a motion to quash. The prosecution will often be able to defeat a motion by amending the indictment to cure the defect.[33] Even if the motion is successful it results only in the discharge, as distinct from the acquittal, of the accused on the charges concerned. It does not operate as a bar to a future prosecution arising out of the same matter. On the other hand a failure to bring a motion to quash a defective indictment can prejudice a subsequent appeal against conviction on the grounds of a miscarriage of justice. The lack of a motion to quash at first instance may be interpreted on appeal as an indication that the accused did not suffer any prejudice as a result of the alleged defect in the indictment.[34]

The prosecution will rarely bring a motion to quash an indictment. Indeed, if the indictment was quashed on the basis of such a motion, it would appear that the committal on which the indictment was framed could not have been used as authority to prefer another indictment for the same offence.[35] A better option, therefore, would be to ask the judge to stay the indictment while the prosecution prepares a fresh indictment which does not suffer from the defect in the first indictment.

---

[30] 2 Hawk. C.25, s.146. A variation on this is the demurrer which is an objection in writing by the accused to the effect that while he admits the facts alleged in the indictment to be true, they do not in point of law render him guilty of an offence sufficiently charged against him. Ryan and Magee suggest that this particular plea is obsolete; *op. cit.*, p. 270. In *R. v. Deputy Chairman of Inner London Sessions, ex p. Commissioner of Metropolitan Police* [1970] 2 Q.B. 80, Lord Parker C.J. expressed the wish that the plea of demurrer should "be allowed to die naturally".

[31] *Attorney General v. Cunningham* [1932] I.R. 28.

[32] *R. v. Jones* (1974) 59 Cr. App. Rep. 120. Note, however, that if the indictment consists only of the committal charges and is properly drafted on its face, the judge will not go behind the indictment to consider whether the evidence upon which the accused was committed for trial was sufficient to disclose a case to answer; *R. v. Chairman, County of London Quarter Sessions, ex p. Downes* [1954] 1 Q.B. 1.

[33] See above, Chap. 15, para 15–52 *et seq.*

[34] *R. v. Thompson* [1914] 2 K.B. 99.

[35] *R. v. Thompson* [1975] 1 W.L.R. 1425, [1975] 2 All E.R. 1028.

The motion to quash is normally made to the court of trial before the accused pleads to the indictment, although it can also be made at any point during the trial. If the case is being tried in the Circuit Court the accused has the alternative of seeking an order of prohibition in the High Court. Where the indictment is clearly bad the court will quash it. In cases of doubt it may prefer to proceed with the trial and leave the accused with the option of seeking a remedy by way of motion in arrest of judgment (see Chapter 19).

D. Pleas of *Autrefois Acquit* and *Autrefois Convict*[35a]

1. Basic Principle

16–10   It has long been established at common law that a person cannot be prosecuted for an offence of which he has already been acquitted or convicted.[36] The reasoning behind this principle is that an individual should not be put at risk of being punished twice for the same infraction. Thus it is commonly known as the rule against double jeopardy. The accused can plead *autrefois acquit* (he has already been tried and acquitted of the offence) or *autrefois convict* (he has already been tried and convicted of the offence). If successful it will be a complete bar to further proceedings with respect to the count in question.

The application of the double jeopardy rule has been specifically extended to statutory offences. The Interpretation Act 1937 provides that where an act or omission constitutes an offence under two or more Acts or under an Act and at common law, the offender shall, unless the contrary intention appears, be liable to be prosecuted and punished under either or any of those Acts, but shall not be liable to be punished twice for the same offence.[37] It has been held that this provision does no more than extend the common law double jeopardy rule to statutory offences.[38]

Technically, it would seem that the pleas of *autrefois acquit* and *autrefois convict* should be applicable only to trials on indictment, at least for common law offences. Historically, they developed along with the plea of pardon as special pleas in bar of indictment.[39] In practice, however they are applied to summary and indictable offences without distinction.[40]

[35a] For a detailed treatment see, P. McDermott, *Res Judicata and Double Jeopardy* (Butterworths, Dublin, 1999), at chaps 21–34.

[36] 2 Hawk. C.35, s.1; 4 Bl Comm. 335.

[37] Interpretation Act 1937, s.14. See *People v. Dermody* [1956] 1 K.B. 26.

[38] *R. v. Miles* [1890] 24 Q.B.D. 423; *R. v. Thomas* [1950] 1 K.B. 26.

[39] The rare cases in which a pardon is granted today are confined to situations where the beneficiary has been convicted and sentenced for the offence concerned. It is most unlikely to feature as a plea in bar of an indictment. Accordingly, it will not be considered here, but see further in Chapter 22 on Appeals.

[40] *Attorney General v. Mallen* [1957] I.R. 344.

2. Same Offence

Lesser Offence Incorporated in Previous Offence

The ease with which the rule against double jeopardy can be stated conceals **16–11** the considerable difficulties that can arise when attempting to apply it in practice to the facts of individual cases. The primary difficulty is in determining whether the offence charged is the same as an offence of which the accused has already been convicted or acquitted. If the offence charged is identical on the law and facts to the previous offence no problem will arise as the situation will attract a straightforward application of the double jeopardy rule. The mere fact that the prosecution has uncovered new evidence would not permit it to commence a fresh prosecution against the accused for the identical offence arising out of the same facts. However, the double jeopardy rule also applies to the situation where the accused has been tried on indictment, acquitted and then subsequently charged with an offence for which the jury could have convicted him in the previous trial. According to Lord Morris of Borth y Gest in the House of Lords in the leading case of *Connelly v. DPP*:[41]

> ". . . one test as to whether the rule applies is whether the evidence which is necessary to support the second indictment, or whether the facts which constitute the second offence, would have been sufficient to procure a legal conviction upon the first indictment either as to the offence charged or as to an offence of which, on the indictment, the accused could have been found guilty . . . "[42]

The learned Lord Justice went on to say that:

> "this test must be subject to the proviso that the offence charged in the second indictment had in fact been committed at the time of the first charge; thus if there is an assault and a prosecution and conviction in respect of it there is no bar to a charge of murder if the assaulted person dies later . . . "[43]

It follows that if a jury has acquitted an accused in circumstances where it was open to it to bring in a verdict of guilty of a lesser offence than that charged the accused cannot be prosecuted subsequently for that lesser offence. For example, an acquittal on a charge of dangerous driving causing death is a bar to a subsequent charge of careless driving in respect of the same incident as section 53(4) of the Road Traffic Act 1961 permits a jury to return a verdict of guilty of careless driving on an indictment for dangerous driving causing death.[44] Similarly, if the jury acquits the accused of murder, he cannot ordinarily be proceeded against for the manslaughter of the same victim. It would appear, however, that if the jury had considered both murder and manslaughter on an indictment for murder and could not agree on the

---

[41] [1964] A.C. 1254. The speech of Lord Morris of Borth y Gest in this case is generally considered to be the foundation of the modern law on the pleas of *autrefois convict* and *autrefois acquit*. He reviewed the old authorities and re-formulated them into nine propositions.

[42] *ibid.* at 1305.

[43] *ibid.*

[44] *Attorney General v. Fitzgerald* [1964] I.R. 458; *Attorney General (McElwain) v. Power* [1964] I.R. 458.

manslaughter question, their verdict of acquittal would not constitute a bar to the subsequent prosecution of the accused for manslaughter.

Pre-requisite Offences

16–12 If an accused has been acquitted of an offence which is a necessary pre-requisite for the commission of another offence, he cannot be charged and convicted subsequently of the latter.[45] Similarly, a conviction or acquittal of one offence will normally preclude a subsequent charge of a more serious offence arising out of the same facts.[46] However, this is subject to the major exception, as noted in the above quotation from Lord Morris of Borth y Gest, that a conviction for assault is no bar to a charge of murder if the victim subsequently dies.

There are circumstances in which an acquittal for one offence will preclude a prosecution for another even though one cannot be said to be subsumed within, or a component of, the other. In the case of an indictment for stealing, for example, statute permits the jury to bring in a verdict of guilty of obtaining by false pretences.[47] Accordingly, an acquittal of larceny will constitute a bar to a charge of obtaining by false pretences based on the same facts.

3. Same Evidence and Witnesses

16–13 It must not be assumed that the rule against double jeopardy will be brought into play in a case where the prosecution pursues a second indictment relying on exactly the same witnesses and exactly the same evidence as had been used in an earlier prosecution which had resulted in the conviction or acquittal of the accused. In *Connelly v. DPP*,[48] for example, the accused was charged with murder and robbery, both charges arising out of the same incident. The prosecution proceeded on the murder count alone, resulting in a conviction which was overturned on appeal. The prosecution then had the accused arraigned on the count of robbery to which he pleaded *autrefois acquit*. Despite the fact that the prosecution was alleging the same facts and relying on the same evidence as it had used in the trial for murder, the House of Lords ruled that the plea of *autrefois acquit* must be rejected. Murder and robbery patently were neither the same nor substantially the same offences. A jury could not lawfully bring in a verdict of guilty of robbery on a count of murder, nor does the prosecution have to prove murder in order to secure a conviction for robbery. Lord Morris of Borth y Gest explained:

---

[45] *People (Attorney General) v. O'Brien* [1963] I.R. 92. An acquittal or conviction of a summary charge of dangerous driving is a bar to an indictment for dangerous driving causing death on the same occasion, since the relevant section of the Road Traffic Act 1961 creates a single offence, with the choice of procedure by indictment where the driving causes death or serious bodily harm; *Attorney General (Ward) v. Thornton* [1964] I.R. 458.

[46] *R. v. Elrington* (1861) 1 B&S 688. But note the situation which arose in *People (Attorney General) v. O'Brien* [1963] I.R. 92 discussed below.

[47] Larceny Act 1916, s.44.

[48] [1964] A.C. 1254.

"It matters not that incidents and occasions being examined on the trial of the second indictment are precisely the same as those which were examined on the trial of the first. The court is concerned with charges of offences or crimes. The test is, therefore, whether such proof as is necessary to convict of the second offence would establish guilt of the first offence or of an offence for which on the first charge there could be a conviction."[49]

Even where the offences are very similar, such as a burglary and larceny arising out of the same incident, an acquittal of one will not necessarily constitute a bar to a prosecution for the other. For example, an acquittal for burglary with intent to steal is not a bar to a subsequent prosecution for larceny arising out of the same facts, and vice versa. The question of a bar will arise only if there could have been a conviction for the second offence on the indictment for the first or if the prosecution have to establish guilt of the first offence in order to secure a conviction for the second.

4. Proceedings in a Foreign Court

An acquittal or conviction by a foreign court, if properly verified, is a bar to an indictment for the same offence in Ireland.[50] There is specific provision in the Criminal Law (Jurisdiction) Act 1976 protecting a person against the risk of being tried again for an offence for which he has already been convicted under the law of Northern Ireland (this Act is discussed in Chapter 2). It reads:

16–14

"It is hereby declared that a person who has been acquitted or convicted of an offence under the law of Northern Ireland is entitled to plead his acquittal or conviction as a bar in any proceedings in the State for an offence consisting of the acts that constituted the offence of which he has been so acquitted or convicted."[51]

5. In Peril of Conviction and Punishment

Conviction and Acquittal on the Merits

Before the double jeopardy rule will come into play it must be established that the accused was actually put in peril of being convicted and punished for the same or a similar offence arising out of the same set of facts. It will not be enough that he was merely tried on indictment for the offence on a previous occasion. He must have been convicted or acquitted on the merits.

16–15

There are many situations in which criminal proceedings against an accused result in something other than a conviction or acquittal on the merits. If, for example, the jury cannot agree and fail to reach a verdict, there is no bar to

---

[49] *Connelly v. DPP* [1964] A.C. 1254, at 1309.
[50] *R. v. Roche* (1775) 1 Leach 134; *R. v. Aughet* (1919) 13 Cr. App. Rep. 101; *Treacy v. DPP* [1971] A.C. 537. However, if the accused has been convicted and sentenced in his absence by a foreign court and there is no realistic possibility of his ever returning to that country to serve his sentence, it would appear that the plea of *autrefois convict* might not apply for the same matter in this State; *R. v. Thomas* [1984] 3 W.L.R. 321.
[51] Criminal Law (Jurisdiction) Act 1976, s.15 see above Chap. 3.

the accused being tried again.[52] Equally, if the previous charge did not proceed to trial because the indictment or summons (as the case may be) was quashed or withdrawn, it will not operate as a bar to fresh proceedings.[53] A withdrawal of a summons in the District Court before the accused pleads to it will not operate as a bar.[54] Similarly, a decision not to return the accused for trial did not amount to an acquittal and, therefore did not operate as a bar to indictment.[55]

A conviction or acquittal which is subsequently quashed as *ultra vires* will not operate as a bar to a new trial for the same offence.[56] For the bar to come into play the conviction or acquittal must be by a court acting within its jurisdiction.[57] Equally, an acquittal by direction due to an insufficient indictment will not be sufficient to raise *autrefois acquit* as the accused in such a case was never in peril of conviction.[58]

Conviction Not Enough

16–16 Even if an accused has been convicted of the same offence on a previous occasion it does not necessarily follow that another prosecution for the same offence is barred. It would appear that the accused would have to be convicted and sentenced for the bar to come into play. Conviction by itself may not be sufficient.[59] It may be that this possibility has little practical relevance today. There have been cases in the past, however, where a summary court of jurisdiction accepted a guilty plea from an accused and proceeded to sentence only to discover that the accused was of such a bad character that he should be dealt with under the sentencing jurisdiction of a higher court. In the absence of a procedure for sending the accused forward for sentencing only, the court of summary jurisdiction proceeded to return him for trial on indictment on the same charges of which the court had already convicted him. Inevitably, a plea of *autrefois convict* was successful in preventing the accused's trial on indictment in such cases. Today, of course, the District Court would deal with such cases by sending the accused forward on a plea of guilty for sentence in the Circuit Court.

There is one situation where even the imposition of sentence is not sufficient to bar prosecution for the same offence. Where an accused has been convicted of an offence and the court takes another offence into consideration

---

52 *DPP v. Nasralla* [1967] 2 A.C. 238; *R. v. Robinson* [1975] Q.B. 508.
53 *R (McDonnell) v. Tyrone JJ* [1912] 2 I.R. 44; *Minister of Supplies v. Connor* [1945] I.R. 231; *State (McLoughlin) v. Shannon* [1948] I.R. 439; *Attorney General (O'Gara) v. Callaghan* 92 I.L.T.R. 74; *State (Hogan) v. Carroll* , unreported, Supreme Court, May 12, 1991.
54 *R. v. Grays Justices, ex p. Law* [1990] Q.B. 54.
55 *State (Shanahan) v. Attorney General* [1964] I.R. 239; *R. v. Manchester City Stipendiary Magistrate, ex p. Snelson* [1977] 1 W.L.R. 911.
56 *R. v. Kent Justices, ex p. Machin* [1952] 2 Q.B. 355.
57 *People (Attorney General) v. O'Brien* [1963] I.R. 92; *R. v. West* [1964] 1 Q.B. 15.
58 *People (Attorney General) v. O'Brien* [1963] I.R. 92; *R. v. Richmond* 1 C & K 240; *Vaux's Case* (1590) 4 Co Rep 44b; *R. v. Greene* (1856) 7 Cox CC 186; *R. v. Marsham* [1912] 2 K.B. 362.
59 *Richards v. The Queen* [1993] A.C. 217, overruling *R. v. Sheridan* [1937] 1 K.B. 223 and *R. v. Grant* [1936] 2 All E.R. 1156.

for the purposes of sentencing, a plea of *autrefois convict* will not necessarily apply to the latter offence.[60] Accordingly, if the accused successfully appeals against conviction and sentence for the primary offence, he is not protected against the possibility of being prosecuted subsequently for the offences which had been taken into consideration in passing sentence.

Certificate of Dismissal

It is worth noting that a certificate of dismissal in a prosecution for a non-fatal offence against the person may be sufficient to prevent a subsequent prosecution for the same offence. Sections 44 and 45 of the Offences against the Persons Act 1861 permit the trial judge to issue a certificate of dismissal in a prosecution for assault or battery where he deems the offence not proved, or justified or so trifling as not to merit any punishment. The certificate releases the party against whom the complaint of assault or battery was made from all further (or other) proceedings in the matter, whether civil or criminal. Although most of the Offences against the Person Act 1861 has been repealed by the Non-fatal Offences against the Person Act 1997, these particular provisions have not been repealed or altered. They only apply where the first prosecution was taken by the victim or someone acting on behalf of the victim; *i.e.* a private prosecution.

16–17

Disciplinary Findings

It is also worth noting that a finding of guilt in disciplinary proceedings followed by the imposition of a penalty does not amount to a conviction sufficient to operate as a bar to criminal proceedings arising out of the same matter.[61]

Acquittal by Direction

One important situation in which the plea of *autrefois acquit* is likely to arise is where the accused has been acquitted by direction of the trial judge. This issue was considered by the Supreme Court in *People (DPP) v. O'Shea*.[62] In that case the court decided by a three to two majority that the DPP could appeal to the Supreme Court against a jury acquittal by direction of the trial judge. Although this controversial decision has since been reversed by legislation[63] the case is still important for its analysis of the rule against double jeopardy. Unfortunately, it does not offer a comprehensive and definitive statement of what is required before an accused will be deemed to have been put in peril of conviction for the purposes of the rule against double jeopardy. In the course of his judgment O'Higgins C.J. took the view that a directed acquittal is not the verdict of a jury and as such results in no trial. Accordingly, the accused has not been placed in peril of conviction. The learned judge

16–18

---

[60]   *R. v. Nicholson* (1947) 32 Cr. App. Rep. 98.
[61]   *R. v. Hogan* [1960] 2 Q.B. 513. Conversely, a conviction of a criminal offence will normally operate as a bar to proceedings for a disciplinary offence arising out of the same matter.
[62]   [1982] I.R. 384.
[63]   Criminal Procedure Act 1993, s.4(1).

found support for this interpretation in *People v. O'Brien*[64] and the judgment of O'Dalaigh J. (as he then was) in *State (Attorney General) v. Binchy*.[65] O'Higgins C.J. was in the majority which decided that the DPP had a right of appeal against a directed acquittal. The two minority judges, Finlay P. (as he then was) and Henchy J., did not address the double jeopardy issue directly. Significantly, however, they rejected the right of the prosecution to appeal on the basis that even if such an appeal was successful the accused could not be re-tried after being acquitted by direction of the judge. It is implicit in their judgments, therefore, that a directed acquittal is sufficient to bring the double jeopardy rule into play. Hederman J., who sided with the majority on the availability of the right of appeal, expressed no view on whether a re-trial might be ordered in the event of the prosecution being successful in their appeal. Nor did he address the issue of double jeopardy directly.

Finality of Verdict

16–19   Closely related to the issue of what constitutes a conviction or acquittal for the purposes of double jeopardy is the requirement that the verdict in the previous proceedings must have been final. If the accused's conviction is quashed on appeal that is normally treated as a jury acquittal sufficient to bring the plea of *autrefois acquit* into play. If, however, the conviction is quashed on appeal and a new trial ordered, the rule against double jeopardy will not apply to bar the new trial.[66]

Charges Not Properly before the Court

An acquittal of a charge which was not properly before the court will not act as a bar to an indictment for a different offence. In *People (Attorney General) v. O'Brien*,[67] for example, the defendant was tried by a jury on one count of manslaughter and two counts of dangerous driving. All three counts arose out of a fatal traffic accident. In the event the jury failed to reach a verdict on the manslaughter count and the trial judge directed a verdict of not guilty on the dangerous driving counts as they were not properly before the court. When the defendant was re-arraigned on the manslaughter count he entered a plea of *autrefois acquit* on the basis that the not guilty verdicts on the dangerous driving counts precluded a trial on the more serious manslaughter charge. On a case stated the Supreme Court accepted that the defendant could not be guilty of the manslaughter charge without also being guilty of dangerous driving. Nevertheless, the not guilty verdicts on the dangerous driving counts were not sufficient to raise *autrefois acquit* as the counts in question were not properly before the court. The accused had not actually been charged in the District Court with the two counts of dangerous driving. Accordingly they could not be included in the indictment pursuant to the terms of section 6 of the Criminal Justice Act 1951.

---

[64]   [1963] I.R. 92.
[65]   [1964] I.R. 395.
[66]   Courts of Justice Act 1928, s.5(2).
[67]   [1963] I.R. 92.

6. Procedure

Timing

The plea of *autrefois acquit* or *autrefois convict* is normally made at the arraignment, but it may be made at any stage of the proceedings.[68] It is made in writing and signed by counsel for the defence. If the accused is unrepresented he may make the plea orally. If the prosecution disputes the plea it should do so by replication. Ryan and Magee suggest that the plea and replication should take the following forms respectively as appropriate:[69]

"Plea
> *The People (Director of Public Prosecutions) v. A.B.*
> *A.B. says that the People ought not further to prosecute the indictment against him because he has been lawfully acquitted (convicted) of the offence charged therein.*
Replication
> *The Director of Public Prosecutions joins issue on behalf of the People."*

16–20

Failure to observe the correct formalities when entering the plea is not fatal to the plea itself.[70]

Proof

Once the issue has been joined a jury must be empanelled to decide the matter.[71] The onus of proof is on the accused who must prove his case on a balance of probabilities.[72] The previous conviction or acquittal can be established by a copy of the record certified by the appropriate officer of the court.[73] However, the accused may introduce further evidence. As explained by Lord Morris of Borth y Gest in *Connelly v. DPP*:

16–21

> " . . . on a plea of *autrefois acquit* or *autrefois convict* a man is not restricted to a comparison between the later indictment and some previous indictment or to the records of the court, but that he may prove by evidence all such questions as to the identity of persons, dates and facts as are necessary to enable him to show that he is being charged with an offence which is either the same or substantially the same, as one in respect of which he could have been convicted . . . "[74]

The dispute usually centres on the legal interpretation to be placed on the facts as opposed to the existence of the facts themselves. In *R. v. Coughlan*[75] the English Court of Appeal approved the practice of counsel reading out to the jury short statements of the material facts about the previous trial and the present case on which they would rely in making their respective submissions. In

---

68   *Connelly v. DPP* [1964] A.C. 1254.
69   Ryan and Magee, *op. cit.*, p. 278.
70   *Flatman v. Light* [1946] K.B. 414.
71   *R. v. Scott* (1785) 1 Leach 401; *People (DPP) v. O'Shea* [1982] I.R. 384, *per* Henchy J.
72   *R. v. Coughlan* (1976) 63 Cr. App. Rep. 33.
73   Evidence Act 1851, s.13.
74   [1964] A.C. 1254 at 1305.
75   *loc. cit.* (1976) 63 Cr. App. R. 33.

that case the court also approved the practice, in cases where the material facts were not in dispute, of the judge giving a strong direction to the jury, bordering on a direction that the plea either has or has not been made out.

Consequences

If the plea succeeds the accused must be discharged in respect of the indictment or in respect of the relevant count in the indictment. If the plea fails the indictment is put in the normal way and the accused can enter a plea of not guilty. Surprisingly, perhaps, it would appear that a new jury does not have to be empanelled to try the charges on the indictment.

7. Issue Estoppel

16–22   Closely associated with the pleas of *autrefois acquit* and *autrefois convict* is the issue estoppel. This would take the form of a submission by the accused that the prosecution is estopped from re-opening a particular issue of fact because it has already been decided in favour of the accused in a previous criminal trial. It might prove a useful option, therefore, in a case where the plea of *autrefois acquit* cannot be established. Although generally recognised as being available for the purposes of a subsequent civil trial (see Chapter 20), its applicability in a subsequent criminal trial has been in some doubt, not least because of the difficulty in determining what issues of fact, if any, the jury has decided in favour of the accused. In England the House of Lords has come down against issue estoppel in the criminal law in *DPP v. Humprhys*.[76]

In that case the accused was acquitted of driving while disqualified on July 18, 1972. He admitted that he was disqualified from driving on July 18, 1972 but gave evidence that he had not driven on that day nor on any other day in 1972. It followed that the only reason for the jury acquittal was that they were not satisfied that the accused was driving on the day in question. He was subsequently prosecuted for perjury. The prosecution case rested on the evidence that it produced at the original trial to prove that the accused had driven on the relevant day, as well as further witnesses, not called at the previous trial, who gave evidence that the accused drove on other days in 1972. The accused was convicted and the House of Lords rejected an appeal based on the argument that the prosecution was estopped from re-opening the issue of whether the accused had driven on the relevant day. Their Lordships ruled that the determination of an issue in favour of the accused at the trial for one offence was no bar to the admission of evidence at a subsequent trial aimed at establishing that the accused had committed perjury in his evidence on the issue in question at the first trial. This was so even where the evidence, if accepted at the second trial, would lead to the inference that the accused was guilty of the offence of which he had been acquitted at the first trial.

---

[76]   [1977] A.C. 1.

It does not follow, however, that the prosecution can always use a charge of **16–23** perjury as a simple device to circumvent a plea of issue estoppel. The majority of the House of Lords in *Humphrys* were of the opinion that the trial judge has a discretion to prevent a prosecution from continuing if it would be an abuse of the process of the court. The discretion might well come into play where the prosecution was using it as a device simply to secure a conviction against the accused for a matter of which he had already been acquitted by a jury. Emmins suggests that the prosecution for perjury in *Humphrys* would have amounted to an abuse of process if it had not been for the fact that the evidence of perjury related not just to the particular day at the centre of the prosecution for driving while disqualified but also extended to other days in 1972.

The ruling in *Humphrys* can also work in favour of the defence. In the earlier case of *R. v. Hogan*,[77] for example, the accused was charged with murder having already been convicted on the same facts of causing grievous bodily harm with intent to the same victim. On appeal against the conviction for murder the Leeds Crown Court ruled that as a result of the earlier conviction the defence were estopped from denying all elements of the prosecution case apart from the causal link between the harm caused and the death of the victim. In deciding that issue estoppel has no place in the criminal law, the House of Lords overruled the decision in *Hogan*.

In Ireland there has been some doubt about the availability of issue estoppel **16–24** in the criminal law, at least up until the decision of the Court of Criminal Appeal in *People (DPP) v. O'Callaghan*.[77a] In *Dublin Corporation v. Flynn*,[78] the Supreme Court reserved its position on whether issue estoppel has absolutely no place in the criminal process.[79] If, however, it had any place in the criminal process the court was of the view that it could operate only for the benefit of the accused. The prosecution could never rely on issue estoppel or *res judicata* in order to avoid the onus of proof in respect of any material issue against the accused. To hold otherwise would be contrary to basic principles of justice. In the words of Henchy J.:

> "It would be contrary to the fundamentals of criminal justice if an accused, because of an estoppel of the kind suggested, were to be debarred from showing in a later trial that the earlier determination of a particular issue was wrong. For one reason or another he may have been prepared to allow the earlier determination to go against him, but there are no reasons of justice why he should be bound to accept that determination for the purposes of a later trial. For example, to avoid undue publicity or to get the matter disposed of quickly or for some other reason, the accused may have been prepared to accept a wrong decision in an earlier prosecution to the effect that he had committed an act of assault or had driven a motor car dangerously; but if a death ensues from the event in question and he is later charged with murder or with the statutory

---

[77] [1974] Q.B. 398.
[77a] unreported, Court of Criminal Appeal, December 18, 2000.
[78] [1980] I.R. 357.
[79] In both Australia (*Mraz v. R.* (No.2) (1956) 96 C.L.R. 62 and the USA (*Sealfon v. United States* (1948) 332 U.S. 575) issue estoppel has been held applicable in criminal cases.

offence of dangerous driving causing death there is no reason why the earlier determination as to assault or dangerous driving should not only relieve the prosecution of proof in that respect but also make it incompetent for the accused to attempt to disprove the correctness of the earlier determination. In such circumstances estoppel would be repugnant to the fair administration of justice because it would deprive the accused of the opportunity of making what might be a good defence. A decision to this effect was given by Mr Justice Gannon in *The State (Brady) v. McGrath* on 25th May, 1979."[80]

The *Flynn* case concerned a prosecution under planning legislation which made it a continuing offence to fail to comply with an enforcement notice duly issued under the legislation. The defendant had been convicted of this offence on five separate occasions in respect of the same enforcement notice. He appealed his last conviction on the ground that the prosecution had not proved the making and service of the enforcement notice. The prosecution contended that the making and service of the notice had been proved against the defendant in a previous prosecution and as such he was estopped from re-opening it in a later prosecution for the same offence. The Supreme Court upheld his appeal on the ground that the prosecution could not rely on issue estoppel to relieve it of the obligation to prove the making and issue of the notice.

In *People (DPP) v. O'Callaghan*[80a] Hardiman J. giving the judgment of the Court of Criminal Appeal, reviewed the English and Irish authorities on issue estoppel in criminal matters. In that case the accused was being tried for a second time following the failure of the jury to agree at his first trial. In the course of the first trial the judge had excluded a particular witness statement as inadmissible on the ground that it was irrelevant. On the second trial the judge admitted the statement in ignorance of the full reasons why his colleague had excluded it at the first trial. The accused was convicted and appealed to the Court of Criminal Appeal on the basis that the decision to exclude the evidence in the first trial should have raised an issue estoppel preventing its use against the accused in the second trial.

Hardiman J. critiqued the reasoning behind House of Lords decision in *Humphrys* and, in particular, its reliance on supposed practical difficulties in applying issue estoppel in criminal proceedings. These difficulties were the notion that it would be rare in a criminal case to be able to identify a precise factual determination capable of giving rise to an issue estoppel, together with the notion that if estoppel was to be available to the defence it would be hard to deny it to the prosecution. Drawing on United States and Canadian authorities, together with academic writings, Hardiman J. exposed the weaknesses inherent in this reasoning. He went on to find that prior to *Humphrys* the common law recognised the availability of issue estoppel in criminal proceedings and that it was essentially an aspect of *res judicata*. He concluded not only that issue estoppel had a place in Irish criminal law but also that the moral integrity of the criminal process required it:

---

[80]   [1980] I.R. 357 at 364–365.
[80a] Court of Criminal Appeal, December 18, 2000.

"Since it seems clearly established at common law, and since its availability in a civil action following a determination of an issue on a criminal case seems established, it appears to this Court that unless and until the Supreme Court is persuaded to give a decision along the lines of *Humphrys*, issue estoppel as between one criminal trial and another should be regarded as available here. It may be noted that in the works of commentators including the authors of the two works mentioned above, various bases in principle are advanced to ground the doctrine of issue estoppel in criminal cases. Many of these relate to the protection of the party who invokes it and to the restriction of repeated litigation on the same issue on the principle *interest rei publicae ut sit finis litium*. There is however, another basis urged namely, the protection of the moral integrity of the criminal process, see, *e.g.*, McDermott *op. cit.* 260. It is this aspect which is, perhaps most relevant here. A notional onlooker in Court seeing the same issue differently decided without hearing evidence, on a reading of a statement, by two different judges sitting in the same courtroom on successive occasions, would not, this Court considers, be confirmed in a favourable view of the criminal process. The difference might be explained by the fact that the second judge was unaware of the first judge's decision or the reasons for it in any detail, but the different results still do not reflect well on the process."

It does not matter that the trial ended inconclusively, so long as there was a clear decision on a relevant issue capable of giving rise to an estoppel with respect to that issue. While this may not happen very often with respect to a jury trial, nevertheless, as is apparent from the facts of *O'Callaghan*, it can happen.

E. Plea of Not Guilty

A plea of not guilty should normally be made by the accused personally and not by counsel on his behalf. The effect of a not guilty plea is to put the entire prosecution case in issue. The prosecution will have to prove each element of the offence against the accused and, generally, will have to negative any defence that might reasonably be open to the accused. To this end a jury will be empanelled to hear and determine the case.   **16–25**

It may happen, however, that the prosecution does not wish to proceed with the case on a plea of not guilty. In this event the prosecution may inform the judge that it does not propose to offer any evidence. The judge may then order that a verdict of not guilty be recorded in respect of the offence or offences in question. In effect this amounts to the equivalent of a jury acquittal. This device has been used regularly in "miscarriage of justice" appeals in England where, as a result of the discovery of new evidence, it transpires that the case against the accused is no longer considered safe.   **16–26**

Where the accused pleads guilty to one or more counts, and not guilty to the rest, the prosecution may ask that the counts to which he has pleaded not   **16–27** guilty be left on the court file.[81] This is most likely to happen in a case where the accused has pleaded guilty to all of the most significant charges on a multi-count indictment. The prosecution may consider that it is not in the public interest to proceed to trial on the subsidiary charges when the sentences, if any, are likely to be minor and imposed to run concurrently with the sentences on the significant charges. Nevertheless, if the evidence on the subsidiary charges is strong the prosecution might prefer to leave them on file, rather than calling no evidence on them. Technically, leaving the counts on file in this manner does not foreclose the possibility of their prosecution being reactivated at some time in the future, but only with the leave of the Court of Criminal Appeal.

It might be considered that leaving counts on the file, with the associated risk of their prosecution being re-activated as some indeterminate time in the future, is unfair to the accused. Arguably the prosecution should be required to elect between proceeding to trial or calling no evidence, except where the accused consents to the counts being left on file. In practice, however, it can be expected that the Court of Criminal Appeal would refuse to give leave to reactivate the prosecution of such counts in any case where the re-activation of the prosecution would be unfair to the accused. That much, and the general nature of the order to leave counts on the file, is made clear in the following quotation from Woolf J. in *Central Criminal Court, ex p. Raymond*:

> "It starts off by having the same effect as an order for an adjournment but an adjournment which it is accepted may never result in a trial. Frequently, the order is made to safeguard the position of the prosecution and the defence in case a defendant, who has been convicted, should appeal, it being the intention of the court if there is no appeal or if the appeal is unsuccessful the defendant should never stand trial. That the defendant can still stand stand trial is indicated by the limits on the discretion of the court (laid down by the House of Lords in *Connolly v. DPP* [1964] A.C. 1254) to prevent the Crown proceeding with a prosecution if it wishes to do so. However, in the majority of cases where such an order is made, there will be no trial and there will certainly come a stage when either the prosecution would not seek a trial or if it did seek a trial, the court would regard it as so oppressive to have a trial that leave to proceed would inevitably be refused."[82]

F. Plea of Guilty

1. Entered Personally

16–28   The majority of cases on indictment result in a plea of guilty. This plea must be entered personally by the accused. It cannot be entered by counsel on his

---

[81]   There is English authority for the proposition that the trial court can order that all of the counts be left on the file; see *Central Criminal Court, ex p. Raymond* [1986] 1 W.L.R. 710 where the accused was convicted of one count on a severed indictment. The court ordered that the remaining counts on that indictment and *all* counts on a separate indictment should remain on the file.

[82]   [1986] 1 W.L.R. 710 at 714–715.

behalf. In *R. v. Williams*[83] the English Court of Appeal explained that the plea of guilty must come from the person who acknowledges guilt. A plea entered by any other person on his behalf is a nullity which will result in the conviction being quashed on appeal and the ordering of a new trial.[84] The decision to plead guilty must also be that of the accused alone. While his legal advisors can advise him in appropriate circumstances that his best course of action would be to plead guilty, they cannot direct him to do so.[85]

2. Guilty to Some Not Guilty in Others

The accused may plead guilty to the indictment as laid. Equally, he may plead guilty to one or more counts on the indictment and not guilty to the others. In this event the trial can proceed on the other count or counts. It may happen, however, that the indictment contains alternative counts arising out of the same matter. For example, the prosecution may frame the indictment to include a count of larceny and a count of handing stolen goods in a situation where it is not sure whether the accused actually stole the goods or merely handled them shortly after they were stolen by someone else. In such a case the prosecution will indicate that it is seeking a conviction on either one or other of the counts. It follows that a plea of guilty to one of the counts and not guilty to the alternative will normally result in the prosecution entering a *nolle prosequi* (see below para 16–49 *et seq.*) on the latter. Nevertheless, the prosecution may prefer a conviction for the other offence. Accordingly, it may proceed to trial on that offence. If it succeeds the accused will normally be sentenced for that offence. His plea of guilty for the alternative offence will remain on the court file but does not amount to a conviction as, technically, a guilty plea does not amount to a conviction until sentence has been passed.[86]

3. Guilty to a Lesser Offence

Another possibility is that the accused will plead guilty to a lesser offence **16–29** than that charged on the indictment. In other words he would plead guilty to a lesser offence which was incorporated within the definition of the offence actually charged in the indictment. Typical examples would be: a plea of guilty of manslaughter to a count of murder, a plea of guilty to larceny to a count of burglary, a plea of guilty of assault to a count of assault causing harm and plea of guilty of careless driving to a count of dangerous driving. The prosecution may accept the guilty plea in which case the accused is acquitted of the more serious offence actually charged on the indictment. Alternatively it may reject the plea and proceed to trial on the offence charged. Moreover, the judge has a discretion to override the prosecution's acceptance of a plea of guilty to a lesser offence.[87] In the "Yorkshire Ripper" case, for example, the

---

[83] [1978] Q.B. 373.
[84] *R. v. Ellis* (1973) 57 Cr. App. Rep. 571.
[85] *DPP v. Lynch* unreported, Court of Criminal Appeal, July 27, 1999.
[86] *R. v. Cole* [1965] 2 Q.B. 388.
[87] *R. v. Soanes* [1948] 1 All E.R. 289; but see *Blackstone's Criminal Practice* (Blackstone Press Ltd, 1997) D10.26.

prosecution was willing to accept a plea of manslaughter on each of the counts of murder. The judge refused to accept the pleas and the trial proceeded on the counts of murder.[88]

16–30   When a plea of guilty to a lesser offence is rejected a plea of not guilty is entered on behalf of the accused and his guilty plea is impliedly withdrawn. The trial proceeds in the normal way and the jury may convict of the offence charged, convict of a lesser offence subsidiary to the offence charged or even acquit the accused altogether. In *R. v. Hazeltine*[89] the accused pleaded not guilty to wounding with intent to cause grievous bodily harm but guilty of unlawful wounding. The plea of guilty to the lesser offence was not accepted and the trial proceeded. The jury acquitted the accused of the offence charged and did not bring in a verdict of guilty to the lesser offence. Nevertheless, the judge proceeded to sentence the accused for the lesser offence on the basis of his plea of guilty to that offence. The English Court of Appeal quashed the sentence on the basis that when the plea of not guilty to the greater offence was entered on behalf of the accused his plea of guilty to the lesser offence was impliedly withdrawn and could not be reinstated by the judge. Emmins explains that the prosecution could not prefer a fresh charge for unlawful wounding simpliciter as that course of action would be countered by the plea of *autrefois acquit*.[90] According to the Court of Appeal the correct course for the prosecution, once it became apparent that the accused was conducting his defence with a view to securing a complete acquittal, would have been to introduce evidence that the accused had pleaded guilty of the lesser offence. Another alternative, perhaps, would have been for the prosecution to seek to have the indictment amended to include separate counts for wounding with intent and unlawful wounding.

4. Guilty to a Different Offence

16–31   It may happen that the accused is prepared to plead guilty to a different offence from that charged on the indictment. A different offence in this context refers to an offence which is not subsidiary to, or subsumed within, any offence charged on the indictment. Section 39(1) of the Criminal Justice Administration Act 1914 makes provision for a guilty plea in such circumstances. It reads:

> "Where a prisoner is arraigned on an indictment for any offence and can lawfully be convicted on such indictment of some other offence not charged in such indictment he may plead not guilty of the offence charged in the indictment, but guilty of such other offence."

The offence to which the accused pleads guilty pursuant to section 39(1) must be one for which he could be found guilty on the indictment. A typical

---

[88]   Emmins, *A Practical Approach to Criminal Procedure* (3rd ed., Financial Training, London, 1985), p. 75.
[89]   [1967] 2 Q.B. 857.
[90]   Emmins *loc. cit.*, p. 76.

example is an indictment charging the accused with simple larceny. By virtue of section 44 of the Larceny Act 1916 an accused can be found guilty of obtaining by false pretences on such an indictment. If the accused pleads guilty to an offence (other than that charged in the indictment) in these circumstances and the prosecution accepts that plea then a verdict of guilty will be recorded for that offence and not guilty for the offence specifically charged on the indictment. If it so happens that the accused could not be found guilty of the other offence on the indictment as framed, it is open to the prosecution to seek to have the indictment amended in order to make this option available.

5. Consequences of Guilty Plea

Where a plea of guilty is accepted the prosecution is released from its **16–32** obligation to prove the case and there is no need to empanel a jury. The court may proceed straight to the sentencing process after having heard an outline of the facts of the case. This outline is normally presented by the police officer in charge of the case. He will also inform the court of the accused's criminal record, where relevant, and any other salient facts. In practice, of course, there is likely to be an adjournment for the purpose of preparing any necessary reports on the accused and/or the victim and to give the parties time to prepare their submissions on sentencing. During the adjournment the accused may be remanded either in custody or on bail.

It may happen that there is a dispute about the facts surrounding the commission of the offence which could affect the nature of the sentence. This is most likely to happen where it is not clear what it is the accused has pleaded guilty to. By pleading guilty the accused is taken to admit the facts set out in the particulars on the indictment. If, however, the particulars are stated in general terms such as " . . . the defendant indecently assaulted . . . " the victim, there will be scope for conflict over what precisely it is that the defendant has admitted to. The nature of the indecent assault, which can vary widely, can have a very significant impact on the sentence. It is important, therefore, that the particulars on the indictment should be sufficiently precise to make clear what it is that the defendant is pleading guilty to.[90a] Where this is not the case and there is conflict over the actual particulars, the prosecution will either have to call evidence in support of their own version or permit sentence to be passed on the basis of the defence version. Where the prosecution does call evidence for that purpose it goes only to the issue of how the offence was committed and not if it was committed. The outcome cannot affect the accused's guilt.

6. Different Pleas from Joint Defendants

If two accuseds are charged in the one indictment and one pleads guilty and the other not guilty, the sentencing of the former will usually be adjourned until

---

[90a] See, for example, *People (DPP) v. Naughton,* Court of Criminal Appeal, February 22, 1999.

the conclusion of the trial of the latter. While the judge retains a discretion to proceed immediately to the sentencing of the accused who pleads guilty,[91] it is expected that he or she will adjourn sentence until such time as the accuseds can be sentenced together. This has the advantage of the judge being in possession of much fuller information about the circumstances in which the crime was committed and the respective contributions of each accused.[92]

7. Accused's State of Mind

16–33   A plea of guilty must be conscious and voluntary. If the accused pleads guilty while under the influence of drugs which render him delusional or prone to making irrational decisions, the plea will be a nullity. In *R. v. Swain*,[93] for example, the accused without any rational explanation changed his plea from not guilty to guilty in the course of the prosecution case. It was subsequently discovered that he was under the influence of the hallucinatory drug LSD at the time. His conviction and sentence were quashed on appeal and a re-trial ordered on the ground that his change of plea was a nullity.

The issue of whether a plea is voluntary can be much more complex. It is firmly established that if an accused pleads guilty when subjected to pressure which is so great that he does not have a genuinely free choice, his plea is a nullity. If, for example, the trial judge tells the accused that he is plainly guilty and is wasting the court's time with a plea of not guilty, a change of plea will be a nullity.[94] The same result will ensue if the accused is given the impression by his counsel that the judge has indicated to him privately that he will impose a non-custodial penalty as distinct from a custodial penalty in return for a change of plea from not guilty to guilty.[95] That is not to say that counsel cannot advise his or her client on what sentence is likely to be imposed and the possible advantages which might accrue from a guilty plea. Indeed, it is accepted that such advice may even be given in forceful terms.[96] So long as that advice is not given in terms or in a manner which effectively takes away the accused's free choice it will not be sufficient to render a guilty plea null and void, even if the guilty plea was offered reluctantly. This issue is considered further below under the heading of plea bargaining.

G. Ambiguous Pleas

16–34   If an accused enters a plea which could be consistent with guilt or innocence it would appear that the court should enter a plea of not guilty on his behalf. The same principle applies to an accused who refused to plead. Where a court proceeds to sentence on a plea which falls short of an unambiguous plea of

---

91   *R. v. Sheffield Crown Court, ex p. Brownlow* [1980] Q.B. 530; *R. v. Palmer* (1994) 158 JP 138.
92   *R. v. Payne* [1950] 1 All E.R. 102; *R. v. Weekes* (1980) 74 Cr. App. Rep. 161.
93   [1986] Crim. L.R. 480.
94   *R. v. Barnes* (1970) 55 Cr. App. Rep. 100.
95   *R. v. Turner* [1970] 2 Q.B. 321.
96   *R. v. Inns* (1974) 60 Cr. App. Rep. 231.

guilt, there will be grounds for appeal against conviction and sentence. In *R. v. Ingleson*,[97] for example, the accused was charged with one count of stealing horses and one count of receiving horses knowing that they were stolen. After pleading guilty he submitted in mitigation of sentence that he did not know the horses were stolen. It was held on appeal that it should have been explained to the accused that the proper plea in the circumstances was not guilty. Accordingly, the plea of guilty was wrongly entered and all proceedings consequent on that plea were bad. A re-trial was ordered.

H. Plea Bargaining

1. Definition

Plea-bargaining is the name given to the negotiation between the State and the accused in which the accused tries to secure a lighter sentence in return for a plea of guilty. It can be further broken down into prosecutorial plea-bargaining and judicial plea-bargaining. The former refers to discussions between the prosecution and the defence over the charges that will be proceeded with in court. Typically, the defence will intimate to the prosecution that the accused is prepared to plead guilty to one or more charges in return for a more serious charge or charges on the indictment being dropped. These discussions will be conducted in private. Judicial plea-bargaining refers to discussions which take place between the prosecution, defence and the judge in the judge's private chambers, usually during the course of the trial. The purpose of such discussions is usually to seek an indication from the judge of the type of sentence he has in mind should the accused be convicted. Any such indication will be used by the defence counsel in advising his client whether to change his plea from not guilty to guilty. As with the prosecutorial plea bargain this form of plea bargain is conducted in private and the results are not normally made public. **16–35**

2. Administration of Justice in Public

Public confidence in the integrity of the criminal process, and the criminal trial in particular, rests substantially on the trial being conducted fully in open court. Indeed, Article 34 of the Constitution stipulates that justice shall be administered in public except in such limited cases as shall be prescribed by law. Similarly the requirement in Article 38 that no person shall be tried on any criminal charge save in due course of law entails, *inter alia*, that a criminal trial shall be held in public, unless there are objective and justifiable reasons why it, or any part of it, needs to be held *in camera*. It follows that in any criminal case the charges formulated against and put to the accused should reflect the nature of admissible evidence available to the prosecution. Where the accused pleads not guilty the evidence against him should be **16–36**

---

[97] [1915] 1 K.B. 512.

presented and tested in open court, the defence arguments and evidence in rebuttal should be presented and tested in open court, the determination by the tribunal of fact should be announced in open court and, where appropriate, the sentencing process should be conducted in open court. The integrity of the process, and public confidence in it, inevitably will be undermined by deals done in private between the players. A secret agreement not to proceed with one or more charges in return for the co-operation of the accused or an agreement to plead guilty in order to wring some concession out of the prosecution would seem to subvert the fundamental principle that not only should justice be done but it should be seen to be done. Carried to extremes the practice of secret deals between the prosecution and the defence would render the criminal trial a sham.

3. Conflicting Interests

16–37   It is also worth bearing in mind that secret deals between the prosecution and the defence will be designed to serve their respective interests. It cannot be assumed, however, that both parties are engaging from positions of equal strength. Almost invariably the prosecution will be playing with a much stronger hand. The implications of this for the practice of plea-bargaining are considered further below. It must also be acknowledged that the prosecution interests when entering into a secret deal with the accused will not necessarily be synonymous with those of the victim. Indeed, it is not difficult to imagine a situation where the victim is keen to see the accused prosecuted in accordance with the full rigour of the law while the bureaucratic convenience of the prosecution, or its perception of the public interest, would be better served by a deal which would cut the proceedings short. Where a secret deal is struck in such circumstances the victim is effectively excluded, resulting in the individual suffering a deep sense of injustice to add to the hurt caused by the crime itself.

4. Benefits of Plea-bargaining

16–38   Despite these inherent dangers the practice of the prosecution and the accused privately negotiating a tacit agreement or understanding concerning their respective approaches to the criminal trial has been a standard feature of the criminal process in Britain for many years. There is no reason to believe that this form of plea-bargaining does not have an equally long pedigree in Ireland. Indeed, it would now appear to be an established feature of the criminal process in this State. The justification for the practice generally rests on the notion that it will not always be in the public interest to pursue all possible criminal charges against an accused through the full rigours of a contested criminal trial. It may be, for example, that the prosecution are not fully confident about securing a conviction for a serious charge on the indictment. Rather than risking the expense and effort of a full criminal trial in an attempt to prove that charge they may be prepared to accept a plea of guilty to a lesser charge. This will free up time and resources which can be used to expedite the trial of other criminal offences. Equally, it may be considered that it is in the public interest to spare a vulnerable victim from the trauma of having to give evidence and submit to cross-examination in a prosecution for a serious sex or child abuse offence when the accused is prepared to plead guilty to a lesser related offence.

5. Prosecutorial Plea-bargaining

Although plea bargaining is an established feature of the criminal process **16–39** today it does not rest on any firm legal foundation. There is no common law or statutory prescription of the situations in which it can be used, the practice that must be followed, the sort of agreements that may be concluded or even the status of any such agreements. The most that can be done here is offer a general description of what happens in practice coupled with an account of the limited judicial guidance which has been offered on what will and what will not be accepted. For the sake of clarity of exposition prosecutorial plea-bargaining will be considered separately from judicial plea-bargaining. It is also necessary to note in advance that a full and accurate account of these practices is hampered by a certain reluctance among practitioners to acknowledge openly that plea-bargaining is a regular feature of the criminal process, let alone to discuss how it operates in practice. Charleton and McDermott suggest that the following colourful description of the attitude that used to prevail in Canada would be descriptive of the present position in Ireland:

> "Professor Graham Parker has observed that as recently as 1965 the whole subject was treated as a 'dirty little secret'. He suggests that most lawyers took the following pharisatic attitude: 'Yes, it probably exists but it is only practised by inferior criminal lawyers. We would rather not discuss it and then, perhaps, it will go away.' It has also been suggested that, until recently, plea bargaining in Canada could be likened to a mysterious ghost freely strolling the halls of our criminal courts, no one knowing exactly what it is or what force it carries, and no-one daring to ask for fear the answer might reveal that which we would rather leave unknown."[98]

Broadly speaking prosecutorial plea-bargaining refers to the process which results in the accused pleading guilty to one or more charges on the understanding that he will benefit from a lighter sentence as a result of the prosecution not proceeding with one or more other charges on the indictment. This can happen where the indictment contains a number of counts arising out of the same incident. Typically, defence counsel will intimate to the prosecution that the accused is prepared to plead guilty to one or more of the lesser charges on the indictment in return for other, more serious, charges being dropped. If the prosecution accepts the offer, it will normally enter a *nolle prosequi* or call no evidence on the other charges. Alternatively, the prosecution may simply ask the

---

[98] Ferguson and Roberts, "Plea Bargaining: Directions for Canadian Reform" (1974) 52 *Canadian Bar Review* 497 at 500, quoted in Charleton and McDermott "Constitutional Implications of Plea Bargaining" (2000) 9 *Bar Review* Vol. 5 476.

judge to leave the other offences on the court file marked not to be proceeded with unless with the leave of the Court of Criminal Appeal. This particular option is subject to the approval of the trial judge, unlike the entry of a *nolle prosequi* which cannot be questioned by the judge. Another possibility is that counsel for the defence will intimate to the prosecution that the accused is prepared to plead guilty to a lesser offence than that charged on the indictment. In this case it is ultimately a matter for the judge to decide whether to accept a plea of guilty to a lesser offence than that charged. Undoubtedly, of course, the prosecution's willingness to accept the plea is an important factor that the judge will take into account in making the determination.

Framing the Indictment

16–40   In these examples of plea bargaining it would be the expectation of the accused that the judge would impose a more lenient sentence for the offence or offences to which he has pleaded guilty than might otherwise have been the case had he been tried and convicted of the other more serious offences on the indictment. Indeed, in many cases the maximum available sentence applicable to the offences to which the accused pleads guilty will be statutorily capped at a level significantly below that applicable to the other more serious offences. It follows that the plea bargaining process is heavily influenced by the manner in which the indictment has been framed. The more counts that there are in the indictment arising out of the same incident, the stronger the prosecution's hand will be in the event of the defence seeking to plea bargain. Similarly, by charging the most serious offence possible on the evidence the prosecution is increasing the pressure on the defence to seek the prosecution's acceptance of a plea of guilty to a lesser charge. It follows that there is potential for the prosecution to frame the indictment deliberately with a view to strengthening its hand in any subsequent plea bargaining. While there is nothing unlawful *per se* in such a practice, difficulties could arise if the prosecution subsequently made the running in seeking a deal whereby they would drop more serious charges in return for a guilty plea to a lesser charge. Ryan and Magee submit that, having once decided to indict the accused for specific offences, the prosecution should never, save in the most exceptional circumstances, offer to accept a plea of guilty to some lesser or alternative offence, or even to invite the defence to treat. Any offer or approach must come from the defence.

16–41   The bargaining between prosecution and defence clearly gives rise to serious issues about the administration of justice being conducted in public. Considerable public disquiet could be generated by a regular practice of serious charges not being pursued in return for guilty pleas to lesser charges.[99]

---

[99] See *e.g.* the DPP's decision to accept a plea of guilty to manslaughter in the trial of persons changed with the murder of Garda Jerry McCabe.

Prior Judicial Approval

Even once off incidents can give rise to concern in high profiles cases.[99] This problem might be averted in some cases by the prosecution seeking the prior approval of the trial judge in open court for their decision to accept a guilty plea to a lesser charge. If the judge does not sanction the arrangement it would appear that the prosecution would have to proceed with the indictment as framed.[100] It does not follow, however, that the prosecution are bound to seek the judge's prior approval. In the absence of a prior request for his approval it would appear that the judge has no power to prevent such an arrangement. Indeed, any attempt by him to force the prosecution to proceed with one or more counts on the indictment against their wishes might undermine the judge's primary status as an independent umpire in the case.[101] In England and Wales when the prosecution do not seek the prior approval of the trial judge for their decision not to proceed with more serious counts in the indictment they will normally explain their reasons in open court.

6. Judicial Plea-bargaining

The Context

Even if the prosecution are not prepared to settle for a plea of guilty to a lesser offence, or in satisfaction of other offences on the indictment, there is still some scope for plea-bargaining. In return for a plea of guilty the prosecution may agree to outline the facts of the case to the judge in a manner which should encourage the judge to be lenient in sentencing. Alternatively, the accused may gamble on a guilty plea simply on the expectation that the judge will impose a lighter sentence than might otherwise be the case if he persisted with a not guilty plea and was convicted by the jury. Of course such a decision may not involve any element of plea bargaining. It may simply be the result of a reasoned assessment by the accused. Equally, however, it may be influenced by the advice of defence counsel who has spoken to the trial judge.

    It is accepted that there are occasions when it may be necessary for counsel for the defence and the prosecution to discuss aspects of the trial with the judge in private whether prior to arraignment or during the trial itself. It may be, for example, that the accused has given valuable assistance to the police in the detection of serious crime on the understanding that his co-operation will be brought to the attention of the judge when considering sentence. The circumstances may be such that the safety of the accused or members of his family may be prejudiced if such co-operation is mentioned in open court. Alternatively, there may be some sensitive personal matters, such as the fact that the accused is suffering from a terminal illness which would be better brought to the attention of the judge in chambers rather than

16–42

---

[100] *R. v. Broad* (1978) 68 Cr. App. Rep. 281.
[101] See the Farquharson Report (1986) on the role of prosecuting counsel as set out in *Archbold* 44th ed., (1992) vol.1, para 4–71 which was approved in *R. v. Grafton* [1993] Q.B. 101.

in open court.[102] On these occasions counsel for both sides should be present, along with the defence solicitor and the court clerk.

In *R. v. Turner*[103] Lord Parker C.J. acknowledged that there must be such freedom of access between counsel and judge. However, he also emphasised that it should be used sparingly:

> "It is of course imperative that, as far as possible, justice must be administered in open court. Counsel should, therefore, only ask to see the judge when it is felt to be really necessary, and the judge must be careful only to treat such communications as private where, in fairness to the accused person, this is necessary."[104]

In practice counsel may take advantage of this access to ascertain whether the judge might consider the imposition of a non-custodial sentence. This, in turn, will influence the advice that counsel will give to the accused on how he should plead to the charges. As will be seen below, however, the extent to which a judicial indication of likely sentence can be used in the plea bargaining process is highly uncertain.

Voluntary Plea

16–43   The legal framework within which the judicial plea bargaining process must operate is vague. To a large extent this derives from the fact that the relevant principles and rules have not been developed to deal specifically with plea bargaining as such. They are concerned instead with the general notion of what constitutes fair procedures in the context of the trial as a whole. This is neatly illustrated by the principle which is most relevant to plea bargaining namely the fundamental principle that the accused's plea must be voluntary. If he is subjected to any improper pressure to plead guilty or to change his plea to guilty from not guilty, the plea will be a nullity. In such circumstances the Court of Criminal Appeal will quash the conviction and order a re-trial. It does not matter whether the improper pressure came from the judge or the accused's own counsel, the result is the same.[105]

This general principle clearly has important implications for plea bargaining. Inevitably, the accused will be heavily dependant on the advice of his counsel on what is the most appropriate course for him to take in the matter of a plea. Counsel will have to assess the strength of the prosecution case and consider the sentence likely to be imposed on conviction after a contested trial compared with what might be imposed on a plea of guilty. He or she must also consider the scope for a plea bargain with the prosecution and what advantage, if any, that might bring for the accused. Weighing up all of these matters counsel must advise the accused on what he or she considers to be the best course of action for the accused in the circumstances, while emphasising

---

[102]   See O'Malley, *Sentencing Law and Practice* (Round Hall Press, Dublin, 2000), at para.10–45.
[103]   [1970] 2 Q.B. 321.
[104]   *ibid.* at 326–327. See also *R. v. Coward* (1980) 70 Cr. App. Rep. 70; *R. v. Llewellyn* (1977) 67 Cr. App. Rep. 149.
[105]   See, *e.g., R v. Barnes* (1970) 55 Cr. App. Rep. 100.

that ultimately it is the accused himself who must take the decision. Although counsel must advise the accused that he must not plead guilty unless he has committed the acts constituting the offence charged he may, in appropriate cases, advise the accused in strong terms of the advantages to be gained from a plea of guilty coupled with a show of remorse. This is the point at which there is a danger that counsel's advice may result in improper pressure being applied on the accused to plead guilty. If the result of counsel's advice is that the accused has effectively lost the power to make a voluntary and deliberate choice his plea of guilty will be a nullity. The difficulty, of course, is in determining when counsel's advice has over-stepped the mark. The leading case on the subject in these islands is the decision of the English Court of Appeal in *R. v. Turner*.[106]

The Turner Case

In that case the accused had pleaded not guilty to theft. During an adjourn- **16–44**
ment in the trial the accused discussed the case with his counsel and solicitor. At one point in the course of this consultation his counsel went to speak with the judge privately. On his return he advised the accused that if he changed his plea to guilty he would receive a non-custodial sentence. If, however, he persisted with his plea of not guilty and was subsequently convicted there was a very real possibility that he would receive a sentence of imprisonment. The circumstances in which this advice was conveyed to the accused led him to believe that his counsel was conveying the views of the judge when in fact counsel was merely expressing his own opinion of what might happen in the case. Accordingly the accused agreed to be re-arraigned and to plead guilty. Although the Court of Appeal accepted that counsel had not exercised any undue influence over the accused it went on to quash the conviction. The fact that the accused believed that counsel was merely passing on the views of the judge meant that the accused was not really exercising a free choice when he changed his plea. In handing down this decision Lord Parker C.J. addressed the constraints within which plea bargaining must operate in the context of private communications between counsel and judge.

> "The judge should, subject to the one exception referred to hereafter, never indicate the sentence which he is minded to impose. A statement that on a plea of guilty he would impose one sentence but that on a conviction following a plea of not guilty he would impose a severer sentence is one which should never be made. This could be taken to be undue pressure on the accused, thus depriving him of that complete freedom of choice which is essential. Such cases however are in the experience of the court happily rare. What on occasions does appear to happen however is that a judge will tell counsel that, having read the depositions and the antecedents, he can safely say that on a plea of guilty he will for instance, make a probation order, something which may be helpful to counsel in advising the accused. The judge in such a case is no doubt careful not to mention what he would do if the accused were convicted following a plea of not guilty. Even so, the accused may well get the impression that the judge is intimating that in that event a severer sentence,

---

[106]   [1970] 2 Q.B. 321.

maybe a custodial sentence would result, so that again he may feel under pressure. This accordingly must also not be done."[107]

It is clear from this passage that there is limited room for manoeuvre in plea-bargaining on the basis of what indication the judge may give in private concerning the likely sentence to be imposed on conviction. Not only can the judge not offer the prospect of a lighter sentence in return for a guilty plea, but he or she must also avoid giving any indication of the likely sentence on a conviction following a plea of not guilty lest this raise the hope of a lighter sentence in return for a plea of guilty. The only exception to this, as Lord Parker C.J. made clear later in his judgment, is that the judge can indicate what form the sentence is likely to take irrespective of whether there is a plea of guilty or not guilty. In other words he can say that the sentence will take the form of a probation order, or a fine or a term of imprisonment or whatever. Such information will, of course be helpful to counsel when advising the accused on the respective merits of a plea of guilty or not guilty. Indeed counsel must disclose to the accused the substance of the private discussion with the judge. Nevertheless, it does not offer any significant scope for the accused to bargain a plea of guilty in return for a lighter sentence.

16–45   It is uncertain whether the decision in *Turner* precludes the possibility of the judge indicating to counsel *in confidence* the approximate level of sentence that he has in mind on the basis of what he has heard so far.[108] Such information would of course be very useful when counsel is advising the accused on the most appropriate course of action with respect to the plea. In *R. v. Cain*[109] the English Court of Appeal held that *Turner* did not preclude this course of action so long as it was understood that counsel would not reveal the judge's guidance as the source of his advice when advising the accused on what sentence he could expect on conviction. It is doubtful, however, that there are any circumstances in which the judge can properly indicate to the counsel that he has one sentence in mind for a conviction following a plea of not guilty and a lesser sentence for a plea of guilty.[110] In *R. v. Inns*,[111] for example, the English Court of Appeal ordered a re-trial where the accused changed his plea from not guilty to guilty after being told that the judge was of a mind to impose a sentence of detention on conviction after a not guilty plea but would consider a lighter sentence on a guilty plea. There was no indication in this case that the judge's advice was given in confidence to counsel and, as such, it was a clear contradiction of the *Turner*

---

[107]   *ibid.* at 327.
[108]   In *R. v. Coward* (1980) 70 Cr. App. Rep. 70 it was said that counsel could not and should not expect a judge, save in wholly exceptional circumstances, to give any guidance whatsoever about the kind of sentence to be passed.
[109]   [1976] Crim. L.R. 464.
[110]   Following the reporting of *R. v. Cain* the English Court of Appeal issued a practice direction [1976] Crim. L.R. stating that if *Cain* is inconsistent with the observations in *Turner* the latter should prevail. See also *R. v. Coward* (1979) 70 Cr. App. Rep. 70 where Lawton L.J. strongly deprecated the notion that counsel could persuade the judge to give an indication of likely sentence on a plea of guilty.
[111]   60 Cr. App. Rep. 231.

guidelines. Nevertheless, even if it had been given in confidence it is submitted that the result would have been the same, particularly where the judge's guidance had come to the attention of the accused.[112]

Case law in England and Wales since *Turner* has consistently reflected opposition to judges either offering, or being seen to offer, a plea bargain to the accused.[113] Where defendants have pleaded guilty as a result of believing that the judge will impose a lighter sentence the appellate courts are likely to quash the conviction and order a re-trial.[114] Similarly, convictions have been quashed where the judge has been seen to resile from an indication of a non-custodial sentence given to counsel in private.[115]

Judicial Plea-bargaining in Ireland

It is unlikely that judicial plea-bargaining is a regular feature of the Irish **16–46** criminal process. Ireland's first DPP is on record as having issued instructions to prosecution counsel not to engage in the practice of accompanying defence counsel to the judge's chamber for the purpose of expressing a view, if asked by the judge, on a sentence which might be imposed.[116] It does not follow, of course, that such discussions never take place. Indeed, the DPP was motivated to issue his instruction by virtue of his discovery that this form of judicial plea-bargaining had taken root. Also it is apparent from a portion of the judgment of the Court of Criminal Appeal in *People (DPP) v. Cox and Keeler*[117] that there were times when counsel for the prosecution and the defence would meet with the trial judge in his chamber before the trial to discuss certain aspects of the trial, including sentence. It is unlikely, however, in the light of the DPP's instruction and the constraints imposed by the Court of Appeal in England and Wales in *Turner* that there will be much scope in this jurisdiction for the accused to trade a plea of guilty in return for the promise of a lighter sentence. Indeed, there is reason to believe that the provisions of the Criminal Justice Act 1993, which enable the DPP to seek a review of sentence on the grounds that it is too light, have severely constrained if not removed, the scope for such bargains. There is nothing in the Act which precludes the DPP from exercising his power to seek a review of a sentence where that sentence accords with the sentence which the judge indicated he would impose should the accused plead guilty. Undoubtedly, if

---

[112] In *R. v. Quartey* [1975] Cr. App. Rep. 592 the Court of Appeal refused to interfere where counsel had been advised by the judge in private that he would impose a sentence of 18 months imprisonment. Subsequently, after hearing more evidence, the judge advised counsel in private that he would impose a sentence of three years imprisonment, but that there would be a reduction if he pleaded guilty.

[113] For a summary see *Blackstone's Criminal Practice* (Blackstone Press Ltd, 1997) D10.43.

[114] *R. v. Ryan* (1977) 67 Cr. App. Rep. 177; *R. v. Grice* (1977) 66 Cr. App. Rep. 167; *R. v. Atkinson* [1978] 1 W.L.R. 425.

[115] *R. v. Bird* (1977) 67 Cr. App. Rep. 203.

[116] Barnes, "Reflections on the Past 24 Years as Director of Public Prosecutions" (1999) 4 *Bar Review* 389 at 393. It would also appear that the DPP issued a general direction in 1998 to circuits outside Dublin that the practice should be discontinued; see *People (DPP) v. Heeney* unreported, Supreme Court, April 5, 2001.

[117] Unreported, Court of Criminal Appeal, May 12, 1998.

the DPP attempted to seek a review in such a case, after having assented to the sentence during the private discussions with the judge and defence counsel, complex issues of basic fairness and estoppel would be raised.[118]

16-47   In *People (DPP) v. Cox and Keeler*,[119] the respondents had been convicted and sentenced after having pleaded not guilty to charges of handling stolen goods. They successfully appealed against both conviction and sentence. At their re-trial they initially pleaded not guilty but changed their plea to guilty on arraignment after their counsel had discussions with prosecution counsel and the trial judge in the judge's chamber. The judge imposed sentences of imprisonment of six years and four years respectively. However, he also suspended the sentences on condition that the respondents entered into a bond to be of good behaviour. The DPP applied to the Court of Criminal Appeal for a review of the sentences under the Criminal Justice Act 1993. The Court concluded that the sentences imposed were unduly lenient having regard to the manner in which the crimes were committed, the amounts involved, the professional nature of the organisation behind them and the criminal records of the accused. Accordingly, the court quashed the sentences and imposed terms of imprisonment of six years and four years respectively.

In the course of the hearing before the Court of Criminal Appeal counsel for one of the respondents very circumspectly drew the attention of the Court to the respondent's change of plea from not guilty to guilty after the pre-trial meeting between both sets of counsel and the judge. Counsel proceeded to argue that in such circumstances there was a grave danger of an injustice being done to the respondents if the court were to exercise its discretion to increase the sentences. The court described this as "a most regrettable situation." It proceeded to explain:

> "The revolutionary changes introduced by s.2 of the Criminal Justice Act, 1993 [empowering the DPP to seek a review of sentence], may put an end to pre-trial discussions between the trial judge, Counsel on behalf of the Director and Counsel for the accused or it may mean that any such discussions will take a different form. Certainly, Counsel must in the future recognise that any sentence imposed by a trial judge (or any sentence that it is anticipated that he may impose) will be subject to review by this court, so that any course of action taken by an accused must have regard to that legal reality."

16-48   Support for this opinion can be found in the decision of the Supreme Court of Victoria in *R. v. Marshall*.[120] In that case the Supreme Court repudiated the practice of asking a judge in open court what the appropriate sentence would be in the event of a plea of guilty. The court's reasoning made it clear that it would be equally unacceptable to ask the judge in private. In the course of its

---

[118]   In the Canadian case, *R. v. Agozzino* [1970] 1 O.R. 480, [1970] 1 CCC 380, the Crown attempted to appeal a sentence on grounds of leniency after it had agreed with the defence not to seek a jail term in return for a plea of guilty. The Ontario Court of Appeal held that the Crown could not repudiate its bargain on appeal.

[119]   *loc. cit.*.

[120]   [1981] V.R. 725.

decision the court explained why it would not consider the English cases, including *Turner*, in any detail. The explanation is of particular significance here:

> "The reason is simply that there is a very important difference between the procedure and administration of the criminal law in England and Victoria. In Victoria the Crown has a right of appeal against a sentence imposed if the Attorney-General considers that a different sentence should have been passed and is satisfied that an appeal should be brought in the public interest: Crimes Act, s.567A. No such right exists in England. Thus if a judge were asked before arraignment to give an indication of the sentence likely to be imposed, the Crown might by its silence give the impression of being content with the indication and yet appeal as soon as the indicated sentence was imposed. In our opinion such a practice would tend to weaken public confidence in the administration of justice."[121]

Admittedly, this reasoning could be used to support the notion that the prosecutor should not appeal a sentence when it accords with the sentence to which he assented in the course of "plea-bargaining" discussions between himself, defence counsel and the judge. In *Murray*, however, the Supreme Court of Victoria relied on this reasoning to support their conclusion that such "plea-bargaining" discussions had no role at all in the criminal process. Given the convergence of Irish law and the law in Victoria on prosecution appeals against sentence, it would appear that the *Murray* decision strengthens the argument that judicial plea-bargaining has no place in the Irish criminal process. Indeed, it also suggests that discussions between the judge and counsel for the defence and prosecution on sentencing matters are unacceptable even if they conform with the Turner guidelines.

Nevertheless, the door has not been closed tightly in Ireland. The matter has come before the Supreme Court recently in *People (DPP) v. Heeney*.[121a] At a pre-trial meeting with counsel for the prosecution and defence the judge indicated the level of sentence he would impose on a guilty plea. Subsequently the defendant pleaded guilty to counts of unlawful carnal knowledge and attempted unlawful carnal knowledge of young girls and was sentenced to terms of imprisonment of 6 years and 3 years respectively. This was increased to ten years by the Court of Criminal Appeal which stated frankly that it could not be fettered in any way by the holding of any private meeting in the judge's chambers or any indication as to the likely sentence given by the trial judge in such a meeting. The Supreme Court was then asked to consider as a point of law of exceptional public importance whether the Court of Criminal Appeal should have regard to the fact that discussion had taken place in chambers prior to the trial between the trial judge and counsel for the prosecution and defence, following which the accused pleaded guilty. The Supreme Court declared that plea-bargaining in the sense of a private arrangement whereby a particular level of sentence will be imposed in return for a plea of guilty has no place in Irish law. That, however, does not preclude

---

[121] *ibid.* at 735.
[121a] Supreme Court, April 5, 2001.

the judge from giving an indication of the difference in level of sentence which a person can on occasion secure in his favour by a plea of guilty. Indeed, the Court went on to rule that the Court of Criminal Appeal was wrong as a matter of law in declining to have regard to the discussions which had taken place prior to the trial. The Supreme Court did not go so far as to say that the Court was bound by the outcome of such discussions where their result was a plea of guilty in return for the effective promise of a significantly lighter sentence. However, the Court was bound to take it into account as a factor in determining whether it would be proper to quash the sentence on the ground that it was unduly lenient. (See further, Chapter 21).

It is also worth noting that Keane C.J., delivering the judgment of the Supreme Court in *Heeney* made it clear that the procedure which had been followed before the trial in this case could not properly be described as 'plea bargaining' in the sense of a bargain in private over matters of plea and sentence. Moreover, if it did take on the trappings of 'plea bargaining' it would be unconstitutional:

> "While the form of procedure adopted in this and other cases has been described as "*plea bargaining*", that appears to me to be a misnomer. Thus, any indication that a trial judge might give as to what sentence he might impose in the event of a plea of guilty would have to be subject to the proviso, express or implied, that he or she might reach a different view depending on the evidence which he or she subsequently heard in open court. As for counsel for the prosecution, while his or her presence is obviously essential if any discussions are going to take place with the judge before the trial, it would not be part of his or her function to enter into any form of "*bargain*" with counsel for the defence as to the appropriate sentence. It must also be emphasised that, while discussions in chambers between judge and counsel are occasionally desirable in the interests of justice, in general, under Article 34.1 of the Constitution, justice must be administered in public. There can thus be no question, in my view, of any form of bargain being entered into in private which would determine in advance the sentence to be imposed by the court. Accordingly, I would agree with the view of the Court of Criminal Appeal that the procedure adopted in this case and in other cases, although it obviously did not amount to any form of "*plea bargain*" and was doubtless, as in other cases, prompted by the best motives, is undesirable and has properly been discontinued by the DPP."

I. *Nolle Prosequi*

1. Timing

16–49   The attorney general had a common law power to stop the prosecution of an accused by entering a *nolle prosequi*. Today it would appear that the source of the power lies in section 12 of the Criminal Justice (Administration) Act 1924 which stipulates that the DPP may enter a *nolle prosequi* at the trial of an accused at any time after the indictment is preferred to the jury and before a verdict is found. The practice at common law had been to enter the *nolle* *prosequi* before the indictment was preferred.[122] Although the exercise of the power under section 12 appears to be confined to the period between the preferment of the indictment and the verdict of the jury, the practice of entering it before the indictment is preferred has continued. In *State (O'Callaghan) v. O hUadhaigh*[123] Finlay P. acknowledged that this practice had continued for 50 years since the enactment of the 1924 Act. Quoting from the judgment of Maguire C.J. in *State (Killian) v. Attorney General*[124] the learned judge took the view that even if the practice was not strictly regular there was no question of the court having any power to interfere with the DPP's decision not to pursue the prosecution. Later, in *State (Coveney) v. The Special Criminal Court*,[125] Finlay P. explained that justice would often be better served by permitting the DPP to enter a *nolle prosequi* before the indictment was preferred:

> "It is difficult to see what end of justice and in particular what right or interest of the accused could be secured by inhibiting the Director of Public Prosecutions as it now is from entering a *nolle prosequi* before the accused had been given in charge to a jury. In many cases as in this case the entry of a *nolle prosequi* before that time expedites the discharge of the accused and, of course, in the very great majority of cases in which a *nolle prosequi* is entered no further proceedings are instituted. In a case such as the present where the entry of a *nolle prosequi* is a precedent to the institution of fresh proceedings in respect of the same charge its early rather than its late entry merely achieves one of the known objectives of justice, namely the speedy dispatch of criminal proceedings. Furthermore, expense incurred by an accused in his own defence and the anxiety associated with a pending criminal charge would be intensified if strict adherence were in all cases paid by the Director of Public Prosecutions to the provisions of the section appearing to provide that it was only when the accused had been put in charge of the jury that he could and should enter a *nolle prosequi*."[126]

Accordingly, despite the formal words of section 12, it is perfectly lawful for the DPP to enter a *nolle prosequi* before the indictment has been preferred.

2. Scope

A *nolle prosequi* entered under section 12 must take the following form: **16–50**

> "On the . . . . day of [20xx] at the trial of AB on the prosecution of the Director of Public Prosecutions on an indictment for . . . . the said Director in his proper person (or by his Counsel) stated to the court that he would not further prosecute the said AB on the said indictment, whereupon it was ordered by the Court that the said AB be discharged of and from the indictment aforesaid."

---

[122] *State (O'Callaghan) v. O hUadhaigh* [1977] I.R. 42; *State (Killian) v. Attorney General* 92 I.L.T.R. 182.

[123] *loc. cit.*

[124] *loc. cit*

[125] [1982] I.L.R.M. 284.

[126] *ibid.* at 288.

Neither common law nor statute offers a definitive list of situations in which the *nolle prosequi* can or cannot be applied. At one time it was often used by the Attorney General to block private prosecutions which were not deemed to be in the public interest. Ever since the private prosecutor lost the power to pursue a prosecution on indictment there has been no need to enter a *nolle prosequi* for this purpose. Today, it is used generally to deal with any situation where, for one reason or another, the DPP considers that the charge in question against the accused should not proceed immediately to trial. This may happen, for example, because information has come to light belatedly suggesting that the accused is not guilty of the offence charged or, for some other reason, that it is not appropriate to put him on trial for the offence. Equally, it may be that the DPP has discovered some flaw in the prosecution case which would result in the case being thrown out should it proceed to trial. Alternatively, the DPP may deem it necessary to enter a *nolle prosequi* and commence fresh proceedings in response to a decision made by the accused. In *State (Coveney) v. The Special Criminal Court*,[127] for example, the accused had been sent forward to the Circuit Criminal Court for sentencing on a plea of guilty. When he changed his plea to not guilty the DPP entered a *nolle prosequi* and instituted fresh proceedings before the Special Criminal Court.

16–51   A *nolle prosequi* may also be entered as a result of a plea bargain between the prosecution and the accused. Indeed, it is worth emphasising in this context that the prosecution does not always have to choose between entering a *nolle prosequi* for the complete indictment and proceeding with the trial on the complete indictment. Despite the actual wording of the form used, it would appear that where the indictment contains a number of counts the prosecution can enter a *nolle prosequi* on one or more counts and proceed to trial on the other count or counts as the case may be.

3. Fresh Proceedings

The circumstances in which a *nolle prosequi* can be entered are closely related to the issue of the consequences or effect of a *nolle prosequi*. The most immediate consequence, of course, is that the prosecution will not proceed on the charge or charges concerned. The courts have no power to compel the DPP to proceed with the prosecution of an offence in any case where he has seen fit to enter a *nolle prosequi*. The more difficult question is whether it is open to the DPP to institute fresh proceedings against the accused in respect of the same charges after having entered a *nolle prosequi*. In *State (Walsh) v. Lennon*[128] the Supreme Court accepted that the entry of a *nolle prosequi* did

---

[127]   [1982] I.L.R.M . 284.
[128]   [1942] I.R. 112. In this case four persons were charged with murder before a Special Criminal Court. While the separate trials of two of the accused were considerably advanced the Attorney General entered a *nolle prosecqui* in respect of all four accused. All four were subsequently tried together for murder in a military court established for that purpose by an executive order made under emergency legislation.

not in itself constitute a bar to further proceedings for the same offence.[129] It does not follow, however, that the DPP has an absolute right to institute fresh proceedings. This much is apparent from the decision of Finlay P. (as he then was) in *State (O'Callaghan) v. O hUadhaigh.*[130]

In *O'Callaghan* the applicant was arrested and charged with four offences arising out of an armed robbery of a post-office. One month later he was arrested and charged with four additional offences of larceny and receiving a motor bicycle and motor vehicle from different places in Dublin. He was returned for trial on each of these counts and the trial was adjourned from time to time on the application of the prosecution. An indictment containing a single charge of receiving in connection with the post office robbery was lodged. Before it came on for trial, however, a further indictment was lodged containing eight counts relating to the post-office robbery, the motor bicycle and motor vehicle, plus a further two counts against another accused. Later, a third indictment was lodged containing a total of 12 counts. When the case finally came on for trial the judge took the view that the only count he had jurisdiction to try was the single count in the first indictment. Counsel for the prosecution entered a *nolle prosequi* on all counts on the three indictments with a view to having the accused re-arrested and re-charged with all the counts on the original charge sheets. When the accused was brought before the District Court on foot of these charges, he commenced an application for an order of prohibition to prevent further proceedings in respect of them.

16–52

On the accused's application for the conditional order of prohibition to be made absolute Finlay P. considered whether it was open to the DPP to institute fresh proceedings for an offence after having entered a *nolle prosequi* in respect of that offence. In particular, he pointed out that if there were no limits on the DPP's power in the matter it would be open to the DPP to avoid the effects of an adverse ruling in the course of proceedings by entering a *nolle prosequi* and re-instituting fresh proceedings which were not affected by the adverse ruling. The oppressive consequences that this might have for the accused are starkly illustrated in the following words of Finlay P.:

> "If the contention of the [DPP] is correct the [applicant], having undergone that form of trial (and remand awaiting trial) and having succeeded in confining the issues to be tried, would be deprived of all that advantage by the simple operation of a statutory power on the part of the Director of Public Prosecutions. In this way the [applicant] would have the entire of his remand awaiting trial set at naught and he would have to start afresh to face a criminal prosecution in which the prosecution, by adopting different procedures, could avoid the consequences of the learned trial judge's view of the law. No such right exists in the accused: if the trial judge makes decisions adverse to the interests of the accused, the latter cannot obtain relief from them otherwise than by appeal from the Central Criminal Court, or by appeal or review in the case of an inferior court."[131]

---

[129] See also *Kelly v. DPP* [1997] 1 I.L.R.M. 69; *State (Coveney) v. The Special Criminal Court* [1982] I.L.R.M. 284.
[130] [1977] I.R. 42.
[131] [1977] I.R. 42

The learned judge went on to conclude that such a power in the hands of the DPP would create "an extraordinary imbalance between the rights and powers of the prosecution and those of the accused respectively". This, in turn, would infringe the basic principles of constitutional fairness which govern criminal procedure. Accordingly, it was not open to the DPP to institute fresh proceedings in respect of those matters which formed the basis of the charges in the three indictments in the case.

16–53 The decision in *O'Callaghan* is heavily predicated on its own special facts and does not provide authority for the proposition that fresh proceedings can never be instituted in respect of charges which have already been the subject of a *nolle prosequi*. Indeed, Finlay P. acknowledged that the entry of a *nolle prosequi* does not necessarily operate as an absolute bar to fresh proceedings, unlike the situation where the DPP indicates that he does not wish to tender any evidence:

> "The existence of this alternative method of procedure [not tendering any evidence], which is sometimes experienced in practice, does tend to suggest that the discharge created by the entry of a *nolle prosequi* under s.12 of the Criminal Justice (Administration) Act 1924 does not of necessity free the accused from anything other than the proceedings under the precise or identical indictment concerned and does not free him from the institution of entirely fresh proceedings arising out of the same alleged offence."[132]

It would operate as a bar only where the institution of fresh proceedings would deprive the accused of his basic right to justice in a criminal trial. In *O'Callaghan*, for example, the trial judge had adjudicated on a significant issue in a manner favourable to the accused and adverse to the contention of the DPP. According to the Supreme Court in *Kelly v. DPP*[133] it would amount to an injustice against the accused if he was deprived of the fruits of that victory by the simple expedient of the DPP starting the proceedings afresh.

16–54 In *Kelly*, in contrast with *O'Callaghan*, there had been no adjudication on any issue and no gain by the applicant which would be lost by the decision to institute fresh proceedings. In that case the applicant was charged with six road traffic offences, including dangerous driving (*simpliciter*), arising out of a fatal accident. Each charge was preferred by way of a District Court summons pursuant to an application made on behalf of the DPP. All six were issued outside the six months time limit applicable to such offences. When they came on for trial they were adjourned to a later date. In the meantime the applicant was arrested and charged with dangerous driving causing death. At the adjourned trial for the six original offences counsel for the defence submitted that they should be struck out as being time-barred. The DPP

---

[132] *ibid.* at 51, approved by the Supreme Court in *Kelly v. DPP* [1997] I.L.R.M. 69 at 78. In *State (Coveney) v. The Special Criminal Court* [1982] I.L.R.M. 284 Finlay P. referred to *State (O'Callaghan) v. O hUadhaigh* and accepted that the entry of a *nolle prosequi* was not a bar in an appropriate case to the institution of fresh proceedings.
[133] [1997] 1 I.L.R.M. 69.

requested that the charge of dangerous driving (*simpliciter*) be struck out and the remaining five charges be adjourned to a later date. Before they came on for trial on the second adjourned date, the DPP informed the applicant that they were being withdrawn. Subsequently, a book of evidence was served on the applicant and he was returned for trial on the charge of dangerous driving causing death. The applicant was given leave to seek an order of prohibition in respect of the trial on the ground, *inter alia*, that the entry of the *nolle prosequi* and institution of fresh proceedings was merely a device to circumvent the problem posed by the summary charges being time-barred. The Supreme Court, however, distinguished the facts of *O'Callaghan*, and concluded that there was nothing inappropriate about the institution of fresh proceedings in this case. There had been no adjudication and no gain by the applicant which was lost by the institution of fresh proceedings.

Another example arose in *State (Coveney) v. The Special Criminal Court*.[134] In that case the accused had pleaded guilty to assault with an offensive weapon with intent to rob and was sent forward for sentence to the Circuit Court. Before he was sentenced he changed his plea to not guilty at which point the DPP entered a *nolle prosequi*. The accused was re-arrested for the same offence and sent forward for trial on the DPP's certificate to the Special Criminal Court. Refusing to make absolute an order of prohibition preventing the trial, Finlay P. distinguished the case on its facts from *O'Callaghan*. In the latter the DPP's entry of a *nolle prosequi* was made in order to avoid a ruling made at the accused's trial. In *Coveney*, however, the DPP was quite properly re-acting to a change of plea by the accused.

J. Change of Plea

1. Change of Plea from Not Guilty to Guilty

It is always open to the accused to change his plea of not guilty to a plea of **16–55** guilty at any time during the trial. The usual practice is for the defence counsel to ask for the indictment to be put again to the accused. When this is done the accused, in person, will plead guilty. The jury must then return a formal verdict of guilty. In the unlikely event that they fail to do so the change of plea is ineffective and the trial is rendered a nullity. In *R. v. Heyes*,[135] for example, the accused changed his plea from not guilty to guilty in the course of the opening of the prosecution's case. Although this occurred in the jury's presence they were not formally asked to return a verdict of guilty. A conviction was recorded on the basis of the accused's change of plea and the trial judge proceeded to sentence. The conviction was quashed on appeal. Lord Goddard in the English Court of Appeal explained that the accused was in the charge of the jury when he changed his plea and as such he could only be convicted or discharged by the verdict of the jury. Since the jury had not been asked to return a verdict the trial was a nullity.

---

[134] [1982] I.L.R.M. 284.
[135] *R. v. Heyes* [1951] 1 K.B. 29.

2. Change of Plea from Guilty to Not Guilty

16–56 The trial judge has a discretion to permit the accused to change his plea from guilty to not guilty at any stage of the trial right up until sentence is passed.[136] So long as the discretion is exercised judicially it is unlikely that a refusal to permit a change of plea from guilty to not guilty could be upset on appeal. There is English authority to suggest that the discretion will be used very sparingly to permit a change of plea. If the accused has understood the nature of the charges against him and entered a clear and informed plea of guilty it is unlikely that the court would permit a change of plea in the course of the trial.[137]

In *R v. South Tameside Magistrates Court, ex p. Rowland*[138] the accused, who was unrepresented, unequivocally pleaded guilty to theft of a handbag and asked for a further similar offence to be taken into consideration. The magistrates indicated that they were considering a custodial sentence and offered her an adjournment to seek legal aid. Taking advantage of this offer she instructed her solicitor in terms which suggested that the bag was actually taken by her co-accused without the knowledge or assistance of the accused herself. Nevertheless the magistrates refused an application for a change of plea from guilty to not guilty. They weighed up the instructions given by the accused to her solicitor against the prospect that she had changed her story because of the risk of a custodial sentence and concluded that the latter was the real motivation for the change of plea. This decision was upheld on Appeal. The magistrates had exercised their discretion judicially. The English Court of Appeal also indicated that the discretion should be exercised to permit a change of plea very sparingly.

Given the constitutional protection afforded to the individual's right to a fair trial in Ireland, it is unlikely that the Irish courts would feel themselves similarly constrained. In *Byrne v. Judge McDonnell*[139] the High Court quashed the conviction and sentence of the accused in the District Court partly on the ground that the District Court judge should have permitted the accused to change his guilty plea to a plea of not guilty after conviction so that he could be legally represented from the beginning of his trial and not merely when it came to sentence. The accused had appeared unrepresented in the District Court and pleaded guilty to failing to pay the correct bus fare. After hearing an outline of the case for the purpose of sentence the judge granted the accused legal aid for a solicitor to make a plea in mitigation on his behalf. The High Court held that once it had become apparent to the District Court judge that a sentence of detention might be appropriate he should have permitted the accused to change his plea of guilty to not guilty so that he could have the benefit of legal aid and legal representation for the whole trial and not just for the purposes of sentencing.

---

[136] *R. v. Plummer* [1902] 2 K.B. 339; *R. v. Dodd* (1981) 74 Cr. App. Rep. 50; *S (an Infant) v. Recorder of Manchester* [1971] A.C. 481.
[137] *R. v. McNally* [1954] 1 W.L.R. 933.
[138] [1983] 3 All E.R. 689.
[139] [1997] 1 I.R. 392.

CHAPTER 17

THE JURY

A. Introduction

The jury is a long-standing and characteristic institution in the criminal   **17–01**
processes of both Ireland and Britain. It can trace its history back to the
thirteenth century in England. It also happens to be one of the most jealously
guarded elements of the criminal justice system. Since 1937 its central
importance in the Irish criminal process has been enshrined in the
Constitution which, subject to a few exceptions, guarantees the right to trial
by jury for non-minor offences. Unfortunately, neither the Constitution nor
statute offers a concise definition of the jury or of the purpose of trial by jury.
In practice the latter gives rise to little difficulty, and is summed up very
neatly in the following quotation from the judgment of the Supreme Court in
O'Callaghan v. Attorney General:

> "The purpose of trial by jury is to provide that a person shall get a fair trial, in
> due course of law, and be tried by a reasonable cross section of people acting
> under the guidance of the judge, bound by his directions on law, but free to
> make their findings as to the facts. The essential feature of a jury trial is to
> interpose between the accused and the prosecution people who will bring their
> experience and common sense to bear on resolving the issue of guilt or
> innocence of the accused."[1]

The jury itself might be described broadly as a body of persons drawn from
the community in a manner which engenders public confidence in their
capacity to hand down an objective verdict in a case after having heard all of
the evidence. In *de Búrca v. Attorney General* Henchy J. described it as:

---

[1] [1993] 2 I.R. 17 at 25.

". . . a group of laymen who, chosen at random from a reasonably diverse panel of jurors from the community, will produce a verdict of guilty or not guilty free from the risks inherent in a trial conducted by a judge or judges only, and which will therefore carry with it the assurance of both correctness and public acceptability that may be expected from the group verdict of such a representative cross-section of the community."[2]

The constitutional support for jury trial on criminal charges, seemingly, does not impose a fixed standard on the methods of selecting a jury or, indeed, on its composition. Even the hallmark of 12 members is not constitutionally ordained.[3] Matters such as minimum standards of competence for prospective jurors, the numerical composition of a jury and the system for the selection of juries are within the discretion of the legislature.[4] It would seem, however, that the system adopted for the selection of juries must be capable of producing juries broadly representative of the community, otherwise it will fall foul of Article 38.5.[5] In *de Búrca*, for example, the Supreme Court ruled unconstitutional certain key provisions of the Juries Act 1927 dealing with the composition of the jury panel. In that case both Henchy J. and Griffin J. considered that the property qualification on eligibility for jury service and the nature of the women's exemption from jury service provided for in the Juries Act 1927 were such as to produce unrepresentative juries. Griffin J. explained that:

> " . . . the jury should be a body which is truly representative, and a fair cross-section of the community. This is widely recognised and accepted in many jurisdictions and, in particular, in the United States, where, by reason of the diversity of the ethnic groups in the population, the question has been considered frequently by the Supreme Court in that country. I would adopt what was stated by the Supreme Court of the United States in *Thiel v. Southern Pacific Company*: –
>> 'Trial by jury presupposes a jury drawn from a pool broadly representative of the community as well as impartial in a specific case. . . . The broad representative character of the jury should be maintained, partly as assurance of a diffused impartiality and partly because sharing in the administration of justice is a phase of civic responsibility.'"[6]

17–02   The Supreme Court reiterated the importance of a jury being representative of the community in *MacCarthaigh v. Éire*.[7] The applicant in that case was charged under the provisions of the Larceny Act 1916. He had been reared through Irish and elected to have the trial conducted through Irish pursuant to his right under Article 8 of the Constitution. Article 8 stipulates that it is the right of every Irish citizen to have proceedings initiated against him or her by

---

[2] [1976] I.R. 38 at 74.

[3] *ibid.* See judgment of Walsh J. at 67.

[4] *ibid.* See judgment of Henchy J. and Walsh J. at 75 and 67 respectively.

[5] This cannot be interpreted as meaning that an accused person has a right to be tried by a jury from the locality in which he or she lives; *State (Hughes) v. Judge Neylon* [1982] I.L.R.M. 108.

[6] *De Búrca v. Attorney General* [1976] I.R. 38 at 82. See also, *State (Byrne) v. Frawley* [1978] I.R. 326.

the State conducted in Irish. The applicant argued that this entailed the right to the selection of a jury composed of individuals who have sufficient knowledge of Irish to understand the evidence and arguments without the aid of a translator. In rejecting this argument the court explained that the jury must represent a true cross-section of the community. It quoted with approval the following passage of the U.S. Supreme Court in *Taylor v. Louisiana*:

> "The purpose of a jury is to guard against the exercise of arbitrary power – to make available the commonsense judgment of the community as a hedge against the overzealous or mistaken prosecutor and in preference to the professional or perhaps over-conditioned or biased response of a judge. *Duncan v. Louisiana* at 155–156. This prophylactic vehicle is not provided if the jury pool is made up of only special segments of the populace or if large, distinctive groups are excluded from the pool. Community participation in the administration of the criminal law, moreover, is not only consistent with our democratic heritage but is also critical to public confidence in the fairness of the criminal justice system. Restricting jury service to only special groups or excluding identifiable segments playing major roles in the community cannot be squared with the constitutional concept of jury trial."[8]

In *MacCarthaigh* the Supreme Court had little difficulty in finding that the exclusion of non-Irish speakers in the selection of a jury would render the jury unrepresentative of the community and, therefore, lacking in one of its most essential characteristics. In Dublin, for example, 75–90 per cent of the community would be excluded from consideration for jury service if non-Irish speakers were excluded. It followed that the applicant's constitutional right to have his criminal trial conducted through Irish could not encompass a right to a jury which excluded non-Irish speakers. While the court acknowledged that the testimony and legal arguments of the accused would lose some of their force and precision when delivered through an interpreter, it nevertheless held that it was more important to the right to a fair trial under Article 38.5 that the jury should represent a true cross section of the community.

Legislation governing the composition and selection of juries must also avoid encroaching on other provisions of the Constitution. In the *de Búrca* case, for example, both O'Higgins C.J. and Walsh J. struck down the property qualification in the 1927 Act on the ground that it infringed the right to equality enshrined in Article 40.1 of the Constitution.[9]

Currently the rules governing eligibility for jury service and the process of selecting a jury are to be found in the Juries Act 1976. It was enacted in response to the Supreme Court's decision in *de Búrca v. Attorney General*[10] declaring certain provisions of the Juries Act 1927 to be unconstitutional. Instead of simply excising the offending parts from the Act, the legislature took the opportunity to replace it in its entirety. The new Act defines those

---

[7] unreported, Supreme Court, July 15, 1998.

[8] 419 U.S. 522 at 530 (1975).

[9] Walsh J. also found the exemption for women unconstitutional on the same basis, while O'Higgins C.J. felt that it was justified in the light of the special place afforded to the role of a woman in the home by Art. 41.2.

821

who qualify for jury service and the procedure which ultimately results in the selection of a jury. Indeed, it would appear that it should be interpreted as "a self contained and all embracing code in relation to juries".[11]

B. Jury Districts

17–03   Association with the local community is a necessary feature of juries. The underlying reason for this was explained by Henchy J. in *State (Byrne) v. Frawley*, as follows:

> "For the formation of a constitutional jury, there must be a valid nexus between juror and jury district. This is needed to ensure that the jury's verdict will have the quality of a community decision; for a jury so constituted will reach its verdict in the knowledge that, in a real and special sense, its members will have to live with that verdict."[12]

Accordingly, where the trial of any issue is to be conducted before a jury, the 1976 Act stipulates that the jury must be called from a panel of jurors drawn from the jury district in which the court is sitting.[13] For this purpose each county constitutes a jury district, and the county boroughs of Dublin, Cork, Limerick and Waterford are treated as part of their respective counties.[14] However, the Minister may, by order, divide a county into two or more jury districts or limit a jury district to a part or parts of a county.[15]

C. Eligibility

17–04   The Juries Act 1976 lays down a very expansive definition of those eligible for jury service. Generally, every citizen is eligible for jury service if he or she is at least 18 years of age and less than 70 years of age, is entered in a register of Dáil electors in a jury district and is not for the time being ineligible or disqualified.[16] The basic preconditions for eligibility therefore are age and registration on the Dáil register of electors for the jury district in question. Unlike the position in Britain,[17] there is no specific residence requirement other than that which follows indirectly from the electoral registration requirement. In order to have one's name qualify for the register of Dáil electors an individual must be "ordinarily resident" in the

---

[10]   [1976] I.R. 38.
[11]   *DPP v. Judge Kevin Haugh* [2000] I.R. 184 *per* Carney J. at 191.
[12]   [1978] I.R. 326 at 347.
[13]   Juries Act 1976, s.5(4).
[14]   *ibid.* s.5(1).
[15]   *ibid.* s.5(2). The Minister may, by order, revoke or vary any such order.
[16]   Juries Act 1976, s.6. The qualification or liability of a person to serve as a juror shall not be affected by the fact that an appeal is pending under s.8 of the Electoral Act 1963 (appeals regarding the register of electors); s.26.
[17]   The Juries Act 1974 (U.K.) imposes a requirement of ordinary residence in the U.K. for any

constituency in question.[18] It does not follow, however, that one must be ordinarily resident in the jury district when called up for jury service. It is quite sufficient that one's name is entered in the register of electors for the jury district in question. The corollary, of course is, that if an individual's name is not entered on the electoral register, even though he satisfied the requirements for registration, he cannot qualify for jury service.

The definition of eligibility for jury service depends heavily on the definitions of those who are ineligible and those who are disqualified. Ineligibility is not defined as such. Instead a list of persons who are ineligible to serve is provided in Part One of the First Schedule to the Act. This list reads:

17–05

"Uachtarán na hÉireann [the President].

Persons concerned with administration of justice
Persons holding or who have at any time held any judicial office within the meaning of the Courts (Establishment and Constitution) Act 1961 (No.38).
Coroners, deputy coroners and persons appointed under section 5(2) of the Local Authorities (Officers and Employees) Act 1926 (No.39) to fill the office of coroner temporarily.
The Attorney General and members of his staff.
The Director of Public Prosecutions and members of his staff.
Barristers and solicitors actually practising as such.
Solicitors' apprentices, solicitors' clerks and other persons employed on work of a legal character in solicitors' offices.
Officers attached to a court or to the President of the High Court and officers and other persons employed in any office attached to a court or attached to the President of the High Court.
Persons employed from time to time in any court for the purpose of taking a record of the proceedings of the court.
Members of the Garda Síochána.
Prison officers and any other persons employed in any prison, Saint Patrick's Institution or any place provided under section 2 of the Prisons Act 1970 (No.11) or in any place in which persons are kept in military custody pursuant to section 2 of the Prisons Act 1972 (No.7) or in any place specified to be used as a prison under section 3 of the latter Act; chaplains and medical officers of, and members of visiting committees for, any such establishment or place.
Persons employed in the welfare service of the Department of Justice, Equality and Law Reform.
A person in charge of, or employed in, a forensic science laboratory.

Members of the Defence Forces
Every member of the Permanent Defence Force, including the Army Nursing Service.
Every member of the Reserve Defence Force during any period during which he is in receipt of pay for any service or duty as a member of the Reserve Defence Force.

---

period of at least five years since attaining the age of 13.

Incapable Persons

A person who because of insufficient capacity to read, deafness[19] or other permanent infirmity is unfit to serve on a jury.

A person who suffers or has suffered from mental illness or mental disability and on account of that condition either (a) is resident in a hospital or other similar institution, or (b) regularly attends for treatment by a medical practitioner."

17–06   The first thing to note about this list is that it drops the property qualification which was found to be unconstitutional in *de Búrca v. Attorney General.*[20] More significant, perhaps, is the fact that it does not attempt to exclude persons who do not possess certain minimum educational qualifications. The potential significance of this omission is increasing as the issues at stake in certain criminal trials become ever more complex. Interestingly, it was intimated in *de Búrca* that it would not necessarily be unconstitutional for the Oireachtas to impose certain minimum standards of ability or competence on qualification for jury service. The Oireachtas, however, has opted for a minimalist approach of excluding persons who are unable to discharge the duties of jury service due to certain physical or mental disabilities or because they cannot read. The legislation does not specifically exclude jurors who do not understand the language in which the proceedings are held. In *Ras Behari Lal v. King-Emperor* the Judicial Committee of the Privy Council set aside convictions for murder after it transpired that one of the jurors did not understand English, the language in which some of the evidence, counsel's address and the judge's charge were given. The Judicial Committee explained that the incompetence of the juror was such as to deny the accused persons an essential part of the protection afforded to them by law.[21]

The other distinctive feature to note about the list of persons ineligible for jury service is the exclusion of a very wide range of persons associated with the administration of justice in either a public or private capacity. This is a well-established feature of jury composition in the common law world. It is, of course, a vital element in protecting the jury's essential image as a representative body of laypersons who provide a critical balance to the legal professionals in the administration of justice. Closely associated with this is the need to avoid the appearance of bias which may result if such personnel were to sit in their capacity as ordinary citizens determining whether their colleagues had proved a case beyond a reasonable doubt. Indeed, it is generally mooted, although the empirical evidence is necessarily lacking, that ordinary laypersons on the jury would be unduly influenced by the views of fellow members who were trained in the law or the administration of justice. At any rate there is no pressure to admit persons concerned in the administration of justice to jury service.

---

[18]   Electoral Act 1963, s.5(1)(b).

[19]   In *Re Osman* (1996) 1 Cr. App. R. 126 a person was discharged from jury service because he could not follow the proceedings in court or the deliberations in the jury room without the assistance of an interpreter in sign language. The court was of the view that it would be an incurable irregularity in the proceedings for the interpreter to retire with the jury when they considered their verdict.

[20]   [1976] I.R. 38.

D. Disqualification

Persons who are otherwise eligible to serve on a jury can be disqualified on   **17–07**
the basis of a criminal record. A person is disqualified if he has, on conviction
for a criminal offence in any part of Ireland, been sentenced to imprisonment
for life or for a term of at least five years, or to detention under section 103 of
the Children Act 1908[22] or its corresponding provisions in Northern Ireland.[23]
It would appear that this disqualification applies for life, irrespective of
whether the full sentence, or any part of it, has been served. Presumably, if
the sentence is suspended the disqualification does not apply. The position
with respect to community service orders is less clear. In Ireland they can be
imposed only as a substitute for a prison sentence with the consent of the
offender. Typically, where the trial judge holds out the possibility of community
service he or she will specify the sentence of imprisonment which will
otherwise apply. While community service is rarely offered as an alternative
to prison terms of five years or more, there is nothing to prevent it.[24]

A person is also disqualified if he has, at any time in the last 10 years,
served any part of a sentence of imprisonment of at least three months in any
part of Ireland, or any part of a sentence of detention of at least three months
in St Patrick's Institution or its equivalent in Northern Ireland.[25] Unlike the
first disqualification, this one has a provisional character in that it expires
after a period of 10 years from the person's release from prison or detention.
Presumably, the disqualification will not apply where the sentence is quashed
on appeal after the individual has served more than three months.

An interesting feature is the extension of the disqualification under these   **17–08**
provisions to cover sentences imposed by a court in Northern Ireland and
sentences served in Northern Ireland. It follows that a person who is sentenced by a court in Northern Ireland and either serves his or her sentence
elsewhere or does not serve it at all may be disqualified under these provisions, depending on the nature and length of the sentence. The same applies
to a person who served a sentence of imprisonment in Northern Ireland.
Arguably this covers persons in respect of time served in Northern Ireland on
foot of a sentence of imprisonment imposed by a court in Great Britain.

Serving a sentence of imprisonment, or being sentenced to a term of
imprisonment, in Great Britain will not normally have any implications for
eligibility for jury service in Ireland. This is despite the fact that it is possible
for a person to be tried, convicted, sentenced and imprisoned in Britain for a
range of offences committed in Ireland.[26] It would appear, however, that there
is no reason why the disqualifications and restrictions on jury service imposed

---

[21] (1933) 50 T.L.R. 1.
[22] The detention of children and young persons convicted of a capital offence.
[23] Juries Act 1976, s.8(a).
[24] See Walsh and Sexton, *A Empirical Study of Community Service Orders in Ireland* (Government
      Stationery Office, Dublin, 1999).
[25] Juries Act 1976, s.8(b).

by the Juries Act 1976 should not apply to a person who has served a portion of his sentence in Ireland or Northern Ireland under the terms of the Transfer of Sentenced Persons Act 1995 or the Crime (Sentences) Act 1997 (UK) as the case may be. Presumably, it is the term of imprisonment to be served in Ireland (or Northern Ireland) which will count towards jury disqualification as distinct from the sentence actually imposed by the court abroad.

E. Excusal

17–09   A person who satisfies the eligibility criteria is qualified and liable to serve as a juror for the trial of all or any issues which are for the time being triable with a jury drawn from that jury district in which he or she is entered in the register of Dáil electors. It does not follow, however, that all such persons must submit to jury service once summoned. There is provision for being excused from jury service. Some persons can be excused as of right while others are excusable at the discretion of the appropriate county registrar.

A person summoned for jury service is entitled to be excused if: (i) he or she is one of the persons specified in Part II of the First Schedule to the 1976 Act and informs the county registrar of his or her wish to be excused; (ii) he or she shows to the satisfaction of the county registrar that he or she has served on a jury, or attended for jury service, in the three years ending with the service of the current summons on him or her; or (iii) he or she shows to the satisfaction of the county registrar that, at the conclusion of a trial, a judge of any court has excused him or her from jury service for a period that has not terminated.[27] If the person concerned satisfies any one of these three criteria the county registrar must excuse him or her from the jury service to which he or she has been summoned. This, of course, does not amount to a disqualification or permanent excusal from jury service. There is nothing to stop a person in any of these three categories from submitting to the summons. Similarly, an excusal from service in response to one summons does not mean that the person will never be summoned again.

17–10   The persons specified in Part II of the First Schedule to the 1976 Act who are entitled to be excused on request include: members of either House of the Oireachtas, members of the Council of State, the Comptroller and Auditor General, the Clerk of either House of the Oireachtas, a person in Holy Orders, a minister of religion, vowed members of certain religious orders, practising medical practitioners (including dentists, nurses and chemists), heads of government departments and offices, chief officers of local authorities, chief officers of health boards, chief officers of harbour authorities, the head of an educational institution, full-time students at an educational institution, the secretary to the Commissioners of Irish Lights, masters of vessels, licensed pilots and persons who are at least 65 years of age and less than 70 years. In addition a range of officers and employees in the Houses of the Oireachtas,

---

[26]   See Criminal Jurisdiction Act 1975 (U.K.).

government departments and offices, the Ministry of Defence, local authorities, health boards, harbour authorities, educational institutions and the Commissioners of Irish Lights are included to the extent that a designated officer in the appropriate institution or body certifies that it would be contrary to the public interest for the individual in question to serve as a juror because he or she performs essential and urgent services of public importance that cannot reasonably be performed by another or postponed.[28]

Clearly this list has been composed with a view to minimising the disruption that would otherwise be caused to the functioning of important public services and institutions if key personnel were absent for a prolonged and indefinite period on jury service. However, if that was the only consideration that had to be taken into account it is likely that the list would be much longer. An excessively long list could create a risk of juries being inherently unrepresentative given a natural tendency for those concerned to exercise their right to be excused. It is significant in this context that the decision of the Supreme Court in the *de Búrca* case was heavily influenced by the fact that women almost invariably failed to exercise their right to opt in to jury service (under the 1927 Act), thereby producing a jury system which was inherently unrepresentative. The Oireachtas would have to be careful, therefore, in any move to extend the list of those who can claim to be excused as of right. The availability of the county registrar's discretion to excuse can ensure that the obligation of jury service does not impact unreasonably either on the interests of the individual or on the interests of the community.

The county registrar may excuse any person whom he has summoned as a juror if the person in question satisfies the registrar that there is good reason why he or she should be excused.[29] The scope of the registrar's discretion in this matter is evident from the fact that the legislation offers no indication of what might qualify as a "good reason" in this context. In practice it seems that parents or guardians caring for a child or children during the hours that the court would be sitting are excused as a general rule. The same applies to individuals who can establish that their businesses or employers would suffer heavily due to their absence on jury business. Illness or some other mental or physical disability which would make it impracticable or unduly discomfiting for the individual to do jury service are also likely to result in a discretionary excusal. Pregnancy may also provide a valid excuse.[30] The registrar's discretion in the matter may be limited by guidance issued by the Minister. The 1976 Act empowers the Minister to issue instructions to county registrars with regard to the practice and procedure to be adopted by them in the discharge of their duties under the Act.[31] The purpose of such instruction is to secure consistency in the administration of the Act. The power cannot be used to

17–11

---

[27] Juries Act 1976, s.9(1).
[28] In the case of officers or employees in educational institutions and the Commissioners of Irish Lights it is sufficient if the certificate states that the person concerned performs services that cannot reasonably be performed by another or postponed.
[29] Juries Act 1976, s.9(2).
[30] *DPP v. Judge Kevin Haugh,* [2000] I.R. 184, *per* Laffoy J. at 201.

issue any instruction concerning whether a particular person or persons should or should not be summoned for, or excused from, jury service. Unfortunately, there is no provision for such instructions to be published.[32]

Judicial guidance on how the power of excusal should be exercised suggests that the key issue is the individual's capacity to discharge his or her duty as an honest and responsible juror. If the individual is affected by factors which call into question his or her capacity to give full attention to the case and to participate in the collective assessment of the evidence the registrar should accede to his or her request to be excused. In *R. v. Guildford Crown Court, ex p. Siderfin*,[33] for example, the applicant was a member of the Plymouth Brethren. In common with other members of the Brethren she took the view that serving on a jury would be contrary to her religious beliefs. Her application to be excused from jury service on the ground of a conscientious objection was refused and her appeal was rejected. On her application for a judicial review of the refusal, Watkins L.J. considered that a conscientious objection on religious grounds was unlikely on its own to amount to a good reason since it would not outweigh the necessity to insist on the observance of the public duty or obligation to perform jury service. However, if her belief would stand in the way of her fulfilling her duty as a juror properly, responsibly and honestly then she should be excused. The applicant had indicated that if forced to serve she would have reached a verdict without reference to the other members of the jury and would have insisted on announcing her verdict separately. The court considered that this attitude would be incompatible with the notion of jurors pooling their ideas and experience in order to reach agreement. Further, since the court below did not seem to have taken on board the applicant's difficulty in co-operating with other jury members, the refusal to excuse her was quashed and the matter remitted to the Crown Court for reconsideration by a different judge.[34]

17–12   In order to benefit from either a compulsory or discretionary excusal the individual concerned must apply to the registrar after having been summoned. This can be done when the individual attends at court in response to the jury summons. Equally, however, there is nothing to prevent an individual submitting a written request to be excused after he or she has received the summons to attend. If an individual who wishes to be excused is not in a position to make an application owing to illness or any other reason, another person may make the appropriate representation on his or her behalf.[35] Where the individual benefits from a compulsory excusal he or she will be excused from the obligation of attendance in response to that particular summons. It offers him or her no protection against any future jury summons.[36] The

---

[31]   Juries Act 1976, s.27.

[32]   In the U.K. guidance is published in the Practice Direction (Jury Service: Excusal) [1988] 1 W.L.R. 1162.

[33]   [1990] 2 Q.B. 683.

[34]   The Crown Court had also erred in refusing to exercise its discretion to adjourn the proceedings to enable the applicant to be legally represented for the hearing of her appeal against the refusal of her application for excusal.

[35]   Juries Act 1976, s.9(3).

[36]   Note, however, that when the registrar is empanelling jurors he can omit persons whom he knows

individual will have to seek an excusal on each occasion that he or she is summoned to attend. The same applies to a discretionary excusal. Indeed, under the discretionary excusal the individual might be excused from attendance at either the whole or a part of the sittings to which he or she has been summoned. Apart from that qualification, it would appear that the excusal provision cannot be used simply to defer the obligation to attend for jury service.[37]

The onus throughout would appear to be on the applicant to satisfy the registrar that he or she either qualifies for excusal automatically or ought to be excused in the exercise of the registrar's discretion. There is no provision for the registrar to question prospective jurors in order to probe their eligibility for jury service or their qualification for excusal. If, however, a person who has been summoned makes representations to the county registrar with a view to having his or her name deleted from the pool, it is implicit that the registrar or his officials may question the person as to his or her qualifications for jury service or his wish or entitlement to be excused.[38] Where the registrar refuses an application for excusal the person concerned may appeal against the refusal to the court at which he or she has been summoned to attend.[39] The decision of the court is final.

The power to excuse at first instance does not reside exclusively in the county registrar. The judge can also excuse a person who is required to be in attendance as a juror during a sitting of the court.[40] Just like the registrar, he must excuse where the person concerned comes with the compulsory excusal category and he or she has a discretion to excuse in all other cases. The judge may also, during the course of a trial and for good reason, excuse a juror from further service as a juror in the trial. Furthermore, at the conclusion of a trial of an exceptionally exacting nature, the judge may excuse members of the jury from jury service for such period as the judge may think fit.[41]

F. Empanelling Jurors

17–13 The task of empanelling a jury falls on the shoulders of county registrars. In each county the process begins with the electoral registration authority[42] delivering copies of the current register of Dáil electors for the county or county borough to the county registrar.[43] The latter must use the current register (or registers) to draw up a panel of jurors for each court.[44] The legislation

---

or believes are not qualified to serve as jurors; Juries Act 1976, s.11.

[37] See *St Albans Crown Court, ex p. Perkins* cited in *Blackstone's Criminal Practice* (Blackstone Press, 1997), D11.4.

[38] *DPP v. Judge Kevin Haugh* [2000] I.R. 184, *per* Laffoy J. at 203.

[39] Juries Act 1976, s.9(4). The procedure for the appeal, including the designation of the judge to hear the appeal, and the time within which and the manner in which it should be brought, shall be as provided by directions of the President of the High Court and the President of the Circuit Court respectively; s.9(5).

[40] Juries Act 1976, s.9(7).

[41] *ibid.* s.9(8).

[42] This will be the county council or, in the case of a county borough, the corporation; see Electoral Act 1963, s.7(1).

[43] Juries Act, 1976, s.10.

does not prescribe any particular method of selection other than that he must use a procedure of random or non-discriminatory selection. The Registrar must also omit persons whom he or she knows or believes are not qualified to serve as jurors. A written summons is then served on each person selected as a juror.[45] Service will be effected either by hand or by post to the juror's address as shown in the current register of Dáil electors.[46] The summons requires the individual concerned to attend as a juror at the named court on the day and time specified and thereafter at the times directed by the court.[47] It will also be accompanied by a notice informing the individual of the effect of the provisions in the 1976 Act concerning qualification, ineligibility, disqualification, excusal and liability for jury service, as well as the consequences of making false statements with respect to the obligation of jury service or serving while ineligible or disqualified.[48] This notice must also inform the individual of his or her right to make representations to the county registrar with a view to obtaining a withdrawal of the summons either on the ground that he or she is not qualified for jury service or that he or she wishes to benefit from a compulsory or discretionary excusal.

The objective in drawing up a panel of jurors is to ensure that there are sufficient jurors to provide juries for the cases to be tried in the jury district over the period in question. There is no fixed quorum applicable to a jury panel. The county registrar will simply exercise his or her own judgement based on experience as to the size of the panel required and the number of jurors that will need to be summoned in order to produce a panel of that size. The Registrar must bear in mind, of course, that not everyone summoned will turn up for service, some of those who do turn up will have to be excused and some will be challenged (see below) in any particular case. The net effect is that both those summoned and those making up the jury panel itself will normally exceed in numbers those actually called to serve in individual cases. It may happen from time to time, however, that there are insufficient numbers to provide a jury for any individual case. In this event, the judge of the court in question may require any persons to be summoned by the county registrar to make up the deficiency.[49] The person or persons in question must be qualified and liable to serve and the judge must specify both the area from which they may be summoned and the method of summons.[50] The names of persons summoned under this provision are added to the panel of jurors summoned through the standard procedure.[51] The persons concerned can apply to the county registrar to be excused in the normal way.[52] However, if the registrar refuses such application, there is no right of appeal to the court against his or her decision. This does not preclude the possibility of being excused by the judge when the court is sitting.[53]

---

44 *ibid.* s.11.
45 *ibid.* s.12(1). See Jury Summons Regulations 1976 for the form of the summons.
46 Juries Act 1976, s.13.
47 *ibid.* ss.12(1) and 34(1).
48 *ibid.* s.12(2).
49 *ibid.* s.14(1).
50 *ibid.* s.14(2).
51 *ibid.* s.14(4).
52 *ibid.* s.14(3).

Compliance with a jury summons can have adverse economic implications for **17–14** the individual concerned. A self employed person can use this as an argument for being excused from service. Employees and apprentices, however, are given more direct protection by the Act. It is provided that a person subject to a contract of employment or apprenticeship (or any agreement collateral to such a contract) shall be treated as employed or apprenticed during any period of absence from his employment or apprenticeship in order to comply with a jury summons.[54] This should ensure that his or her wages, salary and related rights are protected. Any attempt by an employer to include a clause in the contract or agreement excluding or limiting his or her liability to pay wages or salary in such circumstances is countered by rendering the clause void.[55] This, of course, does not offer any protection against loss of over-time or other incidental benefits of employment or apprenticeship.

If a jury panel has been drawn up in a manner which offends against the Constitution then it can be challenged on that ground. A jury drawn from such a panel will be constitutionally infirm even if each member on that jury is lawfully competent to serve on it. If an accused objects to a jury being selected from a panel which has been drawn up in an unconstitutional manner and his objection is denied he will have grounds to appeal against his conviction. Similarly, if he discovers subsequent to his conviction that the jury was drawn from a panel which suffered from a constitutional infirmity it would appear that he also has grounds for appeal so long as he does not delay unduly. In *State (Byrne) v. Frawley*[56] the accused was in the course of being tried for larceny and receiving when the Supreme Court decision in *de Búrca v. Attorney General*[57] was handed down. The jury panel from which the accused's jury had been drawn suffered from exactly the same constitutional infirmity as that at issue in *de Búrca*. The Supreme Court accepted that this gave grounds for appeal against his conviction. On the facts of the case, however, it transpired that the accused was fully aware of the import of the *de Búrca* decision at the time of his trial. Nevertheless, he had opted not to object to the jury at his trial nor in the subsequent appeal against conviction. Accordingly, the Court ruled that he was subsequently debarred from asserting that the jury lacked constitutionality.

G. Jury Selection

The selection process begins with the jury panel present in open court. The **17–15** judge must warn them that they cannot serve if they are ineligible or disqualified and he or she must inform them of the penalty for serving while ineligible or disqualified.[58] The judge must also invite any person who knows

---

[53] *ibid.* s.9(7).
[54] *ibid.* s.29(1).
[55] *ibid.* s.29(2).
[56] [1978] I.R. 326.
[57] [1976] I.R. 38.
[58] Juries Act 1976, s.15(3).

that he or she is not qualified to serve or who has doubts about his or her qualification to communicate this fact to the judge if selected on the jury ballot. The judge must extend a similar invitation to any person who may have an interest in or connection with the case or the parties. The purpose of this invitation is partly to weed out any person from the jury panel who is disqualified or ineligible to serve, and partly to ensure that the jurors empannelled will be disinterested or unbiased. To achieve this latter objective it will normally be necessary for the trial judge to make a brief statement of the nature of the case, including who and what is involved.[59] If any juror discovers that he knows any of the parties involved or that the nature of the case is such that he personally would not be able to bring an open mind to it, he should convey his circumstances to the judge at this point.

Having an interest in the case or with the parties to the case does not automatically disqualify a juror. Indeed, an indirect interest will not of itself render a trial unsatisfactory.[60] Nevertheless, it is a factor which could result in a challenge to the juror or the judge exercising his discretion to exclude a juror.[61] Equally, it can result in the quashing of a conviction where it transpires afterwards that one of the jury members was a victim of the crime charged. In *People (Attorney General) v. Singer*,[62] for example, the accused was charged with a number of offences of fraudulent conversion arising out of a failed investment scheme. The circumstances were such that there was likely to be a large number of victims among members of the public. It transpired that the foreman of the jury was one such victim. In quashing the convictions on appeal the Court of Criminal Appeal said:

> "The possibility of the victim of the accused being impannelled as a juror to try the accused is something which may well be regarded as having lain outside the contemplation alike of legislature and of common law as it developed. Ordinarily, as has been said, the victim's name will be found in the particulars of the offence and he will be a witness at the trial, having made a deposition in the District Court. The victim generally will be known to all, and to none will it occur to think of him as other than standing in a category quite apart from those from among whom the judges of the accused are to be selected. The victim is not to be thought of as indifferent, and his presence on the jury manifestly offends against the concept of fair trial, the essence of which is third-party judgment, however honestly he should strive to discharge his duty as juror. A victim of a crime is by the crime itself set apart from those who may be called upon to try the accused. The crime must be looked upon as disabling the victim from acting as a juror on the trial of the offence. In the opinion of the Court it effects disqualification."[63]

The court specifically declined to state an opinion on what the position would be if the accused knowingly remains silent when one of his victims is empannelled as a juror.

---

[59] *DPP v. Judge Kevin Haugh* [2000] 1 I.R. 184, *per* Carney J. at 192.
[60] *People v. Singer* [1975] I.R. 408.
[61] The judge has a power to excuse or discharge a juror and a power to direct that a juror shall not serve; see Juries Act 1976, ss.9(7), 23 and 24.
[62] 1961 1 Frewen 214.
[63] *ibid.* at 223.

The mere fact that a juror has been a victim of a similar crime in the past will not in itself be sufficient to disqualify a juror. If, however, the experience has been such that the juror could not bring an impartial mind to bear on the determination of the accused's guilt then he or she should bring this matter to the attention of the judge at the outset and he or she will be excluded. A failure to disclose such experience and/or to exclude the juror may result in a conviction being quashed. Past experience as a victim of sexual abuse can cause particular difficulty in this context. In *People (DPP) v. Tobin*[63a] a member of the jury disclosed past experience of sexual abuse during the course of the jury's deliberations on a trial for several rapes and indecent assaults perpetrated on a child over a period of years. The jury foreman brought the matter to the attention of the judge and assured the judge that it would not affect the impartiality of the juror in question. The accused was convicted by a majority verdict. On appeal to the Court of Criminal Appeal the conviction was quashed and a re-trial ordered. The court distinguished the *Singer* case on its facts but went on to hold that where the facts create a risk of even objective bias the conviction cannot stand. In this case, given the particular nature of sexual abuse, a reasonable and fair minded observer would consider that there was a danger that the juror might have been unconsciously influenced by his or her personal experience. That in itself would be sufficient to deny the accused a fair trial. (See further, para. 17–36).

17–16

The actual selection of persons to serve on a jury is normally made by balloting from the jury panel in open court.[64] Balloting is not mandatory in the case of those additional jurors, if any, who were summoned after balloting had begun in order to make up a deficiency in the panel.[65] The term "balloting" is not actually defined in the legislation. In practice, the name of each juror on the panel is put into a box and the registrar of the court pulls names blindly from the box in open court. The names are called out and the persons concerned are asked to step forward to the jury box. It is common practice to call forward more than 12 persons (usually 20) in order to make allowances for challenges and excusals. These are then sworn individually in the order in which they were called until there are twelve sworn jurors. If the full complement is reached without exhausting the total of those called forward, the remainder are sent back to the panel. Conversely, if the total of those called forward is exhausted without producing 12 sworn jurors, the registrar will continue to pull names from the box in open court until the full complement of sworn jurors has been reached.

Each juror is sworn separately,[66] usually by the registrar of the court.[67] The normal practice whenever the issue to be tried is whether the accused is or is not guilty of an offence, is for the registrar to call out the juror's name and

---

[63a] [2001] 3 I.R. 469.
[64] Juries Act 1976, s.15(1).
[65] *ibid.* s.15(2).
[66] *ibid.* s.17(2).
[67] *ibid.* s.17(1).

then to direct him or her to take the Testament[68] in his uplifted hand and say the following words:[69]

> "I swear by Almighty God that I will well and truly try the issue whether the accused is (*or* are) guilty or not guilty of the offence (*or* the several offences) charged in the indictment preferred against him (*or* her *or* them) and a true verdict give according to the evidence."[70]

Where the issue to be tried is whether an accused person is or is not competent to plead, the form of the oath is:

> "I swear by Almighty God that I will well and diligently inquire whether (*stating the name of the accused person*), the prisoner at the bar, be insane or not and a true verdict give according to the evidence."[71]

In any other case the form of the oath is:

> "I swear by Almighty God that I will well and truly try all such issues as shall be given to me to try and true verdicts give according to the evidence."[72]

Generally, the oath must be administered to every juror in this manner unless the juror appears to be physically incapable of doing so, or objects to doing so and satisfies the judge that he or she is entitled to take it in some other manner.[73] The legislation makes only limited provision for alternatives. A juror who states that he or she has a religious belief and is not of the Christian or Jewish faith may be sworn in any manner that he or she states to be binding on him or her if the judge so permits.[74] In the case of a juror who professes to have no religious faith[75] the making of an affirmation will be acceptable in place of the oath.[76] Where a juror objects to taking the oath in the ordinary manner he must make his or her objection known immediately after his or her name is called out and before the administration of the oath actually begins.[77] If he or she refuses to be sworn, or insists on being sworn in a manner not authorised by the 1976 Act, he or she shall not be included in the jury being sworn at that time.[78] He or she will also be committing a criminal offence.[79]

---

[68] For this purpose "Testament" means the New Testament in the case of a person of the Christian faith and the Old Testament in the case of a person of the Jewish faith; Juries Act 1976, s.17(7).

[69] Juries Act 1976, s.18(1).

[70] *ibid.* s.19(1).

[71] *ibid.* s.19(2).

[72] *ibid.* s.19(3).

[73] *ibid.* s.18(4).

[74] *ibid.* s.18(3).

[75] It seems that the ordinary oath will not be invalidated on the ground that the person taking it has no religious belief; see Oaths Act 1888, s.3.

[76] Juries Act 1976, s.18(2). The form of affirmation is: "I, (AB), do solemnly, sincerely, and truly declare and affirm" followed by the words of the appropriate oath; see Oaths Act 1882, s.2.

[77] Juries Act 1976, s.17(3). For this purpose, the administration of the oath is deemed to have begun when the registrar (or other officer) begins to say the words of the oath to the juror being sworn; s.17(6).

[78] *ibid.* s.17(5).

[79] *ibid.* s.37.

H. Challenging Jurors

1. Introduction

The composition of a jury is not entirely a random exercise based on the vagaries of the ballot. In the interval of time between a juror's name being called out and before the administration of the oath to him has commenced, he or she may be challenged by either the prosecution or the defence.[80] Equally, it would appear that the trial judge retains a discretion to exclude a juror. In practice challenges are made by the solicitor for the defence or prosecution as the case may be.

17–17

2. Peremptory Challenge

The prosecution and each accused person can challenge up to a maximum of seven jurors without having to show cause.[81] This is known as the right of peremptory challenge. Any juror challenged pursuant to this right is excluded from serving on the jury.[82] The challenge is usually made as the juror in question is about to take the oath. No reasons are given for such challenges, nor do they involve any question or argument. The challenge normally reflects a subjective assessment of the likely attitude of the juror to the challenger's case, based on matters such as: age, sex, appearance, address or employment. Interestingly, if there is more than one accused in the trial, each enjoys a right of peremptory challenge over seven jurors. The prosecution, however, is always limited to a maximum of seven.

17–18

3. Challenge for Cause

In addition to this right of peremptory challenge, both the prosecution and defence enjoy the right to challenge any number of jurors "for cause shown".[83] If the challenge is successful the juror in question must be excluded from the jury.[84] The legislation does not specify what qualifies as "cause" in this context. It does stipulate, however, that the cause must be shown immediately and the judge will then allow or disallow the challenge "as he shall think proper."[85] Clearly, this will be satisfied by any of the factors which render the juror ineligible to serve. Beyond that there is less certainty. Presumably a juror will be excluded if the party making the challenge is able to put forward cogent reasons why the juror might not discharge the obligations of jury service fairly and impartially. This presupposes something more than a subjective assessment of the juror's likely attitude to the challenger's case based on criteria such as age, sex, social status etc. In order to succeed, it is likely that the challenger will have

17–19

---

[80] *ibid.* s.17(4). In practice the challenges are made by the solicitor for the prosecution or defence, as the case may be.
[81] *ibid.* s.20(2).
[82] *ibid.* s.20(3).
[83] *ibid.* s.21(2).
[84] *ibid.* s.21(4).
[85] *ibid.* s.21(3).

to be able to point to matters personal to the individual which would call into question his or her capacity to function as a capable and impartial juror in the individual case, as distinct from cases generally or cases of any particular category.

The common law authorities suggest that some apparent or actual bias is necessary in order to challenge a juror successfully. If, for example, a juror had expressed hostility to one side or other, was related to or had a material connection with one of the Tr parties or had expressed a wish as to the outcome of the case it is likely that he or she would be excluded.[86] If a jury member is a victim of the offence charged against the accused, he or she should clearly be excluded.[87] It is unlikely, however, that a juror could be challenged successfully on more objective grounds such as, for example, having a past criminal record, being the former victim of a similar crime, being related to a police officer, being a member of a particular ethnic community or having a particular religious belief.[88] Having prior knowledge of the case may be more problematic. Generally, the mere fact that a juror has read, heard or seen previous media coverage of the case will not be sufficient in itself to satisfy cause. Nevertheless, cause may be shown where the nature of that coverage is such that it would prevent the juror from trying the case impartially.

In *R v. Kray*[89] the two accused were before the court on an indictment which included a count of murder. They had also been convicted of murder at an earlier trial. Newspaper coverage of that earlier trial and its result included several prejudicial matters which had not been put in evidence before the court. The defence in the current trial sought to challenge any juror who had read the newspaper articles. The trial judge ruled that a juror would not be disqualified simply because he had read the articles. The position would be different, however, if, as a result of reading the articles, the juror's "mind had become so clogged with prejudice that he was unable to try the case impartially."

17–20   Generally, the courts are extremely reluctant to entertain the argument that there has been so much adverse reporting about a case and/or the defendant that it would be impossible to empanel a jury which would not already have a view on the defendant's guilt. Where a risk of prejudice arises from pre-trial media coverage the court normally deals with it by giving the jury very clear instructions to ignore any information or impressions which they may have acquired from such coverage and to base their decision only on the evidence presented before them in court. In very exceptional circumstances, however, it may be necessary to postpone or drop the prosecution altogether if the media coverage has been such that the accused cannot be assured a fair trial.

---

[86]   *R. v. O'Coigley* (1798) 26 St Tr 1191.
[87]   *People (Attorney General) v. Singer* (1961) 1 Frewen 214.
[88]   In *R v. Ford* [1989] Q.B. 868 Lord Lane C.J. stated that the mere fact that a juror is of a particular race or holds a particular religious belief cannot found a challenge for cause by a party on the ground of bias.
[89]   (1969) 53 Cr. App. R. 412.

In *People (DPP) v. Haughey*,[90] for example, the Circuit Court imposed an indefinite stay on the trial of Charles Haughey for charges of obstructing the McCracken Tribunal which was inquiring into his financial affairs while he was a government minister and Taoiseach. In an earlier application Charles Haughey had sought an adjournment of the trial until some reasonable period after the conclusion and report of the Moriarty Tribunal which was inquiring into, *inter alia*, the operation of certain offshore bank accounts known as the Ansbacher Accounts. The court found that the nature and content of the publicity surrounding these inquiries and charges were such that Mr Haughey's standing and reputation had been seriously injured across a broad front and that he had been exposed to "hatred, ridicule and contempt". In a related decision of a Divisional Court Carney J. commented that no adult resident in the State could but be aware of certain matters, namely that Mr Haughey had for some time been subject to public controversy and adverse publicity and that the mention of his name was liable to engender strong feelings of support and, increasingly, embittered condemnation. Nevertheless, Mr Haughey's application for a postponement of his trial on the grounds that in the prevailing climate of public opinion it would be impossible to empanel an impartial and unbiased jury to try his case was unsuccessful. A subsequent application, however, was successful. The court felt compelled to grant a stay on account of the volume and extent of adverse pre-trial publicity, including a widely broadcast comment by the Tánaiste, Mary Harney, to the effect that Mr Haughey should be jailed. The court felt that this publicity would make it very difficult to empanel a jury which did not include individuals who had already formed a view about Mr Haughey's guilt. This indefinite adjournment was upheld by the High Court on an application for a judicial review in *DPP v. Haugh (No.2)*.[91a]

Re Zoe Developments[91b] is another case in which an adjournment has been used in order to counter the risk of a fair trial being prejudiced through adverse publicity. In that case the judge adjourned the proceedings for six months in order to allow the fade factor to come into play.

4. Procedure

The Juries Act does not prescribe the procedure applicable to a challenge for cause. It merely states that cause must be shown immediately and that the judge will then allow or disallow the challenge as he shall think proper. In practice, once at least 12 jurors have been selected by ballot, each one of them will be asked individually to stand up in turn to take the oath. The challenge to an individual juror must be made before that juror has actually begun to take the oath. It would appear that the judge has a discretion to permit a challenge to be made if the juror has already started to take the oath.[92] A challenge for cause cannot be made after the jury has been sworn in,

17–21

---

[90] See *DPP v. Judge Haugh (No.2)* [2001] 1 I.R. 162.
[91a] *ibid.*
[91b] Unreported, High Court, March 3, 1999.
[92] *R. v. Harrington* (1976) 64 Cr. App. R. 1.

even if information grounding cause only becomes available at that stage. The appropriate course to take in such circumstances is to apply to the judge to exercise his power to discharge the juror.[93]

The party exercising the right to challenge for cause cannot question the juror in order to expose or investigate possible matters which would amount to "cause".[94] In *People (Attorney General) v. Singer*,[95] for example, the Court of Criminal Appeal made it clear that the defendant could not question a juror in order to determine whether he was an investor in the failed investment scheme:

> "In the absence of knowledge on the applicant's part that the juror was an investor and claimant in the liquidation it is clear he could not have discovered his incapacity. The trial judge could not allow jurors to be questioned before challenge with a view to enquiring whether they were investors and claimants in the liquidation: see *People (Attorney General) v. Lehman (No.2)* [1947] I.R. 137 at 141 and the cases there referred to. Moreover for an accused to challenge for cause without information and to call the juror as a witness in support of such challenge in the hope of obtaining proof would amount to an abuse of the process of the Court."[96]

17–22   The court went on to explain that any juror who was an investor in the scheme should have informed the court and that the judge in such cases should have reminded jurors of their duty to disclose any interest that they may have in the prosecution. Similarly, in *People (Attorney General) v. Lehman (No.2)*,[97] the Court of Criminal Appeal ruled that the trial judge had been correct in refusing to permit defence counsel question each juror on whether he had read newspapers reports of the proceedings of the Court of Criminal Appeal which had quashed the defendant's conviction for murder on his first trial.

In England and Wales, by contrast, the defendant is permitted to question the juror directly, but only after he has presented prima facie evidence of his grounds of challenge.[98]

It would appear that the trial judge has an implicit power to put questions to a person on the jury panel in order to verify his or her eligibility or suitability to serve. Section 35(3) of the Juries Act 1976, for example, stipulates:

> "If any person refuses without reasonable cause or excuse to answer, or gives an answer known to him to be false in a material particular, or recklessly gives an answer that is false in a material particular, when questioned by a judge of the court for the purpose of determining whether that person is qualified to serve as a juror, he shall be guilty of an offence and shall be liable in summary conviction to a fine not exceeding £50."

---

[93]   *R. v. Morris* (1991) 93 Cr. App. R. 102.
[94]   *People (Attorney General) v. Singer* (1961) 1 Frewen 214; *People (Attorney General) v. Lehman (No.2)* [1947] I.R. 137; *DPP v. Judge Kevin Haugh* [2000] 1 I.R. 184.
[95]   (1961) 1 Frewen 214.
[96]   *ibid.* at 224.
[97]   [1947] I.R. 137.
[98]   *R v. Dowling* (1848) 7 St Tr NS 382; *R v. Chandler (No.2)* [1964] 2 Q.B. 322; *R v. Broderick* [1970] Crim. L.R. 155. But see, *R v. Kray* (1969) Cr. App. R. 412 where it would appear that the defence was permitted to put certain questions to jurors prior to establishing a prima facie case.

It is clearly implicit in this provision that the trial judge can put questions in open court to a juror or member of the jury panel in order to determine whether that individual is qualified to serve as a juror. Also, section 15(3) of the Juries Act 1976 requires the judge to invite any member of the jury panel who is in doubt about his or her qualifications to serve or who may have an interest in or connection with the case to communicate that fact to the judge. It is implicit from this that the judge can put specific questions to any such member of the panel in order to clarify whether he or she is ineligible or is exposed to a conflict of interest which would render him or her unsuitable to serve on the jury. Undoubtedly, the judge will also have the power to put questions to a juror before exercising his or her power under section 24 of the Act (see below para 17–33) to discharge that juror in the interests of justice.

Just because the trial judge has the power to put questions to members of the jury panel in order to ascertain their eligibility or suitability to serve on a particular jury, it does not follow that he or she can require members to complete a questionnaire with the aim of facilitating the selection of an impartial jury in a controversial case. In *DPP v. Judge Kevin Haugh*,[99] former Taoiseach Charles Haughey sought to have charges against him of obstructing the McCracken Tribunal of Inquiry postponed until a reasonable period after the conclusion and report of the Moriarty Tribunal of Inquiry. His contention was that the nature and extent of the adverse publicity being generated against him by these tribunals created a serious risk of an unfair trial at least until the effects of the publicity had receded. Haugh J., in the Dublin Circuit Criminal Court, was not satisfied that there was a serious risk of an unfair trial as in his experience "persons empanelled to serve on a jury take their oath seriously and conscientiously go about their deliberations in a manner directed by a trial judge's charge." Nevertheless, he considered that the circumstances of this particular case required additional safeguards over and above the norm in the selection of a jury. Accordingly, he ordered that a letter and a question-naire should be sent to each member of the jury panel.

17–23

The letter explained that the member may be called upon to serve on a jury in the prosecution of Charles Haughey and that, given the personality involved and the publicity surrounding the case, special measures were considered necessary to secure a jury which was capable of trying the case in a fair and unbiased manner. Accordingly, each member was asked to fill in the question-naire consisting of 15 questions. All but one of these questions were aimed broadly at ascertaining whether the member had any connection with any of the parties at the centre of the case or the McCracken or Moriarty Tribunals of Inquiry and whether the member had been influenced by the publicity surrounding them and Charles Haughey. The other question asked for the member's date of birth. A numbering system was devised to ensure that only the judge and counsel for the prosecution and defence could connect the information on a completed questionnaire with the individual member who

---

[99]   [2000] 1 I.R. 184.

had completed it. The objective behind the questionnaire was to provide the parties with relevant information which would assist them in making challenges for cause and without cause against individual jurors. The ultimate objective was to enhance the prospects of selecting a jury which would not contain individuals who might not be able to approach the evidence and the issues with an open mind.

17–24   On the application of the DPP a Divisional Court quashed Judge Haugh's order that the letter and questionnaire should be sent out and granted a declaration that the Juries Act 1976 and the common law do not permit the questioning of potential jurors in the manner contemplated by the questionnaire. The President of the Court, Carney J., was of the view that the Juries Act 1976 is a "self-contained and all-embracing code relating to juries both civil and criminal." Within that code section 15(3) provides the final filter to eliminate disqualified and ineligible jurors and to eliminate biased jurors. It is the provision which requires the judge to invite individuals who have been selected to serve on the jury to communicate to him any concerns they may harbour about their eligibility or suitability to sit on the jury in question. Carney J. ruled that there was no provision in the code permitting members of the jury panel to be questioned in advance of being selected to serve on the jury. Accordingly, the trial judge had neither an express nor implied power to issue the questionnaire. Equally, no such power was recognised at common law.[100]

In a similar vein Laffoy J. considered that the whole spirit and manifest intention of the provisions of the 1976 Act were to place openness and transparency at the very heart of the jury selection process. While there was scope for communications between an individual and the country registrar with a view to having an individual exempted or excused from a jury panel, there was no provision or authority to question a person on the panel or require him or her to furnish information in relation to any other matter before he or she attends court in response to the jury summons. Moreover, the facility in section 15(3) for a juror to communicate in writing his or her concerns about his or her eligibility or suitability to serve was, according to the learned judge, intended to protect the privacy and sensitivities of the individual and to avoid embarrassment. It did not detract from the basic rule that the business of selecting a jury for a particular trial was to be conducted *viva voce* in open court. Accordingly, there was no room for the type of questionnaire which had featured in this case.

It has been suggested that one way of limiting damage from adverse pre-trial publicity is to ask prospective jurors at the time of empanelling a jury whether in view of the adverse publicity they would not be able to bring an open mind to the trial. If any of them felt that they would not be able to bring an open mind they could be invited to inform the trial judge upon being chosen.[100a] Indeed, it would appear that that course was followed in the highly

---

[100]   *People (Attorney General) v. Singer* (1961) 1 Frewen 214; *People (Attorney General) v. Lehman (No.2)* [1947] I.R. 137.
[100a]   *DPP v. Haugh (No.2)* [2001] 1 I.R. 162.

publicised trial of Catherine Nevin for the murder of her husband. Several jurors who acknowledged that they did not have open minds were excused.

5. Residual Discretion

It would appear that the trial judge retains a residual discretion to exclude a juror who has been selected by ballot.[101] This discretion is associated with the judge's duty to ensure a fair trial. Accordingly it is to be exercised primarily to exclude individual jurors who appear incompetent to discharge their duties as jurors and who, for some reason, have not been challenged by either the prosecution or the defence. Lord Campbell C.J. stated in *Mansell v. The Queen*[102] that the trial judge has a duty to exclude jurors who are incapable of discharging their duties on account of factors such as drunkenness, mental or physical infirmity or preoccupation with some other pressing matter. In *Ras Behari Lal v. King-Emporor*,[103] for example, the fatal incapacity was the fact that one of the juror's did not understand English in a trial where some of the evidence, counsel's address and the judge's summing up were delivered in English. Further examples would include difficulty in hearing or reading. It would appear, however, that the discretion should not be exercised in a manner which would otherwise interfere with the random nature of the jury. In *R. v. Ford*,[104] for example, the judgment of Lord Lane C.J. in the English Court of Appeal, makes clear that the discretion should not be exercised to exclude competent jurors in order to secure a racially balanced jury or otherwise to influence the overall composition of the jury.

17–25

6. Challenging the Array

At common law either the prosecution or the defence can challenge the whole jury panel summoned for the case on the ground that the person responsible for the summoning acted improperly or was biased.[105] This is known as challenging the array.[106] If, for example, the person responsible for summoning the panel had a personal interest in the outcome of the case, the whole panel might be challenged successfully.[107] Equally, if individuals had been included in the panel at the request of one of the parties or because of their religious or political beliefs the panel would be open to challenge.[108]

17–26

In the absence of bias or improper conduct on the part of the person summoning the jury panel, the panel cannot be challenged on the ground that it is

---

[101] *Mansell v. The Queen* (1857) 8 E & B 54; *R. v. Chandler (No.2)* [1964] 2 Q.B. 322; *R v. Ford* [1989] Q.B. 868.

[102] (1857) 8 E & B 54.

[103] (1933) 50 T.L.R. 1.

[104] [1989] Q.B. 868.

[105] Blackstone's *Criminal Practice* (Blackstone Press, 1997), D11.10.

[106] The Juries Act 1927 abolished the challenge to the array in Ireland. However, the Juries Act, 1976, which has repealed and replaced the 1927 Act did not retain the abolition of the challenge to the array. It is at east arguable, therefore, that the common law right to challenge the array has been resurrected by default.

[107] *R. v. Dolby* (1823) 2 B & C 104.

[108] *R. v. O'Doherty* (1848) 6 St Tr NS 831.

imbalanced on the grounds of race, gender or age,[109] or does not adequately reflect the racial or social mix in the community from which it was drawn.[110] In *R v. Ford*,[111] for example, the appellant challenged his conviction for reckless driving and taking a vehicle without authority on the ground that the trial judge had refused his application for a racially balanced jury. In rejecting the appeal Lord Lane C.J. explained that a challenge to the array of jurors summoned must be on the ground of bias or other irregularity on the part of the summoning officer. The fact that a jury panel contains few if any jurors from the same racial group as the accused cannot of itself found a challenge or justify the judge in discharging the panel and ordering the summoning of a new one. Equally, the judge should not entertain a complaint that the jury panel is not truly random because it contains a lower proportion of persons from a certain race or ethnic group than live in the catchment area for the panel, unless the disproportion can be attributed to bias or impropriety on the part of the summoning officer. If the disproportion may be due to maladministration in the procedures for summoning jurors, that must be corrected by administrative as opposed to judicial intervention.

In *MacCarthaigh v. Éire*,[112] the Supreme Court rejected an application for a jury to be composed only of individuals who had sufficient knowledge of the Irish language to understand the evidence and arguments without the aid of a translator. The applicant had been reared through Irish and elected to have his trial conducted through Irish pursuant to his right under Article 8 of the Constitution. The court rejected the application on the ground that a jury which was selected in a manner so as to exclude non-Irish speakers would not be sufficiently representative of the whole community. That, in turn, would be a breach of the accused's right to a jury trial as guaranteed by Article 38.5 of the Constitution.

7. Standing By

17–27   The Juries Act 1927 gave the Attorney General the right to "stand by" jurors. This right was exercised by the Attorney General, or his representative in court, simply saying "stand by" after a juror's name was called and before the oath was administered. The effect was that the juror in question would be passed over, but not necessarily excluded. If a full jury had not been sworn once the whole panel had been exhausted, the jurors who had been passed by would then be considered again. On this occasion each had to be accepted as called unless challenged successfully. This right of "stand by" was exercisable only by the prosecution and was not positively carried over into the 1976 Act. Nevertheless it is recognised at common law[113] and is still applied in England

---

[109] *R. v. Broderick* [1970] Crim. L.R. 155.
[110] *R. v. Danvers* [1982] Crim. L.R. 680.
[111] [1989] Q.B. 868.
[112] [1999] 1 I.R. 200.
[113] *Mansell v. The Queen* (1857) 8 E & B 54.

and Wales.[114] It is unlikely, however, that it would be recognised as subsisting at common law in Ireland today.[115]

8. Information about Jurors

Successful use of the right to challenge for cause depends heavily on the challenger having relevant information about the jurors on the panel. However, the information available as of right to either side is limited. Every person (whether involved in relevant criminal proceedings or not) is entitled to reasonable facilities to inspect a panel of jurors free of charge.[116] While the panel includes any supplemental panel prepared for the proceedings in question, it is not necessary to indicate that any of the persons named have been excused since the panel was prepared, nor is it necessary to include any persons who have been summoned subsequently to make up an expected deficiency in the numbers.[117] Nevertheless, on request, the right to inspect the panel will extend to the right to be shown all alterations to it and the names of any persons summoned subsequently and to be told of any excusals.[118] A party to any criminal proceedings is also entitled to a copy of the panel of jurors free of charge on application to the county registrar. These rights are exercisable at any time between the issue of the relevant jury summonses and the close of the trial or the time when it is no longer possible to have a trial with a jury.[119]

17–28

The exercise of these rights of inspection will not shed much light on the individual members of the jury panel. The names and addresses of each member will appear as shown on the Dáil register of electors. The notice accompanying the jury summons normally asks the recipient to inform the county registrar of his occupation. Where this information is communicated it will be available to anyone inspecting the jury panel. However, there is no obligation on the juror to supply this information. Apart from these meagre pieces of information the prosecution and defence must rely on their own devices to dig up information which they can use to mount effective challenges to individual panel members.

The prosecution are in a stronger position than the defence to carry out background checks on jurors. In particular they should be able to access the criminal records of members of the jury panel. In England and Wales it is not unusual for the police to check on the criminal records of jurors and to pass the relevant information onto the prosecution who, in turn, use it in the jury selection process. This practice was approved by the Court of Appeal in *R v. Mason*.[120] There is also a practice of "jury vetting" in terrorist cases and cases

17–29

---

[114] Blackstone's *Criminal Practice* (Blackstone Press, 1997), D11.13.
[115] See Finlay P. in *State (O'Callaghan) v. O'hUadhaigh* [1977] I.R. 42.
[116] Juries Act, 1976, s.16(1).
[117] *ibid.* s.16(3).
[118] *ibid.* s.16(4).
[119] *ibid.* s.16(2).
[120] [1981] Q.B. 881. The Association of Chief Police Officers have issued recommendations on when the police should undertake a check on the criminal records of potential jurors; see Blackstone's *Criminal Practice* (Blackstone Press, 1997) Appendix 4.

involving national security in England and Wales. In these cases the checks go beyond criminal records of jurors to include police special branch records and the security services. Such checks may only be made on the personal authority of the Attorney General and are subject to guidelines issued by the Attorney General.[121]

In Ireland there would appear to be little evidence of any serious "jury-vetting". The prosecution does not even appear to make regular use of police and security records.[122] Equally, there are no published guidelines on the subject. As explained earlier, an attempt to elicit further information about prospective jurors by means of a questionnaire was rebuffed by a Divisional Court in *DPP v. Judge Kevin Haugh.*[123]

I. Jury Composition

1. Numerical Composition

17–30 Surprisingly, the Juries Act 1976 does not actually define the composition of a jury in a criminal trial beyond the stipulations on eligibility. Traditionally, the jury in a criminal matter in both Ireland and Britain has been composed of 12 individuals. Indeed, it appears that if less than 12 jurors are sworn in for a case, the resultant verdict will be ineffectual. It follows that the numerical composition of a jury in any individual case is normally settled after 12 individuals have been sworn. Circumstances may arise subsequently, as a result of which the numerical composition will alter. For example, a juror may become ill or be discharged for some other reason.

The 1976 Act does not deal comprehensively with the consequences of one or more jurors dying, being directed not to serve, or being discharged or excused from service after having been sworn in for the purposes of a trial. It does stipulate that a jury depleted as a result of any one or more of these events will remain properly constituted for all the purposes of the trial unless the judge directs otherwise or the number of jurors falls below 10.[124] Where the jury remains properly constituted the trial will proceed and a verdict may be found. What is not so clear is whether deficiencies can be made up in the course of the trial by the addition of substitute jurors as can happen in some other jurisdictions. The implication, however, is that the use of substitute jurors is not permissible and that the only option is to abandon the trial if the number of jurors serving falls below 10. It would appear that it is also open to the judge to abandon the trial if the number falls below 12.

---

[121] Blackstone's *Criminal Practice* (Blackstone Press, 1997) Appendix 4.
[122] Perhaps this can be explained partly by the fact that since 1972 trials in which such sources of information would be most useful have been tried largely in the non-jury Special Criminal Court.
[123] [2000] 1 I.R. 184.
[124] Juries Act 1976, s.23.

2. Composition of the Jury as a Ground of Appeal

At common law the fact that a member of the jury was irregularly appointed, **17–31** is ineligible or otherwise unfit to serve will not generally constitute a ground for appeal against conviction, unless the defence raised the defect in the course of the trial. Even if the defence does not discover the defect until after the trial, there is no ground for appeal.[125] It would appear that the only definite exception is where the defect takes the form of impersonation.[126] In the Irish case of *Attorney General v. Kennedy*[127] the accused was convicted by a jury on a charge of attempted larceny it was discovered the following morning that an under age youth had served on the jury. The youth had responded to a jury summons sent to his father. When his father's name was picked from the ballot box to serve on the jury the youth came forward, took the oath and served on the jury. When the matter was brought to the attention of the judge he expressed the view that on these facts the jury had not been duly empanelled in accordance with the law. Accordingly, the tribunal which tried the accused was not properly constituted and there was no proper verdict to justify the conviction and sentence imposed upon the accused. However, the trial judge also considered that he had no power to interfere with the verdict or sentence, but directed that the matter be reported to the Attorney General. The accused was subsequently directed to be released from custody by direction of the Department of Justice.

It is unlikely, however, that Irish courts would consider themselves bound by the common law where an irregularity in the composition of the jury was not discovered until after the jury had been discharged.[128] If the irregularity is such as to interfere with the individual's constitutional right to a fair trial it can be expected that an appeal will lie against conviction where the defendant was not aware of the defect in the course of the trial. It is also worth noting that the English courts are more inclined to permit an appeal in such circumstances where the irregularity arises from the incapacity of a juror as distinct from the manner of his appointment. Where, for example, it transpires that one of the jurors had made up his mind about the guilt of the accused before the trial the English courts would be prepared to set aside the conviction.[129] However, evidence that the juror knew the accused and had a poor opinion of his character will not necessarily be sufficient in itself.[130]

---

[125] See, *e.g. R v. Chapman* (1976) 63 Cr. App. R. 75 in which it was discovered after conviction that one of the jurors was deaf and had heard only half the evidence. This case was decided on the basis of the Juries Act 1974, s.18 (U.K.) which broadly follows the common law on the subject.

[126] *R v. Tremearne* (1826) 5 B&C 254.

[127] (1956) 90 I.L.T.R. 48.

[128] *People (Attorney General) v. Singer* (1961) 1 Frewen 214.

[129] *R v. Syme* (1914) 10 Cr. App. R. 284; *R v. Box* [1964] 1 Q.B. 430.

[130] *R v. Box* [1964] 1 Q.B. 430. *R v. Pennington* (1985) 81 Cr. App. R. 217; *R v. Bliss* (1986) 84 Cr. App. R. 1.

J. Discharging Individual Jurors

17–32   The Juries Act empowers the trial judge to direct at any stage of the trial that any person summoned or sworn as a juror shall not serve or continue to serve if the judge considers for any stated reason that it is desirable in the interests of justice that he or she should give that direction.[131] The judge may exercise this power on his or her own initiative or in response to a motion from either the prosecution or defence. Equally the judge may, for good reason, excuse a juror during the course of a trial from further service as a juror.[132] This is likely to arise on the application of the individual juror. The Act offers no guidance on the sort of factors that may warrant a direction or an excusal under these two powers. A direction which is desirable in the interests of justice presupposes the existence of some matter which would call into question the juror's capacity to serve ably and impartially. Examples might include: illness, a failure or refusal to observe the evidence and arguments, communication with either party to the case, personal familiarity with a key witness[133] and misconduct. An excusal for good reason, on the other hand, suggests some personal difficulty which would render it impracticable for a juror to continue. Examples might concern a medical condition or domestic or business pressures which were either not foreseen or which are incompatible with the projected length of the trial.[134]

17–33   The trial judge has always possessed a common law power to discharge an individual juror "in cases of evident necessity."[135] Unfortunately, there is little guidance in the authorities on what may qualify as "evident necessity". Undoubtedly, it would cover illness and any other matter which would prevent the juror from discharging his or her duties as a juror impartially and efficiently. It need not, however, amount to an impossible situation. In *R v. Hambery*,[136] for example, it was expected that the hearing would not last beyond Friday. In the event the trial judge did not commence the summing up until Friday and it was obvious that the case would last beyond the weekend. Accordingly, the judge asked the jury members if any of them had made holiday plans. One juror indicated that she was going on holidays that weekend and did not offer to make alternative arrangements. The judge discharged that juror and continued the case with the remaining 11 jurors who ultimately returned a unanimous guilty verdict. On appeal it was argued that

---

[131] Juries Act 1976, s.24.

[132] *ibid.* s.9(7). The judge also has the same duty or discretion as the county registrar to excuse a person from attendance or further attendance where that person is otherwise required to be in attendance as a juror at a court during a sitting.

[133] A juror who knows the accused or knows of his bad character should not serve as a juror; *R. v. Box* [1964] 1 Q.B. 430

[134] In *People (DPP) v. Nevin* unreported, Central Criminal Court, the trial judge discharged the second jury before any evidence was called because one of the jurors discovered she was pregnant and did not feel able to cope with the demands of the trial. The judge decided to discharge the whole jury as the trial promised to be a long one and she felt that it would be better to begin with 12 jurors rather than 11.

[135] *Blackstone's Commentaries* (1857 ed). *Winsor v. R.* (1866) L.R. 1 Q.B.

[136] [1977] Q.B. 924.

the trial judge had no jurisdiction to discharge the juror. Alternatively, it was argued that if he had jurisdiction he had exercised his discretion wrongly on the facts of the case. In rejecting the appeal, Lawton L.J. in the Court of Appeal stated that the trial judge was entitled to take the juror's statement that she was going on holiday as indicating a high degree of need for discharging her. While it might have been better to enquire further into the possibility of postponing the holiday, there were no grounds for ruling that the trial judge did not have a sufficient basis to conclude that there was sufficient necessity to warrant a discharge. Trial by jury depends on the willing co-operation of the public, and if "the administration of justice can be carried on without inconveniencing jurors unduly, then it should be."

Before exercising the power to discharge a juror the judge may need to question the juror or the jury as a whole in order to satisfy himself or herself that there are proper grounds for the discharge. Indeed, in *R. v. Blackwell*[137] the English Court of Appeal stated that the judge had a duty to investigate whether there was any realistic suspicion that a juror had been improperly approached, pressurised or tampered with. Such an investigation would probably require questioning of individual jurors and possibly the jury as a whole.[138] The questioning, however, should be confined to the issue of whether the jury's independence had been compromised and must not extend to their deliberations in the case. As a matter of good practice the judge should also seek the views of the parties before deciding whether to discharge a juror.[139]

Where the trial judge does discharge a juror in the course of a trial the jury shall, unless the judge directs otherwise, remain properly constituted for all the purposes of the trial and the trial shall proceed accordingly.[140] If, however, the number of jurors falls below 10 as a result of one or more being discharged, it would appear that the whole jury must be discharged and the trial aborted. In effect, therefore, the trial judge has a discretion to discharge a maximum of two jurors.

K. Discharging the Whole Jury

1. Appeal against Refusal to Discharge

The Juries Act does not deal directly with the discharge of the whole jury, as distinct from the discharge of one or more individual members. At common law, however, the trial judge has a discretion to discharge the whole jury before they have returned a verdict. Such a discharge does not amount to an acquittal and the accused may be retried before a fresh jury. Nevertheless, it would appear that the judge's decision to discharge the jury cannot be

17–34

---

137 [1995] 2 Cr. App. R. 625.
138 In *R v. Orgles* [1994] 1 W.L.R. 108 the Court of Appeal ruled that where the issue was the capacity of the jury to function as a whole due to an internal conflict between some members, the jury should be questioned as a whole in open court. If the problem had an external source then the individual juror or jurors affected should be questioned separately from the rest.
139 *R v. Richardson* [1979] 1 W.L.R. 1316.
140 Juries Act 1976, s.23.

overturned on appeal.[141] A refusal to discharge the jury on foot of a defence application, on the other hand, can constitute the basis for an appeal against conviction.

Since the decision on whether to discharge the jury is a matter for the discretion of the trial judge, it can be expected that an appeal court will interfere only where there is a serious risk of injustice. The most likely scenario is where the jury's deliberations or view of the case has become tainted as a result of being exposed to third party information or opinion either from the media or from direct contact with third parties. The leading English case is *R v. Sawyer*.[142] In that case three members of the jury had a five minute conversation with two customs officers in the court canteen in the course of a trial for importing cannabis. Although the two officers were witnesses for the prosecution, it was accepted that the conversation had nothing to do with the trial, apart from its probable duration. On these facts the trial judge refused a defence application to discharge the jury. On appeal, Lord Widgery C.J. stated that the correct test to be applied in such cases was whether "there was a real danger that [the accused] was or might have been prejudiced by what had gone on".[143] The court went on to conclude that there was no real danger of prejudice to the accused in this case. Given the length and contents of the conversation it was highly unlikely that it would have the effect of prejudicing the jurors against the accused or influencing their consideration of the evidence.

The Irish Court of Criminal Appeal took a similar approach in *People (Attorney General) v. Quinn*[144] when it quoted with approval the following passage from the judgment in *R v. Twiss*:

> "In those circumstances it is necessary for us to consider whether what the juryman did was of such a character as to lead us to think that there may have been an injustice done to the prisoner. It is not enough that he spoke to someone, and that the person to whom he spoke was a witness, although it makes it necessary to consider the matter more carefully if the person to whom he spoke was a witness; and I hope that nothing decided in this Court today will incline anybody to think that we hold it to be a laudable practice for jurymen to go out and talk to other persons. They had much better keep their own counsel and not speak to anybody else. If they speak to anybody else about the case they certainly ought not to speak to a witness, because if they do, their conduct may be open to grave suspicion."[144a]

It will be a very different matter, of course, if the jury member discusses the case with the witness. Equally, however, the circumstances of the contact between jury members and third parties may be sufficient to convey the appearance that the trial may not be fair, in which case it is likely that the jury will be discharged or a new trial ordered on appeal. In the Irish case of *People*

---

[141] *R v. Gorman* [1987] 1 W.L.R. 545.
[142] (1980) 71 Cr. App. R. 283.
[143] *ibid.* at 285–286. For further elucidation of the "real danger" test see: *R v. Spencer* [1987] A.C. 128; *R v. Gough* [1993] A.C. 646; *R v. Walker* [1996] Crim. L.R. 752.
[144] [1965] I.R. 366.
[144a] *ibid.* at 373, quoting from [1918] 2 K.B. 853 at 859.

(Attorney General) v. Heffernan (No.2)[144b] the Court of Criminal Appeal quashed a conviction for capital murder because of jury contact with third parties. In that case the jury was not permitted to separate from the commencement of the trial which lasted several days, including a weekend during which the proceedings were adjourned. On the Sunday the jury was taken on an outing during a break in the trial. In the course of that outing they were joined by a party of tourists who dined and conversed with them for about six hours. Even though there was no evidence to suggest that the trial was discussed in the course of their conversations or that the accused was prejudiced in any way by the contact, the court felt compelled to quash the conviction and order a re-trial on account of the nature and length of the interaction between the jury and their third parties.[145]

Although the *Heffernan* case might be distinguished from the *Sawyer* case on its facts, it would seem reasonable to suppose that the Irish appellate courts will take a stricter approach than their English counterparts when asserting the integrity of jury deliberations. The constitutional right to trial by jury coupled with the accused's constitutional right to a fair trial compel the appellate courts to err on the side of caution in such matters. Hamilton P. explained the underlying principles succinctly as follows in *Z. v. DPP*:

> "Having regard to the fundamental role of juries in our criminal justice system, it is fundamental that for an accused to have a fair trial, not only that the trial should be conducted in accordance with fair procedures but that the jury should reach its verdict in a criminal case by reference only to the evidence lawfully admitted at the trial and not by reference to facts, alleged or otherwise, statements or opinions gathered from the media or some other outside sources because fair procedures incorporate the requirement of trial by a jury unprejudiced by pre-trial publicity and capable of conducting a fair determination of facts on the evidence as presented by the trial."[146]

2. Exercise of Discretion

Broadly, there are four situations in which the judge may consider exercising **17–35** his discretion to discharge the jury: (i) when the jury has been inadvertently prejudiced against the accused; (ii) misconduct by some jurors; (iii) when jurors have personal knowledge of the accused or of his criminal record; and (iv) when the jury cannot agree on a verdict issue. The fourth situation is dealt with in chapter 19. The first three will be dealt with now in the order in which they are listed. At the outset, however, it must be emphasised that the analysis is based primarily on decisions of appellate courts in the United Kingdom. Since the decision whether to discharge a jury in a particular case is a matter for the discretion of the trial judge, appellate courts will be reluctant to interfere except in extreme cases. It follows that the guidance which can be

---

[144b] [1951] I.R. 206.
[145] The court distinguished the earlier Irish case of *R v. O'Neill* 3 Cr & Dix 146 which appeared to suggest that there would have to be discussion of the trial or prejudice to the accused in order to warrant the quashing of a conviction on the grounds of jury contact with a third party.
[146] [1994] 2 I.L.R.M. 481.

extracted from the case law reflects the sort of situations in which a trial judge must exercise his or her discretion to discharge. In practice it would not be unusual for trial judges to accede to a defence application to discharge a jury in circumstances which are either broader or less extreme than those which would persuade an appellate court to quash the judge's refusal to discharge.[147]

17–36 In the interests of a fair trial it is accepted that the jury must not be informed about unsavoury aspects of the accused's character which might prejudice their impartial and objective assessment of the admissible evidence relevant to the offence actually charged. In particular, the jury should not be informed of the accused's previous criminal record or the fact that he is well-known to the police, except to the extent that he has elected to put his character in issue or the similar fact evidence rule applies. It is recognised that where a jury has improperly heard such evidence, it is very difficult for them to put it out of their minds when considering the accused's guilt.[148] Accordingly, if through inadvertence prejudicial information about the accused's character or past criminal record comes to the attention of the jury improperly, the trial judge will have to consider whether to exercise his or her discretion to discharge the jury.

A considerable body of case law has built up in the United Kingdom on the grounds upon which it would be proper for an appellate court to interfere with the trial judge's exercise of discretion in this matter. Generally, it would appear that an appellate court will consider whether the failure to discharge the jury might have resulted in an injustice having regard to all of the circumstances of the case. In *R v. McCann*,[149] for example, the accused elected not to give evidence in their trial for conspiracy to murder the Secretary of State for Northern Ireland. During the closing stages of the trial the Home Secretary announced to the House of Commons the government's intention to change the law on the right to silence. That same night television interviews with the Secretary of State for Northern Ireland and Lord Denning were broadcast in which they strongly expressed the view that in terrorist cases a failure to answer questions or give evidence was tantamount to guilt. The trial judge refused to exercise his discretion to discharge the jury and the accused were convicted. In allowing the appeal the Court of Appeal explained that its power to interfere with the trial judge's exercise of discretion was not confined to errors of principle or a lack of material facts upon which the judge could have properly arrived at his decision. While it had to give great weight to the trial judge's exercise of discretion, it could nevertheless review all the relevant facts and circumstances. If, having done that, it considered that there was a real risk that the jury had been influenced by the statements resulting in injustice, then the only way in which justice could be done and be seen to be done was by discharging the jury and ordering a new trial.

---

[147] In the *Nevin* case, for *e.g.*, the trial judge discharged the jury when it transpired that the jury deliberations could be overheard in the public gallery of an adjoining courtroom.

[148] *R v. Palmer* (1935) 25 Cr. App. R. 97.

[149] (1991) 92 Cr. App. R. 239.

It would appear that the trial judge's exercise of discretion can be influenced by the manner in which the information came to the attention of the jury. In *R v. Weaver*,[150] for example, the jury became aware that the accused was known to the police as a result of questions persistently put to a police officer in cross examination by defence counsel. In rejecting an appeal based on the trial judge's refusal to discharge the jury, Sachs L.J. gave as one of his reasons the fact that defence counsel was responsible for inviting the answers about which he subsequently complained. Similarly, if evidence of the accused's bad character comes from his co-accused the trial judge's refusal to discharge the jury is unlikely to be upset on appeal in the absence of other relevant factors.[151] If, however, the information comes uninvited from prosecution counsel, a prosecution witness, members of the public or some other source then the prospects for a successful appeal are significantly greater.[152]

The source of the prejudice may be a biased juror or a juror who appears to be biased. In *People (DPP) v. Tobin*[152a] a juror on a sexual abuse trial disclosed, during the course of the jury's deliberations, that he had been the victim of sexual abuse. Nevertheless, the foreman of the jury assured the judge that the juror in question would be able to bring an impartial mind to the determination of the issues in the case. The accused was convicted by a majority verdict. On appeal against conviction the Court of Criminal Appeal had to consider whether the conviction should be quashed on the ground that the jury should have been discharged once the juror disclosed his past experience of sexual abuse. Delivering the judgment of the court, Fennelly J. reviewed the tests laid down by the leading English and Australian authorities as well as the decision of the European Court of Human Rights in *Sander v. United Kingdom*.[152b] In the *Sander's* case it was brought to the trial judge's attention that one of the juror's on the trial of a British national of Asian origin had made racist remarks. The judge proceeded with the trial and directed the jury to disregard any prejudices. All jury members also signed a note disowning any racist remarks or prejudices. Nevertheless, the United Kingdom was found to be in breach of Article 6(1) of the European Convention on Human Rights (right to a fair trial) as an objective observer might reasonably entertain doubts as to the impartiality of the jury in the circumstances.

Fennelly J. preferred this objective approach of the European Court of Human Rights to the approach of the House of Lords in *R v. Gough*[152c] which had advocated a test of whether there was a real danger that the accused might not receive a fair trial. He also found support for this approach in the

---

[150] [1968] 1 Q.B. 353.

[151] *R v. Sutton* (1969) 53 Cr. App. R. 504.

[152] See, *e.g. R v. Blackford* (1989) 89 Cr. App. R. 239; *R v. Boyes* [1991] Crim. L.R. 717; *R v. McCann* (1991) 92 Cr. App. R. 239; *R v. Ricketts* [1991] Crim. L.R. 915; *R v. Maguire* [1996] Crim. L.R. 833; *R v. Dubarry* (1976) 64 Cr. App. R. 7; *R v. Fedrick* [1990] Crim. L.R. 403; *R v. Hutton* [1990] Crim. L.R. 875.

[152a] [2001] 3 I.R. 469.

[152b] Application No.34129/96 (May 9, 2000).

[152c] [1993] A.C. 646.

rich and growing body of Irish case law on bias in judicial and quasi-judicial decision-making bodies. Applying that to the facts of *Tobin* he concluded that:

> " . . . a reasonable and fair minded observer would consider that there was a danger, in the sense of a possibility, that the juror might have been unconsciously influenced by his or her personal experience and, for that reason the appellant might not receive a fair trial. Moreover, even jurors without similar experience of sexual abuse might well be influenced by sympathy for a fellow juror who had suffered, at the hands of another, the type of abuse with which the accused was charged."[152d]

It does not follow that in every case where it transpires that a juror has been the victim of a criminal offence similar to that of which the accused is found guilty that the conviction must be quashed. Fennelly J. emphasised that sexual abuse was in a special category. Moreover, it was significant in this case that the juror had been sufficiently affected by his or her past experience to bring the matter up with the other members of the jury, and the other members of the jury were sufficiently concerned to raise the matter with the judge. Also, Fennelly J. did not rule out the possibility that any prejudice in such cases could be counteracted by a carefully worded special direction to the jury.

The prospects of a successful appeal for a failure to discharge the jury on the ground of prejudicial information improperly coming to their attention will be enhanced if the defence applies for the jury to be discharged in the course of the trial. If the accused is legally represented and fails to seek a discharge in the course of the trial, an appeal against conviction is liable to be dismissed even if the facts were such that an application for discharge would probably have been granted had it been made to the trial judge.[153] If the accused is not legally represented and matters arise which could warrant the jury being discharged, the trial judge should draw the matters to the attention of the accused and invite him to consider making an application to have the jury discharged. The trial judge's failure to do so would be considered a material irregularity which could necessitate the quashing of a conviction on appeal.[154]

17–37   Misconduct by a juror which is sufficient to warrant discharge of the jury normally takes the form of talking about the case to prosecution witnesses or members of the public while the case is ongoing. Once the jury have been empanelled to hear a case they are generally secluded from the parties and the members of the public for the duration of the trial. Up until they actually retire to consider their verdict, however, they are normally permitted to separate during those periods when the case is adjourned. During these periods, in particular, there is ample scope for jury members to discuss the case with third parties. Accordingly, on the first occasion that they separate the trial

---

[152d] *People (DPP) v. Tobin* [2001] 3 I.R. 469 at 478–479.
[153] *R v. Wattam* [1942] 1 All E.R. 178.
[154] *R v. Featherstone* [1942] 2 All E.R. 672.

judge should warn them not to discuss the case with anyone who is not one of their number.[155]

Even though only one juror is shown to have breached the instruction not to discuss the case with third parties, that will normally be sufficient to warrant the discharge of the whole jury. The courts are inclined to take a very strict approach to preserving the integrity of jury deliberations from third party influence. Indeed, in the celebrated *Nevin* case the first jury to be empanelled were subsequently discharged because persons sitting in the public gallery of a court room could overhear their deliberations in the jury room.

If a juror knows the accused or has personal knowledge of his or her bad character, he should not continue as a juror in the case. If the matter is only brought to the attention of the court during the trial, the court will have to consider whether to exercise its discretion to discharge the whole jury. While a failure to discharge the jury in such circumstances will not inevitably result in a conviction being quashed on appeal, it is submitted that this is the most likely result. However, there is common law authority to the effect that an appeal will be rejected if a juror's knowledge of or bias towards the accused is first challenged by the defence after conviction.[156]

L. Offences

The obligations associated with jury service are backed up by a number of criminal offences. Any person who has been duly summoned as a juror is guilty of an offence if he or she fails without reasonable excuse to attend in compliance with the summons or to attend on any day when required by the court.[157] The offence is punishable on summary conviction by a fine not exceeding €63.50. It will be a complete defence that the summons was served less than 14 days before the date specified in it for the person's first attendance.[158] Even if a juror attends in response to a summons, he or she will be guilty of an offence if he or she is not available when called upon to serve as a juror or is unfit for service due to drink or drugs.[159] Once again the offence is punishable on summary conviction by a fine not exceeding €63.50.

Attempts by a person to avoid jury service by making false representations are also penalised by the criminal law. If a person who has been duly summoned as a juror makes a false representation to the county registrar, or any person acting on his behalf, or to a judge with the intention of evading jury service, he commits a criminal offence.[160] A person will also commit the offence if he or she causes or permits the false representation to be made on his or her

17–38

---

[155] *People (DPP) v. McKeever* [1994] 2 I.L.R.M. 186; *R v. Prime* (1973) 57 Cr. App. R. 632.

[156] *R v. Box* [1964] 1 Q.B. 430. But see *People (Attorney General) v. Singer* (1961) 1 Frewen 214 for the position where the juror is one of the victims of the offence or offences with which the accused is charged.

[157] Juries Act 1976, s.34.

[158] *ibid.* s.34(2). This defence does not apply to a juror who has been summoned under s.14 to make up an expected deficiency in a juror panel.

[159] Juries Act 1976, s.34(2).

[160] *ibid.* s.35(1).

behalf. Moreover, if a person makes, or causes or permits to be made, on behalf of another person duly summoned as a juror, a false representation in order to enable that other person to evade jury service, he is guilty of a criminal offence.[161] If the judge questions a person for the purpose of determining whether that person is qualified to serve as a juror, it is an offence to refuse to answer.[162] Similarly it is an offence to give an answer which the person knows to be false in a material particular or recklessly to give an answer which is false in a material particular. In all of these cases the offence is punishable on summary conviction by a fine not exceeding €63.50.

Where a person is called upon to be sworn as a juror and refuses to be sworn in a manner authorised by the 1976 Act or by law, he or she is guilty of an offence punishable on summary conviction by a fine not exceeding €63.50.[163] A person who serves on a jury knowing that he or she is ineligible for service, is guilty of an offence punishable on summary conviction by a fine not exceeding €63.50.[164] If he or she serves knowing that he or she is disqualified, he or she is guilty of an offence punishable on summary conviction by a fine not exceeding €254.[165]

M. Issues to be Tried by a Jury

17–39   The Juries Act 1976 does not define which issues a jury is competent to try in a criminal matter. In addition to the issue of whether the accused is guilty or not guilty, it is well settled in practice that a jury can be sworn in to try whether the accused is insane or not. This is reflected in two of the three forms of the oath prescribed in the Act. However, the Act also prescribes a third form for the oath in which each juror swears to try "all such issues" as shall be given to him or her to try. It follows that a jury can be sworn in to try other matters, besides the guilt or sanity of the accused. In practice, the only other matter which features in this context is the issue of whether the accused is fit to plead.

---

[161]   *ibid.* s.35(2).
[162]   *ibid.* s.35(3).
[163]   *ibid.* s.37.
[164]   *ibid.* s.36(1).
[165]   *ibid.* s.36(2).

CHAPTER 18

TRIAL EVIDENCE

A. Introduction

Although this chapter is titled "Trial Evidence" it must not be viewed as an   **18–01**
attempt to cover all of the evidential matters relevant to a criminal trial. The
law of evidence is a substantial subject in its own right and reference should
be made to specialist texts.[1] What is attempted here is merely a general introduction to the law on some of the main issues of evidence which feature in a
criminal trial, such as competence and compellability, corroboration, identification, the admissibility of documentary evidence, the admissibility of evidence
given through video-link and discovery. Other major issues which are likely
to arise in the criminal trial, such as the admissibility of confession evidence,
the exclusionary rule, the right to silence, alibi evidence and similar fact evidence have been covered in earlier chapters. This chapter, therefore, merely
mops up a number of outstanding issues.

B. Competence and Compellability of Witnesses

1. Introduction

A witness is said to be competent if he or she has the capacity to offer admis-   **18–02**
sible testimony pertaining to an issue in the trial. A witness who fails this test
cannot be called to give evidence in a criminal trial. As a general rule if a
witness is competent he or she can be compelled to attend and give evidence
at a criminal trial either for the prosecution or the defence. However, there are
defined circumstances in which a competent witness cannot be compelled to
attend and give evidence on behalf of the prosecution against the accused.

---

[1] See, *e.g.*, Cannon and Neligan *Evidence* (Round Hall, Dublin, 2002); Fennell, *Law of Evidence in* Ireland
(Butterworths, Dublin, 1992); C. Tapper *Cross and Tapper on Evidence* (Butterworths, London, 1995)
Wigmore A treatise on Evidence; Phipson; Andrews and Hirst *Andrews and Hirst on Criminal Evidence*
(Waterlow, London, 1987).

These will be considered after the elements necessary to satisfy competency are explored more fully.

2. Comprehension

18–03   Generally, if a witness is capable of understanding the nature of the oath and can convey his evidence in a manner which enables the jury and all concerned to follow it, he is competent. Where competency is put in issue it is a matter for the trial judge to determine whether the witness is competent to give evidence. Both sides can examine and cross-examine the witness, with the burden of proving competence remaining throughout on the party tendering the witness.[2] A physical disability such as deafness and/or dumbness will not be fatal so long as the witness concerned is able to communicate his evidence through an interpreter or some other mechanism. Similarly, the competency of a witness does not depend on his capacity to speak English. He may give his evidence in any language so long as it can be interpreted for the benefit of all others concerned in the case. Indeed, it would appear that the witness is entitled to give evidence in his or her own vernacular language irrespective of what language that happens to be, even if the witness is competent in English. In *Attorney General v. Joyce*,[3] for example, Kennedy C.J. was clearly of the view that the importance of permitting a witness to give his evidence in his vernacular language took precedence to any inconvenience that may attach to providing an interpretation:

> "It would seem to me to be a requisite of natural justice, particularly in a criminal trial, that a witness should be allowed to give evidence in the language which is his or her vernacular language, whether that language be Irish or English, or any foreign language and it would follow, if the language used should not be a language known to the members of the Court, that means of interpreting the language to the Court (Judge and jury), and also, in the case of evidence against a prisoner, that means of interpreting it to the prisoner, should be provided."[4]

The accused, of course, enjoys a constitutional right to give his evidence in Irish, irrespective of whether that is his first language. He cannot, however, stand on a right to have all the evidence and proceedings conducted in Irish, as opposed to English, if he is fluent in the use of the English language.

Where there is a need to provide a translation of evidence, even from Irish to English, for the benefit of all concerned it will be unlawful to hear the case without the benefit of an interpreter.[5] Presumably the obligation to provide an interpreter falls on the State.[6] Where an interpreter is required he must be sworn and must interpret the evidence in an unbiased fashion.

---

[2] *People (Attorney General) v. Kehoe* [1951] I.R. 70; *R. v. Hill* (1851) 2 Den 254.
[3] [1929] I.R. 526.
[4] *ibid.* at 531.
[5] *O Monachain v. An Taoiseach* [1986] I.L.R.M. 660.
[6] See Rules of the Superior Court, Ord. 120 for the appointment of interpreters.

3. Understanding the Oath

The mere fact that a witness may be suffering from a defective or below **18–04** average intellect will not be sufficient in itself to render him incompetent. So long as he can understand the nature of the oath the judge may permit him to give evidence.[7] An incapacity to appreciate the nature of the oath will normally render the witness incompetent. This, of course, could give rise to a serious problem with respect to the evidence of young children. There has never been a fixed age threshold below which a child would be deemed incompetent to give evidence in a criminal trial. Traditionally, a child's competence was assessed on his or her capacity to understand the nature of the oath. This is clearly set out in the following passage from the decision of a court of 12 judges in the eighteenth century case of *R v. Brasier*:

> "[A]n infant, though under seven years of age, may be sworn in a criminal prosecution, provided such infant appears, on strict examination by the Court, to possess a sufficient knowledge of the nature and consequences of an oath . . . for there is no precise or fixed rule as to the time within which infants are excluded from giving evidence; but their admissibility depends upon the sense and reason they entertain of the danger and impiety of falsehood, which is to be collected from their answers to questions propounded to them by the Court . . ."[8]

This formulation was basically adopted by the Court of Criminal Appeal in *Attorney General v. O'Sullivan*.[9] In that case the court also held that it was not necessary for the trial court to embark upon an inquiry into the child's understanding of the oath before permitting him to give sworn testimony. The matter could be decided by the judge either in the course of a *voir dire* or in the course of the trial during the relevant examination or even cross-examination of the child on his or her evidence.

Today it is unlikely that the courts will interpret "a sufficient knowledge of the nature and consequences of an oath" as requiring any understanding of divine retribution for a failure to tell the truth. In the Canadian case of *R v. Bannerman*,[10] for example, a 13 year old witness said that he knew it was bad not to tell the truth, but that he did not know what would happen if he did not tell the truth. The court rejected the argument that the boy's failure to appreciate that he will suffer from some form of divine punishment if he broke his oath meant that he did not understand the consequences of the oath. It was quite sufficient that the witness appreciates that he is assuming a moral obligation when he takes the oath. Even the fact that the witness has not heard of God will not in itself render him incompetent to give sworn evidence, so long as he appreciates the solemnity of the occasion and the special responsibility attaching to telling the truth when under oath. In his judgment in the English case of *R v. Hayes* Bridge L.J. put the point very succinctly as follows:

---

[7] The degree of credibility attaching to a witness of defective intellect is a matter for the jury to determine when weighing up the evidence; *R. v. Hill* 2 Den 254; *R. v. Dunning* [1965] Crim. LR. 372.

[8] (1772) 1 Leach 199.

[9] [1930] I.R. 552.

[10] (1966) 55 W.W.R. 257.

"It is unrealistic not to recognise that, in the present state of society, amongst the adult population the divine sanction of an oath is probably not generally recognised. The important consideration, we think, when a judge has to decide whether a child should properly be sworn, is whether the child has a sufficient appreciation of the solemnity of the occasion, and the added responsibility to tell the truth, which is involved in taking an oath, over and above the duty to tell the truth which is an ordinary duty of normal social conduct."[11]

Unsworn evidence of a child

18–05   Even if a child does not qualify to give sworn evidence in an individual case it has been possible since 1908 for the unsworn evidence of "a child of tender years" to be accepted in criminal proceedings.[12] Such evidence, however, suffered from the handicap that it had to be corroborated as a matter of law.[13] This limitation has now been removed by the Criminal Evidence Act 1992[14] which also clarifies and extends the scope of the rule governing the reception of the unsworn testimony of a child witness. Under this Act the evidence of a person under 14 years of age, or a person over that age who is suffering from a mental handicap, may be received in any criminal proceedings otherwise than on oath or affirmation, if the court is satisfied that he is capable of giving an intelligible account of events which are relevant to those proceedings.[15] The focus of the test here is not on the witness' capacity to understand the nature and consequences of an oath, but his capacity to give an intelligible account of the events relevant to the proceedings. Although such evidence will not be sworn, the witness will be guilty of an offence equivalent to perjury if he makes a statement material in the proceedings which he knows to be false or does not believe to true.[16]

4. Spouses

Competency at Common Law

18–06   Competency is not solely a matter of a witness' capacity to understand the nature of an oath or ability to offer an intelligible account of events relevant to the proceedings. The common law, for example, has always adopted a restrictive approach to the competence of a witness to give evidence for the prosecution against his or her spouse in criminal proceedings. The general rule at common law is that one spouse is incompetent to give evidence for the prosecution against the other. Even where there are two or more joint defendants a witness will not be competent to give evidence for the prosecution if one of the accused is his or her spouse. This has been explained on the ground that to permit one

---

[11] [1977] 1 W.L.R. 234 at p.237.
[12] Children Act 1908, s.30, as amended by s.28(2) of the Criminal Justice Administration Act 1914, s.28(2). See now, Criminal Evidence Act 1992, s.27(1).
[13] See *Attorney General v. O'Sullivan* [1930] I.R. 552.
[14] Criminal Evidence Act 1992, s.28(1).
[15] *ibid.* s.27(1)(3).
[16] *ibid.* s.27(2).

spouse to give evidence against the other would seriously threaten the public interest in preserving the peace and unity of the family based on marriage.[17]

Clearly, if the spousal rule on competency was absolute it would constitute a major impediment to the successful prosecution of crimes such as serious spousal assault, incest and child sexual abuse within the family. Not surprisingly, therefore, a number of important exceptions are to be found at common law and in statute. The most important exception at common law concerns a prosecution arising out of personal injury being perpetrated by one spouse upon the other.[18] Personal injury in this context undoubtedly includes sexual offences such as buggery and marital rape.[19]

In *DPP v. J.T.*[20] Walsh J., in the Court of Criminal Appeal, reviewed the common law authorities on this exception and the impact of the provisions in the Constitution which protect the family and the personal rights of the individual. The case in question concerned competency of a wife to give evidence against her husband on charges of incest, buggery and indecent assault against their daughter. Walsh J. concluded:

> "If, as the Court believes to be the case, the common law never envisaged any such prohibition on the competence or compellability of a wife in case of attacks upon her by her husband, the members of the family, as envisaged by the Constitution, can have no lesser claim to have the right to justice vindicated by ensuring that all necessary relevant evidence on which that vindication will depend is available to the courts."[21]

Accordingly, one spouse is competent (and compellable) to give evidence against the other in a criminal trial in respect of an offence involving the infliction of personal injury upon another member of the family. In so far as any provision of the Criminal Justice (Evidence) Act 1924 might have suggest otherwise it was not deemed to have been carried over into Irish law by Article 50 of the Constitution.

Compellability at Common Law

It is worth noting that Walsh J. considered that a spouse is not just competent but also compellable to give evidence against the other spouse pursuant to this exception. The learned judge considered that the constitutional imperative which underpinned the exception demanded that a reluctant spouse should be compelled to give evidence. In this respect he refused to follow the House of Lords decision in *Hoskyn v. Commissioner of the Police for the Metropolis*[22]

---

[17] See, *e.g.*, *Hoskyn v. Commissioner of Police for the Metropolis* 67 Cr. App. Rep. 88, *per* Lord Wilberforce at p.95 quoting Gilbert *Law of Evidence* (3rd ed., 1769) at 136; *Hawkins v. US* 3 Led 2d (1959) 128, *per* O'Connor J. at p.129. See also Walsh J. in *DPP v. J.T.* 3 Frewen 141.

[18] *R. v. Lapworth* [1931] 1 K.B. 117; *R. v. Blanchard* [1952] 1 All E.R. 114. Other common law exceptions include forcible abduction and marriage, *R. v. Wakefield* 2 Lew C.C. 279, *Reeve v. Wood* 5 B & S 364; and possibly high treason, *R. v. Griggs* 2 Hawk c.46, 582, *DPP v. Blady* [1912] 2 K.B. 85.

[19] *R. v. Blanchard* [1952] 1 All E.R.. 114.

[20] 3 Frewen 141.

[21] *ibid.* at 158.

which held that a spouse would be competent but not compellable to give evidence against the other spouse in criminal proceedings for the infliction of personal injury on the former. Walsh J.'s position is now reflected in the Criminal Evidence Act 1992 (see below).

Statutory Provisions on Competency

18–07   Prior to the enactment of the Criminal Evidence Act 1992 there were a number of disparate statutory provisions, including the Criminal Justice (Evidence) Act 1924, which rendered spouses competent, but not compellable, against each other in criminal proceedings for a limited number of offences.[23] These have now been replaced by the 1992 Act. Although the Act does not specifically abolish the common law exceptions, its provisions are likely to render them redundant in practice.

Under the Criminal Evidence Act 1992 a spouse, and a former spouse,[24] of the accused is generally competent to give evidence against him or her at the instance of the prosecution in any criminal proceedings.[25] This reverses the general rule at common law. The primary exception to this provision concerns the situation where the spouses (or former spouses) are charged in the same proceedings. In this event, a spouse (or former spouse) will not be competent to give evidence against the other, unless the former is not, or is no longer, liable to be convicted at the trial either as a result of pleading guilty or for any other reason.[26]

Statutory Provisions on Compellability

In certain limited circumstances the spouse of the accused is also compellable as a witness for the prosecution. This applies if the offence involves violence or the threat of violence to the spouse, to a child of the spouse or of the accused[27] or to any person who was under 17 years of age at the material time.[28] Similarly, the spouse is compellable if the offence is a sexual offence alleged to have been committed against a child of the spouse or of the accused or against a person who was under 17 years of age at the material time.[29]

---

[22] [1978] 2 W.L.R. 695 effectively overruling R. v. Lapworth [1931] 1 K.B. 117.

[23] See Ryan and Magee *The Irish Criminal Process* (Mercier Press, Dublin, 1983), pp.324–325.

[24] A former spouse is defined for this purpose as including a person who, in respect of his or her marriage to the accused, has been granted a decree of judicial separation or has entered into a separation agreement; Criminal Evidence Act 1992, s.20.

[25] Criminal Evidence Act 1992, s.21(a).

[26] *ibid.* s.25.

[27] A child of the spouse or the accused in this context includes a child who has been adopted by the spouse or the accused under the Adoption Acts or, where adopted outside the State, a child whose adoption is recognised by the State by virtue of the Acts. A child in this context also includes a person in relation to whom the spouse or the accused is in *loco parentis*. Criminal Evidence Act 1992, s.22(3).

[28] Criminal Evidence Act 1992, s.22(1)(a). Also covered is an attempt or conspiracy to commit such an offence and aiding, abetting, counselling, procuring or inciting the commission of such an offence; s.22(1)(c).

[29] Criminal Evidence Act 1992, s.22(1)(b). Once again the inchoate offence and secondary participation are covered; s.22(1)(c).

A former spouse of the accused is compellable at the instance of the prosecution in a much broader range of circumstances. As a general rule the former spouse is always compellable for the prosecution unless the alleged offence is one for which a spouse would not be compellable and was committed while the marriage was still subsisting.[30]

In the case of both spouses and former spouses these compellability provisions are qualified by the marital privacy exception in the same manner as the competency provisions.[31] Similarly, a person is not compellable to give evidence for the prosecution against a spouse or former spouse where they are charged in the same proceedings, unless the person concerned is not, or is no longer, liable to be convicted at the trial.[32]

Competence and Compellability at Instance of Accused

The Criminal Evidence Act 1992 renders the spouse or former spouse of an accused competent to give evidence at the instance of the accused or a co-accused.[33] The Act also renders the spouse or former spouse compellable to give evidence at the instance of the accused in any criminal proceedings.[34] The only exception is where the spouse (or former) spouse of the accused is also charged in the same proceedings. In this event the spouse or former spouse is not compellable at the instance of the accused unless the former is not, or is no longer, liable to be convicted at the trial.[35] The spouse or former spouse of an accused is only compellable to give evidence at the instance of a co-accused in circumstances where he or she would be compellable to give evidence at the instance of the prosecution. It is worth noting, however, that the statutory limitations on the compellability of the spouse or former spouse of the accused to give evidence at the instance of a co-accused only apply where the accused and co-accused are charged in the same proceedings. This does not affect the power of the court to order separate trials if it considers that that is desirable in the interests of justice.[36]

It is worth noting that the Act's provisions on the competency and compellability of spouses are specifically subordinated to the right of a spouse or former spouse in respect of marital privacy.[37] This, of course, is a reflection of the constitutional right to marital privacy first recognised in *McGee v. Attorney General*.[38] Nevertheless, it is difficult to predict its effect on the general statutory rule on the competence of spouses. It is at least arguable that it would preclude the competence of one spouse to give evidence in the prosecution of the other spouse concerning offences such as marital rape or the commission of

18–08

---

[30] Criminal Evidence Act 1992, s.22(2). The offence must have been committed at a time when no decree of judicial separation or separation agreement was in force.
[31] Criminal Evidence Act 1992, s.26.
[32] *ibid.* s.25.
[33] *ibid.* s.21(b).
[34] *ibid.* s.23.
[35] *ibid.* s.25.
[36] *ibid.* s.24(2).
[37] *ibid.* s.26.
[38] [1974] I.R. 284.

unnatural acts by one spouse against the other. It is unlikely, however, that such an interpretation would survive Walsh J.'s analysis of the constitutional position in *DDP v. J.T.*[39] (see above).

5. The Accused and Co-Accused

18–09 The accused is not normally a competent witness for the prosecution when he is being tried alone.[40] Similarly, he is not competent to testify against a co-accused where both are being tried in the same proceedings.[41] In this case, however, there are various strategies open to the prosecution to circumvent this incapacity, subject of course to the limitations which apply where the accused and co-accused are spouses or former spouses. If, for example, the prosecution refuses to offer any evidence against an accused a verdict of acquittal will be recorded in respect of the accused. This will render him both competent and compellable to testify against a co-accused. If the prosecution adopt this strategy and subsequently attempt to recommence the prosecution against the accused he could plead *autrefois acquit*. An alternative strategy is for the prosecution to enter a *nolle prosequi* against the accused. Although this will not operate as an absolute bar against the re-institution of proceedings against him it will render him competent and compellable to testify against a co-accused. A third possibility arises where the accused pleads guilty on arraignment. Once he is sentenced he will be competent and compellable to give evidence against the co-accused.[42] The prosecution might manufacture such a situation by entering into a plea bargain with the accused. It would appear, however, that the court has a discretion to admit accomplice evidence where it is given by the accomplice after he has pleaded guilty and before he is sentenced.[43] Finally, the prosecution might secure separate trials for the accused and co-accused. In this event the accused will be competent and compellable to testify against the co-accused once the proceedings against the former have been completed.

6. Diplomatic Immunity

18–10 The Diplomatic Relations and Immunities Act 1967 makes special provision for the compellability of diplomatic agents.[44] These stipulate that a diplomatic agent is not obliged to give evidence as a witness in criminal proceedings.[45] This special privilege extends to the family members of the agent forming

---

[39] 3 Frewen 141.

[40] It would appear, however, that he is both competent and compellable in a prosecution for public nuisance under the Evidence Act 1877; Ryan and Magee, op.cit., p.326.

[41] In *Attorney General v. Ingham* 82 I.L.T.R. 79 Gavan Duffy P applied this rule to render an accused who had been returned for trial incompetent to give evidence for the prosecution on the preliminary examination of a co-accused.

[42] *R. v. Payne* [1950] 1 All E.R.. 102; *People v. Shribman* [1946] I.R. 431.

[43] *People (Attorney General) v. Shribman* [1946] I.R. 431.

[44] This Act gives effect in Irish law to Ireland's obligations under the Vienna Convention on Diplomatic Relations.

[45] Diplomatic Relations and Immunities Act 1967, s.5(1).

part of his household, providing that they are not nationals of the host State. A similar privilege extends to members of the administrative and technical staff of the mission together with members of their families. It would appear that the Convention does not modify the general rules on competence.

C. Corroboration

1. Introduction

Defining Corroboration

As will be explained below there are circumstances where a person cannot be convicted on the basis of uncorroborated evidence and circumstances in which the judge may be required to warn the jury of the dangers of convicting on the basis of uncorroborated evidence. To qualify as corroboration in this context evidence must be independent of that evidence which requires corroboration and it must be evidence which connects the accused or which tends to connect him with the offence in question.[46] It follows that a victim cannot corroborate his own evidence,[47] although evidence of the victim's condition from another witness may corroborate the victim's evidence.[48] Equally, it has been decided that the evidence of accomplices cannot normally provide mutual corroboration (see below).[49] In sexual offence cases evidence of a complaint which is made by the injured party on the first opportunity may be admitted as evidence of the consistency of her story and lack of consent, but it does not amount to corroboration of her evidence.[50] Whether evidence is capable of being corroboration is a question of law to be determined by the trial judge. If the judge finds that evidence can amount to corroboration then it will be a matter for the jury to determine whether it amounts to corroboration in fact.[51]

18–11

Where the unsworn evidence of child has been admitted it may corroborate evidence given by any other person.[52]

Corroboration Requirement

As a general rule a person may be convicted solely on the testimony of a single witness. There is no general requirement that the testimony of one witness should be corroborated by the testimony of another or evidence from another

---

[46] *R. v. Baskerville* [1916] 2 K.B. 658 *per* Reading L.C.J.. at 667; quoted with approval in *People v. Phelan* Frewen 98. See also, *People (Attorney General) v. Williams* [1940] I.R. 195; *People (Attorney General) v. Trayers* [1956] I.R. 110.

[47] *R. v. Christie* [1914] A.C. 557.

[48] *R. v. Zielinski* (1950) Cr. App. Rep. 193.

[49] *R. v. Gay* (1909) 2 Cr. App. Rep. 327; *DPP v. Hester* [1973] A.C. 297; for an exception see *DPP v. Kilbourne* [1973] A.C. 728.

[50] *R. v. Brophy* unreported, Court of Criminal Appeal, January 30, 1992; *R. v. Lillyman* [1896] 2 QB 167; *R. v. Lovell* 17 Cr. App. Rep. 163.

[51] *R. v. Farid* 30 Cr. App. Rep. 168; *People v. Lynch* [1982] I.R. 64.

[52] Criminal Evidence Act 1992, s.28(3).

independent source. However, there are two categories of exception to this rule. First, there is a small number of offences in which the jury must be directed to enter an acquittal where the prosecution case relies solely upon the uncorroborated testimony of a single witness. Perjury is the only such offence remaining at common law, the remainder being found in statutory enactments.[53]

The second category of exception is more important in practice, even though it is not a true exception. It consists of a diverse range of situations in which the judge might be required to warn the jury of the dangers of convicting the accused in the absence of corroborative evidence. While it is open to the jury to convict in such cases in the absence of corroboration, a failure by the judge to give the warning may afford grounds for appeal against conviction. This category can be further broken down into those situations where the judge must give a warning, those where it is desirable to do so and those in which he has a discretion. It is worth exploring each in a little more detail.

2. Compulsory Corroboration

18–12   The evidence of complainants in certain sexual offence cases requires corroboration as a matter of law. The absence of corroboration in such cases must result in the acquittal of the accused. The offences in question are those created by section 3 of the Criminal Law Amendment Act 1885 as amended by section 8 of the Criminal Law Amendment Act 1935 (the procuration of women to have unlawful carnal knowledge or to become prostitutes, and to procure unlawful carnal knowledge by intimidation, false pretences or the administration of drugs). In other sexual offence cases it used to be that the judge had to warn the jury of the dangers of convicting on the evidence of the complainant in the absence of corroboration.[54] Now it is left to the discretion of the trial judge to decide whether a warning is necessary and, if so, what form that warning should take.[55]

It used to be the case that if a child under 14 years of age gives unsworn evidence the accused could not be convicted in the absence of corroboration.[56] This requirement has now been abolished by the Criminal Evidence Act 1992.[57] It also used to be the case that the judge was under an obligation to warn the jury about the dangers of convicting on the sworn evidence of such a

---

[53] See, *e.g.*, Treason Act 1939, ss.1(4) and 2(2); Road Traffic Act 1961, s.105 and Criminal Law Amendment Act 1885, s.3 as amended by Criminal Law Amendment Act 1935, s.8.

[54] *People (DPP) v. Reid* [1993] 2 I.R. 195; *James v. R.* 55 Cr. App. Rep. 299 (rape); *People v. Williams* [1940] I.R. 195, *People v. Powell* [1945] I.R. 305, *People v. Moore* [1950] Ir. Jur. Rep. 45, *People v. Quinn* [1955] I.R. 57, *People v. Trayers* [1956] I.R. 110 (unlawful carnal knowledge); *Attorney General v. Corcoran* 63 I.L.T.R. 145, *People (Attorney General) v. Cradden* [1955] I.R. 130, *People v. Casey* [1961] I.R. 264 (indecent assault); *Attorney General v. O'Sullivan* [1930] I.R. 552, *People v. Troy* 84 I.L.T.R. 193 (sodomy); and *Attorney General v. Duffy* [1931] I.R. 144, *People v. Ward* 78 I.L.T.R. 64 (gross indecency between males).

[55] Criminal Law (Rape)(Amendment) Act 1990, s.7 for discussion see Hanly "Corroborating Rape Charges" (11), (4) (2001) I.C.L.J. 2.

[56] Children Act 1908, s.30, as amended by Criminal Justice Administration Act 1914, s.2. See also *Attorney General v. Sullivan* [1930] I.R. 552.

[57] See s.28(1).

child in a sexual offences case.[58] That requirement has also been abolished by the 1992 Act.[59]

3. Compulsory Warning

Scope

Traditionally the trial judge was under an obligation to give a warning to the jury about the dangers of convicting on the evidence of an accomplice, the sworn evidence of a child or the evidence of a complainant in certain sexual offence cases where the evidence in question was not corroborated. Now the obligation is confined to accomplice evidence and is considered a rule of law.[60] In such cases the judge must warn the jury that it is dangerous to convict the accused on the uncorroborated evidence of a person who was actually involved in the commission of the offence.[61] If, however, after having heard the warning they are satisfied that the accomplice's evidence is true beyond a reasonable doubt they may accept it. A failure to give the warning will result in the subsequent conviction being quashed unless the appellate court applies the proviso in section 5 of the Courts of Justice Act 1928.

18–13

Definition of Accomplice

Unfortunately, the case law does not offer a precise definition of what constitutes an accomplice for the purpose of triggering the warning obligation. In *Attorney General v. Linehan*,[62] for example, Kennedy C.J. said that a "narrow or precise definition" of an accomplice should not be adopted in this context. In that case, for example, the mother of a new born child was considered to be an accomplice to the child's murder immediately after the birth even though she had been acquitted when tried as the first suspect. She had testified at her own trial and at the subsequent trial of her grandmother that the child had been killed by her grandmother and that she herself had taken no part in the killing. Undoubtedly a principal or accessory will qualify as an accomplice, but the term is by no means confined to these.[63] Indeed, it is not necessary that the accomplice should be charged with any offence or even be likely to be charged with an offence arising out of the same matter. The term can extend to a situation where the respective contributions of the parties to the crime might more properly be described as perpetrator and victim. It even

---

[58] *Attorney General v. O'Sullivan* [1930] I.R. 552.

[59] Criminal Evidence Act 1992, s.28(2).

[60] *People (Attorney General) v. Williams* [1940] I.R. 195; *People (Attorney General) v. Phelan* 1 Frewen 98.

[61] *Davies v. DPP* [1954] A.C. 378. See *People (Attorney General) v. Shribman* [1946] I.R. 431 for the difficulties which arise on this issue in respect of a trial before the Special Criminal Court.

[62] [1929] I.R. 19 at 23.

[63] See, *e.g., Attorney General v. Linehan* [1929] I.R. 19; *People (DPP) v. Murtagh* [1990] 1 I.R. 339 (party incited to make a false allegation supporting a criminal complaint); *People v. Shaw* (evidence of a sale of stolen goods to an innocent third party) [1960] I.R. 168; *People v. Ryan* Frewen 304 (friends of the accused who were in the company of the accused but who did not participate in a violent assault on the victim); *People v. Lawless* Frewen 338 (the brother of the recipient of stolen goods); *R. v. Jennings* 7 Cr. App. Rep. 242; *R. v. Dixon* 19 Cr. App. Rep. 36.

seems that the spouse of a witness or an accomplice may be treated as the equivalent of an accomplice in this context.[64] It is also worth noting that the slightest degree of complicity will suffice.[65] The mere fact that the person has already been charged and acquitted will not necessarily disqualify him as an accomplice.[66] On the other hand an *agent provocateur* does not qualify.[67] The judge should not leave it to the jury to decide whether a witness is an accomplice for the purpose of the warning.[68]

Corroboration between Accomplices

The evidence of one accomplice cannot normally provide corroboration for the evidence of another.[69] In sexual assaults against children it has been accepted by the House of Lords that members of one group of children can corroborate members of another group where each group is giving evidence about separate incidents in which they were involved, whereas members of the same group giving evidence about the same incident cannot corroborate each other.[70]

Judge's Direction

When the judge is instructing the jury on what constitutes corroboration of the evidence of an accomplice he or she must be careful to explain that it is not sufficient that there is independent evidence which confirms parts of the accomplice's testimony or that the account which the accomplice is offering is credible. The independent evidence must corroborate that part of the accomplice's evidence which involves the accused in the crime.[71] The degree and gravity of the warning should vary according to the degree of the complicity.[72] In a case where the accused is charged with several counts on the evidence of an accomplice, the judge should make clear to the jury the danger of convicting on the uncorroborated evidence of an accomplice and the need for corroboration on each count.[73] However, evidence given on a count which is subsequently withdrawn can, where appropriate be accepted as corroboration on other counts.[74]

Where the evidence against a person includes a confession which is not corroborated, there is now a statutory requirement on the judge to advise the

---

[64] *Attorney General v. Durnan* [1934] I.R. 308; *People v. Coleman* [1945] I.R. 237.
[65] *People (Attorney General) v. Carney* [1955] I.R. 324 (loaning a van to a lifelong fried which was used, without his knowledge, to transport a stolen safe, and then permitting, under protest, the safe to be buried temporarily in his back garden).
[66] *Attorney General v. Linehan* [1929] I.R. 19.
[67] *R. v. Bickley* 2 Cr. App. Rep. 53.
[68] *People (Attorney General) v. Carney* [1955] I.R. 324.
[69] *People (Attorney General) v. Lawless* 1 Frewen 338; *R. v. Gay* (1909) 2 Cr. App. Rep. 327; *DPP v. Hester* [1973] A.C. 297.
[70] *DPP v. Kilbourne* [1973] AC 728.
[71] *R. v. Baskerville* [1916] 2 K.B. 658; *People (Attorney General) v. Phelan* 1 Frewen 98.
[72] *People (Attorney General) v. Williams* [1940] I.R. 195.
[73] *People (Attorney General) v. Shaw* [1960] I.R. 168.
[74] *ibid.*
[74a] Criminal Procedure Act 1993, s. 10.

jury to have due regard to the absence of corroboration (see chapter 9, para 9–27).[74a]

4. Discretionary Warning

Children's Evidence

It was seen earlier that a child under 14 years of age may be permitted to give **18–14** unsworn testimony if the court is satisfied that he is capable of giving an intelligible account of the relevant events. Prior to the enactment of the Criminal Evidence Act 1992, however, an accused could not be convicted on the basis of such unsworn testimony unless it was corroborated by some material evidence implicating the accused.[75] By comparison, an accused could be convicted on the sworn evidence of a child so long as the judge gave an appropriate warning to the jury about the dangers of convicting in the absence of corroboration.[76]

The 1992 Act has abolished the requirement for corroboration in the case of the unsworn evidence of a child.[77] It follows that a jury may now convict solely on the basis of the unsworn testimony of a child under the age of 14. The Act has also abolished the requirement for a warning of the dangers of convicting on the uncorroborated evidence of a child.[78] In its place the judge is given a discretion to decide, having regard to all the evidence given, whether the jury should be given a warning. Where he or she decides to give a warning it is not necessary for him to use any particular form of words.[79] Moreover, where the unsworn evidence of a child (or mentally handicapped person) is received pursuant to the 1992 Act it may corroborate the sworn or unsworn evidence of any other person.[80]

It is worth noting that the 1992 Act does not impact upon the duty to give a warning in the case of accomplice evidence. It follows that if the child is considered an accomplice in any case the warning must be given.

Sexual Offences

As noted above the compulsory warning about the dangers of convicting for rape or indecent assault in the absence of corroboration has been replaced by a judicial discretion to give a warning.[81] In *People (DDP) v. M.J.M.* Denham J. quoted with approval the following excerpts from the judgment of Lord Taylor C.J. in *R. v. Makanjuola* dealing with the approach which the trial judge should take in his summing up to the jury in a case where the equivalent English legislation had come into play:

---

[75] Children Act 1908, s.30.
[76] *People v. Casey (No.2)* [1963] I.R. 33.
[77] Criminal Evidence Act 1992, s.28(1).
[78] *ibid.* s.28(2)(a).
[79] *ibid.* s.28(2)(b).
[80] *ibid.* s.28(3).
[81] Criminal Law (Rape)(Amendment) Act 1990, s.7. *People (DPP) v. J.E.M.* unreported, Court of Criminal Appeal, February 1, 2000; *People (DPP) v. J.C.* unreported, Court of Criminal Appeal, November 7, 1994; *People (DPP) v. A.M. unreported*, Court of Criminal Appeal, November 3, 1997; *People (DPP) v. M.J.M.* unreported, Court of Criminal Appeal, July 28, 1995.

"(2) It is a matter for the judge's discretion what, if any, warning he considers appropriate in respect of such a witness, as indeed in respect of any other witness in whatever type of case. Whether he chooses to give a warning and in what terms will depend on the circumstances of the case, the issues raised and the content and quality of the witness's evidence.

(3) In some cases, it may be appropriate for the judge to warn the jury to exercise caution before acting upon the unsupported evidence of a witness. This will not be so simply because the witness is a complainant of a sexual offence nor will it necessarily be so because a witness is alleged to be an accomplice. There will need to be an evidential basis for suggesting that the evidence of the witness may be unreliable. An evidential basis does not include mere suggestions by cross-examining counsel.

(4) If any question arises as to whether the judge should give a special warning in respect of a witness, it is desirable that the question be resolved by discussions with counsel in the absence of the jury before final speeches.

(5) Where the judge does decide to give some warning in respect of a witness, it will be appropriate to do so as part of the judge's review of the evidence and his comments as to how the jury should evaluate it rather than as a set-piece legal direction.

(6) Where some warning is required, it will be for the judge to decide the strength and terms of the warning. It does not have to be invested with the whole florid regime of the old corroboration rules.

(7) . . . Attempts to re-impose the straitjacket of the old corroboration rules are strongly to be deprecated.

(8) Finally, this court will be disinclined to interfere with a trial judge's exercise of his discretion save in a case where that exercise is unreasonable in the Wednesbury sense (see *Associated Provincial Picture Houses Ltd v. Wednesbury Corporation* [1947] 2 All E.R. 680)"[82]

Denham J. also quoted with approval the following analysis of Lord Taylor C.J. of the approach the trial judge should take to the exercise of the discretion:

"Given that the requirement of a corroboration direction is abrogated in the terms of s.32(1) [English version], we have been invited to give guidance as to the circumstances in which, as a matter of discretion, a judge ought in summing up to a jury to urge caution in regard to a particular witness and the terms in which that should be done. The circumstances and evidence in criminal cases are infinitely variable and it is impossible to categorise how a judge should deal with them. Bt it is clear that to carry on giving 'discretionary' warnings generally and in the same terms as were previously obligatory would be contrary to the policy and purpose of the 1994 Act [English version]. Whether, as a matter of discretion, a judge should give any warning and if so its strength and terms must depend upon the content and manner of the witness's evidence, and the circumstances of the case and the issues raised. The judge will often consider that no special warning is required at all. Where, however, the witness has been shown to be unreliable, he or she may consider it necessary to urge caution. In a more extreme case, if the witness is shown to have lied, to have made previous false complaints, or to bear the defendant some grudge, a stronger warning may be thought appropriate and the judge

---

[82] Unreported, Court of Criminal Appeal, February 1, 2000 at 17–18, quoting from *R. v. Makanjoula* [1995] 3 All E.R. 730 at 733.

may suggest it would be wise to look for some supporting material before acting on the impugned witness's evidence. We stress that these observations are merely illustrative of some, not all, of the factors which judges may take into account in measuring where a witness stands in the scale of reliability and what response they should make at that level in their directions to the jury. We also stress that judges are not required to conform to any formula and this court would be slow to interfere with the exercise of discretion by a trial judge who has the advantage of assessing the manner of a witness's evidence as well as its content."[83]

It is evident from this extract that the trial judge should not simply give a warning as a matter of course. A warning will be appropriate only where there is present some factor which calls into question the reliability or credibility of the complainant's testimony. Moreover, the contents of the warning may be influenced by the nature and degree of the factors which detract from the reliability and credibility of the complainant's testimony. In *People (DPP) v. Molloy*[84] Flood J. intimated that in a sexual offence case where the charge is essentially supported by the evidence of the complainant alone without collateral forensic evidence or any other form of corroboration it would be prudent practice for the judge to warn the jury that they should be careful not to convict in the absence of corroborative evidence unless they were "very very satisfied with the testimony of the complainant".[85] This would seem to conflict with the approach outlined above. In the *Molloy* case, however, the complainant suffered from a mental handicap which left her with a childlike mind, there was a significant difference in her evidence and that of the only other witness namely her mother and there was an unusual domestic situation in the complainant's house where the offence was alleged to have taken place.[86] Flood J. drew specific attention to these circumstances as supporting the need for a definitive warning. It is also worth pointing out that in this case the jury had returned a verdict of not guilty on the first count and yet a verdict of guilty on the second count despite the fact that the complaints and supporting evidence for both counts were very similar. Flood J. expressed some unease over this outcome.

D. Identification Evidence

1. Introduction

It is well established that visual identification evidence must be treated with caution, particularly in those cases where the only issue in dispute is whether the accused is the person who committed the crime. Mistaken identification

18–15

---

[83] *The People (DPP) v. J.E.M.* unreported, Court of Criminal Appeal, February 1, 2000 *per* Denham J., quoting Lord Taylor C.J. in *R. v. Makanjoula* [1995] 3 All E.R.. 730 at 732–733.
[84] Court of Criminal Appeal, July 28, 1995.
[85] *ibid.* at 6.
[86] Denham J. distinguished this case on these facts in *People (DPP) v. J.E.M.* unreported, Court of Criminal Appeal, February 1, 2000.

evidence is a notable source of miscarriages of justice.[87] The evidence of a victim or independent witness who is certain that he has correctly identified the witness can be very persuasive on the jury. Experience has shown, however, that identification evidence is not always as reliable as it appears to be at first sight. Several factors can operate individually and collectively to undermine the accuracy of an identification. If, for example, the witness had merely a fleeting glimpse of the offender, or made the observation at a distance or in poor light, or suffered from poor eyesight or was intoxicated, exhausted or suffering from trauma at the time, the reliability of the identification would be suspect. Even if the accused was closely familiar to the witness prior to the commission of the offence, these factors would seriously undermine the reliability of the identification. Unfortunately some, perhaps even many, of these factors are frequently operative when a crime is being committed. The reliability of identification evidence can also be undermined by the manner in which it was obtained. If, for example, the police show a witness photographs of suspects, including the accused, prior to conducting an identification parade, it would be difficult to place must confidence in the identification.[88]

2. The Warning

18–16   The courts in this jurisdiction, and in Britain, recognise the risk of wrongful conviction posed by uncritical reliance on identification evidence. Accordingly, they have developed the practice of giving a warning to the jury in all cases which rely wholly or substantially on visual identification evidence. In Ireland the need for the warning and the general form which it should take are laid down in the following passage from the judgment of Kingsmill Moore J. in the leading case of *People v. Casey (No.2)*:

> "We are of the opinion that juries as a whole may not be fully aware of the dangers involved in visual identification nor of the considerable number of cases in which such identification has been proved to be erroneous; and also that they may be inclined to attribute too much probative effect to the test of an identification parade. In our opinion it is desirable that in all cases, where the verdict depends substantially on the correctness of an identification, their attention should be called in general terms to the fact that in a number of instances such identification has proved erroneous, to the possibilities of mistake in the case before them and to the necessity of caution. Nor do we think that such warning should be confined to cases where the identification is that of only one witness. Experience has shown that mistakes can occur where two or more witnesses have made positive identifications. We consider juries in cases where the correctness of an identification is challenged should be directed on the following lines, namely, that if their verdict as to the guilt of the prisoner is to depend wholly or substantially on the correctness of such identification, they

---

[87] In its eleventh report the English Criminal Law Revision Committee cited mistaken identification as by far the greatest cause of actual or possible wrong convictions.

[88] See, for *e.g.* the dispute concerning this in the *Meleady* case which is discussed in Chap. 22 under the heading of "Miscarriages of Justice".

should bear in mind that there have been a number of instances where responsible witnesses, whose honesty was not in question and whose opportunities for
observation had been adequate, made positive identifications on a parade or
otherwise, which identifications were subsequently proved to be erroneous; and
accordingly that they should be specially cautious before accepting such
evidence of identification as correct; but that if after careful examination of
such evidence in the light of all the circumstances, and with due regard to all
the other evidence in the case, they feel satisfied beyond reasonable doubt of
the correctness of the identification they are at liberty to act upon it."[89]

The warning does not advise the jury specifically of the dangers of convicting
on identification evidence in the absence of corroboration. The focus instead
is on the need to take great care in relying on the accuracy of identification
evidence. If the jury is satisfied, after careful consideration that they can rely
on the identification evidence, they can proceed to act upon it. A failure to
give the warning, however, would constitute grounds for quashing the
conviction on appeal.

In the leading English case, *R v. Turnbull*,[90] Widgery L.C.J. went further and   **18–17**
set out in some detail the sort of weaknesses in identification evidence that
the trial judge should draw to the attention of the accused. Indeed, the learned
Lord Chief Justice was also of the view that in a case where the identification
evidence was poor the trial judge should actually withdraw the case from the
jury and direct an acquittal unless there was evidence supporting the
identification. While *Turnbull* has been cited with approval by the Irish courts
there has been no specific consideration of whether the judge should
withdraw a case from the jury where there is no supporting evidence for a
poor identification.

It is important not to view either *Casey (No.2)* or *Turnbull* as offering a
definitive statement of the matters concerning identification evidence that the
trial judge must draw to the attention of the jury. They merely offer statements of
general principle. The application of those principles will have to be sensitive to
the facts of each individual case. Indeed, having given the direction quoted above
from his judgment in *Casey (No.2)* Kingsmill Moore J. went on to say:

"This direction is not meant to be a stereo-typed formula. It may be too
condensed to be fully appreciated by a jury without some further explanation
and the facts of an individual case may require it to be couched in stronger or
more ample terms, as when the witness or witnesses had no previous acquaintance with the appearance of the accused or had only an indifferent opportunity
for observation. It does, however, contain a minimum warning which should be
given in any case which depends on visual identification. No specific reference is
made to 'corroboration in a material particular implicating the accused.' An item
of evidence falling within this formula may, according to its nature, have very
little or very great probative value. This consideration is meant to be covered
by the words, 'in the light of all the circumstances, and with due regard to all

---

[89] [1963] I.R. 33 at 39–40.
[90] [1977] Q.B. 224.

the other evidence in the case,' and it is for the judge to deal with the lesser or greater probative value of any item of corroborative evidence."[91]

Similarly, in *People (DDP) v. O'Reilly*[92] the Supreme Court acknowledged that the warning must not be treated as a stereo-typed formula to be recited irrespective of the facts of the case. The trial judge must draw the jury's attention to the particular facts of the instant case which were relevant to a consideration of the reliability of the identification evidence. In *People (Attorney General) v. Fagan*[93] the Court of Criminal Appeal ruled that the facts of the case required a stronger warning than that which was given in *Casey (No.2)*. In Fagan the accused had been convicted of robbery of a petrol station primarily on the basis of identification by the station attendant. The attendant made the identification after having been brought to a sitting of the Circuit Court where he was told by the gardai either that he would see or might see the person who carried out the robbery.

E. Documentary Evidence

1. Business Records

Introduction

18–18 The rule against hearsay precludes the introduction of documentary evidence as proof of the facts contained in them. This can present particular problems for the prosecution when part of its case rests on information that has been compiled in the course of a business. It may prove impossible to identify, locate or produce the person who compiled the information. Even if this does not cause a problem, it may be that the person who compiled the information had no personal knowledge, or recollection, of the truth of its contents. If an essential element of the prosecution case depends on oral proof of the contents of an individual record in such circumstances it will almost invariably fail.[94] To cope with this situation the Criminal Evidence Act 1992 makes limited provision for the admissibility of certain documentary evidence. It is worth noting at the outset that evidence which satisfies the statutory requirements will be admissible for both the prosecution and the defence.

The Rule

Where information contained in a document[95] was compiled in the course of a business and was supplied by a person who had personal knowledge of the contents, it is generally admissible in any criminal proceedings as evidence of

---

[91] [1963] I.R. 33 at 40
[92] [1990] 2 I.R. 415.
[93] 1 Frewen 375.
[94] See, *e.g., Myers v. DPP* [1964] 2 All E.R.. 881.
[95] A "document" is defined as including (i) a map, plan, graph, drawing or photograph, or (ii) a reproduction in permanent legible form, by a computer or other means (including enlarging), of information in non-legible form; Criminal Evidence Act 1992, s.2(1).

any fact contained in it where direct oral evidence of that information would be admissible.[96] In other words the obstacle to admissibility presented by the fact that the information is contained in a document is removed in certain circumstances in the case of records compiled by a person in the course of a business. This provision extends to documentary information stored in non-legible form[97] which has been reproduced in permanent legible form in the course of the normal operation of the reproduction system concerned. The supplier and compiler of the information need not be the same person. Indeed, it is not even necessary for the information to have been supplied directly. If, however, the information was supplied indirectly each person through whom it was supplied (whether or not he is identifiable) must have received it in the ordinary course of a business.[98]

A "Business"

For the purpose of this general provision a "business" is given a very broad definition. It includes any trade, profession or occupation carried on either within or outside the State. It embraces both public and private, domestic and international, as well as profit and non-profiting-making, bodies. Specifically included are: any person or body remunerated or financed wholly or partly out of moneys provided by the Oireachtas; any institution of the European Communities; any national or local authority in a jurisdiction outside the State; and any international organisation.

Limitations on the Rule

The legislation imposes some specific limitations on the operation of this admissibility rule. It does not apply to information that is privileged from disclosure in criminal proceedings.[99] Nor does it apply to information supplied by a person who would not be compellable to give evidence at the instance of the party wishing to give the information concerned.[100] Information compiled for the purposes of any criminal investigation, statutory investigation or inquiry, civil or criminal proceedings or disciplinary proceedings is not normally covered by the rule.[101]

18–19

Situations where Limitations do not Apply

The limitation pertaining to information compiled for the purpose of any criminal investigation etc does not apply where the information contained in

---

[96] Criminal Evidence Act 1992, s.5(1). It is specifically provided that where a document purports to be a birth certificate issued in pursuance of the Births and Deaths Registration Acts, 1863 to 1987, and a person is named therein as father or mother of the person to whose birth the certificate relates, the document shall be admissible in any criminal proceedings as evidence of the relationship indicated therein; s.5(5).

[97] "Information in non-legible form" is defined as including information on microfilm, microfiche, magnetic tape or disk; Criminal Evidence Act 1992, s.2(1).

[98] Criminal Evidence Act 1992, s.5(2).

[99] *ibid.* s.5(3)(a)

[100] *ibid.* s.5(3)(b).

[101] *ibid.* s.5(3)(c).

the document was compiled in the presence of a judge of the District Court and supplied on oath by a person in respect of whom an offence is alleged to have been committed and who is ordinarily resident outside the State.[102] Similarly, this particular limitation does not apply where it is not possible or practicable to invoke the provisions governing the taking of a sworn deposition or the taking of a person's evidence through a live television link before a judge of the District Court.[103] It does not apply where the person in respect of whom the offence was alleged to have been committed either has died or is outside the State and it is not reasonably practicable to secure his attendance at the criminal proceedings concerned.[104] The limitation also does not apply to certain types of document, namely: a map, plan, drawing or photograph (including any explanatory material in or accompanying the document concerned); a record of a direction given by a member of the Garda Síochána pursuant to any enactment; a record of the receipt, handling, transmission, examination or analysis of any thing by any person acting on behalf of any party to the proceedings; or a record by a registered medical practitioner of an examination of a living or dead person.[105] The net effect of the non-applicability of the limitation to the information in question is that the document will be admissible as evidence of the facts contained within it so long as it satisfies the basic admissibility criteria outlined above.

Explanations

It may happen that information which is admissible in evidence pursuant to these provisions is expressed in terms that are not intelligible without explanation to the average person. In this case an explanation of the information shall also be admissible in evidence if it is given orally by a person competent to do so, or if it is contained in a document and the document purports to be signed by such a person.[106]

Certificate

18–20 Where a party to criminal proceedings wishes to rely on these statutory provisions to introduce documentary evidence he can do so through a certificate which states that the information was compiled in the ordinary course of a specified business, that the information is not of a kind precluded under the provisions, the date or approximate date on which the information was compiled and that the other relevant factors are satisfied.[107] Where appropriate, the certificate must also state that the person who supplied the information cannot reasonably be expected to have any, or any adequate, recollection of the matters dealt with in the information, having regard to the time that has elapsed since he supplied it or to any other specified circumstances. The

---

[102] *ibid.* s.5(4)(a)(i).
[103] *ibid.* s.5(4)(a)(ii), as amended by Criminal Justice Act 1999, s.18(1).
[104] *ibid.* s.5(4)(a)(iii).
[105] *ibid.* s.5(4)(b).
[106] *ibid.* s.5(6).
[107] *ibid.* s.6(1).

certificate must be signed by a person who occupies a position in relation to the management of the business in the course of which the information was compiled or who is otherwise in a position to give the certificate. It shall be sufficient, however, if any matter in the certificate is stated or specified to the best of the knowledge and belief of the person stating or specifying it.[108]

Generally, a certificate which satisfies these statutory requirements is evidence of any matter stated or specified in it. Nevertheless, the court always has a discretion to require oral evidence to be given of any matter stated or specified in a certificate.[109] Where a person makes a statement in a certificate which is given in evidence in any criminal proceedings and he knows that the statement is false or does not believe that it is true, he shall be guilty of an offence if the statement is material to the proceedings.[110]

Serving Documents

Information in a document shall not be admissible in evidence under these provisions without the leave of the court, unless a copy of the document (and certificate, where appropriate) has been served on the accused as required by the Criminal Procedure Act 1967.[111] Alternatively, not later than 21 days before the commencement of the trial, a notice of intention to give the information in evidence (together with a copy of the document and, where appropriate, the certificate) may be served on each of the other parties to the proceedings by the party proposing to give it in evidence.[112] A party on whom notice has been served cannot, without the leave of the court, object to the admissibility in evidence of the information, or any part of it, unless he serves notice of objection on each of the other parties not later than seven days before the commencement of the trial.[113] Where such a notice has been served concerning the information in a certificate, the court must require oral evidence to be given of any matter stated or specified in the certificate.[114]

18–21

A document can be served on any person for the purposes of these provisions by delivering it to him or to his solicitor, by addressing it to him and leaving it at his usual or last known residence or place of business or by addressing it to his solicitor and leaving it at the solicitor's office, or by sending it by registered post to him at his usual or last known residence or place of business or to his solicitor at the solicitor's office.[115] In the case of a body corporate it can be served by delivering it to the secretary or clerk of the body at its registered or principal office or by sending it by registered post to the secretary or clerk of that body at that office.

---

[108] *ibid.* s.6(2).

[109] *ibid.* s.6(3). The court must require oral evidence to be given where a notice has been served pursuant to s.7(2) objecting to the admissibility in evidence of the whole or any specified part of the information concerned.

[110] Criminal Evidence Act 1992, s.6(4).

[111] *ibid.* s.7(1)(a), as amended by Criminal Justice Act 1999, s.18(2).

[112] *ibid.* s.7(1)(b).

[113] *ibid.* s.7(2).

[114] *ibid.* s.6(3).

[115] *ibid.* s.7(3). Where the document is to be served on an accused it must be served personally on him if he is not represented by a solicitor; s.7(4).

Discretion to Exclude

Even if documentary evidence is technically admissible under the statutory provisions outlined above, it or any part of it must be excluded in criminal proceedings if the court is of the opinion that in the interests of justice the information concerned ought not to be admitted.[116] When considering its opinion in the matter the court must have regard to all the circumstances, including: whether having regard to the contents and source of the information and the circumstances in which it was compiled, it is a reasonable inference that the information is reliable; whether having regard to the nature and source of the document containing the information and to any other circumstances that appear relevant to the court, it is a reasonable inference that the document is authentic; and having regard in particular to whether it is likely to be possible to controvert the information where the person who supplied it does not attend to give evidence in the proceedings, the risk that its admission or exclusion will result in unfairness to the accused.[117]

Weight

Documentary evidence which survives this test must still be assessed for weight. In estimating the weight, if any, to be attached to information given in evidence pursuant to these provisions, regard shall be had to all of the circumstances from which any inference can reasonably be drawn as to its accuracy.[118]

Credibility of Person Supplying the Information

The admission of documentary evidence in substitution for the first hand oral version is not meant to reduce the scope for attacking the credibility of the person who supplied the information concerned. Accordingly, it is provided that any evidence is admissible as relevant to the credibility of the person who supplied the information if that evidence would have been admissible had he been called as a witness.[119] Equally, the court may give leave for evidence of any matter to be given where that matter could have been put in cross-examination to the supplier of the information as relevant to his credibility as a witness.[120] Evidence tending to prove that the supplier of information made a statement which is inconsistent with the information supplied is also admissible for the purpose of showing that he contradicted himself.[121]

Copies

Where information contained in a document is admissible in evidence in criminal proceedings, the information may be given in evidence by producing

---

[116] *ibid.* s.8(1).
[117] *ibid.* s.8(2).
[118] *ibid.* s.8(3).
[119] *ibid.* s.9(a).
[120] *ibid.* s.9(b).
[121] *ibid.* s.9(c).

a copy of the document, or the material part of it, authenticated in such manner as the court may approve.[122] It does not matter for this purpose whether the original document still exists.

Other options

It is worth noting that it will not always be necessary to rely on the provisions of the Criminal Evidence Act 1992 to secure the admission of business records. The rule against hearsay will not apply to exclude a business record where a witness can testify that he compiled the record and can identify the record as one which he personally filled in or signed.[123] Moreover, even if the witness did not compile the record it would still be admissible if the record was properly in the custody of the witness as a public officer.[124]

2. District Court Certificates

The provisions governing the admissibility of documentary evidence in the Criminal Evidence Act 1992 do not extend to records made by gardai in the course of a criminal investigation. It follows that individual gardai must be called to give evidence in person of all relevant matters that they saw and did in connection with a criminal investigation which has resulted in a person being charged. Even if these are quite mundane matters which the gardai will have recorded as a matter of standard practice, the individuals in question will have to be called to state them in evidence. This applies irrespective of whether the proceedings are a charge and remand hearing in the District Court, pre-trial proceedings or the trial itself.

18–22

Inevitably, this requirement to appear and give evidence in person tied down a significant amount of Garda manpower at certain times. Where the evidence to be given by a member of the force in such situations was relatively innocuous and uncontroversial, it would seem sensible for it to be submitted in documentary form. This would release the member for more productive duties outside the court without unduly undermining the fairness of the criminal trial. The problem, of course, was that by virtue of the hearsay rule such documentary evidence could not be admitted in order to prove the truth of any facts stated in it. This obstacle has now been removed in certain circumstances by the Criminal Justice (Miscellaneous Provisions) Act 1997. Where these circumstances are present the Garda evidence can be admitted in the form of a District Court certificate or a scene of crime certificate.

A District Court certificate can be tendered in evidence where a person has been arrested without warrant and charged for the first time before the District Court. The certificate will state that the member who signed it did one or

---

[122] *ibid.* s.30.

[123] *People (DPP) v. Byrne* unreported, Court of Criminal Appeal, June 7, 2000.

[124] *ibid.* The case in question concerned the use of a crashed vehicle to provide a new identity for a stolen vehicle. An official of the motor taxation office produced the original records of the registration of a motor vehicle and an officer of the Revenue Commissioners gave evidence of a letter seeking de-registration of the crashed vehicle. Their evidence was held admissible without the need for a certificate under s. 5 or 6 of the 1992 Act.

more of the following with respect to the person concerned, namely: arrested him for a specified offence, charged him with a specified offence or cautioned him on arrest or charge for a specified offence.[125] The signed certificate is then admissible as evidence of the matters stated in it when tendered by a member of the Garda Síochána not below the rank of sergeant.[126] It follows that where a number of individuals are being charged for the first time at the same sitting of the District Court a single member, not below the rank of sergeant, can appear and tender the duly signed and completed certificates of arrest, charge and caution with respect to each accused. There will be no need for the gardai who effected the actual arrests, charges and cautions to appear.

While this may result in the more efficient deployment of Garda resources, it may occasionally prove problematic in practice. For example, a certificate will not be sufficient in itself to establish that the person before the court is the same person named in the certificate. Accordingly, if there is any such dispute over identity it may still be necessary to call the member who effected the arrest etc to prove that the person named in the certificate is the person before the court. This problem will not necessarily be averted by a provision in the 1997 Act which stipulates that where a charge sheet and recognisance is laid before the District Court the person to whom they relate must identify himself when required to do so by the court.[127] Surprisingly, the Act does not impose any penalty for a failure to comply with the court's request in this matter. It is also worth noting that if the use of a certificate in any individual case is likely to be a source of unfairness to any party the court retains a discretion to direct that the matters stated in the certificate should be given through oral evidence. The relevant provision reads:

> "In any criminal proceedings the court may, if it considers that the interests of justice so require, direct that oral evidence of the matters stated in a certificate under this section be given, and the court may for the purpose of receiving oral evidence adjourn the proceedings to a later date."[128]

3. Scene of Crime Certificates

18–23   A scene of crime certificate concerns the evidence of a member who has been deployed to preserve the scene of a crime for investigation. The evidence of a member so deployed will be important to establish when the scene was preserved, the extent to which it was preserved and the identity of all those who had access to the scene during the investigation. In most cases, however, such evidence is uncontentious. It follows that it, too, could be given through the means of a certificate thereby obviating the need for several gardai to spend lengthy and unproductive periods of time in court. By virtue of the 1997 Act a scene of crime certificate, signed by the member who made it,

---

[125] Criminal Justice (Miscellaneous Provisions) Act 1997, s.6(1).
[126] *ibid.* s.6(5).
[127] *ibid.* s.6(6).
[128] *ibid.* s.6(4).

may be tendered in evidence in any criminal proceedings by a member not below the rank of sergeant.[129]

The certificate will state that the member who signed it did one or more of the following at or adjacent to the place where the offence is alleged to have been committed or at a place containing evidence of the alleged offence, namely: commenced duty, or replaced a specified member on duty, at a specified time; and remained on duty until a specified time or until replaced at a specified time by a specified member.[130] Equally, it will state that no person entered the place in question during a specified period without the permission of the member and that no evidence at that place was disturbed while he was on duty there. If a person entered the place when the member concerned was on duty the certificate must state the name of that person and the purpose for which he was permitted to enter.[131]

The signed certificate will be admissible in evidence of the matters stated in it. Accordingly, it will not be necessary for members who merely secured the scene of investigation to attend in person to give evidence in subsequent criminal proceedings arising out of the alleged offence. Their evidence can be submitted in the form of certificates by a member not below the rank of sergeant. It is worth noting that this facility applies to all criminal proceedings arising out of the alleged offence. In that sense it is more substantive than the District Court certificate which applies only when the person arrested is charged for the first time before the District Court. It is worth noting, therefore, that the court's discretion to direct that oral evidence be given of matters stated in a District Court certificate extends also to matters stated in a scene of crime certificate.[132]

4. Fingerprint Certificates

Where part of the prosecution evidence against the accused consists of finger-print or palmprint evidence it will usually be necessary for the member or members who took the accused's prints to appear in court in person to give evidence that the prints before the court are those taken from the accused. Such evidence is rarely contested by the accused. If there is a dispute about fingerprint or palmprint evidence it usually concerns whether the prints actually match those taken from the scene of the crime or from items associated with the commission of the offence. It follows that the requirement to receive oral evidence from the members who took the accused's prints is usually little more than a formality and another example of Garda manpower being tied up in unproductive court duties. The Criminal Justice (Miscellaneous Provisions) Act 1997 seeks to address this problem by permitting an image of fingerprints and palmprints to be proved through the medium of a certificate.

18–24

---

[129] *ibid.* s.6(5).
[130] *ibid.* s.6(2).
[131] *ibid.* s.6(3).
[132] *ibid.* s.6(4).

By virtue of the Act a power to take a person's fingerprints or palmprints now includes the power to record an image of the prints so taken.[133] The recording may be done by electronic or any other means. Where a member of the Garda Síochána records an image of any fingerprint or palmprint pursuant to this provision, he may attach it to, or include it in, a certificate stating that the image is the fingerprint or palmprint, as the case may be, of a specified person and that the image was recorded by the member. The certificate, signed by the member concerned, will be evidence of the matters stated in it unless the contrary is proved.[134] This admissibility provision also extends to a signed certificate stating that a photograph attached to or contained in the certificate is a photograph of a specified person taken by the member who signed it. Where such a certificate is produced it would appear that the onus is on the accused to establish that the image accompanying the certificate is not that of his fingerprints or palmprints. There is no specific provision giving the court a discretion to direct that oral evidence be given of the matters stated in the certificate. It must be noted, however, that the certificate is merely evidence of the facts stated therein. It does not provide conclusive proof.

5. Medical Certificates

18–25   Another certificate worth mentioning is the medical certificate, even though it does not directly concern Garda manpower. The Non-fatal Offences against the Person Act 1997 makes provision for a doctor's certificate to be admitted in evidence of the facts stated therein in any proceedings for an offence alleging the causing of harm or serious harm to a person.[135] This certificate must purport to be signed by a registered medical practitioner and relate to the examination of the person concerned. Such certificate shall, unless the contrary is proved, be evidence of any fact thereby certified without proof of any signature thereon or that any such signature is that of such practitioner. The primary importance of this provision will, of course, be in the context of a medical examination of the accused's alleged victim. It will no longer be necessary to call the doctor who examined the victim to give evidence of the nature or extent of his injuries. The absence of the doctor will render it more difficult for the defence to challenge whether the victim actually suffered harm or serious harm, as the case may be.

Once again it must be noted that the certificate is merely evidence of the matters certified. It does not provide conclusive proof of the matters in question. The accused can always produce evidence in rebuttal either directly or indirectly through the cross-examination of prosecution witnesses.

---

[133] See Chap.6 for the powers to take fingerprints and palmprints.
[134] Criminal Justice (Miscellaneous Provisions) Act 1997, s.11.
[135] Non-fatal Offences against the Person Act 1997, s.25.

6. Others

Drunk Driving Certificates

A certificate satisfying prescribed requirements can be admissible as evidence **18–26** of a specified offence or offences in certain circumstances. The classic example is a certificate of the Medical Bureau of Road Safety stating the level of alcohol in the blood as detected from a blood or urine specimen. Section 23(2) of the Road Traffic (Amendment) Act 1978 stipulates that such a certificate shall be sufficient evidence of the facts stated therein and that it shall, until the contrary is shown, be sufficient evidence of compliance by the Bureau with all of the statutory requirements which the Bureau is required to comply with in the handling and analysis of the sample and in its reporting of that analysis.[136] It follows that a duly completed certificate will be sufficient in itself to substantiate a conviction for drunk driving. There is no need to call direct evidence from those who handled the specimen, carried out the analysis and completed the certificate. Equally, there is no need to call direct evidence about the scientific basis for the methods used to produce the results.

The Road Traffic Act 1994, as amended by the Road Traffic Act 1995 made provision for a new offence of drunk driving which was based on the concentration of alcohol in a person's breath. For this purpose (and other purposes) the concentration of alcohol in a person's breath is measured by a new device called an alcolyser. The person exhales in to the alcolyser which will duly produce a statement of the concentration of alcohol in the breath. When taken pursuant to the prescribed statutory procedures a duly completed statement shall, until the contrary is shown, be sufficient evidence of the facts stated therein in any proceedings under the Road Traffic Acts.[137] Once again there is no requirement to prove the scientific basis upon which the alcolyser works.[138] Equally, the statement constitutes evidence, until the contrary is shown, that the member of the Garda Síochána concerned complied with the statutory requirements for taking the statement. It is always open to the defendant to challenge the accuracy or provenance of the alcolyser or the procedures followed in taking a statement through cross-examination of Garda witnesses and the calling of evidence. In the absence of such challenge, however, it would appear that the statement will in itself be sufficient to ground a conviction. It is also worth noting, although not directly in point, that section 12 of the Road Traffic Act 1994 states that it shall be presumed until the contrary is shown that an apparatus provided to a member of the Garda Síochána is for the purpose of enabling a person to provide a specimen of breath pursuant to that section and is an apparatus for indicating the presence of alcohol in the

---

[136] *State (Murphy) v. Johnston* [1983] I.R. 235. This also happens to be the case in which section 23(1) of the Act referred to Pt III of the Act when Pt V was clearly intended. The Supreme Court ruled that it had no power to read the provision as if it read Pt V. In any event it transpired that s.23(1) was largely superfluous on the facts of the case due to the terms of s.23(2).

[137] Road Traffic Act 1994, s.21(1).

[138] *DPP v. Syron* [2001] 2 I.R. 105.

breath. Accordingly, it is not necessary for the prosecution to lead evidence in each case that the apparatus is as described.[139]

Tax Certificates

The Income Tax code also makes provision for the offence of failing to make a return of income as required by the code to be proved by certain certificates issued by an officer of the Revenue Commissioners. The relevant statutory provisions states that the certificates shall be evidence, until the contrary is proved, of the facts stated therein.[140] The facts averred in the certificate are that the officer has examined his records and that it appears from them that a notice was duly given to the defendant and that the notice had not been complied with. The certificate may be tendered in evidence without proof and shall be deemed until the contrary is proved to have been signed by the officer in question. In *O'Callaghan v. District Justice Clifford*[141] the Supreme Court noted that the offence of failing to make a return of income include a mens rea requirement which could not be satisfied solely by the certificate. It also cautioned that when the State seeks to prosecute offences by way of a certificate which encompasses the entire of the prosecution case, of which a factor or factors are not set out on the certificate, the court has a special duty to ensure that the due process of law is applied. In this case the failure of the District Court judge to grant an adjournment to enable the defendant to be present to defend them was held to vitiate the proceedings.

Others

There are a number of discrete statutory provisions which permit the statement of a member of the Garda Síochána to be admitted in certain circumstances as evidence of its contents even though the statement consists merely of the member's belief or opinion as to the existence of certain facts. An example is to be found in the Proceeds of Crime Act 1996. It makes provision for an affidavit or oral evidence of a member of the Garda Síochána (or an officer of the Revenue Commissioners authorised for the purposes of the Act) to be admitted as evidence in a case where the State is seeking an order under the Act for the seizure of what are believed to be criminal assets. The affidavit or oral evidence must consist of a statement of the member's belief that the respondent is in possession of property which is the proceeds of crime or which has been acquired from the proceeds of crime and has a value of not less than €12,700. Such affidavit or oral evidence can be admitted as proof of its contents in the context of an application for an interim or interlocutory order under the Act.[142] In the case of an interlocutory order only oral evidence will be admissible for this purpose.

---

[139] *Manson v. District Judge O'Donnell et al.* unreported, High Court, January 27, 2000.
[140] Income Tax Act 1967, s.500(4), as inserted by Finance Act 1980, s.57. See now Taxes Consolidation Act 1997, s. 1052(4).
[141] [1993] 3 I.R. 603.
[142] Proceeds of Crime Act 1996, s.8.

F. Evidence through Video and TV Link

1. Introduction

The prosecution of charges involving allegations of child sexual abuse often   **18–27**
involve young children being examined and cross-examined as witnesses in
open court. This can be a terrifying experience for any young child, particularly where, as is normally the case, it involves the child victim having to
confront his or her abuser. Indeed prosecutions have been lost purely as a
result of child witnesses not being able to cope with the demands of the
criminal trial. Many more have not been pursued by the DDP on the basis that
the key child witnesses would not be able to cope with the challenge of
confronting their abuser and giving evidence against him in the unfamiliar
and intimidating environment of the criminal court. Public concern at this
situation eventually resulted in the enactment of measures to protect children
from the obligation of having to confront their abuser and submit to
examination and cross-examination in open court. These measures, contained
in the Criminal Evidence Act 1992, are not confined solely to very young
children nor to the prosecution of charges involving child sexual abuse. It is
also worth noting at the outset that the relevant provisions in the Act only
come into operation on such day or days as may be fixed by order of the
Minister for Justice, Equality and Law Reform.[143] Moreover, any of the
provisions may be brought into force on different days for different courts
and for different circuits and district court districts.

2. Live Television Link

In any case involving a sexual offence[144] or an offence involving violence or   **18–28**
the threat of violence to a person, evidence may be given, whether from within
or outside the State, through a live television link by a person under 17 years
of age.[145] This extends to a person with a mental handicap who has reached

---

[143] Criminal Evidence Act 1992, s.1(3).
[144] This is defined as: rape; an offence under s.3 of the Criminal Law (Sexual Offences) Act 1993;
sexual assault within the meaning of s.2 of the Criminal Law (Rape)(Amendment) Act 1990;
aggravated sexual assault (within the meaning of s. 3 of the 1990 Act); rape under s.4 of the 1990
Act; or an offence under: (i) s.3 (as amended by s.8 of the Criminal Law Amendment Act 1935),
s.6 (as amended by s.9 of that Act) or s.11 of the Criminal Law Amendment Act 1885, (ii) s.4 of
the Criminal Law (Sexual Offences) Act 1993, (iii) s.1 (as amended by s.12 of the Criminal
Justice Act 1993 and s.5 of the Criminal Law (Incest Proceedings) Act 1995) or s.2 (as amended
by s.12 of the Act of 1935) of the Punishment of Incest Act 1908 (now repealed by the Children
Act 2001, but there is comparable provision for a person under 18 years of age in s. 255 of the
2001 Act), (iv) s.17 (as amended by s.11 of the Act of 1935) of the Children Act 1908, or (iv) ss. 1
or 2 of the Act of 1935, or (v) s.5 of the Criminal Law (Sexual Offences) Act 1993. Excluded is an
attempt to commit any such offence. See Criminal Evidence Act 1992, s.2(1), as amended by
Criminal Justice (Miscellaneous Provisions) Act 1997, s.16. But see the immediately proceeding
footnote.
[145] Criminal Evidence Act 1992, s.13(1). Also covered is an offence consisting of attempting or
conspiring to commit, or of aiding, abetting, counselling, procuring or inciting the commission of
a sexual offence or an offence involving violence or the threat of violence to a person; s.12(c). The
inclusion of an attempt to commit a sexual offence would appear to conflict with the definition of
a sexual offence in s.2(1) which excludes an attempt to commit a sexual offence.

the age of 17 years.[146] While the provision clearly covers the child victim it is worth noting that it also extends to any qualifying person irrespective of whether he or she is a witness for the prosecution or the defence. The accused, however, is specifically excluded. Where these requirements are satisfied the witness's evidence can be given through a live television link unless the court sees good reason to the contrary. The court may also give leave for evidence to be given through a live television link by any person (apart from the accused) and for any offence in any other case.[147]

Where evidence is given through a live television link under these provisions neither the judge, nor the barrister or solicitor concerned in the examination of the witness should wear a wig or gown, unless the evidence is given through an intermediary (see below).[148] The evidence must also be video-recorded.[149]

This facility to give evidence through a live television link means that the witness can give his or her evidence without having to be physically present in the courtroom. Apart from that, however, the proceedings will follow their normal course. In the case of the actual trial the witness will give his or her evidence live and will be examined and cross-examined by the prosecution and defence just as if he or she was physically present in the court. The same applies on an application to dismiss charges under section 4E of the Criminal Procedure Act 1967 and where depositions are being taken before a judge of the District Court pursuant to section 4F of the Criminal Procedure Act 1967. Where the evidence is being given in the trial, the witness will normally give the evidence by television link from a room located within the actual court building where the trial is being held. Typically this room will be furnished to make the witness feel at ease. Nevertheless, it may happen that this falls short of what is required to enable the witness to give a full and frank account of his or her evidence. Accordingly, there is provision for the witness to be questioned through an intermediary.

These provisions were brought into force for the Dublin Metropolitan District of the District Court on September 30, 1993 by the Criminal Evidence Act 1992 (Commencement) Order, 1993 (S.I. No.288 of 1993) and for the Central Criminal Court and the Dublin Circuit Criminal Court on February 15, 1993 by the Criminal Evidence Act 1992 (Commencement) Order, 1993 (S.I. No.38 of 1993).

3. Questioning through Intermediary

18–29   Where a person under 17 years of age is giving evidence through a television link pursuant to these provisions, the court may, on the application of the prosecution or the accused, direct that the witness be questioned through an

---

[146] Criminal Evidence Act 1992, s.19.
[147] *ibid.* s.13(1)(b).
[148] *ibid.* s.13(3).
[149] *ibid.* s.13(2).

intermediary.[150] This extends to a person with a mental handicap who has reached the age of 17 years.[151] The court may issue such a direction if it is satisfied that, having regard to the age or mental condition of the witness, the interests of justice require that any questions put to the witness should be put through an intermediary. In this event the questions put to the witness by the intermediary must be put either in the words used by the questioner or in a manner which conveys to the witness, in a way which is appropriate to his or her age and mental condition, the meaning of the questions being asked.[152] The intermediary will be appointed by the court and must be a person who, in its opinion, is competent to act in this capacity.[153]

4. Identifying the Accused

The issue of identification often proves a traumatic experience for a child victim or child witness of sexual abuse, particularly where the accused is another family member. Giving evidence through a live television link will not always be sufficient to protect the witness from the trauma involved. Accordingly, it is provided that where a witness is giving evidence through a live television link in a case where evidence is given that the accused was known to him or her prior to the commission of the alleged offence, the witness shall not be required to identify the accused at the trial of the offence unless the court in the interests of justice directs otherwise.[154] In any other case, evidence given by a person other than the witness that the witness identified the accused at an identification parade as being the offender shall be admissible as evidence that the accused was so identified.[155]

18–30

5. Video-recorded Evidence

The child witness may even be spared the experience of having to give evidence through a live television link during the criminal trial of a sexual offence or an offence involving violence or the threat of violence. A video-recording[156] of his or her evidence or statement will be admissible in certain circumstances once the relevant statutory provisions have been fully brought into force by ministerial order.[157] If a person under 17 years of age has given evidence through a live television link in proceedings to which Part 1A of the

18–31

---

150 *ibid.* s.14(1). These provisions have been brought into effect on March 3, 1997 by Criminal Evidence Act 1992 (Sections 14 and 19)(Commencement) Order 1997.
151 Criminal Evidence Act 1992, s.19.
152 *ibid.* s.14(2).
153 *ibid.* s.14(3).
154 *ibid.* s.18(i). S.18 was brought into effect from February 15, 1993 by the Criminal Evidence Act 1992 (Commencement) Order 1993.
155 Criminal Evidence Act 1992, s.18(ii).
156 "Video-recording" is defined as any recording, on any medium, from which a moving image may by any means be produced and includes the accompanying soundtrack (if any), and cognate words shall be construed accordingly; Criminal Evidence Act 1992, s.2(1).
157 In this context, "statement" includes any representation of fact whether in words or otherwise; Criminal Evidence Act 1992, s.16(4).

Criminal Procedure Act 1967 applies (application to dismiss, or the taking of a deposition before a judge of the District Court), a video-recording of the evidence is generally admissible at the subsequent trial as evidence of any fact stated therein of which direct oral evidence by the witness would be admissible.[158] This extends to a person with a mental handicap who has reached the age of 17 years.[159] In the case of a person under 14 years of age who is the victim of the offence charged (or a victim suffering from a mental handicap who has reached the age of 14 years),[160] a video-recording of his or her statement during an interview with a member of the Garda Síochána, or any other person competent for the purpose, will be admissible on the same terms.[161] In this case, however, the video-recording will be admissible only if the person who made the statement is available at the trial for cross-examination.[162]

The admissibility of a video-recording under these provisions cannot be admitted in evidence if the court is of the opinion that in the interests of justice it ought not to be admitted.[163] This discretion can be applied to exclude the whole recording or any part of it. In considering whether it ought not to be admitted the court must have regard to all of the circumstances, including any risk that its admission will result in unfairness to the accused.[164] Where a video-recording is admitted in evidence the question of what weight should be attached to any statement contained in it will have to be considered. For this purpose regard must be had to all the circumstances from which any inference can reasonably be drawn as to its accuracy.[165] It is also worth noting that if a video-recording is admissible a copy of the video-recording will be admissible where authenticated in such manner as may be approved by the court.[166]

6. Evidence from outside the State

18–32   The benefits of technology can also be used to overcome the problems posed by the fact that a witness is outside the State and will not be available to give evidence in person at the actual trial. If the witness is a person under the age of 17 years and the circumstances come within the provisions described above there will be no problem. His or her evidence can be taken by live television link as described above. In any other case a person (apart from the accused) who is outside the State may, with the leave of the court, give evidence in any criminal proceedings through a live television link.[167] There

---

[158] Criminal Evidence Act 1992, s.16(1)(a), as amended by Criminal Justice Act 1999, s.20(a). This was brought into force for the Dublin Metropolitan District of the District Court on September 30, 1993 by Criminal Evidence Act 1992 (Sections 13, 15(4), 16, 17 and 19)(Commencement) Order, 1993.
[159] Criminal Evidence Act 1992, s.19.
[160] *ibid.* s.19.
[161] *ibid.* s.16(1)(b). This provision has not yet been brought into force.
[162] *ibid.* as amended by Criminal Justice Act 1999, s.20(b).
[163] *ibid.* s.16(2)(a).
[164] *ibid.* s.16(2)(b).
[165] *ibid.* s.16(3).
[166] *ibid.* s.30.
[167] *ibid.* s.29(1). S. 29 was brought into force on October 6, 1997 by the Criminal Evidence Act 1992 (Section 29) (Commencement) Order 1997.

are no restrictions relevant to the nature of the offence charged. Evidence given pursuant to this provision must be video-recorded.[168] If, while giving evidence, the person makes a statement material in the proceedings which he knows to be false or does not believe to be true he shall be guilty of perjury irrespective of his nationality.[169] Proceedings for such perjury may be taken, and the offence may for all incidental purposes be treated as having been committed, in any place in this State.[170]

7. Court Facilities

Clearly, there will have to be appropriate facilities available in the court room **18–33** to receive evidence by live television link or even by video. In the case of a child witness in an abuse case it may also be necessary to have a specially furnished room available in the court building to facilitate the taking of evidence through the live television link. It is for this reason that the relevant provisions of the Criminal Evidence Act 1992 will only come into force by order of the Minister for Justice Equality and Law Reform, and even then at different times for different courts and court locations. The measures can only be applied in those courtrooms where the appropriate facilities are available. At present the provisions have been put into operation for: the Dublin Metropolitan District of the District Court, the Central Criminal Court and the Dublin Circuit Criminal Court.[171] Where proceedings for a relevant offence arise in a circuit or district court area in respect of which the provisions have not been brought into effect, the court may by order transfer the proceedings to another district in which they are in operation.[172] The court may issue such order where it is of the opinion that it is desirable that evidence be given in the proceedings through a live television link or by means of a video-recording. Once the order is made the jurisdiction of the court to which the proceedings have been transferred may be exercised by a judge of the circuit concerned in the case of the Circuit Court, and by a judge for the time being assigned to the district court district concerned in the case of the District Court.

8. Constitutionality of TV Link Provisions

The provisions in the 1992 Act permitting a witness to give evidence through **18–34** a live television link in certain circumstances raise issues of fundamental fairness of procedures in a criminal trial. In particular, they pose the question of whether it is implicit in the notion of fairness to a person accused of criminal behaviour that he be afforded the opportunity to confront his accuser in the physical presence of the tribunal of fact. In *White v. Ireland*[173] Kinlen J.

---

[168] Criminal Evidence Act 1992, s.29(2).
[169] *ibid*. s.29(3)
[170] *ibid*. s.29(4).
[171] Criminal Evidence Act 1992 (Commencement) Order, 1993 (S.I. Nos. 38 and 288).
[172] Criminal Evidence Act 1992, s.17. This was brought into force on September 30, 1993 by the Criminal Evidence Act 1992 (Sections 13, 15(4), 16, 17 and 19)(Commencement) Order 1993.
[173] [1995] 2 I.R. 268.

ruled in the High Court that the accused did not enjoy a constitutional right to an "eye-ball to eye-ball" confrontation with his accuser in the course of the criminal trial. The issue was subsequently considered by the Supreme Court on appeal from the judgment of Costello P. in *Donnelly v. Ireland*.[174] In that case the accused was charged with sexual assault contrary to the Criminal Law (Rape)(Amendment) Act 1990. His victim was a girl who was 14 years of age at the time she came to give evidence in the case. Seven days prior to the trial the prosecution informed the accused that they intended to rely on the provisions of the 1992 Act for the purpose of adducing evidence from the victim by means of a live television link. The accused's objections to the fairness of this procedure were overruled by the trial judge and the victim proceeded to give her evidence through the live television link and the accused was convicted. The accused sought to have the conviction quashed on the ground that the statutory provisions permitting the victim to give evidence through a live television link were unconstitutional. He lost in the High Court and appealed to the Supreme Court.

The fundamental issue for determination by the Supreme Court was whether a person charged with an offence within the scope of section 12 of the 1992 Act has a constitutional right to confront his accuser in open court when the latter is giving evidence at the trial. The Constitution, of course, does not confer such a right explicitly. The question, therefore, was whether it was implicit in the individual's constitutional right to fair procedures guaranteed by Articles 38.1 and 40.3.1°. Hamilton C.J. giving the judgment of the Supreme Court, acknowledged that the words "in due of course of law" in Article 38.1 make it mandatory that every criminal trial shall be conducted in accordance with the concept of justice, that the procedures shall be fair and that the person accused will be afforded every opportunity to defend himself. Quoting from the judgment of Gannon J. in *State (Healy) v. Donoghue*[175] he noted that an essential ingredient in the concept of fair procedures is that an accused person should have the opportunity to hear and test by examination the evidence offered by or on behalf of an accuser. The purpose of such cross-examination was to test the credibility of the witness. The key issue, therefore, was whether the witness' credibility could be tested effectively only if he or she gave evidence and submitted to cross-examination in the physical presence of the accused. Hamilton C.J. ruled that the physical presence of the witness was not essential for this purpose:

> "The court is satisfied, however, that the assessment of such credibility does not require that the witness should be required to give evidence in the physical presence of the accused person and that the requirements of fair procedure are adequately fulfilled by requiring that the witness give evidence on oath and be subjected to cross-examination and that the judge and jury have ample opportunity to observe the demeanour of the witness while giving evidence and being subjected to cross-examination. In this way an accused person's right to a fair trial is adequately protected and vindicated. Such right does not include

---

[174] [1998] 1 I.L.R.M. 402 (SC); unreported, High Court, December 9, 1996.
[175] [1976] I.R. 325.

the right in all circumstances to require that the evidence be given in his physical presence and consequently there is no such constitutional right."[176]

The net effect of the Supreme Court's decision is that an accused does not enjoy a distinct constitutional right to have a witness give evidence and submit to cross examination in his physical presence. Accordingly, the relevant provisions of the 1992 Act were not unconstitutional solely by virtue of the fact that they permitted a child witness to give evidence in certain circumstances through the medium of a live television link.

It does not follow automatically that the procedure for giving evidence through a television link satisfies the constitutional requirement of fair procedures. Indeed, the appellant argued that even if the accused did not enjoy a distinct constitutional right to have prosecution witnesses give evidence in his physical presence, the procedure introduced by the 1992 Act still fell below what was required by fair procedures. In particular, he relied upon the fact that the legislation did not require a case by case determination of whether the prosecution should be permitted to avail of the television link procedure. Closely associated with this was the argument that the legislation placed an unfair onus on the accused by requiring him to establish the witness' competence to undertake a face-to-face confrontation with the accused. Hamilton C.J., however, dismissed these arguments cursorily by stating that in the absence of a specific constitutional right it was a matter for the Oireachtas to determine the circumstances in which evidence could be given other than in the presence of the accused. Such statutory measures would benefit from the presumption of constitutionality and the appellant would have to discharge the heavy burden of establishing clearly that the measures amounted to unfair procedures and were repugnant to the Constitution. The learned Chief Justice ruled that the appellant had failed to discharge this burden with respect to the relevant provisions in the 1992 Act.

Hamilton C.J. did not list the factors which persuaded him that the procedure introduced by the relevant provisions of the 1992 Act were consistent with the constitutional norms governing a fair trial. It is apparent from his judgment, however, that he was heavily influenced by the fact that giving evidence through the live television link procedure would not detract from the fact that the witnesses would still have to give evidence on oath and submit to cross-examination in the sight and sound of the judge and jury. It was only the physical presence of the witnesses that would be lacking. The Chief Justice also referred specifically to the protection afforded the accused by virtue of the fact that the legislation enables a young person to give evidence through a live television link "unless the court sees good reason to the contrary", and that any other person can give evidence in a similar manner only "with the leave of the court". In considering either of these issues a judge would be obliged to have regard to the accused's right to a fair trial.

Surprisingly, perhaps, Hamilton C.J. did not attempt to justify the use of the live television link procedure by reference to the nature of the circumstances

---

[176] [1998] 1 I.L.R.M. 401 at 419–420.

in which it is intended to be used. He did, however, draw strong support for his analysis from the decision of the U.S. Supreme Court in *Maryland v. Craig*.[177] In that case the U.S. Supreme Court was also called upon to consider the constitutionality of legislation which permitted an alleged victim of child abuse to give evidence against the accused through a television link rather than in the physical presence of the accused in open court. Despite the fact that the sixth Amendment to the American Constitution specifically guarantees the accused a right, *inter alia*, "to be confronted with the witnesses against him" the court upheld the constitutionality of the relevant statutory provisions. It ruled that the confrontation clause in the sixth Amendment does not guarantee the accused an absolute right to a face-to-face meeting with prosecution witnesses at the trial. The central concern of this clause was to ensure the reliability of testimony against the accused by subjecting it to a rigorous testing in the context of an adversarial proceeding before the tribunal of fact. The absence of a physical confrontation, therefore, would not automatically amount to an infringement of the confrontation clause in the Sixth Amendment. Nevertheless, the U.S. Supreme Court cautioned that the clause reflects a preference for a face-to-face confrontation at trial, and that this right may not be dispensed with easily. Indeed, it could be excluded only where that was necessary to further an important public policy and only where the reliability of accusatory witnesses is otherwise assured.

---

[177] (1989) 497 US 836.

CHAPTER 19

TRIAL PROCEDURE

A. Introduction

The primary function of the criminal trial is the determination of whether the **19–01** accused is guilty or not guilty of the offence or offences charged. In Ireland, the trial is conducted on an accusatorial and adversarial basis. The onus is on the prosecution to prove the charge or charges against the accused beyond a reasonable doubt. In pursuit of this object counsel for the prosecution must operate within the rules of evidence and trial procedure. The defence, as will be seen later, can leave the prosecution to its proof and opt not to participate in the trial other than by entering a plea of not guilty and testing the prosecution case. If, however, the accused wishes to present a defence he, too, must do so within the relevant rules of evidence and trial procedure.

This chapter will deal primarily with the procedural aspects of the trial while the preceding chapter deals with certain matters of evidence. In practice, of course, it is not always possible to treat the two separately in a clinical fashion. Inevitably, aspects of trial procedure can only be understood meaningfully in the light of matters which might be classified more appropriately as rules of evidence. Accordingly, the division between the two chapters is more a reflection of convenience of exposition rather than any strict doctrinal distinction.

B. The Players

1. The Judge

The primary players in a criminal trial are the judge, the prosecution, the **19–02** defence and, in a trial on indictment in the Circuit Court or the Central

Criminal Court, the jury. The general responsibility to ensure that the trial is conducted in a fair and proper manner falls on the judge. He or she interprets and enforces the rules of evidence and procedure governing the trial. His or her role differs, however, depending on whether the trial is by judge and jury or by a judge sitting alone. In the former the judge presides over the court and determines all matters of law and procedure. He or she will explain the legal principles and rules which the jury must apply in order to decide whether the accused is guilty or not guilty. The actual determination of facts, including the guilt or innocence of the accused, is the preserve of the jury. In a trial by a judge sitting alone the judge is the arbiter of both law and fact.

The judge can call a witness and is entitled to question or cross-examine any witness called by either side, including the accused in a case where he gives evidence on oath. In our adversarial system of trial, however, the primary responsibility for adducing relevant evidence and testing that evidence falls on the prosecution and defence respectively. For the most part the judge plays the role of an umpire interpreting and enforcing the rules of the adversarial contest. Where he or she does intervene to question witnesses for either side it is usually for the purpose of clearing up any ambiguity or misunderstanding.[1] It would be quite improper for the judge to engage in extensive cross-examination of a witness or witnesses or to do so in a manner which usurps the role of the prosecution or defence. Even constant interruptions of the defence case by the judge may constitute grounds to quash a conviction.

19–03 In *People v. McGuinness*[2] the Court of Criminal Appeal had to consider whether a conviction for rape should be quashed due to the nature and extent of the trial judge's interruptions in the examination and cross-examination of witnesses. The accused's defence was consent. At the time of the trial it was permissible to cross-examine the complainant about her character and behaviour in an attempt to show that she would be likely to consent. Kenny J. considered that in such a case the cross-examination of the complainant would be the most important evidential part of the trial. It will have been very carefully planned by counsel in advance and, in the interests of a fair trial for the accused, he must be allowed to follow it without unnecessary interruptions:

> "Counsel for the accused will be severely handicapped if he is diverted from his plan. When the defence to such a charge is consent, the cross-examination of the complainant is the most important evidential part of the trial. It may be long, but counsel should be allowed to return to matters he has already dealt with if he has succeeded in showing that on other matters the witness is not to be believed. The judge must be patient and confine his intervention to the minimum necessary for a fair trial. The judge should intervene only when cross-examining counsel mis-states evidence already given or asks a question which the witness may not understand, or when the judge thinks that the witness has misunderstood the question. When the defence is consent, the

---

[1] See, *e.g., DPP v. Kiely* Unreported Court of Criminal Appeal, March 21, 2001.
[2] *People v. McGuinness* [1978] I.R. 189.

judge must allow unpleasant charges to be made against the complainant in connection with her past: he should not indicate to the jury that he disapproves of this being done."[3]

In this case the cross-examination of the complainant consisted of 423 questions, 123 of which were put directly by the judge and which were not confined to clarifying answers already given or clearing up ambiguities. They included as many as 17 consecutive questions. The judge also made about 60 additional remarks and directions to the jury. The Court of Criminal Appeal considered that:

" . . . the number of questions put by the judge and the many interventions made by him made it impossible for [defence counsel] to conduct a cross-examination on the lines he considered would be most effective and could have had the effect of causing the jury to believe that the judge had formed a definite opinion as to the credibility of the complainant."[4]

In addition the judge asked 20 consecutive questions of the complainant's mother. The court considered that an active participation by a trial judge in the examination-in-chief of witnesses is also undesirable as it may convey the impression to the accused or the jury of a lack of impartiality on his part.

The court felt that the effect of the judge's interventions was to render the trial unsatisfactory, despite the fact that there was ample evidence upon which the jury could have convicted. Accordingly, the court set the conviction aside and ordered a new-trial.

Although the Court of Criminal Appeal emphasised the distinctive nature of a rape trial in which the defence is consent, it is apparent that the general approach of the court in that case to judicial interventions is generally applicable. Indeed, the court approved the following passage from the judgment of Denning L.J. which set out the relevant principles and rationale for those principles in the civil case of *Jones v. National Coal Board*:

19–04

"Now it cannot, of course, be doubted that a judge is not only entitled but is, indeed, bound to intervene at any stage of a witness's evidence if he feels that, by reason of the technical nature of the evidence or otherwise, it is only by putting questions of his own that he can properly follow and appreciate what the witness is saying. Nevertheless, it is obvious for more than one reason that such interventions should be as infrequent as possible when the witness is under cross-examination. It is only by cross-examination that a witness's evidence can be properly tested, and it loses much of its effectiveness in counsel's hands if the witness is given time to think out the answer to awkward questions; the very gist of cross-examination lies in the unbroken sequence of question and answer. Further than this, cross-examining counsel is at a grave disadvantage if he is prevented from following a preconceived line of inquiry which is, in his view, most likely to elicit admissions from the witness or qualifications of the evidence which he has given in chief.

---

[3] *ibid.* at 190–191.
[4] *ibid.* at 191.

Excessive judicial interruption inevitably weakens the effectiveness of cross-examination in relation to both the aspects which we have mentioned, for at one and the same time it gives a witness valuable time for thought before answering a difficult question, and diverts cross-examining counsel from the course which he had intended to pursue, and to which it is by no means easy sometimes to return."[5]

2. Counsel

19–05   In a trial on indictment both the prosecution and the defence are normally represented by counsel. Counsel for the prosecution will be nominated by the DPP, apart from the rare cases in which they must be nominated by the Attorney-General.[6] Although the accused is entitled to conduct his case in person he will almost invariably be represented by counsel. In the District Court the prosecution may be represented by counsel appointed by the DPP or the Chief Prosecution Solicitor. It is also quite common for the local State Solicitor to act in person and, indeed, in some parts of the country many summary prosecutions are conducted by a Garda Superintendent. The accused will frequently be represented by a solicitor in summary proceedings, although it is not unusual for him to be represented by counsel. Where the accused intends to plead guilty at summary trial he may opt not to seek legal representation, particularly where the likely outcome is a small fine.

Although the trial is conducted on an adversarial basis counsel for either side do not have complete freedom over the tactics they may employ in order to secure a victory. Their status as officers of the court tailors, in different ways, the duty that they owe to their respective clients. This is particularly marked in the case of counsel for the prosecution. While his or her immediate role is to present the case for the prosecution with a view to securing a conviction on behalf of the State, this must not be discharged in a manner which conflicts with his or her primary responsibility which is to assist in the administration of justice. It is no part of his or her function to obtain a conviction at all costs. He or she must exhibit all the facts to the jury fairly and impartially by giving them guidance as to the law, subject to the directions of the judge, as may be necessary for them to apply the facts to the case.[7]

19–06   The role of counsel for the defence is very neatly summarised in the following statement of principle by the Chairman of the English Bar in 1976:

"It is the duty of counsel when defending an accused on a criminal charge to present to the court, fearlessly and without regard to his personal interests, the defence of the accused. It is not his function to determine the truth or falsity of that defence, nor should he permit his personal opinion of that defence to influence his conduct of it. No counsel may refuse to defend because of his

---

[5]   *ibid.* at 192–193, quoting from [1957] 2 Q.B. 55 at 65.
[6]   See, *e.g.*, Fisheries Act 1978, s.18.
[7]   *R v. Puddick* 4 F&F 497; *R v. Banks* [1916] 2 K.B. 621. See E Ryan and P Magee *The Irish Criminal Process* (Mercier Press, Dublin, 1983), p.307.

opinion of the character of the accused nor of the crime charged. That is a rule of the Bar, and it would be a grave matter in any free society were it not. Counsel also has a duty to the court and to the public. This duty includes the clear presentation of the issues and the avoidance of waste of time, repetition and prolixity. In the conduct of every case counsel must be mindful of this public responsibility."[8]

Although counsel for the defence clearly enjoys greater latitude than counsel for the prosecution in representing the interests of his or her client, there are limits to the strategies that he can adopt with a view to securing an acquittal.[9] His duty to the court prevents him from asserting anything on behalf of his client which he knows to be a lie. Equally, he or she may not connive at nor attempt to substantiate a fraud. Where counsel knows that his or her client has committed the offence his or her role will be confined largely to putting the prosecution to its proof and making submissions on the law. She must not put her client into the witness box to give evidence which she knows is false, nor may she adduce evidence which she knows to be false. Her duty to the court precludes any such course of action in the interests of her client. For the most part counsel's role in such a case will be confined to raising technical objections to the admissibility of evidence, cross-examining witnesses for the prosecution and making submissions on the relevant law.

In order to fulfil his duty to his client the defence counsel must be properly instructed and have adequate time to prepare the defence. The Bar Council has ruled in this regard that a barrister should not conduct a criminal case on indictment unless given instructions at least one week in advance of the hearing.[10] Instructions in this context include: the book of evidence, a statement from the accused taken by his solicitor, the indictment, the statements of any witnesses to be called on behalf of the accused, and confirmation that any proofs advised by the barrister have been carried out.

3. The Jury

The composition and empanelling of the jury is covered in chapter 17. The essential role of the jury is to determine whether the accused is guilty or not guilty in a case where the accused has pleaded not guilty, or where a plea of not guilty has been entered on his behalf, to one or more counts on the indictment. Once the jury has been empanelled and the trial is ready to begin the accused is given into their charge. The count or counts to which the accused has pleaded not guilty are read over to the jury who are informed that the issue which they have to try with respect to each is whether the accused is guilty or not guilty.

19–07

Typically, the jurors will spend most of their time throughout the trial listening passively to the evidence, the submissions of counsel and the

---

[8] Ryan and Magee *The Irish Criminal Process* (Mercier Press, Dublin, 1983), *op. cit.*, p.309. See 62 Cr.App.R. 193–4.

[9] *ibid.* pp.308–309.

[10] Bar Council Ruling, May 21, 1979; cited in Ryan and Magee, *op. cit.*, p.308; see also, *People (DPP) v. McDonagh* [2001] 3 I.R. 411.

directions of the judge before retiring to consider their verdict in private. It is critically important, of course, that the jury's verdict should not be tainted as a result of having heard or considered inadmissible evidence. Accordingly, the jury will be required to retire temporarily during the course of a trial while arguments over the admissibility of evidence are presented and considered in a *voir dire*. There is also provision for the jury to leave the courtroom to view a specific place. Under the Juries Act 1976 the judge may at any time before the jury have given their verdict direct that the jurors shall have a view of any specific place, which in his or her opinion it is expedient that they should see.[11] To this end the judge may adjourn the trial at such stage and for such time as appears to be convenient. However, the judge may only make an order under this provision on the application of the prosecution or the accused.[12] He or she must also give such directions as appear to him or her to be expedient for the purpose of preventing any undue communication with the jurors during the execution of the order.[13]

The jurors may separate before considering their verdict unless the judge directs otherwise.[14] In a trial lasting more than one day the jurors will normally separate at the end of each day's proceedings. Once they have retired to consider their verdict, however, they must not separate until discharged by the court. In any case where they have not managed to reach a verdict by late evening it is standard practice for the judge to send them to an hotel for the night. Where the judge directs that the jury should not separate, or if they have retired to consider their verdict, they are put in charge of an officer of the court or a police officer.[15] This officer is under a duty not to permit separation or conversation with third parties.

19–08 Whether they have separated or not the jurors will be under strict instructions not to discuss the case with anyone other than themselves.[16] There is always the danger that improper communications between a member or members of the jury and a third party will render the trial unsatisfactory. Where it transpires during the course of the trial that there has been such communication the judge must consider whether in all the circumstances there is a real danger that the accused will be prejudiced by continuing the trial with the jury as originally constituted. The mere fact that there has been communication is not sufficient in itself to constitute prejudice. In *R v. Sawyer*,[17] for example, three jurors had talked to prosecution witnesses in the court restaurant during an adjournment. The English Court of Appeal, however, ruled that there was no prejudice to the accused as their conversation had

---

[11] Juries Act 1976, s.22(1).
[12] *ibid.*, s.22(3).
[13] *ibid.*, s.22(4).
[14] *ibid.*, s.25.
[15] Ryan and Magee, *op. cit.*, p.311.
[16] *R v. Prime* (1973) 57 Cr.App.R. 632.
[17] (1980) 71 Cr.App.R. 283. See also *People v. Quinn* [1965] I.R. 366 where the Supreme Court ruled that a brief conversation between a juror and the accused did not prejudice a fair hearing. For a more extreme example, see *R v. Spencer* [1985] 2 W.L.R. 197.

been about neutral matters unconnected with the trial. It would appear that the courts are more sensitive to improper communications when the jury has not separated. In *People v. Heffernan (No.2)*,[18] for example, the Court of Criminal Appeal accepted that members of the jury mixing with strangers over a prolonged period during a murder trial could be sufficient to render a trial unsatisfactory even though the accused was not shown to have been prejudiced.

Even if the judge concludes that there is a risk of prejudice from the improper communication between a member or members of the jury and a third party it does not follow that he or she must abort the trial. It may be that discharging the juror or jurors in question will be sufficient to protect the accused, so long as there are sufficient jurors left to carry on with the trial. In making this determination the judge will have to consider the extent to which the errant juror or jurors may have influenced their colleagues against the accused by passing on any information or views which they acquired from their third–party communications. In *R v. Spencer*,[19] for example, an individual juror was discharged for having improper conversations with a third party in circumstances which were likely to prejudice him against the accused. After being discharged the juror gave a lift home to three of his former colleagues on the jury for an overnight adjournment. Although the Court of Appeal accepted that the case was discussed on that journey it upheld the trial judge's refusal to discharge the three jurors and thereby abort the trial. The court was of the opinion that it was unlikely that any of the three jurors would have been prejudiced in their subsequent deliberations as a result of their conversation with their discharged colleague. It would appear, therefore, that the court may require more than the appearance of possible prejudice before aborting a trial due to the transgressions of some of the jurors.

4. Language

The proceedings will normally be conducted in the English language. The accused, however, has a constitutional right to give his evidence in Irish and to be cross-examined in Irish. It does not follow that he has a constitutional right to have whole proceedings conducted in Irish. The accused and other witnesses are also entitled to give their evidence in the their own vernacular language. Indeed, the accused has a right to have evidence given against him to be given in his own vernacular language. Where any of these situations arise there is an obligation on the State to provide the necessary interpretation facilities to ensure that the members of the court can follow the evidence. In *Attorney General v. Joyce*, a case in which several witnesses, including the two accused, gave their evidence in the Irish language, Kennedy C.J. explained the position as follows:

---

[18] [1950] I.R. 206, following *R v. Taylor* [1950] N.I. 57.
[19] [1985] 2 W.L.R. 197.

"It would seem to me to be a requisite of natural justice, particularly in a criminal trial, that a witness should be allowed to give evidence in the language which is his or her vernacular language, whether that language be Irish or English, or any foreign language; and it would follow, if the language used should not be a language known to the members of the Court, that means of interpreting the language to the Court (judge and jury), and also, in the case of evidence against a prisoner, that means of interpreting it to the prisoner, should be provided. The Irish language, however, is not merely the vernacular language of most, if not all of the witnesses in question in the present case, but it holds a special position by virtue of the Constitution of the Saorstát, in which its status is recognised and established as the national language of the Saorstát, from which it follows that, whether it be the vernacular language of a particular citizen or not, if he is competent to use the language, he is entitled to do so. Therefore, it may be said that all those who gave their evidence in the Irish language in the present case had, as it were, a double right to do so: first, on general principles of natural justice as their vernacular language; and second, as a matter of Constitutional right."[19a]

Where there is a need to provide a translation of evidence, even from Irish to English, it will be unlawful to hear the case without the benefit of an interpreter.[19b]

C. The Prosecution Case

1. Introduction

19–09   In presenting the case against the accused, counsel for the prosecution must confine himself or herself to evidence which connects the accused with the offence charged. Evidence to the effect that the accused has committed other offences, or has a criminal record, and is therefore the sort of person who would commit the offence charged is generally inadmissible. There are, of course, exceptions such as where the evidence in question qualifies as "system evidence" as distinct from "similar fact evidence" or where the accused has put his own character in issue or attacked the character of prosecution witnesses. The law pertaining to the admissibility of evidence, and related matters, are for the most part dealt with in the preceding chapter 9 and sporadically in some other chapters.

2. Opening

19–10   Counsel for the prosecution opens the case against the accused by giving an oral summary of the facts that he or she intends to prove to the jury. Counsel must be careful in this opening statement to avoid reference to any inadmissible evidence, or evidence the admissibility of which might be challenged by the defence. Where there is doubt over the admissibility of a particular piece

---

[19a] [1929] I.R. 526 at 581.
[19b] *O Monachain v. An Taoiseach* [1986] I.L.R.M. 660.

of evidence it might be considered good practice to sound out the defence on what their attitude is likely to be. If evidence is subsequently ruled inadmissible, the fact that the prosecution has disclosed its existence in the opening summary may result in the jury being discharged and a new trial being ordered.

It is not normally necessary to prove that the accused has been sent forward for trial. Nevertheless, if it is questioned then it should be proved. There is a prima facie presumption of its validity.[20]

3. Prosecution Witnesses

As a general rule evidence for the prosecution must be given orally. While documents which "prove themselves" may be submitted in evidence without the need for direct oral evidence of their contents, this is very much the exception. It was seen in the preceding chapter that recent statutory enactments have expanded the range of situations in which documentary evidence may be submitted in evidence as proof of their contents. For the most part, however, these provisions are confined to uncontentious matters concerning certain formalities done by members of the Garda Síochána during the investigation or pre–trial process. Their purpose is to save gardai from spending valuable time waiting around in court to give evidence which will have little or no substantive bearing on the outcome of the case. In other words they fall very far short of a move towards the sort of written processes which are a feature of the criminal process in civil law jurisdictions. The prosecution case in Irish courts is still presented primarily through the medium of witnesses who are called to give their evidence in person.

19–11

The prosecution should call to give evidence, or make available, all witnesses whom it considers to be material and whose attendance can be secured.[21] This applies even with respect to witnesses whose evidence may not be fully supportive of the prosecution case.[22] Indeed, it is worth remembering in this context that counsel is an officer of the court and his or her primary duty is to assist in the administration of justice rather than to secure a conviction. He or she is generally bound to produce all witnesses who made depositions and, so far as he or she can, to produce for the purpose of the defence any witness whom the accused requires for this purpose.[22a] Nevertheless, it is likely that this duty would not oblige him or her to call witnesses whose evidence he or she considers to be false. Equally, he or she enjoys a wide discretion with respect to the evidence he or she considers material. In *People (Attorney General) v. Kerins*,[23] for example, the Court of Criminal Appeal considered that the prosecutor was justified in not calling evidence of a fingerprint on an automatic pistol which had been found at the scene of a

---

[20] *People v. Hannigan* [1958] I.R. 378; *State (Attorney General) v. Binchy* [1964] I.R. 395; *State (Smith) v. Governor of Mountjoy Prison* 102 I.L.T.R. 93.
[21] *People v. Byrne* [1974] I.R. 1.
[22] *People v. Kerins* [1945] I.R. 339.
[22a] *O'Regan v. DPP* [2002] 2 I.L.R.M. 68.
[23] [1945] I.R. 339.

capital murder. There was no suggestion that the fingerprint had been identified and the only evidence with reference to it was that of the ballistics expert who had stated that so far as he knew the fingerprint was not relative to the inquiry. It is submitted with respect that this is a decision unduly favourable to the prosecution in that evidence of the unidentified print could be relevant in mounting an argument that a third unidentified party might have been present and responsible for the shooting. In the same case the court also accepted the decision of the prosecutor not to call witnesses who failed to identify anyone at an identification parade. Counsel for the defence suggested that these witnesses had an opportunity of seeing the culprits as they cycled away from the scene of the crime. The court, however, accepted that having regard to the circumstances of the crime and the rapid disappearance of the criminals, the persons in question could not give any material evidence.

4. Evidence on Oath

19–12   At common law all evidence in a criminal trial must be given on oath. In practice, however, significant inroads have been made into this requirement by statute in the case of persons with no religious belief or who do not understand the significance of an oath. Where evidence is to be given on oath, the oath is administered by the Registrar of the Court. He or she will ask the witness to hold the New Testament (the Old Testament in the case of a Jew) in his uplifted hand and say the words: "I, (A.B.) swear by Almighty God that the evidence I shall give to the court on this trial shall be the truth, the whole truth and nothing but the truth."[24] Other formats are also possible. For example, a person may swear with uplifted hand in the form and manner usual in Scotland.[25] If the witness is neither a Christian nor a Jew the oath can be administered in any other lawful manner.[26] Indeed, a person is bound by an oath administered in any form which he declares to be binding.[27] A person who objects to be sworn, on the ground that he has no religious belief or that the taking of an oath is contrary to his religious belief, can make a solemn affirmation as follows: "I (A.B.) do solemnly, sincerely and truly declare and affirm that the evidence I shall give to the court on this trial shall be the truth, the whole truth and nothing but the truth".[28] Once an oath has been administered, however, its validity is not affected by the mere fact that the person who took it had no religious belief.[29]

5. Oral Examination

19–13   Once the witness has been duly sworn counsel for the prosecution will begin to elicit the witness's evidence through a process of question and answer

---

[24]   Oaths Act 1909, s.2(1).
[25]   Oaths Act 1888, s.5.
[26]   Oaths Act 1909, s.2(2).
[27]   Oaths Act 1838, s.1.
[28]   Oaths Act 1888, ss.1 and 2. See Quakers and Moravians Acts 1833 and 1839 for versions applicable specifically to Quakers and Moravians.
[29]   Oaths Act 1888, s.3.

known as examination. The task for counsel is to ask questions which prompt the witness to give an account of what he or she knows about the matter in question, without actually influencing the substance of the account in any particular direction by asking leading questions. A leading question in this context is a question which actually suggests the substance of the answer which counsel wants the witness to give. While keeping within the constraints of the leading question rule, counsel should also aim to keep the witness's evidence as close as possible to the contents of his statement in the book of evidence.

Relying on the oral evidence of witnesses, however, inevitably entails a certain amount of unpredictability about the evidence that will actually be given at the trial. It is always possible that a witness will say something significant in the witness box that he had not said in his earlier statement to the police or the prosecution. The admissibility of such material will not be affected merely by the fact that it was not contained in the book of evidence served on the accused. Nevertheless, it is a fundamental tenet of fair procedures that the accused is entitled to know in advance the case he will have to meet at trial. Accordingly, if the new material is prejudicial to the accused, at the very least he should be granted an adjournment to consider its implications. If the material is seriously prejudicial to the accused it may even be necessary to discharge the jury and order a new trial. Where the prosecution wish to introduce evidence which has only become available after the trial has commenced, it will normally be necessary to seek an adjournment so that the new evidence can be served on the accused and he is given an opportunity to consider it.

6. Hostile Witnesses

The prosecution case will normally consist of the evidence freely given by its **19–14** own witnesses under examination coupled with any material exhibits. Invariably the prosecution will know the substance of a witness' evidence in advance. If it happens that the account offered by a witness under examination falls short of prosecution expectations counsel will have to elicit the missing information by questioning which avoids infringement of the rule against leading questions. This need not be an unusual occurrence. It is usually associated with a witness having difficulty recalling the relevant events accurately or simply being intimidated or unnerved by the experience of having to give evidence in a courtroom. It may also happen, however, that the witness is deliberately offering a version which differs in material respects from the statement he or she originally gave to the police. Perhaps he has been intimidated or bribed by the accused in the meantime, or perhaps he has simply had a change of heart about giving evidence for the prosecution. Whatever the reason, if it appears that the witness is deliberately offering a version in the witness box which differs materially from his previous statement, the prosecution can apply to the judge for leave to treat the witness as "hostile" or "adverse":

"A party producing a witness shall not be allowed to impeach his credit by general evidence of bad character; but he may, in case the witness shall, in the opinion of the judge prove adverse, contradict him by other evidence, or by leave of the judge, prove that he has made at other times a statement inconsistent with his present testimony; but before such last-mentioned proof can be given the circumstances of the supposed statement, sufficient to designate the particular occasion, must be mentioned to the witness, and he must be asked whether or not he has made such statement."[30]

Where the prosecution (or the defence) wish to have a witness treated as "hostile" they must submit an application with supporting material to the judge in the absence of the jury.

19–15 The effect of treating a witness as "hostile" is to enable the prosecution to cross-examine the witness about having made a previous statement which does not match what he is now saying in the witness box and, where necessary, to introduce evidence of the previous inconsistent statement. It must be emphasised, however, that the previous written statement does not thereby become evidence of the facts stated in it. The witness' evidence consists of what he says in the witness box. The previous written statement is merely evidence of the fact that he has given a different version from that which he is now offering. In other words it goes to the witness' credibility. It would be difficult to improve on the following lucid account by Walsh J. of the proper procedure to be followed and the consequences which ensue in having a witness declared hostile:

"The proper procedure, if it is desired to have a witness treated as hostile, is make an application to the judge and put before him the material upon which it is sought to have the witness declared to be a hostile witness. This, of course, should be done in the absence of the jury and, if the judge rules that the witness may be treated as hostile, then the witness may be cross-examined. That is something quite different and distinct from the rules and procedure which govern the admissibility of written statements in cross-examination. This particular witness had been allowed to be treated as hostile and, when the jury were recalled to court, the proper procedure for the prosecution was to have put to the witness that she had on another occasion made a statement which differed materially from or contradicted the one she was making in the witness-box. If she were to deny that, then the proper procedure would have been to have her stand down from the box, and to prove in fact that she did in fact make a statement by putting into the box the person who took the statement, proving it in the ordinary way without revealing the contents of the statement at that stage. The earlier witness should then have been put back into the box and the statement put to her for identification, and then her attention should have been directed to the passage in which the alleged contradiction or material variation appears. If she had agreed that there was such a contradiction or material variation, that should have been an end of the matter in so far as the question of impugning her credibility was concerned because there would have been before the jury an admission from the witness

---

[30] Criminal Procedure Act 1865, s.3 (Denman's Act).

to the effect that she had made contrary statements on the same matter. The statement might then be put in evidence, though that would not be strictly necessary at that stage when the admission had been made. If she had persisted in denying the contradiction, then the statement, having already been proved, would have gone in as evidence of the fact that the witness had made a contrary statement.

It must at all times be made clear to the jury that what the witness said in the written statement is not evidence of the fact referred to but is only evidence on the question of whether or not she has said something else – it is evidence going only to her credibility."[31]

7. Cross-examination

Once a prosecution witness has been examined-in-chief he may be cross-examined by the defence. The primary objective of cross-examination is to undermine or cast doubt on the credibility of the witness' evidence. The cross-examiner has greater freedom than the examiner in the sort of questions he or she may put to the witness. Leading questions are permitted, as are questions designed to expose the witness' bad character. In the case of a sexual assault trial, however, certain restrictions apply. Except with the leave of the judge, questions may not be asked in cross-examination nor may evidence be adduced, by or on behalf of the accused, about any sexual experience (other than that to which the charge relates) of the complainant with any person.[32] An application to ask such a question or adduce any such evidence must be made to the judge in the absence of the jury.[33] The judge may give leave only if he or she is satisfied that it would be unfair to the accused to refuse the application. Unfairness in this context refers to the situation where an assumption can be made that if the question or evidence were not allowed the jury might be satisfied that the accused was guilty, whereas if it was allowed the effect might reasonably be that they would not be satisfied.[34] If the judge does give leave the evidence or question must be kept within the limits of the leave given.[35]

19–16

If a prosecution witness gives evidence in the course of examination-in-chief which the defence proposes to challenge by calling evidence in rebuttal, the defence must be careful in putting their version to the prosecution witness in cross-examination so as to give him or her an opportunity to respond to it. Specific provision is made for the situation where the defence contends that the prosecution witness has given evidence which is inconsistent with a previous statement he has made on the matter. If the witness does not admit the previous statement the defence must disclose sufficient particularity about

---

[31] *People v. Taylor* [1974] I.R. 97 at 99.
[32] Criminal Law (Rape) Act 1981, s.3(1), as amended by Criminal Law (Rape)(Amendment) Act 1990, s.13.
[33] *ibid.* s.3(2)(a). Where an application is made by an accused person under this provision in a case involving rape or aggravated sexual assault, the complainant is entitled to be heard in relation to the application and, for this purpose, to be legally represented; Criminal Law (Rape) Act 1981, s.4(A) as inserted by Sex Offenders Act 2001, s.34.
[34] *ibid.* s.3(2)(b).
[35] *ibid.* s.3(3).

the previous occasion to enable the witness to identify it. If he persists in his denial the defence may adduce evidence in due course to prove that he made the previous statement.[36] However, this evidence will only be relevant to the credibility of the prosecution witness, it does not make the previous statement evidence of the truth of its contents. Where the previous statement was made in writing Ryan and Magee suggest that the procedure applicable in the case of a hostile witness should be followed.[37]

8. Re-examination

19–17 Once the defence has completed its cross-examination of a prosecution witness the prosecution may re-examine the witness. The re-examination must be confined to matters which arise from the cross-examination and it must be conducted generally within the same rules as those that apply to the examination-in-chief. For the most part the objective will be to clarify issues that may have been left in some doubt or hanging in the air as a result of answers given to questions asked during the cross-examination. If the prosecution wish to introduce any fresh matter which they may have overlooked, they may do so only with the leave of the judge. Where leave is given, the defence will be able to cross-examine the witness on any new matter introduced.[38]

9. Witnesses in the Courtroom

19–18 There is no rule in Ireland which excludes a witness from the courtroom during a trial in which he is due to give evidence. Indeed, it is common practice for witnesses to sit in the body of the court and observe the progress of the trial before being called. This practice clearly raises the prospect of a prospective witness tailoring his evidence in response to what he has heard from a prior witness under examination or cross-examination. The extent to which he can do so without exposing himself to damaging cross-examination is, of course, limited by the fact that he has already supplied a written statement of his evidence. Nevertheless, it may be appropriate in a particular case to request the judge to exercise his or her discretion to exclude all, or some, of the witnesses from the courtroom during the proceedings until they have given their evidence.

10. The *Voir Dire*

19–19 As a general rule all of the evidence must be given in the presence of the jury.[39] It was seen in the preceding chapter that there is provision for young children and mentally incapacitated persons to give evidence via video-link in certain circumstances. Nevertheless, the jury will still be able to observe these witnesses being examined and cross-examined. The one major exception to

---

[36] Criminal Procedure Act 1865, s.4.
[37] Ryan and Magee, *op. cit.*, p.340.
[38] *ibid. op. cit.*, p.341.
[39] *R v. Reynolds* 34 Cr.App.R. 60.

the rule that evidence must be given in the presence of the jury arises where the accused contests the admissibility of a piece of evidence being offered by the prosecution. If this evidence is of such a nature that the accused risks being prejudiced by the mere fact of the jury becoming aware that it exists, arguments about its admissibility will have to be conducted in the absence of the jury. Typically, although not invariably, the evidence in question will consist of a confession which has been obtained in circumstances which, according to the accused, render it involuntary or amount to a breach of his constitutional rights or otherwise warrant its exclusion in the exercise of the judge's discretion.[40] The very process of challenging the admissibility of the confession will alert the jury to the fact that the accused confessed. Even if the confession is ultimately ruled inadmissible there is an obvious risk that the accused will be unfairly prejudiced as a result of the jury being influenced by what they heard in the course of arguments over the admissibility issue. Accordingly, when the prosecution is about to present evidence the admissibility of which the accused is likely to contest, the usual procedure is for the judge to direct the jury to withdraw from the courtroom. A *voir dire*, or trial within a trial, will then commence in which the sole issue is the admissibility of the contested evidence.

The prosecution will open the *voir dire* by calling evidence of the fact that the accused made the contested statement (where the *voir dire* concerns the admissibility of a confession) and the circumstances in which it was made. Usually this will consist of the examination of police officers who were engaged in the questioning and supervision of the accused and other witnesses, such as doctors, who can offer evidence relevant to the circumstances in which the accused made the confession. Relevant exhibits, if any, can also be presented in evidence. The prosecution witnesses can be cross-examined, and exhibits examined, by the accused in the normal manner. The critical feature, of course, will be the evidence presented by the accused. He will go into the witness box and provide testimony about whether he made a confession and, if so, its contents and the circumstances in which it was made. He can also call witnesses and present exhibits. The accused and his witnesses may be cross-examined by the prosecution who can also examine any exhibits. In addition, both sides can be expected to make legal submissions on the law governing the admissibility of the evidence in question.

The task for the judge at the end of these submissions is to rule on the admissibility of the contested evidence. Where there is a dispute about the facts, as is usually the case with respect to confession evidence, the judge's ruling on admissibility will inevitably involve a determination of fact. It was seen in chapter 9 that this gave rise to the view in some judicial circles that matters of disputed fact should be determined by the jury in the course of the

19–20

---

[40] Other possibilities include: evidence obtained pursuant to an allegedly unconstitutional procedure, evidence of "similar facts" (see paras. 19–35 *et seq* and chapter 14) and evidence of previous criminal record.

voir dire itself. The current position, however, is that the jury have no role to play in the *voir dire* and that all matters of law and fact necessary to determine the admissibility issue should be decided by the judge sitting alone.[41]

If the judge rules that the contested evidence is inadmissible the jury will be recalled and the trial will proceed with no mention of the existence of the inadmissible evidence or of anything that transpired during the *voir dire*. It may be that the trial will collapse at this point, particularly if the prosecution case depended primarily on the excluded evidence. If, however, the judge rules the evidence admissible the jury will be recalled and the trial will proceed with the prosecution introducing the evidence as if for the first time. It follows that the accused will get a second opportunity to attack the evidence. On this occasion, however, he cannot challenge its admissibility. The focus of his attack will be directed at the weight that can be attached to it. He will have to make a tactical decision on whether to go into the witness box to offer evidence in his defence, or whether to rely solely on the cross-examination of prosecution witnesses.

19–21   Before leaving the *voir dire* it is worth noting that it is quite normal for the jury to retire temporarily during the course of prolonged legal argument. It may be, for example, that the case raises complex legal issues on whether the offence charged is known to the law, the competency of a witness, or the legality of a particular procedure. In such circumstances the jury will normally be asked to withdraw until such time as the court is ready to resume hearing evidence. Indeed, the trial judge may, at any stage of the case and without the consent of the defence, require the jury to retire and hear argument and evidence in their absence. In *People (Attorney General) v. O'Brien*[42] it was argued before the Court of Criminal Appeal that the judge should not exclude the jury during arguments over the admissibility of evidence unless the accused either requests or consents to the exclusion of the jury. These arguments were based on dicta in the judgment of Hewart L.C.J. in the English Court of Criminal Appeal decision of *R v. Anderson*[43] and the contents of a passage to similar effect in Archbold. In rejecting these arguments Kenny J. stated:

> "We think that the passage in the judgment of Hewart L.C.J. which I have quoted and the statement of the law in Archbold based on it are completely incorrect and should not now be followed. We find no difficulty in imagining many circumstances in which the trial judge should direct the jury to retire during a criminal case without the consent of the defence so that evidence may be given in their absence. If the prosecution wish to give evidence of a statement made by the accused and if counsel for the defence objects to its admission, the proper course for the judge is to hear all evidence in connection with it in the absence of the jury. If, however, counsel for the defence who is objecting to the admission of the statement, insists on the jury being present

---

[41]   *People v. Conroy* [1988] I.L.R.M. 4.
[42]   1 Frewen 343.
[43]   21 Cr.App.R. 178.

while the evidence is heard, the judge will be compelled to discharge the jury if he rules that the statement should not be in evidence. If the general proposition for which counsel for the accused contends is correct, counsel for the defence could, by tendering inadmissible evidence, have the jury discharged on every occasion on which the trial was held. This is so absurd that we are convinced that the passage relied on in *Anderson's* case 21 Cr.App.R. 178 and the statements in the various editions of Archbold based on it are not correct."[44]

For further discussion on the *voir dire*, etc., see chapter 9 at paras 9–54, etc.

D. Direction to Acquit

At the conclusion of the case for the prosecution the judge may decide to direct the jury as a matter of law to find the accused not guilty of one, several or all of the counts on the indictment. He or she may do this either on his or her own volition or in response to a defence submission of no case to answer. There are several grounds upon which the judge may decide to direct an acquittal. It may be, for example, that the prosecution evidence does not disclose any offence known to the law.[45] An acquittal will also be directed as a matter of law where the judge determines that the prosecution evidence does not establish the offence with which the accused is charged or any other offence of which he could be found guilty on the indictment. Equally, the judge may determine the evidence as it stands is such that no reasonable jury properly charged could convict.[46] This can present particular difficulties where the strength of the prosecution case is dependant upon the view which the jury might take of the reliability of witness testimony or other key elements of prosecution evidence. The classic statement of how a judge should approach an application of no case to answer is that given by Lord Lane C.J. in *R v. Galbraith*:

19–22

> "How then should the judge approach a submission of 'no case'? (1) If there is no evidence that the crime alleged has been committed by the defendant, there is no difficulty. The judge will of course stop the case. (2) The difficulty arises where there is some evidence but it is of a tenuous character, for example because of inherent weakness or vagueness or because it is inconsistent with other evidence. (a) Where the judge comes to the conclusion that the prosecution evidence, taken at its highest, is such that a jury properly directed could not properly convict upon it, it is his duty, upon a submission being made to stop the case. (b) Where however the prosecution evidence is such that its strength or weakness depends on the view to be taken of a witness's reliability, or other matters which are generally speaking within the province of the jury and where on one possible view of the facts there is evidence upon which a jury could properly come to the conclusion that the defendant is guilty, then the judge should allow the matter to be tried by the jury."[47]

---

[44] *op. cit.* at 347.

[45] *Attorney General v. Cunningham* [1932] I.R. 28; *People v. Edge* [1943] I.R. 115.

[46] See, *e.g., People (DPP) v. Higginbotham* unreported, Court of Criminal Appeal, November 17, 2000.

[47] [1981] 1 W.L.R. 1039 at 1042. Quoted with approval by Denham J. in *DPP v. M* unreported, Court of Criminal Appeal, February 15, 2001; Flood J. in *DPP v. Barnwell* unreported, Central Criminal Court, January 24, 1997.

19–23 It can be deduced from this extract of Lord Lane's judgment that mere inconsistencies in the evidence of the key prosecution witness will not necessarily result in a direction of no case to answer where the prosecution case rests on the evidence of that witness. The essential issue to be considered by the judge is whether "on one possible view of the facts there is evidence upon which a jury could properly come to the conclusion that the defendant is guilty." He or she must be careful not to usurp the function of the jury in this matter by making the determination himself or herself. Ultimately, it is for the jury to decide whether such inconsistencies as there are in the witness's testimony render him or her an unreliable witness.[48] If, however, the nature and extent of the inconsistencies were such as to render it unfair to proceed with the trial then the judge should exercise his or her discretion to stop the trial.[49] For this to happen, however, it would seem that there would have to be a doubt whether the crime was committed at all or at least an absolute conflict in the prosecution evidence which could not be resolved.[50]

If a defence submission of no case to answer is refused and the accused is ultimately convicted the judge's refusal to grant a directed acquittal may afford a ground of appeal. Where the prosecution evidence did not disclose a case against the accused, a jury conviction will be over-turned on the basis that the judge should have withdrawn the case from the jury and directed an acquittal. This is so even where the defence offered evidence which supplied what was missing from the prosecution evidence in order to establish a case to answer.[51] The justification arises from the fact that the accused should never have been put to his defence in the first place. Since the presumption of innocence imposes the burden of proving guilt on the prosecution it would be a denial of the accused's right to a fair trial if he was convicted in a case where the prosecution evidence was in itself insufficient in law. However, where the prosecution does establish a case to answer, no matter how weak, the mere fact that it would not have been sufficient to warrant a conviction without the assistance of evidence offered by the defence will not afford grounds for over-turning the jury conviction.[52]

E. The Case for the Defence

1. Options

Introduction

19–24 There are several options available to the accused in the conduct of his defence. The procedure to be followed can differ depending on which

---

[48] *DPP v. M* unreported, Court of Criminal Appeal, February 15, 2001; *DPP v. Nolan* unreported, Central Criminal Court, November 27, 2001.

[49] See, *e.g., DPP v. Morrisey* unreported, Court of Criminal Appeal, July 10, 1998; *DPP v. Barnwell* unreported, Central Criminal Court, January 24, 1997.

[50] *DPP v. Nolan* unreported, Central Criminal Court, November 27, 2001.

[51] *R v. Fraser* 7 Cr.App.R. 99; *R v. Hogan* 16 Cr.App.R. 182; *R v. Power* [1919] 1 K.B. 572; *R v. Garside* 52 Cr.App.R. 85.

[52] *R v. Abbott* [1955] 2 Q.B. 497.

particular option is taken. It has already been seen that the defence may make a submission of no case to answer at the conclusion of the case for the prosecution. This will entail the presentation of legal arguments by the defence followed, usually, by counter arguments from the prosecution. If this submission is successful the accused will be acquitted. Equally, the judge may decide to direct an acquittal on his or her own volition.

Procedure where Accused Represented

Unless an acquittal results from this procedure the trial judge must ask counsel for the defence at the close of the prosecution case if he or she intends to adduce evidence.[53] If no counsel announces an intention to do so, the prosecution may proceed with the summing up of its case to the jury.[54] The Criminal Justice Act 1984 gives the prosecution a right to a closing speech when the accused is represented.[54a] This will be followed by the closing address from the defence. The 1984 Act gives the defence the right to give their closing address after the prosecution in all cases.[54b]

If counsel does intend to call evidence the procedure can differ depending on whether he or she intends to call witnesses to give evidence as to the facts.[55] If he or she intends to call no witnesses as to the facts, other than the accused himself, he or she is not entitled to open the case to the jury in the sense of outlining the substance of the defence case with respect to the facts alleged by the prosecution. Instead he or she must proceed immediately to call the accused to give evidence, and to call any witnesses as to the character of the accused. The prosecution may then sum up its case to the jury followed by the defence's closing address. If, however, counsel for the defence proposes to call witnesses as to the facts other than the accused, he may open the case to the jury, and call his or her witnesses for the purpose of examination, cross-examination and re-examination. This will be followed by the closing address, if any,[55a] for the prosecution, and the closing address for the defence. It is also worth noting in this context that documents put in evidence have the same effect as witnesses to the facts.[56]

It is apparent that the timing of the prosecution's second address or summing up to the jury differs depending on whether counsel for the defence has called witnesses as to the facts, other than the accused. It must also be said, however, that where the prosecution has the right to the last word it should only exercise it in exceptional cases.[57] Moreover, it seldom exercises

---

[53] It would appear that the judge is under a duty to do this where the accused is represented by counsel, but not where the accused is not represented by counsel; see Ryan and Magee, *op. cit.*, p.343.

[54] Criminal Procedure Act 1865, s.2.

[54a] Criminal Justice Act 1984, s.24(1)(a).

[54b] *ibid.* s.24(1)(b).

[55] In this context documents put in evidence have the same effect as witnesses to the facts; Ryan and Magee, *op. cit.*, p.344.

[55a] According to Ryan and Magee, *op. cit.*, p.344 the prosecution seldom exercises its right to address the jury for the second time.

[56] Ryan and Magee, *op. cit.*, p.344.

[57] *R v. Bryant* [1979] Q.B. 108; *People v. Kerins* [1945] I.R. 339.

its right to address the jury for a second time even in those cases where the defence has the right to the last word.[58]

Procedure where accused not represented

19–25   The procedure applicable where the accused is not represented by counsel differs in a few respects. If he wishes to give evidence himself and call other witnesses as to character only, he may do so and then address the jury on his own behalf. There has been some confusion in the past over the prosecution right to a closing address and the order of closing addresses where the accused was not legally represented. In *Attorney General v. Lawless* Hanna J., giving the judgment of the Court of Criminal Appeal explained that it had been the long established practice in Ireland that counsel appearing on behalf of the Attorney General (now the DPP) had the right of final reply where counsel for the accused had called no witnesses. The right of reply, however, whether by counsel for the prosecution or counsel for the accused, was not based on any legal right but had its origin in the discretion of the judge controlling the *cursus curiae* of the trial. Hanna J. considered that section 3 of the Criminal Justice (Evidence) Act 1924 had no application where the prosecution was presented by counsel appearing on behalf of the Attorney General (now the DPP).[59] It is important to note that the accused in *Lawless* was represented by counsel. In *People (Attorney General) v. Thompson*[60] Walsh J., giving the judgment of the Court of Criminal Appeal, appeared to accept the ruling in *Lawless,* but in that case Walsh J. was dealing with a situation where the accused was not legally represented. However, Walsh J. did go on to say that:

> "In practice, however, the 'right of reply' is rarely, if ever, exercised in the case of undefended prisoners calling no evidence and giving no evidence."[61]

The matter would appear to be settled now by section 24 of the Criminal Justice Act 1984. It states that the prosecution has the right to a closing speech except where the accused is not represented and does not call any witnesses other than a witness as to character. It also states that the closing speech for the defence shall be made after that for the prosecution.[61a] It follows that the defence will always have the right to the last word.[61b]

The interpretation of these provisions where the accused dismissed his legal team at the point where the trial judge refused an application for a directed acquittal arose for consideration before the Court of Criminal Appeal in *People (DPP) v. Byrne.*[61c] Giving the judgment of the Court, Barron J.

---

[58]   Ryan and Magee, *op. cit.*, p.344.
[59]   S.3 states: "In cases where the right of reply depends upon the question whether evidence has been called for the defence, the fact that the person charged has been called as a witness shall not of itself confer on the prosecution the right of reply." This has since been repealed by Criminal Justice Act 1984, s.24(2).
[60]   1 Frewen 201.
[61]   *ibid.* at 208.
[61a]   Criminal Justice Act 1984, s.21(1)(a).
[61b]   *ibid.* s.21(1)(b).
[61c]   *People (DPP) v. Byrne* [1998] 2 I.R. 417.

explained that on a literal interpretation of the provisions the prosecution was entitled to a closing address since the accused had been legally represented from the beginning up to the point of a refusal for a direction. The learned judge was also of the view that even on a purposive interpretation it was clear that the intention of the Oireachtas was to provide the prosecution with a right to a closing address in this situation:

"However, even if one were to adopt a purposive rather than a literal construction of the section, it is clear that it cannot have been the intention of the Oireachtas to deprive the prosecution of their right to a closing speech in the circumstances that arose in this case. The object of the section is to give the prosecution a right to a closing speech in circumstances where the accused has been represented by counsel or a solicitor who, as professional advocates, may have exposed what appear to be weaknesses or *lacunae* in the prosecution's case and which the prosecution may wish to deal with before the jury consider their verdict. It was clearly the view of the legislature that it would tilt the balance unfairly in favour of the prosecution if they were to have a similar facility where the accused was not so legally represented and did not call any evidence. It would tilt the balance unfairly in the other direction if an accused person, by discharging his counsel or solicitor after they had tested the strength or otherwise of the prosecution case in full, could deprive the prosecution of the opportunity to make a closing speech."[61d]

If an unrepresented accused wishes to call witnesses as to the facts he may open his case, give evidence and call his witnesses.[62] In this event the prosecution may then sum up its case and the accused may make his closing address to the jury in that order.

It is also worth noting that the trial judge is under a duty to inform the accused of the options available to him, including his right to address the jury on his own behalf where he is not represented by counsel. A failure to inform the accused of his rights in this regard could be grounds for quashing a conviction.[63]

Procedure where Accused does not participate

It may happen that not only is the accused not legally represented but he may decline to participate in the proceedings at all. This was the situation before the Special Criminal Court in *People (Attorney General) v. Kerins*.[64] In that case counsel for the prosecution addressed the court at the close of the evidence for the prosecution. In this address he closed the case for the prosecution and summarised the evidence for the assistance of the court and the accused who was not represented. On his appeal the accused argued that this address was irregular in that section 2 of the Criminal Procedure Act

---

[61d] *ibid.* at 437.

[62] Once again documents put in evidence have the same effect as witnesses to the facts; Ryan and Magee, *op. cit.*

[63] The English case of *R v. Carter* 44 Cr.App.R. 225 holds otherwise, but it is unlikely that this will prevail in Ireland in light of the principles enunciated in *State (Healy) v. Donoghue* [1976] I.R. 325.

[64] [1945] I.R. 339.

1865 only permitted the prosecution to address the jury a second time for the purpose of summing up the evidence against the accused in a case where the accused was represented by counsel. The Court of Criminal Appeal held that the provision was inapplicable on the facts of this case because the prosecution counsel was addressing the court in its capacity as a tribunal of law and not as a tribunal of fact. The purpose of the address was to persuade the court that as a matter of law a *prima facie* case had been established against the accused. It was not the equivalent of an address to the jury to sum up the case for the prosecution and the evidence against the accused for the court as a tribunal of fact.

2. Presumption of Innocence

Background

19–26   Inevitably, the presentation of the defence case benefits from the presumption of innocence. Every accused in a criminal trial enjoys a constitutionally protected right to the presumption of innocence. Although it is not specifically mentioned in the Constitution the courts have had little difficulty in finding that it is implicit in Article 38.1 of the Constitution which states that: "No person shall be tried on any criminal charge save in due course of law".[65] The most obvious consequence in the context of the criminal trial is that the burden of proof is placed firmly on the prosecution. Accordingly, the prosecution must prove beyond a reasonable doubt that the accused is guilty of the offence charged. There is no obligation on the accused to play an active role in countering the case presented by the prosecution. In effect he has the right to remain silent throughout the proceedings. Indeed, there was a time when the accused was legally incompetent to give evidence on oath on his own behalf in a criminal trial.

Prior to 1924 the accused either had to remain silent or make an unsworn statement from the dock.[66] Although framed originally as an obligation to remain silent it has become known as the right to silence, or part of the privilege against self-incrimination. It derived from a perceived need to protect the accused against himself. The low levels of literacy generally associated with accused persons in the seventeenth and eighteenth centuries created a real danger that they could be talked into convicting themselves out of their own mouths. This situation coupled with the gross severity of punishments regularly imposed for relatively minor offences during those centuries meant that artificial measures had to be taken to protect the accused against wrongful conviction and punishment. His or her lack of competence to give evidence on oath was one such device. Gradually, however, it developed into one of the hallmarks of our adversarial system of criminal

---

[65]   In *O'Leary v. Attorney General* [1991] I.L.R.M. 454 Costello J. pointed out that the presumption of innocence was firmly established in the common law and in various international instruments; at 458–459. See also *Rock v. Ireland* [1998] 2 I.L.R.M. 35.

[66]   Criminal Justice (Evidence) Act 1924 renders the accused competent to give evidence on his own behalf. In England this was achieved by the Criminal Evidence Act 1898.

justice. It epitomised the fundamental principle that the onus of proof lay on the prosecution which had to discharge the onus without any assistance from the accused. Accordingly, the accused was entitled to remain silent throughout the criminal trial and thereby put the prosecution to its proof. Even when the Criminal Justice (Evidence) Act 1924 rendered the accused competent to give evidence on oath it did not seek to undermine his substantive right to remain silent. Indeed, the Act sought to protect the accused's right to silence by specifically providing that the failure of the accused (or his or her spouse) to give evidence shall not be made the subject of any comment by the prosecution.

Constitutional Status

This right to remain silent has itself acquired constitutional status and has extended beyond the confines of the trial itself to protect the suspect in police custody and persons under investigation by other officials exercising statutory powers.[67] Like most constitutional rights, however, it is not absolute. The courts have been prepared in certain circumstances to uphold restrictions on the exercise of the right to the presumption of innocence and the right to silence where such restrictions are provided by law and which do not infringe the principle of proportionality (see chapter 6). The main restrictions might be classified as follows: criminalising the failure of a person to answer police questions in certain circumstances; permitting adverse inferences to be drawn at the trial from the failure of an accused to answer certain questions in the course of the police investigation; shifting the evidential burden of proof on to an accused in certain circumstances; and obliging the accused to make advance disclosure of an alibi defence in certain circumstances.

Restrictions

Up until recently, the primary example of a criminal offence consisting of a **19–27** failure or refusal to answer police questions is to be found in section 52 of the Offences against the State Act 1939. Although the constitutionality of this provision was upheld in *Heaney v. Ireland*,[68] it was found by the European Court of Human Rights to be in breach of Article 6 of the European Convention on Human Rights.[69] This case and the issues surrounding the criminalisation of a failure or refusal to answer questions in a pre-trial investigation are dealt with in chapter 6. It is not necessary to say anything more about them here other than to make the obvious point that evidence obtained pursuant to such provisions are generally inadmissible against the accused in a trial for a criminal offence.

Similarly, there is no need to say anything here about the requirement governing advance disclosure of an alibi defence. It is dealt with below under

---

[67] *Heaney v. Ireland* [1997] 1 I.L.R.M. 117; *Rock v. Ireland* [1998] 2 I.L.R.M. 35; *People (DPP) v. Finnerty* [2000] 1 I.L.R.M. 191; *In the matter of National Irish Bank Ltd and the Companies Act 1990* [1999] 1 I.L.R.M. 321.

[68] [1997] 1 I.L.R.M. 117.

[69] *Quinn v. Ireland.* (2001) 33 E.H.R.R. 264.

the heading of advance disclosure. Clearly, it constitutes a further inroad on the accused's right to the presumption of innocence and right to silence.

19–28 There are several statutory provisions which permit the court to draw adverse inferences from the failure of an accused to co-operate in a specified manner with the police investigation into certain offences. The main provisions are to be found in sections 18 and 19 of the Criminal Justice Act 1984, section 7 of the Criminal Justice (Drug Trafficking) Act 1996 and sections 2 and 5 of the Offences against the State (Amendment) Act 1998, all of which are discussed in the context of police interrogation in chapter 6. It is not necessary to add anything further about these provisions here. Nevertheless, it is worth noting that ever since the enactment of the Criminal Justice (Evidence) Act 1924 it has been possible for the trial judge to comment on the accused's failure to give evidence.[70] This right also extends to counsel for any co-accused,[71] but not to counsel for the prosecution.[72] It does not follow, of course, that the comment should be adverse to the accused. Indeed, there is a responsibility on the judge to explain to the jury that the accused's silence does not necessarily signify guilt. The following comment from Lord Parker in *R v. Bathurst*[73] is typical:

> "[The accused] is not bound to give evidence, . . . he can sit back and see if the prosecution have proved their case, and . . . while the jury have been deprived of the opportunity of hearing his story tested in cross-examination the one thing they must not do is to assume that he is guilty because he has not gone into the witness box."[74]

It must also be said, however, that the trial judge can make a stronger comment, adverse to the accused, where the facts of the case warrant it.

Shifting the Evidential Burden

Statutory provisions which appear to shift the burden of proof from the prosecution to the accused are now a regular feature of Irish law. Costello J. in *O'Leary v. Attorney General*[75] listed a number of examples of statutory provisions which might be classified under this heading.[76] Unfortunately, they do not all use a standard form for expressing when and to what extent the burden of proof shifts on to the accused. Nevertheless, they all represent, in one form or another, a restriction on the presumption of innocence. The constitutionality of such restrictions was considered by the High Court and

---

[70] *R v. Rhodes* [1899] 1 Q.B. 77. Decided under the English Criminal Evidence Act 1898.
[71] *R v. Wickham* 55 Cr.App.R. 199.
[72] Criminal Justice (Evidence) Act 1924, s.1(b).
[73] [1968] 2 Q.B. 99.
[74] *ibid.* at 107–108. See also *R v. Mutch* [1973] 1 All E.R. 178.
[75] [1991] I.L.R.M. 454.
[76] Examples are to be found in: the Libel Act 1843, the Explosive Substances Act 1883, the Merchandise Marks Act 1884, the Forgery Act 1913, the Prevention of Corrupt Practices Act 1916, the Criminal Justice (Theft and Fraud Offences) Act 2001, the Offences against the State Act 1939, the Criminal Law (Jurisdiction) Act 1976, the Misuse of Drugs Act 1977 and the Misuse of Drugs Act 1984.

the Supreme Court with specific reference to section 24 of the Offences against the State Act 1939 in the *O'Leary* case.[77]

In this case the applicant had been charged and convicted of membership of an unlawful organisation contrary to section 21 of the Offences against the State Act 1939 and with possession of incriminating documents contrary to section 12 of the same Act. In securing the conviction for membership the prosecution had relied, *inter alia,* on section 24 of the Act which stipulates:

19–29

> "On the trial of a person charged with the offence of being a member of an unlawful organisation, proof to the satisfaction of the court that an incriminating document relating to the said organisation was found on such person or in his possession or on lands or in premises owned or occupied by him or under his control shall, without more, be evidence until the contrary is proved that such person was a member of the said organisation at the time alleged in the said charge."

The applicant sought a declaration that section 24 breached his constitutional right to the presumption of innocence essentially on the ground that it relieved the prosecution of the burden of proving guilt and imposed on the accused the burden of proving his innocence. Before dealing with the particulars of section 24, Costello J. in the High Court drew a critcial distinction between the legal burden of proof and the evidential burden of proof:

> "[I]t is important to bear in mind that the phrase 'the burden of proof' is used in two entirely different senses and that when it is said that a statute 'shifts' the burden of proof onto the accused this may mean two entirely different things. The phrase is used firstly to describe as a matter of substantive law the burden which is imposed on the prosecution in a criminal trial to establish the case against the accused beyond a reasonable doubt. This burden is fixed by law and remains on the prosecution from the beginning to the end of the trial. It is this burden which arises from the presumption of the accused's innocence and it is the removal of this burden by statute that may involve a breach of the accused's constitutional rights. It is usual to refer to this burden as the legal or persuasive burden of proof. But the phrase is also used to describe the burden which is cast on the prosecution in a criminal trial of adducing evidence to establish a case against an accused, a burden which is now usually referred to as the 'evidential burden of proof'. In criminal cases the prosecution discharges this evidential burden by adducing sufficient evidence to raise a prima facie case against an accused. It can then be said that an evidential burden has been cast on to the accused. But the shifting of the evidential burden does not discharge the legal burden of proof which at all times rests on the prosecution. The accused may elect not to call any evidence and will be entitled to an acquittal if the evidence adduced does not establish his or her guilt beyond a reasonable doubt. Therefore if a statute is to be construed as merely shifting the evidential burden no constitutional infringement occurs."[78]

---

[77] [1991] I.L.R.M. 454 (HC); [1995] 2 I.L.R.M. 259 (SC).
[78] [1991] I.L.R.M. 454 at 460.

19–30   It follows that a statutory provision which shifts the legal burden of proof on to the accused will almost inevitably breach his constitutional right to the presumption of innocence. In other words a provision which obliges the court to convict the accused if he fails to adduce exculpatory evidence is likely to be unconstitutional. This result will not necessarily ensue if it is only the evidential burden that is shifted. Even if the effect of the provision is that the accused will be convicted if he does not adduce exculpatory evidence it will not necessarily be unconstitutional. It is only if the statute obliges the court to convict in such circumstances that the constitutional infirmity is likely to arise. If the statute merely gives legal effect to an inference of guilt which it is reasonable to draw from facts which the prosecution must establish then it is unlikely to be struck down as unconstitutional. Costello J. offered the example of section 27A of the Firearms Act 1964 (as inserted by s.8 of the Criminal Law (Jurisdiction) Act 1976) which provides that where a person has a firearm in his possession in such circumstances as to give rise to a reasonable suspicion that he has not or does not possess it for a lawful purpose he shall be guilty of an offence "unless he has it in his possession . . . for a lawful purpose." Since the inference of guilt arises from facts established by the prosecution, as opposed to the terms of the statutory provision, there is no unconstitutionality.

Viewed in this light, section 24 of the Offences Against the State Act 1939 falls well short of what would be required in this context to breach the presumption of constitutionality. Clearly, it involves only a shift in the evidential burden of proof. Possession of an incriminating document is merely evidence from which a court may infer guilt. Even if the accused fails to adduce exculpatory evidence the court will still have to evaluate the evidence pertaining to possession with a view to determining whether it is sufficient to warrant a conviction for membership. Accordingly the High Court and, on appeal, the Supreme Court, refused to grant a declaration that section 24 was unconstitutional.

3. Alibi Evidence

19–31   Consistent with the right to the presumption of innocence and the right to silence is fact that the accused is not obliged to disclose his defence to the prosecution in advance of presenting it in court at the trial. However, just as limited inroads have been accepted on his right to silence during police investigation in certain circumstances, so also have inroads been made on his right to hold back the contents of his defence. This is evident where the accused intends to rely on an alibi defence.

On a trial on indictment the accused cannot, without the leave of the court, adduce evidence in support of an alibi unless he gives notice of particulars of the alibi before the end of the prescribed period.[79] In this context "evidence in support of an alibi" is specifically defined as evidence tending to show that by

---

[79]   Criminal Justice Act 1984, s.20(1).

reason of the presence of the accused at a particular place or in a particular area at a particular time he was not, or was unlikely to have been, at the place where the offence is alleged to have been committed at the time of its alleged commission.[80] The notice of alibi must be given in writing to the solicitor for the prosecution.[81] It must be given before the end of the prescribed period which is defined as: the period of 14 days after the date on which the accused is served with the book of evidence;[82] or, where the accused on being sent forward for sentence changes his plea to one of not guilty, the period of 14 days from the date on which he is served with the book of evidence;[83] or, where the accused is brought before the Special Criminal Court for trial under section 47 of the Offences against the State Act 1939, such period as is fixed by the court when the court fixes the date of trial.[84]

Where a notice is required to be given to the solicitor for the prosecution under these provisions it may be given by delivering it to him, by leaving it at his office or by sending it to him by registered post at his office.[85]

The legislation does not specifically prescribe the form or contents of a notice of particulars of an alibi. However, it does state that even if the accused does give notice of particulars he will not be able to call a witness to give alibi evidence without the leave of the court unless the following requirements are satisfied. First, the notice must include the name and address of the witness or, if the accused does not know the name and address at the time he gives the notice, any information in his possession which might be of material assistance in finding the witness.[86] Second, if the notice does not include the name and address the court must be satisfied that the accused, before giving the notice, took and has continued to take all reasonable steps to secure that the name and address would be ascertained.[87] Third, if the notice does not contain the name and address and the accused subsequently discovers the name and address or receives other information which might be of material assistance in finding the witness, he must immediately give notice of the name and address or other information as the case may be.[88] Fourth, if the accused is notified by or on behalf of the prosecution that the witness has not been traced by the name or at the address given, he must immediately give notice of any such information which is then in his possession or subsequently received.[89]

If the accused does not satisfy the requirements as to giving notice of an alibi defence it does not follow that he is absolutely barred from adducing evidence of the defence at the trial. However, it does mean that he will only

19–32

---

[80] *ibid.* s.20(8).
[81] *ibid.* s.20(6), as amended by Criminal Justice Act 1999, s.16(3)(a).
[82] *ibid.* s.20(8)(a), as amended by Criminal Justice Act 1999, s.16(3)(b).
[83] *ibid.* s.20(8)(c), as amended by Criminal Justice Act 1999, s.16(3)(d).
[84] *ibid.* s.20(8)(d).
[85] *ibid.* s.20(7).
[86] *ibid.* s.20(2)(a).
[87] *ibid.* s.20(2)(b).
[88] *ibid.* s.20(2)(c).
[89] *ibid.* s.20(2)(d).

be able to adduce the evidence with the leave of the court. The court cannot refuse leave if it appears to it that the accused was not informed of the requirements of these provisions by the District Court when he was sent forward for trial[90] or by the trial court when, on being sent forward for sentence, he changed his plea to not guilty[91] or, where he was brought before the Special Criminal Court for trial under section 47 of the 1939 Act, by the court when it fixed the date of trial.[92] Any evidence tendered to disprove an alibi may, subject to any directions by the court as to the time it is to be given, be given before or after evidence is given in support of the alibi.[93]

Any notice under these provisions which purports to be given on behalf of the accused by his solicitor shall, unless the contrary is proved, be deemed to be given with the authority of the accused.[94]

4. Unsworn Statement from the Dock

19–33 Although the accused was not competent to give evidence on oath prior to 1924 he did enjoy the right to make an unsworn statement from the dock. The prosecution did not enjoy a correlative right to cross-examine the accused on any such statement. Nevertheless, it would appear that it had to form part of the transcript of the trial. In *People v. Riordan*,[95] for example, the Court of Criminal Appeal quashed the conviction and ordered a re-trial essentially on the ground that the accused's defence, contained in his unsworn statement, had not been put to the jury and had not been included in the transcript of the trial.

Although the Criminal Justice (Evidence) Act 1924 specifically preserved the accused's right to make an unsworn statement,[96] it has since been abolished by the Criminal Justice Act 1984.[97] Now, if the accused elects to give evidence he must do so on oath and submit to cross-examination.[98] If, however, he is not represented by counsel or a solicitor, he remains free to address the court or the jury, otherwise than on oath, on any matter on which counsel or solicitor could have addressed the court or jury on his behalf.[98a] Equally, the abolition of the right to make an unsworn statement does not

---

[90] *ibid.* s.20(3)(a).
[91] *ibid.* s.20(3)(b).
[92] *ibid.* s.20(3)(c).
[93] *ibid.* s.20(4).
[94] *ibid.* s.20(5).
[95] [1948] I.R. 416.
[96] Criminal Justice (Evidence) Act 1924, s.1(h).
[97] Criminal Justice Act 1984, s.23.
[98] *ibid.* s.23(1).
[98a] In *People (DPP) v. Byrne* [1998] 2 I.R. 417 the accused, who was charged with accomplices, dismissed his legal team at the close of the prosecution case. His accomplices, who were represented, intimated to the judge that they would not be going into evidence. The judge thereupon advised the accused that if he wanted to say anything to the jury about his involvement in the offences charged he would have to do so on oath in the witness box and must do so in the manner that counsel would have done on the evidence given. When it became apparent that the accused was using the opportunity to attempt to have the jury discharged the judge stopped him from proceeding. The Court of Criminal Appeal ruled that this was a matter within the discretion of the trial judge which he had exercised properly on the facts of the case.

prevent him from making an unsworn statement where the statement is one which he is required by law to make personally, or one by way of mitigation before the court passes sentence on him.[99]

5. Cross-Examination of the Accused

Introduction

Where the accused elects to give evidence he is liable to cross-examination by the prosecution and, where applicable, by counsel for any co-accused. The cross-examination, however, must be conducted within certain limits imposed by the Criminal Justice (Evidence) Act 1924. On the one hand the Act removes the privilege against self-incrimination for the accused who exercises his right to give evidence on oath in his own defence. The relevant provision is section 1(e) which reads:

19–34

> "[A] person charged and being a witness in pursuance of this Act may be asked any question in cross-examination notwithstanding that it would tend to criminate him as to the offence charged."

The Shield

The effects of this provision are qualified by the contents of section 1(f) which confer on the accused certain protections which are not available to other witnesses under cross-examination. These protections are commonly referred to as the "shield". This is a reflection of the fact that they can be used by the accused to fend off certain types of question designed to incriminate him by reference to his character or criminal offences distinct from the offence or offences actually charged. Like all shields, however, it can be penetrated or lifted in certain circumstances thereby exposing the accused to the otherwise prohibited questions.

19–35

In order to consider the extent of the shield and the circumstances in which it can be penetrated or lifted it would be as well to quote section 1(f) in full. It states:

> "[A] person charged and called as a witness in pursuance of this Act shall not be asked, and if asked shall not be required to answer, any question tending to show that he has committed or been convicted of or been charged with any offence other than that wherewith he is then charged, or is of bad character, unless:
>
> (i) the proof that he has committed or been convicted of such other offence is admissible evidence to show that he is guilty of the offence wherewith he is then charged; or
>
> (ii) he has personally or by his advocate asked questions of the witnesses for the prosecution with a view to establish his own good character, or has given evidence of his good character, or the nature or conduct of the defence is such as to involve imputations on the character of the prosecutor or the witnesses for the prosecution; or

---

[99] Criminal Justice Act 1984, s.23(2).

(iii) he has given evidence against any other person charged with the same offence."

Clearly, the shield provides the accused with a measure of protection against questions tending to show that he has committed an offence other than that charged or that he has been convicted or charged with an offence other than that charged. Similarly it protects him against questions tending to show that he is of bad character. Prohibited, therefore, are questions about matters such as: previous criminal convictions, alleged criminal activities, association with known criminals and criminal or anti-social reputation. It is also worth noting that "tending to show" in this context means revealing to the jury for the first time.[100] Accordingly, the shield will not protect the accused against questions tending to show facts of which the jury are already aware.

The protection afforded by the shield is not absolute. Paragraphs (i) to (iii) of section 1(f) set out the circumstances in which the protection can be lost. The following paragraphs are intended only as a brief introduction to the scope and limitations of the protection afforded by the shield. For a more detailed account, reference should be made to specialist texts on the law of evidence.[101]

Similar Fact Evidence

Paragraph (i) differs from (ii) and (iii) in so far as its application does not depend on any action or strategy on the part of the accused. It compels the accused to answer questions about his commission or conviction of another offence, apart from that charged, where proof of his commission or conviction of that other offence is admissible to show that he is guilty of the offence charged. In other words, the prosecution can cross-examine the accused about his commission or conviction of another offence where the similarity between it and the offence charged is sufficient to satisfy the similar fact evidence rule.

19–36   The similar fact evidence rule is summed up in the following quotation from Lord Herschell LC in *Makin v. Attorney General*:

> "It is undoubtedly not competent for the prosecution to adduce evidence tending to show that the accused has been guilty of criminal acts other than those covered by the indictment, for the purpose of leading to the conclusion that the accused is a person likely from his criminal conduct or character to have committed the offence for which he is being tried. On the other hand, the mere fact that the evidence adduced tends to show the commission of other crimes does not render it inadmissible if it be relevant to an issue before the jury, and it may be so relevant if it bears upon the question whether the acts alleged to constitute the crime charged in the indictment were designed or accidental, or to rebut a defence which would otherwise be open to the accused."[102]

---

[100]   *Jones v. DPP* [1962] A.C. 635.
[101]   See, *e.g.*, Fennell, *op. cit.*, Tapper, *op. cit.*, Wigmore, *op. cit.*
[102]   [1984] A.C. 57 at 65.

This passage was quoted with approval by Barron J. in the Court of Criminal Appeal in *DPP v. Kelly*.[102a] For the learned judge's analysis of the passage in the light of other Irish, English and commonwealth case law, and further discussion on "similar fact" evidence, see chapter 14.

Clearly the accused cannot be cross-examined about his involvement in offences other than those covered by the indictment. If, however, there is sufficient evidence of similarity between the other offences and those charged, then evidence of the former may be considered sufficiently relevant to render it admissible under section 1(f)(i). For this to happen there must be a sufficient similarity between the nature, or manner of commission, of the alleged previous offences and the offence with which the accused is charged. This similarity would have to reveal a disposition on the part of the accused which is also reflected in the conduct which lies at the heart of the offence charged. In *R v. Smith*,[103] for example, the accused was charged with the murder of a woman with whom he had gone through a ceremony of marriage. Evidence of the deaths of two women with whom he had previously undergone ceremonies of marriage was admitted. In each case the deceased woman was found drowned in her bath, the door of the bathroom would not lock, the defendant had informed a medical practitioner that the victim suffered from epileptic fits and the victim's life was insured for the benefit of the accused. The court held that the degree of similar evidence in the deaths was so striking that the evidence of the previous deaths was admissible on the current charge.[104]

When the prosecution wishes to rely on "similar fact" evidence which the defence challenges as inadmissible, the admissibility should, if possible, be decided in the absence of the jury at the outset of the trial.[104a] If it is ruled inadmissible and the accused is being charged in the same indictment with counts which raise the "similar fact" issue the indictment should be severed and the accused granted separate trials with respect to each of the counts.

Evidence of good character

Paragraph (ii), like paragraph (iii), can come into play only as a result of the manner in which the accused conducts his defence. It is sometimes said, therefore, that their application is dependant on the accused lifting the shield, while paragraph (i) penetrates the shield. There are essentially two ways in which the accused can lose the benefit of the shield under paragraph (ii). First, he may seek to establish his own good character. In this context "character" relates to both moral disposition and general reputation.[105] The

---

[102a] Unreported, Court of Criminal Appeal, December 13, 1999.
[103] (1915) 11 Cr.App.R. 229.
[104] For a case where the similarities were not sufficiently strong, see *Noor Mohamed v. R* [1949] A.C. 182.
[104a] *R v. Boardman* [1975] A.C. 421; *DPP v. Kelly* unreported, Court of Criminal Appeal, December 13, 1999.
[105] *People v. Coleman* [1945] I.R. 237; *Stirland v. DPP* [1944] A.C. 315; *Malindi v. R* [1967] A.C. 439; *Selvey v. DPP* [1970] A.C. 304.

accused may seek to establish his good character under paragraph (ii) either by asking a question of a prosecution witness with a view to establishing his own good character, or by introducing evidence of his own good character. In the former the shield will be lifted only if the *intent* of the person asking the question was to establish the accused's good character. It will not be sufficient merely that the *effect* of the question was to establish his good character. Nevertheless, the following examples from English case law illustrate just how easy it is for the accused to put his character in issue under paragraph (ii):[106] an assertion by the accused that he attended Mass regularly;[107] questions aimed at showing that the accused was a married man with a family and in regular employment;[108] and an assertion by the accused charged with larceny by finding that he had previously found money and returned it to its owners.[109]

Attacking the character of Prosecution witnesses

19–37   The second means by which the accused can lose the benefit of the shield under paragraph (ii) is by attacking the character of the prosecution or witnesses for the prosecution. This can be done either by the defence making allegations in their evidence or by putting allegations to prosecution witnesses in cross-examination. Once again "character" in this context relates to both moral disposition and general reputation. Examples which have been held sufficient to lift the shield include allegations that: a prosecution witness had committed the offence with which the accused was charged;[110] witnesses for the prosecution had taken part in a conspiracy;[111] a prosecution witness (police officer) had fabricated a statement;[112] and a prosecution witness was involved in vice.[113] In *People (Attorney General) v. Coleman*[114] the Court of Criminal Appeal accepted that there was an imputation on the character of two prosecution witnesses where it was put to them in cross-examination that: they, rather than the accused, had unlawfully performed an operation with intent to procure a miscarriage; they conspired to charge the accused with a crime which, to their knowledge, he was innocent; that prior to their marriage one of them had used contraceptives contrary to the teaching of the Church to which she belonged; and that they had married with the intent of defeating the ends of justice.

Even if the nature of the defence necessarily involves an imputation being made about the character of a prosecution witness the benefit of the shield may still be lost,[115] particularly if the proper conduct of the defence did not

---

[106]   These examples are listed in Ryan and Magee, *op. cit.*, p.348, fn.15.
[107]   *R v. Ferguson* 2 Cr.App.R. 250.
[108]   *R v. Coulman* 20 Cr.App.R. 106.
[109]   *R v. Samuel* 40 Cr.App.R. 8.
[110]   *People v. Coleman* [1945] I.R. 237.
[111]   *Attorney General v. Campbell* 62 I.L.T.R. 30.
[112]   *R v. Britzman* [1983] 1 All E.R. 639. This applies only where the allegation is made in the trial itself. It does not apply to the *voir dire*.
[113]   *R v. Bishop* [1974] 3 W.L.R. 308.
[114]   [1945] I.R. 237.
[115]   *Selvey v. DPP* [1970] A.C. 304.

necessitate the imputation.[116] However, an allegation that the victim in a rape case consented will not result in losing the shield.[117] Indeed, the courts will generally permit the accused to probe the veracity of prosecution witnesses by severe cross-examination,[118] even to the extent of calling a prosecution witness a "liar",[119] without removing the protection of the shield.

In *Attorney General v. O'Shea*[120] gardai investigating a murder secreted one **19–38** of their number under a bed in the dwelling of the chief suspect. The purpose was to listen to conversations between the suspect and his sister in the hope that that would reveal inculpatory evidence. Subsequently, in the course of the trial counsel for the defence tested the evidence of this witness in a rigorous and searching cross-examination during which he contradicted his evidence on several occasions. The Court of Criminal Appeal, however, did not accept that this was sufficient to amount to an imputation on the character of the witness sufficient to lose the shield:

> "The effect of the argument, if accepted, would be to put the defence in the position of cross-examining the witnesses for the prosecution in every case at the peril of exposing the accused to evidence of bad character, which was certainly not the intention of the statute. The contradiction of witnesses for the prosecution, the testing of the truth and accuracy of their testimony by legitimate cross-examination, however severe, is not, in the opinion of the court, such a conduct of the defence as to involve imputations on the character of the witnesses for the prosecution within the meaning of section 1(f)(ii) of the Act (No.37 of 1924)."[121]

The court went on to explain that it would be different if the conduct of the cross-examination amounted to the formulation of specific charges against the witness such as that he was giving false evidence in pursuance of a conspiracy to create evidence in order to cover the weakness of the prosecution case at its crucial points.

Consequences of Lifting the Shield

Once the accused has put his own good character in issue under paragraph (ii) the trial judge may exercise his or her discretion to permit the prosecution to put questions which would otherwise have been prohibited by the shield. In this event the prosecution will be able to ask the accused about any other offences which he may have committed, of which he has been convicted or with which he has been charged. This can include an offence which has occurred after the offences charged in the indictment,[122] but probably not an

---

[116] *People v. Coleman* [1945] I.R. 237.
[117] *R v. Turner* [1944] K.B. 463. Note, however, the restrictions imposed on the cross-examination of the victim in a sexual assault offence case by Criminal Law (Rape) Act 1981, s.3, as amended by Criminal Law (Rape)(Amendment) Act 1990, s.13.
[118] *Attorney General v. O'Shea* [1931] I.R. 713.
[119] *R v. Rouse* [1904] 1 K.B. 184.
[120] [1931] I.R. 713.
[121] *ibid.* at 723.
[122] *R v. Wood* [1920] 2 K.B. 179.

offence of which the accused has previously been acquitted[123] or one for which he is currently wanted.[124] The accused may also be asked about his character. It is worth noting that "character" in this context is indivisible. In other words the questions about the accused's character do not have to be directly related to the nature of the offence with which he is charged. So, for example, an accused charged with an offence of dishonesty may find himself questioned about his history of marital infidelity.

19–39 A difficult question concerns the purpose to which evidence of the accused's previous criminal activity or bad character can be put once it has been admitted pursuant to paragraph (ii). The issue was addressed by the Court of Criminal Appeal in *People v. Bond*[125] where the accused coupled his alibi defence with imputations on the character of the prosecution witnesses. The prosecution responded by introducing evidence of the accused's previous convictions. The trial judge did not instruct the jury that such evidence was generally inadmissible and that it was permitted in this case only because the accused had attacked the character of the prosecution witnesses. The Court of Criminal Appeal ruled, in quashing the conviction, that the judge should have explained to the jury why the evidence of the previous convictions was admitted and directed them that it should be used only to consider the credibility of the accused as distinct from the probability of him having committed the offence charged:

> "The way in which this evidence was to be used by the jury was vital to the interests of the applicant. It certainly necessitated a careful direction from the judge as to why it was admitted, and as to how it was to be used; that it went to his credit only, and should on no account be used to show the probability of his guilt."[126]

It follows that the jury is expected to apply the evidence admitted pursuant to section 1(f)(ii) as relevant to the credibility of the accused only, as distinct from his guilt.[127]

Giving Evidence against Co-accused

Paragraph (iii) of section 1(f) comes into play if the accused gives evidence against any other person charged with the same offence. It is not necessary that the accused should formally elect to give evidence against his co-accused on behalf of the prosecution. What matters is the effect of the accused's testimony. Where the accused lifts the shield under this paragraph the trial judge has a discretion to permit the prosecution to ask him the otherwise prohibited questions about previous criminal activity and bad character. Counsel for the co-accused, by comparison, is entitled as of right to put the prohibited questions to the accused in such circumstances. Should counsel for

---

[123] *Maxwell v. DPP* [1935] A.C. 309.
[124] *People v. Havelin* 86 I.L.T.R. 168.
[125] [1966] I.R. 214.
[126] *People v. Bond* [1966] I.R. 214 at 223.
[127] See also, *R v. Vickers* [1972] Crim.L.R. 101.

the co-accused wish to pursue this course, it is nevertheless desirable that he should inform the court and counsel for the accused in advance.[128]

It is worth noting that the accused and his co-accused must actually be indicted on the same charges before the shield can be lifted under paragraph (iii).[129] It is not clear whether it will be sufficient that they are charged with offences arising out of the same set of circumstances.

6. Defence Witnesses

As a general rule any person who can offer testimony relevant to the defence is a competent and compellable witness for the defence. Nevertheless, there are some circumstances in which a witness may not be compelled to testify on behalf of the defence. The defendant, for example, is not compellable in any case where he is being tried jointly with another.[130] If, however, he has been or is to be tried separately from the other person he is a compellable witness for that other person.[131] Similarly, if he is being tried jointly with another person and has pleaded guilty he is a compellable witness for that other person.[132] In practice, of course, it is highly unlikely that the defence will compel an unwilling witness to testify.

19–40

The competency and compellability of witnesses generally in a criminal trial is discussed in the preceding chapter.

F. Further Evidence

Circumstances may arise in which the prosecution may wish to adduce further evidence after it has presented its case. It may happen, for example, that new evidence becomes available at a late stage or that the defence has introduced a matter in evidence which the prosecution wishes to rebut. It may even be that the prosecution has inadvertently omitted to introduce some evidence as part of its case. The question arises whether, and to what extent, the prosecution should be allowed to introduce such evidence after it has closed its case.

19–41

Clearly, there is a possibility of unfairness to the accused if the prosecution is allowed to have a second bite of the cherry after having heard the defence case being presented in full. Accordingly, the general practice is that evidence upon which the prosecution wishes to rely must be adduced before the close of its case. It is, however, a rule of practice only. There is no strict legal prohibition on the tendering of further evidence at a later stage. Indeed, it would appear to be entirely a matter for the discretion of the trial judge to determine whether evidence can be adduced by the prosecution or the defence

---

[128]   Ryan and Magee, *op. cit.*, p.352.
[129]   *R v. Russell* [1971] 1 Q.B. 151.
[130]   Criminal Justice (Evidence) Act 1924, s.1.
[131]   It would appear that he is compellable as a defence witness when being tried jointly with another person on a charge of public nuisance under the Evidence Act 1877; see Ryan and Magee, op. cit.
[132]   *R v. Boal* [1965] 1 Q.B. 402.

after the close of their respective cases.[133] In particular, if the evidence for the defence introduces new matters which the prosecution could not foresee, the trial judge has a discretion to permit rebutting evidence to be introduced by the prosecution.[134] The exercise of this discretion featured occasionally in cases where the accused sprang a surprise alibi. With the provisions on advance disclosure of such a defence it is now less likely to arise in this context.

In *People (DPP) v. Leahy*[134a] the accused was charged with uttering forged documents, including a bank draft. Part of the evidence against him included his fingerprint on the draft. At his trial he gave evidence to the effect that when he was being questioned about another matter by gardai he was shown bank drafts which he had handled. He asserted that this must have included the bank draft containing his fingerprint. Not only could the prosecution not have anticipated this evidence but it would have been highly improper for them to have introduced it as part of their case as it would have alerted the jury to the fact that the accused was being investigated by the gardai in relation to another matter. In these unusual circumstances the Court of Criminal Appeal considered that the trial judge was correct in permitting the prosecution to introduce evidence, after the close of the prosecution case, to the effect that the bank draft which had been produced to the appellant on the previous investigation was not the same bank draft being proffered in evidence:

"In the normal course a trial judge has to be vigilant before allowing in evidence from the prosecution after the prosecution has closed its case. But in this particular case a very strange set of circumstances arose in that part of the evidence against the applicant was what was alleged to be his fingerprint on one of the bank drafts in question. The applicant, when he came to give evidence as he did, explained the presence of his fingerprint on the bank draft by reason of the fact that a Garda officer, when questioning him about another matter, had produced a number of bank drafts to him, and that this must have been one of the bank draft which the Garda officer had produced to him and that it was in that way that his fingerprint came to be on the bank draft. The prosecution could hardly have anticipated that evidence but even if they had anticipated the evidence, it is not evidence which a trial judge would normally have admitted the prosecution to use as part of their case, because it would have told the jury that this particular man, who is being charged in this case, had been investigated in relation to another matter by the gardai. Under these circumstances it appears to us that the trial judge was perfectly entitled , and was being perfectly correct, in the interest of justice, to admit the evidence from Garda Culhane, that the bank draft which he had produced to the applicant on the previous occasion was not the same bank draft as the bank draft before the court in the present case, and therefore that the fingerprint on the bank draft in the present case could not be explained away in that way."

---

[133] See, by analogy, the Supreme Court decision in *People (Attorney General) v. O'Brien* [1963] I.R. 65 dealing with the judicial discretion to recall (discussed below under "Jury Deliberations"). For English examples on how the discretion should be used, see *R v. Rice* [1963] 1 Q.B. 857; *R v. Doran* 56 Cr.App.R. 429; *R v. Kane* 65 Cr.App.R. 270; *R v. Halford* 67 Cr.App.R. 318.

[134] *R v. Whelan* 8 LR Ir 314; *Attorney General v. Gleeson* 64 I.L.T.R. 225.

[134a] Unreported, Court of Criminal Appeal, February 14, 2000.

The trial judge may call a witness who has not been called by either side. Given the adversarial nature of the trial this is a power which should be exercised sparingly, particularly after the case for the defence has closed.[135] Nevertheless, situations will arise where it appears to the court that an identifiable individual may be able to offer critical evidence on the facts at the heart of the case, but for one reason or another neither the prosecution nor the defence are willing to call him. In such circumstances the judge might usefully exercise his or her discretion to call the witness and put relevant questions to him. Although neither the prosecution nor the defence is entitled to cross-examine such a witness as of right, each should be given leave to do so where the witness proves adverse to that party.[136]

G. Closing Addresses

The primary function of the closing addresses to the jury on behalf of the prosecution and defence is to summarise their respective cases in the light of the evidence and arguments adduced at the trial. There are certain limits, however, on the points which can be made by either side. Prosecution counsel is not entitled to comment on the failure of the accused (or the spouse of the accused) to give evidence.[137] Equally he or she should not comment on the failure of the accused to call other witnesses, unless it might fairly be expected that witnesses would be called to support a story presented by the accused. The prosecution must also avoid the argument that an acquittal would damage the character or reputation of the complainant.[138] Counsel for the defence, on the other hand, should not state as fact matters which have not been put in evidence.[139] Nor, in the absence of evidence, should he suggest that the crime was committed by a specific individual who is not on trial.[140] He or she can, however, draw the attention of the jury to any evidence which might reasonably show that some other person was responsible.[141] Counsel should also exercise restraint in referring to the consequences of conviction for a capital crime,[142] and he or she should not invite the jury to add a rider to their verdict.[143] Generally, it might be said that there is merit in keeping the addresses as short as possible.[144]

19–42

---

[135] *R v. Harris* [1927] 2 K.B. 587

[136] *Coulson v. Disborough* [1894] 2 Q.B. 316.

[137] Criminal Justice (Evidence) Act 1924, s.1(b).

[138] *R v. Rudland* 4 F & F 495; *R v. Puddick* 4 F & F 497.

[139] *R v. Shimmin* 15 Cox CC 122.

[140] *Attorney General v. O'Leary* [1926] I.R. 445.

[141] *R v. Wainright* 13 Cox CC 171.

[142] *Attorney General v. O'Leary* [1926] I.R. 445. In this case the defence counsel told the jury "that they would be guilty of judicial murder if they convicted the prisoners, and he threatened them with the terrors of the conscience-stricken in the night"; at 450.

[143] *R v. Black* [1963] 1 W.L.R. 1311.

[144] See the views of Lawton L.J. in the exceptional case of *R v. Landy* [1981] 1 W.L.R. 355 at 363.

H. Summing Up

Purpose

19–43   After counsel for the prosecution and defence have completed their addresses to the jury the judge will normally sum up or charge the jury.[145] There is no absolute requirement for the judge to sum up in every case. It may be that the facts and the law are so straightforward that a summing up is not necessary.[146] Most cases, however, will benefit from a summing up which summarises the evidence presented by either side, the relevant principles and rules of law which must be applied and the function of the jury with respect to the law and facts. The contents and style of a summing up will inevitably differ from case to case. Its overall objective is to assist the jury in its task of determining on the evidence whether the accused is guilty or not guilty of the offence or offences charged. What is required, therefore, is a clear and accurate summary of the relevant evidence for either side and of the relevant legal rules and principles.[147] Excessive detail or prolixity could defeat the purpose. In *R v. Landy*,[148] for example, the judge gave a summing up which lasted for six days after a trial which had taken up 73 days of submissions and evidence followed by 11 days of counsels' speeches to the jury. Lawton L.J., in the English Court of Appeal, took the opportunity to emphasise how the basic objective of the summing up could be defeated by an undue attention to detail:

> "A summing up should be clear, concise and intelligible. If it is overloaded with detail, whether of fact or law and follows no obvious plan, it will not have any of the attributes it should have. This summing up suffered from the fact that the judge was over-conscientious. He seems to have decided that the jury should be reminded of nearly all the details of the evidence and directed as to every facet of the law which applied. He must have spent hours preparing his summing up but in the end he got lost in the trees and missed the wood."[149]

An essential part of any summing up is an explanation of the basic function to be discharged by the jury and the parameters within which they must operate. Accordingly, the judge should instruct the jury that their function is to decide whether the prosecution has proved the charge or charges against the accused. A jury verdict of guilty or not guilty should be unanimous. It will be seen later, however, that there are circumstances in which a majority of 10 will be acceptable. The judge must explain these circumstances to the jury. Equally, he or she should advise the jury that in their deliberations leading to their verdict they should confine themselves to the evidence which has been adduced in court and should ignore what they have heard or read elsewhere.

---

[145]   *R v. Finch* 12 Cr.App.R. 77.
[146]   *R v. Newman* 9 Cr.App.R. 134; *R v. Attfield* [1961] 1 W.L.R. 1135.
[147]   See, *e.g.*, *R v. Landy* [1981] 1 W.L.R. 355 *per* Lawton L.J. at 367; *R v. Lawrence* [1982] A.C. 510 *per* Lord Hailsham LC at 519.
[148]   [1981] 1 W.L.R. 355.
[149]   *R v. Landy* [1981] 1 W.L.R. 355 *per* Lawton L.J. at 367.

In assessing the evidence and its significance they are, of course, entitled to avail of their general knowledge and common sense.[150]

Multiple Counts and Defendants

If there are more than one accused the judge should instruct the jury that they must deal with each one separately and, with respect to any one individual, they should consider only so much of the evidence which is material to his or her guilt. They must not, for example, consider evidence against one accused as indicating the guilt of another. Similarly, if there are several counts the judge should warn the jury that each of them constitutes a separate charge on which they may convict only on so much of the evidence that is material to it. They must not supplement the evidence material to one count with evidence material only to another.[151] So, for example, if the accused is charged with several counts of robbery on different dates, the evidence adduced with respect to one robbery must not be taken into account when considering the accused's guilt with respect to one of the other robberies. It may also happen, however, that the same evidence may be material to more than one count. This is likely to happen where the counts are alleged in the alternative, as in larceny and receiving stolen goods, or where they merely vary in degree, such as murder or manslaughter. In this event it will be perfectly proper for the jury to consider the same evidence on more than one count, so long as it is material in each.

Standard of Proof

One of the most critical directions to the jury concerns the standard of proof. **19–44** The requisite standard, of course, is proof beyond a reasonable doubt. Unfortunately, it is not possible to identify a set formula which should be used by the judge to explain this standard to the jury. Indeed, it has even been suggested that, having observed the jury throughout the trial, the judge should use words which are most appropriate to convey to that particular jury that they must not return a verdict of guilty unless they are sure of the guilt of the accused.[152] While the judge need not tell the jury that they must be "certain" of the accused's guilt before bringing in a verdict of guilty, it would appear that expressions such as "satisfied",[153] "pretty certain", "reasonably sure" and "pretty sure" may not be sufficient. Something stronger is required. In the Court of Criminal Appeal case of *People v. Byrne*, Kenny J. defined the correct approach:

> "The correct charge to a jury is that they must be satisfied beyond reasonable doubt of the guilt of the accused, and it is helpful if that degree of proof is contrasted with that in a civil case. It is also essential, however, that the jury should be told that the accused is entitled to the benefit of the doubt and that

---

[150] *R v. Rosser* 7 C & P 648; *R v. Jones* 54 Cr.App.R. 63.
[151] *People v. Wallace* (1982) 2 Frewen 125.
[152] *Walters v. R* [1969] A.C. 26.
[153] *People v. Byrne* [1974] I.R. 1.

when two views on any part of the case are possible on the evidence, they should adopt that which is favourable to the accused unless the State has established the other beyond reasonable doubt."[154]

It is desirable that the direction should explain to the jury that the benefit of the doubt should always accrue to the defendant in the sense that where there are two conflicting versions of any material fact the jury ought to accept the version favourable to the defendant unless the contrary is proved beyond a reasonable doubt. Nevertheless, a failure to refer specifically to the benefit of doubt accruing to the defendant will not necessarily be fatal so long as the direction taken as a whole adequately conveys to the jury the true meaning of "beyond a reasonable doubt" and the nature of the onus which rests on the prosecution.[155]

Onus of Proof

Closely associated with the standard of proof is the issue of the onus or burden of proof. The judge should direct the jury that the burden of proof rests throughout on the prosecution. They must prove beyond a reasonable doubt that the accused is guilty. Accordingly, the judge should advise the jury that the benefit of any doubt should always be applied in favour of the accused.[156] It does not follow, however, that a verdict of not guilty must be returned automatically in every case where the jury entertains a doubt over the accuracy of prosecution evidence. It may be, for example, that the doubt relates only to one piece of evidence and that the jury are satisfied that the accused is guilty beyond a reasonable doubt on the basis of other evidence. In this event they ought to return a verdict of guilty.

19–45 Problems can arise where the circumstances in which the crime was committed are such that an explanation might reasonably be expected of the accused who asserts his innocence. Cases involving the handling of recently stolen goods offer a convenient illustration. It can happen that when an accused is found in possession of goods which have recently been stolen he offers an explanation of innocent possession which is very difficult for the prosecution to disprove. In such case the trial judge must be careful in his summing up to the jury to avoid conveying the impression that there is any onus on the accused even to raise a doubt in the minds of the jury that his story might be true. The judge must make clear to the jury that the onus throughout is on the prosecution to satisfy them that the accused is guilty beyond a reasonable doubt. If the jury are left with a doubt about the guilt of the accused they must acquit, even if they did not believe the accused's account of how he had come by the goods. Accordingly, in *People (Attorney General) v. Ogleby*[157] the Court of Criminal Appeal quashed the accused's

---

[154] *ibid.* at 9.
[155] See, *e.g.*, *DPP v. Kiely* unreported, Court of Criminal Appeal, March 21, 2001.
[156] See also: *Attorney General v. O'Connor* [1935] Ir. Jur. Rep. 1; *People v. Berber* [1944] I.R. 405; *People v. Quinn* [1965] I.R. 366; *People v. Oglesby* [1966] I.R. 162.
[157] [1966] I.R. 162.

conviction for handling stolen goods because the judge in his direction to the jury had told them that if they rejected the explanation of the accused about how he had come by the goods they were entitled to convict. The Court of Criminal Appeal considered that this might encourage the jury to believe that they should convict if they considered that the accused's explanation was untrue. Their focus would be on whether the accused's account was true or untrue rather than on whether the prosecution had established his guilt beyond a reasonable doubt.

Similar problems have arisen where the accused raised the defence of self defence. In this event the judge must be careful in his directions to the jury not to convey the impression that they should convict unless the accused raises a doubt in their minds that he acted in self defence. In *People (Attorney General) v. Quinn*,[158] for example, the accused pleaded self defence to a homicide. In the course of his charge to the jury the judge gave the impression that there was an onus on the accused to make a sufficient impression in the jury's mind to create at least a doubt about the State's case. The Supreme Court considered this to be a misdirection. In his judgment Walsh J. explained the correct approach for summing up on the onus of proof in a defence of self defence:

"When the evidence in a case, whether it be the evidence offered by the prosecution or by the defence, discloses a possible defence of self-defence the onus remains throughout upon the prosecution to establish that the accused is guilty of the offence charged. The onus is never upon the accused to raise a doubt in the minds of the jury. In such case the burden rests on the prosecution to negative the possible defence of self-defence which has arisen and if, having considered the whole of the evidence, the jury is either convinced of the innocence of the prisoner or left in doubt whether or not he was acting in necessary self-defence they must acquit. Before the possible defence can be left to the jury as an issue there must be some evidence from which the jury would be entitled to find that issue in favour of the appellant. If the evidence for the prosecution does not disclose this possible defence then the necessary evidence will fall to be given by the defence. In such a case, however, where it falls to the defence to give the necessary evidence, it must be made clear to the jury that there is a distinction, fine though it may appear, between adducing the evidence and the burden of proof and that there is no onus whatever upon the accused to establish any degree of doubt in their minds. In directing the jury on the question of the onus of proof it can only be misleading to a jury to refer to 'establishing' the defence 'in such a way as to raise a doubt.' No defence has to be 'established' in any case apart from insanity. In a case where there is evidence, whether it be disclosed in the prosecution case or in the defence case, which is sufficient to leave the issue of self defence to the jury the only question the jury has to consider is whether they are satisfied beyond a reasonable doubt that the accused killed the deceased (if it be a case of homicide) and whether the jury is satisfied beyond reasonable doubt that the prosecution has negatived the issue of self defence. If the jury is not satisfied beyond reasonable doubt on both of these matters the accused must be acquitted."[159]

---

[158] [1965] I.R. 366.
[159] *ibid.* at 382–383.

The presumption that the accused intended the natural and probable consequences of his act on a charge of murder can also present problems on the summing up. The jury must be directed that this presumption will apply unless it is rebutted. The judge must be careful, however, not to convey the impression to the jury that there is an onus on the accused to establish that the killing was accidental. This can prove awkward in a case where the accused elects to give evidence. Inevitably, the judge will want to invite the jury to consider whether the presumption has been rebutted by the accused's evidence or, indeed, other factors which have emerged in the course of the trial. It can be difficult sometimes on the facts of an individual case to come up with a formula which will convey this message to the jury without leaving them with the impression that the onus of proof has shifted from the prosecution to the defence. In *People (DPP) v. Cotter*[159a] Lynch J., giving the judgment of the Court of Criminal Appeal, acknowledged that there was no hard and fast formula for dealing with the presumption that a person is presumed to intend the natural and probable consequences of his or her conduct. Nevertheless, the learned judge proceeded to offer the following as a useful formula for explaining the matter to the jury:

> "If you are satisfied beyond a reasonable doubt that the presumption of intending the natural and probable consequences of conduct has not been rebutted then that presumption applies and you may convict of murder. If, however, you are not so satisfied, then you must have a reasonable doubt as to whether or not the presumption applies and you should acquit of murder. There is no onus on the accused to establish anything. You must consider all the evidence including that of the accused and you ask yourselves has the prosecution satisfied you beyond a reasonable doubt that the presumption has not been rebutted and therefore applies and depending on your answer you proceed accordingly to convict or acquit of murder."

Evidential Burden

19–46   It may happen, of course, that the evidential burden of proof (as distinct from the legal burden of proof) will be shifted by statute from the prosecution to the defence. This is most likely to occur in a statutory offence involving possession.[160] For example, if a person is charged with possession of firearms which have been found concealed on his property or in a car in which he was travelling he assumes the burden of proving that he did not know of their presence. The judge will have to explain to the jury that while the legal burden of proving possession remains on the prosecution throughout, the accused will be assumed to have known of the presence of the firearms unless he can prove that he did not know of their presence.[160a] Where the evidential burden shifts to the accused in this manner it is discharged on the civil standard of a balance of probabilities. The judge's direction to the jury will

---

[159a] Unreported, Court of Criminal Appeal, June 28, 1999.
[160] See, *e.g.*, Criminal Justice (Theft and Fraud offences) Act 2001, s.15 (possession of implement with intention that it be used in the course of or in connection with housebreaking).
[160a] See *People (DPP) v. Byrne* [1988] 2 I.R. 417 for analysis of the appropriate direction in respect of possession under s.29 of the Misuse of Drugs Act 1977.

have to bring out this distinction. The same applies to the defence of insanity which also involves an evidential burden shifting to the accused.

Case for the Defence

Where the judge gives a summing up he or she must be careful to address the case for the defence as well as the prosecution.[161] In particular he or she must put to the jury the defence case as formulated by the defence. Indeed, it is the right of the defence to say what their defence is and to have that put to the jury.[161a] The length and detail of the judge's summing up in relation to the facts, however, will depend very much on the nature of the individual case. The judge can comment on the evidence given. This may even involve a strong expression of his opinion on the facts, providing that he makes it clear to the jury that the responsibility for determining the facts is theirs and that they should ignore his views if they disagree with them.[162] While the judge is entitled to comment adversely on aspects of the accused's explanation for his conduct in the matter charged, he must be careful to avoid stating it in a way which is calculated to discredit it. In *People (Attorney General) v. Oglesby*,[162a] for example, the judge referred to the accused's account of having bought a stolen tape recorder from a man in a pub in mocking terms. This attracted criticism from the Court of Criminal Appeal.

Comment on Failure to give Evidence

Unlike the prosecution the judge can comment on the failure of the accused (or his spouse) to give evidence or to call evidence in respect of some aspect of his defence. There is no obligation on the judge to comment on the failure of the accused to give evidence. He or she has a discretion in the matter which should be exercised discreetly.[163] Where the judge does comment he or she should balance his or her remarks by making it clear that there is no obligation on the accused to go into the witness box. It is not acceptable to state that: "You may take into account that he has not gone into the witness box."[164] Equally, the judge should be careful not to comment on the accused's failure to give evidence in terms which draw attention to the accused's failure to provide an innocent explanation for the presence of incriminating evidence. Not only might this conflict with his right to silence,[165] but it may convey the impression that there is an onus on the accused to provide an innocent explanation.[166]

19–47

By virtue of several statutory enactments the trial judge can invite the jury, in certain circumstances, to draw such inferences as appear proper from the

---

[161] In *R v. Young* [1964] 1 W.L.R. 717 a verdict of guilty brought in by the jury before the judge summed up the defence case was quashed.

[161a] *People (DPP) v. Hanley* unreported, Court of Criminal Appeal, November 5, 1999.

[162] *R v. O'Donnell* 12 Cr.App.R. 219; *R v. Canny* 30 Cr.App.R. 143.

[162a] [1966] I.R. 162.

[163] *People (Attorney General) v. Travers* [1956] I.R. 110.

[164] *ibid.*

[165] *DPP v. Finnerty* [1999] 4 I.R. 364.

[166] See, *e.g., DPP v. Coddington* unreported, Court of Criminal Appeal, May 31, 2001.

failure or refusal of the accused to mention certain facts, give an account of certain matters or consent to the taking of certain samples when required by a member of the Garda Síochána.

Corroboration Warning

Where relevant, the judge must warn the jury of the risks associated with identification error and the danger of convicting on uncorroborated evidence, as well as what may constitute corroboration. The warning need not be expressed in any particular terms. Indeed, its degree and gravity should vary according to the particular circumstances of the case. Where the warning is necessary the judge should convey to the jury that, in the absence of corroboration, they should weigh the evidence of the complainant with great care before they decide to convict.[167] He or she must also explain to the jury that corroboration consists of independent evidence of material circumstances tending to implicate the accused in the commission of the crime with which he is charged. Corroboration on minor details which do not relate directly to guilt is not sufficient.[168]

Judicial Experience

If the case depends on circumstantial evidence the trial judge should warn the jury that they should not convict unless satisfied that it is consistent only with the guilt of the accused.[169] The judge is also entitled to give the benefit of his or her experience, for example, drawing the jury's attention to the fact that the accused, contrary to the usual practice, has not adduced medical evidence to support his plea of insanity.[170]

Directions on the Law

19–48   Another vital feature of the judge's summing up to the jury concerns his or her directions on the law. These must be aimed at helping the jury to reach a verdict in the instant case.[171] Accordingly, the judge should aim to translate the relevant rules and principles into workable standards which could be applied by a layman, and avoid broad disquisitions on the law which are aimed more at an academic or professional audience.[172] Equally a failure to explain fully the legal principles which the jury must apply will provide grounds for appeal.[172a] When dealing with the particular charge he must

---

[167]   *People (Attorney General) v. Williams* [1940] I.R. 195; *State (Attorney General) v. Moore* [1950] Ir.Jur.Rep. 45.

[168]   *People (Attorney General) v. Travers* [1956] I.R. 110.

[169]   *Attorney General v. Finkel* (1951) Frewen 123.

[170]   *People v. Manning* 89 I.L.T.R. 155.

[171]   *R v. Bonnyman* 28 Cr.App.R. 131. They should avoid irrelevant matter such as a disparaging reference to a previous trial and acquittal of the accused; *Attorney General v. Hurley* 71 I.L.T.R. 29.

[172]   See, *e.g., R v. Lawrence* [1982] A.C. 510, *per* Lord Hailsham LC at 519.

[172a]   Sometimes it can be difficult to identify the borderline between an explanation of the law, which is within the judge's province, and a discussion of the merits and facts of the case, which is not; see *DPP v. Donegan* unreported, Court of Criminal Appeal, July 26, 1999.

instruct the jury on the necessary ingredients of the offence,[173] including where relevant any shift in the evidential burden of proof.

The directions on the law pertaining to the offence charged may also have to deal with the possibility of the jury being entitled to bring in a verdict of guilty of a lesser offence than that charged. For the most part this will not pose a problem as the lesser offence is usually an ingredient or element of the more serious offence. In the case of murder, however, it may be open to the jury to bring in a conviction for manslaughter on the grounds of provocation. Where the defence of provocation is raised on a charge of murder the judge should rule on whether there is any evidence of provocation which, having regard to the accused's temperament, character and circumstances might have caused him to lose control of himself at the time of the wrongful act.[174] The judge must bear in mind that the test for provocation is entirely subjective.[175] This requires that there should be some evidence that the actual accused was provoked to the extent of total loss of self control; evidence which may be provided directly from either prosecution or defence witnesses or by inference from such evidence.[176] If there is evidence of provocation the judge must leave the matter for the jury and direct them on the ingredients of the limited defence.[177] Although it was held in *People (DPP) v. Davis*[178] that the defence of provocation cannot be put to the jury unless the defence has raised some evidence of the defence (either at the trial or through earlier explanations of his actions which have been put in evidence by the prosecution), it has not yet been determined whether the judge should leave the defence to the jury where the accused has either not directly relied upon the defence during the course of the hearing before the jury or has relied upon a defence which is inconsistent with provocation.[179]

Exceptionally, on a charge of murder, the judge may direct the jury that on the evidence they cannot as a matter of law, bring in the lesser verdict of manslaughter.[180] In any case where the accused has raised a defence, such as self-defence, duress, intoxication, etc., and has introduced evidence the judge must direct the jury on the relevant law.

19–49

---

173 *R v. Lincoln* [1944] 1 All E.R. 604; *People v. Bristow* (1961) Frewen 249.

174 *DPP v. MacEoin* [1978] I.R. 34.

175 *DPP v. Kelly* [2000] 2 I.R. 1; *DPP v. Mullane* unreported, Court of Criminal Appeal, March 11, 1997; *DPP v. McDonagh* unreported, Court of Criminal Appeal, May 31, 2001; *DPP v. Boyle* unreported, Court of Criminal Appeal, July 29, 1999.

176 The judge need not direct the jury on provocation if there is no evidence of provocation; *People (DPP) v. Davis* [2001] 1 I.R. 146; *DPP v. McDonagh* unreported, Court of Criminal Appeal, May 31, 2001.

177 For discussion of the ingredients of the defence see, F McAuley and P McCutcheon *Criminal Liability* (Dublin, Round Hall, 2000); P Charleton *Offences against the Person* (Dublin, Butterworths, 1992).

178 [2001] 1 I.R. 146.

179 See, *e.g., DPP v. Halligan* unreported, Court of Criminal Appeal, July 13, 1998; *DPP v. McDonagh* unreported, Court of Criminal Appeal, May 31, 2001.

180 *State v. McMullen* [1925] 2 I.R. 9; *People v. Cadden* (1956) Frewen 157; *People v. McGrath* (1960) Frewen 192; *R v. Vickers* 61 Cr.App.R. 48. See also, *People (DPP) v. McDonagh* unreported, Court of Criminal Appeal, May 31, 2001.

Grounds for Appeal

Ultimately, it must be remembered that the judge's summing to the jury is an oral presentation which the members of the jury hear only once. Accordingly, its adequacy and/or accuracy must be assessed on the basis of the impact it can be expected to have had on the jury at the time in the courtroom and not on the basis of a clinical parsing and dissection of words as they appear subsequently on the transcript of the trial. Kennedy C.J. described as follows the approach which should be taken by the Court of Criminal Appeal when considering a ground of appeal based on an alleged misdirection by the trial judge to the jury:

> "In general, this court should not approach the consideration of a trial judge's charge to the jury at the end of a trial as a written document to be read and examined as it appears before us on paper, but we should consider and value it for what it was – the living, spoken word of the judge, addressed to the minds of the jurors through their ears, uttered once only, to produce certain immediate effects and impressions, and delivered in the atmosphere of the trial created by the evidence, the speeches of counsel, and the whole conduct of the proceedings. Such a rule is particularly important in the consideration of the objection with which I am now dealing, an objection not made at the trial."[181]

I. Jury Deliberations

1. Jury Retirement

19–50 At the conclusion of the judge's charge the jury will normally retire to consider their verdict. An officer of the court will be appointed to attend to them and to ensure that no unauthorised person communicates with them during their deliberations. Great care is taken to ensure that the jury's verdict is seen to be the verdict of the members of the jury alone, uninfluenced by anything they may have seen or heard from any unauthorised source after they have retired. Accordingly, once they have retired they cannot separate without the special permission of the court. In practice they are normally kept together until they have reached a verdict or until it is apparent that they will be unable to reach a verdict. On occasions this can mean that they are sent to an hotel overnight or even for several nights.

2. The Issue Paper

When the jury retire they are given an "issue paper" which sets out the charges and an indication of the issues to be determined. It would appear that the judge can submit certain questions for the jury in addition to the issue paper.[182] They also have access to any exhibits which have been put in evidence, including any written statement by the accused. If necessary, the

---

[181] *Attorney General v. O'Shea* [1931] I.R. 713 at 726–727.
[182] *People (Attorney General) v. McCormack* (1944) 1 Frewen 55.

accused's statement can be edited in advance to exclude extraneous matters such as references to previous convictions or a co-accused. Care must also be take to ensure that only documents which have been admitted in evidence are given to the jury. If they are given anything which was not in evidence the trial may be held to be unsatisfactory and a conviction quashed. In *People (Attorney General) v. Moran*,[183] for example, a prosecution witness detracted in his testimony in the witness box from significant parts of his statement to the police in which he had claimed that the accused was present at the scene of the crime. As a result there was no direct evidence given at the trial establishing the presence of the accused at the scene of the crime. By accident a copy of the witness's earlier statement was included with some of the exhibits which were given to the jury when they retired to consider their verdict. The mistake was discovered a short time later and the statement retrieved. Nevertheless, the Court of Criminal Appeal considered that it could not be sure that the jury's assessment of the evidence and determination might not have been affected by the contents of the statements. Accordingly, it quashed the conviction and ordered a re-trial.

3. Further Communications

There may be further communication between the jury and the court even after they have retired to consider their verdict. This, however, should not be used to put questions which could not legally have been put by counsel in his or her examination of those witnesses.[184]

If either the prosecution or the defence wishes to raise an objection to any aspect or part of the judge's charge they should do so by submitting appropriate requisitions to the judge after the jury have retired. A failure by the defence to submit appropriate requisitions at this stage may put it at a disadvantage in making the objection on appeal.[184a] The failure will not necessarily preclude the defence from raising the matter on appeal. If the judge thinks fit he or she may recall the jury and direct them further in the light of any such requisitions.[185] The jury may also ask for further assistance from the judge. In this event the assistance must be given in open court in the presence of counsel.[186] Even without such a request the judge may himself wish to correct some direction he has given.

---

[183] (1974) 1 Frewen 380.

[184] *State v. Kelly and Gorman* [1925] 2 I.R. 73. In this case the questions were put by the jury before the judge's charge in order to clear up some doubts they had about the reliability of identification evidence.

[184a] *People (DPP) v. Noonan* [1998] 2 I.R. 439; *DPP v. Moloney* unreported, Court of Criminal Appeal, March 2, 1992.

[185] *R v. Cocks* 63 Cr.App.R. 79.

[186] *R v. Willmott* 10 Cr.App.R. 173. The furnishing of erroneous information on a matter which the jury clearly considered important will provide grounds for quashing the conviction; *People (DPP) v. McDonald* unreported, Court of Criminal Appeal, January 31, 2000.

4. Recall of Witnesses

19–51   The jury may ask for any witness to be recalled. In *People (Attorney General) v. O'Brien*[187] the Supreme Court was called upon to rule on whether the trial judge could recall a witness to give evidence after the jury had retired. Although previous judgments of the Court of Criminal Appeal suggested that the trial judge enjoyed a discretion in the matter, recent English decisions suggested that the judge had no such power. In giving the judgment of the Supreme Court Davitt P. expressed dissatisfaction with the rigidity of the English approach which prevented the jury from hearing further evidence in an attempt to resolve questions which they felt were left hanging in the air. While accepting that there should not normally be a departure from the usual procedure in which each side's case should be put fully in the time and space allocated to it. Davitt P. was of the view that:

> " . . . procedure is a means to an end and not an end in itself; and that the purpose of formal procedure is to facilitate the orderly and efficient transaction of the business in question. That purpose would be frustrated if, by too rigid an adherence to forms, a proper decision on the matter in hand were to be prevented. Where the business in question is the administration of justice, whether civil or criminal, it is all the more important that procedure should be regarded in true perspective and with a proper sense of proportion; and that where there is a conflict between the requirements of justice and the forms of procedure justice should not be the one to suffer.[188]

The learned judge went on to declare that the trial judge always enjoyed a discretion to recall a witness, or even to call a witness who had not previously been called, and that that discretion could be exercised in appropriate circumstances both before and after the summing up:

> "In this country the proper rule is, in our view, that a trial judge has power in the exercise of his discretion to allow a witness to be recalled and to give evidence at any stage of the case before the jury agrees on a verdict. That discretion must, of course, be judicially exercised. The propriety of recalling a witness and of the questions addressed to him must to a great extent depend upon the course of the trial, the facts of the case, and other matters which can be fully and properly appreciated only by the trial judge himself. His discretion should therefore not be interfered with unless an injustice has resulted from its exercise."[189]

This discretion can be exercised to recall a witness to shed further light on his earlier evidence, even if the effect of that further clarification is to embarrass the defence.[190] It should not be exercised, however, in order to facilitate defence counsel re-calling a witness in order to repair damage which has been done to the defence case as a result of questions from the jury, where the

---

[187]   [1963] I.R. 65.
[188]   *ibid.* at 71.
[189]   *ibid.* at 80.
[190]   *Attorney General v. McDermott* [1933] I.R. 512.

defence questions could and should have been put to the witness in the course of the trial.[191]

5. Deliberations in Secret

It is firmly established that the deliberations of the jury are secret. They **19–52** cannot be questioned subsequently, either as a group or as individuals, about how they reached their verdict. This applies even if there is a legitimate doubt over whether the conviction of the accused is fully in accordance with what the jury agreed. In *People (Attorney General) v. Longe,*[192] for example, the accused was charged on an indictment containing two charges of dangerous driving causing death and dangerous driving simpliciter. In the course of his directions the judge also explained that they could return a verdict of careless driving if they were not satisfied that either of the two counts were made out. The issue paper, as completed by the jury, recorded "disagreed" on count no.1 and "guilty" on count no.2. The judge specifically asked the foreman if it was a verdict of "guilty" to which the foreman replied "yes". The judge proceeded to sentence the accused on the charge of dangerous driving. The next day the foreman appeared in the court to inform the judge that he and the other members of the jury had intended to convict of the lesser charge of careless driving and felt that they had done so. The trial judge considered that he had no power to change the verdict of the jury at that point. On appeal to the Court of Criminal Appeal the accused argued that the court had jurisdiction under section 12 of the Courts (Supplemental Provisions) Act 1961 to investigate the matter. The court, however, considered that any such investigation would inevitably involve the questioning and cross-examination of the jury members about their deliberations. In the opinion of the court, to proceed down this road would "end the finality of a jury verdict and open the way for any juror (bona fide or otherwise), after a correction in a criminal case, to originate an investigation of this kind."[193] It would also run contrary to the well established principle that the nature of the jury deliberation in a criminal case should not be revealed or inquired into. Accordingly, the court rejected the appeal.

6. Overnight Suspension of Deliberation

It used to be the case that the jury were required to continue deliberating until they had reached a verdict or until it became apparent that they would not be able to agree. While this ensured that the jury deliberations would not be influenced by third parties, it carried with it the danger that verdicts would be reached due to exhaustion or a desire to be released back to their ordinary

---

[191] In *State v. Kelly and Gorman* [1925] 2 I.R. 73 the defence were embarrassed as a result of the answers which were given in response to questions put by the jury at the close of the prosecution and defence cases. The Court of Criminal Appeal upheld the trial judge's refusal to recall a witness in order to repair the damage by putting questions that could have been put in the course of the trial.

[192] [1967] I.R. 369.

lives rather than as a result of calm considered reflection on the evidence. Accordingly, the practice developed of sending the jury to a hotel for a meal and overnight stay when they had not completed their deliberations by late evening. They would return to the court the next day to continue their deliberations. One of the primary purposes of this practice would of course be defeated if a tired jury was required or even permitted to continue their deliberations overnight in the hotel. Any encouragement to the jury to pursue this course would be likely to result in the quashing of their verdict. The issue arose in *People (DPP) v. Gavin*[194] where it was dealt with by McGuinness J:

> "It seems clear from this passage that the judge, and indeed counsel for the prosecution, envisaged that the jury would continue their deliberations and the consideration of their verdict at the hotel later that night. In fact, they are being encouraged to take that course. This cannot be right. The practice of suspending the jury's deliberations and sending them to a hotel for the night was introduced in recent years precisely because it was held to be wrong to keep a jury deliberating late at night in their jury room when in fact they had reached the point of exhaustion and could not give proper consideration to the vital questions which they had to decide. The jury was sent to a hotel overnight in order to have a break from their deliberations, to rest and recuperate, so that they could return to their consideration of their verdict the following morning rested and with a fresh mind. All of this laudable purpose is negatived if the jury is encouraged, and virtually instructed, to continue to consider their verdict late at night ... in a hotel after their dinner and possibly some drinks."[195]

J. The Verdict

1. Majority Verdicts

Availability

19–53   At common law the verdict of the jury, whether for conviction or acquittal, had to be unanimous. This remains the position where the jury is composed of only 10 members. The Criminal Justice Act 1984, however, has introduced the option of a majority verdict in certain circumstances. It stipulates that the jury verdict need not be unanimous in a case where there are not fewer than 11 jurors if 10 of them agree on the verdict.[196] In other words acceptable majorities can be: 10 out of 12, 11 out of 12 and 10 out of 11. Where the jury consists of only ten members its verdict must be unanimous.[197]

The effective operation of these provisions is dependant on transparency with respect to the nature of a verdict of guilty. Accordingly, where the jury returns a verdict of guilty in any case the court shall not accept the verdict

---

[193]   *ibid.* at 377.
[194]   Unreported, Court of Criminal Appeal, July 27, 2000.
[195]   *ibid.* at 11–12.
[196]   Criminal Justice Act 1984, s.25(1).
[197]   Where the jury members fall below 10 the trial will have to be abandoned.

unless the foreman has stated in open court whether the verdict is unanimous or by an acceptable majority.[198] If it is a majority verdict he must also specify the number of jurors who agreed to the verdict. If, however, the verdict is one of not guilty the court shall cause it to be taken in such a way that it is not revealed whether it was unanimous or by a majority.[199]

The availability of a majority verdict is subject to certain restrictions in the case of a guilty verdict. In particular, a majority verdict of guilty cannot be accepted by the court unless it appears to the court that the jury have had at least two hours for deliberation.[200] Subject to this absolute minimum of two hours, the court cannot accept a majority verdict of guilty unless it appears to the court that the jury have had such period of time for deliberation as the court thinks reasonable having regard to the nature and complexity of the case. In any individual case this could result in the court requiring the jury to deliberate for a period substantially longer than two hours before it is prepared to accept a majority guilty verdict.

It is also important to emphasise that a majority verdict cannot be accepted unless the foreman of the jury states in open court that it was a majority verdict and the number of jurors who agreed with the verdict. The Court of Criminal Appeal in *People (DPP) v. Ryan*[201] ruled that this requirement was stated in mandatory terms in the Criminal Justice Act 1984. Accordingly, failure to comply with it will inevitably result in the quashing of the conviction.[202]

Failure to Agree

If the jury fail to agree they will be discharged and a new trial ordered. In **19–54** *State v. M'Mullen*[203] the Court of Criminal Appeal had to consider the extent of the judge's discretion to discharge a jury in the event of their failure to agree. In that case the accused was charged with the capital murder of a member of the Garda Síochána who was killed while attempting to arrest the accused in the course of his duty. In his direction to the jury the judge told them that they would have to reach a verdict of murder or nothing; manslaughter was not an option. Over the course of the next two and a half hours the foreman of the jury returned on several occasions to tell the judge that they could not agree on a charge of murder and indicated that they might be able to agree on manslaughter. The judge consistently denied that option and eventually discharged them after two and half hours when the foreman had made it clear that they still could not agree. In his attempt to prevent a re-trial the accused argued, *inter alia*, that the judge had no right to discharge the jury in the circumstances. Kennedy C.J., giving the judgment of the Court of Criminal Appeal, explained that it is a matter for the trial judge to determine when it is appropriate to discharge the jury before they have returned their verdict:

---

[198] Criminal Justice Act 1984, s.25(2).
[199] *ibid.* s.25(4).
[200] *ibid.* s.25(3).
[201] [1925] 2 I.R. 9.
[202] *ibid.* at 19.

"The rule stated in sweeping terms by Coke (Co. Litt. 227 *b*), qualified by Blackstone (4 Bl. Com. 360), and stated by Foster to be exploded (*Kinloch's Case*: Foster's Crown Cases, at p.31), has now given place to the established rule and practice that it is lawful for the judge at the trial to discharge the jury before verdict when necessity, in the sense of a high degree of need, for such discharge is made evident to his mind from facts ascertained by him. The existence of such necessity or high degree of need is a matter for the determination of the judge at the trial, and for him alone, and his decision is not open to review. It is a matter depending upon the exercise of a judicial discretion both as to the facts relevant to be considered in the particular case and as to the effect of those facts. The statement of the result upon the record suffices to establish that the particular order for discharge was lawfully made, see *per* Erle C.J. in *Winsor v. The Queen* L.R. 1 Q.B. 289, 390. If the Judge is satisfied that the jury cannot agree, or that unanimity can only be obtained by coercing some jurors by detention and physical discomforts to sacrifice conscientious convictions, no one would say that, were it open to review, the judge's discretion and authority had been improperly exercised by discharging the jury."[204]

19–55   It is respectfully submitted that the learned judge's reference to the trial judge's exercise of discretion not being open to review does not preclude a higher court considering whether, on the facts of an individual case, the discretion had come into play. Indeed, in *M'Mullen* Kennedy C.J. went on to make it clear that the Court of Criminal Appeal was satisfied that the jury was not able to agree and that the trial judge was best placed to determine that that disagreement was not likely to disappear after deliberation. Accordingly, his decision was not reviewable. If, however, there was no evidence that the jury were having difficulty in their deliberations and no evidence of any other irregularity, then it is submitted that the trial judge would have no discretion to discharge the jury.

Disagreements on Some Counts

If the jury agrees on some counts and disagree on others, there will have to be a new trial with respect to the latter. A new trial will not be necessary, however, if the verdict they have agreed on the former amounts in substance to a conviction or acquittal, as the case may be, on the latter. Equally, the prosecution may be prepared to accept the verdict on the counts on which the jury have agreed, in which case it will enter a *nolle prosequi* on the others.

2. General Verdict

19–56   Where the jury agree on a verdict they may bring in either a general verdict or a special verdict. The former will declare the accused guilty or not guilty. Where there are several counts he will be convicted on all, acquitted on all or found guilty of some and not guilty on others. It may happen that some

---

[203]   Unreported, Court of Criminal Appeal, July 12, 1999.

[204]   See also, *People (DPP) v. Higginbotham* unreported, Court of Criminal Appeal, November 17, 2000.

counts relate to the same type of offence and differ only in degree as, for example, in assault[205] and assault causing harm.[206] In this event if the jury convict on the more serious offence, they should be directed to return no verdict on the lesser.[207] It may also happen that the accused is charged with alternative offences, as in larceny and handling stolen goods. In this event, if the jury convict on one count they may be discharged from returning a verdict on the alternative count. Further complications can arise where several defendants are tried together. Although, as a general rule, some may be found guilty and others not guilty, it may happen that the acquittal of one or some requires the acquittal of another. This can happen where the offence charged requires the involement of at least two persons. If two persons are charged with conspiring with each other (and no-one else), for example, the acquittal of one necessitates the acquittal of the other.

3. Alternative Verdicts

Introduction

At common law there are circumstances in which the jury could find the accused not guilty of the offence charged in the indictment but guilty of some other offence which has not been specifically charged. For the most part these concern situations where the elements of the other offence are encompassed within the elements of the offence charged. The primary example is murder and manslaughter. Where the accused is charged with murder the jury may return a conviction for manslaughter if they are not satisfied that the prosecution has established malice aforethought or if they are satisfied that the accused acted under provocation.[208] Examples which arise more frequently in practice, perhaps, concern situations where statute has prescribed a higher penalty for a common law offence which has been committed with special or aggravating circumstances. In such cases the jury can return a verdict of guilty of the basic common law offence if they are not satisfied that the special or aggravating circumstances charged in the indictment have not been established. To these must be added a motley collection of statutory examples introduced in a piecemeal fashion over many years.[209] Typically, such a statutory provision will stipulate that where a specified offence is charged in the indictment it is open to the jury to find the accused guilty of a different offence specified in the same statutory provision. Almost invariably, the components of the latter offence will be encompassed within the definition of the offence charged.

19–57

---

[205] Non-fatal Offences against the Person Act 1997, s.2.
[206] *ibid.* s.3.
[207] If the jury acquits on the more serious offence it is open to them to convict of the lesser offence.
[208] *People v. White* [1947] I.R. 247.
[209] See examples listed in Ryan and Magee, *op. cit.*, pp.366–370.

The unprincipled growth of these alternative verdict provisions has given rise to problems, particularly in the framing of the indictment.[210] It is not always clear in individual cases whether it will be open to the jury to return a verdict of guilty to a lesser offence than that charged in the indictment. To avoid the injustice of a defendant who is clearly guilty of an offence being acquitted, the prosecution may be tempted to charge not just the serious offence which they feel that they can prove, but also a number of lesser offences representing their fallback position. The net result is an indictment which is longer and more complex than might otherwise have been the case if the jury was free to return a verdict of guilty to a lesser offence, which was necessarily subsumed within the definition of the more serious offence charged. It would appear, however, that the Criminal Law Act 1997 has brought some rationalisation to this area of the law. Indictments for murder, capital murder and other offences are each dealt with separately.

Murder etc.

On an indictment for murder where the evidence does not warrant a conviction for murder, the accused may be found guilty of any of the following offences for which a conviction is warranted: manslaughter or causing serious harm with intent to cause serious harm; any offence of which the accused may be found guilty by virtue of an enactment specifically so providing (including an offence under section 7(3) of the Criminal Law Act 1997);[211] an attempt to commit murder or an attempt to commit any other offence of which the accused might be found guilty under this provision; or an offence under the Criminal Law (Suicide) Act 1993.[212] He may not, however, be found guilty on the same indictment of any offence apart from one of these. Similarly, the accused may be convicted for any of these offences or for murder as an alternative to an offence charged in the indictment as murder under section 3 of the Criminal Justice Act 1990, or for an attempt to commit such murder.[213]

19–58   Where a person is being tried on indictment for any offence (apart from treason, murder to which section 3 of the Criminal Justice Act 1990 applies or murder), and the evidence does not warrant a conviction for the offence

---

[210]   See, *e.g.*, Ryan and Magee, *op. cit.*, pp.370–371.

[211]   S.7(2) of the Criminal Law Act 1997 creates the offence of impeding the apprehension or prosecution of a person who has committed an arrestable offence. S.7(3) permits the conviction of an accused of an offence under s.7(2) as an alternative to a conviction of the substantive arrestable offence charged in the indictment. Where an accused is charged with murder, therefore, s.7(3) permits an alternative verdict of guilty of impeding the apprehension or prosecution of a person for murder to be entered where the evidence so warrants it.

[212]   Criminal Law Act 1997, s.9(2), as amended by Non-fatal Offences against the Person Act 1997, s.29.

[213]   Criminal Law Act 1997, s.9(3). Murder under s.3 of the 1990 Act is: murder of a member of the Garda Síochána or a prison officer acting in the course of duty; murder done in furtherance of an offence under ss. 6–9 of the Offences against the State Act 1939 or in the course or furtherance of the activities of an unlawful organisation; and murder of the head, member of government or diplomatic officer of a foreign state, where the murder was committed within the State for a political motive.

charged, he or she may be found guilty of another offence where the allegations in the indictment amount to or include (expressly or by implication) an allegation of that other offence.[214] Alternatively, he can be found guilty of any offence of which he could be found guilty on an indictment charging that other offence. An allegation of an offence under these provisions includes an allegation of attempting to commit the offence.[215] It follows that a verdict of guilty of an attempt to commit the offence charged may be returned as an alternative to a verdict of guilty of the offence charged, so long as the allegations in the indictment amount to or include (expressly or impliedly) an allegation of attempting to commit that offence. Equally, it would appear that a verdict of guilty of an attempt to commit an offence other than that charged is possible, so long as the allegations in the indictment amount to or include (expressly or impliedly) an allegation of attempting to commit that other offence.

Attempts and Completed offence

The 1997 Act specifically states that where a person is charged in the indictment with attempting to commit an offence, or with any assault or other act preliminary to an offence, but not with the completed offence, the accused may be convicted of the attempt as charged even though he or she is shown to be guilty of the completed offence.[216] In the case of trial by jury, this possibility is subject to the discretion of the court to discharge the jury with a view to the preferment of an indictment for the completed offence.

The Test for an Alternative Offence

Clearly these provisions extend significantly the range of offences of which an accused can be found guilty on an indictment. Just how significant a provision it is will depend on how the courts assess when the allegations in an indictment amount to or include, expressly or impliedly, an allegation of an offence other than that charged.

A count expressly includes an allegation of another offence if what remains, after having struck out from the particulars those allegations which have not been established by the evidence laid before the jury, amounts to valid particulars for the other offence. In *R v. Lillis*[217] (dealing with the equivalent English provision), for example, the accused was charged with burglary in that having entered a building as a trespasser on a certain date he stole a lawnmower. The prosecution evidence revealed that he had permission to enter the building and to borrow the lawnmower. It was just that he had failed to return it when he ought to have returned it. The judge ruled that there was no case to answer with respect to the burglary but invited the jury to consider the possibility of theft on the basis that the accused had appropriated the mower dishonestly by keeping it. The jury convicted the accused of theft. He

---

[214] Criminal Law Act 1997, s.9(4).
[215] *ibid.* s.9(5).
[216] *ibid.* s.9(5).
[217] [1972] 2 Q.B. 236.

appealed arguing that a count which basically alleged that he had stolen a lawnmower inside a building on a certain date should not expose him to the risk of conviction for subsequently stealing the lawnmower outside the building. The Court of Appeal was not persuaded. The allegations in the count still provided the basis for a valid count of theft of the lawnmower even after the matters which the prosecution could not prove were omitted. The only weakness was the fact that the framed count specified the wrong date. The court ruled, however, that a variation between the date laid in the indictment and the evidence as to when the offence occurred will only be a good ground of appeal if the variation prejudiced or embarrassed the accused in the presentation of his defence. The facts in this case did not disclose any such prejudice.

19–59   Unfortunately, the case law does not offer a very clear statement of when a count includes by implication an allegation of another offence. The leading English case is the House of Lords decision in *R v. Wilson; R v. Jenkins*.[218] In that case Lord Roskill held that the previously accepted test laid down by Sachs L.J. in *R v. Springfield*[219] was too restrictive. The *Springfield* test was relatively straightforward. A verdict of guilty for the alternative offence could be returned only where the commission of that other offence was a necessary step towards the commission of the offence charged. In an indictment for robbery, for example, the prosecution must establish that the accused steals and, immediately before or at the time of doing so, and in order to do so, uses force on any person or seeks to put any person in fear of being then and there subjected to force. Clearly, a count charging robbery will not succeed if the prosecution cannot prove that the accused was guilty of stealing. Proof of stealing, therefore, is a necessary step in establishing a count of robbery. Accordingly, a jury may return a verdict of guilty of stealing on a charge of robbery even though the indictment does not contain a specific count of stealing. It is worth emphasising, however, that the "necessary step" test will be satisfied only if the commission of the alternative offence is, as a matter of legal definition, a necessary step towards the commission of the offence charged. It will not be sufficient that the prosecution has led evidence which suggests that the accused committed the alternative offence if the definition of the offence charged in the indictment does not as a matter of law impliedly include the elements of the alternative offence.

19–60   The problem with the "necessary step" test propounded in *Springfield*, as interpreted by Roskill L.J. in *R v. Wilson; R v. Jenkins*, is that a verdict of guilty could not be returned for the alternative offence if, as a matter of law, it was possible to commit the offence charged in the indictment without also committing the alternative offence. In *R v. Wilson; R v. Jenkins* the issue for the House of Lords was whether the appellants had been lawfully convicted of assault occasioning actual bodily harm on counts which charged them with

---

[218]   [1984] A.C. 242.
[219]   (1969) 53 Cr.App.R. 608.

maliciously inflicting grievous bodily harm (contrary to section 20 of the Offences against the Person Act 1861) and entering a building as a trespasser and inflicting grievous bodily harm on a person therein (contrary to section 9(1)(b) of the Theft Act 1968). The issue, therefore, was whether an allegation of inflicting grievous bodily harm impliedly includes an allegation of assault occasioning actual bodily harm. The House of Lords upheld the convictions despite assuming in favour of the appellants that it was possible to inflict harm without actually assaulting the victim. In other words, the conviction for an offence other than that charged in the indictment was upheld, despite the fact that the "necessary step" test was not satisfied. It is not entirely clear from Lord Roskill's judgment, however, how the appropriate test should be formulated. Emmins suggests that a count impliedly includes an allegation of another offence not only when it is a necessary step towards committing the offence charged, but also when in the normal course of events a person committing the latter will also commit the former.[220]

Effect of Conviction of Alternative offence

Where a person charged on indictment with any offence is convicted of some other offence of which he might be found guilty on that charge, conviction of that other offence shall be an acquittal of the offence charged.[221]

Other Provisions

These alternative verdict provisions in the Criminal Law Act 1997 clearly render redundant many of the pre-existing statutory provisions permitting alternative verdicts. The Act, however, does not specifically repeal the other measures. It might not be wise, therefore, to ignore them entirely. Indeed, some of them patently are not subsumed within the provisions of the 1997 Act. Under the Offences against the Person Act 1861, for example, a person charged with the murder of a child may be convicted of concealment of birth.[222]

4. Special Verdict

A special verdict is one in which the jury merely makes a finding as to the facts leaving the legal inferences from those facts to be drawn by the court. Such verdicts are generally quite rare in practice.[223] Ryan and Magee cite the well-known example of *R v. Dudley and Stephens*[224] in which the accused were charged with the murder of a boy while they were all ship-wrecked at sea.[225] The jury found that the accused had killed the boy and ate his flesh in order to save themselves from starvation. It was left to the court to decide whether these facts warranted a conviction for murder.

19–61

---

220   J. Sprack *Emmins on Criminal Procedure* (8th ed., London, Beachstone Press, 2000, p.307.
221   Criminal Law Act 1997, s.9(7).
222   Offences against the Person Act 1861, s.60.
223   Such verdicts should be returned only in the most exceptional cases; *R v. Bourne* 36 Cr.App.R. 125.
224   (1884) 14 Q.B.D. 273.
225   Ryan and Magee, *op. cit.*, p.372.

Where a special verdict is encountered in practice it is most likely to be the verdict of guilty but insane. Technically, the verdict of guilty but insane is a special verdict. If the accused was legally insane at the time he committed the *actus reus* of the offence charged he would have lacked the appropriate *mens rea* and, as such, is not guilty. If, however, the jury is satisfied beyond a reasonable doubt that the accused committed the act or was guilty of the omission charged and it appears to them that he was legally insane at the time of commission or omission, they should return a verdict of guilty but insane.[226] Technically this is an acquittal. What it says is that the accused is guilty of the act or omission alleged against him but that he was insane at the time of commission or omission as the case may be. In such a case the accused will be committed to the Central Mental Hospital where he will be kept in custody at the will and pleasure of the government.[227] Accordingly, it is highly unlikely that the accused will raise a defence of insanity in any case apart from murder. Even then it is rarely raised by the accused. Where he does seek to rely on insanity the onus is on him to establish the defence as a matter of probability. If he succeeds, the onus shifts on to the prosecution to prove beyond a reasonable doubt that the accused was not insane at the time of the commission of the *actus reus*. Equally, however, the issue can be raised by the prosecution.[228] The prosecution is under no obligation to furnish the defence with all medical reports it may have received.[229]

5. Receiving the Verdict

The General Rule

19–62 Generally, the judge will accept the first verdict that the jury returns. Indeed, it would appear that the judge has no discretion to do otherwise where the verdict is clear and unambiguous. He or she should not even ask the jury to reconsider it in such a case.[230] The verdict is not complete, however, until the jury have dealt with all possible alternatives open to them on the indictment.[231] Moreover, even where the verdict is complete there may be circumstances in which it is either possible or desirable for the judge to ask the jury to reconsider their verdict or certain parts of it. If the verdict is ambiguous or inconsistent, for example, the judge may ask the jury to reconsider it in the light of any further directions where necessary.[232] Equally or alternatively, he or she may try to clear up the ambiguity or inconsistency by putting appropriate questions to the jury.[233] It does not follow, however, that an

---

[226] Trial of Lunatics Act 1883, s.2(1).
[227] Criminal Lunatics Act 1800, s.1; Lunacy (Ireland) Act 1821, ss.1 and 8; Central Criminal Lunatic Asylum (Ireland) Act 1845, s.8; Mental Treatment Act 1961, s.39.
[228] *Attorney General v. Boylan* [1937] I.R. 449.
[229] *People v. Kelly* (1962) Frewen 267
[230] *R v. Robinson* [1975] Q.B. 508.
[231] *R v. Carter* [1964] 2 Q.B. 1.
[232] *Attorney General v. Lane* 63 I.L.T.R. 6.
[233] *R v. Hawkes* 22 Cr.App.R. 172; R v. White 45 Cr.App.R. 34; *R v. Larkin* [1943] K.B. 174.

apparently inconsistent verdict cannot stand.[234] If the intention of the jury to convict is clear the Court of Criminal Appeal may decide that no miscarriage of justice has occurred and decline to quash the conviction. On the other hand, if the verdict is such that no judgment can properly be entered a re-trial may be ordered.[235]

Riders

Occasionally, the jury will add a rider to their verdict such as, for example, a recommendation to mercy after a verdict of guilty. This will not normally vitiate the verdict. Similarly, words added to the verdict which do not vary its effect may be disregarded.[236] In *Attorney General v. O'Shea*,[237] for example, the jury returned a verdict of guilty of murder but added the rider: "The jury are of the opinion that this was an unpremeditated crime, committed during a period of mental abnormality, and strongly recommend that special consideration be given to this factor." On appeal it was argued that this amounted to a verdict of not guilty of murder. Kennedy C.J. rejected this argument and expanded on riders to jury verdicts as follows:

> "The arguments on this branch of the appeal are not in the least tenable in the view of the Court. In some respects they run counter to long-settled legal principles. In the first place, unlike some of the cases cited, where the 'rider' was a clear *qualification* of the verdict, and, therefore, necessarily read as part of it (as where the form is, 'guilty, *but* . . .,' etc.), the verdict in the present case is complete in itself, and separate from the 'rider'. No doubt if a 'rider', though separate in form, discovered an error in the verdict, or disclosed a miscarriage of justice involved in the verdict, should it stand alone, the Court would not allow the mere separation of the 'rider' from the verdict in form to bring about injustice. The 'rider' in the present case, however, does not contain anything which constitutes a qualification of the crime of murder, or which would reduce it to manslaughter. 'Premeditation' is not an element of murder, and is a wholly different thing from the essential ingredient of 'malice aforethought'. An unintended homicide, caused while committing a felony with violence against the person (as, for example, rape), is murder in law. The addition to a verdict of a 'guilty of murder' of a statement that it was done 'without premeditation' has actually been held in several cases not to modify a verdict of murder. *Reg v. Doherty* 16 Cox C.C. 306; *R. v. Maloney* 9 Cox C.C. 6; *Fairbrother's Case* 1 Cr.App.R. 233 were cited to us in argument.
>
> With regard to the statement in the 'rider' that the crime was committed 'during a period of mental abnormality,' the court is equally clear that no modification of the verdict of guilty of murder is to be found there. Abnormality is not in law insanity which would relieve the individual of the consequences of his crime. The defence very carefully abstained at the trial from making a case of insanity. No evidence of insanity was offered: and so

---

[234] *R v. Drury* 56 Cr.App.R. 104.
[235] *Attorney General v. O'Connell* [1937] Ir.Jur.Rep. 57.
[236] *R v. Moore* 23 Cr.App.R. 138; *People v. Keogh* [1944] I.R. 309; *People v. E* [1945] Ir.Jur.Rep. 67.
[237] [1931] I.R. 713.

far from intending seriously to argue that case here, *M'Naghten's Case* 10 Cl. & F. 200 was not even cited until the court called for it."[238]

19–63 As Kennedy C.J. intimated above the situation would be different if the rider was at variance with the formal verdict of guilty. In that event, the mere fact that the rider was separate in form from the verdict would not be allowed to bring about a miscarriage of justice. In *People (Attorney General) v. Keogh,*[239] for example, the accused was convicted as a principal in the second degree of the murder and disposal of the body of her new born infant, a charge which at the time was punishable by the death penalty. In returning a verdict of guilty, the jury added the rider: "As the jury are unanimously of the opinion that the accused had, in the circumstances, no option but to aid and abet, they strongly recommend her to the mercy of the court." The Court of Criminal Appeal accepted that the rider was reasonably capable of two interpretations. First, it could mean that the accused was acting under duress which was not a defence to the charge. Alternatively, it could mean that the jury considered that her condition at the time was such that she was physically and mentally unable to make the effort necessary to assist or participate in the principal's criminal act. On this interpretation she would be not guilty of the offence charged. The court ruled that if, as a result of a rider to the verdict, there was a reasonable doubt about the jury's finding of guilt, the conviction would have to be quashed and a new trial ordered:

> "The position of the court in relation to the present verdict, including the rider, is this. This court thinks that upon one reasonably possible, though not the only reasonably possible, interpretation of the rider, the jury intended to express a view of the case which, if properly expressed, would amount in law to a conviction; but that upon another reasonably possible interpretation of the rider, the jury intended to express a view of the case which, if properly expressed, would amount to an acquittal. The result is to leave this court in doubt as to which of these two views the jury really intended to express, and as this court regards both interpretations as reasonably possible, it must likewise regard the doubt as a reasonable doubt. As a jury cannot convict upon a criminal charge if is has a reasonable doubt as to guilt, so this court feels that it cannot hold that the jury intended their verdict and rider taken together to express a view which would amount to a conviction in law, if the court has a reasonable doubt as to whether or not the jury did so intend. Since this court has such a doubt, it is impossible to allow the verdict to stand."[239a]

6. Finality of Verdict

19–64 Once the verdict has been delivered it is entered on the record of the court. The judge, however, may amend it either before it is entered on the record or afterwards so long as the amendment is effected before the jury have left the jury-box. No amendment can be made after the jury have left the box,

---

[238] *ibid.* at 728–729.
[239] [1944] I.R. 309; *R v. Woodfall* 5 Burr. 2661 approved.
[239a] *ibid.* at 316–317.

although the judge may correct the record if there is clear evidence that it does not represent the actual verdict.[240] The necessary evidence for the correction of a verdict which had been delivered, entered on the record and signed by the jury foreman could not be supplied by the unsworn statement of one member of the jury after he had left the jury box, nor by the examination and cross-examination of all jury members under oath.[241] Even if it transpired after conviction and sentence that the jury had been improperly constituted the judge would have no power to correct the verdict.[242]

7. Arrest of Judgment

If the accused is found guilty the next step usually concerns sentencing. However, at any time after conviction and before sentence, the accused may move the court to arrest judgment.[242a] Equally, the court may, on its own initiative, arrest the judgment in an appropriate case. Arrest of judgment has the effect of an acquittal, apart from the fact that it does not operate as a bar to a fresh indictment.[243] It will arise only on account of some defect on the face of the record such as, for example, a want of sufficient certainty in the indictment which has not been amended or a conviction not relating to an offence known to the law.[244] A defect in the evidence or an alleged irregularity at the trial would not be sufficient. In *People (Attorney General) v. Quinn*,[245] for example, defence counsel applied for an arrest of judgment when it transpired that one of the jury members, who was in the company of one of the witnesses, had a verbal altercation with the accused and his sister in the hall of the courthouse. This occurred after the court had adjourned on a Friday evening. The jury returned a verdict of guilty the following day. Defence counsel argued that this constituted an irregularity of such seriousness that the judge should not pass sentence, but should arrest judgment and direct a new trial. The trial judge refused the application. His refusal was upheld by the Court of Criminal Appeal which stated that he had no jurisdiction to set aside the verdict of a jury in a criminal matter. The court did not make clear whether a trial judge never had a jurisdiction to set aside the verdict of a jury in a criminal matter or whether the jurisdiction was just not made out on the facts of this case. Presumably, the latter was intended.

19–65

---

[240] *R v. Virrier* 12 Ad & E 317.

[241] *People v. Longe* [1967] I.R. 369.

[242] *People v. Kennedy* 90 I.L.T.R. 48. Ryan and Magee note that the accused appears to have been released by the Minister for Justice; *op. cit.*, p.375.

[242a] Note, however, that judicial review probably does not lie on a quia timet basis in the interval between a finding of guilty and the recording of a conviction and/or passing of sentence; *Mellett v. Judge Reilly* unreported, High Court, October 4, 2001, *per* Carroll J.

[243] *Vaux's Case* 4 Co Rep 44a.

[244] Ryan and Magee, *op. cit.*, p.375.

[245] [1965] I.R. 366.

8. Acquittal

19–66   If the accused is found not guilty on all counts of the indictment, and is not in custody on any other matter, he is entitled to be discharged immediately.[246]

9. Costs

19–67   The issue of costs does not arise frequently as the accused will often be granted free legal aid. However, the court has jurisdiction to award costs to an accused person who is acquitted.[247] Section 14(2) of the Courts (Supplemental Provisions) Act 1961 and the Rules of the Superior Courts, Ord.99, r.1 confer a discretion on the Central Criminal Court to award costs to an accused who has been acquitted.[248] While costs will normally follow the event, an acquitted accused would have to apply to the court for its discretion to be exercised in his or her favour. It would appear that the Circuit Court Rules 2001, Ord.66, r.1, confer a similar jurisdiction on the Circuit Court.

K. Publicity

1. Introduction

19–68   Article 34.1 of the Constitution stipulates that "save in such special and limited cases as may be prescribed by law, justice shall be administered in public". This reflects a long established tradition in countries based on democracy and the rule of law that justice should be administered in independent courts whose proceedings are open to public scrutiny. Equally, however, it has always been accepted that there are limited circumstances in which the interests of justice and the common good require the exclusion of the public, sections of the public or individuals from court proceedings or from particular parts of court proceedings. In Ireland, apart from circumstances which come within the scope of the court's general contempt jurisdiction or its duty to protect the accused's right to a fair trial, these can be provided for only by an Act of the Oireacthas.[249]

2. *In Camera* Hearings

There are several examples of statutory measures providing for *in camera* hearings in criminal matters. Most of them reflect a concern for the privacy of the family and the rights of children. The public, for example, are excluded from proceedings under the Punishment of Incest Act 1908, apart from the

---

[246]   *Mee v. Cruikshank* 20 Cox CC 210.

[247]   See *People (Attorney General) v. Bell* [1969] I.R. 24 for a detailed historical analysis of the legislation and rules governing the existence of a power to award costs in criminal proceedings on indictment.

[248]   *People (Attorney General) v. Bell* [1969] I.R. 24.

[249]   See *Irish Times Ltd v. Murphy* [1998] 2 I.L.R.M. 161, *per* O'Flaherty J. at 179.

verdict, the verdict or decision and, where relevant, the sentence.[250] In other words, the only persons who may be present are the parties, their legal representatives, the judge, the jury and bona fide representatives of the press. The general public are excluded. Witnesses are present only while giving evidence. In all other criminal proceedings of an indecent or obscene nature, the court may exclude all persons apart from the officers of the court, persons directly concerned in the proceedings, bona fide representatives of the press and such other persons as the court may, in its discretion permit to remain.[251]

Further restrictions apply when persons giving evidence in a criminal case involving conduct contrary to decency or morality are, in the opinion of the court, under 17 years of age. In such a case the court may direct the exclusion of all persons other than members or officers of the court, the parties to the case, their counsel or solicitors, persons not directly concerned in the case and bona fide representatives of the press.[252] This exclusion only applies while the witness is giving evidence. In all of these cases, if the person with or against whom the offence is alleged to have been committed is a female or is under 21 years of age, a parent or other relative or friend is entitled to remain in court during the whole of the hearing.[253] The same entitlement applies for the benefit of the accused where he is under 21 years of age.

19–69

Children under 15 (other than infants in arms) may not be present in court during the trial of other persons except for so long as their presence is required as witnesses or otherwise for the purposes of justice.[254]

The interests of State security provide another source of exclusions. In the course of proceedings for the major offences under the Official Secrets Act 1963, the prosecution can make an application that part of the hearing should be held *in camera* on the ground that the publication of any evidence given or statement made during that part would be prejudicial to the safety or preservation of the State. Where an application is duly made under this provision the court must order that the part of the hearing concerned be held *in camera*.[255] Such an order will be without prejudice to the publication of the verdict and the sentence, if any. There are also provisions permitting the exclusion of members of the general public from a hearing by the Special Criminal Court. These are dealt with in chapter 20.

---

250 Criminal Law (Incest Proceedings) Act 1995, s.2.
251 Criminal Justice Act 1951, s.20(3).
252 Children Act 1908, ss.114 and 131, as amended by the Children Act 1941, s.29. See now Children Act 2001, s.257 for provision to clear the court when a person under 18 years of age is giving evidence.
253 Criminal Justice Act 1951, s.20(4).
254 Children Act 1908, ss.115 and 131, as amended.
255 Official Secrets Act 1963, s.12.

3. Press Reporting

Freedom of the Press

19–70 The constitutional imperative that justice shall be administered in public cannot be satisfied simply by permitting public access to the courtroom when a trial is taking place. It also entails the freedom of the press to issue fair, accurate and contemporaneous reporting of trial proceedings. The importance of press freedom in this context was highlighted by the Supreme Court in *Irish Times Ltd v. Murphy*[256] where it ruled that a trial which was held under the circumstances of a ban on contemporaneous press and media reporting was not a trial held in public within the meaning of Article 34.1 of the Constitution, despite the fact that the public were admitted to the proceedings. Keane J. (as he then was) explained the position as follows:

> " . . . the very fact that physical and other constraints prevent more than a miniscule section of the entire population from being present in court while justice is being administered makes it all the more imperative that the media should have the widest possible freedom to report what happens in court which is consistent with the proper administration of justice. It is manifest that the right of the public to know what is happening in our courts, a right which is clearly recognised and guaranteed by Article 34, would be eroded almost to vanishing point if the public had to depend on the account that might be transmitted to them by such people as happened to gain admission to the courtroom for the trial in question. In modern conditions, the media are the eyes and ears of the public and the ordinary citizen is almost entirely dependant on them for his knowledge of what goes on in court."[257]

Restrictions on Press Freedom

It does not follow, of course, that the right of the press to report fully and contemporaneously on court proceedings is absolute. Just as there are restrictions on the extent to which justice must be administered in public, so also can there be limitations on the press freedom to report. Indeed, there are a number of statutory provisions imposing certain limitations designed for the most part to protect the legitimate interests of one or other parties involved in the proceedings. Where the trial involves offences of a sexual nature, for example, it is often the case that the press are enjoined to report the proceedings in a manner which protects the anonymity of the parties.[258] Equally, it is generally accepted that the requirements of a fair trial require the postponement of the press reporting on certain matters which arise in the

---

[256] [1998] 2 I.L.R.M. 161.

[257] *ibid.* at 187.

[258] The Criminal Law (Rape) Act 1981, *e.g.*, precludes the publication of material likely to identify a complainant in a trial for a sexual assault and the accused in a rape trial; see ss. 7 and 8, as amended by s.17(2) of the Criminal Law (Rape)(Amendment) Act 1990. See also, Criminal Law (Incest Proceedings) Act 1995, s.3 which prohibits the publication of any matter which is likely to lead members of the public to identify either the accused or the alleged victim once an individual has been charged under the Punishment of Incest Act 1908.

course of criminal proceedings. Where the admissibility of evidence is considered in a *voir dire*, for example, the whole purpose of excluding the jury would often be defeated if members of the jury could read the next day what transpired in the *voir dire*. Similarly, where separate trials are ordered for two or more persons who are jointly indicted it will often be necessary to postpone the reporting of evidence given in the trial of one accused which may be incriminatory of an accused who will be tried later.

The extent to which the court of trial can issue an order postponing the contemporaneous reporting of trial proceedings was also considered by the Supreme Court in *Irish Times v. Murphy*.[259] That case concerned the trial of four persons accused of importing and possessing, with intent to supply, the largest consignment of cocaine ever to be seized in the State. All four accused were foreign nationals residing outside the jurisdiction and were remanded in custody. The trial judge was concerned that inaccurate or unfair press reporting of the trial proceedings could result in the trial being aborted at some point, with the result that the accused would have to be remanded in custody for an even longer period pending the outcome of a second trial. Accordingly, he made an order postponing, until the conclusion of the trial, the media reporting of the evidence that would be given in the course of the trial. The only matters which the media could report in the interim were: the fact that the trial was proceeding; the names and addresses of the accused parties; the nature of the crimes alleged in the indictments; the place where the trial was proceeding; and the fact that a fifth accused had pleaded guilty and had been put back for sentence. It seems that the trial judge was motivated to make the order as a result of recent cases in which trials had to be aborted due to inaccurate or unfair press reporting and indications that the reporting of the proceedings in question was not fully accurate. Several media organisations sought unsuccessfully an order in the High Court to quash the judge's order. They appealed to the Supreme Court.

19–71

The Supreme Court had to consider two fundamental issues:

> "1. Whether the trial held before the learned Circuit Court judge was a trial being held in public within the meaning of Article 34.1 of the Constitution by reason of the order made prohibiting the contemporaneous reporting of the details thereof.
> 2. Whether, in the particular circumstances of this case, it was open to the learned Circuit Court judge to prohibit the contemporaneous reporting of the trial by the appellants herein on the grounds that there was a real risk of an unfair trial if such reporting were permitted."

The court concluded, as explained above, that an order prohibiting the contemporaneous reporting of the details of a trial would, in the absence of lawful justification, infringe the requirement in Article 34.1 of the Constitution that justice should be administered in public. The key issues, therefore, was the extent to which a judge could lawfully limit contemporaneous reporting

---

[259] [1998] 2 I.L.R.M. 161.

of a trial without infringing Article 34.1 and whether that limit had been exceeded on the facts of this case.

19–72   The court's starting point for a consideration of these issues was that the constitutional requirement that justice shall be administered in public is not absolute. Inroads are permissible in "such special and limited cases as may be prescribed by law." Accordingly, it is open to the Oireachtas to make specific statutory provisions permitting justice to be administered otherwise than in public in certain limited situations. It does not follow, however, that a court has no power to order a trial otherwise than in public in circumstances which are not covered by a specific statutory enactment. Article 34.1 must be construed in the light of other provisions of the Constitution and, in particular, Article 38.1 which stipulates that no person shall be tried on any criminal charge save in due course of law and Article 40.3 which guarantees the right to fair procedures. If the Article 34.1 requirement that justice be administered in public should conflict with an individual's right to a fair trial under Articles 38.1 and 40.3 then, according to the Supreme Court, the latter must prevail. Accordingly, there is scope in any individual case for the trial judge to impose a ban on the contemporary reporting of the trial proceedings in order to protect the accused's right to a fair trial. Before imposing a ban, however, the judge would have to be satisfied of the following two things:

> "(a) that there is a real risk of an unfair trial, if contemporaneous reporting is permitted, and
>
> (b) that the damage which any improper reporting would cause could not be remedied by the trial judge by appropriate directions to the jury or otherwise."[260]

The court was at pains to emphasise that any risk of an unfair trial flowing from contemporaneous reporting of the proceedings should normally be averted by directions to the jury. Hamilton C.J., for example, made a point of referring to recent trials which were aborted because the trial judge considered that the integrity of the trial process had been infected by the manner in which the proceedings were reported. He cautioned that a risk to a fair trial would arise in such circumstances only if the reporting came to the attention of the jury and contained facts and opinions which were likely to influence the jury in the consideration of their verdict. Even then the trial judge should discharge the jury only if he or she is satisfied that the risk of an unfair trial cannot be avoided by appropriate rulings and directions. That should be an exceptional situation:

> "Save in exceptional circumstances, a trial judge should have confidence in the ability of the jury to understand and comply with such directions, to disregard any inadmissible evidence and to give a true verdict in accordance with the evidence. It is only when this is not possible that the extreme step shall be taken of discharging the jury."[261]

---

[260]   *ibid.* per Hamilton C.J. at 173–174.
[261]   *ibid.* per Hamilton C.J. at 174.

On the facts of the case, the court had little difficulty in concluding that there **19–73** was no evidence before the trial judge which would have justified him in holding that there was a real risk of an unfair trial if contemporaneous reporting of the proceedings was permitted. He could not simply assume that the reporting would be other than fair and accurate. If it subsequently transpired that the reporting was not fair or accurate the court had adequate powers to deal with such a situation either under the contempt of court procedure or through appropriate directions to the jury.

The law of criminal contempt also plays a role in limiting what can and cannot be published in the course of a trial. Contempt in this context is a publication which is calculated to obstruct or interfere with the due course of justice in a criminal trial. In determining whether a particular publication would have that effect in any individual the court would have to balance the need to protect the due administration of justice with the freedom of expression. In *Kelly v. O'Neill*[262] the Supreme Court made it clear that in the event of a conflict between the two the former must prevail. In considering whether the administration of justice was prejudiced the court would have to consider a range of factors such as the timing of the publication relative to the trial, as well as the contents of the publication itself. The mere fact that the publication was made after the jury had returned its verdict and before sentence would not preclude the possibility of contempt.[263] There was always the risk that the judge could be influenced subconsciously by the publication. Equally, contempt is not confined to situations where the decision-maker might be influenced. It will also come into play where a publication undermines public confidence in the administration of justice. Accordingly, if there is the appearance that a sentence might have been influenced by a publication, then that publication may be a contempt of court.

4. Adverse Pre-trial Publicity

The General Principles

Publicity can impact upon a trial even before the trial itself has begun. The **19–74** crime alleged, for example, may have been the subject of extensive media reporting. Equally, the arrest and charging of the accused may receive coverage which goes beyond the mere factual reporting of the events. Inevitably, circumstances will arise from time to time where the accused alleges that the pre-trial publicity will prejudice a jury against him or her to the extent that he cannot be guaranteed a fair trial in accordance with the requirements of Article 38.1 of the Constitution. In this event it is likely that the accused will seek an order prohibiting the trial. In practice, however, the courts are reluctant to grant such an order in the absence of a clear and substantial risk of unfairness to the accused.

---

[262] Unreported, Supreme Court, December 2, 1999.
[263] *Cullen v. Toibin* [1984] I.L.R.M. 577 distinguished.

The Supreme Court had to address the issue in *D v. DPP*.[264] The accused was charged with indecent assault on a female on a date unknown between April and November 1988. The trial was due to take place in January 1993. In August 1992 the Sunday Tribune published a front page story based on an interview with the victim. The contents of the story, including the headline, were calculated to arouse great sympathy for the victim and included material which was both legally inadmissible and highly prejudicial against the accused. However, neither the victim nor the accused were named and nor did the story identify the place or places at which the offences were alleged to have occurred. The issue before the court was whether the contents of the story were sufficient to prejudice a jury against the accused. Although the court appeared to be broadly in agreement on the basic legal principles at issue, it split three to two on their application to the facts of the case.

The fundamental issue was, of course, the accused's right to due process in the trial of a criminal charge as guaranteed by Article 38.1 of the Constitution, and the right to fairness of procedures as guaranteed by Article 40.3. The contents of the latter in this context were summed up by Denham J:

> "Fair procedures incorporate the requirement of a trial by jury unprejudiced by pre-trial publicity. The applicant is entitled to a jury capable of concluding a fair determination of facts on the facts as presented at the trial."[265]

In the event of a conflict between this right to a fair trial and the community's right to prosecute in any individual case, the former must prevail. Accordingly, if the accused can establish that there is a real or serious risk of an unfair trial resulting from the pre-trial publicity then the community's right to prosecute would have to give way. The risk, however, would have to be an unavoidable risk. There is an onus, therefore, on the accused to show that the risk could not be averted by appropriate rulings and directions by the trial judge.[266]

The real difficulty, of course, arises in determining when the accused has managed to establish that there is a real or serious risk. It will not always be sufficient that the jury may have heard or read material sympathetic to the victim and prejudicial to the accused. There would have to be a real likelihood that one or more members of the jury would be influenced in his or her decision on the case as a result of what he or she has seen or heard. In the current case this would mean, in the words of Denham J., that at least one juror:

> "(i)   will have read the article,
> (ii) will remember the article,
> (iii) will connect the applicant to the article,
> (iv) will be prejudiced against the applicant because of the article,
> (v)   will not comply with their oath as jurors, and
> (vi) will not comply with the charge of the trial judge."[266a]

---

[264] [1994] 1 I.L.R.M. 435.
[265] *ibid.* at 442.
[266] *Z v. DPP* [1994] 2 I.R. 476.
[266a] [1994] 1 I.L.R.M. 435 at 443.

In considering these factors it would have to be taken into account that, in his direction to the jury, the judge will have instructed them that they should find facts on the evidence presented to the court alone. Given that the media coverage in this case amounted to a single article in a single Sunday newspaper which does not identify the accused and the fact that it was published five months before the trial which would be held in Dublin, the majority felt that a real risk of unfairness had not been established.

The Judges Rulings and Directions to the Jury

Great confidence is placed in the capacity of the trial judge's rulings and **19–75** directions to ensure that the jury are not tainted in their deliberations by adverse pre-trial publicity about the defendant or his or her guilt. Even where jury members are acknowledged to have heard damning information about the defendant and his guilt from the media it is accepted that the trial judge's rulings and directions can provide adequate protection for the accused. In *Z v. DPP*,[267] for example, the charges against the defendant arose out of the infamous *X Case* which was at the centre of the abortion referendum debates in the 1990s.[268] In referring to the media coverage of the case the President of the High Court said:

> "It is clear from a consideration of this material that this is a case of massive national coverage – of media saturation – a case where a story has been told and retold in all forms of media, repeatedly over a length of time, to the public subsequent to the injunction proceedings, during the referendum debate and the charging in the District Court and the return for trial of the applicant."[269]

Nevertheless, the High Court felt that the accused could be guaranteed a fair trial. Given the special circumstances particular care would have to be taken both in empanelling the jury and in the trial judge's directions to the jury to ensure that they tried the case purely on the basis of the evidence presented in the course of the trial. The court was confident that this could be achieved. Similarly, the Supreme Court was unanimously of the opinion that on the facts of this case the trial judge would be able to direct the jury very clearly that all of the media controversy and issues surrounding the *X Case* were irrelevant to the trial before them and as such must be put completely out of their minds. A jury instructed in such terms could be relied upon to bring an impartial mind to the issues which had to be decided and to confine themselves to the evidence sworn before them. It is also worth noting that the Supreme Court felt that the judge's directions would also be sufficient to offset any prejudice which might result from the widespread pre-trial media reports which had linked DNA evidence to the guilt of the accused.

---

[267] [1994] 2 I.R. 476.
[268] See *Attorney General v. X* [1992] 1 I.R. 1.
[269] *Z v. DPP* [1994] 2 I.R. 476 at 489.

Postponement of Trial

Even if the judge's directions are not sufficient to guard against a jury bias flowing from adverse pre-trial publicity it does not follow that a criminal trial will have to be abandoned. There is always the possibility of adjourning the trial for a period until the effects of the publicity have dissipated. In *Re Zoe Developments*,[270] for example, Geoghegan J. did not think that there was a serious risk of an unfair trial but he nevertheless held an adjournment of six months was necessary to allow the fade factor to come into play. In *DPP v. Haugh (No.2)*[271] an indefinite adjournment was upheld on very special facts. This is dealt with more fully in chapter 17 on The Jury.

Contempt

It should be noted that just because a trial has not been stopped or abandoned because of the publication of matter adverse to the interests of the accused either before or during the trial, it does not follow that the publication will or cannot amount to contempt of court.[272]

L. Record of Trial Proceedings

19–76 There is no specific statutory provision imposing an obligation to record the proceedings in a trial on indictment. The Courts of Justice Act 1924, however, stipulated that any appeal to the Court of Criminal Appeal had to be heard on the basis of a transcript of the evidence.[273] In practice, therefore, it has always been considered necessary to have a stenographer to take a verbatim record of the trial proceedings by shorthand. The original provision in The Courts of Justice Act 1924 has now been substituted by the Criminal Justice (Miscellaneous Provisions) Act 1997 to permit the appeal to be heard and determined on the basis of "a record of the proceedings at the trial and on a transcript thereof verified by the judge before whom the case was tried."[274] Under the substituted version it would appear that an appeal is to be heard on the basis of a record of the trial and a transcript of the record. This would suggest that it is no longer necessary to have a stenographer present in court taking a verbatim record of the proceedings. The record can be taken by other means, such as an electronic tape-recording or audio-visual recording. Indeed, a "record" for this purpose is defined very broadly to include, in addition to a written record:

(a) shorthand notes, or a disc, tape, soundtrack or other device in which information, sounds or signals are embodied so as to be capable (with or

---

[270] Unreported, Supreme Court, March 3, 1999.
[271] [2001] 1 I.R. 162.
[272] See *Kelly v. O'Neill* unreported, Supreme Court, December 2, 1999.
[273] The Courts of Justice Act 1924, s.33.
[274] The Courts of Justice Act 1924, s.33(1)(a), as substituted by Criminal Justice (Miscellaneous Provisions) Act 1997, s.7.

without the aid of some other instrument) of being reproduced in legible
or audible form,

(b) a film tape or other device in which visual images are embodied so as to
be capable (with or without the aid of some other instrument) of being
reproduced in visual form, and

(c) a photograph.

This provision does not specifically dispense with the need for a stenographer **19–77**
or for the preparation of a transcript of the evidence. Indeed, it is still the
practice for the proceedings to be recorded by a stenographer sitting in court
taking shorthand notes. This record will contain the evidence, any objection
to the evidence, the legal arguments, any statement by the accused,[275] the
summing up and the sentence imposed. It will not normally include counsel's
addresses to the jury unless the trial judge directs otherwise. The vital feature
of the record is that it should be a complete and accurate record. If, for
example, the evidence is given in the Irish language this must be reflected by
a verbatim record of the evidence as given in Irish and a record of the
interpretation in English. Referring to a record taken by a stenographer
Kennedy C.J. explained in *Attorney General v. Joyce* that:

> " . . . it is the duty of the official stenographer to report every case fully and in
> every detail, and certainly, in a case where evidence is given in the Irish
> language, it is the duty of the stenographer employed for that purpose to
> record every word of the evidence so given in that language, and if he fails to
> do so, it may have very grave consequences . . . I therefore take this oppor-
> tunity of impressing upon the stenographers the importance of an absolutely
> complete report of the trial, and of every word spoken in the course of it."[276]

In this case the evidence had been given in Irish but recorded in both English
and Irish by the stenographer. The Irish version was subsequently mislaid. It
was held by the Court of Criminal Appeal that a transcript of the translation
was sufficient where there was no question as to its accuracy. Under the
statutory provision if the trial judge is of the opinion that the record or the
transcript does not reflect what took place during the trial, the record and
transcript shall be supplemented by a report by the trial judge setting out the
defects which he or she considers are contained in the record or transcript as
the case may be.[277]

It must be remembered that these provisions governing the taking of a
record and the preparation of a transcript of trial proceedings on indictment
are linked to the possibility of an appeal to the Court of Criminal Appeal.

---

[275] *People v. Riordan* [1948] I.R. 416. In this case the Court of Criminal Appeal criticised the
transcript for its omission of the accused's unsworn statement from the dock.

[276] [1929] I.R. 526 at 533–534.

[277] The Courts of Justice Act 1924, s.33(1)(b), as substituted by s.7 of the Criminal Justice (Misc
ellaneous Provisions) Act 1997. Where the Court of Criminal Appeal is of the opinion that either
the record or the transcript thereof is defective in any material particular, it may determine the
appeal in such manner as it considers, in all the circumstances, appropriate; s.33(2) as substituted
by s.7.

They do not by themselves constitute an absolute duty to take a record or prepare a transcript. It is unlikely, therefore, that the failure to take a contemporaneous record of the proceedings will affect the validity of the trial. It might be argued, of course, that an extensive interpretation of what constitutes an accused's right to a fair trial would embrace the right to have an authoritative and contemporaneous record made of the proceedings.

CHAPTER 20

THE SPECIAL CRIMINAL COURT

A. Introduction

Article 38.3 of the Constitution permits the establishment of special criminal **20–01** courts for the trial of offences in cases where the ordinary courts are deemed inadequate to secure the administration of justice and the preservation of public peace and order. The inadequacy of the ordinary courts in this context must be determined in accordance with law. Similarly, where special criminal courts are established pursuant to Article 38.3 they must be established by law and their constitution, powers, jurisdiction and procedure must be prescribed by law. However, they are not bound by the provisions of Articles 34 and 35 of the Constitution. Broadly speaking, this means that the judges do not have to be appointed strictly in accordance with the terms of the Constitution[1] and the right to jury trial does not apply. Nevertheless, it would appear that the right to be tried "in due course of law", specifically protected by Article 38.1 of the Constitution, does apply to trial in the special criminal courts.

B. Establishment

1. The Power

Section 35 of the Offences against the State Act 1939 confers on the govern- **20–02** ment the power to issue a proclamation which is an essential precondition for the establishment of special criminal courts. It reads:

---

[1] The special criminal courts which sat from 1939 to 1946 and from 1961 to 1962 were composed of military officers. An attempt to challenge the validity of the court on the basis that it was in effect a military tribunal failed in *Re McCurtain* [1941] I.R. 83.

"If and whenever and so often as the Government is satisfied that the ordinary courts are inadequate to secure the effective administration of justice and the preservation of public peace and order and that it is necessary that this Part of this Act should come into force, the Government may make and publish a proclamation declaring that the Government is satisfied as aforesaid and ordering that this Part of this Act shall come into force."[2]

The Part of the Act in question is Part V which makes provision for the establishment of special criminal courts. When the government has issued a proclamation bringing Part V into force it will remain in force until annulled by a resolution of the Dáil,[3] or until the government makes and publishes a proclamation declaring that Part V is no longer in force.[4] The government must do this if it is satisfied that the ordinary courts are adequate to secure the administration of justice and the preservation of public peace and order. The necessary proclamations have been made on three occasions resulting in the establishment of special criminal courts from 1939 to 1946, 1961 to 1962 and from 1972 to date.

Judicial Review

20–03   Although Article 38.3.1° of the Constitution expressly states that special courts may be established by law for the trial of offences ". . . where it may be determined *in accordance with such law* that the ordinary courts are inadequate . . ." (emphasis added), section 35 of the 1939 Act confers a subjective power on the government to decide whether the ordinary courts are inadequate. The legislation does not prescribe the circumstances in which the power may be exercised or the considerations which should inform its exercise. Instead it confers what appears to be an unfettered executive power on the government. Indeed, as will be seen below, the Supreme Court in *Kavanagh v. Ireland*[5] described the power to issue a proclamation as essentially a political act.[6] It is at least arguable, therefore, that section 35 does not satisfy the constitutional requirement that the determination of the inadequacy of the ordinary courts should be "in accordance with law". Just because the power to make the determination is conferred on the government by a statutory provision, it does not follow that the determination is made "in accordance with law" as that phrase is commonly understood in constitutional jurisprudence. Nevertheless, the courts have so far rejected any attempts to challenge the constitutionality or the legality of the proclamation establishing the current Special Criminal Court.[7]

In *Re MacCurtain*[8] Gavan Duffy J. rejected the argument that the Oireachtas could not properly delegate the power to determine the inadequacy of the

---

[2]   Offences against the State Act 1939, s.35(2).
[3]   *ibid.* s.35(5).
[4]   *ibid.* s.35(4).
[5]   [1997] 1 I.L.R.M. 321.
[6]   See also *Savage & McOwen v. DPP* [1982] I.L.R.M. 385.
[7]   In *In re MacCurtain* [1941] I.R. 83 both Gavan Duffy J. in the High Court and O'Sullivan C.J. in the Supreme Court interpreted the provision literally to mean that provision should be made for the determination in the same law which made provision for the establishment of the Special Criminal Court.

ordinary courts to the government under Article 38.3.1°. In doing so he also made it clear that the determination was essentially executive in nature:

> "The Oireachtas clearly considered the Government to be the authority best situated, from its position and the information at its disposal, to determine whether or not the Special Tribunals were necessary in the circumstances set out in the section. In my opinion the provision that the Government may make such a proclamation when satisfied that the ordinary courts are inadequate is clearly meant to be an essentially executive decision of the highest executive authority in the State. In my opinion, the Government, in declaring itself satisfied within the section of the inadequacy of the ordinary Courts and of the necessity to set up Special Courts, cannot be said to be acting either in a judicial or in a legislative capacity. Nor is there any need under the Act for the Government to give its reasons, and it is quite impossible for a Court to impose any such obligation on the Government in connection with this executive act when the statute did not do so. No authority was cited for the proposition that the Oireachtas cannot delegate a decision of this kind. There is, I think, in fact ample authority to the contrary."[9]

In *Kavanagh v. Ireland*[10] the Supreme Court confirmed that a government proclamation bringing Part V of the 1939 Act into force enjoyed the presumption of constitutionality. It also held that the exercise of the power to issue a proclamation bringing Part V of the Act into force is essentially a political act. So long as the government acts *bona fide* in satisfying itself that the ordinary courts are inadequate to secure the effective administration of justice and the preservation of public peace and order the courts have no jurisdiction to interfere.[10a] The position is summarised very neatly by Barrington J. as follows:

> "The question of whether the ordinary courts are or are not adequate to secure the effective administration of justice and the preservation of public peace and order is primarily a political question, and, for that reason, is left to the legislature and the executive. The fact that the control intended is primarily a political control is underlined by s.35(5) which provides that it shall be lawful for Daíl Éireann, at any time where Part V of the Act is in force, to pass a resolution annulling the proclamation by virtue of which Part V was brought into force and that thereupon such proclamation shall be annulled and Part V shall cease to be in force but without prejudice to the validity of anything previously done thereunder.
>
> . . .
>
> In deciding whether to make a proclamation under s.35(2) of the Offences Against the State Act 1939 the government is not acting judicially in the sense that it is adjudicating upon the rights of any particular citizen. Rather it is making a political judgment on the adequacy of the ordinary courts to secure the effective administration of justice and the preservation of public peace and order. It is natural that such a political decision should be primarily subject to political control"[11]

---

[8] [1941] I.R. 83.
[9] *ibid.* at 86.
[10] [1997] 1 I.L.R.M. 321.
[10a] See *Byrne v. Dempsey*, unreported, Supreme Court, March 11, 1999.
[11] *Kavanagh v. Ireland* [1997] 1 I.L.R.M. 321, *per* Barrington J. at 328–329.

20–04   Curiously, Keane J., (as he then was) giving judgment in the same case, did not discount fully the possibility of a judicial review of a proclamation, particularly where the circumstances which had given rise to it had largely dissipated:

> "A decision of this nature taken by the government, as is clear from the authorities already cited, cannot be regarded as forever beyond the reach of judicial control. As has been pointed out in the course of argument, the powers conferred by Part V of the Act are indeed far reaching and allow of the trial of persons on serious offences, not merely without a jury, but by tribunals composed of persons without any legal qualifications. Save in the exceptional circumstances of war and national emergency envisaged by Article 28.3, the courts at all times retain their jurisdiction to intervene so as to ensure that the exercise of these drastic powers to abridge the citizens' rights is not abused by the arm of government to which they have been entrusted."[11a]

Hamilton C.J, O'Flaherty J. and Blayney J. all concurred with Keane J.'s judgment, but they also concurred with the judgment of Barrington J. which considered that the power to issue a proclamation was essentially a political matter and not amenable to judicial control so long as it was exercised *bona fide*. The Committee to Review the Offences against the State Acts, 1939–1998 and Related Matters have expressed the opinion that the practical effects of the decision in *Kavanagh* are to render it all but impossible to mount a legal challenge to a decision by the government to establish or maintain in force a Special Criminal Court.[12] This interpretation of *Kavanagh* also appears to be supported by the Supreme Court's decision in *Gilligan v. Ireland*[13] where the court rejected the applicant's attempt to challenge by way of judicial review the proclamation establishing the Special Criminal Court. Nevertheless, it is worth noting that the Court did not close the door firmly on the scope for a challenge to the legality or constitutionality of the proclamation. The Court felt able to base its decision on the narrow ground that the application was out of time for judicial review. It did indicate, however, that the matter sought to be raised on the judicial review would be more appropriately brought by way of a plenary summons.

Executive Review

20–05   It would appear that the government has been keeping the need for the retention of the Special Criminal Court under review in recent years.[14] Reviews have taken place annually from 1997 to 2000 inclusive involving consultations with the Department of Justice, Equality and Law Reform, the Attorney General, the Director of Public Prosecutions and the Garda Síochána. In each review the retention of the court was considered to be warranted on several

---

[11a] *ibid.* at 338.

[12] *Report of the Committee to Review the Offences against the State Acts, 1939–1998 and Related Matters* (Stationery Office, Dublin, 2002) Chap. 9, para.4.8.

[13] [2001] 1 I.L.R.M. 473.

[14] *Report of the Committee to Review the Offences against the State Acts, 1939–1998 and Related Matters, op.cit.* at Chap. 9, para.6.3.

grounds, including the continuing threat to the security of the State from subversive organisations and the ruthlessness of certain organised criminal gangs operating within the State. The risk of jury and witness intimidation from these sources was considered to be such that the ordinary courts were inadequate to secure the effective administration of justice and the preservation of public peace and order. The Committee to Review the Offences against the State Acts, 1939–1998 and Related Matters considered the need for the retention of the court in the light of the Good Friday Peace Agreement. A majority of the Committee felt that the retention of the court, albeit with some minor modifications, was justified by the threat posed by terrorism and organised crime. A minority advocated the abolition of the court.[15] The majority recommended that a resolution establishing the court should lapse automatically unless positively affirmed by resolutions passed by both Houses of the Oireachtas at three-yearly intervals.[16]

2. Background to the Establishment of the Current Court

It would seem that the government is under an obligation to establish a special criminal court as soon as may be after Part V of the 1939 is brought into force by proclamation.[17] Admittedly, the relevant statutory provision does not actually specify that it is the government which must establish a Special Criminal Court, but the implication is clear from the provisions read as a whole.[18] The legislation does specifically empower the government, whenever it considers it necessary or desirable to do so, to establish such additional number of special criminal courts as it thinks fit.[19] Equally, it may reduce the number of such courts by abolishing those which appear redundant.[20] Nevertheless, it would appear that at least one special criminal court must be retained so long as a proclamation under Part V is in force. Presumably, although it is not specifically stated in the Act any remaining special court or courts will be abolished automatically when Part V is de-activated. Only one court has been established pursuant to the proclamation in 1972.[21]

20–06

The current Special Criminal Court was established on the basis of the proclamation issued in 1972 primarily in response to the spill-over into this jurisdiction of the violent situation in Northern Ireland. Indeed, the vast bulk of the cases coming before the court in the 1970s and 1980s have been associated with the situation in Northern Ireland. Not surprisingly, this gave rise to a general perception that the court was established to deal with subversive crime for which the ordinary courts were inadequate. As the volume of subversive

---

[15] *ibid.*

[16] *ibid.* para.8.4.

[17] Offences against the State Act 1939, s.38(1).

[18] *McGlinchey v. Governor of Portlaoise Prison* [1998] I.R. 671.

[19] Offences against the State Act 1939, s.38(2).

[20] *ibid.* s.38(3).

[21] The government considered establishing a second special criminal court in 1976 to deal with the large backlog of cases which had built up. In the event the suggestion was not proceeded with; see Hogan and Walker *Political Violence and the Law in Ireland* (Manchester University Press, Manchester, 1989) p.239, fn.2.

crime tailed off in the 1990s so also did the case load of the court. Indeed, it became increasingly apparent that organised, as distinct from subversive, crime was providing the court with a significant portion of its caseload. This trend was encouraged by a landmark decision of the Supreme Court in *People (DPP) v. Quilligan*[22] in which Walsh J. took the opportunity to review the general nature and scope of the Offences against the State Act 1939. In the course of his judgment he noted that Parts II, III and IV of the Act were permanent measures which were aimed directly at subversive activities. Part V, by contrast, was more in the nature of temporary emergency legislation and dealt with the adequacy of the ordinary courts to secure the effective administration of justice and the preservation of public peace and order. Critically, the learned judge was of the opinion that Part V was not confined in its operation to subversive crime, but could be deployed against any type of crime which had the capacity to interfere with the proper functioning of the ordinary courts. He explained the implications for the government's power to issue a proclamation bringing Part V into force as follows:

> "Equally it does not follow that the power of the government to issue a proclamation to the effect that the ordinary courts are inadequate to secure the effective administration of justice, the preservation of peace and order must necessarily apply only with reference to the type of offences created by Parts II and III of the Act. It is common knowledge, and indeed was discussed in the debates leading to the enactment of the Act of 1939, that what was envisaged were cases or situations of a political nature where juries could be open to intimidation or threats of various types. However a similar situation could also arise in types of cases far removed from what one would call 'political type' offences. There could well be a grave situation in dealing with ordinary gangsterism or well financed and well organised large scale drug dealing, or other situations where it might be believed or established that juries were for some corrupt reason, or by virtue of threats, or of illegal interference, being prevented from doing justice."[23]

This analysis was adopted by the Supreme Court in *Kavanagh v. Ireland*[24] rejecting an appeal against the High Court's refusal, *inter alia*, to quash the 1972 proclamation. In that case the applicant had been charged with ordinary, as distinct from subversive, offences. He challenged the legality of his trial before the Special Criminal Court on the ground, *inter alia*, that the court had been established for the purpose of dealing with subversive crime only. Both the High Court and the Supreme Court, however, were of the view that what mattered was not the type of crime at issue but the validity of the government's opinion that the ordinary courts were inadequate to secure the effective administration of justice and the preservation of public peace and order.

---

[22] [1986] I.R. 495.
[23] *ibid.* at 509–510.
[24] *op. cit.*

C. Composition

Independence

Each special criminal court must consist of an uneven number of members, **20–07** subject to a minimum of three.[25] Each member must be a judge of the High Court, a judge of the Circuit Court, a judge of the District Court, a barrister or solicitor of not less than seven years standing or an officer of the Defence Forces not below the rank of commandant.[26] Each member is appointed, and is removable at will, by the government.[27] It follows that the members of the court do not enjoy the security of tenure and associated independence which attach to judges in the ordinary courts by virtue of Article 35 of the Constitution. Moreover, the power to fix their remuneration and allowances is vested in the Minister for Finance.[28] Nevertheless, all attempts to challenge the constitutionality of the court on the ground of a lack of independence from the executive have failed.

In *Eccles v. Ireland*,[29] for example, it was argued that section 39 of the Offences against the State Act 1939 (composition of the Special Criminal Court) was unconstitutional in that it afforded the government an unfettered power to interfere with the proceedings and decisions of the court. This argument was based on the proposition that the government could use its power to terminate the appointment of members of the court on the ground that their decisions did not favour the interests of the executive. It was also argued that the power of the Minister for Finance to fix the remuneration of members of the court could constitute an unfettered power to influence the decisions of the court. The net effect of these provisions, it was suggested, would be to deprive the members of the guarantees of judicial independence and deny the accused his or her constitutional right to a trial in due course of law.

Barrington J. felt compelled to dismiss these arguments in the High Court partly because it had not been suggested that the judges displayed a lack of full independence and partly because Article 38.6 of the Constitution specifically excluded the application of Articles 34 and 35 (the judicial independence provisions) of the Constitution from the Special Criminal Court. The Supreme Court also dismissed the challenge, although it preferred to base its decision on the presumption that the powers conferred by section 39 were meant to be exercised in a constitutional manner, as laid down in *East Donegal Co-operative v. Attorney General*.[30] It followed that the powers under section 39

---

[25] Offences against the State Act 1939, s.39(1).

[26] *ibid.* s.39(3). Military officers have not served on the current Special Criminal Court. *The Report of the Committee to Review the Offences against the State Act 1939–1998 and Related Matters,* op.cit at Chap.9, para.9.11 recommends that eligibility to sit on the court should be confined to serving judges of the High Court, Circuit Court and District Court.

[27] This does not preclude the resignation of any member from his or her appointment to the court. At the very least the government's acceptance of any such resignation coupled with the appointment of a replacement can be interpreted as an exercise of the government's power of appointment and removal. See *McGlinchey v. Governor of Portloaise Prison* [1988] I.R. 671.

[28] Offences against the State Act 1939, s.39(4).

[29] [1985] I.R. 545.

[30] [1970] I.R. 317.

could not be exercised to deny the individual his constitutional right to a trial in due process of law as guaranteed by Article 38.1.[31] Accordingly, any attempt by the executive to exercise its powers under section 39 in order to pressurise the Special Criminal Court to reach decisions favourable to it would be restrained by the ordinary courts:

> "If [the executive was] to seek to exercise its power in a manner capable of interfering with the judicial independence of the Court, in the trial of persons charged before it, it would be attempting to frustrate the constitutional right of persons accused before that court to a trial in due course of law. Any such attempt would be prevented and corrected by the courts established under the Constitution. Whilst, therefore, the Special Criminal Court does not attract the express guarantees of judicial independence contained in Article 35 of the Constitution, it does have, derived from the Constitution, a guarantee of independence in the carrying out of its functions."[32]

Following this decision the applicants complained unsuccessfully to the European Commission of Human Rights that the appointments system did not comply with Article 6(1) of the European Convention for the Protection of Human Rights and Fundamental Freedoms.[33] This provision guarantees, *inter alia*, a hearing before an independent and impartial tribunal. The Commission's decision was heavily swayed by the fact that no serving judge of the court had ever been removed against his will. Citing more recent precedent from the Scottish High Court of Justiciary and the European Court of Human Rights,[34] the Committee to Review the Offences against the State Acts, 1939–1998 and Related Matters expressed the view that the new European Court of Human Rights might not follow the decision of the Commission in this case.[35] Accordingly, a majority of the Committee endorsed the recommendation of the Constitution Review Group[36] that Article 38.6 of the Constitution should be amended (with knock on amendments in the Offences against the State Act 1939) so that the guarantees of independence and tenure contained in Articles 34 and 35 of the Constitution would apply to the judges in the Special Criminal Court.[37]

Membership Opt-out

20–08 The fact that membership of the court is confined to government appointees creates the opportunity for a judge serving in the ordinary courts to decline an

---

[31] See also *State (Bollard) v. Special Criminal Court* unreported, High Court, September 20, 1972.
[32] [1985] I.R. 545 at 549.
[33] *Eccles, McPhillips & McShane v. Ireland* (1988) 59 D.R. 212.
[34] *Starrs v. Ruxton, Procurator Fiscal, Linlithgow* (1999) SCCR 1052; *Lauko v. Slovakia* [1998] EHHR IV–2492.
[35] *Report of the Committee to Review the Offences against the State Acts, 1939–1998 and Related Matters* op.cit. at Ch.9, para.9.5.
[36] *Report of the Constitution Review Group* (Stationery Office, Dublin, Pn2632) at 198.
[37] *Report of the Committee to Review the Offences against the State Acts, 1939–1998 and Related Matters* op.cit. at paras.9.11–9.12. See also, The 4th Report of the All-Party Oireachtas Committee on the Constitution *The Courts and the Judiciary* (Stationery Office, Dublin, Pn.7831) at 34–35.

invitation to sit in the Special Criminal Court. When the government of the day was considering the establishment of *Special Courts* in 1931 two members of the Supreme Court informed it that they would resign rather than sit on such a court.[38] The device of government appointments to the court, instead of automatic membership for members of the ordinary courts, helps to avoid the prospect of individual judges having to choose between resignation and sitting on a Special Criminal Court. Nevertheless, a majority of the Committee to Review the Offences against the State Acts, 1939–1998 and Related Matters has recommended that the government should no longer have the power to appoint individual judges to the Special Criminal Court.[39] Instead all serving members of the High Court, Circuit Court and District Court should be liable to serve as members of the Special Criminal Court. The President of the High Court would act ex officio as President of the Special Criminal Court and, having consulted with the Presidents of the Circuit Court and District Court, he or she would be exclusively responsible for the designation of which judge should sit on any particular case.

Membership of Current Court

The current Special Criminal Court, established in 1972, consists of 11 members, made up of: four judges of the High Court, three judges from the Circuit Court and four judges from the District Court. In practice the court sits with the minimum quorum of three drawn from its panel of members. This means that the membership of a panel can vary from case to case even though there is only one court. Accordingly, it is less likely that a member of the court will find himself or herself trying a case against an accused in circumstances where that member had sat in a previous case in which findings prejudicial to the same accused had been made.[40]

    Typically the three members of the court hearing an individual case will comprise one High Court judge, one Circuit Court judge and one District Court judge.[41] There have been occasions, however, where it has transpired that at least one of the members has sat in a trial after he had retired as a judge of the ordinary courts. In *State (Gallagher) v. Governor of Portlaoise Prison*,[42] for example, the presiding judge who sentenced the accused was a retired judge of the High Court. Refusing an application for habeas corpus Henchy J. explained that the Bar Council had certified that, where applicable, judges resumed their status as barristers upon retirement from the bench. He went on to hold that since the retired judge in question satisfied the requirement of

20–09

---

[38] *ibid.* at Chap. 9, para.1.2.

[39] *ibid.* at Chap. 9, para.9.11.

[40] See *McGlinchey v. Ireland* [1990] 2 I.R. 215.

[41] The decision as to who will sit on any particular case is an administrative matter. As such it is not necessary for all the members of the court to sit in open court and debate which of them shall sit on any particular case. Nor is it necessary to have a formal order drawn up and authenticated by the Registrar specifying which of them shall sit. See *McGlinchey v. Governor of Portloaise Prison* [1988] I.R. 671.

[42] Unreported, High Court, July 1983.

seven years standing as a barrister he was qualified to be a member of the Special Criminal Court.[43]

This would appear to be a particularly generous interpretation in favour of the State given that the judge in question was appointed to the Special Criminal Court by virtue of his status as a judge of the High Court, as opposed to his status as a barrister of seven years standing. Nevertheless, a similar result ensued, albeit by a different route, in *McGinchey v. Governor of Portlaoise Prison*.[44] In this case Mr. Justice McMahon, one of the members of the court which tried and convicted the applicant, had retired from the High Court prior to the commencement of the applicant's trial in the Special Criminal Court. It was held by the High Court on an application for habeas corpus that Mr Justice McMahon was a judge of the High Court at the time of his appointment to the *Special Criminal Court*. As such he was qualified for appointment. It was not necessary that his qualifications had to be held for the duration of his membership. Once again this would appear to be an exceptionally favourable interpretation for the State. By giving such an extremely literal interpretation to the words of the statutory provision governing the composition of the court, it is respectfully submitted that the High Court has introduced an artificial distinction between qualifications for appointment and qualifications for membership. The Committee to Review the Offences against the State Acts, 1939–1998 and Related Matters has recommended that eligibility to serve on the court should be confined to serving judges of the High Court, Circuit Court and District Court.[45]

D. Jurisdiction

1. General Jurisdiction

20–10   Since the Special Criminal Court is a creature of statute it has no inherent jurisdiction.[46] The scope of its jurisdiction and powers derive entirely from statute. Its jurisdiction is defined in the Offences against the State Act 1939 as follows:[47]

> "(1) A Special Criminal Court shall have jurisdiction to try and to convict or acquit any person lawfully brought before that Court for trial under this Act and shall also have the following ancillary jurisdictions, that is to say:–
> (a) jurisdiction to sentence every person convicted by that Court of any offence to suffer the punishment provided by law in respect of such offence;

---

[43] See also, *McGlinchey v. Governor of Portlaoise Prison* [1998] I.R. 671 in respect of a judge of the District Court who had retired before his appointment to the Special Criminal Court took effect. His appointment was saved by virtue of the fact that he was a solicitor of seven years' standing on that date.

[44] [1988] I.R. 671.

[45] *op.cit.* at Chap.9, para.9.11.

[46] *People (Attorney General) v. Shribman and Samuels* [1946] I.R. 431.

[47] Offences against the State Act 1939, s.43.

(b) jurisdiction, in lieu of or in addition to making any other order in respect of a person, to require such person to enter into a recognisance before such Special Criminal Court or before a justice of the District Court, in such amount and with or without sureties as such Special Criminal Court shall direct, to keep the peace and be of good behaviour for such period as that Court shall specify;[48]

(c) jurisdiction to order the detention of and to detain in civil or military custody, or to admit to bail in such amount and with or without sureties as that Court shall direct, pending trial by that Court and during and after trial until conviction or acquittal, any person sent, sent forward, transferred, or otherwise brought for trial by that Court;[49]

(d) power to administer oaths to witnesses;

(e) jurisdiction and power to punish, in the same manner and in the like cases as the High Court, all persons whom such Special Criminal Court finds guilty of contempt of that Court or any member thereof, whether such contempt is or is not committed in the presence of that Court;

(f) power, in relation to recognisances and bail bonds entered into before such Special Criminal Court, to estreat such recognisances and bail bonds in the like manner and the like cases as the District Court estreats recognisances and bail bonds entered into before it.

(2) The provisions of this Part of this Act in relation to the carrying out of sentences of imprisonment pronounced by Special Criminal Courts and the regulations made under those provisions shall apply and have effect in relation to the carrying out of orders made by Special Criminal Courts under the foregoing sub-section of this section for the detention of persons in custody, whether civil or military."

2. Scheduled Offences

Current Statutory Offences

The concept of a "scheduled offence" plays a central role in the jurisdiction   **20–11**
of the court. While Part V of the Act is in force, the government may by order declare any offence to be a "scheduled offence" for the purposes of Part V if it is satisfied that the ordinary courts are inadequate to ensure the effective administration of justice and preservation of public peace and order in relation to that offence.[50] Offences currently scheduled pursuant to these provisions are: any offence under the Explosive Substances Act 1883;[51] any offence under the Firearms Acts, 1925–71;[52] any offence under the Offences against the State Act 1939,[53] and any offence under sections 6 to 9 and section 12 of the Offences against the State (Amendment) Act 1998.[54] An attempt,

---

[48] Any recognisance entered into before the Court must be in accordance with Form 15 to the Special Criminal Court Rules or in such similar form as the circumstances require; Offences against the State Acts 1939 to 1972 Special Criminal Court Rules 1975, r.26.

[49] *ibid.*

[50] Offences against the State Act 1939, s.36.

[51] Offences against the State Act 1939 (Scheduled Offences) Order, 1972.

[52] *ibid.*

[53] *ibid.*

[54] Offences against the State (Amendment) Act 1998, s.14(2).

conspiracy or incitement to commit any of these offences is also scheduled, as is aiding or abetting the commission of any such offence.[55]

Also scheduled is any offence under the Malicious Damage Act 1861.[56] However, most of this Act has been repealed and replaced by the Criminal Damage Act 1991. A small number of relatively minor offences survive under the 1861 Act but it is unlikely that they will feature in practice in prosecutions before the Special Criminal Court. Since no offence has been scheduled by specific reference to the Criminal Damage Act 1991 it must be assumed that offences under this Act are not scheduled for the purposes of the 1939 Act even though some of them would have been scheduled in their previous existence under the Malicious Damage Act 1861. An offence under section 7 of the Conspiracy and Protection of Property Act 1875 was also scheduled.[57] However, section 7 has since been repealed and replaced by section 31 of the Non-fatal Offences against the Person Act 1997. Since an offence under the latter provision has not been specifically scheduled it must follow that they are no longer scheduled.

Amended Statutory Offences

It is apparent that all offences which have been scheduled for the purpose of proceedings before the current Special Criminal Court have been scheduled by reference to the statutory provision or provisions which created them. It can assumed, in the absence of specific provision to the contrary, that repeal of the relevant statutory provision will have the effect of de-scheduling the offences in question even if they re-appear in substance under the guise of a different statutory provision. If, however, the statutory provision is merely amended, as distinct from being repealed, it would appear that this will not affect the scheduled status of the offences covered by it. There is no need for the government to issue a new order specifically scheduling the offences under the named statutory provision as amended by the named statutory amendment. Section 3 of the Explosives Substances Act 1883, for example, has been amended by the substitution of a new section 3 by the Criminal Law (Jurisdiction) Act 1976. The government did not issue a new order making it clear that any offence under section 3, as amended, was scheduled for the purposes of Part V of the 1939 Act. Nevertheless, the High Court held in *State (Daly) v. Delap*[58] that the amendment by substitution did not mean that offences under section 3 ceased to be scheduled for the purposes of the original scheduling order. Finlay P. (as he then was) explained that the intention of the legislature in inserting the new offences into the existing legislation was clearly to ensure that the new offences would attract all the features and characters of an offence under that legislation, including scheduling. It follows

---

[55] Offences Against the State Act 1939, s.37.
[56] Offences against the State Act 1939 (Scheduled Offences) Order, 1972.
[57] Offences against the State Act 1939 (Scheduled Offences)(No.2) Order, 1972.
[58] Unreported, High Court, June 30, 1980. Affirmed by the Court of Criminal Appeal in *People (DPP) v. Tuite* 2 Frewen 175.

that the arrest power under section 30 of the 1939 Act extends to any offences inserted in these enactments after the scheduling Order itself was issued.[59]

Non-subversive Offences

The scheduling of the offences by reference to the particular enactments **20–12** which created them is significant for another reason. There is no suggestion in the bare words of the scheduling power or the manner in which it was exercised that the offences in question are scheduled only if they are suspected of having been committed in a subversive context.[60] An individual who is charged with a scheduled offence must be sent for trial to the Special Criminal Court, unless the DPP directs otherwise. It will not matter that the offence was committed as part of an "ordinary" as distinct from a "subversive" criminal act.[61] The terms of the scheduling power are such that the government could decide to schedule offences by reference to any "particular class or kind". So far it has decided not to exercise the power in this manner. It follows that the courts are not sympathetic to the argument that the Special Criminal Court lacks jurisdiction in non-subversive cases. In *People v. Quilligan (No.1)*,[62] as noted above, Walsh J. in the Supreme Court specifically rejected the notion that the power to establish a Special Criminal Court was confined to cases or situations of a political nature where juries could be open to intimidation or threats. The vital issue was not the source of the intimidation or threats, but their likely consequences for the capacity of the ordinary courts to administer justice. Similarly, in *Kavanagh v. Ireland*[63] Barrington J. declared that it was not open to the defendant to argue that the offences with which he was charged before the Special Criminal Court were not of a subversive nature:

> "All of the offences in respect of which the applicant was charged are scheduled offences or offences in respect of which the Director of Public Prosecutions has issued a certificate under section 47(2) of the Act. Under these circumstances it avails the applicant nothing to submit that the offences in respect of which he has been charged are not of a 'subversive' nature, for the issue involved is not the nature of the offences but the adequacy, in the opinion of the Government or the Director of Public Prosecutions, of the ordinary courts to secure the effective administration of justice in relation to them."[64]

Constitutionality of Scheduled Offences

It is at least arguable that the scheduling provision does not accord with the requirements of Article 38.3 of the Constitution. The latter provision allows for the trial of offences in the Special Criminal Court "in cases where it may

---

[59] See also *People (DPP) v. Tuite* 2 Frewen 175 for amendments to offences under the Explosive Substances Act 1883.
[60] *People (DPP) v. Walsh* [1988] I.L.R.M. 137.
[61] *People (DPP) v. Quilligan (No.1)* [1986] I.R. 495.
[62] *ibid.*
[63] [1996] 1 I.R. 321.
[64] *ibid.* at 358.

be determined in accordance with law that the ordinary courts are inadequate to secure the effective administration of justice and the preservation of public peace and order." This can interpreted to confine the constitutional jurisdiction to try an accused in a Special Criminal Court to cases in which individual assessments have been made that the ordinary courts are inadequate. Such individual assessments will not be required where the jurisdiction of the court is triggered by virtue of the fact that the offence in question stands scheduled. Even the DPP's power to send a scheduled offence for trial in the ordinary courts in an individual case will not be sufficient in itself to ensure that a determination on the adequacy of the ordinary courts will be made in each case involving a scheduled offence. A majority of the Committee to Review the Offences against the State Acts, 1939–1998 and Related Matters have responded to this by recommending the abolition of the distinction between scheduled and non-scheduled offences as a basis for triggering the jurisdiction of the Special Criminal Court.[65] In their view it is preferable to base the jurisdiction of the court on the merits of the individual case instead of some pre-conceived statutory assumption that persons charged with certain types of offences should be sent to the Special Criminal Court unless the DPP decides otherwise. It will be seen below that the jurisdiction of the Special Criminal Court can already be triggered by the DPP in the case of non-scheduled offences.

The government is the only authority which can withdraw any offence from the scheduled category. Indeed, it is under an obligation to do so when it is satisfied that the effective administration of justice and the preservation of public peace and order can be secured through the ordinary courts. While the Oireachtas has no power to withdraw offences from the scheduled category directly, it can achieve the same effect indirectly in respect of offences scheduled by enactment by repealing the enactment creating the offence in question. This has been done in respect of many of the offences under the Malicious Damage Act 1861 and section 7 of the Conspiracy and Protection of Property Act 1875.

3. Alternative Verdicts

20–13   The court's jurisdiction is further extended by the Criminal Justice (Verdicts) Act 1976 which was enacted in response to rulings that the court lacked certain powers enjoyed by the Central Criminal Court and the Circuit Court to return a verdict of guilty of an offence other than that charged. The 1976 Act stipulates that where a person is before a court to be tried for an offence and the trial is being or will be held without a jury, the court shall enjoy the same jurisdiction and powers to give any verdict or make any findings as the court would have if the court were sitting with a jury.[65a] Furthermore, if the offence is only triable summarily then the court will enjoy the same jurisdiction and

---

[65] *Report of the Committee to Review the Offences against the State Acts, 1939–1998 and Related Matters* (Stationery Office, Dublin, 2002) at Chap. 9, paras.10.1–10.3.
[65a] Criminal Justice (Verdicts) Act 1976, s.1(1).

powers with respect to the verdict and findings as it would if the offence were triable on indictment. Enactments and rules of law relating to the verdict of the jury shall apply with any necessary modifications.

These provisions in the 1976 Act clearly go beyond the immediate objective of putting the Special Criminal Court on the same footing as the ordinary courts with respect to alternative verdicts in trials on indictment. At the very least it appears that they extend these powers to the District Court. The 1976 Act goes on to provide that where a person is lawfully before a court charged with an offence and pleads guilty to that offence, the court shall have jurisdiction to convict him of another offence with which he is not specifically charged and of which he could be convicted by that court after trial for the offence specifically charged.[65b] Ryan and Magee say that this replaces the more limited provisions of s.39(1) of the Criminal Justice Administration Act 1914.[66]

Every order, conviction or sentence made or pronounced by the Special Criminal Court has the same consequences in law as a like order, conviction or sentence made or pronounced by the Central Criminal Court.[67]

4. Sentencing

The Special Criminal Court has jurisdiction to sentence every person con-   **20–14**
victed by it of any offence to suffer the punishment provided by law in respect of such offence.[68] The various forms of punishment provided for by Irish law are dealt with in Chapter 21. Nevertheless, there are two issues which are best dealt with here; namely the government's power to remit or defer a sentence, and the statutory provisions governing forfeiture of certain public offices and employments.

Remission or Deferral of Sentence

The government enjoys a very broad statutory power to remit or defer any punishment imposed by the Special Criminal Court. This extends to fines and terms of imprisonment, the only exception being the sentence imposed in a capital case. The relevant provision gives the government an absolute discretion at any time to ". . . remit in whole or in part or modify (by way of mitigation only) or defer any punishment imposed by a Special Criminal Court."[69] Where the government exercises this power to remit or defer a punishment it may attach such conditions, if any, as it may think proper.[70] In the event of a deferral of a sentence of imprisonment, the person concerned shall be bound to serve the deferred sentence, or part of it, when it comes into operation.[71] For that purpose he may be arrested without warrant.

[65b] *ibid.* s.1(2).
[66] Ryan and Magee, The Irish Criminal Process (Mercier Press, Cork, 1983), p.386.
[67] Offences against the State Act 1939, s.50(2).
[68] *ibid.* s.43(1).
[69] *ibid.* s.33(3).
[70] *ibid.* s.33(2).
[71] *ibid.* s.33(3).

Forfeiture of Public Office, Employment, etc.

20–15   Section 34 of the Offences against the State Act 1939 stipulates that where a person is convicted of a scheduled offence[72] by a Special Criminal Court and at the time of the conviction holds "an office or employment remunerated out of the Central Fund or moneys provided by the Oireachtas or moneys raised by local taxation, or in or under or as a paid member of a board or body established by or under statutory authority", he shall immediately upon such conviction forfeit the office, employment, place or emolument.[73] Similarly, any such person who is in receipt of a pension or superannuation allowance payable from such sources shall forfeit it immediately upon the conviction and it will cease to be payable forthwith.[74] The Act goes on to provide that any person who is convicted of a scheduled offence by a Special Criminal Court shall be disqualified for holding any such office or employment within seven years of the date of the conviction.[75] Moreover, he is also disqualified from receiving or being granted, at any time after the date of the conviction, any pension, superannuation allowance or gratuity from such source in respect of any service rendered before the date of the conviction.[76]

Clearly, these provisions are draconian by any standards. In effect they impose a secondary punishment of loss of office, employment, pension and superannuation allowance on any person convicted of a scheduled offence by a Special Criminal Court while employed, or having been employed, in the public service. Equally, they act as a seven year bar to employment in the public service for any person so convicted. The severity of these provisions is compounded by their exceptionally broad definition of employment in the public service. Not only do they cover employment in central and local government but they also affect employment in the hugely diverse range of commercial and non-commercial bodies which have been set up under statutory authority. Their effect is not rendered any less draconian by the inclusion of a provision which gives the government an absolute discretion to remit, in whole or in part, any forfeiture or disqualification incurred under them and to restore or revive, in whole or in part, the subject of such forfeiture as from the date of such remission.[77] It is also stated that where any forfeiture or disqualification is quashed or annulled the quashing or annulment shall take effect from the date of the conviction.[78] If the convicted person is granted a free pardon any such forfeiture or disqualification shall be annulled from the date of the pardon.

The constitutionality of these forfeiture and disqualification provisions were successfully challenged in *Cox v. Ireland*[79] in both the High Court and,

---

[72] Meaning an offence scheduled for the purposes of Pt V of the Offences against the State Act 1939.
[73] Offences against the State Act 1939, s.34(1).
[74] *ibid.* s.34(2).
[75] *ibid.* s.34(3)(a).
[76] *ibid.* s.34(3)(b) and (c).
[77] *ibid.* s.34(5).
[78] *ibid.* s.34(4).
[79] [1992] 2 I.R. 503. The ruling in this case attracted a number of civil actions for damages by individuals who had suffered the punishment in the past. Many of these were unsuccessful due to delay; *McDonnell v. Ireland* [1998] 1 I.R. 134; *Murphy v. Ireland* [1996] 2 I.L.R.M. 461.

on appeal, the Supreme Court. The plaintiff was a teacher in a vocational school. He was convicted of a firearms offence on a plea of guilty in the Special Criminal Court and sentenced to two years imprisonment. On his release the board of management of the school were willing to re-instate him but were advised by an officer of the Minister for Education that section 34 of the Offences against the State Act 1939 must be applied to the plaintiff. The plaintiff challenged the constitutionality of the provisions in section 34 on the grounds that they constituted unfair discrimination contrary to Article 40.1 of the Constitution, did not comply with the Article 38 requirement that the trial of a criminal offence should be in due course of law and constituted an administration of justice in breach of Article 34 of the Constitution.

The High Court ruled that the disabilities imposed upon the plaintiff by section 34 amounted to a punishment, as opposed to a mere matter of contract between employer and employee. As such it was part of the administration of justice within the meaning of Article 34 of the Constitution. Nevertheless, it rejected the plaintiff's argument that there was a breach of Article 34 of the Constitution in this case. The fact that the plaintiff was tried before the Special Criminal Court (and therefore exposed to the mandatory penalty) was the result not of the direction of the DPP but of the Oireachtas. However, the court went on to consider whether the Oireachtas had acted fairly and even-handedly in enacting section 34. It found that the penalty does not apply to all offences under the 1939 Act, it does not apply unless Part V is in operation, it does not apply to scheduled offences where the DPP directs trial in the ordinary courts, it does not apply to persons convicted in the Special Criminal Court who is not employed in the public sector, it is limited to persons in receipt of (or entitled to) remuneration or benefits from public funds, its scope extends beyond loss of office or employment to pension rights already earned prior to conviction, it has a profound effect on the personal rights of those within its ambit and there is nothing in the section or elsewhere in the Act to suggest that its provisions are in the interests of the common good. Accordingly, the judge, Mr Justice Barr, concluded:

> "In the light of these factors I have no doubt that the penalties imposed by s.34 of the Act of 1939 on those within its compass are patently unfair and capricious in nature. They amount to an unreasonable and unjustified interference with the personal rights, to which I have already referred, of those within its ambit, which are guaranteed by Article 40.3 of the Constitution as unspecified personal rights. . . . The provisions of the section also amount to unfair discrimination under Article 40, s.1, which guarantees equality before the law . . . It follows that s.34 of the Offences against the State Act 1939, in its entirety is unconstitutional and void"[80]

The Supreme Court reached a similar decision on appeal. It also emphasised, however, the legitimate interest of the State in relying on onerous and far-reaching penalties and forfeitures to protect its fundamental interests: **20–16**

---

[80] *ibid.* at 513–514.

> "The Court is satisfied that the State is entitled, for the protection of public peace and order, and for the maintenance and stability of its own authority, by its laws to provide onerous and far-reaching penalties and forfeitures imposed as a major deterrent to the commission of crimes threatening such peace and order and State authority, and is also entitled to ensure as far as practicable that amongst those involved in the carrying out of the functions of the State, there is not included persons who commit such crimes."[81]

Nevertheless the Court went on to hold that in section 34 had gone beyond what was required to protect these fundamental objectives and had failed to protect the constitutional rights of the citizen. The provisions of section 34 were "impermissibly wide and indiscriminate". The sort of offences which would be caught differed widely in their seriousness. Equally, they applied exclusively and absolutely to offences committed by persons who happened to hold a public office or be in public employment even though they could establish that their motive or intention in committing the offence, and the circumstances surrounding its commission, bore no relation at all to any question of the maintenance of public peace and order or the authority or stability of the State. In effect the provisions were disproportionate to the objects to be secured.[82] It is worth noting, however, that the ruling in *Cox* would not necessarily prevent an employer from dismissing an employee simply on the basis that he or she had been convicted of a scheduled offence.[83]

There is provision for the annulment of a forfeiture or disqualification in the event of the quashing or annulment of the associated conviction or where the individual concerned is granted a free pardon.[84] Similarly, the government has a power to remit any such forfeiture or disqualification.[85] In the light of the decision in *Cox* these provisions have no current practical relevance.

5. Contempt

20–17   It would appear that the Special Criminal Court has the same powers as the Central Criminal Court to punish contempt in the face of the court. In *In the Matter of the Sentence of Kevin O'Kelly for Contempt of Court by the Special Criminal Court*,[86] for example, a journalist was convicted and sentenced to imprisonment for contempt by the Special Criminal Court. He had been called as a witness by the prosecution and had refused to answer a question in the witness box abut the identity of a person with whom he had conducted an interview. On appeal against sentence the Supreme Court elaborated upon the duty of journalists to give evidence in court about their sources. However, it did not question the jurisdiction of the court to punish contempt in such cases.

---

[81] *ibid. per* Finlay C.J. at 522–523.
[82] See *People (DPP) v. W.C.* [1994] 1 I.L.R.M. 321.
[83] See *McDonnell v. Ireland* [1998] 1 I.R. 134.
[84] Offences against the State Act 1939, s.34(4).
[85] *ibid.* s.34(5).
[86] 1 Frewen 366.

E. Invoking the Jurisdiction of the Special Criminal Court

1. Introduction

The Special Criminal Court has jurisdiction to try and to convict or acquit any **20–18** person ". . . lawfully brought before that Court for trial . . ." under the Offences against the State Act 1939. Since the court is a creature of statute and has no inherent jurisdiction of its own it follows that its jurisdiction can be invoked in any individual case only where a person has been brought before it in accordance with the requisite statutory procedures. These are set out in sections 45 to 48 inclusive of the Offences against the State Act 1939. They prescribe three methods for invoking the jurisdiction of the court: the accused may be charged directly before the court; he may be returned for trial by the District Court to the Special Criminal Court; and the High Court may order that a case awaiting trial in either the Central Criminal Court or the Circuit Court should be transferred to the Special Criminal Court. Each of these situations are dealt with below.

It will also be seen that the DPP plays a critical role in determining whether an accused is tried in the Special Criminal Court or the ordinary courts. His role will be considered more fully after the three routes to the Special Criminal Court have been discussed. It is also worth noting that the Offences against the State Act 1939 permits the establishment of more than one Special Criminal Court. Section 49 makes provision for the selection of the Special Criminal Court by which an individual accused will be tried where more than one is sitting. The details will not be pursued here as only one such court has been established since 1972 and this situation is not likely to change in the foreseeable future.

2. Cases Originating in the District Court

Scheduled Offences to be Tried on Indictment

The procedure applicable to cases originating in the District Court differs **20–19** depending on whether the offences in question are scheduled or non-scheduled. Where a person is charged before a District Court with a scheduled offence which is an indictable offence, and the judge sends him forward for trial on the charge, he must send him forward for trial to the Special Criminal Court unless the DPP directs otherwise.[87] In effect, therefore, where a scheduled offence is to be tried on indictment the DPP enjoys a power to divert it away from the Special Criminal Court. In any such case where he decides not to exercise this power, the accused will be sent forward for trial to the Special Criminal Court. If the accused is being sent forward for trial to the Special Criminal Court under this provision, the District Court must send him forward

---

[87] Offences against the State Act 1939, s.45(2). The section actually refers to "a" special criminal court. However, a District Court order which sent the accused forward to "the" special criminal court is valid where there is only one Special Criminal Court; *State (Littlejohn) v. Governor of Mountjoy Prison,* unreported, Supreme Court, March 18, 1976.

in custody, unless the DPP gives consent to bail. Where the DPP does not consent and the accused is sent forward in custody he can apply to the High Court for bail.[88]

Scheduled Offences Triable Summarily

Where a person is brought before the District Court charged with a scheduled offence which that court can dispose of summarily, the judge must, if the DPP so requests, send the person for trial to the Special Criminal Court.[89] In this situation the DPP will have to act positively in order to ensure that the accused is sent forward for trial in the Special Criminal Court. If he fails to act, or decides not to act, the accused may be dealt with in the District Court even though he is charged with a scheduled offence. It is also worth noting that this provision would appear to cover not just summary offences but also those indictable offences which the judge can deal with summarily. Even if the accused wishes to plead guilty it would appear that the District Court judge is required to send him forward to the Special Criminal Court when the DPP so requests. Where the accused is sent forward for trial to the Special Criminal Court at the behest of the DPP under this provision, it would appear that the District Court retains its power to grant bail. If the District Court refuses bail and sends the accused forward in custody he may apply to the High Court for bail.[90]

Issuing Directions

The DPP's power to issue directions in a case where the accused is charged with a scheduled offence clearly differs depending on whether the accused is to be tried summarily or on indictment. With respect to the former the accused will be sent forward for trial in the Special Criminal Court only if the DPP issues positive directions to that effect. With respect to the latter, by contrast, he will be sent forward for trial in the Special Criminal Court automatically unless the DPP issues positive directions to the contrary. Surprisingly, perhaps the legislation does not specify how the appropriate directions should be given in any case. In *State (Bollard) v. Special Criminal Court*[91] Kenny J. accepted a verbal communication of the fact that the Attorney General (now the DPP) had certified in writing that the ordinary courts were in his opinion inadequate to secure the effective administration of justice and the preservation of public peace and order. By implication it would seem that verbal communication of the issue of the necessary directions would also be sufficient. Ryan and Magee state that in practice such directions are often communicated verbally to the judge of the District Court by counsel conducting the case on behalf of the DPP[92] They further submit that it is desirable that any order returning an accused for

---

[88] Offences against the State Act 1939, s.45(3).
[89] *ibid.* s.45(1).
[90] *ibid.* s.45(3).
[91] Unreported, High Court, September 20, 1972.
[92] Ryan and Magee, *The Irish Criminal Process* (Mercier Press, Dublin, 1983) p.378.

trial on a scheduled offence to the Central Criminal Court or to the Circuit Court should show on its face that the appropriate direction from the DPP has been given. If the order returning the accused for trial contains no reference to such a direction it may prove necessary at a later stage to provide oral evidence that the direction was communicated to the District Court judge in order to establish the validity of the return for trial. Where the DPP's direction is submitted in writing verified by his signature, it would appear that the court can take judicial notice of the fact that the person whose signature appears on the direction was the DPP at the time he signed it.[93] The court will not question the authenticity of the signature in the absence of evidence calling it into question.

Non-scheduled Offences

If an accused is charged with a non-scheduled offence, whether triable summarily or on indictment, he will not normally be sent forward for trial to the Special Criminal Court. However, the DPP may act to ensure that he is sent forward for trial to the Special Criminal Court. The position differs slightly depending on whether the accused is charged with an offence triable summarily or an offence to be tried on indictment.

20–20

Where a person appears before the District Court charged with a non-scheduled, indictable offence, and the judge sends him forward for trial on the charge, the judge must send him forward for trial before the Special Criminal Court if the DPP so requests.[94] In this case, however, the DPP's request must be grounded on his written certificate that the ordinary courts are in his opinion inadequate to secure the effective administration of justice and the preservation of public peace and order in relation to the trial of such person on such charge. Where the accused is sent forward for trial by the Special Criminal Court pursuant to this provision he must be sent forward in custody unless the DPP consents to bail. If the DPP does not consent and the accused is sent forward in custody he may apply to the High Court for bail.[95]

Where the accused is charged before the District Court with a non-scheduled offence which the court has jurisdiction to deal with summarily the judge must send him forward for trial by the Special Criminal Court on that charge if the DPP so requests.[96] Once again, the DPP's request must be grounded on his written certificate that the ordinary courts are in his opinion inadequate to secure the effective administration of justice and the preservation of public peace and order in relation to the trial of such person. Indeed, the only difference between this situation and that where the accused is sent forward to the Special Criminal Court for a non-scheduled indictable offence is that in this case the District Court would appear to retain its power to grant bail. If the Court

---

[93] *Re MacCurtain* [1941] I.R. 83.
[94] Offences against the State Act 1939, s.46(2).
[95] *ibid.* s.46(3).
[96] *ibid.* s.46(1). As is the case with a scheduled offence which is triable summarily, it would appear that this provision extends to an indictable offence triable summarily and to a situation where the accused intends to plead guilty.

sends the accused forward in custody he may apply to the High Court for bail.[97] Once again it is worth noting that the Court will take judicial notice of the fact that the person whose signature appears on the direction was the DPP at the time he signed it, and the court will not question the authenticity of the signature in the absence of evidence calling it into question.[98]

The scope of the DPP's power to certify the inadequacy of the ordinary courts is considered further below under the heading "Reviewing the DPP's Directions".

3. Sending Forward on a Plea of Guilty

20–21   The relevant provisions in the Offences against the State Act do not deal specifically with the situation where a person has pleaded guilty in the District Court to a scheduled, indictable offence or any other offence in respect of which the DPP requests that he be sent forward for trial to the Special Criminal Court. The relevant provisions refer only to the accused being sent forward for trial by the Special Criminal Court, as distinct from being sent forward for sentencing only. The question arises, therefore, whether the accused who pleads guilty to an indictable offence can be sent forward for sentencing to the Special Criminal Court. Given that the jurisdiction of the

20–22   court derives solely from statute it might be thought that the answer would have to be no in the absence of a specific provision in the legislation conferring such jurisdiction.[99] However, when the issue arose in *State (Littlejohn) v. Governor of Mountjoy Prison*[100] the Supreme Court ruled in favour of the Special Criminal Court having jurisdiction. In that case the applicant had appeared before a District Court judge charged with armed robbery, a non-scheduled, indictable offence. The Attorney General[101] certified that the ordinary courts were inadequate to secure the effective administration of justice and the preservation of peace and order in relation to the trial of the accused and duly requested that he be sent forward for trial to the Special Criminal Court. Although the applicant pleaded guilty the District Court judge sent him forward for sentence to the Special Criminal Court. In seeking an order of *habeas corpus* the applicant argued that the District Court order sending him forward was bad as the Attorney General's certificate was ineffective to secure his return to the Special Criminal Court for sentence only, as distinct from trial. The Supreme Court dismissed this argument on the basis that the word "trial" also encompassed a sentence, unless the context of a particular statute required otherwise.[102] The Court could find nothing in the relevant statutory provision which would require the word to be confined to a judicial hearing of the issue of guilt or innocence as opposed to the issue of sentence.

---

[97] Offences against the State Act 1939, s.46(3).

[98] *Re MacCurtain* [1941] I.R. 83.

[99] See, *e.g. People (Attorney General) v. Shribman and Samuels* [1946] I.R. 431; *People (DPP) v. Rice* [1979] I.R. 15; *State (DPP) v. Special Criminal Court* unreported, High Court, May 18, 1983.

[100] Unreported, Supreme Court, March 18, 1976.

[101] At that time his functions in this matter had not been transferred to the DPP.

[102] The Court accepted that Criminal Procedure Act 1967, s.13(2)(b) was an example of a provision which did require an opposite interpretation. See *State (Williams) v. Kelly (No.2)* [1970] I.R. 271.

4. Transfer to the Special Criminal Court

The prosecution can secure the transfer of a trial on indictment to the Special Criminal Court even after the accused has been returned for trial to the Central Criminal Court or the Circuit Court, as the case may be.[103] For this to happen the DPP would have to certify that the ordinary courts are, in his opinion, inadequate to secure the effective administration of justice and the preservation of public peace and order in relation to the trial of the accused on the charge in question. If he so certifies he must cause an application to be made to the High Court, grounded upon his certificate, for an order transferring the trial of the accused on the charge to the Special Criminal Court. When presented with such an application it would appear that the High Court must issue the order requested.[104] An attempt to challenge the exercise of this power as an unwarranted intrusion upon the powers of the High Court was rejected by Carroll J. in *O'Reilly and Judge v. DPP*:[105]

> ". . . the function of the High Court sitting as the Central Criminal Court to try an offence ceases when the DPP has certified under s.48 of the Offences against the State Act 1939, and makes application to the court to transfer to the Special Criminal Court. The trial of the individual concerned must thenceforth be in the Special Criminal Court. Such trial is authorised directly by Article 38(3). In my opinion the constitutional jurisdiction of the High Court is limited by the operation of Article 38(3) and the mandatory order sending the accused forward for trial to the Special Criminal Court is not an unwarranted intrusion of the powers of the High Court. On the contrary, it is constitutionally justified under Article 38(3)."

With respect it is submitted that this explanation does not directly address the point at issue which is the manner in which the case is brought before the Special Criminal Court. There is nothing in Article 38.3 which suggests that an agent of the executive enjoys an unfettered discretion to deprive the High Court of jurisdiction in a case of which it is already seised. In any event, once a transfer order has been issued the accused is deemed to have been sent forward to the Special Criminal Court for trial on the charge in question.[106]

Where a transfer order has been made under this provision a copy must be served on the accused by a member of the Garda Síochána and a copy sent to the appropriate county registrar.[107] The Special Criminal Court will fix the time and place of trial. If the accused is in custody when the order is made he shall remain in custody until brought before the Special Criminal Court for trial. Equally, if he is on bail at the time the order is made, such bail shall be deemed to be for his attendance before the Special Criminal Court for trial at the time and place directed by that court.

---

[103] Offences against the State Act 1939, s.48.
[104] *State (Coveney) v. Special Criminal Court* [1982] I.L.R.M. 284, *per* Finlay P at 286.
[105] [1984] I.L.R.M. 224, *per* Carroll J. at 230.
[106] Offences against the State Act 1939, s.48(a).
[107] *ibid.* s.48(b).

5. Cases Originating in the Special Criminal Court

The Power

20–23 There is provision for a person to be brought directly before the Special Criminal Court for charge and trial. The procedure differs slightly depending on whether it is intended to charge a scheduled offence or a non-scheduled offence. Where it is intended to charge a person with a scheduled offence the DPP may direct that, instead of charging the person with the offence before a judge of the District Court, he should be brought before the Special Criminal Court and charged with the offence.[108] When such a direction is given, the person concerned must be brought directly before the Special Criminal Court where he shall be charged with and tried for the offence.[109] This provision will also apply to a non-scheduled offence, but only if the DPP certifies that the ordinary courts are, in his opinion, inadequate to secure the effective administration of justice and the preservation of public peace and order in relation to the trial of such person on such charge.[110]

The Procedure

The DPP's direction in the case of a scheduled offence must be conveyed to the court in writing signed by the DPP or orally by a person appearing on his behalf or prosecuting in his name.[111] There is no specific provision governing the communication of the direction and certification in the case of a non-scheduled offence, but the strong implication is that the same procedure applies as for a scheduled offence. In *People (DPP) v. Eccles, McPhilips and McShane*[112] the accused were before the Special Criminal Court charged with the non-scheduled offence of capital murder. The DPP's certificate on the inadequacy of the ordinary courts had been signed by a professional officer of the DPP and communicated to the court by a solicitor for the prosecution. In the course of the trial prosecution counsel stated orally to the court that the DPP's function in giving the certificate was performed on his behalf by the professional officer in question. The accused appealed against conviction on the ground, *inter alia*, that the certificate had not been sufficiently proved in order to invoke the jurisdiction of the court. They also asserted that the certificate should have been proved at their first appearance before the court. In rejecting the first argument the Court of Criminal Appeal referred to section 4(1)(a) of the Prosecution of Offences Act 1974 which permits the

---

[108] Offences against the State Act 1939, s.47(1). It is worth noting that the obligation to take the suspect directly before the Special Criminal Court in such a case applies even in a case where the provisions of the Criminal Law (Jurisdiction) Act 1976 may be invoked. The provisions of ss.47 and 30(4) of the 1939 Act are not impliedly amended by ss.14 and 20 of the 1976 Act to create a the situation whereby a suspect arrested under s.30 for a matter within the scope of the 1976 Act would invariably have to be brought before a District Court. See *Sloan v. Special Criminal Court* [1993] 3 I.R. 528.

[109] *People (Attorney General) v. Doyle and Maher* 1 Frewen 39.

[110] Offences against the State Act 1939, s.47(2).

[111] Offences against the State Act 1939 to 1972 Special Criminal Court Rules 1975, r.17(3).

[112] 3 Frewen 36.

DPP to authorise any of his professional officers to perform on his behalf any of his functions in relation to a particular case or cases. Section 4(3) stipulates that the performance of any of the DPP's functions, either personally or under his authority by one of his professional officers, may be established without further proof in any proceedings by a statement of that fact made in writing and signed by the DPP or orally to the court concerned by a person appearing on behalf of the DPP The Court of Criminal Appeal found that these requirements had been satisfied on the facts of this case. The Court also rejected the argument that the necessary proof of the issuing of the certificate should have been presented on the first appearance of the accused. While the issuance of the certificate is a necessary precondition to the jurisdiction of the court in the case of a non-scheduled offence, the fact that it has issued can be proved in the requisite manner at any time before the close of the prosecution case.

Warrant for Arrest

Where a person is required to be brought before the Special Criminal Court to   **20–24**
be charged under these provisions that court may issue a warrant for his arrest with a view to having the person brought before it.[113] In the case of a non-scheduled offence, however, the warrant for arrest can issue only after the DPP has duly certified to the court that the ordinary courts are in his opinion inadequate to secure the effective administration of justice and the preservation of public order in relation to the case in hand.[114] In the case of both scheduled and non-scheduled offences the relevant statutory provision merely states that it shall be lawful for the court to issue a warrant whenever the person in question is required to be brought before the court to be charged with the offence. In that respect it differs from most other judicial powers to issue warrants in that it does not specifically require the court to be satisfied upon information that there are reasonable grounds to suspect the person of having committed the offence in question. It would appear, therefore, that a warrant can issue so long as the court is presented with evidence to the effect that the DPP has issued the appropriate direction in respect of the accused and, in the case of a non-scheduled offence, a certificate as to the inadequacy of the ordinary courts. In practice, the prosecution will normally present evidence linking the accused to the offence, but there is no requirement for this evidence to be sufficient to establish a reasonable suspicion against the accused.[115]

Summons for Appearance

The Special Criminal Court Rules also make provision for the issue of a summons to compel the appearance of a person where the DPP has directed that he be charged before the court. Unlike the situation with respect to the

---

[113] Offences against the State Act 1939, s.47(3). It would appear that Form 5 or 6 of the Schedule of Forms in the Special Criminal Court Rules should be used; Offences against the State Acts 1939 to 1972; Special Criminal Court Rules 1975, r.17(4).

[114] *McElhinney v. Special Criminal Court* [1990] 1 I.R. 405.

[115] *McMahon v. Special Criminal Court* unreported, High Court, August 30, 1998.

warrant, they specifically state that the court may, on information or evidence relating to the offence being given before it, order the issue of a summons ordering the person in question to attend before the court and there to be charged with the offence.[116] It follows that for a summons to issue the prosecution will have to present information or evidence relating to the offence itself. This, however, does not require the presentation of evidence sufficient to leave the court satisfied that there are reasonable grounds to suspect that the accused committed the offence.[117]

The Rules go on to say that where the person fails to appear in answer to a summons duly served upon him, his appearance may be procured by the issue of a warrant under an order of the court.[118] It is at least arguable, therefore, that the court should proceed by summons in the first instance in any individual case unless there is reason to believe that a summons will not be effective to secure his appearance. This argument is not necessarily defeated by the fact that the Rules also state that nothing in them shall be construed as prohibiting the court from ordering the issue of a warrant whether or not a summons has already been issued.[119] It is also worth noting that when a person is brought before the Special Criminal Court by summons for the purpose of being charged before the court the Chief Prosecution Solicitor must furnish him and the court with a summary of the evidence to be given at his trial.[120]

6. Compliance with Statutory Procedures

20–25   Since the Special Criminal Court has no inherent jurisdiction of its own it follows that compliance with the relevant statutory procedures are essential in order to invoke its jurisdiction in any individual case. Just because its jurisdiction can be invoked in certain circumstances by charging a person directly before the court, it does not follow that a person can be lawfully tried simply by taking advantage of his voluntary presence or appearance in the court. The relevant statutory provisions stipulate that the court has jurisdiction to try any person "lawfully brought before that court for trial under [the 1939 Act]."[121] As seen above the Act provides only three methods by which the person can lawfully be brought before the court for the purpose of trial. Two of these methods involve the person either being sent for trial by a judge of the District Court or being transferred by order of the court of trial. The third involves the person being charged directly before the court. Even here it would appear that the person must be brought before the court in accordance with the relevant statutory provisions. If the person is brought before the court pursuant to a warrant for the purpose of being charged and it transpires that the warrant was

---

[116] Offences against the State Acts 1939 to 1972 Special Criminal Court Rules, 1975, r.17(1). For this purpose Form 16 or such similar form as the circumstances require should be used.

[117] *McMahon v. Special Criminal Court* unreported, High Court, August 30, 1998.

[118] Offences against the State Acts 1939 to 1922 Special Criminal Court Rules 1975. r.17(2). Form 17 should be used for the arrest warrant.

[119] *ibid.* r.17(4).

[120] *ibid.* r.17(6).

[121] Offences against the State Act 1939, s.43(1).

issued without jurisdiction, the procedural lacuna cannot be made good by the actual presence of the person before the court.[122] The situation is not analogous to that in District Court proceedings whereby the District Court can acquire jurisdiction in a case by taking advantage of a person's presence before the Court. However, if a person has been lawfully brought before the court in respect of one charge it would appear that the court can take advantage of his presence there to charge him with a further offence, even though it would not have had jurisdiction in respect of the latter had the person not been brought before the court in respect of the former charge.

In *McElhinney v. DPP*[123] the accused was charged with a scheduled offence and a non-scheduled offence. The DPP issued a direction that the person should be charged directly before the Special Criminal Court. He was brought before the court on foot of two warrants issued by the court. It transpired that the warrant charging him with the non-scheduled offence was not validly issued as prior to its issue the DPP had not properly certified that the ordinary courts were in his opinion inadequate to secure the effective administration of justice in respect of the case in accordance with the relevant statutory requirement. The other warrant was validly issued. The accused secured an order for separate trials for the two offences. He subsequently objected to the trial for the non-scheduled offence on the ground that he had not been lawfully brought before the court in respect of that charge due to the defect in the warrant. This objection was rejected by the court which proceeded to try and convict him for the offence. The accused successfully obtained an order of certiorari in the High Court quashing the warrant and his conviction and sentence. Gannon J. was of the opinion that the jurisdiction of the Special Criminal Court in respect of each offence was dependant on full compliance with the relevant procedures. Since the warrant for the non-scheduled offence had been issued without jurisdiction it followed that it could not provide a proper basis for bringing him before the court in respect of that offence.

The High Court's decision in *McElhinney* was overturned on appeal to the Supreme Court which, following the decision of the Court of Criminal Appeal in *People (DPP) v. Pringle*,[124] took a very literal approach to what was meant by "brought before a Special Criminal Court". The Supreme Court accepted that a person could not be charged before the Special Criminal Court purely on the basis of his voluntary presence before the court. However, it went on to hold that the court would acquire jurisdiction to charge the person and proceed to trial so long as the person had been lawfully brought before it for some purpose. In this case the person had been lawfully brought before the court to be charged with the scheduled offence. As such he was a person lawfully brought before the court. Since the charge pertaining to the non-scheduled offence was put to him at that point, the requirements for invoking the jurisdiction of the court were satisfied. It was not absolutely necessary that the accused should have been brought before the court specifically or solely for the purpose of being charged

---

[122] *McElhinney v. Special Criminal Court* [1990] 1 I.R. 405.
[123] [1990] 1 I.R. 405.
[124] (1981) 2 Frewen 77–57.

with the scheduled offence. It was sufficient that he was lawfully brought before the court.

The Supreme Court in *McElhinney* did not directly address the question of what was meant by "lawfully" brought before the court. In that case there was a valid warrant in respect of the scheduled offence so it did not have to consider the position which would have arisen if both warrants had been invalid. Nevertheless, it would seem implicit in the judgment of the court that if there was no valid warrant, the accused would not have been lawfully before the court and, as a result, the court would have lacked jurisdiction. Support for this view can be found in the approach of the Court of Criminal Appeal in *People (DPP) v. Caffrey*.[125] In that case the accused was tried and convicted before the Special Criminal Court having been arrested and detained under section 30. He appealed his conviction on the ground that he had not been lawfully arrested and detained under section 30 and that, as such, the jurisdiction of the Special Criminal Court had not been lawfully invoked. It is not clear from the judgment in the case whether the accused had been brought directly before the court for the purpose of being charged. Nevertheless the Court of Criminal Appeal dealt with the appeal explicitly on the basis that it was common ground that the jurisdiction of the Special Criminal Court was dependant on a lawful arrest under section 30.[126]

20–26   Unfortunately, the clarity of this position is thrown into some doubt by the decision of the Court of Criminal Appeal in *People v. Kehoe*.[127] In that case the Court of Criminal Appeal addressed the issue of whether the Special Criminal Court would have jurisdiction in a case where the accused was not in lawful custody at the time he was brought before it. The accused had been brought directly before the Special Criminal Court to be charged pursuant to the direction of the DPP At the time he was in Garda custody having been arrested and detained under section 30 of the Offences against the State Act 1939. He submitted that his arrest and detention under section 30 was tainted with illegality with the result that he was in unlawful custody when brought before the Special Criminal Court. He further submitted that that would be sufficient to deprive the court of jurisdiction in his case. In rejecting these arguments the Court of Criminal Appeal explained that the jurisdiction of the court was triggered by the DPP directing that the accused should be brought before the court to be charged. Its jurisdiction did not depend on the technical validity of the manner in which the accused was brought before the court. It may be, of course, that the application of unfair procedures or a breach of the constitutional rights of the accused up to that point would be sufficient to invalidate a subsequent trial. The time to make that case, however, was when the accused was first brought before the court. If the point was not taken then it cannot be relied upon subsequently to deny the jurisdiction of the court.

---

[125] [1986] I.L.R.M. 687.

[126] In *People v. Campbell* 2 Frewen 131 the Court of Criminal Appeal specifically declined to determine whether persons not lawfully arrested, but brought in Garda custody before the Special Criminal Court for the purpose of being charged, can be lawfully tried by the Court.

[127] [1985] I.R. 444.

In some respects the analysis of the law in *Kehoe* sits uneasily with the analysis in *McElhinney*. In the latter the Supreme Court accepted that the Special Criminal Court could not acquire jurisdiction simply by virtue of the fact that the accused was physically present before the court. Jurisdiction would be dependant on the accused having been lawfully brought before the court pursuant to the relevant statutory requirements. In *McElhinney* these requirements were a direction by the DPP and a valid warrant issued by the court itself. In *Kehoe* there was no warrant and no need to rely on a warrant issued by the court. Accordingly, the accused was lawfully brought before the court, for the purpose of invoking the court's jurisdiction, simply if he was brought there pursuant to the lawful direction of the DPP So long as that direction had issued lawfully and the accused had been brought before the court pursuant to it, the court would have jurisdiction in the case. The fact that there may have been some illegality in the arrest and detention of the accused *en route* to the court would not deprive the court of actual jurisdiction in the case, unless the accused raised the matter on his first appearance and established that the illegality was such that it would invalidate his subsequent trial.

While the divergent analyses in *McElhinney* and *Kehoe* might be accommodated on the basis that the court was addressing two different factual situations, it cannot be gainsaid that the difference between them is very thin. Indeed, it might seem perverse to the layman that the jurisdiction of the court can be denied in a case where the accused is brought before it on a warrant which had been issued by the court without jurisdiction, but not where the accused has been brought before it having been unlawfully arrested and detained under section 30. It would seem preferable to adopt the approach implicit in *McElhinney*, and supported by *Caffrey*, that the jurisdiction of the court is dependant on the accused having been lawfully brought before it in the sense that he has been brought before it pursuant to a lawful arrest or in response to the issue of a valid summons.

F. Reviewing the DPP's Direction

Introduction

It is apparent that the DPP plays a major role in determining whether an **20–27** accused will be tried in the Special Criminal Court. The only offences which will be tried automatically in the Special Criminal Court are those which are both scheduled under the Offences against the State Act and are to be tried on indictment. Even then the DPP has a role to play in that he can divert any individual case from the Special Criminal Court to the Central Criminal Court or the Circuit Court as the case may be. Of greater significance, of course, is the fact that by issuing the appropriate certificate or direction he can ensure that the trial of any other offence at all, whether scheduled or non-scheduled, will be held in the Special Criminal Court as distinct from the ordinary courts. In the case of a non-minor offence this will have the effect of denying the accused his constitutional right to trial by jury. This is a most serious matter in any circumstances, but particularly where the offence in question has not been scheduled under the Offences against the State Act. At least where the offence in question is scheduled it is known in advance that a person charged with it is liable to be tried in the Special Criminal Court. Moreover, the decision to schedule it will have been taken by the government pursuant to a power specifically conferred upon it by the Offences against the State Act 1939. Before exercising the scheduling power the government will have to be satisfied that the ordinary courts are inadequate to ensure the effective administration of justice and the preservation of public peace and order in relation to the offence in question. The government is democratically accountable to the Daíl for any such decision. The DPP also must be of the opinion that the ordinary courts are inadequate to secure the effective administration of justice etc before sending for trial in the Special Criminal Court a person charged with a non scheduled offence. The DPP, however, is not democratically accountable for his actions, nor does he have a democratic mandate. It might be expected, therefore, given the important constitutional ramifications of his decision in any individual case, that the courts would have been active in ensuring that the DPP exercised his discretion judiciously and reasonably in these matters. Surprisingly, perhaps, the courts have so far declined all attempts at persuading them that they have a jurisdiction to review the DPP's decisions in these matters.

Scope of DPP's Discretion

In *State (Littlejohn) v. Governor of Mountjoy Prison*[128] the applicant pleaded guilty to a non-scheduled offence and was sent forward for sentence to the Special Criminal Court on the Attorney General's certificate. The applicant challenged the validity of the certificate on the ground of unreasonableness. He argued that since the Special Criminal Court was composed of a High Court judge, a Circuit Court judge and a District Court judge it was unreasonable to certify that a court consisting of any one of them sitting alone was inadequate to secure the effective administration of justice. Henchy J, in the Supreme Court, intimated that the courts could not go behind the certificate to examine the grounds upon which the Attorney General had formed his opinion about the inadequacy of the ordinary courts. Nevertheless, he also made it clear that while the threat of jury intimidation in the ordinary courts was certainly one ground upon which the Attorney General could exercise the power of certification it was by no means the only one. In this case, for example, it was perfectly legitimate for the Attorney General to form the requisite opinion on the basis that the individual and collective standing of three judges from the ordinary courts when sitting as a Special Criminal Court were distinguishable from their function and standing as members of the ordinary courts. The judges' decisions on verdict and sentence in the Special Criminal Court were collective decisions. Unlike the position which prevails in the ordinary courts it would not be possible to determine which, if any, of the members sitting in an individual case had agreed with or dissented from the collective decision of the court.

---

[128] Unreported, Supreme Court, March 18, 1976.

It does not follow, however, that the DPP could not form the opinion in any individual case that the ordinary courts were inadequate to secure the effective administration of justice in the trial by jury of the accused but adequate for the purposes of sentencing only. In *State (Coveney) v.* Special Criminal Court,[129] for example, the accused was sent forward on a plea of guilty to the Circuit Court where he changed his plea to not guilty. The DPP responded by providing the necessary certificate to have the case transferred to the Special Criminal Court. The argument that the DPP had acted *ultra vires* in issuing the certificate was rejected by Finlay P.:

> "There appears to me to be nothing patently incorrect in a view if it were held . . . that for the purpose of sentence only on a plea of guilty the ordinary courts were adequate but for the purpose of trial by jury on evidence they were inadequate."[130]

Further evidence of judicial reluctance to review the basis on which a certificate was issued is to be found in the decision of the Supreme Court in *Re Article 26 and the Criminal Law (Jurisdiction) Bill*.[131] Counsel had argued that the commission of an offence outside the State could not affect the effective administration of justice or the preservation of public peace or order within the State. Accordingly, the DPP could not legitimately form the opinion that the ordinary courts would be inadequate to secure the effective administration of justice in this State in the trial of an offence which had been committed outside the State. In rejecting this argument O'Higgins C.J. stated that the correct test to be applied was whether it was impossible to envisage circumstances in which the DPP could not properly form the opinion that the ordinary courts were inadequate to deal with extra-territorial offences created by the Bill. While this does not preclude the possibility for judicial review, it leaves very little room for it.[132] Indeed, O'Higgins C.J. had no difficulty in envisaging circumstances in which the DPP could properly form the necessary opinion with respect to extra-territorial offences.

Beyond Judicial Review

The issue of whether the DPP's certification is subject to judicial review was addressed directly in *Savage and Owen v. DPP*.[133] In that case the applicants had been sent for trial to the Special Criminal Court on non-scheduled offences pursuant to the requisite certificates issued by the DPP They sought a declaration from the High Court to the effect that the certificates were void and, in consequence, that the District Court order sending them forward for trial to the Special Criminal Court was void. The central issue in the case was whether the exercise of the DPP's certification power was open to review. Finlay P held that it was not. So long as the DPP had formed the requisite

20–28

---

[129] [1982] I.L.R.M. 284.
[130] *ibid.* at 286.
[131] [1977] I.R. 129.
[132] The court specifically declined to express an opinion on whether a certificate could be subjected to judicial review as it felt that it was not necessary to express an opinion on the point.
[133] [1982] I.L.R.M. 385.

opinion in the case at hand, the courts could not examine the basis upon which it was formed. In reaching this conclusion the learned judge was heavily influenced by the nature of the Special Criminal Court and the purposes for which it was established. He noted, in particular, that the court was established in response to circumstances which endangered the very existence of the State and which rendered special methods of trial necessary for the preservation of public peace and order. Their establishment by government proclamation was not susceptible to judicial review. Only the Daíl could annul such a proclamation. Equally the courts had no jurisdiction to review the exercise of the government's power to declare an offence to be scheduled. Finlay P went on to interpret the DPP's power to certify in the case of scheduled offences as a graft on the government's power to schedule. As such it, too, was beyond the scope of judicial review. The courts could not review the DPP's decision to require the trial of a person on a summary scheduled offence to be held in the Special Criminal Court, nor could they review his decision to abstain from directing the trial of a person on an indictable scheduled offence to be held in the ordinary courts as opposed to the Special Criminal Court.

On the question of the DPP's power to certify in the case of non-scheduled offences, which was the specific point at issue in the case, Finlay P. noted that the terms of the relevant statutory provision did not appear to envisage judicial review of the DPP's decision. He went on to declare that serious consequences would ensue if it was subject to judicial review. In particular, the learned judge considered that it could result in the DPP having to reveal in open court all of the information, knowledge and facts upon which he formed his opinion. Given that the court was established to deal with persons seeking to overthrow the established organs of the State this would create insuperable security difficulties. Accordingly, Finlay P. concluded that to subject the DPP's certification power to judicial review would be to render the whole Special Criminal Court machinery in Part V inoperable:

> "If the contention made on behalf of the plaintiffs in this case was correct and if the opinion of the DPP necessary for a certificate issued by him pursuant to section 46 subsection 2 of the Act of 1939 were reviewable by a court then upon a *prima facie* case being established in pleadings by any person returned for trial pursuant to such a certificate that some of the matters of which the section demands should be the opinion of the DPP were not true, or that the opinion was one which was based on false information or an erroneous inference from facts established or made known to the DPP, it would be necessary for the director in order to uphold the certificate he issued and for the Special Criminal Court to have jurisdiction over the case which on his certificate has been sent forward for trial by it to reveal in open court in litigation at the instance of the accused person himself all the information, knowledge and facts upon which he formed his opinion. This would obviously, as a practical matter, entirely make impossible the operation of Part V of the Act of 1939 for the trial of any non-scheduled offence by the Special Criminal Court whilst it is established and in existence. The revealing of such information in open court under conditions under which persons seeking to overthrow the established organs of the State would be a

security impossibility and to interpret section 46 subsection 2 of the Act of 1939 so as to make that necessary would be to vitiate the entire of that sub-section."[134]

Both the decision and reasoning employed by the High Court in *Savage and McOwen* has attracted considerable criticism.[135] Certainly, the notion of an unreviewable discretionary power vested in a public body, such as the DPP, sits uneasily with the firmly established trend in favour of subjecting the exercise of public powers to judicial review.[136] It has even been accepted that the DPP's power to decide whether or not to prosecute in an individual case is amenable to judicial review.[137] It is difficult, therefore, to appreciate why the exercise of a discretionary power which can deprive the individual of his constitutional right to trial by jury should be unreviewable. Nevertheless, when the issue arose again before the High Court in *O'Reilly & Judge v. DPP*[138] Carroll J. also rejected the contention that the DPP's decision was subject to judicial review. In this case the DPP had directed that the accused should be charged and tried before the Special Criminal Court in respect of one offence and that his trial in respect of other offences should be transferred from the Central Criminal Court to the Special Criminal Court. The issues were effectively the same as those in *Savage and McOwen*. Indeed, Carroll J. adopted similar reasoning to that used by Finlay P. in *Savage and McOwen* in reaching the conclusion that the DPP's decision was unreviewable. It would appear that the courts view the opinion of the DPP as to the adequacy of the ordinary courts in securing the effective administration of justice as being one of exceptional importance and confidentiality.[139]

In *Kavanagh v. Ireland*[140] the Supreme Court confirmed that the exercise of the DPP's power of certification was effectively beyond the reach of judicial scrutiny, although it did intimate that it could be challenged on the basis of mala fides. In the words of Barrington J: **20–29**

> "This judgment has attempted to stress that the primary control over the powers of the Government under Article 38, s.3 of the Constitution and under Part V of the Offences Against the State Act 1939, is a political control. This means that normally the proclamation of the Government under section 35(2) and (4) of the Offences Against the State Act 1939, or the certificates or directions of the DPP under section 47 of the same Act will not be subject to judicial review in the absence of mala fides."[141]

---

[134] *ibid. per* Finlay P. at 389.
[135] See, *e.g.* Hogan and Walker, *op.cit.* at p.235; Byrne, "Judicial Reviewability of a Prosecutorial Discretion" (1981) *Irish Jurist* 86; Byrne, "The Director of Public Prosecution's Power to Refer Cases to the Special Court" 6 (1984) D.U.L.J.; Pye, "Judicial Review of Discretionary Powers under Pt V of the Offences against the State Act 1939" 3 (1985) D.U.L.J. 65.
[136] See Hogan and Morgan, *Administrative Law in Ireland* (3rd ed., Round Hall Sweet & Maxwell, Dublin, 1998) at 617–690 for the trend in favour of judicial review.
[137] *State (McCormack) v. Curran* [1987] I.L.R.M. 225.
[138] [1984] I.L.R.M. 224.
[139] See also, Barrington J., *obiter*, in *State (Smith & Fox) v. Governor of the Curragh Military Detention Barracks* [1980] I.L.R.M. 208; and Gavan Duffy J. in *Re MacCurtain* [1941] I.R. 83 at 87.
[140] [1996] 1 I.R. 321.
[141] *ibid.* at 360.

Nevertheless, it is worth pointing out that the substance of the relevant part of Barrington J.'s judgment is directed at the power to establish the Special Criminal Court by proclamation. He does not specifically address the nature of the DPP's certification power. Instead, for the purposes of judicial review, he treats it as *ad idem* with the government's power to establish the Special Criminal Court. In the later case of *Byrne and Dempsey v. The Government of Ireland*[142] the Supreme Court, citing its own decision in Kavanagh as authority, confirmed that the exercise of the DPP's certification power was unreviewable in the absence of a prima facie case of mala fides. In that case the Supreme Court refused to look behind the DPP's decision to certify the inadequacy of the ordinary courts in respect of three accused persons, despite the fact that he permitted the trial of six of their co-accused to go ahead in the ordinary courts.

Consequences of Unreviewable Power

20–30   An inevitable and important consequence of the courts refusal to subject the DPP's certification power to judicial review is that the DPP enjoys virtually unlimited freedom over the sort of cases which he can send for trial to the Special Criminal Court. It might have been supposed, reasonably, that the certification power was intended to be exercised only in those cases which entailed a subversive element. Indeed, Finlay P. found support for his decision in *Savage and McOwen* in the fact that the Special Criminal Court was established to deal with persons seeking to overthrow the established organs of the State. In the absence of judicial review, however, it would appear that there is no legal mechanism which can be used to restrain the DPP from sending a case to the Special Criminal Court even though it lacks a subversive element. So long as the DPP actually forms the opinion that the ordinary courts are inadequate to secure the effective administration of justice or the preservation of public peace or order with respect to the trial of the accused on the charge in question, his decision to send it to the Special Criminal Court would appear to be beyond attack. It would not matter that the case in question lacked any subversive connotations.

Much of the workload of the Special Criminal Court over the past decade or more has stemmed from the organised crime sector as opposed to the subversive sector. Many of these cases have been sent to the Special Criminal Court pursuant to the exercise of the DPP's certification power.[143] The legality of this practice was upheld by the Supreme Court in *Kavanagh v. Ireland*[144] where it was acknowledged that the jurisdiction of the Special Criminal Court was not confined to subversive crime. Significantly, the accused was charged with both scheduled and non-scheduled offences which had no subversive connotations and was tried in the Special Criminal Court pursuant to a certificate from the DPP to the effect that the ordinary courts were inadequate

---

[142] Unreported, Supreme Court, March 11, 1999.
[143] *O'Reilly and Judge* was actually dealt with on the basis that the applicant was not a member of any subversive organisation.
[144] [1997] 1 I.L.R.M. 321.

to secure the effective administration of justice in that case. The court rejected a challenge to, *inter alia*, the lawfulness of the DPP's decision to issue the certificate.

Constitutional Challenge

It is also worth noting that attempts have been made to challenge the constitutionality of the DPP's certification powers. As with the attempts to establish the availability of judicial review, these have proved unsuccessful. In *State (Bollard) v.* Special Criminal Court,[145] for example, the High Court decided that the power of the Attorney General (now the DPP) to compel a judge of the District Court to send a person for trial to the Special Criminal Court on a scheduled offence, which could be disposed of summarily, was an exercise of the judicial power. The exercise of the power, in the words of Kenny J., "did not decide the innocence or guilt of the accused."[146] Kenny J. also rejected the argument that a decision not to direct the trial of the accused before the ordinary courts in the case of an indictable scheduled offence involved an exercise of the judicial power. By implication the DPP's power to certify the inadequacy of the ordinary courts to secure the effective administration of justice did not amount to an exercise of the judicial power of the State. Similarly, Carroll J., in *O'Reilly and Judge v. DPP*,[147] was not persuaded that the DPP's certification power represented an unjustified intrusion into the judicial domain by virtue of the fact that it could be used to compel the High Court to transfer the trial of a case from the Central Criminal Court or the Circuit Court to the Special Criminal Court. The learned judge was of the opinion that the jurisdiction of the High Court had already been limited in this matter by Article 38.3 of the constitution.[148] Carroll J. also rejected the argument that the DPP's power to have an accused charged and tried directly before the Special Criminal Court infringed the accused's constitutional right to a preliminary examination. She found that there was no such right.

20–31

The UN Human Rights Committee

The role of the DPP in triggering the jurisdiction of the Special Criminal Court has been challenged successfully before the UN Human Rights Committee. In *Kavanagh v. Ireland*[149] the applicant was tried and convicted before the Special Criminal Court on charges arising out of a kidnapping and armed robbery. It was common ground that an organised crime gang was behind the planning and execution of the offences and that there was no terrorist involvement. The applicant was charged with one scheduled offence and several non-scheduled offences. The DPP certified with respect to the non-scheduled offences that the ordinary courts were in his opinion inadequate

20–32

---

[145] Unreported, High Court, September 20, 1972. See also *Re MacCurtain* [1941] I.R. 83.
[146] *ibid.* at 3–4.
[147] [1984] I.L.R.M. 224.
[148] See also *Tormey v. Ireland* [1985] I.R. 289, *per* Henchy J. at 295.
[149] UN Committee on Human Rights *Communication No.819/1998* (April 4, 2001).

to secure the effective administration of justice in relation to the trial of the applicant on the charges. Accordingly, the applicant was sent for trial to the Special Criminal Court. He challenged the DPP's power of certification before the Human Rights Committee on the ground, *inter alia*, that it breached Article 26 of the UN Covenant on Civil and Political Rights. Article 26 reads:

> "All persons are equal before the law and are entitled without any discrimination to the equal protection of the law. In this respect the law shall prohibit any discrimination and guarantee to all persons equal and effective protection against discrimination on any ground such as race, colour, sex, language, religion, political or other opinion, national or social origin, birth or other status."

The Committee accepted that trial before the Special Criminal Court did not of itself constitute a violation of the right to a fair hearing. However, it was of the opinion that the differences in trial procedure between the Special Criminal Court and the ordinary courts were such that the State was under an obligation to justify the decision to try the applicant before the former rather than the latter:

> "The DPP's decision to charge the author before the Special Criminal Court resulted in the author facing an extra-ordinary trial procedure before an extraordinarily constituted court. This distinction deprived the author of certain procedures under domestic law distinguishing the author from others charged with similar offences in the ordinary courts. Within the jurisdiction of the State party, trial by jury in particular is considered an important protection generally available to accused persons. Under Article 26, the State party is therefore required to demonstrate that such a decision to try a person by another procedure was based upon reasonable and objective grounds."

The Committee went on to find that the State had "failed to demonstrate that the decision to try the author before the Special Criminal Court was based upon reasonable and objective grounds. As such the State was in breach of its obligations under Article 26. Critical to the Committee's finding was the fact that no reasons are required to be given for the DPP's decision that the ordinary courts were inadequate or that trial in the Special Criminal Court was proper. Equally no reasons were provided to the Committee in the particular case. The Committee was also influenced by the fact that "judicial review of the DPP's decisions is effectively restricted to the most exceptional and virtually undemonstrable circumstances.

Committee to Review the Offences against the State

Since the UN Committee's decision in *Kavanagh* was handed down the Committee to Review the Offences against the State legislation has published a majority interim report on the Special Criminal Court.[150] This interim report acknowledges the difficulties posed by the unfettered and unreviewable discretion of the DPP to direct trial before the Special Criminal Court for non-scheduled offences. The majority, however, also experienced great

---

[150] *Committee to Review the Offences against the State Acts, 1939–1998 and Related Matters Interim Report* (2001).

difficulty in developing a mechanism which would balance the State's interest in maintaining the confidentiality of its sources and the accused's interest in being provided with sufficient relevant information to be able to challenge the DPP's decision.

The majority considered four options for accommodating the concerns of the UN Human Rights Committee in the *Kavanagh* case.[151] The first is an *inter pares* hearing before the High Court to approve the decision to send the accused for trial before the Special Criminal Court. The decision would be upheld if the High Court was satisfied that there was valid grounds for the decision in the sense that there was a real or significant risk that the ordinary courts would be inadequate to deal with the case by reason of the threat of intimidation of actual or potential jurors. If the High Court was not so satisfied trial would be before the ordinary courts. The primary difficulty with this approach, from the perspective of the majority, was the risk that sensitive security information would be revealed to the accused. This would not necessarily be avoided by holding the proceedings *in camera*. The majority did accept that this difficulty could be averted by the use of an independent counsel procedure (see below).

The second option is an *ex parte* application before the High Court sitting *in camera*. The majority's concern about this option was the appearance of unfair procedures for the accused who would be denied the opportunity to participate in the proceedings. As with option one this risk could be reduced by the use of an independent counsel procedure.

The third option is an administrative review of the DPP's decision by a retired judge, along the lines of the review process under the Interception of Postal Packets and Telecommunications Messages (Regulation) Act 1993. The retired judge would have access to the entire file and would have the right to pose questions to the DPP and his staff regarding the decision. Unless the retired judge was satisfied that the DPP's decision was based on reasonable and objective grounds then he would be obliged to have the case transferred to the ordinary courts. The majority's concern with this option was that it was not sufficiently objective or transparent. They also considered that it might be open to the criticism that it amounted to the administration of justice in private.

The fourth option, and the one recommended by the majority, is review by a serving member of the Supreme Court. Under this option the DPP would submit the decision to refer a case to the Special Criminal Court and accompanying reasons to a judge of the Supreme Court nominated for that purpose by the Chief Justice. If the judge was satisfied after reviewing the decision that it was based upon reasonable and objective grounds he would certify accordingly and the trial could proceed before the Special Criminal Court. If the judge refused to so certify the trial could proceed only before the ordinary courts. The majority acknowledged that this option suffered from the same sort of weaknesses as are apparent in the second and third options. However, they suggest that these can be alleviated by the use of a independent counsel

---

[151] *Report of the Committee to Review the Offences against the State Acts, 1939–1998 and Related Matters* (Stationery Office, Dublin, 2002), Chap.9, para.11.1–11.13.

999

procedure. This would involve the case against trial before the Special Criminal Court being argued by a court-appointed independent counsel. Such counsel would represent the interests of the accused but would not act for him. He, unlike the accused, would be appraised of material upon which the prosecution based its decision. He would then argue the case on behalf of the accused in an *in camera* hearing from which the accused was excluded.

G. Practice and Procedure

1. Introduction

20–33 When the court is sitting in the exercise of its jurisdiction or function the members present at and taking part in such sitting must consist of an uneven number, not less than three.[152] In practice the court normally sits with three members. Subject to the requirement of an uneven number (not less than three) present at and taking part in a sitting, the court may exercise any power, jurisdiction or function vested in it notwithstanding one or more vacancies in its membership.[153] The court has absolute control over the times and places of its sittings and enjoys control over its own procedure in all respects. With the agreement of the Minister for Justice, Equality and Law Reform it may make rules regulating its practice and procedure and these rules may provide, in particular, for the issuing of summonses, the procedure for bringing (in custody or on bail) persons before it for trial, the admission or exclusion of the public to or from its sittings, the enforcing of the attendance of witnesses and the production of documents.[154] Subject to these provisions the rules of evidence and, as far as practicable, the practice and procedure applicable to the trial of a person on indictment in the Central Criminal Court apply to the trial of a person in the Special Criminal Court.[155]

Distinction between Jurisdiction and Procedure

20–34 It is important in this context, however, to distinguish between the practice and procedure of the court on the one hand and its jurisdiction on the other. Since the court is purely a creature of statute it does not enjoy any inherent jurisdiction. Its jurisdictional powers are conferred exclusively by statute. Accordingly, it has been held that, in the absence of appropriate statutory provisions, the Special Criminal Court is under no obligation to deliver a

---

[152] Offences against the State Act 1939, s.41(2).

[153] *ibid.* s.41(3).

[154] *ibid.* s.41(1) empowers the Special Criminal Court to make, with the concurrence of the Minister of Justice, Equality and Law Reform, rules regulating its practice and procedure. The current rules are the Special Criminal Court Rules 1975 (S.I. No.234 of 1975) (as amended by Offences against the State Acts 1939–1998 (Special Criminal Court Rules) 2001(S.I. No. 536 of 2001). These Rules revoke the 1972 Rules (S.I. No.147 of 1972).

[155] *ibid.* s.41(4). It has been suggested that if the legislation provided for special rules of evidence in the Special Criminal Court it would be unconstitutional; see *Report of the Committee to Review the Offences against the State Acts 1939–1998 and Related Matters* (Stationery Office, Dublin, 2002), Chap.9, para.2.7, citing *Cox v. Ireland* [1992] 2 I.R. 532.

reasoned verdict,[156] had no power to return alternative verdicts[157] and has no power to accept amendments rectifying errors in an indictment.[158] Since these all go to the jurisdiction of the court, as opposed to matters of practice and procedure, the legislative lacunae are not filled by the general provision in the Offences against the State Act to the effect that the practice and procedure applicable to a trial on indictment in the Central Criminal Court applies, as far as practicable, to a trial in the Special Criminal Court.

A matter going to the jurisdiction of the court can be distinguished from mere practice and procedure by virtue of the fact that the latter is part of the actual determination in the case, as opposed to a step in the process leading to that determination. In *People (DPP) v. Rice*,[159] for example, the Court of Criminal Appeal had to decide whether the statutory power conferred on a jury by section 44(1) of the Larceny Act 1916 to return a verdict of guilty of assault with intent to rob as an alternative to robbery was a matter of jurisdiction as opposed to a matter of practice and procedure. In holding that it was very definitely the former, Henchy J. explained that:

> "[Even] if a jury in the Central Criminal Court, in the absence of section 44(1) of the Act of 1916, were held to have power under common law to bring in such an alternative verdict, it could not be said that such power derives from the practice and procedure of the court. In no way could such a power be held to be merely a step in the process leading to the determination of the proceedings. It is part of the determination itself. Therefore, it is a matter of jurisdiction. While the inclusion of alternative counts in an indictment is procedural, the power to return a verdict of guilty of an offence which is not charged is a matter of jurisdiction which must be shown to exist under common law or statute. As the Special Criminal Court is a creature of statute such jurisdiction could be found only in the statutory provisions which invest it with jurisdiction.[160]

It followed that the general provision in the Offences against the State Act to the effect that the practice and procedure applicable to a trial on indictment in the Central Criminal Court shall also apply, as far as practicable, to a trial in the Special Criminal Court, was not sufficient to confer on the latter the former's powers to return alternative verdicts. Accordingly, it was necessary to enact the Criminal Justice (Verdicts) Act 1976 to remedy the deficiency in the powers of the Special Criminal Court (see above).

The Rules

The rules governing practice and procedure before the Special Criminal Court are to be found primarily in the Offences against the State Act 1939 and, more particularly, the Special Criminal Court Rules 1975 as amended.[161] It is

---

[156] *People (Attorney General) v. Shribman and Samuels* [1946] I.R. 431.

[157] *People (DPP) v. Rice* [1979] I.R. 15; *People v. Yates,* unreported, Supreme Court, November 12, 1975). This deficiency has been remedied by the Criminal Justice (Verdicts) Act 1976.

[158] *State (DPP) v. Special Criminal Court,* unreported, High Court, May 18, 1983.

[159] [1979] I.R. 15.

[160] *ibid.* at 19–20.

[161] The full title is Offences against the State Acts 1939 to 1972 Special Criminal Court Rules 1975.

worth noting at the outset that non-compliance with any of the Rules will not render any proceedings void.[162] In the event of any non-compliance, however, the court may direct that the proceedings be treated as void or set aside in part as irregular, or that they be amended or otherwise dealt with in such manner or in such terms as it sees fit. Equally, a departure from any of the Court Forms scheduled to the Rules will not vitiate or make void the proceedings or matter to which such Forms relate, so long as the form or the words used are otherwise sufficient in substance and effect.[163]

2. Court Sittings

20–35   Both the Act and the Rules stipulate that the sittings of the court shall be held at such places and at such times as the court itself shall decide.[164] Notice of the time and place of a sitting shall be given to relevant parties by the Registrar.[165] The Office of the Registrar is located at Green Street Courthouse, or at such other place as shall be fixed by the court from time to time.[166] The Registrar shall keep custody of all documents transmitted to or received by him in his capacity as Registrar and all exhibits directed by the court to be retained by him.[167] He must also keep a register containing particulars of all cases for trial by the court.[168]

The court will decide which member shall preside at a sitting.[169] It is the presiding member who pronounces the decision of the court at the end of the trial or proceedings.[170] Although, Article 34.1 of the Constitution, which prescribes that justice shall be administered in public does not apply to the Special Criminal Court, it rarely sits *in camera*.[171] The Rules stipulate that the court sittings are open to the public, subject to the court's powers to exclude certain categories of persons and to impose certain restrictions on the reporting of its proceedings in an individual case.[172] The court generally may impose conditions and limitations on public access from time to time. In particular, it may limit the numbers of members of the public (other than bona fide representatives of the press) who may have access to a sitting, either generally or in relation to a particular trial or trials.[173] It also has the power to authorise members of the Garda Síochána to prevent from attending any sitting any

---

[162] r.31(1).
[163] r.31(2).
[164] Offences against the State Act 1939, s.41(1); r.4.
[165] r.5; see Form 2. Service may be effected either by serving it on the accused personally or by sending it by prepaid ordinary post addressed to him at his last or usual place of abode or to his solicitor, and thereupon it shall be deemed to have been served at the time at which it would have been delivered in the ordinary course of post; r.22(1).
[166] r.27(1).
[167] r.27(2).
[168] r.27(3).
[169] r.6(1).
[170] r.6(2).
[171] In a trial under the Official Secrets Act 1963 the Court sat *in camera* pursuant to s.12 of the 1963 Act; see *People (Attorney General) v. Crinnion* [1976] I.R. 29.
[172] r.7(1).
[173] r.7(2).

person where the court has reason to believe that that person is likely to interfere with its proceedings, and it can direct the removal from the court of any person interfering with its proceedings. Moreover, the court may exclude from any hearing, or part of a hearing, the public or any members of the public (other than bona fide representatives of the press) where it is satisfied that such a course of action is desirable in the interests of justice or for the protection of the accused or any other person.[174]

The court may also act to conceal the identity of witnesses and other persons mentioned in evidence. It may permit a witness to give his name and address in writing to the court and it may permit a witness, including the accused, to give the name and address of any person mentioned in his evidence in writing to the court.[175] The court may prohibit the publication of the name and address of a witness or the evidence, or any part of the evidence of a witness.[176] The court may also direct that a witness shall not remain in court while the evidence of another witness is being given, and it may make provision for the separation of witnesses from each other.[177]

3. Transmission and Supply of Documents

Indictable Offences

The Rules make provision for the transmission to the Special Criminal Court **20–36** of all relevant documents and material evidence necessary for the trial in any individual case.[178] In indictable cases where the accused has been sent forward from the District Court or transferred from the Central Criminal Court or the Circuit Court, these include provision for the person charged to be supplied with a copy of the indictment, copies of the depositions, any further witness statements and a list of any further exhibits.[179] Where the person is charged with an indictable offence directly before the Special Criminal Court the Chief Prosecution Solicitor shall furnish him with: a list of the charges to be preferred against him, a list of the witnesses to be called, a statement of the evidence that is to be given by each of them and a list of the exhibits.[180] Copies of these documents are also supplied to the court.[181] In any case where the DPP proposes to call further witnesses or to adduce further evidence from listed witnesses he must furnish the accused and the court with a list of the further witnesses and statements of the further evidence.[182] The same applies to any further exhibits that will be produced. The Chief Prosecution Solicitor must also file a copy of the indictment with the Registrar and the accused is entitled to a copy free of charge on application.[183]

---

[174] r.7(3).
[175] r.7(4).
[176] r.7(5).
[177] r.8.
[178] rr.9 and 13.
[179] rr.11 and 12
[180] r.15(1).
[181] r.15(3).
[182] rr.12, 13, 15(4).
[183] rr.10, 11 and 15(5).

Offences Triable Summarily

Where a judge of the District Court has sent a person forward for trial to the Special Criminal Court on a charge which he had jurisdiction to dispose of summarily, the Chief Prosecution Solicitor must, within seven days of the order sending the person forward for trial, furnish him with a list of the charges to be preferred and a summary of the evidence to be given at the trial.[184] This summary, however, will not preclude the production of further evidence by the prosecution at the trial. The clerk of the District Court area where the order sending the accused forward was made must, within the same time limit, transmit to the Registrar: a statement of the charges upon which the person was sent for trial; the order of the District Court judge sending the person forward for trial; any recognisance taken by the judge in the case; any exhibit handed into the District Court; any sworn information in writing upon which the proceedings were initiated.[185]

Charged before the Court

Where a person is charged with a summary offence directly before the Special Criminal Court he is treated the same as if he was charged directly before the court with an indictable offence.[186] If he is charged with an indictable offence and a summary offence he may, unless the court orders otherwise, be indicted at his trial on an indictment which includes a count in respect of the summary offence.[187] It is also worth noting that when a person is brought before the Special Criminal Court by summons for the purpose of being charged before the court the Chief Prosecution Solicitor must furnish him and the court with a summary of the evidence to be given at his trial.[188]

4. Securing Attendance before the Court

The Accused

20–37   The Rules include specific provisions to secure the attendance at court of a person to be charged or tried before the Special Criminal Court. Where the person concerned is to be charged directly before the Special Criminal Court and an information or evidence relating to the offence is laid before the court, the court may order the issue of a summons ordering the person to attend before the court to be charged with the offence.[189] If the persons fails to attend in response to the summons his attendance may be secured by the issue

---

[184] r.14(a). If the person is brought before the court pursuant to a summons issued pursuant to the Rules, the Chief Prosecution Solicitor must furnish him and the court with a summary of the evidence to be given at the trial; r.17(6).

[185] r.14(b).

[186] r.16(a).

[187] r.16(b).

[188] r.17(6).

[189] r.17(1); see Form 16. The summons shall be served either by a member of the Garda Síochána, or by such other person as the court may direct, by delivering a copy to the person concerned or by leaving a copy at his usual or last place of abode or at his office or place of business, with a family member or relation, or with his agent, clerk or servant, not being under the age of 16 years, unless

of a warrant.[190] The court also has the power to issue a warrant for the arrest of a person who is to be charged directly before the court.[191] There is no specific obligation on it to proceed initially with the issue of a summons. Where the person is before the court, pursuant to a summons or warrant, the court may commit him to prison or to military custody to be kept there until his trial for the offence with which he is charged.[192] Alternatively, it may admit him to bail in such recognisances and with such sureties as the court shall direct.

Where the person concerned is in custody at the relevant time his attendance at the court for trial may be secured by an appropriate warrant directed to his custodian.[193] If he is on bail at the time he must surrender himself to the custody of such persons as the court may direct at the place and time specified in the appropriate Notice sent to him by the Registrar.[194] On surrendering he shall be searched and detained in custody or released on bail as the court shall direct. If he fails to surrender the court may issue a warrant for his apprehension and detention in prison pending his trial or until further order of the court.[195] During any adjournment of the trial or postponement of verdict or sentence, the court may order the detention of the person concerned in custody.[196]

Witnesses

The Rules make provision for the attendance of witnesses in court. Where it appears to the Registrar that any person is able to give material evidence either for the prosecution or the defence on any trial, he may issue a summons to such person requiring him to attend at a specified time and place to give evidence at the trial and to produce such documents in his possession as the Registrar deems necessary.[197] If, however, the court is satisfied by evidence on oath that it is probable that such person will not attend to give evidence unless compelled, the court may issue a warrant to arrest him and to bring him before the court to give evidence and produce such documents as may be required.[198] Similarly, if a person fails to comply with a witness summons, or

20–38

---

personal service is specifically required by the court; r.22(2)(a). Where the person to be charged is a body corporate the summons shall be served by leaving a copy at or by sending a copy by prepaid ordinary post to the registered office of the body corporate within the State or any such office or place within the State at which the body trades or carries on business, or by such other form of substituted service as the court may direct; r.22(2)(b).

[190] r.17(2); see form 17. This warrant is served in the same manner as the summons; r.22(2).

[191] r.17(4); a variation of Form 5 or 6 can be used. It is served in the same manner as the summons; r.22(2).

[192] r.17(5); see Form 10. It is served in the same manner as the summons; r.22(2).

[193] r.18(1); Form 1 is used where the person is sent forward or transferred to the court for trial. Where he is to be brought before the court to be charged and tried a variation of Form 7 or 8 should be used; r.18(2).

[194] r.19(1); see Form 2. Service may be effected either by serving it on the accused personally, or by sending it by prepaid ordinary post addressed to the accused at his last or usual place of abode, or to his solicitor, thereupon it shall be deemed to have been served at the time at which it would have been delivered in the ordinary course of post; r.22(1).

[195] r.19(2). A variation of Form 3 or 4 should be used.

[196] r.20; See Form 11.

[197] r.21(1). See Form 12. Where the person is in prison Form 9 should be used; r.21(3).

[198] r.21(1). See Form 13.

if the court is satisfied upon evidence on oath that the person is evading service, the court may issue a warrant for his arrest.[199] A witness summons issued under these provisions shall be served by a member of the Garda Síochána, or by such other person as the court may direct, by delivering a copy to the person concerned or by leaving a copy at his last place of abode or at his office or place of business with a family member or relation or with his agent, clerk or servant, not below the age of 16 years.[200] If the person to be charged is a body corporate it can be served by leaving a copy at, or sending a copy by prepaid ordinary post to, the registered office of the body corporate within the State or any such office or place within the State at which such body trades or carries on business, or by such other form of substituted service as the court may direct.[201]

Proof of Service

Proof of service of a summons or notice pursuant to these provisions may be given by statutory declaration of the person effecting the service, made before a person authorised by law to take and receive statutory declarations.[202] Such declaration shall be endorsed upon the back of the original summons. The court, however, may always require the person who had effected the service to attend before it to give evidence touching such service.

5. Administering the Oath and Related Matters

20–39   The oath is administered to witnesses in the presence of the court and on behalf of the court by the Registrar, or such other person as the court shall direct.[203] The court may grant free legal aid under the Criminal Justice (Legal Aid) Act 1962 and Regulations made pursuant to it as if it was the Central Criminal Court and the accused had been returned for trial to the Central Criminal Court.[204] If the accused is not defended at his trial before the Special Criminal Court, the presiding member of the court must inform him at the close of the case for the prosecution that either he may give evidence in his defence on oath in which case he would be liable to be cross-examined and to be questioned by the court, or he may make no statement.[205] He must also be informed that he may address the court in his defence and may call witnesses in his defence.

---

[199] r.21(2).
[200] r.22(2)(a).
[201] r.22(2((b).
[202] r.23. See Form 14.
[203] r.28.
[204] r.30.
[205] r.24. Originally, there was a third option namely to make a statement not on oath in which case he would not be liable to be cross-examined or to be questioned by the court. However, the right to make an unsworn statement was abolished generally by the Criminal Justice Act 1984, s.23.

6. Standing Mute

The Offences against the State Act 1939 makes specific provision for the situation where the accused stands mute or refuses to plead. If the accused stands mute when called upon to plead to the charge made against him, the court must hear such evidence (if any) relevant to the issue as to whether he is mute of malice or mute by visitation of God.[206] If the court is satisfied on the evidence presented that the accused is mute by visitation of God, the same consequences ensue as if he had been found mute by visitation of God by a judge sitting in the Central Criminal Court (see Chapter 16). If, on the other hand, no evidence is presented or if the court is not satisfied that the accused is mute by visitation of God, it must direct a plea of "not guilty" to be entered for that person. Similarly, if the accused fails or refuses to plead otherwise than by standing mute the court must direct a plea of "not guilty" to be entered in his behalf.[207] This situation is most likely to arise where the accused refuses to recognise the authority of the court. However, the Act also stipulates that if by any act or omission at any stage of his trial a person refuses to recognise the authority or jurisdiction of the court, or does any act which in the opinion of the court is equivalent to a refusal to recognise the court or its authority or jurisdiction, he shall be guilty of contempt of court and may be punished accordingly.[208] There is, of course, an exception for a person who contests in due form of law the jurisdiction of the court to try him.

20–40

7. Trial Procedure in the Absence of the Jury

The trial procedure and rules of evidence applicable to the trial of a person on indictment in the Central Criminal Court apply generally to a trial in the Special Criminal Court, unless otherwise prescribed in the Offences against the State Act 1939.[209] As explained earlier, it would also appear that the Special Criminal Court has the same powers as the Central Criminal Court to punish contempt in the face of the court.[210]

20–41

Absence of the Jury

The major difference between the procedure before the Special Criminal Court and that before the Central Criminal Court stems from the absence of the jury in the former.[210a] This is particularly evident in the context of a

20–42

---

206 Offences against the State Act 1939, s.51(1). See Chapter 16 for an explanation of "mute of malice" and "mute by visitation of God".

207 *ibid* s.51(2).

208 *ibid* s.51(3).

209 *ibid* s.41(4). Henchy J. explained the purpose of this provision as follows:
"The Special Criminal Court will operate its jurisdiction according to the known pattern of the Central Criminal Court, and thus escape the hazards of the unknown and the uncertainty that would beset a new court, such as the Special Criminal Court, with no ancestry of precedent behind it." *People (DPP) v. Rice* [1979] I.R. 15 at 18.

210 *Re Matter of the Sentence of Kevin O'Kelly for Contempt of Court by the Special Criminal Court* 1 Frewen 366.

210a For a comparison between the Special Criminal Court and the non-jury "Diplock Court" in Northern Ireland, see P. Charleton and P. McDermott, "Constitutional Aspects of Non-Jury Courts" (2000) 6 *Bar Review* 106 at 142.

challenge to the admissibility of confession evidence. It has already been seen in Chapter 9 that arguments over the admissibility of such evidence are normally conducted in the absence of the jury in the Central Criminal Court. Witnesses for both sides will be examined and cross-examined as to what happened in the interrogation room and the judge will make a ruling on the admissibility of the confession. If the judge rules the confession admissible the trial will resume in the presence of the jury and the prosecution will usually call its witnesses to testify once again as to the circumstances in which the confession was given. The witnesses will then be cross-examined once again by the defence with the objective of persuading the jury not to place much weight on the reliability of the confession. In the Special Criminal Court, however, there is no jury. The question arises, therefore, whether it is necessary for the prosecution to examine its witnesses again where the Special Criminal Court has ruled a confession admissible after hearing the witnesses being fully examined and cross-examined and the arguments of both sides.

This issue arose in *People (DPP) v. McGowan*[211] where the court conducted a *voir dire* and ruled a confession admissible. The prosecution then recalled its witnesses who had given evidence during the voir dire and simply asked each if he affirmed his evidence in the *voir dire* to be true and correct. Counsel for the defence was given the opportunity to cross-examine each witness but declined. It was argued on appeal that this procedure did not accord fully with that in the Central Criminal Court. However, Griffin J., delivering the judgment of the Court of Criminal Appeal, held that the deviation from the procedure applicable in the Central Criminal Court could be explained by the absence of the jury. Since the procedure actually adopted in this case before the Special Criminal Court conformed as nearly as possible with that in the Central Criminal Court it satisfied the requirements of the Offences against the State Act.

Hearing Inadmissible Evidence

The absence of the jury in the Special Criminal Court can also result in a situation where the tribunal of fact hears inadmissible evidence. This is less likely to happen in the Central Criminal Court as arguments over admissibility are normally conducted in the absence of the tribunal of fact. In the Special Criminal Court, however, the members of the court are the tribunal of fact and, as such, will hear all of the evidence irrespective of whether parts of it are subsequently ruled inadmissible. Surprisingly, perhaps, the court is not required to disqualify itself from a case where it has heard inadmissible evidence prejudicial to the accused. In *People (DPP) v. McMahon*,[212] for example, during the course of the trial the court heard inadmissible evidence which was highly prejudicial to the accused. Despite the fact that the accused would have been entitled to a discharge of the jury in such circumstances if the evidence had been given in the presence of a jury in the Central Criminal Court, the Special Criminal Court refused to disqualify itself in this case. The

---

[211] [1979] I.R. 45.
[212] [1984] I.L.R.M. 461.

question arose, therefore, whether this was a breach of the requirement in the Offences against the State Act that the practice and procedure applicable in a trial before the Special Criminal Court should apply, as far as practicable, to a trial on indictment in the Central Criminal Court. Hederman J., in the Court of Criminal Appeal, held that it was not necessary for the court to disqualify itself in these circumstances. He based his finding on a controversial distinction between the capacity of the judges and a jury as follows:[213]

> "Clearly, it is impracticable – indeed impossible – to import a rule, however, valuable, governing the conduct of jury trial into a trial by a non-jury court. This analogy is not valid. In the present case the Special Criminal Court was made up of three experienced judges who clearly recognised the highly prejudicial nature of the evidence and they asserted in open court that they were capable of excluding that evidence from their minds. Furthermore, this court cannot ignore the acceptance by counsel for the applicant at the trial that the judges hearing the case were capable of so doing."[214]

The court, however, has a discretion to disqualify itself in such circumstances. In *DPP v. Corrigan*,[215] for example, the court disqualified itself even though counsel had not specifically applied for disqualification.[216]

The issue of the court hearing or seeing prejudicial material against the accused will also arise where the prosecution claims privilege in respect of documents in the case of opposition from the defence. In *DPP v.* Special Criminal Court[217] the Supreme Court accepted that the prosecution could claim privilege in respect of the statement of an informer who would be at risk if his identity was revealed. In the event of a conflict between the informer's right to life and the defendant's right to a fair trial, the solution was for the trial court to inspect the documents in question and determine whether they contained matters useful to the defence. In the case of a trial before the Special Criminal Court it is quite likely that this will result in the members of the court becoming aware of inadmissible material highly prejudicial to the defendant. Nevertheless, neither the Special Criminal Court, the High Court nor the Supreme Court in that case felt that it was necessary for the trial to be conducted by members of the court other than those who had inspected the documents.

The fact that the DPP's application for a judicial review in *DPP v.* Special Criminal Court was entertained reflects another possible distinction between a criminal trial in the Special Criminal Court and that before a judge and jury. Technically the application was made once the trial had started. Once a trial has started the courts will not normally entertain a break for the purpose of initiating proceedings before another court. This is especially so with respect

---

213 See criticism in Hogan and Walker, *op.cit*, p. 231.
214 [1984] I.L.R.M. 461 at p.467. For criticism of this reasoning, see Hogan and Walker, *op.cit.*, p. 231.
215 Unreported case cited in *McMahon*.
216 In *McGlinchey v. Ireland* [1990] 2 I.R. 215, O'Hanlon J. in the High Court left open the issue of what the position would be if a member of the court trying a case against an accused had been a member of the panel hearing a previous case in which prejudicial findings on matters currently before the court were made against the same accused.
217 [1999] 1 I.R. 60.

to a jury trial due to the undesirability of having the jury waiting around for weeks or even months for the proceedings to resume. The criminal trial is meant to be a seamless, unbroken procedure. While acknowledging the force of the conventional position the Supreme Court was prepared to make an exception in this case due to the exceptional circumstances. Given the absence of the jury the court felt able to treat the proceedings as being more like a pre-trial application.

Counsel's Address

20–43   The procedure governing counsel's right to address the jury is another trial feature which might be affected by the absence of the jury. In *People (Attorney General) v. Kerins*[218] the accused appealed against his conviction in the Special Criminal Court. He had refused to recognise the authority of the court during his trial and had declined legal representation. At the close of the prosecution case counsel for the prosecution summarised the prosecution evidence for the purpose of, in his words, ". . . the assistance of the court and, also, I think, for the assistance, perhaps, of the accused, who is not defended." In seeking leave to appeal against conviction, the accused argued, *inter alia*, that this address was highly improper. There was no provision for it in the Offences against the State Act 1939 or in the Rules adopted by the Special Criminal Court. He also submitted that, pursuant to the Criminal Procedure Act 1865, no such address could have been made to the jury in the Central Criminal Court. In rejecting this submission the Court of Criminal Appeal took the view, *obiter*, that it would not be practicable to apply to the Special Criminal Court the provisions of the 1865 Act dealing with counsel's address to the jury. It did not explain why the judges in the Special Criminal Court could not be treated as the jury for this purpose. In any event the Court of Criminal Appeal went on to find that counsel's address in this case was an address to the court on a matter of law as distinct from the equivalent of an address to the jury on the facts. As such the 1865 Act was irrelevant.

Reasoned Verdict

The fact that the determination of guilt is made by the court, instead of a jury, has an effect on the form of the determination. In a jury trial the verdict will normally be returned as guilty or not guilty. The jury does not explain its decision. It does not detail its findings on specific facts which were in dispute; nor does it specify what facts it considered to be relevant, what inferences it drew from those facts or what weight it gave to certain pieces of evidence. All of these matters are rolled up into a simple verdict of guilty or not guilty. Although it is under no statutory obligation to do so,[219] the Special Criminal Court delivers a verdict supported by a reasoned judgment as a matter of

---

[218] [1945] I.R. 339.

[219] In *People (Attorney General) v. Shribman and Samuels* [1946] I.R. 431 the Court of Criminal Appeal ruled that the Special Criminal Court was under no statutory obligation to deliver a reasoned verdict. Although the Court also seemed to suggest that it could not be compelled to deliver a reasoned verdict, it is possible that a different view would be taken of this matter today; see *R. v.*

practice.[220] This judgment, which is a collective judgment of the court, will offer a reasoned explanation of the verdict. It will set out the findings of fact and the inferences drawn from those facts. This, of course, is very useful for a person who has been found guilty and who is considering an appeal against his conviction. Equally, the Court of Criminal Appeal will be able to examine the court's detailed findings of fact and inferences drawn from those facts when considering the soundness of the conviction.

Collective Verdict

The verdict in the Special Criminal Court also differs from a jury verdict in that there cannot be a hung verdict. As explained below the decision in the Special Criminal Court is by a majority of the members sitting in the case. It follow that a majority in favour of a guilty verdict will result in a guilty verdict, while a majority in favour of a not guilty verdict will result in an acquittal. There is no provision for a failure to reach a decision.

Other Matters

It will be seen below that the DPP cannot exercise his power under section 34 of the Criminal Procedure Act 1967 to refer a question of law to the Supreme Court where that question of law has resulted in a verdict in favour of the accused by direction of the trial judge.[221]   **20–44**

8. Verdict

The verdict of the Special Criminal Court in every case, and the determination of every question, shall be by a majority of the members present and taking part in the case or determination.[222] No member or officer of the court shall disclose whether any such determination was or was not unanimous or, where the determination was not unanimous, the opinion of any individual member of the court. Every decision of the court shall be pronounced by a member specifically designated by the court and no other member may pronounce or indicate his concurrence or dissent.[223] As has been seen, this collective nature of the court's decisions was one of the factors which persuaded Henchy J. in the *Littlejohn* case that the three judges sitting together in the Special Criminal Court could be distinguished both individually and collectively from their standing and function as members of the ordinary courts.

Knightsbridge Crown Court, ex p. International Sporting Ltd [1982] QB 304; *State (Daly) v. Minister for Agriculture* [1987] I.R. 165; *State (Creedon) v. Criminal Injuries Compensation Tribunal* [1988] I.R. 51; *Breen v. Minister for Defence* [1994] 2 I.R. 34; *Ni Eili v. Environmental Protection Agency* unreported, Supreme Court, July 31, 1999; *Orange Communications Ltd v. Director of Telecommunications Regulation* unreported, Supreme Court, May 18, 2000.

220   A majority of the Committee to Review the Offences against the State Acts, 1939–1998 and Related Matters recommended that this should be formally provided for in law; *op.cit.* at Chap. 9, paras.14.1–14.2.

221   *People (DPP) v. Crinnion* [1976] I.R. 29.

222   Offences against the State Act 1939, s.40(1).

223   *ibid.* s.40(2).

A majority of the Committee to Review the Offences against the State Acts 1939–1998 and Other Related Matters are unhappy about the possibility of convictions being by a majority. They are of the view that a requirement of unanimity for conviction in a three judge court would not be unreasonable and would provide an extra protection for the accused. Accordingly, they recommend that no person should be convicted by the Special Criminal Court unless there is unanimity on this issue on the part of the three judges trying the case.[224] If all members of the court cannot agree on guilt then the court would have jurisdiction to order one further re-trial before a differently composed panel of the court. If, following the re-trial, there was still a lack of unanimity then the accused must be acquitted. In a case where a majority were of the view that the accused should be acquitted, the majority of the Committee are content with the current position, namely that the verdict must be one of acquittal.

9. Status and Implementation of Court Orders

20–45   Every order, conviction or sentence made or pronounced by the Special Criminal Court has the same consequences in law as a like order, conviction or sentence made or pronounced by the Central Criminal Court.[225] Unless provided otherwise by regulations made under section 50(1) of the Offences against the State Act 1939 every order made or sentence pronounced by the Special Criminal Court shall be carried out by the same authorities and officers who are required by law to carry out a like order or sentence of the Central Criminal Court.[226] They must also carry out the order or sentence in the same manner that a like order or sentence of the Central Criminal Court is required by law to be carried out. In carrying out the sentence or order of the Special Criminal Court they shall enjoy the same protections and immunities as are conferred by law on persons carrying out a like order or sentence of the Central Criminal Court.[227]

Every order or other act of the Special Criminal Court shall be authenticated by the signature of the Registrar of that court.[228] A document signed by the Registrar and purporting to be an order or other act of the Special Criminal Court shall be received in evidence in all courts and be deemed to be such an order or other act without proof of the signature.[229]

10. Adjournments and Extension of Time

20–46   The court may abridge or extend the time for doing any act. It may also adjourn the hearing of any trial or application to the court or postpone verdict or sentence as it shall think fit.[230]

---

[224] *Report of the Committee to Review the Offences against the State Acts, 1939–1998 and Related Matters* (Stationery Office, Dublin, 2002), Chap.9, paras.13.1–13.4.
[225] Offences against the State Act 1939, s.50(2).
[226] *ibid.* s.50(1).
[227] *ibid.* s.50(2).
[228] *ibid.* s.42(1).
[229] *ibid.* s.42(2).
[230] r.29.

11. Official Record of Proceedings

The Special Criminal Court Rules make provision for the taking of an official **20–47** record of proceedings before the court. They stipulate that an official stenographer, appointed for the purpose by the Minister for Justice, Equality and Law Reform, shall sign the shorthand note taken by him of any trial or proceeding in the Special Criminal Court.[231] He must also certify that the note is a complete and correct shorthand note of the proceedings which it covers and he must lodge it with the Registrar. For the purposes of an appeal to the Court of Criminal Appeal, the stenographer's shorthand note shall consist of the evidence, any objection taken in the course of the evidence, any statement made by the accused person and the verdict and sentence of the court.[232] It shall not include any part of the speeches of counsel or solicitor unless otherwise ordered by the court.

In *Kelly v. Ireland*[233] (see further below) it was argued in the High Court that the record of proceedings taken pursuant to these provisions could be used only for the purpose of appeals or applications for leave to appeal to the Court of Criminal Appeal, and that it could not be used for the formal proof in later civil proceedings of decisions taken in the course of the criminal trial before the Special Criminal Court. In the course of the trial before the Special Criminal Court the court had refused an application from counsel for the accused to see the transcript after the court had ruled on the admissibility of statements. In the related High Court proceedings for assault arising out of the same issues which had been before the Special Criminal Court, O'Hanlon J. acknowledged that the Special Criminal Court could control its own procedures. Nevertheless he went on to express the opinion, *obiter*, that ". . . where it [was] necessary for the purpose of doing justice in a case involving litigation between contesting parties, an extract from the transcript of the proceedings before the court would be made available or its production could be compelled should it become necessary to do so."[234]

H. Right to Appeal

Where the Special Criminal Court has convicted a person of any offence or **20–48** sentenced him to suffer any punishment, the person concerned may appeal against such conviction or sentence to the Court of Criminal Appeal if he obtains a certificate from the Special Criminal Court that the case is a fit case for appeal.[235] If the court refuses the necessary certificate the person may appeal to the Court of Criminal Appeal which may grant him leave to appeal against the conviction or sentence. In practice the hearing of an application for leave to appeal will be treated as the hearing of the substantive appeal on

---

[231] r.25(1).
[232] r.25(2).
[233] [1986] I.L.R.M. 318.
[234] *ibid.* at 323.
[235] Offences against the State Act 1939, s.44.

its merits. In practice, therefore, there is an automatic right of appeal to the Court of Criminal Appeal. A majority of the Committee to Review the Offences against the State and Other related Matters recommended that the formal position in law should be brought into line with the position in practice by giving persons convicted by the Special Criminal Court a full right of appeal against conviction and sentence without the necessity for prior leave to appeal.[236]

The Record

For the purposes of an appeal to the Court of Criminal Appeal, as noted above, the stenographer's shorthand note shall consist of the evidence, any objection taken in the course of the evidence, any statement made by the accused person and the verdict and sentence of the court.[237] It shall not include any part of the speeches of counsel or solicitor unless otherwise ordered by the court.

Approach of Court of Criminal Appeal

The approach of the Court of Criminal Appeal to appeals from the Special Criminal Court is basically the same as its approach to appeals from the Circuit Court or Central Criminal Court. Indeed, the main statutory provisions governing appeals to the Court of Criminal Appeal, including its jurisdiction in relation to such appeals, are specifically extended to appeals from the Special Criminal Court.[237a] The Court of Criminal Appeal's approach is summarised in the following passage from the judgment of O'Higgins C.J. in *People v. Madden*:

> "In the appeals now before this court, we have transcripts of the rulings of the Special Criminal Court made in the course, and at the end, of the trial on questions of law and findings of facts in relation to the admissibility of evidence, the sufficiency or cogency of the evidence, and the reasons for the rulings and verdicts given. Therefore, subject to the grounds of appeal, it would seem to be the function of this court to consider the conduct of the trial as disclosed in the stenographer's report to determine whether or not the trial was satisfactory in the sense of being conducted in a constitutional manner with fairness, to review so far as may be required any rulings on matters of law, to review so far as may be necessary the application of the rules of evidence as applied in the trial, and to consider whether any inferences of fact drawn by the court of trial can properly be supported by the evidence; but otherwise to adopt all findings of fact, subject to the admonitions in the passages cited above."[238]

This passage was cited with approval in *People (DPP) v. Tuite* by the Court of Criminal Appeal with the following addendum:

---

[236] *Report of the Committee to Review the Offences against the State Acts, 1939–1998 and Related Matters* (Stationery Office, Dublin, 2002), Chap.9, paras.12.1–12.4.
[237] r.25(2).
[237a] Offences against the State Act 1939, s.44(2), as amended by Criminal Procedure Act 1993, s. 3(8). Note that the text of the amendment refers to s.34 of the Criminal Justice Act 1924 and s.5 of the Criminal Justice Act 1928 when it should read s.34 of The Courts of Justice Act 1924 and s.5 of the Courts of Justice Act 1928 respectively. The statutory provisions in question are: ss.28 to 30, 32, 33 and 35 of the Courts of Justice Act 1924, ss.6 and 7 of the Courts of Justice Act 1928 and s.3 of the Criminal Procedure Act 1993.
[238] [1977] I.R. 336 at 340.

"This Court would add to these observations the view that, subject always to the overriding demands of justice, this Court will not entertain submissions, critical of the Special Criminal Court, where such submissions were not made to that Court at the trial."[239]

As is evident from the first passage above the Court of Criminal Appeal, when considering an appeal from the Special Criminal Court, will have before it not just conclusions of law and fact, but also the reasoned judgment explaining how those facts, including the issue of guilt, were determined. By contrast, in appeals from jury trials the court will not have the benefit of a reasoned judgment to support the jury's determination of guilt. It follows that the Court of Criminal Appeal can subject the Special Criminal Court's determination of guilt to closer scrutiny relative to a jury determination. In particular, it can assess the soundness of the court's reasoning, including its findings of fact and the inferences it drew from those facts, in reaching its determination of guilt. This facility is not available in respect of jury determinations of guilt. In *Madden*, for example, there was no appeal against the court's statement of the principles of law governing the liability of accomplices. However, one of the grounds of appeal was that the court had misdirected itself in applying those principles to the evidence before it.

Further Appeal

Where the accused's appeal has been dismissed he may appeal to the Supreme Court if a certificate is granted that the case involves a point of law of exceptional public importance. The certificate may be granted only by the Court of Criminal Appeal, the Attorney General or the DPP.[240] The prosecution does not enjoy a right of appeal to the Court of Criminal Appeal against an acquittal in the Special Criminal Court. Equally, it cannot appeal from the Court of Criminal Appeal to the Supreme Court.[241]

I. References under Section 34 of the Criminal Procedure Act 1967

Section 34 of the Criminal Procedure Act 1967 makes provision for the DPP **20–49** to refer a question of law to the Supreme Court for determination where a verdict in favour of the accused has been found by direction of the trial judge. The purpose of the referral is to appeal the judge's ruling on the question of law which resulted in the direction. A decision in favour of the DPP will be without prejudice to the verdict in favour of the accused.

The section 34 procedure is clearly applicable to trial by judge and jury. In *People (Attorney General) v. Crinnion*,[242] however, the Supreme Court ruled that it did not extend to trial before the Special Criminal Court. The wording of the provision clearly presupposes a trial before judge and jury. It refers to a

---

[239] 2 Frewen 175.
[240] Courts of Justice Act 1924, s.31 and the Prosecution of Offences Act 1974, s.5.
[241] *People (Attorney General) v. Kennedy* [1946] I.R. 517.
[242] [1976] I.R. 29.

verdict in favour of the accused being found on a direction by the trial judge given on a question of law. This, as explained by O'Higgins C.J. is inapplicable to trial before a Special Criminal Court:

> "For the section to apply, there must first be a question of law upon which a direction is given by the trial judge in pursuance of which a verdict is founded. It seems to me to be an abuse of the language used to seek to apply it to a trial without a jury before three judges whose function is to announce, at the end of the case, a finding of guilty or not guilty. A direction of the trial judge presupposes the existence of some body whom he can direct, and whose duty it is to find a verdict. Beyond the slightest shadow of doubt these words describe a criminal trial with a jury, and no other form of trial."[243]

In the same case Henchy J. found support for this decision in the fact that the DPP can consult with the trial judge, and include any observations which the judge may have, for the purpose of settling the statement of the question to be referred. This would not be workable in respect of the Special Criminal Court where there are three judges who speak with one voice when giving their decision and are barred from disclosing their individual opinions. Henchy J. also drew attention to the different wording of the comparable provision in England and Wales and Northern Ireland. There the referral procedure was not confined to a case in which a verdict had been directed by the trial judge or to the point of law which had directly resulted in the acquittal.

J. Immunities

20–50   The members of the Special Criminal Court enjoy the same immunities in the discharge of their functions as those attaching to judges of the ordinary courts. No action, prosecution or other proceeding, civil or criminal, shall lie against any member of the court in respect of any order made, conviction or sentence pronounced, or other thing done by that court.[244] This immunity extends to anything done by a member in the course of the performance of his duties or the exercise of his powers as a member of the court or otherwise in his capacity as a member, irrespective of whether the thing in question was necessary to the performance of such duties or the exercise of such powers. Similarly, no action, prosecution or other proceeding, civil or criminal, shall lie against any registrar, clerk or servant of the court in respect of anything done by him in the performance of his duties as such registrar, clerk or servant, whether such thing was or was not necessary to the performance of such duties.[245] Persons giving evidence before the Special Criminal Court or for use in proceedings before the court also enjoy immunity from an action in defamation in respect of anything written or said by them in giving evidence, whether written or oral.[246]

---

[243] *ibid.* at 33.
[244] Offences against the State Act 1939, s.53(1).
[245] *ibid.* s.53(3).
[246] Offences against the State Act 1939, s.53(2).

K. Issue Estoppel in Subsequent Civil Proceedings

20–51

The question whether decisions taken in the course of a criminal trial before the Special Criminal Court could be re-opened in subsequent civil proceedings arising out of the same set of facts was considered by the High Court in *Kelly v. Ireland*.[247] In that case the applicant had been convicted before the Special Criminal Court, largely on the basis of admissions obtained from him in disputed circumstances while in Garda custody. The Special Criminal Court rejected his contention that admissions had been obtained by force and oppression and ruled that they were given voluntarily. The applicant subsequently brought an action for assault in respect of the manner in which the admissions had been obtained. arising out of his alleged treatment in Garda custody. The allegations at the heart of his civil case were virtually identical to those on which he had relied in challenging the admissibility of the admissions in the course of the criminal trial. The State sought to prohibit the civil action on the grounds that the applicant was estopped from raising these matters anew as they were *res judicata* and that the initiation of the civil proceedings in these circumstances was an abuse of the process of the court.

In his judgment O'Hanlon J. surveyed the English authorities, including the House of Lords decision in the "Birmingham Six" case which involved a very similar set of circumstances, and found that they placed a heavy emphasis on certainly and finality in litigation. As such, they were very reluctant to countenance the re-opening in subsequent civil proceedings of decisions which had been taken in the course of criminal proceedings. The basis of these decisions, however, was an abuse of process as distinct from issue estoppel. The English courts were generally of the view that issue estoppel had no place in criminal law, largely because of the differences in the approach to the finding of fact in the civil and criminal processes. In the latter there were no pleadings and no judgments explaining how the issues were decided, Even if it was possible to identify the individual issues which had to be determined it would be difficult, if not impossible, to do more than guess how the jury had decided any individual issue beyond the general issue of guilty or not guilty.

Confining himself very specifically to the issue of whether decisions decided in the course of criminal proceedings (as distinct from the fact of conviction) could give rise to an issue estoppel in subsequent civil proceedings, O'Hanlon J. felt able to distinguish the English authorities in the specific context of the Special Criminal Court. Of critical importance here was the fact that decisions in cases before the Special Criminal Court were taken by the court itself and not by a jury. Moreover, the decision of the court was delivered in the form of a reasoned judgment. Accordingly, the difficulties which stem from a jury trial in this context will not necessarily be applicable:

> "The same difficulty was mentioned in the judgments in *McIlkenny*, namely, that even a decision of a judge on the issue of admissibility of statements was merged in a later verdict of a jury which had to consider what weight they should give to statements which were admitted. This problem does not arise,

---

[247] [1986] I.L.R.M. 318.

however, in the case of the Special Criminal Court where the decision on the preliminary issue and the final verdict is given by the court itself, sitting without a jury, and where a judgment can be and is given, defining the issue and explaining how it has been decided."[248]

20–52   It does not follow, of course, that matters which have arisen for determination in the course of proceedings before the Special Criminal Court cannot be re-opened in subsequent civil proceedings. Issue estoppel may also arise where the issue in question is clear and it has been decided against a party to those proceedings in a reasoned judgment. While O'Hanlon J. considered that it would be a rare case where these requirements would be satisfied, nevertheless he would be prepared in such a case to find an issue estoppel:

> "In the rare case where a clearly identifiable issue has been raised in the course of a criminal trial and has been decided against a party to those proceedings by means of a judgment explaining how the issue has been decided, I would be prepared to hold that such decision may give rise to issue estoppel in later civil proceedings in which that party is also involved. Such estoppel would arise, not only in relation to the specific issue determined (in this case, whether the statement was made freely and voluntarily) but also to findings which were fundamental to the court's decision on such issue."[249]

O'Hanlon J. went on to hold on the facts of the present case that an issue estoppel arose with respect to the circumstances in which the admissions had been obtained from the applicant. The learned judge did not feel compelled to decide whether privity of parties in the criminal and civil proceedings was a condition precedent for issue estoppel. He considered that there was privity between the People at the suit of the DPP as prosecutor in the criminal proceedings on the one hand, and on the other hand the People as identified with the State who must bear responsibility for the tortious acts committed by servants of the State in the course of the execution of their duties.

It is also worth noting that O'Hanlon J. considered that it would be an abuse of the process of the court to permit the applicant to re-open in the civil proceedings the determination of the Special Criminal Court with respect to the manner in which the admissions had been obtained. In this respect the Irish decision was fully in line with the approach taken by the English Court of Appeal and House of Lords in respect of the "Birmingham Six" case:

> "Apart altogether from the concept of issue estoppel in the circumstances of the present case, I would also hold, as did the House of Lords in *Hunter*, (upholding, in this respect, the decision of the Court of Appeal in *McIlkenny*), that in the absence of special circumstances, an effort to challenge the correctness of a decision made by a court of competent jurisdiction against a party in the course of a criminal trial, by means of civil proceedings instituted by such person after that decision has been made, should normally be restrained as an abuse of the court."[250]

---

[248] *ibid.* at 328.
[249] *ibid.*
[250] *ibid.* at 330.

CHAPTER 21

SENTENCE

A. Introduction

1. Scope of chapter

This chapter offers a descriptive outline of the primary sentencing options   **21–01**
available to the courts, the general rules and principles applied by the courts
when imposing sentence and the procedure typically followed in sentencing.
It does not attempt to analyse sentencing policy and practice with respect to
individual offences, nor does it offer a critique of sentencing policy and
practice. It is based primarily on a survey of Irish case law and legislation.
For a broader and deeper treatment of the subject, reference should be made
to specialist texts on the subject and in particular, to Tom O'Malley's
Sentencing Law and Practice.[1]

2. Limits on the District Court

Sentencing is a matter for the judge as opposed to the jury. The judge,
however, is not entirely free to decide on what punishment to impose in any
individual case. In the District Court, for example, the level of punishment
which the judge may impose on indictable offences which are tried summarily is statutorily restricted to 12 months, or an aggregate of two years
where consecutive sentences are imposed.[2] Although there is no general
statutory provision governing the judge's sentencing powers for summary
offences, they are implicitly limited by the constitutional link between summary offences and minor offences. If the offence in question is a non-minor

---

[1] Round Hall Sweet and Maxwell, Dublin, 2000.
[2] Criminal Justice Act 1951, s.5, as amended by Criminal Justice Act 1984, s.12(1). The
constitutionality of this provision was upheld by the High Court in *Meagher v. O'Leary* [1998] 1
I.L.R.M. 211.

offence the accused has a constitutional right to trial by jury. Case law has established that the severity of punishment which may be imposed on conviction for a particular offence is a vital factor in determining whether that offence is a non-minor offence. Generally, it might be said that a possible maximum prison sentence of two years would take an offence out of the minor category and into the non-minor category while a maximum of 12 months would not.[3] The picture is less certain with respect to fines. A maximum fine of €1,500 in today's value is unlikely to be sufficient to cross the line but it is difficult to be precise about the point at which the courts are likely to consider that the line has been crossed. In any event, the net effect is that the sentencing powers of the District Court for summary offences might be considered to be a maximum sentence of 12 months imprisonment and/or a maximum fine of €2,500, subject to the caveat that the monetary maximum has not been the subject of recent judicial decision.

3. Limits on Indictment

Much greater difficulty can be encountered in identifying the scope of the judge's discretion in sentencing an offender who has been convicted on indictment.[4] For some offences, most notably murder, there is no discretion as the sentence is mandatory. For most offences, however, the judge will enjoy considerable discretion over the sentence to impose in any individual case. At common law, for example, there was no limit to the term of imprisonment which the judge could impose.[5] This is still the position generally with respect to common law offences today.[6] In practice, however, the judge's discretion is limited either by legislation covering broad categories of offences or by statutory provisions dealing with specific offences which, more often than not, are created by the same provisions. In either case these statutory provisions will normally fix the maximum term of imprisonment and/or fine which may be imposed for a defined category of offences or for an individual offence, as the case may be. Some also set a minimum sentence. Where appropriate the legislation will set different maximum sentences for summary conviction and for conviction on indictment. Generally, the judge's sentencing discretion is also limited by the distinction drawn between adult and child offenders. Further complications are added by the fact that ancillary punishments, such as disqualification and forfeiture, are available for some offences.

4. The Statutory Parameters

21–02   It follows that in order to identify the sentencing options available to the judge in any particular case it will be necessary, as a first step, to check the

---

[3]   *Melling v. O'Mathghamhna* [1962] I.R. 1, *Mallon v. Minister for Agriculture* [1996] 1 I.R. 517.
[4]   A person sent forward for sentence on a plea of guilty from the District Court may be dealt with in all respects as if he had been convicted on indictment; Criminal Law Act 1997, s.10(5).
[5]   *R v. Castro* 5 (1880) Q.B.D. 490.
[6]   *People v. Giles* [1974] I.R. 422; *R v. Morris* [1951] 1 K.B. 394.

legislation creating the offence, assuming that it is a statutory offence. If there is no such legislation, or if it does not define the range of punishments available, one must look to any general statutory provisions applicable to the offence in question. Indeed, even if the legislation specifically defines the range of punishments available for that offence, it may still be necessary to check other relevant statutory provisions, such as those dealing with the sentencing of children. Up until very recently, it could happen that there was no specific maximum term of imprisonment applicable to a particular statutory offence. With the enactment of the Criminal Law Act 1997, however, this is no longer the case. That Act, which has abolished the distinction between felony and misdemeanour, stipulates that where a person is convicted on indictment of a statutory offence punishable with imprisonment and for which no particular maximum term is specified, the maximum prison term to which the person is liable shall be two years.[7]

It is also worth noting at this point that even where statute specifies a maximum sentence for an offence, it does not follow that a judge is free in any individual case to impose whatever sentence he or she pleases within that maximum. The judge must exercise his or her discretion fairly. Over the years case law and judicial practice have thrown up a number of distinct principles and factors which should inform the imposition of sentence in an individual case. A failure to follow these principles or to take these factors into account can form the basis for a successful appeal against sentence. These principles and factors will be outlined after the range of primary and ancillary sentencing options have been identified.

B. Primary Sentencing Options

1. The Death Penalty

History

Prior to the enactment of the Criminal Justice Act 1964 the death penalty was available as a punishment in Ireland for treason, murder and piracy. The 1964 Act replaced the death penalty with penal servitude for life for all offences with the exception of: treason under the Treason Act 1939, capital murder and certain offences committed by a person under military law.[8] By far the most important of these offences in practice was capital murder. It embraced the following: the murder of a member of the Garda Síochána acting in the

21–03

---

[7] Note also that the 1997 Act repeals s.1 of the Penal Servitude Act 1891 which had made provision for minimum periods of penal servitude of three years (which could be substituted by a prison sentence of two years) and a maximum term of five years penal servitude for those statutory offences in respect of which there was no specific statutory maximum. The maximum term of imprisonment for these offences is now five years.

[8] Criminal Justice Act 1964, ss.1(1) and 2 . The offences against military law are set out in s.124 (certain offences committed by commanders when in action) , s.125 (certain offences committed by any person in relation to the enemy), s.127 (certain offences related to prisoners of war) and s.128 (mutiny with violence) Defence Act 1954.

course of duty; the murder of a prison officer acting in the course of duty; murder committed in the course or furtherance of certain offences under the Offences against the State Act 1939 or in the course or furtherance of the activities of an unlawful organisation within the meaning of that Act; and the murder of the head of a foreign State, or of a member of the government or diplomatic mission of a foreign State, when committed within the State for a political motive.[9]

Abolition

The death penalty in Ireland was abolished entirely by the Criminal Justice Act 1990.[10] The 1990 Act also abolished the distinct offence of capital murder and introduced in its place a new offence of "murder to which section 3 applies".[11] Section 3 defines a range of offences which are almost identical to those previously embraced by capital murder: the murder of a member of the Garda Síochána acting in the course of duty;[12] the murder of a prison officer acting in the course of duty; murder committed in the course or furtherance of certain offences under the Offences against the State Act 1939[13] or in the course or furtherance of the activities of an organisation rendered unlawful by that Act;[14] and the murder of the head of a foreign State, or a member of the government or diplomatic mission of a foreign State, when committed within this State for a political motive.[15] The primary difference between this definition and the definition of capital murder is that section 3 specifically includes an attempt to commit murder in any of these circumstances. The Act also makes it clear that murder (and an attempt to commit murder) to which section 3 applies is a distinct offence from murder.[16] Accordingly, a person accused of murder within the scope of section 3 must be charged in the indictment specifically with murder (or attempt to commit murder as the case may be) to which section 3 applies.[17]

Murder to which Section 3 Applies

21–04 A person cannot be convicted of murder to which section 3 applies (or an attempt to commit such murder) unless it is proved that he knew of the

---

[9] Criminal Justice Act 1964, s.1(1)(b).
[10] Criminal Justice Act 1990, s.1.
[11] *ibid.* s.3. The law and procedure relating to murder and to attempt to commit murder shall apply generally to murder (and the attempt) to which s.3 applies, save as otherwise provided in the Act; s.3(2)(b).
[12] See *People (DPP) v. Murray* [1977] I.R. 360 for an analysis of the ingredients of this offence.
[13] The offences in question are set out in s.6 (usurpation of functions of government); s.7 (obstruction of government); s.8 (obstruction of the President); and s.9 (interference with military or other employees of the State).
[14] S.18 of the Offences against the State Act 1939 defines organisations as unlawful by reference to their activities. However, s.3 of the Criminal Justice Act 1990 does not include murder (or an attempt) committed in the course or furtherance of the activities of an unlawful organisation within the meaning of s.18(f) of the 1939 Act; *i.e.* an organisation which promotes, encourages or advocates the non-payment of moneys payable to the Central Fund or any other public fund or the non-payment of local taxation.
[15] Criminal Justice Act 1990, s.3(1).
[16] *ibid.* s.3(2).
[17] *ibid.* s.6(1).

existence of each ingredient of the offence specified in section 3(1) or was reckless as to whether or not that ingredient existed. The inclusion of this provision clears up any confusion that may have lingered in the aftermath of the Supreme Court's decision in *People (DPP) v. Murray*.[18] In the case of the murder of a member of the Garda Síochána, therefore, the prosecution would have to prove that the accused either knew or was reckless as to whether or not his victim was a member of the Garda Síochána and was, at the time, acting in the course of duty. Although it is not absolutely certain, it is submitted that this provision does not apply to the murder itself. In other words the standard *mens rea* for murder or attempted murder, as the case may be, remains unaffected and must be proved. The statutory requirement to prove knowledge or recklessness applies only to the existence of the additional ingredients, namely membership and acting in the course of duty. It is further submitted that recklessness in this context connotes subjective recklessness of the *Cunningham* variety.[19]

Where a person is indicted for murder to which section 3 applies and the evidence does not warrant a conviction for that offence he may be found guilty of murder alone if the evidence warrants such a conviction.[20] Similarly, if the evidence does not warrant a conviction for murder but does warrant a conviction for manslaughter, he may be found guilty of manslaughter.[21] If a person is indicted for an attempt to commit murder to which section 3 applies and the evidence does not warrant a conviction for such an attempt but does warrant a conviction for an attempt to commit murder, he may be found guilty of an attempt to commit murder.[22]

The vital distinction between murder to which section 3 applies and ordinary murder concerns sentence. Although the former no longer attracts the death penalty which attached to its predecessor, capital murder, it is not punished simply by the mandatory life sentence applicable to murder. The Act stipulates that a person convicted of murder must be sentenced to imprisonment for life.[23] It goes on to say, however, that where a person, other than a child or young person (a person under 17 years of age), is convicted of a murder to which section 3 applies, the court when passing sentence must specify a minimum period of imprisonment of at least 40 years to be served by that person.[24] Where the court has convicted the person of an attempt to commit such murder it must impose a minimum sentence of 20 years imprisonment and must specify a minimum period of imprisonment of at least 20 years to be served by that person.[25]

---

[18] [1977] I.R. 360.
[19] See J. McAuley & P. McCutchean *Criminal Liability: a Grammar* (Round Hall Sweet & Maxwell, Dublin, 2000), pp.282–290, for discussion of *Cunningham* recklessness.
[20] Criminal Justice Act 1990, s.6(2)(a).
[21] *ibid*. s.6(2)(b).
[22] *ibid*. s.6(3).
[23] *ibid*. s.2.
[24] *ibid*. s.4(a).
[25] *ibid*. s.4(b).

Minimum Sentences of Imprisonment for murder to which Section 3 Applies

21–05   It is also worth noting that the abolition of the death penalty for treason in the Criminal Justice Act 1990 is balanced by provision for minimum periods of imprisonment. In fact it is dealt with in almost identical terms to the substantive murder offences. Accordingly, a person convicted of treason shall be sentenced to imprisonment for life and, unless the person concerned is a child or young person, the court must specify a minimum period of imprisonment of at least 40 years to be served by that person. There is no such provision with respect to the offences against military law or those under the Offences against the State Act 1939 which had previously attracted the death penalty.

Where a person is sentenced under these provisions to life imprisonment, subject to a minimum of 40 or 20 years, as the case may be, he cannot benefit from the statutory power to commute or remit punishment before the end of the minimum period specified by the court (see later).[26] Similarly, temporary release may not be granted before the end of the minimum period unless for "grave reasons of a humanitarian nature". However, it would appear that the prisoners in question can still earn remission for good behaviour under the Prison Rules (see later). For this purpose the minimum period is deemed to be a determinate sentence and the remitted period is calculated accordingly. Typically, this can result in the time actually served for a forty year period being reduced to 30 years.

2. Imprisonment

Different Modes of Imprisonment

21–06   Up until very recently Irish enactments in force recognised several different forms of sentence involving deprivation of liberty. In addition to imprisonment, there was penal servitude, imprisonment with hard labour and imprisonment without hard labour.[27] Penal servitude was introduced generally as a substitute for deportation to the colonies. Technically, it was quite distinct from a sentence of imprisonment with or without hard labour. Indeed, the Minister for Justice, Equality and Law Reform had the power by order to set apart places of confinement for prisoners under sentence of penal servitude.[28] These were to be described as "convict prisons". In practice, however, no such order was ever made and, in terms of custodial treatment, persons sentenced to penal servitude have been treated generally the same as persons sentenced to imprisonment. Similarly, offenders sentenced to imprisonment with hard labour or without hard labour have been treated, since the establishment of this State, in the same manner as offenders sentenced to imprisonment *simpliciter*. It is also worth noting that the sentence of penal servitude differed from imprisonment in that it could not be interrupted once it had commenced. It follows that if the prisoner was released from prison for a period in the

---

[26]   *ibid.* s.5.

[27]   See generally, E Ryan and P Magee *The Irish Criminal Process* (Mercier Press, Dublin, 1983), pp.395–398.

course of serving his sentence that would not stop time running for the purpose of calculating the remaining time he had to serve.[29] His release date on returning to prison at the end of the period would be exactly the same as it was when he was released at the beginning of the period.

Abolition of Penal Servitude and Hard Labour

The concepts of penal servitude and imprisonment without hard labour have now been abolished by the Criminal Law Act 1997.[30] Similarly, the notion of classifying offenders in prison into separate divisions has been abolished.[31] Any person who, immediately before the commencement of the Act, was undergoing or was liable to undergo a term of penal servitude shall be treated as if he was undergoing or was liable to undergo imprisonment, instead of penal servitude, for that term.[32] Similarly, any person who has been sentenced to imprisonment with hard labour for a term which has not expired at the commencement of the Act shall, for the remainder of that term, be treated as though he had been sentenced to imprisonment without hard labour.[33] However, the replacement of a sentence of penal servitude to one of imprisonment does not change the rule stated above that a sentence of penal servitude, unlike a sentence of imprisonment, cannot be interrupted once it has commenced. A very clear statement of intent in the Criminal Law Act 1997 to abandon this rule with respect to current sentences of penal servitude would be required before that result could be achieved. In *DPP v. Murphy*[34] O'Donovan J. ruled that there was no such clear statement of intent in the Act. Accordingly, while a sentence of penal servitude imposed before the coming into force of the relevant provisions of the 1997 Act would be treated for all other purposes as a sentence of imprisonment, it could not be interrupted by any period during which the prisoner was released from prison while serving the sentence.

21–07

Having replaced penal servitude and hard labour with imprisonment the Act goes on to make consequential provision with respect to maximum sentences. It stipulates that every enactment conferring a power on a court to pass a sentence of penal servitude or imprisonment with hard labour shall be treated as empowering the court to pass a sentence of imprisonment for a term not exceeding the maximum term of penal servitude or imprisonment with hard labour, as the case may be, for which a sentence could have been passed in that case immediately before the commencement of the Act.[35] It follows, therefore, that it is still necessary today to look to enactments which made provision for penal servitude and/or imprisonment with hard labour and

---

[28]   Prisons (Ireland) Act 1856, s.2.
[29]   *State (Woods) v. Governor of Portlaoise Prison* 108 I.L.T.R. 57; *State (Langan) v. Donohue* [1974] I.R. 251.
[30]   Criminal Law Act 1997, s.11(1) and (3). The expressions "with or without hard labour", "with hard labour", "without hard labour", and corresponding expressions wherever occurring in any enactment prescribing the punishment for an offence are repealed.
[31]   Criminal Law Act 1997, s.11(4).
[32]   *ibid.* s.11(5).
[33]   *ibid.* s.11(6).
[34]   Unreported, High Court, November 20, 2000.
[35]   Criminal Law Act 1997, s.11(2) and (3).

which were in force immediately prior to the enactment of the 1997 Act. Maximum and minimum terms of penal servitude and/or imprisonment with hard labour set for specific offences by these enactments will continue to apply to the offences in question, subject to the qualification that the terms in question refer to imprisonment as opposed to penal servitude or imprisonment with hard labour.

Maximun Sentences

21–08   Most statutory enactments specify a maximum and/or minimum term of imprisonment which may be imposed on conviction for an offence or offences created by the enactments in question. The specification of maximum punishments in this context is much more common than minimum punishments. The Non-fatal Offences against the Person Act 1997, for example, specifies maximum terms of imprisonment for a number of offences where the offender is convicted on indictment. These range from a term of five years to life imprisonment. Indeed, a maximum term of five years imprisonment would appear to be a notional benchmark separating serious offences from lesser offences for certain purposes. Offences which can be punished by a sentence of five years or more might be classed as serious offences. Significantly, the definition of an arrestable offence for the purposes of arrest without warrant and detention is an offence which can be punished on conviction for a term of five years imprisonment or by a more severe penalty. Where a person is convicted on indictment of an offence for which there is no specified maximum sentence of imprisonment, the maximum period of imprisonment which can be imposed is two years.

Minimum Sentences

The statutory prescription of minimum sentences of imprisonment is now quite rare. Ryan and Magee, however, state that many of the older statutes prescribe that an offence shall be punishable by penal servitude for a term of not less than three years or imprisonment, with or without hard labour, for a term not exceeding two years.[36] It is not clear to what extent such provisions remain applicable today. Certainly, by virtue of the Criminal Law Act 1997, the minimum three year term of penal servitude must be interpreted as a three year term of imprisonment, while the maximum term of two years hard labour must be treated as a two year term of imprisonment. It would appear, however, that most, and possibly all, of the offences subject to a minimum three year term of imprisonment have since been replaced by statutory enactments which provide only for maximum terms of imprisonment. Nevertheless, the concept of a minimum term of imprisonment would appear to be set to make a comeback, at least in modified form. As noted above, when the Criminal Justice Act 1990 abolished the death penalty for treason and capital murder it created new offences of treason and murder within the scope of

---

[36]   Ryan and Magee, *op. cit.*, pp.397–398.

section 3 of the Criminal Justice Act , 1990 (formerly capital murder). The Act goes on to provide that where a person has been convicted of either of these offences, the judge is required to specify a minimum sentence of at least 40 years imprisonment which must be served where the person in question is not a child or young person.[37] In the case of a conviction for an attempt to commit murder within the scope of section 3 of the 1990 Act, the minimum sentence is 20 years.[38] Once again the judge is required to specify a minimum term of imprisonment of at least 20 years which the offender must serve.

The Criminal Justice Act 1999 has introduced a more controversial minimum sentence for certain drug offences. The Act creates a new offence of possession of a controlled drug for sale or supply where the market value of the drugs in question amounts to €13,000 or more.[39] It also stipulates that where a person (not being a child or young person) is convicted of such an offence the court shall, when imposing sentence, specify a period of not less than 10 years as the minimum period of imprisonment to be served by the person.[40] This requirement does not apply where the court is satisfied that there are exceptional and specific circumstances relating to the offence, or the person convicted, which would make a minimum sentence of 10 years unjust in all the circumstances.[41] In determining whether such circumstances exist, the court may have regard to any matters it considers appropriate, including whether the person pleaded guilty and, if so, when he indicated an intention to plead guilty and the circumstances in which the indication was given, as well as whether the person materially assisted in the investigation of the offence. Where a minimum 10 year sentence is imposed pursuant to these provisions it cannot be reduced below 10 years by an exercise of the powers of remission and commutation under the Criminal Justice Act 1951.[42] Equally, the prisoner concerned cannot normally benefit from temporary release under the Criminal Justice Act 1960 before 10 years have been served.[43] However, he can benefit from remission for good behaviour.[44] It is also worth noting that if the prisoner is a drug addict and the addiction was a substantial factor in the commission of the offence, the court can list the sentence for review after one half of the sentence has been served.[45]

Even if the sentencing court decides that the minimum sentence provision does not apply because the circumstances of the offence or the offender would render it unjust, it would appear that the existence of the minimum sentence provision will influence the court's determination of an appropriate sentence in the case. In *People (DPP) v. Renald*[46] the Court of Criminal

21–09

---

[37] Criminal Justice Act 1999, s.4(a).
[38] *ibid.* s.4(b).
[39] Misuse of Drugs Act 1977, s.15A, as inserted by Criminal Justice Act 1999, s.4.
[40] Misuse of Drugs Act 1977, s.27(3B), as inserted by Criminal Justice Act 1999, s.5.
[41] *ibid.* s.27(3C), as inserted by Criminal Justice Act 1999, s.5.
[42] *ibid.* s.27(3D), as inserted by Criminal Justice Act 1999, s.5.
[43] *ibid.* s.27(3F) and (3J), as inserted by Criminal Justice Act 1999, s.5.
[44] *ibid.* s.27(3E), as inserted by Criminal Justice Act 1999, s.5.
[45] *ibid.* s.27(3G) and (3H), as inserted by Criminal Justice Act 1999, s.5.
[46] Unreported, Court of Criminal Appeal, November 23, 2001.

Appeal stated that the existence of any such statutory minimum was an important guide for the court when assessing the gravity of the offence in a case where the minimum did not apply owing to exceptional circumstances. However, the statutory minimum should not be used as a benchmark against which the court could make reductions or discounts.[47] The court would have to take into account all of the relevant circumstances, including the maximum permissible sentence and the existence of the statutory minimum.[48] Moreover, just because there may be circumstances which render it unjust to impose the statutory minimum, the existence of these circumstances does not reduce the inherent seriousness of the offence.

Mandatory Sentences

Some offences attract a mandatory sentence of imprisonment. As referred to above, for example, the sentence for murder and treason is statutorily fixed as life imprisonment.[49] The judge has no discretion in the matter. A sentence of life imprisonment is technically a sentence of imprisonment for life. In practice, it is most unusual for a prisoner subject to a life sentence to be kept in prison for the remainder of his natural life. Although he is not eligible for remission for good conduct under the Prison Rules he may be considered for release on licence by the Minister for Justice, Equality and Law Reform after he has served a minimum term of seven years in prison. In practice, such prisoners are not released until they have served at least nine years.[50] Although released on licence, the life sentence remains. If the licence is revoked for a reason the person in question can be taken back into prison.

No Maximum or Minimum

21–10 Some statutory enactments create or define criminal offences and do not specify a maximum sentence of imprisonment which can be imposed on conviction. These situations are now covered by several statutory provisions which, unfortunately, do not correlate smoothly with each other. A sentence of penal servitude could not be imposed for a term longer than seven years, in the absence of specific statutory authority authorising a longer term.[51] Where an offence was declared to be a felony by any statute in force on 5th August 1891 (when the Penal Servitude Act 1891 came into force) and no punishment was specifically provided for it, the effect of the material enactments would appear to be that the offence was punishable with penal servitude for any period not exceeding seven years.[52] If, however, an offence (whether felony

---

[47] *People (DPP) v. Duffy* unreported, Court of Criminal Appeal, December 21, 2001.
[48] A plea of guilty and cooperation with the investigation will not necessarily result in a sentence of less than 10 years; *People (DPP) v. Hogarty* unreported, Court of Criminal Appeal, December 21, 2001.
[49] Criminal Justice Act 1990, s.2
[50] See O'Malley, *op. cit.*, p.289.
[51] Criminal Law (Ireland) Act 1828, s.15; Penal Servitude Act 1857, s.2; Penal Servitude Act 1891, s.1.
[52] Ryan and Magee, *op. cit.*, p.396.

or misdemeanour) was declared to be punishable with penal servitude, the maximum term was five years, unless a particular statute authorised a longer term. These provisions must now be considered in the light of the Criminal Law Act 1997. Not only does it replace penal servitude with imprisonment but it also stipulates that the maximum sentence of imprisonment which may be imposed by a court *in lieu* of penal servitude for any offence cannot exceed the maximum term of penal servitude which could have been imposed for that offence immediately before the commencement of the 1997 Act.[53] In the case of an offence declared to be a felony by any statute in force on the 5th August 1891 for which no punishment was specifically provided, the maximum term would appear to be seven years. For any offence which was declared to be punishable by penal servitude the maximum term would appear to be five years, unless a particular statute authorised a longer term.

Unfortunately, the relative clarity of these provisions has been clouded by a further provision which states that in the case of any enactment in force on August 5, 1891 whereby a court had, immediately before the commencement of the 1997 Act, power to pass a sentence of penal servitude, the maximum term of imprisonment which can be imposed shall not exceed five years or any greater term authorised by the enactment. It is not clear whether this is simply a restatement of the five year limit provision or whether it is intended to reduce the seven year limit to a five year limit. The general sense of the words used would suggest that the latter is the correct interpretation.

To complicate matters further, it must be acknowledged that the Penal **21–11** Servitude Act 1891 empowered a court to impose a sentence of imprisonment with or without hard labour for a term not exceeding two years as a substitute for a sentence of penal servitude, except where an Act provided otherwise.[54] This option has special relevance for offences created by statutory enactments which did not specify a maximum term of penal servitude. It is difficult to know what to make of this provision in the light of the substitution of imprisonment for sentences of penal servitude and imprisonment with or without hard labour. The Criminal Law Act 1997 states that ". . . every enactment conferring a power on a court to pass a sentence of imprisonment with hard labour in any case shall operate so as to empower that court to pass a sentence of imprisonment for a term not exceeding the term for which a sentence of imprisonment with hard labour could have been passed in that case immediately before the commencement of this Act . . ."[55] There is nothing to preclude this provision applying to a sentence of imprisonment with hard labour as a substitute for a sentence of penal servitude. While there might have been some merit in permitting a court to impose a sentence of imprisonment with hard labour for a maximum period of two years as a substitute for a longer term of penal servitude, the same hardly applies where

---

[53] Criminal Law Act 1997, s.11(2).
[54] Penal Servitude Act 1891, s.1(2). *People v. Power* unreported, Court of Criminal Appeal, July 31, 1975.
[55] Criminal Law Act 1997, s.11(3).

imprisonment with hard labour and penal servitude have been replaced by the common currency of imprisonment. It hardly makes sense to give a court discretion to sentence an offender to imprisonment for a maximum term of two years as a substitute for a sentence of imprisonment for a longer term. It is submitted, therefore, that the discretion conferred in this matter by the Penal Servitude Act 1891 is now defunct.

Even before the abolition of penal servitude and imprisonment with or without hard labour many statutory offences were punishable by imprisonment *simpliciter*. Typically, these were misdemeanours triable on indictment. The Criminal Law Act 1997 imposes a maximum term of imprisonment which can be imposed on conviction on indictment for such offences where a maximum has not already been fixed by some other statutory enactment. It stipulates that where a person is convicted on indictment for an offence against any enactment for which he is liable to be sentenced to imprisonment, the maximum term of imprisonment that may be imposed for the offence is two years.[56] This, of course, does not apply where some other enactment limits the maximum sentence to a specified term or extends it to imprisonment for life.

Attempts

At common law, the maximum sentence applicable to an attempt to commit a statutory offence cannot exceed that applicable to the substantive offence.[57] The same applies generally with respect to conspiracy. The Criminal Law Act 1997 extends this rule, at least as far as attempts are concerned, to any offence for which a maximum term of imprisonment or a maximum fine is provided by any enactment.[58]

Concurrent and Consecutive Sentences

21–12 Where an offender is sentenced to imprisonment on a number of counts in the same indictment, or on more than one indictment at the same sitting, it is quite normal for the court to direct that the sentences should be served concurrently. In effect, therefore, the prisoner's term of imprisonment will be equivalent to the longest single term imposed for any of the counts or on any of the indictments.[59] Similarly, if the offender is already serving a sentence at the time he or she is convicted of another offence it would not be unusual for the court to pass a sentence of imprisonment to run concurrently with that already being served. Equally, however, it is open to the court in any of these situations to pass a sentence of imprisonment which is to run consecutively with another term imposed or currently being served.[60] The effect is that the former will commence automatically when, and not before, the latter has

---

[56] *ibid.* s.10(1).
[57] *R v. Pearce* [1952] 2 All E.R. 718; *Verrier v. DPP* [1967] 2 A.C. 195.
[58] Criminal Law Act 1997, s.10(2).
[59] *State (Brien) v. Kelly* [1970] I.R. 69.
[60] *State (Jones) v. O'Donovan* [1973] I.R. 329; *State (McNally) v. O'Donovan* [1974] I.R. 272; *R v. Hemming* 7 Cr.App.R.236.

ended. In some circumstances the court is actually obliged to order a sentence of imprisonment to run consecutively with another sentence. Any sentence of imprisonment passed on a person for an offence committed while he or she was on bail, for example, must be consecutive on any sentence passed on him or her for a previous offence.[61] If he or she has been sentenced for two or more previous offences the sentence to be passed shall be consecutive on the last sentence to expire. Similarly, any sentence of imprisonment or detention in Saint Patrick's Institution passed on a person for an offence committed while he or she is serving any such sentence shall be consecutive on the sentence that he or she is serving.[62] If he or she is due to serve more than one sentence then the sentence to be passed shall run consecutively on the sentence due to expire last.

The concept of consecutive sentences of imprisonment can pose a difficulty for the District Court. Generally, it is accepted that the maximum single sentence of imprisonment which can be passed by the District Court is twelve months. In the case of indictable offences triable summarily this limit is imposed by statute. In summary offences it results from the interpretation of a minor offence in the context of the constitutional right to trial by jury for non-minor offences. Inevitably, the question arises, can the District Court circumvent these limits on its sentencing powers by passing sentences of imprisonment to run consecutively? The answer is a qualified yes. The Criminal Justice Act 1951 stipulates that where two or more sentences passed by the District Court are ordered to run consecutively the aggregate term of imprisonment (or detention in Saint Patrick's Institution as the case may be) shall not exceed two years.[63] Similarly, where the court is obliged to order sentences to run consecutively it is standard for an aggregate limit of two years to be imposed.[64] The net result, therefore, is that a court of summary jurisdiction can sentence an offender to a lengthy aggregate period of imprisonment.

Calculating Period of Imprisonment

The imposition of a specified sentence of imprisonment in any individual case naturally presupposes clear rules for determining when a sentence begins and ends. Surprisingly, perhaps, there are no comprehensive rules dealing with such matters in Ireland. It would appear, as a general rule, that a sentence imposed in the Central Criminal Court commences on the day that it is issued.[65] In the case of the Circuit Court, Ryan and Magee submit, by analogy from the practice in the days of assize and gaol delivery, that a sentence commences from the first

21–13

---

[61] Criminal Justice Act 1984, s.11(1). This does not apply where any such sentence is one of imprisonment for life or is a sentence of detention under s.103 of the Children Act 1908.

[62] Criminal Law Act 1976, s.13(1). Once again, this does not apply in any case where the sentence being served or to be passed is a sentence of life imprisonment; s.13(2).

[63] Criminal Justice Act 1951, s.5, as amended by Criminal Justice Act 1984, s.12(1).

[64] Criminal Justice Act 1984, s.11(1); Criminal Law Act 1976, s.13(1) as amended by Criminal Justice Act 1984, s.12(2).

[65] RSC Ord.9, r.85 states that every order of the Central Criminal Court, when drawn up, shall be dated the day of the week, month and year in which it was made, unless that Court shall direct otherwise, and shall take effect accordingly.

day of the sitting in question, unless otherwise stated.[66] In practice, of course, a sentence of imprisonment is often made retrospective, particularly where the offender has been in custody awaiting trial.

There is no statutory provision in Ireland governing the calculation of time spent in prison for the purpose of serving a sentence of imprisonment. In England, the day on which a sentence of imprisonment begins is counted as part of the term. Months are calculated as calendar months. If the last day of the term of imprisonment falls on a Sunday, Christmas Day or Good Friday the prisoner must be released on the immediately preceding day. Account must also be taken of periods of remission earned by the prisoner for good behaviour.

3. Suspended Sentence

Introduction

21–14   There is no statutory authority in Ireland enabling a court to suspend the operation of a prison sentence.[67] In practice, the courts have always assumed such a power and the imposition of a "suspended sentence" is quite common.[68] A "suspended sentence" is the expression used to refer generally to the situation where the court, having passed a sentence of imprisonment for a specified term, suspends its operation. Any criminal court may suspend a prison sentence unless the sentence is required by law (*e.g.* life imprisonment for murder). This does not necessarily preclude the suspension of one or more sentences which are required by law to run consecutively.

Standard Form

The net effect of suspending a prison sentence is that time begins to run from the imposition of the sentence and if the offender does not do anything which results in another appearance before the court in a criminal matter the sentence will expire at the end of its specified term without the offender spending a day in prison. Typically the sentence of imprisonment will be suspended upon the offender entering into a recognisance, with or without sureties, to keep the peace and be of good behaviour for a specified period.

Further conditions may also be added. In the case of foreign nationals, for example, it is not unusual for the court to attach a condition that the offender leave the country and not re-enter for a specified period of years.[69] It is worth noting, however, that in appropriate circumstances such a condition can give

---

[66]   Ryan and Magee, *op. cit.*, p.399.

[67]   Ironically, there is provision preventing a court from suspending a sentence imposed for certain offences; see, *e.g.* hijacking and endangering aircraft under the Air Navigation and Transport Acts 1973 and 1975.

[68]   *State (McIlhagga) v. Governor of Portlaoise Prison* unreported, Supreme Court, July 29, 1971. See, generally, N Osborough *A Damocles Sword Guaranteed Irish* (1982) Irish Jurist 221, in which the author traces the development of the suspended sentence as an invention of the Irish judiciary. The Supreme Court fully endorsed the suspended sentence in *O'Brien v. Governor of Limerick Prison* [1997] 2 I.L.R.M. 349.

[69]   See O'Malley, *op. cit.*, for some recent examples.

rise to issues under the European Convention on Human Rights, European Union law on the free movement of persons and the Constitution.

If the offender breaches his or her recognisance then the sentence comes into full operation without the need for any further order.[70] In practice, what usually happens is that the offender appears before the court during the period of the suspended sentence charged with another offence. If convicted he will be sentenced for that other offence and the suspended sentence will also be activated.

Although the suspended sentence is a sentence in its own right it must be remembered that it is intimately associated with a sentence of imprisonment. If the defendant breaches the terms of suspension he is liable to be ordered to serve the full term of the sentence. It is important, therefore, that the sentencing should begin by deciding whether a prison sentence is appropriate and, if so, what length of sentence is appropriate. Only then should it considered whether there are circumstances which warrant a suspension of the sentence. A suspended sentence should never be imposed in a case where the gravity and circumstances of the offence taken by themselves would not have warranted a prison sentence.

"Butler Orders"

A variation of the suspended sentence which has proved increasingly popular is the imposition of a lengthy custodial sentence with a direction that the offender should be brought back before the court after having served a specified portion of the sentence. At that point the court will consider suspending the remainder of the sentence subject to the accused entering into a recognisance to keep the peace for the remaining period of the sentence.[71] If the accused is subsequently convicted of an offence committed during that period the remainder of the sentence will be activated.[72] The hallmark of this type of sentence is that the judge retains seisin of the case. The accused is brought back before the court after he has served the specified portion of the sentence and it is a matter for the judge to decide what should be done about the remaining portion of the sentence. This form of sentence is colloquially referred to as a "Butler Order" having been fashioned by Butler J. in *State (Woods) v. Attorney General*.[73] It is wholly separate from the executive power to remit or commute sentence.

21–15

The "Butler Order" has proved attractive as a means of building in an element of rehabilitation to a custodial sentence, particularly in respect of a young person or a person with an addiction or behavioural problem which needs to be addressed.[74] Indeed, there is authority to the effect that it should be used

---

[70] *R v. Spratling* [1911] 1 K.B. 77.

[71] This form of sentence is colloquially referred to as a "Butler Order" having been first introduced by the late Butler J.; see *State (Woods) v. Attorney General* [1969] I.R. 385.

[72] See, for example, *People (DPP) v. Aylmer* [1995] 2 I.L.R.M. 624. Note, however, that it is not every trivial breach which will be sufficient to activate the suspended portion of the sentence; *per* Hederman J. at 638.

[73] [1969] I.R. 385.

[74] See Denham J. in *People (DPP) v. Sheedy* [2000] 2 I.R. 184 at 194.

only in such cases.[75] It was also a means whereby the sentencing judge could ensure that the convicted person actually served a specified minimum term during a period when pressure on prison space was resulting in wholesale early releases. Equally, however, the "Butler Order" has come in for criticism, particularly in the Court of Criminal Appeal.[76] It is also worth noting that difficulties can arise as a result of the wording of the order in any individual case.

21–16   In *O'Brien v. Governor of Limerick Prison*,[77] for example, Lavan J. sentenced the accused to 10 years imprisonment with a further stipulation to the effect that the last six years of the sentence should be suspended upon the accused entering into a bond to keep the peace for that six year period. This differed from the typical "Butler Order" in that it took the form of a period of imprisonment at the end of which the prisoner would be released automatically subject to a suspended sentence of six years. This form of sentence creates particular difficulties with respect to remission for good behaviour. Under the terms of the Prisons (Ireland) Act 1907 and the Rules for the Government of Prisons 1947, a prisoner can earn remission of a portion of his imprisonment for good behaviour. The question arises, therefore, with respect to the type of sentence imposed in *O'Brien's* case, whether the prisoner can earn remission during the period of imprisonment and, if so, whether it must be offset against the mandatory period of imprisonment imposed. In *O'Brien* it was quite clear that the sentencing judge's intention was that the prisoner should serve a minimum of four years before being released. That, however, would preclude the benefit of remission earned during that four year period. The Prison Rules on remission clearly envisage that the period of imprisonment will be identical with the period of the sentence. Equally, the Prison Rules stipulate that a prisoner's sentence is deemed to have expired on his discharge. This is inconsistent with a period of imprisonment remaining suspended over a prisoner's head after his release pursuant to the Rules. Accordingly, the Supreme Court ruled that the particular form of sentence applied in *O'Brien* is incompatible with the Prisons Act and the Prisons Rules and, as such, should not be imposed. It should be noted, however, that this does not affect the propriety of a typical "Butler Order".

Status of "Butler Orders"

The Supreme Court has yet to rule authoritatively on the validity of "Butler Orders". In *People (DPP) v. Aylmer*,[78] the Supreme Court refused to quash the form of "Butler Order" imposed in that case, while declining to express an opinion on its desirability.[79] In *People (DPP) v. Finn*,[80] however, the

---

[75]   *People (DPP) v. Sheedy* unreported, Court of Criminal Appeal, October 15, 1999.

[76]   See, *e.g. People (DPP) v. Fagan* unreported, Court of Criminal Appeal, November 7, 1977; *People (DPP) v. O'Toole* unreported, Court of Criminal Appeal, May 26, 1978; *People (DPP) v. Cahill* [1980] I.R. 8.

[77]   [1997] 2 I.L.R.M. 349.

[78]   [1995] 2 I.L.R.M. 624.

[79]   See also, *O'Brien v. Governor of Limerick Prison* [1997] 2 I.L.R.M. 349.

[80]   [2001] 2 I.R. 25.

Supreme Court addressed the validity of the orders directly, albeit *obiter*, in **21–17** the context of a challenge to the DPP's application for a review of sentence (see later). Keane C.J., giving the judgment of the court, considered that the judge's final order on the review date was, in all but name, the exercise of the power of commutation or remission of sentence. Article 13.6 of the Constitution vests the power of commutation or remission in the President and makes provision for the power to be conferred by law on other authorities. The Criminal Justice Act 1951 expressly conferred the power on the government and, where it had so delegated its power, the Minister for Justice, Equality and Law Reform. There is no similar provision conferring such a general power on the courts.[81] Accordingly, for the courts to suspend a sentence when it came up for review on a "Butler Order" is in effect an unlawful encroachment upon the executive power. Equally, the operation of a "Butler Order" seemed to be at variance with the appeal structure as reflected in the Rules of the Superior Courts. They required an application for a certificate that the case is a fit case for appeal to be made at the close of the trial or within three days thereafter. If the close of trial was to be interpreted as the date when sentence was imposed, and the sentencing process was not completed until the review date, the accused would be deprived of his or her right of appeal against sentence until such time as he or she had served a significant portion of his or her sentence. While this analysis was delivered *obiter*, the clear message is that the Supreme Court in *Finn* considered "Butler Orders" to be invalid.[82] Keane C.J. also expressed the desire for any such power of commutation or remission to be placed on a clear and transparent basis. This would require legislative intervention to create a parole board or other such entity which would operate in accordance with prescribed procedures.

Adjournment of Sentence

Another possibility which, strictly speaking, is not a suspended sentence as defined above is for the court to adjourn sentence for a certain time to see how the offender behaves. Usually, there will be an expectation in such cases that the offender will take some restorative action such as paying compensation to the victim, or rehabilitative action such as undergoing a detoxification programme. When the court comes to reconsider the matter it can proceed to the imposition of the sentence which it would otherwise have passed if it is not satisfied with the offender's performance in the interim. This practice has no statutory foundation and has not yet been the subject of a judicial ruling. This is dealt with further under "Sentencing Principles".

---

[81] There are provisions, such as that concerning certain drugs offences in the Criminal Justice Act 1999.

[82] It is also worth noting that a majority of the Law Reform Commission recommended that the reviewing function inherent in this form of sentence should be removed from the courts and left with the executive; Law Reform Commission Report on Sentencing (Dublin, LRC 53, 1996).

4. Community Service Orders

Function

21–18   There are obvious advantages to a punishment which requires the offender to do something positive on behalf of the community as an alternative to being incarcerated in prison for a period of time. The community benefits not just from the positive work done by the offender but also from being spared the expense of keeping him or her in prison. The offender benefits not just because he or she retains his or her freedom but also from the satisfaction of making amends for the wrongdoing. In some cases it can result in the offender keeping his or her employment which otherwise would have been lost consequent on his or her imprisonment. The offender's family also benefits from being spared the adverse consequences that typically follow when one of its members, perhaps the primary income source, is imprisoned. It is not surprising, therefore, that the concept of sentencing an offender to a programme of work in the community, as an alternative to a term of imprisonment, has taken firm root in many jurisdictions around the world in the second half of the twentieth century. It was adopted in Ireland in the mid-1980s.[83]

Jurisdiction

The Criminal Justice (Community Service) Act 1983[84] provides courts with the power to sentence offenders to a community service order in certain circumstances. All courts exercising criminal jurisdiction enjoy this power, with the exception of the Special Criminal Court. It is only available, however, in respect of an offender who is over 16 years of age and has been convicted of a criminal offence.[85] Moreover, the court can only impose an order as an alternative to a sentence of imprisonment or detention in Saint Patrick's Institution. Technically, therefore, the court should not consider a community service order in any case where it would otherwise have imposed a fine or a probation order or any other punishment short of imprisonment or detention. In practice, however, it seems that community service orders are sometimes perceived as an attractive and appropriate form of punishment for many cases which would never have attracted a custodial sentence.[86] On the other hand, courts cannot impose a community service order for an offence for which the sentence is fixed by law.

Length

A community service order will oblige the offender to complete a specified number of hours of unpaid work in the community under the supervision of a

---

[83]   See the Criminal Justice (Community Service) Act 1983 and the Criminal Justice (Community Service) Regulations 1984. For background material see White Paper on Community Service Orders issued by the Minister for Justice (PRI. 9930, 1981).

[84]   The Act was brought into force in December 1984 by the Criminal Justice (Community Service) Act 1983 (Commencement) Order 1984. However, it did not become operational until February 1984.

[85]   Criminal Justice (Community Service) Act 1983, s.2.

[86]   See D Walsh and P Sexton *An Empirical Study of Community Service Orders in Ireland* (Dublin, Stationery Office, 1999).

probation officer. The minimum number of hours which can be imposed is 40 while the maximum is 240.[87] Where the offender is convicted of two or more offences the court may apply community service orders in respect of each and direct that they shall run concurrently or consecutively.[88] Similarly, if there is already an order in force in respect of the offender at the time the court imposes a further order, it may direct that the latter shall run either concurrently with or consecutively to the latter.[89] In any case, where orders run consecutively the aggregate must not exceed 240 hours.

The Community Service

Neither the Act nor the regulations specify the nature of the work which would be suitable or unsuitable for a community service order. The policy behind the legislation is that the offender should be required to perform tasks which will benefit his or her own local community. This might take the form of helping out at an old people's home or recreational centre, working with the handicapped or helping out in a youth club. It could also involve labouring work in the form of renovating community buildings or improving the environment. Clearly, there is a risk that the orders could be perceived as a form of punishment by compulsory labour which could be in breach of the European Convention on Human Rights. Accordingly, the court's power to apply a community service order is exercisable only where the offender in question gives his consent.[90] The court must also be satisfied of the offender's ability and suitability to perform the community service order.[91] To this end it must consider the offender's individual circumstances and a report on him or her prepared by a probation officer. In so far as practicable, the work should avoid any interference with the time the offender normally works or attends an educational or training establishment.[92] Before imposing the order the court must also explain to the offender that he will be guilty of an offence if he or she fails to perform the required work. Generally the work must be performed within one year, although this may be extended in certain circumstances.[93] In any event the order remains in force until the offender has worked the number of hours specified in it.

21–19

Supervision of Probation Officer

An offender subject to a community service order must serve out the order under the supervision of a probation officer appointed by the court. This does not mean that the officer functions as the offender's employer with respect to the work. In practice the offender will work under the immediate direction of an employer in the community. It is the role of the probation officer, however,

---

[87]   *Criminal Justice (Community Service) Act 1983*, s.3(2).
[88]   *ibid.* s.5(2).
[89]   *ibid.* s.5(3).
[90]   *ibid.* s.4(1)(vi). See *Scully v. District Judge Crowley* unreported, Supreme Court, May 3, 2001.
[91]   *ibid.* s.4(1)(i).
[92]   *ibid.* s.7(3).
[93]   *ibid.* s.7(2).

to supervise the implementation of the order. In other words he or she must ensure that the offender is actually fulfilling the terms of the order. To this end he or she will be in regular contact with the offender while the offender is working under the order and with the offender's employer. The probation officer reports directly to the court on the performance of the offender in fulfilling the terms of the order. If the offender breaches the terms of the order he commits an offence for which he can be fined up to a maximum of €381. Equally, where the officer reports to the court that the offender has breached the terms of the order, the court may revoke the order and deal with the offender for the original offence as if the community service order had never been made.[94] Strictly speaking, if it takes this approach the court should impose a custodial sentence as community service orders ought to be applied only in those cases where the court would otherwise have imposed a custodial sentence.

Practice

21–20   Although the Circuit Court and the Central Criminal Court have jurisdiction to apply community service orders, in practice the vast majority are applied by the District Court.[95] To some extent this might be explained by the fact that offenders coming before the District Court are deemed generally more suitable for community service orders than those who come before the other courts. Undoubtedly, there is also a greater resistance to the notion of applying a non-custodial sentence to the serious offences tried on indictment than would be the case for the offences dealt with at District Court level. Nevertheless, it is submitted that at least part of the reason why District Courts are more frequent users of community service orders is the perceived attractiveness of this option compared to probation, fines and other such non-custodial sentences. In other words the stipulation that the order should be applied only as a substitute for a custodial sentence is not always followed rigorously.[96]

Procedure

The normal procedure in any case where the judge is considering the possibility of a community service order is for the judge to indicate the length of prison sentence or sentence of detention which he or she has in mind and the number of hours community service which he or she would impose instead.[97] The defendant will then be asked whether he or she consents to community service. If the answer is in the affirmative the judge will then adjourn the proceedings for the preparation of a report on the defendant's suitability for community service and the availability of a suitable community service project. At the resumed hearing the judge will consider the report and

---

[94]   *ibid.* s.7(4).
[95]   See D Walsh and P Sexton, *op. cit.*
[96]   *ibid.*
[97]   *ibid.* for a discussion of this practice. See also *Scully v. District Judge Crowley* unreported, Supreme Court, May 3, 2001.

may take oral evidence from the probation officer and any other relevant person. If the judge is satisfied that the defendant is fit for community service and that a suitable project is available he or she will impose a sentence of community service at that point.

Part 9 of the Children Act 2001 makes separate provision for the imposition of community sanctions on children of 16 and 17 years of age. However, the provisions have not yet been fully brought into force.

5. Fines

Power to Impose Fines

Although fines are a standard form of punishment imposed by courts today, the power to impose fines has developed in a haphazard manner. In the case of a conviction for felony, for example, a court had no general power to pass a sentence consisting of a fine.[98] By contrast a court had a power at common law to impose a fine on conviction for any misdemeanour.[99] The Criminal Law Act 1997 has abolished the distinction between felonies and misdemeanours.[100] It has also imposed a general rule to the effect that on all matters where a distinction had previously been made between felonies and misdemeanours, the law and practice applicable to misdemeanours at the commencement of the Act shall now apply to all offences.[101] It is arguable that this provision is sufficient to extend to felonies the power to impose a fine for misdemeanours. The better view, it is submitted, is that it falls short. In any event there is a provision later in the Act which goes a long way to providing the courts with a general power to impose a fine on conviction for an offence which used to be classed as a felony. It stipulates:

> "Where a person is convicted on indictment of any offence other than an offence for which the sentence is fixed by law, the court, if not precluded from doing so by its exercise of some other power, may impose a fine in lieu of or in addition to dealing with the offender in any other way in which the court has power to deal with him or her, subject however to any enactment limiting the amount of the fine that may be imposed or requiring the offender to be dealt with in a particular way."[102]

This combined with the court's power to impose a fine for any misdemeanour should provide sufficient legal basis for fines in respect of all offences, apart from those where the sentence is fixed by law. The general power, of course, may be limited by specific statutory provision which requires an offender to be dealt with in a particular way.

There remains the critical issue of the limits, if any, to a fine which may be imposed as punishment on conviction for any particular offence. At common

21–21

---

[98] There was an exception for manslaughter; see Offences against the Person Act 1861, s.5.
[99] Ryan and Magee, *op. cit.*, p.402.
[100] Criminal Law Act 1997, s.3(1).
[101] *ibid.* s.3(2).
[102] *ibid.* s.10(3).

law there did not appear to be any limit on the amount of a fine which could be imposed by a court on conviction for a misdemeanour.[103] In practice, of course, it was quite normal for statutory enactments to specify maximum fines which could be imposed on conviction for an offence or offences created by, or referred to in, the enactments concerned. Moreover, these provisions often set different maximum fines depending on whether the offender was convicted on indictment or summarily. This continues as standard practice today. In the case of summary offences, however, the legislature must be careful not to specify a fine that is so high that it has the effect of converting the offence in question into a non-minor offence within the meaning of Article 38 of the Constitution. If the offence is classified as non-minor the accused will have a constitutional right to trial by jury. The current practice is to specify a maximum fine of €1,905 for a summary conviction. There is no reason to believe from the extant case law that this figure is so high as to classify the offence concerned as non-minor. The problem does not arise with respect to indictable offences.[104] When creating offences the legislature does not always specify a fine as a possible punishment on conviction on indictment. Where it does it is likely that no limit will be specified. Even in those cases where the legislation does not prescribe a fine as a possible sentence a court, as has been seen above, will be able to impose a fine either in substitution for or in addition to the prescribed punishment, unless the punishment is fixed by law.[105]

The net effect is that for most statutory criminal offences which come before the courts today, for which the sentence is not fixed by law, the court will have the power to impose a fine and there may be a statutory ceiling on the amount of fine that may be imposed. Where there is such a statutory maximum, more often than not it will be laid down in the enactment creating the offence in question. For summary offences the maximum will have to be set at or below a level which does not bring the offence into the non-minor category. As yet there is no provision for linking fines to the wealth of offenders by means of a formula which would result in a wealthier offender paying a higher fine than a poorer offender for an identical offence.[106] Nevertheless, it would appear that a court should have regard to the means of the offender when it is tailoring a fine to suit the circumstances of an individual case. The District Court Rules specifically require the District Court, when fixing the amount of the penalty, to take into consideration, amongst other things, the means of the accused so far as they are known at the time. It can be expected that the higher courts will adopt a similar approach in any case where a fine is deemed the appropriate punishment.

---

[103] Ryan and Magee, *op. cit.*, p.402.

[104] €1,270 is specified as the maximum fine which may be imposed on summary conviction of certain indictable offences; see Criminal Justice Act 1951, s.4(1) and Criminal Procedure Act 1967, s.13(3)(a), as amended by Criminal Justice Act 1984, s.17.

[105] Criminal Law Act 1997, s.10(3).

[106] This possibility has been considered by the Law Reform Commission which expressed some doubts about its constitutionality in respect of minor offences being tried summarily; Law Reform Commission *Report on the Indexation of Fines* (Dublin, LRC 37, 1991)

It is also worth noting that where the court has the option of imposing a fine **21–22** on conviction, it will usually be free to impose a fine either by itself or in addition to some other punishment, including imprisonment. Typically, when an enactment is creating a criminal offence it will stipulate that any person found guilty of the offence shall be liable on conviction to imprisonment for a term not exceeding a specified period and/or a fine not exceeding a specified amount. The clear implication is that it is open to the court to impose both a fine and a term of imprisonment, subject to the specified maximum figures. Even without such clear statutory authority for the offence in question it is generally accepted that a court can impose a sentence consisting of both a fine and a term of imprisonment for any offence where it has the power to impose both sentences separately.[107] The major exception, of course, is any offence for which the sentence is fixed by law.

Children

Child and young offenders pose a special problem with respect to fines. Since they are less likely than adults to have an independent source of income there are obvious difficulties in using the fine as a suitable punishment. Nevertheless, child or young offenders can be fined within certain limits, and there is provision for the fines, etc., to be paid by parents or guardians. Currently, the relevant law is to be found in a confusing combination of the Summary Jurisdiction Over Children (Ireland) Act 1884, the Children Act 1908 and the Children Act 2001. The first two will be repealed by the 2001 Act as soon as the relevant provision comes into force. Until that happens, however, it is necessary to outline the relevant provisions of all three enactments. Indeed, it is worth noting that the substantive provisions of the 2001 Act concerning fines are almost wholly in force, although the provisions repealing the 1884 and 1908 Acts are not. Reference should also be made to the Criminal Justice Act 1993 which makes provision for compensation orders against offenders. It is dealt with more fully below under the heading of "Compensation".

The Summary Jurisdiction Over Children (Ireland) Act 1884 provides that the **21–23** maximum punishment for a child (under 15 years of age) convicted of a summary offence is a fine of €2.54.[108] Similarly, under the Children Act 1908, where a child is dealt with for an indictable offence in the District Court he or she may be fined or ordered to pay damages or costs which must be paid by the child's parent or guardian. Once again the maximum fine in respect of the child is €2.54. Where relevant, the amount of costs must not exceed the amount of the fine and fees paid by the prosecutor. If the parent or guardian can be found, and the court is not satisfied that he has not contributed to the commission of the offence through neglect, the court need not proceed to a

---

[107] See, in particular, Criminal Law Act 1997, s.10(3).
[108] S.6. The possibility of imprisonment up to a period of one month was removed by the Children Act 1908, s.134.

conviction.[109] If the charge against the child is proved, the parent or guardian may be required to pay damages or costs and to give security for the good behaviour of the child. The primary provisions governing the liability of the parents or guardian are set out in section 99 of the Children Act 1908.[110] As noted below, however, these have now been amended by the Criminal Justice Act 1993 which deals with compensation orders generally in criminal proceedings. The 1993 Act stipulates that the references to damages in section 99 of the 1908 Act shall be construed as including references to a compensation order under the 1993 Act.

These provisions with respect to children apply with only slight variations in respect of young offenders (15–17 years of age). Where a fine is imposed the young offender can be required to pay only if his parent or guardian cannot be found, or has not contributed to the commission of the offence by neglecting to exercise due care of the child. If the parent or guardian can be found, and the court is not satisfied that he has not contributed to the commission of the offence through neglect, the fine, etc., is paid by the parent or guardian. The maximum amount of fine or damages in respect of a young offender convicted summarily of an indictable offence is €12.70. No general limit is imposed in respect of summary offences.

The parent or guardian must be given an opportunity to attend court and be heard. Where a fine is imposed on a parent or guardian it may be recovered by distress or imprisonment as if the order had been made against the parent or guardian for an offence committed by them.[111]

These provisions with respect to child and young offenders, which are set to be repealed by the Children Act 2001, must be read in conjunction with the following provisions of the Children Act 2001 which are currently in force. In so far as there is any conflict or inconsistency between the provisions under the 2001 Act and the preceding provisions, the former must prevail as having been enacted later in time.

The Children Act 2001

21–24   Under the Children Act 2001 a fine is one of the options which the court can impose on a child (under 18 years of age) where it is satisfied of his or her guilt. Where the court has dealt with a child summarily for any offence and is of the opinion that the appropriate penalty is or includes a fine, the fine shall not exceed half of the amount which the District Court could impose on a person of full age and capacity on summary conviction for such an offence.[112] In effect, this is a substantial increase in the amount of a fine which can be imposed on a child. Many statutory offences carry a possible maximum fine of

---

[109] Children Act 1908, s.99.

[110] References to the maintenance debtor in the Family Law (Maintenance of Spouses and Children) Act 1976, in a case where s.99 of the Children Act 1908 applies, shall be construed as references to his parent or guardian; Criminal Justice Act 1993, s.7(2).

[111] If the parent is on service with the Defence Forces any such fines or costs may not be recovered by distress or imprisonment; Defence Act 1954, s.107(4).

[112] Children Act 2001, s.108.

€1,905 on summary conviction. It follows that the maximum fine which can be imposed on a child in summary proceedings for such an offence is €952.

When determining the amount of a fine to be imposed on a child the court, in addition to any other considerations, must have regard to the child's present and future means in so far as they appear or are known to the court.[113] For that purpose the court may require the child to give evidence as to those means and his or her financial commitments. The court must also have regard to these considerations when determining whether to award costs against a child and the amount of any such costs.[114] These provisions apply whether the court is dealing with the case summarily or on indictment.

Where a court orders a child to pay a fine, costs or compensation and the child is in default, the court shall not order the child to be detained in any case where the child would be liable to be committed to prison if he or she were a person of full age and capacity.[115] At first sight this would appear to be a rather peculiar way of stating that a court shall not order a child to be detained for non-payment of a fine, costs or compensation. Presumably, the intention is to make it clear that in respect of children there is no detention equivalent to committal to prison for adults in default. It does not follow that no further action can be taken against children in default. The legislation goes on to state that "*in lieu* of such an order" (presumably of detention) the court may make one or more of the following orders: (i) in the case of a fine, an order reducing its amount; (ii) an order allowing time, or further time, for payment of the fine, costs or compensation; and (iii) an order imposing a community sanction appropriate to the age of the child.[116] It is worth emphasising, however, that one or more of these options can be imposed only if the child would have been liable to be committed to prison if he or she was a person of full age and capacity.

Where an order is made under these provisions in respect of non-payment it **21–25** shall be deemed to be an order made on a finding of guilt.[117] Presumably a finding of guilt in this context includes the situation where the court is satisfied as to the defendant's guilt without actually proceeding to a conviction. Under the Children Act 2001 (and the Probation of Offenders Act 1907), a court can deal with a child offender in certain ways without actually proceeding to a conviction so long as it is satisfied as to his or her guilt.

Enforcement

Fines are payable to the Exchequer unless an order has been made directing that they be paid to some other body.[118] There is also provision enabling a

---

[113] *ibid.* s.109(a).
[114] *ibid.* s.109(b).
[115] *ibid.* s.110(1)(a).
[116] *ibid.* s.110(1)(b). This third option is not yet in force.
[117] *ibid.* s.110(2).
[118] Court Officers Act 1926, s.26. See J. Woods *District Court Practice and Procedure in Criminal Cases* (Woods, Limerick, 1994) at pp.236–238 for a list of such orders.

court to award part or all of a fine to an injured party who has instituted proceedings in certain consumer matters.[119] Failure to pay a fine can result in the defaulter being committed to prison if he or she is 18 years of age or older. The position with respect to children is noted above. In the case of summary conviction the periods of imprisonment relative to the amount of fine are as follows:[120]

Amount of fine	*Period of imprisonment*
Not exceeding €63.50	5 days
Exceeding €63.50, but not exceeding €317.50	15 days
Exceeding €317.50 but not exceeding €635	45 days
Exceeding €635	90 days

A fine for this purpose includes any compensation, costs or expenses, in addition to the fine itself. Where the fine is imposed on a corporate body following summary conviction and the body defaults in payment, the fine may be levied by distress and sale of its goods.[121]

6. Entering into a Recognisance

Jurisdiction

21–26   Courts of summary jurisdiction have long exercised a jurisdiction to bind persons over to keep the peace.[122] This jurisdiction has now been statutorily extended to judges of the Supreme Court and High Court, and to judges of the Circuit and District Court within their circuits or districts as the case may be.[123] Technically, the person concerned is asked to enter into a recognisance, with or without sureties, to keep the peace for a specified period. A refusal to do so will result in imprisonment for a defined period.[124] Failure to abide by the terms of the undertaking can result in the person concerned being brought back before the court for punishment and/or the forfeiture of the sum involved. The exercise of this jurisdiction is not predicated on a conviction. Indeed, it is frequently used as a means of dealing with a situation which has arisen and which may result in the commission of one or more criminal offences, usually breach of the peace.

Consequent on Conviction

Entering into a recognisance can be used either in addition to or instead of any other penalty in certain circumstances where there has been a conviction.[125] A

---

[119] Consumer Information Act 1978, s.17(3). See *Director of Consumer Affairs v. Sunshine Holidays* [1984] I.L.R.M. 551.

[120] Courts (No.2) Act 1986, s.2 and District Court Rules 1997, Ord.23.

[121] O'Malley, *op. cit.*, p.317.

[122] See O'Malley, *op. cit.*, pp.295–296 for background.

[123] Courts (Supplemental Provisions) Act 1961, s.54.

[124] *Gregory v. Windle* [1995] 1 I.L.R.M. 131.

[125] The Criminal Law Act 1997, s.10(4) confirms that on the conviction of a person for an offence incircumstances where the court has the power to bind the offender over to keep the peace or to be

distinction was drawn in this regard between felonies and misdemeanours. A person convicted of a felony (apart from murder) could be required, in addition to any other penalty imposed, to enter into a recognisance, with or without sureties, to keep the peace.[126] If he failed to find sureties, when required, it appears that he could be sentenced to imprisonment for a period not exceeding one year. Any person convicted of a misdemeanour could be required to enter into a recognisance, with or without sureties, to be of good behaviour for a reasonable time.[127] Once again he could be sentenced to imprisonment for up to one year if he failed to find sureties when required in the case of any offence under certain statutes authorising this procedure in the case of felony.[128]

Instead of Sentence

Where a person has been convicted on indictment the court has a jurisdiction   **21–27** at common law to release him without sentence on condition that he enters into a recognisance to appear before the court for sentencing on a certain day or on a day to be notified to him.[129] This option is available only with the consent of the offender in question.[130] It is most likely to be used in a case where, on the one hand, a custodial sentence might be appropriate given the track record of the accused in committing similar offences and, on the other hand, circumstances have arisen where there are real prospects that the accused will reform if given another chance. By inviting the offender to enter into a recognisance as an alternative to the immediate imposition of a custodial sentence the court can give him the breathing space necessary to build a new future for himself. At the same time by attaching strict conditions to the recognisance, thereby tailoring it to the particular circumstances that have arisen in the case, the court can ensure that society reaps the benefits while shouldering little of the risk. If the offender fails to abide by the conditions he will be brought back to court to be sentenced. If he abides by the conditions of the recognisance for the period specified the sentence will not be imposed at all.

A recognisance often features in the context of the exercise of the court's statutory jurisdiction to impose a probation order on an offender. This jurisdiction is considered next under the sub-heading of probation.

Procedure

Since binding over constitutes an interference with liberty, the court will have   **21–28** to follow appropriate fair procedures before using it in any individual case.

---

of good behaviour, the court can bind him over without sentencing him to a fine or imprisonment.

[126] Ryan and Magee, *op. cit.*, p.402.

[127] *R v. Dunn* 12 Q.B. 1026; *R v. Edgar* 23 Cox CC 558.

[128] Ryan and Magee cite the following statutory provisions: Malicious Damage Act 1861, s.73; Coinage Offences Act 1861, s.38; Offences against the Person Act 1861, s.71; Forgery Act 1913, s.12; and the Larceny Act 1916, s.37(5).

[129] *R v. Hodges* (1967) 57 Cr.App.R. 361. See also Probation of Offenders Act 1907, s.1(2).

[130] The co-operation of others may also be required depending on the particular conditions that the

The person affected must be given the opportunity to be heard and witnesses should normally be heard with a view to establishing the relevant facts.[131] Indeed, the Criminal Justice Administration Act 1914 states that in District Court proceedings where binding over orders are being considered the defendants are entitled to call witnesses and tender evidence.[132]

Constitutionality

Given the nature of a binding over order, particularly in respect of a person who has not been convicted of an offence, it might be thought that it constitutes an unconstitutional form of preventative detention. This issue was addressed by the High Court in *Gregory Windle*,[133] albeit in the context of defendants who were convicted of offences. In that case the defendants were convicted of public order offences and were ordered to enter into recognisances with personal and independent sureties to keep the peace and be of good behaviour for six months. They were to be imprisoned until they entered into the recognisance. Failure to enter into the recognisance or to comply with its terms would result in imprisonment for one month. On an application for judicial review of the order the defendants argued that it amounted to an unconstitutional form of preventative detention in that it was punishing them for offences which they might commit in future. They relied by analogy on the decision of the Supreme Court in *People (Attorney General) v. O'Callaghan*,[134] which declared that a denial of bail in order to prevent the commission of offences in the future was unconstitutional. However, O'Hanlon J. found that there were circumstances in which it would be justifiable to deprive the individual of his or her liberty even though such action was not consequential on a criminal conviction. He considered that the power to bind over was beneficial and necessary to give effect to court orders. When exercised with prudence and discretion it would not give rise to any conflict with the constitution.

7. Probation

Introduction

21–29 The Probation of Offenders Act 1907 empowers courts to impose a probation order on an offender in certain circumstances. Broadly speaking, a probation order is a formal warning to a person that if he does not keep the peace and abide by conditions imposed by the court for a specified period he is liable to be brought before the court for punishment. Typically, but not invariably, the court will appoint a probation officer to supervise the person's compliance with the terms of his or her probation order, to report to the court on his or her

---

court might wish to impose on a recognisance in any individual case; see, *e.g.*, *R v. Williams* (1982) 75 Cr.App.R. 378.
[131] *Clarke v. Hogan* [1995] 1 I.R. 318.
[132] Criminal Justice Administration Act 1914, s.43(13).
[133] [1995] 1 I.L.R.M. 131.
[134] [1966] I.R. 501.

progress, to provide advice and guidance and to help him or her find employment.

On Conviction on Indictment

Where a person is convicted on indictment of any offence punishable by imprisonment, the Probation of Offenders Act 1907 gives the court the power to discharge the offender conditionally on his or her entering into a recognisance, with or without sureties, to be of good behaviour and to appear for sentence when called upon at any time during such period, not exceeding three years, as may be specified in the order. [135] This option is generally available where the court is of the opinion that it is inexpedient to inflict any punishment, or anything other than a nominal punishment, or that it is expedient to release the offender on probation. When considering whether to exercise the option the court will have regard to: the character, antecedents, age, health or mental condition of the person concerned and the trivial nature of the offence or the extenuating circumstances under which the offence was committed. While the use of a probation order is clearly feasible in the case of a serious offence, it is much more likely to feature where the commission of the offence has not caused serious harm. Equally, there is no absolute rule against the repeated use of a probation order to deal with the same offender.[136] However, the Court of Criminal Appeal has advised against such a practice where the offences in question are serious.[137] Although it is not specifically stated in the Act, it is apparent that a probation order cannot be issued where the punishment for the offence in question is fixed by law. Moreover, some enactments creating new criminal offences specifically stipulate that the terms of the Probation Act cannot be applied to them.[138] It is also worth noting that a probation order can be applied to a corporate body.[139]

Summary Jurisdiction

The District Court can also deal with an offender on conviction by means of a **21–30** probation order. Equally, where a person appears before the District Court charged with an offence punishable by that court, and the court thinks that the charge is proved it may, without proceeding to conviction, make an order dismissing the charge or discharging the offender conditionally on his or her entering into a recognisance, with or without sureties, to be of good behaviour and to appear for conviction and sentence when called upon at any time during such period, not exceeding three years, as may be specified in the

---

[135] Probation of Offenders Act 1907, s.1(2).

[136] Equally, the absence of a previous conviction does not confer an entitlement to dismissal or discharge under s.1(1) of the Probation Act 1907 in the District Court; *Gilroy v. Brennan* [1926] I.R. 482.

[137] *People v. Buckley* (1959) Frewen 190.

[138] See, *e.g.* hijacking and endangering aviation under the Air Navigation and Transport Acts 1973 and 1975; drink driving and related offences under the Road Traffic Act 1961, ss.49 and 50 and Road Traffic Act 1994, ss.13–15. For further examples, see Woods at p.406. Also certain summary offences cannot benefit from the terms of the Act.

[139] *Shannon Regional Fisheries Board v. Cavan County Council* [1996] 3 I.R. 267.

order.[140] These options are available to the court where it is of the opinion having regard to: (a) the character, antecedents, age, health or mental condition of the person charged, (b) the trivial nature of the offence, or (c) the extenuating circumstances under which the offence was committed, that it is inexpedient to inflict any punishment other than a nominal punishment, or that it is expedient to release the offender on probation.[141] If the accused fails to abide by the terms of the order he or she may be brought back before the court for punishment. It is worth emphasising that the District Court can impose a probation order without actually proceeding to a formal conviction. It is sufficient that the court thinks the charge is proved. Equally, it can dismiss the charge altogether in such circumstances without imposing a probation order.[142]

Court Order

In any case where the court exercises the probation option it will make an order discharging the offender on condition that he or she enter into a recognisance with or without sureties, to be of good behaviour and to appear for sentence when called on at any time during such period, not exceeding three years, which may be specified in the order.[143] In addition to any such order the court may order the offender to pay such damages for injury or compensation for loss, and to pay such costs of proceedings, as the court thinks reasonable.[144] The court may also impose a condition that the offender be placed under the supervision of a person named in the order for the period of the order and it may impose further conditions to secure that supervision.[145] In addition, the court may impose conditions with respect to residence, abstention from intoxicating liquor and any other matters as the court may, having regard to the particular circumstances of the case, consider necessary for the prevention of a repetition of the same offence or the commission of other offences.[146] The court must supply the offender with a notice stating in simple terms any conditions he is required to observe under the order.[147]

Supervision

21–31 Where an offender is dealt with by way of a probation order he will be allocated to the supervision of a probation and welfare officer for the period specified in the order. There is no precise definition of what this supervision actually entails. However, an accurate picture is reflected in the supervisory duties of a probation officer as set out in section 4 of the Probation of Offenders Act 1907. They are:

---

[140] Probation of Offenders Act 1907, s.1(1).

[141] Any one of these circumstances will suffice; see *McClelland v. Brady* [1918] 2 I.R. 63.

[142] This is not the equivalent of an acquittal; *Attorney General v. Cullen* (1951) 86 I.L.T.R. 26; *Mulhall v. O'Donnell* [1989] I.L.R.M. 367; Courts of Justice Act 1953, s.33.

[143] Probation of Offenders Act 1907, s.1(1) and (2).

[144] *ibid.* s.1(3), and Criminal Justice Act 1993, 6(12(b).

[145] *ibid.* s.2(1).

[146] *ibid.* s.2(2), as amended by Criminal Justice Administration Act 1914, s.8.

[147] *ibid.* s.2(3).

(a) to visit or receive reports from the person under supervision at such reasonable intervals as may be specified in the probation order or, subject thereto, as the probation officer thinks fit;

(b) to see that he observes the conditions of his recognisance;

(c) to report to the court as to his behaviour;

(d) to advise, assist, and befriend him, and, when necessary, to endeavour to find him suitable employment.[148]

Flexibility

Clearly, the probation order imposed on conviction is an exceptionally flexible sentencing instrument designed to cater specifically for the rehabilitative needs of the individual offender and society's interest in preventing any further offending by the person subject to the order. The court has the power to mould the order to cater for the particular circumstances of each individual case. It may happen, of course, that subsequent events necessitate some alteration to the order to take account of the new developments. Accordingly, there is provision for the court to vary its order in a case where the offender is under the supervision of a probation officer. If it appears to the court, on the application of the probation officer, that the terms of the recognisance should be varied, it may summons the offender before it and vary the terms of the recognisance unless the offender shows cause on why the variation should not be made. The variation may extend (up to a maximum of three years from the original order), or diminish the duration, alter the conditions or insert new conditions. Equally, the court may discharge the recognisance if it is satisfied that the conduct of the offender has been such as to make it unnecessary that he or she be kept under supervision any longer.[149] Any such variation can be effected only consequent to an application by the probation officer.

Breach

Ultimately, a probation order is a mechanism whereby the offender is given a **21–32** chance to avoid a more punitive form of sanction. In order to get that chance he or she must enter into certain undertakings with respect to his or her future behaviour. It follows that if the offender subsequently breaches that undertaking, not only is he or she in breach of a court order but he or she is also exposed to punishment for the original offence. Accordingly, if information is sworn that an offender has failed to observe any of the conditions of his or her recognisance the court which bound him or her over, or any District Court judge, may issue a warrant for arrest or summons him or her and his or her sureties, if any, to attend before the court. If the offender is arrested and

---

[148] For more on the role of a probation officer, see *First Report of the Expert Group on the Probation and Welfare Service* (Government Stationery Office, Dublin, 1998).

[149] Probation of Offenders Act 1907, s.5; as substituted by Criminal Justice Administration Act 1914, s.9.

brought first before the District Court he or she may be remanded in custody or on bail to appear before the court which bound him or her over.[150] The District Court may then proceed to sentence him or her for the original offence if it is satisfied that he or she has failed to observe any condition of his or her recognisance.[151] Equally, it may send the offender to an industrial school if he or she is within the appropriate age group.

Children and Young Offenders

Finally, it is worth mentioning two probation options which apply specifically to young offenders (under 17 years of age), in addition to the provisions of the Probation of Offenders Act 1907 generally as discussed above. First, a child or young person may be placed in the care of the Court Probation Officer.[152] In the case of a child (under 15 years of age), the officer must be named in the order, unless there is good reason to the contrary. The second option consists of Probation Hostels for young persons. These cater primarily for boys and girls aged between 14 and 16 years old, who have appeared before the courts on criminal charges and have been given the benefit of the Probation Act. If the offender agrees to reside in one of these hostels under the supervision of trained staff, the court may apply the Probation Act on condition that he or she actually resides in the hostel. Schooling, where applicable, will continue as normal. If the individual concerned has left school a programme of work or apprenticeship will be provided. Where an individual is resident in one of these hostels he or she will continue to be subject to the supervision of the court through the Probation Liaison Officer. In practice, this tends to mean that most of these cases arise from the District Court.

Part 9 of the Children Act 2001 introduces a range of probation options for children (under 18 years of age) but the relevant provisions are not yet in force.

8. Detention of Young Offenders

Introduction

21–33   There are a number of restrictions applicable to the imprisonment or detention of young offenders which do not apply to adult offenders. Equally, there are a number of detention options available for young offenders which are not applicable to adults. These are based primarily in the Children Act 1908, as amended. Although the current measures governing custodial sentences for young offenders are set to be repealed and replaced by the Children Act 2001, the relevant provisions in the 2001 Act have not yet been brought into force. Accordingly, the current law in force will be described first, followed by an outline of the relevant provisions in the 2001 Act.

---

[150] *ibid.* s.6.
[151] *ibid.* s.6(5). *R v. Spratling* [1911] 1 K.B. 77.
[152] Probation of Offenders Act 1907, s.2.

Age Categories

At the outset it is necessary to identify the various categories of young offenders as particular options and restrictions normally apply by reference to distinct categories. Generally, a distinction is drawn in the legislation between "children" and "young persons". A child is a person under the age of 15 years, while a young person is a person of at least 15 years of age and under the age of 17. Although they are not given a distinct title there is distinct statutory provision for the punishment of young offenders between the ages of 17 and 19 years. There are also some provisions making specific provision for age bands which straddle two or more of these categories.

Where it is necessary to determine the age of an offender in the context of punishment the relevant date appears to be that on which the sentence is passed and not the date of the actual crime.[153] The court should hear evidence on oath as to the age of the offender.[154] However, the order of the court will not necessarily be invalidated where the age is incorrectly stated, even if the court has been misled. Its determination of age would appear to be final.[155]

Detention in Industrial and Reformatory Schools

Certified industrial schools (generally referred to as 'residential homes') and reformatory schools provide the primary custodial options for offenders under 17 years of age. Their primary function is education and rehabilitation, and as such they can be distinguished from prison or even detention in St Patrick's Institution (see below).[156] Industrial schools were established originally for children in need of care. They still have that mission today, although they also accommodate child offenders.[157] Reformatory schools by comparison cater solely for offenders. Nevertheless, there is no essential difference between them in terms of their primary purpose.[158]

21–34

An industrial school provides the only custodial option for a child under 12 years of age. The court can send an offender below 12 years of age to an industrial school if it thinks it is expedient to deal with him or her in that manner without proceeding to convict him or her. An offender between the ages of 12 and 15 years may be sent to an industrial school, but only if: he or she has not been convicted previously, the manager of the school is willing to receive him or her, and the court is satisfied that his or her character and antecedents are such that he or she will not exercise an evil influence over other children in the school.[159] Otherwise the option is a reformatory school.

---

[153] *R v. Fitt* [1919] 2 I.R. 35.
[154] Children Act 1908, s.123(1), as amended by the Children Act 1941, s.27. See Children Act 2001, s.269. See also, *State (Kenny) v. O'hUadhaigh* [1979] I.R. 1.
[155] Children Act 1908, s.123(1), as amended by the Children Act 1941, s.27. See also, *State (Kenny) v. O'hUadhaigh* [1979] I.R. 1.
[156] See the description of Trinity House Reformatory School given by Barr J. in *J v. Delap* [1989] I.R. 167 at 169–170. But note *State (Sheerin) v. Kennedy* [1966] I.R. 379 where it was held that there was no practical difference between imprisonment and detention in St Patrick's Institution.
[157] There are only two certified industrial schools for boys, St Joseph's in Clonmel and St Lawrence's in Finglas. There are none for girls.
[158] *McM v. Manager of Trinity House* [1995] 2 I.L.R.M. 546.
[159] Children Act 1908, s.58(1).

Where the child has been sent to an industrial school as an alternative to a reformatory school, the manager of the school can ask the Minister for Education and Science for an order transferring the child to a reformatory school.[160]

Where a child is sent to an industrial school it can be for such period as the court deems proper. However, he may not be detained there beyond the age of 16 years unless the Minister for Education and Science, with the consent of the child's parents or guardian, directs that he should stay on for a further year for the purpose of completing his education.[161]

An offender between the ages of 12 and 17 years may be sent on conviction to a certified reformatory school.[162] The legislation imposes minimum and maximum periods of detention in these schools of two years and four years respectively. However, a person cannot be detained there beyond his or her 19th birthday.[163] This may be extended up to a maximum of 21 years of age in any individual case where the Minister for Justice, Equality and Law Reform feels that it is necessary for his or her protection and welfare. If there is no place for an offender in a reformatory school the offender must be brought back before the court for a further order.[164] It would appear, however, that the only options in such a case are: detention for a maximum period of one month in a place of detention, but only if the offence in question is punishable with imprisonment or the offender is in default of fines, damages or costs for which he or she could be imprisoned if he or she were an adult;[165] detention in St Patrick's Institutions if the offender is male and at least 16 years of age; and imprisonment, but only if the offender is so depraved or unruly as to be unfit for detention elsewhere.

Detention in St Patrick's Institution

21–35   Detention in St Patrick's Institution, a former borstal institution located beside Mountjoy Prison in Dublin, is an option for offenders between the ages of 17 and 21 years.[166] There are several possibilities for committal to St Patrick's. Under the Criminal Justice Act 1960 a person between the ages of 17 and 21 years who has been convicted of an offence for which he is liable

---

[160] Under s. 69 of the Children Act 1908 the Minister has the power to transfer persons from one industrial school to another and from one reformatory school to another. He can transfer an offender under the age of 14 years from a reformatory to an industrial school. He can also transfer a child over 12 years of age from an industrial school to a reformatory school where the child is found to be exercising an evil influence over the other children in the school. This last option was considered in some detail and found to be constitutional in *McM v. Manager of Trinity House* [1995] 2 I.L.R.M. 546.

[161] Children Act 1908, s.65 as extended; Children Act 1941, s.12 and Children (Amendment) Act 1949, s.6.

[162] Children Act 1908, ss.57 and 58, as amended by the Children Act 1941, s.10.

[163] Children Act 1908, ss.65 and 68, as amended by the Children Act 1941, ss.11 and 14. Since detention in a reformatory is not the equivalent of imprisonment the statutory limit of one year (or aggregate of two years) imprisonment on the jurisdiction of the District Court does not apply; *J v. Delap* [1989] I.R. 167.

[164] Children Act 1908, s.57.

[165] *ibid.* s.106. O'Malley notes that places of detention under this provision were intended as remand centres for children and young persons, but they are being used as a stop-gap measure for convicted offenders; *op. cit.*, at 228.

[166] Criminal Justice Act 1960, s.12.

to be sent to prison may be sent instead to St Patrick's for the period for which he would otherwise have been sent to prison.[167] A person between the ages of 16 and 17 years may also be sent to St Patrick's in these circumstances provided the court considers that none of the other methods for dealing with the case are suitable.[168] The most likely situation here is the unavailability of a suitable place in a reformatory school. There is another variation for an offender between the ages of 16 and 21 years who has been convicted on indictment. He may be sentenced to a minimum of two and a maximum of three years in St Patrick's if it appears to the court that by reason of his criminal habits or tendencies or associations with persons of bad character it is expedient that he should be subject to such detention for such term and under such instruction and discipline as appears most conducive to his reformation and the repression of crime.[169] This last option is only available when the qualifying circumstances are present. Where they are present the court may apply the minimum and maximum option, but it is not bound to do so.[170] It can still resort to the other options which are not subject to a minimum and maximum.

St Patrick's Institution is a custodial unit whose primary mission is the reform of offenders sent to it.[171] It is an alternative to, as opposed to the equivalent of, imprisonment.[172] The intention is that each offender will benefit from a programme of training which caters for his particular circumstances and is aimed at steering him away from future criminal activity. Accordingly, a judge must exercise discretion in sentencing an offender to a term of detention in St Patrick's. Just because the offender falls within the eligible age category it does not follow that such a sentence would be appropriate. The judge should satisfy himself or herself that the particular offender would be likely to benefit from the curriculum in St Patrick's and would not prevent other inmates from benefiting from it.[173] For this reason a sentence of detention should not be ordered to commence from the expiry of a sentence of imprisonment currently being served. By the time the offender had completed the sentence of imprisonment he might not satisfy the criteria for detention in St Patrick's.

Although detention in St Patrick's Institution can be distinguished from imprisonment on the basis of its emphasis on rehabilitation and reform. It **21–36**

---

[167] *ibid.* s.13(1). See *People (Attorney General) v. Boylan* [1963] I.R. 238.

[168] *ibid.* s.13(2).

[169] Prevention of Crime Act 1908, s.1(1), as amended by Criminal Justice Administration Act 1914, s.11(1).

[170] *People (Attorney General) v. Boylan* [1963] I.R. 238.

[171] See *State (White) v. Martin* (1977) 111 I.L.T.R. 21.

[172] In *State (White) v. Martin* (1977) 111 I.L.T.R. 21 it was held that detention was radically different from imprisonment. But note *State (Sheerin) v. Kennedy* [1966] I.R. 379 where it was held that there was no practical difference between detention and imprisonment. Gannon J. in *State (Craven) v. Frawley* [1980] I.R. 1 attempts to reconcile the two by pointing out that the Supreme Court in *White* was emphasising that detention should be chosen only in special circumstances. Equally, it may be that the Supreme Court in *Sheerin* was merely stating the obvious, namely that both options involved deprivation of liberty within a disciplined regime.

[173] See Henchy J. in *State (White) v. Martin* [1977] 111 I.L.T.R. 21 at p.24.

does not follow that a longer sentence might be imposed in order to promote those objectives. The judge should first decide the term of imprisonment that would be appropriate in the case having regard to the offence. This term should not be exceeded if he or she then decides that detention in St Patrick's would be a more appropriate option than prison for the offender.[174]

Detention for Female Offenders

As noted above, St Patrick's Institution caters only for male offenders. As yet, there is no equivalent provision for female offenders. Accordingly, once they have reached the age of 17 years they must either be sent to prison or released. Indeed, the lack of places in certified schools for females between the ages of 15 and 17 years means that they too can find themselves in prison solely because there is no other suitable accommodation available.

Re-routing to Prison

A juvenile offender who has been sentenced to a period of detention in St Patrick's Institution can be re-routed to prison in certain circumstances. There are at least two possibilities. First, whenever the Minister for Justice, Equality and Law Reform is of the opinion that it is necessary to do so for the purpose of relieving congestion in St Patrick's Institution he may direct the transfer to prison of any offender, not under 17 years of age, serving a sentence in St Patrick's, whose transfer is in his opinion necessary.[175] Where the Minister exercises this power in any individual case he must commute the unexpired residue of the term of detention to such term of imprisonment as he may determine, not exceeding the unexpired residue. It must be noted, however, that this transfer power is operative only for such period as the Minister may specify after consultation with the Visiting Committee of St Patrick's Institution.

21–37   The second possibility arises where a person detained in St Patrick's Institution is reported by the Visiting Committee to be incorrigible or to be exercising a bad influence on other inmates of the Institution. In this event, the Minister for Justice, Equality and Law Reform may commute the term of detention to a term of imprisonment, not exceeding the residue of the term of detention.[176] In *State (Craven) v. Frawley*,[177] the High Court considered that the transfer power may be necessary in the interests of the health of the prisoner or the better administration of the prisons. As such it was of an administrative as distinct from a judicial character. The vesting of the power in the Minister did not involve a constitutional conflict with the judicial function in the administrative of justice. Before exercising the power,

---

[174] *People (Attorney General) v. Boylan* [1963] I.R. 238; *State (White) v. Martin* [1977] 111 I.L.T.R. 21. But *State (Clinch) v. Connellan* [1985] I.R. 597 can be interpreted as raising a doubt over whether this point has been finally settled.

[175] Prisons Act 1970, s.7.

[176] Prevention of Crime Act 1908, s.7, as adapted. See also, *State (Holden) v. Governor of Portlaoise Prison* [1964] I.R. 80; *State (Dickenson) v. Kelly* [1974] I.R. 73.

[177] [1980] I.R. 1.

however, the Minister must have received an informed decision from the Visiting Committee, as distinct from a personal recommendation from the chairman of the committee.[178] Moreover, the Minister's order must correlate with the report of the Visiting Committee. In *State (Brien) v. Kelly*,[179] for example, an order was quashed because it purported to be made on the basis that the offender was incorrigible while the Visiting Committee's report was to the effect that he was exercising a bad influence over the other inmates. The Minister's order must also reflect the commutation of the unexpired residue of the term of detention to a term of imprisonment.[180] It is worth noting that a commutation order cannot be made retrospectively. The offender must actually be serving a sentence of detention at the time it is commuted to a sentence of imprisonment.

It is also worth noting that the Minister has a general power to transfer prisoners from one prison to another, from a prison to a place of detention and from a place of detention to a prison.[181] This would appear to permit the Minister to transfer an offender from St Patrick's Institution to prison without any preconditions or strings attached. It is submitted, however, that this general power must be interpreted subject to the specific provisions dealing with the transfer of offenders from St Patrick's to prison. To hold otherwise would deprive the more specific provisions of any meaningful effect.

Unruly or Depraved Character

A child (under 15 years of age) cannot be sentenced to a term of imprisonment under any circumstances. A young person (between 15 and 17 years of age) may not be sentenced to imprisonment, or committed to prison in default of payment of a fine, damages or costs,[182] unless the court certifies that the young person is of so unruly a character that he or she cannot be detained in a place of detention provided under Part V of the Children Act 1908, or that he or she is so depraved in character as not to be a fit person to be detained under the Act.[183] These provisions are interpreted strictly in the sense that a young person cannot be sentenced to imprisonment unless a certificate has been duly issued. In *Greene v. Governor of Mountjoy Prison*,[184] for example, the Supreme Court quashed a District Court order sentencing a young person to imprisonment because the certificate stated that she was so depraved a character as not to be a fit person to be detained under Part V of

---

[178] *State (Holden) v. Governor of Portlaoise* [1964] I.R. 80; *State (Dickinson) v. Kelly* [1964] I.R. 73.

[179] [1970] I.R. 69.

[180] *State (Holden) v. Governor of Portlaoise* [1964] I.R. 80.

[181] Prisons Act 1970, s.5.

[182] See now Children Act 2001, s.110 which precludes detention for default and provides other means with dealing with default.

[183] Children Act 1908, s.102(3). The constitutionality of this provision was upheld in the High Court in *J.G. v. Governor of Mountjoy Prison* [1991] 1 I.R. 373 essentially on the ground that it could be seen as protecting the rights of children by prohibiting their imprisonment except in limited circumstances. On appeal the constitutional issue was specifically left open by the Supreme Court which disposed of the case on other grounds.

[184] [1996] 2 I.L.R.M. 16.

the Act, whereas it should have stated that she was not a fit person to be detained under the Act. This decision seems to imply that a young person cannot be sentenced to imprisonment on the ground that he or she is of so unruly a character that he or she cannot be detained under the Act, but could be sentenced to imprisonment on the ground that he or she is of so unruly a character that he or she cannot be detained in a place of detention under Part V of the Act. Equally, the young person could not be sentenced to imprisonment on the ground that he or she was so depraved a character that he or she could not be detained in a place of detention under Part V of the Act, but could be sentenced to imprisonment if he or she was so depraved a character that he or she was not a fit person to be detained under the Act. Whatever the rational justification for these fine distinctions, they do attach some importance to the distinction between an unruly character and a depraved character.[185]

21–38   In *State (Holland) v. Kennedy*,[186] the Supreme Court considered the requirements for a certificate of unruliness of character. In that case a District Court judge had issued a certificate without conducting any enquiry or receiving any evidence as to the general character of the accused. The judge based the certificate on the circumstances and nature of the vicious assault for which the accused was before the court. In quashing the certificate, the Supreme Court explained the correct approach to the issuing of a certificate:

> "What the respondent had to be satisfied of before she could sentence this young person to prison was that he *is* of so unruly a character (not that he *has been* so unruly) that he *cannot* be (not that he *ought not* to be) detained in the provided place of detention. The only evidence bearing on that question was evidence of the part played by him in the assault. While that evidence showed that on that occasion he had been unruly, indeed violently aggressive, there was no evidence that at the time of sentence he was of so unruly a character that he could not be detained in the place of detention provided under the statute . . . The bare facts of the assault, unrelated to any evidence of a behavioural pattern, could not justify what was in effect a prognosis that this young person would not be amenable [to the regime in the place of detention]."[187]

The court clearly emphasised the importance of considering the character of the offender at the time of sentencing. This cannot be determined solely on the basis of the facts of the offence for which he was before the court. Moreover, it is not sufficient that the offender ought not to be detained in the place of detention. His unruly character must be such that he cannot be detained there.

21–39   The meaning of a "depraved character" was considered by the High Court in *J.G. v. Governor of Mountjoy Prison*.[188] Drawing on dictionary definitions Blayney J. seemed to accept an interpretation which depicted a depraved

---

[185] See comment of O'Malley, *op. cit.*, p.234.
[186] [1977] I.R. 193.
[187] [1977] I.R. 193 at 200–201.
[188] [1991] I.R. 373.

person as being "morally bad" or "immoral, unprincipled, vicious, wicked". The learned judge went on to conclude that the District Court judge was correct in finding that the two 15 year old girls in question were of depraved character. This finding appears to be based on the fact that one girl had 14 previous convictions and the other girl had 12, all for property and assault offences. In light of the decision in *State (Holland) v. Kennedy*,[189] it is at least arguable that such facts are insufficient in themselves to establish that an offender is so depraved a character as not to be a fit person to be detained under the 1908 Act. It is respectfully submitted that it would be necessary for the judge to go further and consider not just whether the criminal records were an accurate reflection of the girls' characters at the time of sentencing and whether they were such that they could not be detained under the 1908 Act. It may be, of course that the District Court judge pursued this course in the instant case.

It is apparent from *State (Holland) v. Kennedy*,[190] that a court should hear sworn evidence before proceeding to certify a young person to be of an unruly or depraved character. Reports from social workers may also be considered with the consent of the defence so long as they are made available to the defence for comment and submission. Equally, if the District Court or Circuit Court proceeds to certify a young person to be of such a character in this context without first hearing sworn evidence, its decision and sentence may be quashed by certiorari.[191] Conditional reports from social workers may also be considered with the consent of the defence, so long as they are made available to the defence for comment and submission.

Limits on Term of Imprisonment

Where a court sentences a young person to imprisonment on the grounds of an unruly or depraved character, the maximum term of imprisonment prescribed by section 106 of the Children Act 1908 does not apply (where no place available in a certified reformatory). However, if the offender (under 17 years of age) is dealt with in the District Court for an indictable offence, the maximum term of imprisonment that may be imposed is three months.[192] It is worth noting in this context that the District Court has jurisdiction to deal with a child or young person for any indictable offence, apart from homicide.[193] Surprisingly, there is no similar restriction on the length of prison sentence which a District Court may impose on an offender under 17 years of age for a summary offence. It would appear that in these cases the normal limits on the jurisdiction of the District Court apply irrespective of the age of the offender.

---

[189] [1977] I.R. 193.

[190] [1977] I.R. 193. See also, *State (Donoghue) v. Kennedy* [1979] I.L.R.M. 109.

[191] *ibid.* In the case of the Central Criminal Court the remedy would be by way of appeal or an application for habeas corpus.

[192] Summary Jurisdiction Over Children (Ireland) Act 1884, s.5(1).

[193] *ibid.* s.5(1), as amended by Children Act 1908, s.133(6).

Sentence for Murder

21–40   The sentencing of a person under 17 years of age for murder is a special case. Section 103 of the Children Act 1908, as originally formulated, stated that a court should not pronounce a sentence of death against a person under 17 years of age. Instead, it should order that he or she be detained during His Majesty's pleasure. In effect this was an indefinite sentence. In *State (0) v. O'Brien*,[194] the Supreme Court upheld the constitutionality of section 103 but only on the basis that it was to be interpreted as authorising the court to determine the length of the prison sentence. The offender shall be detained in such place and on such conditions as the Minister for Justice, Equality and Law Reform may direct, but the sentence itself was an indeterminate sentence which could be brought to an end at any time by the court. The offender was being detained at the pleasure of the court, not the executive.[195] While the sentence could be remitted pursuant to Article 13 of the Constitution and related statutory provisions, it could not be commuted by the executive.

It now appears that a court can also impose a determinate sentence in the case of a young person convicted of murder. In *People (DPP) v. Sacco and a Minor*,[196] the defendants, one of whom was under 17 years of age, were charged with murder. The Central Criminal Court sat to consider as a preliminary issue its sentencing powers with respect to a young person convicted of murder. It concluded that it had the power to sentence a young person under section 103 to an indeterminate sentence, in which case it would retain *seisin*, or to a determinate sentence. In the event the young person pleaded guilty and the court proceeded to sentence her to seven years detention. Accordingly, she was committed to Oberstown House Reformatory School, where she could be detained until her seventeenth birthday (about ten weeks later). After that the only custodial option was prison as there was no female equivalent to St Patrick's Institution where the offender could be detained until her twenty-first birthday. When the case came before the Court of Criminal Appeal, the court confirmed that a determinate sentence was an available option.[197] However, given the absence of a suitable place for the detention of the offender between her seventeenth and twenty-first birthdays, the court suspended the balance of the seven year term and ordered that a programme of rehabilitation be put in place for her with the aid of the probation service and her family. From a jurisprudential perspective the key point is the recognition that a determinate sentence is now an available option for young persons convicted of murder.

9. Reforms under the Children Act 2001

Introduction

21–41   The provisions in the Children Act 1908 (as amended) and the Summary Jurisdiction Over Children Act 1884 governing the detention, imprisonment

---

[194] [1973] I.R. 50.
[195] See also, *Gallagher v. DPP* [1991] 1 I.R. 31.
[196] Unreported, Central Criminal Court, March 23, 1998.
[197] *People (DPP) v. a Minor* unreported, Court of Criminal Appeal, July 13, 1998.

and custodial sentencing powers with respect to children and young persons are set to be repealed once the relevant provisions of the Children Act 2001 come into force. In their place will come a new body of provisions offering the courts a wide range of non-custodial options and fewer (but very familiar) custodial options. The custodial options are detention in a children detention school (nearest equivalent to St Patrick's) or in a children detention centre (direct replacement of industrial and reformatory schools). Imprisonment is not available as an option for children under 18 years of age.

General Principles

The Act sets out a number of general principles to guide courts in dealing with children who are either charged with or found guilty of criminal offences. These principles apply to all courts and not just the Children Court. These principles are heavily biased towards the rehabilitation as distinct from the punishment of child offenders. At the same time they do not ignore the interests of the victim and the need to respect the fundamental rights of the child as an autonomous citizen.

Although the principles are not specifically presented in any hierarchical order it is worth noting that the first one concerns the court's duty to respect the rights of the child as an autonomous individual. Any court, when dealing with children charged with offences must have regard to the principle that children have rights and freedoms before the law equal to those enjoyed by adults.[198] In particular, they have the right to be heard and/or participate in any proceedings of the court that can affect them. A related principle is that criminal proceedings cannot be used solely to provide any assistance or service needed to care for or protect a child.[199] It follows that a child cannot be treated as a criminal even to ensure his or her basic entitlements of bodily safety, food, clothing, shelter, medical care, education and a modicum of family life. Equally, the child's rights to due process in criminal proceedings cannot be set aside or watered down in order to pursue paternalistic goals of rehabilitation which are likely to be in the longer term interests of the child.

Rehabilitation takes centre stage in the punishment of a child for a criminal offence. It would appear that the following principles apply not just in respect of sentencing in a court but also in the formulation of an action plan by a family conference. Any penalty imposed on a child for an offence should cause as little interference as possible with the child's legitimate activities and pursuits.[200] It should take the form most likely to maintain and promote the development of the child and the least restrictive form that is appropriate in the circumstances. Clearly, the emphasis should be on community sanctions which can be integrated with the child's normal and healthy development and activities. Equally, any penalty should be positive rather than negative in terms of the child's development. A period of detention should be imposed only as a last resort.

---

[198] Children Act 2001, s.96(1)(a).
[199] *ibid.* s.96(1)(b).
[200] *ibid.* s.96(2).

Unusually, the legislation actually sets out the reasons why such a rehabilitative approach to the punishment of a child is desirable wherever possible. Presumably, these reasons should also be used as a guide to the matters that should be taken into account when designing a penalty to meet the objectives set out above. They are: to allow the education, training or employment of children to proceed without interruption; to preserve and strengthen the relationship between children and their parents and other family members; to foster the ability of families to develop their own means of dealing with offending by their children; and to allow children reside in their own homes.

21–42   Although rehabilitation is clearly a primary aim in the sentencing of child offenders this should not stop a court from imposing a lighter sentence on a child than it would on an adult for a similar offence. The legislation specifically permits a court to take into consideration as mitigating factors a child's age and level of maturity in determining the nature of any penalty, unless the penalty is fixed by law.[201] It goes on to say that the penalty imposed on a child should be no greater than that which would be appropriate in the case of an adult who commits an offence of the same kind, and may be less where so provided for by Part 9 of the Act.[202] The implication of these two provisions, when read together with the provisions described above, is that in pursuing the primary objective of rehabilitation the court should not lose sight of the fact that it is dealing with a child as distinct from an adult offender and that it should continue to treat the child more leniently in the matter of sentencing than might be the case in respect of an adult.

The legislation specifically states that any measures for dealing with offending by children shall have due regard to the interests of any victims of their offending.[203] The wording of the provision and the fact that it appears last in the list of relevant considerations conveys the impression that it is of secondary importance to the objective of rehabilitation. Nevertheless, the fact that they are specifically mentioned as having to be taken into account in dealing with child offenders ensures that the interests of victims cannot be ignored and that sentencing children cannot be an exercise solely in rehabilitation. Indeed, the reference to the interests of victims would appear to be broad enough to cover not just the direct and immediate victim of the offence, but also any indirect victims including, in appropriate cases, the local community and even the State. This preserves the possibility of an element of retribution and/or deterrence where that is deemed necessary. However, the interests of victims do not have to be interpreted solely in that context. It may be, for example, that the interests of the direct victim in an individual case are best served by an apology and reparation.

---

[201] *ibid.* s.96(3).
[202] *ibid.* s.96(4).
[203] *ibid.* s.96(5).

The wording of the relevant provision is also peculiar. It refers to "any measures" as distinct from any penalty imposed by a court. It follows that it embraces not just court imposed penalties, but also actions agreed upon at a family conference and a family welfare conference. It is also broad enough to cover any relevant regulations issued by a Minister or policies or actions adopted by the Diversion Programme, the management of a children detention school and so on.

Children Detention Orders

A court cannot pass a sentence of imprisonment on a child or commit a child to prison.[204] It may, however, impose on a child a period of detention in a children detention school or in a children detention centre.[205] In such a case the order is a children detention order. Such an order is intended as a last resort. It cannot be imposed unless the court is satisfied that detention is the only suitable way of dealing with the child.[206] Also, if the child is under the age of 16 years the court must also be satisfied that there is a place available for him or her in a children detention school before it can make the order. In any case where the court imposes a children detention order it shall state its reasons in open court.[207]

21–43

Deferring the Order

A court may defer the making of a detention order if a place is not available for the child in a detention school or for any other sufficient reason.[208] It is not at all clear how this relates to the provision prohibiting the court from making an order in the first place in respect of a child under 16 years of age where a place is not available for him or her in a children detention school. In the absence of clear words to the contrary, it is at least arguable that the prohibition still stands and that the deferment option is not available in respect of a child under the age of 16 in respect of whom a place is not available at the time of making the order. An alternative interpretation is that the deferment option operates to postpone the making of the order, as distinct from its application. Accordingly, there would be no inconsistency between the prohibition on the making of a detention order in respect of a child under 16 years when no place was available for him or her in a children detention school, and the power to defer the making of the order until such a place becomes available. It would appear that the latter interpretation is more consistent with the scheme of the legislation.[209]

Before a court can make a deferment order it must have considered a probation officer's report or any other report compiled pursuant to the

---

[204] *ibid.* s.156.
[205] *ibid.* s.142.
[206] *ibid.* s.143(1).
[207] *ibid.* s.143(2).
[208] *ibid.* s.144(1).
[209] S.145 presupposes the possibility of a deferral of the making of a detention order in respect of a

provisions of Part 9.[210] It must also have heard evidence from any person whose attendance it may have requested, including any person who made a report.[211] In addition, it must have given the parent or guardian of the child (or spouse of the child if applicable) an opportunity to give evidence.[212] If such person is not present the court must give an adult relative of the child or other adult accompanying the child in court an opportunity to give evidence. It is also important to note that a deferment order can be made only if the court is of the opinion that the appropriate way of dealing with the child would be to make a children detention order. It is not available as a sort of half-way house in a case where the court would not be minded to impose a full order. Even where these preconditions have been satisfied the court can make a deferment order only if it is satisfied that it would be in the interests of justice to do so having regard to the nature of the offence and the age, level of understanding, character and circumstances of the child concerned.[213]

21–44   Where the court defers the making of a child detention order it shall adjourn the hearing and order that the child be placed under the supervision of a probation and welfare officer.[214] If the order was deferred due to the unavailability of a place in a children detention school, the court shall order the director of that school to apply to the court to make the children detention order when a place becomes available.[215] In any other case the court shall state in open court: the period of detention that is being deferred; the date of the resumed hearing; and that at the resumed hearing the court will take into account the information contained in the probation and welfare officer's report concerning the child's conduct in the meantime and the information on the child's conduct after the finding of guilt, including the extent to which the child has complied with any conditions suggested by the court; any change in the child's circumstances; and on any reparation by the child to the victim, together with any other information which the officer considers relevant.[216]

When deferring a children detention order the court must explain to the child in open court and in language appropriate to the child's level of understanding: why the making of the order is being deferred and for what period; any of the conditions which can be attached to a community sanction and which the court suggests should be complied with by the child during that period; the expectation of the court that the child will be of good conduct during that period and the possible consequences of a failure to comply with any conditions imposed; and the expectation of the court that the child's

---

child under 16 years of age in respect of which a place in a children detention school was not immediately available.
[210] *ibid.* s.144(1)(a).
[211] *ibid.* s.144(1)(b).
[212] *ibid.* s.144(1)(c).
[213] *ibid.* s.144(2).
[214] *ibid.* s.144(3).
[215] *ibid.* s.144(4).
[216] *ibid.* s.144(5).

parents or guardian will help and encourage the child to comply with any conditions imposed and not commit any further offences.[217]

Where the making of a children detention order has been deferred and the hearing adjourned, the probation officer supervising the child must prepare a report on the child for consideration by the court at the resumed hearing.[218] The report shall contain information on the child's conduct after the finding of guilt, including the extent to which the child has complied with any conditions suggested by the court, any change in the child's circumstances and on any reparation by the child to the victim, together with any other information which the officer considers relevant.[219] The officer must make all reasonable efforts to ensure that the report is lodged with the clerk or other proper officer of the court at least four working days before the date of the resumed hearing.[220]

The resumed hearing must take place not later than one year from the date of the adjourned hearing, and it may take place even though the child has attained the age of 18 years in the meantime.[221] At that hearing the court will consider the probation officer's report and, if the court thinks it necessary, will hear evidence from the officer. It has three options for disposing of the case. It can: impose the period of detention which it had deferred or any shorter period; suspend the whole or any portion of the period of detention; or impose a community sanction appropriate to the age of the child concerned.[222] The possibility of a further deferral at this point is specifically precluded.[223] The court must explain to the child in open court the reasons for its decision in language which the child understands.

It may happen, of course, that the director of a children detention school will apply to the court for the making of the detention order on a place having become available in the school. It is not clear whether the court must make a detention order in this event or whether any of the three options described above are still available to it. Since the legislation does not specifically preclude the court from taking one of these options in this case it is submitted that they remain available even where the director has applied for the detention order to be made. Indeed, it is arguable, that the hearing may be resumed and the child dealt with in accordance with one of these options even though the director has not made an application. It may happen that a place does not become available within the one year time limit on resumed hearings. If the court could not deal with the child by any one of the other options during this period the case would be left in a legal limbo. The legislation does not make any other specific provision for this event. The only sensible solution would appear to be that the court always retains the option

21–45

---

[217] *ibid.* s.144(6).
[218] *ibid.* s.144(7)(a).
[219] *ibid.* s.144(7)(b).
[220] *ibid.* s.144(7)(c).
[221] *ibid.* s.144(8).
[222] *ibid.* s.144(9).
[223] *ibid.* s.144(11).

to deal with the case on the basis of one of the three options described above, even if it is a case where the making of the order was deferred until a place became available in a children detention school. What is clear is that the court does not have the discretion to make a further deferral at this point where a director has applied to the court for the making of the detention order on a place having become available.[224]

Where the court proposes to make a detention order on the application of the director it may issue a summons requiring the child to appear before it. If the child does not appear it may issue a warrant for his or her arrest.[225]

There is a further alternative in respect of a child under 16 years of age for whom no place is immediately available in a children detention school. Instead of deferring the making of a detention order in respect of the child until a place becomes available, the court may make an order imposing the community sanction it considers most appropriate for the child.[226] The court may do this where it is satisfied that it would not be appropriate in the particular case to defer the making of a children detention order.

21–46 The period of deferment may be cut short if the child is found guilty of any offence before the expiry of that period. In this event the court may make the detention order (which had otherwise been deferred) before the end of the period of deferral.[227] It is worth noting that this option arises where the child is found guilty of an offence during the period of deferral. Interpreted literally this means that the detention order can be activated early even if the offence in respect of which the child was found guilty was committed before the period of deferral began. Conversely, the fact that the child committed an offence during the period of deferral will not be sufficient to trigger this provision if the child was not actually found guilty of the offence during the deferral period. It may be, of course, that the legislative intention was to empower the court to cut a period of deferment short where the child was found guilty of an offence committed during the deferral period.

Where the court proposes to make a detention order, either at the end of the full or truncated deferral period it must issue a summons requiring the child to appear before it.[228] If the child does not appear the court may issue a warrant for his or her arrest.

Detention in a Children Detention School

Where the court imposes a children detention order there are two possibilities depending on the age of the child. If the child is under the age of 16 years the court must order that he or she be detained in a children detention school.[229]

---

[224] *ibid.* s.144(11).
[225] *ibid.* s.144(10)
[226] *ibid.* s.145.
[227] *ibid.* s.146(a).
[228] *ibid.* s.146(b).
[229] *ibid.* s.147(a).

If the child is between the ages of 16 years and 18 years the court must order that he or she be detained in a children detention centre.[230]

The period of detention in a children detention school which a court may impose shall not be less than three months nor more than three years.[231] Any such period of detention may be consecutive on any period imposed for a previous offence or offences. However, where two or more consecutive periods are imposed the aggregate period cannot exceed three years.[232] As a general rule the period of detention in a children detention school shall not extend beyond the date on which the child attains the age of 18 years. [233] Where a child reaches that age without completing his or her period of detention the child shall, if practicable, be placed out under supervision in the community in accordance the community supervision scheme. These provisions are without prejudice to the court's power to impose a period of detention for longer than three years in certain circumstances. Such a period can be served in a children detention school until the child has reached the age of 16 years and thereafter in another designated place.

Where a child is ordered to be detained in a children detention school, a certified copy of the order shall be delivered with the child to the director of the school specified in the order.[234] This is sufficient authority for the detention of the child in the school for the period specified.

Detention in a Children Detention Centre

The Minister for Justice, Equality and Law Reform may by order designate as a children detention centre any institution (or part of such institution) or other place which in his opinion is suitable for the detention of offenders between 16 years and 18 years of age.[235] The order must specify the date on which it came into force.[236] It may also specify the class or classes of children who may be detained in a children detention centre by reference to age or sex.[237] Where any such specifications are made in respect of an individual detention centre a person not satisfying the specifications cannot be detained in that centre.[238] However, any such order will not affect the lawfulness of the detention of any person who was detained in the institution or place concerned immediately before the order came into force.[239] The Minister may amend or revoke orders made under these provisions.[240]

21–47

It would appear that a person cannot be sentenced by a children court to detention in a children detention centre for an offence for longer than the term

---

[230] *ibid.* s.147(b).
[231] *ibid.* s.149(1).
[232] *ibid.* s.149(2).
[233] *ibid.* s.149(3).
[234] *ibid.* s.148.
[235] *ibid.* s.150(1).
[236] *ibid.* s.150(3).
[237] *ibid.* s.150(4)(a).
[238] *ibid.* s.150(4)(b).
[230] *ibid.* s.150(5).
[240] *ibid.* s.150(6).

of imprisonment which the court could have imposed on a person of full age and capacity who is convicted of the offence in question.[241]

Appeal

In any case where a children court or the District Court commits a child to a children detention school or a children detention centre an appeal against the order shall lie to the Circuit Court.[242]

Supervision Order

21–48   A court can combine a supervision element with a detention order in respect of a child who is between the ages of 16 and 18 years. This is possible only where the court is satisfied that detention is the only suitable way of dealing with the child. Instead of making the detention order the court may make a detention and supervision order.[243] This shall provide for detention in a children detention centre followed by supervision in the community.[244] Generally, half of the period for which the order is in force shall be spent in the detention centre and half under supervision in the community.[245] However, where the child is released from detention on earning remission of sentence by industry or good conduct or on being given temporary release under the sections 2 and 3 of the Criminal Justice Act 1960, supervision shall be deemed to commence on the child's release.[246] It is not at all clear whether the period of supervision will then continue for the full length of the original order or whether it will be confined to the period which the child actually spent in the detention centre; presumably it is the latter.

Supervision under this order shall be carried out by a probation and welfare officer, while the detention is treated for all purposes as detention under a children detention order.[247] The order may also specify any of the conditions which may be attached to a community sanction order as the court considers necessary for helping to ensure that the child would be of good behaviour and for reducing the likelihood of the child's committing any further offences.[248]

The court which made the detention and supervision order may also take action where it appears to the court, on the application of the probation and welfare officer supervising the child, that the child has failed without reasonable cause to comply with the order or any condition attached to it. In

---

[241] *ibid.* s.150(2). This would appear to be a poorly drafted provision. It refers to a sentence of detention imposed by the Children Court under "this section", but the section in question does not refer to the Children Court imposing a sentence of detention.

[242] *ibid.* s.265.

[243] *ibid.* s.151(1).

[244] *ibid.* s.151(2).

[245] *ibid.* s.151(3).

[246] *ibid.* s.151(4). The subsection merely refers to ss. 2 or 3 of the Act of 1960, without specifying which Act of 1960. It would appear that the "Act of 1960" is not defined elsewhere in the 2001 Act. It is presumed that the reference is to the Criminal Justice Act 1960.

[247] *ibid.* s.151(5) and (6).

[248] *ibid.* s.151(7).

this event the court may direct the child to comply with the order or attached condition to the extent that it has not been complied with.[249] Alternatively, it may revoke the order and substitute another detention and supervision order or any other community sanction. A third option is to revoke the order and deal with the case in any other way in which it could have been dealt with before the order was made. Among the matters which the court should take into account when making such a decision are the extent to which and the period during which the child has complied with the original order and any attached conditions. Where the court proposes to exercise its power under these provisions the court shall summon the child to appear before it. If the child does not appear the court may issue a warrant for his or her arrest.

Detention for Certain Indictable Offences

There is provision for the detention of a child under the age of 16 years for longer than the maximum period of three years. If such a child is convicted of an indictable offence and the court is of the opinion that one of the other ways in which the case may be dealt with is inadequate, it may by order impose on the child a period of detention in excess of three years.[250] The term of detention imposed cannot be for longer than the term of imprisonment which the court could have imposed on a person of full age and capacity who is convicted of the offence in question.[251] When the court imposes a sentence of detention exceeding three years it shall give its reasons in open court.[252]

21–49

Where a period of detention is imposed under this provision it shall be served initially in a children detention school.[253] When the child has attained the age of 16 years the place or places in which it will be served depends on the age of the child and other circumstances.

The child may be detained in a children school until he or she has reached the age of 18 years and six months.[254] However, when a child has been detained under these provisions the director of the school in which the child is detained may, once the child has attained the age of 16 years or at any time thereafter, apply in writing to the court in question to have the child transferred to a children detention centre.[255] Any such application in respect of a child under the age of 18 years shall set out the reasons for the application. If the court is satisfied that those reasons would justify the transfer of the child to a children detention centre, it may order that the application be granted.[256]

Where an application is made under these provisions in respect of a child who has attained the age of 18 years the transfer shall be to a prison or a place

---

[249] *ibid.* s.151(8).
[250] *ibid.* s.155(1).
[251] *ibid.* s.155(7).
[252] *ibid.* s.155(8).
[253] *ibid.* s.155(1).
[254] *ibid.* s.155(2).
[255] *ibid.* s.155(3).
[256] *ibid.* s.155(4).

of detention provided for under section 2 of the Prisons Act 1970.[257] The same applies where a child who has attained the age of 18 years is transferred from a children detention centre for any other reason

Any statutory provisions, rules or regulations applying to persons serving a sentence in a children detention centre, in a prison or in a place of detention provided for by section 2 of the Prisons Act 1970 shall, as appropriate, apply with any necessary modification to children transferred pursuant to these provisions.[258]

There are specific provisions governing the transfer of children from one place of detention to another. Unfortunately, they are not always very clear about who can authorise the transfers or when the transfers can take place. It is specifically stated that Minister for Justice, Equality and Law Reform may direct the transfer of a child from a children detention centre to another such centre to serve the whole or any part of the unexpired residue of his or her period of detention.[259] There is no indication of when the Minister can or cannot take such action. Since the transfers are between children detention centres it must be assumed that the intention is not to impose limits on the power.

Transfers

21–50 The legislation stipulates that a child may be transferred from a children detention centre to a prison or a place of detention only upon reaching the age of 18 years.[260] The wording of the provision, coupled with the fact that it does not specify who may authorise the transfer or the grounds and procedure applicable to such a transfer, suggests that it is merely intended to prevent a child under the age of 18 years being transferred under some other provision. It is not actually conferring a power of transfer itself. There is, however, provision authorising the transfer of a child of 16 or 17 years of age to be transferred to a children detention centre from a prison or place of detention under section 2 of the Prisons Act 1970.[261] It, too, does not specify who may authorise the transfer or the grounds or procedure applicable to such a transfer. Nevertheless, the measure is clearly worded in permissive terms.

A child cannot normally be transferred from a children detention school to a children detention centre.[262] The exception arises in the context of punishment for indictable offences. Also, no child can be transferred from any place of custody to a prison or a place of detention provided under section 2 of the Prisons Act 1970.[263] A place of custody in this context means a junior remand centre, a remand centre, a children detention school or a children detention centre.[264]

---

[257] *ibid.* s.155(5).
[258] *ibid.* s.155(6).
[259] *ibid.* s.152(1).
[260] *ibid.* s.152(5).
[261] *ibid.* s.152(6).
[262] *ibid.* s.152(4).
[263] *ibid.* s.152(2).
[264] *ibid.* s.152(3).

10. Corporal Punishment

Although it has long fallen into disuse in this country statutory authority for a **21–51** sentence of corporal punishment for male offenders existed right up until 1997. Adult males could suffer a sentence of whipping when found guilty of certain offences,[265] while males under the age of 16 years could also be sentenced to whipping for certain specified offences. The Rules for the Government of Prisons, 1947 made provision for how the punishment was to be inflicted.[266] Birching was available generally for a male child found guilty of an indictable offence in the District Court. In such cases the Court could, instead of any other punishment, direct that he receive not more than 6 strokes of the birch to be inflicted privately by a police officer in the presence of a senior police officer, the Governor and Medical Officer of the Prison and, if he wishes to be present, the parent or guardian of the child.[267]

Of course any attempt to implement these provisions would be contrary to the **21–52** European Convention on Human Rights to which Ireland is bound in international law. In *Tyrer v. United Kingdom*[268] the European Court of Human Rights had to consider whether the practice of birching as a punishment for certain young offenders in the Isle of Man was compatible with the Convention. The rules and procedures applicable to birching in the Isle of Man were quite similar to those in Ireland. The Court ruled that the practice amounted to degrading treatment and, as such, was in breach of Article 3 of the Convention. The terms of the Court's reasoning were such as to leave little scope within the Convention for any form of corporal punishment to be inflicted as part of a sentence for a criminal offence. Indeed, the Court has gone on since to declare the parental beating of a child incompatible with the Convention.[269] Although the Court's decision in *Tyrer* was handed down in 1978 it was not until 1997 that the effect of the Irish statutory provisions authorising the use of whipping and birching was formally abolished. The Criminal Law Act 1997 stipulates that:

> "No person shall be sentenced by a court to whipping, and so far as any enactment confers power on a court to pass a sentence of whipping it shall cease to have effect."[270]

---

[265] Ryan and Magee, *op. cit.*, p.401, fn.2 cite the following examples: Offences against the Person Act 1861, s.21; and Garroters Act 1863, s.1 (attempting to choke, etc., with intent); Criminal Law Amendment Act 1885, s.2 (procuration of women) as amended by the Criminal Law Amendment Act 1912, s.3 and the Criminal Law Amendment Act 1935, s.7; Inebriates Act 1898, s.1 (pimps) as extended by the Criminal Law Amendment Act 1912, s.7(5).

[266] Rules for the Government of Prisons 1947 (S.I. No. 320 of 1947), rr.72–73.

[267] Summary Jurisdiction over Children (Ireland) Act 1884, s.4(1) as adapted; Children Act 1908, s.128(1); and Children Act 1941, s.28; Rules for the Government of Prisons 1947 (S.I. No. 320 of 1947). See Ryan and Magee, *op. cit.*, p.411.

[268] (1978) 2. E.H.R.R. 1.

[269] *A v. U.K.* No. 25599/94, September 23, 1998.

[270] Criminal Law Act 1997, s.12(1).

While this provision does not specifically abolish birching the section in question goes on to provide:

> "Corporal punishment shall not be inflicted in any place to which the Prisons Acts, 1826 to 1980, or section 13 of the Criminal Justice Act 1960 apply."[271]

This provision is primarily concerned with the equally significant objective of prohibiting the use of any form of corporal punishment as part of internal discipline within prisons, detention centres or reformatory schools. Nevertheless, in so far as birching had to be administered in a prison it clearly has the incidental effect of outlawing birching. In any event the statutory provision authorising a District Court to pass a sentence of birching on an adult male is one of the many specifically repealed by the 1997 Act.[272]

C. Ancillary Punishments and Orders

1. Introduction

21–53   It often happens that a court will have a power, and/or a duty, to apply a penalty in addition to the primary punishments available on conviction of a criminal offence. Typically, each of these additional or ancillary penalties will have a close association with the nature of the particular offence to which it attaches. Quite often the object of the ancillary penalty will be to deprive the offender of the fruits of his crime or to render it more difficult or painful for him to repeat the offence at some point in the future. Indeed, they are particularly prevalent in the context of regulatory offences. There is also a trend in favour of ordering an offender to make reparation or pay compensation to his victim. While technically this does not qualify as an ancillary penalty, the offender will often perceive it as such. It is apparent, therefore, that the range of such penalties and remedial orders that the court can make is quite extensive. The most that can be done here is to identify the main forms that they take and to describe some of those which feature most frequently in practice.

2. Disqualification

21–54   Many economic and social occupations can be pursued lawfully only when the operator holds an appropriate licence. In addition the law will often prescribe certain standards which must be observed in the conduct of such licensed occupations. Frequently, the licence requirement and associated standards are enforced through the criminal law. A breach of such criminal laws will be punishable by the usual sanctions of a fine, or even imprisonment. In addition, however, the legislation may, and often does seek to promote standards in the licensed occupations by including provision for the

---

[271] *ibid.* s.12(2).
[272] Criminal Law Act 1997, s.16 and Third Schedule.

suspension or revocation of the offender's licence, the imposition of disabilities on the licence or even a prohibition on him acquiring a licence. The classic example is, of course, the driving licence.

Where a person is convicted of an offence under certain provisions of the Road Traffic Acts the court may make an order disqualifying him from holding a driving licence for such period as the court thinks fit.[273] In some cases, most notably, drunk driving, the court is obliged to disqualify the offender from holding a driving licence for a specified minimum period.[274] The court may also impose a disqualification on a person convicted of an offence where a motor vehicle was used in the course of committing the offence.[275] It must be emphasised, however, that a disqualification in any of these situations, although commonly classed as a punishment, is not a primary or direct punishment. Its nature is neatly summed up in the following passage from the decision of the Supreme Court in *Conroy v. Attorney General*:

> "One must not lose sight, however, of the real nature of the disqualification order which is that it is essentially a finding of unfitness of the person concerned to hold a driving licence. Apart from the statutory minimum which is imposed in certain cases, this is a matter which must be determined by the court in the light of evidence which it hears on this aspect of the case and in the light of that evidence it may determine what period of disqualification will be appropriate. A motor car, if not driven properly, is a potential danger not merely to the driver himself but to all other persons using the highway. It is obvious that the protection of the common good requires that the right to drive a motor car cannot be unrestricted. The right may therefore be lost if a court, on a consideration of the relevant facts and materials, determines that the person concerned, by reason of his general recklessness or thoughtlessness or of his propensity to drink, or by reason of disease or other disability or his abuse of the right by exercising it in the furtherance of criminal activities, is unfit to exercise the right to drive a motor car. Such disqualification is not a punishment notwithstanding that the consequence of such finding of unfitness might be both socially and economically serious for the person concerned."[276]

It is normal practice, therefore, for the court to consider as a separate matter, and after hearing appropriate evidence, the issue of whether the person concerned is unfit to hold a driving licence before imposing a disqualification.[277] It does not follow, however, that there must be a separate hearing. It will be sufficient that there is evidence before the judge sufficient to allow him or her reach a conclusion as to the defendant's fitness to drive.[278]

The Road Traffic Act 2002 makes provision for the introduction of a "penalty points system" for certain driving offences. The basic idea is that certain driving offences attract penalty points on the offenders driving licence. When a person is convicted of such an offence or pays an "on the spot fine"

---

[273] Road Traffic Act 1961, ss. 26 and 27.
[274] *ibid.* ss.26 and 27.
[275] *ibid.* s.27.
[276] [1965] I.R. 411 at 441–442.
[277] *People v. Poyning* [1972] I.R. 402; *People v. Hogan* (1972) Frewen 360.
[278] *Glynn v. Hussey* [1996] 1 I.L.R.M. 235.

for such an offence the specified number of penalty points will be endorsed on his or her licence. When the total number of penalty points equals or exceeds 12 the person concerned is disqualified from holding a licence for a period of six months and his or her licence is suspended for that period. At the end of the period of disqualification the points are removed from the licence. Apart from that eventuality, penalty points endorsed on a licence normally remain for three years. At the time of writing the introduction of the penalty points system was imminent.

21–55   Although, strictly speaking, it is not an aspect of sentencing, it is worth noting that certain disqualifications may follow automatically or in consequence of a criminal conviction which has resulted in a sentence of imprisonment. Anyone who has been sentenced to a term of imprisonment or detention, for example, will be disqualified from jury service depending on the length of the sentence and/or when it was passed.[279] Similarly, anyone serving a sentence of imprisonment of more than six months imposed by a court in the State is disqualified from being elected to the Oireachtas.[280] Significantly, the disqualification does not extend to anyone serving a sentence of imprisonment imposed by a court outside the State, including a court in Northern Ireland. Statutes establishing public bodies often include a provision disqualifying from membership persons who have certain types of criminal records. A criminal record can also disqualify a person from pursuing certain professions or vocations.[281] In some cases the disqualification is imposed by statute while in others it is the result of self-regulation by the professional bodies concerned. In all of them the disqualification applies as a matter of law or practice. It does not normally feature as a distinct part of the sentencing process in any individual case, although it can be taken into account when the judge is considering factors in mitigation of sentence (see later). It is also worth noting the provisions governing the disqualification of company directors. Where a company director is convicted on indictment of any offence in relation to a company involving fraud or dishonesty he or she will be disqualified from being concerned in the management, either as director or otherwise, of any company for up to five years.[282] The court can impose a different period of disqualification on the application of the DPP and having regard to all the circumstances of the case. It is possible that this discretion is not confined to the length of the order in that it can extend to the imposition of the disqualification itself. The statutory provision in question is poorly drafted.

3. Forfeiture of Property

21–56   At one time a conviction for treason or felony entailed the forfeiture of the convict's property. Although forfeiture in these terms was abolished by the

---

[279] Juries Act 1976, s.8.
[280] Electoral Act 1923, ss.51(2)(a) and 57(2)(a).
[281] Auctioneers and House Agents Act 1947, s.18; Veterinary Surgeons Act 1931, s.34, as amended by Veterinary Surgeons Act 1960, s.1; Solicitors Act 1954, s.34.
[282] Companies Act 1990, s.160(1); Building Societies Act 1976, ss.42 and 68; Unit Trust Act 1972,

Forfeiture Act 1870, forfeiture still plays a significant role in the aftermath of a conviction for certain criminal offences. A number of statutes provide for the forfeiture of property connected with the commission of a criminal offence. For the most part the wording of the relevant provisions will differ in detail. Generally, however, they form a pattern of which section 30 of the Misuse of Drugs Act 1977 is typical:

> "(1) Subject to subsection (2) of this section, a court by which a person is convicted of an offence under this Act may order anything shown to the satisfaction of the court to relate to the offence to be forfeited and either destroyed or dealt with in such other manner as the court thinks fit.
>
> (2) A court shall not order anything to be forfeited under this section if a person claiming to be the owner of or otherwise interested in it applies to be heard by the court, unless an opportunity has been given to him to show cause why the order should not be made."

This provision was considered by the High Court in *Bowes v. Devally*.[283] In that case the accused was convicted of unlawful possession of drugs. In addition to the imposition of a fine the trial court also ordered the forfeiture of a sum of £890 which was found in the same room as the drugs. Forensic evidence revealed small traces of cannabis resin on the notes in the applicant's possession. The applicant, however, had given evidence that the money was the property of her mother and that she was simply minding it. Accordingly, she sought an order of certiorari quashing the forfeiture order. Geoghegan J. noted that the forfeiture is part of the penalty and, as such, the circumstances in which it can be made must be strictly construed. Moreover, it must relate to the particular offence for which the applicant was convicted. In this case there was no evidence that it was related to the offence of possession. It would not be sufficient that the money might be used to buy drugs in the future. Even if it might have been the proceeds of selling drugs it could not be lawfully forfeited in this case as the accused had been convicted of possession as opposed to selling. Since the forfeiture had to be considered as an integral part of the penalty it could not be severed from the fine.[284] The learned judge had no option, therefore, but to quash the sentence and exercise his discretion under Order 84, r.26(4) of the Rules of the Superieur Courts to refer the matter back to the Circuit Court with a direction to reach a decision in accordance with the findings of the court.

The Criminal Justice Act 1994 provides a much more wide ranging forfeiture power. It stipulates that when a person is convicted of an offence and the court is satisfied that any property which has been lawfully seized from him or her, or which was in his or her possession or under his or her control at the time of apprehension or summons, has been used for the purpose of facilitating the commission of any offence or was intended by him or her to be used for that purpose, the court may make a forfeiture order in respect of that property.[285] One

---

s.16. See Murray *Director Disqualification and the Criminal Law* (1992) 2 I.C.L.J. 165.

[283] [1995] 2 I.L.R.M. 148.

[284] See *State (Kiernan) v. De Burca* [1963] I.R. 348.

[285] Criminal Justice Act 1994, s.61.

of the striking features of this provision is that it applies in respect of any offence, not just the offence of which the person stands convicted by the court. Also included is any property used to dispose of property relating to the offence or for the purpose of enabling any other person to avoid apprehension or detection. Where the offence consists of unlawful possession of property which was lawfully seized from the offender or which was in his or her possession or control at the time of his or her apprehension or summons, an order may also be may in respect of that property.

21–57   The forfeiture power under the 1994 Act is discretionary.[286] The court is not bound to issue an order in any case. However, in considering whether to issue an order the court must have regard to the value of the property and the likely financial and other effects on the offender, including the cumulative impact of any other order or orders which the court is minded to impose. Where a forfeiture order is imposed under these provisions the effect is to deprive the offender of his rights in the property. Any person claiming to be the owner of the property must be given an opportunity to be heard on request and the order must not be put into full effect until the ordinary appeal procedures, if activated, have been exhausted. A person, other than the offender, who claims to be the owner of the property can rely on the Police Property Act 1897 to recover the property.[287] He or she must show either that he did not consent to the offender having possession of the property or that he did not know, and had no reason to suspect, that the property was likely to be used in connection with crime.

O'Malley draws attention to the similarity of the general forfeiture provisions of the 1994 Act and those in comparable English legislation.[288] He suggests that the English case law is a useful guide, particularly with its emphasis on the totality of the punishment in any individual case. The courts must be careful not to "overdo" the punishment through a combination of a prison sentence, etc., and forfeiture orders.

4. Confiscation of the Proceeds of Crime

Criminal Justice Act 1994

21–58   In addition to the forfeiture provisions contained in diverse statutes the State now has very broad powers at its disposal to target the assets of criminals or suspected criminals. The Criminal Justice Act 1994, for example, makes provision for the court which has sentenced or otherwise dealt with an offender in respect of a drug-trafficking offence to make a determination on

---

[286] See s.17 of the Offences against the State (Amendment) Act 1998 which renders a forfeiture order obligatory under certain circumstances in respect of certain firearms and explosive offences.

[287] There is provision in s.56 of the Criminal Justice (Theft and Fraud Offences) Act 2001 for property to be restored to its owner following a successful prosecution by or on behalf of the owner. There are limits on the extent to which a criminal court is either able or prepared to make orders under this provision; see, e.g., *Curtis v. Brennan* [1997] 1 I.L.R.M. 344.

[288] O'Malley, *op. cit.*, pp.333–334.

whether the offender has benefited from the offence. The court is normally obliged to make such a determination in respect of a drug-trafficking offence. It has a discretion to make a similar determination in respect of offences other than drug-trafficking offences.[289] If the court makes a determination under these provisions it shall determine the amount to be recovered and make a confiscation order requiring the offender to pay that amount. Although the order is not treated as a sentence any other penalty, including other forfeitures and compensation payments, imposed on the offender in respect of the offence must be taken into account in calculating the amount. A failure to pay the required amount will result in a prison sentence graduated in accordance with a scale based on the amount of the order. The Proceeds of Crime Act 1996 goes one step further in that it provides for confiscation orders in respect of the seizure of assets which can be identified as the proceeds of crime even though no individual has actually been convicted of the crime in question.[290]

Interim Orders

The 1996 Act powers the High Court to issue interim, interlocutory and disposal orders in certain circumstances. An interim order can be issued prohibiting the respondent, or any specified person having notice of the order, from disposing of or otherwise dealing with specified property or diminishing its value during the period of 21 days from the date of the order.[291] The application is heard *ex parte* and in private. The court may issue an order under these provisions where it is shown to its satisfaction that a person is in possession of the property concerned and that it constitutes, directly or indirectly, the proceeds of crime or was acquired, in whole or in part, with or in connection with property that, directly or indirectly, constitutes the proceeds of crime and the value of the property is not less than €13,000. In the course of the application, or while an interim order is in force, the court may grant an application compelling the respondent to file information on his or her assets and income (see below). Equally, once an interim order has been issued the court may appoint a receiver to manage or deal with the property (see below).

The net effect of the order is to ensure that the property in question is available for confiscation at a later date should that prove necessary. Its singular nature is emphasised by the ease with which it can be obtained, the potentially far reaching scope of the order and the extent to which it encroaches upon the property rights of the individual. There is provision for the respondent (or any person claiming an interest in the property) to challenge an order after the event. However, the onus will be on the individual to satisfy the court that the property, or any part of it, is not the proceeds of

---

[289] As a result of an amendment effected by s.25 of the Criminal Justice Act 1999 the court does not have to proceed to a determination of the benefits in question if, having regard to the means of the offender, the amount likely to be recovered would be insufficient to justify the making of an order.

[290] See P McCutcheon and D Walsh *The Confiscation of Criminal Assets: Laws and Practice* (Round Hall, Dublin, 1999).

[291] Proceeds of Crime Act 1996, s.2.

crime or that its value is less than €13,000. If the applicant succeeds the court may vary or discharge the order.

Interlocutory Orders

An interim order lapses automatically after 21 days unless an application for an interlocutory order is brought within that period. An interlocutory order can be issued where the applicant tenders admissible evidence to the effect that a person is in possession or control of property which constitutes the proceeds of crime and which has a value of not less than €13,000.[292] Notice of the application must be given to the person or persons concerned unless the court is satisfied that it is not reasonably possible to ascertain their whereabouts.

A feature of this provision is that the case for an order can be made out simply by a member of the Garda Síochána not below the rank of Chief Superintendent or an authorised officer of the Criminal Assets Bureau stating, either in an affidavit or in oral evidence, his or her belief that: (i) the respondent is in possession or control of specified property and that the property constitutes directly or indirectly the proceeds of crime; or (ii) that the respondent is in possession or control of specified property and that the property was acquired in whole or in part with or in connection with property that directly or indirectly constitutes the proceeds of crime; and (iii) that the value of the property is not less than €13,000. Where such evidence is placed before the court it must grant the order unless the respondent introduces evidence to the contrary or the court is satisfied that there would be a serious risk of injustice.

As with the procedure for an interim order, an application can be made to the court for an order compelling the respondent to file an affidavit in the Central Office of the High Court specifying the property in his or her possession or control or his or her income or sources of income during such period as the court may specify. The period may not exceed 10 years ending on the date of the application. It is worth bearing in mind in this context that the respondent need not have been charged with, let alone convicted of, a criminal offence. When this provision is combined with the provision on the acceptability of opinion evidence it is clear that the 1996 Act places the State in a very strong position to deprive suspected criminals of the proceeds of their crime. Astute use of these provisions can place such persons in a position where they effectively have to establish that their assets have been acquired legitimately.

The interlocutory order has much the same effect on the property as an interim order, subject to the critical difference that it can last much longer. Unless a person concerned establishes at some point that the property does not satisfy the criteria for an interlocutory order, the order will remain in force until the determination of an application for a disposal order. Such an application can be made only after an interlocutory order has been in force for at least seven years. The court, however, also retains the power to vary the order during this period. Equally, it may make orders enabling the respondent

---

[292] *ibid.* s.3.

to discharge out of the property reasonable living or other necessary expenses and/or to carry on a business, trade or profession to which any of the property relates. The court may also appoint a receiver at any time when an inter-locutory (or an interim) order is in force.[293] He or she may be given such powers as the court thinks appropriate in individual cases, including such powers to take possession of the property to which the order relates and to manage or otherwise deal with it in accordance with the court's directions.

Disposal Orders

After an interlocutory order has been in force in respect of specified property for a period of at least seven years, an application can be made for a disposal order in relation to that property.[294] The application is made to the High Court, with due notice to the respondent and other such persons as the court should order. The court must grant the disposal order unless it is shown to its satisfaction that the property is not the proceeds of crime. The court cannot make the order if it is satisfied that there would be a serious risk of injustice. Any person claiming ownership of any of the property must be given an opportunity to show cause why a disposal order should not be made.

Once granted, the order deprives the respondent of his or her rights in the property which automatically transfers to the Minister for Justice, Equality and Law Reform or such other person to whom the order relates. Where property vests in the Minister pursuant to these provisions he or she can sell or otherwise dispose of it and the proceeds of any such disposition (or moneys transferred to him) are for the benefit of the Exchequer.

There are provisions for the payment of compensation to persons who suffer loss as a result of orders being issued under these provisions in respect of property which does not constitute directly or indirectly the proceeds of crime, or which was not acquired in whole or in part with or in connection with such property.[295] Compensation can be awarded where the applicant shows to the satisfaction of the court that he or she is the owner of the property in question and that the order has been discharged or varied or has lapsed. Where compensation is awarded it is paid by the Minister for Justice, Equality and Law Reform.

5. Forfeiture of Office or Employment

Up until very recently a conviction for treason or felony could also result in the forfeiture of certain public offices.[296] Now, of course, with the abolition of the distinction between felonies and misdemeanours, that is no longer the case.[297] The Offences against the State Act 1939 also makes provision for the

21–59

---

[293] *ibid.* s.7.
[294] *ibid.* s.4.
[295] *ibid.* s.16.
[296] Forfeiture Act 1870, s.2.
[297] Criminal Law Act 1997, s.3. The Forfeiture Act 1870 is repealed in its entirety by Criminal Law Act 1997, s.16 and the Third Schedule.

forfeiture of certain public offices and employments upon conviction. These provisions were struck down as unconstitutional in *Cox v. Ireland*[298] (see chapter 20).

6. Compensation

Introduction

21–60   When imposing sentence on an offender the judge will often have jurisdiction to order him or her to pay compensation to the victim either *in lieu* of, or in addition to, any punishment it may impose. For example, the court may supplement a probation order with an order directing the offender to pay such damages for injury or compensation for loss, and such costs of proceedings, as the court thinks reasonable.[299] Strictly speaking, the compensatory nature of such payments is that they ought not to be considered as part of the punishment. In practice, of course, they will be perceived as part of the punishment, not least because of the fact that they are ordered by the court immediately upon conviction and in the context of passing sentence. It would seem appropriate, therefore, to deal with them here.

Jurisdiction

The Criminal Justice Act 1993 makes general provision for compensation orders on conviction.[300] It stipulates that on conviction of an offender[301] the court may, unless it sees reason to the contrary, make an order requiring him or her, or where appropriate, his or her parent or guardian,[302] to pay compensation for any personal injury or loss resulting from the offence to any person who has suffered such injury or loss.[303] This order may be in addition to, or in place of, any other order the court may make with respect to the offender. The power extends to compensation orders in respect of any injury or loss resulting from offences taken into consideration by the court in determining sentence. Loss resulting from the offence is given an extended definition where the commission of the offence by the convicted person involved the taking of property out of the possession of the injured party.[304] Where the property has been recovered any loss occurring to the injured party

---

[298] [1992] 2 I.R. 503.

[299] Probation of Offenders Act 1907, s.1(3).

[300] These provisions are without prejudice to any other enactment which provides for the payment of compensation by a person convicted of an offence or otherwise proved to have committed an offence; Criminal Justice Act 1993, s.6(10).

[301] References to conviction of a person includes references to dealing with a person under section 1(1) of the Probation of Offenders Act 1907; see Criminal Justice Act 1993, s.6(12)(b).

[302] Criminal Justice Act 1993, s.6(12)(c). See Children Act 1908, s.99 for the situations where the order will be addressed to a parent or guardian.

[303] Criminal Justice Act 1993, s.6(1). In any case where death has resulted from an offence "loss" means any matter (including mental distress resulting from the death and funeral expenses) for which damages could be awarded in respect of the death by virtue of Pt V of the Civil Liability Act 1961, and "injured party" includes a dependant (within the meaning of the said Pt V) of the deceased person concerned; see s.6(12)(a).

[304] Criminal Justice Act 1993, s.6(3).

as a result of the property being damaged while out of his or her possession shall be treated, for the purposes of a compensation order under these provisions, as having resulted from the offence. It does not matter how the damage was caused or who caused it. The net effect is that the offender may be liable for compensation even though he did not personally damage the property in question. This will cover damage to a vehicle where the offence involves the taking of that vehicle.[305] However, it will not otherwise cover any injury or loss resulting from the use of a vehicle in a public place unless it appears to the court that the use of the vehicle by the convicted person was in breach of the road traffic compulsory insurance provisions.[306]

Where a compensation order is addressed to a parent or guardian under these provisions it shall not of itself give rise to any other liability on the part of the parent or guardian in respect of the injury or loss.[307]

Relevant factors

In determining whether to make a compensation order under these provisions, **21–61** and the amount if any, the court must have regard to the means and financial commitments of the person concerned, or the means and financial commitments of a parent or guardian where the court is empowered to require a parent or guardian to pay.[308] To this end the court may require the convicted person, or his parent or guardian as the case may be, to give evidence as to his means and financial commitments. Where an order is made it shall be of such amount as the court considers appropriate, having regard to any evidence and to any representations that are made by or on behalf of the convicted person, his parent or guardian (where relevant), the injured party or the prosecutor.[309] However, it cannot exceed the amount of damages which, in the opinion of the court, the injured party would be entitled to recover in a civil action against the convicted person in respect of the injury or loss concerned. An order made by the District Court must not exceed such amount as may stand prescribed for the time being by law as the limit of that court's jurisdiction in tort. Currently, the limit of this jurisdiction is €6,350 (there is provision to increase it to €20,000; Court, and Court Officers Act 2002, s.14 but it is not yet in force).

---

[305] *ibid.* s.6(4)(b). In this event the amount of compensation may include an amount representing the whole or part of any loss of or reduction in preferential rates of insurance resulting from the use of the vehicle.

[306] Criminal Justice Act 1993, s.6(4)(a).

[307] *ibid.* s.6(11).

[308] *ibid.* s.6(5) and (13). See Children Act 1908, s.99 for the court's power to require a parent or guardian to pay any fine, damages or costs imposed on or awarded against a child or young person. The references to damages in s.99 shall be construed as if they included references to compensation under a compensation order and subss. (5) and (6) of s.99 shall not apply in relation to an order; see Criminal Justice Act 1993, s.6(9).

[309] Criminal Justice Act 1993, s.6(2).

Flexibility

The Act leaves the court with considerable flexibility over the terms of a compensation order. The order, for example, may provide for payment of compensation by instalments at such times as the court shall in all the circumstances consider reasonable.[310] Moreover, in any case where the court considers it appropriate to impose both a fine and a compensation order, and the convicted person has insufficient means to pay an appropriate fine and appropriate compensation, the court may, if it is satisfied that the person's means are sufficient, make a compensation order. If it is further satisfied that it is appropriate to do so having regard to the person's means remaining after compliance with the order, the court may impose a fine.[311] When assessing the person's means in this context the court must also take into account his or her financial commitments.[312]

Variation

21–62 There is provision for the variation of a compensation order at any time after the order has become operable and before it has been fully satisfied.[313] The convicted person (and/or his or her parent or guardian where relevant) may apply for a variation to the District Court or, where the amount payable under the order exceeds the current limit of that court's jurisdiction in tort, to the court which imposed the order. If the court is satisfied that the injured party concerned has been given the opportunity of making representations to the court on the issue, and having regard to any such representations which are made, the court may vary any instalment or direct that no further payments be made.[314] This can be done where it appears to the court that because of a substantial reduction in the means of the convicted person (and/or his or her parent or guardian where relevant) his means are insufficient to satisfy the order in full. By the same token, the court may increase the amount to be paid, the amount of any instalment or the number of any instalments on the application of the injured party concerned.[315] On this occasion the court must be satisfied that the convicted person (and/or his or her parent or guardian where relevant) has been given an opportunity of making representations to the court on the issue and it must have regard to any such representations that are made. Before making the increase it must appear to the court that as a result of a substantial increase in the means of the convicted person his or her means are sufficient for this purpose, and that the increased amount to be paid would not exceed the lesser of (i) the amount of damages that the injured party concerned would be entitled to recover in a civil action against the convicted person in respect of the injury or loss concerned, or (ii) such

---

[310] *ibid.* s.6(6).
[311] *ibid.* s.6(7).
[312] *ibid.* s.6(13).
[313] The order becomes operable in this context after it ceases to be suspended by virtue of s.8 of the Act; see below.
[314] Criminal Justice Act 1993, s.6(8)(a).
[315] *ibid.* s.6(8)(b).

amount as may stand prescribed for the time being by law as the limit of the court's jurisdiction in tort.[316]

Enforcement

Payments under a compensation order must be made to a District Court clerk as may be determined from time to time by the court which made the order.[317] From there they go to the injured party concerned. The machinery for the enforcement of maintenance orders under the Family Law (Maintenance of Spouses and Children) Act 1976, including in particular the provisions on attachment of earnings, are extended, subject to the necessary modifications, to the compensation orders.[318]

Appeal

The operation of a compensation order is suspended until the expiry of the ordinary time for giving notice of an appeal, or of an application for leave to appeal, against conviction and/or sentence.[319] Where notice of appeal is given within the permitted time, or such extended time as the court may allow, the order is suspended until the appeal (or any further appeal) is finally determined or abandoned or until the time for instituting any further appeal has expired.[320] The order shall not take effect if the conviction is reversed on appeal.[321] Moreover, a court hearing an appeal against conviction or sentence may annul or vary the order.[322] A person against whom an order has been made may appeal against the order to the court to which an appeal against the conviction may be brought.[323] The court may annul or vary the order. Pending the determination of the appeal, or any further appeal, the order will be suspended.

21–63

Impact on Civil Award

Clearly, the making of a compensation order has implications for the assessment and award of damages in civil proceedings in respect of the same injury or loss. If damages are assessed in such circumstances in an amount which exceeds the amount paid under the compensation order, the damages awarded shall not exceed the amount of that excess.[324] Equally, if the amount paid under the order exceeds the amount in which damages are assessed, the court may order that the excess be repaid to the person against whom the

---

[316] It is not entirely clear whether the reference to the court's jurisdiction in tort is a reference to the jurisdiction of the District Court or that of the court which imposed the order.

[317] Criminal Justice Act 1993, s.7(1).

[318] *ibid.* s.7((2).

[319] *ibid.* s.8(1)(a). For the purpose of these provisions a reference to conviction include references to dealing with a person under s.1(1) of the Probation of Offenders Act 1907; see s.8(6).

[320] Criminal Justice Act 1993, s.8(1)(b).

[321] *ibid.* s.8(2). Also, where an order has been made against a person in respect of an offence taken into consideration in determining his sentence, the order shall cease to have effect if he successfully appeals against his conviction of the offence of which he was convicted in the proceedings in which the order was made; s.8(5)

[322] Criminal Justice Act 1993, s.8(3).

[323] *ibid.* s.8(4).

[324] *ibid.* s.9(i).

order was made.[325] The compensation order shall cease to have effect upon the award of damages by the court.

7. Naming and Shaming

21–64   In sexual offence cases it is becoming increasingly common for victims to waive their right to anonymity so that the defendant might be "named and shamed". While this does not qualify as a formal method of punishment, almost inevitably it will have a punitive effect on the defendant. Indeed, that is usually the victim's motivation in waiving anonymity. The courts do not grant these applications as a matter of routine. The wishes of the victim are, of course, a precondition for lifting the prohibition on publishing the identity of the defendant where that might lead to the identification of the victim. If there are several victims and even one does not support the public exposure of the defendant then the court will not lift the prohibition.[326]

Sex Offenders Register

Although it is not the full equivalent of naming and shaming it is worth mentioning, under this general heading, the recent introduction of a sex offenders register in Ireland. The Sex Offenders Act 2001, which came into effect on September 27, 2001,[327] makes provision for certain sex offenders to notify the Garda Síochána of their identities and movements. Persons concerned are those convicted of a relevant offence after the Act came into force, or who are sentenced for a relevant offence after the Act came into force, or who are the subject of a current sentence for a relevant offence when the Act came into force.[328] The relevant sexual offences are set out in the Schedule to the Act.[329] A person satisfying these requirements must notify the Garda Síochána of his or her name (and any other names which he or she uses), and his or her home address.[330] This information must be notified within seven days of the date of conviction or commencement of the Act, whichever is appropriate.[331] Similarly, if the person changes his or her name or address, he or she must notify the change to the Garda Síochána within seven days. If he or she intends to leave the State for a continuous period of seven days or more, he or she must notify the Garda Síochána of that intention and, if known, the address outside the State at which he or she will stay. Notification can be given in person at a Garda station or by post. There is provision for the application of these provisions to a person within the State who has been convicted of a relevant offence outside the State.[332] The period during which a notification requirement subsists can vary from indefinite duration to a

---

[325] *ibid.* s.9(ii).

[326] *People (DPP) v. JM* unreported, Court of Criminal Appeal, February 22, 2002.

[327] Sex Offenders Act 2001 (Commencement) Order 2001 (S.I. No. 426),

[328] Sex Offenders Act 2001. S.7.

[329] Note the exceptions in s.2 of the Act.

[330] Sex Offenders Act 2001, s.10. See s.10(6) for details.

[331] Periods when the person is in custody are disregarded for the purposes of the time limit.

[332] Sex Offenders Act 2001, s.13.

minimum of five years (two and a half years for a person under 18 years of age) depending on the nature of the sentence imposed.[333]

Where the conviction of a person gives rise to a notification requirement under the 2001 Act, the court before which the person is convicted (or before which the sentence is subsequently imposed) shall issue a certificate stating that the person has been convicted of the offence, the sentence imposed and that the person is subject to the notification requirement.[334] In the event of the conviction being quashed (or sentence varied), the court which quashes the conviction or varies the sentence shall issue a certificate stating that the conviction has been quashed or sentence varied as the case may be. In either of these situations the certificate is issued to the Garda Síochána, the person convicted and, where appropriate, the person in charge of the place where the person is ordered to be imprisoned or the probation and welfare service.

Where a person subject to the notification requirement is ordered to be imprisoned in respect of an offence, the person in charge of the place where he or she is imprisoned must notify the person in writing that he or she is subject to the notification requirement before the date on which the sentence expires or the date of release.[335] At least 10 days before his or her release the person in charge must also inform the Commissioner of the Garda Síochána of this information.

Failure to comply with the notification obligations is a criminal offence.[336] There is provision for a person subject to the notification obligation for indefinite duration to apply to the court to have it discharged after a period of 10 years.[337]

Sex Offender Orders

The 2001 Act makes provision for a court to issue a sex offenders order in respect of a person.[338] The effect of such an order is to prohibit the person from doing a thing or things as the court considers necessary for the purpose of protecting the public from serious harm. An order can be issued in a private hearing on the application of a member of the Garda Síochána not below the rank of chief superintendent.[339] The court must be satisfied on a balance of probabilities[340] on the basis of evidence tendered by the applicant that the person concerned has been convicted in the State of a sexual offence, or has been convicted in a place outside the State of an offence consisting of an act which if done within the State would constitute an sexual offence within the Act.[341] The court must also be satisfied on the basis of the evidence tendered that the person concerned has behaved on one or more occasions since his or her release from prison in such a way as to give reasonable grounds for

---

[333] *ibid.* s.8.
[334] *ibid.* s.14.
[335] *ibid.* s.9.
[336] *ibid.* s.12.
[337] *ibid.* s.11.
[338] *ibid.* s.16.
[339] *ibid.* s.16(1).
[340] *ibid.* s.21.
[341] *ibid.* s.16(2) and (3).

believing that an order is necessary to protect the pubic from serious harm. The order as issued will specify one or more things which the person concerned is prohibited from doing in order to protect the public from serious harm.[342] It takes effect upon notification to the person concerned,[343] and shall remain in force for a period of five years or such longer period as the court may prescribe.[344] During this period the person concerned is also subject to the notification requirements outlined above.[345] There is provision for appeal against an order and for an application to discharge or vary the order.[346]

Notifying an Employer

Where a person has been convicted in the State of a sexual offence, or has been convicted in a place outside the State of an offence consisting of an act which if done within the State would constitute an sexual offence within the Act, the person may be under an obligation to inform a prospective employer about the conviction.[347] This obligation arises on taking up a contract of employment, entering into a contract for services, applying for employment or applying to do work on another person's behalf where the work in any of these situations consists mainly of the person concerned having unsupervised access to or contact with a child or a mentally impaired person. Failure to inform is a criminal offence.

Post-release Supervision of Sex Offenders

The 2001 Act empowers a court to consider whether to impose a sentence involving post-release supervision when it is determining the sentence to be imposed on a sex offender in respect of the sexual offence concerned.[348] In considering the matter the court must have regard to: the need for a period after the offender has been released into the community during which his or her conduct is supervised by a reasonable person; the need to protect the public from serious harm; the need to prevent the commission by the offender of further sexual offences; and the need to rehabilitate or further rehabilitate the offender. If it thinks it necessary the court may receive evidence or submissions from any person concerned when considering these matters.

The court may impose on a sex offender a sentence involving post-release supervision.[349] This is a sentence of imprisonment followed by the imposition of a period post-release when the offender shall be under the supervision of a probation officer. The offender will also be required to comply with such conditions as are specified in the sentence for securing that supervision. The inclusion of a period of supervision shall not result in the imposition of a

---

[342] *ibid.* s.16(4).
[343] *ibid.* s.17.
[344] *ibid.* s.16(6).
[345] *ibid.* s.16(7).
[346] *ibid.* ss.18 and 19.
[347] *ibid.* s.26.
[348] *ibid.* s.28.
[349] *ibid.* s.29.

lesser term of imprisonment than would otherwise have been imposed, but the aggregate of the two periods cannot exceed the maximum term of imprisonment that could have been imposed for the offence. In determining the period of supervision, the court shall have regard to the criteria relevant to its consideration of whether to include an element of post-release supervision. The court can also include conditions which it considers appropriate for these purposes and for the needs of the sex offender.[350] When imposing a post-release supervision element in the sentence, the court must explain the effect of the sentence to the offender, the consequences of a failure to comply with it and the fact that the court may vary or discharge the order on the application of the offender or a probation and welfare officer.[351]

8. Deportation

Deportation cannot properly be described as an available punishment for criminal wrongdoing. Nevertheless, it does feature from time to time in the sentencing of non-nationals who have not established a permanent residence here.[352] The usual pattern is that the offender will be charged with an offence which will attract a prison sentence or a fine which he is unable to pay. Typical examples are: public order offences, criminal damage, larceny or even drug offences. The offender will be required to enter into a recognisance which involves a condition that he will leave the State at the first practical opportunity and not re-enter the State for a specified period. This form of sanction can, in appropriate circumstances, fall foul of European Community law on the free movement of persons where the offender is a national of another E.U. State.[353] Equally, there is the possibility that it could breach the rights of the individual under the European Convention on Human Rights or, despite the fact that the offender will be a non-national, the Constitution.

21–65

9. Drug Court

Finally, it is worth drawing attention to the introduction of a "drug court". In effect, this represents a novel approach to dealing with certain categories of offender whose offending is driven by a drug habit. Such a court has been introduced on a trial basis in Dublin. An outline account is offered in chapter 2 in the section dealing with the District Court.

D. Sentencing Principles

1. Introduction

The determination of what sentence to impose in any individual case is an exercise of judicial power. As such it is primarily a matter for the judge to

21–66

---

[350] *ibid.* s.30.
[351] *ibid.* s.31. See s.32 for discharge or variation of order and s.33 for penalties for non-compliance.
[352] See O'Malley, *op. cit.*, pp.337–339.
[353] *R v. Bouchereau* [1977] E.C.R. 1999.

determine, subject to limits prescribed by law for the offence in question. It does not follow, however, that the judge can act arbitrarily in deciding what sentence to impose in any individual case. The Irish courts have developed a body of sentencing principles to guide judges in the exercise of their discretion in individual cases. A flagrant disregard of these principles can result in a sentence being varied on appeal by the defence or the prosecution. It is worth noting at the outset that these principles do not extend to a set of sentencing tariffs for particular offences committed in specified circumstances. While the courts accept that there must be equity in sentencing between cases, and for this purpose they will occasionally look at sentences handed down in similar cases, they stress the need to tailor a sentence to suit the facts of the individual cases.[354] So far this has precluded the judicial promulgation of sentencing guidelines for particular offences.[355] Even in respect of rape where, arguably, they have come closest, they have declined to follow their English counterparts in recommending a range or tariff of appropriate sentences for rape, preferring instead to leave the determination of sentence to the judge in each individual case.[356]

2. Objectives

It is generally accepted that the objectives of sentencing are to punish the offender for the crime, to deter him or her and others from committing that type of offence in the future and to rehabilitate the offender. In *State (Stanbridge) v. Mahon*,[357] for example, Gannon J. summarised the objectives of sentencing:

> "The first consideration in determining the sentence is the public interest, which is served not merely by punishing the offender and showing a deterrent to others but also by affording a compelling inducement and an opportunity to the offender to reform. The punishment should be appropriate not only to the offence committed but also to the particular offender."[358]

It is noteworthy that this statement does not include prevention as an object of sentencing. Indeed, it would seem that it is not open to a judge to impose a long custodial sentence on the offender for the purpose of preventing him from committing such offences in the future. In *People (DPP) v. Carmody*,[359] for example, two offenders were sentenced to imprisonment for six years each after pleading guilty to charges of burglary. In imposing such a severe sentence the judge was motivated by the fact that they were professional

---

[354] See, *e.g.*, *People (DPP) v. Gallagher* unreported, Court of Criminal Appeal, March 4, 1994; *People (DPP) v. Z* unreported, Court of Criminal Appeal, March 14, 1995; *People (DPP) v. Power* unreported, Court of Criminal Appeal, March 3, 1997; *People (DPP) v. Sheedy* unreported, Court of Criminal Appeal, October 15, 1999.

[355] See, *e.g.*, *People (DPP) v. Sheedy* unreported, Court of Criminal Appeal, October 15, 1999.

[356] A recommended tariff for rape was laid down in *R v. Billam* [1986] 1 All E.R. 985. However, the Irish Supreme Court in *Tiernan* declined the invitation to adopt a similar approach. See also *DPP v. R O'D* unreported, Court of Criminal Appeal, May 25, 2000.

[357] [1979] I.R. 214.

[358] [1979] I.R. 214 at 218, citing *R v. Ball* 35 Cr.App.R. 164.

[359] [1988] I.L.R.M. 370.

burglars who showed no intention of abandoning their life of crime. One offender had 130 previous convictions going back to 1961 for which he had served a total of over 20 years imprisonment. The other, his brother, had a record about twice as long. On appeal, however, the Court of Criminal Appeal substituted sentences of three years imprisonment on the basis that the only justification for the six year sentences were "an understandable attempt to procure reform by prevention." Since preventative justice has no place in our legal system the court ruled that this did not provide an acceptable basis for the sentences imposed.

Interestingly, the Court of Criminal Appeal in *Carmody* referred to section 10 **21–67** of the Prevention of Crime Act 1908 which provides for the preventative detention of an habitual criminal for not more than ten years and not less than five. Surprisingly, perhaps, the Court seems to have proceeded on the basis that this would have provided a sound basis for the sentences handed down in this case were it not for the fact that there were no facilities in the State for such detention. It is respectfully submitted, however, that there must be a question mark over the constitutionality of section 10 in so far as it provides for the incarceration of an offender in order to prevent him from re-offending as distinct from punishing him for an offence or offences committed. Support for this argument can be found in the judgment of Denham J. in *People (DPP) v. M*, where she quoted with approval the following passage from the judgment of Walsh J. in *People (Attorney General) v. O'Callaghan*:

> "In this country it would be quite contrary to the concept of personal liberty enshrined in the Constitution that any person should be punished in respect of any matter upon which he has not been convicted or that in any circumstances he should be deprived of his liberty upon only the belief that he will commit offences if left at liberty, save in the most extraordinary circumstances carefully spelled out by the Oireachtas and then only to secure the preservation of public peace and order or the public safety and the preservation of the State in a time of national emergency or in some situation akin to that."[360]

A bald statement of the objectives of sentencing offers very little insight into what sentence will be appropriate in any individual case. The factual circumstances surrounding the commission of an offence and the personal circumstances of an offender will differ from case to case. The fact that the sentence imposed must be appropriate not only to the offence committed, but also to the particular offender suggests that the sentence imposed in any individual case must of necessity be unique to that case. Nevertheless, the appropriateness of a sentence may be challenged on the basis of matters such as the process followed by the sentencing judge, the factors taken into account and the weight attributed to those factors.

---

[360] [1966] I.R. 501 quoted in *People (DPP) v. M* [1994] 2 I.L.R.M. 541 at 549.

3. Sentence Based on Offence of Conviction

21–68   As a general rule the court will consider first what the sentence should be in principle having regard to the gravity of the offence and then it will go on to consider mitigating factors.[361] This, of course, is only a rough guide and, quite frequently, the two steps will overlap. Nevertheless, this two-step approach will be adopted here to facilitate explication of the factors which a judge should take into account in determining the appropriate sentence to impose in any individual case. At the outset, however, it would do no harm to emphasise the rather obvious point that, except where it is taking other offences into consideration, the court must be careful to sentence an offender only for the offence of which he has been convicted or to which he has pleaded guilty. This can assume some importance where the defendant has been convicted of one offence but acquitted on more serious offences arising out the same incident. In *People (DPP) v. M*,[362] for example, the Court of Criminal Appeal reduced a four year sentence of imprisonment for sexual assault to two years because it appeared that the sentencing judge may have been unduly influenced by the facts of a count of rape against the same victim on which the defendant was acquitted. Significantly, it appears that the victim impact report in this case suggested that the offender had engaged in full intercourse and oral sex with the victim without her consent. It is a useful reminder, therefore, of how alert defence counsel must be to ensure that the sentencing process is not prejudiced by technically extraneous material in such reports.

Sometimes the notoriety of the defendant or of the broader context in which the offence was committed can create a risk of the defendant's sentence being influenced by other crimes for which he is not before the court. In *People (DPP) v. Holland*,[363] for example, the applicant was sentenced to the exceptionally long sentence of 20 years for possessing cannabis for the purpose of sale or supply. This was reduced to eight years by the Court of Criminal Appeal partly because the severity of sentence may have been influenced by references in the course of the trial to the defendant being involved in other crimes including murder. However, an inadmissible reference to the defendant being well known to the Garda National Drug Unit in the sentencing stage for a drugs offence will not be sufficient to vitiate the sentence where there is no evidence that such a comment had any effect on the severity of the sentence.[364]

21–69   The sentencing of an offender on specimen counts can also cause difficulties in this context, particularly in child sexual abuse cases. There is always the risk that the severity of sentence will be influenced by the fact that the defendant has a long history of abusing children, even though he is only before the court on one or more specimen counts. While the matter has yet to

---

[361] See, *e.g.,* the approach of Denham J. in *People (DPP) v. M* [1994] 2 I.L.R.M. 541.
[362] Unreported, Court of Criminal Appeal, January 18, 1997.
[363] Unreported, Court of Criminal Appeal, June 15, 1998.
[364] *People (DPP) v. Murray* unreported, Court of Criminal Appeal, May 16, 2001.

be fully addressed by the Irish courts, it would seem on the basis of principle that the defendant should be sentenced only for the offences of which he has been convicted or on which he has pleaded guilty. Moreover, the severity of sentence should not be affected by the knowledge that they are only a small part of the true scale of offending. In *People (DPP) v. B*,[365] for example, the defendant pleaded guilty to 10 sample counts of sexual offences against his daughter. There was a total of 70 counts on the indictment and it was acknowledged that the true total may run into hundreds. The Court of Criminal Appeal felt that the judge may have taken more than the 10 sample counts into account when he imposed a sentence of 15 years. Accordingly, the court reduced it to 11 years. This does not prevent the sentence being influenced by the history of abuse indirectly by, for example, the court taking into account the impact of the offence on the victim.

Just as the defendant should be sentenced only for the offence for which he is before the court, so also must he be sentenced for each offence of which he has been convicted or to which he has pleaded guilty. This is so even if one of the offences captures the essence of the criminal conduct and the others are merely subsidiary to it, or if the intention is to impose concurrent sentences for the others. This must be distinguished from the situation in which the court accedes to an application to take other offences into consideration when imposing sentence for the offence or offences for which the defendant is before the court.[366] The court does not record a separate sentence for each of the other offences. Instead they are reflected in the sentence imposed in respect of the offence or offences for which the defendant is before the court.

4. Gravity of the Crime

Focus on Facts of Individual Case

In considering what sentence would be appropriate in principle the court must **21–70** have regard to the gravity of the crime. In particular there must be proportionality between the severity of the sentence and the gravity of the crime.[367] Some crimes, for example, are so grave that they will almost invariably call for an immediate and substantial term of imprisonment. Typically, these will include crimes involving serious violence to the person, most terrorist offences, robbery involving the use of a weapon or violence, larceny of property valued at a substantial amount of money, serious damage to property, rape and child sexual abuse. In *DPP v. Tiernan*,[368] for example, Finlay C.J. explained, with respect to rape, that the character of the offence and the impact it has on the victim are so grave that a substantial period of imprisonment is warranted on conviction even in the absence of aggravating factors:

> "Whilst in every criminal case a judge must impose a sentence which in his opinion meets the particular circumstances of the case and of the accused

---

[365] Unreported, Court of Criminal Appeal, December 14, 1998.
[366] See, *e.g.*, *People (DPP) v. Higgins* unreported, Supreme Court, November 22, 1995.
[367] *People (DPP) v. M* [1994] 2 I.L.R.M. 54 at 547.
[368] [1989] I.L.R.M. 149.

person before him, it is not easy to imagine the circumstance which would justify departure from a substantial immediate custodial sentence for rape and I can only express the view that they would probably be wholly exceptional."[369]

Nevertheless, as noted above, the Irish courts have declined to follow their English counterparts and recommend a range or tariff of appropriate sentences for rape, preferring instead to leave the determination of sentence to the judge in each individual case.[370] There have even been cases where a non-custodial sentence has been imposed.[371] In *DPP v. R O'D*,[372] the Court of Criminal Appeal emphasised the need to address the particular circumstances of each individual case. It also drew attention to the huge growth in the number of convictions for rape and sexual assault cases since the decision in *Tiernan*. Many of these were committed within family situations a long time ago. In some of these cases factors such as the circumstances in which the offence was committed, the low risk of repetition, and the benefits of rehabilitation can combine to render a custodial sentence undesirable.

While the courts accept that there must be equity in sentencing between cases and that information on sentencing in similar cases is useful, they continue to emphasise the need to tailor a sentence to suit the facts of the individual cases. They are generally reluctant to lay down sentencing guidelines for particular offences.[373]

Maximum Available Sentence

21–71   A key indicator of the gravity of the crime is the maximum available sentence for that crime. Typically, the sentencing court will identify the maximum available sentence available for the crime and then use that as a base line to identify a sentence which would be proportionate to that maximum having regard to the gravity for the offence. It would be most unusual, but not unprecedented, for the maximum to be imposed in any individual case. As a general rule the maximum sentence should be reserved for the worst reasonably imaginable variation of the offence.[374] Even in such extreme cases it would be unusual not to find a basis for some reduction, however small. Nevertheless, there is legislative encouragement for the imposition of the maximum sentence in appropriate circumstances. The Criminal Justice Act 1999 provides that a court shall not be precluded from imposing a maximum sentence if satisfied that exceptional circumstance relating to the offence so warrant.[375] This seems to suggest that even if the defendant pleads guilty at an early stage,

---

[369] *ibid.* at 151. Note also *Attorney General v. Conroy* [1965] I.R. 411 where the Supreme Court stated that the nature of the offence was such as to render unconstitutional any statutory provision which could permit it ever to be regarded as a minor offence.

[370] A recommended tariff for rape was laid down in *R v. Billam* [1986] 1 All E.R. 985. However, the Irish Supreme Court in *Tiernan* declined the invitation to adopt a similar approach.

[371] See, *e.g., People (DPP) v. WC* [1994] 1 I.L.R.M. 321 where a suspended sentence of nine years was imposed.

[372] Unreported, Court of Criminal Appeal, May 25, 2000.

[373] See, *e.g., People (DPP) v. Sheedy* unreported, Court of Criminal Appeal, October 15, 1999.

[374] O'Malley, *op. cit.*, p.140.

[375] Criminal Justice Act 1999, s.29.

which as will be seen later normally earns an automatic deduction, the court could still impose the maximum applicable sentence to reflect the exceptional circumstances relating to the commission of the offence.

When the court is considering the gravity of the offence by reference to the maximum available sentence, it is the maximum sentence at the time of the commission of the offence that is relevant, as distinct from the maximum available at the date of conviction or sentence.[376] The court will also take into account when the maximum sentence was fixed. While maximum penalties fixed for an offence many years ago may not be a reliable guide to the gravity of that offence today, more recent statutory enactments will be interpreted as a sure guide to the legislature's policy in the matter.[377] The Misuse of Drugs Act 1977, for example, fixed maximum penalties of 14 years imprisonment and a fine of £3,000 for possession of controlled drugs for sale or supply. In 1984 these penalties were increased to life imprisonment and an unlimited fine. In *People (DPP) v. Gethins*,[378] the Court of Criminal Appeal commented that these substantial increases in comparatively recent years "is the clearest possible indication, not merely to the judiciary, but also to the community as a whole, of how serious these offences are, and how damaging the use of drugs, and the evil traffic which it generates, can be and has been to society."[379] Even if the maximum sentence for an offence has not been increased in recent years, a court may be inclined to impose a relatively severe sentence to reflect judicial concern at the increased prevalence of the offence in recent times.

Statutory Minimum Sentence

The existence of a statutory minimum sentence for an offence is also an important guide for the courts in determining the gravity of the offence and the appropriate sentence to impose for its commission.[380] The court, however, should not take a statutory minimum as the starting point for determining the appropriate sentence. Other relevant factors must be considered, including the maximum sentence.

Impact on Victim

The general impact on the victim is relevant to an assessment of the gravity of the crime. If the victim has been severely traumatised and will suffer serious, long-term adverse effects as a result of the crime then this is likely to be reflected by a more severe sentence. On the other hand, if the victim has made a speedy recovery with no likelihood of long-term effects it can be expected that this will result in a more lenient sentence. These remarks must be qualified by the general principle that sentencing is primarily a matter

21–72

---

[376] See, *e.g., People (DPP) v. Bartley* unreported, Court of Criminal Appeal, June 13, 1997.

[377] See, *e.g., People (DPP) v. Sheedy* unreported, Court of Criminal Appeal, October 15, 1999; *People (DPP) v. DH* unreported, Court of Criminal Appeal, February 1, 2000.

[378] Unreported, Court of Criminal Appeal, November 23, 2001.

[379] *ibid.* at 3. See also *People (DPP) v. Renald* unreported, Court of Criminal Appeal, November 23, 2001.

[380] *People (DPP) v. Renald* unreported, Court of Criminal Appeal, November 23, 2001; *People (DPP) v. Hogarty* unreported, Court of Criminal Appeal, December 21, 2001.

between the accused and the State as opposed to an exercise in retaliation by the victim.[381] Equally, however, it must be noted that in the case of a sexual offence within the meaning of the Criminal Evidence Act 1992, or an offence involving violence or the threat of violence to a person, the sentencing court is obliged to take into account any effect (whether long-term or otherwise) of the offence on the person in respect of whom it was committed.[382] The choice of this form of words suggests that it is the impact on the direct victim of the offence which matters, as distinct from the impact on indirect victims such as family members. In order to assess the victim impact it may necessary to receive evidence or submissions concerning any such impact. Indeed, when requested by the victim, the court must hear the evidence of the victim as to the effect of the offence on him or her.[383]

When a victim is giving evidence about the impact of the crime he or she will not be permitted to express views on what a proper sentence might be.[384] The same applies to the relative of a victim and a relative of the accused. However, the court will admit a mercy plea from a victim, a relative of a victim or a relative of an accused. In *DPP v. R O'D*,[385] for example, both the sentencing court and the Court of Criminal Appeal attached great importance to the wishes of the two victims that their brother, the accused, should not be given a prison sentence for sexual assaults committed upon them some years previously.

Aggravating factors

21–73 The presence of aggravating factors typically will result in a custodial sentence for offences which might not otherwise have attracted such a sentence, or an even longer sentence for those offences for which a substantial and immediate custodial sentence is appropriate. In *Tiernan*, for example, aggravating factors present were that: the rape was a gang rape carried out by three men; the victim was raped on more than one occasion; the rape was accompanied by acts of sexual perversion; violence in addition to the sexual acts was inflicted; the rape was performed by an act of abduction and the imprisonment of the victim's boyfriend in the boot of their car; the victim suffered from a serious nervous disorder as a result of the rape; and the accused had a criminal record of violence and indecency. On these facts the Supreme Court held that a sentence of 21 years was not wrong in principle, although it proceeded to reduce it to 17 years as the trial judge and the Court of Criminal Appeal had not given sufficient credit for the accused's admission and plea of guilty. Similarly, in *People (DPP) v. M*,[386] the Supreme Court held that sentences ranging from 18 years penal servitude to fours years imprisonment for 68 charges of illicit sexual activities on boys in a school in which the accused was a

---

[381] *People (DPP) v. M* [1994] 2 I.L.R.M. 541, *per* Denham J. at 548.
[382] Criminal Justice Act 1993, s.5(1).
[383] *ibid.* s.5(3).
[384] *DPP v. R O'D* unreported, Court of Criminal Appeal, May 25, 2000.
[385] Unreported, Court of Criminal Appeal, May 25, 2000.
[386] [1994] 2 I.L.R.M. 541.

teacher was not wrong in principle. The facts of the case indicated grave offences by a person in a position of trust committed over years in an escalating cycle of abuse against six boys. It was a planned system of extensive child abuse typical of the compulsive behaviour found in paedophilia. In this case also, the Supreme Court imposed significant reductions in the sentences in order to take account of certain mitigating factors.

Specific aggravating factors which feature in the case law include the use of firearms or gratuitous violence in the commission of the offence, group violence, the invasion of the victim's home and breach of trust between the offender and the victim.[387] Pursuant to the Criminal Justice Act 1984 the courts are obliged when determining sentence for an offence committed while on bail, to treat the fact that the offence was committed while on bail as an aggravating factor and to impose a heavier sentence for it than would otherwise have been imposed in the absence of this factor.[388] This requirement does not apply when the sentence for the first offence is a life sentence. Also, it does not apply in any case where the court considers that there are exceptional circumstances justifying a departure from it.

Just as the gravity of the offence may be increased by aggravating factors, so also may it be reduced by mitigating factors. It will be seen later that mitigating factors relevant to the individual offender can result in a reduction of the sentence that might otherwise have been imposed for the offence. There may also be mitigating factors arising from the circumstances in which the offence itself was committed. These can be taken into account when the court is determining the sentence that would be proportionate to the gravity of the offence. Relevant factors in this context are: provocation, the commission of the offence under circumstances of duress or emotional stress, intoxication as a factor in inducing the commission of the offence,[389] entrapment by the police or third parties, a mistake of law or fact which resulted in the defendant not being aware that his actions amounted to an offence and actions or circumstances which technically satisfy the offence but which constitute a very minor example of the offence (what O'Malley refers to as marginal offending).[390]

Other factors

When determining the sentence that would be appropriate to the gravity of the offence the court should not take into account the possibility of remission for good behaviour under the Prison Rules, or the scope for temporary or early release as a result of executive action.[391] There are grounds, however, to argue that the courts should resort to imprisonment as a last resort. The enactment of the Criminal Justice (Community Service) Act 1983 signalled a

---

[387] O'Malley, *op. cit.*, pp.158–162.

[388] Criminal Justice Act 1984, s.11(3), as amended by the Bail Act 1997, s.10. This was brought into force on June 2, 1998.

[389] This can also act as an aggravating factor where the drunken state of the accused added to the trauma suffered by the victim.

[390] O'Malley, *op. cit.*, pp.151–157.

[391] *ibid.* at 145–146.

shift in public policy in favour of non-custodial sentencing. Similarly, the Children Act 2001 has made provision for a whole range of non-custodial options for the punishment of young offenders.

Manslaughter

21–74
Manslaughter is a crime which can give rise to difficulties in determining the sentence appropriate to the gravity of the offence in any individual case. The maximum sentence available is, of course, life imprisonment. Subject to that, however, the sentencing judge has a discretion over the sentence to impose on conviction for manslaughter in any individual case. Given that the factual circumstances resulting in culpable homicide can vary so immensely it should come as no surprise that sentences imposed for manslaughter can also vary enormously. Indeed, it is not unusual for a non-custodial sentence to be imposed.[392] At the other end of the scale there have been cases in which the maximum life sentence might be considered appropriate, even where the offender has pleaded guilty to manslaughter as a lesser offence to murder.[393] In *People (DPP) v. Conroy*,[394] for example, the Supreme Court held that a maximum sentence of life imprisonment was not necessarily wrong in principle in such circumstances. In that case, Finlay C.J. explained the impact upon sentence of a plea of guilty to a lesser offence than that charged:

> "In general a court is obliged to have regard, where a person charged on an indictment pleads guilty to a lesser offence than might have been available on conviction after trial, to the acceptance of that plea by the prosecuting authority. There could not be any principle which inhibited the court in such an event from imposing a sentence which was lawful for the crime to which the plea of guilty has been entered, merely on the basis that no greater sentence was lawful in respect of the crime for which if the plea had not been accepted the accused could have been convicted. Having regard to the multiple factors which enter into consideration of sentence in the case of a homicide, there would not appear to me to be any grounds for a general presumption that the crime of manslaughter may not, having regard to its individual facts and particular circumstances be in many instances, as, or more, serious from a sentencing point of view than a crime consisting of murder."[395]

5. Personal circumstances and mitigating factors

Introduction

21–75
Once the judge has determined the gravity of the offence and the nature of the punishment in principle he or she should turn to consider the appropriateness of the sentence in view of the particular circumstances of the case. Once

---

[392] O'Malley suggests that there is a general tendency towards leniency in the form of a suspended sentence where there is severe provocation or where it takes the form of prolonged physical or sexual abuse of the offender; *op. cit.* at 152.

[393] *People (DPP) v. McAuley and Walsh* unreported, Court of Criminal Appeal, October 25, 2001.

[394] [1989] I.L.R.M. 139.

[395] *ibid.* at 142.

again proportionality is relevant. In this context, however, it is proportionality between the nature of the sentence and the personal circumstances of the accused which are at issue. The essence of the discretionary nature of sentencing is that the personal situation of the accused must be taken into consideration by the court:

> "The objects of passing sentence are not merely to deter the particular criminal from committing a crime again but to induce him in so far as possible to turn from a criminal to an honest life and indeed the public interest would be best served if the criminal could be induced to take the latter course. It is therefore the duty of the courts to pass what are the appropriate sentences in each case having regard to the particular circumstances of that case – not only in regard to the particular crime but in regard to the particular criminal."[396]

It is in this context that the court considers mitigating factors. A failure by the judge to take account, or to take sufficient account, of recognised mitigating factors in determining the length of a prison sentence is an error of principle which can result in the sentence being reduced or varied on appeal. Some mitigating factors are relevant to all offences while others are particular to specific types of offence.

Plea of Guilty

The most important and general mitigating factor is a plea of guilty. The courts invariably give a discount for an early plea of guilty. Not only does this save the State and the witnesses the expense and inconvenience of a trial, but it also spares the victim from the trauma of having to relive the experience of the crime by being subjected to examination and cross-examination in public.[397] The court must be careful, however, not to punish the accused for exercising his constitutional right to plead not guilty and put the prosecution to the test.[398] It does not follow, however, that the court must ignore the manner in which the accused conducted his defence. When imposing sentence in a rape case, for example, the court is not bound to disregard the fact that the defendant based his defence on an allegation that the victim was to blame for, or was the instigator of, what transpired between them.[399]

Early Admission

Closely related to a plea of guilty is an early admission. This is particularly important in rape or sexual abuse cases. The courts acknowledge the importance of sparing victims of such crimes, particularly children, from the trauma of anticipating the appearance in court and from the associated legal procedures.[400] It is also interpreted as a sign of remorse which is also a

---

[396] *People (Attorney General) v. O'Driscoll* (1972) 1 Frewen 351, *per* Walsh J. at 359; approved by the Supreme Court in *People (DPP) v. M* [1994] 2 I.L.R.M. 541, *per* Denham J. at 547–548.
[397] *People (DPP) v. Tiernan* [1988] I.R. 250; *People (DPP) v. M* [1994] 3 I.R. 306.
[398] *People (DPP) v. Connaughton* unreported, Court of Criminal Appeal, April 5, 2001.
[399] *People (DPP) v. Sheehy* unreported, Court of Criminal Appeal, July 12, 1999.
[400] *People (DPP) v. Tiernan* [1989] I.L.R.M. 149; *DPP v. G* [1994] 1 I.R. 587; *People (DPP) v. M* [1994] 2 I.L.R.M. 541; *DPP v. Byrne* [1995] 1 I.L.R.M. 279.

positive factor in mitigation of sentence.[401] Accordingly, an admission and an early indication that a guilty plea will be entered will normally earn a reduction in sentence. The courts have consistently given greater credit for an early admission. While late admissions will carry some value the courts are less generous to guilty pleas which are entered at a very later stage with a view to securing a tactical advantage in terms of sentence. This approach has now been implicitly endorsed by the legislature in that the Criminal Justice Act 1999 provides that the sentencing court, if it considers it appropriate to do so, shall take account of the stage at which the person indicated an intention to plead guilty and the circumstances in which the indication was given.[402]

21–76 The size of the reduction for an early admission will also depend on the circumstances onf the individual case. A substantial reduction might be appropriate in a case where the prosecution would have experienced serious difficulty in securing a conviction on a plea of not guilty. On the other hand very little, or perhaps no reduction, might be appropriate where the accused was caught *in flagrante delicto*. Equally, a plea of guilty in circumstances where the accused had little to lose and the victim or the State little to benefit is unlikely to secure a reduction. In *People (DPP) v. Conroy*,[403] the Supreme Court upheld the refusal of the trial judge to grant a reduction in the sentence imposed on a conviction for manslaughter. The accused pleaded guilty to manslaughter only after he was indicted for murder for the third time. The first trial was aborted as a result of a jury disagreement. His conviction for murder in the second trial was set aside by the Supreme Court on a point of law. The victim, naturally, was unavailable to give evidence at any of the trials. In these circumstances Finlay C.J. was satisfied that the plea of guilty to manslaughter was only a negligible mitigating factor which did not afford a valid ground of appeal.

Co-operation with Gardaí

It would appear that a discount is also appropriate where the defendant has co-operated fully with gardaí in the investigation of a crime in which he or she may have been only a minor player.[404] Conversely, a failure by the defendant to give information when called upon to do so by the court will not warrant an actual increase in the severity of sentence.[405]

---

[401] See, *e.g., People (DPP) v. F* unreported, Court of Criminal Appeal, July 5, 1997; *People (DPP) v. S* unreported, Court of Criminal Appeal, July 4, 1994.
[402] Criminal Justice Act 1999, s.29.
[403] [1989] I.L.R.M. 139.
[404] See comments of Murphy J. in *DPP v. Warren et al* unreported, Court of Criminal Appeal, July 5, 1999 where he referred with approval to the decision of the New Zealand Court of Appeal in *Rex v. Ulrich* [1981] 3 N.Z.L.R. 310.
[405] *DPP v. Maloney* 3 Frewen 267.

Rehabilitation

Another very important factor of general application is rehabilitation. The court must consider the chances of the accused being rehabilitated into society at the end of his sentence. If rehabilitation is reasonably possible then the court should take this into account in determining the sentence. An integral part of rehabilitation is light at the end of the tunnel. The accused should be left with an element of hope and something to look forward to by way of motivation towards self-improvement and rehabilitation. The courts have acknowledged the importance of this factor, particularly where the gravity of the crime calls for a long custodial sentence.[406] Once again the size of reduction which may be appropriate under this heading will vary with the facts of each individual case. If, for example, the accused is getting on in years and there is a real risk that he will die in prison a more substantial reduction might be applied under this heading than would have been the case had he been younger.

There may be a public as well as a private aspect to rehabilitation, particularly **21–77** in respect of an offender whose criminal activity is driven by the need to feed a drug addiction. Clearly, the private welfare of such an individual will be served by rehabilitation. Given the huge volume of crime that is drug related it is equally evident that the public also has a very keen interest in the rehabilitation of drug offenders. The matter was put thus by Geoghegan J. in the Court of Criminal Appeal in *People (DPP) v. Dreeling and Lawlor*:

> "This court agrees with these principles provided that under the heading 'Rehabilitation' there may be a public aspect as well as a private aspect. The private welfare of the accused is something which any sentencing court is entitled to take into account provided it balances it against other factors including the public outrage at the offence, but rehabilitation is not necessarily just in the private interest of a particular accused. In drug cases in particular there is a very substantial public interest in the rehabilitation of the offender. A huge percentage of crime today including violent crime is drug related but worse still as the learned judge adverted to, the drug taking does not stop at the prison gates. In that respect drink related crime is not really analogous. It has always been accepted by the courts that whereas drink may be an explanation for crime it is not an excuse and in such a case prison may be positively beneficial to an alcoholic accused. But with drugs the position is often quite the reverse. There is grave danger that continued drug taking in prison will lead to worse crimes when the prisoner is ultimately released."[407]

It may be, therefore, that in many drug-related cases the court will be inclined to impose a non-custodial sentence, or even postpone sentence for a period to see how the accused responds to treatment, when a custodial sentence might have been imposed for a similar offence committed with no drug abuse context.

---

[406] See, for example, *People (Attorney General) v. O'Driscoll* (1971) 1 Frewen 351; *People (Attorney General) v. Poyning* [1972] I.R. 402; *People (DPP) v. Conroy* [1989] I.L.R.M. 139; *People (DPP) v. M* [1994] 2 I.L.R.M. 541; *People (DPP) v. MS* [2000] 2 I.L.R.M. 311.

[407] Unreported, Court of Criminal Appeal, November 13, 2001 at 7.

While sexual offence cases will raise different issues the Court of Criminal Appeal has drawn attention to the public dimension to the rehabilitation of the sex offender:

> "Rehabilitation is not just a private benefit conferred on the accused. There is a very substantial public interest in a sex offender being rehabilitated so that he will not commit such an offence again. It is well known that in the case of paedophiles rehabilitation giving rise to any guarantee or near guarantee that there will not be a repetition of the offences can in many instances be almost impossible. But in other cases where there has been a history of sexual abuse within a family many years ago the perpetrator is not a paedophile in the classic sense of that term and could usefully avail of treatment."[408]

Similarly in *People (DPP) v. MS*,[409] Denham J. stressed the benefits accruing to both the defendant and society when a defendant successfully undergoes a treatment programme in prison to address the circumstances of an addiction or dysfunctional personal or family relationship connected with his or her criminal behaviour. This is an important factor which can help persuade the court to suspend the remainder of a custodial sentence on condition that the defendant is subject to a programme of supervision in the community.

21–78 The courts are reluctant to give a discount for the absence of appropriate rehabilitative facilities in prison. This is particularly relevant in the context of sexual offenders. The courts acknowledge, for example, that treatment in prison for paedophiles is very basic. Nevertheless, they will not normally suspend part of a custodial sentence with a view to the offender securing appropriate treatment in an outside facility.[410] They take the view that the provision of such treatment and opportunities for prisoners to avail of it is a matter for the Minister for Justice, Equality and Law Reform.[411] That, however, does not preclude sentence discounts for other factors associated with a paedophile condition. It is worth noting that in some recent cases of child sexual abuse involving members of religious orders, the courts have accepted in mitigation factors such as: the unnatural and isolated life-style in which the accused spent his youth, and the willingness of the order to look after the accused and ensure that he is never again in a position of power and trust with respect to children.[412]

The desire to encourage rehabilitation can result in the court adjourning the case for an extended period before imposing sentence.[413] The object is to see to how the defendant responds to treatment in the meantime. This is not unusual in cases where the offence is connected with the defendant's drug

---

[408] *DPP v. R O'D* unreported, Court of Criminal Appeal, May 25, 2000.

[409] [2000] 2 I.L.R.M. 311.

[410] See, however, *People (DPP) v. Byrne* unreported, Court of Criminal Appeal, January 31, 2000.

[411] *People (DPP) v. Payne* unreported, Court of Criminal Appeal, July 27, 1999. Note, however, the exceptional circumstances of *DPP v. R O'D* unreported, Court of Criminal Appeal, May 25, 2000 in which the prospect of rehabilitation was a significant factor in persuading the Court to impose a suspended sentence.

[412] See, *e.g.*, *People (DPP) v. M* [1994] 2 I.L.R.M. 541.

[413] See N Osborough *Deferment of Imposing Sentence* (1981) 16 Irish Jurist 262, for a discussion of the power to defer sentence to see how the defendant behaves in the meantime.

addiction or where it involves a sexual offence within the family.[414] Even if
the defendant responds well to treatment in the meantime there is no
guarantee that a custodial sentence will not still be imposed at the end of the
adjournment in any case where a custodial sentence is otherwise appropriate.
However, the defendant can reasonably expect that a lengthy adjournment
during which he has responded well to treatment will result in a reduced or
more lenient sentence. [415] The personal circumstances of the accused are also
relevant. Inevitably, these will vary from case to case. The sort of factors
which may be relevant are: remorse, past criminal record, family commitments, attitude of family members, attitude of employer, a commitment to
reform and a low risk of re-offending. Some of these factors might be
considered as equally relevant to the gravity of the crime.

First time Offender

As a general proposition it can be said that a court will not normally impose a   **21–79**
sentence of imprisonment for a first criminal offence, unless the circumstances of the offence are particularly serious.[416] Equally, a first offence
typically will warrant a lighter sentence than might have been applied for the
same offence committed by an offender with a long criminal record.[417] Where
the defendant has a past criminal record that is a factor which the court must
take into account when determining the appropriate sentence.[418] A criminal
record in this context refers only to convictions recorded against the
defendant before the commission of the offence in question as distinct from
before the imposition of sentence for that offence.[419] While the existence of
such a criminal record is undoubtedly relevant to the determination of
sentence it is difficult to be prescriptive about exactly how it is relevant.[420]
The most likely impact is on the extent to which a court is willing to give a
reduction for mitigating factors. The longer and more persistent the record,
particularly for offences similar to that before the court, the less likely the
court will be to give any reduction for mitigating factors. Conversely, a minor
or stale criminal record, or one which bears no similarity to the offence before
the court, is likely to have little impact in this direction. The age of the
offender is also a factor in that the courts are more inclined to give a young
offender a chance to reform even if he has built up a fairly long criminal

---

[414] See O'Malley, *op. cit.*, p.318 for details of two unusual cases in which sentencing was deferred in
respect of two defendants convicted of terrorist type offences. In one case the defendant was an
elderly man who was described by the court as an "old fool" in the circumstances surrounding the
commission of the offence while the other concerned a 17 year old with a mental age of age of 11
and no previous convictions.
[415] *DPP v. McBride* unreported, Court of Criminal Appeal, July 5, 1999.
[416] *People (Attorney General) v. McClure* [1945] I.R. 275; *People (Attorney General) v. Thomas*
[1945] I.R. 319.
[417] *People (DPP) v. Sherin* unreported, Court of Criminal Appeal, July 28, 1999; *People (DPP) v.
Burke* unreported, Court of Criminal Appeal, July 28, 1999.
[418] *People (Attorney General) v. Poyning* [1972] I.R. 402.
[419] *Attorney General (McConville) v. Brannigan* [1962] I.R. 370.
[420] See discussion in O'Malley, *op. cit.*, pp.189–191.

record.[421] Indeed, the courts will not necessarily confine this possibility to minors.[422]

Age

Age can be a significant factor in sentencing generally. The Children Act 1908 and, more particularly, its successor the Children Act 2001, reflect a preference for non-custodial sentences for children, while the courts tend to apply more leniency in the sentencing of minors compared with adult offenders. Age can also be a significant factor at the other end of the scale. The courts do take into account the relatively severe impact that a custodial sentence can have on defendants of advanced years. Accordingly, they are more likely to give a larger discount than might otherwise have been the case for a younger defendant.[423] In appropriate cases custodial terms will be suspended.[424] In *People (DPP) v. JM*,[425] for example, the sentencing court imposed a custodial term of three years on a retired primary school teacher who had pleaded guilty to a series of sexual assaults against his pupils in the past. The court considered that an eight year term would have been appropriate but taking into account the fact that the defendant was 84 years of age and in poor mental and physical health the court decided that a proportionate sentence would be three years imprisonment. On appeal, the Court of Criminal Appeal accepted that a sentence of eight years would have been appropriate given the nature of the offences. Equally, the sentencing court was correct in reducing the sentence to three years. However, the Court of Criminal Appeal went on to rule that the sentencing court erred in failing to suspend the sentence, taking into account the advanced old age and deteriorating health of the defendant together with his remorse and social disgrace to which he would be subject in his local community as a result of the conviction.

21–80   It does not follow, of course, that the courts will never impose a prison sentence on a defendant who is in his or her eighties and who is suffering from certain medical conditions. Much depends on the particular circumstances of each case. Giving judgment in *People (DPP) v. PH*,[426] on the same day as *JM* the same Court of Criminal Appeal upheld a sentence of three years imprisonment in which the last year only was suspended. The defendant in that case was 87 years of age and was convicted of serious indecent assaults against young friends of his granddaughter. In this case, however, the

---

[421] The Children Act 2001, s.258 makes provision for the effective deletion of certain offences from a child's criminal record after 3 years in certain circumstances.

[422] *People (DPP) v. Jennings* unreported, Court of Criminal Appeal, February 15, 1999.

[423] *DPP v. K* unreported, Court of Criminal Appeal, March 20, 1991; *People (DPP) v. Doyle* unreported, Court of Criminal Appeal, March 24, 1994; *People (DPP) v. PH* unreported, Court of Criminal Appeal, February 22, 2002.

[424] *DPP v. Doyle* unreported, Court of Criminal Appeal, March 24, 1999.

[425] Unreported, Court of Criminal Appeal, February 22, 2002.

[426] Unreported, Court of Criminal Appeal, February 22, 2002. See also *DPP v. Warren et al* unreported, Court of Criminal Appeal, July 5, 1999.

defendant was in stronger health than the defendant in *JM*, his guilty plea came late and his actions had a very serious detrimental effect on one of his victims.

Disability and Illness

Disability and illness can influence sentencing in an individual case, primarily because a custodial sentence will almost invariably have a harsher impact upon a person suffering from disability or illness compared with a healthy offender. Equally, in appropriate cases, a court will take into account the fact that the defendant may not have fully appreciated the harm he was causing due to a mental disorder.[427] While factors such as religious, racial, national or ethnic origins should never be equated with a disability, the reality is that offenders can suffer on these grounds in prison either as a result of direct victimisation or, where their home is abroad, because they are cut-off from family contact and support. It is not unusual for a court to make allowances for such additional hardships in appropriate cases.[428] Similarly, the courts have been known to give sentencing discounts for offenders who are at high risk of victimisation in prison because of their occupation. While there may be a popular perception that female offenders benefit from greater leniency in sentencing than that applied to males, there is no hard evidence to support it.[429]

Other Penalties

It would appear that the sentencing court can take into account other penalties already incurred by the defendant as a result of being found guilty and other adverse consequences which will flow from the conviction. Where the court is calculating the amount of a fine to impose, for example, it will take into account any related disqualifications or financial penalties which the defendant will incur as a result of the conviction.[430] Similarly, when the court is deciding to impose a custodial sentence or the length of a custodial sentence and whether it should be suspended it will normally take into account, where relevant, factors such as loss of pensionable employment, adverse effect on business, break-up of marriage and loss of social standing in the community suffered by the defendant as a result of the conviction.[431] While the court can take account of these other adverse consequences in mitigation, it must be careful not to invite the defendant to waive a legal right, such as the right to sue gardai, in return for a lighter sentence.[432] A

---

[427] *DPP v. Smith* unreported, Court of Criminal Appeal, November 22, 1999.
[428] *People (DPP) v. Clarke* unreported, Court of Criminal Appeal, November 17, 1997; *People (DPP) v. Isenborger* unreported, Court of Criminal Appeal, January 25, 1999.
[429] See O'Malley, *op. cit.*, pp.182–183.
[430] *DPP v. Redmond* unreported, Court of Criminal Appeal, December 21, 2000.
[431] See, for example, *People (DPP) v. Brophy* [1992] I.L.R.M. 709; *People (DPP) v. O'S* unreported, Court of Criminal Appeal, June 13, 1994; *People (DPP) v. Z* unreported, Court of Criminal Appeal, March 14, 1995.
[432] *Mellett v. Judge Reilly* unreported, High Court, October 4, 2001.

punishment beating administered in the community has also been taken into account in mitigation.[433]

Information on character of offender

21–81 The court must be careful not to be prejudiced against the defendant by information about his or her character which is not directly relevant to the offence before which he or she is before the court. In *DPP v. Redmond*,[434] for example, the defendant had been the subject of some notoriety for allegedly taking bribes from property developers in his position as a senior local government official in Dublin. The offence for which he was before the court was only very loosely and indirectly connected with those alleged activities. The offence was a failure to make tax returns. Accordingly, the sentencing judge was very careful not to have any regard to the publicity surrounding the defendant's alleged role in taking the bribes when determining the appropriate sentence. Equally, the court must not take into account material prejudicial to the character of the accused which is not directly relevant to the commission of the offence, but which has been offered by a witness without being invited.[435] Conversely, there are examples of judges giving the defendant credit for good deeds after the commission of the offence and before the imposition of sentence. Typically, these will involve making restitution or paying compensation to the victim, actions which also help demonstrate the defendant's remorse. However, there have also been cases of the defendant getting credit for more socially beneficial activities such as rescuing people in danger, or even just fulfilling his family responsibilities or finding employment.

Historical environment in which offence is committed

Where the offence or offences were committed a long time ago in circumstances which were different from those prevailing today the courts will be favourably disposed towards leniency. This has been a feature in some of the cases involving sexual offences against children by persons in positions of authority over the victims. The courts tend to treat these offences against the social and legal context which prevailed at the time they were committed rather than on the basis of current norms.[436]

Individualised sentencing

21–82 The close association between mitigating factors and the personal circumstances of an offender ensures that it will always be difficult to make exact meaningful comparisons between the sentence handed down in one case and that in another. Meaningful comparisons are also rendered difficult by virtue

---

[433] *People (DPP) v. D* unreported, Court of Criminal Appeal, December 20, 1993; *People (DPP) v. Hamilton* unreported, Court of Criminal Appeal, January 25, 1999.
[434] unreported, Court of Criminal Appeal, December 21, 2000.
[435] In *People (DPP) v. Murray* unreported, Court of Criminal Appeal, May 16, 2001 the sentencing judge very properly ignored a remark by the Garda witness that the defendant who had just been convicted of a drugs offence was well known to the Garda National Drug Unit.
[436] See, *e.g., People (DPP) v. J(T)* unreported, Court of Criminal Appeal, November 6, 1996.

of the fact that the circumstances surrounding the commission of one offence will always differ in some respect from another. It follows that even when two or more accused are jointly indicted and convicted for the same offence, it cannot be assumed that they will all receive the same sentence. The point is well made by Walsh J. in the Court of Criminal Appeal in *People (Attorney General v. Poyning*:

> "When two prisoners have been jointly indicted and convicted and one of them receives a light sentence, or none at all, it does not follow that a severe sentence on the other must be unjust. If in any particular case one of such joint accused has received too short a sentence, that is not *per se* a ground on which this court would necessarily interfere with the longer sentence passed on the other. Of course, in any particular case the court must examine the disparity in sentences where, if all other things were equal, the sentences would be the same; it must examine whether the differentiation in treatment is justified. The court, in considering the principles which should inform a judge's mind when imposing sentence and having regard to the differences in the characters and antecedents of the convicted persons, will seek to discover whether the discrimination was based on those differences.[437]

6. Concurrent or Consecutive Sentences

Where the accused has been convicted of two or more offences for which the court imposes custodial sentences, the question arises whether the sentences should run concurrently or consecutively. It is not seriously questioned that the court has the power to order sentences to run consecutively,[438] although an exceptionally long cumulative total in any individual case would give rise to an issue of constitutionality. In practice concurrent sentencing is the norm.

As a general principle where the court is imposing custodial sentences for more than one offence in the same proceedings, it will order the sentences to run concurrently where the offences arise out of the same incident. In effect this means that the sentence to be served is that for the count which attracted the longest custodial sentence. While the court will always have a discretion to impose consecutive sentences in respect of separate charges, in the absence of specific statutory provision to the contrary that discretion will not normally be exercised unless the charges relate to separate victims in respect of different crimes.[439] Even then it would not be unusual for the sentences to be ordered to run concurrently. In *DPP v. Byrne*,[440] for example, the accused was sentenced on a plea of guilty to the rape of two women committed at two

---

[437] [1972] I.R. 402 at 408; quoted with approval by Finlay C.J. in the Supreme Court in *People (DPP) v. Conroy* [1989] I.L.R.M. 139 at 143.

[438] O'Malley cites common law, s.20 of the Criminal Law (Ireland) Act 1828, s.5 of the Criminal Justice Act 1951 and rulings of Lynch J. in *State (Dixon) v. Martin* [1985] I.L.R.M. 240 and *State (O'Donoghue) v. District Justice for Limerick City* unreported, High Court, April 17, 1986 as authorities for the power to impose consecutive sentences.

[439] *People (DPP) v. Coogan* unreported, Court of Criminal Appeal, July 29, 1997; *People (DPP) v. Z* unreported, Court of Criminal Appeal, March 14, 1995.

[440] [1995] 1 I.L.R.M. 279.

different places 24 hours apart. The judge sentenced him to two terms of imprisonment of 10 years each to run concurrently. The DPP applied to the Court of Criminal Appeal for a review of the sentence on the ground of leniency. The basis of the application was that the sentences were unduly lenient as they were imposed to run concurrently. In effect, therefore, there was no additional penalty for the second rape. The court, however, refused to interfere with the sentence, holding that the trial judge had not erred in principle.

21–83   In any case where concurrent or consecutive sentencing is an issue it will clearly be helpful to determine whether the offences arose out of the same transaction. In many situations this will not prove problematic as the offences will have clearly arisen out of wholly separate transactions. Difficulties will arise, however, where the same offence is committed repeatedly on separate occasions in the same circumstances or against the same victim. In *Meagher v. O'Leary*,[441] the applicant was found guilty on several counts of possessing illegal growth promoters. All of the substances were found on the applicant's premises and in two cars. Concurrent sentences were imposed on 11 of the counts, but consecutive sentences were imposed in respect of the substances in one of the cars. The consecutive sentences were upheld on a judicial review. Moriarty J. considered that the two substances in question clearly differed in form and colour and as such could properly be viewed as constituting two separate offences. The learned judge also suggested that a useful test for determining whether or not offences were separate would be to decide whether or not an acquittal in respect of a charge confined to one of them would be a bar to a prosecution for any of the others.

In *People (DPP) v. Z*,[442] the Court of Criminal Appeal seemed to accept that consecutive sentences in sexual offence cases could be warranted only where the accused had committed the offences against different victims over a relatively long period of time. Equally, or alternatively, that the individual offences should be accompanied with circumstances of depravity. In that case, the court quashed consecutive sentences of seven years penal servitude which had been imposed on the defendant in respect of two counts of unlawful carnal knowledge against a girl under the age of 15 years. It does not follow, however, that consecutive sentences are never appropriate in respect of a series of sexual offences against the same victim. In *People (DPP) v. TB*, the Court of Criminal Appeal upheld consecutive sentences of four years imprisonment imposed on a father in respect of two counts of sexual assault against his daughter. The indictment actually charged 32 counts of sexual assault against the daughter and two against another victim. The court held that it was within the discretion of the sentencing judge to impose the consecutive sentences as the offences were committed at intervals over many years. The court was also influenced by the fact that the maximum

---

[441] [1998] 2 I.L.R.M. 481.
[442] Unreported, Court of Criminal Appeal, March 14, 1995. The victim in this case became pregnant as a result of the offences and her pregnancy was at the centre of the *X* abortion case.

sentence available for sexual assault was five years imprisonment, a limit which did not offer sufficient scope to reflect the gravity of the total criminal behaviour in this case.

The Court of Criminal Appeal was motivated by similar considerations when **21–84** it substituted two consecutive sentences of three years imprisonment for concurrent sentences of three years in *People (DPP) v. McKenna*.[443] In that case the defendant had been found guilty of serious sexual offences committed on a regular basis against his daughter over two long periods of time. The court justified the consecutive sentences by reference to the circumstances of depravity which surrounded the commission of the offences and the undue leniency of three years imprisonment given the nature and extent of the offences.

If the defendant is already serving a prison sentence at the time of conviction for another offence, it would appear that a consecutive sentence is appropriate.[444] Otherwise the second offence will effectively go unpunished. The same applies to an offence committing while incarcerated in prison.[445]

As a general principle a court must have regard to the total punishment when imposing custodial sentences to run consecutively. If the total is excessive relative to the overall gravity of the offending behaviour appropriate reductions should be made. This could, of course, result in the abandonment of the consecutive sentence and the imposition of suitable sentences to run concurrently.[436] It is quite likely that a trial court in this country would be restrained from imposing consecutive sentences, the cumulative total of which rendered it inevitable that the offender would spend the rest of his life in prison. It is also worth noting that the District Court should not impose consecutive sentences in respect of different summonses or charges arising out of the same criminal transaction in a manner which results in an aggregate custodial sentence in excess of 12 months,[447] unless they involve offences committed while the defendant is on bail (see below).

When a court imposes a consecutive sentence the order will specify when the consecutive sentence is to begin. Normally this will be on the expiry of the first or longest of the consecutive sentences imposed. If, however, the sentence is to run consecutively to a sentence or sentences currently being served then the order should state clearly which sentence already imposed on him or her is the sentence to which the new sentence is to run consecutively.[448]

There are some situations in which a court is obliged to impose consecutive **21–85** sentences. Section 11 of the Criminal Justice Act 1984 stipulates that a

---

[443] Unreported, Court of Criminal Appeal, May 9, 2002.

[444] *People (DPP) v. Murphy* unreported, Court of Criminal Appeal, February 1, 1999.

[445] O'Malley, *op. cit.*, p.175.

[446] See, *e.g., People (DPP) v. O'Shea and Conroy* unreported, Court of Criminal Appeal, February 17, 1997.

[447] *Meagher v. O'Leary* [1998] 1 I.L.R.M. 211.

[448] *State (Gleeson) v. Martin* [1985] I.L.R.M. 577; *State (Dixon) v. Martin* [1985] I.L.R.M. 240.

sentence of imprisonment imposed on a person who is on bail must be consecutive to any sentence passed on him for a previous offence. If he is sentenced for two or more previous offences then it must run consecutively to the last due to expire. This requirement does not apply where any of the sentences involved is life imprisonment or indefinite detention under section 103 of the Children Act 1908. Where the sentences are imposed by the District Court the aggregate cannot exceed two years. Although it is not specifically stated in the Criminal Justice Act 1984 which introduced this consecutive sentencing requirement, it would seem that the sentencing court must have regard to the total sentence relative to the gravity of the criminal behaviour involved:

> "the sentencing court should determine the sentence appropriate to the offence or offences on the indictment to which the section applies, without regard to the fact that it must be a consecutive sentence under the provisions of section 11, and direct that such sentence shall be consecutive on any sentence for a previous offence. That is not to say, in a proper case, the sentencing court, in the case of grave offences, should not adjust the sentence downwards where not to do so would impose a manifestly unjust punishment on the accused."[449]

The Court of Criminal Appeal has held that, in an appropriate case, a court may suspend a consecutive sentence imposed pursuant to the requirement in section 11 of the 1984 Act.[450] On one view this would appear to defeat the policy behind section 11. Indeed, it is worth noting that the Bail Act 1997 has now introduced a requirement that the court should normally treat the fact that the offence was committed on bail as an aggravating factor and therefore should impose a heavier sentence than might otherwise have been the case.[451] While this does not preclude the court from suspending the consecutive sentence, it might be interpreted as narrowing the scope for such a result.

Another statutory provision requiring a sentence to be ordered to run consecutively is to be found in section 19(4) of the Criminal Justice Act 1994. It states that a prison sentence imposed in default of the payment of a confiscation order must be ordered to run consecutively to any term of imprisonment for which the defendant is liable under the sentence for the offence in question. However, the length of the consecutive sentence shall be reduced in proportion to any sum or sums recovered under the order. The Act provides, *inter alia*, for the imposition of confiscation orders in the amount that the defendant is estimated to have benefited from drug dealing.

It is also worth noting section 13 of the Criminal Law Act 1976 which stipulates that a custodial sentence imposed on a defendant for an offence committed while serving another prison sentence must be consecutive to the latter sentence. If two or more sentences are being served then it must be consecutive to the last to expire. This provision does not apply when the sentence being served is a life sentence.

---

[449] *People (DPP) v. Healy* [1990] 1 I.R. 388 at 392.
[450] *People (DPP) v. Dennigan* 3 Frewen 253; *People (DPP) v. Farrell* [1992] 2 I.R. 32.
[451] Criminal Justice Act 1984, s.11(3), as amended by Bail Act 1997, s.10.

7. Taking other offences into consideration

Closely related to concurrent sentencing is the subject of taking offences into consideration for the purpose of sentencing. This arises where the accused has been convicted of an offence and, before sentence is imposed, he or she pleads guilty to other offences and asks the court to take them into account when imposing sentence. Normally the power is used only in respect of offences of which the accused has not actually been charged, although there seems no reason in principle why a court, having convicted an accused of one offence, could not accede to his or her request to take other similar offences on the charge sheet into consideration for the purpose of sentence.[452] The necessary jurisdiction is to be found in section 8 of the Criminal Justice Act 1951 which reads:

21–86

> "(1) Where a person on being convicted of an offence admits himself guilty of any other offence and asks to have it taken into consideration in awarding punishment, the court may take it into consideration accordingly.
>
> (2) If the court takes an offence into consideration, a note of the fact shall be made and filed with the record of the sentence, and the accused shall not be prosecuted for that offence, unless his conviction is reversed on appeal.

The DPP's consent is required before the court can accede to the defendant's request to take other offences into consideration.[453]

Where the court accedes to a request under this provision it will normally impose a stiffer sentence than it might otherwise have imposed.[454] Just how much stiffer the sentence will be depends on the number of extra offences involved. Presumably, the gravity of the additional offences will also be a factor. However, it does not follow that a sentence should be increased significantly simply because the offences being taken into consideration involve serious matters.[455] The advantage to the offender is that the sentence imposed will inevitably be less than the cumulative total of individual sentences which would have been imposed had he or she been charged separately for each of the offences. It also means that he or she is protected against further prosecution for the offences. The State benefits from savings in the investigation and prosecution of these offences.

Although section 8 does not specifically impose any limitation on the nature of the offences which can be taken into consideration for the purpose of sentencing, there are implied limits. A court, for example, cannot take into consideration offences over which it has no jurisdiction. Equally, it would be inappropriate to apply the provision with respect to very serious offences. Also excluded are offences which carry a mandatory penalty. The obvious

21–87

---

[452] See, however, *DPP v. Higgins* unreported, Supreme Court, November 22, 1995 where Finlay C.J. was critical of this practice on the ground that a conviction on the count on which a sentence was imposed might be overturned on appeal on a technicality.

[453] Criminal Justice (Miscellaneous Provisions) Act 1997, s.9.

[454] *People (DPP) v. Gray* [1987] I.L.R.M. 4.

[455] *People (DPP) v. McAuley and Walsh* unreported, Court of Criminal Appeal, October 25, 2001.

example is murder. In *DPP v. Gray*,[456] however, the Supreme Court ruled that a District Court judge was wrong to apply section 8 to excise offences which carried mandatory financial penalties. The accused in that case was charged with 17 separate charges of having breached the betting duty regulations. Each charge consisted of a repetition of the same conduct on different occasions. The legislation, however, imposed a mandatory penalty of £800 for each breach of the regulations, with provision for mitigation to a sum not below £400. The District Court judge proceeded to convict the accused on the first charge and took the others into consideration for the purpose of sentence which he fixed at £800. The Supreme Court ruled that he had no power to do this as section 8, *inter alia*, had no application to offences carrying a mandatory penalty. In the words of Griffin J:

> "In my opinion s.8(1) of the Criminal Justice Act 1951 can have no application where the offence in respect of which the accused person has been convicted is one carrying a mandatory penalty. Where the court can impose only one penalty for that offence, any other offence of which the accused admits himself guilty is in such case incapable of being 'taken into consideration in awarding punishment' within the meaning of the section. The purpose of the section is in my opinion clear – to enable the judge, in passing sentence, where offences other than those for which an accused person has been convicted had been committed by him, and were still untried and were admitted by him, to impose a sentence appropriate to the offence of which he was convicted having regard to and taking into account the other offences of which he then admitted his guilt. As the Chief Justice has pointed out, this the judge cannot genuinely and *bona fide* do where only one penalty can be imposed for the convicted offence."[457]

Griffin J. went on to state *obiter* that the section could not be used in respect of offences which carried mandatory consequential orders, such as the disqualification attaching to a conviction for drink driving.

E. Procedure

1. Introduction

21–88 The question of what sentence to impose once the offender has been convicted can be the subject of a hearing in itself. Indeed, in a case where the judge is minded to impose a custodial sentence it would not be unusual for him or her to adjourn the case to facilitate a full hearing on the question of sentence. Even in minor cases in the District Court where the accused has pleaded guilty the judge will consider any plea of mitigation submitted by or on behalf of the offender and the previous criminal record of the accused before imposing sentence.

As outlined above the critical factors which the judge will take into account when determining sentence are: the gravity of the offence, the personal

---

[456] [1987] I.L.R.M. 4.
[457] *ibid.* at 13.

circumstances of the accused, his or her reaction to having committed the offence, his or her criminal record, if any, the facts surrounding the commission of the offence and the impact on the victim. The relative importance of these factors in any individual case will help shape the form and substance of the sentencing hearing.

2. Relevant Factors

Circumstances of the offence

In the interests of transparency and fair procedures the judge should at least **21–89** outline the salient facts surrounding the offence, the circumstances of the offender, the impact upon the victim and any other factor which he or she has taken into account in determining the sentence. Where the defendant pleaded not guilty most, if not all, of the relevant facts surrounding the commission of the offence will have been established in the course of the trial. Nevertheless, it may still be necessary to establish further facts for the purpose of sentence. It may be, for example, that the offence was one of strict liability in which it was not necessary to prove the defendant's state of mind with respect to a key ingredient of the *actus reus*. Since such matters can have a significant impact on sentence it will normally be necessary to engage in further fact-finding with respect to them at the sentencing stage. If the defendant has pleaded guilty it will be necessary to furnish the judge with an account of the surrounding facts for the purpose of determining the appropriate sentence. This is normally done by a police officer familiar with the case relaying the basic facts to the court. However, the defendant must be given an opportunity to contest the version presented by the police officer.[458] The victim also has a right to give evidence about what happened to him or her.[459]

Character and antecedents of the offender

Fact-finding may also be necessary in respect of the character and antecedents of the defendant.[460] His or her previous criminal record will be provided by a member of the Garda Síochána, usually the same member who gives an outline of the facts in an uncontested case. This must not include information about other complaints against the defendant.[461] The defence may also wish to lead evidence of previous good character.[462] To this end they may call witnesses who can testify to the accused's good character. These witnesses will go into the witness box, take the oath and submit to examination and cross-examination in the same manner as any witness heard during the trial. The only difference is that their testimony will relate only to their acquaintance with the character of the offender.

---

[458] *State (Stanbridge) v. Mahon* [1979] I.R. 214.
[459] *DPP v. Quilligan* unreported, Court of Criminal Appeal, May 17, 1999.
[460] *People (Attorney General) v. Poyning* [1972] I.R. 402.
[461] *People v. Riordan* [1948] I.R. 416.
[462] *People (Attorney General) v. Poyning* [1972] I.R. 402.

Reports

In addition, the court may be supplied by one or more reports concerning the defendant and/or the victim. The judge may call for probation, medical and/or psychiatric reports on the defendant before proceeding to sentence. Equally, if the offence is a sexual offence or involves personal violence or the threat of violence the court must take into account any effect of the offence on the victim.[463] To this end it may, where necessary, receive evidence or submissions concerning any such effect. Frequently this is done through the submission of a victim impact report which, at least on some occasions, is prepared by the Garda Síochána with the assistance of the victim. However, the court must also hear the victim's evidence as to the effect of the offence where the victim so requests.

Status of Victim's Evidence

21–90   Flood J. considered the status of the victim's evidence at the sentencing stage in *People (DPP) v. MC*.[464] The learned judge pointed out that the victim was not a witness for the prosecution in this context. The victim has the right to the assistance of his own solicitor and counsel for the purpose of giving evidence as to the effect of the offence, but only through examination-in-chief. He or she does not have the right to make submissions on the appropriate sentence. While the victim does not constitute a separate party in the sentencing process, both the prosecution and defence counsel have the right to cross-examine him or her on the evidence given. It is also worth noting that Flood J. commented as follows on how the victim's evidence (or decision not to give evidence) at the sentencing stage should be assessed:

> "The court, where evidence has been heard under the provisions of section 5, has a duty to take this evidence into account in determining the sentence to be imposed on the accused. This evidence is to be weighed in the same way as any other portion of evidence considered by the court in the sentencing hearing. It is also important to note that any evidence given under section 5 is subject to the same rules as to admissibility, and weight, as any other evidence in a criminal case. The fact that an injured party has elected to give evidence pursuant to section 5 is not to be treated, of itself, as either an aggravating factor or a mitigating factor in determining sentence. Section 5 cannot, and does not, purport to make any change to the manner in which a court is obliged to carry out its constitutional duty to independently select an appropriate sentence for a particular accused."[465]

Views of Prosecution

As a long standing matter of practice the prosecution does not seek a particular sentence in any individual case, nor does it make representations to

---

[463] Criminal Justice Act 1993, s.5(1).
[464] Unreported, Court of Criminal Appeal, June 16, 1995.
[465] *ibid.*

the trial judge on what an appropriate sentence might be. It would appear, however, that prosecution counsel (and defence counsel) is under a professional duty to draw the court's attention to any statutory provisions or common law authorities relevant to sentencing in the particular case where the judge seems to have overlooked them.[466] It will be seen later that the prosecution can seek a review of sentence on the grounds of undue leniency. It has been suggested in some quarters that a logical corollary would be for the prosecution to offer a view on sentencing at first instance.[467] O'Malley also points out that counsel representing the State are routinely asked to comment when defence appeals against sentence are being heard in the Court of Criminal Appeal.[468]

Conflict over Facts

It may happen that there is a dispute over facts at the sentencing stage. Where this relates to the circumstances in which the offence was committed it would appear that the appropriate course of action is for the judge to determine the facts after having listened to evidence presented by each side. This is known in England as a "Newton" hearing after the name of the leading case on the subject.[469] Clearly, this will rarely occur where the defendant was convicted on a not-guilty plea, unless the case concerns a strict liability offence. If the defendant disputes any part of the criminal record the prosecution will have to prove it formally through, for example, the production of relevant court orders. Where the defendant calls character witnesses these can be cross-examined by the prosecution. Similarly, where the victim gives evidence on the effect of the offence, he or she can be cross-examined by both the prosecution and the defence. It is not the practice for the prosecution to call witnesses to give evidence in rebuttal of character evidence led by the defence.

    Where there is a dispute between the parties over the facts surrounding the commission of an offence on a plea of guilty, a question arises over the standard of proof which the prosecution must meet. The importance of this matter is enhanced by the fact that sentencing is the only element which really matters to the defendant in a case where he or she has pleaded guilty. It is essential, therefore, that the prosecution should be held to the same high standard that they would have to satisfy for proof of guilt in a contested case. O'Malley points to convincing Canadian authority which suggests that the appropriate standard is proof beyond a reasonable doubt.[470]

21–91

---

[466] *People (DPP) v. Dennigan* 3 Frewen 253.
[467] *Attorney General's Reference (No.7 of 1997)* [1997] Crim.L.R. 908. See also O'Malley at p.354.
[468] O'Malley, *op. cit.*, p.354.
[469] See O'Malley, *op. cit.*, p.344.
[470] *R v. Gardiner* [1982] 2 SCR 368. See O'Malley, *op. cit.*, p.346.

3. Transparency

Public Hearing

21–92   Transparency is a vital incident of fairness in the sentencing process. It is important, therefore, that any report made available to the judge for sentencing purposes should also be made available to the parties. Similarly, the trial judge should never meet in chambers alone with a probation officer or other professional person to discuss any aspect of sentencing in an individual case. The Court of Criminal Appeal, in what O'Malley describes as in effect a practice direction,[471] offered this guidance:

> "By virtue of the obligation under the Constitution, and in order to ensure that justice is done, a criminal trial must be held in public, and the accused should always be present during all of a criminal trial on indictment which includes sentencing. It is not in accordance with law that any part of a criminal trial should be held in a judge's chamber and in the absence of the accused. Nor would it be proper though it did not occur in this instance, for any report to be made available to the judge which was not also available to the parties, and in particular to the defence. Justice must be administered in open court and everything pertaining to a criminal trial and to the sentencing of a person who has been convicted must be in open court."[472]

Presumably, this does not affect the legality of the practice whereby defence counsel seeks guidance from the judge in chambers (with prosecution counsel present) as to what sentence he or she had in mind. Such guidance can prove useful for defence counsel in giving advice to his or her client on whether to plead guilty. Given the presence of counsel for both sides in such discussions, plus the fact that they do not involve bargaining over sentence, it is at least arguable that they do not amount to sentencing in private. Although the courts have occasionally deprecated the practice it seems that it still occurs.

Presence of Defendant

21–93   It is explicit in the quotation above from the Court of Criminal Appeal that sentencing should normally be conducted in the presence of the defendant. He or she has a constitutional right to be present and to follow the whole of the criminal proceedings, including sentencing.[473] It is not an absolute right. It must give way to the need to protect the order of court proceedings in any case where the defendant is proving too disruptive. Equally, it cannot prevent the court from proceeding with sentence in any case where the accused has absconded. It is difficult, however, to envisage circumstances in which a court would be justified in not pronouncing sentence in public. Indeed, the Supreme Court has declared on several occasions the importance of pronouncing sentence in open court.[474] It follows that when a court pronounces sentence

---

[471] O'Malley, *op. cit.*, p.356.
[472] *People (DPP) v. McGinley* 3 Frewen 251 *per* Hederman J. at 252.
[473] *Lawlor v. Hogan* [1993] I.L.R.M. 606.
[474] *State (Kiernan) v. de Burca* [1963] I.R. 348; *Molly v. Sheehan* [1978] I.R. 438.

and subsequently alters sentence before the sitting has ended, it must pronounce the alteration in open court.[475]

Statement of Reasons

The statement of reasons for a sentence would also seem to be an essential ingredient of transparency. Indeed, this would seem to be particularly important given the scope for divergence in the sentences handed down for what appears superficially to be similar offences. Also for the defendant who pleads guilty, the sentence and the factors which have been taken into account are the most important aspects of the whole process. A statement of reasons in each case will also facilitate the appellate process and help generate consistency and public confidence in the system. It might seem surprising, therefore, that there is no statutory requirement to give reasons for the particular sentence handed down in each case. In practice, it would appear that reasons are normally given, at least where the defendant has been charged on indictment. This is in keeping with the developing jurisprudence which requires the giving of reasons for administrative decisions which impact upon the rights and liabilities of the individual.

Sentencing Accomplices

Where a number of defendants are charged jointly and one of them pleads guilty he should not be sentenced until the trial of the others has concluded. Only then will the court be able to assess the relative culpability of all the parties. It may happen, of course, that the defendant who has pleaded guilty will give evidence for the prosecution against his former accomplices. In this event the better practice is to sentence the defendant on his guilty plea before he gives evidence. This is necessary to avoid the appearance or reality of his evidence being affected by a desire for a lenient sentence. In *People (Attorney General) v. Poyning*,[476] O'Dalaigh C.J., giving the judgment of the Supreme Court distinguished the situation in which the co-accused's were charged on different counts or, indeed, where they all pleaded guilty.

4. Executing Warrants of Imprisonment or Detention

Form of Warrant

The warrant of imprisonment or detention, as the case may be, constitutes the legal authority for the imprisonment or detention of the offender who has been sentenced to a term of imprisonment or detention.[477] To be valid the warrant must be engrossed by the sentencing judge. It will recite the name of the offender, and other details necessary for his or her identification, the

21–94

---

[475] *State (Kiernan) v. de Burca* [1963] I.R. 348. It seems that the District Court, at least, has jurisdiction to alter sentence before the sitting in question has ended, but not thereafter; *R (Burke) v. Cork Justices* [1905] 2 I.R. 309.

[476] [1972] I.R. 402.

[477] Criminal Justice Administration Act 1914, s.3 and District Court Rules 1997, Ord.26, r.9.

offence, the court, the date of issue, the sentence and the place of detention (where relevant). It must also state the date on which the sentence is to begin or provide sufficient information by which the date can be identified.[478] The validity of the warrant will not be affected by a clerical error which does not affect the nature and substance of the warrant. In *O'Driscoll v. Governor of Cork Prison*,[479] for example, the High Court refused to quash a warrant which incorrectly stated the date of the relevant court order.

Where a sentence has been upheld or varied on appeal the original warrant can still provide the necessary authority to hold the offender, subject only to such variation as may follow from the decision of the appellate court. In *Application of McLoughlin*,[480] for example, where the Court of Criminal Appeal reduced a sentence of 10 years imprisonment to six years, the Supreme Court held that it was not necessary for the Court of Criminal Appeal to issue a new warrant. The original warrant constituted good authority for the detention of the appellant. It was not necessary for the alteration in the sentence to be embodied in a new warrant.[481]

Date of Commencement

The date on which a prison sentence commences is considered to be equally as important as the length of the sentence.[482] Normally the sentence will commence on the date on which it is pronounced. Accordingly, the warrant of committal should be issued and executed immediately. If it is not executed immediately, it will be sent to the superintendent or inspector of the Garda Síochána in charge of the area where the warrant is issued, or any superintendent or inspector who acts for any other part of that district. If necessary, the warrant may be transmitted to officers in any other part of the State where the person may be found.[483] Delay in the execution of the warrant will not necessarily invalidate the warrant.[484] However, an unreasonable delay or unexplained delays between the imposition of the sentence and the execution of the warrant can result in the warrant being quashed.[485]

In the absence of specific statutory provision to the contrary, a court can order a prison sentence to take effect later than the date on which it is pronounced.[486] This can happen where the sentence is to run consecutively to a prison sentence currently being served. Equally, however, the sentence can be ordered to take effect from a later date in response to the personal circumstances of the offender. In *Meagher v. O'Leary*,[487] for example, the court deferred a

---

[478] See, *e.g.*, *State (McNally) v. O'Donovan* [1964] I.R. 272; *Re Tynan* [1969] I.R. 273.
[479] [1989] I.L.R.M. 239.
[480] [1970] I.R. 197.
[481] See also, *People (Attorney General) v. Poyning* [1972] I.R. 402.
[482] See *State (Flynn and McCormick) v. Governor of Mountjoy Prison* unreported, High Court, May 6, 1997, *per* Barron J.
[483] District Court Rules 1997, Ord.26, r.7.
[484] *O'Driscoll v. Governor of Mountjoy Prison* [1989] I.L.R.M. 239.
[485] *Dalton v. Governor of Training Unit* [1999] 1 I.L.R.M. 439.
[486] See *State (Jones) v. O'Donovan* [1973] I.R. 329 and *State (McNally) v. O'Donovan* [1974] I.R. 272 for examples concerning sentences of penal servitude.
[487] [1998] 2 I.L.R.M. 481.

sentence of imprisonment from March 13, 1997 to May 1, 1997 to enable the defendant, a farmer, to make arrangements for the management of the farm in his absence.

Stale Warrants

A prison governor will be justified in refusing to receive a prisoner who has **21–95** been sentenced to a term of imprisonment, but in respect of whom the warrant of committal to prison has not yet issued.[488] Equally, he will be justified in refusing to receive a prisoner where the warrant has become stale.[489] A stale warrant does not provide legal authority for the detention of the person concerned. A warrant will become stale if it has not been executed within the time limit fixed by the warrant itself. If no such time limit is specified it will become stale if it has not been executed within a reasonable time or, at any rate, after a period of six months. In the case of an unexecuted District Court warrant the person to whom it was addressed should return it to the issuing judge with a certificate stating the reason for non-execution. The warrant can then be re-issued, unless the delay or reasons for the delay are such as to render such a course of action unjust. The following extract from *State (McCarthy) v. Governor of Mountjoy Prison* suggests that non-execution within a reasonable time does not automatically protect the defendant against the issue and execution of a fresh warrant:

> ". . . the court's duty and power to see that its orders are executed can be in no way dependent upon the default of a third party. The party against whom execution has not yet been made suffers no hurt; rather has he enjoyed what has been described as an unwarranted respite. A new warrant will be appropriate when the original warrant has been destroyed or lost and also, although not necessarily so, when a new bailiff is chosen. But in all other cases reason and principle, economy and dispatch, indicate that the original warrant should be re-issued. The re-issued warrant with the date of re-issue endorsed thereon is given a new lease of life as from the date of the duration specified [in the District Court Rules]."[490]

F. Prosecution Application for Review of Sentence

1. Introduction

A distinctive feature of the sentencing process in Ireland is the fact that the **21–96** prosecution does not seek a particular sentence nor does it make representations to the court on what the appropriate sentence might be.[491] The fact that the victim can now be heard in the matter of sentencing in respect of certain offences does not alter this position. While this remains true for the impo-

---

[488] See, *e.g., O'Driscoll v. Governor of Cork Prison* [1989] I.L.R.M. 239.
[489] *Healy v. Governor of Cork Prison* [1997] 2 I.L.R.M. 357.
[490] [1997] 2 I.L.R.M. 361 at 368, quoted with approval in *Healy v. Governor of Cork Prison* [1997] 2 I.L.R.M. 357 at 360. For cogent criticism of this approach see O'Malley, *op. cit.*, p.366.
[491] See, *e.g., People (DPP) v. Sheedy* unreported, Court of Criminal Appeal, October 15, 1999.

sition of sentence at first instance, there is now provision under the Criminal Justice Act 1993 for the prosecution to seek a review of sentence imposed on conviction on indictment. There are no comparable provisions for the prosecution to seek a review of sentence imposed on summary conviction.

2. Scope of Power

Time Limit

The DPP may apply to the Court of Criminal Appeal to review a sentence imposed on conviction on indictment if it appears to him that the sentence was unduly lenient.[492] An application must be brought within 28 days from the day on which the sentence was imposed and notice must be given to the convicted person. It is not entirely clear whether notice of the application must also be given within the 28 day period, but that would appear to be the legislative intention. Moreover, there is no specific requirement that the notice should be lodged with the office of the Court of Criminal Appeal within the 28 days. Indeed, there are no Rules of Court dealing specifically with the procedure applicable to an application by the DPP for review of sentence. It would appear that the practice is to apply by analogy the Rules of the Superior Courts to appeals to the Court of Criminal Appeal.[493] This requires notice of the application to be served on the registrar. The notice can be served by delivery to the proper officer at the Office of the Court within the 28 day time limit.

There is no specific provision for the 28 day limit to be exceeded. Given the implications of any such application by the DPP for the rights and freedom of the convicted person, it can be assumed, therefore, that the time limit will be applied strictly.[494]

Sentence or Other Order

The application can only be taken after sentence has been imposed. In *People (DPP) v. Murphy*,[495] Lynch J. expressed the view, *obiter*, that the procedure is not applicable in a case where the judge has merely postponed sentence, even if the postponement is for a period of one year followed by a further one year period. In *People (DPP) v. Dreeling and Lawlor*,[496] however, the Court of Criminal Appeal had to decide whether an application could be brought at the point where the judge defers sentence for one year to see how the defendants responded to treatment for drug addiction and supervision by the probation and welfare service in the meantime. The judge qualified this by saying that he was not holding out any promise that a prison sentence would not be

---

[492] Criminal Justice Act 1993, s.2(1).
[493] *DPP v. McKenna* unreported, Court of Criminal Appeal, February 6, 2002.
[494] Criminal Justice Act 1993, s.2(2).
[495] Unreported, Court of Criminal Appeal, April 29, 1997.
[496] Unreported, Court of Criminal Appeal, February 27, 2001.

imposed on the adjourned date. The key issue to be determined by the Court of Criminal Appeal was whether the judge's order could qualify as the imposition of sentence for the purpose of initiating a prosecution review. The court looked to the definition of "sentence" in the 1993 Act and found that it specifically included a sentence of imprisonment and any other order made by a court in dealing with a convicted person other than an order under section 17 of the Lunacy (Ireland) Act 1821 or section 2(2) of the Trial of Lunatics Act 1883, or an order postponing sentence for the purpose of obtaining a medical or psychiatric report or a report by a probation officer. The court attached particular importance to the fact that the definition included not just a sentence of imprisonment but also "any other order" made by the court in dealing with a convicted person. While this would not include any short adjournment to enable the judge gather all the evidence necessary to determine sentence, the court felt confident that the legislative intention was to include any order concerning the manner in which the convicted person was to be dealt with, even if that involved a deferment of final sentence. The court found support for this interpretation in the express exclusion of a postponement for the purpose of obtaining reports. The implication was that any postponement of a final sentence which involved an actual dealing with the convicted person also qualified as a sentence. Accordingly, the DPP could bring an application to review a sentence where the judge had postponed a final determination for a period to see how the accused behaved in the meantime.

Discretion

Significantly, when the Court of Criminal Appeal came to consider the merits of the case in *Dreeling and Lawlor*,[497] it emphasised that its power to refuse the DPP's application was wholly dependent on a determination of the merits. It always retained a discretion in the matter. In exercising that discretion an important factor to be taken into account was the undesirability of it effectively acting as a court of first instance in imposing sentence. This is always likely to be a danger in a case where the sentencing judge postpones sentence for a period to see how the accused behaves in the meantime. If the DPP seeks a review of the order at that point and the Court of Criminal Appeal accedes to the application, that court will effectively become the sentencing court at first instance. Since this is likely to happen at a time when the case would otherwise have come back to the sentencing judge for review, the better course will often be to allow the sentencing judge make a final order in the matter.

21–97

3. Application in Postponed Sentences

Adjourned Sentence

The court in *Dreeling and Lawlor* did not specifically address the issue of whether the DPP would still have the power to seek a review of sentence at

---

[497] *People (DPP) v. Dreeling v. Lawlor* unreported, Court of Criminal Appeal, November 13, 2001.

the point where the judge imposes a final sentence in any case where the DPP had the option of seeking a review at the point of postponement. It would seem at least potentially unfair to give the DPP two bites of the cherry in this matter. Indeed, oppression on the accused was a factor which weighed heavily on Lynch J. in refusing the DPP's application for a review of sentence when it was finally imposed in *Murray* more than two years after the conviction. On the other hand, it could be that the sentence as finally imposed is considered unduly lenient by the DPP in which case the legislative intention would be defeated if the DPP could not take an application at that point. The issue has not yet been addressed directly by the Court of Criminal Appeal although, as will be seen, the Supreme Court has commented upon it *obiter* in *People (DPP) v. Finn.*[498] However, in *DPP v. Kennedy and Wills,*[499] an application was entertained when the judge imposed a final, non-custodial sentence one year after the conviction. In that case, the sentencing judge indicated that a sentence of five years in prison would be appropriate but proceeded to adjourn the case for one year to see how the defendants behaved in the meantime and what compensation they would collect for the defendant. When the case came back before the judge one year later he imposed a suspended sentence of five years. The DPP brought an application for review at that point, the result of which was that the sentence was quashed and replaced with a sentence of five years, with the first four years and six months being suspended.[500]

Butler Orders

21–98 A "Butler Order" poses further problems for the timing of a review application under these provisions. A "Butler Order", as explained above, is a sentencing order in which the judge imposes a term of imprisonment and states that he will review it after the defendant has served a specified period. The usual context is that if the defendant has been of good behaviour while in prison during that period and availed of whatever treatment is available the judge will suspend the remainder of the sentence when it comes back before him for review. The question arises, therefore, whether the DPP can seek a review of the sentence on the ground of undue leniency at the time the original order is imposed, at the time of the judge's final order on review, or both.

The Supreme Court addressed this specific question in *People (DPP) v. Finn.*[501] In giving the judgment of the Supreme Court, Keane C.J. was of the view that the legislative intention was to enable a review application to be brought at the point where the judge made the original order. Echoing the reasoning of the Court of Criminal Appeal in *Dreeling and Lawlor*, Keane C.J. explained that the definition of a sentence in the statutory provisions extended beyond an absolute and complete sentence to orders which deferred

---

[498] [2001] 2 I.R. 25.
[499] Unreported, Court of Criminal Appeal, February 27, 2001.
[500] See also *People (DPP) v. Connolly* unreported, Court of Criminal Appeal, November 25, 1996 where an application was entertained by the Court of Criminal Appeal at this point without question.
[501] [2001] 2 I.R. 25.

a final decision on a possible custodial sentence until the court had an opportunity to assess the defendant's rehabilitation. Accordingly, the DPP could bring an application for review at the point where the decision to defer was taken. Equally, as was seen above in *Dreeling and Lawlor*, he could bring an application at the point where the actual sentence was imposed at the end of the period of deferral. It did not follow, however, that an application could be brought at the point where the court settled the final sentence in a "Butler Order". This was not quite the same thing as the imposition of a sentence at the end of a period of deferral. With the "Butler Order" the sentence is already fixed in the original order. The length of custodial term and the period which would have to be served is known, and the likelihood of the remainder being suspended at the end of that period in certain circumstances is also known at the outset. It is not a situation in which the DPP was not in a position to know the nature of the sentence as originally imposed on conviction. It follows that the time to seek a review is no later than 28 days after the original order. To permit the DPP to bring two separate applications, the second being when the judge reviews the operation of the original sentence, would constitute a significant encroachment upon the finality of a judicial decision in favour of a convicted person. Keane C.J. could find no support for such a facility in the statutory provisions. The definition of "sentence" had to be interpreted in the context of the statute as a whole. This made it clear that the legislative intention was to permit a prosecution application in respect of a sentence imposed on conviction, and not on a review of sentence which is the position in respect of a "Butler Order".

The decision in *Finn* offers implicit support for the notion that the DPP can have two bites of the cherry in a case where sentence has been deferred. In respect of a "Butler Order", however, he can only bring an application within 28 days of the imposition of the original sentence. The judge's decision on a review of sentence is beyond the DPP's reach. In practice, of course, this should prove of more academic than practical significance given the views which the Supreme Court expressed about the validity of "Butler Orders" in *Finn*.

4. DPP's Decision

Assessment of "Unduly Lenient"

The DPP can make an application for review only if it appears to him that the sentence imposed was unduly lenient. How the Court of Criminal Appeal has interpreted "unduly lenient" on these applications is dealt with below. The legislation, however, does not specify any factors which the DPP should take into account, nor the sources of information which he should access, when deciding whether a sentence is unduly lenient.[502] Undoubtedly, he will be guided by the practice of the Court of Criminal Appeal on such applications

21–99

---

[502] O'Malley suggests that there is evidence that the DPP may be coming under undue pressure from public opinion in deciding to seek a review in individual cases; *op. cit.*, pp.384–385.

and the accumulated knowledge within his office on the sort of sentences which are typically imposed for the same offences committed by similar individuals in similar circumstances. He can also consider the reports or any relevant documents which were considered by the sentencing court before it imposed sentence in the case at hand. Indeed, the registrar of that court is obliged to give a copy of such reports or documents to the DPP on request. It is also worth noting that the registrar must give a copy of any such reports or documents to the convicted person and the Court of Criminal Appeal where the DPP has made an application for review of sentence.[503]

Prohibition on Representation

The DPP enjoys some statutory protection against representations aimed at influencing his decision for or against a review application. The provisions in section 6 of the Prosecution of Offences Act 1974 which prohibit certain communications in relation to criminal proceedings are specifically applied to the sentence review application process.[504] Accordingly, there is a general prohibition on communications with the DPP (and the Attorney General, the acting DPP, a member of the Garda Síochána or a solicitor acting for the Attorney General or DPP in their official capacities), for the purpose of influencing him in the making of a decision in relation to an application for sentence review under these provisions. This prohibition does not extend to communications made by the convicted person or by a person involved in the matter, either personally or as a legal or medical adviser to the person, or as a social worker or a family member. Presumably, a "person involved" in this context includes any victim of the offence in question.

5. Jurisdiction of Court of Criminal Appeal

Scope

21–100 The Court of Criminal Appeal may either refuse an application for review,[505] or quash the sentence and in its place impose on the convicted person such sentence as it considers appropriate, so long as it is a sentence which could have been imposed on the offender by the sentencing court concerned.[506] The legislation does not specifically state that the Court of Criminal Appeal on such an application can quash a sentence and impose another sentence only if it is satisfied that the original sentence was unduly lenient. The only specific restriction is that it cannot quash the original sentence and impose another sentence which could not have been imposed on the offender by the sentencing court. It would appear, therefore, that the court could act on an application under these provisions even if it was not satisfied that the original

---

[503] Criminal Justice Act 1993, s.4(1)(b).
[504] *ibid.* s.2(4).
[505] *ibid.* s.2(3)(b).
[506] *ibid.* s.2(3)(a).

sentence was unduly lenient. Indeed, it might even impose a lesser sentence. In practice, of course, such applications can only be brought if the DPP feels that the original sentence was unduly lenient. Moreover, the Court of Criminal Appeal takes the view that the issue it has to determine on such an application is whether a sentence was unduly lenient.[507] It follows that the focus in these applications is on whether the original sentence was unduly lenient and, more particularly, how the Court of Criminal Appeal determines whether or not a stiffer sentence is warranted.

Guidelines on Court's Approach

In the first review application to come before the Court of Criminal Appeal, **21–101**
DPP v. Byrne,[508] the court took the opportunity to offer the following guidance on how the relevant provisions should operate:

> "In the first place, since the Director of Public Prosecutions brings the appeal the onus of proof clearly rests on him to show that the sentence called in question was 'unduly lenient'.
>
> Secondly, the court should always afford great weight to the trial judge's reasons for imposing the sentence that is called in question. He is the one who receives the evidence at first hand; even where the victims chose not to come to court as in this case – both women were very adamant that they did not want to come to court – he may detect nuances in the evidence that may not be as readily discernible to an appellate court. In particular, if the trial judge has kept a balance between the particular circumstances of the commission of the offence and the relevant personal circumstances of the person sentenced: what Flood J. has termed the 'constitutional principle of proportionality' (see *People (DPP) v. W.C.* [1994] 1 I.L.R.M. 321), his decision should not be disturbed.
>
> Thirdly, it is in the view of the court unlikely to be of help to ask if there had been imposed a more severe sentence, would it be upheld on appeal by an appellant as being right in principle? And that is because, as submitted by Mr Grogan S.C., the test to be applied under the section is not the converse of the enquiry the court makes where there is an appeal by an appellant. The inquiry the court makes in this form of appeal is to determine whether the sentence was 'unduly lenient'.
>
> Finally, it is clear from the wording of the section that, since the finding must be one of undue leniency, nothing but a substantial departure from what would be regarded as the appropriate sentence would justify the intervention of this court."[509]

6. Undue Leniency

Degree of Divergence

It is clear from these guidelines that the Court of Criminal Appeal will not **21–102**
interfere with the original sentence simply because it is lenient or even

---

[507] *People (DPP) v. Cox and Keeler* unreported, Court of Criminal Appeal, October 12, 1998.
[508] [1995] 1 I.L.R.M. 279.
[509] *ibid.* at 287.

because a stiffer sentence would not have been upset on appeal.[510] The court will have to be persuaded that the sentence imposed falls far below what would have been appropriate in all of the circumstances. These include the particular circumstances of the individual offender. The matter was put by Barron J. in *DPP v. McCormack*:

> "In the view of the Court, undue leniency connotes a clear divergence by the court of trial from the norm and would, save in exceptional circumstances, have been caused by an obvious error in principle. Each case must depend upon its special circumstances. The appropriate sentence depends not only upon its own facts but also upon the personal circumstances of the accused. The sentence to be imposed is not the appropriate sentence for the crime, but the appropriate sentence for the crime because it has been committed by that accused. The range of possible penalties is dependent upon these two factors. It is only when the penalty is below the range as determined on this basis that the question of undue leniency may be considered."[511]

Moreover, the court will give great weight to the sentencing court's interpretation of the relevant circumstances.[512] It will be very slow to overrule the balance which that court has stuck between the circumstances of the offence and the circumstances of the offender.[513] On the facts of *Byrne* itself, for example, the court refused to interfere with the trial judge's discount of four years for the defendant's early admission of guilt in what would otherwise have been 14 year sentences for a double rape. The court was not deterred from that conclusion by the fact that the trial judge had ordered the sentences to run concurrently, even though each rape would have merited a 10 year sentence on its own.

Error of Principle

It is also worth emphasising that undue leniency will not be satisfied by a mere difference in opinion between the sentencing court and the Court of Criminal Appeal on what the appropriate sentence is on the particular circumstances of the case. The inadequacy in the sentence must be such as to raise an error of principle. In *DPP v. Kennedy and Wills*,[514] for example, the Court of Criminal Appeal found that the sentencing judge had been guilty of an error of principle in adjourning the case to see what compensation the defendants would collect for the victim. While compensation could be accepted as a sign of contrition or remorse it could not be applied in a manner which conveyed a sense of the defendants buying their way out of a sentence.

---

[510] *People (DPP) v. McAuley and Walsh* unreported, Court of Criminal Appeal, October 25, 2001.
[511] Unreported, Court of Criminal Appeal, April 18, 2000.
[512] In *People (DPP) v. Crowley* unreported, Court of Criminal Appeal, January 31, 2000 the sentencing judge was influenced by the young age of the defendant, the opportunity for reforming him, his remorse, payment of compensation and behaviour since the offence when imposing a suspended sentence for a vicious drunken assault. The Court of Criminal Appeal refused to interfere with the sentencing judge's assessment and sentence,
[513] *DPP v. Naughton* unreported, Court of Criminal Appeal, May 18, 1999; *DPP v. Xhafa* unreported, Court of Criminal Appeal, June 21, 1999.
[514] Unreported, Court of Criminal Appeal, February 7, 2001.

A gross departure from the norm may also be sufficient to raise an error of principle, but it will not be satisfied simply because the members of the Court of Criminal Appeal would have imposed a heavier sentence in the case.[515]

Proportionality

In *People (DPP) v. Connolly*,[516] the court applied what Flood J. referred to in *People (DPP) v. W.C.*[517] as the principle of proportionality in assessing whether the sentencing court had been too lenient. In that case the defendant had been convicted of killing a 25 year old woman who had six children and a 60 year old man by dangerous driving. He was sentenced to three years imprisonment to be reviewed five months later. On review the judge suspended the remainder of the sentence. The Court of Criminal Appeal found, balancing the proportionality of the circumstances of the offence and the harm done to the victims against the impact of the sentence on the personal circumstances of the accused, that the suspension of the balance of the sentence was lenient. However, it was not so lenient as to justify interference by the Court of Criminal Appeal. In reaching this decision the court also took into account the delay that there had been in reaching finality with respect to the sentence. It took almost one year for the review application to be heard. During that period the applicant was out of custody and in a state of uncertainty about his sentence. This coupled with the effect that his five months in prison had on him persuaded the court that the sentence taken as a whole in all of the circumstances was not unduly lenient.

21–103

Rehabilitation

There is some evidence that the Court of Criminal Appeal will be particularly reluctant to interfere with a sentence designed to rehabilitate a drug addict. This is particularly so where the DPP's application is taken against a deferment of sentence so as to enable the sentencing judge assess the accused's response to treatment for his or her addiction. The Court of Criminal Appeal takes the view that there is a very substantial public interest in the rehabilitation of drug users. A sentence which might be unduly lenient in the case of one offender, therefore, might not be unduly lenient in the case of another where it was motivated by the prospects of weaning the latter of his or her addiction.[518]

The issue of rehabilitation has also arisen in the context of sex offenders. In *People (DPP) v. Payne*,[519] the Court of Criminal Appeal considered that the absence of appropriate therapy or rehabilitative facilities in prison for sex offenders was not a factor which the sentencing court should take into account when determining sentence. In that case, the court quashed a

---

[515] *DPP v. Redmond* unreported, Court of Criminal Appeal, December 21, 2000.
[516] Unreported, Court of Criminal Appeal, November 25, 1996.
[517] [1994] 1 I.L.R.M. 321.
[518] See, *e.g., People (DPP) v. Dreeling and Lawlor* unreported, Court of Criminal Appeal, November 13, 2001.
[519] Unreported, Court of Criminal Appeal, July 27, 1999.

sentence of six years imprisonment in which the balance was suspended after two years and then imposed a full six year term. However, the court felt able to distinguish *Payne* on its facts in *DPP v. R O'D*.[520] The former case concerned a paedophile priest who had abused altar boys and who continued the abuse even after a complaint had been lodged. *R O'D*, however, concerned a brother abusing younger sisters several years previously. The abuse had ceased, the brother was responding very well to treatment and the sisters had made it clear that they did not want a custodial sentence to be imposed. In these exceptional circumstances, the Court of Criminal Appeal felt that the rehabilitation of the defendant through a non-custodial sentence with strict conditions attached would be more in the public interest than retribution through the imposition of a custodial sentence.

Severity of Sentence

21–104   The closer the sentence is to the top of the scale the more difficult it will be to persuade the Court of Criminal Appeal that it is unduly lenient. In *People (DPP) v. McAuley and Walsh*,[521] for example, the Court of Criminal Appeal refused to quash sentences of over 15 years imprisonment for the manslaughter of a detective garda in particularly callous circumstances. The court explained that such sentences were amongst the longest imposed in modern times for the offence of manslaughter. Accordingly, it would be very difficult to establish that they were unduly lenient as distinct from merely lenient. The Court was also not deterred from its view by the fact that the defendants had some serious offences taken into consideration for the purpose of their sentences.

Examples of Undue Leniency

There have been several cases in which the Court of Criminal Appeal has been persuaded that the original sentence was unduly lenient. In *DPP v. G*,[522] for example, the court converted a suspended sentence of five years for rape and indecent assault to an actual sentence of five years imprisonment. The offender had raped his sister over a 40 year period of time and had committed indecent assaults on his niece much more recently. The trial judge justified his highly unusual step of suspending the sentence by reference to the offender's advanced age, the traumatic effect that the conviction would have on his otherwise highly respected family, his plea of guilty and the fact that the rapes of his sister took place a long time ago and that the sister had made a very good recovery. Having regard in particular to the defendant's indecent assaults on his niece much more recently and the traumatic effect that they had on her, the Court of Criminal Appeal was not satisfied that these factors were sufficient to bring the case into the highly exceptional category in which a non-custodial sentence might be imposed for rape. It considered that the

---

[520] Unreported, Court of Criminal Appeal, May 25, 2000.
[521] Unreported, Court of Criminal Appeal, October 25, 2001.
[522] Unreported, Court of Criminal Appeal, February 8, 1999.

appropriate sentences for the rapes and indecent assaults would have been in the region of six to 10 years imprisonment. Accordingly, the sentence actually imposed was unduly lenient. Significantly, the court felt able to reach this decision despite noting that the defendant was not in custody and in a state of uncertainty about the sentence for a period of 17 months after the sentence was imposed.

In *People (DPP) v. Power*,[523] the court increased a sentence for rape from four years to six years. The rape in that case was aggravated by a number of serious bodily injuries to the victim which, in themselves according to the Court of Criminal Appeal, might have warranted a sentence of four years. While it agreed with the trial judge that the defendant's early plea of guilt and genuine remorse merited a substantial reduction, it concluded nevertheless that the four year sentence was much too low. It was fortified in this conclusion by a comparison of the facts and sentence in *Byrne* and a review of over 40 cases where sentences were imposed on pleas of guilty to rape over the previous three years.

An excess of judicial compassion proved fatal to suspended sentences handed down in respect of offences for handling stolen property worth over £100,000 in *People (DPP) v. Cox and Keeler*.[524] In that case the trial judge opted to give the defendants a chance, having noted that they were married with families, had not been before the courts on a criminal matter for several years, had their original convictions quashed on appeal, had honoured their bail and pleaded guilty at their re-trial. The Court of Criminal Appeal, however, considered that even allowing for these factors suspended sentences were out of all proportion to the seriousness of the offences, the professional nature of the criminal operation and the criminal records of the two accused. Accordingly, the court imposed the sentences which had been suspended by the trial judge. In this case there was also a strong suspicion that the accused pleaded guilty as part of a plea-bargaining negotiation. While the Court of Criminal Appeal indicated that any future plea-bargaining would have to take place against the reality that it would have no currency with the court on a sentence review application, the court further ordered that in order to avoid any possible injustice in the case it should be brought back before the sentencing court after one year for review.

In *DPP v. Dodd*,[525] the defendant's previous criminal record, including a conviction in England for causing death by dangerous driving five years previously, were major factors in persuading the court in a very short judgment to impose a stiffer sentence for the offence of dangerous driving causing serious harm. The court was also influenced by the fact that the Oireachtas had recently increased the maximum sentence for this offence from a term of five years to a term of 10 years imprisonment. In *McDonagh v.*

21–105

---

[523] Unreported, Court of Criminal Appeal, March 3, 1997.
[524] Unreported, Court of Criminal Appeal, October 12, 1998.
[525] Unreported, Court of Criminal Appeal, April 19, 1999.

DPP,[526] the court also increased a sentence from six to 10 years. The offence in this case concerned the possession of explosives. The court concluded that the original sentence was unduly lenient by reference to one other similar case in which the sentence was 15 years. Despite acknowledging that the sentences in both cases were handed down by experienced Special Criminal Courts, the Court of Criminal Appeal decided that the appropriate sentence in the comparator case should have been 10 years instead of 15 years imprisonment. Accordingly, it increased the sentence in the case before it to 10 years imprisonment.

A peculiar situation arose in *People (DPP) v. Murphy*,[527] where the accused received a suspended sentence of six months imprisonment. Although the Court of Criminal Appeal considered that the sentence was too lenient it refused to interfere with it essentially because it felt that the accused had suffered enough. In that case the victim refused to make any input into the original sentencing decision while the accused provided a very impressive body of testimonials about his good character. Among these were representations from his fellow workers at An Post which suggested that the accused would be sacked and lose all the pension and other entitlements which had been built up over 25 years. Accordingly, the judge postponed sentence for one year until An Post clarified its position on the accused's future status with them. With no clarification having been received by the end of that year the judge postponed sentence for another year. Eventually sentence was imposed over two years after conviction.

21–106   There is some evidence to support O'Malley's concern that review applications are being brought with undue frequency. Similarly, there is reason to believe that the Court of Criminal Appeal, perhaps influenced by the frequency of applications, is becoming more inclined to approach these cases on the basis of what sentence it would have considered appropriate rather than on the basis of whether the sentence actually imposed was so excessively lenient that it merited interference. In *DPP v. Seery and Ferncombe*,[528] for example, the court doubled a sentence of three years imprisonment to six year imprisonment in almost summary fashion. The sentence in question was imposed for acts of violence against prison officers in the course of a prison disturbance and was ordered to run consecutively to the term which the prisoner was already serving. Similarly, in *DPP v. Melia*,[529] the Court of Criminal Appeal decided to increase concurrent sentences of eight years and three years imprisonment for aggravated sexual assaults to concurrent sentences of 12 years imprisonment. In reaching this decision, the court did not make comparisons with the sort of sentences which were being imposed for other similar offences or for aggravated rapes, nor did it explain fully why a sentence of eight years imprisonment could be considered to be not just lenient

---

[526] Unreported, Court of Criminal Appeal, May 19, 2000.
[527] Unreported, Court of Criminal Appeal, April 29, 1997.
[528] Unreported, Court of Criminal Appeal, July 29, 1999.
[529] Unreported, Court of Criminal Appeal, November 29, 1999.

but unduly lenient. It seemed to be heavily influenced by the fact that the offender had been previously convicted of rape for which he received a sentence of six years imprisonment and was considered to be a disturbed and dangerous person. These factors would also have been known to the trial judge.

Discretion

It is worth bearing in mind that the Court of Criminal Appeal retains a discretion to refuse an application for review even where the sentence in question might be considered unduly lenient in itself.[530] The discretion, of course, must be exercised properly. Nevertheless, it can result in applications being refused due to a long lapse of time between the original order and the hearing of the review application, or because of other circumstances in which it would be oppressive to subject the offender to a stiffer sentence than that originally opposed.

21–107

7. Relevance to Developments post Sentence

Current Circumstances

In *DPP v. Egan*,[531] the Court of Criminal Appeal made it clear that when considering what sentence would be appropriate on an application for review under these provisions, the court had to consider the circumstances as they were at the time of the review hearing. These circumstances could be quite different from those confronting the sentencing court. The defendant might have been released back into the community having served a period of time in prison, he may have lost a permanent pensionable employment, his family and social circumstances may have changed for the worse, he may have made reparation to the victim, he may be responding very well to treatment and so on. The court, therefore, might be persuaded that the sentence originally imposed was unduly lenient, but taking into account the circumstances as they are at the date of the hearing it may not be appropriate to impose a stiffer sentence or make an order that would result in the defendant being sent to, or back to, prison. This is particularly so where the defendant is a first offender of previous good character.

Uncertainty

An inevitable consequence of the review process is that conviction and sentence might not necessarily bring finality for the offender. If the prosecution seeks a review of the sentence the offender will be left in a state of uncertainty until the Court of Criminal Appeal has handed down its decision in the matter. In some cases this can be well over one year for the date of the original sentence. This can be particularly harsh on an offender who has been given a non-custodial sentence or who has completed his or her

---

[530] *DPP v. Murphy* unreported, Court of Criminal Appeal, April 20, 1997; *People (DPP) v. Dreeling and Lawlor* unreported, Court of Criminal Appeal, November 13, 2001.
[531] Unreported, Court of Criminal Appeal, December 18, 2000.

prison sentence before the hearing in the Court of Criminal Appeal. Such an offender will be left facing the prospect that he or she might after all be sent to prison, or have to return to prison. As has been seen above, particularly in *People (DPP) v. Connolly*,[532] these are factors which the Court can take into account in deciding not to interfere with a sentence which is considered lenient. In *People (DPP) v. Sullivan*,[533] a delay of 16 months from the DPP's application to the actual hearing by the Court of Criminal Appeal was the dominant factor in persuading the court not to interfere with the non-custodial sentence originally imposed in respect of indecent assaults against two young children.

21–108 It does not follow that the court will never send a defendant back to prison or convert a suspended sentence into a full sentence in any case where it considers that that is merited. In *People (DPP) v. Isenborger*,[534] for example, the court considered the circumstances of the offence and the severity of the injuries to the victims to be such that a prison sentence of seven to 10 years could be warranted. Accordingly, it substituted a sentence of five years imprisonment for a suspended sentence of four years. Similarly, in *People (DPP) v. Gethins*,[535] the court converted a three year suspended sentence into a sentence in which only the first two years were suspended. The defendant, a mother of six children the youngest of whom was two years of age, had acted as the courier in an elaborate scheme which involved the importation of a very substantial amount of cannabis resin. What might be considered a particularly harsh outcome for the defendants occurred in *DPP v. Kennedy and Wills*.[536] In that case the sentencing judge adjourned sentence for one year to see how the defendants behaved and to give them an opportunity to collect compensation for the victim. At the end of the year the judge, being satisfied with the defendants' behaviour and the compensation, imposed a suspended five year sentence. The DPP brought a review application at this point, the outcome of which was that the defendants' had to serve the first six months of the five year sentence with the remainder suspended. This was over four years after the offence and almost two years after the sentencing judge made the initial order.

Implications of Plea Bargain

The implications of a review of sentence at the suit of the prosecution are particularly severe in a case where the accused has pleaded guilty after having been advised by his counsel, following a private meeting with the judge, of the sort of sentence he is likely to get on a plea of guilty. It was seen above that the Court of Criminal Appeal indicated in *People (DPP) v. Cox and Keeler*[537] that a reduced sentence which had been imposed as the result of any

---

[532] Unreported, Court of Criminal Appeal, November 25, 1996.
[533] Unreported, Court of Criminal Appeal, January 18, 1999.
[534] Unreported, Court of Criminal Appeal, January 25, 1999.
[535] Unreported, Court of Criminal Appeal, November 23, 2001.
[536] Unreported, Court of Criminal Appeal, February 27, 2001.
[537] Unreported, Court of Criminal Appeal, October 12, 1998.

form of "plea bargain" resulting from private discussions between counsel and the judge was at risk of being set aside on a sentence review application. The Court of Criminal Appeal would not be bound by any understanding reached in the private discussions nor would it inquire into the discussions between counsel and client which ensued consequent on counsels' private discussions with the judge. In effect this should have spelled the end of the practice of counsel seeking an indication from the judge as to the sort of sentence he had in mind for a plea of guilty and then using that information to advise his client on a plea. The attractions of such a practice would be seriously compromised by the knowledge that any perceived gains on sentence reduction were liable to be lost on an application for review. Nevertheless, the practice seems to have carried on, at least on the Dublin Circuit, as the matter came before the Supreme Court in the subsequent case of *People (DPP) v. Heeney*.[538]

In *Heeney*, counsel for the prosecution and defence met the judge in chambers **21–109** prior to the beginning of the trial. At that meeting the judge indicated the level of sentence he would impose on a guilty plea. Subsequently, the defendant pleaded guilty to counts of unlawful carnal knowledge and attempted unlawful carnal knowledge of young girls and was therefore sentenced to terms of imprisonment of six years and three years respectively. This was increased to 10 years by the Court of Criminal Appeal which stated frankly that it could not be fettered in any way by the holding of any private meeting in the judge's chambers or any indication as to the likely sentence given by the trial judge in such a meeting. The Supreme Court was then asked to consider as a point of law of exceptional public importance whether the Court of Criminal Appeal should have regard to the fact that discussion had taken place in chambers prior to the trial between the trial judge and counsel for the prosecution and defence, following which the accused pleaded guilty. The Supreme Court declared that plea-bargaining in the sense of a private arrangement whereby a particular level of sentence will be imposed in return for a plea of guilty has no place in Irish law. That, however, does not preclude the judge from giving an indication of the difference in level of sentence which a person can on occasion secure in his favour by a plea of guilty. Moreover, and more importantly for the narrow point at issue, is the factual question of whether the defendant pleaded guilty having been led to believe that the overwhelming likelihood was that he would have received the sentences which were actually imposed. Accordingly, the Court of Criminal Appeal was wrong as a matter of law to decline to have regard to the discussions which had taken place prior to the trial. The Supreme Court did not go so far as to say that the Court was bound by the outcome of such discussions where their result was a plea of guilty in return for the effective promise of a significantly lighter sentence. However, the Court was bound to take it into account as a factor in determining whether it would be proper to quash the sentence on the ground that it was unduly lenient.

---

[538] [2001] 1 I.R. 736.

Double Jeopardy

21–110   Another factor which, arguably, should be taken into account by the Court of Criminal Appeal when reviewing a sentence under these provisions is the element of double jeopardy involved. At its most extreme, this argument is that a defendant having been convicted and sentenced once should not be placed in jeopardy of being sentenced again for the same offence on foot of a prosecution application for review of sentence. The Supreme Court considered and rejected this argument in the *Heeney* case on the ground that double jeopardy has application only to the risk of being tried again for an offence in respect of which he has already been convicted or acquitted. It has no application to an adjudication by the Court of Criminal Appeal in a sentence review application. Nevertheless, the Supreme Court went on to suggest that on such an application the Court of Criminal Appeal could, and possibly should, take into account:

> "... any additional stress or trauma which it considers may have been caused to the defendant by his or her being subjected to an additional sentencing process ..."[539]

However, the degree to which that factor, if it arises at all, should have any impact on its decision is entirely a matter for the court.

8. Sentencing Powers

Scope

Where the Court of Criminal Appeal has quashed a sentence under these provisions it can impose any sentence which the sentencing court could have imposed on the offender. As explained above, this could actually result in a more lenient sentence, although such an outcome is most unlikely. In determining the appropriate sentence the court is constrained not just by the general jurisdictional limits of the sentencing court in respect of the offence in question, but also any limits which arise from the status of the individual offender. If the offender is a child or young person, for example, the court will be constrained by the limits on the sentencing court's powers in respect of the punishment of children or young persons.

Impact on Victim

When deciding what sentence to impose in place of the quashed sentence in a case concerning certain sexual offences or offences involving violence or the threat of violence against the person, it would appear that the Court of Criminal Appeal is bound to take into account the impact of the offence on the victim. This statutory requirement, introduced by the Criminal Justice Act 1993, applies where a court is determining the sentence to be imposed in a

---

[539] *ibid.* at 740.

relevant case (see earlier).[540] There is no suggestion that it is confined to the court of trial. It must be assumed, therefore, that it applies to the Court of Criminal Appeal when it is determining what sentence to impose after having quashed a sentence on a review application. Indeed, in all the cases to date it is apparent that the court pays due regard to the impact of the offence on victims when deciding whether to interfere with the sentence originally imposed. It is also worth noting that in making a determination in such a case the court must, on the application of the victim, hear the evidence of the victim as to the effect of the offence on him or her.[541]

9. Procedure

Onus on DPP

An application for review of sentence is taken by the DPP. It follows that the onus is on the DPP to persuade the Court of Criminal Appeal that the sentence imposed by the sentencing court was unduly lenient and as such should be replaced by a stiffer sentence.[542] The DPP cannot satisfy this requirement simply by asserting that the sentence was unduly lenient. He must be able to show on the basis of specific submissions of law or fact that the sentence was tainted by an error of principle.[543]

21–111

Legal Aid

The DPP must notify the convicted person of the making of any such application.[544] A legal aid (appeal) certificate is deemed to have been granted for the purposes of the Criminal Justice (Legal Aid) Act 1962 to the convicted person for the purposes of the application.[545] In effect this means that if the convicted person was legally aided at his trial he will be automatically granted the benefits of legal aid appropriate for an appeal without having to apply for them. In particular, he or she is entitled to free legal aid in the preparation and conduct of his case before the Court of Criminal Appeal, and to have a solicitor and counsel assigned to him or her for that purpose in the manner envisaged by section 10 of the 1962 Act.[546]

It can be expected, therefore, that the vast majority of defendants in sentence review applications under these provisions will be legally aided. However, for those few that are not the Court of Criminal Appeal has jurisdiction to award costs in their favour and costs will normally follow the event.[547]

---

[540] Criminal Justice Act 1993, s.5(1).
[541] *ibid.* s.5(2).
[542] *DPP v. Byrne* [1995] 1 I.L.R.M. 279; *People (DPP) v. Cox and Keeler* unreported, Court of Criminal Appeal, October 12, 1998.
[543] *DPP v. Redmond* unreported, Court of Criminal Appeal, December 21, 2000.
[544] Criminal Justice Act 1993, s.2(2).
[545] *ibid.* s.4(2)(a).
[546] *ibid.* s.4(2)(b).
[547] *People (DPP) v. Redmond* unreported, Court of Criminal Appeal, March 29, 2001; *DPP v. Hughes* unreported, Court of Criminal Appeal, March 27, 2000.

10. Appeal

21–112　Either the convicted person or the DPP can appeal to the Supreme Court against the determination of an application for review of sentence by the Court of Criminal Appeal. Such an appeal is possible only if the Court of Criminal Appeal, the Attorney General or the DPP certifies that the Court of Criminal Appeal's determination involves a point of law of exceptional public importance and that it is desirable in the public interest that an appeal should be taken to the Supreme Court.[548] Irrespective of who initiates the appeal the convicted person is automatically granted a legal aid (Supreme Court) certificate for the purposes of the appeal.[549] Once again he or she is entitled to free legal aid in the preparation and conduct of his or her case before the Supreme Court and to have a solicitor and counsel assigned for that purpose in the manner prescribed by section 10 of the 1962 Act.[550]

On an appeal under these provisions the Supreme Court may, for the purposes of its decision, remit the case to be dealt with by the Court of Criminal Appeal, or it may deal with the case itself and for that purpose exercise any powers of the Court of Criminal Appeal.[551] In particular, the Supreme Court may quash any sentence imposed by the Court of Criminal Appeal and in its place impose on the convicted person such sentence as it considers appropriate, so long as it is a sentence which could have been imposed on the offender by the sentencing court. Subject to this restriction, the Supreme Court quite clearly can impose either a stiffer or more lenient sentence than any imposed by the Court of Criminal Appeal in the case.

G. Pardon, Commutation and Remission

1. Pardon and Commutation

21–113　Article 13.6 of the Constitution confers on the President the right of pardon and the power to commute or remit punishment imposed by any court exercising criminal jurisdiction. However, the President can act in these matters only on the advice of the government.[552] Moreover, the right of pardon and the powers of commutation and remission can also be conferred by law on other authorities besides the President.[553] Indeed, the Criminal Justice Act 1951 permits the government to commute or remit in whole or in part any punishment imposed by a court exercising criminal jurisdiction, subject to such conditions as they may think proper, and may remit in whole or in part any forfeiture or disqualification imposed by such a court and

---

[548] *ibid.* s.3(1).

[549] *ibid.* s.4(2)(a).

[550] *ibid.* s.4(2)(b).

[551] *ibid.* s.3(2).

[552] Bunreacht na hÉireann, Art. 13.9.

[553] The right of pardon or the powers of commutation and remission in capital cases cannot be conferred by law on other authorities. However, this limitation has probably lost its practical

restore or revive, in whole or in part, the subject of the forfeiture.[554] The government is also expressly empowered to delegate these powers by order to the Minister for Justice, Equality and Law Reform and, where relevant, to revoke such delegation by order.[555]

There are significant differences of substance between pardon, commutation and remission. A pardon can absolve the offender not just from the punishment imposed for the offence in question but also from the guilt itself. It is not clear, however, whether a pardon automatically achieves the latter in every case. There is authority in the U.S. Supreme Court to the effect that a pardon reaches both punishment and guilt.[556] The English Court of Appeal, by contrast, takes the view that a free pardon does not eliminate a conviction, merely the pains, penalties and punishments that ensue therefrom.[557] In Ireland, the presidential pardon has been exercised only very rarely.[558] On each occasion the wording used has made it clear that the offender was exonerated from both punishment and guilt. The most recent occasion for its use was in the Nicky Kelly case.[559] The government's official statement on the pardon in that case stated: "The effect of the pardon will be to put Mr Kelly in the same position as he would have been in if he had not been convicted of the charges in question."[560]

21–114 The distinction between commutation and remission is less clear-cut and, indeed, the two terms are often used inter-changeably. Commutation of punishment generally denotes the situation where the offender is absolved from punishment which had otherwise been imposed. It does not affect the offender's guilt. Prior to the abolition of the death penalty in 1990, it was standard practice for the President to commute the death penalty imposed on anyone convicted of capital murder. In these cases a punishment of 40 years imprisonment was substituted. There is no requirement, however, for a lesser punishment to be substituted for the one commuted. Nor is it necessary to commute a sentence before the sentence has commenced. There is no reason why the remainder of a sentence cannot be commuted after the offender has satisfied part of it.

---

significance with the abolition of the death penalty by the Criminal Justice Act 1990, although it is arguable that the power cannot be conferred on other authorities in respect of murder to which s.3 of the Act applies.

[554] Criminal Justice Act 1951, s.23.

[555] Criminal Justice Act 1951, s.23, as amended by Criminal Justice (Miscellaneous Provisions) Act 1997, s.17 In *Brennan v. Minister for Justice* [1995] 2 I.L.R.M. 206 at 211, Geoghegan J. queried whether Art 13 permitted the government to delegate the power to commute or remit punishment.

[556] See Field J. in *ex p. Garland* (1886) 71 US (4 Wall) 330.

[557] See, for example, *R v. Foster* [1984] 2 All E.R. 679; see J Casey *Constitutional Law in Ireland* (2nd ed., London, Sweet & Maxwell, 1992), pp.70–71.

[558] See *Report of Committee to Enquire into Certain Aspects of Criminal Procedure* (Government Stationery Office, Dublin, 1990), pp.16–18.

[559] See D Walsh *Miscarriages of Justice in the Republic of Ireland* in C Walker and K Starmer (eds) *Justice in Error* (2nd ed., London, Blackstone Press, 1999).

[560] *The Irish Times*, April 29, 1992.

2. Remission

21–115   Remission of punishment signifies the situation where a portion of the offender's punishment is discounted. Typically, this will arise as a reward for good behaviour on the part of the offender, although it should be distinguished from the situation where the judge imposes a term of imprisonment subject to the proviso that he or she will consider suspending the remainder of it after the offender has served a specified period. The Prisons (Ireland) Act 1907 permits provision to be made in the Prison Rules for a prisoner to earn remission of a portion of his imprisonment by special industry and good conduct.[561] On his discharge the remitted portion of the sentence is deemed to have expired.

The key provision governing remission is to be found in Rule 38 of the Rules for the Government of Prisons which states that:

> "A convicted prisoner sentenced to imprisonment, whether by one sentence or cumulative sentences, for a period exceeding one calendar month, shall be eligible, by industry and good conduct, to earn a remission of a portion of his imprisonment, not exceeding one-fourth of the whole sentence, provided that the remission so granted does not result in the prisoner being discharged before he has served one month."

New draft prison rules published in 1994 by the government in *The Management of Offenders: A Five Year Plan*[562] state that remission will not apply to sentences for non-payment of debt or contempt of court. Subject to any such exceptions it follows that a prisoner who behaves well in prison can expect to serve no more than three quarters of the prison term imposed. It would appear, however, that there is a practice of granting up to 50 per cent remission in some prisons, including Portlaoise and Shelton Abbey.[563] The legal basis for such a practice is uncertain.

3. Release on Licence

21–116   Persons serving a life sentence do not qualify for remission under the Prison Rules. However, they and others serving long-term sentences can expect to be released on licence by the Minister for Justice, Equality and Law Reform after having served a significant number of years. A Sentence Review Group was established in 1989 to advise the Minister in these cases.[564] This has now been replaced by a parole board which has been established on a non-statutory basis. All prisoners who have served seven years or more of their sentence may apply to have their cases considered by the Review Group. Among the recommendations which the group can make are outright release, short periods of release, escorted outings, transfer to another institution and the provision of

---

[561] Prisons (Ireland) Act 1907, s.1.
[562] Stationery Office, Dublin, 1994.
[563] *Dempsey v. Minister for Justice* [1994] 1 I.L.R.M. 401.
[564] See *The Management of Offenders: a Five Year Plan* (Government Stationery Office Dublin) at 153.

appropriate therapy.[565] The decision in any individual case is a matter for the Minister.

4. Remission and Commutation by Order of the Minister

Remission and commutation of punishment can also arise in the context of the Minister for Justice, Equality and Law Reform exercising his delegated powers under section 23 of the Criminal Justice Act 1951. Indeed, up until recently it was common practice for the Minister to remit a portion of a fine imposed by the District Court in response to representations from the accused. Frequently, these representations will be supported by a member of the Dáil for the accused's constituency and/or the Garda Superintendent from the area in question. Almost invariably, they will seek a reduction in the fine and/or prison sentence on the grounds of personal or family hardship. In 1993, for example, the Minister dealt with 4,050 petitions for the remission of fines and the remission or commutation of prison sentences. The number refused was 1,767; an extension of time for payment was granted in 604 cases, full remission was granted in 98 cases and a partial mitigation of fines was granted in 1,580 cases. Clearly, the exercise of the Minister's powers of remission and commutation under the 1951 Act was quite significant. Nevertheless, the whole process was conducted as a private matter between the accused and/or his representative in the Oireachtas on the one hand and the Minister on the other. The judge who had imposed the sentence in any particular case was not consulted and there was no publication of the decision and supporting reasons in any individual case. It was almost as if a private system of justice was operating alongside the public system. Although the former was clearly limited in extent, nevertheless it had the effect of overriding key decisions taken in the latter.

Constitutionality

The constitutionality and legality of the ministerial practice of remitting fines and remitting or commuting prison sentences was challenged in *Brennan v. Minister for Justice*.[566] In that case a District Court judge sought an order of certiorari to quash the Minister's action in reducing the fines (and extending the time for payment) imposed by the judge in a number of cases. Geoghegan J., in the High Court, rejected the argument that the power to remit punishment, as derived from Article 13.6, forms part of the administration of justice. He considered that the power to determine an appropriate sentence and the power to remit or reduce a sentence were wholly different kinds of power. The former was clearly a judicial power[567] while the latter lacked the characteristics of the administration of justice identified by Kenny J. in

21–117

---

[565] See O'Malley, *op. cit.*, pp.289–290.
[566] [1995] 2 I.L.R.M. 206.
[567] See *State (O) v. O'Brien* [1973] I.R. 50.

McDonald v. Bord na gCon.[568] Instead, it corresponded to what was formerly the royal prerogative of mercy and as such was an executive function.[569] Equally, the exercise of the power of remission did not require a hearing in public, nor prior consultation with the judge who imposed the sentence. Nevertheless, the learned judge went on to hold that the manner in which the Minister had been exercising the power was *ultra vires* the 1951 Act and Article 13.6 of the Constitution. The nature of the power was such that it could be exercised only in exceptional circumstances. The Minister, however, had been exercising it in a manner which resulted in the establishment of a parallel system of justice:

> "I am quite satisfied that Article 13.6 of the Constitution was never intended to create a parallel or alternative system of justice than that provided for by Article 34. Yet that is precisely what is happening in these cases. There is no evidence that the minister found exceptional or unusual circumstances to justify her modifying the judge's order. The kind of points put forward either by the petitioning TD or by the garda superintendent in his respective reports or by the petitioner himself are all points which either were or could have been put before the judge when he was considering sentence. There was nothing in any of the reports before the minister to indicate that that was not done and, if so, that it could not have been done. I am not necessarily suggesting that the minister can only exercise her power if there is a change of circumstances following on the district judge's order. Indeed, I think it would be unwise to attempt any definition of what precisely the exceptional circumstances would have to be to justify remission of a fine. I think that in very exceptional cases a minister might be able to exercise his or her power in circumstances where he or she believed the judge's decision was wholly insupportable. But it is not easy to conceive of circumstances where that would be justified even on an exceptional basis in the case of a district judge's order which can be appealed to the Circuit Court, which court must in turn embark on a complete rehearing. Even though the appeal to the Circuit Court would be final, a Circuit Court judge who acted wholly irrationally would be subject to judicial review by the higher courts. It would seem to me, therefore, that it would be only in the rarest of circumstances (and I cannot conceive of what they might be) that the minister can modify a district judge's order imposing a fine on the basis of what he or she thought that the decision was wrong. There might be circumstances where some genuine unintended mistake was made by the judge which would lead to a legitimate exercise of the power. But in general it would seem to me that having regard to the clear provisions of the Constitution relating to the courts, the power under Article 13.6 must have been intended to be exercised sparingly."[570]

Transparency

21–118   It is apparent, therefore, that an accused who is unhappy about the sentence imposed in any individual case should seek a remedy through the normal

---

[568] [1965] I.R. 217, as approved by the Supreme Court in *Goodman International v. Hamilton* [1992] 2 I.R. 542.

[569] See, however, the analysis of Walsh J. *obiter* in *State (O) v. O'Brien* [1973] I.R. 50.

[570] [1995] 2 I.L.R.M. 206 at 220–221.

judicial process. Only in the most exceptional of circumstances would it be proper for the Minister to override that process on a petition from the accused. Moreover, in any case where the Minister does exercise the power to commute or remit he should record the facts of the case and his reasons for exercising the power:

"Although the exercise of the power by the minister need not be exercised in public as I indicated, it is constitutionally necessary, in my view, that all the evidence and information leading up to and the reasons for the exercise of the power be recorded. This is a logical consequence of the special nature of the power which would have been envisaged as to be exercised only in special cases. But for the exercise of any power, whether constitutional, statutory or otherwise, some accountability is essential. There has been a long established practice that the minister does not answer questions in Dáil Éireann relating to individual instances of the exercise of this power. That being so, the only way that the minister can in practice be made accountable for the proper exercise of the power is by means of judicial review in an appropriate case. But a proper judicial review would be frustrated unless there were stated reasons recorded for the exercise of the power together with all the information on which it was based. In the case of remission of fines, I would envisage that the most common instance of a legitimate exercise of the power would be some relevant change of circumstance since the court decision and outside the time for normal appeal. But as I have already indicated, I am not attempting to define what exactly the reasons must be and specifically I am not considering remission in the context of lack of prison accommodation as that did not arise in any of the four cases."[571]

As this quotation illustrates the legitimate exercise of the power is most likely to concern factors which arise after the court decision and outside the normal time for appeal. In the case of a sentence of imprisonment this may include a shortage of prison accommodation, although the learned judge refrained from expressing a view on that possibility.

5. Temporary Release

Introduction

There is provision for the Minister for Justice, Equality and Law Reform to make rules for the temporary release of prisoners or persons detained in St Patrick's Institution.[572] The operation of any such rules may be subject to statutory restrictions in respect of certain offences.[573] Where the power is available, the Minister may also also suspend, wholly or in part, the currency of the sentence of the person released under such rules.[574] Where the currency of the sentence is suspended during the period of temporary release it has the

21–119

---

[571] *ibid.* at 221.
[572] Criminal Justice Act 1960, s.2. These is also provision for the temporary release of criminal lunatics held in District Mental Hospitals or the Central Mental Hospital rules; s.3.
[573] See, for example, treason or murder contrary to s.3 of the Criminal Justice Act 1990 and certain drug offences (Criminal Justice Act 1999).
[574] Criminal Justice Act 1960, s.5.

effect of stopping the sentence from running during the period of suspension. In other words, the time on temporary release while the currency of the sentence suspended is not included in calculating how long the prisoner has left to serve when he returns to prison. It is possible, therefore, that a prisoner might be on temporary release for most of his sentence and then be brought back into custody to serve the remainder of his sentence after the date on which the sentence would normally have expired. However, undue delay in revoking a temporary release in such circumstances without adequate delay might be deemed unfair by the courts.[575] It should also be noted that the currency of the sentence will be suspended during the period of temporary release only if the rules specifically require it or if the Minister has positively directed a suspension.

The Rules

The temporary release scheme is governed primarily by the Prisoners (Temporary Release) Rules 1960. These confer the power to grant temporary release on the governor of the institution concerned, although the exercise of the power is always subject to the directions of the Minister and to any exceptions which may be specified in ministerial directions. Apart from certain statutory restrictions applicable to specified offences, there are no formal grounds for granting or refusing temporary release. However, the rules do provide for the attachment of conditions including, in particular, a requirement for the person in question:

(a) to keep the peace and be of good behaviour during the period of release;

(b) to be of sober habits; and

(c) not to communicate with, or publish or cause to be published any matter by means of, newspapers or any other publishing medium or engage in public controversy.[576]

As O'Malley points out the third of these requirements is so broad and so blatantly in conflict with common-sense and current norms of freedom of expression that it must be legally and constitutionally doubtful.[577]

Effect of Temporary Release

21–120   Where a person has been given temporary release he is deemed to be lawfully at large and entitled to remain so for the period of his release provided he observes the conditions of his release. He is deemed to be unlawfully at large if his period of release has expired or if he breaches any condition of his release.[578] In this event the currency of his sentence must be suspended for all of the period during which he was unlawfully at large. A member of the

---

[575] *Cunningham v. Governor of Mountjoy Prison* [1987] I.L.R.M. 33.
[576] Prisoners (Temporary Release) Rules 1960, r.5.
[577] O'Malley at p.283.
[578] Criminal Justice Act 1960, s.6.

Garda Síochána may also arrest any person whom he or she suspects on reasonable grounds to be unlawfully at large.[579]

Revocation

A temporary release can be revoked. It would appear, however, that this can only happen where the person in question has broken one of the conditions of his release. Moreover, the existence of any such breach must be determined in accordance with fair procedures. While this does not require a judicial determination it does nevertheless require an inquiry into whether there was a breach, and the person concerned should be heard in any such inquiry.[580] The mere fact that he has been charged with a criminal offence while on temporary release will not in itself be sufficient to justify automatic revocation.

Right to Continued Temporary Release

It would appear that a person who has been granted successive periods of temporary release does not enjoy a right to be heard before a decision is taken to refuse him a further period of temporary release.[581] His situation can be distinguished from that of a person whose temporary release is revoked. It may be, however, that a person has been granted successive periods of temporary release over such a long period of time that he acquires a legitimate expectation that that will continue. In *Sherlock v. Governor of Mountjoy Prison*,[582] for example, the applicant was given a life sentence for murder in 1970. He was granted temporary release in 1978 and this continued from time to time up until 1990 when he was suddenly taken back into prison without explanation. In this case, it was held that the applicant had acquired a legitimate expectation to continued temporary release to the extent that he should have been given reasons why it was not granted and an opportunity to make representations.

6. Release Pursuant to the Multi-Party Agreement

The Multi-Party Agreement (generally known as the Good Friday Agreement or the Peace Agreement) entered into between the British and Irish governments and most of the political parties in Northern Ireland with a view to a settlement of the conflict in Northern Ireland, contains provisions on the release of prisoners. These are scheduled to the Criminal Justice (Release of Prisoners) Act 1998 and are worth setting out in full:

21–121

> "1. Both Governments will put in place mechanisms to provide for an accelerated programme for the release of prisoners, including transferred prisoners, convicted of schedule offences in Northern Ireland or, in the case of those sentenced outside Northern Ireland, similar offences (referred to

---

[579] *ibid.* s.7.
[580] *State (Murphy) v. Kielt* [194] I.R. 458.
[581] *Ryan v. Governor of Limerick Prison* [1988] I.R. 198.
[582] [1991] 1 I.R. 451.

hereafter as qualifying prisoners). Any such arrangements will protect the rights of individual prisoners under national and international law.

2. Prisoners affiliated to organisations which have not established or are not maintaining a complete and unequivocal ceasefire will not benefit from the arrangements. The situation in this regard will be kept under review.

3. Both Governments will complete a review process within a fixed time frame and set prospective release dates for all qualifying prisoners. The review process would provide for the advance of the release dates of qualifying prisoners while allowing account to be taken of the seriousness of the offences for which the person was convicted and the need to protect the community. In addition, the intention would be that should the circumstances allow it, any qualifying prisoners who remained in custody two years after the commencement of the scheme would be released at that point.

4. The Governments will seek to enact the appropriate legislation to give effect to these arrangements by the end of June 1998.

5. The Governments continue to recognise the importance of measures to facilitate the re-integration of prisoners into the community by providing support both prior to and after release, including assistance directed towards availing of employment opportunities, re-training and/or re-skilling and further education."

These provisions have been implemented in Ireland by the Criminal Justice (Release of Prisoners) Act 1998. This Act provides for the establishment of an independent Commission to advise the Minister for Justice, Equality and Law Reform on the exercise of his powers of release with respect to any persons specified to be "qualifying prisoners" for the purpose of the scheme set out above. The Minister must have regard to the provisions of the scheme as set out above and to the advice of the Commission. The Act does not actually confer any additional powers of release on the Minister. If he decides to release a prisoner pursuant to these provisions he must act in accordance with his existing powers of release, such as those found in the Offences against the State Act 1939, the Criminal Justice Act 1951 or the Prisoners (Temporary Release) Rules 1960. In so far as any of these powers of release are conferred on the government, the advice conveyed by the Commission is given to the Minister with a view to the Minister communicating it to the other members of government so that the government can decide whether to exercise its power of release.

21–122   It would appear, therefore, that the primary determination on whether a prisoner qualifies for release under the scheme is essentially a matter for the Minister, having regard to the terms of the scheme as set out above. Having determined that a prisoner does qualify he must then consider the advice of the Commission before deciding whether to release (or to advise the government to release) the prisoner. The criteria which the Minister applies to determine whether a prisoner is a "qualifying prisoner" under the terms of the scheme arose for decision in *Doherty v. Governor of Portlaoise Prison*.[583] In that case the applicant had been an active member of paramilitary organisations

---

[583] Unreported, High Court, November 24, 2000.

involved with the conflict in Northern Ireland and had served prison sentences arising out of such activities. At the time of his application he was serving a prison sentence for firearms offences committed at a time when he was no longer a member of a paramilitary organisation. His application to the Minister to be considered for release under the terms of the 1998 Act was refused because his offence had not been committed in connection with the situation in Northern Ireland and because he was no longer a member of a paramilitary organisation on ceasefire.

Reviewing the *vires* of the Minister's grounds for refusing the request, McKechnie J. explained that the 1998 Act should not be construed strictly in the manner normally applicable to criminal legislation which created offences, provided for sanctions, or restricted rights and freedoms. The 1998 Act, unlike the others, confers a privilege. Accordingly, there was more scope to interpret its key provisions in their broader context. In particular, they had to be interpreted in light of the relevant provisions of the Multi-party Agreement. Taking this approach, McKechnie J. concluded that it was not necessary for a prisoner to be a member of a paramilitary organisation in order to benefit from the scheme. Prisoners were specifically excluded under the scheme only if they were members of paramilitary organisations not on ceasefire. It did not follow that it was necessary for a prisoner to be a member of a paramilitary organisation on ceasefire in order to qualify. Not only is the Minister bound to take this into account when making his decision, but the imposition of any precondition of membership would be in breach of the terms of the scheme and unlawful on grounds of public policy.

McKechnie J. had greater difficulty with the argument that the scheme was confined to prisoners who were serving sentences in respect of offences committed in connection with the situation in Northern Ireland. Neither the 1998 Act nor the terms of the scheme itself made this a specific precondition. It was enough that the prisoner was convicted of a schedule offence in Northern Ireland or similar offences in the case of those sentenced outside Northern Ireland. Since the firearms offences of which the prisoner was sentenced would be schedule offences in Northern Ireland, McKechnie J. accepted that that requirement was satisfied. However, the learned judge went on to hold that it was open to the Minister to require a connection between the offence and the situation in Northern Ireland. He supported this conclusion by reference to the fact that the scheme emanates from the Multi-Party Agreement which was designed to deal with the situation in Northern Ireland. No intention was expressed in the scheme itself or in the 1998 Act to extend it beyond that context. Indeed, resort to such a literal interpretation could result in the absurdity of prisoners who had committed offences for personal gain taking advantage of the scheme. Accordingly, it is not enough simply that the prisoner was convicted in the Special Criminal Court for an offence which would be a schedule offence in Northern Ireland. There would have to be a connection between the offence and the situation in Northern Ireland.

H. Transfer of Prisoners

1. Domestic Transfers

21–123   When a judge sentences an offender to a term of imprisonment he or she does not normally specify the prison in which the sentence is to be served. The place of incarceration would appear to be an executive matter, subject to legislative enactments which either prohibit or require the imprisonment or detention of specified categories of offender in specified locations. Generally, prisoners may be committed to such prisons as the Minister for Justice, Equality and Law Reform may direct.[584] The Minister also has the power to transfer prisoners from one prison to another. The position with respect to young offenders is set out above. Nevertheless, it is worth noting that the Minister can direct the transfer of detainees who are not under 17 years of age from St Patricks Institution to a prison in order to relieve overcrowding in St Patricks.[585]

The ministerial power of transfer is often used to transfer prisoners from secure prisons to prisons with a more relaxed regime in order prepare them for release. It can equally be used in the other direction, particularly if a prisoner takes advantage of the more relaxed regime to escape or proves unduly disruptive. It is likely, however, that an executive transfer to a prison regime which subjects the prisoner to a different form of punishment than that imposed by the courts would be considered unlawful.[586]

2. Transfers into and out of the State

The Transfer of Sentenced Persons Act, as amended by the Transfer of Sentenced Persons (Amendment) Act 1997, implements in Ireland the provisions of the Convention on the Transfer of Sentenced Prisoners 1983.[587] A prisoner wishing to be transferred from Ireland to his or her home State (the administering State) may submit a request to the Minister for Justice, Equality and Law Reform. The Minister must satisfy himself that the prisoner is a national of the administering State, that a final sentence has been imposed and that the sentence is within the scope of the Convention. The administering State must also be informed of the transfer request and consent to the transfer. Where the transfer request is granted the transfer is effected by the issue of a warrant by the Minister. The detailed arrangements for the transfer are set out in the Act.

Once the prisoner has been transferred into the custody of the administering State the enforcement of the sentence stands suspended in Ireland. Moreover, it cannot be enforced in Ireland after the time that the

---

[584] Criminal Justice Administration Act 1914, s.17(3).

[585] Prisons Act 1970 , s.7. This section is operational only for such periods as are specified by the Minister. Prisons Act 1970 (Section 7) Order 2001 (S.I. No. 97) – 24 months from June 28, 2001.

[586] *State (Boyle) v. Governor of Curragh Military Detention Barracks* [1980] I.L.R.M. 242.

[587] This is a Council of Europe Conventions which facilitates the transfer of citizens from the State in which they have been sentenced to imprisonment to their home State for the purpose of serving out the remainder of their sentence in their home State. It came into force on July 1, 1985.

administering State considers the enforcement of the sentence to have been completed. For the purposes of enforcing the sentence the administering State has a choice. It can continue the enforcement of the sentence immediately or through a court or administrative order. If it takes this course it is bound by the legal nature and duration of the sentence imposed in Ireland. Alternatively, it may convert the sentence through a judicial or administrative procedure into a decision of the administering State. This will have the effect of substituting the Irish sentence for a sentence prescribed by its own law for the offence in question. If it takes this course it will be bound by the findings of fact as they appear in the judgment of the Irish court: it cannot convert a custodial sentence into a pecuniary sentence, it must deduct the time already served, it cannot aggravate the punishment and it is not bound by any minimum sentence which its law provides for the offence in question. The administering State may also grant any pardon, amnesty or commutation of sentence in accordance with its own laws. However, the Irish courts retain the sole right to determine any application for review of judgment in the case. Where applicable, the administering State shall cease to enforce the sentence as soon as it is informed by the Irish authorities of any decision or measure which renders the sentence unenforceable.

21–124 Prisoners sentenced and incarcerated in other signatory countries to the Convention can seek to be transferred to serve their sentences in Ireland so long as they can show close ties with the State. A request must be made by the sentencing State or by or on behalf of the prisoner. The conditions outlined above for a transfer out also apply to a transfer in. Once an appropriate request has been received the Minister will normally apply to the High Court for a warrant to have the prisoner brought into the State. The application will be granted where the court is satisfied that the conditions outlined above are satisfied. In this event, the court may specify the place in which the prisoner is to be held. Its order is authority for the continued enforcement of the sentence. If the sentence is incompatible with Irish law the Minister may decide whether an application can be made for an order adapting it to what the appropriate penalty would be for a similar offence committed here. However, a sentence adapted pursuant to these provisions cannot aggravate the original sentence in terms of its nature or duration. These adaptation provisions have particular significance in respect of sentences of imprisonment imposed in the United Kingdom which are longer than any that could be imposed in Ireland for similar offences.

21–125 There is provision for the Minister to vary or revoke a warrant issued by him and to apply to the High Court for a variation or revocation of its order authorising the transfer of a prisoner into the State. In either case, the variation or revocation can be effected only in order to give effect to the provisions of the Convention.

The Act includes a general non-discrimination provision. It provides that in deciding on applications for transfer into or out of the State, the Minister shall not without good reason discriminate between applicants on the grounds of marital status, racial origin, age, political opinions or religious or other beliefs, health or sexual life, taking into account the operational requirements of the prison service and the welfare of the applicant. Moreover, if he refuses an application the Minister should give reasons for his decision where that is practicable and where the interests of justice do not preclude it.

CHAPTER 22

APPEALS

A. Introduction

The common law does not recognise a right of appeal from decisions of   **22–01**
courts exercising criminal jurisdiction.[1] Accordingly, one must look to the
Constitution or statute to determine the extent to which the defence and/or the
prosecution can appeal decisions of courts exercising criminal jurisdiction.
The Constitution does not address the subject directly. Apart from providing a
right of appeal to the Supreme Court from all decisions of the High Court, it
has nothing specific to say about appeal in criminal matters. The relevant
legislative provisions deal separately with appeals at different levels of the
court hierarchy. They also distinguish between making an appeal and a case
stated. Beginning with appeals from the District Court, this chapter will deal
with each tier of the appeal process in turn, followed by the procedure for
dealing with miscarriages of justice.

    Apart from appeals by way of case stated this chapter does not address the
broader subject of seeking a remedy in criminal matters by way of judicial
review. It often happens that in the circumstances of an individual case an
application for judicial review offers a more appropriate remedy than an
appeal, or may be the only remedy immediately available to the accused, in a
criminal matter. Equally, the circumstances may be such that the accused will
have a choice between an appeal and a judicial review.[1a] The High Court will
entertain applications for judicial review in criminal matters in appropriate
cases. It is reluctant, however, to entertain an application for leave to apply
for a judicial review when an appeal is pending or is a more appropriate

---

[1] *People v. Kennedy* [1946] I.R. 517; *People v. O'Shea* unreported, Supreme Court, November 2,
1982.
[1a] Note, however, that judicial review probably does not lie on a *quia timet* basis in the interval
between a finding of guilty and the recording of a conviction and/or passing of sentence; *Mellett v.
Judge Reilly* High Court, October 4, 2001, *per* Carroll J.

remedy.[1b] Nevertheless, it will not necessarily refuse such applications where judicial review is clearly an appropriate remedy in the circumstances of the case. Equally, the mere fact that a right of appeal is available in a case is not an obstacle to an application for judicial review.[1c] For a treatment of judicial review in criminal matters reference should be made to a specialist text in public law.[1d]

B. Appeals from the District Court

1. Legal Basis

22–02   Appeals from the District Court can take the form of a straightforward appeal to the Circuit Court, a case stated to the High Court or a consultative case stated to the High Court. Each will be dealt with in turn.

There is no constitutional or common law right of appeal from the District Court to the Circuit Court. There is, however, a statutory right of appeal for the benefit of a convicted person by virtue of section 18(1) of the Courts of Justice Act 1928. It stipulates that any person who has been convicted of a criminal offence in the District Court may appeal against conviction or sentence or both to the Circuit Court. This right of appeal extends to any order of the District Court dismissing the case under the Probation of Offenders Act 1907,[2] and an order for the payment of a penal or other sum, the doing of anything involving expense, the estreating of any recognizance or for the undergoing of any term of imprisonment by the person against whom the order was made. An order in this context also includes an order committing a person to a certified school within the meaning of the Childrens Act, 1908 to 1949, or to a borstal institution or to a place of detention provided under Part V of the Children Act 1908.[3] A person who has been convicted and committed to prison under section 10 of the Criminal Justice Administration Act 1914 without sentence until the next sitting of the Circuit Court can appeal.[4] Section 18(1) of the Courts of Justice Act 1928 specifically excludes orders binding a person to the peace or to be of good behaviour or both from the right of appeal to the District Court. However, the Criminal Justice Act 1951 makes provision for an application to the Circuit Court to be released from the obligations imposed by such an order.[5]

[1b] *Buckley v. Kirby* [2000] 3 I.R. 431; *Killeen v. DPP* [1997] 3 I.R. 218; *DPP v. Kelliher* unreported, Supreme Court, June 24, 2000.

[1c] *Nevin v. Crowley* [2001] 1 I.R. 113.

[1d] See, for example, Hogan and Morgan *Administrative Law* (3rd ed., Round Hall Sweet & Maxwell, Dublin, 1998).

[2] Courts of Justice Act 1953, s.33.

[3] Criminal Justice Act 1951, s.24. This is set to be replaced by Children Act 2001, s.265 which makes provision for appeal to the Circuit Court from orders of the Children Court or the District Court committing a child to a detention school or place of detention. See also ss.111–114 for appeals against other orders.

[4] Criminal Justice Administration Act 1914, s.43(12).

[5] Criminal Justice Act 1951, s.16.

There is no right of appeal for a complainant who is ordered to pay costs on the dismissal of his complaint. According to *Clifford v. Foley*[6] an order for costs in this situation is not an order for a "penal or other sum" within the meaning of section 18(1) of the Courts of Justice Act 1928.

2. Prosecution Appeals

The right of appeal conferred by section 18(1) of the Courts of Justice Act 1928 is clearly confined to a person convicted. As such, it does not extend to a right of appeal by the prosecutor against an acquittal. Indeed, there is no statutory provisions conferring a general right of appeal against acquittals. There are, however, a few statutory provisions that confer a right of appeal against an acquittal in certain limited contexts.[7] The constitutionality of one of these was challenged in *Considine v. Shannon Regional Fisheries Board*.[8] In that case the defendant had been acquitted of a number of offences under the Fisheries (Consolidation) Act 1959. Relying on the terms of section 310(1) of the Act the prosecutor appealed these convictions to the Circuit Court. The defendant challenged the constitutionality of this provision in so far as it purported to confer a right of appeal against an acquittal. In rejecting the challenge both the High Court and the Supreme Court relied on Article 34.3.4° of the Constitution which reads: "The Courts of First Instance shall also include Courts of local and limited jurisdiction with a right of appeal as determined by law." The Supreme Court ruled that this provision must be interpreted literally to mean that there was no constitutional bar against the Oireachtas creating a statutory right of appeal from a decision of the District Court (or the Circuit Court), even where that decision was an acquittal. Article 38.1 of the Constitution, which states that no person shall be tried on any criminal charge save in due course of law, does not necessarily preclude a right of appeal against an acquittal.[9] Accordingly, it was open to the Oireachtas to make provision by law for a right of appeal against an acquittal in the District Court.

3. Locus of Appeal

An appeal under any of the provisions described above lies to the judge of the Circuit Court within whose circuit lies the district or any part of the district of the judge from whose decision the appeal is taken.[10] There are slight variations in respect of convictions of licence-holders for pubs and clubs.[11] The appropriate Circuit Court for the hearing of the appeal is that which is

22–03

---

[6] (1946) Ir Jur Rep 53.
[7] See, *e.g.*, Fisheries Act 1850, ss. 51, 53 and 54; Inland Revenue (No.2) Act 1861, s.19; Fisheries Act 1939, s.100; and Fisheries (Consolidation) Act 1959, s.310(1).
[8] [1997] 2 I.R. 404, [1998] 1 I.L.R.M. 11.
[9] *People v. O'Shea* [1982] I.R. 384 cited with approval.
[10] Courts of Justice Act 1928, s.18(3).
[11] See J. Woods *District Court Practice and Procedure in Criminal Cases* (Woods, Limerick, 1994) p. 450.

held in the nearest town in the Circuit to the courthouse at which the decision was given, unless the Circuit judge orders otherwise.[12]

4. Initiating an Appeal

Notice

An appeal to the Circuit Court from a decision of the District Court must be by notice of appeal signed by the appellant or his solicitor.[13] According to Woods, defendants who have been jointly charged may serve joint notice of appeal even though there have been separate convictions.[14] Similarly, one of several joint defendants may appeal without the concurrence of the others.[15]

Service of Notice and other Documents

22–04   The notice of appeal must be served upon every party directly affected by the appeal within 14 days from the date on which the decision appealed from was given. Although not specifically stated, the clear implication is that this obligation rests upon the appellant.[16] Within this 14-day period the appellant must also lodge the original of the notice of appeal, together with a statutory declaration as to service, with the clerk for the court area within which the case was heard. Where the party wishing to appeal is in custody at the time, he shall be supplied with the necessary forms by the governor of the prison or other place of detention or, if in the custody of the Garda Síochána, by the relevant superintendent or inspector.[17] When completed, the forms must be transmitted immediately by the governor, superintendent or, inspector, as the case may be, to the clerk. The notice of appeal to be served upon the opposing party must be served by a member of the Garda Síochána who shall make the statutory declaration of service. This declaration must be lodged with the clerk.

Whenever the party to be served with a notice of appeal has appeared by a solicitor at the hearing, all notices and other documents to be served upon him may be served upon the solicitor that appeared for him.[18] Service may be effected by leaving the documents at the solicitor's office. Where the party has not appeared by a solicitor, notice of appeal shall be served upon him personally or by leaving it with a clerk, servant, spouse, child or other person over the age of 16 years of age at the party's residence, office or place of business.[19] It may also be served by posting it in a registered envelope addressed to the party at his or her last known residence, office or place of business. Proof of service shall be by statutory declaration which, when made, shall be lodged with the clerk.

---

[12]   Circuit Court Rules, 2001, Ord.41, r.2.
[13]   District Court Rules 1997, Ord.101, r.1. See Form 101.2 Schedule D.
[14]   Woods at 451. See *R v. Oxfordshire Justices* (1842) 12 LJMC 40.
[15]   *Ibid. R (Gibson) v. Fermanagh Justices* [1897] 2 I.R. 603.
[16]   The situation is different if the appellant is in custody at the time he wishes to appeal; see below.
[17]   Circuit Court Rules 2001, Ord.41, r.7.
[18]   *ibid.* r.8.
[19]   *ibid.* r.9.

Lodging Documents

Where any document is required or authorised to be lodged with the clerk, or any notice is required or authorised to be given to the clerk, in any of the situations described above, it may be lodged or given by leaving it with the clerk or by forwarding it by prepaid post to the clerk.[20] Where the prepaid post method is used, the date of lodgment or receipt shall be the day of the actual receipt of the document or notice by the clerk.

Certificate of Appeal

The clerk must sign and transmit to the County Registrar the certificate of appeal to the Circuit Court.[21] This certificate must be accompanied by: a certified copy of the conviction or order,[22] the original notice of appeal, the depositions (if any), the statement of the accused in writing (if any), the recognisance (if any), the original summons or other document by which the proceedings have been instituted, and the bond or other security given in the District Court (if any).[23] In practice any bail money lodged by a party to the recognisance is also forwarded with these documents.[24]

Recognisances

The District Court judge has a discretion to seek a recognisance for the purpose of the appeal,[25] subject to the fact that a recognisance cannot be required from the Attorney General, the DPP, the Director of Consumer Affairs,[25a] any Minister of the Government or Minister of State or any officer of such Minister, an officer or member of the Garda Síochána acting in an official capacity or an officer of the Revenue Commissioners acting in an official capacity.[26] An application to have recognisances fixed in the event of an appeal is generally made at the conclusion of the case, but it may be made *ex parte* at any time within 14 days from the date of the decision.[27] Where the

---

[20] *ibid.* r.10.

[21] *ibid.* r.12. See Form 101.7 Sched.D.

[22] Note s.14 of the Courts Act 1971 which reads: "In any legal proceedings regard shall not be had to any record (other than an order which, when an order is required, shall be drawn up by the district court clerk and signed by a justice or a copy thereof certified in accordance with the rules of court) relating to a decision of a justice of the District Court in any case of summary jurisdiction."

[23] Circuit Court Rules, 2001, Ord.41, r.1(ii).

[24] Woods at p.456.

[25] Circuit Court Rules, 2001, Ord.41, r.4. There is authority to the effect that a judge of the District Court does not have jurisdiction to refuse to fix recognisances for an appeal, but merely the amount of such recognisances; see *People v. Paul McCormack, re bail motion* unreported, High Court 1972; and Carroll J. in *M.D. v. G.D.* unreported, High Court, July 30, 1992. See Woods at p.452. Presumably these have been superseded by the terms of r.4.

[25a] The District Court Rules 1997 refer to the office as the Director of Consumer Affairs and Fair Trade. The correct title is the Director for Consumer Affairs. The responsibility for fair trade existed only for a few years by virtue of the Restrictive Practices (Amendment) Act 1987 before being transferred to the Competition Authority by the Competition Act 1991. I am indebted to Aengus O'Hanrahan B.A., LL.M for pointing this out.

[26] District Court Rules 1999, Ord.12, r.20.

[27] Woods at p.452.

court does require a recognisance, it shall fix the amount in which the appellant and the surety or sureties, if any, are to be bound. A sum of money equivalent to the amount of the recognisance may be accepted *in lieu* of a surety or sureties. Any such recognisance must be entered into within the 14-day period permitted for the service of notice of appeal.[28] Proceedings for the estreatment of any such recognisance must be taken in the Circuit Court.[29]

5. Stay of Execution

22–05 An appeal normally operates as a stay of execution.[30] However, in cases where the court requires a recognisance the appeal will not operate as a stay of execution unless the recognisance is entered into within the specified period of 14 days. Where the appellant is in custody he shall be released once the notice of appeal has been given and the recognisance, if any, entered into. In any case where a monetary penalty has been imposed on the appellant, the court may issue the warrant of committal in default of payment upon expiry of the time allowed by order for payment, unless the appellant has entered into the recognisance. Where an order affecting the holding of a driving licence has been imposed consequential upon conviction, it shall be suspended following lodgment of notice of appeal and entry of the recognisance within the 14-day period.[31]

Where an appeal is lodged and the recognisance, if any, entered into and the warrant to execute the District Court order has not issued, the warrant shall not issue until the appeal has been decided or the appellant has failed to perform the condition of the recognisance.[32] If the warrant has been issued but not executed, the clerk shall immediately notify the relevant superintendent that an appeal has been lodged and a recognisance, if any, entered into. In this event the superintendent shall return the warrant to the clerk for cancellation by the court.

6. Enlargement of Time

22–06 The District Court Rules 1997 make general provision for the enlargement or abridgement of the time for doing any act or taking any proceeding. The relevant rule states:

> "Save where such time is appointed by statute, and subject to paragraph (2) of this rule, a Judge may upon such terms as he or she thinks fit enlarge or abridge the time appointed by these Rules, or fixed by the Judge under this rule, for doing any act or taking any proceeding, and any such enlargement or abridgement may be made although the application for the same is not made until after the expiration of the time appointed or fixed. The Judge may declare

---

[28] See District Court Rules 1997, Ord.101, r.4 and Sched.D Forms 101.4 and 101.6.

[29] Criminal Procedure Act 1967, s.32. The court also has the power to substitute a new recognisance for a defective one: Civil Bill Courts Procedure Amendment (Ir) Act 1864, s.50.

[30] District Court Rules 1997, Ord.101, r.6.

[31] Road Traffic Act 1961, s.30(3) as substituted by Road Traffic Act 1968, s.20.

[32] District Court Rules 1997, Ord.101, r.11.

any step taken or act done to be sufficient even though not taken or done within the time or in the manner prescribed by these Rules."[33]

It would appear that this Rule applies to the 14-day period for the lodging of notice of appeal and entry into the associated recognisance.[34] At least that has been the practice of the District Court in respect of the predecessor to the Rule.[35] The Circuit Court Rules also make provision for the extension of time limits in respect of appeals from the District Court as follows:

"The Court may, upon such terms (if any) as it may think reasonable extend the time for all appeals to be taken pursuant to the provisions of the Rules of this Order."[36]

It is not clear from the bare words of the Rule or the provisions of the remainder of the Order whether this applies to the time limits laid down by the District Court Rules. If it does apply, it is equally unclear how the jurisdictions of the Circuit Court and the District Court are to function with respect to each other in the matter.[37] In practice, it would appear that an application to extend time limits is made in the District Court in the first instance.[38] If that court refuses the application, an appeal against such refusal can be taken to the Circuit Court, or a fresh application made to that court.

In *State (O'Sullivan) v. Buckley*[39] it was stated, *per* Lavery J., that the principles enunciated in *Eire Continental Trading Co Ltd v. Clonmel Foods Ltd*,[40] although laid down in a civil case, were equally applicable to applications for an extension of time for appeals from the District Court in a criminal matter. The principles in question would appear to be that: (i) the applicant must show that he had a bona fide intention to appeal formed within the permitted time; (ii) he must show the existence of something like mistake, and that mistake as to procedure, and in particular, the mistake of counsel or solicitor as to the meaning of a relevant rule, was not sufficient; and (iii) he must establish that an arguable ground of appeal exists.[41] However, in *People v. Kelly*[42] the Supreme Court, with specific reference to the test laid down in *Eire Continental Trading Co Ltd*, declared that:

---

[33] District Court Rules 1999, Ord.12, r.3(1). Paragraph (2) specifically excludes the times limited by the Rules for lodging a notice requiring a case stated and for entering into a recognisance conditioned to prosecute without delay such case stated.

[34] Presumably, it does not extend to lodgment of notice of appeal and entry into the associated recognisance in order to secure the suspension of a disqualification etc order from holding a driving licence, as the time period for such lodgment etc is imposed by statute.

[35] *State v. Wade* (1957) 91 I.L.T.R. 76; see Woods at p.454.

[36] Circuit Court Rules 2001, Ord. 41, r.9.

[37] In *State (O'Sullivan) v. Buckley* (1964) 101 I.L.T.R. 152, dealing with the predecessors of the current Rules, Lavery J. considered that an application to extend time to appeal to the Circuit Court should be made in the Circuit Court and not in the District Court. He felt that this was especially so when leave to appeal is sought after the time limited for appeal has expired. Since the point was not raised and argued he declined to express a firm opinion on the matter.

[38] Woods at p.455.

[39] (1964) 101 I.L.T.R. 152.

[40] [1955] I.R. 170.

[41] Woods at p.455.

[42] [1982] I.L.R.M. 1.

". . . such tests or criteria are inappropriate to a consideration whether an enlargement of time should be allowed for an appeal or an application for leave to
appeal in a criminal case."[43]

Although the Supreme Court in *Kelly* was dealing with the relevant provision
in the Rules of the Superior Courts which permits the court to enlarge the
time for an appeal to the Court of Criminal Appeal "upon such terms (if any)
as the justice of the case may require",[44] it is submitted that its general
approach in the matter is equally applicable to an interpretation of the District
Court Rules on the enlargement of time for an appeal to the Circuit Court.
O'Higgins C.J. explained the correct approach as follows:

". . . the court's approach must be flexible and its discretion guided not by any
general test or criterion but by what, on the particular facts of the case in
question, appears to be just and equitable. To apply to the exercise of its
jurisdiction to entertain a late appeal the criteria applied in the present case
[i.e. the *Eire Continental Trading* criteria] is to destroy this flexibility and to
impose on the applicant an onus which is not justified. I would fear also that
the application of such criteria could lead, at times, to manifest injustice."[45]

An application to extend time for service and lodgment of a notice of appeal
cannot be granted on an *ex parte* application. In *State (O'Sullivan) v. Buckley*[46] it
was held that to grant such an application on an *ex parte* basis would violate
the fundamental principle of judicial proceedings that the other party should
be heard.

7. Adjournment

22–07   Where an appeal has been adjourned to a later sitting of the court, there is no
obligation on the Circuit Court office to inform an appellant personally of the
particular date on which his appeal is listed for hearing at that later hearing.
In *McCann v. Judge Groarke*[47] the appeal had been adjourned by consent to
the March 2000 sitting of the Circuit Court in Dundalk. The appellant did not
appear when the appeal was called on March 21 and it was duly struck out.
Neither the appellant nor his solicitor had consulted *Iris Oifigúil* or the Law
Society Directory for 2000 which stated March 21 as the first day of the
March sitting of the court in Dundalk. It transpired that the solicitor may have
been depending on an informal practice whereby the court office in Dundalk
would inform "out-of-town" solicitors of the date when their appeal was going
to come up. This practice helped to avoid the inconvenience of "out-of town"
solicitors and their clients coming to Dundalk on the first day of the sitting when
their case might not be heard until some days later. In this case, however, it
seems that the notification was not sent. Nevertheless, on an application to the
High Court for a judicial review, Herbert J. ruled that reliance on such a

---

[43]   *ibid.* at 5.
[44]   RSC, Ord.86, r.8.
[45]   [1982] I.L.R.M. 1 at 5.
[46]   (1964) 101 I.L.T.R. 152.
[47]   Unreported, High Court, May 3, 2001.

practice was no excuse for a non-appearance. The onus of finding out the date on which an appeal would be called and being present on that date was a matter for the appellant and his solicitor:

> "In my judgment it was at all times the duty of the Applicant and therefore of his Solicitors to prosecute this Appeal and to take active measures to appraise themselves of the adjourned date for hearing in March 2000 and to be present on that date and on any other date to which the Court might have occasion to further adjourn the Appeal. The Circuit Court Office in Dundalk was under no duty whatsoever to assume the function of a watchdog for the Applicant or his Solicitors as regards the date of the Appeal.
>
> In my judgment, an informal general practice of notification of this nature to what are termed 'out of town Solicitors', of the, 'for mention', 'call over' or hearing dates of matters listed before the Circuit Court sitting in Dundalk does not justify a legitimate expectation in such persons that notice will always be given and in time and to the correct party so as to render any vigilance in their part unnecessary. In my judgment a voluntary laudable practice of this nature, even if its sole purpose and object was, 'to allow for the effective and efficient administration of justice by the Court', could not in itself reverse the role of the Appellant and the person whose obligation is to do all things necessary to prosecute his Appeal and for this purpose to take active steps to ascertain the hearing date and to ensure his presence before the Court on that date."[48]

8. Re-Hearing

Full re-hearing of the Issues

Where the appeal is against conviction the Circuit Court must conduct a full rehearing of the case on both the facts and the law.[49] In *State (McLoughlin) v. Shanahan*[50] the appellant had been convicted and fined in the District Court for the offence of dangerous driving under section 51 of the Road Traffic Act 1933 (as it then was). Although section 51 created two separate offences, the District Court judge's order did not specify the offence in respect of which the conviction was entered. On appeal the Circuit Court affirmed the conviction and varied the judge's order to show a conviction and fine for each offence. On an application to the High Court for an order of certiorari to quash the Circuit Court order, Davitt J. explained that even if the District Court judge's order was bad, the Circuit Court had jurisdiction to vary it on appeal, as the appeal was a re-hearing of the matter:

> "It seems to me that when a defendant, aggrieved by the decision of a District Justice in a criminal case, takes an appeal therefrom to the Circuit Court he seeks, and obtains, a hearing of the case *de novo*. He, in effect, asks the Circuit Judge to hear the whole matter again and to substitute for the order made by the District Justice (of which he disapproves) the order of the Circuit Court (of which he hopes he can approve). He impliedly admits the jurisdiction of the Circuit Court to substitute its own order for that of the District Court."[51]

---

[48] *Ibid.*
[49] *State (Attorney General) v. Connolly* [1948] I.R. 176.
[50] [1948] I.R. 439.
[51] *ibid.* at 449. See also *State (Roche) v. Delap* [1980] I.R. 170.

Similarly, in *Ex parte McFadden*[52] Palles C.B. observed that:

> "... although the word used in the section is 'Appeal', still, reading that word in the light of the numerous cases on the subject that have been decided since the time of Lord Raymond, there is no doubt that it means that you are to have a 'new trial' – a new investigation of your guilt, with an opportunity to both parties to bring forward new evidence, and a decision upon that evidence by an independent tribunal and an independent mind."[53]

The court may also amend a defective summons on appeal,[54] permit the substitution of a new recognisance for a defective one,[55] and amend a defective District Court order.[56]

New Evidence and Issues

22–08   All questions of law and fact are open to review on the appeal. Either party can call fresh evidence in addition to that adduced in the District Court proceedings. In *State (Aherne) v. Cotter*[57] Walsh J, in deciding that the Circuit Court could increase a sentence imposed by the District Court in a case where the appellant purported to appeal against conviction only, explained that "[a]n appeal by way of retrial enables a totally different case to be made by either side or both."[58]

The learned judge went on to say that:

> "The retrial commences on an assumption that the accused is innocent until he is proved guilty on the re-trial: it would appear somewhat unusual if the new trial were to start with the question of his sentence being treated as already determined so that the only remaining question was whether it should be enforced or not, depending upon conviction."[59]

Arguments not raised in the District Court can be relied upon in the Circuit Court appeal. In *DPP (Nagle) v. Flynn*,[60] for example, the appellant had been convicted in the District Court on a number of road traffic summonses. After his conviction and before the hearing of his appeal the Supreme Court handed down its decision in *State (Clarke) v. Roche*[61] invalidating the procedure used to issue the type of summonses in the appellant's case. The appellant then sought to raise on appeal the validity of the complaint on foot of which the summonses had issued in his case, although he had not challenged the validity of the complaint in the District Court proceedings. Finlay C.J., giving the judgment of the Supreme Court, held that the appellant could challenge

---

52   *Judgments of the Superior Courts in Ireland*, 1988 ed., at 165 cited in *Re G. (an Infant)* [1960] N.I. 35.
53   *ibid.* at 170.
54   County Officers and Courts (Ir) Act 1877, s.76.
55   Civil Bill Courts Procedure Amendment (Ir) Act 1864, s.49.
56   *ibid.* s.49. See Woods at p.457.
57   [1982] I.R. 188.
58   *ibid.* at 198.
59   *ibid.* But see comment of Griffin J. in *Attorney General (Lambe) v. Fitzgerald* [1973] I.R. 195 quoted below.
60   [1987] I.R. 534.
61   [1986] I.R. 619.

the validity of the complaint on the appeal. Since the appeal was by way of re-hearing he could not be debarred from raising points in his defence solely because they had not been relied upon by him in the District Court.

Change of Plea

There is also authority for the proposition that an appellant who pleaded guilty in the District Court may change his plea to not guilty on an appeal to the Circuit Court against conviction.[62] In dealing with such a case in *Attorney (General) v. Lambe*[63] Griffin J. acknowledged that the appeal was by way of a hearing *de novo* and said:

    22-09

> "The defendant appealed against the whole of the order of the District Court and so it is irrelevant, so far as the question of the jurisdiction of the Circuit is concerned, that he pleaded guilty in the District Court. That he did so may, of course, affect his credit on the re-hearing, and therefore go to the issue of his guilt, but it in no way ousts his right to a new hearing on the matters appealed against, namely his conviction and sentence."[64]

The learned judge's comment about the impact of his earlier guilty plea on the defendant's credit on the appeal sits uneasily with Walsh J.'s comment on the assumption that he is innocent until proved guilty on the retrial. It is respectfully submitted that the latter position is more consistent with principle.

Differences from Hearing at First Instance

It does not follow that the appeal hearing is identical in all respects to a criminal trial before the Circuit Court. The court, for example, sits without a jury when hearing the appeal. Equally it must be borne in mind that the appellant has been convicted in the District Court. He comes before the Circuit Court in order to challenge that conviction and/or sentence, rather than to plead to the charges. Lavery J. in *Attorney General v. Mallen*[65] explained that the appeal ". . . is a true appeal though by way of rehearing and is not a re-trial except in form."[66] In that case the appellant had been convicted of dangerous driving on one summons in the District Court, but acquitted on lesser charge of careless driving on another summons. He appealed against the conviction. On his appeal he argued the preliminary point that any further prosecution for dangerous driving was barred by the fact of his acquittal for the lesser offence. In rejecting this argument on a case stated from the Circuit Court, Lavery J. explained that the District Court judge's order convicting the appellant retains its character as such unless and until it is confirmed or varied by the Circuit Court. Its character is not altered by the mere fact that the appeal was conducted by way of a complete re-hearing. The re-hearing is not a re-trial in the sense of commencing a prosecution for the offence anew.

---

[62] *Attorney General (Lambe) v. Fitzgerald* [1973] I.R. 195.
[63] [1973] I.R. 195.
[64] *ibid.* at 198.
[65] [1957] I.R. 344.
[66] *ibid.* at 352.

Non-Appearance

It is also worth noting that where the appellant does not appear, the appeal should be struck out.[67] In this event, or where the appellant does not otherwise prosecute the appeal, the Circuit Court judge may order the appellant to pay to the party receiving notice of appeal such costs and expenses as shall seem just to the judge.[68] The judge may direct the County Registrar to issue all warrants necessary and proper to enforce payment of such costs.[69] Similarly, the necessary warrant or warrants for the enforcement of the original order may be issued by the County Registrar. Where the respondent does not appear, the appellant is entitled to have the order of the District Court reversed.[70] Woods notes that, unlike the Superior Courts Rules, the Circuit Court Rules do not provide for notice of abandonment of appeal.[71]

Procedure

22–10   Apart from the variations noted above and those outlined below with respect to an appeal against sentence only, the normal Circuit Court procedure applies on an appeal. Witnesses are called for the purpose of examination, cross-examination and re-examination. The court can remand the accused from time to time, and in doing so is not bound by the limitations applicable to the District Court under the Criminal Procedure Act 1967.[72] The Circuit Court judge can award costs of any proceedings in that court free from the prohibition on a District Court judge awarding costs and witness expenses against the Attorney General, the DPP or a member of the Garda Síochána when acting in the discharge of his or her duties as a police officer.[73] The District Court Rules Committee has no power to make rules affecting the jurisdiction of the Circuit Court to hear and determine an appeal from the District Court.[74]

Where the appeal is taken against sentence only, there is no need to conduct a full re-hearing of the case. Section 50 of the Courts (Supplemental Provisions) Act 1961 stipulates that where the appeal is against sentence only, the Circuit Court cannot re-hear the case except to the extent necessary to enable the court to adjudicate on the question of sentence. It follows that the re-hearing will be confined to those matters which would impinge upon the severity of sentence. This, of course, will vary from case to case, and can involve calling witnesses for the purposes of examination and cross-examination.

---

[67]   *R (McMonagle) v. Donegal Justices* [1905] 2 I.R. 644.
[68]   Circuit Court Rules 2001, Ord.41, r.4.
[69]   *ibid.* r.5.
[70]   *R v. Surrey Justices* [1892] 2 Q.B. 719.
[71]   Woods at p.458.
[72]   *Maguire v. Judge O'Hanrahan* [1988] I.L.R.M. 243.
[73]   *State (DPP) v. Judge Roe* [1985] I.R. 307.
[74]   *State (Aherne) v. Cotter* [1982] I.R. 188.

9. The Decision

In determining the appeal the Circuit Court judge may confirm, vary or reverse the order of the District Court judge.[75] With respect to sentence, however, the Circuit Court judge is bound by the same limitations as apply to the District Court by virtue of section 5 of the Criminal Justice Act 1951, as amended. The order made by the Circuit Court judge must be one which could validly be made by a District Court judge.[76] Subject to that, the Circuit Court judge has jurisdiction to increase the sentence imposed in the District Court.[77] It would also appear that the Circuit Court judge has a discretion to grant or withhold costs to either side on the appeal.[78]

The decision of the Circuit Court judge on the appeal is "final and conclusive and not appealable".[79] Not only does that preclude an appeal to a higher court, but the Circuit Court judge has no jurisdiction to reinstate an appeal which he has already dismissed.[80] Nevertheless, the option of judicial review remains intact. Where, for example, the Circuit Court judge has affirmed the District Court order, the appellant can seek an order of certiorari to quash both the Circuit Court order and the original District Court order.[81] It would appear, however, that an application for certiorari cannot be taken while an appeal to the Circuit Court is pending.[82] It is also worth noting that the Circuit Court judge can state a case for the opinion of the Supreme Court on a question of law arising on the appeal before he or she gives judgment in the case.[83] (see paras 22–65 *et seq.*)

10. Execution of Court Order

Where the District Court order has been confirmed or varied, or if the appeal is not prosecuted, the Circuit Court judge may direct the issue by the County Registrar of all warrants necessary and proper for the execution of the original order or of such varied order.[84] The same applies with respect to a order for the payment of costs. According to Woods, County Registrars have been instructed that where an order of the District Court, as confirmed or varied on appeal, directs the imprisonment of the defendant and the defendant is not committed by the Circuit Court pursuant to this provision, notification of the result of the appeal should issue to the District Court clerk concerned on the day of the appeal hearing or, at the latest, on the morning of the following day.[85]

22–11

---

[75] Petty Sessions (Ir) Act 1851, s.24(6).
[76] *State (White) v. Judge Martin* unreported, Supreme Court, October 21, 1976.
[77] *State (Aherne) v. Cotter* [1982] I.R. 188; *State (O'Rourke) v. Martin* [1984] I.L.R.M. 333.
[78] Circuit Court Rules 2001, Ord.66 and Ord.41, r.5.
[79] Courts of Justice Act 1928, s.18.
[80] *State (Dunne) v. Martin* [1982] I.R. 229.
[81] *State (Quinn) v. Mangan* [1945] I.R. 532.
[82] *State (Roche) v. Delap* [1980] I.R. 170. But see comments in *Buckley v. Kirby* [2000] 3 I.R. 431 and *Nevin v. Crowley* [2001] 1 I.R. 113.
[83] Courts of Justice Act 1947, s.16. See *Doyle v. Hearne* [1988] I.L.R.M. 318.
[84] Circuit Court Rules 2001, Ord.41, r.5.
[85] Woods, at p. 459.

Where the order of the District Court, as confirmed or varied on appeal, directs the imprisonment of any person, the Circuit Court judge may direct that such person be taken into custody immediately, or detained in custody, and imprisoned pending the issue of the warrant for the execution of the order.[86] This direction can be given either at the time the judge confirms or varies the District Court order or at any time before the issue of the relevant warrant by a judge of the District Court or the County Registrar. According to Woods, where a defendant has been committed by the Circuit Court pursuant to this provision, County Registrars have been requested in instructions to indicate to the District Court clerk that the defendant has been committed on foot of a "temporary" warrant.

The Circuit Court may issue the necessary instrument to enforce its decision on the appeal.[87] Equally, it may allow the same to be issued by the District Court in accordance with section 23 of the Courts of Justice (District Court) Act 1946. For this purpose an "instrument to enforce its decision" does not include a direction to detain the defendant in custody pending the issue of a formal warrant.[88] The County Registrar must certify to the appropriate District Court clerk the purport of every order made by the Circuit Court on the appeal, and return to the clerk the original summons or other documents by which the proceedings were instituted.[89]

22–12   Once the appeal has been determined and the certificate of appeal returned with the County Registrar's certificate duly completed on it,[90] the clerk shall immediately prepare the necessary warrant or warrants to enforce the order unless the Circuit Court judge has already issued the necessary warrant.[91] Where the clerk has prepared the necessary warrant or warrants, the District Court shall issue them and take all further steps required for the execution of the conviction or order as confirmed or varied by the Circuit Court judge. This extends to the enforcement of payment of any costs, compensation or expenses awarded by the Circuit Court judge. The relevant superintendent of the Garda Síochána shall inform the clerk of any case in which the Circuit Court judge has not caused the necessary warrant to be issued. The return of the certificate of appeal, with the County Registrar's certificate duly completed on it, is a condition precedent for the jurisdiction of the District Court judge to issue the necessary warrants of execution.[92]

Where the Circuit Court judge does not cause the necessary warrant to be issued giving effect to his or her order on the determination of the appeal, the relevant superintendent of the Garda Síochána must inform the relevant District Court clerk of that fact. The Rules do not specifically state that this should be done immediately, but fair procedures require that it should be done

---

[86] Circuit Court Rules 2001, Ord.41, r.6.
[87] *Ibid*, r.7.
[88] *State (Caddle) v. McCarthy* [1957] I.R. 361.
[89] Circuit Court Rules 2001, Ord.41, r.8.
[90] See District Court Rules 1997, Sched.D Form 101.7.
[91] District Court Rules 1997, Ord.101, r.13.
[92] *State (Maguire) v. O'Reilly* (1947) 81 I.L.T.R. 1.

promptly.[93] In practice it would appear that notification is not actually effected by the superintendent but by the return of the charge sheet. The Rules do require the District Court judge to issue the necessary warrant immediately where it has not been issued by the Circuit Court judge. Delay in issuing the warrant can provide grounds for depriving it of substantive effect. In *Dutton v. District Justice O'Donnell*,[94] for example, the defendant withdrew his appeal, but the Circuit Court judge did not cause the necessary warrant to issue for the execution of the original District Court order sentencing him to a term of detention. Moreover, the judge was not informed that the defendant was in custody at the time, serving a sentence of detention on another matter. Had the judge been informed of this fact, it is likely that he would have issued the warrant so that the sentence would be served concurrently with the sentence which the defendant was serving at the time. Owing to a subsequent delay, the warrant was not issued by the District Court judge until four and a half months later. By this time the defendant had served the sentence for the other offences and was now facing into a new term of detention pursuant to the delayed warrant. The High Court ruled that in the interests of protecting the constitutional rights of the defendant, the warrant must be considered as if it had issued at the time of the determination of the appeal by the Circuit Court. The net effect was that it was now spent. In giving the judgment of the Court, Barron J. also intimated that where the defendant was serving a sentence of imprisonment at the date of the confirmation of the District Court sentence, the Circuit Court must be informed of this circumstance. The Court should then cause the necessary warrants to be issued there and then, unless it decides that sentences should be consecutive or for some similar reason.

It does not follow that delay in the issuing of the warrant or in its execution **22–13** will invariably result in it losing its efficacy. All depends on the facts and circumstances of each individual case.[95] In *O'Driscoll v. Governor of Cork Prison*,[96] for example, there was a delay of three months in its execution of the warrant giving effect to the Circuit Court order affirming the sentence of imprisonment handed down in the District Court. In this case the Circuit Court had granted a delay in the execution of the warrant so that it was not to commence before a specified date. As a result of administrative rearrangements the warrant was not actually executed until three months after that specified date. Lynch J. acknowledged that warrants must be executed within a reasonable time, but that in the circumstances of this case there was no unreasonable delay on the part of the State:

---

[93] *Dutton v. District Justice O'Donnell* [1989] I.R. 218.
[94] [1989] I.R. 218.
[95] For other cases in which delay was found sufficient to deprive the warrant of effect, see *Cunningham v. Governor of Mountjoy Prison* [1987] I.L.R.M. 33; *State (McCormick) v. Governor of Mountjoy Prison* unreported, High Court, May 6, 1987.
[96] [1989] 1 I.L.R.M. 239.

"I am also satisfied that the warrants as drawn up and engrossed do not confer an unfettered discretion on the executive as to when the imprisonment will commence. The warrants must be executed within a reasonable time and in the circumstances of this case I am satisfied that there was no unreasonable delay on the part of the State authorities and that the warrants were accordingly executed within a reasonable time."[97]

Where the Circuit Court dismisses an appeal in terms which confirm the order of the District Court, it is unnecessary for the Circuit Court to issue an order, except for the purpose of giving immediate effect to a punishment pending the issue of a warrant from either the District Court or the Circuit Court.[98] The original order of the District Court is affirmed and the instrument necessary to enforce it may be issued either by the District Court or the Circuit Court.

The order recording the Circuit Court's decision on the appeal must concord with the contents of the decision announced in Court. In *State (Kiernan) v. District Justice De Burca*,[99] for example, the Circuit Court affirmed the appellant's conviction on one count while dismissing his conviction on other counts. In pronouncing the decision in court the judge made an order as to the amount of the fine and expenses to be paid, but did not specify a term of imprisonment to be imposed in the alternative or in default of payment of the fine. The order as issued by the County Registrar, however, provided that in the event of default in payment of the fine, the defendant should be imprisoned for a period of six months without hard labour unless the sums in questions were paid sooner. The Circuit Court order was quashed by the Supreme Court as the order as issued did not correspond with that pronounced in court. The Supreme Court also ruled that it was not possible to sever that portion of the order with respect to imprisonment for default, as an order in a criminal matter may not be severed.

C. Case Stated under Summary Jurisdiction Act 1857

1. Introduction

22–14 Either party to summary criminal proceedings in the District Court may request the judge to state a case for the opinion of the High Court on any question of law. Technically, this is not an appeal, although in practice it will often have a similar effect to an appeal. While applications are confined to questions of law, as distinct from questions of fact, it must be remembered that the question whether a finding of fact (including a finding of guilt) is based on sufficient evidence is in itself a question of law.

There are two types of case stated: a case stated under the Summary Jurisdiction Act 1857 and a consultative case stated. Each will be dealt with in turn.

---

[97] *ibid.* at 242
[98] *State (O'Dare) v. Sheehy* [1984] I.L.R.M. 99.
[99] [1963] I.R. 348. See also *State (O'Dare) v. Sheehy* [1984] I.L.R.M. 99.

2. Basis

Introduction

A case stated under the Summary Jurisdiction Act 1857 can be submitted where one of the parties to the proceedings is dissatisfied with the judge's determination on a point of law. Section 2 of the 1857 Act, as extended by section 51 of the Courts (Supplemental Provisions) Act 1961,[100] stipulates that after the hearing and determination by a judge of the District Court of any proceedings, other than proceedings relating to an indictable offence not dealt with summarily,[101] any party may apply to the judge to state and sign a case setting forth the facts and grounds of his decision for the opinion of the High Court. Since the application can be made by any party to the proceedings, it follows that the facility can be availed of to appeal against an acquittal as well as a conviction.[102] It is also available in respect of a dismissal under section 1(1) of the Probation of Offenders Act 1907.[103] Even if none of the parties to the proceedings ask the judge to state a case it would appear that the judge can state a case on his or her own initiative. This would be particularly relevant where the judge harbours a doubt about his or her jurisdiction to hear the proceedings.

22–15

Point of Law

A case can only be stated on a point of law. This can include a ruling on the admissibility of evidence,[104] but it cannot extend to an issue about the constitutionality of a post-1937 statute.[105] Equally, the case stated cannot be used to pose questions that indirectly raise the constitutionality of a post-1937 statutory provision.[106] It would appear, however, that it is possible to seek a ruling on the constitutionality of a pre-1937 statute (see below under "Consultative Case Stated").[107] The District Court judge's findings of fact underpinning the case stated are conclusive, unless it appears that there is no evidence to support them.[108] However, the existence of evidence to support the judge's findings of fact, including a finding of guilt, is in itself a question

22–16

---

[100] Sullivan P. in *State (Reilly) v. District Justice for Clones* [[1935] I.R. 908 was of the opinion that ss.2, 3 and 4 of the 1857 Act had been impliedly repealed by ss.83 and 86 of the Courts of Justice Act 1924. This would appear now not to be the case. Not only does s.51 of the 1961 formally acknowledge the continued application of s.2 of the 1857 Act, but s.3 of the 1961 Act explicitly repeals ss.82 and 83 of the 1924 Act. See Murnaghan J. in *Attorney General (Fahy) v. Bruen* [1936] I.R. 750 for a discussion of the background to section 2 of the 1857 Act and the difference between it and s.83 of the 1924 Act.

[101] This does not exclude the possibility of appeal by way of case stated in the context of extradition proceedings for an indictable offence; see *McMahon v. McDonald* unreported, Supreme Court, July 27 1989.

[102] *DPP v. Nangle* [1984] I.L.R.M. 171.

[103] *Oaten v. Auty* (1919) 83 JP 173.

[104] *Dwyer v. Larkin* 5 N.I.J.R. 25.

[105] *Minister for Labour v. Costello* [1989] I.L.R.M. 485; *Foyle Fisheries Commission v. Gallen* (1960) Ir. Jur. Rep. 35.

[107] *DPP v. Dougan* [1997] 1 I.L.R.M. 550.

[108] *DPP (Stratford) v. O'Neill* [1998] 1 I.L.R.M. 221.

of law which can be the subject of a case stated.[109] Similarly, the question of whether there is sufficient evidence to warrant a conviction is a question of law.[110] Nevertheless, it must be said that the High Court is reluctant to upset an acquittal on the grounds that it was unsupported by the evidence.

In *DPP v. Nangle*,[111] for example, an off-duty member of the Garda Síochána was acquitted in the District Court on a charge of assault occasioning actual bodily harm. The injured party did not give evidence but three witnesses testified that they saw the defendant turn and swing a blow with his hand striking the injured party. In cross-examination they said that they did not see the injured party provoking the defendant in any way, but accepted that it was possible that the injured party made an attempt to strike the defendant that they did not see. In his evidence the defendant claimed that the injured party had made an offensive remark and raised his left hand. The defendant claimed that he put out his right hand in self-defence and it connected with the injured party's jaw. The DPP appealed against the acquittal by way of a case stated on the ground that the defendant's evidence was so incredible that it was a perverse decision to permit that evidence to raise a doubt in the mind of the learned District Court judge.

Costello J. accepted the general principle that where a District Court judge reaches a determination that is unsupported by any evidence before him, that constitutes good grounds for setting aside the decision on a case stated. While this holds true for appeals against acquittals as against convictions, it is subject to the qualification that ". . . in the case of an appeal against acquittal the onus of proof beyond a reasonable doubt rests upon the prosecution and that includes, as occurred in this case, the onus of negativing by a standard of proof beyond a reasonable doubt a defence such as self-defence."[112] Costello J. accepted that there was a clear air of implausibility about the account given of the incident. Nevertheless, he did not feel that the circumstances were such as to warrant interference with the judge's determination:

> "I am satisfied, however, that it would constitute an unwarranted interference by me in a proceeding which is exclusively confined to correcting errors of law by an inferior court in the determination of proceedings before it, to hold that evidence so summarised, could not have raised a doubt in the mind of the district justice. He had the opportunity of hearing the witnesses in this case and of listening to their answers to questions both in direct and cross-examination dealing no doubt in significant detail with the incidents which occurred. One could well conceive that the case might have taken a completely different course had the injured party been available as a witness but it would be quite improper for a court to convict an accused person on any speculation as to what an absent witness might have said. In these circumstances I am satisfied that there are no grounds on which I should interfere with the decision of the

[109] *Donaghy v. Walsh* [1914] 2 I.R. 261; *Minister for Industry and Commerce v. Healy* [1941] I.R. 545.
[110] *State (Turley) v. O'Floinn* [1968] I.R. 245.
[111] *ibid.*
[112] *DPP v. Nangle* [1984] I.L.R.M. 171.

learned district justice and that this appeal by way of case stated must be dismissed."[113]

Obligation

Generally, the judge is under a duty to state a case when requested unless he considers the application to be frivolous (see below).[114] If the judge gives no reason for his refusal to state a case, it will be assumed that he or she was of the opinion that the application was merely frivolous.[115] It would also appear that a judge can refuse to state a case where no doubtful or difficult question of law is involved,[116] or the point of law at issue is well settled,[117] or the point cannot assist the applicant even if it is decided in his favour.[118]

22–17

Where an application to state a case is made by the Attorney General, the DPP, a Government Minister, a Minister of State or the Revenue Commissioners, the judge of the District Court is obliged to accede to it, according to the terms of section 4 of the 1857 Act and the District Court Rules 1997.[119] In *Fitzgerald v. DPP*,[120] however, the High Court declared these provisions unconstitutional in that they constituted an unwarranted interference in the judicial domain and were discriminatory. The net effect of this ruling is to give the judge of the District Court the same limited discretion in dealing with an application for an appeal by way of case stated from the DPP and the other specified bodies as he or she enjoys with respect to such applications from other parties.

Where a District Court judge strikes out a case on the ground that he has no jurisdiction to hear it, he cannot refuse an application to state a case on whether his determination was correct in law. In *Sports Arena Ltd v. O'Reilly*[121] it was argued that where a judge strikes out a case on the basis that he has no jurisdiction to hear it, it must necessarily follow that he has no jurisdiction to state a case. To hold otherwise would involve the judge assuming jurisdiction to deal in a certain manner with the case after having decided that he lacked jurisdiction. In rejecting this argument Blayney J. explained:

> "Where an order striking out an application is made, there are obviously two possible positions: either it was correctly made, in which case the District Justice had no jurisdiction to hear the case and so would have no jurisdiction to state a case; or it was wrongly made, in which case the District Justice had jurisdiction to hear the case and likewise would have jurisdiction to state a case. When an application is made in such circumstances for a case stated, it is made for the purpose of challenging the order, so it is made on the basis that the order was wrongly made. But if it was wrongly made, the District Justice

---

[113] *ibid.* at 172.
[114] *ibid.* at 173.
[115] Summary Jurisdiction Act 1857, s.4. Ryan and Magee *The Irish Criminal Process* (Mercier Press, Dublin, 1983) state that where the application is made by the DPP the District Court judge must state a case; *op.cit.*, p.417.
[116] *Sports Arena Ltd v. O'Reilly* [1987] I.R. 185.
[117] *Crick v. Crick* (1856) 6 W.R. 594; see Woods at p.469.
[118] *R v. Newport Justices* (1929) 93 J.P. 179; see Woods at p.469.
[119] *R (Murphy) v. Cork Justices* [1914] 2 I.R. 249.
[120] District Court Rules 1997, Ord.102, r.15.

had jurisdiction to deal with the case, and also necessarily has jurisdiction to state a case for the opinion of the High Court. It follows in my opinion that the District Justice is not entitled to refuse to state a case in such circumstances on the grounds that he has no power to do so. If the applicant obtains a favourable decision on the question raised in the case stated, that will necessarily involve a decision that the District Justice had the power to state the case."[122]

Blayney J. distinguished the High Court decision in *Attorney General v. Byrne*.[123] In that case it was held that an application for a case stated under section 2 cannot be used to challenge the jurisdiction of the District Court judge to determine the case or rulings of the judge which go to his jurisdiction. The proper remedy in such circumstances was an application for an order of *certiorari*. Blayney J. explained that the decision in Beirne was confined to its own special facts which were that the applicant for a case stated had objected to the jurisdiction of the judge in the matter. Accordingly, it is only authority for the proposition that a District Court judge is entitled to refuse to state a case at the request of a party who is contending that the judge has no jurisdiction to hear the case.

Mandamus

22–18   Where the judge refuses an application, the applicant can apply to the High Court for an order of mandamus to compel the judge to state a case.[124] The High Court will not interfere where the effect of its intervention would merely be to overturn a decision that the District Court judge had reached within the exercise of his or her discretion. If, for example, the judge formed the view that the application was frivolous and that there was a basis for his or her decision, the High Court will not interfere even if it would have exercised the discretion differently in the matter.[125] If, however, the judge's refusal to state a case is tantamount to a refusal or failure to exercise his or her discretion in the matter, the High Court will normally issue an order of mandamus.[126] In *State (Turley) v. O'Floinn*,[127] for example, a District Court judge had refused to state a case on the ground that there was no question of law involved in the determination of the charge against the defendant. The High Court found that the facts of the case raised a number of important questions of law and issued an order of mandamus compelling the judge to state a case. This decision was upheld by the Supreme Court.

22–19   It would appear that the High Court retains a general discretion not to compel a District Court judge to state a case. In *R. (Murphy) v. Justices of Cork*,[128] for example, the High Court refused to order the justices to state a case in circumstances where a decision on the point at issue in favour of the applicant

---

[121] unreported, High Court, May 4, 2001.
[122] [1987] I.R. 185.
[123] ibid. at p.191.
[124] [1943] I.R. 480.
[125] Summary Jurisdiction Act 1857, s.5.
[126] *State (Reilly) v. District Justice of Clones* [1935] I.R. 908.
[127] *Prendergast v. Porter* [1961] I.R. 440.
[128] [1968] I.R. 245.

would not have affected the ultimate determination in the case. Cherry L.C.J. explained the matter thus:

> "It is true that the section which requires justices to state a case upon questions of law is mandatory in its character ; and they are bound to do so unless they consider the application frivolous. But it has always been held that this Court has a discretion as to making an order to compel justices to state a case. Where the determination of the real question at issue between the parties would not be affected by the answers to the questions suggested for consideration, an order ought not, in my opinion, to be made commanding them to state a case. This principle, to my mind, applies with peculiar force to a criminal charge of a serious character where the accused has been already acquitted by the justices."[129]

3. Timing

The application to the judge must be made in writing within 14 days after the determination. The immediate effect of an application is to suspend the determination of the proceedings in the District Court.[130] The availability of appeal by way of case stated is not precluded by a statute that makes a decision of a District Court in a particular matter final and unappealable.[131]

A distinctive feature of the application for a case stated under section 2 of the 1857 Act is that it is available only after the judge has given his decision in the case. In other words, it has all the appearance and substance of an appeal on a point of law. Indeed, the party requesting the case stated, who can be any party who was entitled to be heard and was actually heard in the proceedings,[132] is described as the appellant.[133] The District Court judge's findings of fact underpinning the case stated are conclusive, unless it appears that there is no evidence to support them.[134] While the findings of fact will have a decisive influence on the point of law to be considered, the High Court is not confined to consideration of the particular matter of law referred by the judge. It may consider other arguments, provided they are compatible with the evidence adduced in the District Court.[135]

4. Procedural Formalities

Compliance

The relevant statutory procedure for a case stated must be followed strictly in order for the High Court to have jurisdiction to entertain the case.[136] It would

---

[129] *R. (Murphy) v. Cork Justices* [1914] 2 I.R. 249.
[130] *ibid.* at 259.
[131] Courts (Supplemental Provisions) Act 1961, s.51(2). The suspension applies until the application has been refused or, if granted, until the case stated has been determined by the High Court.
[132] In *Murphy v. Bayliss* unreported, Supreme Court, July 22, 1976 it was stated that this merely closes off one form of appeal, namely an appeal to the Circuit Court.
[132] Courts (Supplemental Provisions) Act 1961, s.51(4).
[133] Summary Jurisdiction Act 1857, s.2.
[134] *Donaghy v. Walsh* [1914] 2 I.R. 261; *Minister for Industry and Commerce v. Healy* [1941] I.R. 545.
[135] *Revenue Commissioners v. Bradley* 76 I.L.T.R. 87.
[136] *Thompson v. Curry* [1970] I.R. 61; *DPP v. Galvin* [1999] 4 I.R. 18, [1999] 2 I.L.R.M. 277.

also appear, however, that the High Court has discretion, in the exercise of its inherent jurisdiction, to waive strict compliance with procedural requirements in appropriate circumstances. In *DPP (Gannon) v. Conlon*[137] the High Court had to deal with the argument that it lacked jurisdiction to deal with the case stated owing to a failure to comply strictly with certain procedural requirements. Giving the judgment of the Court Finnegan J. explained:

> ". . . the Court has a general or inherent jurisdiction to operate the provisions of the 1857 Act section 2: *O v. M* [1977] I.R. 33. The High Court exercises full judicial power in all matters concerning the general administration of justice and has unrestricted and unlimited powers in all matters except insofar as that has been taken away in unequivocal terms by statutory enactment and the Court may exercise its inherent jurisdiction in respect of matters which are regulated by Statute or Rule of Court: *Willis v. Earl Beauchamp* (1886) 11 P.D. 59 at 63."

Exercising this inherent jurisdiction in the case, Finnegan J. discounted the fact that the appellant had used the old form for the notice of application as distinct from the new form. Both forms were virtually identical in substance. The learned judge also discounted the fact that, due to a typographical error, the notice was addressed to the District Court clerk for District Court No.6 instead of District Court No.10. In fact, the notice had been sent to the correct District Court clerk. However, he was not prepared to waive compliance with the requirement in the Rules to serve a copy of the notice personally on the party within three days of receiving the case (see below). While he felt that he had a discretion to extend the time for compliance with this requirement, there were not special circumstances on the facts of the case that warranted exercise of the discretion in favour of the appellant.

5. Application Notice

Notice of an application for a case stated must be signed and lodged by the applicant or his solicitor with the clerk for the court area in which the proceedings were heard and determined.[138] This must be done within 14 days of the determination. It used to be that this 14-day period could not be enlarged by the judge,[139] but the relevant provision has been omitted from the 1997 version of the District Court Rules.[140] A copy of the notice must also be served by registered post upon every other party to the proceedings within 14 days after the determination.[141] This has been interpreted to mean personal

---

[137] Unreported, High Court, December 20, 2001.

[138] District Court Rules 1997, Ord.102, r.8(2). The Notice must be in the Form 102.3; see r.8(1) and Sched.D. Note exercise of discretion to accept the old form in *DPP (Gannon) v. Conlon* unreported, High Court, December 20, 2001.

[139] Woods p.470.

[140] It would appear that the High Court has an inherent jurisdiction in this matter; *DPP (Gannon) v. Conlon* unreported, High Court, December 2001.

[141] District Court Rules 1997, Ord.102, r.8(3). The High Court has a discretion to waive the requirement of service by registered post where the notice is actually received by the party's solicitor; *DPP (Gannon) v. Conlon* unreported, High Court, December 20, 2001.

service.[142] While the High Court has a discretion in its inherent jurisdiction to accept service on a solicitor retained by the other party, it will not normally exercise this discretion in the absence of circumstances that rendered it difficult or impossible to effect personal service.[143]

Recognisance

Within the 14-day period the appellant must enter into a recognisance before a judge of the District Court, with or without sureties and in such sum or sums as the judge may determine.[144] This requirement does not apply where the appellant is the Attorney General, the DPP, the Director of Consumer Affairs, any Minister of the Government or Minister of State or officer of any such Minister, an officer or member of the Garda Síochána acting in a official capacity or an officer of the Revenue Commissioners acting in an official capacity.[145] The recognisance is conditioned for the appellant to prosecute the case stated without delay, to submit to the judgment of the High Court and to pay such costs as may be awarded by the High Court. If the appellant is in custody at the time of the application, the judge may release him and the recognisance will be conditioned for his appearance before the judge at the sitting of the District Court for the area in question to be held after the expiration of 14 days from the day upon which the decision of the High Court is given, unless the determination appealed against is reversed.

22–20

Suspension of Determination

Once an application has been made, the determination in respect of which it is made shall be suspended.[146] Where the judge grants the application, the suspension lasts until the case stated has been heard and determined. If he refuses the application, the suspension lasts only until the time of refusal. Where the application is granted, the determination of the proceedings in the District Court are suspended until the case stated has been determined by the High Court.[147] Moreover, there can be no further findings of fact in the proceedings after the High Court has determined the point of law at issue.[148]

22–21

6. Preparing the case stated

The Format

Where a judge grants an application for a case stated, he or she shall prepare and sign the case stated within six months from the date of the application.[149]

---

[142] *DPP (Gannon) v. Conlon* unreported, High Court, December 20, 2001.
[143] *ibid.* See also *Crowley v. McVeigh* [1990] I.L.R.M. 220; *Hill v. Wright* (1896) 60 JP 312; *Syred v. Carruthers* (1858) 22 J.P. 399; *Clarke v. Maguire* [1909] 2 I.R. 681.
[144] District Court Rules 1997, Ord.102, r.9.
[145] *ibid.* and Ord. 12, r.20. The recognisance shall be in Form 102.4 Sched.D. Note that the correct title is the Office of Director of Consumer Affairs, and not (as in the District Court Rules 1997) the office of the Director of Consumer Affairs and Fair Trade. See para. 22–04.
[146] *ibid.* r.10.
[147] Courts (Supplemental Provisions) Act 1961, s.51(2).
[148] *M.T.T. v. N.T.* unreported, Supreme Court, April 1, 1982.
[149] District Court Rules 1997, Ord.102, r.12.

In order to secure agreement between the parties on the facts of the case stated, the judge may, if he or she thinks fit, submit a draft of the case stated to the parties or receive a draft from the parties within two months of the date of the application. In the event of a dispute between the parties as to the facts, the facts shall be found by the judge. Typically, the case stated will set out in paragraphs the facts of the case, the contentions of the parties and the District Court judge's finding of fact, any inferences or conclusions of fact which he drew from the facts as found by him, and a statement of the ruling at issue.[150]

Where a judge has refused to state a case on the ground that he considers it frivolous, he shall on request of the appellant sign and cause to be delivered to him or her a certificate of refusal and cause a copy to be served upon every other party to the proceedings.[151]

Signature

It would appear that a case stated must be signed by the District Court judge who heard the case and that he or she must be a judge of the District Court when he or she signed it. If either of these requirements is not satisfied, the High Court will have no jurisdiction to entertain the case. In *DPP v. Galvin*[152] the DPP appealed an acquittal in the District Court by way of case stated. The judge who heard the case in the District Court was made a Circuit Court judge before he signed the case stated. Accordingly he signed the case stated as "judge of the Circuit Court" and not, as required by section 2 of the 1857 Act (as amended), as judge of the District Court. Geoghegan J., in the High Court, ruled that it was imperative that at the time of signing the case stated the judge continued to be a judge of the District Court. Not only was this implicit in the words of the statutory provision, but it was also necessary for the case to be sent back to the same judge for determination consequent upon the High Court's ruling. If the judge was no longer a judge of the District Court, he would not have jurisdiction to make a final determination in the case. The learned judge declined to express a view as to the legal effect of his decision with respect to whether the acquittal stood, whether it permanently remained an undecided case or whether there was some other way in which the appellant could secure a rehearing in the District Court. He did acknowledge that this could be highly unjust in the event of an appeal against conviction by way of case stated that could not proceed because the executive had appointed the judge to a higher court in the interim.

7. Notification

To the Other Party

22–22   Once the case has been stated and signed by the judge, the appellant shall receive the case stated from the clerk.[153] He must transmit the case stated to

---

[150] *Emerson v. Hearty* [1946] N.I. 35. See also Woods at pp.474–475.
[151] District Court Rules 1997, Ord.102, r.15. Such certificate shall be in the Form 102.6 Sched.D.
[152] [1999] 4 I.R. 18, [1999] 2 I.L.R.M. 277.
[153] District Court Rules 1997, Ord.102, r.13.

the High Court within three days of receiving it. Before transmitting it to the High Court he must give notice of the appeal in writing,[154] together with a copy of the case stated duly signed, to the other party to the proceedings. It is imperative that notice is given in writing to the other party before the case is transmitted to the High Court. Failure to do so will render the case stated *ultra vires*.[155] The defect cannot be made good by notice after the case has been transmitted. While the High Court has a power to extend the three-day period for transmission,[156] it would appear that this cannot be used for the purpose of effecting personal service on the other party.[157] Service on the other party normally means personal service, but it may be sufficient to serve it on an agent of the party in certain circumstances where strenuous efforts to effect personal service have proved unsuccessful.[158]

Where the judge states a case on his or her own initiative (without a prior request from one of the parties), the clerk shall give notice in writing forthwith to each party in the proceedings and shall then transmit the case stated to the Central Office of the High Court.[159]

Lodgment of Documents

The Rules of the Superior Courts state that at any time within 10 days of the date of transmission the clerk shall lodge with the proper officer one or more copies of the case stated and any documents as may be required for the use of the Court.[160] Any party to the proceedings is entitled to obtain, on application to the proper officer and upon payment of the prescribed fee, one or more copies of the case stated and documents, if any.[161] Once the case has been transmitted to the Central Office, the proper officer shall immediately file it and set it down for hearing.[162] However, it shall not appear in the list for hearing until the expiration of 10 days after it has been received.

22–23

8. Delay

Undue delay in the prosecution of an appeal by way of case stated can result in the High Court refusing to deal with it. Hederman J. made the point succinctly in *DPP v. Flahive*:

> "In my view any party seeking a case stated to the High Court has an obligation to diligently prosecute the appeal and if there is any undue delay, I am of the opinion that the High Court would be entitled to refuse to deal with

---

[154] What constitutes notice in writing is interpreted strictly; see *DPP v. O'Connor* unreported, High Court, May 9, 1983; *Little v. Donnelly* [1871] I.R. 5 CL 1; Woods p.474.

[155] *Thompson v. Curry* [1970] I.R. 61.

[156] *Attorney General v. Shivnan* [1968] I.R. 369; *DPP (Murphy) v. Regan* [1993] 1 I.L.R.M. 335.

[157] *DPP (Murphy) v. Regan* [1993] I.L.R.M. 335.

[158] *Crowley v. McVeigh* [1990] I.L.R.M. 220; *Hill v. Wright* (1896) 60 J.P. 312; *Syred v. Carruthers* (1858) 22 J.P. 399; *Clarke v. Maguire* [1909] 2 I.R. 681.

[159] District Court Rules 1997, Ord.102, r.14, Such notice to the parties shall be in Form 102.5 Sched.D.

[160] Rules of the Superior Courts, Ord.62, r.6.

[161] *Ibid.*, r.7.

[162] *Ibid.*, r.4.

the case, and where the High Court was of opinion that to deal with the case after a long delay would be prejudicial or unjust to the other party, should refuse to entertain the case."[163]

In *DPP v. Rice*[164] there was a delay of four years in bringing proceedings by way of case stated to the High Court. In this case the DPP was appealing by way of case stated against the acquittal of the defendant. The incident which resulted in the criminal proceedings occurred one year earlier. Noting that the delay in prosecuting the appeal had not been justified, Kelly J. considered that the defendant's constitutional right to a trial in due course of law would be jeopardised if the case stated was entertained. In effect it would be tantamount to putting him in jeopardy in respect of matters which had occurred five years previously and of which he had been acquitted four years ago.

9. The High Court Hearing

Scope

22–24 Where a case has been duly stated to the High Court under section 2 of the 1857 Act, that Court must hear and determine the question or questions of law arising on it.[165] Naturally, this includes the point or points of law specifically referred by the judge of the District Court, but it is not necessarily confined to them. Any point taken in the District Court may be relied on in the High Court even though it is not referred to by the judge in the case stated.[166] Equally, it may consider other arguments which had not been raised in the District Court, provided they are compatible with the evidence adduced in the District Court.[167] The jurisdiction of the District Court in the matter in question can be raised even though it was not raised in the lower Court or specifically mentioned on the case stated.[168]

The Determination

The High Court can reverse, affirm or amend the determination of the District Court judge in the case stated.[169] Equally it may state its opinion on the matter referred and remit that opinion to the District Court judge, or it may make such other order in relation to the matter as it thinks fit. This includes such orders as to costs as the Court shall think fit, although no order for costs can be made against the District Court judge.[170] The High Court can also send the case back for amendment or further findings of fact.[171] In this event

---

[163] Unreported, Supreme Court, October 29, 1986.
[164] [2000] 2 I.L.R.M. 393.
[165] Summary Jurisdiction Act 1857, s.6.
[166] *Revenue Commissioners v. Bradley* (1942) 76 I.L.T.R. 87; Woods p.476.
[167] *Revenue Commissioners v. Bradley* (1942) 76 I.L.T.R. 87; *Attorney General v. Bruen* (1937) 71 I.L.T.R. 94.
[168] *People (Attorney General) v. Downes* (1944) Ir. Jur. Rep. 40.
[169] Summary Jurisdiction Act 1857, s.6.
[170] *Ibid.*
[171] *ibid.* s.7.

the District Court judge should give the parties the opportunity of being heard on the matter.[172]

Final and conclusive

The High Court's decision on a case stated is final and conclusive on all parties.[173] This, however, does not override the constitutional right of appeal from all decisions of the High Court to the Supreme Court. In *Attorney General (Fahy) v. Bruen*[174] the Supreme Court found that the right of appeal from decisions of the High Court to the Supreme Court under the 1922 Constitution could be limited only by legislation enacted after the adoption of the Constitution. Since the 1857 Act did not satisfy this requirement, it followed that an appeal lay to the Supreme Court from the High Court's decision on a case stated under section 2 of the 1857 Act. Since the 1937 Constitution makes identical provision to the 1922 Constitution in the matter of appeals from decisions of the High Court to the Supreme Court, the same rule applies today. By contrast, it will be seen below that an appeal from a decision of the High Court on a consultative case stated under the Courts (Supplemental Provisions) Act 1961 is available only by leave of the High Court.[175]

Implementing the Determination

Once a case stated has been remitted to the District Court judge, the judge must proceed to deal with it in accordance with the direction or opinion of the High Court.[176] There can be no further findings of fact in the proceedings after the High Court has determined the point of law at issue.[177] Typically the effect of the High Court's ruling in the case stated will be to confirm or quash the District Court's determination in the case. The District Court judge has the same jurisdiction to enforce the order of the High Court as he would have had to enforce his original order.[178]

22–25

Any person who appeals by way of a case stated under section 2 of the 1857 Act is taken to have abandoned any right of appeal to the Circuit Court.[179] However, it would appear that where a case stated is remitted to the District Court judge with a direction to convict, and the judge convicts in obedience to that direction, the conviction can be appealed to the Circuit Court.[180]

---

[172] *Forte v. McAllister* (1917) 2 I.R. 387.
[173] Summary Jurisdiction Act 1857, s.6.
[174] [1936] I.R. 750.
[175] Courts (Supplemental Provisions) Act 1961, s.52(2); see also *Minister for Industry and Commerce v. Healy* [1941] I.R. 545.
[176] In *DPP v. Corbett* unreported, Supreme Court, October 16, 1992, Finlay C.J. rejected the argument that delay arising from two separate and distinct cases stated in the proceedings would provide a basis for the District Court judge to dismiss the prosecution.
[177] *M.T.T. v. N.T.* unreported, Supreme Court, April 1, 1982.
[178] Summary Jurisdiction Act 1857, s.9.
[179] *ibid.* s.14.
[180] *R. (Drohan) v. Waterford Justices* (1900) 2 I.R. 307.

D. Consultative Case Stated

1. Jurisdiction

Introduction

22–26 The second method for stating a case from the District Court to the High Court is generally known as the consultative case stated. It is provided for by section 52 of the Courts (Supplemental Provisions) Act 1961.[181] The distinctive feature about this option is that the case may be stated before the judge has given his or her decision in the case. In other words the proceedings can be interrupted in mid-stream for the purpose of getting a ruling on the point of law from the High Court. When the High Court's ruling is pronounced the proceedings in the District Court will resume on the basis of the law as declared by the High Court.

Obligation

Section 52 stipulates that a judge of the District Court shall, if requested by any person who has been heard in any proceedings whatsoever before him, refer any question of law arising in those proceedings to the High Court for determination. This power does not extend to proceedings relating to an indictable offence which is not being dealt with summarily by the court.[182] Where one of the parties requests the judge to make the referral it seems that the judge is under an obligation to refer, unless he or she considers the request frivolous. In the absence of a request from the parties the judge has a discretion to refer.

Point of Law

The discussion above on what constitutes a point of law for the purpose of a case stated applies equally with respect to a consultative case stated. The same applies to the discussion of when a District Court judge can refuse to state a case on the ground that it is frivolous.

Constitutionality of Statute

As noted above, the question of law cannot concern the constitutionality of a post 1937 statute.[183] The District Court judge can only state a case on matters which he is competent to determine himself. Since Article 34.3.2° confines the jurisdiction to rule on the constitutionality of a post 1937 statute to the High Court, it follows that a District Court judge is not competent to rule on

---

[181] This largely reproduces s.83 of the Courts of Justice Act 1924 which was repealed by the 1961 Act. The Supreme Court in *Attorney General (Fahy) v. Bruen* [1936] I.R. 750 considered that s.83 of the 1924 introduced a new jurisdiction in addition to that provided by s.2 of the Summary Jurisdiction Act 1857.

[182] As noted above in the "Case Stated" this does not preclude resort to the consultative case stated procedure in extradition proceedings for an offence which will be dealt with on indictment in the foreign jurisdiction.

[183] See *Minister for Labour v. Costello* [1988] I.R. 235, [1989] I.L.R.M. 485.

such matters.[184] The District Court cannot circumvent this prohibition by presenting questions which, while not directly questioning the constitutionality of a statutory provision, produce that effect indirectly. In *DPP v. Dougan*,[185] for example, the District Court stated a case for the opinion of the High Court on whether certain offences under the Road Traffic Act 1994 were minor offences. Since the Act made no provision for these offences to be tried on indictment, it followed that the Court was really being asked to rule on whether the offences were unconstitutional having regard to Article 38.5 of the Constitution. Geoghegan J. ruled in the High Court that the District Court had jurisdiction to state the case but that it was not entitled to specific answers to the questions, as the net effect of the questions was to raise the constitutionality of the relevant provisions in the Act. In *DPP (Stratford) v. O'Neill*[186] Smyth J. acknowledged that Article 34.3.2° of the Constitution prevents the District Court from entering into an adjudication on the constitutionality of a post-1937 statute directly, or indirectly by way of case stated.

It would appear that the prohibition does not extend to pre-1937 statutes. Accordingly, a District Court could, where necessary, enter into an adjudication on the constitutionality of such a statute both directly and indirectly, including by way of a consultative case stated.

2. Determination of Facts

Woods suggests that, by analogy with a case stated by a Circuit Court judge to the Supreme Court, it is a matter for the judge to decide the time at which a case will be stated.[187] However, if he decides to state a case for the opinion of the High Court, he must do so before finally giving his decision in the case.[188] As a general proposition it is desirable that all material facts should be found and the evidence concerning them heard before a question of law is raised for determination by the High Court.[189] Indeed, a judge cannot use the case stated procedure to ask the High Court to define the meaning of expressions used in a statute generally without reference to particular facts.[190] Moreover, where a case has been stated and a determination given by the High Court, a second case stated cannot be submitted in the same proceedings.[191]

In *DPP (Travers) v. Brennan*[192] a District Court judge submitted a consultative case stated without first hearing the evidence and finding the facts relevant to the point of law in issue. When the case came before the Supreme Court by way of appeal from the decision of the High Court Lynch J., giving the

22–27

---

[184] See *State (Sheerin) v. Kennedy* [1966] I.R. 379.

[185] [1997] 1 I.L.R.M. 550.

[186] [1998] 1 I.L.R.M. 221.

[187] Woods at p.478.

[188] *Attorney General v. Simpson* [1959] I.R. 335.

[189] *Doyle v. Hearne* [1988] I.L.R.M. 318.

[190] *O'Neill v. Butler* unreported, High Court, November 26, 1979; *Attorney General v. McLoughlin* [1931] I.R. 430.

[191] *Gavin Low Ltd v. Field (No.2)* [1942] I.R. 610.

[192] [1998] 4 I.R. 67.

judgment of the Court, indicated that this was irregular. The learned judge went on to describe the correct approach as follows:

> "The proper procedure leading to the stating of a consultative case for the opinion of the Superior Courts is for the District Judge to hear all the evidence relevant to the point of law arising, to find the facts relevant to such point of law in the light of such evidence, then to state the case posing the questions appropriate to elucidate the point of law and finally, on receiving the answers to those questions to decide the matter before him on the basis of those answers. See the cases of *Mitchelstown Co-op Society v. Comr. For Valuation* [1989] I.R. 210; *Doyle v. Hearne* [1987] IR 601 and *Dolan v. Corn Exchange* [1973] I.R. 269."[193]

3. Adjournment and Consequential Orders

22–28   Where the judge refers a question of law to the High Court under section 52 he or she must adjourn the proceedings.[194] The adjournment is to the next sitting of the District Court to be held in the court area in question after 14 days from the day on which the decision of the High Court is given. Before adjourning the proceedings the judge may require the party requesting the case stated to enter into a recognisance before the judge.[195] Where applicable, the recognisance shall be with or without sureties and in such sum or sums as the judge may determine.[196] When completed the recognisance shall be lodged with the clerk. The parties who are exempt from the recognisance requirement in a case stated under section 2 of the Summary Jurisdiction Act 1857 (see above) are also exempt for the purposes of the procedure under section 52 of the 1961 Act.

Where a party to the proceedings is in custody when the judge adjourns the proceedings under these provisions he or she may release that party or commit him to prison by warrant.[197] Alternatively the judge may discharge the party on his entering into a recognisance, with or without sureties, and in such sum or sums as the judge shall determine. Once completed the recognisance shall be lodged with the clerk.[198]

4. Submission of case stated

22–29   Where a judge grants an application for a case stated, or decides to make a referral without such a request, he or she shall prepare and sign the case stated within six months from the date of the application.[199] In order to secure

---

[193] *ibid.* at 70.
[194] District Court Rules, 1997, Ord.102, r.11(1).
[195] *Ibid.,* r.11(2).
[196] *ibid.* The recognisance shall be in the Form 102.4 Sched.D.
[197] *Ibid.,* r.11(3).
[198] *ibid.* The recognisance shall be in the Form 102.4 Sched.D.
[199] *ibid.* r.12. Note that the case stated must be signed by the judge hearing the proceedings and that he must continue to be a judge of the District Court at the time he signs it; see *DPP v. Galvin* [1999] 4 I.R. 18, [1999] 2 I.L.R.M. 277, discussed above.

agreement between the parties on the facts of the case stated the judge may, if he or she thinks fit, submit a draft of the case stated to the parties or receive a draft from the parties within two months of the date of the application. In the event of a dispute between the parties as to the facts, the facts shall be found by the judge. Typically, the case stated will set out in paragraphs the facts of the case, the contentions of the parties and the District Court judge's finding of fact and a statement of the questions on which the judge has reserved his or her decision pending the opinion of the High Court.[200]

Once the case has been stated and signed by the judge, the party requesting the case stated shall receive the case stated from the clerk.[201] The case may then be transmitted to the Central Office of the High Court by the party in question or by the District Court.[202] Where the judge states a case on his or her own initiative refers (without a prior request from one of the parties) the clerk shall give notice in writing forthwith to each party in the proceedings and shall then transmit the case stated to the Central Office of the High Court.[203]

The Rules of the Superior Courts state that at any time within ten days of the date of transmission the clerk shall lodge with the proper officer one or more copies of the case stated and any documents as may be required for the use of the Court.[204] Any party to the proceedings is entitled to obtain, on application to the proper officer and upon payment of the prescribed fee, one or more copies of the case stated and documents if any.[205] Once the case has been transmitted to the Central Office the proper officer shall immediately file it and set it down for hearing.[206] However, it shall not appear in the list for hearing until the expiration of ten days after it has been received.

5. Appeal

An appeal lies by leave of the High Court to the Supreme Court from any determination of the High Court on a consultative case stated.[207] Since the 1961 Act is a post 1937 statute it follows that the specific inclusion of the requirement for leave to appeal qualifies the constitutional right of appeal to the Supreme Court from all decisions of the High Court. It is also worth noting that a party's right of appeal against the District Court judge's final determination in the case is not prejudiced by his having exercised the option of requesting a consultative case stated in the course of the proceedings in the District Court.

---

[200] See Woods p.481.
[201] District Court Rules, 1997, Ord.102, r.13.
[202] Rules of the Superior Courtss, Ord.62, r.3.
[203] District Court Rules, 1997, Ord.102, r.14, Such notice to the parties shall be in Form 102.5 Sched.D.
[204] Rules of the Superior Courts, Ord.62, r.6.
[205] *ibid.* Ord.62, r.7.
[206] *ibid.* Ord.62, r.4.
[207] Courts (Supplemental Provisions) Act 1961, s.52(2).

E. Appeals to the Court of Criminal Appeal

1. Introduction

22–30   The Court of Criminal Appeal was established by the Courts of Justice Act 1924[208] and re-established by the Courts (Establishment and Constitution) Act 1961.[209] The jurisdiction of the former Court was transferred to the present Court by the Courts (Supplemental Provisions) Act 1961.[210] It is purely a creature of statute and is set to be abolished with the establishment of two or more panels in the Supreme Court.[211]

A person convicted on indictment in the Circuit Court or the Central Criminal Court may appeal against conviction and/or sentence to the Court of Criminal Appeal.[212] Similarly, a person convicted of an offence in the Special Criminal Court may appeal against conviction and/or sentence to the Court of Criminal Appeal.[213] A person may also appeal to the Court against sentence where he has pleaded guilty in the District Court and been returned to the Circuit Court for sentence.[214] It would appear that an accused cannot secure leave to appeal against a verdict of guilty but insane. Technically, such a verdict is an acquittal and, therefore, not appealable.[215] It is also worth noting that the prosecution has no right of appeal against an acquittal to the Court of Criminal Appeal, nor can it be granted leave to appeal. However, there are circumstances in which it may be able to refer a point of law for the consideration of the Court.[216] This is dealt with later.

2. Leave to Appeal

The Requirement

22–31   There is no absolute right of appeal to the Court of Criminal Appeal for the defendant who has been convicted. A prospective appellant must first obtain leave to appeal. He must apply in the first instance to the trial judge for a certificate that the case is a fit case for appeal.[217] If this application is refused, he may apply to the Court of Criminal Appeal for leave by way of an appeal against the refusal.[218] It would appear from the relevant statutory provision that the trial court's refusal to grant a certificate is a pre-requisite for an application for leave to appeal to the Court of Criminal Appeal.

---

[208] Courts of Justice Act 1924, s.8.
[209] Courts (Establishment and Constitution) Act 1961, s.3.
[210] Courts (Supplemental Provisions) Act 1961, ss.12 and 48.
[211] See the Courts and Court Officers Act 1995.
[212] Courts of Justice Act 1924, s.63.
[213] Offences against the State Act 1939, s.44(1).
[214] Criminal Procedure (Amendment) Act 1973, s.1; nullifying the effect of *People v. Tyrrell* [1970] I.R. 294.
[215] *Felstead v. R.* [1914] AC 534.
[216] Criminal Procedure Act 1967, 34(1).
[217] Courts of Justice Act 1924, s.31(i).
[218] *ibid.* s.31(ii).

Time Limits

The application for a certificate from the trial judge that the case is a fit case **22–32** for appeal must be made at the close of the trial or within three days thereafter.[219] In *People v. Cronin*[220] it was held by the Supreme Court that the Court of Criminal Appeal has no jurisdiction to extend the time for making such an application. Its jurisdiction is confined to an appeal against a refusal by the trial court to grant a certificate. Accordingly, an application for enlargement must be taken in the trial court, unless for some reason outside the appellant's control that machinery becomes inoperable. Where the application to enlarge is refused in the Central Criminal Court, the refusal can be appealed to the Supreme Court by virtue of Article 34.4.3° of the Constitution. This option is not available, however, in respect of a refusal by the Circuit Court and, presumably, the Special Criminal Court.[221] As a rule of thumb, therefore, it would be standard procedure to lodge an application for a certificate in any case where an appeal might be considered.[222]

Enlargement of time

The strictness of the ruling in *Cronin* must be in some doubt in the light of the Supreme Court's interpretation of the Rules of the Superior Courts in *People v. Kelly*.[223] The Rules make specific provision for an extension of time to be granted for the purpose of an appeal to the Court of Criminal Appeal. They stipulate that, except in any case where steps are required by statute to be taken in the Central Criminal Court or in the Circuit Court, the Court of Criminal Appeal may enlarge the time appointed by the Rules for doing any act or taking any proceeding upon such terms (if any) as the justice of the case may require.[224] Any such enlargement may be ordered even if the application for enlargement is not made until after the expiration of the time appointed by the Rules. The application must specify the grounds upon which the application is based and the grounds on which the applicant proposes to base his appeal or application for leave.[225] The Court's jurisdiction to grant an extension of time is also enhanced indirectly by the terms of rule 38 of RSC Order 86 (previously rule 40). It stipulates that non-compliance on the part of the appellant with the rules of Order 86, or with any rule of practice for the time being in force, shall not prevent the further prosecution of his appeal or application, unless the Court shall so direct, but such appeal or application may be dealt with on such manner and upon such terms as the Court shall think fit.

---

[219] Rules of the Superior Courts, Ord.86, r.3. Where a certificate is granted it may be in Form No.1.

[220] [1972] I.R. 159.

[221] There may be a doubt with respect to the Special Criminal Court given that the procedures before it are meant to follow, as closely as possible, those before the Central Criminal Court.

[222] Note, however, that a solicitor should not lodge an appeal without the authority of his client; *R v. McCready* [1978] 1W.L.R. 1376; *R v. Jones* [1971] 2 Q.B. 456.

[223] [1982] I.R. 90.

[224] Rules of the Superior Courts, Ord.86, r.8(1)

[225] *ibid.* r.8(3). An application for an enlargement of time within which notice of appeal or notice of application for leave to appeal may be served shall be in Form No.5; r.8(2).

22–33   It cannot be assumed that the Court of Criminal Appeal will readily grant an extension of time to facilitate the late prosecution of an appeal. In *People v. Kelly*[226] the appellant was tried with two co-accused on charges of larceny of mail bags and of stopping a mail train with intent to rob the mail. The appellant absconded to the U.S.A. before the conclusion of his trial. He was convicted and sentenced to 12 years penal servitude in his absence and his two co-accused were convicted and sentenced to terms of 12 years and nine years respectively. The two co-accused appealed their conviction to the Court of Criminal Appeal which quashed them primarily on the ground that their confessions should have been excluded at the trial due to the circumstances in which they were obtained. Since the appellant's confession had been obtained in similar circumstances he returned to the jurisdiction and sought leave from the Court of Criminal Appeal for an enlargement of time within which to bring an application for leave to appeal against his conviction. The Court refused to grant leave but it did accede to the appellant's application for a certificate that its decision to refuse leave involved a point of law of exceptional public importance and that it was desirable in the public interest that an appeal should be taken to the Supreme Court. The point of law concerned the criteria which should be applied in determining an application for leave for an enlargement of time within which to bring an application for leave to appeal against conviction.

The Supreme Court upheld the appeal on the ground that the test applied by the Court of Criminal Appeal was that appropriate to a civil matter as opposed to a criminal matter.[227] The Supreme Court held that in considering whether to grant an application for enlargement of time the Court of Criminal Appeal must be guided by what is required by the justice of the case. It should exercise its power flexibly, unrestricted and unhampered by any consideration other than that which is required by the justice of the particular case in which the application is made. The Court also ruled that by virtue of Order 86, rule 38 of the Rules of the Superior Courts the appellant could have applied directly to the Court of Criminal Appeal for leave to appeal without first seeking an enlargement of time.[228] Once again, in considering any such application the Court must be flexible and exercise its discretion in accordance with what appears to be just and equitable on the particular facts of the case in question. The mere fact that the appellant did not evidence an intention to appeal immediately or soon after conviction is not sufficient in itself to refuse his application. Even, as in this case, his "reprehensible and dishonourable" conduct in fleeing from justice is not necessarily fatal. If the application raises a question which merits investigation justice requires that the application should be granted. The appellant succeeding in doing that by establishing the

---

[226] [1982] I.R. 90.

[227] Basically the Court of Criminal Appeal had applied the test laid down in *Eire Continental Trading Co. Ltd v. Clonmel Foods Ltd.* [1955] I.R. 170. In essence this permitted leave to be granted only where an intention to appeal existed at the time of or immediately after conviction and where there were grounds of appeal which could be described as arguable or substantial.

[228] The court split 3:2 on this point.

very close similarity between the essential facts of his case and that of two co-accused whose convictions had been quashed on appeal:

> "That factor is that the evidence on which his conviction rests was a self-incriminating admission made in circumstances akin to those in which his two co-accused made admissions which led to their convictions, but which admissions were later held by the Court of Criminal Appeal to have been unfairly obtained so that their convictions and sentences were quashed. The self-incriminating admissions of all three accused appear to have been made in the same place of detention, during the same period of detention and as a result of methods of interrogation which had certain common features. The appellant's two co-accused had their convictions quashed for different reasons, but each reason amounted to a finding that, in regard to their alleged admissions, they had been denied basic fairness of procedures. Because of the apparently close connection between the circumstances in which self-inculpatory statements were obtained from all three accused, the suspicion remains that the appellant may be able to show, for one or other reasons which availed his co-accused or for some other reason, that the confessional evidence (without which his conviction would, apparently, not have resulted) should have been ruled inadmissible."[229]

In the light of the decision in *Kelly* it would appear that the three day rule for seeking an appeal certificate from the trial judge might be circumvented by applying directly to the Court of Criminal Appeal for an enlargement of time in which to seek an application for leave to appeal. It must said, however, that none of the judgments in *Kelly* adverted to the fact that the relevant statutory provision only provides for an application to the Court of Criminal Appeal for leave to appeal where the appellant is appealing against the trial court's refusal to grant an appeal certificate. It would appear that the appellant in *Kelly* had neither sought an appeal certificate from the trial court nor sought an enlargement of time from the trial court to apply for a certificate. Moreover, it would appear that the Supreme Court's previous decision in *Cronin* was not cited to the court in *Kelly*.

Notice

Where an appellant has been granted a certificate by the trial judge he must serve a notice of appeal setting out the grounds of appeal within 14 days of the date on which the certificate was granted.[230] If he has been refused a certificate he must serve a notice of application for leave to appeal. This, too, must set out the grounds of appeal and must be served within seven days from the date of the refusal of the certificate.[231] If the application for leave is granted the original notice is deemed to be the notice of appeal.[232] Every notice of appeal

22–34

---

[229] *People v. Kelly* [1982] I.R. 90, *per* Henchy J. at 115–116.
[230] Rules of the Superior Courts, Ord.86, r.4. This must be in the Form No.2. The grounds of appeal may be amended or added to by leave of the court; *People v. Kerins* [1945] I.R. 339; *People v. Hughes* 92 I.L.T.R. 179.
[231] *ibid.* This must be in the Form No.3.
[232] Rules of the Superior Courts, Ord.86, r.6.

under section 29(6) of the Road Traffic Act 1961 must be served on the Registrar within seven days from the date of the order appealed against.[233]

Signature

The notice of appeal or application for leave to appeal must normally be signed by the appellant, unless he is unable to write or is alleged to be insane at the time or is a body corporate.[234] If the appellant cannot write he may affix his mark on the notice in the presence of a witness who shall attest it.[235] Where it is alleged that he is insane at the time, the notice may be given and signed by a solicitor or other person on his behalf.[236] In the case of a body corporate it will be sufficient if the notice is signed by the secretary, clerk, manager or solicitor of such body.[237] Any other notice, apart from a notice of appeal or notice of application for leave to appeal, must be in writing and signed by the person giving the notice or by his solicitor.[238]

Serving Notice

22–35 Notice of appeal and notice of an application for leave to appeal must be served on the Registrar of the Court of Criminal Appeal.[239] The Registrar must give notice of the appeal or application for leave to appeal to: the Chief State Solicitor; the proper officer of the court of trial;, the Commissioner of the Garda Síochána; and, where the appellant is in prison or has been released on bail, the Governor of the prison and the Secretary of the Department of Justice, Equality and Law Reform.[240] Notice of every other application to the court shall be served on the Registrar and the Chief State Solicitor or appellant (as the case may be) and such other person, if any, as the court may direct.[241]

In every case where an appellant is not in prison or is represented by a solicitor, his notice of appeal or notice of application for leave to appeal must be served on the Registrar personally or by delivering it to the proper officer at the Office of the Court at the Four Courts in Dublin.[242] In all other cases not specifically provided for, service of any notice or other document may be effected personally or by sending it by pre-paid post addressed to the person on whom it is to be served. Where any notice is required or authorised to be

---

[233] *ibid.* Ord.86, r.5. This notice must be in the Form No.27.
[234] *ibid.* Ord.86, r.31(1).
[235] *ibid.* r.31(2).
[236] *ibid.* r.31(3).
[237] *ibid.* r.31(4).
[238] *ibid.* r.31(1).
[239] *ibid.* r.4. Form No.2 must be used for notice of appeal and Form No.3 must be used for notice of application for leave to appeal.
[240] *ibid.*, r.7. This must be in the Form No.4. Notice to the Governor of a prison is not necessary if the appellant's notice of appeal or notice of application for leave to appeal was forwarded to the Registrar by the Governor.
[241] *ibid.* r.29. Such notice shall be in accordance with the Form No.26.
[242] *ibid.* r.31(6).

given to the court under these provisions it shall be addressed to and served upon the Registrar, The Court of Criminal Appeal, Four Courts, Dublin.[243]

The time limits specified for service of the notice of appeal or notice of application for leave to appeal can be enlarged pursuant to an application under Order 86, rule 8 of the Rules of the Superior Courts. Presumably, any such application for enlargement will be considered in accordance with the principles in *Kelly* as outlined above.

Statement of Grounds of Appeal

The notice of appeal will set out the grounds of appeal. Given the time constraints within which the notice must be served it is usually the case that the grounds of appeal will be formulated before the full transcript of the trial becomes available. This can work to the disadvantage of the accused if his appeal is confined to the grounds originally set out on the notice of the appeal. It may be, for example, that the subsequent perusal of the transcript will reveal further grounds of appeal which did not occur to the defence at the time they prepared the notice of appeal.

While the court discourages the practice of scrutinising the transcript with a view to formulating grounds of appeal,[243a] it is generally willing to permit the appellant to raise grounds of appeal at the hearing which were not specifically stated in the notice of appeal as served on the other side.[243b] If, however, counsel seeks to raise points on the appeal which were not canvassed at the trial, the court will normally look for an explanation as to why it was not made at the trial.[243c] O'Flaherty J. put the matter bluntly as follows in *People (DPP) v. Moloney*:

> "We would wish to re-iterate the jurisprudence of the Court which has been in place for many years that there is an obligation on counsel on both sides, the prosecution and the defence, to bring to the attention of the trial judge any inadequacies they perceive in his directions to the jury. If an appeal is brought before this Court on a point that has not been canvassed at trial this Court will regard any person making such a new point as having an obligation to explain why it is sought to be made on appeal when not made at the trial."[243d]

The Court is more hostile to attempts by the DPP to change its stance from the trial to the appeal. In *People (DPP) v. McHugh*,[243e] for example, the DPP assumed the burden of proving that not only did the defendant know that goods were stolen but that in fact the goods were stolen for the purposes of establishing guilt of a money laundering offence. On the appeal by the defendant against his conviction, however, the DPP argued that it was only

---

[243] *ibid.* r.31(5).

[243a] *People (Attorney General) v. Coughlin* [1968] 1 Frewen 325.

[243b] See, for *e.g., DPP v. Moloney* unreported, Court of Criminal Appeal, March 2, 1992.

[243c] In *People (DPP) v. Noonan* [1998] 2 I.R. 439 the primary ground of appeal had not been raised in the requisitions at the trial. Nevertheless, the Court of Criminal Appeal entertained the appeal as it concluded that the omission related to such a fundamental aspect of the defence that it must have been due to an oversight.

[243d] Unreported, Court of Criminal Appeal, March 2, 1992.

[243e] Unreported, Court of Criminal Appeal, February 12, 2002.

necessary to prove that the defendant knew that the goods were stolen. Responding to this change of strategy, Fennelly J. said that in the normal course of events the prosecution should not be allowed to alter its stance for the purpose of the hearing of the appeal. However, since the defendant suffered no inherent prejudice in the criminal trial itself nor any procedural disadvantage in the appeal as a result of the DPP's strategy, the Court entertained the DPP's submissions on the matter.

Even if the grounds of appeal are more suitable to be raised by way of plenary proceedings, the court has demonstrated a willingness to entertain the appeal where it considers that that is necessary in order to do justice for the accused. In *DPP v. Lynch*,[243f] for example, the Court entertained an appeal against a conviction for murder where the grounds of appeal were an allegation that the accused had pleaded guilty as a result of improper pressure from his legal advisors. In effect the dispute was not between the accused and the DPP, but between the accused and his own legal advisors. What the Court of Criminal Appeal was being asked to do was not only to resolve that dispute but to decide whether in all the circumstances there would be a lacking in the principle of fairness to refuse the accused a trial on the merits. Giving the judgment of the Court, Barron J. explained:

> "While obviously all this can be achieved in plenary proceedings, it is more appropriate to invoke the jurisdiction of this Court to determine the matter. While the facts involved in the issue of duress might be better determined in fresh proceedings, the more fundamental issue, whether the appellant should in all the circumstances be allowed to change his plea and obtain a trial on the merits is more properly a matter for this Court. The Director of Public Prosecutions must be heard on such an issue, but would not automatically be a party to declaratory proceedings."

The Decision

Leave to appeal shall be granted by the Court of Criminal Appeal in cases where it is of the opinion that a question of law is involved, or where the trial appears to the Court to have been unsatisfactory or where there appears to the Court to be any other sufficient ground of appeal.[244] However, if the appellant pleaded guilty on arraignment, for example, he will not normally be granted leave in the absence of exceptional circumstances. In *People v. Marshall*[245] the court accepted that entering a plea of guilty under a misapprehension amounted to exceptional circumstances for this purpose. In that case the Court accepted that the accused was confused and did not understand the charge to which he had pleaded guilty. He intended to plead guilty to a less serious charge on the indictment when he was arraigned. The court granted leave to appeal, treated the application for leave as the appeal and quashed the conviction.

[243f] Unreported, Court of Criminal Appeal, July 27, 1999 and December 14, 1998.
[244] Courts of Justice Act 1924, s.32.
[245] [1956] I.R. 79.

3. Consequential Orders

Postponment of Sentence

Where a person seeks leave to appeal against conviction and/or sentence it will usually be necessary to make certain further orders pending the outcome of the application or appeal. The court has the power to make whatever consequential orders it may think fit.[246] The most immediate issue, of course, will concern the sentence, if any. Where the person has been sentenced on conviction to the payment of a fine (with imprisonment in default) the person lawfully authorised to receive such fine shall, on receiving it, retain it until the determination of the appeal.[247] If the appellant is in custody in default of payment he will be deemed to have been sentenced to a term of imprisonment.[248] The trial judge, however, when granting a certificate of appeal also has a power to order that the payment of a fine imposed on conviction should be postponed until the final determination of the appeal.[249] This option will be available where the person concerned intimates to the trial judge that he is desirous of appealing to the Court of Criminal Appeal and applies for a certificate. If he or she gives the certificate the judge may order the person to enter into recognisances immediately, with or without sureties, to prosecute his appeal.[250] If, after entering into such recognisances, the person fails to serve notice of appeal within the time allowed, the Registrar shall certify such failure and shall send the certificate, together with the recognisances, to the proper officer of the court of trial. The trial judge may then make such order for the estreat of the recognisances, payment of the fine and otherwise as he or she may think fit.[251]

An appellant who has paid the fine to which he was sentenced shall, in the event of a successful appeal, be entitled to the return of the sum to him, subject to any order of the court.[252]

Suspension of Orders for Costs and Compensation

Where the trial judge makes an order on conviction requiring the person convicted to pay the whole or part of the costs of the prosecution, or compensation to the victim or award to another third party, there is provision for it to be suspended pending the outcome of an appeal.[253] The operation of any such order is automatically suspended for 21 clear days after the day on which it was made. The same applies to any order affecting the rights or property of the convicted person. Where notice of appeal, or notice of application for

22–36

22–37

---

[246]   Courts of Justice Act 1924, s.32, as amended by the Criminal Procedure Act 1993, s.3(6).
[247]   Rules of the Superior Courts, Ord.86, r.9(1).
[248]   *ibid.* r.9(2).
[249]   *ibid.* r.9(3).
[250]   The recognisances shall be in the Forms Nos. 6 and 7. A surety bound by recognisances under this provision shall have all of the powers of a surety "under rule 20". Presumably this should read "rule 19". See Rules of the Superior Courts, Ord.86, r.9(3).
[251]   Rules of the Superior Courts, Ord.86, r.9(4).
[252]   *ibid.* r.9(5).
[253]   *ibid.* r.11(1).

leave to appeal, is served within the 21 day period, the operation of the order shall be suspended until the determination of the appeal or application. Where an order is made the judge shall give such directions as he or she thinks right as to the retention by any person of any money or valuable securities belonging to the person convicted which has been seized from him or which is in the possession of the prosecution proper.[254] Such directions shall last for a period of 21 clear days or, in the event of an appeal or application for leave to appeal, until the determination of the appeal or application. If any property or subject matter connected with the prosecution is ordered to be destroyed or forfeited on conviction, the operation of the order shall be suspended for the period of 21 clear days from the close of the trial.[255] In the event of an appeal, or an application for leave to appeal, the order shall be suspended until the determination of the appeal or the application. A similar suspensory provision applies to any claim or proceedings which may be taken under statute against the convicted person in consequence of the conviction,[256] and to any order of restitution.[257] Moreover, if the trial judge is of the opinion that the title to any property, the subject of an order of restitution made on conviction, is not in dispute and that such property is reasonably necessary for the appeal hearing, he shall give such directions or impose such terms on the person in whose favour the order of restitution was made as he or she shall think right in order to secure its production at the appeal hearing.[258]

Where the trial judge makes any order for the payment of money by the convicted person, or any other person, and the order would normally be suspended as a result of these provisions, the judge may direct that the order should not be suspended unless the person concerned shall give security by way of an undertaking for the payment of the amount in question to the person in whose favour the order was made.[259] The judge shall determine the manner and time in which the security should be given.

Certificate of Conviction

22–38   The clerk of the court, or other officer having custody of the records, shall not issue a certificate of conviction of any person convicted on indictment in the court for a period of 21 clear days after the day on which the trial concluded.[260] If a notice of appeal, or an application for leave to appeal is lodged, such notice shall not issue until the determination of the appeal or application. Where an application for a certificate is made to the clerk, or other such officer, after the 21 day period he or she will have to be satisfied before issuing the certificate that no appeal or application for leave to appeal is

---

[254] *ibid.* r.11(2).

[255] *ibid.* r.11(4).

[256] *ibid.* r.11(5).

[257] *ibid.* r.12.

[258] *ibid.* r.10. This also applies to any property to which the provisions of s.24(1) of the Sale of Goods Act 1893 applies.

[259] *ibid.* r.11(3).

[260] *ibid.* r.13(1). In this context "conviction" means the verdict or plea of guilty and any final judgment passed thereon.

pending in the court against the conviction.[261] After the expiration of two months from the date of conviction a certificate may be issued, except in those cases where an appeal or application for leave to appeal is still undetermined.[262]

4. Bail

If the appellant is in custody as a result of his conviction he may wish to apply for bail pending his appeal (or any re-trial). The Court of Criminal Appeal has power to admit the appellant to bail pending the determination of his appeal or application for leave to appeal.[263] The principles and procedures governing this jurisdiction are dealt with in chapter 10 on Bail.

22–39

5. Notifying the Parties

The Registrar must keep a register of all cases in which he has received a notice of appeal or a notice of application for leave to appeal.[264] He must also prepare from time to time a general list of cases to be dealt with by the court.[265] This list must be published in such a manner as shall be convenient for giving due notice to any parties interested in the hearing of such cases. If the appellant is in custody the registrar must also notify him and his solicitor (if any), the Governor of the prison and the prisons section of the Department of Justice, Equality and Law Reform of the probable day on which his appeal will be heard.[266] Where necessary, the Department must take steps to transfer the appellant to a prison convenient for his appearance at such a reasonable time before the hearing to enable him to consult his legal adviser. Once the date of the hearing has been fixed the Registrar must give notice to the appellant and his solicitor (if any) and the Chief State Solicitor.[267]

22–40

6. Presence of the Appellant and other Parties

An appellant who is in custody is entitled, if he so desires, to be present in person at the hearing of his appeal or application for leave to appeal and, subject to the prior consent of the court, at all related interlocutory applications.[268] If he has been admitted to bail he must, when his case is called on before the court, surrender himself to such persons as the court shall from time to time direct.[269] He may be searched by such persons and is deemed to be in their lawful custody until further released on bail or otherwise dealt with as the

22–41

---

[261] *ibid.* r.13(2). To this end a person is entitled to obtain from the registrar a certificate in Form No.8 for the purpose of satisfying the clerk, or other officer, that no such appeal or application is pending.

[262] *ibid.* r.13(2).

[263] Courts of Justice Act 1924, s.32, as amended by the Criminal Procedure Act 1993, s.3(6).

[264] Rules of the Superior Courts , Ord.86, r.20(1). The register is open to public inspection.

[265] *ibid.* r.20(2).

[266] *ibid.* r.22(1).

[267] *ibid.* r.22(2).

[268] *ibid.* r.25(1). This also applies to an application for enlargement of time; r.25(2).

[269] *ibid.* r.19(8).

court shall direct. If an appellant who is free on bail fails to appear, the court may dismiss the appeal and issue a warrant for his apprehension.[270]

Where a restitution order has been made by the court of trial, the person in whose favour the order was made, the appellant and, with the leave of the Court of Criminal Appeal, any other person shall be entitled to be heard before any order is made by the court annulling or varying the order.[271]

7. Documents for the Appeal

Scope

22–42　An appeal is normally heard and determined on the basis of a record of the trial proceedings and a transcript of the record verified by the trial judge.[272] The record in this context includes, in addition to a written record and a photograph, any shorthand notes, disc, tape, soundtrack or other device in which information, sounds or signals are embodied so as to be capable (with or without the aid of some other instrument) of being reproduced in legible or audible form.[273] Equally, it includes a film tape or other device in which visual images are embodied so as to be capable (with or without the aid of some other instrument) of being reproduced in visual form. If the trial judge is of the opinion that the record or transcript does not reflect what took place at the trial the appeal may also be based on (in addition to the record and transcript) a report by the judge as to the defects which he or she considers such records or transcript contains.[274] The court may also hear new or additional evidence and may refer any matter for report by the trial judge. Indeed, in relation to any appeal or application for leave to appeal, the court may direct the Registrar to request from the trial judge a written report giving his or her opinion on the case generally or upon any point arising from it.[275] The judge is under a duty to provide the report as requested. If the court is of the opinion that either the record or the transcript is defective in any material particular, it may determine the appeal in such manner as it considers appropriate in all the circumstances.[276]

---

[270] *ibid.* The warrant is in the Form No.15. It shall be deemed for all purposes to be a warrant issued by a judge of the District Court for the apprehension of a person charged with any indictable offence under the provisions of the Petty Sessions (Ireland) Act 1851, or any amending statute; see Rules of the Superior Courts, Ord.86, r.36.

[271] Rules of the Superior Courts, Ord.86, r.27.

[272] Courts of Justice Act 1924, s.33(1)(a), as substituted by the Criminal Justice (Miscellaneous Provisions) Act 1997, s.7

[273] *ibid.* s.33(3).

[274] *ibid.* s.33(1)(b).

[275] Rules of the Superior Courts, Ord. 86, r.18(1). The report of the trial judge under this provision shall be made to the court of Criminal Appeal and, except by leave of the court, the registrar shall not furnish any part of it to any person; r.18(2).

[276] Courts of Justice Act 1924, s.33(2), as amended by Criminal Justice (Miscellaneous Provisions) Act 1997, s.7.

The Transcript

The combined effect of these provisions has a knock on effect on the sort of documents relevant to the appeal hearing. In most cases, however, the transcript of the trial will be the central material on the appeal. At the conclusion of the trial the stenographer must sign the shorthand note and certify that it is complete and correct.[277] At the request of the Registrar the stenographer shall furnish to him a report comprising the original shorthand note and a transcript of the whole of such note or of such part as may be required.[278] The stenographer's report must contain the evidence, including any objection taken in the course of the evidence, any statement made by the accused, the summing up and the sentence of the trial judge.[279] Unless otherwise ordered by the trial judge it shall not include any part of the speeches of counsel or solicitor, nor even a plea in mitigation of sentence. The transcript of the shorthand note may be made either by the official stenographer who took the shorthand note or by another competent person.[280] It must be typewritten and certified by the person making it to be a correct and complete transcript of the whole of the shorthand note taken by the stenographer or of such part of it as may be required.[281] Before the stenographer submits his report to the Registrar he must submit the transcript to the trial judge to be certified by him or her.[282] Any party interested in an appeal or application for leave to appeal may obtain from the Registrar a copy of the transcript of the whole or any part of the shorthand note as relates to the appeal or application on payment of the proper charges.[283]

Normally, the Registrar will obtain the transcript of the shorthand note for any application for leave to appeal which he has listed.[284] He must also obtain and lay before the court in proper form all documents, exhibits and other things relating to the proceedings in the court of trial which are necessary for the proper determination of the appeal or application for leave to appeal.[285]

Securing Documents and Exhibits

22–43

Documents and exhibits used at the original trial will also be relevant to the appeal. Accordingly, when the Registrar receives notice of appeal or a notice of application for leave to appeal he must apply to the proper officer of the court of trial for the original depositions of witnesses examined at the committal hearing (presumably this must now be taken to refer to depositions

---

[277] Rules of the Superior Courts, Ord.86, r.14(1).
[278] *ibid.* r.14(2).
[279] *ibid.* r.14(7).
[280] *ibid.* r.14(5).
[281] *ibid.* r.14(6).
[282] *ibid.* r.14(3).
[283] *ibid.* r.14(4).
[284] The registrar may list a case for hearing without obtaining the transcript of the shorthand note if it appears to him that the notice of application for leave to appeal does not show any substantial ground of appeal; Criminal Procedure Act 1993, s.5(1) and Rules of the Superior Courts, Ord.86, r.26.
[285] Rules of the Superior Courts, Ord.86, r.21.

taken before the District Court pursuant to an order of the trial court), the indictment or indictments against the appellant, a copy of the record of the appellant's trial from the Trials Book, any exhibit or exhibits retained by such officer and a list of the exhibits.[286] The court officer is under to a duty to comply with such a request.[287] Moreover, the Registrar may, on an application made to him by the appellant or the DPP, obtain and keep available for use by the court any documents, exhibits or other things relating to the appeal proceedings.[288] He is under a duty to do so when directed by the court or where he considers the subject matter to be necessary for the proper determination of any appeal or application. Pending the determination of the appeal proceedings the subject matter in question shall be open, as and when the Registrar may arrange, for the inspection of any party concerned.

Some documents or exhibits connected with the appeal proceedings may be in the custody of a third person. Where this situation arises the court may, on the application of the appellant or the DPP, order any such document, exhibit or other such thing to be produced to the Registrar by any person having the custody or control of it.[289]

Service of any order under these provisions relating to the retention of documents or exhibits is personal unless the court orders otherwise.[290]

It is also worth noting that where a person is convicted and an order of restitution is made in respect of any property, the judge of the court of trial has a power to give directions as he or she shall think right to a person in whose favour the order of restitution is made in order to secure the production of the property (or a sample, portion or facsimile representation thereof) for use at the hearing of any appeal.[291] This power arises where the judge is of the opinion that the title to the property is not in dispute and the property is reasonably necessary to be produced for use at the hearing of any appeal.

On the hearing of an appeal or, as the case may be, of an application for leave to appeal, against conviction or sentence the Court of Criminal Appeal has a general power to order the production of any document, exhibit or other thing connected with the proceedings.[292]

Obtaining copies of Documents or Exhibits

22–44　At any time after the notice of appeal, or notice of application for leave to appeal, has been served the appellant or the DPP, or their respective solicitors or persons representing them, may obtain from the Registrar copies of any documents or exhibits in his possession for the purposes of the appeal or

---

[286] *ibid.* r.15.

[287] Upon the final determination of the appeal or application for leave to appeal, the registrar shall return the documents to the court officer concerned.

[288] Rules of the Superior Courts, Ord.86, r.16(1).

[289] *ibid.* r.16(2).

[290] *ibid.* r.16(3). For the purpose of effecting service the Registrar may require the assistance of the Garda Siochana, and it shall be their duty to carry out any directions of the Registrar under this rule.

[291] *ibid.* r.10. This also applies to property to which the provisions of s.24(1) of the Sale of Goods Act 1893 apply.

[292] Criminal Procedure Act 1993, s.3(3)(b).

application.[293] Such copies shall be supplied at the proper charges, although there are situations in which they may be supplied free of charge. A transcript of the shorthand notes taken of the proceedings at the trial of an appellant shall be supplied by the Registrar free of charge to an appellant who has been granted a legal aid certificate and to any other appellant by order of the court.[294] Where an appellant requires from the Registrar a copy of any document or exhibit in his custody for the purposes of the appeal, and he is either not legally represented or has been granted a legal aid (appeal) certificate, the copy shall be supplied free of charge where the Registrar considers proper to supply it.[295]

8. Fresh Evidence

Application for Leave

The appeal is normally conducted on the basis of the evidence submitted at the trial. However, there is a procedure to facilitate the submission of fresh evidence in suitable cases. If the appellant wishes to call evidence which was not adduced at the trial he must apply to the court for leave. The application for the attendance and examination of any witness before the court must be made in the appropriate form.[296] This form will state the name and address of the witness, whether he was examined at the trial, the reason why he was not examined (if relevant) and the matters on which it is proposed to examine him. Annexed to this form will normally be a statement, signed by the witness, setting out his evidence and the reason why he did not give such evidence at the trial.[297] The court may dispense with the need for this form.

22–45

Assessment Criteria

It is not possible to state absolutely and precisely what criteria the court will apply when determining whether to admit new evidence on appeal. On the one hand the court is mindful of the need to ensure that an innocent person is not convicted. Accordingly, it will often give the appellant the benefit of the doubt with respect to the admission of new evidence even in cases where the arguments in favour of admission appear weak. On the other hand the court is keen to avoid the appeal being turned into a re-run of the trial. As a general rule it can be said that if the fresh evidence was available at the time of the trial and was not used it will not be admitted.[298] Even then there are

---

[293] *Ibid,* r.17(1).

[294] *ibid.* r.17(2).

[295] *ibid.* r.17(3).

[296] Rules of the Superior Courts, Ord.86, r.24(1). The form is Form No.21. It seems that the application must be made at the hearing of the appeal, or the application for leave to appeal, as the case may be. It cannot be made as a preliminary application; Ryan and Magee, *op.cit.,* at p.428. Moreover, if an application for leave to appeal has been refused it cannot be reinstated for the purpose of seeking to adduce fresh evidence; *State v. Killian* (1951) Frewen 115.

[297] If the appellant is legally represented it would appear that the statement should be taken by the appellant's solicitor; *Attorney General v. McGann* [1927] I.R. 503.

[298] *Attorney General v. McGann* [1927] I.R. 503; *People v. Keane* 110 I.L.T.R. 1.

exceptions. Ultimately, much will depend on the particular circumstances of the case. The court may also have regard to the credibility of the evidence when deciding whether to admit it.[299]

Further Garda Inquiries

22–46 Where the appeal is based on new or additional evidence the court may direct the Commissioner of the Garda Síochána to have such inquiries carried out as the court considers necessary or expedient for the purpose of determining whether further evidence ought to be adduced.[300] It is worth noting the parameters to any such inquiry. The power cannot be used to authorise the conduct of a general inquiry into any allegations which have given rise to the appeal. The court should specify the particular matters which it wants to have investigated, and the Commissioner should confine the inquiry to the question of determining whether further evidence ought to be produced. The inquiry cannot be used as a vehicle to determine the facts surrounding the allegations. That is a matter for the court.

Taking new Evidence

22–47 Where the court decides in favour of admitting the new evidence it will issue an order for the attendance and examination of the witness (or witnesses, as the case may be).[301] It shall be served upon the witness and shall specify the time and place at which he is to attend to give evidence.[302] Usually, the new evidence will be taken by the court itself.[303] However, it may order the examination of the witness to be conducted otherwise than before the court, in which case it will specify the person appointed as examiner and the place of examination.[304] In this event the Registrar must supply to the examiner any documents, exhibits or any other material relating to the said appeal as and when requested to do so.[305] When the examiner has appointed a date and time for the examination he shall request the Registrar to give notice of them to the appellant, the DPP, their legal representatives and (where relevant) the Governor of the prison in which the appellant is held.[306] The Registrar must serve the proper notice on every witness to be examined.[307] Service of the notice must be personal unless the court orders otherwise.[308] For this purpose the Registrar may require the assistance of the Garda Síochána.

---

[299] *R v. Hamilton* 13 Cr. App. Rep. 32; *Braddock v. Tillotson's Newspapers Ltd* 65 T.L.R. 553.
[300] Criminal Procedure Act 1993, s.3(3)(a).
[301] Rules of the Superior Courts, Ord.86, r.24(2). The court may order the expenses of the witness to be defrayed as part of the costs of the State in the appeal; r.24(8).
[302] It shall be in Form No.22.
[303] The court has a general power to receive the evidence, if tendered, of any witness. See the Criminal Procedure Act 1993, s.3(3)(d).
[304] Rules of the Superior Courts, Ord.86, r.24(3).
[305] *ibid.* r.24(4). After the examination these documents and exhibits and other material shall be returned to the Registrar by the examiner, together with any depositions taken by him.
[306] Rules of the Superior Courts, Ord.86, r.24(5).
[307] This notice shall be served in the Form No.23; Rules of the Superior Courts, Ord.86, r.24(5).
[308] Rules of the Superior Courts, Ord.86, r.16(3).

The conduct of the examination of a witness by an examiner under these **22–48** provisions is similar to the taking of depositions before a judge of the District Court for the purpose of a preliminary examination.[309] The witness, unless not required to be sworn if giving evidence at the trial on indictment, must give his evidence upon oath to be administered by the examiner.[310] The examination is taken in the form of a deposition and, unless otherwise ordered, shall be taken in private.[311] The appellant and the DPP, or counsel or solicitor on their behalf, are entitled to be present at and take part in any examination of the witness.[312] Depositions taken by the examiner must be submitted to the registrar at the conclusion of the examination.[313]

The Court enjoys a general power to order any person who would have been a compellable witness in the proceedings from which the appeal lies to attend for examination, and to be examined, before the court whether or not he was called in those proceedings.[314] This power would appear to be expressed in terms sufficiently broad to enable the court to call for examination witnesses who have not been called by the appellant. Where a witness is required for examination under this provision the court may order the examination to be conducted, in a manner provided by rules of the court, before any judge or officer of the court or other person appointed by the court for the purpose.[315] It may also allow the admission of any depositions so taken as evidence before the court.

Impact of New Evidence

Where the court has admitted fresh evidence and assessed its credibility it may **22–49** either affirm the conviction, quash it entirely or allow the appeal and order a re-trial on the grounds that the weight of the evidence ought to be determined by a jury rather than by the court itself.[316] In reaching this decision the court must conduct an objective evaluation of the new evidence with a view to determining whether in the light of it the conviction was unsafe and unsatisfactory.[317] It cannot reach this conclusion based solely on the course which the defence took at the trial. It must consider the course the defence might have taken had it been aware in advance of the existence of the new evidence and whether a different approach by the defence might have led to an acquittal.

9. Jurisdiction of the court

In theory the jurisdiction of the court will depend on whether it is dealing **22–50** with an actual appeal or an application for leave to appeal. In practice, the

---

[309] See Rules of the Superior Courts, Ord.86, r.24(7).
[310] *ibid.* r.24(6).
[311] *ibid.* r.24(7). The caption in the Form No.24 shall be attached to any such deposition.
[312] *ibid.* r.24(10).
[313] *ibid.* r.24(4).
[314] Criminal Procedure Act 1993, s.3(3)(c).
[315] *ibid.* s.3(4).
[316] *Attorney General v. Kelly* [1937] I.R. 315.
[317] *People (DPP) v. Gannon* [1997] I I.R. 40.

merits of an appeal are normally considered on an application for leave to appeal so that the distinction between the two proceedings is more apparent than real.[318]

On the hearing of an appeal against conviction there are four options available to the court. First, it may affirm the conviction.[319] It may do this even if it is of the opinion that a point raised in the appeal might be decided in favour of the appellant, if it considers that no miscarriage of justice has occurred.[320] Second, it may quash the conviction and make no further order.[321] Third, it may quash the conviction and order the appellant to be re-tried for the offence.[322] Where the court takes this option in respect of an appellant who had been granted legal aid at his original trial, the legal aid certificate for his trial shall have effect as if it had been granted also in relation to his re-trial.[323] Fourth, it may quash the conviction and substitute a verdict of guilty of another offence.[324] It can do this where it appears to the court that the appellant could have been found guilty of the other offence and that the jury must have been satisfied of facts which proved him guilty of the other offence.[325] In this event, the court may impose such sentence in substitution for that imposed at the trial as may be authorised by law for the other offence, so long as it is not a sentence of greater severity.[326]

When hearing an appeal against sentence the court may quash the sentence and in its place impose such sentence or make such order as it considers appropriate.[327] However, it must be a sentence or order which could have been imposed on the convicted person for the offence at the court of trial.

In addition, the court may make such order as may be necessary for the purpose of doing justice in the individual case.[328] This may entail an order for costs including, in exceptional cases, the costs of the trial itself unless the appellant is covered by a legal aid certificate.[329] In *People (DPP) v. Redmond*[329a] the Court of Criminal Appeal ruled that it also had jurisdiction to award costs to a defendant where the prosecution exercised its power to seek a review of the sentence on the grounds of undue leniency (see chapter 22).

---

[318] Report of Committee to Inquire into Certain Aspects of Criminal Procedure (Stationery Office, Dublin, 1990), p.6. The *Report of the Committee to Review the Offences against the State Acts, 1939 to 1998 and Related Matters* recommends the abolition of the requirement to seek leave, and the provision of an untrammelled right of appeal against conviction and sentence for persons convicted of serious offences; paras. 9.78–9.81.

[319] Criminal Procedure Act 1993, s.3(1)(a).

[320] Presumably, this refers to the sort of situations which would attract the proviso as distinct from those which would not qualify for compensation (see later).

[321] Criminal Procedure Act 1993, s.3(1)(b).

[322] *ibid.* s.3(1)(c).

[323] *ibid.* s.3(7).

[324] *ibid.* s.3(1)(d)(i). See the Criminal Law Act 1997, s.9, for the powers of the trial court with respect to alternative verdicts.

[325] Where the trial was conducted before a court sitting without a jury, the reference to the jury in this provision must be construed as a reference to the court of trial; Criminal Procedure Act 1993, s.3(5).

[326] *ibid.* s.3(1)(d)(ii).

[327] *ibid.* s.3(2).

[328] *ibid.* s.3(3)(e). See also *People v. Bell* [1969] I.R. 24.

[329] Criminal Justice (Legal Aid) Act 1962, s.8; *People v. Harte* [1946] I.R. 110.

[329a] Unreported Court of Criminal Appeal, March 29, 2001.

It is open to the court, in a suitable case, to substitute a verdict of guilty but **22–51** insane for a verdict of guilty. If it appears to the court that although the appellant was guilty of the act or omission charged against him, he was insane at the time the act was done or omission made so as not to be responsible according to law for his actions, the court may quash the sentence passed at the trial and order the appellant to be kept in custody as a criminal lunatic, in the same manner as if such a verdict had been found by the jury.[330] Technically, of course, this is an acquittal. Accordingly, the court will quash the sentence imposed and order that the appellant be detained in the Central Mental Hospital at the will and pleasure of the government. In practice, the court will be most reluctant to adopt this course as it would involve the court usurping the function of the jury. In *People v. Fennell*,[331] for example, the court declined an invitation to substitute a verdict of guilty but insane for a verdict of guilty. Its decision was based partly on the evidence and partly on its unwillingness to perform the function of the jury in the matter.

10. Summary Determination

It is worth noting that it will not always be necessary for the court to move to **22–52** a full hearing of an appeal or application for leave to appeal. There is pro-vision for a summary determination. If the court considers that the application is frivolous or vexatious and that it can be determined without adjourning it for a full hearing, the court may dismiss the application summarily without calling on anyone to attend the hearing or to appear on behalf of the prosecution.[332] The court may exercise this jurisdiction by a single judge and the convicted person may appeal to the court against the summary deter-mination of his application.[333]

If it appears to the Registrar that a notice of an application for leave to appeal does not show any substantial ground of appeal he may, without calling for the report of the official stenographer, list the case for hearing without obtaining a transcript of the shorthand note taken by the stenographer at the trial.

11. Quashing the Conviction

Error of Law or Procedure

The grounds upon which the court may quash a conviction are not set in **22–53** stone. However, a useful summary of them is provided as follows by the court itself in *People v. Madden* where it explained that its role was:

> "to review as far as may be required any rulings on matters of law, to review as far as may be necessary the application of the rules of evidence as applied in the trial, and to consider whether any inferences of fact drawn by the court

---

[330] Courts of Justice Act 1924, s.35.
[331] [1940] I.R. 445.
[332] Criminal Procedure Act 1993, s.5(1).
[333] Criminal Procedure Act 1993, s.5(2).

of trial can properly be supported by the evidence; but otherwise to adopt all findings of fact."[334]

In practice, however, the most likely grounds will concern an error of law or procedure at the trial. This could take the form of a misdirection on the law to the jury. The judge, for example, may have erred in his or her explanation of what must be established in order to satisfy the constituent elements of the offence charged. Equally, in a case involving a challenge to the admissibility of evidence, the judge may have erred in deciding to admit a particular piece of evidence which the Court of Criminal Appeal determines is legally inadmissible. A quite different possibility is the discovery that one or more members of the jury had contact with witnesses for the prosecution during the course of the trial. These, of course, are only a few examples. It would be quite difficult, if not impossible, to offer a comprehensive list of the possible errors of law and procedure which could result in the quashing of a conviction on appeal.

Finding of fact

Even in the absence of an error of law or procedure in the course of the trial, a conviction may still be quashed. This can happen if the Court of Criminal Appeal considers that the verdict of the trial court is unreasonable or cannot be supported having regard to the evidence. To succeed under this heading, however, it will not be sufficient that the court itself may have reached a different verdict from that of the jury or the court (where it is sitting without a jury). The court will have to be satisfied that no reasonable jury or court, as the case may be, could have reached the decision in question on the basis of the evidence before it. In other words the verdict would have to be perverse. The fact that the fact-finder, unlike the Court of Criminal Appeal, had the opportunity to see and hear the witnesses at first hand and to assess their credibility will be an important factor which the court will bear in mind when deciding whether it should upset the verdict under this heading.

22–54   Sometimes the jury, or the court sitting without a jury, must make one or more findings of fact preparatory to its determination of guilt. This is particularly likely to happen in confession cases where the judge has to decide whether the accused was subjected to a fear of prejudice or hope of advantage held out by a person in authority or to oppressive treatment. The prospects of an appellant persuading the Court of Criminal Appeal that the judge or the jury (as the case may be) erred in its findings of fact in such circumstances are low. As a general rule the Court of Criminal Appeal will adopt the findings of fact by the trial court. It will not upset them unless they are "so clearly against the weight of testimony as to amount to a defeat of justice."[335] If anything this reflects a greater reluctance on the part of the court to question the findings of fact than to upset the verdict.

---

[334] [1977] I.R. 336 at 340.
[335] *People v. Madden* [1977] I.R. 336 at 339.

Fresh Evidence

It may happen, of course, that the reliability of the conviction is thrown into doubt as a result of the emergence of fresh evidence. As noted above, where new evidence is presented on an appeal the court must conduct an objective evaluation of the new evidence with a view to determining whether in the light of it the conviction was unsafe and unsatisfactory.[336] If it concludes that the new evidence renders the conviction unsafe and unsatisfactory it must quash the conviction and, in appropriate circumstances, order a re-trial.

12. The Proviso

Even if the appellant succeeds on one or more grounds of appeal it will not necessarily result in the quashing of the verdict. There is provision for the court to dismiss the appeal, notwithstanding the fact that it is of the opinion that a point raised in the appeal might be decided in favour of the appellant, if it considers that no miscarriage of justice has actually occurred.[337] This is generally referred to as the proviso. The nature of this jurisdiction is such that it is not always possible to predict when the court will exercise it. Inevitably, each case must be treated on its own facts and the weight of the evidence presented. It follows that even a substantial error may not always be sufficient to overcome the proviso. In *Attorney General v. Doyle*,[338] for example, the proviso was applied to uphold a conviction despite the fact that the trial judge had wrongly directed the jury that certain evidence amounted to corroboration. Similarly, in *Attorney General v. Richmond*[339] a conviction was upheld where the trial judge had failed in his direction to the jury sufficiently to distinguish between preparation for and an attempt to commit a crime.

Generally, it might be said that when the court is considering whether to apply the proviso it will consider whether "in the face of the volume of the evidence which was given at the trial, an overwhelming case was proved which the jury could not, without perversity, have ignored so as to find an acquittal."[340] While this helps explain why even substantial errors will not always be sufficient to overcome the proviso, it also holds out the possibility of relatively minor errors being sufficient in certain circumstances. The Court of Criminal Appeal, for example, could be persuaded to quash a conviction in the face of a relatively minor error if it harboured doubts about the weight and volume of the evidence. In *Attorney General v. McLoughlin*,[341] the court quashed a conviction on the ground that evidence of a complaint of sexual assault was wrongly admitted at the trial as it had not been made sponta-

22–55

---

[336] *People (DPP) v. Gannon* [1997] I I.R. 40.
[337] Criminal Procedure Act 1993, s.3(1); previously Courts of Justice Act 1928, s.5. The corresponding English provision, found in s.2(1) of the Criminal Appeal Act 1968, is generally referred to as the proviso.
[338] 75 I.L.T.R. 41.
[339] (1935) Frewen 28.
[340] *Attorney General v. Hurley* 71 I.L.T.R. 29, *per* Kennedy C.J. at 34.
[341] 71 I.L.T.R. 247.

neously or as soon as practicable after the assault. This was a case in which the evidence of guilt generally was not overwhelming.

It can be difficult to persuade the court to quash a conviction on account of the conduct of the judge during the trial. Even if the court accepts that the judge intervened too frequently during the presentation of the defence case or made disparaging remarks about the accused in the presence of the jury it is more likely to apply the proviso than quash the conviction.[342] Nevertheless, there have been cases where the court has refused to apply the proviso on the grounds that the judicial interventions were of such a magnitude as to impede the fair presentation of the defence case or such as to fatally prejudice the accused in the eyes of the jury.

13. Re-trial

22–56 If the court quashes the conviction it does not follow that the criminal proceedings in the matter are closed. The court may order a re-trial for the same offence. Whether the court makes such an order will depend very much on the facts of the individual case and the grounds upon which the conviction was quashed. If, for example, the court quashes the conviction on the ground that evidence was wrongfully admitted at the trial, there is no point in ordering a re-trial unless there is other cogent, admissible evidence of the appellant's guilt. This situation is most likely to arise where the case against the accused is based primarily or exclusively on a confession, an identification or forensic evidence which the Court of Criminal Appeal rules has been wrongfully admitted at the trial.[343] If, however, the defect which resulted in the quashing of the conviction is such that it can be corrected at a new trial, without unfairness to the accused, it is quite likely that the court will order a re-trial. An improper jury direction, for example, would fall into this category. If the court considers that the jury might still convict if properly directed then it is quite likely that it will order a re-trial.[344] Similarly, a re-trial may be ordered where the conviction was quashed due to an irregularity at the trial which could be corrected at a re-trial without unfairness to the accused. In *People v. Heffernan (No.2)*,[345] for example, a re-trial was ordered when the conviction was quashed on the ground that there had been contact between the jury and the public.[346] However, a re-trial should not be ordered if the conviction is quashed because of the failure of the prosecution to adduce an essential proof at the trial.[347]

---

[342] In *Attorney General v. Hurley* 71 I.L.T.R. 29 the court declined to quash the conviction even though it held that the trial judge should not have made certain disparaging remarks about a previous acquittal of the accused.

[343] In *Attorney General v. Cleary* 72 I.L.T.R. 84 a re-trial was ordered even though the court ruled that the accused's confession should have been excluded at the trial. In that case, however, other evidence of guilt had been adduced at the trial

[344] *Au Pui-Kuen v. Attorney General of Hong Kong* [1979] 1 All E.R. 769.

[345] [1951] I.R. 206.

[346] A similar result ensued in *People v. Moran* (1979) Frewen 380, where inadmissible statements were inadvertently given to the jury on retirement.

[347] *People v. Griffin* [1974] I.R. 416.

Where the court does order a re-trial the person concerned may, notwith- **22–57**
standing any rule of law, be indicted and tried and, if found guilty, sentenced
for the offence in question.[348] When exercising this power to order a re-trial it
would appear that the court may confine the re-trial to certain counts on the
indictment.[349] It may not, however, order a re-trial on different charges.[350]
Where a legal aid certificate does not apply the court may order the costs of
the appeal and the re-trial to be paid by the State, unless it is of the opinion
that the necessity for the new trial has been caused or contributed to by the
defence.[351] The court may also remand the appellant in custody or on bail on
such terms as it thinks fit,[352] and order that any property or money forfeited,
restored or paid by virtue of the conviction or of any order made on
conviction be retained pending the re-trial.[353]

14. Appeal against Sentence

The Court of Criminal Appeal has jurisdiction to affirm or vary the sentence **22–58**
imposed by the lower court. Its jurisdiction to vary sentence includes the
power to increase as well as to reduce the severity of punishment imposed. It
cannot, however, impose a more severe sentence than that which the lower
court could have imposed. Where the Court exercises its jurisdiction to
suspend a prison sentence which has been imposed by a lower court it has no
further function in policing compliance with the terms or conditions of the
suspension.[354] An application to activate the suspended sentence will have to
be taken to the original sentencing court.

As a general rule the Court of Criminal Appeal is reluctant to interfere
with a sentence imposed by a lower court. Even where the court would have
been inclined to impose a greater or lesser sentence than the lower court it
will not normally interfere unless it considers that the sentencing court has
erred in principle or was misinformed as to some material fact relevant to
sentence.[355] It can also prove difficult to persuade the court that the lower
court has erred in the matter of sentence. In *People v. Poyning*,[356] for example,
the court held that the fact that a co-accused had received a sentence which
was too lenient was not a ground for interfering with the sentence properly
imposed on the appellant.

The jurisdiction of the Court of Criminal Appeal to vary sentence was
addressed by the Court itself in *People (DPP) v. MS*.[357] In that case the

---

[348] Criminal Procedure Act 1993, s.4(1).
[349] *People v. Singer* (1961) Frewen 214. S.3 and 4 of the Criminal Procedure Act 1993 would appear
to contemplate a re-trial on the original charge or charges only.
[350] *People v. Gilmore* 85 I.L.T.R. 99.
[351] Criminal Procedure Act 1993, s.4(2)(a). Costs were refused in *People v. Hopkins* (1953) Frewen
142 and *People v. Moran* (1974) Frewen 380; see Ryan and Magee, *op.cit.*, at p.432, fn.29.
[352] Criminal Procedure Act 1993, s.4(2)(b).
[353] Criminal Procedure Act 1993, s.4(2)(c).
[354] *Attorney General v. Carolan* unreported, Court of Criminal Appeal, April 24, 1994; *People
(Attorney General) v. Grimes* [1955] I.R. 315.
[355] *People v. Earls* [1969] I.R. 414.
[356] [1972] I.R. 402.

appellant had been convicted of rape and sentenced to six years imprisonment. While in prison he made excellent progress under the sex offenders programme and other programmes run by the probation and welfare service. There was a view, which was accepted by the Court, that it would be in the interests of both the defendant and the public at large for the defendant to be released early under a programme of supervision in the community rather than be required to serve the full term of his sentence. Normally, this type of case is provided for in advance by the trial judge imposing a custodial sentence and fixing a review date when the case can be brought back before him for consideration. Alternatively, it can be dealt with by the executive in the context of the early release programme. Neither option was present in this case. The trial judge had not fixed a review date and the early release programme was not applied to sex offenders. The question to be decided, therefore, was whether the Court of Criminal Appeal would have jurisdiction on appeal against a sentence of imprisonment to suspend the balance of a sentence immediately or at a specified date in the future on account of the defendant' progress while in prison.

The primary argument against the Court of Criminal Appeal exercising such jurisdiction is that it would involve the Court stepping into the shoes of the sentencing court conducting a review of sentence at the review date. Typically, the Court would have to seek and consider reports on the defendant and witnesses would have to be examined and cross-examined as if the matter was being determined at first instance. It would also encourage prisoners who had progressed well in prison to seek early release from the Court of Criminal Appeal rather than through the executive programme of early release.

In giving the judgment of the Court, Denham J. emphasised that the fundamental jurisdiction of the Court of Criminal Appeal was to do justice in the case before it. Justice in this case meant a just sentence for the victim, the defendant and society. The victim did not object to the sentence being reduced so long as the defendant did not interfere with her or her children. The defendant had successfully completed a programme of treatment to the extent that release under supervision would be more beneficial to the defendant and society than release at the end of his sentence with no supervision. An element of rehabilitation is also beneficial to both the defendant and the community. On the basis of these factors, Denham J. concluded that the Court of Criminal Appeal did have jurisdiction to suspend part of the sentence on condition that the defendant would be under a programme of supervision in the community.

The Criminal Justice Act 1993 has introduced a novel procedure whereby the DPP may apply to the Court of Criminal Appeal for a review of a sentence on the ground that it was unduly lenient.[358] This procedure is dealt with in chapter 21 on sentencing.

22–59   Where an application (or associated appeal) is made under these provisions a legal aid (appeal certificate) or, as the case may be, a legal aid

---

[357] [2000] 2 I.L.R.M. 311.
[358] Criminal Justice Act 1993, s.2(1).

(Supreme Court) certificate shall be deemed, for the purposes of the Criminal Justice (Legal Aid) Act 1962, to have been granted in respect of the person whose sentence is the subject of the application (or appeal).[359] Moreover, the person concerned shall be entitled to free legal aid in the preparation and conduct of his case before the Court of Criminal Appeal or the Supreme Court, and to have a solicitor and counsel assigned to him for that purpose in the manner prescribed by regulations under the 1962 Act.[360]

15. The Judgment of the Court

Pronouncement

The judgment of the court is pronounced by the President of the Court or by such other member of the court as he may direct.[361] It is normally issued as a single judgment reflecting the opinion of the majority of the members present.[362] Unless the court directs otherwise, no judgment with respect to the determination of any question may be pronounced separately by any other member.

22–60

Any interlocutory application in relation to an appeal or to an application for leave to appeal may be dealt with by the Chief Justice or by a judge of the Supreme Court designated by him.[363]

Giving notice of the Decision

When the court has made an order refusing an application for leave to appeal, or finally determining an appeal, the Registrar must give notice of that decision to the following persons: the appellant; the proper officer of the court of trial; the Commissioner of the Garda Síochána; the Governor of the prison (if the appellant is in prison or has been released on bail); and the Secretary of the Department of Justice, Equality and Law Reform.[364] The proper officer of the court of trial, on receiving notice, shall enter the particulars on the records of that court.[365]

Costs

The jurisdiction of the Court of Criminal Appeal to award costs on an appeal was clearly stated in section 34 of the Courts of Justice Act 1924. That section has since been repealed by the Criminal Procedure Act 1993 which, in turn, provides that the Court has jurisdiction, *inter alia*, to:

> "generally make such order as may be necessary for the purpose of doing justice in the case before the Court".[366]

---

[359] *ibid.* s.4(2)(a).

[360] *ibid.* s.4(2)(b).

[361] The President of the Court is the member who is entitled to precedence over the other members.

[362] Courts of Justice Act 1924, s.28.

[363] Courts of Justice Act 1928, s.7. See *Attorney General v. Scuffil* [1936] I.R. 469.

[364] Rules of the Superior Courts, Ord.86, r.28(1). Notice does not have to be given to the appellant if was present or legally represented at the hearing.

[365] Rules of the Superior Courts, Ord.86, r.28(2).

[366] Criminal Procedure Act 1993, s.3(3)(e).

Presumably that is sufficient to confer the necessary jurisdiction to award costs. In any event it would appear that there is no doubt that the Court has such jurisdiction.[367]

16. Abandonment of Appeal

22–61   The appellant always has the option of formally abandoning his appeal at any time after he has served notice of appeal or of application for leave to appeal or for enlargement of time.[368] To do this he should serve notice on the Registrar in the appropriate form not later than ten days before the date fixed for the hearing.[369] The Registrar must then notify the persons affected.[370]

17. Miscellaneous

22–62   It is worth noting the following miscellaneous provisions in the Rules of the Supreme Court which cannot easily be accommodated under any of the headings above.

Issue of Forms and Instructions

The Registrar shall furnish the necessary forms and instructions in relation to notices of appeal or notices of application to any person who demands them and to officers of the courts, Governors of prisons and such other officers or persons as he thinks fit.[371] The Governor of a prison shall cause those forms and instructions to be placed at the disposal of the prisoners desiring to make any application, and shall cause any such notice given by a prisoner in his custody to be forwarded on behalf of the prisoner to the Registrar.

Means and Circumstances of the Appelant

It is the duty of the Garda Síochána of the district in which the appellant resided before his conviction, or of the district from which he was committed, to enquire as to and report to the Registrar, when required by him, upon the means and circumstances of any appellant where such a question arises.[372]

Allocation of Prison officers

The Prisons Section of the Department of Equality and Law Reform shall, on notice from the Registrar, cause from time to time such sufficient number of male and female officers to attend the sittings of the court as, having regard to

---

[367] See, for *e.g.*, judgment of Hardiman J. in *People (DPP) v. Redmond* unreported, Court of Criminal Appeal, March 29, 2001.
[368] Rules of the Superior Courts, Ord.86, r.23(1).
[369] The appropriate form is Form No.20.
[370] Rules of the Superior Courts, Ord.86, r.23(2).
[371] *ibid.* r.32.
[372] *ibid.* r.33.

the list of appeals and applications for leave to appeal, the Department shall consider necessary.[373]

Enforcement of Duty

The performance of any duty imposed upon any person by the Rules of the Superior Courts dealing with the Court of Criminal Appeal may be enforced by order of the court.[374]

Date of orders

Every order of the court, when drawn up, shall be dated the day of the week, month and year on which it was made, unless the court shall direct otherwise.[375] It shall take effect accordingly and shall be issued out of the Office of the Court.

Non-Compliance with Rules

Non-compliance on the part of an appellant with the Rules of the Superior Courts dealing with the Court of Criminal Appeal, or with any practice for the time being in force, shall not prevent the further prosecution of his appeal or application unless the court shall so direct.[376] Such appeal or application may be dealt with in such manner and upon such terms as the court shall think fit.

F. Appeal to the Supreme Court

1. Introduction

There are several routes through which a determination in a criminal trial can find its way to the Supreme Court. Article 34.4.3° of the Constitution provides that the Supreme Court shall, with such exceptions and subject to such regulations as may be prescribed by law, have appellate jurisdiction from all decisions of the High Court. As will be seen below, up until the enactment of the Criminal Procedure Act 1993 this provided a constitutional basis for an appeal direct to the Supreme Court for a person convicted in the Central Criminal Court. Article 34.4.3° also stipulates that the Supreme Court shall have appellate jurisdiction from such other courts as may be prescribed by law. It follows that recourse to the Supreme Court to challenge the decision of any other court in a criminal matter is available only to the extent specifically prescribed by statute.[377] There are three such possibilities. First, the DPP may refer a question of law to the Supreme Court where the accused has been acquitted by direction of the trial judge. Secondly, a Circuit Court judge has jurisdiction to refer a question of law to the Supreme Court. Thirdly, a case

22–63

---

[373] *ibid.* r.34.
[374] *ibid.* r.35.
[375] *ibid.* r.37.
[376] *ibid.* r.38.
[377] *State (Browne) v. Feran* [1967] I.R. 147.

can come to the Supreme Court from the Court of Criminal Appeal where the DPP certifies that the decision of the former involves a point of law of exceptional public importance and that it is desirable in the public interest that an appeal should be taken. Each of these possibilities will be considered in turn, followed by an appeal from the Central Criminal Court.

2. References by the DPP

Scope

22–64   Section 34(1) of the Criminal Procedure Act 1967 states:

> "Where, on a question of law, a verdict in favour of an accused person is found by direction of the trial judge, the [DPP] may, without prejudice to the verdict in favour of the accused, refer the question of law to the Supreme Court for determination."

This provides a mechanism whereby the DPP can challenge the trial judge's determination on a point of law which led directly to the acquittal of the defendant. It would appear, however, that the determination must relate to a question of law on which the verdict of the jury was directed by the trial judge. It is doubtful whether it can be used to challenge a ruling which impacted upon the evidential content of the trial as distinct from the question whether on the evidence as it stood at the close of the case for the prosecution it was open to the court to acquit the accused. Admittedly, in *People v. Cummins*[378] the Supreme Court considered the trial judge's ruling on the admissibility a confession on a section 34 reference. In that case, however, the issue of whether the court had jurisdiction in the matter was not argued. In *People v. Crinnion*,[379] however, Henchy J. expressed the view, *obiter*, that the reference procedure could not be used to challenge rulings on the admissibility of evidence:

> "As I read s.34, it limits the [DPP's] power of reference to a question of law on which the verdict of the jury was directed by the trial judge; it does not apply to prior questions of law which, because of their effect on the evidential content of the trial, may have a bearing on that point of law. Otherwise, any ruling of the trial judge which specifically excludes, or has the effect of excluding, evidence could be made the subject matter of a reference under the section if in the result a direction was given because of insufficiency of evidence resulting from an earlier ruling. Such an extended interpretation of what the legislature intended by the question of law on which the jury's verdict was directed would be an unwarranted straining, if not a violation, of the meaning of plain words, and would be out of keeping with the rule of interpretation that, for the reasons I have given earlier, this section should be construed strictly."[380]

---

[378] [1972] I.R. 312.
[379] [1976] I.R. 29.
[380] *ibid.* at 36.

Limited to Trial by Jury

The referral option is available only in respect of a direction given by the judge in a jury trial. In *People v. Crinnion*,[381] the Supreme Court decided that the procedure was not applicable in respect of a trial without a jury:

> "The section refers to a verdict in favour of an accused person being found on the direction by the trial judge in pursuance of which a verdict is founded. It seems to me to be an abuse of language used to seek to apply it to a trial without a jury before three judges whose function is to announce, at the end of the case, a finding of guilty or not guilty. A direction of the trial judge presupposes the existence of some body whom he can direct, and whose duty it is to find a verdict. Beyond the slightest shadow of doubt these words describe a criminal trial with a jury, and no other form of trial."[382]

The question of Law

The statement of the question of law to be referred must be settled by the DPP in consultation with the trial judge.[383] It must include any observations which the judge may wish to add. The Supreme Court must assign counsel to argue in support of the decision of the trial judge.[384]

Effect of Decision

Finally, it is important to emphasise that the finding of the Supreme Court on a referral under section 34 is without prejudice to the verdict in favour of the accused. It follows that even if the Supreme Court rules that the judge erred in his or her direction the accused will not be deprived of the benefit of his acquittal.

3. Case Stated from Circuit Court

Statutory Source

There is statutory provision for the submission of a consultative case stated from the Circuit Court to the Supreme Court. Section 16 of the Courts of Justice Act 1947 states:

22–65

> "A Circuit Judge may, if an application in that behalf is made by any party to any matter (other than a re-hearing, under section 196 of the Income Tax Act, 1918, of any such appeal as is referred to in the said section) pending before him, refer, on such terms as to costs or otherwise as he thinks fit, any question of law arising in such matter to the Supreme Court by way of case stated for the determination of the Supreme Court and may adjourn the pronouncement of his judgment or order in the matter pending the determination of such case stated."

---

[381] [1976] I.R. 29.
[382] *ibid.* at 33.
[383] Criminal Procedure Act 1967, s.34(2).
[384] *ibid.* s.34(3).

The purpose of the section 16 procedure is neatly described in the following extract from the judgment of Budd J. in *People (Attorney General) v. McGlynn*:

> "Viewing the section in the light of the law as it stood at the time when it was enacted, the remedial object would appear to be to provide a convenient and speedy method of having a difficult point of law, arising in a matter pending before a Circuit Judge, determined in the correct fashion while the matter is still pending before him rather than as would have been the position theretofore, to have the whole case relitigated on appeal before the High Court on Circuit with the possibility, at that later stage, of having a case stated to the Supreme Court."[385]

Jurisdictional Limits

The bare terms of section 16 do not specifically confine the procedure to civil cases. In practice, however, its application would give rise to major difficulty in criminal cases heard before a judge and jury. This issue was addressed by the Supreme Court in *People (Attorney General) v. McGlynn*.[386] In that case defence counsel wished to address the jury on a modified version of the *M'Naghten* rules on insanity. The Circuit Judge preferred the version proposed by counsel but felt constrained by the law as it stood to direct the jury on the *M'Naghten* rules. In the event of an unfavourable verdict for the defence they could always pursue the possibility of an appeal to the Court of Criminal Appeal with the further possibility of an appeal to the Supreme Court on a point if law of exceptional public importance. The judge acceded to the submission of defence counsel that he could circumvent these lengthy and uncertain possibilities by stating a case under section 16. As a preliminary matter, therefore the Supreme Court had to decide whether it had jurisdiction to hear an application under section 16 from a Circuit Judge conducting a criminal trial before a jury.

Since an application under section 16 must be made while the case is pending before the court and before judgment has been given in the case, considerable practical difficulties will arise in a criminal matter being heard before a jury. These are illustrated in the following passage from the judgment of Budd J:

> "When one considers what is bound to happen if such a course is taken in any trial and, indeed, what did happen in the case of this particular trial, it would seem reasonably clear that neither the interests of justice nor the convenient conduct of a criminal prosecution before a judge and jury will be forwarded or advanced if the particular procedure is adopted in such a case. As has happened in this case, the jury must be sent home. Some considerable time must inevitably elapse before the decision of the Supreme Court can be given and before the trial can be continued. During that interval it is almost bound to happen that the jury will forget a great deal of the evidence given before them, and the difficulties of recalling the evidence to their minds must be very great,

---

[385] [1967] I.R. 232 at 242.
[386] [1967] I.R. 232.

if it can be done satisfactorily at all. The danger of the case being discussed by members of the jury with other persons, despite any admonition to the contrary given by the trial judge, increases with the length of the adjournment. The danger of the jury forgetting, over a long interval of adjournment, portions of the evidence given is something which also may well militate against the interests of the accused person."[387]

In order to avoid these difficulties the jury trial must be conducted as far as possible without any lengthy interruptions.   **22–66**

As O'Dalaigh C.J. explained:

"The nature of a criminal trial by jury is that, once it starts, it continues right through until discharge or verdict. It has the unity and continuity of a play. It is something unknown to the criminal law for a jury to be recessed in the middle of a trial for months on end, and it would require clear words to authorise such an unusual alteration in the course of a criminal trial by jury."[388]

Not only are there no clear words applying the section 16 procedure to criminal trials by jury, but the Supreme Court found clear indications in the wording of the section itself to the effect that it was never intended to be exercisable in a criminal trial in the period after an accused had been given in charge to the jury and before verdict:

"This examination seems to my mind to show that the power conferred by s.16 is not exercisable in respect of questions of law arising after an accused has been given in charge to the jury and before verdict; and, accordingly, in my judgment the Case stated by the President of the Circuit Court was stated without jurisdiction and this Court cannot, therefore, entertain it."[389]

Walsh J. was prepared to entertain the possibility of a case stated being submitted pursuant to section 16 before the accused is given in charge to the jury or in respect of any matter arising after the jury had returned its verdict and before the judge had finally disposed of the case. The other judges, however, declined to express an opinion on this. It is also worth noting that the section 16 procedure would not be available in respect of trial without a jury in the Special Criminal Court. Section 16 expressly confines the procedure to referrals by a Circuit Judge in respect of proceedings pending before him or her.

Cases Stated from District Court Appeals

The difficulties associated with a section 16 reference in the context of a criminal trial before a jury do not apply to District Court appeals in the Circuit Court. Although such appeals are by way of a re-hearing, they are heard before a Circuit Court judge sitting without a jury. Accordingly, there is no insuperable obstacle to the submission of a consultative case stated from the Circuit Court to the Supreme Court in respect of a point of law which has emerged in the course of the hearing of an appeal from the District Court.   **22–67**

---

[387] *ibid.* at 242–243.
[388] *ibid.* at 239
[389] *Ibid.*

The same might be said of the Special Criminal Court in so far as it sits without a jury. In *DPP v. Special Criminal Court*,[390] however, the Supreme Court made it clear that the continuity of a criminal trial before a jury was a precept which was equally applicable to a trial before the Special Criminal Court. The mere fact that the Court sat without a jury did not mean that it was more acceptable to interrupt the trial after it had started for the purpose of a judicial review. While a judicial review application was permitted in that case after the prosecution had opened its case, the Supreme Court explained that in the circumstances it was more in the nature of a pre-trial application. The prosecution had been invited to open its case in order to facilitate a full consideration of the judicial review application.

Judicial Discretion

A Circuit Court judge enjoys a discretion over whether to accede to a request to submit a consultative case stated to the Supreme Court pursuant to section 16. In *McKenna v. Deery* the Supreme Court offered the following guidance on how this discretion should be exercised:

> "The discretion conferred on the Circuit Court judge by s.16 of the Act of 1947 is in terms unlimited but all discretions conferred on courts must be exercised judicially. Nevertheless, consultative cases stated are primarily for the guidance and assistance of the judge who is asked to state such a case and if the judge is quite clear in his own mind as to the proper decision in the case, *prima facie* he is entitled to refuse the application and to go ahead and decide the case in accordance with his firm and positive views. The superior courts should be slow to interfere in such a case and should only do so if there is not merely an arguable case, but substantial, weighty and solid grounds calling for a decision by the Supreme Court on the question or questions of law the subject matter of the application by one of the parties to the proceedings."[391]

In this case the applicant had been convicted of certain gaming offences in the District Court. He appealed the convictions to the Circuit Court. In the course of the appeal hearing the judge refused the applicant's request to state a case for the opinion of the Supreme Court on certain matters. The High Court, on a judicial review of this refusal, granted an order of mandamus compelling the judge to state a case for the Supreme Court. The judge appealed success-fully to the Supreme Court which found that the points of law raised by the applicant did not arise on the facts as found by the judge. Accordingly, any case stated on these points would have been moot.

---

[390] [1999] 1 I.R. 60.
[391] [1998] I.R. 62 at 75. The standard test laid down in *McHale v. Devally* unreported, High Court, May 20, 1993 was criticised as setting too low a threshold.

4. Appeal from Court of Criminal Appeal

Statutory Source

The decision of the Court of Criminal Appeal on appeal from a lower court is **22–68**
final. However, an appeal may be taken to the Supreme Court on a point of
law. Section 29 of The Courts of Justice Act 1924 states:

> "The determination by the Court of Criminal Appeal of any appeal or other
> matter which it has power to determine shall be final, and no appeal shall lie
> from that court to the Supreme Court, unless that court or the [DPP] shall
> certify that the decision involves a point of law of exceptional public
> importance and that it is desirable in the public interest that an appeal should
> be taken to the Supreme Court, in which case an appeal may be brought to the
> Supreme Court, the decision of which shall be final and conclusive."

The procedure is triggered by either the Court of Criminal Appeal or the DPP
certifying that the decision of the court in the case at hand involves a point of
law of exceptional public importance and that it is desirable in the public
interest that an appeal should be taken to the Supreme Court whose decision
shall then be final. The Supreme Court has no jurisdiction to grant the
certificate.[392] It follows that if the Court of Criminal Appeal refuses the
application the accused cannot appeal the refusal to the Supreme Court. It
would appear, however, that the DPP can still exercise his power to issue a
certificate in case where the Court of Criminal Appeal has already refused to
issue a certificate.[393]

Limits of the Appeal

Section 29 can be used to pursue an appeal against conviction or sentence or
both.[394] Although the bare words of section 29 do not preclude the possibility,
it would appear that an appeal cannot be taken under this provision where the
Court of Criminal Appeal has quashed the conviction.[395] The matter was
considered by the Supreme Court in *People (Attorney General) v. Kennedy*.[396]
In that case the defendant's convictions in the Special Criminal Court were
quashed on appeal by the Court of Criminal Appeal. The Attorney General
issued a certificate that the court's decision involved a point of law of
exceptional public importance for the purpose of an appeal to the Supreme
Court. He also served notice of appeal against the quashing of the conviction.
The Supreme Court considered as a preliminary matter the question whether
section 29 encompassed the possibility of an appeal against an order quashing
a conviction.

---

[392] *Attorney General v. Murray* [1926] I.R. 300.
[393] See, *e.g., People (Attorney General) v. Giles* [1974] I.R. 422.
[394] See the examples listed by Walsh J. in *People (Attorney General) v. Giles* [1974] I.R. 422.
[395] Such a case was entertained by the Supreme Court in *People (Attorney General) v. Harte* [1946] I.R. 110, but the subject of the appeal was an order for costs in favour of the appellant and not the quashing of the conviction.
[396] *People (Attorney General) v. Kennedy* [1946] I.R. 517.

The court found, by a majority of four to one, that it was not open to the Attorney General (now the DPP) to use the provisions of section 29 to appeal against an order of the Court of Criminal Appeal quashing a conviction. The majority based their decision on an interpretation of the words of section 29 in the context of the Act as a whole and the long line of established authority which precluded the possibility of an appeal against a substantive acquittal. It was clear from the authorities that:

> ". . . it was the established policy of the law that a decision of acquittal by a Court of competent jurisdiction could not again be brought before any other Court, and that, in order to show a right of appeal, the words must 'be clear, express, and free from any ambiguity.'"[397]

The terms of section 29 did not clearly and unequivocally confer a right of appeal on the prosecution against an order quashing the conviction. In the words of Black J:

> "The giving of an appeal even to a convicted party, as in the English Act of 1907 and our Act of 1924, was a fundamental innovation. The giving of an appeal against an acquittal would be an even more fundamental innovation. It would mean what Lord Halsbury, in *Cox v. Hakes* said affected the right of personal freedom and a reversal of the policy of centuries. I could not believe that our Legislature intended to introduce such a revolutionary reversal of the policy of centuries and one gravely affecting personal freedom, by a section expressed in such terms as s.29 and subject to such an ambiguity."[398]

Although the point was not specifically decided by the court it would seem to follow that the DPP cannot avail of section 29 to appeal against a decision of the Court of Criminal Appeal to quash or reduce a sentence imposed on the appellant. That, of course, does not affect the possibility of an appeal to the Supreme Court under the provisions of the Criminal Justice Act 1993 (see Chapter 21 on Sentencing).

Scope of Points of Law

22–69   Section 29 does not require that the point of law of exceptional public impor-
tance should be stated in the certificate. Indeed, it has been the practice in this country not to state the point of law in the certificate.[399] This opens up the possibility of raising points of law before the Supreme Court additional to that on which the certificate was granted by the Court of Criminal Appeal or DPP.[400] In *People (Attorney General) v. Giles*[401] Walsh J. explained that an appeal under section 29 lies against the decision of the Court of Criminal Appeal, not the determination of the court on the point of law upon which the certificate was based. Once the certificate had issued the appeal is treated the

---

[397] *ibid.* at 529, *per* Murnaghan J. referring to Palles C.B. in *R (Kane) v. Chairman and Justices of Co. Tyrone* 40 I.L.T.R. 181.
[398] *ibid.* at 538.
[399] *Per* Walsh J. in *People (Attorney General) v. Giles* [1974] I.R. 422 at 427.
[400] *People v. Giles* [1974] I.R. 422; *People (DPP) v. Shaw* [1982] I.R. 1; *People v. Kelly (No.2)* [1982] I.R. 90.
[401] [1947] I.R. 422.

same as any other appeal. The normal practice is to serve a notice of appeal and to set out the grounds of appeal. Not only are these not confined to the point of law upon which the certificate was granted, but they can be amended in the course of the hearing. Even if the appellant has appealed against conviction only he can subsequently apply to amend his grounds of appeal to include an appeal against sentence, and *vice versa*. The only limitation is that the section 29 appeal cannot stray beyond the parameters of the appeal in the Court of Criminal Appeal. If the earlier appeal was against conviction only, it could not be expanded to include an appeal against sentence, and vice versa.

The Decision

If the point is decided in favour of the accused it is likely that the court will quash the conviction and/or quash or reduce the sentence. It would appear that the court has all the powers of the Court of Criminal Appeal in disposing of such an appeal. It can affirm or reverse the conviction in whole or in part; and it can remit, reduce or increase or otherwise vary the sentence.[402] Where it reverses a conviction in whole or in part it can order a re-trial. Equally, if it is of the opinion that a point raised in the appeal might be decided in favour of the appellant, it may still dismiss the appeal if it considers that no miscarriage has actually occurred.

5. Appeal from the Central Criminal Court

Introduction

Article 34.4.3° of the Constitution stipulates that the Supreme Court shall, **22–70** with such exceptions and subject to such regulations as may be prescribed by law, have appellate jurisdiction from all decisions of the High Court. It goes on to say that the Supreme Court shall also have appellate jurisdiction from such decisions of other courts as may be prescribed by law. Apart from the limited situations described above the Oireachtas has not conferred appellate jurisdiction on the Supreme Court from the decisions of any lower courts in criminal matters. The Central Criminal Court, however, is the High Court exercising its criminal jurisdiction.[403] It follows that, by virtue of Article 34.4.3°, there is a right of appeal directly to the Supreme Court from all decisions of the Central Criminal Court. The scope of this appeal must now be considered, including the extent to which it has been limited or regulated by the Oireachtas.

Defendant's Right of Appeal under Art 34.4.3°

The issue of whether the accused has an automatic right of appeal against conviction arose indirectly in *People v. Conmey*.[404] In that case the accused

---

[402] Courts of Justice Act 1928, s.5, as re-enacted by the Courts (Supplemental Provisions) Act 1961, s.48.
[403] Courts (Supplemental Provisions) Act 1961, s.11(1).
[404] [1975] I.R. 341.

had been convicted in the Central Criminal Court. He appealed against both conviction and sentence to the Court of Criminal Appeal which dismissed the appeal and refused to grant a certificate of leave to appeal to the Supreme Court. The accused then sought to appeal his conviction in the Central Criminal Court direct to the Supreme Court. To that end he applied to the Supreme Court for an order extending the time for appeal. His application was dismissed on the ground that, having already appealed to the Court of Criminal Appeal, his appellate rights were exhausted. However, three of the five judges expressed an opinion on whether the Constitution conferred a right on an accused to appeal to the Supreme Court against a conviction in the Central Criminal Court. All three were of the view that the Constitution did confer such a right.[405] Such a right of appeal against both conviction and sentence has been exercised and approved on a number of occasions, but without ever being the subject of an authoritative decision by the Supreme Court.[406] In *People v. O'Shea*,[407] however, the issue of whether the DPP could appeal an acquittal in the Central Criminal Court to the Supreme Court had to be determined. The majority decision in favour of the DPP's right of appeal pursuant to Article 34.4.3 (see below) provides further support for the proposition that the accused has a right of appeal against both conviction and sentence. Indeed, O'Higgins C.J. (with whom Walsh J. and Hederman J. agreed) declared that *People v. Conmey* was a clear authority for the accused's right of appeal.

Prosecution Right of Appeal under Art. 34.4.3°

Much more controversial is the notion that, in the absence of qualifying legislation, Article 34.4.3 confers on the prosecution the right of appeal against an acquittal in the Central Criminal Court. This, of course, is in marked contrast to the position in the Circuit Court where the prosecution cannot appeal against an acquittal to the Supreme Court. The existence of the prosecution's right of appeal under Article 34.4.3° was declared by a majority of three to two in the Supreme Court in *People v. O'Shea*.[408] The majority relied variously on the clear words of Article 34.4.3° and the injustice that would flow from a failure to correct jury verdicts which were flawed as a result of some defect in the trial. The latter point is well made in the following quotation from the judgment of O'Higgins C.J.:

> "It should be remembered that the Constitution is concerned with justice, and in the context of this case, with criminal trials being fairly conducted in due course of law. While these considerations provide safeguards for the person accused they also guarantee to the State, which accuses him and which has a duty to detect and suppress crime, that he will in fact be tried fairly and

---

[405] The three judges in question were: O'Higgins C.J., Walsh J. and Doyle J. (who agreed with Walsh J.). The two judges who expressed no opinion were Griffin J. and Budd J.

[406] See, e.g., *People (DPP) v. Shaw* [1982] I.R. 1; *People (DPP) v. Lynch* [1982] I.R. 64; *People (DPP) v. Quilligan (No.2)* [1989] I.R. 46.

[407] [1982] I.R. 384.

[408] *ibid.*

properly on the evidence adduced against him and in accordance with law. If, as a result of an error made by the trial judge, the jury is not permitted to consider the evidence of the charge brought against him or to pronounce on his guilt or innocence, can it be said that justice has been accorded to the State and to society? In my view, it cannot and, if this be so, a situation would exist which the Constitution prohibits."[409]

The implication is that there should be a right of appeal against acquittal in all jury trials, not just those in the Central Criminal Court. The difficulty with this, of course, is that Article 34.4.3 only covers appeals from the Central Criminal Court. Legislation would be required to extend the right to trials in the Circuit Court. Such legislation would overturn centuries of practice in which the prosecution was not permitted to appeal against the decision of a court at any level acquitting a person tried on a criminal charge before a jury.[410]

Statutory Abolition of Rights of Appeal

When the Oireachtas did eventually legislate on the subject it opted to abolish **22–71** both the prosecution's and the defence's right of appeal against acquittal and conviction/sentence respectively direct from the Central Criminal Court to the Supreme Court. Section 11(1) of the Criminal Procedure Act 1993 stipulates that:

> "The right of appeal to the Supreme Court, other than an appeal under section 34 of the Criminal Procedure Act, 1967, from a decision of the Central Criminal Court is hereby abolished."

Section 11(2) goes on to say that this does not apply to a decision of the Central Criminal Court in so far as it relates to the validity of any law having regard to the provisions of the Constitution. The net effect is that an accused who has been convicted and sentenced in the Central Criminal Court is placed in much the same position as an accused convicted in the Circuit Court. He can seek leave to appeal to the Court of Criminal Appeal, with the possibility of a further appeal to the Supreme Court on a point of law of exceptional public importance. An additional possibility, which is not available to the accused in the Circuit Court, is to appeal to the Supreme Court against a decision of the Central Criminal Court on the constitutional validity of any law which was relevant to his conviction. The prosecution, on the other hand, has lost the right of appeal to the Supreme Court from an acquittal in the Central Criminal Court. However, it retains the power to refer a question of law decided in favour of the accused in the Central Criminal Court (and in the Circuit Court) to the Supreme Court for determination, without prejudice to the verdict in favour of the accused.

These provisions would appear to be quite consistent with Article 34.4.3° of the Constitution. The Supreme Court's decision in *O'Shea* did not establish the existence of an absolute constitutional right to appeal against acquittal in

---

[409] *ibid.* at 405.
[410] See Finlay P. in *People (DPP) v. O'Shea* [1982] I.R. 384 at 413 quoting from Palles C.B. in *Great Southern & Western Railway Co. v. Gooding* [1908] 2 I.R. 429 at 431 who was, in turn, quoting from Lord Coleridge C.J. in *The Queen v. Duncan* (1881) 7 Q.B.D. 198.

a jury trial. It merely held that the provision in Article 34.4.3° of a right of appeal to the Supreme Court against all decisions of the High Court extends to appeals by the prosecution against jury acquittals in the Central Criminal Court. The right of appeal, however, is specifically subject to such exceptions and regulations as may be prescribed by law. Section 11 of the Criminal Procedure Act 1993 is such an exception.

It must be remembered that the Central Criminal Court is the High Court exercising its criminal jurisdiction. It may happen, therefore, that interlocutory decisions taken in the course of proceedings before the Central Criminal Court are in reality decisions taken in the exercise of the jurisdiction of the High Court in which case the restriction imposed by section 11(1) of the 1993 Act on appeals to the Supreme Court does not apply. In *People (DPP) v. Sweeney*,[411] Smyth J. made a non-party order of discovery against the Rape Crisis Centre in a rape case before the Central Criminal Court. On an appeal against this order one of the issues which the Supreme Court had to consider was whether section 11(1) precluded the possibility of an appeal in the case. Giving the judgment of the Court, Geoghegan J. explained that, despite appearances, the order of discovery was not made by the High Court in the exercise of its criminal jurisdiction. In fact the High Court had no jurisdiction to issue an order of discovery in a criminal case. The High Court only has civil jurisdiction to issue an order of discovery. In so far as Smyth J. made the order in the course of the criminal proceedings, he was exercising the civil jurisdiction of the High Court. This substantive reality was not affected by the fact that administratively the order was issued through the office of the Central Criminal Court. It follows that the restriction on appeals from the Central Court to the Supreme Court imposed by section 11(1) had no application in this case.

Interestingly, Geoghegan J. also drew attention to another possible limitation on the restriction imposed by section 11(1), namely whether it was confined to final decisions of the Central Criminal Court:

> "I do not propose to express an opinion on the important matter which was argued before the court as to whether section 11(1) applied only to final decisions of the Central Criminal Court on the basis that it was intended merely to repeal the decision of this court in *People (DPP) v. O'Shea* [1982] I.R. 384; [1983] I.L.R.M. 592 or whether it was intended to apply to interlocutory orders by the court as well. Under the conventional rules of the common law for statutory interpretation there is a strong case in favour of the latter argument, but given that it has long been held that the right of appeal to the Supreme Court under the Constitution can only be removed by clear words, I would leave open to be determined on another occasion the question of what view the court should take if on a contextual interpretation it was clearly not intended by the Oireachtas to abolish the right of appeal in all cases."[412]

---

[411] [2002] 1 I.L.R.M. 532.
[412] ibid. at 533–534.

G. Miscarriages of Justice

1. Introduction

It can happen that new facts or evidence emerge which cast doubt upon the reliability of a conviction after the trial and appellate procedures have been exhausted. Prior to 1993 there was no procedure through which such cases could be re-opened by the courts. The only option available to the accused was to seek a pardon and/or remission or commutation of sentence. In the late eighties and early nineties a whole string of miscarriages of justice were exposed and rectified in Britain. These included high profile cases such as the Birmingham Six, the Guildford Four and the Maguire Seven as well as several other cases where the police had fabricated evidence against the accused.[413] With the release of the Birmingham Six and the Guildford Four, in particular, questions were being asked whether there were sufficient safeguards within the Irish criminal justice system to prevent such cases from arising or to provide a remedy for those cases which slipped through the net. Public unease over cases such as *Meleady and Grogan*[414] and *Nicky Kelly* gave force to these questions.[415] The government responded in 1989 by establishing a committee of inquiry under the chairmanship of Judge Frank Martin Its terms of reference were:

22–72

"(1) To examine whether there is a need for a procedure whereby persons who have exhausted the normal appeals procedure can have their cases further reviewed, and if so, to make recommendations as to what procedure should be provided and in what circumstances it should apply, and

(2) given that uncorroborated inculpatory admissions made by an accused to the Garda Síochána can be sufficient evidence to ground a conviction, to examine whether additional safeguards are needed to ensure that such admissions are properly obtained and recorded and to make recommendations accordingly."

Although the committee reported in March 1990,[416] its recommendations on a review procedure were not implemented until December 1993 in the form of the Criminal Procedure Act 1993, while its recommendations on the electronic recording of confessions were not acted upon until March 1997 in the form of the Criminal Justice Act 1984 (Electronic Recording of Interviews) Regulations 1997. The former is dealt with here while the latter are considered in chapter 6.

---

[413] See Walker and Starmer (eds.) *Justice in Error* (2nd ed., Blackstone Press, London, 1999).

[414] [1995] 2 I.R. 517 (CCA); [1997] 2 I.R. 249 (SC).

[415] See Walsh, "Miscarriages of Justice in the Republic of Ireland" in Walker and Starmer (eds.) *Justice in Error* (2nd ed., Blackstone Press, London, 1999).

[416] *Report of Committee to Inquire into Certain Aspects of Criminal Procedure* (Stationery Office, Dublin, 1990).

2. Invoking the Procedure

Introduction

22–73   The Criminal Procedure Act 1993 makes provision for the Court of Criminal Appeal to review alleged miscarriages of justice in cases where the court has previously rejected an appeal or an application for leave to appeal in the case.[417] The jurisdiction of the court can be invoked by a person who has been convicted of an offence either on indictment or after signing a guilty plea and being sent forward for sentence under section 13(2)(b) of the Criminal Procedure Act 1967.[418] Such a person can invoke the procedure where he still stands convicted of the offence after an appeal to the Court of Criminal Appeal (including an application for leave to appeal), and any subsequent re-trial, and no further proceedings are pending in relation to the appeal. It would appear, therefore, that if the person is convicted on a re-trial following upon a successful appeal, he does not have to appeal his conviction again to the Court of Criminal Appeal in order to invoke the procedure. Moreover, the requirement that no further proceedings should be pending in relation to the appeal is a reference to separate proceedings in the nature of a criminal appeal being pursued simultaneously. It does not necessarily preclude the possibility of a civil action being pursued simultaneously in respect of the same matters.[419]

Where these conditions are satisfied and the person alleges that a new or newly discovered fact shows that there has been a miscarriage of justice in relation to the conviction or that the sentence is excessive, he may apply to the Court of Criminal Appeal for an order quashing the conviction or reviewing the sentence.[420] The application will be treated for all purposes as an appeal to the court against the conviction or sentence.[421]

New Evidence

At the heart of this procedure is the allegation that new evidence has emerged which suggests that there may have been a miscarriage of justice or that the sentence is excessive. The new evidence must take the form of a new fact or a newly discovered fact.[422] A "new fact" in this context means a fact which was known to the convicted person at the time of the trial or appeal proceedings the significance of which was appreciated by him, where he alleges that there is a reasonable explanation for his failure to adduce evidence of that fact.[423] A "newly-discovered fact" is a fact discovered by, or coming to the notice of, the convicted person after the relevant appeal proceedings have been finally

---

[417]   These provisions extend to the Courts-Martial Appeals Court; Criminal Procedure Act 1993, s.6.
[418]   Criminal Procedure Act 1993, s.2(1)(a).
[419]   *People (DPP) v. Pringle* [1995] 2 I.R. 547.
[420]   Criminal Procedure Act 1993, s.2(1)(b).
[421]   *ibid.* s.2(2).
[422]   See the Criminal Procedure Act 1993, s.2(3) for the definition of a "new fact" and s.2(4) for the definition of a "newly-discovered" fact.
[423]   Criminal Procedure Act 1993, s.2(3).

determined, or a fact the significance of which was not appreciated by the convicted person or his advisers during the trial or appeal proceedings.[424] There is no requirement on the applicant to allege that there is a reasonable explanation for his failure to adduce evidence of the newly-discovered fact in the earlier proceedings.

Prior Assessment of new evidence

There is no executive or judicial filter which an applicant must survive in order to have his case referred to the court under this procedure. Whether there is new facts or newly discovered facts to trigger the jurisdiction of the Court of Criminal Appeal under the 1993 Act is a matter for the court itself. It is not a matter which can be dealt with by the High Court on an application for habeas corpus.[425] However, where the appeal is based on new or additional evidence the court can direct the Commissioner of the Garda Síochána to have such inquiries carried out as the court considers necessary or expedient for the purpose of determining whether further evidence ought to be adduced.[426] As noted earlier, the purpose of any such inquiries is merely to help the court determine whether any further evidence ought to be adduced. It cannot take the form of a wide ranging inquiry aimed at determining the facts.

22–74

3. Approach of the Court

The New Facts

The application is treated for all purposes as an appeal to the Court of Criminal Appeal against conviction or sentence.[427] Accordingly the powers and jurisdiction of the court with respect to ordinary appeals against conviction or sentence, as discussed above under the heading of appeals to the Court of Criminal Appeal, apply to these appeals. In addition, however, the court is under a particular obligation to consider the new facts or newly discovered facts on the basis of which the appeal has been brought. In *People (DPP) v. Gannon*,[428] for example, the Court of Criminal Appeal had to consider whether there was a miscarriage justice in respect of a conviction for rape. The newly discovered facts concerned evidence of discrepancies in the victim's description of her attacker. These discrepancies were contained in documents which were not disclosed to the defence at the time of the trial or first appeal. The Court of Criminal Appeal dismissed the miscarriage of justice application as it considered that the documents in question would not have influenced the conduct of the defence even if they had been available to the defence at the time of the trial. It concluded that the newly discovered facts

---

[424] *ibid.* s.2(4).
[425] *Holland v. Governor of Portlaoise Prison* unreported, High Court, March 8, 2001.
[426] Criminal Procedure Act 1993, s.3(3)(a).
[427] *ibid.* s.2(2).
[428] [1997] 1 I.R. 40.

did not render the conviction unsafe and unsatisfactory having regard to the course which the defence took at the trial. The court reached this conclusion on the basis that the defence did not cross-examine the complainant on the divergencies with respect to identification which were apparent between her evidence in chief and her statement in the book of evidence.

On appeal against this dismissal to the Supreme Court, Blayney J. explained that the obligation on the Court of Criminal Appeal when considering a miscarriage of justice application was to embark on an objective evaluation of the newly-discovered facts to determine whether they were such as to render the conviction unsafe and unsatisfactory. The court could not simply assume that the new facts would have had no impact upon the outcome of the trial having regard to the strategy actually employed by the defence at the original trial:

> ". . . the question whether a newly-discovered fact has rendered a conviction unsafe and unsatisfactory, cannot be determined by having regard to the course taken by the defence at the trial. What the Court is required to do is to carry out an objective evaluation of the newly-discovered fact with a view to determining in the light of it, whether the applicant's conviction was unsafe and unsatisfactory. The Court cannot have regard solely to the course taken by the defence at the trial."[429]

The Supreme Court went on to consider the significance of the new facts in the light of the other evidence presented at the trial and concluded that the new information added nothing to the case either way. The discrepancies in the identification evidence were minimal. Accordingly, it upheld the Court of Criminal Appeal's rejection of the miscarriage of justice application.

Comparison with ordinary Appeals

22–75   It is worth noting that a miscarriage of justice application will not necessarily be identical in all respects to an appeal or application for leave to appeal to the Court of Criminal Appeal. The former can be brought only on the basis of a new fact or a newly-discovered fact. Moreover, there will already have been an unsuccessful appeal (or application for leave to appeal) to the Court of Criminal Appeal on the facts and/or questions of law. The very strong implication, therefore, is that a miscarriage of justice application cannot be taken purely on a question of law. This assertion, however, must be qualified by the possibility that new facts could raise new issues of law which were not raised in the earlier proceedings or could impact upon how issues of law were dealt with in those proceedings. Presumably, such matters could be dealt with on a miscarriage of justice application. Equally, it may happen that the interpretation of the law as applied in the earlier proceedings is shown subsequently to have been in error as a result, for example, of a decision of the Supreme Court or a ruling of the European Court of Justice. It is at least arguable that any such decision of the Supreme Court or the European Court of Justice could qualify as a new fact or newly discovered fact for the purpose of a miscarriage of justice application.

---

[429] *ibid.* at 48.

It is also arguable that on an application under these provisions the court can entertain grounds of appeal additional to those based on the new or newly discovered facts. The legislation merely requires that an applicant should allege that a new or newly discovered fact shows that there has been a miscarriage of justice or that the sentence is excessive. This is required in order to give the court jurisdiction in the matter. It does not follow that the court must confine its review of the soundness of the conviction or sentence to the issues raised by the new or newly discovered fact. If the soundness of the conviction or sentence is called into question during the proceedings as a result of facts, other than the new or newly discovered fact specifically alleged, or even points of law, it is at least arguable that the court would have jurisdiction to entertain them. The legislation does not specifically confine the review to the new or newly discovered fact. Indeed, it states that an application under these provisions shall be treated for all purposes as an appeal against conviction or sentence.

Procedure

22–76

Since miscarriage of justice applications are treated for all intents and purposes as appeals it can be assumed that the normal appeals procedure generally applies, subject to the requirement that there must be evidence of new facts or newly discovered facts. In the *Meleady* case (see paras. 22–78, and 22–83 *et seq.*) the application was supported by substantial written submissions in which it was argued that the evidence relating to the thumb print and the existence of the memo were newly discovered facts, the non-disclosure of which had rendered the trial and convictions so unsatisfactory as to amount to a miscarriage of justice. These arguments were countered by a substantial written submission from the DPP. These submissions were expanded upon orally at the hearing and oral evidence was adduced with respect to the memo.

It would appear that the court prefers these applications to be conducted in a spirit of mutual cooperation with each side making prior disclosure of evidence to be given at the hearing relevant to new or newly discovered facts. If it appears that the State was not cooperating fully, it would be prepared make an order for discovery including, if necessary, an order permitting the use of materials which had become available as a result of discovery in civil proceedings. This preference for an open approach is evident from the following passage of the judgment of the court in the *Pringle* case:

> "It was clear from the outset that oral evidence would be required to be called by both sides and so the Court stipulated that each side should serve on the other, in advance of the hearing, a statement containing an outline of the evidence that would be given by each proposed witness; further, each side was required to set forth in advance, in summary form, the submissions that would be elaborated upon later in Court.
>
> On the 2nd December, 1994, the Court ordered that full discovery of all documents and files in the possession of the State relevant to the proceedings should be made. The Court had initially stipulated that the matter could be dealt with in a spirit of mutual cooperation between the parties and without a

formal order for discovery but when an allegation was made on behalf of the applicant that the State was withholding relevant information the Court took the view that the best course was to make a formal order for discovery. It made no finding then, not does it now, that there was anything in the point that the State had not cooperated fully but, in any event in due course, a stage was reached where the parties were satisfied that the order of discovery was complied with. The Court also made clear, by way of exception to the general rule, that documents that had become available on discovery in the civil proceedings could be used in these present proceedings."[430]

4. The Issue to be Determined

Scope

In the applications which have been brought to date the focus has been purely on the existence of new or newly discovered facts and whether they were sufficient to establish that there might have been a miscarriage of justice. A miscarriage of justice in this context has not been confined to the situation where the defendant was convicted of a crime which he did not commit. The court has interpreted it to extend to the situation whereby the soundness of the conviction has been called into question. This could be because a material irregularity in the trial, including the non-disclosure of material by the prosecution to the defence, has rendered the conviction unsafe and unsatisfactory. Equally, it could be because the court cannot be sure that the jury would have convicted had the new facts been available at the time of the trial. This could be because of the effect that the new facts might have had on the jury or because of the difference it might have made to the manner in which the defence conducted their case.

Whether there might be a miscarriage of Justice

The court does not have to determine at this point whether there actually has been a miscarriage of justice. It will be quite sufficient if it is satisfied that there might have been a miscarriage of justice sufficient to warrant the quashing of the conviction with or without an order for a re-trial or a review of the sentence. This aspect is emphasised in the following passage from the judgment of the Court of Criminal Appeal in *People (DPP) v. Meleady* which was also cited with approval in *People (DPP) v. Pringle*,[431] the first two cases in which convictions were quashed pursuant to a miscarriage of justice application:

> ". . . the Court takes it as clear at the outset that its jurisdiction in a case such as the present is properly invoked where a convicted person who has previously appealed unsuccessfully against his conviction alleges that a new or newly-discovered fact shows that there has been a miscarriage of justice in relation to the conviction and applies to the court for an order quashing the conviction.

---

[430] [1995] 2 I.R. 547 at 554.
[431] [1995] 2 I.R. 547 at 567–568.

Thereafter, the application is to be treated "for all purposes" as an appeal to the court against the conviction. In the result, the court is empowered to affirm or quash the conviction or to order a re-trial, as though it were dealing with an appeal by the well-established machinery already in existence. There is nothing in the wording of s.2 or s.3 to suggest that the applicant under s.2, in addition to alleging that a newly-discovered fact shows that there has been a miscarriage of justice, must satisfy the court that such a miscarriage has actually occurred before it proceeds to exercise the powers to quash the conviction or to quash and order a re-trial.

Nor is there any reason for such a requirement: the mischief which this legislation was designed to remedy was not simply the non-disclosure to the court of trial of facts which, if available, would have conclusively demonstrated the innocence of the accused. It was also to provide redress, hitherto not available, in cases where facts came to light for the first time after the appeal to this Court which showed that there might have been a miscarriage of justice. The power to order a re-trial in cases under s.2 would be inappropriate if relief under that section was only intended to be available to those who could satisfy this Court that a miscarriage of justice had actually occurred. It seems clear to this Court that it was also intended to afford relief to those who could point to materials which, if they had been available at the trial, might – not necessarily would – have raised a reasonable doubt in the mind of the jury."[432]

It will be seen later that the court might be called to go further and certify that there has been a miscarriage of justice for the purpose of a compensation claim.

The Meleady and Pringle Cases

In *People (DPP) v. Meleady,*[433] the Court of Criminal Appeal quashed a conviction on an application for a miscarriage of justice. In this case the appellant had been identified as the front seat passenger in a car which had been unlawfully taken and driven away. He denied that he was the front seat passenger and his denial was supported by the evidence of another party who claimed that he was the front seat passenger. The latter was convicted in separate proceedings on the basis that he was the back seat passenger. It subsequently transpired that the thumb print of this individual had been discovered on the front passenger window of the vehicle. This fact had not been revealed to the defence. The Court of Criminal Appeal ruled that the non-disclosure of this fact to the defence prior to his trial rendered the appellant's conviction unsafe and unsatisfactory. The court also found that the conviction was unsafe and unsatisfactory by virtue of the non-disclosure to the defence of the existence of a memo by a solicitor in the Chief State Solicitor's Office which suggested that the main prosecution witness had been shown a book of photographs before making his subsequent identification of the appellant at a court house. In reaching this conclusion the court did not consider it necessary to resolve the conflict in the evidence as to whether the main witness actually had been shown a book of photographs before making the identification. It

---

[432] [1995] 2 I.R. 517 at 540–541.
[433] [1995] 2 I.R. 517.

was quite sufficient that the defence was denied the opportunity of pursuing the evidence which suggested that this might have happened.

In *People (DPP) v. Pringle*[434] the applicant had been convicted by the Special Criminal Court and had appealed unsuccessfully to the Court of Criminal Appeal. Subsequently evidence came to light which raised an issue as to the credibility of one of two members of the Garda Síochána who had taken an inculpatory statement from the applicant while being interrogated in Garda custody. This statement was central to the prosecution case. At his trial and on his appeal the applicant contested the accuracy of the statement as recorded by the member in question. In his application for a miscarriage of justice the Court of Criminal Appeal accepted that had the evidence relating to the credibility of the member of the Garda Síochána who took the contested statement been available at the time of the trial it might have been used to raise a reasonable doubt in the mind of the court. The Court of Criminal Appeal went on to find that this was sufficient to render the conviction unsafe and unsatisfactory. It was not necessary for the court to be satisfied that the newly discovered fact would have raised a reasonable doubt in the mind of the court. It was sufficient that it might. Accordingly, the court quashed the conviction and order a re-trial. The DPP entered a *nolle prosequi* in respect of the re-trial.

5. Further Applications

22–79   If a person still stands convicted after the miscarriage of justice application (including any re-trial) has run its course he may apply again for an order quashing the conviction or reviewing the sentence on the basis of new evidence. This will be possible where the person alleges that a fact discovered by him or coming to his notice after the hearing of the first application (and any subsequent re-trial), or a fact the significance of which was not appreciated by him or his advisers during the hearing of the application (and any subsequent re-trial) shows that there has been a miscarriage of justice in relation to the conviction or that the sentence was excessive.[435] The second application will be treated for all intents and purposes as an appeal to the Court of Criminal Appeal against conviction and sentence. Indeed, it would appear that there is nothing to prevent an appellant making successive applications under these provisions until he is eventually successful, so long as each successive application is supported by appropriate new evidence.

6. Petition for Grant of Pardon

Introduction

22–80   The miscarriage of justice measures in the 1993 Act also include provisions on a petition for the grant of a pardon. Although this could be dealt with

---

[434] [1995] 2 I.R. 547.
[435] Criminal Procedure Act 1993, s.2(5).

under the heading of pardon, commutation and remission in chapter 21 it is convenient to deal with it here given the connection with a miscarriage of justice.

Initiating the Procedure

The 1993 Act makes provision for a petition to the Minister for Justice, Equality and Law Reform with a view to the government advising the President to grant a pardon under Article 13.6 of the Constitution.[436] A person can invoke these provisions if he has been convicted of an offence, has appealed unsuccessfully against the conviction (and no further proceedings are pending in relation to the appeal) and alleges that a new or newly discovered fact shows that a miscarriage of justice has occurred in relation to the conviction.[437] A "new fact" in this context is a fact known to the convicted person at the time of the trial or appeal proceedings the significance of which was appreciated by him, where he alleges that there is a reasonable explanation for his failure to adduce evidence of it.[438] A "newly discovered fact", on the other hand, is a fact discovered by, or coming to the notice of, the convicted person after the relevant appeal proceedings have been finally determined, or a fact the significance of which was not appreciated by the convicted person or his advisers during the trial or appeal proceedings.[439]

Ministerial options on a Petition

Where a petition is lodged under these provisions the Minister shall make, or cause to be made, such inquiries as he considers necessary. If, however, he forms the opinion that the matters dealt with in the petition could be dealt with appropriately by an appeal to the Court of Criminal Appeal under the miscarriage of justice machinery described above, he shall inform the petitioner accordingly and take no further action.[440] If he is of the opinion that a case has not been made out that a miscarriage of justice has occurred and that no useful purpose would be served by further investigation, he shall inform the petitioner accordingly and take no further action in the case.[441] In any other case, the Minister must recommend to the government either that it should advise the President to grant a pardon in respect of the offence of which the applicant was convicted,[442] or that it should appoint a committee (see below) to inquire and report on the case.[443] It is worth noting that the Minister must take either of these actions even though he may not have formed the opinion that a miscarriage of justice has occurred. The duty will arise so long as he

---

[436] These provisions are quite separate from, and do not affect, any functions of the Minister in relation to a petition to him from a person, other than a person defined in these provisions, with a view to the government advising the President to grant a pardon under Article 13.6 of the Constitution; Criminal Procedure Act 1993, s.7(6).

[437] Criminal Procedure Act 1993, s.7(1).

[438] *ibid.* s.7(3).

[439] *ibid.* s.7(4).

[440] *ibid.* s.7(2)(a)(i).

[441] *ibid.* s.7(2)(a)(ii).

[442] *ibid.* s.7(2)(b)(i).

[443] *ibid.* s.7(2)(b)(ii). S.8 makes provision for the establishment of such a committee.

has not formed an opinion that a case has not been made out that a mis-carriage of justice has occurred and has not formed the opinion that the matter would be handled more appropriately through the appeals procedure.

Committee of Inquiry

22–81 For the purpose of enabling it to decide whether or not to advise the President to exercise the right of pardon under Article 13.6 of the Constitution, the gov-ernment may establish a committee to inquire into any or all of the matters dealt with in a petition for the grant of a pardon and to report whether, in the opinion of the committee, the President should be so advised.[444] It would appear that the government's power to establish such a committee is not con-fined to petitions submitted pursuant to the procedure in the 1993 Act. Certainly, there are no specific words in the legislation which confine the committee to such petitions. In any event, the committee shall be a tribunal within the meaning of the Tribunals of Inquiry (Evidence) Acts, 1921 and 2002.[445] It can consist of one member or a plurality of members. Where the latter is the case the government shall designate one of the members to be chairman.[446] This member must be either a judge or former judge or a practising barrister or solicitor of not less than ten years standing.[447] Where the committee is composed of a single member he or she must satisfy these qualifications. In conducting an inquiry under these provisions a committee may receive such evidence and other information as it sees fit, whether or not that evidence or information is or would be admissible in a court of law.[448]

7. Compensation

Scope of the Scheme

22–82 One of the vital ingredients of the new procedure is the provision for com-pensation. The question of compensation will arise where a person's conviction has been quashed pursuant to the miscarriage of justice procedure or on appeal, or where a person has been acquitted in any re-trial.[449] It is worth noting here that the compensation scheme is not confined to cases in which there has been a successful application under the miscarriage of justice procedure or a pardon. It also extends to cases in which the conviction has been quashed on appeal. This encompasses cases in which the conviction was quashed on first appeal, without having to resort to the miscarriage of justice or pardon procedures. In *Connell v. DPP*,[450] for example, the applicant had been convicted of murder in 1991. His conviction was quashed by the Court of Criminal Appeal in 1995. In 1997 the applicant sought compensation under

---

[444] *ibid.* s.8(1).
[445] *ibid.* s.8(2).
[446] *ibid.* s.8(3).
[447] *ibid.* s.8(4).
[448] *ibid.* s.8(5).
[449] *ibid.* s.9(1).
[450] [1999] 4 I.R. 1.

the 1993 Act in respect of the quashing of his conviction in 1995. The court addressed, as a preliminary matter, the issue of whether it could entertain an application consequent upon its quashing of a conviction pursuant to an ordinary appeal, as distinct from its quashing of a conviction on an application pursuant to the 1993 Act. The court confirmed that the correct interpretation of the relevant statutory provision was that a person could seek compensation under the 1993 Act in respect of a conviction which was quashed through the ordinary appeals procedure.

The quashing of a conviction is not in itself sufficient to give rise to a right to compensation. There is the additional requirement of a finding of a miscarriage of justice. Just because there are grounds for quashing the conviction, it does not follow that there has been a miscarriage of justice within the statutory scheme. Under the scheme the Minister for Justice, Equality and Law Reform must pay compensation in any such case where the Court of Criminal Appeal (or the court of trial in the event of a re-trial) has certified that a newly-discovered fact shows that there has been a miscarriage of justice.

Triggering the Scheme

The compensation scheme is triggered by reference to a "newly discovered fact" as distinct from a "new fact". The definition of a "newly discovered fact" for the purpose of the compensation scheme is virtually identical to that for the purpose of invoking the jurisdiction of the Court of Criminal Appeal to quash the conviction pursuant to the miscarriage of justice procedure. For the purposes of the Compensation Scheme a "newly discovered fact" is a fact which was discovered by the convicted person or which came to his notice after the relevant appeal proceedings had been finally determined, or a fact the significance of which was not appreciated by the convicted person or his advisers during the trial or appeal proceedings.[451]

Where an applicant, having satisfied the necessary pre-requisites, applies to the Court of Criminal Appeal for a certificate of a miscarriage of justice, he or she is entitled to have the court enter on an inquiry as to whether a "newly discovered fact" shows that there has been a miscarriage of justice. No distinction can be drawn between those whose convictions have been quashed on appeal and those who have been acquitted on a retrial. The Court of Criminal Appeal cannot refuse a certificate of a miscarriage of justice simply because the "newly discovered fact" has not been considered by a jury. So held the Supreme Court in upholding an appeal against the Court of Criminal Appeal's refusal to grant a certificate in *People (DPP) v. Meleady (No.2)*.[452]

The Meleady *case*

The *Meleady* case was one of the first cases on the miscarriage of justice **22–83** procedure to be considered by the Supreme Court. It concerned convictions

---

[451] *ibid.* s.9(6)(a).
[452] [1997] 2 I.R. 249.

based on a possible mistaken identification.[453] The facts were that some youths took a car at night from the driveway of the owner's home. As the car was being driven away the owner jumped onto the bonnet. He managed to hold on for a few minutes, even though the front seat passenger was trying to knock him off with articles taken from inside the car. Subsequently, at the request of the police, both the owner and his son who had witnessed the incident, attended a sitting of the District Court where they identified Joseph Meleady and Bernard Grogan as the persons responsible. Both defendants were convicted of assault and malicious damage arising out of the incident and were sentenced to five years imprisonment. A re-trial was ordered on appeal as a result of new evidence given by a third party that he had been present in the vehicle, that a fourth party was in the front passenger seat and that neither Meleady nor Grogan had been in the car.[454] The fourth party had been charged with being in the car and was convicted on a plea of guilty in separate proceedings. At Meleady and Grogan's re-trial their lawyers conducted the defence on the basis of legal argument and did not call the defendants to give evidence. They were convicted again.[455] The conviction, however, was based solely on an identification,[456] which in turn was based essentially on what the owner could see at night looking through the windscreen of a moving car while lying on its bonnet and being subjected to attempts to force him off. The third party was charged with perjury on the basis of the evidence he had given on the first appeal. The jury disagreed but he was convicted on a re-trial.

Meleady and Grogan always protested their innocence. Initially they were supported only by local opinion in their own neighbourhood, and by a few senior politicians and churchmen who took an active interest in their case. The public appeal of their case was boosted considerably by an RTÉ investigative documentary programme, broadcast in 1990, which revealed that fingerprint evidence found in the car was more consistent with the presence of three other individuals who actually claimed that they were the culprits. At the original trial one of these persons (the fourth party) had given evidence that he was in the front seat of the car and that neither Meleady nor Grogan had been in the car. Although the prosecution did not lead any forensic evidence from the car, they put to the witness in cross-examination that his fingerprint had been found on a back seat window of the car. In fact, the forensic examination had revealed that the witness" fingerprint was on a front seat window.[457]

---

[453] The Committee set up by the Minister for Justice, Equality and Law Reform in 1989 to inquire into certain aspects of criminal procedure accepted that mistaken identification had given rise to wrongful convictions in the past. See *Report of Committee to Inquire into Certain Aspects of Criminal Procedure,* op.cit, pp. 9–10.

[454] A re-trial was ordered because at the appeal a third youth, Paul McDonnell, gave evidence that he, and not Meleady and Grogan, was in the car on the relevant night. Subsequently, McDonnell was charged and convicted of perjury.

[455] The third party was subsequently charged with perjury. The jury disagreed on the first trial, but he was convicted on the second trial.

[456] It is permissible to convict solely on the basis of identification evidence. However, the judge is obliged to deliver a strongly worded warning to the jury on the dangers of convicting on the basis of identification alone; *People v. Casey (No.2)* [1963] I.R. 33 at 39.

[457] This information was only revealed in the course of the cross-examination of a Garda witness during the second perjury trial of the third party.

Neither this critical information, nor the fact that the car had been subjected to forensic examination, was revealed to the defence. It followed that the defence were not made aware of the fact that no fingerprints from either Meleady or Grogan were found in the car.

In 1991, an internal investigation in the Chief State Solicitors office resulted **22–84** in the discovery of a memo (the Walker memo) written by a solicitor in the office in preparation for the committal proceedings against Meleady and Grogan on May 18, 1984. The memo stated that the car owner, and chief prosecution witness, had been shown a book of 50 photographs, in which he picked out one of the accused, before the official identification. This information, which has always been contested by the witness and member of the Garda in question, had not been disclosed to the defence nor was it revealed during the trial.

The dilemma facing the government was how to respond to these developments. At the time there was no formal mechanism by which the case could be referred back to the courts for further consideration. The only option was a straight choice between direct executive interference in the administration of justice[458] or doing nothing. Eventually, after much prevarication,[459] the Minister compromised by remitting the remaining seven months of Meleady's five-year sentence of imprisonment. Grogan had already served his sentence by this time.

In February 1994 the *Meleady* case was taken to the Court of Criminal Appeal pursuant to the provisions of the 1993 Act.[460] The court concluded that the non-disclosure of the fingerprint evidence and the existence of the Walker memo to the defence rendered the convictions unsafe and unsatisfactory. Accordingly it quashed the convictions and sentences without ordering a retrial. Surprisingly, perhaps, the court refused the defence application for a certificate that there had been a miscarriage of justice. Without this certificate Meleady and Grogan could not receive compensation for the five years which each had served in prison. The court reasoned that the quashing of a conviction on appeal was not always synonymous with a miscarriage of justice. Even where a conviction was quashed without an order for a retrial it did not inevitably follow that there had been a miscarriage of justice within the scope of the 1993 Act. In the *Meleady* case the court concluded that a certificate could not issue because the evidence of the chief prosecution witness had not been considered by a jury in a trial untainted by the irregularities revealed by the newly-discovered facts.

The defence appealed the refusal of the certificate to the Supreme Court which ruled that the Court of Criminal Appeal had erred in finding that a certificate could not issue simply because the newly-discovered material had

---

[458] The Minister has the power, delegated by the government, to remit or commute sentences imposed by the courts; Criminal Justice Act 1951, s.23 as amended by the Road Traffic Act 1961, s.124. The government can advise the President to exercise the right to pardon and to remit or commute punishment imposed by the courts; Arts. 13.6 and 13.9 of the 1937 Constitution.

[459] As late as February 1990 the Minister asserted that he could see no grounds for intervening in the case of Meleady who was still serving his sentence. In 1988 he had rejected a petition for Grogan's release.

[460] *People (DPP) v. Meleady* [1995] 2 I.R. 517.

not been considered by a jury.[461] Once an applicant has had his or her conviction quashed on appeal or has been acquitted on a retrial, he or she is entitled to have the Court of Criminal Appeal enter on an inquiry as to whether a newly-discovered fact shows that there has been a miscarriage of justice. No distinction can be drawn between those whose convictions have been quashed on appeal, and those who have been acquitted on a retrial. Accordingly, the Supreme Court remitted the case back to the Court of Criminal Appeal to consider whether there had been a miscarriage of justice.[462] As will be seen below the Court of Criminal Appeal subsequently granted a certificate of a miscarriage of justice.[463]

Establishing a Miscarriage of Justice

In delivering the unanimous judgment of the Supreme Court in *Meleady* Blayney J. emphasised that just because a newly-discovered fact has resulted in the quashing of a conviction without an order for a retrial, it does not automatically follow that a miscarriage of justice certificate must issue. Apart from declaring that a certificate was not dependant upon a jury having had an opportunity to consider the "newly discovered fact" he did not elaborate on what constituted a miscarriage of justice for the purpose of the compensation procedure. Some further clarification was offered by the Supreme Court in its judgment in *People (DPP) v. Pringle*[464] handed down on the same day as its judgment in the *Meleady* case.

In *Pringle* the applicant had been convicted of capital murder and robbery and sentenced to death (later commuted to 40 years' imprisonment) in November 1980. In 1995 he appealed his conviction and sentence to the Court of Criminal Appeal under the terms of the 1993 Act. The basis of the appeal was new evidence which cast doubt on the credibility of one of two Garda officers who had taken a confession from the applicant while he was in police custody. The court quashed the conviction and ordered a retrial.[465] The DPP entered a *nolle prosequi* in respect of the retrial and the applicant applied unsuccessfully to the Court of Criminal Appeal for a miscarriage of justice certificate. On the appeal against this refusal the Supreme Court confirmed that the onus was on the applicant to prove positively and on a balance of probabilities that a newly-discovered fact showed that there had been a miscarriage of justice. The mere fact of the conviction being quashed without an order for a retrial was not sufficient in itself. Because this requirement may not have been fully appreciated on account of the newness of the procedure, the Supreme Court remitted the case back to the Court of Criminal Appeal so that the applicant could argue his case on this basis.[466]

---

[461] *People (DPP) v. Meleady* (No.2) [1997] 2 I.R. 249.

[462] In December 1996 the owner of the car involved was awarded £452,000 criminal injuries compensation for mental injuries and stress resulting from the case.

[463] Unreported, Court of Criminal Appeal, March 20, 2001.

[464] [1997] 2 I.R. 225.

[465] *People (DPP) v. Pringle* [1995] 2 I.R. 547.

[466] Instead of pursuing this option the plaintiff brought an action for damages for negligence, breach of duty and a failure to vindicate his constitutional rights; see *Pringle v. Ireland* [1999] 4 I.R. 10.

The Supreme Court in *Pringle* explained that the miscarriage of justice procedure was a civil, as distinct from a criminal proceeding. Accordingly, the onus is on the applicant to establish on the civil standard of proof that there has been a miscarriage of justice. The fact that his conviction has been quashed, whether on appeal or by a jury in a re-trial, is not sufficient in itself to establish that there has been a miscarriage of justice. Equally, the fact that his presumption of innocence is restored is irrelevant, as the presumption of innocence is fundamental to a criminal trial and has no place in a civil inquiry into whether there was a miscarriage of justice.

In parts of his judgment in *Pringle* Lynch J. appears to suggest that a miscarriage of justice certificate should issue only where an applicant has established on a balance of probabilities and on the basis of relevant and admissible evidence that he is innocent of the offence. Blayney J., with whom the other judges in the court, agreed did not go that far. Indeed, he specifically refrained from offering a definition of a miscarriage of justice.

When *Meleady and Grogan* returned to the Court of Criminal Appeal, that court preferred the approach of Blayney J. It could envisage insuperable problems if the applicants in that case had to prove, as a matter of probability, that they were innocent of the offence in the popular meaning of that term. Instead the applicants would have to prove on a balance of probabilities that there had been a miscarriage of justice. That, however, could not be done simply by establishing that there was a reasonable possibility that a jury would acquit on a re-trial when presented with the newly discovered fact. This would not establish a probability, as distinct from a possibility, that the newly discovered fact would lead to an acquittal. Equally, it would not be sufficient where there was a possibility of a re-trial that it would not have been appropriate to apply the proviso. Something stronger is required. In *Meleady and Grogan* the newly discovered facts were such that, had they been known at the time of the trial, it is likely that the trial judge would have exercised his discretion to exclude the identification evidence. Since the case depended on that evidence it follows that there would have been no evidence of guilt to be put before the jury. Accordingly, the court proceeded to find that there had been a miscarriage of justice. While, it is dangerous to draw general conclusions from the facts of an individual case, it would appear that the circumstances must be such that the defendant should not have been put on trial before the Court of Criminal Appeal will find a miscarriage of justice. It must also be said that there are indications in the judgment of the court in *Meleady and Grogan* that the deliberate suppression of evidence by the prosecution or a deliberate denial of the defendant's constitutional rights might also produce the same result.

22–85

Admissible Evidence

The Court of Criminal Appeal in *Meleady and Grogan* gave some consideration to the issue of what evidence, if any, it should hear on the application for a certificate of a miscarriage of justice. It made provisional rulings to the effect that the defendants could be called, but that they would be confined in their evidence to matters relevant to the newly discovered facts. On the facts of this particular case the court also accepted that they would be allowed to deny their involvement in the crime as they had failed to take the opportunity to do so at their second trial. The court was also willing to hear evidence from the fourth party (described above) as he had not been called to give evidence in the second trial. However, the court made a provisional ruling against hearing alibi witnesses. It was agreed on both sides that the court could have regard to a considerable amount of documentary material, including: four State files relating to the case; the transcript of the evidence heard before the Court of Criminal Appeal on the previous occasion the case came before it; and the transcript of the evidence at the second trial. It was apparent that had the court wished further material, such as the transcript of the first trial and the transcripts of the perjury trials, it would have been made available. Since there was openness on all sides about the production of documentary materials the court did to have to make any formal determination as to what materials should be before a differently composed court dealing with an application for a certificate of a miscarriage of justice to that which dealt with an application to review the conviction.

Payment of Compensation

22–86　Where the court certifies that there has been a miscarriage of justice the compensation is paid to the convicted person or, if he is dead, to his legal representatives.[467] The amount of compensation, which is only payable on application,[468] is at the Minister's discretion.[469] However, any person dissatisfied with the amount awarded may apply to the High Court to determine the amount which must be paid.[470] The duty to pay compensation under these provisions does not arise if the non-disclosure of the operative fact in time is wholly or partly attributable to the convicted person.[471]

　　Compensation is also payable on the same terms where a person convicted of an offence has been pardoned as a result of a petition submitted under the 1993 Act and the Minister for Justice, Equality and Law Reform is of the opinion that a newly-discovered fact shows that there has been a miscarriage of justice.[472] A pardon by itself does not qualify the convicted person for compensation.

Other Compensation Options

It would appear that the initiation of an application for compensation under the 1993 Act will not always preclude the possibility of a claim for damages

---

[467] Criminal Procedure Act 1993, s.9(1).
[468] *ibid.* s.9(3).
[469] *ibid.* s.9(4).
[470] *ibid.* s.9(5).
[471] *ibid.* s.9(1).
[472] *ibid.* s.9(1)(b).

under some other heading. In *Pringle v. Ireland*,[473] for example, the High Court had to consider a claim for damages from the plaintiff for negligence, breach of duty and failure to vindicate his constitutional rights. The claim arose out of the same matters that had formed the basis of the plaintiff's application for compensation under the 1993 Act. The High Court had to decide as a preliminary matter whether the plaintiff's claim in the current proceedings were barred by his exercise of the option to seek compensation under the 1993 Act. In deciding in favour of the plaintiff the Hugh Court found that there were three pre-requisites for a successful claim under the 1993 Act, namely: a conviction, the quashing of the conviction and the issuance of a certificate of a miscarriage of justice. Since the Court of Criminal Appeal had refused to issue the certificate one of the essential pre-requisites was missing. While the Supreme Court permitted the plaintiff to renew his application before the Court of Criminal Appeal, the plaintiff had declined to do so. Instead he had initiated these proceedings. It follows that he was not maintaining two actions for compensation in respect of the same matter.

---

[473] [1999] 4 I.R. 10 [2000] 2 I.L.R.M. 161.

INDEX